# University Casebook Series

# INTERNATIONAL COMMERCIAL ARBITRATION

## CASES, MATERIALS AND NOTES ON

## THE RESOLUTION OF

## INTERNATIONAL BUSINESS DISPUTES

**W. MICHAEL REISMAN**
Hohfeld Professor of Jurisprudence, Yale Law School

**W. LAURENCE CRAIG**
Member of the New York Bar; *Avocat*, Paris; Former Member
of the Court of Arbitration of the International Chamber of
Commerce, Paris; Partner, Coudert Frères, Paris

**WILLIAM PARK**
Professor of Law, Boston University; Counsel, Ropes & Gray,
Boston

**JAN PAULSSON**
Member of the Connecticut Bar; *Avocat*, Paris; Partner,
Freshfields, Paris

WESTBURY, NEW YORK
THE FOUNDATION PRESS, INC.
1997

 TEXT IS PRINTED ON 10% POST CONSUMER RECYCLED PAPER

# PREFACE

Advising and assisting in the planning and structuring of a wide range of international commercial transactions are increasingly routine tasks in the general corporate practice of American lawyers. In the allocation of tasks among the members of the teams that design these multi-jurisdictional transactions, responsibility for the anticipation of disputes and the provision for planned dispute resolution is a unique and particularly important legal contribution. With increasing frequency, arbitration is being selected as the contractual method of dispute resolution in these transactions. There are a number of reasons: the neutrality and malleability of arbitration, the establishment of multilateral international conventions that make arbitration agreements effective and awards economically enforceable, and the increasing willingness of national courts, including United States courts, to transfer international commercial cases to arbitral jurisdictions abroad.

Despite the increasing importance of this technique in practice and the growing interest in alternative dispute resolution in scholarly and legislative circles, teaching materials that incorporate a wide range of foreign and domestic decisions on international commercial arbitration are not readily available in the United States. In part, this is due to the inaccessibility of documents relating to key parts of the arbitral process. In many cases, records of pleadings are not kept. If they are kept, they are treated as confidential. Many important awards are unpublished or, at least, not published in their entirety. In addition, because arbitration is a genuinely international enterprise, many awards, appearing in languages other than English, remain inaccessible to the general American practitioner.

This book and the accompanying volume of rules, treaties and statutes, undertakes to remedy this deficiency. The materials have been designed (i) to acquaint the American student and practitioner with the conditions that make international commercial arbitration an attractive option in responding to jurisdictional problems and a viable solution to certain challenges to clients; (ii) to track and provide detailed legal material for the sequential phases of international commercial arbitration, from the design of an arbitration agreement, through the initiation and conduct of the arbitration proceedings to arbitration's relation to national courts, control mechanisms, and the review and enforcement of arbitral awards; and (iii) to identify and equip the practitioner and student to appraise those major policy issues with which this area of the law must deal and which necessarily figure prominently, if not centrally, in the hardest cases. Because a significant proportion of international commercial transactions involve governments, their agencies or instrumentalities, special attention is accorded to issues of sovereign immunity.

While the materials are concerned primarily with preparing the American practitioner for effective participation in international commercial arbitration, foreign materials which are ordinarily inaccessible to American lawyers but which, in the view of the authors, are indispensable for such practice, have been included. Mastery of these materials will acquaint the student with the process of international commercial arbitration, the major legal, strategic and professional ethical problems likely to be encountered in practicing it, and some of the important policy issues that are likely to reshape it in the coming decades.

These materials have been prepared for use by practitioners and for a two- or three-hour course in a single semester. As they presuppose some familiarity with a number of areas of commercial law and civil procedure, it has been assumed that students taking the course will be in their second or third year of law school. In such advanced courses, time is often the scarcest resource. Since the context and processes of international commercial arbitration are quite different from their domestic counterparts and their exposition takes much time, the editors felt that valuable classroom time could be saved by setting much of this material out in a rather direct presentation which can be mastered by the student studying alone. The Introduction has been designed to be read by the students before the first class along with a section of Chapter 1.

# ACKNOWLEDGEMENTS

The assistance we received in the preparation of this book was of the highest order. The editors particularly wish to thank Marcilyn Burke, Jennifer Bender, Bethany Berger and Mark Wiedman for their research assistance. Mark Wickersham and Adam Farlow were also helpful in the final stages of preparation. Cheryl A. DeFilippo supervised the preparation of the manuscript and reviewed virtually every phase of preparation. We owe a special debt of thanks to her. Gene Coakley of the Yale Law Library worked, beyond the call, to find the material needed. Dean Anthony T. Kronman provided generous support.

For permission to reprint excerpts under copyright, the editors wish to thank:

American Arbitration Association, for permission to reprint from CODE OF ETHICS FOR ARBITRATORS IN COMMERCIAL DISPUTES (1977); Rosemary S. Page, *Res Judicata, Collateral Estoppel, Arbitration Awards*, AAA ANNUAL REPORT: ARBITRATION AND THE LAW (1987-88), page 39.

American Journal of International Law and Professor Hans Smit, editor, for permission to reprint *The State of Israel v. Desert Exploration 1976 Incident*, summarized in Lawrence F. Ebb, *A Tale of Three Cities: Arbitrator Misconduct by Abuse of Retainer and Commitment Fee Arrangements*, THE AMERICAN REVIEW OF INTERNATIONAL ARBITRATION: ESSAYS IN HONOR OF HANS SMIT 3, 177, 181-90 (1992).

American Society of International Law, for permission to reprint selections from *Wintershall A.G. v. Government of Qatar*, Ad Hoc Arbitral Final Award 28 I.L.M. 833 (1989).

Arbitration International and the London Court of International Arbitration for permission to reprint selections from Albert Jan van den Berg, *Non-domestic Arbitral Awards Under the 1958 New York Convention*, Volume 2 (1986), page 191; E. Allan Farnsworth,

*Punitive Damages in Arbitration*, Volume 7 (1991), pages 3, 5-8; Pierre Mayer, *Mandatory Rules of Law in International Arbitration*, Volume 2 (1986), pages 274, 275-77; Pierre Yves Tschanz, *International Arbitration in the U.S.: The Need for a New Act*, Volume 3 (1987), pages 309, 314-19; W. Michael Tupman, *Staying Enforcement of Arbitral Awards under the New York Convention*, Volume 3 (1987), pages 209, 215-17.

Association suisse de l'arbitrage, for permission to reprint Swiss Intercantonal Arbitration Convention: Concordat suisse sur l'arbitrage (1974).

British Institute of International and Comparative Law, for permission to reprint selections from International & Comparative Law Quarterly, Michael Kerr, *Arbitration and the Courts: The UNCITRAL Model Law*, Volume 34 (1985), page 1; William W. Park, *The Lex Loci Arbitri and International Commercial Arbitration*, Volume 32 (1983), page 21; Jan Paulsson, *Delocalization of International Commercial Arbitration: When and Why It Matters*, Volume 32 (1983), page 53.

Brooklyn Journal of International Law, for permission to reprint selections from William W. Park, *Private Adjudicators and the Public Interest: The Expanding Scope of International Arbitration*, Volume 12 (1986), pages 629-40, 646-48, 664-67.

Butterworth & Co. (Publishers) Ltd., for permission to reprint selections from Michael J. Mustill and Stewart C. Boyd, THE LAW AND PRACTICE OF COMMERCIAL ARBITRATION IN ENGLAND (2d ed. 1989), pages 646-48, 554-55.

Cambridge University Press and Judge Stephen M. Schwebel, to reprint selections from Stephen M. Schwebel, INTERNATIONAL ARBITRATION: THREE SALIENT PROBLEMS (1987), pages 1-6; *Iran v. United States*, 5 Iran-United States Claims Tribunal Reports, Volume 5 (1984), page 131.

Duke University Press, for permission to reprint selections from W. Michael Reisman, SYSTEMS OF CONTROL IN INTERNATIONAL ADJUDICATION AND ARBITRATION: BREAKDOWN AND REPAIR (1992), pages 1-10, 50-86, which reserves all rights.

George Washington University, for permission to reprint selections from the George Washington Journal of International Law & Economics, Allen B. Green & Deneice Jordan-Walker, *Alternative Dispute Resolution in International Government Contracting: A Proposal*, Volume 20 (1987), pages 419, 435-38.

Harvard Law Review Association, for permission to reprint selections from Arthur T. von Mehren & Donald T. Trautman, *Recognition of Foreign Adjudications: A Survey and a Suggested Approach*, 81 HARVARD LAW REVIEW (1968), page 1601.

International Bar Association, for permission to reprint selections from RULES OF ETHICS FOR INTERNATIONAL ARBITRATORS.

ICSID Review, for permission to reprint selections from *Maritime International Nominees Establishment (MINE) v. Guinea*, 1 FOREIGN INVESTMENT L.J. (ICSID Rev.) (1986), pages 380, 383-91.

International Chamber of Commerce, to reprint selections from Eric A. Schwartz, *International Conciliation and the ICC*, ICC INTERNATIONAL COURT OF ARBITRATION BULLETIN (November 1994), page 5.

Kluwer Law International, for permission to reprint selections from Albert Jan van den Berg, THE NEW YORK ARBITRATION CONVENTION OF 1958 (1981), pages 56-71; for permission to reprint selections from Journal of International Arbitration, Georges Delaume, *SEEE v. Yugoslavia: Epitaph of Interlude*, Volume 4 (1987), pages 3, 25; Stephen R. Bond, *How to Draft an Arbitration Clause*, (June, 1989), page 65; for permission to reprint selections from Arbitration International, Kazuo Iwasaki, *Selection of Situs: Criteria and Priorities*, Number 2 (1986), pages 57, 64-67; Andreas F. Lowenfeld, *Lex Mercatoria: An Arbitrator's View*, Number 6 (1990), pages 133, 137-40; Lord Justice Mustill, *The New Lex Mercatoria: The First Twenty-Five Years*, Number 4 (1988), pages 86, 108; Jan Paulsson, *May a State Invoke Its Internal Law to Repudiate Consent to International Commercial Arbitration?*, Number 2 (1986), pages 90, 102-03; for permission to reprint selections from Yearbook of Commercial Arbitration, Partial Final Award No. 1510 (Nov. 28, 1980), Volume 7 (1982), pages 151-55; ICC Arbitration No. 5029, Interim Award, (July 16, 1986), Volume 12 (1987), page 113; ICC Arbitration No.

6281, Award (Aug. 26, 1989), Volume 15 (1990), page 96; ICC Arbitration No. 1512, Final Award (Mar. 1, 1971), Volume 1 (1976), page 128; French Construction Co. A v. Iranian Gov't Org. B, Volume 10 (1985), page 47; Society of Maritime Arbitrators, Inc., Interim Award No. 2015 (Aug. 24, 1985), Volume 11 (1986), page 209; ICC Arbitration No. 4402, Partial Award (Mar. 17, 1983), Volume 9 (1984), page 138.

Litec Librairies Techniques, for permission to reprint selections from Arthur T. von Mehren, *To What Extent is International Commercial Arbitration Autonomous?* in Le Droit des relations économiques internationales (Etudes offertes à Berthold Goldman (Editions Litec 1983), page 217.

Mealey Publications, Inc., Wayne, PA, for permission to reprint selections from Mealey's International Arbitration Report, ICC Arbitration No. 6401, Preliminary Award (Dec. 19, 1991), Volume 7 (1992); J. Gillis Wetter, *Arbitration in the New Europe*, Volume 5 (November, 1990), pages 13, 16-18; Jan Paulsson, *The New York Convention's Misadventures in India*, Volume 6 (June, 1992), pages 3-8.

Oceana Publications, Inc. for permission to reprint selections from Craig, Park & Paulsson, INTERNATIONAL CHAMBER OF COMMERCE ARBITRATION (2d ed. 1990), pages 269-70, 614-19; Austria: Code of Civil Procedure, Fourth Chapter, Arbitration Procedure; Austria: Judicature Act; Austria: Federal Statute on Private International Law; Italy: The Italian Arbitration Law Reform, The New Text of the Code of Civil Procedure as Amended by Law No. 25 of 5 January 1994, Unofficial Translation by the Milan Chamber of Commerce; J. Gillis Wetter, THE INTERNATIONAL PROCESS: PUBLIC AND PRIVATE, Volume 1 (1979), pages 441, 444-56.

Oxford University Press and Professor Pierre Lalive, for permission to reprint selections from Lalive, *The First "World Bank" Arbitration (Holiday Inns v. Morocco) - Some Legal Problems*, 51 BRITISH YEARBOOK OF INTERNATIONAL LAW (1982), page 123.

The Parker School of Foreign and Comparative Law and Dr. Vratislav Pechota, for permission to reprint selections from the translation by Luigi Fernando and Frank Koerner of Germany's Gesetz

Gegen Wettbewerbsbeschräankungen (Kartell Gesetz), Section 91, (BGBI 1957 I at 1801.

Queen Mary College and Julian D.M. Lew, for permission to reprint from Julian D.M. Lew, CONTEMPORARY PROBLEMS IN INTERNATIONAL ARBITRATION (1987), pages 104-12.

Revue de l'Arbitrage, for permission to reprint selections from Pierre Bellet, *The Dutco Case, Siemens A.G. & BkMI Industrielagan GmbH v. Dutco Construction Co.* Revue de l'Arbitrage (1992), page 470.

Professors Pieter Sanders and Albert Jan van den Berg for permission to reprint their translations of the arbitration laws of Belgium, Germany, The Netherlands and Switzerland in INTERNATIONAL HANDBOOK ON COMMERCIAL ARBITRATION.

Schulthess Verlag, Zurich for permission to reprint selections from Adam Samuel, JURISDICTIONAL PROBLEMS IN INTERNATIONAL COMMERCIAL ARBITRATION (1989), pages 82-83, 106-17, 307-09.

Stockholm Chamber of Commerce, for permission to reprint selections from the translation of The Swedish Arbitration Act of 1929 (as amended and in force on January 1 1984); The Swedish Act of 1929 Concerning Foreign Arbitration Agreements Arbitration and Awards (as amended and in force on 1 January 1984).

Sweet & Maxwell, for permission to reprint selections from F.A. Mann, *Private Arbitration and Public Policy*, 4 CIVIL JUSTICE (1985), pages 257, 262; Alan Redfern & Martin Hunter, LAW AND PRACTICE OF INTERNATIONAL COMMERCIAL ARBITRATION (2d ed. 1991), pages 15-16, 194-96, 297-98.

Tulane Law Review, for permission to reprint selections from William W. Park, *National Law and Commercial Justice: Safeguarding Procedural Integrity in International Arbitration*, pages 699-703, 694-95, 684-89, 663-70, originally published in 63 TULANE LAW REVIEW 647 (1989).

University of Minnesota Law School, for permission to reprint selections from Jay L. Westbrook, *The Coming Encounter:*

*International Arbitration and Bankruptcy*, 67 MINNESOTA LAW REVIEW (1983), pages 595, 642-44.

Virginia Journal of International Law, for permission to reprint selections from Lionel Kennedy, *Enforcing International Commercial Arbitration Agreements & Awards not Subject to the New York Convention*, Volume 23 (1982), pages 85-100; Jan Paulsson, *The Role of the Swedish Courts in Transnational Commercial Arbitration*, Volume 21 (1981), pages 244-48.

The Yale Law Journal Company and Fred B. Rothman & Company, for permission to reprint selections from Leonard V. Quigley, *Accession by the U.S. to the U.N. Convention on the Recognition and Enforcement of Foreign Arbitral Awards*, Volume 70 (1961), pages 1049-82.

Yearbook Commercial Arbitration, for permission to reprint from the International Handbook on Commercial Arbitration, Belgium: Code Judiciaire, Sixth Part: Arbitration, Articles 1676 to 1723 (1996); Germany: German Code of Civil Procedure, Book X Arbitration Procedure, Articles 1025 to 1048 (1987) and Law On the Recognition and Enforcement of Foreign Arbitral Awards (1984); The Netherlands Arbitration Act (1987) and Code of Civil Procedure, Book Four: Arbitration, Articles 1020 to 1076 and Miscellaneous Provisions, Including Transitional Law, Articles II - VI (1987); Swiss Private International Law Act, Chapter 12: International Arbitration, Articles 176 to 194 (1988).

# SUMMARY OF CONTENTS

*

# TABLE OF CONTENTS

# TABLE OF CASES

## I.  UNITED STATES CASES.

## III.    DECISIONS OF ARBITRAL AND INTERNATIONAL TRIBUNALS.

*

# INTRODUCTION

## How Does a Typical Arbitration Work?

How does a typical international commercial arbitration usually work? Each international commercial arbitration varies according to factors such as the rules adopted, the venue selected and the facts of the actual dispute, but the most basic, recurring features may be sketched in general terms. This sketch will be detailed and refined as we proceed through the book.

### 1. The Sequences of an Arbitration

### The Arbitration Clause:

Two parties, in drafting an international contract, anticipate that disputes between them may arise concerning the performance of the contract. For whatever reason, they prefer that those disputes not be decided by the courts. Hence they provide in the contract that any or certain prescribed categories of dispute will be referred to arbitration. The formula they use is often referred to as a "dispute resolution mechanism" or more concisely an "arbitration clause," a "jurisdictional clause" or a future disputes clause.[1] Alternatively, but less frequently, parties who have not inserted a jurisdictional clause in their contract may decide after a dispute has erupted that they will submit their specific dispute to arbitration rather than go to court. This type of arrangement is sometimes called a "submission agreement." Parties who have decided in favor of arbitration — whether in anticipation or after the eruption of a dispute — may incorporate any of a number of systems of procedural rules, some associated with specific arbitral institutions.

---

[1] Note the distinction in French between a *clause compromissoire* and a *compromis*. A *compromis* is a "submission agreement" for the reference of a dispute to arbitration or judicial settlement: a negotiated document setting forth precisely the issues to be determined.

SETTING UP THE TRIBUNAL:

With some variations the sequence of events on the eruption of a dispute will essentially be as follows. One party will inform the other that it wishes to arbitrate a particular matter and will indicate the nature of the subject matter and at the same time suggest an arbitrator for the panel. Within a prescribed period of time, the other party is expected to appoint an arbitrator. The parties or these two arbitrators proceed to choose a third arbitrator who serves as the Chairman of the tribunal. When one of the parties does not cooperate in selecting a Chairman, many institutional systems provide for an "appointing authority" to perform this indispensable function. Without a tribunal, an arbitration obviously could not proceed.

THE ARBITRATION:

Thereafter, operating under one common set of arbitral rules, the parties meet with the tribunal to agree upon or have the tribunal frame the key issues to be resolved, set time tables, and determine other matters pertinent to the conduct of the arbitration. In accordance with the timetable, the parties submit documents and at the appropriate time hold the arbitral trial at which witnesses may be called and evidence adduced in ways comparable to procedures in domestic courts. Thereafter the arbitrators deliberate and render their decision which is known as an arbitral award.

THE NOTIFICATION:

In the case of an institution like the International Chamber of Commerce, the award is reviewed by an internal "Court," essentially for matters of form, and then the parties are notified. In non-institutional arbitration, the tribunal itself notifies the parties of the award.

ENFORCEMENT OF THE AWARD:

If the award is not complied with, the winning party normally seeks enforcement in those national jurisdictions where the losing party has assets, usually relying on treaties facilitating the enforcement of such international arbitral awards. The losing party may seek to have these same national courts annul the award or refuse its enforcement on the limited number of grounds which arbitration law makes available.

## 2.    WHY DO PARTIES SELECT ARBITRATION?

The available statistics, though far from complete, indicate that use of the arbitral method for resolving international disputes between entities involved in international commerce is increasing. Viewed from the international standpoint, this trend is hardly surprising. Trade and investment across state lines is on the rise, and parties from different jurisdictions who engage in such activity frequently seek the comparative neutrality of a non-state tribunal to resolve their differences. Parties to a transaction from different states may be reluctant to submit to the jurisdiction of the courts of the other. This reluctance may arise from lack of enthusiasm about operating in another language, or according to the procedures and, insofar as it infiltrates procedure, the substantive law of another state. In some circumstances, one party may fear that the courts of the other may have a preference for their own nationals, may share a dislike of a particular foreign nationality or may, in cases involving very large amounts of money, lean toward finding in favor of their national because of the consequences for their national economy and political system. Where one of the parties is a state or state agency, a non-state party may prefer arbitration to submitting a dispute to the courts of the other contracting party. Arbitration may thus serve to "equalize" the non-state entity by transferring the dispute to a setting which may be designed to minimize or ignore the sovereign character of one of the parties rather more than would a national court.

Arbitration may also be utilized because the various national laws which might be relevant have not developed enough to treat problems raised in a pioneer industry. Thus issues regarding intellectual property rights in computer software of companies from different states may be submitted to arbitration as a way of resolving a dispute by shaping new law on the matter. In some circumstances potential litigants may also seek out arbitration because it is touted as more rapid, private and cheaper than domestic adjudication, though many of these characteristics of international commercial arbitration may be relative and sometimes overstated.

International commercial arbitration is also on the increase because many national court systems not only help international arbitration but appear anxious to externalize a larger amount of the disputes that are formally within their jurisdiction. The willingness of national courts to compel parties who have made prior commitments to engage in private arbitration and then to enforce the awards that ensue, subject only to limited judicial review, increases the likelihood that parties will resort to that mode of dispute resolution.

3. THE LEGAL BASIS OF INTERNATIONAL ARBITRATION: A PARTIAL EXPLANATION

Arbitration, whether national or international, is a contractual creature in two senses. First, it cannot take place if the parties do not agree to it. Second, the parties may largely shape the features of their specific arbitration to meet their particular needs. But like contracts themselves, arbitration, as a set of practices, is also shaped by law. In international arbitration, the laws that perform this function are international and national, public and private. This point must be explored briefly.

We have observed that arbitration is a contractual method for the relatively private settlement of disputes. Parties have the competence under the legal system or systems that are pertinent to them to contract with regard to certain matters. The legal system may also permit them to include in their contract a provision for resolving any disputes that may arise by agreeing beforehand to accept the decision of a designated third party. The procedures by which that decision is made may be freely selected by the parties or prescribed in part by the state. They may be extremely simple and informal or may approximate all of the more complex arrangements found in courts of advanced legal systems. The result of an arbitration, the award, is ostensibly part of the contract of the parties, but is usually enforceable by national courts in more summary procedures than would be available for an ordinary contractual dispute. When enforcement is sought, a variety of defenses may be available to the award debtor, the side that has lost. These defenses are theoretically different from an appeal. They are not supposed to raise alleged mistakes of fact or law or to challenge the general wisdom of the award, but only to allege that the award and the procedures for reaching it violated the contractual limits set by the parties or that its enforcement would contravene some critical public policies of the national forum in which enforcement is sought.

From this very brief description, it is clear that arbitration, despite its supposed "contractual," "private" and "autonomous" character, is effectively inoperable, if not inconceivable, without the tolerance and contingent support of the usual national judicial institutions. To mention only a few examples, national courts may be necessary:

- to compel the arbitration, in the event a party refuses to comply with its contractual obligation to repair to arbitration at the instance of the other party;

- to issue subpoenas or otherwise aid in the gathering of evidence;

- to enforce or refuse to enforce an award.

The brief description we have essayed should also demonstrate the limits of an exclusively "contractual" explanation of arbitration. It is not true that anything susceptible to private contract can be arbitrated. A legal system may permit contracts about labor conditions or interspousal responsibilities for children, but set severe limitations on the possibility of private arbitration of disputes that arise from these contractual arrangements.

For these reasons, we propose to refer to arbitration as a legally authorized method of dispute resolution, which is optional to the parties, subject to legal regulation, and contingent on judicial supervision and enforcement. International commercial arbitration is subject to legal regulation by a number of national legal systems and by international law and generally incorporates the judicial supervision and enforcement of more than one national legal system.

### 4.    INTERNATIONAL VS. NON-INTERNATIONAL ARBITRATION

International arbitration must be distinguished from non-international (also called "national" or "domestic") arbitration. Despite variations in terminology and practice in many national systems, the central, common feature distinguishing international from national arbitration is the diversity of nationality of the litigants or, minimally, the fact that the arbitrating parties are not nationals of the arbitral forum. (Let us overlook for the moment the public international legal question of which law and which institutions determine nationality.)

Given the role of governments, their agencies and instrumentalities in international economic exchanges, it is no surprise that they too now figure prominently as litigants in international arbitration. For the moment, let us treat governments, their agencies and their instrumentalities as a single class, though, as we will see, each may require different treatment in some jurisdictions and in some arbitral phases.

## 5. TYPES OF "PRIVITY" IN COMMERCIAL ARBITRATION

As will become clear in the materials that follow, the identity of the litigant is an important factor in the different phases of arbitration. There are three possible types of arbitral privity at the international commercial level. Each type has different and sometimes important consequences for different phases of the arbitral process.

A. State/state arbitrations
B. State/non-state arbitrations
C. Non-state/non-state arbitrations

When a state entity is a defendant, issues of sovereign immunity may arise in the initiating phase, the jurisdictional phase, during the actual procedure of the arbitration and in the nullification and enforcement phases. It is possible that "Act of State" issues may also arise, though they are equally available to non-state defendants. Another jurisdictional problem that may arise when state entities are parties is that the competence of a governmental agency or instrumentality, and indeed the government itself, to agree to arbitrate may be subject to constitutional and statutory limitations which must be considered from an international legal standpoint.

## 6. INTERNATIONAL ARBITRAL INSTITUTIONS

In theory the parties in international arbitrations can tailor every aspect of a procedure to the special needs of their case. But this imposes a tremendous burden, time-wise and money-wise, on the lawyers designing the arbitration and on the litigants. Consequently, a large volume of international arbitration now takes place within the framework of a number of specialized institutions. Even in *ad hoc* arbitrations, parties frequently take advantage of a variety of existing arbitral institutions and/or procedures, which are adopted, in whole or in part, for particular arbitrations. All of the major institutions with their specialized procedures will be examined in this book.

The materials that follow are designed to explore many of these matters in the context of the phases of arbitration. You may wish to study the Table of Contents carefully before beginning the first chapter in order to gain a sense of the structure of the book. The Supplement contains the major rules of arbitration and a selection of national arbitration statutes and pertinent treaties. The material in the Supplement is keyed to pertinent parts of the text.

*

# CHAPTER 1

# JURISDICTIONAL PROBLEMS AND SOLUTIONS IN INTERNATIONAL COMMERCIAL TRANSACTIONS

## INTRODUCTION

Consider three hypothetical cases:

1. Furniture Corporation (Furncorp) of Jackson, Mississippi, produces moderately-priced furniture which it ships to dealers throughout the United States. In general, it averages a 20% profit on gross sales. Furncorp has received its first order from abroad, $50,000 worth of furniture to be shipped to Lima, Peru. Furncorp uses its usual order form, which does little more than identify the purchaser and call for net payment in 30 days. When the purchaser in Lima fails to pay, Furncorp discovers that it must retain Peruvian counsel, sue in Lima and that the initiation of a suit will require providing a bond to the Peruvian court system for court costs.

2. New York Construction Company (NYCCO) enters into a 10-year joint venture with Italian Construction Company (ICO) to construct large-scale port facilities in Tunis. Two years into the project, fundamental disagreements between NYCCO and ICO develop. ICO commences suit in Italy, obliging NYCCO to conduct the suit there.

3. Texas Oil Company (TOC) and British Petroleum (BP) contract to develop jointly an oil field in Libya. BP insists that key circumstances it had relied on in concluding the contract have changed and seeks renegotiation, but TOC insists on compliance with the original contract. BP commences suit in London, relying, for jurisdiction, on an English long-arm statute and on an idiosyncratic English statute on frustration of contracts.

## THE PROBLEM

I.      THE NECESSITY OF PLANNING JURISDICTION IN INTERNATIONAL COMMERCIAL TRANSACTIONS

Cases like these and many others involve international transactions in which the parties did not agree, beforehand, as to <u>where</u> and <u>how</u> disputes that might arise between them might be heard, *i.e.*, they did not decide on what is often called in these transactions "jurisdiction." This would not have been a serious oversight in a purely domestic transaction, for even in the absence of prior agreement on where disputes between them should be decided, both parties would be subject to the same compulsory court system. In the sorts of international commercial transactions hypothesized above, however, not deciding on jurisdiction beforehand can be serious, and even calamitous, for one of the parties. In the absence of an agreement about where and how disputes are to be resolved, the party that initiates the suit first has the option of choosing the forum which it believes is most favorable to it — whether procedurally, substantively or tactically — or at least most costly and difficult for the other party.

This plaintiff's option, sometimes referred to as "forum shopping," can be a successful litigative or negotiating strategy for the party using it if (i) international law's rules on jurisdiction do not assign exclusive and predictable jurisdiction to one particular forum, and/or (ii) the forum which has been selected by the plaintiff is willing and able, by its own law, to accept and effectively exercise jurisdiction. Some judges and jurisdictions entertain the notion that they have been assigned a special mission in this regard. In a well-known English admiralty case, the *Atlantic Star*, [1973] Q.B. 364, Lord Denning said,

> No one who comes to these courts asking for justice should come in vain. . . . This right to come here is not confined to Englishmen. It extends to any friendly foreigner. He can seek the aid of our courts if he desires to do so. You may call this "forum shopping" if you please, but if the forum is England, it is a good place to shop in, both for the quality of the goods and the speed of service.

Where conditions allow forum shopping, the plaintiff has the option of selecting, among a number of potential fora, the one most likely to discriminate in its favor and against that of the defendant. Even where the substantive law has been internationalized and is substantially the same in each forum, procedural differences among fora may tip the scales in favor of one party or the other. In this sort of situation, each party has an incentive to initiate suit before the other, a dynamic that can polarize the parties and push them past accommodation and to litigation. Jurisdictional certainty or uncertainty must therefore be taken into account when structuring an international transaction and planning for the resolution of potential disputes. A number of trends in international and national judicial theory are critical for these calculations and are explored in the materials that follow.

A.   INTERNATIONAL   LAW   AND   THE   THEORY   OF CONCURRENT JURISDICTION

1.    *The S.S. "Lotus"* (Fr. v. Turk.), 1927 P.C.I.J. (ser. A) No. 10, at 18-19 (Sept. 7, 1927).

[This dispute arose from a maritime collision in international waters between a French steamer, the *Lotus* and a Turkish collier, the *Bozcourt*. After the collision the French ship entered a Turkish port. The question submitted to the Permanent Court of International Justice was whether Turkey had violated international law in initiating criminal proceedings against the officer of the watch on the French ship.]

International law governs relations between independent States. The rules of law binding upon States therefore emanate from their own free will as expressed in conventions or by usages generally accepted as expressing principles of law and established in order to regulate the relations between these co-existing independent communities or with a view to the achievement of common aims. Restrictions upon the independence of States cannot therefore be presumed.

Now the first and foremost restriction imposed by international law upon a State is that — failing the existence of a permissive rule to the contrary — it may not exercise its power in any form in the territory of another State. In this sense jurisdiction is certainly territorial; it cannot be exercised by a State outside its territory except by virtue of a permissive rule derived from international custom or from a convention.

It does not, however, follow that international law prohibits a State from exercising jurisdiction in its own territory, in respect of any case which relates to acts which have taken place abroad, and in which it cannot rely on some permissive rule of international law. Such a view would only be tenable if international law contained a general prohibition to States to extend the application of their laws and the jurisdiction of their courts to persons, property and acts outside their territory, and if, as an exception to this general prohibition, it allowed States to do so in certain specific cases. But this is certainly not the case under international law as it stands at present. Far from laying down a general prohibition to the effect that States may not extend the application of their laws and the jurisdiction of their courts to persons, property and acts outside their territory, it leaves them in this respect a wide measure of discretion which is only limited in certain cases by prohibitive rules; as regards other cases, every State remains free to adopt the principles which it regards as best and most suitable.

This discretion left to States by international law explains the great variety of rules which they have been able to adopt without objections or complaints on the part of other States; it is in order to remedy the difficulties resulting from such variety that efforts have been made for many years past, both in Europe and America, to prepare conventions the effect of which would be precisely to limit the discretion at present left to States in this respect by international law, thus making good the existing lacunae in respect of jurisdiction or removing the conflicting jurisdictions arising from the diversity of the principles adopted by the various States.

In these circumstances, all that can be required of a State is that it should not overstep the limits which international law places upon its jurisdiction; within these limits, its title to exercise jurisdiction rests in its sovereignty.

It follows from the foregoing that the contention of the French Government to the effect that Turkey must in each case be able to cite a rule of international law authorizing her to exercise jurisdiction, is opposed to the generally accepted international law. . . .

## Notes and Questions

1. While every national legal system has its own body of private international law or conflicts of law, it is important to bear in mind that public international law, which operates on all states, itself prescribes fundamental jurisdictional rules which limit what individual states may do. This public international legal dimension of private international law is frequently overlooked. *See generally* MYRES S. MCDOUGAL & W. MICHAEL REISMAN, INTERNATIONAL LAW IN CONTEMPORARY PERSPECTIVE Part V (1981).

2. If international law contemplates different states having concurrent jurisdiction over the same dispute, is there any international legal objection to ICO initiating suit against NYCCO in an Italian court, in the second hypothetical at the beginning of this chapter?

3. At international law, a state is liable to another state under the law of State Responsibility if it deprives the national of the other state of some internationally guaranteed right. If there are clear principles of jurisdiction at the international level and a state permits itself to be the forum for a "hijacked" case, as it were, a claim of State Responsibility might lie on behalf of the state whose national has been injured. The effectiveness of this claim depends, however, upon the operation of State Responsibility, which is notoriously slow, as well as upon the clarity of the relevant principles of international jurisdiction involved which are often concurrent and sometimes uncertain.

2. INTERNATIONAL CONVENTION ON CERTAIN RULES CONCERNING CIVIL JURISDICTION IN MATTERS OF COLLISION, ARTICLES 1 AND 2

. . .

## Article 1:

(1) An action for collision occurring between seagoing [sic] vessels, or between sea going vessels and inland navigation craft, can only be introduced:

    (a) either before the court where the defendant has his habitual residence or a place of business;

    (b) or before the court of the place where arrest has been effected of the defendant ship or of any other ship belonging to the defendant which can be lawfully arrested, or where arrest could have been effected and bail or other security has been furnished;

(c)        or before the court of the place of collision when the collision has occurred within the limits of a port or in inland waters.

.        .        .

(2)        It shall be for the plaintiff to decide in which of the courts referred to in (1) of this article the action shall be instituted.

.        .        .

(3)        A claimant shall not be allowed to bring a further action against the same defendant on the same facts in another jurisdiction, without discontinuing an action already instituted.

.        .        .

3.        RESTATEMENT OF THE LAW THIRD: THE FOREIGN RELATIONS LAW OF THE UNITED STATES (1987) SECTION 421

### Jurisdiction to Adjudicate

(1) A state may exercise jurisdiction through its courts to adjudicate with respect to a person or thing if the relationship of the state to the person or thing is such as to make the exercise of jurisdiction reasonable.

(2) In general, a state's exercise of jurisdiction to adjudicate with respect to a person or thing is reasonable if, at the time jurisdiction is asserted:

(a)        the person or thing is present in the territory of the state, other than transitorily;

(b)        the person, if a natural person, is domiciled in the state;

(c)     the person, if a natural person, is resident in the state;

(d)     the person, if a natural person, is a national of the state;

(e)     the person, if a corporation or comparable juridical person, is organized pursuant to the law of the state;

(f)     a ship, aircraft or other vehicle to which the adjudication relates is registered under the laws of the state;

(g)     the person, whether natural or juridical, has consented to the exercise of jurisdiction;

(h)     the person, whether natural or juridical, regularly carries on business in the state;

(i)     the person, whether natural or juridical, had carried on activity in the state, but only in respect of such activity;

(j)     the person, whether natural or juridical, had carried on outside the state an activity having a substantial, direct, and foreseeable effect within the state, but only in respect of such activity; or

(k)     the thing that is the subject of adjudication is owned, possessed, or used in the state, but only in respect of a claim reasonably connected with that thing.

(3) A defense of lack of jurisdiction is generally waived by any appearance by or on behalf of a person or thing (whether as plaintiff, defendant, or third party), if the appearance is for a purpose that does not include a challenge to the exercise of jurisdiction.

### Notes and Questions

1. International law operates, as we have seen, on a theory of concurrent jurisdiction, in which the courts of several different states may be deemed to be equally competent to seize jurisdiction of the same case. Therefore, in the absence of contrary contractual restriction, a party to an international transaction is entitled, under international law, to select the forum which is most favorable to it, both procedurally and substantively. What are the consequences of these options on the negotiation of the transaction, on its performance, and on the predictability of judicial outcomes?

2. What remedies are theoretically available to a party to an international transaction if it believes that it has been "hijacked" into a forum which is either without jurisdiction or is essentially unfair? What remedies are practically available?

3. The International Convention on Certain Rules Concerning Civil Jurisdiction on Matters of Collision was the determinative factor in persuading the English Court to accept jurisdiction over the dispute in the notable case *Owners of the Motor Vessel "Atlantic Star" v. Owner of the Motor Vessel "Bonn Spes" (infra* p. 91).

B.     THEORIES OF JUDICIAL JURISDICTION IN THE UNITED STATES

American Courts have claimed that they must effect Congressional intention without regard to its possible incompatibility with international law.

*Strathearn Steamship Company v. Dillon*, 252 U.S. 348 (1920).

Mr. JUSTICE DAY delivered the opinion of the Court.

This case presents questions arising under the Seamen's Act of March 4, 1915, c. 153, 38 Stat. 1164. It appears that Dillon, the respondent, was a British subject, and shipped at Liverpool on the eighth of May, 1916, on a British vessel. The shipping articles provided for a voyage of not exceeding three years, commencing at Liverpool and ending at such port in the United Kingdom as might be required by the master, the voyage including ports of the United States. The wages which were fixed by the articles were made payable at the end of the voyage. At the time of the demand for one-half wages, and at the time of the beginning of the action, the period of the voyage abroad had not been reached. The articles provided that no cash should be advanced abroad or liberty granted other than at the pleasure of the master. This, it is admitted, was a valid contract for the payment of wages under the laws of Great Britain. The ship arrived at the Port of Pensacola, Florida, on July 31, 1916, and while she was in that port, Dillon, still in the employ of the ship, demanded from her master one-half part of the wages theretofore earned, and payment was refused. Dillon had received nothing for about two months, and after the refusal of the master to comply with his demand for one-half wages, he filed in the District Court of the United States a libel against the ship, claiming $125.00, the amount of wages earned at the time of demand and refusal.

The District Court found against Dillon upon the ground that his demand was premature. The Circuit Court of Appeals reversed this decision, and held that Dillon was entitled to recover. 256 Fed. Rep. 631. A writ of certiorari brings before us for review the decree of the Circuit Court of Appeals.

In *Sandberg v. McDonald*, 248 U.S. 185 (1918), and *Neilson v. Rhine Shipping Co.*, 248 U.S. 205 (1918), we had occasion to deal with §11 of the Seamen's Act, and held that it did not invalidate advancement of seamen's wages in foreign countries when legal where made. The instant case requires us to consider now §4 of the same act. That section amends §4530, Rev. Stats., and so far as pertinent provides: "Sec. 4530. Every seaman on a vessel of the United States shall be entitled to receive on demand from the master of the vessel to which he belongs one-half part of the wages which he shall have then earned at every port where such vessel, after the voyage has been commenced, shall load or deliver cargo before the voyage is ended and all stipulations in the contract to the contrary shall be void: <u>Provided</u>, Such a demand shall not be made before the expiration of, nor oftener than once in five days. Any failure on the part of the master to comply with this demand shall release the seaman from his contract and he shall be entitled to full payment of wages earned. . . . <u>And provided further</u>, That this section shall apply to seamen on foreign vessels while in harbors of the United States, and the courts of the United States shall be open to such seamen for its enforcement."

·    ·    ·

The section, of which the statute now under consideration is an amendment, expressly excepted from the right to recover one-half of the wages those cases in which the contract otherwise provided. In the amended section all such contract provisions are expressly rendered void, and the right to recover is given the seamen notwithstanding contractual obligations to the contrary. The language applies to all seamen on vessels of the United States, and the second proviso of the section as it now reads makes it applicable to seamen on foreign vessels while in harbors of the United States. The proviso does not stop there, for it contains the express provision that the courts of the United States shall be open to seamen on foreign vessels for its enforcement. The latter provision is of the utmost importance in determining the proper construction of this section of the act. It manifests the purpose of Congress to give the benefit of the act to seamen on foreign vessels, and to open the doors of the federal courts to foreign seamen. No such provision was necessary as to American seamen, for they had the right independently of this statute to seek redress in the courts of the United States, and, if it were the intention of Congress to limit the provision of the act to American seamen, this feature would have been wholly superfluous.

It is said that it is the purpose to limit the benefit of the act to American seamen, notwithstanding this provision giving access to seamen on foreign vessels to the courts of the United States, because of the title of the act in which its purpose is expressed "to promote the welfare of American seamen in the merchant marine of the United States." But this title is more than this, and not only declares the purposes to promote the welfare of American seamen but further to abolish arrest and imprisonment as a penalty for desertion and to secure the abrogation of treaty provisions in relation thereto; and to promote safety at sea. But the title of an act cannot limit the plain meaning of its text, although it may be looked to to aid in construction in cases of doubt. *Cornell v. Coyne*, 192 U.S. 418, 530 (1904), and cases cited. Apart from the text, which we think plain, it is by no means clear that, if the act were given a construction to limit its application to American seamen only, the purposes of Congress would be subserved, for such limited construction would have a tendency to prevent the employment of American seamen, and to promote the engagement of those who were not entitled to sue for one-half wages under the provisions of the law. But, taking the provisions of the act as the same are written, we think it plain that it manifests the purpose of Congress to place American and foreign seamen on an equality of right in so far as the privileges of this section are concerned, with equal opportunity to resort to the courts of the United States for the enforcement of the act. Before the amendment, as we have already pointed out, the right to recover one-half the wages could not be enforced in face of a contractual obligation to the contrary. Congress, for reasons which it deemed sufficient, amended the act so as to permit the recovery upon the conditions named in the statute. In the case of *Sandberg v. McDonald*, 248 U.S. *supra*, we found no purpose manifested by Congress in §11 to interfere with wages advanced in foreign ports under contracts legal where made. That section dealt with advancements, and contained no provision such as we find in §4. Under §4 all contracts are avoided which run counter to the purposes of the statute. Whether consideration for contractual rights under engagements legally made in foreign countries would suggest a different course is not our province to inquire. It is sufficient to say that Congress has otherwise declared by the positive terms of this enactment, and if it had authority to do so, the law is enforcible [sic] in the courts.

We come then to consider the contention that this construction renders the statute unconstitutional as being destructive of contract rights. But we think this contention must be decided adversely to the petitioner upon the authority of previous cases in this court. The matter was fully considered in *Patterson v. Bark Eudora*, 190 U.S. 169 (1903), in which the previous decisions of this court were reviewed, and the conclusion reached that the jurisdiction of this Government over foreign merchant vessels in our ports was such as to give authority to Congress to make provisions of the character now under consideration; that it was for this Government to determine upon what terms and conditions vessels of other countries might be permitted to enter our harbors, and to impose conditions upon the shipment of sailors in our own ports, and make them applicable to foreign as well as domestic vessels. Upon the authority of that case, and others cited in the opinion therein, we have no doubt as to the authority of Congress to pass a statute of this sort, applicable to foreign vessels in our ports and controlling the employment and payment of seamen as a condition of the right of such foreign vessels to enter and use the ports of the United States.

.     .     .

## Notes and Questions

1. *Strathearn* apparently holds that U.S. courts must give effect to Congressional intention without regard to its possible incompatibility with international law. This does not mean that domestic courts are oblivious to international law. Where there is a clear conflict between domestic legislation and an international prescription, courts usually seek to find an interpretation which will minimize or obviate the conflict. See, for example, Judge Palmieri's opinion in *United States v. Palestine Liberation Organization*, 347 U.S. 483 (1954), discussed in W. Michael Reisman, *An International Farce: The Sad Case of the PLO Mission*, 14 YALE J. INT'L L. 412 (1989).

2. Does the Supreme Court inquire as to possible international legal limitations on what Congress may do? If such limitations were pleaded and established, does *Strathearn* indicate that the Court would give effect to them?

3. If there are no international legal limitations or, at least, if national courts, following the Supreme Court, do not give effect to them when they conflict with domestic legislative instructions, what prohibits the United Kingdom from (i) passing legislation comparable to that in operation in the United States but reflecting its own policy; (ii) passing domestic legislation permitting the British defendant to sue the American plaintiff in British courts for the amount of the award plus interest and costs, in a British court? Consider, in this regard, the British Protection of Trading Interests Act (1980 c. 11).

I.--(1) If it appears to the Secretary of State--

> (a) that measures have been or are proposed to be taken by or under the law of any overseas country for regulating or controlling international trade; and
> (b) that those measures, in so far as they apply or would apply to things done or to be done outside the territorial jurisdiction of that country by persons carrying on business in the United Kingdom, are damaging or threaten to damage the trading interests of the United Kingdom,

the Secretary of State may by order direct that this section shall apply to those measures either generally or in their application to such cases as may be specified in the order.

(2) The Secretary of State may by order make provision for requiring, or enabling the Secretary of State to require, a person in the United Kingdom who carries on business there to give notice to the Secretary of State of any requirement or prohibition imposed or threatened to be imposed on that person pursuant to any measures in so far as this section applies to them by virtue of an order under subsection (1) above.

(3) The Secretary of State may give to any person in the United Kingdom who carries on business there such directions for prohibiting compliance with any such requirement or prohibition as aforesaid as he considers appropriate for avoiding damage to the trading interests of the United Kingdom.

(4) The power of the Secretary of State to make orders under subsection (1) or (2) above shall be exercisable by statutory instrument subject to annulment in pursuance of a resolution of either House of Parliament.

(5) Directions under subsection (3) above may be either general or special and may prohibit compliance with any requirement or prohibition either absolutely or in such cases or

subject to such conditions as to consent or otherwise as may be specified in the directions; and general directions under that subsection shall be published in such manner as appears to the Secretary of State to be appropriate.

(6) In this section "trade" includes any activity carried on in the course of a business of any description and "trading interests" shall be construed accordingly.

## II.   DUE PROCESS: LIMITATIONS ON THE ASSERTION OF JURISDICTION

A.   *International Shoe Co. v. Washington*, 326 U.S. 310 (1945).

MR. CHIEF JUSTICE STONE delivered the opinion of the Court.

The questions for decision are (1) whether, within the limitations of the due process clause of the Fourteenth Amendment, appellant, a Delaware corporation, has by its activities in the State of Washington rendered itself amenable to proceedings in the courts of that state to recover unpaid contributions to the state unemployment compensation fund exacted by state statutes, Washington Unemployment Compensation Act, Washington Revised Statutes, § 9998-103a through § 9998-123a, 1941 Supp., and (2) whether the state can exact those contributions consistently with the due process clause of the Fourteenth Amendment.

. . . .

The facts as found by the appeal tribunal and accepted by the state Superior Court and Supreme Court, are not in dispute. Appellant is a Delaware corporation, having its principal place of business in St. Louis, Missouri, and is engaged in the manufacture and sale of shoes and other footwear. It maintains places of business in several states, other than Washington, at which its manufacturing is carried on and from which its merchandise is distributed interstate through several sales units or branches located outside the State of Washington.

Appellant has no office in Washington and makes no contracts either for sale or purchase of merchandise there. It maintains no stock of merchandise in that state and makes there no deliveries of goods in intrastate commerce. During the years from 1937 to 1940, now in question, appellant employed eleven to thirteen salesmen under direct supervision and control of sales managers located in St. Louis. These salesmen resided in Washington; their principal activities were confined to that state; and they were compensated by commissions based upon the amount of their sales. The commissions for each year totaled more than $31,000. Appellant supplies its salesmen with a line of samples, each consisting of one shoe of a pair, which they display to prospective purchasers. On occasion they rent permanent sample rooms, for exhibiting samples, in business buildings, or rent rooms in hotels or business buildings temporarily for that purpose. The cost of such rentals is reimbursed by appellant.

The authority of the salesmen is limited to exhibiting their samples and soliciting orders from prospective buyers, at prices and on terms fixed by appellant. The salesmen transmit the orders to appellant's office in St. Louis for acceptance or rejection, and when accepted the merchandise for filling the orders is shipped f.o.b. from points outside Washington to the purchasers within the state. All the merchandise shipped into Washington is invoiced at the place of shipment from which collections are made. No salesman has authority to enter into contracts or to make collections.

The Supreme Court of Washington was of opinion that the regular and systematic solicitation of orders in the state by appellant's salesmen, resulting in a continuous flow of appellant's product into the state, was sufficient to constitute doing business in the state so as to make appellant amenable to suit in its courts. But it was also of opinion that there were sufficient additional activities shown to bring the case within the rule frequently stated, that solicitation within a state by the agents of a foreign corporation plus some additional activities there are sufficient to render the corporation amenable to suit brought in the courts of the state to enforce an obligation arising out of its activities there . . . . The court found such additional activities in the salesmen's display of samples sometimes in permanent display rooms, and the salesmen's residence within the state, continued over a period of years, all resulting in a substantial volume of merchandise regularly shipped by appellant to purchasers within the state. The court also held that the statute as applied did not invade the constitutional power of Congress to regulate interstate commerce and did not impose a prohibited burden on such commerce.

Appellant's argument, renewed here, that the statute imposes an unconstitutional burden on interstate commerce need not detain us. For 53 Stat. 1391, 26 U.S.C. § 1606(a) provides that "No person required under a State law to make payments to an unemployment fund shall be relieved from compliance therewith on the ground that he is engaged in interstate or foreign commerce, or that the State law does to distinguish between employees engaged in interstate or foreign commerce and those engaged in intrastate commerce." It is no longer debatable that Congress, in the exercise of the commerce power, may authorize the states, in specified ways, to regulate interstate commerce or impose burdens upon it. . . .

Appellant also insists that its activities within the state were not sufficient to manifest its "presence" there and that in its absence the state courts were without jurisdiction, that consequently it was a denial of due process for the state to subject appellant to suit. It refers to those cases in which it was said that the mere solicitation of orders for the purchase of goods within a state, to be accepted without the state and filled by shipment of the purchased goods interstate, does not render the corporation seller amendable to suit within the state. . . . And appellant further argues that since it was not present within the state, it is a denial of due process to subject it to taxation or other money exaction. It thus denies the power of the state to lay the tax or to subject appellant to a suit for its collection.

Historically the jurisdiction of courts to render judgment *in personam* is grounded on their de facto power over the defendant's person. Hence his presence within the territorial jurisdiction of a court was prerequisite to its rendition of a judgment personally binding him. *Pennoyer v. Neff*, 95 U.S. 714, 733. But now that the *capias ad respondendum* has given way to personal service of summons or other form of notice, due process requires only that in order to subject a defendant to a judgment *in personam*, if he be not present within the territory of the forum, he have certain minimum contacts with it such that the maintenance of the suit does not offend "traditional notions of fair play and substantial justice." *Milliken v. Meyer*, 311 U.S. 457, 463. . . .

Since the corporate personality is a fiction, although a fiction intended to be acted upon as though it were a fact, *Klein v. Board of Supervisors*, 282 U.S. 19, 24, it is clear that unlike an individual its "presence" without, as well as within, the state of its origin can be manifested only by activities carried on in its behalf by those who are authorized to act for it. To say that the corporation is so far "present" there as to satisfy due process requirements, for purposes of taxation or the maintenance of suits against it in the courts of the state, is to beg the question to be decided. For the terms "present" or "presence" are used merely to symbolize those activities of the corporation's agent within the state which courts will deem to be sufficient to satisfy the demands of due process. L. Hand, J., in *Hutchinson v. Chase & Gilbert*, 45 F.2d 139, 141. Those demands may be met by such contacts of the corporation with the state of the forum as make it reasonable, in the context of our federal system of government, to require the corporation to defend the particular suit which is brought there. An "estimate of the inconveniences" which would result to the corporation from a trial away from its "home" or principal place of business is relevant in this connection. *Hutchinson v. Chase & Gilbert*, *supra*, 141.

"Presence" in the state in this sense has never been doubted when the activities of the corporation there have not only been continuous and systematic, but also give rise to the liabilities sued on, even though no consent to be sued or authorization to an agent to accept service of process has been given . . . . Conversely it has been generally recognized that the casual presence of the corporate agent or even his conduct of single or isolated items of activities in a state in the corporation's behalf are not enough to subject it to suit on causes of action unconnected with the activities there . . . . To require the corporation in such circumstances to defend the suit away from its home or other jurisdiction where it carries on more substantial activities has been thought to lay too great and unreasonable a burden on the corporation to comport with due process.

While it has been held, in cases on which appellant relies, that continuous activity of some sorts within a state is not enough to support the demand that the corporation be amenable to suits unrelated to that activity . . . there have been instances in which the continuous corporate operations within a state were thought so substantial and of such a nature as to justify suit against it on causes of action arising from dealings entirely distinct from those activities . . . .

Finally, although the commission of some single or occasional acts of the corporate agent in a state sufficient to impose an obligation or liability on the corporation has not been thought to confer upon the state authority to enforce it, *Rosenberg Bros. & Co. v. Curtis Brown Co.*, 260 U.S. 516, other such acts, because of their nature and quality and the circumstances of their commission, may be deemed sufficient to render the corporation liable to suit. . . . True, some of the decisions holding the corporation amenable to suit have been supported by resort to the legal fiction that it has given its consent to service and suit, consent being implied from its presence in the state through the acts of its authorized agents. . . . But more realistically it may be said that those authorized acts were of such a nature as to justify the fiction. . . .

It is evident that the criteria by which we mark the boundary line between those activities which justify the subjection of a corporation to suit, and those which do not, cannot be simply mechanical or quantitative. The test is not merely, as has sometimes been suggested, whether the activity, which the corporation has seen fit to procure through its agents in another state, is a little more or a little less. . . . Whether due process is satisfied must depend rather upon the quality and nature of the activity in relation to the fair and orderly administration of the laws which it was the purpose of the due process clause to insure. That clause does not contemplate that a state may make binding a judgment *in personam* against an individual or corporate defendant with which the state has no contacts, ties, or relations . . . .

But to the extent that a corporation exercises the privilege of conducting activities within a state, it enjoys the benefits and protection of the laws of that state. The exercise of that privilege may give rise to obligations, and, so far as those obligations arise out of or are connected with the activities within the state, a procedure which requires the corporation to respond to a suit brought to enforce them can, in most instances, hardly be said to be undue. . . .

Applying these standards, the activities carried on in behalf of appellant in the State of Washington were neither irregular nor casual. They were systematic and continuous throughout the years in question. They resulted in a large volume of interstate business, in the course of which appellant received the benefits and protection of the laws of the state, including the right to resort to the courts for the enforcement of its rights. The obligation which is here sued upon arose out of those very activities. It is evident that these operations establish sufficient contacts or ties with the state of the forum to make it reasonable and just, according to our traditional conception of fair play and substantial justice, to permit the state to enforce the obligations which appellant has incurred there. Hence we cannot say that the maintenance of the present suit in the State of Washington involves an unreasonable or undue procedure.

We are likewise unable to conclude that the service of the process within the state upon an agent whose activities establish appellant's "presence" there was not sufficient notice of the suit, or that the suit was so unrelated to those activities as to make the agent an inappropriate vehicle for communicating the notice. It is enough that appellant has established such contacts with the state that the particular form of substituted service adopted there gives reasonable assurance that the notice will be actual. . . . Nor can we say that the mailing of the notice of suit to appellant by registered mail at its home office was not reasonably calculated to apprise appellant of the suit. . . .

.     .     .

Appellant having rendered itself amenable to suit upon obligations arising out of the activities of its salesmen in Washington, the state may maintain the present suit *in personam* to collect the tax laid upon the exercise of the privilege of employing appellant's salesmen within the state. For Washington has made one of those activities, which taken together establish appellant's "presence" there for purposes of suit, the taxable event by which the state brings appellant within the reach of its taxing power. The state thus has constitutional power to lay the tax and to subject appellant to a suit to recover it. The activities which establish its "presence" subject it alike to taxation by the state and to suit to recover the tax. . . .

### Notes and Questions

1. *International Shoe*, particularly as illuminated in some of the subsequent cases considered below, provides criteria for determining whether a state within the United States federal union can assert jurisdiction over persons, things or events that are simultaneously or sequentially subject to jurisdictional claims of other states. But does it provide criteria for determining whether one foreign jurisdiction or another should exercise jurisdiction? Assuming that the notion of "due process" is not

idiosyncratically American but has cognates in other systems, does *International Shoe* really instruct a court as to which jurisdiction is entitled to exercise jurisdiction? Affirmatively, the Supreme Court said, "Whether due process is satisfied must depend rather upon the quality and nature of the activity in relation to the fair and orderly administration of the laws which it was the purpose of the due process clause to ensure." Negatively, the Court says only that a state may not make a binding judgment *in personam* if it has "no contacts, ties, or relations with the defendant." This appears to be a formula consistent with a theory of concurrent jurisdiction, in which many fora could claim jurisdiction over the same persons, things or events. Hence, the pressure for a "race to the courthouse" in international disputes is not substantially lessened by the *International Shoe* standard.

    2. *International Shoe* establishes jurisdiction by reference to contacts that "were neither irregular nor casual." Suppose that the activity for which jurisdiction was sought was "irregular" but had great and foreseeable effects on the forum: could the exercise of jurisdiction be justified by *International Shoe*?

    B.      *Shaffer v. Heitner*, 433 U.S. 186 (1976).

    [Shareholders in the Greyhound Corp., a Delaware company, brought a derivative suit against the non-resident directors of the corporation. The Delaware court assumed jurisdiction under a state statute which made Delaware the situs of the intangible stock interest and allowed in rem actions to be brought against non-resident directors who had no other connection with the state. The Supreme Court of Delaware affirmed the assertion of jurisdiction.]

                            .       .       .           .

    The case for applying to jurisdiction *in rem* the same test of "fair play and substantial justice" as governs assertions of jurisdiction *in personam* is simple and straightforward. It is premised on recognition that "[t]he phrase, 'judicial jurisdiction over a thing,' is a customary elliptical way of referring to jurisdiction over the interests of persons in a thing." Restatement (Second) of Conflict of Laws §56, Introductory Note (1971) (hereafter Restatement). This recognition leads to the conclusion that in order to justify an exercise of jurisdiction *in rem*, the basis for jurisdiction must be sufficient to justify exercising "jurisdiction over the interests of persons in a thing." The standard for determining whether an exercise of jurisdiction over the interests of persons is consistent with the Due Process Clause is the minimum-contacts standard elucidated in *International Shoe*.

This argument, of course, does not ignore the fact that the presence of property in a State may bear on the existence of jurisdiction by providing contacts among the forum State, the defendant, and the litigation. For example, when claims to the property itself are the source of the underlying controversy between the plaintiff and the defendant, it would be unusual for the State where the property is located not to have jurisdiction. In such cases, the defendant's claim to property located in the State would normally indicate that he expected to benefit from the State's protection of his interest. The State's strong interests in assuring the marketability of property within its borders and in providing a procedure for peaceful resolution of disputes about the possession of that property would also support jurisdiction, as would the likelihood that important records and witnesses will be found in the State. The presence of property may also favor jurisdiction in cases, such as suits for injury suffered on the land of an absentee owner, where the defendant's ownership of the property is conceded but the cause of action is otherwise related to rights and duties growing out of that ownership.

It appears, therefore, that jurisdiction over many types of actions which now are or might be brought *in rem* would not be affected by a holding that any assertion of state-court jurisdiction must satisfy the *International Shoe* standard. For the type of *quasi in rem* action typified by *Harris v. Balk* and the present case, however, accepting the proposed analysis would result in significant change. These are cases where the property which now serves as the basis for state-court jurisdiction is completely unrelated to the plaintiff's cause of action. Thus, although the presence of the defendant's property in a State might suggest the existence of other ties among the defendant, the State, and the litigation, the presence of the property alone would not support the State's jurisdiction. If those other ties did not exist, cases over which the State is now thought to have jurisdiction could not be brought in that forum.

Since acceptance of the *International Shoe* test would most affect this class of cases, we examine the arguments against adopting that standard as they relate to this category of litigation. Before doing so, however, we note that this type of case also presents the clearest illustration of the argument in favor of assessing assertions of jurisdiction by a single standard. For in cases such as *Harris* and this one, the only role played by the property is to provide the basis for bringing the defendant into court. Indeed, the express purpose of the Delaware sequestration procedure is to compel the defendant to enter a personal appearance. In such cases, if a direct assertion of personal jurisdiction over the defendant would violate the Constitution, it would seem that an indirect assertion of that jurisdiction should be equally impermissible.

The primary rationale for treating the presence of property as a sufficient basis for jurisdiction to adjudicate claims over which the State would not have jurisdiction if *International Shoe* applied is that a wrongdoer

> "should not be able to avoid payment of his obligations
> by the expedient of removing his assets to a place where
> he is not subject to an in personam suit." Restatement §
> 66, Comment a.

. . . This justification, however, does not explain why jurisdiction should be recognized without regard to whether the property is present in the State because of an effort to avoid the owner's obligations. Nor does it support jurisdiction to adjudicate the underlying claim. At most, it suggests that a State in which property is located should have jurisdiction to attach that property, by use of proper procedures, as security for a judgment being sought in a forum where the litigation can be maintained consistently with *International Shoe*. . . . Moreover, we know of nothing to justify the assumption that a debtor can avoid paying his obligations by removing his property to a State in which his creditor cannot obtain personal jurisdiction over him. The Full Faith and Credit Clause, after all, makes the valid *in personam* judgment of one State enforceable in all other States.

It might also be suggested that allowing *in rem* jurisdiction avoids the uncertainty inherent in the *International Shoe* standard and assures a plaintiff of a forum. . . . We believe, however, that the fairness standard of *International Shoe* can be easily applied in the vast majority of cases. Moreover, when the existence of jurisdiction in a particular forum under *International Shoe* is unclear, the cost of simplifying the litigation by avoiding the jurisdictional question may be the sacrifice of "fair play and substantial justice." That cost is too high.

We are left, then, to consider the significance of the long history of jurisdiction based solely on the presence of property in a State. Although the theory that territorial power is both essential to and sufficient for jurisdiction has been undermined, we have never held that the presence of property in a State does not automatically confer jurisdiction over the owner's interest in that property. This history must be considered as supporting the proposition that jurisdiction based solely on the presence of property satisfies the demands of due process, cf. *Ownbey v. Morgan*, 256 U.S. 94, 111 (1921), but it is not decisive. "[T]raditional notions of fair play and substantial justice" can be as readily offended by the perpetuation of ancient forms that are no longer justified as by the adoption of new procedures that are inconsistent with the basic values of our constitutional heritage. Cf. *Sniadach v. Family Finance Corp.*, 395 U.S., at 340; *Wolf v. Colorado*, 338 U.S. 25, 27 (1949). The fiction that an assertion of jurisdiction over property is anything but an assertion of jurisdiction over the owner of the property supports an ancient form without substantial modern justification. Its continued acceptance would serve only to allow state-court jurisdiction that is fundamentally unfair to the defendant.

We therefore conclude that all assertions of state-court jurisdiction must be evaluated according to the standards set forth in *International Shoe* and its progeny.

### Notes and Questions

1. The holding in *Shaffer*, by expanding the general application of *International Shoe*, makes it even more difficult to find clear guidelines concerning the boundaries of international jurisdiction. In *Shaffer*, the Court eliminates the heretofore exclusivity of jurisdiction based on the location of property within a territory. In a national system, presided over by a Supreme Court of compulsory jurisdiction, the resulting concurrent jurisdictional theory that emerges can be controlled. Can it be controlled in a coarchical international system in which there is no such presiding court? Discuss.

2. In *Shaffer*, the Court makes the ultimate determination of assertions of jurisdiction by one state over another turn on "the basic values of our constitutional heritage." Are these values sufficiently precise to be presented, in some codified form, to foreign jurisdictions for their acceptance? Or are they essentially open-ended, determined on a case-by-case basis by the Supreme Court itself? Are the "basic values of our constitutional heritage" shared by other states? Discuss.

C.       *Asahi Metal Industry Co., Ltd. v. Superior Court of California, Solano County*, 480 U.S. 102 (1987).

[An American was injured and his wife killed in a motorcycle accident in California, allegedly caused by the failure of a defective tire made in Taiwan and incorporating some components from Japan. Suit was based on California's long-arm statute which authorizes jurisdiction "on any basis not inconsistent with the Constitution of this State or of the United States." The Taiwanese manufacturer settled with the American claimant and then continued the suit, now for indemnity, against Asahi, the Japanese manufacturer. Though Asahi's sales to the Taiwanese manufacturer were less than two percent of its total volume in 1981 and less than one-half of one percent of its volume in 1982, the first instance court confirmed jurisdiction: "Asahi obviously does business on an international scale. It is not unreasonable that they defend claims of defect in their product on an international scale." Jurisdiction was quashed by the Court of Appeals of California on the ground that "it would be unreasonable to require Asahi to respond in California solely on the basis of ultimately realized foreseeability that the product into which its component was embodied would be sold all over the world including California." The California Supreme Court reversed and confirmed jurisdiction essentially on the ground that Asahi's intentional act of putting its components into the stream of commerce via Taiwan, and its awareness that some of its products would be sold in California, fulfilled constitutional due process requirements for the exercise of state jurisdiction.]

.     .     .

The Due Process Clause of the Fourteenth Amendment limits the power of a state court to exert personal jurisdiction over a nonresident defendant. "[T]he constitutional touchstone" of the determination whether an exercise of personal jurisdiction comports with due process "remains whether the defendant purposefully established 'minimum contacts' in the forum State." *Burger King Corp. v. Rudzewicz*, 471 U.S. 462, 474 (1985), quoting *International Shoe Co. v. Washington*, 326 U.S. at 316. Most recently we have reaffirmed the oft-quoted reasoning of *Hanson v. Denckla*, 357 U.S. 235, 253 (1958), that minimum contacts must have a basis in "some act by which the defendant purposefully avails itself of the privilege of conducting activities within the forum State, thus invoking the benefits and protections of its laws." *Burger King*, 471 U.S., at 475.

"Jurisdiction is proper . . . where the contacts proximately result from actions by the defendant himself that create a 'substantial connection' with the forum State." *Ibid.*, quoting *McGee v. International Life Insurance Co.*, 355 U.S. 220, 223 (1957) (emphasis in original).

Applying the principle that minimum contacts must be based on an act of the defendant, the Court in *World-Wide Volkswagen Corp. v. Woodson*, 444 U.S. 286 (1980), rejected the assertion that a consumer's unilateral act of bringing the defendant's product into the forum State was a sufficient constitutional basis for personal jurisdiction over the defendant. It had been argued in *World-Wide Volkswagen* that because an automobile retailer and its wholesale distributor sold a product mobile by design and purpose, they could foresee being haled into court in the distant States into which their customers might drive. The Court rejected this concept of foreseeability as an insufficient basis for jurisdiction under the Due Process Clause. *Id.*, at 295-296. The Court disclaimed, however, the idea that "foreseeability is wholly irrelevant" to personal jurisdiction, concluding that "[t]he forum state does not exceed its powers under the Due Process Clause if it asserts personal jurisdiction over a corporation that delivers its products into the stream of commerce with the expectation that they will be purchased by consumers in the forum State." *Id.*, at 297-298 (citation omitted). The Court reasoned:

> "When a corporation 'purposefully avails itself of the privilege of conducting activities within the forum State,' *Hanson v. Denckla*, 357 U.S. [235,] 253 [(1958)], it has clear notice that it is subject to suit there, and can act to alleviate the risk of burdensome litigation by procuring insurance, passing the expected costs on to customers, or, if the risks are too great, severing its connection with the State. Hence if the sale of a product of a manufacturer or distributor . . . is not simply an isolated occurrence, but arises from the efforts of the manufacturer or distributor to serve, directly or indirectly, the market for its product in other States, it is not unreasonable to subject it to suit in one of those States if its allegedly defective merchandise has there been the source of injury to its owners or to others." *Id.*, at 297.

In *World-Wide Volkswagen* itself, the state court sought to base jurisdiction not on any act of the defendant, but on the foreseeable unilateral actions of the consumer. Since *World-Wide Volkswagen*, lower courts have been confronted with cases in which the defendant acted by placing a product in the stream of commerce, and the stream eventually swept defendant's product into the forum State, but the defendant did nothing else to purposefully avail itself of the market in the forum State. Some courts have understood the Due Process Clause, as interpreted in *World-Wide Volkswagen*, to allow an exercise of personal jurisdiction to be based on no more than the defendant's act of placing the product in the stream of commerce. Other courts have understood the Due Process Clause and the above-quoted language in *World-Wide Volkswagen* to require the action of the defendant to be more purposefully directed at the forum State than the mere act of placing a product in the stream of commerce.

The reasoning of the Supreme Court of California in the present case illustrates the former interpretation of *World-Wide Volkswagen*. The Supreme Court of California held that, because the stream of commerce eventually brought some valves Asahi sold Cheng Shin into California, Asahi's awareness that its valves would be sold in California was sufficient to permit California to exercise jurisdiction over Asahi consistent with the requirements of the Due Process Clause. The Supreme Court of California's position was consistent with those courts that have held that mere foreseeability or awareness was a constitutionally sufficient basis for personal jurisdiction if the defendant's product made its way into the forum State while still in the stream of commerce. . . .

Other courts, however, have understood the Due Process Clause to require something more than that the defendant was aware of its product's entry into the forum State through the stream of commerce in order for the State to exert jurisdiction over the defendant. In the present case, for example, the State Court of Appeal did not read the Due Process Clause, as interpreted by *World-Wide Volkswagen*, to allow "mere foreseeability that the product will enter the forum state [to] be enough by itself to establish jurisdiction over the distributor and retailer." App. to Pet. for Cert. B5. In *Humble v. Toyota Motor Co.*, 727 F.2d 709 (CA8 1984), an injured car passenger brought suit against Arakawa Auto Body Company, a Japanese corporation that manufactured car seats for Toyota. Arakawa did no business in the United States; it had no office, affiliate, subsidiary, or agent in the

United States; it manufactured its component parts outside the United States and delivered them to Toyota Motor Company in Japan. The Court of Appeals, adopting the reasoning of the District Court in that case, noted that although it "does not doubt that Arakawa could have foreseen that its product would find its way into the United States," it would be "manifestly unjust" to require Arakawa to defend itself in the United States. *Id.*, at 710-711, quoting 578 F.Supp. 530, 533 (ND Iowa 1982). See also *Hutson v. Fehr Bros., Inc.*, 584 F.2d 833 (CA8 1978); see generally *Max Daetwyler Corp. v. R. Meyer*, 762 F.2d 290, 299 (CA3 1985) (collecting "stream of commerce" cases in which the "manufacturers involved had made deliberate decisions to market their products in the forum state").

We now find this latter position to be consonant with the requirements of due process. The "substantial connection," *Burger King*, 471 U.S., at 475; *McGee*, 355 U.S., at 223, between the defendant and the forum State necessary for a finding of minimum contacts must come about by *an action of the defendant purposefully directed toward the forum State. Burger King, supra*, at 476; *Keeton v. Hustler Magazine, Inc.*, 465 U.S. 770, 774 (1984). The placement of a product into the stream of commerce, without more, is not an act of the defendant purposefully directed toward the forum State. Additional conduct of the defendant may indicate an intent or purpose to serve the market in the forum State, for example, designing the product for the market in the forum State, advertising in the forum State, establishing channels for providing regular advice to customers in the forum State, or marketing the product through a distributor who has agreed to serve as the sales agent in the forum State. But a defendant's awareness that the stream of commerce may or will sweep the product into the forum State does not convert the mere act of placing the product into the stream into an act purposefully directed toward the forum State.

Assuming, *arguendo*, that respondents have established Asahi's awareness that some of the valves sold to Cheng Shin would be incorporated into tire tubes sold in California, respondents have not demonstrated any action by Asahi to purposefully avail itself of the California market. Asahi does not do business in California. It has no office, agents, employee, or property in California. It does not advertise or otherwise solicit business in California. It did not create, control, or employ the distribution system that brought its valves to

California. Cf. *Hicks v. Kawasaki Heavy Industries*, 452 F.Supp. 130 (MD Pa. 1978). There is no evidence that Asahi designed its product in anticipation of sales in California. Cf. *Rockwell International Corp. v. Costruzioni Aeronautiche Giovanni Agusta*, 553 F.Supp. 328 (ED Pa. 1982). On the basis of these facts, the exertion of personal jurisdiction over Asahi by the Superior Court of California exceeds the limits of due process.

B

The strictures of the Due Process Clause forbid a state court from exercising personal jurisdiction over Asahi under circumstances that would offend "'traditional notions of fair play and substantial justice.'" *International Shoe Co. v. Washington*, 326 U.S., at 316, quoting *Milliken v. Meyer*, 311 U.S., at 463.

We have previously explained that the determination of the reasonableness of the exercise of jurisdiction in each case will depend on an evaluation of several factors. A court must consider the burden on the defendant, the interests of the forum State, and the plaintiff's interest in obtaining relief. It must also weigh in its determination "the interstate judicial system's interest in obtaining the most efficient resolution of controversies; and the shared interest of the several States in furthering fundamental substantive social policies." *World-Wide Volkswagen*, 444 U.S., at 292 (citations omitted).

A consideration of these factors in the present case clearly reveals the unreasonableness of the assertion of jurisdiction over Asahi, even apart from the question of the placement of goods in the stream of commerce.

Certainly the burden on the defendant in this case is severe. Asahi has been commanded by the Supreme Court of California not only to traverse the distance between Asahi's headquarters in Japan and the Superior Court of California in and for the County of Solano, but also to submit its dispute with Cheng Shin to a foreign nation's judicial system. The unique burdens placed upon one who must defend oneself in a foreign legal system should have significant weight in assessing the reasonableness of stretching the long arm of personal jurisdiction over national borders.

When minimum contacts have been established, often the interests of the plaintiff and the forum in the exercise of jurisdiction will justify even the serious burdens placed on the alien defendant. In the present case, however, the interests of the plaintiff and the forum in California's assertion of jurisdiction over Asahi are slight. All that remains is a claim for indemnification asserted by Cheng Shin, a Taiwanese corporation, against Asahi. The transaction on which the indemnification claim is based took place in Taiwan; Asahi's components were shipped from Japan to Taiwan. Cheng Shin has not demonstrated that it is more convenient for it to litigate its indemnification claim against Asahi in California rather than in Taiwan or Japan.

Because the plaintiff is not a California resident, California's legitimate interests in the dispute have considerably diminished. The Supreme Court of California argued that the State had an interest in "protecting its consumers by ensuring that foreign manufacturers comply with the state's safety standards." 39 Cal. 3d, at 49, 702 P.2d, at 550. The State Supreme Court's definition of California's interest, however, was overly broad. The dispute between Cheng Shin and Asahi is primarily about indemnification rather than safety standards. Moreover, it is not at all clear at this point that California law should govern the question whether a Japanese corporation should indemnify a Taiwanese corporation on the basis of a sale made in Taiwan and a shipment of goods from Japan to Taiwan. *Phillips Petroleum v. Shutts*, 472 U.S. 797, 821-22 (1985); *Allstate Insurance Co. v. Hague*, 449 U.S. 302, 312-13 (1981). The possibility of being haled into a California court as a result of an accident involving Asahi's components undoubtedly creates an additional deterrent to the manufacture of unsafe components; however, similar pressures will be placed on Asahi by the purchasers of its components as long as those who use Asahi components in their final products, and sell those products in California, are subject to the application of California tort law.

*World-Wide Volkswagen* also admonished courts to take into consideration the interests of the "several States," in addition to the forum State, in the efficient judicial resolution of the dispute and the advancement of substantive policies. In the present case, this advice calls for a court to consider the procedural and substantive policies of other <u>nations</u> whose interests are affected by the assertion of jurisdiction by the California court. The procedural and substantive interests of other nations in a state court's assertion of jurisdiction over an alien defendant will differ from case to case. In every case, however, those interests, as well as the Federal Government's interest in its foreign relations policies, will be best served by a careful inquiry into the reasonableness of the assertion of jurisdiction in the particular case, and an unwillingness to find the serious burdens on an alien defendant outweighed by minimal interests on the part of the plaintiff or the forum State. "Great care and reserve should be exercised when extending our notions of personal jurisdiction into the international field." *United States v. First National City Bank*, 379 U.S. 378, 404 (1965) (Harlan, J., dissenting). See Born, *Reflections on Judicial Jurisdiction in International Cases*, to be published in 17 Ga. J. Int'l & Comp. L. 1 (1987).

Considering the international context, the heavy burden on the alien defendant, and the slight interests of the plaintiff and the forum State, the exercise of personal jurisdiction by a California court over Asahi in this instance would be unreasonable and unfair.

.    .    .

[Justices Brennan, White, Marshall, Blackmun and Stevens concurred in the Judgment and in parts of the reasoning.]

#### Notes and Questions

1. *Asahi* concerned a suit between a Taiwanese company and a Japanese company for indemnification. The Court states: "Because the plaintiff is not a California resident, California's legitimate interests in the dispute have considerably diminished." If the case had been between *Asahi* and the injured American plaintiff, would the reasoning of the Court have applied and jurisdiction also been rejected? (See the selection from "Restatement Third," *supra* p. 6.) If not, does *Asahi* really provide instruction as to U.S. attitudes toward judicial jurisdiction when the plaintiff is American?

2. Assume, in this regard, that the plaintiff in *Asahi* was a resident of Washington state, where the injury took place. Do you think the Court would have been disposed to allow California to exercise jurisdiction?

D.    *Helicopteros Nacionales de Colombia, S.A. v. Hall*, 466
      U.S. 408 (1984).

JUSTICE BLACKMUN delivered the opinion of the Court.

.    .    .

Petitioner Helicopteros Nacionales de Colombia, S.A. (Helicol),
is a Colombian corporation with its principal place of business in the
city of Bogota in that country. It is engaged in the business of
providing helicopter transportation for oil and construction companies
in South America. On January 26, 1976, a helicopter owned by Helicol
crashed in Peru. Four United States citizens were among those who lost
their lives in the accident. Respondents are the survivors and
representatives of the four decedents.

At the time of the crash, respondents' decedents were employed
by Consorcio, a Peruvian consortium, and were working on a pipeline
in Peru. Consorcio is the alter ego of a joint venture named Williams-
Sedco-Horn (WSH). The venture had its headquarters in Houston, Tex.
Consorcio had been formed to enable the venturers to enter into a
contract with Petro Peru, the Peruvian state-owned oil company.
Consorcio was to construct a pipeline for Petro Peru running from the
interior of Peru westward to the Pacific Ocean. Peruvian law forbade
construction of the pipeline by any non-Peruvian entity.

Consorcio/WSH needed helicopters to move personnel,
materials and equipment into and out of the construction area. In 1974,
upon request of Consorcio/WSH, the chief executive officer of Helicol,
Francisco Restrepo, flew to the United States and conferred in Houston
with representatives of the three joint venturers. At that meeting, there
was a discussion of prices, availability, working conditions, fuel,
supplies, and housing. Restrepo represented that Helicol could have the
first helicopter on the job in 15 days. The Consorcio/WSH
representatives decided to accept the contract proposed by Restrepo.
Helicol began performing before the agreement was formally signed in
Peru on November 11, 1974. The contract was written in Spanish on
official government stationery and provided that the residence of all the
parties would be Lima, Peru. It further stated that controversies arising
out of the contract would be submitted to the jurisdiction of Peruvian
courts. In addition, it provided that Consorcio/WSH would make

payments to Helicol's account with the Bank of America in New York City. App. 12a.

Aside from the negotiation session in Houston between Restrepo and the representatives of Consorcio/WSH, Helicol had other contacts with Texas. During the years 1970-1977, it purchased helicopters (approximately 80% of its fleet), spare parts, and accessories for more than $4 million from Bell Helicopter Company in Fort Worth. In that period, Helicol sent prospective pilots to Fort Worth for training and to ferry the aircraft to South America. It also sent management and maintenance personnel to visit Bell Helicopter in Fort Worth during the same period in order to receive "plant familiarization" and for technical consultation. Helicol received into its New York City and Panama City, Fla., bank accounts over $5 million in payments from Consorcio/WSH drawn upon First City National Bank of Houston.

Beyond the foregoing, there have been no other business contacts between Helicol and the State of Texas. Helicol never has been authorized to do business in Texas and never has had an agent for the service of process within the State. It never has performed helicopter operations in Texas or sold any product that reached Texas, never solicited business in Texas, never signed any contract in Texas, never had any employee based there, and never recruited an employee in Texas. In addition, Helicol never has owned real or personal property in Texas and never has maintained an office or establishment there. Helicol has maintained no records in Texas and has no shareholders in that State.[2] None of the respondents or their decedents were domiciled in Texas, Tr. of Oral Arg. 17, 18,[3] but all of the decedents were hired in Houston by Consorcio/WSH to work on the Petro Peru pipeline project.

---

[2] [4] The Colombian national airline, Aerovias Nacionales de Colombia, owns approximately 94% of Helicol's capital stock. The remainder is held by Aerovias Corporation de Viajes and four South American individuals. . . .

[3] [5] Respondents' lack of residential or other contacts with Texas of itself does not defeat otherwise proper jurisdiction. *Keeton v. Hustler Magazine, Inc.*, 465 U.S. 770, 780 (1984); *Calder v. Jones*, 465 U.S. 783, 788 (1984). We mention respondents' lack of contacts merely to show that nothing in the nature of the relationship between respondents and Helicol could possibly enhance Helicol's contacts with Texas. The harm suffered by respondents did not occur in Texas. Nor is it alleged that any negligence on the part of Helicol took place in Texas.

Respondents instituted wrongful-death actions in the District Court of Harris County, Tex., against Consorcio/WSH, Bell Helicopter Company, and Helicol. Helicol filed special appearances and moved to dismiss the actions for lack of *in personam* jurisdiction over it. The motion was denied. After a consolidated jury trial, judgment was entered against Helicol on a jury verdict of $1,141,200 in favor of respondents.

[On appeal, the only question was whether it was consistent with the Due Process Clause for the Texas courts to assert *in personam* jurisdiction over Helicol.]

The Due Process Clause of the Fourteenth Amendment operates to limit the power of a State to assert *in personam* jurisdiction over a nonresident defendant. *Pennoyer v. Neff*, 95 U.S. 714 (1878). Due process requirements are satisfied when *in personam* jurisdiction is asserted over a nonresident corporate defendant that has "certain minimum contacts with [the forum] such that the maintenance of the suit does not offend 'traditional notions of fair play and substantial justice.'" *International Shoe Co. v. Washington*, 326 U.S. 310, 316 (1945), quoting *Milliken v. Meyer*, 311 U.S. 457, 463 (1940). When a controversy is related to or "arises out of" a defendant's contacts with the forum, the Court has said that a "relationship among the defendant, the forum, and the litigation" is the essential foundation of *in personam* jurisdiction. *Shaffer v. Heitner*, 433 U.S. 186, 204 (1977).[4]

Even when the cause of action does not arise out of or relate to the foreign corporation's activities in the forum State,[5] due process is

---

[4] [8] It has been said that when a State exercises personal jurisdiction over a defendant in a suit arising out of or related to the defendant's contacts with the forum, the State is exercising "specific jurisdiction" over the defendant. *See* Von Mehren & Trautman, Jurisdiction to Adjudicate: A Suggested Analysis, 79 Harv. L. Rev. 1121, 1144-64 (1966).

[5] [9] When a State exercises personal jurisdiction over a defendant in a suit not arising out of or related to the defendant's contacts with the forum, the State has been said to be exercising "general jurisdiction" over the defendant. *See* Brilmayer, How Contacts Count: Due Process Limitations on State Court Jurisdiction, 1980 S. Ct. Rev. 77, 80-81; Von Mehren & Trautman, *supra* note 8, at 1136-44; *Calder v. Jones*, 465 U.S., at 786.

not offended by a State's subjecting the corporation to its *in personam* jurisdiction when there are sufficient contacts between the State and the foreign corporation. *Perkins v. Benguet Consolidated Mining Co.*, 342 U.S. 437 (1952); see *Keeton v. Hustler Magazine, Inc.*, 465 U.S. 770, 779-780 (1984). In *Perkins*, the Court addressed a situation in which state courts had asserted general jurisdiction over a defendant foreign corporation. During the Japanese occupation of the Philippine Islands, the president and general manager of a Philippine mining corporation maintained an office in Ohio from which he conducted activities on behalf of the company. He kept company files and held directors' meetings in the office, carried on correspondence relating to the business, distributed salary checks drawn on two active Ohio bank accounts, engaged an Ohio bank to act as transfer agent, and supervised policies dealing with the rehabilitation of the corporation's properties in the Philippines. In short, the foreign corporation, through its president, "ha[d] been carrying on in Ohio a continuous and systematic, but limited, part of its general business," and the exercise of general jurisdiction over the Philippine corporation by an Ohio court was "reasonable and just." 342 U.S., at 438, 445.

All parties to the present case concede that respondents' claims against Helicol did not "arise out of," and are not related to, Helicol's activities within Texas.[6] We thus must explore the nature of Helicol's

---

[6] [10] See Brief for Respondents 14; Tr. of Oral Arg. 26-27, 30-31. Because the parties have not argued any relationship between the cause of action and Helicol's contacts with the State of Texas, we, contrary to the dissent's implication, *post*, at 419-40, assert no "view" with respect to that issue.

The dissent suggests that we have erred in drawing no distinction between controversies that "relate to" a defendant's contacts with a forum and those that "arise out of" such contacts. *Post*, at 420. This criticism is somewhat puzzling, for the dissent goes on to urge that, for purposes of determining the constitutional validity of an assertion of specific jurisdiction, there really should be no distinction between the two. *Post*, at 427-428.

We do not address the validity or consequences of such a distinction because the issue has not been presented in this case. Respondents have made no argument that their cause of action either arose out of or is related to Helicol's contacts with the State of Texas. Absent any briefing on the issue, we decline to reach the questions (1) whether the terms "arising out of" and "related to" describe different connections between a cause of action and a defendant's contacts with a forum, and (2) what sort of tie between a cause of action and a defendant's contacts with a forum is necessary to a determination that either connection exists. Nor do we reach the question whether, if the two types of relationship differ, a forum's exercise of personal jurisdiction in a situation where the cause of action "relates to," but does not

contacts with the State of Texas to determine whether they constitute
the kind of continuous and systematic general business contacts the
Court found to exist in *Perkins*. We hold that they do not.

It is undisputed that Helicol does not have a place of business
in Texas and never has been licensed to do business in the State.
Basically, Helicol's contacts with Texas consisted of sending its chief
executive officer to Houston for a contract-negotiation session;
accepting into its New York bank account checks drawn on a Houston
bank; purchasing helicopters, equipment, and training services from
Bell Helicopter for substantial sums; and sending personnel to Bell's
facilities in Forth Worth for training.

The one trip to Houston by Helicol's chief executive officer for
the purpose of negotiating the transportation-services contract with
Consorcio/WSH cannot be described or regarded as a contact of a
"continuous and systematic" nature, as *Perkins* described it, see also
*International Shoe Co. v. Washington*, 326 U.S., at 320, and thus
cannot support an assertion of *in personam* jurisdiction over Helicol by
a Texas court. Similarly, Helicol's acceptance from Consorcio/WSH
of checks drawn on a Texas bank is of negligible significance for
purposes of determining whether Helicol had sufficient contacts in
Texas. There is no indication that Helicol ever requested that the
checks be drawn on a Texas bank or that there was any negotiation
between Helicol and Consorcio/WSH with respect to the location or
identity of the bank on which checks would be drawn. Common sense
and everyday experience suggest that, absent unusual circumstances,[7]
the bank on which a check is drawn is generally of little consequence
to the payee and is a matter left to the discretion of the drawer. Such
unilateral activity of another party or a third person is not an
appropriate consideration when determining whether a defendant has
sufficient contacts with a forum State to justify an assertion and
jurisdiction. See *Kulko v. California Superior Court*, 436 U.S. 84, 93
(1978) (arbitrary to subject one parent to suit in any State where other
parent chooses to spend time while having custody of child pursuant to

---

"arise out of," the defendant's contacts with the forum should be analyzed as an
assertion of specific jurisdiction.

[7] [11] For example, if the financial health and continued ability of the bank to
honor the draft are questionable, the payee might request that the check be drawn on
an account at some other institution.

separation agreement); *Hanson v. Denckla*, 357 U.S. 235, 253 (1958) ("The unilateral activity of those who claim some relationship with a nonresident defendant cannot satisfy the requirement of contact with the forum State"); see also Lilly, Jurisdiction Over Domestic and Alien Defendants, 69 Va. L. Rev. 85, 99 (1983).

The Texas Supreme Court focused on the purchases and the related training trips in finding contacts sufficient to support an assertion of jurisdiction. We do not agree with that assessment, for the Court's opinion in *Rosenberg Bros. & Co. v. Curtis Brown Co.*, 260 U.S. 516 (1923) (Brandeis, J., for a unanimous tribunal), makes clear that purchases and related trips, standing alone, are not a sufficient basis for a State's assertion of jurisdiction.

The defendant in *Rosenberg* was a small retailer in Tulsa, Okla., who dealt in men's clothing and furnishings. It never had applied for a license to do business in New York, nor had it at any time authorized suit to be brought against it there. It never had an established place of business in New York and never regularly carried on business in that State. Its only connection with New York was that it purchased from New York wholesalers a large portion of the merchandise sold in its Tulsa store. The purchases sometimes were made by correspondence and sometimes through visits to New York by an officer of the defendant. The Court concluded: "Visits on such business, even if occurring at regular intervals, would not warrant the inference that the corporation was present within the jurisdiction of [New York]." *Id.*, at 518.

This Court in *International Shoe* acknowledged and did not repudiate its holding in *Rosenberg*. See 326 U.S., at 318. In accordance with *Rosenberg*, we hold that mere purchases, even if occurring at regular intervals, are not enough to warrant a State's assertion of *in personam* jurisdiction over a nonresident corporation in a cause of action not related to those purchase transactions.[8] Nor can

---

[8] [12] This Court in *International Shoe* cited *Rosenberg* for the proposition that "the commission of some single or occasional acts of the corporate agent in a state sufficient to impose an obligation or liability on the corporation has not been thought to confer upon the state authority to enforce it." 326 U.S., at 318. Arguably, therefore, *Rosenberg* also stands for the proposition that mere purchases are not a sufficient basis for either general or specific jurisdiction. Because the case before us is one in which there has been an assertion of general jurisdiction over a foreign

we conclude that the fact that Helicol sent personnel into Texas for training in connection with the purchase of helicopters and equipment in that State in any way enhanced the nature of Helicol's contacts with Texas. The training was a part of the package of goods and services purchased by Helicol from Bell Helicopter. The brief presence of Helicol employees in Texas for the purpose of attending the training sessions is no more a significant contact than were the trips to New York made by the buyer for the retail store in *Rosenberg*. See also *Kulko v. California Superior Court*, 436 U.S., at 93 (basing California jurisdiction on 3-day and 1-day stopovers in that State "would make a mockery of" due process limitations on assertion of personal jurisdiction).

[Justice Brennan dissented: "In contrast, I believe that the undisputed contacts in this case between petitioner Helicol and the State of Texas are sufficiently important, and sufficiently related to the underlying cause of action, to make it fair and reasonable for the State to assert personal jurisdiction over Helicol for the wrongful-death actions filed by the respondents. Given that Helicol has purposefully availed itself of the benefits and obligations of the forum, and given the direct relationship between the underlying cause of action and Helicol's contacts with the forum, maintenance of this suit in the Texas courts "does not offend [the] 'traditional notions of fair play and substantial justice,'" *International Shoe Co. v. Washington*, 326 U.S. 310, 316 (1945) (quoting *Milliken v. Meyer*, 311 U.S. 457, 463 (1940)), that are the touchstone of jurisdictional analysis under the Due Process Clause. I therefore dissent."]

### E.    STATE LONG-ARM STATUTES

Within the due process framework established by the Constitution and applied by the Supreme Court, state legislatures have developed and applied a variety of long-arm statutes to obtain jurisdiction over out-of-state defendants. Consider some examples:

---

defendant, we need not decide the continuing validity of *Rosenberg* with respect to an assertion of specific jurisdiction, *i.e.*, where the cause of action arises out of or relates to the purchases by the defendant in the forum State.

1.    CALIFORNIA CIVIL PROCEDURE CODE (CAL. CIV. PROC. CODE §410.10 (West 1994)).

A court of this state may exercise jurisdiction on any basis not inconsistent with the Constitution of this state or of the United States.

2.    NEW JERSEY CIVIL PRACTICE (N.J. CIV. PRAC. 4:4-4(e) (1988)).

(e) **Substituted Service on Certain Individuals**. On the filing of an affidavit of the attorney for the plaintiff or of any person having knowledge of the facts, that, after diligent inquiry and effort, an individual cannot be served in this State under any of the preceding paragraphs of this rule, then, consistent with due process of law, service may be made by mailing, by registered or certified mail, return receipt requested, a copy of the summons and complaint to the individual addressed to his dwelling house or usual place of abode or, with postal instructions to deliver to addressee only, to his place of business or employment. If the addressee refused to claim or to accept delivery of registered or certified mail, service may be made by ordinary mail addressed to him at his dwelling house or usual place of abode. The party making service may, at his option, make service simultaneously by registered or certified mail and ordinary mail, and if the addressee refuses to claim and accept delivery of registered mail and if the ordinary mailing is not returned, the simultaneous mailing shall constitute effective service. If for any other reason delivery cannot be made, then service may be made outside the State as provided in R. 4:4-5(a) upon any person upon whom service is authorized by the law of this State or of the state wherein service is effected.

3.    TEXAS CIVIL PRACTICE AND REMEDIES CODE ANNOTATED (TEX. CIV. PRAC. & REM. CODE ANN. §17.043 (West 1986)).

In an action arising from a nonresident's business in this state, process may be served on the person in charge, at the time of service, of any business in which the nonresident is engaged in this state if the nonresident is not required by statute to designate or maintain a resident agent for service of process.

4.      NEW YORK CIVIL PRACTICE LAW AND RULES
        (N.Y. CIV. PRAC. L. & R. §302 (McKinney
        1976)).

**(a) Acts which are the basis of jurisdiction**. As to a cause of
action arising from any of the acts enumerated in this section, a court
may exercise personal jurisdiction over any non-domiciliary, or his
executor or administrator, who in person or through an agent:

1.      transacts any business within the state; or

2.      commits a tortious act within the state, except as to a
        cause of action for defamation of character arising from
        the act; or

3.      commits a tortious act without the state causing injury to
        person or property within the state, except as to a cause
        of action for defamation of character arising from the
        act, if he

        (i)     regularly does or solicits business, or engages in
                any other persistent course of conduct, or derives
                substantial revenue from goods used or
                consumed or services rendered, in the state, or

        (ii)    expects or should reasonably expect the act to
                have consequences in the state and derives
                substantial revenue from interstate or
                international commerce; or

4.      owns, uses or possesses any real property situated within
        the state.

**(b) Personal jurisdiction over non-resident defendant**. A
court in any matrimonial action or family court proceeding involving
a demand for support or alimony may exercise personal jurisdiction
over the respondent or defendant notwithstanding the fact that he or she
no longer is a resident or domiciliary of this state, or over his or her
executor or administrator, if the party seeking support is a resident of
or domiciled in this state at the time such demand is made, provided
that this state was the matrimonial domicile of the parties before their

separation, or the defendant abandoned the plaintiff in this state, or the obligation to pay support or alimony accrued under the laws of this state or under an agreement executed in this state.

(c) **Effect of appearance**. Where personal jurisdiction is based solely upon this section, an appearance does not confer such jurisdiction with respect to causes of action not arising from an act enumerated in this section.

## F.    CONCLUSION

Within the highly permissive framework of international law, United States courts have accorded themselves broad discretion to seize jurisdiction over international transactions in which the defendant has not consented to jurisdiction. It would be wrong to conclude that United States courts have been unduly aggressive in reaching out and expanding national jurisdiction. Some limitative doctrines do emerge in the case law. But given the varieties of long-arm statutes in the various states, the ultimate criterion of reasonableness prescribed by the Restatement and the as-yet unresolved question of the dominant theory of jurisdiction in the Supreme Court, there are considerable incentives for forum-shopping plaintiffs to select the United States when they think it serves their purposes. When they do this, the outcome is uncertain. Born & Weston, in their study INTERNATIONAL CIVIL LITIGATION AND UNITED STATES COURTS 118 (1989) observe:

> Particularly in light of the expansive theories of personal jurisdiction now embraced by U.S. courts, it is sometimes difficult for foreign defendants to resist jurisdiction successfully.

A second consequence of United States expansive jurisdictional practices is that of encouraging other jurisdictions to follow suit or, at least, not restrain their own expansive jurisdictional practices.

III.    ENGLISH THEORIES OF JUDICIAL JURISDICTION

A.    HISTORIC PRACTICE

*Sirdar Gurdyal Singh v. Rajah of Faridkote*, 1894 App. Cas. 670, 684 (P.C.) (appeal taken from Punjab).

"[A] decree pronounced *in absentem* by a foreign Court, to the jurisdiction of which the defendant has not in any way submitted himself, is by international law an absolute nullity."

B.    CURRENT PRACTICE: ORDER 11: RULES OF THE SUPREME COURT (RSC) (Rules of the Supreme Court, S.I. 1965, No. 1776).[9]

SERVICE OF PROCESS, ETC., OUT OF THE JURISDICTION

*Principal cases in which service of writ out of jurisdiction is permissible*

1.—(1)  Subject to rule 3 and provided that the writ does not contain any such claim as is mentioned in Order 75, rule 2(1)(a), service of a writ, or notice of a writ, out of the jurisdiction is permissible with the leave of the Court in the following cases, that is to say—

. . .

(f)    if the action begun by the writ is brought against a defendant not domiciled or ordinarily resident in Scotland to enforce, rescind, dissolve, annul or otherwise affect a contract, or to recover damages or obtain other relief in respect of the breach of a contract, being (in ether case) a contract which—

(i)    was made within the jurisdiction, or

---

[9] This rule was subsequently and frequently amended after 1965. The most important amendment was made in 1983. RSC (Amendment No. 2, 1983) S.I. 1983, No. 1181 (1.21). The amendment recast the rule but left substantively unchanged the provisions with which the following case is concerned.

. . .

(iii)    is by its terms, or by implication governed by English law;

(g)    if the action begun by the writ is brought against a defendant not domiciled or ordinarily resident in Scotland or Northern Ireland, in respect of a breach committed within the jurisdiction of a contract made within or out of the jurisdiction, and irrespective of the fact, if such be the case, that the breach was preceded or accompanied by a breach committed out of the jurisdiction that rendered impossible the performance of so much of the contract as ought to have been performed within the jurisdiction;

\*    \*    \*

This Order has been characterized even by English courts as jurisdictionally exorbitant.[10]

1.    *BP Exploration Co. (Libya) v. Hunt*, 3 All E.R. 879 (Q.B. 1976).

[Hunt, a U.S. national and Texas citizen, was granted an oil concession by Libya. In 1960, Hunt concluded a "farm-in" agreement with British Petroleum, with the consent of Libya, for the joint development of a concession. BP agreed to pay all of Hunt's expenses and costs until export of petroleum from the concession commenced. At that point, BP would be reimbursed by 3/8 of Hunt's one-half share of the petroleum until BP's total outlay had been repaid. But if the concession proved unproductive, BP would have no claims against Hunt. This agreement was signed in London. In 1967, another agreement amending the 1960 agreement was initialled in Texas. In 1971, the new Qaddaffi Government in Libya nationalized BP, allegedly for acts of the British Government in the Persian Gulf. Hunt continued to exploit the concession on his own account until his interests were nationalized in 1973. BP exercised an arbitration clause against Libya and secured an

---

[10] The expansive nature of jurisdiction under R.S.C. Ord. 11 is analyzed in detail in *Amin Rashid Shipping Corp. v. Kuwait Ins. Co.* (*infra* p. 53).

award against Libya, though Libya never participated in the arbitration. Thereafter, BP settled separately with Libya and Hunt settled separately with Libya. After the settlements, BP commenced a suit against Hunt in London, claiming that the contracts were governed by English law, that they had been frustrated by the nationalization and that under the English Law Reform (Frustrated Contracts) Act of 1943, Hunt was obliged to pay whatever he had received in settlement from Libya to BP. The determinative issue in the case was whether jurisdiction could be founded under Order 11. Kerr, J. delivered the opinion.]

·     ·     ·

. . . The writ was issued on 2nd May 1975 . . . .

·     ·     ·

Mr. Hunt declined to accept service of the writ through agents or solicitors in the country, and attempts to serve him personally during a short visit here proved unsuccessful. On 19th June 1975 BP then obtained leave to serve notice of this writ on Mr. Hunt by post in Dallas as already mentioned. However, on 10th June 1975 Mr. Hunt had meanwhile himself instituted proceedings against BP in the Northern District Court of Texas for a declaration that he was under no liability to BP. Mr. Hunt therefore brought his proceedings in Texas after BP had brought this action in England; he did so before service of the English proceedings was effected on him but after he had become aware that they had been brought. His summons to set aside the service of notice of the writ and all subsequent proceedings, which is now before me, was then issued on 23rd July 1975. . . .

*Contentions in support of the application to set aside*

Leave to serve outside the jurisdiction was given on the basis of an affidavit by Mr. John Gauntlett of BP's solicitors, his contention being that the court had jurisdiction under RSC Ord 11, r 1(1)(f)(i) and/or (iii), viz that the 1960 agreement had been made within the jurisdiction and or was by implication governed by English law. On behalf of Mr. Hunt, a large number of contentions were put forward by counsel in support of the present application. These can conveniently be grouped as follows. (1) The court has no jurisdiction because the case does not fall within RSC Ord 11, r 1. (2) Even if there is jurisdiction, the service should be set aside because BP's claim is bound to fail in any event. (3) The case is not a proper one for service outside the jurisdiction, as required by RSC Ord 11, r 4(2), because London is not the forum conveniens. (4) The service should in any event be set aside because Mr. Gauntlett's affidavit failed to give a sufficiently full and fair account of the position, as required by the rule.

I will accordingly deal with these contentions in turn. In doing so I bear in mind the three well-known criteria relating to the exercise of this jurisdiction as summarised by Farwell LJ in The Hagen and often restated since, viz that the jurisdiction is to be exercised with caution; that any doubts should be resolved in favour of the foreigner, bearing in mind that the case must not only fall within the letter but also within the spirit of the sub-paragraphs; and that an insufficiently full and fair disclosure of the material circumstances in BP's affidavit in support of the ex parte application would justify the discharge of the order granting leave, even though BP may be in a position to make another application.

*Jurisdiction under RSC Ord 11, r 1(1)(f)*

Counsel for Mr. Hunt took two points which logically precede the question whether the contract was made in London and whether the proper law was English under RSC Ord 11, r 1(1)(f). He submitted that the relief claimed by BP under paras (i) and (ii) of the writ did not fall within r 1(1)(f) at all, because this is not an 'action begun . . . to enforce, rescind, dissolve, annul or otherwise affect a contract . . .'

In relation to the claim for a declaration under para (i) of the writ that the contract had become frustrated, it was accepted by counsel for BP that BP could only rely on the word of sub-para (f) 'or otherwise affect the contract.' However, counsel for Mr. Hunt submitted that a claim for a declaration that a contract has been discharged by frustration -- and indeed any claim relating to an allegedly frustrated contract -- cannot fall even within these words, since ex hypothesi there no longer is any contract, because on BP's case it has been discharged by frustration. He said, in effect, that on BP's own contention the court is dealing with an ex-contract, a corpse and that there is therefore no longer any contract which can be 'affected.' I cannot accept this contention. The words 'or otherwise affect' are very wide; indeed, almost as wide as they can be. A claim for a declaration that a contract has become discharged, whether as the result of frustration, repudiation or otherwise, is in my view a claim which affects the contract in question. The contrary construction would have serious and highly inconvenient consequences. For instance, a contract might be entirely English, made here, governed by English law, and broken here, but on this submission our courts would nevertheless be obliged to decline jurisdiction and to leave it to a foreign court to declare whether according to English law the contract had for some reason become discharged. I think that the wide words 'or otherwise affect' were deliberately included to prevent a result such as this, and I therefore reject this contention.

In my view, similar considerations equally apply to counsel for Mr. Hunt's second point under this head, viz that the claim under para (ii) of the writ for relief under the Law Reform (Frustrated Contracts) Act 1943, is not within any of the sub-paragraphs of r 1(1). In this connection I must first set out certain provisions of this Act. Section 1(1) reads:

> 'Where a contract governed by English law has become impossible of performance or been otherwise frustrated, and the parties thereto have for that reason been discharged from the further performance of the contract, the following provisions of this section shall, subject to the provisions of section two of this Act, have effect in relation thereto.'

The Act therefore only applies to contracts governed by English law. I have to deal with the question of the proper law hereafter, but for present purposes I will assume that this requirement is satisfied, since otherwise cadit quaestio. I need not read any of the other provisions of s 1 save to state that BP's claim under para (ii) of the writ which I have quoted is founded on s 1(3) of the 1943 Act, the provision dealing with pre-frustration benefits conferred by one party on the other. The alleged benefits in question, as I understand, are all the installations and activities by means whereof Mr. Hunt's concession 65 was exploited, and the oil in the ground converted into marketable oil delivered at the Libyan seaboard.

Subsections (1), (2) and (3) of §2 of the 1943 Act each refer to 'contracts' to which the Act applies, notwithstanding that the Act only applies 'where a contract . . . has become impossible of performance or been otherwise frustrated'. This is of some relevance to counsel for Mr. Hunt's first argument with which I have already dealt, since it shows that the 1943 Act itself is drafted on the basis that contracts, albeit frustrated, are to be affected by the provisions of the Act. I set out in this connection s 2(3), since this is also material to another point on which counsel for Mr. Hunt relies, and to which I turn hereafter:

> 'Where any contract to which this Act applies contains any provisions which upon the true construction of the contract, is intended to have effect in the event of circumstances arising which operate, or would but for the said provision operate, to frustrate the contract, or is intended to have effect whether such circumstances arise or not, the court shall give effect to the said provision, and shall only give effect to the foregoing section of this Act to such extent, if any, as appears to the court to be consistent with the said provision.'

If one then asks oneself: is a claim under the 1943 Act one which 'affects' a contract which has been (allegedly) frustrated?, it seems to me that the answer must be in the affirmative as a matter of ordinary English, and indeed on the basis of the language of the 1943 Act itself. The dictionary meaning of the verb 'to affect' in this context is 'to produce a material effect' on something. It seems to me that this is precisely what the 1943 Act is doing in relation to a frustrated contract governed by English law. Section 1(1) provides that as regards such a contract 'the following provisions of this section shall . . . have effect in relation thereto'. The word 'thereto' can in my view only relate to the frustrated contract, in the same way as the word 'thereto' a little earlier in the same sentence. It follows that the Act provides that s 1(3) is to have effect in relation to a frustrated contract governed by English law. In these circumstances, it appears to me that a claim under this subsection is clearly one which 'affects' such a contract. Here again, the contrary construction would produce undesirable results, which I do not think can have been intended. The consequence would be that an English court would have jurisdiction to give leave to serve a defendant out of the jurisdiction where the plaintiff claims that a contract governed by English law has become frustrated, but, if this issue is decided in favour of the plaintiff, that the English court would then have to leave it to a foreign court to decide the consequences between the parties which flow from the 1943 Act.

I think that this is the short answer to counsel for Mr. Hunt's point on the relief claimed under para (ii) of the writ and that it really stands or falls with his point on para (i). In my view, the court's powers to determine the issues which 'affect' a contract falling within RSC Ord 11, r 1(1)(f), do not cease by reason of the frustration of the contract, and they include the application of the 1943 Act to the extent that its provisions have effect in relation to the contract. I therefore also reject this contention.

.     .     .

I now turn to the remaining questions under sub-para (f), viz whether the contract was made within the jurisdiction or impliedly governed by English law. The issue as to the proper law is of greater importance because it also concerns the applicability of the 1943 Act and the question of forum conveniens, and I therefore begin with this.

Neither the 1960 agreement nor the 1967 amendment contains any express term about the governing law or the jurisdictional venue in the event of dispute. The operating agreement contains an arbitration clause providing for the appointment of an arbitrator by each of the parties and of a referee to be appointed, in default of agreement between the arbitrators, by the President of the International Court of Justice, but without any indication of the law to be applied or of the country in which the arbitration is to take place. Both parties have evidently ignored this arbitration clause, as they are entitled to do. BP contends that the proper law is English. The position taken in the affidavits supporting Mr. Hunt's application to set the service aside, is that the proper law was either Libyan or Texan. However, when counsel for Mr. Hunt opened the case, he disclaimed reliance on Libyan law so far as the letter agreement was concerned, but maintained it in relation to the operating agreement. He invited me to 'split' the proper law in this way as between Texas law and Libyan law. He said, and counsel for BP agreed, that as a matter of business reality the parties could not have intended that the whole of their contractual relations should be governed by Libyan law. But counsel for Mr. Hunt subsequently resiled from this position and submitted that Libyan law might also be applicable to the letter agreement and, further, that it was in any event sufficient for present purposes if I decided that the proper law was not English law. I cannot accept any of these contentions. First, I think that I should decide what in my view the proper law is, not what it is not. Secondly, it is in my view clearly impossible to 'split' the proper law in this case between the different parts of the contract. The letter agreement refers to the operating agreement in many of its provisions and expressly requires both to be read together. The 1967 amendment refers to both and amends both. In my judgment, counsel for Mr. Hunt's first reaction was the right one and effect can be given to it without any 'splitting' of the proper law. It is perfectly possible for two parties in different countries, who are engaged on a joint venture in some third country, to provide that their contractual relations concerning the joint venture should be governed by the law of one of them, or indeed by some other system of law, but subject to the proviso that to the extent that performance is to take place in the country of the joint venture, and therefore requires compliance with the local law, that country's system of law is to be applicable. Indeed, in relation to a joint venture in what may be called a developing country between two parties with multifarious international interests this would be a sensible and businesslike arrangement. I think that this is the position here. If one simply asks oneself: with which country, or with the system of law of which country, is the totality of the contractual arrangements between the parties most closely connected? I think that the answer would be Libya. But if in all the circumstances the court is convinced that it was nevertheless not the intention of these parties that their contract in relation to the sharing of concession 65 should in all respects be governed by the law of Libya, then it is in my view open to the court to exclude the law of Libya as the proper law, leaving it only applicable insofar as concerns the performance of obligations in Libya which are necessarily subject to Libyan law, and then to determine the intended proper law objectively as between other systems of law.

Quite apart from the fact that this appears to me to be the most businesslike approach in this case, as it did to both counsel, there are also intrinsic indications to the same effect in the evidence. First, in 1964, when some question evidently arose about the extent to which further exploration should be carried out in concession 65, Mr. Hunt wrote the following to BP in a letter of 21st April:

'I still have the feeling that the Anglo-Saxon system of justice and jurisprudence is superior to the system we frequently encounter in the Middle East and South America, and I hope that BP feel likewise.'

I know that there are technical reasons for ignoring post-contractual statements, but it seems to me to fly in the face of common sense nevertheless, and on other equally technical grounds, to attribute an intention to Mr. Hunt to subject his rights under the 1960 agreement to Libyan law. Secondly, I think that cl 1(b) and 14 of the letter agreement are of considerable significance in this connection, and I have already summarised their effect. They clearly show that it was the common intention of both parties to seek to maintain and bring to fruition their agreement to share concession 65 even if the Libyan authorities should refuse consent or withhold their approval of the assignment of 50 per cent of Mr. Hunt's share to BP. They therefore intended, if necessary and so far as possible, to circumvent Libyan law in order to achieve their objective. Finally, though perhaps of lesser force, is the last part of cl 18 of the letter agreement which I have also already quoted. If it had been intended that the whole arrangement should be governed by Libyan law, then this would have been unnecessary. As it is, it suggests that the parties intended some other system of law to be applicable, provided only that if and insofar as this might involve a forfeiture or breach of concession 65 under Libyan law, any particular provision should to this extent be void and of no effect.

For all these reasons I consider that Libyan law must be rejected as the intended proper law of the contract and that a choice must be made between the English law and the law of Texas. The question is then, as posed by both counsel: with which of these systems of law did the transaction have its closest and most real connection? (see *Bonython v. Commonwealth of Australia*, per Lord Simonds). As to this, the answer is clearly and overwhelmingly in favour of English law. Apart from the fact that a Dallas address is given for Mr. Hunt, I do not think that the 1960 agreement contains any reference to Texas. It contains references to the revenue authorities of the United States, but equally to the Bank of England. Counsel for Mr. Hunt's only real point in support of a connecting factor with Texas was, as he put it, that this was an agreement relating to 'a Texan concession'. However, it was not a Texan concession, but a concession in Libya granted to a resident of Texas. The connecting factors in favour of English law are overwhelming in comparison. First, the 1960 agreement was executed in England. This, of course, is far from conclusive, but is still a factor to be weighed in the balance and pointing in the direction of English law. The fact that the 1967 amendment was initialled in Texas is of no relevance to the question of the proper law, because the parties could not have intended by a limited amendment to alter in 1967 whatever had been the proper law since 1960. Next, there is the important fact that BP was to be 'the Operator' under the 1960 agreement and was so described throughout. All the principal and active obligations were to be performed by BP. Counsel for BP is right in saying that as between England and Texas the former was clearly intended to be the centre of gravity of the contractual arrangements and the primary place of performance. Admittedly, the principal centre of gravity and place of performance was obviously to be Libya itself, but I have already dealt with the purely Libyan aspect of the arrangements. It is also true that for the performance of the contract BP employed considerable Libyan and ex-patriate staff in Libya and presumably hardly any staff in London, and this was envisaged. But the fact that, as one would expect, much of the administration and ancillary activities relating to the contract with Mr. Hunt would take place in London is made clear by a provision in one of the exhibits to the operating agreement. This provides under the heading 'Administrative Overhead London':

> 'Operator shall have the right to assess against the joint property covered hereby the appropriate proportion of London management and administrative overhead charges . . .'

It then proceeds to define these, including inter alia technical and advisory services. Finally, there is the point that, apart from the initial payment of $2,000,000, the 1960 agreement provided that all payments were to be made and received in sterling, with detailed provisions as to how the rate of exchange was to be computed. Taking the agreement as a whole, it is therefore clear that sterling was to be the money of account.

In all these circumstances I conclude that the proper law of the contract is English law, with the consequence that the case falls within RSC Ord 11, r 1(1)(f)(iii).

. . . During the argument it seemed to me that the answer to this contention was that the contract includes the 1967 amendment, that this was made in Dallas (though remaining to be mutually confirmed by telex), and that the contract sued on as a whole was therefore made partly in London and partly in Dallas, and accordingly not within the jurisdiction. On further consideration, however, I have come to the conclusion that this is not the right approach. I think that the correct analysis is that the contract was made in London and amended in Dallas; not that it was made partly in London and partly in Dallas, or elsewhere. The 1967 amendment could not stand alone; it merely amended certain provisions of the 1960 agreement. The position would, of course, have been different if the 1967 amendment had operated as a discharge of the 1960 agreement and substituted a fresh agreement. The foregoing analysis is also in accord with what Denning L.J. appears to have thought in *Entores Ltd v. Miles Far East Corpn*, where he preferred the view that an agreement made in one country and amended in another should be regarded as not having been made in the latter country. Secondly, even if this analysis be wrong, I think that it is sufficient for the purposes of the rule if the contract which is the subject-matter of the action was *substantially* made within the jurisdiction. Otherwise the effect of the rule could be voided by some very minor subsequent amendment or addendum executed abroad. This analysis is consonant with what was the position relating to successive contractual breaches outside and within the jurisdiction before the adoption of the present wording of sub-para (g), i.e. before the addition of the words 'irrespective of the fact . . . that the breach was preceded or accompanied by a breach committed out of the jurisdiction . . .' In relation to the earlier wording of the corresponding paragraph it was held sufficient to attract jurisdiction if a substantial part of the contract had to be performed within the jurisdiction and if there was a breach of that part: see *Rein v. Stein*. As I read the decision of the House of Lords in *Johnson v. Taylor Bros & Co. Ltd.*, this also approved the principle that a sufficient ground to found jurisdiction existed under the former wording if a substantial breach had occurred within the jurisdiction, though not if this merely resulted inevitably in consequence of a breach outside. I accordingly hold that leave to serve out of the jurisdiction was also justified on the basis of RSC Ord 11, r 1(1)(f)(i), because the contract was made within the jurisdiction.

.     .     .

## Forum conveniens

It was submitted on behalf of Mr. Hunt that London is not the forum conveniens for this action, but that Texas is. Counsel for Mr. Hunt countered the evidence that BP's voluminous records and numerous witnesses relevant to the issues are in England and cannot conveniently be called in Texas by other evidence to the effect that Mr.

Hunt's equally voluminous documents are in Dallas and that he, like BP, would wish to call witnesses who can much more easily be called in his own jurisdiction than in that of the other side. He also relied on evidence to show that Mr. Hunt is not geared to fighting a major action in London, although he and some of his companies operate through an office here, whereas BP's worldwide organisation, including its office or offices in the United States, would find it less of a burden to fight in Texas. But although these contentions are entitled to some weight they are far from determinative. Any country exercising jurisdiction over a foreigner inevitably subjects him to greater inconvenience and expense than if he could contest the action within his own jurisdiction. As in football, each side prefers to play at home. In many, and probably most, cases the foreign defendant would have no office or other organisation in the country whose 'long-arm jurisdiction' (to use the American term) calls on him to come to contest a claim. In the present case, Mr. Hunt is at least to some limited extent more favourably placed than many foreign defendants, though he may well be inconvenienced to a considerable extent.

However, in my view these kinds of considerations do not represent the right approach, or at any rate represent only a secondary approach, to the question of what is the forum conveniens. The primary question is: what is the most appropriate tribunal to try the issues in the interest of justice in all the circumstances? In this connection I respectfully adopt and follow the remarks of Buskley J. in *Re Kernot (an infant)* where he said:

> 'In considering questions of forum conveniens I think that the court has to take into consideration not only such matters as the physical convenience of the parties and the witnesses and matters attendant on the trial and things of that kind, but also the system of law which is to be applied, and must consider what court is really the appropriate tribunal to reach a proper answer in applying that system of law. That seems to me as much relevant for consideration as are considerations of personal convenience and questions of expense.'

Having arrived at the conclusion that the proper law to be applied in the present case is English law, I consider that this is the predominating factor to be borne in mind. Unless there be other considerations of overwhelming weight which militate against the

English courts, which in my view do not exist in the present case, I think that the appropriate forum for deciding the rights of the parties under English law are the courts of this country. In Texas it would be necessary to adduce expert evidence on English law. Furthermore, since BP was the 'Operator' in relation to the joint venture, and since the evidence shows that, as one would expect, a great deal of the planning, research and administration was to be done in this country, this country is the natural centre of gravity as against Texas to determine whether or not, and if so to what extent, the operations under the contract have conferred valuable benefits on Mr. Hunt which might give rise to some monetary claim under English law. In relation to a claim of this kind one would expect the bulk of the evidence to be here rather than in Texas. In these circumstances I have no hesitation in rejecting the contention that if this court otherwise has jurisdiction in relation to the present claim, the discretion to exercise this jurisdiction should be renounced because London is not the forum conveniens. On the contrary, putting it positively, I consider that as between England and Texas the English courts clearly are the forum conveniens.

.    .    .

[Jurisdiction was confirmed at every instance of appeal and the House of Lords confirmed a judgment against Hunt of $42 million. Hunt sought to challenge the judgment under Protocol I of the European Convention on Human Rights, but the European Commission declared his application inadmissible. *H. v. United Kingdom*, App. No. 10000/82, 33 Eur. Comm'n H.R. Dec. & Rep. 247 (1983).]

### Notes and Questions

1. Ironically, Hunt's contract with BP had included an arbitration clause which, for reasons that are not clear, his lawyers did not insist upon. If they had done so in timely fashion, it is difficult to see how the unusual and quite unexpected result in this judgment would have eventuated.

2. *BP v. Hunt* is particularly instructive about the uncertainty of the exercise of national jurisdiction in international transactions and, as a related matter, the surprises latent in such jurisdiction with regard to the application of substantive law. Discuss.

3. After Mr. Hunt lost his case in the House of Lords and failed to have it admitted before the European Commission on Human Rights, what alternatives were available to him?

2.  *Amin Rasheed Shipping Corp. v. Kuwait Ins. Co.*, 1 App. Cas. 50, 58-73 (1983).

LORD DIPLOCK. My Lords, the plaintiff/appellant ("the assured") is a shipping company incorporated in Liberia, but having its head office and carrying on its business in Dubai. It is the owner of a cargo vessel of the landing craft type, the *Al Wahab* ("the vessel") which, at the relevant time, traded in Arabian Gulf waters only. In these proceedings, the assured seeks to litigate in the English commercial court its claim against the defendants/respondents ("the insurers") for a constructive total loss of the vessel which was insured under a hull and machinery policy of insurance against marine and war risks ("the policy") that had been issued in Kuwait by the insurers who have their head office there and branch offices elsewhere in the Gulf, including Dubai, but have no office or representative in England.

The policy was on the insurers' standard printed form of hull policy. It was in the English language only. The wording followed meticulously (with minor and in my view immaterial omissions of express references to London) that of the Lloyd's S.G. policy scheduled to the Marine Insurance Act 1906, but adapted by typewritten insertions for use as a time, instead of a voyage, policy, and excluding references to "goods and merchandise." It incorporated in the body of the policy the usual F.C. & S. clause from what at that time was the Standard English Marine Policy; but, by a typewritten insertion, was expressed to be "Subject to Institute War and Strikes Clauses Hulls dated 1.10.70 as attached"; and a print of those clauses without any additions or amendments was attached to the policy. The policy was expressed to be issued in Kuwait on April 28, 1979, and claims (if any) expressed to be payable in Kuwait.

In order to achieve its object of pursuing its claim against the insurers in the English court, rather than a Kuwaiti court, the assured had two obstacles to overcome:

First, it had to bring the case within R.S.C., Ord. 11, r. 1 (1), in order to obtain leave to serve a writ on the insurers out of the jurisdiction. Although the assured had originally asserted that the contract of insurance had been made on its behalf by an agent trading in England, this failed on the facts; and in this House the only provision of rule 1 (1) that was relied upon by the assured was that contained in subparagraph (f) (iii) of which the relevant wording is:

> "if the action begun by the writ is brought against a defendant not domiciled or ordinarily resident in Scotland to enforce. . .a contract. . .being. . .a contract which. . .(iii) is by its terms, or by implication, governed by English law; . . ."

I will call this first obstacle the jurisdiction point.

The second obstacle is that the assured must satisfy the requirements of rule 4 (2) which provides:

> "No such leave shall be granted unless it shall be made sufficiently to appear to the court that the case is a proper one for service out of the jurisdiction under this Order."

I will call this second obstacle the discretion point.

.    .    .

The jurisdiction point on which judicial opinion in the courts below was evenly divided is one which is of considerable importance in transnational commercial contracts, and the approach in modern times to the exercise of the discretion in cases falling within R.S.C., Ord. 11, r. 1 (1) (f), is also deserving of re-examination. So, in spite of the unanimity of the result in both courts below, leave to appeal from the decision of the Court of Appeal was given by that court.

*The jurisdiction point*

My Lords, the jurisdiction point is one that falls to be determined by English law and by English law alone. The relevant rules to be applied to its determination are the English rules of conflict of laws, not the conflict rules of any other country—which may or may not be the same as those of England. In particular, so far as the jurisdiction point itself is concerned, it is immaterial whether the courts of the only obvious rival forum, a Kuwaiti court, would take the same view as an English court as to what was the proper law of the policy. The relevance of this only arises if and when one reaches the discretion point.

The applicable English conflict rules are those for determining what is the "proper law" of a contract, i.e., the law that governs the interpretation and the validity of the contract and the mode of performance and the consequences of breaches of the contract: *Compagnie Tunisienne de Navigation S.A. v. Compagnie d'Armement Maritime S.A.* [1971] A.C. 572, 603. To identify a particular system of law as being that in accordance with which the parties to it intended a contract to be interpreted, identifies that system of law as the "proper law" of the contract. The reason for this is plain; the purpose of entering into a contract being to create legal rights and obligations between the parties to it, interpretation of the contract involves determining what are the legal rights and obligations to which the words used in it give rise. This is not possible except by reference to the system of law by which the legal consequences that follow from the use of those words is to be ascertained. In *Vita Food Products Inc. v. Unus Shipping Co. Ltd.* [1939] A.C. 277, 298, Lord Wright said in a passage cited by Upjohn J. in *In re Claim by Helbert Wagg & Co. Ltd.* [1956] Ch. 323, 341:

> "There were certain differences between [*The Torni* [1932] P. 78] and the present. One was that the bills of lading had a clause providing that they were "to be construed in accordance with English law" not as in the present case "shall be governed by English law." In their Lordships' judgment that distinction is merely verbal and is too narrow to make a substantial difference. The construction of a contract by English law involves the application to its terms of the relevant English statutes, whatever they may be, and the rules and implications of the English common law for its construction, including the rules of the conflict of laws. In this sense the construing of the contract has the effect that the contract is to be governed by English law."

My Lords, R.S.C., Ord. 11, r. 1 (1)(f)(iii), states as the test that is relevant to the jurisdiction point in the instant case that the policy "is by its terms, or by implication, governed by English law." English conflict rules accord to the parties to a contract a wide liberty to choose the law by which their contract is to be governed. So the first step in the determination of the jurisdiction point is to examine the policy in order to see whether the parties have, by its express terms or by necessary implication from the language used, evinced a common intention as to the system of law by reference to which their mutual rights and obligations under it are to be ascertained. As Lord Atkin put it in *Rex v. International Trustee for the Protection of Bondholders Aktiengesellschaft* [1937] A.C. 500, 529:

> "The legal principles which are to guide an English court on the question of the proper law of a contract are now well settled. It is the law which the parties intended to apply. Their intention will be ascertained by the intention expressed in the contract if any, which will be conclusive. If no intention be expressed the intention will be presumed by the court from the terms of the contract and the relevant surrounding circumstances."

Lord Atkin goes on to refer to particular facts or conditions that led to a prima facie inference as to the intention of the parties to apply a particular system of law. He gives as examples the lex loci contractus or lex loci solutions, and concludes:

> "But all these rules but serve to give prima facie indications of intention: they are all capable of being overcome by counter indications, however difficult it may be in some cases to find such."

There is no conflict between this and Lord Simonds's pithy definition of the "proper law" of the contract to be found in *Bonython v. Commonwealth of Australia* [1951] A.C. 201, 219 which is so often quoted, i.e. "the system of law by reference to which the contract was made or that with which the transaction has its closest and most real connection." It may be worth while pointing out that the "or" in this quotation is disjunctive, as is apparent from the fact that Lord Simonds goes on immediately to speak of "the consideration of <u>the latter question</u>." If it is apparent from the terms of the contract itself that the parties intended it to be interpreted by reference to a particular system of law, their intention will prevail and the latter question as the system of law with which, in the view of the court, the transaction to which the contract relates would, but for such intention of the parties have had the closest and most real connection, does not arise.

One final comment upon what under English conflict rules is meant by the "proper law" of a contract may be appropriate. It is the substantive law of the country which the parties have chosen as that by which their mutual legally enforceable rights are to be ascertained, but excluding any renvoi, whether of remission or transmission, that the courts of that country might themselves apply if the matter were litigated before them. For example, if a contract made in England were expressed to be governed by French law, the English court would apply French substantive law to it notwithstanding that a French court applying its own conflict rules might accept a renvoi to English law as the lex loci contractus if the matter were litigated before it. Conversely, assuming that under English conflict rules English law is the proper law of the contract the fact that the courts of a country which under English conflict rules would be regarded as having jurisdiction over a dispute arising under the contract (in casu Kuwait) would under its own conflict rules have recourse to English law as determinative of the rights and obligations of the parties, would not make the proper law of the contract any the less English law because it was the law that a Kuwaiti court also would apply.

I can state briefly what Lord Atkin refers to as the relevant surrounding circumstances, at the time the policy was issued before I come to deal with its actual terms; since although the policy contains no express provision choosing English law as the proper law of the contract, nevertheless its provisions taken as a whole, in my opinion, by necessary implication point ineluctably to the conclusion that the intention of the parties was that their mutual rights and obligations under it should be determined in accordance with the English law of marine insurance.

The policy was the second renewal of similar policies on the vessel of which the first was issued on April 29, 1977. The assured by 1977 carried out the insurance of its ships through the London office of an English company that was a member of the Rasheed Group. As brokers for this purpose it used J.H. Minet & Co. Ltd. ("Minets") who also acted as re-insurance brokers for the insurers. Premiums were paid to Minets in London, policies were issued by the insurers in Kuwait and sent on by them to Minets who passed them on in London to the English company. Claims, though expressed by the policies to be payable in Kuwait, were in practice settled in running accounts in sterling in London between Minets and the insurers and between Minets and the assured.

I mention, in passing, that in these days of modern methods of communication where international contracts are so frequently negotiated by telex, whether what turns out to be the final offer is accepted in the country where one telex is situated or in the country where the other telex is installed is often a mere matter of chance. In the result the lex loci contractus has lost much of the significance in determining what is the proper law of contract that it had close on 50 years ago when Lord Atkin referred to it in the passage that I have cited. As respects lex loci solutionis the closeness of the connection of the contract with this varies with the nature of the contract. A contract of insurance is performed by the payment of money, the premiums by the assured, claims by the insurers, and, in the case of marine insurance, very often in what is used as an international rather than a national currency. In the instant case, the course of business between the insurers and the assured established before the policy now sought to be sued upon was entered into, ignoring, as it did, the provision in the previous policies that claims were payable in Kuwait, shows how little weight the parties themselves attached to the lex loci solutionis.

The crucial surrounding circumstance, however, is that it was common ground between the expert witnesses on Kuwaiti law that at the time the policy was entered into there was no indigenous law of marine insurance in Kuwait. Kuwait is a country in which the practice since 1961, when it began to develop as a thriving financial and commercial centre, has been to follow the example of the civil law countries and to embody the law dealing with commercial matters, at any rate, in written codes. In Kuwait there had been in existence since 1961 a Commercial Code dealing generally with commercial contracts but not specifically with contracts of marine insurance. The contract of marine insurance is highly idiosyncratic; it involves juristic concepts that are peculiar to itself such as sue and labour, subrogation, abandonment and constructive total loss; to give but a few examples. The general law of contract is able to throw but little light upon the rights and obligations under a policy of marine insurance in the multifarious contingencies that may occur while the contract is in force. The lacuna in the Kuwaiti commercial law has since been filled in 1980 by the promulgation for the first time of a code of marine insurance law. This code does not simply adopt the English law of marine insurance; there are significant differences. However, it did not come into operation until August 15, 1980, and it is without retrospective effect. It does not therefore apply to the policy which was entered into at a time before there was any indigenous law of marine insurance in Kuwait.

I add here, in parenthesis, that this does not mean that before the Marine Insurance Code was promulgated Kuwaiti courts were disabled from trying cases involving contracts of marine insurance, any more than the Commercial Court in England is disabled from trying a case involving a contract whose proper law is French law. A number of claims under marine insurance policies were in fact tried in Kuwaiti courts before the Kuwaiti code of marine insurance came into effect. The courts were able to undertake this task because the legal system of Kuwait includes a Code of Conflict of Laws. This incorporates article 59 which deals with determining the proper law of a contract. The article provides that in the case of a trans-national contract it

> "shall, from the standpoint of the substantive conditions governing it and the effects ensuing from its conclusion, be subject to the law of the state...where the contract is concluded...unless the contracting parties agree to the application of another law or *circumstances suggest that another law is the one contemplated for application.*"

This article expressly recognizes the duty of the Kuwaiti courts to give effect to the substantive law of some state other than Kuwait even where the contract is concluded in Kuwait if circumstances suggest that the law of that other state was the one contemplated for application; and, as will be seen when I come to the discretion point, a relevant circumstance in the case of contracts of marine insurance entered into in Kuwait before the promulgation of the Kuwaiti Marine Insurance Code was the non-existence in Kuwait of any indigenous marine insurance law.

Turning now to the terms of the policy itself, the adoption of the obsolete language of the Lloyd's S.G. policy as scheduled to the Marine Insurance Act 1906 makes it impossible to discover what are the legal incidents of the mutual rights and obligations accepted by the insurers and the assured as having been brought into existence by the contract, unless recourse is had not only to the rules for construction of the policy contained in the first schedule, but also to many of the substantive provisions of the Act which is (accurately) described in its long title as: "An Act to codify the law relating to marine insurance." To give some examples: the policy is a valued policy; the legal consequences of this in various circumstances are prescribed by sections 27, 32, 67 and 68. The policy contained two type-written insertions "Warranted Lloyd's class to be maintained throughout the policy period" and "Warranted trading in Arabian Gulf waters only"; the legal consequences of the use of these expressions in a policy of insurance is laid down in sections 33 to 35. On the other hand, the printed words include the so-called memorandum: "N.B. The ship and freight are warranted free from average under three pounds per cent. unless general, or the ship be stranded, sunk or burnt," where "warranted" is used in a different sense; to ascertain the legal effect of the expression in this context recourse must be had to sections 64 to 66 and 76. The legal effect of the sue and labour clause included in the policy is laid down in section 78. These are but a few examples of the more esoteric provisions of the policy of which the legal effect is undiscoverable except by reference to the Marine Insurance Act 1906; but the whole of the provisions of the statute are directed to determining what are the mutual rights and obligations of parties to a contract of marine insurance, whether the clauses of the contract are in the obsolete language of the Lloyd's S.G. policy (which, with the F.C. & S. clause added, is referred to in the Institute War and Strikes Clauses Hull-Time, as "the Standard Form of English Marine Policy"), or whether they are in the up-to-date language of the Institute War and Strike Clauses that were attached to the policy. Except by reference to the English statute and to the judicial exegesis of the code that it enacts it is not possible to interpret the policy or to determine what those mutual legal rights and obligations are. So, applying, as one must in deciding the jurisdiction point, English rules of conflict of laws, the proper law of the contract embodied in the policy is English law.

How then did it come about that two such experienced commercial judges as Robert Goff L.J. and Bingham J. came to the conclusion that the contract embodied in the policy was *not* governed by English law? There was evidence, and even in the absence of evidence your Lordships could I think take judicial notice of the fact, that the Standard Form of English Marine Policy together with the appropriate Institute Clauses attached, was widely used on insurance markets in many countries of the world, other than those countries of the Commonwealth that have enacted or inherited statutes of their own in the same terms as the Marine Insurance Act 1906. The widespread use of the form in countries that have not inherited or adopted the English common law led both Bingham J. and Robert Goff L.J. to conclude that the Standard Form of English Marine Policy and the Institute Clauses had become internationalised; the "lingua franca" and the "common currency" of international insurance were the metaphors that Bingham J. used to describe it; while Robert Goff L.J. [1983] 1 W.L.R. 228, 249, identified what he described as the basic fallacy in the argument of counsel for the assured as being:

> "that, although the historical origin of the policy may be English and although English law and practice may provide a useful source of persuasive authority on the construction of the policy wherever it may be used, nevertheless the use of a form which has become an international form of contract provides of itself little connection with English law for the purpose of ascertaining the proper law of the contract."

My Lords, contracts are incapable of existing in a legal vacuum. They are mere pieces of paper devoid of all legal effect unless they were made by reference to some system of private law which defines the obligations assumed by the parties to the contract by their use of particular forms of words and prescribes the remedies enforceable in a court of justice for failure to perform any of those obligations; and this must be so however widespread geographically the use of a contract employing a particular form of words to express the obligations assumed by the parties may be. To speak of English law and practice providing a useful source of *persuasive* authority on the construction of the policy wherever it may be used, begs the whole question: why is recourse to English law needed at all? The necessity to do so is common ground between the experts on Kuwaiti law on either side; it is because in the absence of an indigenous law of marine insurance in Kuwait English law was the only system of private law by reference to which it was possible for a Kuwaiti court to give a sensible and precise meaning to the language that the parties had chosen to use in the policy. As the authorities that I have cited earlier show, under English conflict rules, which are those your Lordships must apply in determining the jurisdiction point, that makes English law the proper law of the contract.

In agreement with Sir John Donaldson M.R. and May L.J. I would accordingly decide the jurisdiction point in favour of the assured.

## The discretion point

My Lords, the jurisdiction exercised by an English court over a foreign corporation which has no place of business in this country, as a result of granting leave under R.S.C., Ord. 11, r. 1 (1)(f) for service out of the jurisdiction of a writ on that corporation, is an exorbitant jurisdiction, i.e., it is one which, under general English conflict rules, an English court would not recognize as possessed by any foreign court in the absence of some treaty providing for such recognition. Comity thus dictates that the judicial discretion to grant leave under this paragraph of R.S.C., Ord. 11, r. 1(1) should be exercised with circumspection in cases where there exists an alternative forum, viz. the courts of the foreign country where the proposed defendant does carry on business, and whose jurisdiction would be recognised under English conflict rules. Such a forum in the instant case was afforded by the courts of Kuwait.

In order to decide whether a Kuwaiti court, as well as having jurisdiction, is also a forum conveniens for the dispute, one must start by seeing what are likely to be the issues between the parties in the proposed action. The assured's claim is for a constructive total loss of the vessel in circumstances briefly narrated by Bingham J. [1982] 1 W.L.R. 961, 964:

"On February 28, 1980 the vessel entered Ras Al Khafji, a small port in Saudi Arabia, just south of Kuwait. The master and crew were seized by the Saudi Arabian authorities and imprisoned. The crew were released in August 1980 and the master in April 1981. The vessel remained where it was with no crew on board, apparently confiscated. It appears, although the evidence is scant and the Saudi Arabian decision as translated in evidence before me is somewhat opaque, that the master was thought to be using the vessel to try and smuggle diesel oil from Saudi Arabia to the United Arab Emirates. This accusation is strongly denied by [the assured] and the truth of it is likely to be a central issue in the action. Neither [the assured] nor, it would seem [the insurers], feel it prudent to visit Saudi Arabia to inspect the vessel or investigate the matter. [The assured] gave notice of abandonment of the vessel to [the insurers] on October 31, 1980, and again on April 28, 1981.

On each occasion [the insurers] rejected the notice but agreed to treat the case as if a writ had been issued on that date."

The central issue in the litigation, as the judge points out, would appear to be one of fact: was the vessel engaged in smuggling when she was seized by the Saudi Arabian authorities? If she was, the loss was excluded by the exception in clause 4 (1) (e) of the Institute War and Strikes Clauses attached to the policy: "arrest, restraint or detainment...by reason of infringement of any customs regulations." Whether she was or not is a question of fact, which involves Saudi Arabian law. The principal witnesses as to what the vessel was doing, and as to whether what happened after it was seized amounted to a constructive total loss, would be those who were the master and crew of the vessel at the time of her seizure. They are Indian and Bangladesh nationals and upon release by the Saudi Arabian authorities they were repatriated to their native countries where, it appears, they now are. Other principal witnesses would be the Saudi Arabians who seized and detained the vessel and Saudi Arabian officials; they are in Saudi Arabia. Kuwait being on international air routes between Europe and India and the Far East is readily accessible to those potential witnesses and to the only potential witnesses who are said by the assured to be in England: the persons between whom it is said an oral charter of the vessel had been entered into which she was performing at the time of the seizure.

Bingham J. was of opinion that the factual question could be determined as well in Kuwait as in England, possibly better, and with no clear overall balance of convenience. His own view that the proper exercise of his discretion would be to refuse leave to serve the writ out of the jurisdiction, even if the proper law of the policy were English law, was influenced largely by the fact that the jurisdiction sought to be invoked by the assured is an exorbitant jurisdiction, and that he had "been given no reason to doubt that a Kuwaiti judge would set himself thoroughly and justly to determine the truth in this case." ([1982] 1 W.L.R. 961, 971) To this I myself would add that a Kuwaiti judge would be likely to have greater familiarity even than the Commercial Court in England with the sort of thing that goes on in purely local trading in the Arabian Gulf, to which the vessel was by express warranty confined.

Although the issues would appear to be primarily issues of fact, questions of law will also be involved relating to notice of abandonment and constructive total loss which are governed by sections 60 to 63 of the Marine Insurance Act 1906. But, as already mentioned, it is common ground between the expert witnesses on Kuwaiti law that Kuwaiti judges in deciding those questions would, under the Kuwait Code of Conflict of Laws, apply English law as the proper law of any policy of marine insurance entered into in Kuwait before August 15, 1980, if it were in the terms of the Standard Form of English Marine Policy with Institute War and Strike Clauses attached. Like Bingham J., I see no reason why a Kuwaiti court should find any difficulty in applying the relevant English law to the facts once they had been found.

My Lords, it was urged upon this House, as it had been urged upon the courts below, that since Kuwait is one of those countries whose courts adopt the practice and procedure that is followed in countries whose legal systems are derived from the civil law and not from the English common law, the ability of a Kuwaiti court to decide matters of disputed fact is markedly inferior to that of the Commercial Court in England. None of the judges in the courts below accepted this invitation to embark on the invidious task of making a comparison of the relative efficiency of the civil law and common law procedures for the determination of disputed facts. In my opinion, it would have been wholly wrong for an English court, with quite inadequate experience of how it works in practice in a particular country, to condemn as inferior to that of our own country a system of procedure for the trial of issues of fact that has long been adopted by a large number of both developed and developing countries in the modern world. So a natural prejudice in favour of a procedure with which English lawyers are familiar is not a consideration to which any weight ought to be given in determining whether a Kuwaiti court or the Commercial Court in England is the forum conveniens for the present litigation.

Nor, with respect, can I accept the suggestion of Sir John Donaldson M.R. that, for the purposes of the application by national courts of the doctrine of comity between one national court and another, the Commercial Court in London is far more than a national or domestic court; it is an "international commercial court" and that Bingham J. erred in regarding it otherwise. True it is that either directly through a choice of forum clause in commercial contracts or indirectly through an English arbitration clause, the Commercial Court in London is much resorted to by foreign nationals for resolution of disputes; and true it is that its judges have acquired unrivalled expertise in such matters, including marine insurance where that insurance is governed by English law. The latter fact no doubt accounts for the popularity of the court with foreign litigants, but their submission to its jurisdiction in the case of contracts which contain such clauses is voluntary and not, as in the instant case, sought to be forced upon an unwilling defendant in the exercise by an English court of what can be classified only as an exorbitant jurisdiction which it does not recognize as possessed by foreign courts.

My Lords, the onus under R.S.C., Ord. 11, r. 4(2) of making it "sufficient to appear to the court that the case is a proper one for service out of the jurisdiction under this order" lies upon the would-be plaintiff. Refusal to grant leave in a case falling within rule 1 (1) (f) does not deprive him of the opportunity of obtaining justice, because ex hypothesi there exists an alternative forum, the courts of the country where the proposed defendant has its place of business where the contract was made, which would be recognised by the English courts as having jurisdiction over the matter in dispute and whose judgment would be enforceable in England.

The exorbitance of the jurisdiction sought to be invoked where reliance is based exclusively upon rule 1 (1)(f)(iii) is an important factor to be placed in the balance against granting leave. It is a factor that is capable of being outweighed if the would-be plaintiff can satisfy the English court that justice either could not be obtained by him in the alternative forum; or could only be obtained at excessive cost, delay or inconvenience. In the instant case, the assured failed to satisfy Bingham J. that any of these factors in favour of granting leave to compel the insurers to submit to the exorbitant jurisdiction of the English court were of sufficient moment to satisfy the onus. May L.J., applying the principles laid down by this House in *Hadmor Productions Ltd. v. Hamilton* [1983] 1 A.C. 191, saw no grounds for interfering with the way in which Bingham J. had said that he would exercise his discretion, but May L.J. added that if he had thought that he himself had an independent discretion he too would have exercised it in the same way.

I too see no reason for differing from Bingham J. on the discretion point; while, for reasons I have given, I think that Sir John Donaldson M.R. was wrong in supposing that Bingham J. erred in failing to regard the Commercial Court in London as an international commercial court and not simply a national court of England. I would therefore dismiss the appeal.

LORD WILBERFORCE. My Lords, the question in this appeal is whether service of a writ upon the respondents outside the jurisdiction of the English courts should be set aside. The provision in the Rules of the Supreme Court which is relied upon as justifying such service is that contained in R.S.C., Ord. 11, r. 1 (1)(f)(iii), which requires, in the case of an action being brought to enforce a contract, that the contract: "is by its terms, or by implication, governed by English law." The contract in question is a policy of marine insurance, dated April 28, 1979, between the appellants and the respondents, and the first question is, therefore, whether this contract comes within the quoted words. If it is held so to do, so that the court has jurisdiction to order service of the writ in Kuwait, a second question arises whether it should do so in the circumstances of the case.

It has been generally accepted, in my opinion rightly, that the formula used in paragraph (f)(iii) above is equivalent to a requirement that the proper law of the contract should be English law. This involves treating the words "by implication" as covering both the situation whether the parties' mutual intention can be inferred and the situation where, no such inference being possible, it is necessary to seek the system of law with which the contract has its closest and most real connection. Although these situations merge into each other, I regard this case as falling rather within the latter words since I can find no basis for inferring, as between the parties to this contract, an intention that the contract should be governed either by English law or by the law of Kuwait. (I should add here that, as was indicated during the hearing, we cannot, consistently with recent authority, have regard to conduct of the parties subsequent to the making of the contract—here the original policy of 1977.) The court's task must be to have regard objectively to the various factors pointing one way or the other and to estimate, as best it can, where the preponderance lies.

The search is for the "proper law": the law which governs the contract and the parties' obligations under it; the law which determines (normally) its validity and legality, its construction and effect, and the conditions of its discharge. It is clear that, as regards this contract, there are only two choices, English law and the law of Kuwait. It is worth considering at the outset what these alternatives involve.

The Lloyd's S.G. form of policy, which the policy in this case is with insignificant departures, its obsolete and, in parts, unintelligible language, is one which has been used for centuries, almost without change. The Marine Insurance Act 1906, a codification Act, passed after 12 years of gestation, which schedules the Lloyd's S.G. policy as a permissible form of policy, also provides in the Schedule a number of definitions. These definitions may be regarded as a form of glossary based on established law, and the substantive provisions in the Act (binding by statutory force only if the proper law is English), as evidence of the established and customary law of marine insurance. I think that we can accept that if Kuwaiti law were regarded as the proper law, it would resort to the definitions and would have regard to commercial custom as (inter alia) manifested by the Act. The expert evidence, in my opinion, establishes so much in relation to the relevant law of Kuwait prior to 1980 when Kuwait introduced its own insurance legislation. Thus, whether English or Kuwaiti law is the proper law, the terms of the contract would be given the meaning ascribed to them by English statute, custom, and decisions.

There is nothing unusual in a situation where, under the proper law of a contract, resort is had to some other system of law for purposes of interpretation. In that case, that other system becomes a source of the law upon which the proper law may draw. Such is frequently the case where a given system of law has not yet developed rules and principles in relation to an activity which has become current, or where another system has from experience built up a coherent and tested structure--as, for example, in banking, insurance or admiralty law, or where countries exist with a common legal heritage such as the common law or the French legal system. In such a case, the proper law is not applying a "conflicts" rule (there may, in fact, be no foreign element in the case) but merely importing a foreign product for domestic use.

There is evidence before us that in relation to insurance, and in particular to cases where Lloyd's S.G. policies are used, courts in Europe do this, and that the courts in Kuwait would act in a similar way, resorting, as to a source of their own domestic law, to English law directly or indirectly via Turkish law.

So returning to the choice before us, it is between the proper law being English law, or the proper law being Kuwaiti law, drawing in part at least on English interpretations. This analysis, if correct, thus early in the discussion calls in question the validity of one line of argument used to support the appellants' case (that the governing law is English law). That argument is simply (I am tempted to say simplistically) that since this contract is in English language and form and embodies many technical expressions which can only be explained by resort to English law, that shows that the proper law, the law governing the contract, must be English law. There are three reasons why this cannot be correct:

(1) As a matter of reasoning it inverts the process which has to be followed. Instead of arguing from the proper law to that which governs interpretation it does the reverse. The form of the contract may indeed be a factor to be considered in the search for the proper law—it is so here, and an important one, but one to be considered with other factors.

(2) It is inconsistent with authority including that of this House. In *Whitworth Street Estates (Manchester) Ltd. v. James Miller & Partners Ltd.* [1970] A.C. 583 the question for decision was whether the proper law was that of England or of Scotland. The contract was on an English R.I.B.A. form which had "many connections with English law" (Lord Hodson, p. 606). It had, in fact, been built up and amended from time to time as the result of English decisions. The decision, by a scarcely discernible majority, was that the proper law was English, but this decision was arrived at by a careful weighing of factors, including the nature and origin of the form. There can be little doubt that on either view, whichever the proper law was held to be, the contract would have fallen to be interpreted according to English law, but this circumstance alone was not regarded as decisive. Similarly, in *Compagnie Tunisienne de Navigation S.A. v. Compagnie d'Armement Maritime S.A.* [1971] A.C. 572, the use of an English form of charter was regarded as a factor to be considered, and the decision was that the proper law was French. Reliance was placed on some observations of Lord Wright in the Privy Council case of *Vita Food Products Inc. v. Unus Shipping Co. Ltd.* [1939] A.C. 277, 298. The passage is quoted in part by my noble and learned friend, Lord Diplock. But, as I understand him, Lord Wright was concerned only with the difference in terminology between that case and *The Torni* [1932] P. 78. I do not read his observations as equating the law governing construction with the proper law; if they were so intended, I could not, with respect, agree with them.

(3) The simple proposition that because a form of contract has to be interpreted in accordance with English rules, or even decisions, the proper law must be English law would have very unfortunate consequences. It is well known, and not disputed, that this Lloyd's S.G. policy is widely used, not only in the British Commonwealth, or countries under British influence, but elsewhere, including countries in Europe. It is regularly used in the Middle East and in the Arabian Gulf. It is a strong thing to say that, in the absence of an express choice of law clause, the proper law of all such policies is to be regarded by an English court as English.

The wide use made of this form of policy calls, on the contrary, for a careful examination in each case of the question what proper law is appropriate, the English law form or derivation of the form being an (important) factor. I do not believe, with respect, that this argument, which both Bingham J. and Robert Goff L.J. regarded as important, can be disposed of by describing it as contending for an internationalised, or floating, contract, unattached to any system of law--to do so does not do it justice. The argument is that the Lloyd's S.G. form of policy is taken into a great number of legal systems, sometimes by statute, as in Australia, sometimes as a matter of commercial practice, as in Belgium or Germany, or in the Arabian Gulf, and that in such cases, though their legal systems may, and on the evidence do, resort to English law in order to interpret its terms, the contract may be regarded as an Australian, Belgian, German, etc. contract. What has to be done is to look carefully at all those factors normally regarded as relevant when the proper law is being searched for, including of course the nature of the policy itself, and to form a judgment as to the system of law with which that policy in the circumstances has the closest and most real connection.

In my opinion, therefore, the classic process of weighing the factors must be followed, with all the difficulties inherent in the process. They are well and clearly listed in the judgment of Sir John Donaldson M.R. I agree with him that the majority of the ingredients said to connect the policy with English law are irrelevant or lacking in weight—these include payment of premiums in sterling in London and the use of J.H. Minet & Co. Ltd., London brokers. The significant factors remain: (1) the use of this form of policy expressed in the English language and requiring interpretation according to English rules and practice; (2) the nationality of the parties, the defendants being incorporated and carrying on business in Kuwait and the plaintiffs being Liberian and resident in Dubai (i.e. neither in England nor in Kuwait); (3) the use of English sterling as the money of account; (4) the issue of the policy in Kuwait—this I regard as of little weight; (5) provision in claims to be paid in Kuwait. This, too, is of minor consequence in view of the practice, established at the time of contracting, of settling claims in London. I think also, for myself, that it is not without importance that the policy contains no choice of law clause. With a policy in a form so essentially English, the absence of such a factor leaves the form and language, as a pointer towards English law, without what one would consider as its natural counterweight. I agree that omission of the Lombard Street or Royal Exchange or London clause is insignificant, but I regard the incorporation of the Institute Clauses, with express reference to English law provisions, as important. With no great confidence, and reluctantly differing as to the ultimate conclusion from Bingham J. and Robert Goff L.J., whose reasoning in principle I approve and follow, I have reached the conclusion that English law is the proper law of this particular contract.

That makes it necessary to decide whether, even so, service of this writ outside the jurisdiction should be allowed to stand. R.S.C., Ord. 11, r. 1 merely states that, given one of the stated conditions, such service is permissible, and it is still necessary for the plaintiff (in this case the appellant) to make it "sufficiently to appear to the court that the case is a proper one for service out of the jurisdiction under this Order" (r. 4 (2)). The rule does not state the considerations by which the court is to decide whether the case is a proper one, and I do not think that we can get much assistance from cases where it is sought to stay an action started in this country, or to enjoin the bringing of proceedings abroad. The situations are different: compare the observations of Stephenson L.J. in *Aratra Potato Co. Ltd. v. Egyptian Navigation Co. (The El Amria)* [1981] 2 Lloyd's Rep. 119, 129. The intention must be to impose upon the plaintiff the burden of showing good reasons why service of a writ, calling for appearance before an English court, should, in the circumstances, be permitted upon a foreign defendant. In considering this question the court must take into account the nature of the dispute, the legal and practical issues involved, such questions as local knowledge, availability of witnesses and their evidence and expense. It is not appropriate, in my opinion, to embark upon a comparison of the procedures, or methods, or reputation or standing of the courts of one country as compared with those of another (cf. *The El Amria* [1981] 2 Lloyd's Rep. 119, 126 per Brandon L.J.). In this case, Bingham J. having first decided there was no jurisdiction to order service in Kuwait, then proceeded, after a review of the factors, to express the opinion that, if there was jurisdiction, he would not consider that it should be exercised. This in my opinion was a substantive decision on the point, viz. an alternative ground of decision of the case before him, not a mere obiter dictum. It is, of course, appealable and was considered, without definitive result, by the Court of Appeal. Having weighed the factors involved and having the benefit of the analysis of them by my noble and learned friend, Lord Diplock, I have come to the conclusion that his decision on this point was right.

For this reason I would dismiss the appeal.

[Lords Roskill, Brandon of Oakbrook and Brightman concurred.]

*        *        *

C.    THE SITUATION IN ENGLISH LAW: SOME CONCLUDING
      OBSERVATIONS

Even in the absence of tangible commercial contacts with the forum, English courts appear disposed to find judicial jurisdiction over cases if the contract is drafted in English, or the currency is in Sterling. English Law will probably be used to supplement any gaps in the contract. Although *Amin Rasheed* rejected English jurisdiction, it is worth bearing in mind that Lord Wilberforce listed the significant factors establishing a connection between the English legal system and a transnational contract between parties of diverse nationality as including an insurance policy in English and the use of English Sterling as the money of account, while dismissing the importance of the place in which the contract was concluded, in this case Kuwait. In the absence of a choice of law by the parties, these factors seem to point toward English law: "With policy in a form so essentially English, the absence of such a factor leaves the form in language, as a pointer towards English law, without what one would consider as its natural counterweight." (*Infra* p. 70) These broad tendencies in favor of judicial jurisdiction are only partially controlled by tempering the discretion involved in the application of this long-arm statute. Thus, the probability of an unwilling defendant prevailing against an asserted jurisdiction by a forum-shopping plaintiff who has selected England would appear no higher than for a defendant in a comparable dilemma in a United States court.

## IV.    OVERALL CONSEQUENCES OF INTERNATIONAL JURISDICTIONAL UNCERTAINTY AND SOLUTIONS

The interaction of an international law that permits concurrent national jurisdiction for the same events with national practices of long-arming means that, in the absence of an anticipatory contractual limitation, either party to an international transaction may potentially initiate suit in a wide range of national fora. Such a structural option has consequences both for the transaction itself as well as the generation and the resolution of disputes.

1.  There is symmetrical pressure on each party to use the initiation of suits as a means of forcing renegotiation of contracts.

2.  Uncertainty with regard to legal regimes of the various optional fora and, as a result, the instability of contractual expectations press both parties to initiate suit in the most preferred forum whether in terms of procedural law, substantive law, or other tactical advantages, if only to preempt the other from doing the same first.

3.  As a result, races to the courthouse and initiation of defensive suits are likely to proliferate.

4. It is difficult to say where a case (such as the hypotheticals at the beginning of this chapter) will be heard and, as a consequence, what mixture of procedural and substantive law will apply.

In light of these circumstances, the planning of jurisdiction in international transactions presents an unavoidable problem which the responsible practitioner must address and solve in the course of structuring international transactions.

A.    SOLUTION NUMBER 1: PLANNING JURISDICTION BY
      CONTRACTUAL PROVISION FOR NEGOTIATION,
      MEDIATION, CONCILIATION OR MINI-TRIALS

Considerations such as the increasing costs of both litigation and
arbitration along with the tendency of such procedures to freeze parties
into adversarial relationships have given rise to interest in and public
support for alternative dispute resolution (ADR). In general, ADR
refers to modalities for resolving disputes which are not affiliated with
the apparatus of the state and which may or may not yield a binding
and enforceable outcome. This section addresses the utility of
contractual commitments to negotiation, mediation, conciliation and the
so-called "mini-trial" as "solutions" to the problem of jurisdictional
uncertainty in international transactions.

1.    NEGOTIATION

Throughout the performance of any contract, parties are
involved in constant exchanges about the meaning of the agreement and
its application and adaptation to unforeseen circumstances. When acute
disagreements emerge, it is usually in the common interest of the
parties to arrive at some sort of accommodation.

In this context, negotiation can be viewed as a form of alternate
dispute resolution, and is sometimes the terminal form in the sense that
it resolves the dispute. In addition, exhaustion of negotiation efforts is
frequently *required* by law, as a pre-condition for the initiation of
formal or state-related third-party dispute resolution mechanisms. For
example, many systems insist that parties seek to negotiate in good
faith before they can invoke an arbitration clause, while in some
national systems, e.g., Japan, there may be mandatory third-party
supervised negotiations. Even in the absence of such requirements,
judges may "urge" the parties to renew efforts to reach a negotiated
solution.

Negotiation, as opposed to arbitration and adjudication, does not
have an explicit substantive or procedural framework. In practice,
however, the process of negotiation exhibits certain implicit
fundamental norms, which tend to be oriented toward accommodation
and resolution of disputes and not necessarily strict application of law.
Thus, although parties, in the course of negotiation, frequently invoke
legal positions, there is no expectation or demand that a negotiated

solution be consistent with prior understandings of an agreement. Indeed, one party is usually pressing *de facto* for some modification of the existing agreement.

Negotiation is usually the preferred modality of the functionally stronger party in a relationship. In some cases parties that anticipate that they will be in a functionally stronger position for the duration of the agreement or life of the transaction and believe that, even if a dispute arises, the interests of all the parties in continuing the operations of the transaction will ensure that operations will not be disrupted, may have a rational incentive *not* to incorporate a third-party dispute resolving mechanism in the agreement. Even where the functionally stronger party decides that it wishes to submit to some binding mechanism as a back-up form of dispute resolution, its functionally dominant position may still permit it, in the negotiations prior to such dispute resolution, to prescribe or inflect certain features of the dispute resolution mode in ways that are likely to discriminate in its own favor.

Negotiation, as does the mini-trial *infra*, may require a party to reveal its legal case before it wants to. Contractually mandated requirements for negotiation are least likely to arise where parties cannot determine in advance which of them will be functionally stronger or whether disputes are likely to disrupt the continuing operation of the transaction. In such cases, the parties share an incentive to establish some explicit modality for resolving potential disputes, rather than relying on an internal negotiation procedure. Variable features such as the certainty of the operation of such a mechanism and the rapidity with which it can be put into operation can be negotiated in advance. Similarly, parties can, by advance agreement, limit potential remedies to the chosen means of dispute resolution, a factor which may be of interest to one or more of the parties.

## 2. MEDIATION

Although mediation in the domestic context typically refers to a mechanism for resolving labor disputes, in the international context it typically refers to intervention to resolve a conflict between states. If the parties in disputes are purely commercial actors, one would expect the dispute resolution mechanism to more closely approach mediation in a domestic context. In such an instance,

[e]ither the parties voluntarily submit the matter to a public or private dispute resolution organization, or a court may suggest or order the parties to submit to mediation. Mediators generally are process-oriented. Their responsibilities include arranging meetings between the parties, assisting in the exchange of information, and relaying the parties' interests and positions. In fulfilling this role, mediators may conduct private meetings with the parties to facilitate the negotiations, and may participate actively by proposing settlements.[11]

In contrast, mediators in disputes involving two states typically play a more active role. Not only may the mediator serve as an aid in communication between the parties and as a source of compromises, but the mediator may take on the role of manipulating the parties into agreement.

In addition to helping adversaries communicate (providing "good offices") and endeavoring to change their images of each other (conciliation), mediators often suggest compromises and may negotiate and bargain with adversaries in an attempt to induce them to change their stance. Mediation is distinct from arbitration, which involves judicial procedure and results in a verdict the parties have committed themselves to accept. Mediation, on the other hand, is basically a political process; there is no advance commitment by the parties to accept the mediator's ideas.

.    .    .

In some situations, position and communication may not be enough to bring about reduction of conflict .  .  .  . The mediator may have to use its position and other available resources to manipulate the parties into agreement, or perhaps into a particular agreement that

---

[11] Eldon H. Crowell & Charles Pou, Jr., *Appealing Contract Decisions: Reducing the Cost and Delay of Procurement Litigation with Alternative Dispute Resolution Techniques*, 49 MD. L. REV. 183, 228 (1990).

appears to the mediator to be the most stable or most favorable. <u>The mediator as a manipulator</u> requires leverage—resources of power, influence, and persuasion that can be brought to bear on the parties to move them to agreement. Leverage is the most elusive element of mediation . . . .[12]

### 3.    CONCILIATION

Eric A. Schwartz, *International Conciliation and the ICC*, ICC INT'L CT. ARB. BULL., Nov. 1994, at 5.

The search for quicker and cheaper means of resolving business disputes has, in recent years, given rise to increased interest in alternatives to both traditional litigation and arbitration, particularly in the United States and other common law jurisdictions sometimes criticised for their "litigious excesses." In Europe, the promotion of alternative dispute resolution techniques other than arbitration ("ADR") has, until now, been much less pronounced, although ADR, in various forms, has long existed there and in other parts of the world. Of course, in Asia, ADR is well known to be firmly rooted in the local landscape.

There are powerful forces that militate in favour of ADR. The conduct of formal litigation, or even arbitration, may, in addition to being costly and possible time-consuming, entail considerable disruption and distraction for the parties involved. Ultimate victory may therefore often be obtained at what, in retrospect, appears to the winning party to be a disproportionately high cost. Indeed, practitioners realise that most commercial disputes can best be resolved through negotiation, and, in fact, the great majority (approximately two-thirds) of the arbitrations administered by the ICC are settled by the parties prior to completion. In many countries, moreover, judges and arbitrators regard it as their duty to try to help the parties settle their dispute before proceeding with a case.

.    .    .

---

[12] INTERNATIONAL MEDIATION IN THEORY AND PRACTICE 7, 13 (Saadia Touval & I. William Zartman, eds. 1985).

## I - THE ICC RULES OF OPTIONAL CONCILIATION

The first and possibly most significant feature of the Conciliation Rules is that they nowhere state what conciliation is or what precisely an ICC conciliator is required to do. Although the Rules (Article 11) envisage that the conciliator may put forward proposals, which the parties are free either to accept or reject (Article 7), for the settlement of the dispute in question, they do not require the conciliator to do so. How conciliators conduct the conciliation and whether or not they make any recommendations to the parties are matters left entirely to the conciliators' discretion (Article 5), the result being that "conciliation" under the Conciliation Rules can reasonably embrace any process in which a third-party neutral assists parties to settle a dispute amicably.

For all practical purposes, therefore, no particular significance need be attached to the use in the rules of the word "conciliation," as opposed, for example, to "mediation." Although "conciliation" and "mediation" are often distinguished, the Conciliation Rules are so broadly drafted that they should permit an ICC conciliator to "conciliate" or to "mediate," no matter how those respective terms may be understood.

.    .    .

The Rules are, first of all, extremely concise, with only eleven articles.

An ICC conciliation proceeding is commenced by the submission to the Secretariat of the ICC International Court of Arbitration of a conciliation application (together with a payment of U.S. $ 500) (Conciliation Rules, Article 2). The application is required to set out "succinctly" the purpose of the request. However, no particular documents or other information are required to be included, as in the case of an ICC Request for Arbitration.

There is also no requirement, as already stated, that there be a previous agreement between the parties to conciliate their disputes. Rather, the conciliation is set in motion if the other party agrees to participate within 15 days after having been notified of the conciliation request (Conciliation Rules, Article 3).

If the parties agree to attempt conciliation, the Secretary General of the ICC Court then appoints a conciliator. Unlike in ICC arbitration, only the Secretariat of the ICC Court and not the ICC Court itself has any involvement in the process. Thus, the Secretary General (rather than the ICC Court) designates the conciliator and fixes the conciliator's remuneration as well as the ICC's administrative charge. The Rules (Article 4) also provide for a sole conciliator (although they do not exclude the possible appointment of more than one conciliator should this be the parties' wish).

The Rules do not lay down any condition or requirements concerning the conciliator to be appointed. Once appointed, the conciliator is to conduct the proceedings as he or she thinks fit (Article 5).

.    .    .

The drafters of the Conciliation Rules assumed that, before agreeing to participate in a conciliation proceeding, parties will normally wish to be sure that they do not risk prejudicing themselves in the event that the conciliation is not successful and subsequent arbitration or judicial proceedings are instituted. The Conciliation Rules therefore provide (see Article 6) that:

> "The confidential nature of the conciliation process shall be respected by every person who is involved in it in whatever capacity."

The confidentiality of any agreement reached by the parties during the conciliation is, moreover, expressly protected (Conciliation Rules, Article 7), and Article 11 further provides that

> "The parties agree not to introduce in any judicial or arbitration proceeding as evidence or in any manner whatsoever:
>
> a) any views expressed or suggestions made by any party with regard to the possible settlement of the dispute;
>
> b) any proposals put forward by the conciliator;
>
> c) the fact that a party had indicated that it was ready to accept some proposal for a settlement put forward by the conciliator."

The Conciliation Rules (Article 10) also prohibit the conciliator from acting "in any judicial or arbitration proceeding relating to the dispute which has been the subject of the conciliation process whether as an arbitrator, representative or counsel of a party" or as a witness, unless the parties otherwise agree.

The Conciliation Rules therefore clearly envisage the complete separation of the conciliation and arbitration processes, unless the parties have otherwise agreed, in contrast to ADR schemes where the conciliator (or mediator) would carry on as an arbitrator if the conciliation (or mediation) attempt were to fail. The ICC Rules of Arbitration, moreover, do not make any provision for possible conciliation during the ICC arbitral process, unlike under certain other regimes where conciliation may be integrated into the arbitral process.

It is to be noted that the provisions on confidentiality relate, by their terms, only to the conciliation process itself and, thus, may not necessarily bar any reference, in a subsequent arbitration or judicial proceeding, to the fact that conciliation may have been requested by a party, but refused by the other. Nor does Article 11 expressly bar the introduction in subsequent judicial or arbitration proceedings of evidence provided to a party by the other during a conciliation. (Evidentiary submissions may arguably be protected, however, by the general confidentiality rule set forth in Article 6.)

.    .    .

During the six-year period between January 1, 1988, when the current version of the Conciliation Rules entered into force, and December 31, 1993, the ICC received 54 Requests for Conciliation, and, out of that relatively small number of applications, an agreement to attempt conciliation was reached in 16 cases. Of those 16 cases, however, only ten actually went forward (of which one is still pending). Five of the other six cases were withdrawn — in four of them by the party who initiated the procedure — before the appointment of a conciliator. The sixth case was settled by the parties directly without recourse to the conciliator appointed.

.    .    .

A typical example is a recently completed conciliation involving a dispute between parties from Switzerland and Monaco. The dispute concerned a contract for the joint commercialisation of a product developed by one of the two companies concerned ("ABC") and the related use of its trademark. The other company ("XYZ") was obligated to pay FF 10,000,000 to ABC, purchase product from ABC and develop a large number of outlets for the sale of the product in question over a ten-year period. After one year XYZ came to the conclusion that the contract was not commercially viable for various reasons and sought either to renegotiate certain financial arrangements or terminate it. ABC, however, was unwilling to accept any of XYZ's proposals. The contract provided for the resolution of all disputes by ICC arbitration.

On March 11, 1992, counsel for XYZ submitted a Request for Conciliation to the ICC (although this was not provided for in the contract itself). XYZ's counsel stated, in its Request, that

> "Given the deterioration in the relations between the parties, which is manifested by the fact that they now only communicate by registered letter, it is clear that they cannot possibly successfully complete their initial project.

> "In these circumstances ... [XYZ] wishes the conciliation of the International Chamber of Commerce of Paris in order to bring to an end the contract tying it to ... [ABC]"

By letter, dated March 27, 1992, ABC agreed to attempt to conciliate. A conciliator was then appointed by the Secretary General of the ICC Court and an advance on costs was fixed (in the amount of U.S.$ 13,000) by April 15, 1992. The advance was payable by the parties in equal shares, and, upon receipt of the full payment, the ICC submitted the file to the conciliator on May 13, 1992. The conciliator immediately contacted the partes in order to give them an opportunity to make written submissions and to fix a "hearing" date on July 9, 1992. At the July 9, 1992 hearing, which lasted six hours, a settlement agreement was reached providing for certain payments by XYZ to ABC and the termination of the contract. The dispute was thus resolved within two months of the conciliator's receipt of the file. The total cost to the parties (exclusive of their own legal expenses) was U.S.$ 13,000 (U.S.$ 2,000 for the ICC's administrative charge and U.S.$ 11,000 for the conciliator's fees and expenses), substantially less than they might have been expected to pay had the case gone to ICC arbitration.

.    .    .

In some cases, the settlement proposals of the conciliator have been submitted to the parties in writing with an analysis of the relevant facts and law, much in the manner of an arbitration award. In fact, one such proposal so closely resembled an award that the parties were identified as "claimant" and "defendant," terms that the Conciliation Rules carefully and appropriately avoid as the proceedings are not intended to be adversarial. (The conciliator's proposals in that one case, moreover, while well motivated, were not accepted by the "defendant," who, the conciliator suggested, should pay to the "claimant" essentially all that it was claiming.)

ICC conciliators have also been notably reluctant to meet (or "caucus") separately with the parties during the conciliation process. In the only case in which this was proposed, the conciliator, a non-lawyer from a common law jurisdiction, invited the parties

> "... to consider whether it would be their wish that the ... [conciliator] can interview the Parties separately during the conciliation proceedings. If this is the wish of the Parties, then any factual information given or allegations made by a party in such separate interviews may be disclosed to the other party for comment, but only with the consent of the disclosing party. If consent is withheld, then the ... [conciliator] would have to seek, by his own questions, ways to give the other party the opportunity to provide their point of view on the disclosed material."

In response, both parties indicated that they did not object to the conciliator interviewing the parties separately during the conciliation proceedings. However, they both insisted that any information given, or allegation made, by a party in such an interview should be disclosed to the other party for comments. In addition, it was proposed that the counsel of the party being interviewed should always be present.

Thus, even in that one instance, the participants in the conciliation were reluctant to jettison those elements of arbitral procedure that they regarded as fundamental to ensuring that they would have an opportunity both to present their case and to answer the case being made against them.

\*     \*     \*

### a.     ICC CONCILIATION RULES

## Rules of Optional Conciliation

.     .     .

Article 2: The party requesting conciliation shall apply to the Secretariat of the Court of the International Chamber of Commerce setting out succinctly the purpose of the request and accompanying it with the fee required to open the file, as set out in Appendix III hereto.

Article 3: The Secretariat of the Court shall, as soon as possible, inform the other party of the request for conciliation. That party will be given a period of 15 days to inform the Secretariat whether it agrees or declines to participate in the attempt to conciliate.

If the other party agrees to participate in the attempt to conciliate it shall so inform the Secretariat within such period.

In the absence of any reply within such period or in the case of a negative reply the request for conciliation shall be deemed to have been declined. The Secretariat shall, as soon as possible, so inform the party which had requested conciliation.

Article 4: Upon receipt of an agreement to attempt conciliation, the Secretary General of the Court shall appoint a conciliator as soon as possible. The conciliator shall inform the parties of his appointment and set a time limit for the parties to present their respective arguments to him.

Article 5: The conciliator shall conduct the conciliation process as he thinks fit, guided by the principles of impartiality, equity and justice.

With the agreement of the parties, the conciliator shall fix the place for conciliation.

The conciliator may at any time during the conciliation process request a party to submit to him such additional information as he deems necessary.

The parties may, if they so wish, be assisted by counsel of their choice.

Article 6: The confidential nature of the conciliation process shall be respected by every person who is involved in it in whatever capacity.

Article 7: The conciliation process shall come to an end:

a) Upon the parties signing an agreement. The parties shall be bound by such agreement. The agreement shall remain confidential unless and to the extent that its execution or application require disclosure.

b) Upon the production by the conciliator of a report recording that the attempt to conciliate has not been successful. Such report shall not contain reasons.

c) Upon notification to the conciliator by one or more parties at any time during the conciliation process of an intention no longer to pursue the conciliation process.

Article 8: Upon termination of the conciliation, the conciliator shall provide the Secretariat of the Court with the settlement agreement signed by the parties or with his report of lack of success or with a notice from one or more parties of the intention no longer to pursue the conciliation process.

.   .   .

Article 11: The parties agree not to introduce in any judicial or arbitration proceeding as evidence or in any manner whatsoever:

a) any views expressed or suggestions made by any party with regard to the possible settlement of the dispute;

b) any proposals put forward by the conciliator;

c) the fact that a party had indicated that it was ready to accept some proposal for a settlement put forward by the conciliator.

### Notes and Questions

1. Note that ICC conciliation is optional. If the party against which a conciliation is sought declines to participate there can be no conciliation.

2. Note also that ICC conciliation makes no reference to application of law. Instead, the rules appear to contemplate an amiable composition of differences without recourse to specific legal standards. Who benefits from this procedure?

3. Discuss the reasons for holding admissible or inadmissible in a subsequent judicial or arbitral proceeding, views, proposals by parties or settlement proposals by conciliators expressed in the conciliation phase.

### b.    UNCITRAL CONCILIATION RULES OF JULY 23, 1980

In June 1973, the United Nations Commission on International Trade Law (UNCITRAL) decided to include among its programs a procedure for the conciliation of international trade disputes. Previous discussions had revealed that conciliation, due to its non-adversarial nature, was sometimes preferred over arbitration by parties from countries which do not favor a strongly adversarial system for internal dispute resolution. The Conciliation Rules are based on the assumption that arbitration is an adversarial procedure and, in contrast, emphasize the non-adversary nature of the conciliation process. Thus, the conciliator is empowered only to suggest ways to settle the dispute which may be rejected by either party or be modified jointly by the parties; moreover, conciliation proceedings can be terminated by a unilateral declaration by either party (Conciliation Rules, Art. 15).

### c.     ICSID CONCILIATION

[ICSID provides for a conciliation procedure under Articles 28-35 of the ICSID Convention (Supplement at p. 101-04).]

### 4.     MINI-TRIALS

Allen B. Green & Deneice Jordan-Walker, *Alternative Dispute Resolution in International Government Contracting: A Proposal*, 20 G.W.J. INT'L L. & ECON. 419, 435-38 (1987).

In recent years, mini-trials have become an increasingly popular ADR method in international commercial and government contracts disputes. Mini-trials are considered to be a viable alternative to lengthy and costly litigation and arbitration proceedings.[13] The Zurich Chamber of Commerce announced in October 1984 that the mini-trial would be available to the international business community as a method for resolving international disputes.[14] Similarly, the U.S. Army Corps of Engineers in March 1985 instituted a pilot mini-trial program for the resolution of disputes involving contract appeals by domestic and foreign contractors.[15] Several multinational corporations also have used mini-trials to resolve their disputes.[16]

---

[13] *See generally* J. HENRY & J. LIEBERMAN, [THE MANAGER'S GUIDE TO RESOLVING LEGAL DISPUTES] 36-47 (1985) . . . (discussing seven advantages of a mini-trial). The advantages of a mini-trial include cost reduction, creative problem-solving, preservation of continuing business relationships, choice of a neutral advisor, tailor-made process, maintenance of confidentiality, and time savings. *Id.*

[14] *See* Desax, *The Zurich Mini-Trial: A New Option for International Dispute Resolution*, 3 ALTERNATIVES 1, 3 (Jan. 1985).

[15] *See Army Engineers Succeed in 1st Mini-Trial*, 3 ALTERNATIVES 3 (Mar. 1985).

[16] The CPR Legal Program at 1 (Mar. 1985) (available at the Center for Public Resources, New York) [hereinafter CPR Legal Program]. Allied Corporation, American Can Company, Austin Industries, Borden, Control Data Corporation, Intel, Shell Oil Company, Space Communications Company, Standard Oil of Indiana, Telecredit, Texaco, TRW, Union Carbide, and Wisconsin Electric Power Company are among the corporations using mini-trials to resolve disputes. *Id.* at 1.

## 1.     Avoidance of Litigation

The purpose of a mini-trial is to resolve business disputes through out-of-court settlements.[17] The mini-trial involves a one to three day presentation by senior executives of the disputing parties summarizing the strengths and weaknesses of each party's position. A neutral advisor normally presides over the presentation.[18] The presentation is followed by negotiations between the executives, who have the authority to settle the dispute.[19] The formality of the proceedings depends on both the procedures adopted by the forum conducting the mini-trial[20] and the mini-trial agreement between the parties.[21]

While a mini-trial is not "really a trial at all,"[22] and therefore not a hostile dispute resolution method, the proceedings are not entirely free of adversity. The presentation, which is a key part of the mini-trial, is made on behalf of the parties by their respective representatives who act as advocates for their client's interests. As such, these representatives present, in the form of pleadings and testimonial or documentary evidence, the strengths of their client's case while

---

[17] *Id.*

[18] *See generally* J. HENRY & J. LIEBERMAN, *supra* note 13[1], at 32-33 (discussing seven advantages of a third-party neutral advisor). There are several reasons why parties generally prefer that a neutral third-party advisor moderate the proceedings. The advisor can facilitate the exchange of information between the parties and encourage the parties to consider joint gains. In addition, the advisor can create the proper procedural background for negotiation and assist the parties in determining reasonable prices. The advisor also can advise the parties when they are acting unreasonably or maintaining unreasonable positions and can keep negotiations going when they otherwise would break down. Finally, the advisor can explain the reasons for an agreement, thereby encouraging acceptance of settlement. *Id.*

[19] *See generally Id.* at 30-32 (discussing the advantages of appointing executives to settle a dispute).

[20] *See, e.g.*, Rules of Procedure for the Zurich Mini-Trial, *reprinted in* Desax, *supra* note 14[12] . . ., at 4-5.

[21] The advantage of the mini-trial procedure is its informality and flexibility. J. HENRY & J. LIEBERMAN, *supra* note 13[1], at 30.

[22] CPR Legal Program, *supra* note 16[14] . . ., at 1.

accentuating the weaknesses of the opponent's position.[23] In this respect, the presentation may closely resemble litigation.[24]

Most mini-trial proceedings result in private settlement of disputes rather than subsequent litigation despite this element of adversariness.[25] This high settlement rate is due in part to the substitution of highly qualified and motivated business executives for lawyers and other third parties during negotiations. These executives enter the proceedings with the objective of reaching a mutually beneficial settlement in order to avoid litigation. The mini-trial process also encourages the parties to consider the long-term mutual benefits of maintaining their established business relationships and the value of making certain tradeoffs in order to preserve these relationships.[26]

2.      Expense

The costs associated with a mini-trial proceeding appear to be substantially lower than either litigation or arbitration.[27] This lower cost is due primarily to the mini-trial's relatively expeditious resolution of disputes and the elimination of costs inherent in litigation and arbitration, such as court costs and attorneys' fees.

The pilot mini-trial program currently being tested by the U.S. Army Corp of Engineers illustrates the cost advantages of the mini-trial. The Corps of Engineers recently settled a $630,000 claim with a construction contractor in a mini-trial proceeding that lasted only two

---

[23] For a contrary view, see Crowell, [*Arbitrating Commercial Disputes: More Problems than Promise*, 15 NAT'L CONT. MGMT. J. 1, 10 (1981)] . . . .

[24] Transnational Corporate Disputes Workshop, Second Annual Corporate Dispute Resolution Institute 2 (Nov. 10-11, 1983) (available at the Center for Public Resources, New York).

[25] CPR Legal Program, *supra* note 16[14] . . ., at 1.

[26] *See* Carter, [*Litigation Alternatives For Companies,* NAT'L L. J., Jan. 16, 1984, at 20] . . . .

[27] According to the cases cited in THE MANAGER'S GUIDE TO RESOLVING LEGAL DISPUTES, the costs of a mini-trial appear to be much less than the costs had those cases been litigated. *See* J. HENRY & J. LIEBERMAN, *supra* note 13[1], at 36-39.

and one half days.[28] The presentation of each party's position, cross examinations, and a discussion by the neutral facilitator took two days. The subsequent negotiations between the executives of the government and the contractor lasted less than twelve hours.[29] If the case had been litigated, there likely would have been several weeks of hearings before the Army Corps of Engineers Board of Contract Appeals or the Armed Services Board of Contract Appeals.[30] The Corps of Engineers also settled a $45 million claim in June 1985 with the Morrison-Knudsen Company in a five-day mini-trial proceeding.[31] The costs of both of these proceedings appear to have been much less than if the disputes had been fully litigated.

## 3.      Confidentiality and Neutrality

Mini-trials generally are considered to be private proceedings.[32] The mini-trial, like other ADR techniques, involves the problem of selecting an impartial advisor. The potential damage to the integrity of the mini-trial proceeding from selecting a biased advisor, however, is significantly less than it is to an arbitration proceeding. A mini-trial advisor, unlike an arbitrator, is not the ultimate decisionmaker. The advisor merely facilitates a settlement as agreed to by the parties, and if the dispute proceeds to trial, the advisor may provide an advisory opinion on the outcome of the dispute.[33] The opinion is neither binding nor legally enforceable.

---

[28] *See Army Engineers Succeed in 1st Mini-Trial, supra* note 15[13] . . ., at 1.

[29] *Id.*

[30] *Id.*

[31] Ruttinger, *Army Corps of Engineers Settles $45 Million Claim at Mini-Trial*, 3 ALTERNATIVES 1, 2 (Aug. 1985).

[32] *See* J. HENRY & J. LIEBERMAN, *supra* note 13[1], at 45-46. The mini-trial proceeding is held in secrecy. *Id.* at 45. Information about the proceeding need not be disclosed and documents remain the property of the parties. *Id.*

[33] Carter, *supra* note . . . 26[24], at 20-21 . . . .

4.      Preservation of Business Relationships

The use of the mini-trial can preserve business relationships for several reasons. First, mini-trials resolve disputes expeditiously, thereby reducing the amount of time for tension and discord to build. Second, mini-trials require senior executives of the disputing parties to maintain meaningful dialogue with an aim toward reaching a mutually advantageous business solution. And finally, mini-trials encourage the parties to focus on the economically sound objective of maintaining a business relationship that can produce a "shared stream of benefits over a long period."[34]

Notes and Questions

1. Consider the following hypothetical: You are counsel for a large American computer company and are negotiating a long-term joint venture with a Japanese company of approximately the same size. Counsel for both companies have agreed on an arbitration clause, but in an informal discussion, your counterpart observes that in some circumstances an arbitration, which could extend over several years, could impede the fulfillment of the contract and the common interests of the parties that it expresses. The idea of developing some sort of mini-trial procedure as a preliminary or substitute for an international arbitration is raised. Prepare a memorandum for your client evaluating the advantages and disadvantages of this technique and, if it is selected, its relationship to a conventional arbitration clause. Draft an international "mini-trial" clause that would address the issues your memorandum has raised and would be acceptable to both parties.

2. Note that the mini-trial, like some of the other modalities, may require a party to reveal its legal case before it wishes to.

5. CONCLUSION

Contractual requirements to negotiate, mediate, or conciliate disputes may provide additional dispute resolution options and serve as some restraint on judicial hijacking, but cannot, by themselves, prevent it. Such procedures are non-binding. Should they prove unsuccessful, they do not provide, in the absence of a contractually-mandated back-

---

[34] *Id.* at 20 . . . . For a discussion of the success of the mini-trial in preserving important business relationships, see J. HENRY & J. LIEBERMAN, *supra* note 1[1], at 42-44.

up procedure, any concrete jurisdictional solution, and thus can allow one party to engage in judicial hijacking.

### B.    SOLUTION NUMBER 2: PLANNING JURISDICTION BY FORUM SELECTION CLAUSES

A surer method available to parties to international transactions for minimizing the jurisdictional uncertainty of these transactions is to agree, at the time of the drafting of the contract, that in case of a dispute arising on or about the contract, a particular national court will be deemed to have jurisdiction. Ideally, selection by the parties of a particular forum will result in a truly neutral court. Even when asymmetrical bargaining positions permit one of the parties to choose a more favorable forum, however, the uncertainties of where an international transaction without such a jurisdiction selection will be adjudicated are minimized.

#### 1.    EXAMPLES OF FORUM SELECTION CLAUSES

A generic forum selection clause in a transnational contract may provide as follows:

> All disputes arising under, on or in connection with this agreement shall be decided by [a specific court in a specific jurisdiction]. The parties hereby accept jurisdiction, for all matters related to any such possible disputes, in this designated forum and waive any rights they may have to bring such an action or related parts of it in any other courts.

As is apparent, the generic clause set out above is designed to restrict every phase of a dispute to the designated forum. Some forum selection clauses are less comprehensive in their ambit and can, theoretically, allow for prejudgment attachments of property in other jurisdictions and enforcement of judgments in other jurisdictions, while respecting the contractual selection of the forum for the primary adjudication.

#### 2.    CONSEQUENCES OF FORUM SELECTION CLAUSES

Forum selection clauses are effective only if the designated forum accepts the parties' choice, other potential fora respect that choice, and all potential fora interpret the clause as comprehensive and not allowing certain types of suits to proceed despite the clause.

There exists some controversy among English judges regarding deference to forum selection clauses. In *Atlantic Star* below, the methodology is not based on forum selection by the parties but whether the choice by the plaintiff of an English forum would work a hardship for the defendant. Consider whether this mode of analysis makes English courts "too" receptive to plaintiffs' initiations.

a. THE RECEPTIVENESS ON THE PART OF THE SELECTED FORUM

*Owners of the Motor Vessel "Atlantic Star" v. Owner of the Motor Vessel "Bona Spes,"* 1 Q.B. 367 (Eng. C.A. 1972).

. . .

LORD DENNING M.R.

1. *Introduction*

[The *Atlantic Star* is a ship owned by the Dutch company, the Holland-American Line, flying the Dutch flag. On January 28, 1970, the ship was proceeding in Belgian waters towards Antwerp when suddenly the fog thickened and became dense. The ship expected to have the help of three tugs to dock, but these tugs were called to help another vessel. The ship attempted to enter the locks without the aid of the tugs. Although the radar was operative, the ship did not see two small vessels moored at the entrance to the lock because they were below the levels of the wall. One vessel was the Dutch motor-barge, the *Bona Spes* and the other one was the Belgian dumb barge, the *Hugo van der Goes*. The *Atlantic Star* crashed into these two vessels and sunk them with their cargoes.]

. . . Two men on board the *Hugo van der Goes*, the skipper and a sailor, were drowned. The wall of the quay was badly damaged. The port authorities were put to expense in clearing the channel. The Belgian National Insurance paid compensation to the relatives of the dead men. All these were innocent of any fault. The question arose at once: was the *Atlantic Star* to blame?

The Commercial Court of Antwerp has a procedure in such a case. On the application of anyone concerned, it can appoint a nautical surveyor to hold an inquiry. On January 29, 1970, the owners of the Belgian barge *Hugo van der Goes* made application. On February 16, 1970, the owner of the Dutch barge *Bona Spes* followed suit. On the same day the President of the court appointed Captain Van Clemens, a qualified master mariner, to carry out an investigation into the circumstances and causes of the collision.

.     .     .

In about February 1971 the surveyor made his report. The trend of it was that the *Atlantic Star* was not at fault, because she had done her best in the dense fog without tugs.

Two of the Belgian claimants started proceedings in the Commercial Court of Antwerp. They were Belgian owners of the *Hugo van der Goes*, and the Belgian accident insurers who paid the dependents of the dead skipper and sailor. Later on the owners of the cargoes on both ships brought proceedings in the court. . . .

But the Dutch owner of the *Bona Spes* brought proceedings in England. In June 1971 he got to know that the *Atlantic Star* was shortly due in Liverpool. On June 15, 1971, he began an action in rem in the High Court of Admiralty in England. The Dutch owners — the Holland-American Line — in order to avoid arrest of the vessel, accepted service of the writ and arranged for a guarantee of £80,000 in respect of the claim. They entered a conditional appearance and applied to stay the action. The Admiralty judge refused to stay. The *Atlantic Star* appeals to this court.

2. *The Cross Undertakings*

While the argument was going on in England, the Dutch owner of the *Bona Spes* became concerned. If his English action was stayed, on the ground that he ought to bring proceedings at Antwerp, there was a two years' limitation. In order to guard against this contingency, on January 21, 1972 the owner of the *Bona Spes* began proceedings in the

Commercial Court of Antwerp against the *Atlantic Star*. The judge found that "this action was begun solely to preserve the time limit in Belgium in case the action here should be stayed." . . .

. . .

### 3. *The Jurisdiction to Stay*

The High Court has jurisdiction to stay proceedings if it thinks fit to do so in any cause or matter pending before it. That appears from section 41 of the Supreme Court of Judicature (Consolidation) Act 1925. The way in which this jurisdiction is to be exercised was stated by Scott L.J. in *St. Pierre v. South American Stores (Gath & Chaves) Ltd.* [1936] 1 K.B. 382, 398:

> "The true rule about a stay under section 41, so far as relevant to this case, may I think be stated thus: (1) A mere balance of convenience is not a sufficient ground for depriving a plaintiff of the advantages of prosecuting his action in an English court if it is otherwise properly brought. The right of access to the King's court must not be lightly refused. (2) In order to justify a stay two-conditions must be satisfied, one positive and the other negative: (a) the defendant must satisfy the court that the continuance of the action would work an injustice because it would be oppressive or vexatious to him or would be an abuse of the process of the court in some other way; and (b) the stay must not cause an injustice to the plaintiff. On both the burden of proof is on the defendant."

. . .

The reasoning which lies behind these rules appears from the cases. When a plaintiff comes as of right to the courts of this country — without having to ask for leave of anyone — and seeks redress from a defendant who is here, or whose ship is here, it is the duty of the courts to award him the redress to which he is entitled: see *McHenry v. Lewis* (1882) 22 Ch.D. 397; *Peruvian Guano Co. v. Bockwoldt* (1883) 23 Ch.D. 225 and *Ionian Bank Ltd. v. Couvreur* [1969] 1 W.L.R. 781. It may be that the plaintiff is able to catch the defendant here when he is on a short visit, as at the Ascot Races (see *Baroda (Maharanee of) v. Wildenstein* [1972] 2 Q.B. 283); or to arrest his ship when it puts into an English port for a few hours. But so long as he can catch him here, or his ship here, he is entitled as of right to bring his action here; and to pursue it to its conclusion. No one who comes to these courts asking for justice should come in vain. He must, of course, come in good faith. He must not do it from an unworthy motive, such as to vex or harass his opponent: see *Logan v. Bank of Scotland (No. 2)* [1906] 1 K.B. 141 and *In re Norton's Settlement* [1908] 1 Ch. 471. Nor must he act oppressively. He must not, in seeking justice himself, treat the defendant unjustly. At any rate, the judges will not allow him to go on, if it would work an injustice to the defendant without doing the plaintiff any advantage. It may be very inconvenient to the defendant to have to contest the action here. But inconvenience falling short of injustice is not sufficient to stay the action: see *St. Pierre v. South American Stores (Gath & Chaves) Ltd.* [1936] 1 K.B. 382. In this respect the law of England is different from that of Scotland: for that law has an established plea of forum non conveniens: see *Societé du Gaz de Paris v. Societé Anonyme de Navigation "Les Armateurs Français,"* 1926 S.C.(H.L.) 13. It is also different from that of the United States: for their courts recognise an unqualified discretion to decline jurisdiction between two foreign vessels: see *Canada Malting Co. Ltd. v. Paterson Steamships Ltd.* (1932) 285 U.S. 413. But we in England think differently. If a plaintiff considers that the procedure of our courts, or the substantive law of England, may hold advantages for him superior to that of any other country, he is entitled to bring his action here — provided always that he can serve the defendant, or arrest his ship, within the jurisdiction of these courts — and provided also that his action is not vexatious or oppressive. It is so stated by Dr. J.H.C. Morris in DICEY'S CONFLICT OF LAWS, 8th ed. (1967), p. 1081. This right to come here is not confined to Englishmen. It extends to any friendly foreigner. He can seek the aid of our courts if he desires to do so. You may call this "forum-shopping" if you please, but if the forum is England, it is a good place to shop in, both for the quality of the goods and the speed of service.

### 4. *The Admiralty Cases*

These principles are borne out by the cases in Admiralty. The owners of ships who engage in international trade are especially vulnerable. Any of their vessels is liable to arrest in any of the ports to which they go. If one of their vessels is involved in a collision, it is open to the plaintiff to arrest her in rem, or any ship of the same owner — (so long as it is one ship only: *The Banco* [1971] P. 137) — in any port where she may be. The plaintiff, naturally enough, decides to arrest her in that country which he considers gives the greatest advantage to him. It is his choice and the shipowner cannot gainsay it. The shipowner will, of course, obtain the release of the vessel by giving security: and, on giving it, he will not be called upon to put it up in another country; see *The Putbus* [1969] P. 136. The action goes for trial in the country thus selected by the plaintiff. He is committed to that country and so long as he pursues it there, after accepting security, he will not be allowed to pursue his claim in another country: see *The Christiansborg* (1885) 10 P.D. 141; *The Soya Margareta* [1961] 1 W.L.R. 709; *The Lucile Bloomfield* [1964] 1 Lloyd's Rep. 324.

Such being the law, the plaintiff chooses the country which suits him best. He may, for instance, find that in one country the limitation fund is higher than in another; and so forth. But he must elect, sooner or later, to sue in one country only. If he brings an action in personam in one country, that does not by itself amount to an election. He may be permitted in proper cases to discontinue that action and pursue his claim in another country: see *The Janera* [1928] P. 55; *The Hartlepool* (1950) 84 L.l.L. Rep. 145; *The Soya Margareta* [1961] 1 W.L.R. 709, 711. But once he arrests the ship or accepts security in lieu, he has made his election.

## 5. *The International Convention*

Although the rules which I have stated seem to give a special advantage to a plaintiff who brings proceedings in the English Court of Admiralty, they cannot be said to be a breach of international comity: for they have received international recognition. There is an international convention [International Convention on Certain Rules Concerning Civil Jurisdiction in Matters of Collision] (May 10, 1952) made in Brussels in 1952 which gives effect to this. It has been ratified by the United Kingdom and Belgium (and others). It says:

*Article 1:*

"(1) An action for collision occurring between sea-going vessels, or between sea-going vessels and inland navigation craft, can only be introduced: (a) either before the court where the defendant has his habitual residence or a place of business; (b) or before the court of the place where arrest has been effected of the defendant ship or of any other ship belonging to the defendant which can be lawfully arrested, or where arrest could have been effected and bail or other security has been furnished; (c) or before the court of the place of collision when the collision has occurred within the limits of a port or in inland waters."

Applying that articles to this case, an action could be brought by the owner of the *Bona Spes* (a) before the courts of the *Netherlands* where the Holland-America Line have their habitual residence; or (b) before the courts of *England*, where arrest could have been effected and security has been furnished; or (c) before the Commercial Court of *Antwerp* where the collision took place.

*Article 1(2):*

"It shall be *for the plaintiff* to decide in which of the courts referred to in (1) of this article, the action shall be instituted."

So the Dutch owner of the *Bona Spes* has the right to decide whether to institute the action in the Netherlands or in England or in Antwerp. If he decides to bring it in England, it is not for the English courts to deny him that right.

*Article 1(3):*

"A claimant shall not be allowed to bring a further action against the same defendant on the same facts in another jurisdiction, without discontinuing an action already instituted."

So the Dutch owner of the *Bona Spes*, having brought an action in England, was not at liberty to bring an action in the Commercial Court of Antwerp without discontinuing the English action. He has never discontinued the English action. So he should not be allowed to bring an action in the Commercial Court of Antwerp. Seeing that the

United Kingdom and Belgium have each ratified this convention, it may be that the court of Antwerp might not allow the *Bona Spes* to obtain judgment in that court, unless it first discontinued the English action.

The important thing to notice about our English law and the International Convention is that it gives the plaintiff the right to decide in which court to bring his action; and, in particular, to arrest one of the defendant's ships at whatever port it happens to call. It is, however, a matter of election, which, once made, cannot be retracted. Once the plaintiff has arrested a ship or obtained security in lieu of arrest, the plaintiff has made his election. He cannot arrest any other ship in any other port, nor obtain security elsewhere.

## 6. *Convenience*

The judge found in terms that so far as convenience is concerned the Commercial Court of Antwerp is by far the most appropriate forum. He pointed out that the collision occurred in the Port of Antwerp; that the navigation there was governed by Belgian law and local regulations; but there had already been a preliminary inquiry there with witnesses by an expert nautical surveyor; that there were five other claims arising out of this collision already pending in the Commercial Court of Antwerp; and that the case had no connection with England at all.

But, given all that convenience, the judge refused to stay the action in this country: and I agree with him. It is plain that the plaintiff honestly believes that there are substantial advantages to him in taking proceedings in England. One advantage is the rule of the English Court of Admiralty that if you run into a ship at anchor, that is prima facie evidence of negligence: see *The Merchant Prince* [1892] P. 179. Another advantage is that the Commercial Court of Antwerp does not see or hear the witnesses itself, not does it have the assistance of assessors. The Antwerp court gives great weight to the report of the nautical surveyor and is very unlikely to depart from it. Whereas, in the English Court of Admiralty, the court will have a double advantage. It will have the statements taken by the nautical surveyor, and the other material before him. But it will also have the benefit of seeing and hearing the witnesses, and having their evidence tested by cross-examination. At any rate, if the plaintiff considers these to be advantages, he is entitled to bring his proceedings here. I would quote Bowen L.J. in *Peruvian Guano Co. v. Bockwoldt*, 23 Ch.D. 225, 234:

> "It seems to me we have no sort of right, moral or legal, to take away from a plaintiff any real chance he may have of an advantage."

We should not stay the action of the plaintiff on the ground that it would be highly convenient to the defendant to be sued in Belgium.

Test it this way: When the plaintiff brought his action in rem and the defendants put up security, the plaintiff had an undoubted right to carry on the action to its conclusion, no matter that it might be overwhelmingly more convenient for proceedings to be heard in Belgium. If this be so, I do not see why he should lose that right simply because the defendant offers to provide reasonable security in Belgium. That offer cannot make the action vexatious or oppressive when it was not so beforehand. In *Chaney v. Murphy*, 64 T.L.R. 489, an offer on somewhat similar lines was held to be quite insufficient to warrant a stay: see p. 492. So here. This offer to provide security in Belgium cannot take away the right the plaintiff obtained to carry on the action in England.

The Holland-America Line say that this gives the plaintiff an unfair advantage. He applies to the Antwerp court for a nautical surveyor. If the report is in his favour, he will take proceedings in the court at Antwerp. If it is against him he will throw it over and take proceedings in England. This is a forceful comment. But, it was made equally in *The Janera* [1928] P. 55: and it did not prevail. Disasters are often followed by inquiries. Whatever their outcome, they cannot take away the right of a plaintiff to pursue his remedy in the courts of his choice.

Mr. Thomas also stressed the multiplicity of proceedings. He said that five claims are already instituted in the Commercial Court of Antwerp: and that this one should not be allowed to continue here with possibly different results. If that be so, it is unfortunate: but, again, it does not affect the plaintiff's right to seek justice here. As it happens, we are told that those other claims are standing still, waiting for the result of this application. If the action of the *Bona Spes* continues in the Admiralty Court here, all the others will discontinue their proceedings there and come here. So there will be no divergence.

### 7. *Conclusion*

My conclusion is that this should proceed in England and that the plaintiff should discontinue his proceedings in the Commercial Court of Antwerp. I would like to assure that court, which we hold in high esteem, that we mean by this no discourtesy to them. All that we do is to give effect to the Convention between our two countries, which says that: "It shall be for the plaintiff to decide in which of the courts the action shall be instituted." In this case the plaintiff has decided to arrest the defendants' vessel in England and take security. That gives him the right to come to these courts, and we cannot say him nay. I would dismiss the appeal.

PHILLIMORE L.J. I agree but I have found this case less easy than have my Lords, Lord Denning M.R. and Cairns L.J. In expressing my agreement I am yielding to the authority afforded by so many decisions of this court over many years, whereas if the problem could be treated as res integra I should wish to allow this appeal. . . .

.    .    .

I think that in the interests of justice regarded objectively a stay should be granted so that this case in all its aspects can be disposed of in the Commercial Court of Antwerp. The only real argument for a contrary decision must be that that court cannot be trusted to arrive at a right decision, whereas the Admiralty Court in London can be so trusted. This line of argument does not commend itself to me.

CAIRNS L.J. When an action is properly brought in an English court and the defendant is within the jurisdiction and is duly served, some special circumstances must exist before the action can be stayed. The same applies to an action in rem when service is effected on the defendant's vessel within the jurisdiction or when, as in this case, service has been accepted by solicitors in order to avoid the risk of arrest. Section 41 (a) of the Supreme Court of Judicature Act 1925 preserves for the court wide powers to stay proceedings, but obviously the power is not unfettered. So far as is relevant to this appeal, the type of case in which the grant of a stay falls to be considered is one where it is alleged by the defendant that for some reason the issues should be decided in a foreign court and not here. The decision whether or not to grant a stay is ultimately dependent on the exercise of discretion, but the discretion is not unlimited. While judicial precedents cannot in any discretionary matter lay down precise rules for the exercise of the discretion (for that would be to destroy the discretion) some guide lines can be established by authority. It would be quite possible for the law of England to have developed in such a way that any action could be stayed if the balance of convenience was in favour of trial in a foreign court. But a consistent line of authority from 1882 to 1972 makes it quite clear that some stronger reason must be shown in this country for depriving a plaintiff of the right to proceed in the court of his choice.

.　　.　　.

That being so, I am entirely satisfied that the jurisdiction to stay ought not to be exercised unless the action can be said to be vexatious of or oppressive of the defendant or unjust to him or an abuse of the process of the court.

.　　.　　.

Mr. Thomas's argument was directed not so much to showing that the English law was the same as that of Scotland, but rather to the proposition that where there is not a "mere" balance of convenience in favour of a foreign court (in the sense of a balance that just tips the scales that way) but an overwhelming balance, then that in itself can make it oppressive to compel the defendant to defend an action in England. I can conceive of cases where inconvenience might be so great as to amount to oppression. I cannot see that the inconvenience here is of that degree. It is by no means uncommon for different causes of action arising out of the same casualty to lead to two actions in different countries. I cannot see that the multiplicity of actions at Antwerp adds much to the inconvenience to the defendants. The fact that witnesses are not within the jurisdiction of the English court and may not be compellable to give evidence here is a common enough feature of Admiralty actions. In my view any inconvenience to the defendants here falls far short of oppression or vexation or injustice.

Nor can I accept that there is no real or substantial advantage to the plaintiff in suing in the English court. I do not consider that there is any onus on the plaintiff to show that he could not get a fair trial in a foreign court in order to justify his suing in England. It is sufficient to avoid the charge of vexation if he can point to some grounds on which a reasonable man might prefer to bring his action here. It might be that the high standing among all maritime people of the English Admiralty Court would be sufficient without more. If more is needed, the plaintiff can reasonably maintain that a trial by a judge who will see and hear the witnesses is more satisfactory than a trial at which the court would be presented with a report resulting from an informal inquiry and would probably use that report as the main basis of its judgment.

I do not consider that international comity would be promoted by the staying of this action. In this connection it is I think appropriate to have in mind that the bringing of the action here was entirely in accordance with the International Convention on Civil Jurisdiction (1952) article 1 (1) and (2) and it is quite immaterial that for special reasons the plaintiff has, since the action was started, done something which was not in accordance with article 1 (3).

b.      RESPECT FOR THE EXCLUSIVITY OF THE
        FORUM SELECTION CLAUSE BY OTHERS

The case popularly known as *Zapata*, which arose in the United States and the United Kingdom, represented a major change in United States judicial policy with regard to accepting and giving effect to contractually designated forum selection clauses.

*The Bremen v. Zapata Off-Shore Co.*, 407 U.S. 1 (1972).

. . . .

. . . Plainly, the courts of England meet the standards of neutrality and long experience in admiralty litigation. The choice of that forum was made in an arm's-length negotiation by experienced and sophisticated businessmen, and absent some compelling and countervailing reason it should be honored by the parties and enforced by the courts.

The argument that such clauses are improper because they tend to "oust" a court of jurisdiction is hardly more than a vestigial legal fiction. It appears to rest at core on historical judicial resistance to any attempt to reduce the power and business of a particular court and has little place in an era when all courts are overloaded and when businesses once essentially local now operate in world markets. It reflects something of a provincial attitude regarding the fairness of other tribunals. No one seriously contends in this case that the forum-selection clause "ousted" the District Court of jurisdiction over Zapata's action. The threshold question is whether that court should have exercised its jurisdiction to do more than give effect to the legitimate expectations of the parties, manifested in their freely negotiated agreement, by specifically enforcing the forum clause.

There are compelling reasons why a freely negotiated private international agreement, unaffected by fraud, undue influence, or overweening bargaining power,[35] such as that involved here, should be given full effect. In this case, for example, we are concerned with a far from routine transaction between companies of two different nations contemplating the tow of an extremely costly piece of equipment from Louisiana across the Gulf of Mexico and the Atlantic Ocean, through the Mediterranean Sea to its final destination in the Adriatic Sea. In the course of its voyage, it was to traverse the waters of many jurisdictions. The *Chaparral* could have been damaged at any point along the route, and there were countless possible ports of refuge. That the accident occurred in the Gulf of Mexico and the barge was towed to Tampa in an emergency were mere fortuities. It cannot be doubted for a moment that the parties sought to provide for a neutral forum for the resolution of any disputes arising during the tow. Manifestly much uncertainty and possibly great inconvenience to both parties could arise if a suit could be maintained in any jurisdiction in which an accident might occur or if jurisdiction were left to any place

---

[35] [14] The record here refutes any notion of overweening bargaining power. Judge Wisdom, dissenting, in the Court of Appeals noted:

"Zapata has neither presented evidence of nor alleged fraud or undue bargaining power in the agreement. Unterweser was only one of several companies bidding on the project. No evidence contradicts its Managing Director's affidavit that it specified English courts 'in an effort to meet Zapata Off-Shore Company half way.' Zapata's Vice President has declared by affidavit that no specific negotiations concerning the forum clause took place. But this was not simply a form contract with boilerplate language that Zapata had no power to alter. The towing of an oil rig across the Atlantic was a new business. Zapata did make alterations to the contract submitted by Unterweser. The forum clause could hardly be ignored. It is the final sentence of the agreement, immediately preceding the date and the parties' signatures...." 428 F.2d 888, 907.

where the *Bremen* or *Unterweser* might happen to be found.[36] The elimination of all such uncertainties by agreeing in advance on a forum acceptable to both parties is an indispensable element in international trade, commerce, and contracting. There is strong evidence that the forum clause was a vital part of the agreement,[37] and it would be unrealistic to think that the parties did not conduct their negotiations, including fixing the monetary terms, with the consequences of the forum clause figuring prominently in their calculations. Under these circumstances, as Justice Karminski reasoned in sustaining jurisdiction over Zapata in the High Court of Justice, "[t]he force of an agreement for litigation in this country, freely entered into between two competent parties, seems to me to be very powerful."

Thus, in the light of present-day commercial realities and expanding international trade we conclude that the forum clause should control absent a strong showing that it should be set aside. Although their opinions are not altogether explicit, it seems reasonably clear that the District Court and the Court of Appeals placed the burden on Unterweser to show that London would be a more convenient forum than Tampa, although the contract expressly resolved that issue. The

---

[36] [15] At the very least, the clause was an effort to eliminate all uncertainty as to the nature, location, and outlook of the forum in which these companies of differing nationalities might find themselves. Moreover, while the contract here did not specifically provide that the substantive law of England should be applied, it is the general rule in English courts that the parties are assumed, absent contrary indication, to have designated the forum with the view that it should apply its own law. See, e.g. *Tzortzis v. Monark Line A/B*, [1968] 1 W.L.R. 406 (C.A.); see generally 1 T. Carver, Carriage by Sea 496-497 (12th ed. 1971); G. Cheshire, Private International Law 193 (7th ed. 1965); A. Dicey & J. Morris, The Conflict of Laws 705, 1046 (8th ed. 1967); Collins, Arbitration Clauses and Forum Selecting Clauses in the Conflict of Laws: Some Recent Developments in England, 2 J. Mar. L. & Comm. 363, 365-370 and n. 7 (1971). It is therefore reasonable to conclude that the forum clause was also an effort to obtain certainty as to the applicable substantive law. . . .

[37] [16] See nn. [14-15], *supra*. Zapata has denied specifically discussing the forum clause with Unterweser, but, as Judge Wisdom pointed out, Zapata made numerous changes in the contract without altering the forum clause, which could hardly have escaped its attention. Zapata is clearly not unsophisticated in such matters. The contract of its wholly owned subsidiary with an Italian corporation covering the contemplated drilling operations in the Adriatic Sea provided that all disputes were to be settled by arbitration in London under English law, and contained broad exculpatory clauses. App. 306-311.

correct approach would have been to enforce the forum clause specifically unless Zapata could clearly show that enforcement would be unreasonable and unjust, or that the clause was invalid for such reasons as fraud or overreaching. Accordingly, the case must be remanded for reconsideration.

We note, however, that there is nothing in the record presently before us that would support a refusal to enforce the forum clause. The Court of Appeals suggested that enforcement would be contrary to the public policy of the forum under *Bisso v. Inland Waterways Corp.*, 349 U.S. 85 (1955), because of the prospect that the English courts would enforce the clauses of the towage contract purporting to exculpate Unterweser from liability for damages to the *Chaparral*. A contractual choice-of-forum clause should be held unenforceable if enforcement would contravene a strong public policy of the forum in which suit is brought, whether declared by statute or by judicial decision. See, e.g., *Boyd v. Grand Trunk W.R. Co.*, 338 U.S. 263 (1949). It is clear, however, that whatever the proper scope of the policy expressed in *Bisso*, it does not reach this case. *Bisso* rested on considerations with respect to the towage business strictly in American waters, and those considerations are not controlling in an international commercial agreement.

.    .    .

Courts have also suggested that a forum clause, even though it is freely bargained for and contravenes no important public policy of the forum, may nevertheless be "unreasonable" and unenforceable if the chosen forum is *seriously* inconvenient for the trial of the action. Of course, where it can be said with reasonable assurance that at the time they entered the contract, the parties to a freely negotiated private international commercial agreement contemplated the claimed inconvenience, it is difficult to see why any such claim of inconvenience should be heard to render the forum clause unenforceable. We are not here dealing with an agreement between two Americans to resolve their essentially local disputes in a remote alien forum. In such a case, the serious inconvenience of the contractual forum to one or both of the parties might carry greater weight in determining the reasonableness of the forum clause. The remoteness of the forum might suggest that the agreement was an adhesive one, or that the parties did not have the particular controversy in mind when they made their agreement; yet even there the party claiming should bear a heavy burden of proof.[38] Similarly, selection of a remote forum to apply differing foreign law to an essentially American controversy might contravene an important public policy of the forum. For example, so long as *Bisso* governs American courts with respect to the towage business in American waters, it would quite arguably be improper to permit an American tower to avoid that policy by providing a foreign forum for resolution of his disputes with an American towee.

This case, however, involves a freely negotiated international commercial transaction between a German and an American corporation for towage of a vessel from the Gulf of Mexico to the Adriatic Sea. As noted, selection of a London forum was clearly a reasonable effort to bring vital certainty to this international transaction and to provide a neutral forum experienced and capable in the resolution of admiralty litigation. Whatever "inconvenience" Zapata would suffer by being forced to litigate in the contractual forum as it agreed to do was clearly foreseeable at the time of contracting. In such circumstances it should be incumbent on the party seeking to escape his contract to show that trial in the contractual forum will be so gravely difficult and inconvenient that he will for all practical purposes be deprived of his day in court. Absent that, there is no basis for concluding that it would be unfair, unjust, or unreasonable to hold that party to his bargain.

In the course of its ruling on Unterweser's second motion to stay the proceedings in Tampa, the District Court did make a conclusory finding that the balance of convenience was "strongly" in favor of litigation in Tampa. However, as previously noted, in making that finding the court erroneously placed the burden of proof on Unterweser to show that the balance of convenience was strongly in its

---

[38] See, e.g., Model Choice of Forum Act § 3(3), *supra*, n. 13, comment: "On rare occasions, the state of the forum may be a substantially more convenient place for the trial of a particular controversy than the chosen state. If so, the present clause would permit the action to proceed. This result will presumably be in accord with the desires of the parties. It can be assumed that they did not have the particular controversy in mind when they made the choice-of-forum agreement since they would not consciously have agreed to have the action brought in an inconvenient place."

favor.[39] Moreover, the finding falls far short of a conclusion that Zapata would be effectively deprived of its day in court should it be forced to litigate in London. Indeed, it cannot even be assumed that it would be placed to the expense of transporting its witnesses to London. It is not unusual for important issues in international admiralty cases to be dealt with by deposition. Both the District Court and the Court of Appeals majority appeared satisfied that Unterweser could receive a fair hearing in Tampa by using deposition testimony of its witnesses from distant places, and there is no reason to conclude that Zapata could not use deposition testimony to equal advantage if forced to litigate in London as it bound itself to do. Nevertheless, to allow Zapata opportunity to carry its heavy burden of showing not only that the balance of convenience is strongly in favor of trial in Tampa (that is, that it will be far more inconvenient for Zapata to litigate in London than it will be for Unterweser to litigate in Tampa), but also that a London trial will be so manifestly and gravely inconvenient to Zapata that it will be effectively deprived of a meaningful day in court, we remand for further proceedings.

Zapata's remaining contentions do not require extended treatment. It is clear that Unterweser's action in filing its limitation complaint in the District Court in Tampa was, so far as Zapata was concerned, solely a defensive measure made necessary as a response

---

[39] [19] Applying the proper burden of proof, Justice Karminski in the High Court of Justice at London made the following findings, which appear to have substantial support in the record:

"[Zapata] pointed out that in this case the balance of convenience so far as witnesses were concerned pointed in the direction of having the case heard and tried in the United States District Court at Tampa in Florida because the probability is that most, but not necessarily all, of the witnesses will be American. The answer, as it seems to me, is that a substantial minority at least of witnesses are likely to be German. The tug was a German vessel and was, as far as I know, manned by a German crew. . . . Where they all are now or are likely to be when this matter is litigated I do not know, because the experience of the Admiralty Court here strongly points out that maritime witnesses in the course of their duties move about freely. The homes of the German crew presumably are in Germany. There is probably a balance of numbers in favour of the Americans, but not, as I am inclined to think, a very heavy balance." App. 212.

It should also be noted that if the exculpatory clause is enforced in the English courts, many of *Zapata's* witnesses on the questions of negligence and damage may be completely unnecessary.

to Zapata's breach of the forum clause of the contract. When the six-month statutory period for filing an action to limit its liability had almost run without the District Court's having ruled on Unterweser's initial motion to dismiss or stay Zapata's action pursuant to the forum clause, Unterweser had no other prudent alternative but to protect itself by filing for limitation of its liability. [footnote omitted] Its action in so doing was a direct consequence of Zapata's failure to abide by the forum clause of the towage contract. There is no basis on which to conclude that this purely necessary defensive action by Unterweser should preclude it from relying on the forum clause it bargained for.

## Notes and Questions

1. Forum selection clauses are assumed by many international counsel to be more reliable than an international arbitration clause. In fact, a forum selection clause's success depends upon the willingness of the court that has been designated to give effect to it. Unless counsel carefully study the putative forum's jurisprudence on the relevant subject matter and personal jurisdiction before they settle on it, there may be unpleasant surprises. Should the court of the forum which has been selected by the parties in a forum selection clause decline to take jurisdiction, the result is a contract with no dispute resolution mechanism, and the technique for deciding the dispute will be up for grabs.

2. What considerations might have led the parties to choose London as the forum in the original contract?

3. The district court in Florida required a security bond. Did the security bond have tactical significance for each of the parties?

## 3.    STATUTORY PROVISIONS ON FORUM SELECTION CLAUSES

In drafting an arbitration agreement, counsel must be careful to make certain that the terms of the agreement do not violate any of the statutory constraints of the chosen forum. If counsel does not take such precautions, the dispute may ultimately find its way to the national court system, vitiating much of the advantage of initially having expended the money and the leverage to obtain an arbitration agreement with a forum selection clause. Consider again the problem in *Atlantic Star*, *supra* p. 91, as you read the following provisions of the state of New York.

NEW YORK GENERAL OBLIGATIONS LAW (N.Y. GEN. OBLIG. LAW §5-1402 (McKinney 1989)).

1. Notwithstanding any act which limits or affects the right of a person to maintain an action or proceedings, including but not limited to, paragraph (b) of section thirteen hundred fourteen of the business corporation law and subdivision two of section two hundred b of the banking law, any person may maintain an action or proceeding against a foreign corporation, non-resident, or foreign state where the action or proceeding arises out of or relates to any contract, agreement or undertaking for which a choice of New York law has been made in whole or in part pursuant to section 5-1401 and which (a) is a contract, agreement or undertaking, contingent or otherwise, in consideration of, or relating to any obligation arising out of a transaction covering in the aggregate, not less than one million dollars, and (b) which contains a provision or provisions whereby such foreign corporation or non-resident agrees to submit to the jurisdiction of the courts of this state.

2. Nothing contained in this section shall be construed to affect the enforcement of any provision respecting choice of forum in any other contract, agreement or undertaking.

### Notes and Questions

1. The New York statute literally requires a choice of New York law as well as a selection of the New York forum.

2. Note Rule 327 "Inconvenient Forum" of the N.Y. C.P.L.R. which provides: "(b) Notwithstanding the provisions of subdivision (a) of this rule, the court shall not stay or dismiss any action on the ground of inconvenient forum, where the action arises out of, or relates to a contract, agreement or undertaking to which section 5-1402 of the general obligations law applies, and the parties to the contract have agreed that the law of their state shall govern their rights or duties in whole or in part." What effect does this have on §5-1402?

3. On the difficulties in enforcing court selection clauses in American jurisdictions other than New York state, see WILLIAM W. PARK, INTERNATIONAL FORUM SELECTION (1995).

4.      ENFORCEMENT OF JUDGMENTS SECURED UNDER
        FORUM SELECTION CLAUSES

In the absence of a bilateral judgment enforcement treaty, judgment creditors, even when they have benefitted from a forum selection clause, must rely upon national law to secure judgment enforcement.

a.      Arthur T. von Mehren & Donald T. Trautman, *Recognition of Foreign Adjudications: A Survey and a Suggested Approach*, 81 HARV. L. REV. 1601 (1968).

.     .     .

## A. General Theory

Recognition and enforcement practices vary widely. Near one extreme is the Dutch approach, which in principle seems to deny preclusive effects to foreign judgments.[40] However, at least when merely recognition — as distinguished from enforcement — is involved, a policy to protect the successful litigant from the harassing or evasive tactics of his previously unsuccessful opponent can overcome this general Dutch attitude against recognition. Especially when a party has availed himself of foreign process, or acquiesced therein, he may be regarded as having no standing to challenge the resulting judgment; and it will be recognized even though direct enforcement might be denied.[41]

At perhaps the other extreme is the practice in the United States. Doubtless influenced by interstate practice as shaped by constitutional compulsions, a state ordinarily recognizes and enforces an internationally foreign judgment to the extent that the judgment was enforceable in the rendering country, if in its view that country had

---

[40] *See* R. KOLLEWIJN, AMERICAN-DUTCH PRIVATE INTERNATIONAL LAW 34-38 (Bilateral Studies in Private Int'l Law No. 3, 2d ed. 1961). *See generally* Smit, *International Res Judicata in the Netherlands: A Comparative Analysis*, 16 BUFFALO L. REV. 165 (1966).

[41] *See* R. KOLLEWIJN, *supra* note 3[8], at 34-38.

adjudicatory jurisdiction in the international sense[42] and utilized fair procedures. Such practice reflects not only a policy against harassing or evasive tactics but also other relevant policies discussed below, including that of fostering the elements of stability and unity essential to an international order in which many aspects of life are not confined within the limits of any single jurisdiction. . . .

The theories typically advanced to explain recognition practice contribute little to any real understanding of what should control. For example, American courts often talk about recognition of foreign judgments in terms of "comity,"[43] a general mode of expression that at most expresses an attitude or disposition[44] and on analysis is simply circular. The typical English formulations — perhaps suggestive of a rather strong policy in favor of recognition but ultimately even less helpful in providing guidance — are in terms of the "legal obligation" of foreign money-judgments; under this approach, the test for determining whether recognition should be accorded is whether a court of competent jurisdiction has adjudicated that a legal obligation exists to pay a sum of money.[45]

The ultimate justification for according some degree of recognition is that if in our highly complex and interrelated world each community exhausted every possibility of insisting on its parochial interests, injustice would result and the normal patterns of life would be disrupted.

.     .     .

---

[42] That is, it was appropriate for the country to adjudicate the particular dispute. For a discussion of our reasons for using this term, see von Mehren & Trautman, *Jurisdiction* 1124-25.

[43] *See, e.g.*, Hilton v. Guyot, 159 U.S. 113, 163-64 (1895).

[44] For an early American criticism of the concept of "comity," in the context of choice of law but at least equally pertinent to recognition, see S. LIVERMORE, DISSERTATIONS ON THE QUESTIONS WHICH ARISE FROM THE CONTRARIETY OF THE POSITIVE LAWS OF DIFFERENT STATES AND NATIONS 26-28 (1828), reprinted in VON MEHREN & TRAUTMAN, MULTISTATE PROBLEMS 32 n.*.

[45] Godard v. Gray, L.R. 6 Q.B. 139, 148 (1870). *See generally*, G. CHESHIRE, PRIVATE INTERNATIONAL LAW 537-38 (7th ed. 1965) [hereinafter cited as CHESHIRE]; A. DICKEY & J. MORRIS, THE CONFLICT OF LAWS 967-68 (8th ed. 1967).

We believe that at least five policies are important: a desire to avoid the duplication of effort and consequent waste involved in reconsidering a matter that has already been litigated; a related concern to protect the successful litigant, whether plaintiff or defendant, from harassing or evasive tactics on the part of his previously unsuccessful opponent; a policy against making the availability of local enforcement the decisive element, as a practical matter, in the plaintiff's choice of forum; an interest in fostering stability and unity in an international order in which many aspects of life are not confined to any single jurisdiction; and, in certain classes of cases, a belief that the rendering jurisdiction is a more appropriate forum than the recognizing jurisdiction, either because the former was more convenient or because as the predominantly concerned jurisdiction or for some other reason its views as to the merits should prevail.

The weight which a recognizing jurisdiction will give to each of these policies will depend in part upon attitudes it holds on related questions. To illustrate, the policy against duplication of effort should presumably be measured against a system's domestic procedural thinking about "splitting" a controversy that could conveniently be handled as a single matter. Procedural thinking in the United States tends toward enlarging the dimensions of a lawsuit: consider especially the broad notion of "cause of action" and the federal rules respecting compulsory counterclaims. Many countries, however — for example, Germany and France — are prepared to allow the parties, if they desire, to fragment a controversy that could be handled as a single matter. A jurisdiction like those in the United States presumably puts a fairly high general value on avoiding duplication of effort while jurisdictions like France and Germany assign a lower value. The former group's recognition practice will to this extent accord broader preclusive effects than the latter's.

Views diverge on the weight to be assigned to international order and stability and to the appropriateness or concerns of the rendering forum. Again, relevant information is to be found in the recognizing jurisdiction's general thinking underlying problems of choice of law and jurisdiction to adjudicate. Does that thinking attempt to contribute to the growth of international order? And does it attach substantial value to social and economic ties that transcend the traditional national political units? At the least, the recognizing jurisdiction can be expected to be consistent — in the sense that the views of general policy underlying the rules and principles in those two areas are compatible with those underlying the recognition of foreign adjudications.

Finally, the significance of the basic policies just discussed should be assessed in the context of the total situation relating the recognizing jurisdiction to the underlying litigation. For example, recognition may be made to depend upon whether the defendant is a member of the rendering community or of the community asked to recognize. Again, an adjudication that applies the same rule of decision as would have been applied by the recognizing community involves fewer difficulties than an adjudication in which a different regulating rule has been applied.

\* \* \*

b. *Hilton v. Guyot*, 159 U.S. 113 (1895).

[In a suit to enforce in the United States a French court's judgment against a New York resident from a transaction in France, the Supreme Court said]

> Where there has been opportunity for a full and fair trial abroad before a court of competent jurisdiction, conducting the trial upon regular proceedings, after due citation of voluntary appearance of the defendant, and under a system of jurisprudence likely to secure an impartial administration of justice between the citizens of its own country and those of other countries, and there is nothing to show either of prejudice in the court or in the systems of laws under which it was sitting, or fraud in procuring the judgment, or any special reason why the comity of this nation should not allow it full effect, the merits of the case should not, in an action brought in this country upon the judgment, be tried afresh, as on a new trial or an appeal, upon the mere assertion by the party that the judgment was erroneous in law or in fact.

c.      *Ackermann v. Levine*, 788 F.2d 830 (2d. Cir. 1986).

[Levine, an American businessman, consulted Ackermann, a lawyer in West Berlin, for which the German lawyer billed him approximately $100,000. Levine refused to pay and Ackermann sued and received a default judgment in Germany. He then commenced an action for enforcement of the foreign judgment in the U.S. District Court for the Southern District of New York. Levine appeared in the district court. The district court refused enforcement on the ground that service of process violated the pertinent international convention and due process, and that recognition and enforcement of the judgment would violate New York public policy. Ackerman appealed.]

.    .    .

To be subject to *in personam* jurisdiction,[46] a defendant must have had certain "minimum contacts" with the forum state, *see, e.g.*, *International Shoe v. Washington*, 326 U.S. 310, 316, 66 S.Ct. 154, 158, 90 L.Ed. 95 (1945); *Milliken v. Meyer*, 311 U.S. 457, 463-64, 61 S. Ct. 339, 342-43, 85 L.Ed. 278 (1940) ("connections"), and reasonable notice of the pendency of the action, *see, e.g.*, *Mullane v. Central Hanover Trust Co.*, 339 U.S. 306, 313-14, 70 S.Ct. 652, 656-57, 94 L.Ed. 865 (1950). We agree with the district court that under the "minimum contacts" test of *International Shoe* and its progeny, Levine had sufficient contacts with West Germany such that he was "avail[ing] himself" of the privileges arising therein, *Hanson v. Denckla*, 357 U.S. 235, 253, 78 S.Ct. 1228, 1240, 2 L.Ed.2d 1283 (1958), so that the exercise of *in personam* jurisdiction would not offend "traditional notions of fair play and substantial justice," *Millikan v. Meyer*, 311 U.S. at 462-64, 61 S.Ct. at 342-43. . . .[47]

---

[46] [5] As to the issue of subject matter jurisdiction, which appellee does not contest, this case arose under the district court's diversity jurisdiction. The Regional Court of Berlin apparently had jurisdiction in Germany to hear actions arising under the BRAGO statute. *See* Certified Translation, Final Judgment in Default, File Nr.: 82 0.39/79 (Dec. 19, 1980), *reprinted in* Jt.App. A-9, at A-14, *citing* art. 29 ZPO.

[47] [6] Specifically, those contacts were: (1) Levine's late May or early June 1979 visit to Germany, during which he consulted with Ackermann; (2) Levine's letter to Ackermann, authorizing him to negotiate on his behalf; (3) several contacts between Levine in New York and Ackermann and others in Germany via telephone and telex;

[The Court found that process was lawfully served.]

There is no basis to believe that the German judgment was fraudulently obtained. Defendant-appellee has offered no basis for us to question the district court's finding of fact that "neither plaintiffs nor defendant acted dishonestly." Op. at 646, or the court's corollary conclusion of law that the German judgment was not fraudulently obtained. *Id.* at 646, *citing Fairchild*, 470 F.Supp. at 615 (alleged fraud "must relate to matters other than issues that could have been litigated and must be a fraud on the court") (quoting *Overmyer v. Eliot Realty*, 83 Misc.2d 694, 371 N.Y.S.2d 246, 258 (Sup.Ct.Westchester Co. 1975)).

## III.

The district court held that, based on the undisputed fact that Ackermann never discussed fees with Levine, the German judgment was rendered unenforceable as violative of New York's public policy that "the attorney, not the client, must ensure the fairness, reasonableness and full comprehension by the client of their compensation agreement." *See Op.* at 646-647 (citing New York cases). On that basis, the district court declined enforcement of the entire award of approximately $100,000.

A judgment is unenforceable as against public policy to the extent that it is "repugnant to fundamental notions of what is decent and just in the State where enforcement is sought." *Tahan v. Hodgson*, 662 F.2d 862, 864 (D.C. Cir.1981) (quoting Rest.2d Conflict of Laws § 117, comment c (1971)). The standard is high, and infrequently met. As one court wrote, "[o]nly in clear-cut cases ought it to avail defendant." *Tahan*, 662 F.2d at 866 n.17 (citing von Mehren & Trautman, *Recognition of Foreign Adjudications: A Survey and a Suggested Approach*, 81 Harv.L.Rev. 1601, 1670 (1968); Paulsen & Sovern, *"Public Policy" in the Conflict of Laws*, 56 Colum.L.Rev. 969, 980-81, 1015-16 (1956)). In the classic formulation, a judgment

---

and (4) Levine's second visit to Germany in August, during which he did not speak with Ackermann but did pursue German investors for the Edgewater Project. The district court also noted that pursuant to contact (2), Ackermann, acting for Levine, personally dealt with two banks in Germany. Also, Levine himself, during his first visit, attended a meeting with representatives of the Grundkreditbank.

that "tends clearly" to undermine the public interest, the public confidence in the administration of the law, or security for individual rights of personal liberty or of private property is against public policy.
. . .

The narrowness of the public policy exception to enforcement would seem to reflect an axiom fundamental to the goals of comity and res judicata that underlie the doctrine of recognition and enforcement of foreign judgments. As Judge Cardozo so lucidly observed: "We are not so provincial as to say that every solution of a problem is wrong because we deal with it otherwise at home." *Loucks*, 224 N.Y. at 110-11. Further, the narrowness of the public policy exception indicates a jurisprudential compromise between two guiding but sometimes conflicting principles in the law of recognition and enforcement of foreign judgments: (1) res judicata, *see* Reese, *The Status in this Country of Judgments Rendered Abroad*, 50 Colum.L.Rev. 783, 797 (1950); Paulsen & Sovern, *supra*, 56 Colum.L.Rev. 969; and (2) fairness to litigants, *see* von Mehren & Patterson, *Recognition and Enforcement of Foreign Country Judgments in the United States*, 6 L.Pol'y in Int'l Bus. 37, 38 (1974), or fairness regarding the underlying transaction, *see* Ehrenzweig, Private International Law § 56, at 202-03 & n.11 (1967).

The question presented here involves the extent to which local public policy will permit recognition and enforcement of a foreign default judgment. Since a foreign default judgment is not more or less conclusive but "*as* conclusive an adjudication" as a contested judgment, *Somportez*, 453 F.2d at 442-43 & n. 13 (citing authority) (emphasis added), the district court quite properly afforded Levine the same opportunity to contest the enforceability of the German judgment in light of the public policy issue.[48] We disagree with dicta in *Tahan*,

---

[48] [12] Under the Uniform Foreign Judgments Recognition Act, 13 U.L.A. 417 (1980) which New York has adopted, *see* N.Y.C.P.L.R. §§ 5301-5309 (McKinney's 1986), a plaintiff seeking enforcement of a foreign country judgment granting or denying recovery of a sum of money must establish *prima facie*: (1) a final judgment, conclusive and enforceable where rendered; (2) subject matter jurisdiction; (3) jurisdiction over the parties or the *res*; and (4) regular proceedings conducted under a system that provides impartial tribunals and procedures compatible with due process. These requirements approximate those required at common law. *See, e.g., Hilton v. Guyot*, 159 U.S. 13, 16 S.Ct. 139, 40 L.Ed. 95 (1895); *see also* Bishop & Burnette, *United States Practice Concerning the Recognition of Foreign Judgments*,

662 F.2d at 867, suggesting that a defendant may not raise a public policy defense once he has defaulted in the foreign adjudication. By defaulting, a defendant ensures that a judgment will be entered against him, and assumes the risk that an irrevocable mistake of law or fact may underlie that judgment. Cf. *Clarkson v. Shaheen*, 544 F.2d 624 (2d Cir.1976); *Ingenohl v. Walter E. Olsen & Co.*, 273 U.S. 541, 544, 47 S.Ct. 451, 452, 71 L.Ed. 762 (1927); *Hilton v. Guyot*, 159 U.S. 113, 203, 16 S.Ct. 139, 158, 40 L.Ed. 95 (1895) (mere mistake of law or fact will not render judgment unenforceable). We see no reason to further penalize such a defendant, or to forsake the legitimate public policy interests of the state in which enforcement is sought.

However, we believe that the district court erred in holding that the failure of German law regarding attorneys fees to meet our more rigorous principles of fiduciary duties sufficiently offended local public policy as to justify nonenforcement of the entire judgment, and thus total vitiation of the values of comity and res judicata that enforcement would promote. We so hold in light of the consistency with which *stare decisis* has followed Judge Cardozo's maxim, *Loucks*, 224 N.Y. at 110-11, 120 N.E. 198, that mere variance with local public policy is not sufficient to decline enforcement.

The narrow public policy exception to enforcement is not met merely because Ackermann did not inform Levine of the BRAGO billing statute. See *Compania Mexicana Radiodifusora Franteriza v. Spann*, 41 F.Supp. 907 (N.D.Tex.1941), *aff'd. sub nom*, *Spann v. Compania Mexicana Radiodifusora Fronteriza*, 131 F.2d 609 (5th Cir.1942) (exception not met where a foreign attorney had failed to apprise his American client of Mexico's rule that a losing plaintiff's liability for costs is proportionate to the amount of relief originally sought). Nor is the exception met in the event that Ackermann's bill should exceed the amount which American lawyers might reasonably have charged. *See Somportex* 453 F.2d at 443 (exception not met where a British default judgment of $94,000 against an American defendant to a contract action included in substantial part damages for loss of good will and for attorneys fees and other costs, none of which would be awarded by Pennsylvania, the state in which enforcement was granted). Certainly it is not enough merely that Germany provides a

---

16 Int'l L. 425, 429-32 (1982). A defendant may then raise, e.g., fraud and public policy. *See* Bishop & Burnette, *supra*, at 434-37.

billing scheme by statute rather than by contractual arrangements subject to an attorney's fiduciary duties. We note that even New York policy permits statute-based billing systems in certain instances. *See, e.g., In re Anninger's Estate*, 35 Misc.2d 493, 230 N.Y.S.2d 910 (Sup.Ct., N.Y.Co.1962) (approving fee of 10% of net recovery from Foreign Claims Settlement Commission, even if there had been no agreement on the fee, where statute so provided); *cf. Compania Mexicana*, 41 F.Supp. at 909, *aff'd.*, 131 F.2d 609 (federal court noting federal and state statutes providing for recovery of attorneys fees). Nor can we say that the German judgment is unenforceable because the attorney-client relationship herein was not structured commensurate with the New York policy favoring, though not requiring, written retainer agreements. It is not enough merely that a foreign judgment fails to fulfill domestic practice or policy. *See Tahan*, 662 F.2d at 867 & n.20 (general rule against compelling losing side in litigation to pay attorneys fees of the winning side) (citing *Somportex*, 453 F.2d at 443).[49]

We hold that the public policy that charges an American lawyer with ensuring fair and reasonable compensation, fully disclosed to and understood by the client, does not warrant nonenforcement of the German judgment, given that there was no finding of "fraud, overreaching or bad faith" on the part of Ackermann, the foreign lawyer, *cf. Spann*, 131 F.2d at 611, and that Levine, the American client, was a sophisticated business person with access to competent American international legal counsel. *Compare In re Schanzer's Estate*, 7 A.D.2d 275, 182 N.Y.S.2d 475, 477-79 (1st Dep't (1959)), *aff'd.*, 8 N.Y.2d 972, 204 N.Y.S.2d 349, 169 N.E. 11 (1960) (attorney breaches retainer agreement with "somewhat illiterate" client). Germany's choice to regulate attorneys fees by statute rather than by fiduciary principles, and to vest the Regional Courts with jurisdiction to ensure the proper application of the BRAGO statute, did not lead to treatment of Levine that could be considered so "repugnant to fundamental notions of what is decent and just," *Tahan*, 662 F.2d at

---

[49] [13] Indeed, in some cases a foreign judgment may be enforceable even though the underlying cause of action does not exist in the state of enforcement, *see Neporany v. Kir*, 5 A.D.2d 438, 173 N.Y.S.2d 146, *appeal dismissed*, 7 A.D.2d 836, 184 N.Y.S.2d 559 (1st Dep't 1959) (action for seduction and criminal conversion), or itself offends the public policy of the state of enforcement, *see, Intercontinental* [sic] *Hotels v. Golden*, 15 N.Y.2d 9, 254, N.Y.S.2d 527, 203 N.E.2d 210 (1964) (action to recover gambling debts).

864, as to warrant nonenforcement of the default judgment in its entirety.

Thus, we think that the district court erred in holding the judgment unenforceable as offensive to New York's public policy that lawyers discharge their fiduciary duty to ensure fair and reasonable fees, fully disclosed to and understood by their clients. However, that this broad, fiduciary-based public policy does not render the judgment unenforceable does not preclude the possibility that a narrower, evidentiary-based public policy might render the judgment unenforceable.

We hold that the applicable theory of public policy requires that recovery of attorneys fees be predicated on evidence of, at a minimum, (1) the existence of some authorization by the client for the attorney to perform the work allegedly performed . . . and (2) the very existence of that work, . . . .

In applying this evidentiary-based public policy, we note that courts are not limited to recognizing a judgment entirely or not at all. Where a foreign judgment contains discrete components, the enforcing court should endeavor to discern the appropriate "extent of recognition," *cf.* 18 C. Wright & A. Miller, Federal Practice and Procedure § 4473, at 745 (1981), with reference to applicable public policy concerns.

Ackermann has laid the predicate in support of his bill for "detailed discussions with prospective buyers" and for the related travel and office expenses, but he has not done so for the "basic fee for the study of the project files, [and] discussion with client and his counsel." As for the discussions and related expenses, there was evidence of authorization in Levine's letter to Ackermann of June 8, 1979 and his telephone response to Ackermann's telex of June 14, 1979, confirming authorization as to the second bank.[50] There was undisputed evidence

---

[50] [14] We recognize that the district judge found that Levine "believed that Mr. Ackermann was acting in the capacity of a broker." Op. at 647. However, Levine specifically requested or assented to Ackermann's discussions with prospective buyers, for which Ackermann is recovering herein. In this sense, Levine authorized the performance of this work, and it is irrelevant to this issue whether Levine so authorized while believing that Ackermann would be acting as a lawyer or a broker. Further, both Ackermann's billing letter to Levine and the complaint in the German

that Ackermann did negotiate with representatives from the two banks in West Berlin and Frankfurt.

Recognition of the foreign judgment to this extent is consonant with the evidence that Levine engaged Ackermann's services and benefited therefrom. Although it was not Levine who brought suit in Germany, he did invoke the law of that nation by seeking counsel with a view toward negotiating a contract with German investors. Levine clearly would have benefited from German law had his work with Ackermann proved fruitful. *Cf. Compania Mexicana*, 41 F.Supp. at 908 (American client "went to Mexico and chose his own attorney and entered into a written power-of-attorney with him" before foreign counsel brought action on his behalf). He thus "finds himself in the quite unenviable position of trying to take the good without the bad, the sweet without the bitter." *Spann*, 131 F.2d at 611.

As to the fifteen to twenty days of work that comprise the bulk of the "basic fee for study of the project files," the record reflects no evidence of an authorization to do such work or of the existence of any work product. The mere fact that Ackermann possessed the project files is inconsequential since Levine did not know that Bauer had given those files to Ackermann. Nor do we find authorization in the office visit of late May or early June, 1978, since the district court found that visit had accomplished only the creation of a misunderstanding. Even if there had been an authorization, there was not a scintilla of evidence of work product. Ackermann offered no client memoranda, no memoranda to his files, no handwritten notes, no markings on the papers that Bauer had given him, and no other indicia of actual performance. Indeed, when his deposition was taken, Ackermann conceded that he prepared no formal memoranda and that he did not believe that there was any work product whatsoever in his files. We do not challenge the district court's finding as to Ackermann's character. However, we need not say that an attorney acted fraudulently or dishonestly to hold, as we do here, that the failure to adduce any evidence of work product requires disallowance of claimed legal fees.

---

court unambiguously stated that Ackermann was seeking *legal fees* for these services. Thus, well before the German default judgment was entered, Levine knew or should have known that the subject dispute involved legal fees. If Levine believed that Ackermann had been acting as a broker, he should have so argued in the German lawsuit; he did not do so, and accordingly may not raise this issue in the enforcement proceeding.

*Newman v. Silver*, 553 F.Supp. at 497, *modified on other grounds*, 713 F.2d 14 (1983).[51]

. . . [W]e hold the German judgment to be enforceable in all respects except for the first item of DM 89.347,50 for the "[b]asic fee for the study of project files, discussion with client and his counsel," for which there was no evidence of authorization or of work product. The judgment of the district court is accordingly, affirmed in part and reversed in part, and the cause is remanded to the district court for entry of an order not inconsistent with this opinion.[52]

### Notes and Questions

1. In *Hilton*, the Court refused enforcement on the grounds that the French courts did not reciprocate for comparable American judgments. Today federal and most state courts no longer require reciprocity in order to enforce foreign judgments.

2. Note that the foreign judgment in *Ackermann v. Levine* was not entitled to direct enforcement but required, for partial enforcement, an extensive and expensive relitigation of the key issues in front of the United States court. The absence of a direct enforcement mechanism and the possibility of a *de novo* hearing in the enforcement jurisdiction represents a major drawback to the effectiveness of forum selection clauses.

3. What dispute resolution options might have been available to Ackermann which would have been more efficient than the one he selected?

4. National courts will normally not enforce foreign judgments predicated upon violations of another country's criminal laws, or upon foreign tax laws (the "Revenue Rule"). While the Full Faith and Credit Clause of the United States Constitution requires that U.S. courts honor all judgments, including penal and tax, rendered by any state court, the prohibition against enforcing criminal and tax judgments retains its vitality with respect to judgments rendered in jurisdictions outside the United States, *Queen v. Gilbertson*, 597 F.2d 1161 (9th Cir. 1979), and the enforcement mechanism established by the Uniform Foreign Money-Judgments

---

[51] [15] That portion of the fee that reflects the initial consultation is also untenable. First, Ackermann provides no mechanism by which this court could separate this de minimis aspect of the "basic fee" from the fifteen to twenty days of subsequent work. Second, we again can discern no evidence in the record of an authorization to consult for payment.

[52] [16] Since the district court did not reach the issues of interest and exchange rates in its opinion, we leave those issues for the district judge to resolve on remand.

Recognition Act, (*see infra* pp. 123-25), specifically excludes enforcement of foreign penal, tax, and matrimonial judgments. As a result, the careful practitioner, in deciding whether to utilize a contractual forum selection clause, must take into account whether any potential disputes arising from a transaction might implicate foreign criminal or tax laws, and thus result in unenforceable judgments.

The rationale commonly given for non-enforcement of foreign penal and tax judgments is that criminal and tax laws are so intimately connected to a state's public policy that it is improper to permit a non-domestic court to decide on enforceability, since such a determination would ultimately force the court to substitute its own domestic notions of proper policy for those of the state where judgment was given. For a fuller explanation of this rationale, see Judge Learned Hand's discussion in *Moore v. Mitchell*, 30 F.2d 600, 604 (2d Cir. 1929). Is this rationale still cogent? Discuss.

> d.  EUROPEAN COMMUNITY CONVENTION ON JURISDICTION AND ENFORCEMENT OF JUDGMENTS IN CIVIL AND COMMERCIAL MATTERS (Brussels, Sept. 27, 1968).

.   .   . .

Article 25. The word "decision" within the meaning of this Convention means any decision rendered by a court of a Contracting State regardless of its designation, such as decree, judgment, order, or writ of execution, as well as a determination of the court costs by the clerk of the court.

Article 26. Decisions rendered in one Contracting State shall be recognized in the other Contracting States, without requiring special proceedings for this purpose.

Where the recognition of a decision is contested, any party asserting recognition may, under the procedure provided by Chapters 2 and 3 of this title, request a ruling to the effect that the decision be recognized.

If recognition is asserted in a dispute before a court of a Contracting State whose decision depends upon the recognition, such court shall be competent to decide.

Article 27. A decision shall not be recognized:

(1) if it is contrary to the public policy of the State in which recognition is sought;

(2) if a defendant who did not enter an appearance in the proceedings was not properly served with a summons initiating the action or was not served in time to prepare his defense;

(3) if the decision conflicts with a decision rendered between the same parties in the State in which recognition is sought;

(4) if the court of the State where the decision was rendered, in rendering a decision on a preliminary question relating to the status, the legal capacity or legal representation of a natural person, the marital property system, or wills and inheritances, has contravened the provisions of international private law of the State in which recognition is sought, unless the same result would be reached if the international private law provisions of such State had been applied.

Article 28. A decision shall further not be recognized if it contravenes the provisions of Chapters 3, 4 and 5 of Title II or in the case set forth in Article 59.

In determining the jurisdiction referred to in the preceding paragraph, the court or authority of the State in which recognition is sought shall be bound by the factual findings on the basis of which the foreign court assumed jurisdiction.

Subject to the provisions of paragraph 1, the jurisdiction of the foreign court may not be reviewed; the provisions relating to jurisdiction do not concern public order within the meaning of Article 7, paragraph 1.

Article 29. Under no circumstances shall a foreign judgment be subject to a review for legality.

Article 30. A court of a Contracting State in which recognition of a decision rendered in another Contracting State is sought may stay the proceedings if the decision has been appealed.

Article 31. Decisions rendered in a Contracting State that are enforceable therein may be enforced in another Contracting State after a writ of execution has been issued upon request of the interested party.

.   .   .

       Article 33. The terms and conditions for the request shall be governed by the law of the State in which enforcement is sought.

       The petitioner must establish domicile in the place where the court has jurisdiction. If, however, the law of the State in which enforcement is sought does not require the establishment of domicile, the petitioner must designate a representative *ad litem*.

\*    \*    \*

     e.      UNIFORM FOREIGN MONEY-JUDGMENTS RECOGNITION ACT, 13 U.L.A. 261 (1986).[53]

§1.     As used in this Act:

       (1) "foreign state" means any governmental unit other than the United States, or any state, district, commonwealth, territory, insular possession thereof, or the Panama Canal Zone, the Trust Territory of the Pacific Islands, or the Ryukyu Islands;

       (2) "foreign judgment" means any judgment of a foreign state granting or denying recovery of a sum of money, other than a judgment for taxes, a fine or other penalty, or a judgment for support in matrimonial or family matters.

     §2.     This Act applies to any foreign judgment that is final and conclusive and enforceable where rendered even though an appeal therefrom is pending or it is subject to appeal.

     §3.     Except as provided in section 4, a foreign judgment meeting the requirements of section 2 is conclusive between the parties to the extent that it grants or denies recovery of a sum of money. The

---

[53] As of 1994, 25 states have adopted the Act verbatim or with minor modifications.

foreign judgment is enforceable in the same manner as the judgment of a sister state which is entitled to full faith and credit.

§4.     (a) A foreign judgment is not conclusive if

(1) the judgment was rendered under a system which does not provide impartial tribunals or procedures compatible with the requirements of due process of law;

(2) the foreign court did not have personal jurisdiction over the defendant; or

(3) the foreign court did not have jurisdiction over the subject matter.

(b) A foreign judgment need not be recognized if

(1) the defendant in the proceedings in the foreign court did not receive notice of the proceedings in sufficient time to enable him to defend;

(2) the judgment was obtained by fraud;

(3) the [cause of action] [claim for relief] on which the judgment is based is repugnant to the public policy of this state;

(4) the judgment conflicts with another final and conclusive judgment;

(5) the proceeding in the foreign court was contrary to an agreement between the parties under which the dispute in question was to be settled otherwise than by proceedings in that court; or

(6) in the case of jurisdiction based only on personal service, the foreign court was a seriously inconvenient forum for the trial of the action.

§5.     (a) The foreign judgment shall not be refused recognition for lack of personal jurisdiction if

(1) the defendant was served personally in the foreign state;

(2) the defendant voluntarily appeared in the proceedings, other than for the purpose of protecting property seized or threatened with seizure in the proceedings or of contesting the jurisdiction of the court over him;

(3) the defendant prior to the commencement of the proceedings had agreed to submit to the jurisdiction of the foreign court with respect to the subject matter involved;

(4) the defendant was domiciled in the foreign state when the proceedings were instituted, or, being a body corporate had its principal place of business, was incorporated, or had otherwise acquired corporate status, in the foreign state;

(5) the defendant had a business office in the foreign state and the proceedings in the foreign court involved a [cause of action] [claim for relief] arising out of business done by the defendant through that office in the foreign state; or

(6) the defendant operated a motor vehicle or airplane in the foreign state and the proceedings involved a [cause of action] [claim for relief] arising out of such operation.

(b) The courts of this state may recognize other bases of jurisdiction.

§6.    If the defendant satisfies the court either that an appeal is pending or that he is entitled and intends to appeal from the foreign judgment, the court may stay the proceedings until the appeal has been determined or until the expiration of a period of time sufficient to enable the defendant to prosecute the appeal.

§7.    This Act does not prevent the recognition of a foreign judgment in situations not covered by this Act.

> f.      *Banque Libanaise Pour le Commerce v. Khreich*, 915 F.2d 1000 (5th Cir. 1990).

[Appeal from a federal district court's refusal to recognize and enforce a money judgment of a court in Abu Dhabi.]

.      .      .

The Bank argues that the district court abused its discretion when it declined to recognize the Abu Dhabi Judgment, finding that Abu Dhabi does not recognize judgments rendered by Texas courts or other courts of the United States. In Texas the Uniform Foreign Country Money-Judgment Recognition Act (the "Texas Recognition Act") controls this issue. Tex.Civ.Prac. & Rem.Code §§ 36.001-36.008 (Vernon 1986 & Supp.1990). The Texas Recognition Act provides that a foreign country money-judgment which is final, conclusive and enforceable where rendered is enforceable in Texas in the same manner as a judgment of a sister state that is entitled to full faith and credit. § 36.004. Historically foreign country judgments have not been entitled to full faith and credit, but only to comity. . . .

Section five of the Texas Recognition Act contains mandatory and discretionary grounds for non-recognition of a foreign country money-judgment. The three criteria listed in section 36.005(a) are mandatory in nature. [footnote omitted] In comparison, a court *need not* recognize a foreign country money-judgment if any of the seven grounds listed in section 36.005(b) are proven.

Section five of the Texas Recognition Act specifically provides that a court need not recognize a foreign country money-judgment if it is "established that the foreign country in which the judgment was rendered does not recognize" Texas judgments. Tex.Civ.Prac. & Rem.Code Ann. § 36.005(b)(7). Since the Texas Recognition Act clearly gives judges discretion in deciding whether to refuse to recognize foreign judgments due to lack of reciprocity, the decision not to recognize the Abu Dhabi Judgment can only be set aside upon a clear showing of abuse of that discretion. . . .

Khreich argues that the district court correctly refused to recognize the Abu Dhabi Judgment on the grounds of non-reciprocity.[54]

.     .     .

Although the Bank cited the district court to relevant Abu Dhabi law regarding the enforcement of foreign judgments, Feulner's affidavit states that in his experience valid concerns exist whether Abu Dhabi courts would actually exercise their discretion to recognize an American judgment. Feulner indicates that Abu Dhabi courts demonstrate "a certain skepticism towards the unquestioning application of legal principles adopted from the developed Western nations, at least where these appear to work to the disadvantage of local parties." R. at

---

[54] [4] Khreich also argued that the district court should not recognize the Abu Dhabi judgment because Abu Dhabi procedures do not comport with the requirements of due process of law. Due to our decision on the reciprocity issue, we need not address this issue.

573-74. Given this evidence, the district court's refusal to recognize the Abu Dhabi Judgment does not constitute an abuse of discretion. Therefore we affirm the district court's refusal to recognize the Abu Dhabi Judgment.

### Notes and Questions

1. Comparable foreign acts may be found in the British Foreign Judgments (Reciprocal Enforcement) Act of 1933. The International Law Association produced a Model Act in 1960.

2. Note that the grounds for challenging the enforcement of a foreign judgment in Sections 4 and 5 provide the resisting defendant with a wide range of substantive and procedural grounds with which to defend itself. This may increase the costs of the judgment creditor who initiates the suit for enforcement and may even require substantial rehearing of many of the issues that had been *res judicata* in the first forum. Such additional costs must be set off against the value of a foreign judgment secured by a forum selection clause.

3. Note that under Article 4(5), violation of a forum selection clause would be admissible as a defense against the enforcement of the foreign judgment. However, the act does not give explicit preference for judgments that emerge from forum selection clause actions. On the other hand, a forum selection clause may be deemed a waiver to objections to jurisdiction.

## 5.    CONCLUSION

The device of a forum selection clause is, at best, only a partial solution to the jurisdictional problem in international transactions. In the absence of an international convention enjoying wide subscription and requiring recognition and enforcement of forum selection clauses, defendants who seek to enforce such clauses when the plaintiff has sought to hijack a case to another jurisdiction must rely on the local case law, which, as has been seen, allows a rather broad discretion to the forum as to whether to honor the clause in that particular dispute. In addition, counsel for defendants will often be obliged to weigh the cost of lodging timely counter-claims against the possible effects of such counter-claims as a waiver to objections to jurisdiction. Counsel will also have to make certain that the selected forum will be competent to accept the case referred to it. Finally, there is no international convention enjoying wide subscription which secures the enforcement of foreign judgments under prescribed conditions.[55] A judgment creditor may therefore still have to face long and costly litigation before enforcement is secured. Moreover, the grounds for non-recognition of the foreign judgment may vary from jurisdiction to jurisdiction and local courts may enjoy considerable discretion in enforcement.

C.    SOLUTION NUMBER 3: PLANNING JURISDICTION BY SELECTION OF ARBITRATION

Another solution to the jurisdictional problems of international transactions is the selection of arbitration which is effected by insertion in the contract of an arbitration clause.

Examples:

Any disputes arising on or about this contract shall be settled by arbitration.

All controversies in connection with this contract shall be settled, on the application of either party, by arbitration in accord with the rules set out hereinafter.
. . .

All disputes arising in connection with the present contract shall be finally settled under the Rules of Conciliation and Arbitration of the International Chamber of Commerce by one or more arbitrators appointed in accordance with the said Rules. (Standard ICC Arbitration Clause)

All disputes, controversies, or differences which may arise between the parties, out of or in relation to or in connection with this contract, or for the breach thereof, shall be finally settled by arbitration in Seoul, Korea in accordance with the Commercial Arbitration Rules of

---

[55] Such a convention does exist within the European Union. Under the Brussels Convention of 1968, the courts of a member country have exclusive jurisdiction where the parties to an agreement have so provided (Article 17). Under Article 26, any judgment then granted would be entitled to immediate recognition in other European Union countries.

the Korean Commercial Arbitration Board and under the Laws of Korea. The award rendered by the arbitrator(s) shall be final and binding upon both parties concerned. (<u>Standard Arbitration Clause of the Korean Commercial Arbitration Board</u>)

Any dispute arising out of or in connection with this contract, including any question regarding its existence, validity or termination, shall be referred to and finally resolved by arbitration under the Rules of the London Court of International Arbitration, which Rules are deemed to be incorporated by reference into this clause. (<u>Recommended Arbitration Clause of the London Court of International Arbitration</u>)

Any controversy or claim arising out of or relating to this contract, or the breach thereof, shall be settled by arbitration in accordance with the Commercial Arbitration Rules of the American Arbitration Association, and judgment upon the award rendered by the arbitrator(s) may be entered in any court having jurisdiction thereof. (<u>Standard Arbitration Clause of the American Arbitration Association</u>)

The [Government]/[<u>name of constituent subdivision or agency</u>]/ of <u>name of Contracting State</u> (hereinafter the 'Host State') and <u>name of investor</u> (hereinafter the 'Investor') hereby consent to submit to the jurisdiction of the International Centre for Settlement of Investment Disputes (hereinafter the 'Centre') all disputes arising out of this agreement [or relating to any investment made under it], for settlement by [conciliation]/[arbitration]/[conciliation] followed, if the dispute remains unresolved within <u>time limit</u> of the communication of the report of the Conciliation Commission to the parties, by arbitration] pursuant to the Convention on the Settlement of Investment Disputes between States and Nationals of Other States (hereinafter the 'Convention'). (A clause recommended for ICSID arbitration, <u>ICSID/5 Model Clauses Recording Comment to Jurisdiction</u>)

## 1. THE EFFECT OF THE ARBITRATION AGREEMENT

Thanks to the 1958 Convention on the Recognition and Enforcement of Foreign Arbitral Awards, often called the "New York Convention," all subscribing states undertake to give effect to these awards and not to permit the initiation of suits before their courts, the classic form of judicial hijacking.

### a. ARTICLE 2 OF THE NEW YORK CONVENTION

1. Each Contracting State shall recognize an agreement in writing under which the parties undertake to submit to arbitration all or any differences which have arisen or which may arise between them in respect of a defined legal relationship, whether contractual or not, concerning a subject matter capable of settlement by arbitration.

2. The term "agreement in writing" shall include an arbitral clause in a contract or an arbitration agreement, signed by the parties or contained in an exchange of letters or telegrams.

3. The court of a Contracting State, when seized of an action in a matter in respect of which the parties have made an agreement within the meaning of this article, shall, at the request of one of the parties, refer the parties to arbitration, unless if [sic] finds that the said agreement is null and void, inoperative or incapable of being performed.

\* \* \*

States-parties also oblige themselves to enforce the award.

### b. ARTICLE 3 OF THE NEW YORK CONVENTION

Each Contracting State shall recognize arbitral awards as binding and enforce them in accordance with the rules of procedure of the territory where the award is relied upon, under the conditions laid down in the following articles. There shall not be imposed substantially more onerous conditions or higher fees or charges on the recognition or enforcement of arbitral awards to which this Convention applies than are imposed on the recognition or enforcement of domestic arbitral awards.

c.      ENFORCEABILITY OF AGREEMENTS TO ARBITRATE

The operative presumption created by Article 2 in United States courts has been concisely stated in *Marchetto v. DeKalb Genetics Corp.*

(i)      *Marchetto v. DeKalb Genetics Corp.*, 711 F.Supp. 936 (N.D. Ill. 1989).

[Plaintiffs, Marchetto, claimed breach of and tortious interference with an agreement which included a clause calling for arbitration in Italy. Defendants moved to dismiss the claim, alleging that the arbitration was required. Plaintiffs responded by alleging that the arbitration clause was inoperable.]

.      .      .

The Federal Arbitration Act ("the Arbitration Act"), 9 U.S.C. § 1 *et seq.*, governs the enforcement, interpretation and validity of arbitration clauses in commercial contracts. *Moses H. Cone Memorial Hospital v. Mercury Construction Corp.*, 460 U.S. 1, 24-25, 103 S.Ct. 927, 941, 74 L.Ed.2d 765 (1983); *Snyder v. Smith*, 736 F.2d 409, 417 (7th Cir.1984); *Zell v. Jacoby-Bender, Inc.*, 542 F.2d 34, 37 (7th Cir.1976). The Arbitration Act provides that arbitration agreements "shall be valid, irrevocable, and enforceable, save upon such grounds as exist at law or equity for the revocation of any contract." 9 U.S.C. § 2. This language creates a presumption in favor of arbitration. *Mitsubishi Motors Corp. v. Soler Chrysler-Plymouth*, 473 U.S. 614, 625, 105 S.Ct. 3346, 3353, 87 L.Ed.2d 444 (1985); *Moses H. Cone Memorial Hospital*, 460 U.S. at 24-25, 103 S.Ct. at 941-42; *Snyder*, 736 F.2d at 417; *In re Oil Spill by Amoco Cadiz*, 659 F.2d 789, 796 (7th Cir.1981). This means courts must vigorously enforce arbitration clauses in commercial contracts. *Id.* Any doubts regarding the validity of an arbitration clause must be resolved in favor of arbitration. *Id.*

The federal policy favoring arbitration applies with special force in the area of international commerce. *Mitsubishi Motors Corp.*, 473 U.S. at 629-31, 105 S.Ct. at 3355-56; *Scherk v. Alberto-Culver Co.*, 417 U.S. 506, 516-17, 94 S.Ct. 2449, 2455-56, 41 L.Ed.2d 270 (1974); *In re Oil Spill by Amoco Cadiz*, 659 F.2d at 795; *Karlberg European Tanspa, Inc. v. JK-Josef Kratz Vertriebsgesellschaft*, 618 F.Supp. 344, 347 (N.D.Ill.1985). In 1970, the United States became a party to the Convention on the Recognition and Enforcement of Foreign Arbitral Awards ("the Convention"). 3 U.S.T. 2517, T.I.A.S. No. 6997 reprinted in 9 U.S.C. § 201 (1980 Supp.); *Scherk*, 417 U.S. at 520 n. 15, 94 S.Ct. at 2457-58 n. 15. The Convention and its enabling legislation, 9 U.S.C. § 201 *et seq.*, were designed to encourage the arbitration of international commercial disputes and to unify the standards by which agreements are enforced. *Scherk*, 417 U.S. at 520 n. 15, 94 S.Ct. at 2457-58 n. 15. By acceding to the Convention, the United States joined other signatory nations in proclaiming a willingness to enforce arbitration clauses in international commercial agreements. *Id.* at 516 n. 10, 94 S.Ct. at 2451 n. 10. *Rhone Mediterranee Compagnia v. Achille Lauro*, 712 F.2d 50, 53-54 (3d Cir.1983).

The strong presumption favoring enforcement of arbitration clauses in international commercial agreements divests this court of substantial discretion in deciding whether to order arbitration. *Sedco v. Petroleos Mexicanos Mexican Nat'l Oil Co.*, 767 F.2d 1140, 1144-45 (5th Cir.1985); *Snyder*, 736 F.2d at 418, 419; *Ledee v. Ceramiche Ragno*, 684 F.2d 184, 186-87 (1st Cir.1982); *In re Oil Spill by Amoco Cadiz*, 659 F.2d at 795-96. The Convention requires this court to inquire whether (1) there is a written arbitration agreement; (2) the agreement provides for arbitration in a signatory country; (3) the agreement arises out of a commercial legal relationship; and (4) the commercial transaction has a reasonable relationship to a foreign state. *Sedco*, 767 F.2d at 1144-45; *Ledee*, 684 F.2d at 186-87. If these factors are met, arbitration is mandatory. *Id.*

There is no dispute that these factors are present in this case. Italy is a signatory country. 9 U.S.C. § 201. The shareholder agreement unquestionably embodies a legal relationship. The arbitration clause was incorporated into this agreement through a written amendment. Moreover, the allegedly unlawful transfers of DeKalb Italiana stock have a reasonable relationship to Italy because they involve an Italian company and allegedly damaged an Italian shareholder group.

The Marchettos ignore these factors. They argue that the arbitration clause is unenforceable under Article II(3) of the Convention. 9 U.S.C. § 201. Article II(3) provides:

> The court of a Contracting State, when seized of an action in a matter in respect of which the parties have made an agreement within the meaning of this article, shall at the request of one of the parties, refer the parties to arbitration, unless it finds that said agreement is null and void, inoperative or incapable of being performed.

*Id.* The Marchettos contend this arbitration clause is incapable of performance because Italian law will not enforce an arbitration agreement where, as here, three of the four defendants are not parties to the agreement. They also argue that their claim for tortious interference in Count II is nonarbitrable under Italian law because it is beyond the scope of the arbitration clause.

These arguments are without merit. The possibility that Italian law might divest a panel of Italian arbitrators of jurisdiction is not determinative of this court's duty to enforce an otherwise valid arbitration agreement. *Mitsubishi Motors Corp.*, 473 U.S. at 629-31, 105 S.Ct. at 3355-56; *Scherk*, 417 U.S. at 517-19, 94 S.Ct. at 2456-57; *Rhone Mediterranee Compagnia*, 712 F.2d at 53-54. Section 203 of the Act provides that:

> [a]n action or proceeding falling under the Convention shall be deemed to arise under the laws and treaties of the United States.

9 U.S.C. § 203. This means that the validity of an arbitration agreement is determined by reference to the Arbitration Act and the federal substantive law of arbitrability. *Moses H. Cone Memorial Hospital*, 460 U.S. at 24, 103 S. Ct. at 941; *Scherk*, 417 U.S. at 520,

94 S.Ct. at 2457; *Rhone Mediterranee Compagnia*, 712 F.2d at 54; *Zell*, 542 F.2d at 37.

.   .   .

The Marchettos respond by arguing that even under federal law, this arbitration clause is unenforceable. They rely on *Volt Information Sciences, Inc. v. Board of Trustees of Leland Stanford Junior Univ.*, 489 U.S. 468, 109 S.Ct. 1248, 103 L.Ed.2d 488 (1989), for the proposition that an arbitration agreement is unenforceable where claims are asserted against entities that are not formal parties to the agreement. In *Volt*, the Supreme Court affirmed a California court's decision to stay arbitration pending resolution of related litigation involving entities that were not parties to the arbitration agreement. *Id.* 109 S.Ct. at 1254-55. The California court based its decision on the California rules of arbitration. *Id.* at 1253. The Supreme Court held that the California rules were not preempted by the Arbitration Act because the parties specifically incorporated the California rules into their arbitration agreement. *Id.* at 1254-55. *Volt* reaffirms the established principle that arbitration agreements are contracts, enforceable according to their terms. *Id.* It does not upset the rule that non-parties to an arbitration agreement may participate in arbitration proceedings. *Moses H. Cone Memorial Hospital*, 460 U.S. at 20, 103 S.Ct. at 939; *C. Itoh & Co.*, 552 F.2d at 1231-32. Accordingly, *Volt* is restricted to its facts and has no bearing on this dispute.

Finally, the Marchettos argue that federal law prohibits the enforcement of an arbitration agreement where it is clear foreign law divests the arbitrators of jurisdiction. This is another way of saying that the validity of an arbitration agreement is determined by the law of the place of arbitration. The Supreme Court has addressed this argument and flatly rejected it:

> There is no reason to assume at the outset of the dispute that international arbitration will not provide an adequate mechanism. To be sure, the international arbitral panel owes no prior allegiance to the legal norms of particular states; hence it has no direct obligation to vindicate their statutory dictates. The tribunal, however, is bound to effectuate the intentions of the parties.

*Mitsubishi Motors Corp.*, 473 U.S. at 636, 105 S.Ct. at 3358-59. Underlying the Supreme Court's willingness to enforce arbitration agreements is the assumption that signatory nations to the Convention will honor arbitration agreements and reject challenges to arbitration based on legal principles unique to the signatory nation. *Scherk*, 417 U.S. at 520 n. 15, 94 S.Ct. at 2457-58; *Rhone Mediterranee Compagnia*, 712 F.2d at 53-54. Italy is a signatory nation and presumably will honor this arbitration clause. *Rhone Mediterranee Compagnia*, 712 F.2d at 54; *Matter of Ferrara S.p.A.*, 441 F.Supp. 778, 781 (S.D.N.Y.1977).

This conclusion is reinforced by the defendants' Italian law expert who states that Italian courts recognize that the Convention vests Italian arbitration panels with plenary jurisdiction over international commercial disputes. Defendants' Reply Mem., Ex. A ¶ 8. Once an Italian arbitration panel asserts jurisdiction in an international commercial matter, Italian courts lose their concurrent jurisdiction. *Id.* The Marchettos also rely on an affidavit of an Italian law expert. Their affidavit alleges that an Italian arbitration panel would not exercise jurisdiction over this dispute. Marchetto Response Mem. Ex. C. At most, this affidavit creates a question of fact regarding the arbitration panel's jurisdiction. This is a subject that must be addressed by the Italian arbitration panel. . . .

### Notes and Questions

1. As noted in *Marchetto*, in *Volt v. Stanford* the Supreme Court, deferring to the operation of California law in an entirely domestic case, suspended arbitration pending resolution of a matter which California law apparently referred to adjudication. (*Volt* is excerpted in Chapter 4, *infra* pp. 421-33). Would the Supreme Court have deferred arbitration had the transaction been international and governed by Article 2 of the 1958 New York Convention?

2. What is the significance of the Court's observation that "the unlawful transfers have a reasonable relationship to Italy?" Is that required by the Convention?

3. Arbitration as a mode of dispute resolution in international commercial transactions has costs, compared to other options. Judgments by national courts are part of a hierarchical control system in which successive appeals are designed to increase the likelihood of a final decision which closely approximates the law relevant to the facts of the case. Awards rendered in international commercial arbitration, which is designed to avoid courts insofar as possible, will be enforced abroad for the most part under the regime provided by Article V of the New York Convention

(Supplement at p. 42-43) in which a national court is authorized only to examine whether the procedures by which the arbitration tribunal reached its award were appropriate, the arbitrators' comportment met minimum standards of fairness, and, in certain exceptional circumstances, that enforcement of the award would not violate local public policy. At favored international arbitration venues modern arbitration statutes have similarly restricted the power of reviewing courts at the seat of arbitration. Thus Craig has written: "What the [New York] Convention did not do, however, was provide any international mechanism to insure the validity of the award where rendered. This was left to the provisions of local law". W. Laurence Craig, *Some Trends and Developments in the Laws and Practice of International Commercial Arbitration*, 30 TEX. INT'L L.J. 1, 11 (1995). This radically reduced judicial supervision is an indispensable part of the international arbitration mechanism but it can be costly to a losing party which is convinced that the award that was rendered is legally wrong. The costs to the forum of exporting the dispute to arbitration in another jurisdiction were relatively low in *Marchetto v. DeKalb*, for no major U.S. policy appeared to have been engaged in the dispute. In contrast, in *Mitsubishi v. Soler* (1985), discussed in detail in Chapter 3, the Supreme Court compelled arbitration on the basis of Article 2 of the 1958 Convention even though a statutory anti-trust claim, not contemplated in the arbitration clause, had been raised by the defendant, who, at the very least, sought to have those issues separated from the arbitration and litigated in the United States.

4. Does the Convention fail to impose any restraint on judicial review at the seat of arbitration? It is true that the Convention in general aims not only at foreign arbitrations but also arbitrations which are not considered domestic where rendered. Nevertheless, the Convention has no language aimed at review as opposed to refusal of recognition and enforcement. There is thus an anomaly where an award is rendered in the United States in an international matter. It would appear to be the case that in setting aside proceedings the losing party could raise all grounds for setting aside provided in chapter 1 of the FAA while if the winning party counterclaimed for enforcement it could insist that no ground could be used for refusal of enforcement other than those specifically set out in the Convention. Discuss.

We will consider many of the problems raised by this dimension of arbitration in the final chapter. For the moment, however, consider the important decision of *Parsons & Whittemore v. RAKTA*.

(ii)    *Parsons & Whittemore Overseas Co., Inc. v. Societe Generale De L'Industrie Du Papier (RAKTA),* 508 F.2d 969 (2d Cir. 1974).

## J. JOSEPH SMITH, Circuit Judge:

Parsons & Whittemore Overseas Co., Inc., (Overseas), an American corporation, appeals from the entry of summary judgment on

February 25, 1974, by Judge Lloyd F. MacMahon of the Southern District of New York on the counter-claim by Societe Generale de L'Industrie du Papier (RAKTA), an Egyptian corporation, to confirm a foreign arbitral award holding Overseas liable to RAKTA for breach of contract. RAKTA in turn challenges the court's concurrent order granting summary judgment on Overseas' complaint, which sought a declaratory judgment denying RAKTA's entitlement to recover the amount of a letter of credit issued by Bank of America [footnote omitted] in RAKTA's favor at Overseas' request. Jurisdiction is based on 9 U.S.C. § 203, which empowers federal district courts to hear cases to recognize and enforce foreign arbitral awards, and 9 U.S.C. § 205, which authorizes the removal of such cases from state courts, as was accomplished in this instance.[56] We affirm the district court's confirmation of the foreign award. Since it has been established that RAKTA can fully satisfy the award out of a supersedeas bond posted by Overseas, we need not and do not rule on RAKTA's appeal from the adjudication of its letter of credit claim.

In November 1962, Overseas consented by written agreement with RAKTA to construct, start up and, for one year, manage and supervise a paperboard mill in Alexandria, Egypt. The Agency for International Development (AID), a branch of the United States State Department, would finance the project by supplying RAKTA with funds with which to purchase letters of credit in Overseas' favor. Among the contract's terms was an arbitration clause, which provided a means to settle differences arising in the course of performance, and a "force majeure" clause, which excused delay in performance due to causes beyond Overseas' reasonable capacity to control.

Work proceeded as planned until May, 1967. Then, with the Arab-Israeli Six Day War on the horizon, recurrent expressions of Egyptian hostility to Americans—nationals of the principal ally of the Israeli enemy—caused the majority of the Overseas work crew to leave Egypt. On June 6, the Egyptian government broke diplomatic ties with the United States and ordered all Americans expelled from Egypt except those who would apply and qualify for a special visa.

---

[56] [2] Overseas initiated suit in New York Supreme Court and the case was removed to federal court on RAKTA's petition.

Having abandoned the project for the present with the construction phase near completion, Overseas notified RAKTA that it regarded this postponement as excused by the force majeure clause. RAKTA disagreed and sought damages for breach of contract. Overseas refused to settle and RAKTA, already at work on completing the performance promised by Overseas, invoked the arbitration clause. Overseas responded by calling into play the clause's option to bring a dispute directly to a three-man arbitral board governed by the rules of the International Chamber of Commerce. After several sessions in 1970, the tribunal issued a preliminary award, which recognized Overseas' force majeure defense as good only during the period from May 28 to June 30, 1967. In so limiting Overseas' defense, the arbitration court emphasized that Overseas had made no more than a perfunctory effort to secure special visas and that AID's notification that it was withdrawing financial backing did not justify Overseas' unilateral decision to abandon the project.[57] After further hearings in 1972, the tribunal made its final award in March, 1973; Overseas was held liable to RAKTA for $312,507.45 in damages for breach of contract and $30,000 for RAKTA's costs; additionally, the arbitrators' compensation was set at $49,000, with Overseas responsible for three-fourths of the sum.

Subsequent to the final award, Overseas in the action here under review sought a declaratory judgment to prevent RAKTA from collecting the award out of a letter of credit issued in RAKTA's favor by Bank of America at Overseas' request. The letter was drawn to satisfy any "penalties" which an arbitral tribunal might assess against Overseas in the future for breach of contract. RAKTA contended that the arbitral award for damages met the letter's requirement of "penalties" and counterclaimed to confirm and enter judgment upon the foreign arbitral award. Overseas' defenses to this counterclaim, all rejected by the district court, form the principal issues for review on this appeal. Four of these defenses are derived from the express language of the applicable United Nations Convention on the Recognition and Enforcement of Foreign Arbitral Awards (Convention), 330 U.N. Treaty Ser. 38, and a fifth is arguably implicit in the Convention. These include: enforcement of the award would violate the public policy of the United States; the award represents an

---

[57] [3] RAKTA represented to the tribunal that it was prepared to finance the project without AID's assistance.

arbitration of matters not appropriately decided by arbitration; the tribunal denied Overseas an adequate opportunity to present its case; the award is predicated upon a resolution of issues outside the scope of the contractual agreement to submit to arbitration; and the award is in manifest disregard of law. In addition to disputing the district court's rejection of its position on the letter of credit, RAKTA seeks on appeal modification of the court's order to correct for an arithmetical error in the sum entered for judgment, as well as an assessment of damages and double costs against Overseas for pursuing a frivolous appeal.

## I. OVERSEAS' DEFENSES AGAINST ENFORCEMENT

In 1958 the Convention was adopted by 26 of the 45 states participating in the United Nations Conference on Commercial Arbitration held in New York. For the signatory states, the New York Convention superseded the Geneva Convention of 1927, 92 League of Nations Treaty Ser. 302. The 1958 Convention's basic thrust was to liberalize procedures for enforcing foreign arbitral awards: [sic] While the Geneva Convention placed the burden of proof on the party seeking enforcement of a foreign arbitral award and did not circumscribe the range of available defenses to those enumerated in the convention, the 1958 Convention clearly shifted the burden of proof to the party defending against enforcement and limited his defenses to seven set forth in Article V. *See* Contini, International Commercial Arbitration, 8 Am.J.Comp.L. 283, 299 (1959). Not a signatory to any prior multilateral agreement on enforcement of arbitral awards, the United States declined to sign the 1958 Convention at the outset. The United States ultimately acceded to the Convention, however, in 1970, [1970] 3 U.S.T. 2517, T.I.A.S. No. 6997, and implemented its accession with 9 U.S.C. §§ 201-208. Under 9 U.S.C. § 208, the existing Federal Arbitration Act, 9 U.S.C. §§ 1-14, applies to the enforcement of foreign awards except to the extent to which the latter may conflict with the Convention. *See generally*, Comment, International Commercial Arbitration under the United Nations Convention and the Amended Federal Arbitration Statute, 47 Wash.L.Rev. 441 (1972).

### A. *Public Policy*

Article V(2)(b) of the Convention allows the court in which enforcement of a foreign arbitral award is sought to refuse enforcement, on the defendant's motion or *sua sponte*, if "enforcement of the award would be contrary to the public policy of [the forum] country." The legislative history of the provision offers no certain guidelines to its construction. Its precursors in the Geneva Convention and the 1958 Convention's ad hoc committee draft extended the public policy exception to, respectively, awards contrary to "principles of the law" and awards violative of "fundamental principles of the law." In one commentator's view, the Convention's failure to include similar language signifies a narrowing of the defense. Contini, *supra*, 8 Am.J.Comp.L. 283 at 304. On the other hand, another noted authority in the field has seized upon this omission as indicative of an intention to broaden the defense. Quigley, Accession by the United States to the United Nations Convention on the Recognition and Enforcement of Foreign Arbitral Awards, 70 Yale L.J. 1049, 1070-71 (1961).

Perhaps more probative, however, are the inferences to be drawn from the history of the Convention as a whole. The general pro-enforcement bias informing the Convention and explaining its supersession of the Geneva Convention points toward a narrow reading of the public policy defense. An expansive construction of this defense would vitiate the Convention's basic effort to remove pre-existing obstacles to enforcement. *See* Straus, Arbitration of Disputes between Multinational Corporations, in New Strategies for Peaceful Resolution of International Business Disputes 114-15 (1971); Digest of Proceedings of International Business Disputes Conference, April 14, 1971, in *id.* at 191 (remarks of Professor W. Reese). Additionally, considerations of reciprocity—considerations given express recognition in the Convention itself[58]—counsel courts to invoke the public policy defense with caution lest foreign courts frequently accept it as a defense to enforcement of arbitral awards rendered in the United States.

---

[58] [4]      A Contracting State shall not be entitled to avail itself of the present Convention against other Contracting States except to the extent that it is itself bound to apply the Convention.

Article XIV. *Cf.* Comment, *supra*, 47 Wash.L.Rev. 441 at 486-87:

[I]n a system based upon reciprocity any tendency to take an overly narrow view of foreign arbitral awards will be balanced by a desire to obtain the widest acceptance of America's awards among the courts of other signatory states, which also have the public policy loophole available to them.

We conclude, therefore, that the Convention's public policy defense should be construed narrowly. Enforcement of foreign arbitral awards may be denied on this basis only where enforcement would violate the forum state's most basic notions of morality and justice. *Cf.* 1 Restatement Second of the Conflict of Laws § 117, comment c, at 340 (1971); Loucks v. Standard Oil Co., 224 N.Y. 99, 111, 120 N.E. 198 (1918).

Under this view of the public policy provision in the Convention, Overseas' public policy defense may easily be dismissed. Overseas argues that various actions by United States officials subsequent to the severance of American-Egyptian relations — most particularly, AID's withdrawal of financial support for the Overseas-RAKTA contract — required Overseas, as a loyal American citizen, to abandon the project. Enforcement of an award predicated on the feasibility of Overseas' returning to work in defiance of these expressions of national policy would therefore allegedly contravene United States public policy. In equating "national" policy with United States "public" policy, the appellant quite plainly misses the mark. To read the public policy defense as a parochial device protective of national political interests would seriously undermine the Convention's utility. This provision was not meant to enshrine the vagaries of international politics under the rubric of "public policy." Rather, a circumscribed public policy doctrine was contemplated by the Convention's framers and every indication is that the United States, in acceding to the Convention, meant to subscribe to this supranational emphasis. *Cf.* Scherk v. Alberto-Culver Co., 417 U.S. 506, 94 S.Ct. 2449, 41 L.Ed.2d 270 (1974).[59]

To deny enforcement of this award largely because of the United States' falling out with Egypt in recent years would mean converting a defense intended to be of narrow scope into a major loophole in the Convention's mechanism for enforcement. We have little hesitation, therefore, in disallowing Overseas' proposed public policy defense.

---

[59] [5] Moreover, the facts here fail to demonstrate that considered government policy forbids completion of the contract itself by a private party.

## B. *Non-Arbitrability*

Article V(2)(a) authorizes a court to deny enforcement, on a defendant's or its own motion, of a foreign arbitral award when "[t]he subject matter of the difference is not capable of settlement by arbitration under the law of that [the forum] country." Under this provision, a court sitting in the United States might, for example, be expected to decline enforcement of an award involving arbitration of an antitrust claim in view of domestic arbitration cases which have held that antitrust matters are entrusted to the exclusive competence of the judiciary. *See, e.g.*, American Safety Equipment Corp. v. J.P. Maguire & Co., 391 F.2d 821 (2d Cir. 1968). On the other hand, it may well be that the special considerations and policies underlying a "truly international agreement," Scherk v. Alberto-Culver Co., *supra*, 417 U.S. 506 at 515, 94 S.Ct. 2449, call for a narrower view of non-arbitrability in the international than the domestic context. *Compare id. with* Wilko v. Swan, 346 U.S. 427, 74 S.Ct. 182, 98 L.Ed. 168 (1953) (enforcement of international, but not domestic, agreement to arbitrate claim based on alleged Securities Act violations.)

Resolution of Overseas' non-arbitrability argument, however, does not require us to reach such difficult distinctions between domestic and foreign awards. For Overseas' argument, that "United States foreign policy issues can hardly be placed at the mercy of foreign arbitrators 'who are charged with the execution of no public trust' and whose loyalties are to foreign interests" Brief for Appellant at 23, plainly fails to raise so substantial an issue of arbitrability. The mere fact that an issue of national interest may incidentally figure into the resolution of a breach of contract claim does not make the dispute not arbitrable. Rather, certain *categories* of claims may be non-arbitrable because of the special national interest vested in their resolution. *Cf.* American Safety Equipment Corp., *supra*, 391 F.2d 821 at 826-27. Furthermore, even were the test for non-arbitrability of an ad hoc nature, Overseas' situation would almost certainly not meet the standard, for Overseas grossly exaggerates the magnitude of the national interest involved in the resolution of its particular claim. Simply because acts of the United States are somehow implicated in a case one cannot conclude that the United States is vitally interested in its outcome. Finally, the Supreme Court's decision in favor of arbitrability in a case far more prominently displaying public features than the instant one, Scherk v. Alberto-Culver Co., *supra*, compels by analogy the conclusion that the foreign award against Overseas dealt with a subject arbitrable under United States law.

The court below was correct in denying relief to Overseas under the Convention's non-arbitrability defense to enforcement of foreign arbitral awards. There is no special national interest in judicial, rather than arbitral, resolution of the breach of contract claim underlying the award in this case.

## C. *Inadequate Opportunity to Present Defense*

Under Article V(1)(b) of the Convention, enforcement of a foreign arbitral award may be denied if the defendant can prove that he was "not given proper notice . . . or was otherwise unable to present his case." This provision essentially sanctions the application of the forum state's standards of due process. *See* Quigley, *supra*, 70 Yale L.J. 1049 at 1067 n. 81; Quigley, Convention on Foreign Arbitral Awards, 58 A.B.A.J. 821, 825 (1972); Aksen, American Arbitration Accession Arrives in the Age of Aquarius, in New Strategies, *supra*, at 48.

Overseas seeks relief under this provision for the arbitration court's refusal to delay proceedings in order to accommodate the speaking schedule of one of Overseas' witnesses, David Nes, the United States Charge d'Affairs in Egypt at the time of the Six Day War. This attempt to state a due process claim fails for several reasons. First, inability to produce one's witnesses before an arbitral tribunal is a risk inherent in an agreement to submit to arbitration. By agreeing to submit disputes to arbitration, a party relinquishes his courtroom rights — including that to subpoena witnesses — in favor of arbitration "with all of its well known advantages and drawbacks." Washington-Baltimore Newspaper Guild, Local 35 v. The Washington Post Co., 143 U.S.App.D.C. 210, 442 F.2d 1234, 1238 (1971). Secondly, the logistical problems of scheduling hearing dates convenient to parties, counsel and arbitrators scattered about the globe argues against deviating from an initially mutually agreeable time plan unless a scheduling change is truly unavoidable. In this instance, Overseas' allegedly key witness was kept from attending the hearing due to a prior commitment to lecture at an American university — hardly the type of obstacle to his presence which would require the arbitral tribunal to postpone the hearing as a matter of fundamental fairness to Overseas. Finally, Overseas cannot complain that the tribunal decided the case without considering evidence critical to its defense and within only Mr. Nes' ability to produce. In fact, the tribunal did have before it an affidavit by Mr. Nes in which he furnished, by his own account, "a good deal of the information to which I would have testified." Appendix to Brief of Appellant at 184a. Moreover, had Mr. Nes wished to furnish *all* the information to which he would have testified, there is every reason to believe that the arbitration tribunal would have considered that as well.

The arbitration tribunal acted within its discretion in declining to reschedule a hearing for the convenience of an Overseas witness. Overseas' due process rights under American law, rights entitled to full force under the Convention as a defense to enforcement, were in no way infringed by the tribunal's decision.

### D. *Arbitration in Excess of Jurisdiction*

Under Article V(1)(c), one defending against enforcement of an arbitral award prevail by proving that:

> The award deals with a difference not contemplated by or not falling within the terms of the submission to arbitration, or it contains decisions on matters beyond the scope of the submission to arbitration. . . .

This provision tracks in more detailed form § 10(d) of the Federal Arbitration Act, 9 U.S.C. § 10(d), which authorizes vacating an award "[w]here the arbitrators exceeded their powers." Both provisions basically allow a party to attack an award predicated upon arbitration of a subject matter not within the agreement to submit to arbitration. This defense to enforcement of a foreign award, like the others already discussed, should be construed narrowly. Once again a narrow construction would comport with the enforcement-facilitating thrust of the Convention. In addition, the case law under the similar provision of the Federal Arbitration Act strongly supports a strict reading. *See, e.g.*, United Steelworkers of America. v. Enterprise Wheel & Car Corp., 363 U.S. 593, 80 S.Ct. 1358, 4 L.Ed.2d 1424 (1960); Coenen v. R.W. Pressprich & Co., 453 F.2d 1209 (2d Cir.), cert. denied, 406 U.S. 949, 92 S.Ct. 2045, 32 L.Ed.2d 337 (1972).

In making this defense as to three components of the award, Overseas must therefore overcome a powerful presumption that the arbitral body acted within its powers. Overseas principally directs its challenge at the $185,000 awarded for loss of production. Its jurisdictional claim focuses on the provision of the contract reciting that "[n]either party shall have any liability for loss of production." The tribunal cannot properly be charged, however, with simply ignoring this alleged limitation on the subject matter over which its decision-making powers extended. Rather, the arbitration court interpreted the provision not to preclude jurisdiction on this matter. As in United Steelworkers of America v. Enterprise Wheel & Car Corp., *supra*, the court may be satisfied that the arbitrator premised the award on a construction of the contract and that it is "not apparent," 363 U.S. 593 at 598, 80 S.Ct. 1358, that the scope of the submission to arbitration has been exceeded.

The appellant's attack on the $60,000 awarded for start-up expenses and $30,000 in costs cannot withstand the most cursory scrutiny. In characterizing the $60,000 as "consequential damages" (and thus proscribed by the arbitration agreement), Overseas is again attempting to secure a reconstruction in this court of the contract—an activity wholly inconsistent with the deference due arbitral decisions on law and fact. *See generally*, Bernhardt v. Polygraphic Company of America, Inc., 350 U.S. 198, 203 & n. 4, 76 S.Ct. 273, 100 L.Ed. 199 (1956). The $30,000 in costs is equally unassailable, for the appellant's contention that this portion of the award is inconsistent with guidelines set by the International Chamber of Commerce is twice removed from reality. First of all, contrary to Overseas' representations, these guidelines (contained in the Guide to ICC Arbitration and reproduced in relevant part in Appendix to Brief of Appellant at 408a) do not require, as a pre-condition to an award of expenses, express authority for such an award in the arbitration clause. The arbitration agreement's silence on this matter, therefore, is not determinative in the case under review. Secondly, since the parties in fact complied with the *Guide's* advice to reach agreement on this matter prior to arbitration—*i.e.*, the request by each for such an award for expenses amounts to tacit agreement on this point—any claim of fatal deviation from the *Guide* is disingenuous to say the least.

Although the Convention recognizes that an award may not be enforced where predicated on a subject matter outside the arbitrator's jurisdiction, it does not sanction second-guessing the arbitrator's construction of the parties' agreement. The appellant's attempt to invoke this defense, however, calls upon the court to ignore this limitation on its decision-making powers and usurp the arbitrator's role. The district court took a proper view of its own jurisdiction in refusing to grant relief on this ground.

E. *Award in "Manifest Disregard" of Law*

Both the legislative history of Article V, *see supra*, and the statute enacted to implement the United States' accession to the Convention[60] are strong authority for treating as exclusive the bases set forth in the Convention for vacating an award. On the other hand, the Federal Arbitration Act, specifically 9 U.S.C. § 10, has been read to include an implied defense to enforcement where the award is in "manifest disregard" of the law. Wilko v. Swan, 346 U.S. 427, 436, 74 S.Ct. 182, 98 L.Ed. 168 (1953); Saxis Steamship Co. v. Multifacs International Traders, Inc., 375 F.2d 577, 582 (2d Cir. 1967); Amicizia Societa Navegazione v. Chilean Nitrate and Iodine Sales Corp., 274 F.2d 805, 808 (2d Cir. 1960).

This case does not require us to decide, however, whether this defense stemming from dictum in *Wilko*, *supra*, obtains in the international arbitration context. For even assuming that the "manifest disregard" defense applies under the Convention, we would have no difficulty rejecting the appellant's contention that such "manifest disregard" is in evidence here. Overseas in effect asks this court to read this defense as a license to review the record of arbitral proceedings for errors of fact or law—a role which we have emphatically declined to assume in the past and reject once again. "[E]xtensive judicial review frustrates the basic purpose of arbitration, which is to dispose of disputes quickly and avoid the expense and delay of extended court proceedings." Saxis Steamship Co., *supra*, 375 F.2d 577 at 582. *See also*, Amicizia Societa Navegazione, *supra*, 274 F.2d 805 at 808.

Insofar as this defense to enforcement of awards in "manifest disregard" of law may be cognizable under the Convention, it, like the other defenses raised by the appellant, fails to provide a sound basis for

---

[60] [6] . . . The court shall confirm the award unless it finds one of the grounds for refusal or deferral of recognition or enforcement specified in the said Convention. . . .

vacating the foreign arbitral award. We therefore affirm the district court's confirmation of the award.

RAKTA does not frame its appeal from the district court's decision disallowing collection on the letter of credit as contingent upon our reversing the district court's confirmation of the award. Nevertheless, since RAKTA can fully satisfy the award out of a supersedeas bond posted by the appellant, we consider RAKTA's appeal no longer to require resolution and therefore decline to rule on it.[61]

### Notes and Questions

1. Imagine yourself the General Counsel of Parsons & Whittemore. As the Six Day War becomes imminent, you decide that the risks of staying in Egypt and the possible liability of your company to workers if a war eventuates is so great that you must invoke the *force majeure* clause. On June 1, events prove the wisdom of your choice. Within two weeks, the war seems to be over but you continue to be somewhat concerned. As a result, you decide not to send your people back into Egypt to complete the contract, still relying on the *force majeure* clause. Egypt, in the meanwhile, insists on completion of the project. Shortly thereafter, Egypt sinks an Israeli cruiser, off Port Said and Israel retaliates with a bombardment of an industrial area along the Canal. Once again, you feel events have vindicated your judgment. But an arbitration tribunal, provided for by a clause in your contract, rules that you are liable to RAKTA for almost $400,000.00. In a court setting, you would be entitled to appeal to a higher court, raising many of the issues of law and, to an extent, of fact which you think were improperly decided by the court of first instance. In an international commercial arbitration, as *Parsons & Whittemore* indicates, you are limited to the defenses available under Article V of the 1958 New York Convention.

---

[61] [7] In view of the general rule requiring strict conformity with the terms of a letter of credit, however, Venizelos, S.A. v. Chase Manhattan Bank, 425 F.2d 461, 464-465 (2d Cir. 1970); Banco Espanol de Credito v. State Street Bank & Trust Co., 385 F.2d 230, 234 (1st Cir. 1967), cert. denied, 390 U.S. 1013, 88 S.Ct. 1263, 20 L.Ed.2d 163 91968); Marine Midland Grace Trust Company of New York v. Banco del Pais, S.A., 261 F.Supp. 884, 889 (S.D.N.Y. 1966), we do register doubts about the force of RAKTA's claim. For while the letter provides, in relevant part, that payment to RAKTA awaits presentation of "[a]n award issued by arbitrators . . . indicating the amount of the penalty due," the award itself was written in terms of "damages" rather than "penalties." But we refrain from passing on this admittedly complex issue and limit our affirmance to the district court's confirmation of the foreign award.

2. In attempting to avail yourself of the Convention in a case like this, you will seek to expand the largely procedural protections in Article V to cover substantive issues. Analyze *Parsons & Whittemore's* defenses in this regard. Are they procedural or under the guise of procedure, do they seek to introduce the substantive issues that might be raised on an appeal? Discuss.

3. Look at the matter from the perspective of the judges in a case like this. They understand their role in the arbitration scheme and appreciate that if they expand interpretatively the grounds in Article V of the Convention to do justice in this particular case, they will, in the longer run, be undermining the arbitral control mechanism.

## V.     SUMMARY AND CONCLUSIONS

Given the current practices in national fora with regard to jurisdiction over international commercial transactions, the prudent practitioner must consider and plan for the possibility of disputes and try to limit the uncertainty as to where a potential dispute may be resolved. Forum selection clauses, one solution, have an inherent weakness in that their effectuation depends upon national courts, which are not bound by any international obligations and therefore retain some discretion in deciding whether to honor forum selection clauses. Non-binding modalities of dispute resolution such as negotiation, mediation, conciliation, or mini-trials may defer a judicial hijacking to an unfriendly forum but do not *per se* prevent it. Nor do they necessarily yield a binding resolution of a dispute. Arbitration clauses, in contrast, appear to have a higher probability of being effected, because the discretion of the national courts which may become involved is limited by an international convention that limits the matters that the national court may take account of in staying arbitration. On the other hand, this very limitation on the role of national courts may lead to the enforcement of an award that would not have passed judicial muster were there an appeal. Thus, there are benefits and costs to the use of arbitration as a dispute resolution mechanism in international transactions. Nevertheless, the selection of arbitration as a solution to the jurisdictional problem provides a restraint on efforts at judicial hijacking and may be viewed as a particularly attractive solution to the jurisdictional problem in international transactions.

## CHAPTER 2

# DESIGNING AN ARBITRATION REGIME

## I.    INTRODUCTION

Once the decision has been made to incorporate arbitration as a dispute resolution mechanism, more is required than simply inserting a pre-packaged arbitration clause. The responsible lawyer has a wide range of arbitral institutions from which to select, each with its own set of rules, or the lawyer may design a tailor-made arbitration. In addition, choices must be made (to name only a few) about the substantive law to be used in construing the contract, the language to be used in an arbitration process, the place or venue in which arbitration is to be conducted and, if a government or its agency or instrumentality is a party, the anticipation of special issues that arise from sovereign immunity.

No single set of arbitral rules can apply to all arbitrations, for differences in the contract and in the disputes likely to arise, in the nationalities of the parties and in the orientations of different legal systems which may affect the arbitration must be taken into account. Hence, prior to designing an arbitration agreement for a particular transaction, the responsible lawyer must have a thorough understanding of the commercial venture being planned and an appreciation of the types of pathologies that are likely to develop out of the transaction. Not every theoretical hazard is a practical hazard for which a provision must be laboriously negotiated. For example, expropriation, a major threat to direct foreign investments in developing countries, against which it might be prudent to negotiate a stabilization clause or secure appropriate insurance, is not a factor in a conventional trading contract between similarly situated exporting states. A refined understanding of the nature of the transaction and its potential pathologies may be gained by a thorough discussion with the client and a study of the appropriate documents.

A second feature of the design of an international commercial arbitration agreement is the unique character of competition and cooperation between the parties engaged in establishing an arbitral regime. More than most other areas of the law, the creation of an arbitration jurisdiction in a contract requires competitors — whose interests momentarily converge but who anticipate conflict in the future — to cooperate in the design of a dispute resolution mechanism that is, at least, minimally fair to both parties. At the same time, each party seeks to anticipate problems and to incorporate features into the arbitral process which are likely to discriminate in its favor should a dispute eventuate. This characteristic of "competitive cooperation" means that parties must often settle for second-best arrangements, since the other party will usually object to the first preference. Another factor pressing for second-best arrangements is the transaction costs of getting an optimal clause. Where the value of the transaction or a conflict about it is small relative to the costs of negotiating an optimal dispute resolution mechanism arrangement, pre-packaged, "off-the-shelf" clauses recommend themselves.

Even the adoption by the parties of a standardized arbitration clause leaves open certain choices: for example, choice of venue and governing law. Many of these choice dimensions have been mentioned earlier. In this chapter we consider them systematically, exploring the various options available when drafting an arbitration clause, choosing venue for arbitration, choosing substantive law, choosing procedural law, and choosing arbitration rules, as well as special problems inherent in state contracts.

II.     CONSIDERATIONS AND OPTIONS IN DRAFTING THE ARBITRATION
        CLAUSE

    A.     Stephen R. Bond, *How to Draft an Arbitration Clause*,
        J. INT'L ARB., June 1989, at 65.[62]

The subject of "How to draft an arbitration clause" is one about which much has been written. Numerous articles analyze the essential ingredients for an arbitral clause and sometimes conclude with the presentation of the "miracle clause" that will solve almost every problem inherent in an arbitration. However, there are several difficulties in putting most of these miraculous clauses into practice.

---

[62] *See also* Stephen R. Bond, *How to Draft an Arbitration Clause (Revisited)*, 1 ICC INT'L CT. ARB. BULL. 14 (1990).

First, too often, as has been said, the dispute resolution clause is done as an afterthought, and without very much thought. Preparation and study of the matter is essential.

Second, the other party may have very different ideas as to what constitutes an ideal clause. The relative bargaining strength of the parties comes into play and the negotiator must know what is essential to his interests and what can safely be given up.

Third, the all-purpose clause may not, in fact, be suitable for all situations. For example, it is all very well to provide clearly in the ideal arbitration clause for payment of interest, but if you ever have to execute upon an award based on such a clause in Saudi Arabia or certain other Muslim countries, the mention of interest may render the entire arbitration clause and award invalid. So too, it is generally preferable to indicate in the arbitration clause the place of arbitration. However, if that place is in a particularly unstable country so that there is a chance that when a dispute arises it might not be possible, for political or security reasons, to hold the arbitration in the place designated, the result may be to render the clause unworkable and to forfeit the right to arbitrate.

Still, the fact remains that because of the consensual nature of arbitration and the various requirements for the validity of the arbitral clause, if you desire that arbitration be the method of dispute resolution between yourself and a business partner, you will have to have an arbitral clause. It is also true that many of the difficulties that most often complicate and delay an arbitral proceeding and the possible enforcement of an arbitral award can be removed or diminished by a well-drafted arbitration clause.

Also, the more effective the arbitration clause you negotiate, the less likely it is that it will ever be used. This is because an ineffective dispute resolution clause will be less of a deterrent to a party that is considering a breach of contract. So, even businessmen who wish to deal with lawyers as little as possible have a major interest in involving an attorney in the negotiation of the dispute settlement provision, unless those businessmen wish to prove, once again, the old adage that arbitration is a procedure that has too few lawyers in the beginning (when the clause is drafted) and too many in the end (when an arbitration is actually under way).

I would like to present some thoughts as to elements which should be considered in drafting and negotiating an arbitration clause. In addition, to make this presentation as pragmatic as possible, I have analysed the arbitration clauses contained in the 237 arbitration cases presented last year to the ICC's Court of Arbitration. From these 237 clauses, some practical lessons can be learned as to what elements the parties themselves consider important and where improvements in arbitration clauses might most usefully be suggested.

.  .  .

Of the 237 cases submitted to the ICC Court last year, *only four* of them resulted from a *compromis*, that is, an agreement to submit an already-existing dispute to arbitration. The other 233 cases arose from *clauses compromissoires*, that is, an arbitration clause agreeing to submit *future* disputes to arbitration. The reasons are obvious. Once a dispute arises, in most instances the parties can no longer agree on anything, including how to resolve their dispute. Rather, each rushes to the national court where it believes it is most advantaged. Any previous oral agreement to go to arbitration is virtually worthless, if only because to benefit from the New York Convention on the Recognition and Enforcement of Foreign Arbitral Awards an arbitration clause must be in writing. . . .

.  .  .

An arbitration clause need not be lengthy or complicated, but if it is to be effective it must be clear. Ambiguity is the worst enemy to be imagined, for it may either render an arbitration clause ineffective or, at the very least, create complications that cost both time and money and thus defeat part of the very reasons that lead the parties to select arbitration.

Frederic Eisemann, for many years the Secretary General of the ICC Court, called these unfortunate clauses "pathological" and such clauses are found every year at the ICC. In 1987, for example, the ICC Court was faced with some 16 clauses—7% of the total—which misidentified the ICC Court, most often by referring to the ICC "of Zürich" or "Geneva." It can be seen as flattering that the ICC is considered to be as neutral, trustworthy and respected as Switzerland, but there is, in fact, only one International Chamber of Commerce in the world and it is headquartered in Paris. This seemingly harmless error can create serious difficulties. In one case last year the claimant actually commenced an *ad hoc* arbitration involving the Zürich Chamber of Commerce before agreeing to the defendant's view that the clause in fact was intended to be for ICC arbitration. In another case, the defendant vigorously contested the competence of the ICC, asserting that the clause was intended to mean an arbitration following the Rules of the Zürich Chamber of Commerce.

Yet another of last year's clauses refer[r]ed to "arbitration in Seoul, Republic of Korea, before the Korean Commercial Arbitration Tribunal in accordance with the Rules of Conciliation and Arbitration of the International Chamber of Commerce". The parties could not agree which arbitral institution was meant and after several actions before Korean courts, the arbitral tribunal appointed by the ICC had to issue a partial award on the point.

One classic arbitral clause illustrates that clarity is far more important than eloquence. It read "English law—arbitration, if any London according ICC Rules." U.K. courts held this to be a valid arbitration agreement providing for the arbitration of any disputes in London in accordance with ICC Rules with English law governing the contract. The court even held that this clause constituted an "exclusion agreement," excluding any appeal to the courts, a subject which will be discussed later.

## 1. *AD HOC* OR INSTITUTIONAL ARBITRATION

. . .

It appears that to shift from *ad hoc* arbitration clause to one specifying an institution is extremely difficult once a dispute has broken out. Accordingly, wisdom and prudence — two watchwords of good attorneys — mandate an effort to incorporate institutional arbitration into the clause. Then, after a dispute arises, if for any reason it subsequently appears desirable for the parties actually to resort to *ad hoc* arbitration experience indicates that the parties can often reach agreement to do this.

A note of caution here, however, is raised by ICC Case 3383. Here, the parties commenced arbitration based on an ICC clause. They then decided to shift to *ad hoc* arbitration, using the same arbitral tribunal and drafted a *compromis* which, *inter alia*, required that an award be issued within three months of its date, which term could be extended four times. Defendant then challenged the legality of this arrangement under its domestic law and refused to agree to any extension. The arbitral tribunal declared that its mandate had expired. The claimant thereafter tried to recommence ICC arbitration but the ICC's sole arbitrator held that the *compromis* had superseded the original ICC clause and that, consequently, there was no longer a valid arbitration clause between the parties giving competence to the ICC.

## 2. THE STANDARD ARBITRATION CLAUSE

The choice of an institution naturally presents you with the standard or model arbitration clause advocated by the chosen institution. The ICC, for example, has the following model clause:

> All disputes arising in connection with the present contract shall be finally settled under the Rules of Conciliation and Arbitration of the International Chamber of Commerce by one or more arbitrators appointed in accordance with the said Rules.

It is short, simple, but contains what has been called the three "essential elements" to any effective arbitral clauses. "All disputes" . . . "in connection with" . . . "finally settled." How often is this standard clause actually used? Of 1987's 237 arbitration clauses, the standard clause, word-for-word, was used exactly once. Does this mean that the clause is valueless? Not at all. It is a basic clause, intended to create an enforceable agreement to arbitrate. However, many parties wish to add elements to it. In fact, the publication containing the amended ICC Arbitration Rules in force from 1 January 1988 itself notes, following the standard clause, that

> Parties are reminded that it may be desirable for them
> to stipulate in the arbitration clause itself the law
> governing the contract, the number of arbitrators and the
> place and language of the arbitration.

Thus, in 1987 the standard ICC clause, with perhaps minor variations of wording, was used in 47 arbitration clauses (20%), generally with the addition of the place of arbitration.

Let us return to the standard ICC clause, which has certainly withstood the test of time, to examine some of its basic elements.

*Scope of the Clause: "In connection with"*

The standard ICC clause refers to all disputes "in connection with" the contract.  Many of the arbitration clauses submitted to the ICC refer to disputes "arising out of or related" to the contract, disputes "arising under" the contract, disputes "related directly and/or indirectly to the performance" of the contract, etc.

These various phrases may all appear to you to mean about the same thing. However, a line of legal analysis has developed that draws a sharp distinction between a so-called "narrow" arbitration clause and a "broad" arbitration clause. A "broad" arbitration clause is more clearly "separable" from the contract in which it is contained so that even when there is an allegation that the contract itself is null and void because, for example, it was induced by fraud, the "broad" arbitration clause permits the arbitral tribunal to retain jurisdiction in order to determine its own competence.

In one U.S. case, a Federal District Court found that the phrase "arising hereunder" was "relatively narrow as arbitration clauses go" and the relevant arbitration was considered by this Court to be restricted solely to "disputes and controversies relating to the interpretation of the contract and matters of performance." Under such an interpretation, matters relating to fraud in the inducement, for example, could not be examined by the arbitral tribunal.

In a more recent U.S. case, a Federal District Court concluded, relying on the case just cited, that the phrase "in connection with this Agreement" in an ICC clause should be "somewhat narrowly read" and excluded one of the nine categories of disputes between the parties. This was reversed on appeal, with the Court of Appeals stating that "the ICC's recommended clause must be construed to encompass a broad scope of arbitration issues. . . . It embraces every dispute between the parties having a significant relationship to the contract regardless of the label attached to the dispute."

This language and the surrounding reasoning clearly demonstrate the advantages of utilizing the key phrases of the ICC clause as well as referring arbitration to a widely-used arbitration institution well-known by judges in national courts.

Thus, parties should be extremely careful not to narrow inadvertently the scope of the arbitration clause by restricting the clause simply to disputes "arising under" the contract or "related to execution or performance" of the contract.

*"Finally settled"*

This point is considered below.

*"The International Chamber of Commerce"*

Difficulties arising from incorrect references to the ICC are discussed below.

.    .    .

## 3. THE PLACE OF ARBITRATION

The importance of the place of arbitration cannot be overestimated. Its legislation determines the likelihood and extent of involvement of national courts in the conduct of the arbitration (either for judicial "assistance" or "interference"), the likelihood of enforceability of the arbitral award (depending on what international conventions the *situs* State is a party to), and the extent and nature of any mandatory procedural rules that you will have to adhere to in the conduct of the arbitration. (For example, in Saudi Arabia, the arbitrators must be Muslim and male.) Such factors are of far greater importance than the touristic attractions of any particular place that sometimes appear to be the decisive factor in making this decision. Parties generally appear to be aware of the importance of the *situs*, at least if one can judge by the fact that in 1987 some 136 arbitration clauses (57%) specified the city or country in which any arbitration held pursuant to the clause would take place. This mention of *situs* is, after the choice of applicable law, the element most often added to the basic ICC arbitration clause. The choice of the place of arbitration may literally determine the outcome of the case. In one ICC arbitration between a Finnish corporation and an Australian corporation, London was selected as the place of arbitration in the arbitration clause. The case involved royalty payments allegedly not made and the purported cancellation of the relevant agreement in 1976. In 1982 the licensor initiated arbitration. The arbitrator found that because the arbitration was taking place in England, the statute of limitations contained in the U.K. Limitation Act had to be applied. So, even assuming that Finnish law was applicable and Finnish law had no comparable statute of limitations, the arbitrator applied the relevant U.K. 6-year statute of limitations and barred all claims arising prior to 1976, which effectively meant all claims.

Yet a final example, to show that even this simplest of choices cannot be made lightly. A recent case in a United States Federal Court involved an arbitration clause in a contract between American and Iranian parties drafted before the Iranian Revolution which had fixed Iran as the site of the arbitration. The U.S. Court refused to accept a request by one of the parties to the contract to shift the *situs* of the arbitration to the United States. The Court stated that it had

> no statutory or equitable mandate that allows us to redraft the agreement premised on the convenience of the parties *ex post* . . . There is neither doctrine nor policy that supplies (the Iranian party) a polestar with which to circumnavigate the plain language of its forum selection clause and thereby avoid its initial, unequivocal and contractually chosen course.

I would like to add here a special comment related to the choice of a place of arbitration. In 57 (24%) of the arbitration clauses submitted to the ICC last year, reference was made not simply to the ICC, but to the ICC "in" Paris or "of" Paris or *de* Paris. This is, in fact, unnecessary as there is only one "International Chamber of Commerce" in the world. Understandably, however, many parties feel more comfortable with this additional clarification. (Indeed, in one ICC award on jurisdiction issued recently, the arbitrator's award on jurisdiction had to deal with a defendant's allegation that the arbitration clause was not intended to refer to ICC arbitration precisely because it did not specify "in Paris" and because there were, defendant alleged, "a large number of international chambers of commerce in the world." The arbitral tribunal quite correctly dismissed this line of reasoning.)

Parties should be aware, however, that reference to the ICC "of" Paris or "in" Paris will be interpreted by the ICC Court of

Arbitration as an indication of the intended place of arbitration, unless another *situs* is clearly indicated in the clause (as does often happen).

This, "rule of interpretation" is equally applied when an arbitration clause mistakenly refers to the ICC "of" Geneva, or "in" Zürich or any other place. After all, as there is only one ICC, the reference to another city can, logically, have no other meaning. (This position of the ICC Court has been given solid support in several ICC awards).

## 4. APPLICABLE LAW

While the choice of the law to be applied by the arbitrators to determine the substantive issues before them is not an element necessary for the validity of an arbitration clause, it is certainly desirable for the parties to agree upon the applicable law in the arbitration clause if at all possible. Failure to do so is a significant factor in increasing the time and cost of an arbitration. Moreover, the decision of the arbitral tribunal on the matter (for it is an issue to be decided by the arbitrators, even if institutional arbitration is used) may bring an unpleasant surprise to one of the parties. Finally, where an institution is to select the chairman or sole arbitrator it is, as a practical matter, far easier to appoint the best possible person when it is known in what country's law the arbitrator should be most expert.

For these reasons, the element most often added to the contract, often directly in the arbitration clause itself, is that of the law applicable to the contract. In 1987 some 178 contracts (75%) contained reference to a specific applicable law, either by naming the law of a particular country or of the country of one of the parties (e.g. "law of seller's country.") The applicable law was included in the arbitration clause itself some 81 times. Also of interest is the rarity of clauses which authorize the arbitral tribunal to resolve the dispute on the basis of equity, amiable composition, *ex aequo et bono*, or with the arbitrators acting as mediators. In 1987, only some 9 clauses (3%) incorporated any such basis for resolving the dispute. (Some other clauses specifically forbade amiable composition, although in ICC arbitration the arbitral tribunal may not act as *amiable compositeur* unless specifically authorized to do so by the parties.)

So too, only one clause, in a contract between Yugoslavian and Kenyan parties, provided that any dispute should be settled "on the basis of international law." No clause in 1987 mentioned *lex mercatoria*.

While the object of this article is certainly not to examine the "philosophy" of arbitration, I cannot help but note that the statistics just cited support the view that arbitration is generally not sought by the parties because they wish an "extra-legal" resolution to their disputes. Rather, the parties appear to desire a resolution based on a specified, predictable legal system. What they clearly do not want is such a legal system being applied by the national court of the other party.

A few points should be borne in mind in deciding upon an applicable law and I will very briefly mention them.

Firstly, it is preferable that the legal system you agree upon in fact is developed in regard to the specific issues likely to arise.

Secondly, you may wish to exclude the conflict of laws principles of the chosen law, either explicitly or by specifying the "substantive law" of the particular country concerned.

Thirdly, be sure that the law you choose considers the subject matter of the contract to be arbitrable. Copyright or patent law questions, anti-trust matters, etc. are often not permitted to be resolved by arbitration, but only in the national courts.

## 5. COMPOSITION OF THE ARBITRAL TRIBUNAL

The next element which should be given the most serious attention is that of the composition of the arbitral tribunal. How many arbitrators do you want? How should they be selected? Should they have any particular qualifications? No broad generalities can cover all the situations likely to arise.

Regarding the number of arbitrators, in 1987's arbitration clauses some 58 (24%) specified either one or three arbitrators. Of these, 11 specified one arbitrator and 59 clauses specified three. It is interesting to note that in some 83 cases where the arbitration clause did not determine the number of arbitrators, the parties were able to reach agreement between themselves on the point prior to the ICC Court having to make a decision. This would indicate that, as a practical matter, it will often be possible to reach agreement on this element even after a dispute has developed. Consequently, it is less urgent to reach agreement on this point in negotiating the arbitration clause than on certain others.

Four of the arbitration clauses specified one arbitrator if the parties could agree upon him, otherwise there would be three arbitrators. Although on the basis of four clauses, no general conclusions can be drawn, these four provide, I believe, a key to a major concern of the parties, namely the need to have an arbitral tribunal in which the parties can have confidence. Confidence is present either by knowing and agreeing upon an individual or, if this cannot be done, by having a three-person tribunal, one of whom can be proposed by each party. Probably for these reasons the ICC's experience has been that parties from developing countries and Eastern European countries have a strong preference for three-person arbitral tribunals. They seem to believe that even though coarbitrators must, pursuant to the ICC Rules, be independent of the party proposing them, a coarbitrator of the same nationality can explain to his fellow arbitrators the legal, economic, and business context within which that party operates.

Of course, three-person arbitral tribunals are more expensive and the arbitration tends to take longer, considerations that cannot be ignored when drafting the arbitration clause.

Arbitration clauses tend to include no mention of other elements relating to the arbitral panel. Only three clauses in 1987 specified the nationality of the chairman and each time he had to be Swiss. Only a single clause set out professional qualifications, namely that the chairman should be "fully educated and trained as a lawyer."

It may well be that ICC clauses are not typical in this regard because parties know that the quality of ICC arbitrators is excellent and the ICC Rules require an arbitrator from a country other than those of the parties. Thus, with regard to the selection of arbitrators, confidence in the arbitral institution may well have reduced the amount of detail parties would otherwise have put in an *ad hoc* arbitration clause, for example.

## 6. LANGUAGE OF THE ARBITRATION

Many parties may mistakenly believe that the language in which the contract is written will automatically be the language of any arbitration arising out of that contract. It is true that the ICC Rules, for example, state in Article 15(3) that the arbitrator shall give "due regard . . . in particular to the language of the contract" in determining the language of the arbitration. It will, however, be for the arbitral tribunal to decide the question should the parties not have agreed on it.

As can well be imagined, simultaneous interpretation at hearings and translation of all documents into two or more languages are enormously expensive and time-consuming. If it is not possible to agree on a language in the arbitration clause then it would be desirable to try to agree either that costs for interpretation and translation are shared or else borne by the party requiring the interpretation or translation. However, not a single clause in 1987 contained such a provision, although some 32 (13.5%) of the clauses did select a language, 25 of them specifying English, 6 French and 1 of them French and/or English.

## 7. WAIVER OF APPEAL/"EXCLUSION AGREEMENT"

A primary advantage of arbitration is that it is, in principle, essentially free from judicial involvement during the arbitration itself and an arbitral award is "final" in the sense that it is intended to be free from judicial examination of its substance. Article 24 of the ICC Rules provides that "the arbitral award shall be final" and the parties are deemed to waive their right to any appeal insofar as such waiver can validly be made. Despite this language, some 49 arbitration clauses (24%) in 1987 specifically provided, in essence, that the award issued is to be "Final and binding upon the Parties who agree to waive all right of appeal thereon."

Depending on the nationalities of the parties, the place of arbitration and the location of assets that may need to be used to satisfy the award, such a specific waiver of appeal in the arbitration clause could well be useful. For example, the U.K. requires an "exclusion agreement" between the parties if they desire to ensure the ouster of court jurisdiction to review the award.

As already noted, the U.K. courts have interpreted an ICC arbitration clause itself as constituting such an exclusion of merits appeal in the light of Article 24 of the ICC Rules. However, the courts of certain other countries may be influenced by the presence or absence of an expressly stated exclusion agreement. Perhaps most importantly in this regard, the draft Swiss law on international arbitration that should, by the end of the year, replace the *Concordat* for international arbitrations, require an "express" waiver of the right of appeal. Every Swiss arbitration expert I have spoken to believes that an ICC clause alone, without such an additional express waiver, would not be sufficient to constitute an exclusion agreement under the draft Swiss law.[63]

### 8. ENTRY OF JUDGMENT STIPULATION

In the U.S., arbitration clauses often provide that judgment may be entered upon the award in any court of competent jurisdiction. The model clause of the AAA contains language to this effect and it has been said that it is better to include such a phrase in clauses with U.S. parties or where execution may be sought in the U.S. Some 31 cases (13%) in 1987 had such a stipulation, and not always where U.S. parties were involved.

### 9. OTHER MATTERS

Much could be said about the advantages of including various other elements in the arbitration clause where, according to circumstances, they could prove useful in facilitating a less expensive and time-consuming arbitration. However, in 1987 these other elements were virtually never mentioned. This does not, of course, detract from their utility, but is probably a reflection of the practical difficulties of negotiating a too-detailed arbitration clause and of the fact that it takes the incentive and stimulation of an actual arbitration before most minds can adequately focus on such matters.

Nevertheless, for the sake of completeness I will list these other elements so that they may be borne in mind should the occasion arise where one or more of them might one day prove to be important in a

---

[63] The texts of the Concordat and the Law of Private International Law, now in force, are reproduced in the Supplement at p. 393.

particular arbitration. (The number of times each element was included in an arbitration clause in 1987 is also noted.)

(a) The applicable procedural law (1).
(b) Power of the arbitrator to adapt the contract (1, refusing any such power).
(c) Extent of discovery and cross-examination (1).
(d) Waiver of sovereign immunity (0).
(e) Accommodation for multiparty disputes (4).
(f) Mandatory conciliation (1).
(g) Division of costs of arbitration between parties (6).
(h) Partial awards either forbidden or required (0).

\*  \*  \*

B.     INSTITUTIONAL ARBITRATION CLAUSES

Consider the following institutional arbitration clauses:

American Arbitration Association

Any controversy or claim arising out of or relating to this agreement, or the breach thereof, shall be settled by arbitration in accordance with the Commercial Arbitration Rules and supplementary procedures for international commercial arbitrations of the American Arbitration Association, and judgment upon the award rendered by the Arbitrator(s) may be entered in any court having jurisdiction.

International Chamber of Commerce

All disputes arising in connection with the present contract shall be finally settled under the Rules of (Conciliation and) Arbitration of the International Chamber of Commerce by one or more arbitrators appointed in accordance with the said Rules.

International Centre for the Settlement of Investment Disputes

The parties hereto consent to submit to the International Centre for Settlement of Investment Disputes any dispute relating to or arising out of this Agreement for settlement by arbitration pursuant to the Convention on the Settlement of Investment Disputes between States and Nationals of Other States.

London Court of International Arbitration

Any dispute arising out of or in connection with this contract, including any question regarding its existence, validity or termination, shall be referred to and finally resolved by arbitration under the Rules of the London Court of International Arbitration, which Rules are deemed to be incorporated by reference into this clause.

### C.    PATHOLOGICAL COMPROMISSORY CLAUSES

There is a rich literature on so-called pathological compromissory clauses. Consider one example from a contract for the publication of Christian books in the United States.

III. MANUSCRIPT    Author agrees to deliver to Publisher no later than Midnight, <u>July 24, 1989</u>, one finally revised copy of the manuscript . . .

.    .    .

[IV] B. Moral
Turpitude    Notwithstanding the foregoing, in the event that Author is publicly accused of an act of moral turpitude, the violation of any law or any other conduct which subjects or could be reasonably anticipated to subject Author or Publisher to public ridicule, contempt, scorn, hatred or censure or could materially diminish the potential sales of the Work, Publisher shall have the right to terminate the terms of this agreement upon written notice to Author given within 60 days following receipt by Publisher of knowledge of public disclosure of such

conduct or alleged conduct. In the event that Publisher shall terminate the terms hereof pursuant to this paragraph, Author will pay to Publisher a sum equal to the advance paid to Author prior to said termination which have not been recouped by Publisher as provided herein as the date of such termination. Author will make such payment within 15 days following Author's receipt of an accounting statement for such period reflecting an unrecouped advance balance. Upon Publisher's receipt of such payment, all such rights granted to Publisher in the Work shall terminate and vest exclusively in Author provided that Publisher shall have the right to sell or otherwise dispose of all remaining copies of the Work published by Publisher under this agreement in any manner Publisher shall deem appropriate.

.     .     .     .

## XVII. MEDIATION AND ARBITRATION

The parties agree that God, in His Word, forbids Christians to bring lawsuits against other Christians in secular courts of law (1 Corinthians 6:1-8), and that God desires that Christians be reconciled to one another when disputes of any nature arise between them (Matthew 5:21-24 6:9-15; 18:5-20.). Because the parties hereto desire to honor and glorify the Lord Jesus Christ in their resolution of any disputes that my [sic] arise under this Agreement, each party agrees that the provisions for mediation and arbitration set forth in this section shall be the sole and exclusive remedy for resolving any disputes between the parties arising out of or involving this Agreement. It is further agreed that each party hereby waives whatever rights he might otherwise have to maintain a lawsuit against another party hereto in a secular court of law, on any disputes arising out of or involving this agreement.

A. Spiritual
Concern

The principals of the parties are brothers in Christ. Each principal of the parties desires that the relationship in Christ, through the Holy Spirit, be preserved, honored and uplifted, and that the unity of the Spirit be preserved in the bond of peace, and be sought after more than any personal gain or right. The principals of the parties desire to be humbled and taught by the Holy Spirit; to confess bitterness and anger one may hold for another, to the other; to forgive, to make right any wrong, and to to [sic] accept the decision of the mediators/arbitrators as the voice and decision of one chosen to be the spiritual authority and judge in a controversy, and whose decision will be accepted and honored, and by which the parties are bound before God to follow.

B. Mediation

Therefore, the principals of the parties agree that each shall take the following steps in order presented, to reconcile any differences or disputes relating to this Agreement.

1. First Step: ("Moreover, if thy brother shall trespass against thee, go and tell him this fault between thee and him alone; if he shall hear thee, thou has gained a brother." Matthew 18:15) The two should meet, pray together, purpose to be reconciled and should be alone. ("He that passeth by, and meddleth with strife belonging not to him, is like one that taketh a dog by the ears." Proverbs 26:17).

2. Second Step: If the disputing parties fail to reconcile their differences as outlined above: ("But if he will not hear thee, then take with thee one or two more, that in the mouth of two or three witnesses every work may be established." Matthew 18:16). The witnesses taken may be percipient witnesses with

knowledge of actual facts of the dispute, or persons with knowledge which would be helpful in resolving the dispute (e.g., could be a lawyer, or wise counselor.) The brothers and witnesses should pray together, and purpose to be reconciled.

3.  Third Step: If the disputing brothers fail to reconcile their differences by either means outlined above, the disputing brothers shall each appoint a man of wisdom, who is himself in submission to Jesus Christ as Lord and Savior, who believes the Bible to be the inspired Word of God, who holds fast to the doctrines of historic Christianity as set forth in the Apostles' and Nicene Creed, who is an active member in good standing of a church, and who is not related to any party by blood or marriage, as mediators. The two men so appointed shall likewise appoint a third man of like character and position to serve as a third mediator. In the event the mediators cannot decide on a neutral third person, then the third mediator shall be appointed by the Christian Legal Society.

   a)  Each party shall submit to the mediators, but not to the other party, his written statement of the facts, contentious [sic] and summary of the settlement discussions to date.

   b)  The mediator(s) shall set a date for a meeting of the parties and their counsel, if any, which shall take place no later than thirty (30) days after the selection of the mediator(s).

   c)  The hearing shall be conducted in a spirit of prayer, for the purpose of hearing, discussing the facts and disputes, with a goal of seeking reconciliation of the brothers and resolution of the dispute which is reducible to writing and acceptable to the disputants.

d)    The mediator(s) shall seek to discern the spiritual needs and weaknesses of the parties as such matters relate to the manner in which the parties view their dispute and the rights each believes he has in the matter.

e)    The mediator(s) should prayerfully seek an application of the principles of the Word of God to the parties and the problem, so that the dispute is resolved in a manner that restores brotherly love and unity, ministers to the spiritual needs revealed by the dispute, and resolves the conflict fairly and equitably. A party should not be permitted, as a "decision" of the mediators to accede to the demands of the other, if the mediators discern that the acceding party's decision is based upon a decision "to be defrauded rather than participate in the dispute," or "to give his shirt also when his coat is demanded," in lieu of honest, spirit-filled and spirit-led mediation.

f)    If a party will not cooperate, or refuses to mediate, or if the mediator(s) cannot lead the parties to a resolution of the conflict through mediation, such result will be considered to be a spiritual defeat to the same parties, and binding arbitration in the manner set forth below shall then be conducted to impose and enforce a settlement. Mediation under this paragraph may be waived by either party and a refusal to follow the procedures required herein within five (5) days after written notice of demand for mediation hereunder shall be deemed to be such a waiver.

C. Arbitration          If mediation fails to achieve a resolution of the dispute, or is waived by either party, the parties shall submit the dispute to the consideration and award of the mediators, who shall then serve as Arbitrators. If any of the mediators who are as such unable or unwilling to serve as Arbitrators, a man with the qualifications described for a mediator shall be selected in the manner described for selecting a mediator within ten (10) days of the notice of the declining mediator of his unwillingness or inability to serve. The person or persons who appointed the declining mediator shall so appoint the new Arbitrator.

1.     Law and Procedure:

The Arbitrators shall apply the substantive Law of God found in the Old and New Testaments in considering the facts and determining the contentions being arbitrated.
. . .


.     .     .


If three Arbitrators are selected under the foregoing procedure but two of the three fail to reach an agreement in the determination of the matter in question, the matter shall be decided by three new Arbitrators who shall be repeated until a decision is finally reached by two of the three Arbitrators selected.

2.     Refusal to Arbitrate

If any party refuses to arbitrate under the terms of this agreement, he agrees that an award may be entered against him by the decision of the Arbitrators provided that the refusing party received notices of each hearing, was given reasonable opportunity to participate, and a written decision was rendered and a notice of said decision is given to the party refusing to participate. If the party refusing to arbitrate also has failed or refused to appoint an arbitrator within ten (10) days after written notice has been given by the other party, nonrefusing party shall appoint a sole arbitrator who shall determine and resolve the dispute.

3.     Judgement

The decision or award entered by the Arbitrators may be entered as a judgment in any Court of competent jurisdiction for the enforcement thereof, although such result would be considered unspiritual defeat and the same of the non-complying party. `

a.     The Arbitrators shall appoint a time and place for the hearing and cause notice thereof to be served personally or by registgered [sic] or certified mail on the parties to the arbitration not less than seven (7) days before the hearing. Appearance at the hearing waives the right to notice.

b.     The Arbitrators may adjourn the hearing from time to time, as necessary. On request of a party to the arbitration for good cause, or upon their own determination, the Arbitrators may postpone the hearing.

c.     The Arbitrators shall preside at the hearing, shall rule on the admission and exclusion of evidence and on questions of hearing procedure and shall exercise all powers relating to the conduct of the hearing. The Arbitrators may select one of the Arbitrators to preside at the hearing if there is more than one Arbitrator.

d.     The parties to the arbitration are entitled to be heard, to present evidence and to cross-examine witnesses appearing at the hearing, but rules of evidence and rules of judicial procedure need not be observed. On request of any party to the arbitration, the testimony of witnesses shall be given under oath.

e.    If the Arbitrators intend to base an award upon information not obtained at the hearing, they shall disclose such information to all parties to the arbitration and give the parties an opportunity to meet it.

f.    The intentions expressed in paragraphs XVIII-A and XVIII-B of Section XVIII shall be of utmost importance in the conduct and tenor of the hearings and spiritual issues should be discussed and dealt with, and God's counsel and wisdom should be frequently and openly sought.

g.    The Arbitrators shall determine and resolve the dispute by majority vote of the Arbitrators. The Arbitrators shall determine, as part of their decision, how the fees and expenses of the parties incurred as a result of any mediation or arbitration hereunder are to be paid. A written decision shall be rendered and signed by a majority of the Arbitrators within thirty (30) days after the final hearing on the matter.

.   .   .

**XX. GOVERNING LAW; JURISDICTION**    This agreement has been entered into in the state of Massachusetts and shall be construed in accordance with the laws of said state if necessary.

### Notes and Questions

1. Bond, then Secretary General of the International Chamber of Commerce, argues in his article that there are great advantages to adopting an institutional arbitral system by incorporating one of their clauses. What are the disadvantages of such an option?

2. Bond urges that many items be negotiated by the parties in the drafting of the arbitration clause. If the parties neglect to stipulate those various items, who decides them? When?

3. In the 1989 contract with a Christian publishing house, what pathologies can you identify? Are there other functional problems with this arbitration clause?

4. If the intent to arbitrate is clear, should a court (or arbitrators) "repair" the clause so the arbitration can proceed and the parties' intentions are fulfilled?

## III.     CONSIDERATIONS AND OPTIONS IN CHOOSING THE VENUE

In most situations, parties are free to choose the place where the arbitration will be held. The choice is consequential. Generally speaking, it should be made at the time that the original agreement to arbitrate is concluded; once a dispute has arisen, it is vastly more difficult to agree to a mutually acceptable venue.

Questions of practical convenience are certainly relevant. For example, the chosen venue must be readily accessible for all parties. The necessary administrative support must be available. At the economic level, it must be possible to transfer funds to and from the country concerned, and import and export necessary documents and other exhibits. However, in the final analysis, legal considerations should weigh most heavily, because the law governing the arbitration (the so-called *lex arbitri*) is typically considered to be the law of the country where the proceedings are held and the award rendered. Thus, if no thought is given to whether a particular legal environment is appropriate, the consequences could be drastic: the procedural rules adopted by the tribunal may not be to the liking of the parties, the local courts may be more (or less) interventionist than desired and, ultimately and most significantly, enforcement of the award may be jeopardized.

In negotiating their chosen venue, the parties have a wide range of options. They must weigh many factors in making their choice.

A.  ALAN REDFERN & MARTIN HUNTER, LAW AND PRACTICE OF INTERNATIONAL COMMERCIAL ARBITRATION 295-97 (2d ed. 1991).

Parties to an international commercial arbitration are generally free to choose for themselves where that arbitration should take place. The failure to make a clear choice of the place of arbitration in the arbitration clause of a contract may lead to unexpected results. A court in the United States ordered an arbitration to proceed in California under the AAA Rules where the arbitration clause did not specify a place of arbitration even though a separate clause in the contract specified that if an arbitration was necessary and was to be held in Peking it was to be subject to the Rules of Procedure of the Foreign Trade Arbitration Commission in Peking.

The parties may make the choice of a place at any time before the arbitration begins; or they may leave it to be made on their behalf by an arbitral institution (if the arbitration is to be conducted under institutional rules) or by the arbitral tribunal itself. At some stage, however, a choice will have to be made. The question which then arises is where should an international commercial arbitration be held? Should it, for example, be held in London or Washington, Paris or Geneva, Cairo or Kuala Lumpur?

There is no simple or universal answer to this question. The nationality of the parties to the arbitration will have to be taken into account, since the general practice is to hold an arbitration in a country which is neutral, in the sense that it is not the country of any of the parties to the dispute. The usual residence or place of business of the parties must be taken into account too, because of the need to cut down as far as possible on the expense and inconvenience of travelling. There are political factors, such as the general acceptability of the particular location to the parties and, in particular, the question of whether any restriction is likely to be imposed on the entry of the arbitral tribunal, the parties, their advisers and witnesses.

There are economic factors, such as freedom to transfer the necessary funds to and from the country concerned. There may well be a need for skilled local support—from lawyers competent to advise on matters relevant to the conduct of the arbitration, or from engineers, surveyors, accountants and other professional men to provide expert assistance and evidence. Such assistance is less expensive if it is available at the place of arbitration.

There are other practical considerations too, such as the availability of suitable rooms for the hearing, and suitable accommodation for the parties, their advisers and witnesses. Some major cities experience an acute shortage of hotel accommodation at certain times of the year. Other relevant requirements include good transportation facilities, by rail or by air; good communications, by telephone, fax and telex; and support facilities, in terms of shorthand writers, interpreters and so on. These services and facilities form part of the infrastructure of an arbitration. The suitability of a particular place for an international arbitration will depend in part on whether there is a sufficient infrastructure to accommodate the parties; but the more important considerations have to do with the legal environment of the prospective place of arbitration. This will be relevant both to the conduct of the arbitration and to the enforceability of any award rendered.

*     *     *

The following case and excerpt demonstrate that the parties' attitudes are likely to be affected by whether they envisage (if they can) being claimants or respondents in any dispute.

B.     *Klöckner Industrien-Anlagen GmbH v. Kien Tat Sdn Bhd & Anor*, 3 MALAYAN L.J. 183 (1990).

[Zakaria Yatim, J: Application to transfer a dispute in arbitration to the jurisdiction of the court which could then provide other remedies.]

.     .     .

The applicant and the first respondent are parties to a contract dated 25 May 1985 relating to the installation of a pulp and paper mill in Sipitang, Sabah, Malaysia. A dispute arose between the parties, and according to cl 37 of the contract the dispute has to be settled by arbitration in accordance with the Rules for Arbitration of the Regional Centre for Arbitration in Kuala Lumpur (hereinafter referred to as 'the Arbitration Centre'). Clause 37 states as follows:

Settlement of Disputes

Any dispute, controversy or claim arising out of or relating to this contract, or the breach, termination or invalidity thereof, shall be settled by arbitration in accordance with the Rules for Arbitration of the Kuala Lumpur Regional Arbitration Centre.

The appointing authority shall be the Kuala Lumpur Regional Arbitration Centre.

The number of arbitrators shall be three according to art 7 of the Rules.

The place of arbitration shall be Kuala Lumpur. The language to be used in the arbitral proceedings shall be English.

The arbitrators are bound to observe the terms of the contract. The law applicable to this contract shall be that of Switzerland.

Pursuant to the above clause, the parties submitted their dispute to the Arbitration Centre for arbitration. The arbitrators were duly appointed and the parties filed their pleadings. On 15 September 1989, the arbitrators made an award on a preliminary point, namely, on security for costs. The award made was based on the consensus of the parties.

During the adjournment of the arbitration proceedings, the applicant filed the present application on a certificate of urgency.

The question for the court to consider is whether it has the power to make an order as prayed for [in] the application?

The arbitration centre is an independent international institution. See my paper in Seminar on International Commercial Arbitration, Kuala Lumpur 2-3 November 1982 p 9 and my article, 'Settlement of Commercial Disputes, Malaysia' [1983] 1 MLJ cxviii at cxxiv. It was established in Kuala Lumpur pursuant to an agreement between the government of Malaysia and the Asian African Legal Consultative Committee (AALCC) through an exchange of letters in March 1978. It was a term of the agreement that the Arbitration Centre would function as an independent institution under the auspices of the AALCC. See my article, 'The Regional Centre for Arbitration, Kuala Lumpur' [1978] 2 MLJ lxxx at lxxxi.

As an international arbitral institution, the Arbitration Centre has its own rules for arbitration. According to the rules, disputes shall be settled in accordance with the arbitration rules made by the United Nations Commission On International Trade Law (hereinafter referred to as 'UNCITRAL Arbitration Rules') as modified by the Rules of the Arbitration Centre. See 'Arbitration Under the Auspices of the Kuala Lumpur Centre'.

Having stated the status of the Arbitration Centre as an independent international institution, I shall now consider whether the court has jurisdiction to exercise supervisory function over arbitration proceedings held under the Rules of the Centre. Section 34 of the Arbitration Act 1952 provides:

> (1)      Notwithstanding anything to the contrary in this Act or in any other written law but subject to subsection (2) in so far as it relates to the enforcement of an award, the provisions of this Act or other written law shall not apply to any arbitration held under the Convention on the Settlement of Investment Disputes Between States and Nationals of Other States 1965 or under the United Nations Commission on International Trade Law Arbitration Rules 1976 and the Rules of the Regional Centre for Arbitration at Kuala Lumpur.

> (2)      Where an award made in an arbitration held in conformity with the Convention or the Rules specified in subsection (1) is sought to be enforced in Malaysia, the enforcement proceedings in respect thereof shall be taken in accordance with the provisions of the Convention specified in subsection (1) or the Convention on the Recognition and Enforcement of Foreign Arbitral Awards 1958, as may be appropriate.

> (3)      The competent court for the purpose of such enforcement shall be the High Court.

Mr. Cecil Abraham, counsel for the applicant, submitted that the first respondent was under receivership in January 1988 and on 14 August

1989 it was compulsively wound up under s 218 of the Companies Act 1965. He referred to the debentures under which the receivers and managers were appointed. He then asked the court to consider under what authority and power the receivers and managers continued with the arbitration. According to him, the right to proceed with arbitration depended solely on the construction of the debentures and s 34 did not apply. He submitted that the words 'other written law' could not be given a wide interpretation. According to him, the section only precludes the application of the Arbitration Act 1952, but does not extend to question of capacity or competence of the receivers and managers to continue with the arbitration. He therefore contended that the question[s] of capacity has to be determined by the court.

Datuk Dominic Puthucheary, counsel for the respondents, on the other hand submitted that s 34 clearly ousted the supervisory role of the court under all laws in force in Malaysia. He said that the words in s 34 are 'plain, clear and precise'. He contended that since the Arbitration Centre served the Asian and the Pacific Region it was only logical that the Arbitration Centre be excluded from any supervisory function of the municipal courts in Malaysia. It would be impossible, he said, for the Arbitration Centre to function as an international arbitral institution if Malaysian laws were applicable in a supervisory capacity or in any other way. Datuk Dominic Puthucheary then submitted that the question of locus standi raised by Mr. Abraham should be determined by the arbitrators.

In my opinion the crucial words in s 34 are '. . . the provisions of this Act and other written law shall not apply to any arbitration held under . . . the Rules of the Regional Centre for Arbitration at Kuala Lumpur'. It is clear that under the section, the court cannot exercise its supervisory function as provided in the Arbitration Act 1952, in respect of such arbitration. Neither can the court exercise its supervisory function over such arbitration under any other written law. The words "written law" has been defined in s 3 of the Interpretation Act 1967, to mean the Federal Constitution and State Constitutions, Acts of Parliament and subsidiary legislation made thereunder; ordinances and enactments and subsidiary legislation made thereunder; and any other legislative enactments or legislative instruments. 'Written Law', therefore, includes the Companies Act 1965.

It has been said that the jurisdiction of the courts must not be taken to be excluded unless there is quite clear language in the Act to have that effect. See dictum of Evershed MR in *Goldsack v. Shore* at p 712. In the present case, I agree with Datuk Dominik Puthucheary that the words in s 34 are 'plain, clear and precise'. Reading the clear language of the section I am of the view that the section excludes the court from exercising its supervisory function under the Arbitration Act 1952 or under any other written law, including the Companies Act 1965, in respect of arbitrations held under the Rules of the Arbitration Centre.

Therefore, the question of capacity or locus standi of a party to the arbitration, the question of security for costs, or the issue of pleadings before the arbitral tribunal, cannot be determined by the court by virtue of s 34. These are issues which the arbitral tribunal has to decide and the court cannot and will not interfere with the proceeding of the tribunal. The function of the court is confined only to the enforcement of the arbitral award if the award is sought to be enforced in Malaysia.

Mr. Cecil Abraham, in the course of his submission seemed to suggest that under art 26(3) of the UNCITRAL Arbitration Rules, the applicant was entitled to seek the relief sought in the application. Article 26(3) reads:

> A request for interim measures addressed by any party to a judicial authority shall not be deemed incompatible with the agreement to arbitrate, or as a waiver of that agreement.

It will be noted that art 26 is under the heading of 'Interim Measures of Protection'. What para 3 of art 26 means is that a party to an arbitral proceeding, may if he so desires, apply to an appropriate judicial authority, to take interim protective measures in order to protect the subject matter of the dispute. See UNITED NATIONS COMMISSION ON INTERNATIONAL TRADE LAW, YEARBOOK Vol VII, 1976, p 176. But, with respect, the present application is not an application to take interim protective measures within the meaning of art 26(2).

Mr. Cecil Abraham also referred to art 33(1) of the UNCITRAL Arbitration Rules. Article 33(1) reads:

> The arbitral tribunal shall apply the law designated by the parties as applicable to the substance of the dispute. Failing

such designation by the parties, the arbitral tribunal shall apply the law determined by the conflict of laws rules which it considers applicable.

The paragraph speaks for itself. If the parties do not designate the applicable law, the arbitral tribunal shall apply the law in accordance with the principles of conflict of laws. In the present case, the parties have designated the applicable law in the arbitration clause quoted above and therefore the question of invoking art 33(1) does not arise.

For the reasons stated above, I conclude that the court has not jurisdiction to make an order in respect of any of the prayers in the application. I therefore dismiss the application with costs.

*   *   *

The hands-off attitude of this Malaysian court should be contrasted with the parochialism evidenced in other legal systems where the temptation to interfere in the international arbitral process has extended to the exclusion of the parties' legal representatives on the grounds that they were not qualified members of the local bar. *See infra* Chapter 7.

C.   ALAN REDFERN & MARTIN HUNTER, LAW AND PRACTICE OF INTERNATIONAL COMMERCIAL ARBITRATION 297-98 (2d ed. 1991).

Whether or not a particular legal environment is right for the conduct of an international arbitration is as much a matter of personal judgment as legal analysis. There are certain minimum requirements on which most arbitrators and practitioners agree. For instance, the local law must be prepared to uphold the efficacy of international arbitration agreements in line with the New York Convention. It must be prepared, if necessary, to assist in the constitution of the arbitral tribunal; and to give that arbitral tribunal, either directly or through its courts, such powers as it may need to carry out its task efficiently and effectively. Again, it must be prepared to recognise and enforce foreign arbitral awards, if it expects awards made on its own territory to be recognised and enforced in other countries.

Beyond such minimum requirements as these, however, there is room for different points of view as to what does and what does not constitute a suitable legal environment for the conduct of an international commercial arbitration. Moreover, the point of view is likely to change according to whether the interest represented is that of claimant, respondent or arbitrator.

## Degree of Control

The claimant in an arbitration, having decided to embark upon arbitral proceedings in order to secure what he considers to be his due, will usually want those proceedings to be carried out as quickly and cheaply as possible. Any assistance which the local law is prepared to give to this end, either directly or through its courts, will no doubt be welcomed; but any intervention by these courts at the suit of the respondent is likely to be seen as judicial interference, which merely adds to the length (and cost) of the proceedings.

The position looks different from the point of view of the respondent. Unless he has a substantial counterclaim to put forward, a respondent has little to gain and much to lose as a result of proceedings against him, whether these are brought before a court or before an arbitral tribunal. At best, his defence to the proceedings will be sustained and his honour satisfied. At worst, he may be faced with being ordered to pay damages, interest and costs. In these circumstances, the speed and economy with which the proceedings are likely to be conducted will be of less interest to him than the assurance that they will be conducted *properly*, and that he will be given a full and proper opportunity to present his case. If such an assurance is built in to the local law, by means of some form of review procedure, the respondent is likely to be more satisfied than if his only remedy is to submit to a process which he regards as unfair and then to attempt to resist recognition and enforcement of the consequent arbitral award - for instance, on the basis that he was unable to present his case.

The arbitral tribunal is likely to adopt a position nearer to that of the claimant than of the respondent, in its view of what constitutes a suitable legal environment. An arbitral tribunal will usually want to carry out the task for which it has been appointed as quickly and as efficiently as possible.

No ideal legal environment exists for the conduct of an international commercial arbitration. No system of law will satisfy the often conflicting requirements of the claimant and the respondent. Further, the position of the state cannot be ignored, since from time to time the state is called upon to lend its authority to the recognition and enforcement of arbitral award. The best that can be done is to find some balance between these different (and competing) interests.

\* \* \*

In practice, neither party anticipates a dispute arising at the time that they are negotiating the agreement. What factors should they therefore consider?

D.    Kazuo Iwasaki, *Selection of Situs: Criteria and Priorities*, 2 ARB. INT'L 57, 64-67 (1986).

*(1) Availability of enforcement of the award*

There are a number of reasons why parties to an international contract may prefer arbitration rather than resorting to the courts of either country.

Perhaps the most obvious advantage of arbitration proceedings compared to court procedure is the possibility of having the award enforced in various jurisdictions; in contrast, the possibility is very limited when it comes to a court judgment.

Accordingly it is submitted that the first standard for the parties' selection of the place of arbitration should be the enforceability of the award both in the country where the award is to be made and countries where the other party has assets against which the award may be enforced.

It is also to be noted that the increased importance of international commercial arbitration during the 1970's took place simultaneously with an expansion of trade involving new countries and between industrial and developing countries. Usually governmental agencies or public or semi-public agencies and institutions are involved in such trade. They may be immune to court proceedings under principles of state or sovereign immunity. Accordingly, arbitration is the only mutually acceptable and practical means of dispute resolution in their dealings with private parties from other countries, although if the government is of a Latin American country that adheres strictly to the Calvo Doctrine, the negotiation of arbitration clause may be almost impossible.

Regarding the enforcement of awards in the country where awards are made, the provisions of the *lex arbitri* relating to grounds for challenging awards, provisional remedies for the future enforcement of awards, and sovereign immunity from execution against the asset of the foreign government or governmental agency or organisation should be taken into consideration.

Concerning the enforcement of an award abroad, the most important question is whether the country where the award is to be made is a contracting state of the 1958 New York Convention. Awards made in a contracting state are enforceable in the sixty-odd countries which have ratified or adhered to the Convention and include most countries involved in international transactions.[64]

If a party to an arbitration agreement is a contracting state or its agency or organisation, any resulting awards made in that or another contracting state have a good chance to be enforceable against the assets of the state party in the United States, since US District Court decided that a country's accession to the 1958 New York Convention should preclude assertion of the sovereign immunity defence in enforcement action under the Convention in *Ipitrade International SA v. Federal Republic of Nigeria*, the US Government supported this decision in its amicus brief on appeal to the DC Circuit Court in *Libyan American Oil Co v. Socialist Libyan Arabic Popular Jamahiriya*.

## (2) Enforceability of the arbitration agreement

Article II(3) of the 1958 New York Convention obliges a Contracting State to enforce arbitration or submission agreements and to refer the parties to arbitration at the request of one of them in the event that the other party has instituted proceedings in a court.

---

[64] *See* Supplement at p. 50.

Therefore, if the arbitration site is located in a contracting state of the Convention and the arbitration or submission agreement falls within the Convention, that agreement is enforceable both in the country of the place of arbitration and in other contracting states, and court action will be stayed or rejected in these countries.

If the place of arbitration is not located in a contracting state of the Convention, the enforceability of the arbitration or submission agreement depends on the *lex arbitri*. And if the requirements of the *lex arbitri* are rigid, the parties will be involved in court litigation in spite of the fact that they once agreed to avoid court litigation.

Such being the case, the question whether the situs is in a contracting state of the Convention, or whether the *lex arbitri* provides for easy enforcement of the arbitration or submission agreement, should be considered in selecting arbitral venue.

### (3) Predictability of outcome

The predictability of the outcome of an international commercial arbitration is essential for the parties to any international business transaction. But it depends on what law the arbitral tribunal applies for its decision.

As explained in the foregoing discussion, it is to be expected that the arbitral tribunal will apply the municipal law determined by the private international law of the arbitration situs.

Accordingly the question whether the private international law in force at the place of arbitration accepts the application of the parties' designated substantive law (party autonomy) should be considered in the selection of the arbitration site.

### (4) Availability of proper and speedy outcome of arbitration

The proper and speedy outcome of the arbitration are the most basic requirements for arbitration. They will be determined mostly by the arbitrators' competence, as well as the arbitration institution's competence in case of administered arbitration.

In addition, court assistance to the arbitration process at the arbitration situs is of great help to expedite the outcome of arbitration, as shown in such matters as the constitution and filling of vacancies of the arbitral tribunal, or the calling of witnesses.

On the other hand, if judicial review of arbitral awards is available under the *lex arbitri*, it sometimes will take a considerable time for such review of an arbitral award by the local court.

Therefore the availability of competent arbitrators, impartial and reliable institutions, court assistance to the arbitration process, and judicial review of arbitral awards under the lex arbitri should be considered in selecting the arbitration situs.

*  *  *

Ultimately, the best advice may be to choose a known venue. Even adopting this cautious approach, problems may still emerge. For instance, in an ICC arbitration between a Finnish company and an Australian company, London was chosen by the parties as the place of arbitration. The parties commenced an arbitration in 1982 involving royalty payments allegedly due in the early 1970's. As the arbitration was taking place in England, could the licensee rely on the limitation periods contained in the English Limitation Act 1980?

> E. *Licensor Oy (Finland) v. Licensee Pty. (Australia)*, Int'l Com. Arb., *reported in* 2 J. INT'L ARB. 75, 76 (1985) (report & comment by Sigvard Jarvin, General Counsel, ICC Court of Arbitration).

[Extracts from Award in ICC Case 4491]

The Plaintiff submits that the Defendant cannot do so because Finnish law is the relevant law, and that, as there is no Limitation Act under Finnish law, no question of the claim being barred arises. However, the arbitration is taking place in London, and English law is the *lex fori*. In questions of limitation the provisions of the *lex fori* must be taken into account — see for example *British Linen Co. v. Drummond* 10 B.&C. 903 at p. 912. The Limitation Act 1980 applies the Act and any other limitation enactment to English arbitrations. I must apply the Limitation Act 1980 even though Finnish law has no such enactment - assuming for this purpose, that Finnish law is the proper law of the licensing agreement. The relevant period for a contractual claim or for an account is six years from the date on which the cause of action accrued: sections 5 and 23 of the Limitation Act 1980. The arbitration must therefore have been commenced within six years of the date when the cause of action accrued.

\*     \*     \*

The claimants in ICC Case 4491, therefore, failed without the merits of the case being considered (although it is to be noted that the outcome of the case would now be different as a result of the Foreign Limitation Periods Act 1984, which provides that where foreign law governs the dispute the foreign limitation period will apply). Detailed consideration should therefore be given to the choice of venue. Will failure to do so be recognised as an act of professional negligence? Gillis Wetter provides one answer in the following except.

F.     J. Gillis Wetter, *Arbitration in the New Europe*, 5 INT'L ARB. REP. 13, 16-18 (1990).

It is universally agreed that selection of a proper venue is a most important choice that the draftsman must make at the time of writing the arbitration agreement. This has been increasingly recognised in practice. Thus, e.g., the ICC Court nowadays has to choose a venue much less frequently than was the case in the past (in 14 per cent of the cases as compared to 50 per cent five years ago).

.     .     .

At the outset, draftsmen must evaluate the broad characteristics of optionally available arbitration locations. Is, for instance, the highly advertised new Swiss arbitration act in and of itself really a sufficiently certain and adequate basis for major arbitral proceedings in Switzerland, or ought contracts providing for arbitration in that jurisdiction to be substantially expanded by the incorporation of rules and detailed contractual regulations?

Even more basic — because the inherent characteristics of certain systems are hidden from sight and rarely, if ever, brought out in the limelight — are unarticulated habits and attitudes such as a deep inclination in certain jurisdictions towards an extreme inquisitorial (or, for that matter, an extreme adversarial) view of the conduct of arbitral proceedings. Should lawyers accept to have their disputes resolved in jurisdictions which do not allow party representatives (including corporate executives) to testify, censure cross-examination, restrict oral hearings to a minimum and forbid dissenting opinions?

Let me mention one other such extreme which has never been sufficiently observed. In the Federal Republic of Germany (and **perhaps**, it is said, also in some neighbouring jurisdictions) the rule in the courts is that the first and foremost duty of judges is to actively promote the settlement of disputes by all means at their disposal throughout the proceedings. I am told that American lawyers sometimes experience such an attitude in their own courts. Surprisingly, however, in Germany the same rule is deemed to apply in arbitral proceedings. This means that at every point in the processing of a case, arbitrators will be prepared to **and in fact are ordained by the legal system to act as conciliators** and to engage in misconduct by compromising themselves in such an alien role. The feature is viewed as basic and as a great attraction in German jurisprudence and practice. However, it is inherently alien to arbitration and tends to jeopardise the integrity of arbitrators. The lawyers who draft international arbitration clauses must determine in their own minds whether they wish to provide for arbitration in jurisdictions which are permeated by such attitudes and philosophies in the realm of the international arbitral process.

.     .     .

Turning from the level of the necessary initial, general assessment of the adequacy of the legal regime operating in a contemplated forum, we arrive at more specific questions. In my submission considerable emphasis should be given to **pre-award and post-award interest[,] the composition and allocation of costs in the arbitration** (both the costs of the tribunal and those of the parties, including fees and disbursements of the lawyers), **available substantive remedies** (including different kinds of damages) and the **assessment of damages**. At the end of the day, the issues in commercial arbitration relate exclusively to money, and all of the indicated issues are crucial to the monetary outcome of any case. In some jurisdictions, those issues are deemed to be governed by the proper law of the contract, i.e. substantive law, in others they are deemed to be governed by the curial law, i.e. normally the law of the forum, in still others related matters are largely unsettled. A choice of forum which is not based on proper advance analysis therefore may be found at the time of litigation to cost a client millions of dollars and to ruin an entire case. The point is that the associated problems are not unforeseeable but often become problems simply because they have not been adequately analysed at the time of the drafting of the arbitration agreement. All jurisdictions unite in one respect: the parties' autonomy in prescribing rules on all the stated specific subjects is virtually unfettered.

Thus the task of the lawyer drafting a contract must be twofold: **firstly** to select a venue which on an overall basis is suitable, or at least less unsuitable than other options, and secondly to supplement the arbitration agreement with specific provisions on a number of procedural subjects which in the judgment of the draftsman are vital. Failure of the lawyer to devote sufficient attention to these tasks is inexcusable and will no doubt increasingly be widely recognised as an act of professional negligence.

\*       \*       \*

Negotiators of arbitration agreements may properly ask how they should decide on a venue. It is clearly impossible to know all relevant rules in all jurisdictions. Should the parties call on the expertise of an arbitral institution? There is, of course, no guarantee that by leaving the choice to the institution, some unexpected problem, such as the local limitation period discussed above, not arise. However, it is the case that such institutions have the resources to keep abreast of developments in different jurisdictions, not to speak of the day to day experience of supervising arbitrations in them. Thus, Article 12 of the ICC Rules and Article 7.1 of the LCIA Rules provide, respectively:

> The place of arbitration shall be fixed by the Court, unless agreed upon by the parties.

> The parties may choose the place of arbitration. Failing such a choice, the place of arbitration shall be London, unless the Tribunal determines in view of all the circumstances of the case that another place is more appropriate.

However much thought goes into the choice of venue, an unpredictable supervening event may still render that choice an unfortunate one. Consider *NIOC v. Ashland*.

G.    *National Iranian Oil Co. [NIOC] v. Ashland Oil, Inc.*, 817 F.2d 326 (5th Cir. 1987).

[In the course of the Iranian Revolution, two Ashland Oil Company subsidiaries received almost $300 million of oil from the National Iranian Oil Co. (NIOC) but did not pay. The arbitration clause in the agreement called for arbitration in Iran, but Ashland refused to arbitrate there because of danger to Americans. It also refused to arbitrate elsewhere, as suggested by NIOC. NIOC sued in Mississippi for breach of contract and to compel arbitration. The District Court found it lacked power to compel arbitration in Mississippi because the contract designated Iran as the venue. NIOC appealed, *inter alia*, claiming that the parties had waived the forum selection clause.]

Section 4 of the Act provides in relevant part that:

> A party aggrieved by the alleged failure, neglect or refusal of another to arbitrate under a written agreement for arbitration may petition any United States district court . . . for an order directing that such arbitration proceed in the manner *provided for in the agreement.* . . . The court shall hear the parties, and upon being satisfied that the making of the agreement for arbitration or the failure to comply therewith is not in issue, the court shall make an order directing the parties to proceed to arbitration *in accordance with the terms of the agreement.* The hearing and proceedings, under such agreement, *shall be within the district in which the petition for an order directing such arbitration is filed.*

9 U.S.C. § 4 (emphasis added). Section 4 thus facially mandates that two conditions must be met before a district court may compel arbitration: (1) that the arbitration be held in the district court in which the court sits; *and* (2) that the arbitration be held in accordance with the agreement of the parties. In this case the forum selection clause, found in Article X of the April contract, provides that "the seat of

arbitration shall be in Tehran, unless otherwise agreed by the parties."
Rec. at 28. Relying on *Snyder v. Smith*, 736 F.2d 409 (7th Cir.), *cert.
denied*, 469 U.S. 1037, 105 S.Ct. 513, 83 L.Ed.2d 403 (1984), the
district court reasoned that the language of section 4 deprived it of the
power to compel arbitration in Mississippi, because to order arbitration
in Mississippi would violate the forum selection clause and thus would
not be "in accordance with the terms of the agreement". 9 U.S.C. § 4.

In *Snyder*, the Seventh Circuit reversed an order of the district
court ordering arbitration in its district in the face of a forum selection
clause designating Houston, Texas as the agreed-upon site of any
arbitral proceeding. The court reasoned that section 4 mandates that
arbitration be compelled only in accord with the terms of the contract,
and one "term of the agreement" was the forum selection clause.

> The right and duty to arbitrate disputes is purely a
> matter of contractual agreement between the parties. . .
> . An arbitration agreement, including its forum selection
> clause is a freely-negotiated contract between the
> parties. Courts must give effect to such freely negotiated
> forum selection clauses.

*Id.* at 419 (citing *M/S Bremen v. Zapata Off-Shore Co.,* 407 U.S. 1,
15-18 . . . (1972)) . . . .

·       ·       ·

Apparently, contrary to some other courts, we have not taken
such a literal approach to the two part mandate of section 4. In
*Dupuy-Busching General Agency, Inc. v. Ambassador Ins. Co.*, 524
F.2d 1275 (5th Cir. 1975) (per curiam), a party to a contract
containing a forum selection clause providing for arbitration in New
Jersey brought suit in Mississippi requesting the court to enjoin
arbitration. The district court ordered arbitration in New Jersey, and
we affirmed the order of the district court compelling arbitration
outside its own district. We did so, however, in accord with the forum
selection clause. Noting the tension in the two conditions of section 4,
we reasoned that "where a party seeking to avoid arbitration brings a
suit for injunctive relief in a district court other than that in which
arbitration is to take place ... the party seeking arbitration may assert
its sect. 4 right to have the arbitration performed in accordance with

the terms of the agreement." *Id.* at 1278; *see also Continental Grain*, 118 F.2d at 969 (ordering arbitration in its own district despite forum selection clause designating New York as the situs of arbitral proceedings, because the plaintiff effectively waived the forum selection clause by bringing suit in Oregon seeking to compel arbitration in New York).

Thus, *Dupuy-Busching* suggests that the language of section 4 need not be applied literally, that there may be some cases in which district courts are empowered to compel arbitration notwithstanding the parties' contractually established forum or outside of the district in which the courts sit. *See Municipal Energy Agency*, 804 F.2d at 344. But this is not such a case. By bringing suit in a district other than the districts designated in the forum selection clause, the plaintiff in *Dupuy-Busching* in effect had waived the right to its bargain. Contrary to NIOC's contention, there has been no such waiver here.

NIOC contends that since it is not seeking to compel arbitration in Iran, it has waived its right to the benefit of the forum selection clause. Further, NIOC argues that Ashland also has waived the "benefit" of such clause by refusing to participate in an arbitral proceeding in Tehran or elsewhere. NIOC therefore concludes that, because the putative waivers render the forum selection clause nugatory, we are free to order arbitration in Mississippi without contravening the contract's terms. This argument rings hollow.

. . .

. . . Because a waiver is a voluntary relinquishment of a known right, *see, e.g., Watkins v. Fly*, 136 F.2d 578, 580 (5th Cir.) (on petition for hearing), *cert. denied*, 320 U.S. 769, 64 S.Ct. 80, 88 L.Ed. 459 (1943); *Restatement (Second) of Contracts*, § 84, comment b (1981), and because NIOC has nothing that it could relinquish in a U.S. court, NIOC could not have waived its "right" to the benefit of the forum selection clause. Moreover, Ashland contends and NIOC does not dispute that NIOC has attempted, and still may be attempting, to compel arbitration through the court system in Iran. Thus, NIOC has not waived its contractual right to arbitration in Iran. NIOC, at most, simply and pragmatically has recognized that it has no legal right in the U.S. courts to compel arbitration in Tehran.

. . .

NIOC also argues that, because it may be "inconvenient" for Ashland to participate in an arbitral proceeding in Iran, this impossibility (or commercial impracticability) renders the forum selection clause without force. Appellant's brief at 23. NIOC, relying on *Snyder*, 736 F.2d at 419, and *The Bremen*, 407 U.S. at 10-12, 92 S.Ct. at 1913-14, therefore asserts that the forum selection clause should be severed and Ashland compelled to perform the essential term of the bargain, *viz.* to participate in an arbitral proceeding (in Mississippi). The syllogism too is fatally flawed.

. . . In *The Bremen*, 407 U.S. at 10-12, 92 S.Ct. at 1913-14, the Supreme Court held, in the context of an international admiralty dispute, that forum selection clauses must be strictly enforced, unless the enforcement would be "unreasonable," or unless the resisting party could show "countervailing" or "compelling" reasons why it should not be enforced. But the forum selection clause at issue in the *The Bremen* did not relate to the choice of situs in an arbitral proceeding, rather it related to the parties' contractual choice of arbitration as opposed to litigation to resolve its disputes. Thus, in *Sam Reisfeld & Son Import Co. v. S.A. Eteco*, 530 F.2d 679 (5th Cir. 1976), we held that the test in *The Bremen* was inapposite respecting the enforcement of the choice of situs expressed in an arbitration agreement. In *Reisfeld*, a U.S. company argued that a forum selection clause designating Belgium as the situs of arbitration should not be enforced because "it is so unreasonable that it either vitiates the arbitration clause altogether or requires a transfer to a more neutral situs." *Id.* at 680. We held that the forum selection clause contained in an arbitration provision must be enforced, even if unreasonable. A forum selection clause establishing the situs of arbitration must be enforced unless it conflicts with an "explicit provision of the Federal Arbitration Act." *Id.* at 680-81.

> Under the Act, a party seeking to avoid arbitration must allege and prove that the arbitration clause itself was a product of fraud, coercion, or "such grounds as exist at law or in equity for the revocation of the contract."

. . . NIOC does not assert that it has been a victim of fraud or coercion, and its assertion of inconvenience or impossibility fails as a "legal ground" for vitiating the freely chosen forum selection clause.

. . . Under traditional principles of contract law, NIOC's argument that the political atmosphere in Iran renders arbitration there impossible or impracticable certainly supplies an adequate predicate for finding the forum selection clause unenforceable and without effect. . . . But impracticability is an argument upon which NIOC may not rely.

In order to assert the doctrine of impossibility or commercial impracticability, the party wishing to assert such a defence must meet two conditions. First "[t]he affected party must have no reason to know at the time the contract was made of the facts on which he [or she] relies." . . . That NIOC—an instrumentality of the Islamic Republic of Iran—could not reasonably have foreseen in April 1979 that an American entity might find it impracticable to participate then or in the near future in an arbitral proceeding in Tehran defies credulity.

By January 16, 1979, the Shah had departed, and by February 1, the Ayatollah Khomeini had returned triumphantly to Iran. On February 14, the American Embassy was attacked for the first time, killing one Iranian civilian employee, wounding an American Marine, and taking some 100 Americans hostage, including Ambassador Sullivan, for approximately two hours. In short, by April 1979, when the contract was executed, the revolutionary government was in place—the same government that took power largely by "mobilizing millions of Iranians against an America equated with satan." B. Rubin, *Paved With Good Intentions: The American Experience and Iran* 255 (1980). Thus, it simply is unimaginable that NIOC, part of the revolutionary government, could not reasonably have foreseen that Tehran would become a forum in which it is indisputably impossible for Americans to participate in any proceedings. *See, e.g.*, *McDonnell Douglas Corp. v. Islamic Republic of Iran*, 758 F.2d 341, 345-46 (8th Cir. 1985) (taking judicial notice of the grave difficulties that would confront an American entity were it forced to litigate a dispute in Iran, and collecting cases).

Second, a party may not rely on the doctrine of impossibility or impracticability "[i]f the event is due to the fault of the . . . [party] himself [or herself]." *Restatement (Second) of Contracts* at § 261, comment d; . . . . Yet, as part of the revolutionary Government, NIOC certainly bears responsibility for creating the chain of events making it impossible for an American entity reasonably to travel to and to engage in quasi-judicial proceedings in Iran. Thus, NIOC cannot assert the doctrine of impossibility.

. . . Even were NIOC able to rely on the fact that it is now impossible for Ashland to arbitrate in Iran, thus vitiating the forum selection clause, NIOC must show that the venue provision is severable from the rest of the arbitration agreement. Whether the agreement to arbitrate is entire or severable turns on the parties' intent at the time the agreement was executed, as determined from the language of the contract and the surrounding circumstances. *See, e.g., Prospero Associates v. Burroughs Corp.*, 714 F.2d 1022, 1026-27 (10th Cir. 1983); *Pollux Marine Agencies, Inc. v. Louis Dreyfus Corp.*, 455 F.Supp. 211, 219 (S.D.N.Y. 1978). NIOC must therefore show that the essence, the essential term, of the bargain was to arbitrate while the situs of the arbitration was merely a minor consideration. *See Restatement (Second) of Contracts* at § 184, comment a; § 185(1) & comment b.

. . . But the language of the standard form document—drafted by NIOC—belies any such argument. Not only did NIOC choose Tehran as the site of any arbitration, but the contract also provides that Iranian law governs the interpretation and rendition of any arbitral awards. The arbitration agreement also provides that, should one of the parties fail to appoint an arbitrator or should the two arbitrators fail to agree on a third arbitrator, "the interested party may request the *President of the Appeal Court of Tehran* to appoint the second arbitrator or the third arbitrator, as the case may be." Rec. at 27 (emphasis added). Indeed, the contract expressly provides that the entire agreement is to be interpreted by reference to Iranian law. The language of the contract thus makes self-evident the importance of Iranian law and Iranian institutions to NIOC. Therefore, the document plainly suggests that the situs selection clause was as important to NIOC as the agreement to resolve disputes privately through arbitration. The language of the contract demonstrates that the parties intended the forum selection clause and the arbitral agreement to be entire, not divisible.

Finally, even where the forum selection clause is severable, we are still not informed how the parties intended to arbitrate in *Mississippi*. NIOC contends, somewhat disingenuously, that because Ashland's corporate offices are in Kentucky, Jackson is far more convenient to Ashland than to NIOC. But NIOC does not dispute Ashland's allegation that NIOC ran to Mississippi because it is one of the few jurisdictions with a six-year, rather than four-year, limitations period for contracts' claims. Thus, by filing when it did in Mississippi,

NIOC was able to assert its claim before the statute of limitations had run, and simultaneously to argue that that statute of limitations had run on to Ashland's counterclaim, which had accrued earlier.

. . . Notwithstanding considerations of "convenience," one cannot reasonably argue that the parties' contract contemplates arbitration in Mississippi. The contract's provision that arbitration was to be in Tehran "unless otherwise agreed" suggests that, were Iran to become inconvenient or unacceptable to one or both parties, no other forum was to be available unless mutually agreed upon. Because arbitration is a creature of contract, we cannot rewrite the agreement of the parties and order the proceeding to be held in Mississippi. . . .

NIOC could have chosen to negotiate a forum selection clause with a situs in any one of the 65 nations that are signatories to the Convention, thereby permitting extra-territorial enforcement by U.S. courts. It also could have selected any one of 50 states in this country in which we could have compelled Ashland to arbitrate. But it did not. It selected a situs that was unenforceable *ab initio*, and we have no statutory or equitable mandate that allows us to redraft the agreement premised on convenience of the parties *ex post*. *See Prima Paint*, 388 U.S. at 404 n. 12, 87 S.Ct. at 1806 n. 12 (purpose of Act "was to make arbitration agreements as enforceable as other contracts, but not more so"); *Robin v. Sun Oil Co.*, 548 F.2d 554, 557 (5th Cir. 1977) (courts may not redraft the parties' agreement in the absence of clear and convincing evidence of mutual mistake).

. . . . .

. . . NIOC points to the weighty congressional policy favoring the use of arbitration if the parties have contractually agreed to resolve their disputes in this manner. . . . This policy acquires special significance in the international context where, because of transnational fora and concomitant conflicts of laws problems, arbitration appears a more inviting forum. . . . Thus, there is a strong, congressionally ordained presumption in favor of arbitrability. Therefore, we have repeatedly held that "arbitration should not be denied 'unless it can be said with positive assurance that an arbitration clause is not susceptible of an interpretation which would cover the dispute at issue.'" *Phillips Petroleum*, 794 F.2d at 1081 (quoting *Wick v. Atlantic Marine, Inc.*, 605 F.2d 166, 168 (5th Cir. 1979)). At the same time, a corollary "of th[is] principle [] is that the duty to submit a dispute to arbitration arises from contracts, therefore a party cannot be compelled to arbitrate a dispute if he has not agreed to do so." *Lodge No. 2504*, 812 F.2d at 221; *see also* H.R.Rep. No. 96, 68th Cong., 1st Sess. 1 (1924) ("Arbitration agreements are purely matters of contract, and the effect of the bill is simply to make the contracting party live up to his agreement"); H.R.Rep. No. 91-702, 91st Cong., 2d Sess. 6 (1970) (bill implementing the Convention has the same purpose). Thus, NIOC's appeal to congressional policy will not suffice to transform the plain words of the parties' agreement to arbitrate in Tehran, Iran to arbitrate in Jackson, Mississippi.

There is also a countervailing policy concern evoked by this case. When the United States adhered to the Convention, it expressly chose the option available in Article I(3), to "apply the Convention, on the basis of reciprocity, to the recognition and enforcement of *only* those awards made in the territory of another Contracting State." Declaration (emphasis added). While the House and Senate Committee reports do not inform us as to the purpose of adopting this reservation, its purpose seems obvious. Concerned with reciprocity, Congress must have meant only to allow signatories to partake of the Convention's benefits in U.S. courts and thus to give further incentives to non-signatory nations to adhere to the Convention. Were we now to order arbitration in Mississippi, despite the forum selection clause designating Tehran into an agreement as the site of arbitration, we would do great violence to this obvious congressional purpose. Were we to order arbitration in the U.S. in the face of a forum selection clause designating a non-signatory forum, which was unenforceable *ab initio*, the non-signatory would have little reason to leave the Hobbesian jungle of international chaos for the ordered and more predictable world of international commercial law.

.     .     .

IV.     CONSIDERATIONS AND OPTIONS IN DISPENSING WITH LAW BY AUTHORIZING DECISION *EX AEQUO ET BONO*

Parties to a modern contract usually view the contractual rights that they have secured from the other party as entitling them to full and strict performance. While many disputes about such contracts are frequently described by one or both parties as disagreements about the meaning of the terms of the agreement, an observer will often see them as a conflict in which one party seeks strict performance while the other, invoking some principle or rule of the governing law, seeks to justify non-performance and/or a change in its obligations. In short, one party seeks implementation of the contract and the other seeks relief from it. When the governing law does not permit such relief, the party seeking it is, in effect, requesting an equitable solution. Equity, in this contractual context, means a renegotiation of the benefits and burdens in ways that are different from those originally expressed in the agreement.

In the absence of a direct contractual authorization or an authorization in the governing law, arbitrators are expected to provide a legal application of the contract and not to renegotiate it on behalf of the parties. When arbitrators are authorized to make a decision which departs from the terms of the contract and/or the governing law, they are usually described as deciding *ex aequo et bono*, or according to equity. These are terms of art which are misleading in their ordinary connotation. For historic reasons, common law lawyers contrapose "law" and "equity," a distinction which implies that law is not equitable. That is quite misleading. Agreements which are freely reached between parties in positions of power parity are not necessarily inequitable. Indeed, it would appear to be inequitable not to give effect to them. A decision *ex aequo et bono* does not import an absolute conception of equity but simply an instruction to arbitrators to ignore the existing terms of a contract and/or those parts of the governing law which are dispositive and to refashion the contract in ways that appear to them to be appropriate.

Under diverse national laws, there may be substantial differences in the powers actually available to arbitrators who have been authorized by the parties to decide *ex aequo et bono*. In some cases, anything the arbitrator wishes may be acceptable. In other cases, the governing law may establish limitations on arbitral competence under this mode of decision. While the identity and quality of the arbitrator is a critical factor in every arbitration, it is obvious that a profound understanding of the nature of the industry in question and of the spectrum of obligations and benefits to be found in the particular transaction is a prerequisite skill for the arbitrator deciding *ex aequo et bono*.

A decision *ex aequo et bono* is a relatively rare occurrence in international commercial arbitration, but it is not unknown. Consider the case of *IBM v. Fujitsu*, decided in 1987, on the basis of arbitration *ex aequo et bono*.

IBM first accused Fujitsu of copying IBM's software in 1982. Fujitsu, as a maker of IBM-compatible mainframes, imitated several features of IBM's software in order to run its own mainframes efficiently. Fujitsu claimed that unless it was able to make similar software IBM would have a monopoly on mainframe software. The following year Fujitsu paid IBM an undisclosed, yet substantial sum as a settlement, and the two companies also set ground rules for the use of the software.

The 1983 agreement quickly collapsed. The arbitrators described the collapse as the almost unavoidable consequence of poor drafting, particularly in the defining of technical terms and in the choice of law clauses.

In 1985, IBM requested arbitration. The tribunal began unsuccessfully, however, in a formal, trial-like manner. Many lawyers and officers for each side were involved in each session. When the representatives from each side decreased in number, however, the arbitrators were able to make some progress. IBM and Fujitsu later signed an agreement which set up a coerced-licensing system for five to ten years. The arbitrators were to oversee any disputes between the parties concerning mainframe operating-system software for the next 15 years, assessing penalties for any infractions of the licensing agreement.

The following passage is the official announcement of the arbitral award.

ANNOUNCEMENT OF IBM/FUJITSU DISPUTE
RESOLUTION
by the American Arbitration Association Commercial
Arbitration Tribunal

in the matter of
International Business Machines Corporation, Claimant
- against -
Fujitsu Limited, Respondent and Counterclaimant
Arbitrators' Report Sept. 15, 1987

On Sept. 15, 1987, we issued an Order and Opinion in an arbitration
between International Business Machines Corporation (IBM) and
Fujitsu Limited (FJ) under the auspices of the American Arbitration
Association (AAA). The parties by agreement have empowered us to
resolve their dispute.

The parties' primary dispute concerns FJ's use of IBM information in
FJ's development of IBM-compatible mainframe operating system
software. IBM claims that FJ copies IBM operating system programs
in violation of IBM's copyrights. FJ maintains that it has only used
IBM information unprotected under copyright law.

In 1983, the parties executed agreements to resolve this dispute. FJ has
made very substantial payments to IBM under these agreements.
However, these agreements were unsuccessful because they failed to
establish adequate protective procedures for the ongoing use of IBM
information in FJ software development and payment for such use.

The Order, binding on both parties, establishes a framework for a
comprehensive resolution of this dispute.

## RESOLUTION OF PAST DISPUTES

The Order will resolve all disputes between the parties with respect to
programs previously released by FJ. FJ will make a lump sum payment
to IBM and will receive immunity, release and waiver of all IBM
claims. We will determine the amount of the lump sum payment during
the coming year. This lump sum payment will be made in lieu of FJ's
obligation under the 1983 agreements to make very substantial
payments to IBM for certain programs designated by FJ for immunity.

Under the Order, FJ and its customers may continue to use existing FJ operating system software without interruption.

## SECURED FACILITY REGIME

To provide FJ a reasonable opportunity to independently develop and maintain operating system software, the Order will allow FJ, during a five to 10-year period (the exact duration to be determined by us) to examine IBM programs in a Secured Facility, and, subject to strict and elaborate safeguards, to derive and document information in accordance with rules specified in written Instructions. FJ may use such information, with immunity, in its software development. FJ will fully and adequately compensate IBM for such access and immunity.

The Order also gives IBM a reciprocal right to establish a Secured Facility if it wishes to examine FJ programs for IBM software development.

## THE BASIC PRINCIPLES OF THE SECURED FACILITY REGIME ARE:

## 1. ACCESS IN EXCHANGE FOR ADEQUATE COMPENSATION

Specified personnel of a party, not otherwise engaged in software development, will have access in a Secured Facility to programming material of the other party (including source code whether or not generally available to customers) from which they may derive, and place on survey sheets, only such interface specifications and any other information specified in the Instructions. A party will have to pay the other party, fully and adequately, for its access to such information.

## 2. INDEPENDENT COMPLIANCE MONITORING

Compliance with Instructions and procedures relating to the Secured Facility will be strictly monitored by an independent and technically expert Facility Supervisor under our guidance and authority. No material will be removed from a Secured Facility except as permitted by the Instructions and approved by the Facility Supervisor. Before any survey sheet is released from a Secured Facility, the Facility Supervisor will transmit copies of such a survey sheet to representatives of the other party who will have an opportunity to object to the inclusion of any specific information. Each party may review for compliance any finished product developed by the other party during this period as a result of the Secured Facility regime. Any such compliance review must take place in a Secured Facility.

## 3. IMMUNITY

A party may use information placed on approved survey sheets in its development of operating system software and the other party may not challenge such use.

## 4. LIMITED DURATION

A party's right to examine deposited programming material of the other party, and to extract information specified in the Instructions, will end after the completion of a five to 10-year period (the exact duration to be determined by us). The Order replaces prior 1983 agreements that required each party to provide "External Information" to the other until at least the year 2002.

### CROSS-LICENSING OF SOFTWARE

We believe that the Order will foster competition with respect to IBM-compatible mainframe hardware systems and products. In the past, FJ has only licensed its operating system software to run on FJ hardware. The Order gives users of each party's mainframe processors the right to license the other party's software products in countries where those products are offered.

As a result, for the first time, customers may license FJ operating system software to operate on IBM machines.

### DISCLOSURE

The parties have agreed that there be no disclosure of agreements or disputes by either party, absent prior written agreement by both parties. They have authorized us to make such disclosure as we deem appropriate.

We believe it is appropriate to disclose the Order and Opinion to the public. We intend to make further disclosures at appropriate times in the future. Meanwhile, the parties and their counsel remain obligated to make no disclosure concerning the arbitration proceedings.

The Order and the Instructions, rules, guidelines and procedures established pursuant to it, will exclusively define the rights and obligations of each party with respect to the use of the party's programming material during this period, notwithstanding copyright decisions of U.S. or Japanese courts or previous agreements of the parties.

The Order also creates a transition period for FJ to establish procedures and policies that will effectively protect IBM's intellectual property after the period expires and FJ's Secured Facility shuts down. After that time, FJ will have access only to IBM programming material generally available to customers and it will be able to use information in its independent software development only in accordance with then applicable copyright law.

### Notes and Questions

1. The WALL STREET JOURNAL reported that the proposal for the unusual procedure in this case actually came from the two arbitrators — one a Professor at Stanford Law School, the other a retired computer executive — after they had worked on the case for about a year.

One of the most extraordinary provisions of the decision gives the two arbitrators sweeping powers to shape future software relations between IBM and Fujitsu. The two men will, in their own words, "constitute the intellectual property law between these two companies".

The resolution — giving Fujitsu access to IBM software, but under strict control and at a potentially enormous price — also promises to strongly affect the $20 billion mainframe-computer market. It will assure IBM of a vigorous rival in one of the market's most profitable segments, where the Armonk, N.Y., giant currently faces little competition: the software at the heart of its mainframes. Depending on the arbitration's monetary terms, which so far haven't been set, it may also saddle Fujitsu with a heavy financial burden and give IBM a huge new source of revenue.

.    .    .

The IBM/Fujitsu arbitrators will be able to decide which IBM software Fujitsu can look at, how much it can copy and what it must pay IBM — an extraordinary arrangement that the arbitrators admit amounts to a "coerced license." They have already said Fujitsu will be able to look at something IBM usually doesn't show rivals — the so-called source code, which reveals exactly how its software is programmed.

Michael W. Miller, *High-Tech World Sees IBM Case as a Way Out of the Copyright Maze*, WALL ST. J., Sept. 18, 1987, at 1.

2. Under what circumstances and what contingencies (if any) would you advise a client to insert, in an arbitration clause, an authorization to the arbitrators to decide *ex aequo et bono*?

3. Under what circumstances and what contingencies would you advise a client to propose or agree to the other party's proposal, after a dispute had arisen, to set aside a choice of law clause in the arbitration agreement and to authorize the arbitrators to decide *ex aequo et bono*?

4. In *IBM v. Fujitsu*, the tribunal was composed of only two party-appointed arbitrators. They may have, in effect, negotiated as proxies for the parties. If there had been a third, neutral arbitrator, would the essential character of this particular *ex aequo et bono* exercise been different? Would this have influenced the parties willingness to authorize arbitration *ex aequo et bono*?

5. What controls exist to restrain arbitrators when an *ex aequo et bono* competence is assigned to them? For example, if the arbitrators in the case had done something one party considered grossly inequitable or beyond the scope of the agreement, what remedies would have been available?

## V.     *LEX MERCATORIA*: CONTENT AND IMPLICATIONS

Each party to an international contract tends to recoil, almost instinctively, from having the other party's national law govern the contract. Therefore, many international contracts adopt, as an alternative, the "neutral" laws of a third country. But the "choice" of a law which may be unknown to both parties may contain any number of substantive and procedural items which one or both parties may not have wanted.

Hence this uncertainty is one impetus to create a universal common law of international contracts, a new law merchant akin to the one that governed the itinerant tradesmen of medieval times. The sources of such a *lex mercatoria* could be various: principles of law common to most national legal systems (or at least to those relevant to the contract in question), norms set down in widely accepted international treaties, trade usages of the relevant transnational sectors, and, indeed, international arbitral awards.

The following three disputes involved ICC awards decided under non-national norms. Two of them explicitly referred to *lex mercatoria*, the third to "internationally accepted principles of law governing contractual relations."

A.      *Pabalk Ticaret Ltd. Sirketi v. Norsolor S.A.*, 11 YEARBOOK OF COMMERCIAL ARBITRATION. 484 (1986).

[Decision of Court of Appeal of Paris and the French Supreme Court, introduced and excerpted in English.]

On 1 June 1971, the French company Ugilor, which became Norsolor on 1 January 1977, concluded with the Turkish company Pabalk an agency agreement under which Pabalk was to receive commissions for the delivery of acrymythile to the Turkish company Aska.

As a result of difficulties which had arisen between Ugilor and Aska, Ugilor terminated the agreement of 1 June 1971 with Pabalk. The termination prompted Pabalk to resort to arbitration at the International Chamber of Commerce (ICC) as provided for in the agreement, on 1 April 1977, claiming unpaid and unearned commissions and damages.

The Court of Arbitration of the ICC fixed Vienna as place of arbitration. The parties had not authorised the arbitrators to act as *amiables compositeurs*.

By an award dated 26 October 1979 the arbitration (B. Cremades, chairman, J. Ghestin, and R. Steiner) held with respect to the applicable law:

Faced with the difficulty of choosing a national law the application of which is sufficiently compelling, the Tribunal considered that it was appropriate, given the international nature of the agreement, to leave aside any compelling reference to a specific legislation, be it Turkish or French, and to apply the international *lex mercatoria*.

One of the principles which inspires the latter is that of the good faith which must preside over the formation and the performance of contracts. The emphasis placed on contractual good faith is moreover one of the dominant tendencies revealed by 'the convergence of national laws on the matter' (G. Cornu, 'Regards sur le titre III du Livre III du Code Civil: des contrats et des obligations conventionnelles en général,' Cours D.E.A. Droit privé, Paris II, 1976-77, p. 200, no. 260).

Good faith expresses not only a state of mind, the knowledge or ignorance of a fact, but also 'reference to customs, to an ethical rule of conduct. . .' (G. Cornu, op. cit., no. 290). It thus expresses a required conduct which can be linked to the general principles of responsibility.

In accordance with the principle of good faith which inspires the international *lex mercatoria*, the Tribunal sought to determine whether, in the present instance, the breach of the agency was attributable to the conduct of one of the parties and whether it had caused damage to the other which would thus be without justification and which equity would hence require to be remedied.

On these bases, the arbitrators examined whether the termination of the agreement was attributable to the conduct of one of the parties and whether it had caused damages to the other party which "equity would hence require to be remedied." They found that the conduct of Ugilor "was scarcely compatible with maintaining good relations" and therefore had to be held responsible for breach of the agency. The arbitrators also held that Ugilor was liable for damages to Pabalk. They found these damages extremely difficult to calculate and therefore "evaluated in equity by way of a global sum" the amount of damages at FFr. 800,000.

The arbitral decision consisted of four points, *viz.*

(I) Ugilor/Norsolor shall pay Pabalk FFR 3,965.97, US Dollars 12,429.65 and 1,320.02 as well as interest of 6 per cent per year as from 1 April 1977, for unpaid commissions;

(II) Ugilor/Norsolor shall pay Pabalk FFR 22,650, for unearned commissions because of firm sales which had partially not been executed during 1973;

(III) Ugilor/Norsolor shall pay Pabalk FFR 800,000 as damages for terminating the agreement;

(IV) Each party shall pay half the cost of the arbitration (*i.e.*, US Dollars 50,000).

The award (ICC no. 3131) is reported in YEARBOOK Vol. IX (1984) pp. 109-111.

In Austria Norsolor sought to set aside the award, inter alia, on the ground that the arbitrators had acted beyond the limits of the arbitration agreement by deciding in equity without authorisation to do so.

The action gave rise to the preliminary question of which court in Austria was competent to deal with the action, Norsolor and Pabalk both having a place of business outside Austria. The Austrian Supreme Court decided on 1 February 1980 that the arbitral award was a domestic (Austrian) award because it had been rendered in Austria, and designated the Commercial Court of First Instance of Vienna as the competent court. An extract of this decision is reported in YEARBOOK Vol. VII (1982) pp. 312-315 (Austria no. 4) with a comment by Dr. Werner Melis.

By a judgment dated 29 June 1981, the Commercial Court of First Instance of Vienna dismissed the action to set aside the award.

In the meantime, in France, Pabalk requested leave for enforcement of the award before the President of the *Tribunal de grande instance* [Court of First Instance] of Paris. The President granted leave for enforcement on 4 February 1980.

The granting of leave for enforcement was upheld in full by the Court of First Instance of Paris on 4 March 1981. The Court considered that the arbitrators in conformity with Art. 13 of the Arbitration Rules of the ICC applied the law designated as the proper law by the rule of conflict which they deemed the most appropriate, which in this case was the general principles of obligations generally applicable to international commerce and that even if they had twice in their reasoning used the term "equity," they had not decided as *"amiables compositeurs."* The Court of First Instance of Paris also held that it was not qualified to examine whether the arbitrators had correctly applied the rule of law which they had found applicable and had made an error in assessment of damages.

Norsolor appealed the decision of the Court of First Instance to the Court of Appeal of Paris. Pending this appeal, an appeal lodged by Pabalk to the Court of Appeal of Vienna to set aside the award was also pending.

By a decision of 15 December 1981, the Court of Appeal in Paris adjourned its decision on enforcement until the Court of Appeal of Vienna had given the decision on Pabalk's appeal. The decision of the Paris Court of Appeal is reported in YEARBOOK Vol. VIII (1983) pp. 362-364 (France no. 5).

On 29 January 1982 the Court of Appeal of Vienna partially set aside the arbitral award (*i.e.*, decision nos. III and IV, see above) because the arbitral tribunal had exceeded the limits of its authority by basing its decisions on equity. The decision of the Vienna Court of Appeal is reported in a Note in YEARBOOK Vol. VII (1983) p. 365.

On 19 November 1982 the Court of Appeal of Paris decided that the 29 January 1982 Vienna Court of Appeal's decision setting aside the award should lead to a refusal of enforcement of decisions nos. III and IV of the award on the ground mentioned in Art. V(1)(e) of the New York Convention ("enforcement may be refused . . . if the award . . . has been set aside ... by a competent authority of the country in which . . . the award was made"). The judgment of the Paris Court of Appeal is reported below.

In the meantime, Norsolor had taken recourse to the Austrian Supreme Court against the decision of the Vienna Court of Appeal setting aside the award. On 18 November 1982, *i.e.*, one day before the Paris Court of Appeal decision just mentioned, refusing enforcement of the award, the Austrian Supreme Court reversed the Vienna Court of Appeal judgment, by holding that the arbitrators had not exceeded their authority.

The judgment of the Austrian Supreme Court is reported in YEARBOOK Vol. X (1985) pp. 159-161 with a note by Dr. Werner Melis.

The judgment of the Austrian Supreme Court, upholding the validity of the award, resulted in a granting of the enforcement of the award by the Court of First Instance of Paris on 20 June 1983.

However, Pabalk had also taken recourse to the French Supreme Court against the judgment of the Paris Court of Appeal of 19 November 1982. On 1 October 1984 the French Supreme Court reversed the judgment of the Paris Court of Appeal. The reasons of the French Supreme Court are also reproduced below.

## COURT OF APPEAL OF PARIS, 19 NOVEMBER 1982

*Applicable international convention*

Considering that under the terms of Art. I of the Convention signed at Geneva on 21 April 1961, the latter applies:

(a) to arbitral agreements concluded for the purpose of settling disputes arising from international trade between physical or legal persons having, when concluding the agreement, their habitual place of residence or their seat in different Contracting States;

(b) to arbitral procedures and awards based on agreements referred to in paragraph (a) above.

Considering that it is not disputed that at the date of the arbitration agreement, the Pabalk company had its seat in Turkey;

That this State has not expressly ratified the Geneva Convention as provided by Art. 10 thereof;

That the said Convention, the applicability of which requires the habitual place of residence or the seat of the parties to the arbitration agreement to be in the territory of Contracting States, thus does not apply in this case;

Considering on the other hand, that the Convention signed in New York on 10 June 1958 applies, according to the terms of Art. I thereof, 'to the recognition and enforcement of arbitral awards made in the territory of a State other than the State where the recognition and enforcement of such awards are sought, and arising out of differences between persons, whether physical or legal,' as well as to 'arbitral awards not considered as domestic awards in the State their recognition and enforcement are sought';

That this latter Convention was ratified both by France and Austria, in whose territory the award in question was made; that, furthermore, this award, as was made clear in the judgment of this Chamber of 15 December 1981, cannot be considered as being French.

That the New York Convention therefore applies in the present case.

On the effect on the present proceedings of the judgment of the Court of Appeal of Vienna

Considering that it has not been established, or even argued, that under Austrian procedural law an appeal to the Supreme Court operates to suspend execution with regard to the subject matter before the Vienna Court, and that, from then on, the judgment of that Court of 29 January 1982, does not have the effect of *res judicata* which would attach in the same circumstances to the decision of a French court of appeal by virtue of Arts. 500 and 589 of the N.C.P.C.;

Considering that the jurisdiction of the Vienna Court of Appeal to adjudicate upon the appeal lodged in Austria by the Norsolor company is not disputed;

Considering that there is no doubt, in the light of that Court's judgment, that it annulled points III and IV of the award, since the word '*cassée*' appears in the *dispositif* of the judgment - a word which, in the translation on file in the present proceedings - is evidently used as synonymous with the term '*annullée*,' used in the reasoning;

That, from that moment on, in accordance with Art. V(1)(e) of the New York Convention of 10 June 1958, the order of the President of the Court of First Instance in Paris, dated 4 February 1980, must be retracted in so far as it grants enforcement of points III and IV of the dispositing of the award;

Considering, on the other hand, that there are no grounds for the retraction of the said enforcement order as to point I and II, which were not annulled by the Vienna Court, and which have not been attacked by Norsolor during the present proceedings, since the reliance by that company on Art. 1028(1) of the old Code of Civil Procedure was directed only at point III of the award, that is, the determination by the arbitrators of the principle of liability incurred as a result of the breach of the contract, and the assessment of the damage resulting from that breach;

Considering that the annulment granted by the Vienna Court and its implications for the present proceedings render moot the contention of the Pabalk company that the enforcing judge would lack jurisdiction to adjudicate 'on a ground involving the wrongful interpretation by the arbitrators of their powers' since any such contention on the part of the appellee exclusively concerns the decision of the arbitrators as to the breach of the contract (point III of the award).

On the additional claims made by the Pabalk company in their submissions of 26 October 1981

Considering that the claim for damages for abuse of process, which was instituted by the unsuccessful appellee, must be rejected;

Considering that the Pabalk Company has requested that the amount awarded it by the arbitral tribunal should bear interest at the rate under French law starting from the date of the enforcement order;

Considering that this claim must be rejected as to the sum of FFr 800,000 mentioned in point III of the award, the enforcement of which is refused for the reasons set out above;

Considering as to the other amounts awarded to the appellant, that it should first be noted that those set out in point I of the award were fixed by the arbitrators at an annual rate of interest of 6 per cent from 1 April 1977;

That, moreover, interest not expressly granted by the arbitral tribunal cannot run from the date of the enforcement order, in which the President of the Court granting it confined himself to declaring that the award as rendered by the arbitrators was enforceable;

That it is up to the Pabalk company, if it wants to start interest running at the statutory rate as it thinks it has a right to do, to summon Norsolor, if it has not already done so, to pay in accordance with the conditions set out in Art. 1153 of the Civil Code.

That the appellant company must, as a result, fail in its additional claims.

## SUPREME COURT, 9 OCTOBER 1984

Considering jointly Art. VII of the Convention on the Recognition and Enforcement of Foreign Arbitral Awards, signed in New York on 10 June 1958, and Art. 12 of the New Code of Civil procedure.

Whereas, according to Art. VII of the New York Convention, the Convention does not deprive any interested party of any right he may have to avail himself of an arbitral award in the manner and to the extent allowed by law or the treaties of the country where such award is sought to be relied upon; as a result, the judge cannot refuse enforcement when his own national legal system permits it, and, by virtue of

Art. 12 of the New Code of Civil Procedure, he should, even *ex officio*, research the matter if such is the case.

Whereas Pabalk Ticaret Limited Sirketi (Pabalk), a Turkish company incorporated in Turkey, and Ugilor, a company incorporated in France, which has since become Norsolor, were parties to an agency agreement which contained an arbitration clause referring to the Rules of the Court of Arbitration of the International Chamber of Commerce (ICC) and in particular to Art. 13 of these Rules, prescribing that in the absence of any indication by the parties as to the applicable law, the arbitrators shall apply the law designated as the proper law by the rule of conflict which they deem appropriate, it being specified that they shall take account of the provisions of the contract and the relevant trade usages.

Whereas, Ugilor having terminated the agreement, Pabalk resorted to the Court of Arbitration of the ICC on 1 April 1977, and the Court of Arbitration determined that arbitration was to take place in Vienna, Austria.

Whereas in their award rendered on 26 October 1979, the arbitrators stated that, faced with the difficulty of choosing a national law, the application of which is sufficiently compelling, it was appropriate, given the international nature of the agreement, to leave aside any compelling reference to a specific legal system, be it Turkish or French, and to apply the international *lex mercatoria*, of which one of the fundamental principles is that of good faith which must govern the formation and performance of contracts.

Whereas the arbitral tribunal found that the termination of the agreement was attributable to Ugilor and that Ugilor's conduct caused unjustified damages to Pabalk, which equity required to be compensated.

Whereas this award, in its four-points decisional part, ordered Norsolor to pay various sums to Pabalk.

Whereas the award was held enforceable in France by an order dated 4 February 1980 of the President of the Court of First Instance of Paris, which Norsolor sought to attack on the basis of Art. 1028 of the Code of Civil Procedure, since repealed but nonetheless applicable here, claiming that the arbitrators had acted as *amiables compositeurs* and thus had exceeded the limits of their authority.

Whereas by judgment dated 4 March 1981 the Court of First Instance [in full] rejected the demand that the enforcement be retracted.

Whereas, in amending this decision and retracting the order in which it granted enforcement of point III and IV of the arbitral award, the judgment under attack applied Art. V(1)(e), of the New York Convention, ratified both by Austria and France, and according to which the recognition and enforcement of an award would be refused only if the award had been set aside by a competent authority of the country in which, or under the law of which, that award was made, and the judgment under attack relied on the fact that these points III and IV of the decisional part of the award had been set aside by a decision dated 29 January 1982 of the Vienna Court of Appeal on the ground that the arbitral tribunal, in violation of Art. 13 of the Rules for the ICC Court of Arbitration, had not determined the national law applicable and limited themselves to refer to international *lex mercatoria*, a 'world law of questionable validity'.

Whereas by ruling in this manner, where a Court of Appeal had a duty to determine, even *ex officio*, if French law would not allow Pabalk to avail itself of the award at stake, the Court of Appeal violated the above-mentioned provisions.

For these reasons we reverse and set aside the decision rendered 19 November 1982 by the Court of Appeal in Paris and send the case to the Court of Appeals of Amiens. . ."

\*       \*       \*

B.       *Compania Valenciana de Cementos Portland S.A. v. Primary Coal, Inc.*, 16 YEARBOOK OF COMMERCIAL ARBITRATION 142 (1991).

[Decision of Paris Court of Appeal, introduced and excerpted in English.]

Valenciana and Primary concluded several contracts, under which Primary was to deliver certain quantities of South African coal to Valenciana's cement plant in Spain for a period of three years. One of the contracts, dated 8 January 1985, contained an ICC arbitration clause.

A dispute arose concerning the execution of the contracts, and was referred to ICC arbitration. The parties signed the Terms of Reference on 3 May 1988.

On 1 September 1988, the sole arbitrator rendered a partial award on the law applicable to the dispute, holding that the dispute would be solved according to the usages of international trade, *i.e.*, *lex mercatoria*. The award is published, in French in Revue de l'arbitrage (1990) pp. 701-712.

Valenciana sought to have the partial award set aside (*recours en annulation*) under Art. 1502(3) and (4) of the New Code of Civil Procedure.

The Court of Appeal of Paris rejected the petition on the following grounds.

*Excerpt*

[With the first ground], it is contended that the arbitrator exceeded the terms of his reference, as defined in the Terms of Reference signed on 3 May 1988. He allegedly failed to choose a conflict of laws rule in order to determine the law applicable to the dispute — while he is deemed to do so under the ICC Rules — and did not explain the appropriateness of *lex mercatoria* — also merely defined as trade usages — with respect to the nature of the dispute (Art. 1502(3)).

The Terms of Reference of 3 May 1988 provide under the heading procedural law . . . that the arbitrator apply, apart from the ICC Arbitration Rules, the provisions of the New CCP applicable to international arbitration.

As far as the law applicable to substance is concerned . . . the Terms of Reference provide that 'if the law applicable to the solution of a dispute between the parties is not indicated in the contract or in any document of an earlier date than this arbitration . . . the law applicable to substance shall be determined by a partial award.'

Art. 13 of the ICC Arbitration Rules, to which the Terms of Reference refer, provides that if the parties have not indicated the applicable law — as is the case here — the arbitrator applies the law designated by the rule of conflict which he deems appropriate, taking into account in all cases the provisions of the contract and the usages of trade.

According to Art. 1496 New CCP, in the present case the arbitrator must decide the dispute according to the rules which he deems appropriate, taking into account in all cases the usages of trade.

In order to decide in this case that *lex mercatoria* was the most appropriate law — being, in the award's own words . . . the body of rules and principles consecrated as rules of law in international trade — the arbitrator first examined and rejected as insufficient the objective connecting factors arising under the two national laws which could be deemed to be applicable, i.e., Spanish law and the law of the State of New York. He then interpreted the tacit intention of the parties and rendered a final decision that they had intended to exclude the application of both Spanish law and the law of the State of New York and even of English law in general.

The law applicable to substance is determined according to rules of conflict.

According to the above-mentioned ICC Rules, in the case at hand the arbitrator was not required to make use of a conflict rule belonging to a given legal system in order to determine the law applicable to substance, but was free to refer to the principles governing this matter.

The arbitrator applied these principles and determined the most characteristic factor connecting the dispute to a body of rules of substantive law, taking into account the nature of the dispute. He examined the connecting factors invoked, rendered a final decision that none of them justified the application of a [national] law, and decided to apply the body of principles and trade usages called *lex mercatoria*, *i.e.*, international norms which can apply to the solution of such a dispute in the absence of a determined [national] jurisdiction.

By so deciding, the arbitrator conformed to his terms of reference. This [first] ground must be rejected.

[With the second ground], it is contended that the arbitrator failed to respect the principle of adversarial process (principe de la contradiction), by deciding ex officio to apply *lex mercatoria* without hearing the parties (Art. 1502(4)).

It appears from the award . . . and from the documents of the arbitral proceedings that Primary subsidiary invoked the applicability of *lex mercatoria* to the substance of the dispute . . . and that in its reply . . . Valenciana implicitly rejected this applicability. . . .

Hence, the issue of the application of *lex mercatoria* to the dispute was raised during the proceedings and the principle of adversarial process has been respected. This ground must be rejected.

*       *       *

C.      *Deutsche Schachtbau-und Tiefbohrgesellschaft m.b.H. v. Ras Al Khaimah Nat'l Oil Co. and Shell Int'l Petroleum Co., Ltd.*, 2 Lloyd's Rep. 246, 248-54 (1987), *rev'd on other grounds*, 2 Lloyd's Rep. 293 (1988).

The Geneva award is a "Convention Award" within the meaning of the Arbitration Act 1975, being an award made in pursuance of an arbitration agreement in the territory of a State, other than the United Kingdom, namely Switzerland, which is a party to the New York Convention on the Recognition and Enforcement of Foreign Arbitral Awards. It follows that it is enforceable in England either by action or under Sect. 26 of the Arbitration Act 1950 and that such enforcement is mandatory, save in the exceptional cases listed in Sect. 5 of the 1975 Act.

.     .     .

[Counsel] for Rakoil takes a number of points which can be consolidated under five heads:

(a)      Is the arbitration agreement subject to the law of Ras Al Khaimah and void under that law?

(b)      Can Rakoil rely upon the decision of the court of Ras Al Khaimah without regard to English rules on the recognition of foreign judgments?

(c)      Did the award exceed the scope of the submission and, if so, can enforcement be refused in whole or in part (sub-ss. (2)(d) and (4) of s. 5 of the Arbitration Act, 1975)?

(d)      Would it be contrary to public policy to enforce the award?

(e)      Are the answers to these questions so clear that there ought to be summary  judgment, as contrasted with leaving D.S.T. to sue on the award?

*The proper law of the arbitration agreement*

It is common ground that this falls to be ascertained by the application of the English rules for the resolution of conflict of laws, since the instant proceedings are in the English courts.

The agreement to arbitrate is contained in art. XXI of the contract and is in the  following terms:

1      All disputes arising in connection with the interpretation or application of this  Agreement shall be finally settled under the Rules of Conciliation and Arbitration of the International Chamber of Commerce by three arbitrators appointed in accordance with the Rules.

2      The arbitration shall be held in Geneva, Switzerland and shall be conducted in the English language.

[Counsel for Rakoil] submits that the proper law of this agreement to arbitrate is that which applies to the wider (substantive) agreement in which it is contained and that, applying the rule that, in the absence of indications of some different choice by the parties, the proper law of a contract is that system of law with which the transaction has the closest and most real connection, the relevant law is that of Ras Al Khaimah (*Compagnie d'Armement Maritime v. Compagnie Tunisienne de Navigation S.A.*, [1970] 2 Lloyd's Rep. 99, [1971] A.C. 572).

[Counsel] appearing for D.S.T., however, rightly points out that an arbitration agreement constitutes a self-contained contract collateral or ancillary to the substantive agreement (*Bremer Vulkan Schiffbau und Maschinenfabrik v. South India Shipping Corporation Ltd.*, [1981] 1 Lloyd's Rep. 253; [1981] A.C. 909) and that it need not be governed by the same law as that agreement (*Hamlyn & Co. v. Talisker Distillery,* [1894] A.C. 202, and *Black Clawson International Ltd. v. Papierwerke Waldhof-Aschaffenburg A.G.*, [1981] 2 Lloyd's Rep. 446). Furthermore, the rules for the ICC court of arbitration of which the parties must be deemed to have been aware, contemplate by art. 8.4 that the arbitrator—

> . . . shall not cease to have jurisdiction by reason of any claim that the contract is null  and void or allegation that it is inexistent provided that he upholds the validity of the agreement to arbitrate. He shall continue to have jurisdiction, even though the contract itself may be inexistent or null and void, to determine the respective rights of the parties and to adjudicate their claims and pleas.

The intention of the parties that the agreement to arbitrate shall be an independent and collateral contract could not be more clearly indicated.

Looking at the arbitration agreement in isolation, there can only be one answer,  namely, that it is governed by Swiss law. Of course it is not permissible to do this and regard must be had to all the surrounding circumstances, including the proper law governing the substantive contract and to the fact that the contract was to be performed in Ras Al Khaimah. However, in view of the international character of the enterprise, it is far from self-evident that the substantive contract is governed by the law of Ras Al Khaimah. As is not unusual in the oil industry, it involved parties of differing nationalities, using United States dollars as the money of account, who have chosen a neutral forum for the resolution of disputes and may well be thought to have chosen a neutral law to govern their rights and liabilities. This probability becomes all the stronger when reference is made to art. 13.3 of the ICC Rules which provides that:

> The parties shall be free to determine the law to be applied by the arbitrator to the merits of the dispute. In the absence of any indication by the parties as to the applicable law, the arbitrator shall apply the law designated as the proper law by the rule of conflict which he deems appropriate.

This suggests that the parties intended to delegate to the arbitrators the choice of law governing the substantive contract, applying what they considered to be appropriate principles and, in the event, the arbitrators did not hold that the contract was governed by the law of Ras Al Khaimah.

Giving the fullest possible weight to any argument favouring the law of Ras Al Khaimah as the proper law of the substantive contract and to the fact that it was undoubtedly the law of the place of performance, I find myself in complete agreement with Mr. Justice Leggatt that the proper law of the arbitration is Swiss.

*Effect of the judgment of the Court of Ras Al Khaimah*

Once it is decided that the agreement to arbitrate is governed by Swiss law, the judgment becomes irrelevant to the validity of that agreement, whether the judgment is viewed as a judgment of a court of competent jurisdiction or as an expert opinion upon the law of Ras Al Khaimah. In terms of Swiss law, which is the only relevant law in the context of the validity of the arbitration agreement, the affidavit evidence of Professor Pierre Lalive is that the arbitration agreement is valid and that this validity is unaffected by any question as to the validity of the contract of which it forms part. This evidence stands uncontradicted. Furthermore, no application was made to cross-examine him on his affidavit.

The bringing of proceedings by Rakoil in the Court of Ras Al Khaimah was a breach of the arbitration agreement, whose scope was amply wide enough to cover all matters in dispute in those proceedings, and accordingly the judgment cannot be recognised or enforced. It follows that Mr. Justice Leggatt was right  to set aside the leave to serve the writ out of the jurisdiction and the Ras Al Khaimah judgment disappears from the scene.

*The scope of the award and of the arbitration agreement*

[Counsel for Rakoil] submits that the award deals with a difference or differences not contemplated by, or not falling within, the terms of the submission to arbitration or contains decisions on matters beyond the scope of the submission to arbitration and that it is not possible to separate such matters from those falling within the true scope of the agreement. Accordingly enforcement should be refused (sub-ss. (2)(d) and (4) of s. 5 of the Arbitration Act, 1975) or at the very least there should not be summary enforcement.

The claim in the arbitration was made by D.S.T. on its own behalf and as agent for and representative of a group of companies including a German company to which I will refer as "Deminex." Deminex, unlike the other companies in the group, does not appear to have been a party to the arbitration agreement. The award also mentioned a company called "Sea & Land" and notes that it had a contract with the Government of Ras Al Khaimah which had not been submitted to arbitration. It appears from the award that both Deminex and Sea & Land were members of a consortium of which D.S.T. was the leader.

The interest of Deminex was challenged in a letter to the Secretary General of the I.C.C. dated Apr. 5, 1979 from the English solicitors of Rakoil. That letter was brought to the attention of the arbitrators and is mentioned in the award. They were also aware that Sea & Land was not a party to the dispute and it is not apparent to me that D.S.T. was ever claiming on behalf of Sea & Land.

Rakoil has never denied the fact that D.S.T. was a party to the arbitration agreement and the award determines only the rights of D.S.T. and Rakoil inter se. It makes no award in favour of Deminex or Sea & Land and makes no determination of the rights of Deminex or Sea & Land against D.S.T.. If the arbitrators have erred in the amount awarded to D.S.T., because they have wrongly taken account of the interests of Deminex or Sea & Land, that is a matter which should have been the subject of a claim to relief from the Swiss Court. No such application has been made. The burden of proving any excess of jurisdiction lies on the person seeking to resist the enforcement of the award. In the light of the failure to apply to the Swiss Courts, of the evidence of Professor Pierre Lalive as to the wide powers of arbitrators under Swiss law, of the fact that the award is made solely in favour of D.S.T. and of the terms of the award itself from which it seems that the arbitrators have held that D.S.T. had independent rights as 'the    Operator', I am not satisfied that there has been any excess of jurisdiction. This objection therefore fails.

*Public policy in relation to the enforcement of the award*

In pursuance of their duty under art. 13.3 of the I.C.C. rules, the arbitrators determined that the proper law governing the substantive obligations of the parties was "internationally accepted principles of law governing contractual relations". The arbitrators prefaced this decision with the following statement:

The arbitration tribunal holds that:

The Concession Agreement, the Assignment Agreement and the 1976 Operating Agreement are contracts between, on the one hand, a number of companies organised under various laws, and, on the other hand, a State respectively a company which is actually an agency of such state.

Reference either to the law of any one of the companies, or of such State, or of the State on whose territory one or several of these contracts were entered into, may seem inappropriate, for several reasons.

The Arbitration Tribunal will refer to what has become common practice in international arbitrations particularly in the field of oil drilling concessions, and especially to arbitrations located in Switzerland. Indeed, this practice, which must have been known to the parties, should be regarded as representing their implicit will. Reference is made in particular to the leading cases of *Sapphire International Petroleum Ltd. v. National Iranian Oil Company* (International Law Reports 1967, 136ff), *Texaco Overseas Petroleum Company v. The Government of the Libyan Arab Republic* (International Law Reports 1979, 389ff). . . .

[Counsel for Rakoil] submits that it would be contrary to English public policy to enforce an award which holds that the rights and obligations of the parties are to be determined, not on the basis of any particular national law, but upon some unspecified, and possibly ill defined, internationally accepted principles of law.

.    .    .

In my judgment there are three questions which the court has to ask itself when confronted with a clause which purports to provide that the rights of the parties shall be governed by some system of "law" which is not that of England or any other State or is a serious modification of such a law:

1.    *Did the parties intend to create legally enforceable rights and obligations?*

If they did not, there is no basis for the intervention of the coercive power of the State to give effect to those "rights and obligations." An intention not to create legally enforceable rights and obligations may be expressed — "this agreement is binding in honour only" — or it may be implied from the relationship between the parties or from the fact that the agreed criteria for the determination of the parties' rights and obligations are too vague or idiosyncratic to have been intended as a basis for the creation of such rights and obligations.

.    .    .

3.    *Would it be contrary to public policy to enforce the award, using the coercive powers of the State?*

Consideration of public policy can never be exhaustively defined, but they should be approached with extreme caution. As Mr. Justice Burrough remarked in *Richardson v. Mellish* (1824) 2 Bing. 229

at p. 252 "It is never argued at all but when other points fail." It has to be shown that there is some element of illegality or that the enforcement of the award would be clearly injurious to the public good or, possibly, that enforcement would be wholly offensive to the ordinary reasonable and fully informed member of the public on whose behalf the powers of the State are exercised.

Asking myself these questions, I am left in no doubt that the parties intended to create legally enforceable rights and liabilities and that the enforcement of the award would not be contrary to public policy. That only leaves the question of whether the agreement has the requisite degree of certainty. By choosing to arbitrate under the Rules of the ICC and, in particular, art. 13.3, the parties have left proper law to be decided by the arbitrators and have not in terms confined the choice to national systems of law. I can see no basis for concluding that the arbitrators' choice of proper law — a common denominator of principles underlying the laws of the various nations governing contractual relations — is outwith the scope of the choice which the parties left to the arbitrators.

                    *       *       *

D.      Lord Justice Mustill, *The New Lex Mercatoria: The First Twenty-Five Years*, 4 ARB. INT'L 86, 108 (1988).

[The *Deutsche Schachtbau-und Tiefbohrgesellschaft* case] is an important case for an English lawyer, as regards both the recognition by the court of a doctrine of *competenz competenz* applicable under the *lex fori*, and also the application of a narrow view of English public policy. The significance so far as regards the *lex mercatoria* is, however, substantially less than might at first sight appear. The starting-point of the judgment was a decision that the agreement to arbitrate was governed by the law of Switzerland. Since the oil company did not participate in the arbitration, there had been no contest on the propriety of a choice of general principles under that law. The company had not sought to set the award aside in Switzerland, nor did it offer any evidence to contradict the expert evidence of Swiss law tendered by the claimants to the effect that the general principles were a valid choice under the ICC choice of law clause. Thus, the English court could accept that the decision to apply the general principles was a permissible performance of the arbitrators' mandate under the choice of law clause according to both the *lex fori* and the *lex causae*. Against this background there was nothing in English public policy to preclude enforcement of the award in England.

Thus far, the import of the decision is clear, and it must greatly hearten the mercatorists. The wider implications, so far as concerns English law, will require careful analysis. As an immediate reaction, the present author would venture the following tentative observations.

(i) The case was not concerned with transnationalism. The claimant's evidence proceeded on the assumption that Swiss law was the *lex causae*. Nobody suggested that there was no national *lex causae*.

(ii) Although the judgment contains a discussion of two English decisions on the effect on a contract of including various types of 'general principles' clauses, this was probably obiter, since (a) there was no such clause in the contract, (b) English law was neither the *lex causae*, the *lex fori*, nor the 'putative proper law,' and (c) the issue had not been argued.

(iii) The judgment did not address the question whether, under English law, when a contract does not contain any explicit choice of the 'general principles' the arbitrators can validly purport to apply them. This extremely important question did not arise in the Court of Appeal, and could not have been decided without reference to certain reported cases, not cited in the judgment.

\*   \*   \*

If the worldwide trend is not to review arbitral awards for errors of substantive law, why all the fuss about *lex mercatoria*? If an award is to be upheld no matter how it misapplied the national law it declares to be applicable, why should another award — no matter how cogently reasoned, or how consistent in its outcome under any conceivably relevant national law — be refused recognition only because it purported to apply anational or transnational norms?

If cases like those excerpted above suggest that enforcement jurisdictions can in fact live with awards applying *lex mercatoria*, the question remains whether parties are well-advised to opt for such general principles when specifying the law applicable to their contract. There is little evidence that the drafters of international contracts in fact explicitly stipulate *lex mercatoria* as the exclusive governing law. This may have to do with the issue of predictability, which is especially troublesome with respect to an alleged body of law which is fragmentary, mostly incapable of being restated in any but the most general and abstract terms. Lord Justice Mustill, now of the House of Lords, is credited with having made the best effort at answering in specific terms the question "what are the rules of the *lex mercatoria*," which he did as follows:

> Plainly, it would be of great practical importance to the hypothetical adviser to know whether in any published work, and particularly in any published award, the view had been expressed that a particular rule forms part of the *lex mercatoria*. Setting aside for a moment the difficulties of time and access to the literature which the adviser would be likely to encounter, it seems that he would be able to put together a list somewhat on the following lines, as representing a tolerably complete account of the rules which are said to constitute the *lex mercatoria* in its present form.

> 1.    A general principle that contracts should *prima facie* be enforced to their terms: *pacta sunt servanda*. The emphasis given to this maxim in the literature suggests that it is regarded, not so much as one of the rules of the *lex mercatoria*, but as the fundamental principle of the entire system.

> 2.    The first general principle is qualified at least in respect of certain long-term contracts, by an exception akin to *rebus sic stantibus*. The interaction of the

principle and the exception has yet to be fully worked out.

3. The first general principle may also be subject to the concept of *abus de droit*, and to a rule that unfair and unconscionable contracts and clauses should not be enforced.

4. There may be a doctrine of *culpa in contrahendo*.

5. A contract should be performed in good faith.

6. A contract obtained by bribes or other dishonest means is void, or at least unenforceable. So too if the contract creates a fictitious transaction designed to achieve an illegal object.

7. A State entity cannot be permitted to evade the enforcement of its obligations by denying its own capacity to make a binding agreement to arbitrate, or by asserting that the agreement is unenforceable for want of procedural formalities to which the entity is subject.

8. The controlling interest of a group of companies is regarded as contracting on behalf of all members of the group, at least so far as concerns an agreement to arbitrate.

9. If unforeseen difficulties intervene in the performance of a contract, the parties should negotiate in good faith to overcome them, even if the contract contains no revision clause.

10. 'Gold clause' agreements are valid and enforceable. Perhaps in some cases either a gold clause or a 'hardship' revision clause may be implied.

11. One party is entitled to treat itself as discharged from its obligations if the other has committed a breach, but only if the breach is substantial.

12.   No party can be allowed by its own act to bring about a non-performance of a condition precedent to its own obligation.

13.   A tribunal is not bound by the characterisation of the contract ascribed to it by the parties.

14.   Damages for breach of contract are limited to the forseeable consequences of the breach.

15.   A party which has suffered a breach of contract must take reasonable steps to mitigate its loss.

16.   Damages for non-delivery are calculated by reference to the market price of the goods and the price at which the buyer has purchased equivalent goods in replacement.

17.   A party must act promptly to enforce its rights, on pain of losing them by waiver. This may be an instance of a more general rule, that each party must act in a diligent and practical manner to safeguard its own interests.

18.   A debtor may in certain circumstances set off his own cross-claims to extinguish or diminish his liability to the creditor.

19.   Contracts should be construed according to the principle *ut res magis valeat quam pereat*.

20.   Failure by one party to respond to a letter written to it by the other is regarded as evidence of assent on its terms.

This list, incomplete as it may be, seems rather a modest haul for 25 years of international arbitration. The reader must form his own conclusions. The following comments may, however, suggest themselves.

First, the reported awards do not in all cases seem to sustain the wealth of commentary based upon them. By no means all of them make explicit reference to the *lex mercatoria* as an independent system of law. Those instances in which reference is made to commercial usage are equally explicable on the ground that the usage controlled the meaning of the contract, an approach which is just as consistent with national as with anational legal systems. Second, it may be said that 'whilst there can be found an abundance of sweeping formulation of legal principles, these are of little use for legal analysis.' Third, where the rules are expressed more specifically, they cannot in every case be derived from any world-wide generalisation of national laws.

### Notes and Questions

1. Does the state have an interest in which law applies in a private dispute, especially one between foreigners?

2. How useful are abstract restatements of the rules of *lex mercatoria* in deciding concrete issues? While a rule such as Mustill's item 7 or item 16 may be concrete enough, how would one synthesize paragraphs 1 to 16?

3. May *lex mercatoria* be applied in a supplementary fashion, as evidence of international trade practices relevant to the interpretation of contracts?

E.    W. LAURENCE CRAIG, ET AL., INTERNATIONAL CHAMBER OF COMMERCE ARBITRATION 614-19 (2d ed. 1990).

*Lex mercatoria* in this modest sense may thus be seen essentially as an expansion of the notion of usages to encompass particular contracts whose specificity is that they are international. According to this view, the interpretation of international contracts requires recognition of the transnational context of the underlying transactions. The practical justification is not difficult to grasp. If international trade is to be facilitated, the regime of international contracts should not be a minefield of hidden provisions of national law. It is easy to say that no one should enter into a contract governed by, say, Finnish or Korean law without getting reliable and comprehensive legal advice, but if one adopts a position of absolute rigidity in this respect one is furthering the cause of lawyers rather than that of commerce. To do so would result in a situation where parties would view any foray into the international field as high adventure, particularly where the governing law is not specified in the contract. And as for parties who are active in a great number of countries, such as the licensor of widely desired technology, is it not healthy to start with the postulate that detailed standard contracts, developed over years of experience in various jurisdictions, should if at all possible be interpreted in a uniform manner, even though the judges of countries X, Y, and Z might have viewed the contracts differently if they had been concluded as a matter of purely domestic commercial relations between fellow nationals?

It would appear particularly appropriate to avoid unexpected peculiarities of a national law in the case where parties have not chosen the applicable law. In such situation, one may often reasonably conclude that the parties have made a "negative choice." Each party proposed its own law, but each proposal was rejected; and finally neither law was stipulated. An arbitrator who then gives one of those laws primacy is in a sense doing just what the parties resolved should not be done. Another situation where the dominance of any national law seems doubtful is that of a contract to be performed in several countries.

National laws often give the judge (and by extension the arbitrator who may be applying them) wide powers to interpret contractual provisions and to apply them to the fact pattern at hand. When an international arbitrator exercises that authority, for example to establish the effect of an amendment on a prior contract or to determine whether an alleged event of force majeure was truly unavoidable, he does so (in conformity with whatever national law may be relevant) in light of all the circumstances. When those circumstances pertain to an international transaction, involving foreign states, foreign law, foreign languages, and foreign currencies — not to mention foreigners — a type of jurisprudence is generated, by repeated decisions dealing with similar transnational fact patterns, which by definition cannot be derived from a purely national context. This, in the present authors' opinion, is a convincing rationale for the reference in ICC awards to arbitral precedents.

\*   \*   \*

F.    *Interim Award in ICC Case 4131*, 7 YEARBOOK OF COMMERCIAL ARBITRATION 131, 132-33, 135-37 (1982).

In 1965, DOW CHEMICAL (Venezuela) entered into a contract with the French Company Boussois-Isolation, whose rights and obligations were subsequently assigned to ISOVER SAINT GOBAIN, for the distribution in France of thermal isolation equipment.    DOW

CHEMICAL (Venezuela) itself subsequently assigned the contract to DOW CHEMICAL A.G. (Claimant no. 3), a subsidiary of DOW CHEMICAL COMPANY (Claimant no. 1).

In 1968, a second distribution agreement was entered into by DOW CHEMICAL EUROPE (Claimant no. 4), a subsidiary of DOW CHEMICAL A.G., with three other companies (including Boussois-Isolation) whose rights and obligations were later assigned to ISOVER SAINT GOBAIN (Defendant) for the distribution of essentially the same products in France.

Both the 1965 and the 1968 agreements, which contained ICC arbitration clauses, provided that deliveries could be made by DOW CHEMICAL FRANCE or any other subsidiary of the DOW CHEMICAL COMPANY. DOW CHEMICAL FRANCE did in fact effectuate the deliveries contemplated in the contracts.

Several actions (not described in the interim award) were brought before French courts against companies of the DOW CHEMICAL Group relating to difficulties in connection with one of the products ("Roofmate").

On the basis of the arbitration clause contained in the contracts with DOW CHEMICAL A.G. and DOW CHEMICAL EUROPE (Claimants no. 3 and 4) the Claimants instituted arbitral proceedings against Defendant alleging that Defendant alone was liable for damages resulting from the use of Roofmate in France.

Defendant raised two preliminary objections, formulated as follows in the Terms of Reference signed by the parties.

(1)     Does the arbitral tribunal have competence to render an award between DOW CHEMICAL FRANCE and DOW CHEMICAL COMPANY on the one hand and ISOVER SAINT GOBAIN on the other?

(2)     In case the arbitral tribunal has no jurisdiction in respect of DOW CHEMICAL FRANCE and DOW CHEMICAL COMPANY (the first two Claimants), should it then not reject the claim of DOW CHEMICAL A.G. and DOW CHEMICAL EUROPE (the Claimants under 3 and 4) for reasons of lack of

direct interest in the cause of action? (In French: à raison de ce qu'elles invoquent un préjudice qui ne serait qu'éventuel?)

It was decided at a preparatory hearing that the arbitral tribunal would first of all render an interim award on these two questions.

> That it thus appears, as was the case with respect to the conclusion and performance of the distribution agreements, that DOW CHEMICAL FRANCE played an essential role in the termination of the 1968 contract, which had been substituted for the 1965 contract; that all of these factors permit the conclusion that DOW CHEMICAL FRANCE was a party to each of these contracts and, consequently, to the arbitration clauses they contained;

> That the same conclusion should be reached with respect to DOW CHEMICAL COMPANY (USA) by reason of its ownership of the trademarks under which the products were marketed, and its absolute control over those of its subsidiaries that were directly involved, or could under the contracts have become involved in the conclusion, performance, or termination of the litigious distribution agreements.

> Considering that the Defendant adopted the same position in its brief of 1 July 1980 before the Court of Appeal of Paris, in support of its motion for the compulsory joinder of inter alia DOW CHEMICAL COMPANY (USA)

> That the Defendant there in fact wrote as follows:

>> 'Whereas DOW CHEMICAL COMPANY, owner of the patents and organizer of the manufacturing and distribution of Roofmate, decided and conceived the modalities of the manufacturing and distribution of said product, thus engaging its direct liability.' (Translated from French - Gen. Ed.)

Considering that in the circumstances of this case, the application of the arbitration clauses to DOW CHEMICAL COMPANY (USA) may also be justified, as we shall now show, by the fact that the contracts containing these clauses concern, in the context of a group of companies, a parent company and certain of its subsidiaries. The same fact could justify, if necessary, the application of the arbitration clause to DOW CHEMICAL FRANCE.

## D.  The Group of Companies

Considering that it is indisputable — and in fact not disputed — that DOW CHEMICAL COMPANY (USA) has and exercises absolute control over its subsidiaries having either signed the relevant contracts or, like DOW CHEMICAL FRANCE, effectively and individually participated in their conclusion, their performance, and their termination;

Considering that irrespective of the distinct juridical identity of each of its members, a group of companies constitutes one and the same economic reality (*une réalité économique unique*) of which the arbitral tribunal should take account when it rules on its own jurisdiction subject to Article 13 (1955 version) or Article 8 (1975 version) of the ICC Rules.

Considering, in particular, that the arbitration clause expressly accepted by certain of the companies of the group should bind the other companies which, by virtue of their role in the conclusion, performance, or termination of the contracts containing said clauses, and in accordance with the mutual intention of all parties to the proceedings, appear to have been veritable parties to these contracts or to have been principally concerned by them and the disputes to which they may give rise.

Considering that ICC arbitral tribunals already pronounced themselves to this effect (see the awards Case No. 2375 of 1975, *Journal du droit international* 1976.973; and in Case No. 1434 of 1975, *id* at 978).

The decisions of these tribunals progressively create caselaw [sic] which should be taken into account, because it draws conclusions from economic reality and conforms to the needs of international commerce, to which rules specific to international arbitration, themselves successively elaborated should respond.

Considering that it is true that in another award (Case No. 2138 of 1974, *Journal du droit international* 1975.934) the arbitral tribunal refused to extend an arbitration clause signed by one company to another company of the same group. However, in so doing it based itself on the factor 'that it was not established that Company X' (which the tribunal had determined was neither a signatory nor a party to the contract) 'would have accepted the arbitration clause if it had signed the contract directly.'

Considering that in the absence of such a showing, the tribunal did not allow application of the arbitration clause; but that in the present case, the circumstances and the documents analyzed above show that such application conforms to the mutual intent of the parties.

That it is not without interest to recall that an American arbitral tribunal recently reached a similar result, referring to U.S. national court decisions and observing that 'it is neither sensible nor practical to exclude (from the arbitral jurisdiction) the claims of companies who have an interest in the venture and who are members of the same corporate family.' (Society of Maritime Arbitrators, Inc., New York, Award Service, Fourth Distribution, Fiscal Year 6/1/80-5/31/81, Awards no. 1486-1514 inclusive. Partial Final Award No. 1510, 28 November 1980, VII YEARBOOK COMMERCIAL ARBITRATION, American Awards, p. 151 (1982).)

Considering finally that in a matter directly connected with the issues litigated in the present arbitration, the Court of Appeal of Paris on 5 February 1982 held that it lacked jurisdiction to hear ISOVER SAINT GOBAIN's motion for the compulsory joinder of not only DOW CHEMICAL EUROPE (which signed the 1968 distribution contract), but also DOW CHEMICAL COMPANY (USA) and (referred) ISOVER SAINT GOBAIN cannot dispute the fact that the litigation is pending and that its claims against DOW COMPANY and DOW EUROPE in their relations inter se flow directly from the two contracts (of 1965 and 1968);

It is true that by the same decision the Court reached a decision on the merits as regards DOW CHEMICAL FRANCE. However, in that case, the said company had been sued on the grounds of quasi-tortious liability, and did not invoke the arbitration clauses and did not contest jurisdiction.

In conclusion it is appropriate for the tribunal to assume jurisdiction over the claim brought not only by DOW CHEMICAL AG (Zürich) and DOW CHEMICAL EUROPE, but also by DOW CHEMICAL COMPANY (USA) and DOW CHEMICAL FRANCE.

\*　　\*　　\*

G.　　Andreas F. Lowenfeld, *Lex Mercatoria: An Arbitrator's View*, 6 ARB. INT'L 133, 137-40 (1990).

My own view of *lex mercatoria* is somewhat different from those both of its critics and of its proponents, though closer to the latter. It may be useful to begin with some illustrations, both from my own experience and from that of others, and then attempt to resume the doctrinal debate.

First, Lando gives the illustration of the Danish seller who has sold goods to a German buyer but delivered them after the last date specified. Under Article 27 of the Scandinavian Sale of Goods Act as in force in Denmark, a buyer who seeks to make a claim arising out of late delivery must give notice immediately on arrival of the goods. No such rule applies in Germany or (so far as appears) in other nations. An arbitral tribunal faced with a claim based on late delivery and no law designated in the contract should not devote its energies to the question of whether seller's law (Danish) or buyer's law (German) applies to the controversy: The Scandinavian rule is an internal one, not fit for international sales. Whether Danish or German law applies to other aspects of the contract, the German buyer should not be defeated by failure to give immediate notice, as long as he has complied with the general commercial rule requiring notice within a reasonable period of time. Use of *lex mercatoria* yields the correct solution: the German buyer prevails.

Confidence in the solution is here strengthened by the fact that the Vienna Convention on Contracts for the International Sale of Goods provides in Article 49(2)(a), that notice must be given within a reasonable time after the buyer has become aware that delivery has been made. But the case as posed by Lando is not one of the application of a treaty. At the time Lando was writing the Vienna Convention was not in effect for any country, and even today, when the Convention has entered into effect, it is not clear that it would be binding on the contract in question. Nevertheless jurists coming from different countries and sitting as arbitrators in Paris or Zurich or Geneva — or indeed in Copenhagen — can draw comfort and support from the fact that their understanding of international commercial law/practice is consistent with the United Nations Convention designed to reflect international consensus.

Secondly, a similar case, in which I served as one of the arbitrators, may serve further to illustrate the uses of *lex mercatoria*, though the case is more complicated and perhaps more controversial. The claimant was a French company which asserted that it had entered into a contract with an Austrian company for the long-term supply of a commodity produced in a developing country. It was clear that there had been no performance, both the Austrian company, the respondent, maintained that the contract had not been validly concluded, and that even if it had been, the formalities required to constitute a valid agreement to arbitrate had not been complied with. The document asserted to embody the contract — some twenty pages of detailed clauses negotiated over several months — had been signed at a hotel in New York by the two principal negotiators, Mr. A for the claimant and Mr. B for the respondent. The respondent, however, pointed out that under Austrian law (at least Austrian internal law) an agent's power to bind a corporation depends on the corporate resolutions inscribed in the Commercial Register, and that Mr. B was listed in the Register as having only collective and not individual signing authority. The document stated that it was to be governed by New York law, and that any disputes that could not be resolved by negotiation were to be submitted to arbitration in Geneva under the rules of the ICC.

The claimant argued for application of New York law as the place of execution and the law chosen by the parties, pointing out that New York not only had no double signature requirement but also had a well developed doctrine of apparent authority. The respondent had two main arguments: first that the issue was one of capacity and that capacity of a corporation is determined by the law of the place of incorporation — here Austria; and second, that if the Austrian law were not applied directly by the arbitrators, it should be applied on the basis of the conflict of laws rules applicable at the seat of the arbitration, *i.e.*, Switzerland. The claimant and the respondent each produced an expert opinion on Austrian law, one showing the importance of Austria's rule on authority to bind a corporation, especially in the context of derogating from jurisdiction of the courts (*i.e.*, agreements to arbitrate), the other suggesting that the rule might not apply to international contracts entered into abroad. Both parties also produced expert opinions on Swiss law, one stating that under Swiss law the authority of a person to bind a corporation depended on the law of the corporation's *siège social*, the other stating that the rule with respect to inscriptions in the commercial register applied to domestic transactions — *i.e.*, between different cantons — but probably not to international transactions or to agreements to arbitrate governed by the New York Convention, which requires only that an agreement to arbitrate be in writing. It was also unclear from the expert reports whether Swiss law would regard the validity of the agreement to arbitrate as governed by the law of the chosen forum, here Geneva, or by the proper law of the contract, whatever that might be. Nor, of course, was it clear that the arbitrators should look to Swiss law for choice of law purposes — the ICC rules suggested the reverse.

Thus the dispute in its preliminary phase — long before issues such as excuse for non-performance, interpretation of the obligations undertaken, or duty to mitigate damages were addressed — could be governed by the law of three different states: New York, Austria and Switzerland, plus the conflict of laws rules of Switzerland or New York and a question of interpretation of the Austrian law.

As it happened, I do not know whether by coincidence or by design, two of the arbitrators were experts in conflict of laws, and we managed to find our way to what I believe was a principled and technically correct solution. I cannot be certain however, whether we decided first on the solution and then found a way to achieve it, or whether we set out on a truly unguided journey and ended up with the right result. It is fair to add that the arbitrators had heard testimony and had studied the prior relations of the parties, so that they had some feeling for the transaction beyond the abstract contract and conflict of laws issues they were required to decide.

My feeling is that wholly neutral principles of conflict of laws are an illusion, but that an understanding of reasonable behavior and expectations of major commercial enterprises can be defined with a fair degree of precision, focusing on such issues as the customs of the particular trade, justified expectations of the parties in the light of the prior and current communications between them, the obligation of good faith dealings, and evidence of reliance. Of course these concepts are not precise in the same way as the number of grams in a kilogram, but they are everywhere the stuff of contracts, the kinds of issues on which arbitrators, and judges, are competent to pass. The suggestion is that whether or not the two parties before the tribunal had concluded a contract could and probably should have been decided by reference to *lex mercatoria*, rather than by elaborate exercises in comparative conflict of laws.

### Notes and Questions

1. Does the last paragraph of the example Lowenfeld uses about the French and Austrian companies suggest that the arbitrators used *lex mercatoria* or simply applied principles of conflicts of laws?

2. The last pargraph also suggests that Lowenfeld believes that the same legal values underpin many different legal systems.  Discuss.

## VI.    CHOOSING ARBITRATION RULES

The proliferation of international commercial arbitral rules and institutions, each of which varies in some significant way from its competitors, means that parties and their lawyers contemplating arbitration, whether by insertion of a general arbitral clause in a contract or by special agreement, have opportunities to select rules and/or institutions which are favorable to them in the case at hand or which are at least even-handed as between the parties. A failure to consider this aspect of commercial arbitration may allow the other party to select rules and/or institutions which discriminate in its favor.

The following rule systems are embedded in an institutional structure, which supervises their implementation:

1.    The International Chamber of Commerce (ICC)
2.    The American Arbitration Association (AAA)
3.    The London Court of International Arbitration (LCIA)
4.    The International Centre for the Settlement of Investment Disputes (ICSID)
5.    The Arbitration Institute of the Stockholm Chamber of Commerce (SCC)

The following is a set of rules which is not embedded in a particular institution:

6.    The United Nations Commission on International Trade Law (UNCITRAL)

To better understand the differences between various forms of arbitration, so as to be able to select the form most advantageous to a client, a brief review of the major arbitral institutions may be helpful.

A.    THE INTERNATIONAL CHAMBER OF COMMERCE (ICC)

The International Court of Arbitration of the International Chamber of Commerce (ICC), was established in 1923. It is an integral part of the ICC which was set up in 1919, with headquarters in Paris, under the French Law of 1901 governing membership associations. The membership of the ICC is composed of national committees in some 60 states whose goal is to favor and promote world commerce. Since its inception, the ICC Court has handled business disputes of an international character. ICC arbitration is designed, according to its own promotional literature, to result in an arbitral award which, by virtue of its soundness in form and substance, will induce parties to honor it voluntarily while being able to withstand efforts to have it set aside by national courts.

Although the ICC Court and its Secretariat are headquartered in Paris, the ICC has no special links to any country or government. In an ICC arbitration, the arbitrators may be of any nationality, the arbitration proceedings may take place anywhere in the world, in any language agreed to by the parties. The Court of Arbitration itself is composed of members from about forty different countries, each member having a legal background and expertise in international business law and dispute resolution. The Secretariat of the Court is also composed of personnel from some ten different countries, speaking various languages. Nonetheless, the ICC has a decided European flavor.

The ICC Court of Arbitration does not itself conduct hearings or decide cases. Resolution of disputes is within the exclusive competence of the one or three arbitrators who hear the parties, assess the merits of the case and make the award. The Court simply supervises the arbitration conducted by tribunals set up in accordance with its rules. Its pertinent functions will be considered below.

### B.      THE AMERICAN ARBITRATION ASSOCIATION (AAA)

The American Arbitration Association (AAA) was founded on January 29, 1926, as a public service, non-profit, membership organization dedicated to the resolution of disputes of all kinds through the use of arbitration and other voluntary methods. It is incorporated under the Not-for-Profit Corporation Law of the State of New York and has its head office at 140 West 51st Street, in New York City.[65] The AAA's objectives are broadly spelled out in the purposes clause of its by-laws:

> The objectives of the Association are for the benefit and education of the general public and interested parties, to study, research, promote, establish and administer procedures for the resolution of disputes of all kinds through the use of arbitration, mediation, conciliation, negotiation, democratic elections and other voluntary procedures, together with such other objects and purposes as are set forth in the certificate of incorporation as consolidated and amended.

---

[65] There are also regional offices in over 20 major cities throughout the United States.

In addition to a broad educational program, the AAA concentrates its efforts on dispute resolution in the fields of labor relations, family disputes, insurance claims and even criminal cases. Commercial arbitration is only one, and by no means the most important, of the AAA's activities.

The AAA provides administrative services for arbitrating many different kinds of disputes at comparatively reasonable fees. In commercial arbitration cases, its main function is to appoint the sole arbitrator or third arbitrator and to organize the arbitration proceedings administratively. It does not decide cases itself. It simply supplies a list from which the parties mutually select their own arbitrators. Arbitration is conducted by specific rules and procedures which are considered below.

### C. THE LONDON COURT OF INTERNATIONAL ARBITRATION (LCIA)

The London Court of Arbitration (LCIA), one of the oldest arbitration bodies in the world, was established in 1892 on the initiative of the Corporation of the City of London. On inauguration in 1892, it was known as the London Chamber of Arbitration and adopted its current name in 1903. In 1986 the LCIA was incorporated as a company limited by guarantee under the control of a Board of Directors. These are all highly experienced in international arbitration and mostly drawn from the LCIA's three constituent bodies, with which it still maintains a formal link through a Joint Consultative Council (JCC) - the Corporation of the City of London, the London Chamber of Commerce and Industry and the Chartered Institute of Arbitrators.

The main function of the LCIA is to appoint arbitrators and to carry out the necessary administrative functions pertaining to the arbitrations. It provides rules, services and facilities for the settlement by arbitration of any dispute, commercial or otherwise, and wherever occurring, which may properly be submitted to arbitration. The international arbitration rules of the LCIA are designed for use under any legal system.

The LCIA has a panel of arbitrators from which appointments are made. The extensive and varied nature of the panel enables the Court to provide appropriate arbitrators for disputes of any magnitude and complexity ranging from small consumer claims to major international commercial disputes. Under the rules of the LCIA, appointment of arbitrators may be made by the President of the LCIA, the parties themselves or other appointing authorities, depending on the circumstances of the case involved.

### D.    THE INTERNATIONAL CENTRE FOR THE SETTLEMENT OF INVESTMENT DISPUTES (ICSID)

The International Center for the Settlement of Investment Disputes (ICSID) was established by the Washington Convention of 1965.[66] The United States is a party. ICSID is based at the principal office of the World Bank in Washington, D.C. It has full international legal personality.[67]

ICSID was established, *inter alia*, "to promote a climate of mutual confidence between states and investors that would be conducive to an increasing flow of resources to developing countries." ICSID promotes the settlement of investment disputes by means of conciliation and arbitration. Its jurisdiction is strictly circumscribed by the Convention: the parties must have agreed to submit their dispute to ICSID; the dispute must be between a Contracting State (or one of its subdivisions or agencies) and a national of another Contracting State, and it must be a legal dispute arising directly out of an "Investment,"[68] which is, itself, carefully defined.

Unless otherwise stated by the parties, prior consent to ICSID arbitration usually implies consent to arbitration as the exclusive remedy. Under the ICSID Convention, the award of an arbitration tribunal is final and binding on the parties.[69] In contrast to other forms of arbitration, ICSID awards are not subject to review by any

---

[66] Convention on the Settlement of Investment Disputes Between States and Nationals of Other States, Mar. 18, 1965, 575 U.N.T.S. 160 (1966) [hereinafter ICSID Convention].

[67] ICSID Convention, Art. 18.

[68] *Id.* at Art. 25.

[69] *Id.* at Art. 53.

national court.[70] ICSID maintains a panel of arbitrators and conciliators and exclusively applies its own rules to proceedings which it conducts.[71]

### E.    THE ARBITRATION INSTITUTE OF THE STOCKHOLM CHAMBER OF COMMERCE (SCC)

The Arbitration Institute of the Stockholm Chamber of Commerce (SCC Institute) is an organization within the Stockholm Chamber of Commerce created in 1917. The SCC Institute was officially organized in 1949 for the purpose of settling disputes associated with trade, industry and shipping.

The Institute is composed of a Secretariat and a Board of three members each appointed for a three-year period by the Executive Committee of the SCC. Of the three Board members, one (the chairman) is to be a judge having experience in disputes of a commercial or industrial nature, one is to be a practicing lawyer, and one is to be a person who enjoys the confidence of the business community.

The SCC Institute adopted revised rules (Rules of the Arbitration Institute of the Stockholm Chamber of Commerce) as of January 1, 1988 designed to take into account Sweden's increasing role as a neutral venue for international arbitration, particularly arbitrations involving East-West trade and commercial transactions with China. Pursuant to its Rules, it acts essentially as an appointing authority and does not administer arbitration in the same way as the ICC and the AAA. In addition to appointing arbitrators under its own Rules, it is willing to act as appointing authority under the UNCITRAL Rules.

---

[70] However, under Art. 52 of the ICSID Convention, there are a few grounds on which a party may seek annulment of an award. These include corruption on the part of a tribunal member, *excès du pouvoir* on the part of the tribunal, a failure to state the reasons on which the award is based, and a serious departure from a fundamental rule of procedure.

[71] In 1978, ICSID adopted the so-called "Additional Facility Rules." These Rules provide for the administration by ICSID of proceedings which fall outside the scope of the ICSID Convention, *e.g.*, because the dispute is not an investment dispute, or the State Party is not a Contracting State. However, since proceedings under the Additional Facility Rules are outside the purview of the ICSID Convention, they depend on national, rather than international, law for their efficacy.

The 1988 revision was adopted after a study of other modern institutional rules including those of the ICC (1975), UNCITRAL (1976), the LCIA (1985) and the AAA (Commercial Arbitration Rules) (1986). Amongst the changes made was the elimination of a provision of the previous rules that "[T]he Swedish law of arbitration shall apply with the additions and modifications stated in these Rules". It was thought that this reference was confusing to foreign parties and tended to overemphasize the role of Swedish procedural law. In fact, Swedish law permits the parties to agree on arbitral procedures to be followed, such as those set out in the SCC Rules, and only a very few mandatory provisions of arbitration law apply.

In addition to its functions under its own Rules as appointing authority, the SCC Institute arranges for secretarial and other assistance in connection with arbitrations and other hearings or meetings. The SCC Institute has increasingly been used as a major international arbitration center. This may be attributable to Sweden's claimed familiarity with and experience in the arbitration process, and perhaps in some cases, to its traditional foreign policy position of neutrality.

F.    THE UNITED NATIONS COMMISSION ON INTERNATIONAL TRADE LAW (UNCITRAL)

The United Nations Commission on International Trade Law (UNCITRAL) is not an arbitration institution but brief reference may be made to it in this context. UNCITRAL was established by the General Assembly in December, 1966 for "the progressive harmonization and unification of the law of international trade."[72] In addition to coordinating the work of organizations active in the international trade field, UNCITRAL also prepares and promotes the adoption of new conventions, laws and codification of international trade terms, customs, and practices. In the conduct of its work, UNCITRAL draws on the expertise and practical know-how of businessmen and lawyers, and cooperates with other international arbitration institutions, such as the ICC, the AAA and the International Council for Commercial Arbitration (ICCA).

---

[72] G.A. Res. 2205, 21 U.N. GAOR, Annex 3, U.N. Doc. A/6396 and (Add. 1&2) (1966), *reprinted in* 1 Y.B. U.N. COMM'N. INT'L. TRADE L. 65 (1968-70), U.N. Doc. A/CN.9/SER.A/1970.

Membership in UNCITRAL is restricted to states. The Commission maintains close links with other United Nations agencies such as the United Nations Conference on Trade and Development (UNCTAD). Since its creation in 1966, some of UNCITRAL's significant contributions to dispute resolution have been its adoption of Arbitration Rules in 1976,[73] Conciliation Rules in 1980,[74] Guidelines for Administering Arbitration under the UNCITRAL Arbitration Rules in 1982, and the Model Law on International Commercial Arbitration in 1985.[75]

## VII. SYSTEMATIC COMPARISON OF INSTITUTIONS AND RULE SYSTEMS

The nature of a contract, the type of contractual disputes likely to arise, and the sorts of interim and final remedies likely to be sought are factors which must be taken into account in selecting one of the available systems of rules. In some cases, political considerations may also play a role. For example, it has been reported that for years the People's Republic of China adamantly refused to use ICC Rules because the ICC is organized on the basis of national committees, one of which is Taiwan's. In comparing the relative advantages and disadvantages of each set of arbitral rules, the prudent lawyer must focus on the way in which each set of rules will interact with the unique components of the specific contract and the specific parties.

---

[73] U.N. Doc. Sales No. E.7 v. 6 (1977). The Arbitration Rules were drafted in consultation with leading arbitration experts from various states. Although designed for worldwide use in "*ad hoc* arbitration," the Rules are also applied in institutional arbitration. Various arbitration centers administer arbitrations under the UNCITRAL Arbitration Rules. Prominent among them is the AAA. The Rules have also been substantially adopted by the Inter-American Commercial Arbitration Commission and some Regional Arbitration centers established under the auspices of the Asian-African Legal Consultative Committee, such as Kuala Lumpur in Malaysia and Cairo in Egypt.

[74] U.N. Doc. A/35/17 (1980). These Rules are designed to assist parties in their endeavors to amicably settle disputes with the help of an impartial, independent conciliator.

[75] Annex 1 to U.N. Doc. A/40/17. Although the Model Law was prepared with the understanding that it would apply to "international commercial arbitration," there is nothing to stop national legislatures from giving it a more extensive application. *See* ALAN REDFERN & MARTIN HUNTER, INTERNATIONAL COMMERCIAL ARBITRATION 389 (1986).

In this section, reference will be made to the rules of the various arbitration systems, which are set out in their entirety in the Supplement. It is expected that review of the material in the textbook will be conducted with continuous reference to the rules themselves.

## A. METHODS OF APPOINTMENT

All arbitrations are susceptible to defection by one party after a dispute has arisen but before an arbitral tribunal has been established, and in some types of contracts and relationships, the probability of such non-appearance may be quite high. Failure of a party to appear before a court will not affect the court's "existence" or capacity to decide. However, because arbitrators are ordinarily appointed by the parties in each dispute, the refusal by one party to appoint its arbitrator could prevent the tribunal from coming into existence. In cases of party non-cooperation, the method and consequences of institutional appointment of an arbitral tribunal becomes very important, and at times can be outcome determinative. There are striking differences between the various sets of rules in this regard.

### 1. ICC

The ICC appointment procedure is relatively standard in cases in which the parties cooperate. The parties may prescribe a tribunal of a single arbitrator or of three arbitrators. If they do not indicate the number, the ICC Court appoints a sole arbitrator unless it believes that "the dispute is such as to warrant the appointment of three arbitrators." Under Article 2 of the ICC Rules, in a three-person arbitration, the party requesting arbitration nominates its arbitrator in the request itself. The request is submitted to the Secretariat of the ICC Court directly or through the National Committee. In either case, the Secretariat notifies the National Committee. The Defendant, under Article 4, must appoint its arbitrator within 30 days of the receipt of the documents from the Secretariat, subject to certain possibilities for extension.

The procedure, insofar as it proceeds amicably, provides a slight advantage to the defendant party, which is informed of the identity of the plaintiff's arbitrator and has at least 30 days to assess him or her and to make an informed choice of an arbitrator likely to counter-balance him. In some circumstances, the position of being the party to choose its arbitrator second can be valuable.

If the defendant refuses to appoint an arbitrator or if the defendant appoints an arbitrator but thereafter the parties prove unable to select a chairman jointly, the Court of the ICC makes the appointment, but it does not make the appointment directly. Under Article 2, it chooses a National Committee, which is the national committee of neither of the parties and is usually the committee of the venue of the arbitration.[76] The National Committee makes a proposal to the ICC. The proposal is usually of a national of that particular country. The Court then reviews the proposal and in most cases confirms it.

The back-up appointment procedure of the ICC has a number of advantages. One advantage, as in all institutional arbitration, is that it increases the probability that a chairman will be appointed and the tribunal will operate. Secondly, it permits the parties to predict, with a rather high degree of probability, the nationality of the chairman in case the parties cannot agree upon one. Since the ICC Court will almost invariably turn to the National Committee of the venue, a designation of venue in an ICC arbitration clause creates a high probability that the chairman will be selected from that jurisdiction. In cases between developing countries and multinational corporations from capital-exporting countries, this assurance can be particularly useful to the private party.

## 2.    AAA

There are three methods of AAA arbitral appointment for domestic arbitration.

If the parties have not appointed an arbitrator or provided for a method of appointment, the dispositive AAA method applies. Rule 13 provides

> If the parties have not appointed an Arbitrator and have
> not provided any other method of appointment, the
> Arbitrator shall be appointed in the following manner:

---

[76] However, in suitable circumstances and provided that neither of the parties objects, the sole arbitrator or the Chairman of the arbitral tribunal may be chosen from a country of which any one of the parties is a national. *See* Art. 2 of ICC Rules.

Immediately after the filing of the Demand or Submission, the AAA shall submit simultaneously to each party to the dispute an identical list of names of persons chosen from the Panel. Each party to the dispute shall have seven days from the mailing date in which to cross off any names objected to, number the remaining names to indicate the order of preference, and return the list to the AAA. If a party does not return the list within the time specified, all persons named therein shall be deemed acceptable. From among the persons who have been approved on both lists, and in accordance with the designated order of mutual preference, the AAA shall invite the acceptance of an Arbitrator to serve. If the parties fail to agree upon any of the persons named, or if acceptable Arbitrators are unable to act, or if for any other reason the appointment cannot be made from the submitted lists, the AAA shall have the power to make the appointment from among other members of the Panel without the submission of any additional list.

Note that the universe of potential arbitrators under this procedure is predetermined by the AAA. Parties may strike the names of unacceptable arbitrators in a peremptory fashion. Statistically, the more names one party strikes, the greater the probability that some of the remaining names will be appointed, and those names themselves may be of only relative desirability. Note also that, in contrast with the ICC, the appointment procedures by the AAA do not include the relative *locus* predictability considered earlier.

In the standard AAA single-person arbitration, there is obviously no place for the classic "party-arbitrator," whom a party may contact about the case and about the candidate's views before the decision to appoint him has been made.[77] The AAA Rules, however, also permit the parties to provide in the contract for the appointment of party-arbitrators who may, within a specified time, appoint a third neutral arbitrator. If the party-arbitrators fail to make the appointment within the dispositive seven-day time limit, the AAA does. Instead of

---

[77] For discussion of the law and professional ethics in this regard, see Chapter 5 *infra*.

having the party arbitrators appoint a neutral colleague, the parties may ask the AAA to appoint the neutral arbitrator directly. In both of these cases, the list method described above will be used. In cases of international arbitration, the parties may prescribe that the neutral arbitrator not be a national of the country of either of the parties, but in contrast to the ICC, there is no way of predicting from what country or legal system the AAA will select a neutral arbitrator.

The conventional AAA single arbitrator procedure seems best designed for two types of cases. First are the highly routinized disputes, where the possible outcomes are limited and losses are usually small and discounted beforehand. In such cases, speed and reliability are most important and the relatively high transaction costs involved in selecting and appointing a three-member panel make little sense. Why generate, for example, $30,000 of expenses in scanning potential arbitrators and making a selection if the dispute itself involves only $25,000? The second case involves disputes where there is high and symmetrical agreement about getting an arbitral solution. In contrast, the conventional AAA procedure would seem inappropriate for "big-ticket" cases, where a direct role in the fashioning of the tribunal is an important factor for the parties. While AAA procedures allow such an expanded role for the parties to be written in, it is important to note that it does not apply automatically upon selection of AAA rules. If such an expanded role is important to one of the parties, it must be secured in prior negotiation and will presumably exact a significant price.

In 1992, the AAA adopted special rules for international arbitration. Parties selecting AAA Rules may appoint their arbitrator or adopt several other methods of appointment. The AAA also has made itself available as the appointing authority under the UNCITRAL Rules. Under the 1992 International Arbitration Rules, Article 6 allows the parties to agree mutually upon "any procedure for appointing arbitrators." If the parties have not mutually agreed on a procedure within 60 days after the commencement of the arbitration, the AAA, as the administrator, appoints, at the request of any party, the arbitrator and arbitrators and designates the President of the tribunal. If the parties have agreed on a procedure for appointing the tribunal but the appointments have not been made within the time limits in that procedure, the AAA, as administrator, will perform the function provided for in the procedure. Article VI(4) states that "in making such appointments, the administrator, after inviting consultation with the parties, shall endeavor to select suitable arbitrators." Thus a very broad discretion is assigned to the AAA and arbitral appointments. If an arbitrator withdraws or dies, a substitute is appointed under the same procedures.

### 3.     LCIA

The London Rules permit parties to prescribe in their agreement that they will appoint the party-arbitrators or to delegate responsibility for selecting party-arbitrators and/or the chairman of the tribunal to the London Court itself. Where parties fail to select their party arbitrators or no consensus can be reached on appointing a chairman, the back-up appointment function under the London Rules is performed by the Court. Article 3.3 of the Rules indicates the criteria which will be applied in selection.

> . . . In selecting arbitrators consideration will be given, so far as possible, to the nature of the contract, the nature and circumstances of the dispute, and the nationality, location and languages of the parties. Where the parties are of different nationalities, then unless they have agreed otherwise, sole arbitrators or chairmen are not to be appointed if they have the same nationality as any party (the nationality of parties being understood to include that of controlling shareholders or interests). If the parties have agreed that they are to nominate arbitrators themselves, or to allow two arbitrators, or a third party, to nominate an arbitrator, the court may refuse to appoint such nominees if it determines that they are not suitable or independent or impartial. In the case of a three-member Tribunal the Court will designate the Chairman, who will not be a party-nominated arbitrator.

Other than the negative injunction of not appointing as Chairman or sole arbitrator a person of the same nationality as one of the parties, it is difficult to predict who will be selected by the London Court, in contrast with ICC where some guidelines provide a degree of predictability.

### 4. ICSID

As explained, ICSID is available only for arbitrations concerning investment disputes between states parties to the ICSID Convention and nationals of another contracting party. In the absence of agreement by the parties to the contrary, an ICSID tribunal will consist of three arbitrators, one appointed by each of the parties and the third appointed by agreement.[78]

If the tribunal has not been constituted, the Chairman of the ICSID Centre proceeds to appoint the arbitrator or arbitrators who have not yet been appointed.[79] The general requirement of national heterogeneity applies to ICSID. While ICSID has a panel of arbitrators, recommended to the Secretary-General of ICSID by the contracting states, appointments by the parties are not restricted to the panel. Yet when the Secretary-General of ICSID acts as the default appointing authority under Article 38, he is obliged by Article 40(1) to select the arbitrators from the members of the list. Insofar as the Secretary-General strictly follows Article 40(1), parties may have some idea of the limits of the universe of potential arbitrators. Note also that Article 38 requires the appointing authority to consult with both parties "as far as possible" before appointing.

ICSID presents certain advantages over some of the other appointment procedures. While the parties may not dictate the identity of the chairman or veto a proposal, the consultation procedure undertaken by the appointing authority means that the appointing authority will probably not designate unacceptable or problematic individuals.

### 5. SCC

Under the Stockholm Rules, the Board of the Institute plays a somewhat larger role in appointments than in other rule systems. The Board is entirely Swedish, composed of three persons appointed for three-year terms. The parties may appoint equal numbers of arbitrators, but the Chairman of the tribunal is appointed by the Institute, giving

---

[78] ICSID Convention, Art. 37(2)(b).

[79] *Id.* at Art. 38.

the party somewhat less control over the composition of the tribunal than in ICC arbitration. The back-up procedure in cases of failure of a party to appoint an arbitrator is assigned to the Institute which makes the appointment. The Stockholm Rules allow a party to reappoint an arbitrator if its designated arbitrator has died, but if the designated arbitrator resigns or is discharged for some reason of disqualification, the Institute makes the next appointment.

## 6.     UNCITRAL

UNCITRAL, as explained above, is comprised of a set of Rules attached to no specific institution. Since one of the main problems of international commercial arbitration is to secure the establishment of a tribunal in the absence of cooperation of one of the parties, UNCITRAL—lacking its own institutional appointing authority—adopts a two-stage solution. In the first stage, parties adopting UNCITRAL Rules may select their own appointing authority to perform this general function. A number of arbitral institutions have agreed to act as appointing authorities for parties arbitrating under the UNCITRAL Rules, for example, the American Arbitration Association, the London Court of Arbitration and the ICC. This appointing authority, or A.A. as it is commonly referred to, acts (i) the parties are either unable to agree, or (ii) the parties request the A.A. to appoint a single arbitrator, or (iii) when one of the parties has not appointed its arbitrator in accord with the agreement, or (iv) when both of the parties have appointed party-arbitrators but either through them or operating directly on their own behalf are unable to appoint the third arbitrator. In all of these circumstances, the appointing authority is expected to complete the tribunal, under the procedures which the parties have established.

In the second step of the process, should the contractually designated appointing authority fail to make its appointment within the designated period, or if the parties have not designated an appointing authority, a back-up A.A. is provided in the UNCITRAL Rules themselves, in the person of the Secretary-General of the Permanent Court of Arbitration (PCA) at The Hague. The appointment procedure, prescribed in Article 6(3), bears a certain similarity to the back-up appointment procedure under the AAA. Unless the parties agree otherwise or the A.A. determines that it is inappropriate, the appointing authority prepares a list of at least three names which is circulated to both parties. Within fifteen days, each party may return the list deleting the names it finds objectionable and numbering the remaining names in order of preference. After the fifteen days have elapsed, the appointing authority selects the sole arbitrator or, as the case may be, the unappointed party-arbitrator or chairman, from the remaining names. If the procedure does not work, Article 6(3)(d) authorizes the appointing authority to select according to its discretion. As set out in Article 6(2) of the Rules, the Secretary General does *not* appoint arbitrators; he "designate[s] an appointing authority", *e.g.*, the ICC, the LCIA or the SCC, or, as he did in challenges arising under the Iran-U.S. Claim cases, the presiding judge of the Supreme Court of the Netherlands. This discretion is limited, if at all, only in the most general terms. Article 6(4) provides:

> In making the appointment, the appointing authority shall have regard to such considerations as are likely to secure the appointment of an independent and impartial arbitrator and shall take into account as well the advisability of appointing an arbitrator of a nationality other than the nationalities of the parties.

Resort to this second stage procedure can, with a high degree of probability, be avoided by selecting a well-established arbitration institute to serve as appointing authority under the UNCITRAL regime. Nevertheless, it should be borne in mind that it may not always be possible in this manner to exclude using the UNCITRAL backup regime, and that the operation of this regime is one over which the parties will have relatively little control; in particular, the *locus* predictability provided by the ICC procedures will be absent.

The relative unpredictability of the back-up A.A. under the UNCITRAL Rules is aggravated by the nature of the Permanent Court of Arbitration. The PCA, at the time of its creation, was a public international arbitral institution limited to disputes between states, and in the post-war period, its competence was expanded to performing a variety of functions for arbitrations between states and private parties. Since its formation in 1899, it has conducted relatively few arbitrations and its work has largely been superseded by the International Court of Justice and *ad hoc* arbitration. Thus, although it has performed well in a number of cases, it is essentially an unknown quantity with relatively little case-law which might permit one to make projections as to how it will operate in the future. In addition, in contrast to the private international arbitral institutions, the PCA is less likely to have a current list of arbitrators specialized in international trade with whom the PCA itself has had experience.

Having now reviewed the uncertainties of arbitration under UNCITRAL, one should note that the parties can circumvent entirely by agreement the appointment procedures of the UNCITRAL Rules. Such circumvention is necessarily an additional item on the negotiating agenda, and parties concluding a complex agreement may not wish to add that burden at the final stage. Moreover, there are some asymmetries in selecting UNCITRAL Rules and then trying to negotiate away part of the dispositive system UNCITRAL provides. One party may find it to its advantage to resist and take its chances with the Permanent Court of Arbitration's back-up procedure.

### Notes and Questions

1. As counsel for a major national insurance company based in Connecticut but doing business throughout North America, you are responsible for dealing each month with approximately 1,500 new claims from standard home-owner's policies which limit payout to $50,000 for accidents or injuries covered by the policies. On average, about half of the monthly claims are challenged by your office and go to court.

    a.      What are the advantages of inserting a standard arbitration clause in each policy?

    b.      Evaluate the arbitration systems considered above and weigh the relative advantages and disadvantages of each for you in this case.

2. As counsel for the same company, you are also responsible for selecting an arbitral system for international insurance contracts, each of whose policies has a maximum pay-out of $200 million. Discuss the relative utilities of the different rule systems in terms of their contrasting appointment and back-up appointment procedures.

3. For other comparisons, see Susan Tiefenbrun, *A Comparison of International Arbitral Rules*, 15 B.C. INT'L & COMP. L. REV. 25 (1992) (comparing UNCITRAL, ICC and AAA); *see also* FREDERICK BROWN, AN OVERVIEW OF THE BASIC RULES OF SELECTED INTERNATIONAL ARBITRATION FORA (1991); JAMES J. MYERS, COMPARISON OF MAJOR INTERNATIONAL ARBITRATION RULES (1983).

### B.    METHODS OF CHALLENGING ARBITRATORS

The different rule systems provide different methods for appraising the impartiality of arbitrators and, where appropriate, challenging them.

In three-party arbitration, it is expected that the party-appointed arbitrator will, within the bounds of discretion, be sympathetic to the case presented by the party having appointed him. In cases in which that sympathy exceeds the bounds of discretion, the other party must weigh the tactical advantages of exchanging one predisposed arbitrator for another, who will be entitled and likely to have the same predisposition, against the injury to the process and the special stresses which are placed upon the neutral chairman in such a procedure. Nevertheless, there are cases in which the balance of considerations tips in favor of challenging a party-appointed arbitrator. In contrast, suspicion of a defect in the neutrality or impartiality of the chairman is more urgent and would, in virtually all cases, incite the party suffering discrimination to lodge a challenge.

The different systems of rules provide entirely different methods for challenge. Challenge under the ICC system is to the Court of the ICC.[80] As there is a body of partially accessible case-law on the Court's approach to this problem, some predictability is available. The ICC method also has the advantage of internalizing this challenge procedure in a private arbitral institution and preventing it from moving into national courts.

Under the 1992 International Arbitration Rules of the AAA, a party may challenge an arbitrator "whenever circumstances exist that give rise to justifiable doubts as to the arbitrator's impartiality or independence." The challenge is lodged with the AAA, as the administrator. If the other parties to the arbitration agree with the challenge, the arbitrator is withdrawn. The arbitrator may also voluntarily withdraw. If the other party or parties do not agree to the challenge or the challenge as arbitrated is not withdrawn, Article 9 provides "the decision on the challenge shall be made by the administrator in its sole discretion." If a withdrawal is effected, the procedures for appointment are followed again.

---

[80] ICC Rules, Art. 2.

The London Court of International Arbitration internalizes the challenge procedure in a comparable fashion. Under the London Rules, an arbitrator may be challenged if the circumstances give rise to doubts about his impartiality or independence.[81] The same criteria may be applied by a party to the arbitrator which it itself appointed, if the reasons for its doubts become apparent only after the appointment has been made.[82] Within fifteen days of the establishment of the tribunal or of notice of the circumstances warranting a challenge, the protesting party must send a written statement to the Court,[83] and the Court makes the final decision.[84]

If the London Court determines that a nominee is not suitable due to lack of independence or impartiality, the Court determines in its discretion whether to follow the original nominating process, which allows some participation by the parties, or whether to reappoint directly.

All of the above methods have the common advantage of conducting the challenge procedure without reference to the arbitral tribunal. Disputes about members of the tribunal which must be decided by the tribunal itself create special stresses on the neutral chairman and they may have some influence on the ultimate outcome of the arbitration.

Under the Stockholm Rules, a party may allege disqualification of an arbitrator on grounds specified in the Swedish Arbitration Act. The alleged disqualification ground must be lodged within 30 days from the time that it became known to the party making the motion. The Institute then makes the decision. If there is a disqualification, the Institute, not the appointing party, appoints the replacement arbitrator.

---

[81] LCIA Rules, Art. 3.7.

[82] *Id.*

[83] *Id.* at Art. 3.8.

[84] *Id.* at Art. 3.9.

The UNCITRAL Rules refer challenges to the appointing authority.[85] When a challenge has been lodged and the other party does not agree to the challenge or the arbitrator does not voluntarily withdraw, a decision is to be made by the party-designated appointing authority or by an authority to be designated by the Secretary-General of the Permanent Court of Arbitration. Where the appointing authority is an existing institution, one may make certain inferences about its likely behavior on the basis of its past behavior. Where the appointing authority is, however, the Secretary-General of the Permanent Court of Arbitration, some uncertainty remains as to how the language of the UNCITRAL Rules will be interpreted.

Under the ICSID Convention, parties lodge challenges to a particular arbitrator with the other members of the tribunal who decide whether or not to disqualify the challenged arbitrator.[86] This procedure may create a curious situation in which the party-appointed arbitrator of the opposing and now challenging side can have a large role in effecting the recusal of the other party-appointed arbitrator. If the two remaining arbitrators do not agree, the decision rests with the Chairman of the Administrative Council of ICSID. When a party challenges a sole arbitrator, the chairman obviously must make the decision directly.

### Notes and Questions

1. Verdi Industries of Milan and Green Company of London have a contract which incorporates an ICC clause that specifies a three-person tribunal with Zurich as the place of arbitration. When a dispute over performance of part of the contract develops, Verdi initiates arbitration and names its arbitrator. Green's counsel interviews possible arbitrators in London and Brussels. They also interview a prominent attorney and well-known arbitrator, Herr Grütli, over lunch in Zurich. Green ultimately appoints a London solicitor as its arbitrator. Subsequently Verdi and Green cannot agree on the appointment of a chairman. The National Committee of Switzerland appoints Herr Grütli as Chairman. Grütli has disclosed the interview and the lunch and the Committee feels that it is no impediment to his appointment. Discuss the possible implications of this appointment from the perspectives of Verdi and Green and consider what options the ICC rules give each party. Weigh the utility of the options for each party.

---

[85] UNCITRAL Rules, Art. 12.

[86] ICSID Convention, Art. 58.

2. You are counsel for Government X in a case before ICSID. You learn early in the arbitration that the arbitrator that Corporation Y appointed, a Singapore attorney, gave some tax advice to Corporation Y for several years but did not state this connection when she accepted the appointment. Discuss your legal options and weigh their strategic utilities.

## C.    THE LAW TO BE APPLIED

There are significant variations with regard to which law the tribunal is to apply. The AAA Rules for domestic arbitration do not address this subject at all. In addition, the AAA is known to discourage its arbitrators from writing reasoned opinions. The absence of any reference to law, however, does not necessarily mean that AAA arbitrations turn on the predilections of the arbitrators. Since the rules appear to have been drafted originally for arbitration within the United States, the assumption may have been that United States law would apply. Under the 1992 International Arbitration Rules of the AAA, Article 29 provides

> 1. The tribunal shall apply the substantive law or laws designated by the parties as applicable to the dispute. Failing such a designation by the parties, the tribunal shall apply such law or laws as it determines to be appropriate.

> 2. In arbitrations involving the application of contract, the tribunal shall decide in accordance with the terms of the contract and shall take into account usages of the trade applicable to the contract.

> 3. The tribunal shall not decide as *amiable compositeur* or *ex aequo et bono* unless the parties have authorized it to do so.

In contrast to the Domestic Rules, the AAA's International Rules establish as the default procedure that the tribunal shall state the reasons upon which the award is based, unless the parties have agreed that no reasons need be given.

In contrast, the ICC, having been designed as an international arbitral institution from its inception, manifests great concern with regard to the law to be applied. Under Article 13, the parties are free to determine the law to be applied to the merits. If the parties do not specify the applicable law, Article 13(3) provides that "the arbitrator shall apply the law designated as the proper law by the rule of conflict which he deems appropriate." Note that ICC Rules apparently give broad authority to the arbitrator to determine which system of conflicts of law he will apply to find the "proper law." This relatively broad discretion should be contrasted with the probable procedure of a court in whatever venue the arbitration is taking place. A national court would presumably apply its own conflicts of law as a procedural element. In contrast because the ICC Rules seem to free the arbitrator from this requirement, choice of law in the absence of agreement under ICC Rules is difficult to predict. It is reasonable to presume that it will be the conflicts rules of the venue, but the Rules do not require it.

Of great importance in the ICC Rules is the sixth paragraph of Article 13, which obliges, in mandatory terms, the arbitrator to take account of "relevant trade usages." Reference to trade usages may prove useful in cases in which one of the parties wishes to overcome a rule of national law designated by the agreement.

UNCITRAL Rules appear to have been influenced by the ICC Rules in the discretion given to the tribunal in deciding which law to apply to the arbitration this regard. In the absence of agreement, the UNCITRAL Rules, like those of the ICC, enjoin the Tribunal to "apply the law determined by the conflict of laws rules which it considers applicable."[87] Unlike the ICC Rules, there is no reference in the UNCITRAL Rules to "proper law," and one may perhaps find in the words "considers applicable" a stricter test than the words "deems appropriate" of the ICC Rules which might be construed as giving greater discretion to the arbitrator. These linguistic differences might be important in some cases, but one should be wary of exaggerating their importance. Note that neither ICC nor AAA Domestic Rules addresses the case where several systems of law are simultaneously applicable. The 1992 AAA Rules do treat this. Several systems of law are likely to apply simultaneously in disputes about concession agreements, where international law, one or more systems of foreign law, trade usages and local law (*e.g.*, for the securing of entry permits, etc.) would all apply.

---

[87] UNCITRAL Rules, Art. 33(1).

Since the Stockholm Rules presume arbitration in Stockholm, the range of choice of the parties with regard to procedural and substantive law depends upon the Stockholm Rules and Swedish law. Rule 5 of the Stockholm Rules prescribes that the Swedish law of arbitration applies, subject to changes in the Rules. As Swedish law permits the parties to select their own substantive law, they may make a choice of law. It should be remembered, however, that as the venue is Sweden, any supplementary application of the law of the venue will be Swedish.

Like the ICC Rules, UNCITRAL also obliges the tribunal to take account of trade usages.[88] But the UNCITRAL Rules require that the trade usages in question be "applicable to the transaction." The ICC Rules, in contrast, ask only that the trade usages be "relevant." Thus an ICC arbitrator might be authorized to consider trade usages not directly applicable to the case at hand, while an UNCITRAL arbitrator might not have this option. The 1992 AAA International Rules enjoin the tribunal to "take into account usages of the trade applicable to the contract," but this is only in arbitrations involving the application of contracts, a condition which makes the AAA Rules somewhat narrower in this regard.

The London Rules do not address the question of governing law directly. But references in the Rules to "applicable law"[89] suggest that the drafters assumed that there was a correct applicable law and that the arbitrators would determine and apply it.

ICSID permits the parties to select their law; the arbitrators, according to Article 42(1), are to decide according to the parties' selection. In the absence of an agreement by the parties, "the Tribunal shall apply the law of the Contracting State party to the dispute (including its rules on the conflict of laws) and such rules of international law as may be applicable."

The contingent arrangement in ICSID Article 42 represents a compromise between the two interest groups responsible for the Convention — capital-exporting states, on the one hand, and developing

---

[88] *Id.* at Art. 33(3).

[89] *See, e.g.*, LCIA Rules Arts. 3.9; 5.2; 13.1(a) & (b).

states, on the other. The government of the developing state may find it advantageous in negotiations to resist agreement on choice of law, hoping to count on the fall- back provision which then applies its own law. The case law of ICSID has tempered that advantage, however, by interpreting Article 42(1) as requiring that the national law be consistent with international law.

### D.    EQUITY

On occasion, parties decide to authorize arbitrators to renegotiate or, in effect, to negotiate supplementary agreements, which reflect what the arbitrators deem appropriate rather than an interpretation of existing contractual language or the application of the governing law to the original agreements. This function is generally referred to as "equity," a term which is quite misleading in that it implies that decisions made according to law or the contract are necessarily or have somehow become inequitable. It is also referred to as decision *ex aequo et bono* or *amiable composition*.

Obviously, there is an element of equitability in every contractual interpretation, in that, within the bounds of language, the arbitrator tries to reach the most equitable possible construction of the instruments in question. There is also likely to be an element of compromise in most arbitrations where two of the arbitrators are party-appointed. The compromise arises from the interests of the chairman in securing, insofar as possible, a unanimous award, thereby increasing the likelihood of its acceptability and its effectiveness. In some circumstances, however, a *clear departure* is authorized. It is unlikely that such an authority will be assigned to any tribunal other than one composed for a special case.

The ICC Rules simply authorize arbitrators to resort to equity if the parties agree to it.[90] UNCITRAL Rules include the same competence but subject it to the applicable law.[91] In other words, even if the tribunal has been authorized by the parties to decide *ex aequo et bono*, it may do so only if and to the extent that the applicable law permits this type of arbitration. The AAA Domestic Rules do not

---

[90] ICC Rules, Art. 13.

[91] UNCITRAL Rules, Art. 33(2).

discuss this matter but AAA Rule 43 provides that "the arbitrator may grant any remedy or relief which the Arbitrator deems just and equitable and within the scope of the agreement of the parties, including, but not limited to, specific performance of a contract." This suggests a residual equitable competence by virtue of the rules even in the absence of authorization by the parties. The London Rules do not address the matter explicitly, but authorize the tribunal to correct a contract or arbitration agreement if the tribunal determines that a "mistake" is common to all the parties.[92] But this rectificatory competence is operable only if the governing law permits it.

The ICSID Convention authorizes the tribunal to decide a dispute *ex aequo et bono* if the parties agree.[93] In addition, the Convention seems to give each tribunal an implied competence if not obligation to decide according to equity. Article 42(2) prohibits a tribunal from returning a finding of *non liquet* in certain prescribed contingent circumstances. (*Non liquet*, literally, "it is not clear" is a hypothetical judicial response to a situation in which there is no explicit legal answer for the question before the judges. The judges note the *lacuna* or gap in the law and refuse to render judgment on the matter.) That prohibition would seem to imply a decision comparable to that of one based on equity. This particular competence is unlikely to be abused as it is particularly vulnerable to attack in the unique nullification phase provided by the ICSID Convention.

### E.    COMPETENCE TO DETERMINE JURISDICTION

Other than in the most amicable arbitrations, at least one party may be expected to raise questions as to the jurisdiction of the tribunal. The challenge may be general, *i.e.*, that the tribunal completely lacks jurisdiction to hear the particular case, or specific, *i.e.*, that the tribunal is competent for part but not all of the case. The various Rules exhibit a certain diversity with regard to the methods for determining jurisdiction. The ICC Rules provide for initial review of a jurisdictional objection concerning the existence or validity of the agreement to arbitrate by the ICC Court. If the Court finds that there is a *prima facie* agreement, it refers the matter to arbitration without in any way

---

[92] LCIA Rules, Art. 13.1(b).

[93] ICSID Convention, Art. 42(3).

prejudicing the competence of a tribunal to decide the jurisdictional question. Under the ICC Rules, an arbitrator continues to have jurisdiction "to determine the respective rights of the parties and to adjudicate upon their claims and pleas," even if the contract itself proves to be "inexistent" or "null and void."[94]

This rule is not felicitous. Plainly, an international commercial arbitral tribunal must have the competence to arbitrate agreements which have been effectively but unlawfully terminated by one party, for example, the termination of a concession agreement by legislation of the host state. The tribunal is then in fact providing a contractual remedy for the violation of the agreement. The language of Article 8 of the ICC Rules is broader and could be subject to misinterpretation. Indeed, on a few occasions in the past decade, tribunals may have reached for jurisdiction beyond the perimeter of the agreement.

Under the Stockholm Rules, initial application for arbitration is made to the Institute. If it is obvious that there is no jurisdiction, the Institute dismisses the case immediately. Although the Rules do not address subsequent procedural phases, challenges to jurisdiction may also be lodged with the tribunal, once it is formed. The tribunal is authorized under Rule 18 to issue separate awards and could issue an award on jurisdiction.

UNCITRAL's procedures with regard to challenges to jurisdiction are more precise. The competence to rule on objections to jurisdiction is assigned to the tribunal itself.[95] An arbitration clause which is valid is deemed to survive an invalid agreement. Claims to jurisdiction must be raised not later than in the statement of defense or in the reply to the counter-claim.[96] Jurisdiction is a preliminary question, though a tribunal may proceed and rule on such a plea in its final award.[97]

---

[94] ICC Rules, Art. 8.

[95] UNCITRAL Rules, Art. 21(1).

[96] *Id.* at Art. 21(3).

[97] *Id.* at Art. 21(4).

The AAA Domestic Rules do not address the question of jurisdiction. The 1992 International Arbitration Rules of the AAA assign the tribunal the power to rule on its own jurisdiction and to determine the existence or validity of both the arbitration agreement and the contract of which it is a part. Nevertheless, the arbitration clause is treated as independent of the other terms of the contract.

The London Rules assign the power to rule on jurisdiction to the tribunal and insulate the arbitration clause from the possible invalidity of the contract.[98] Pleas as to jurisdiction are to be raised not later than in the statement of defense.[99] A plea that the tribunal is exceeding the scope of its authority in any other matter must be raised "promptly" after the tribunal has indicated its intention to decide on the matter which one of the parties now alleges extends beyond the scope of its authority.[100] Note that these provisions are not, in fact, rigid, and the tribunal is explicitly accorded a competence to admit a late plea.

As ICSID is both a set of rules and an arbitral institution, a two-phased examination of jurisdiction occurs. When an initial request for arbitration is submitted to ICSID, the Secretary-General must make an initial determination of whether the bare minima of jurisdiction are present. Thus if the defendant state is not a party to the ICSID Convention or, though a party, has signed no document indicating acceptance of jurisdiction for the particular case, the Secretary-General would not convene a tribunal to which the request for arbitration would be passed. The performance of this function should be essentially clerical. Any challenges to ICSID jurisdiction are to be considered promptly, but the tribunal is given the competence to determine whether to deal with them as a preliminary question or to join them to the merits of the dispute.[101]

---

[98] LCIA Rules, Art. 14.1.

[99] *Id.* at Art. 14.2.

[100] *Id.*

[101] ICSID Convention, Art. 41(2).

## F.    PROCEDURE

There is considerable variation among the rules with regard to the procedures to be employed. In ICC arbitration, the ICC Rules govern the proceedings and where those Rules are silent, any rules that the parties (or, failing these, the arbitrator) may settle.[102] These rules need not be based on any particular provision of municipal procedural law, but an ICC arbitral tribunal will need to examine whether any mandatory provisions of the procedural law at the place of arbitration apply.[103] In the absence of agreement, it will be recalled, venue is set by the ICC Court. Where both municipal law and the ICC Rules are silent on a procedural matter, they may be supplemented by the agreement of the parties or, failing such an agreement, the tribunal decides the matter.

UNCITRAL is more open textured with regard to procedure. Procedural questions are entirely subject to the tribunal's judgment, with the proviso that the parties be treated with equality and that, at every stage of the proceedings, each party be given a full opportunity to present its case.[104] While this is a much broader mandate than the ICC formulation and no reference is made to the law of the place of arbitration, it is plain that its mandatory procedural provisions will apply. UNCITRAL has also produced a model law for adoption by states which goes far toward reducing the opportunity for idiosyncratic national procedures from applying to an international arbitration conducted within its jurisdiction.

The AAA Domestic Rules do not address this question. The 1992 International Arbitration Rules of the AAA assign to the tribunal the competence to conduct the arbitration "in whatever manner it considers appropriate," provided that certain basic rules of natural justice are respected.

---

[102] ICC Rules, Art. 11.

[103] Article 11 makes a passing reference to the possible relevance of municipal procedural law and Article 26 (the "General Rule") provides that the arbitrator "shall make every effort to make sure that the Award is enforceable at law."

[104] UNCITRAL Rules, Art. 15(1).

The London Rules provide that in the absence of agreement by the parties or some rules contained within the London Rules themselves, the tribunal has the widest discretion allowed to use such laws as may be applicable to insure the just, expeditious, economical and final determination of the dispute.[105]

As mentioned earlier, Rule 5 of the Stockholm Rules establishes that Swedish law of arbitration, along with the Rules, is the effective applicable law.

ICSID provides for procedures as set out in the Convention. A detailed set of rules has been prepared and these apply as well, unless the parties agree otherwise. As this is a public international arbitral institution, the procedural law of the venue will not apply. Any question about procedure which is not addressed by the Convention or Rules is to be decided by the tribunal.[106]

With the exception of ICSID, which is a self-contained international arbitral system, all the rules balance, in one fashion or another, the application of their own procedure and that of the venue in which the arbitration takes place. In this respect, comparisons concerning procedure under the different sets of rules must take into account the venue where the arbitration is planned. Inevitably, some local arbitration procedure will infiltrate proceedings other than those undertaken by ICSID. On the other hand, a number of jurisdictions have passed international arbitration statutes which purport to reduce the role of national law and procedure to the vanishing point.

## G.     EXAMINATION *IN LOCO*

A number of specific procedural options are available in only some of the rules. For example, examinations *in loco*, which may be quite important in international construction contracts, are authorized under some systems of rules. Neither American Arbitration Association Domestic Rules (Rule 33) nor the International Rules authorize such examinations. They are not explicitly authorized, however, under ICC Rules. The London Rules do not explicitly authorize a tribunal to make

---

[105] LCIA Rules, Art. 5.2.

[106] ICSID Convention, Art. 44.

an examination *in loco*; however, Article 13.1(f) authorizes the tribunal to "conduct such inquiries as may appear to the tribunal to be necessary or expedient." Subsection (g) authorizes the tribunal to "order the parties to make any property or thing available for inspection, in their presence, by the tribunal or any expert." Rule 15 of the Stockholm Rules provides that "the tribunal may, particularly during the preliminary proceedings, empower the chairman of the tribunal to take any necessary action for the conduct of the proceedings." Tribunal competence to conduct examinations *in loco* will depend on Swedish procedural law. Article 43 of the ICSID Rules explicitly authorizes the tribunal to conduct an examination *in loco*, unless the parties otherwise agree.

## H.    INTERIM MEASURES

In international commercial arbitration, even more than in domestic litigation, temporary restraining orders of various sorts are often indispensable if an award subsequently rendered is to be effective. All such temporary orders, whether conservatory attachments, injunctions, or other restraints, are referred to in international arbitration as "interim measures." That term is preferred because the issue of the jurisdiction of the tribunal has frequently not yet been heard at the time that a party requests some interim measure. Interim measures are terminated by a finding of lack of jurisdiction or by an order of the tribunal.

The ICC Rules do not authorize the tribunal to issue interim measures. Article 8, paragraph 5 authorizes the parties to apply "to any competent judicial authority for interim or conservatory measures, and they shall not by so doing be held to infringe the agreement to arbitrate or to affect the relevant powers reserved to the arbitrator." Resort to a judicial authority is not an optimal solution, because the issuing of temporary restraining orders in many jurisdictions (particularly in the United States) is preceded by a rather careful examination on the part of the court as to whether the order is justified. Having to resort to the national courts for interim measures thus frustrates one of the main objectives of arbitration which is to keep disputes out of national courts. Moreover, a number of jurisdictions will refuse to provide this service for parties under an arbitration agreement on the logical, if not necessarily persuasive, ground that to do so would require a national court to intervene in the case.

The UNCITRAL Rules incorporate the ICC approach insofar as they permit the parties to have recourse to a judicial authority without thereby waiving their rights under the arbitration agreement. However, UNCITRAL also authorizes the tribunal itself to issue "any interim measures it deems necessary in respect of the subject-matter of the dispute."[107] The interim measures issued under the UNCITRAL Rules are deemed to be an award and consequently should benefit from the enforcement procedures of the New York Convention.

As mentioned, Rule 15 of the Stockholm Rules authorizes the chairman "particularly during the preliminary proceedings" to take any necessary action for the conduct of the proceedings.

The AAA Domestic Rules authorize the tribunal "to issue such orders as may be deemed necessary to safeguard the property which is the subject-matter of the arbitration without prejudice to the rights of the parties or to the final determination of the dispute." (Rule 34) The International Arbitration Rules of the AAA provide the most elaborate regime for interim measures of protection. At the request of any party, the tribunal may take "whatever interim measures it deems necessary in respect of the subject-matter of the dispute, including measures for the conservation of the goods which are the subject-matter in dispute, such as ordering their deposit with a third person or the sale of perishable goods." The International Rules specify that the interim measures may take the form of an interim award and that the tribunal may require security for the costs of such measures. In addition, the Rules provide that a request for interim measures by a party to a judicial authority shall not be deemed incompatible with the agreement to arbitrate or a waiver of the right to arbitrate. The London Rules authorize the tribunal to "order the preservation, storage, sale or other disposal of any property or thing under the control of any party."[108]

Article 47 of the ICSID Convention provides that "[e]xcept as the parties otherwise agree, the Tribunal may, if it considers that the circumstances so require, recommend any provisional measures which should be taken to preserve the respective rights of either party." The provision is elaborated in Rule 39 of the ICSID Rules.

---

[107] UNCITRAL Rules, Art. 26.

[108] LCIA Rules, Art. 13.1(h).

## I.    SUBPOENA *DUCES TECUM*

Insofar as the production of documents by the parties to an arbitration is concerned, institutional rules vary widely in their specificity.

The ICC Rules do not explicitly authorize the tribunal to require the submission of documents. The parties may include such an authorization in their agreement in accord with Article 11 which also gives general powers to the arbitrator in procedural matters. In the absence of specific powers given to the arbitrator by municipal procedural law for the production of documents the arbitrator would only, in appropriate circumstances, be able to draw limited adverse inferences from a party's non-production of documents ordered to be produced.

Similarly, the AAA Rules depend upon local law. Rule 15 of the Stockholm Rules would appear to be general authority for this power, subject to Swedish procedural law.

UNCITRAL Article 24(3) gives the tribunal broad competence to require the production of documents.

The London Rules in Article 13.1(g), authorize the tribunal to "order the parties to make any property or thing available for inspection, in their presence, by the Tribunal or any expert."

ICSID Article 43(a) authorizes the tribunal to "call upon the parties to produce documents or other evidence."

## J.    DEFAULT PROCEDURES

It is not uncommon for a defendant not to appear in an international arbitration. This is not a violation of law and in certain circumstances, may be a tactical move which is sometimes prudent and wise (and sometimes very risky). Because this is not an infrequently used tactic, it is important to compare the default procedures of the different rule systems.

The ICC Rules are quite laconic with regard to default. Article 15, paragraph 2 authorizes the arbitrator to proceed with the arbitration as long as he is satisfied that the summons was duly received and the absence is without an excuse. The ICC Rules do not specify a burden of proof.

The AAA Domestic Rules are more precise on this point. Like the ICC Rules, they authorize the tribunal to proceed in the absence of a party but they add that "[a]n award shall not be made solely on the default of a party. The Arbitrator shall require the party who is present to submit such evidence as the Arbitrator may require for the making of an award."[109] The AAA's International Rules imply a subtle penalty for the defaulting party. Article 24(3) provides

> If a party, duly invited to produce evidence, fails to do so within the time established by the tribunal without showing sufficient cause for such failure, as determined by the tribunal, the tribunal may make the award on the evidence before it.

A prudent tribunal could interpret this provision to require it to satisfy itself as to the sufficiency of the evidence with regard to the claim lodged before it. But the language is not without ambiguity and Article 24(3) could be interpreted as an authority to render an award on the basis of the applicant's claim, even though the evidence is not sufficient.

The UNCITRAL Rules are somewhat less clear. Article 28(2) authorizes a tribunal to continue in the absence of the defendant while Article 24(1) assigns the burden of proof with regard to facts to whichever party is relying on those facts, whether claimant or defendant. Article 28(3) authorizes the tribunal to render an award on the evidence before it if one of the parties fails to produce documentary evidence.

The London Rules, in Article 14.3, authorize the tribunal to proceed in the absence of the defendant.

The Stockholm Rules do not address this problem.

The ICSID Rules are most developed with regard to intentional non-appearance. Article 45(1) states that the failure of a party to appear

---

[109] AAA Rule 30.

or to present its case is not deemed an admission of the other party's assertions.

### K.    METHODS OF RENDERING DECISIONS

In three-arbitrator tribunals in which two of the arbitrators are selected by the parties and will often espouse their appointing party's position, it is possible that there will be three different viewpoints among the three members. The ICC Rules provide, in Article 19, that if there is no majority, the award is to be made by the chairman of the tribunal. This means, effectively, that it is the chairman of an ICC three-member tribunal who has the competence to make the decision. The power of the chairman is amplified further by a practice unique to ICC arbitration, known as the "Terms of Reference." Article 13(1) requires the arbitrator to draw up a document defining his Terms of Reference. Much of this material is clerical and no more than a transposition from pleadings and written statements submitted up until that time by the parties. Beyond this clerical function, the Terms of Reference also include a "definition of the issues to be determined." The power to define the issues to be determined and the authority to make an award in the absence of a majority underscores the preeminent competence assigned to the chairman in ICC arbitration. Thus in cases of dispute about what is in dispute, the neutral chairman will determine what is at issue even before the arbitration commences.

In contrast, UNCITRAL Rules require, in Article 31(1), that the award be made by majority. This requirement substantially reduces the power of the chairman, who must adapt his decision to one of the other arbitrators.

Similarly, AAA Domestic Arbitration Rule 28 requires a decision by majority. AAA International Arbitration Rule Article 27 also adopts a majority decision method, but allows the parties or the tribunal to authorize decisions or rulings on questions of procedure by the presiding arbitrator. But such decisions or rulings are subject to revision by the plenary tribunal.

The London Rules, in Article 16.3, provide for majority decision. In the absence of a majority, "the Chairman of the Tribunal shall make the award alone as if he were the sole arbitrator."

The Stockholm Rules provide that if the appointed arbitrators do not agree, the opinion of the chairman prevails.

ICSID Tribunals decide, in accord with Article 48(1), by majority.

Decision-making dynamics are an important consideration in the selection of rules. Rule systems requiring majority decision enhance the power of the party-appointed arbitrators. Rule systems in which the chairman either immediately or in the absence of a majority renders the decision alone proportionately reduce the power of the party-appointed arbitrators. In systems in which the principle of majority rule does not govern, the identity of the chairman and the methods by which he is selected become even more important.

### Notes and Questions

1. As counsel for an international construction company, you are concluding a contract with the Government of Thailand for construction of an airport outside of Bangkok. Both parties agree that there must be provision for arbitration. Consider the rules that would best serve your purposes.

2. You are counsel to a producer of widgets that arranges regional distribution agreements around the world. Distributors in different regions want an arbitration clause. Analyze and explain the interests of your client in this matter.

3. You are counsel to a developing country that is negotiating a substantial direct investment by Klug Corporation of Germany. The investment involves building and managing a factory to produce fertilizers, constructing a railroad to link the factory and the coast, building a deep-water port and managing the railroad and port for ten years. Discuss your arbitration options. (Please note the plural.)

4. The ICC rule system which assigns the ultimate decision power to the chairman of the tribunal in circumstances in which the two party-appointed arbitrators do not agree is, obviously, heavily weighted in favor of the chairman. Since the chairman also has the same power in the decision about conclusion of the "Terms of Reference," the power of the party-appointed arbitrators can sometimes be reduced to the vanishing point. This limits some of the advantageous features of three-party arbitration but, it should be noted, also avoids anomalous situations in which the decision is to be made by majority but all three arbitrators disagree. This situation was presented in a public international arbitration in 1991. In a maritime boundary dispute between Guinea-Bissau and Senegal, which was submitted to three-party arbitration under rules which required a simple majority, the operative question was phrased in the following terms:

The Tribunal is requested to decide in accordance with the norms of international law on the following questions:

> 1. Does the Agreement concluded by an exchange of letters of 26 April 1960, and which relates to the maritime boundary, have the force of law and the relations between the Republic of Guinea-Bissau and the Republic of Senegal?

> 2. In the event of a negative answer to the first question, what is the course of the line delimiting the maritime territories appertaining to the Republic of Guinea-Bissau and the Republic of Senegal respectively?

The party-appointed arbitrator of Guinea-Bissau, Judge Mohammed Bedjaoui, was of the opinion that the 1960 Agreement did not have the force of law in the relations between the two countries. The Senegalese-appointed arbitrator, Judge André Gros, was apparently of the opinion that the Agreement did have the force of law for some of the maritime boundaries but that the tribunal should not advance and answer the second, contingent question posed in the *compromis*. The president of the tribunal, Professor Barberis, agreed with Judge Gros with regard to the validity as between the parties of the 1960 Agreement, but because it addressed only some maritime boundaries, Barberis felt the Tribunal should advance to the second question. Yet since the rules provided that "decisions of the Tribunal . . . shall be taken by a majority of its members" (Article 4), Professor Barberis apparently felt that he had to join with Judge Gros in order to establish a majority. In the Award of July 31, 1989, Professor Barberis added a declaration in which he stated, in effect, that the tribunal should have proceeded to the second question because the answer to the first question was partially negative. Guinea-Bissau then challenged the validity of the award and asked the International Court of Justice to annul it. Although the Court refused, the anomalous situation created by the application of the rules in this case proved quite problematic.[110]

Do you think there may have been a way by which Professor Barberis, as president of the tribunal, could have had the tribunal advance to the second question?

## VIII. CONSIDERATIONS AND OPTIONS IN DESIGNING AN *AD HOC* ARBITRATION

### A. *AD HOC* ARBITRATION: "DOING YOUR OWN THING"

In some circumstances, parties may choose to design an independent arbitral procedure not associated with any of the existing

---

[110] *See* Case Concerning the Arbitral Award of 31 July 1989, 1991 I.C.J. 53.

institutions. Alternatively, they may design an arbitral procedure and incorporate another institution only for a single matter, for example by designating the President of the International Court of Justice as the entity competent to choose a third arbitrator or, on default of one of the parties, a second and third arbitrator. The advantages of preparing a tailor-made arbitration clause, like the advantage of tailor-made clothing, is a "fit" that is perfect, but there are considerable disadvantages. For example, every feature of the arbitration procedure becomes a subject of negotiation and the time and legal costs involved in the transaction may become substantial. Moreover, the more the parties depart from routinized forms which have been tested by time, the more likely they are to encounter unexpected consequences. For example, dispensing with one of the appointing authorities in existing rule systems and selecting an untried appointing authority for an *ad hoc* arbitration runs the risk that the designated appointing authority may not perform as expected. The need to negotiate every aspect may also mean that, on balance, parties lose as much as they gain, for each gain secured from the other party comes with the cost of a concession made to it. The design of an *ad hoc* arbitration is worthwhile when for one or both of the parties there is some feature which is so critical that if it cannot be secured, the advantage of arbitration substantially diminishes.

Some sense of the challenges and implications of creating an *ad hoc* arbitration may be gained from the arbitration between Kuwait and the American Independent Oil Company. The dispute concerned alleged expropriation of concessionary rights, with claims for many billions of dollars and, ultimately, an award for almost $1.5 billion. Although the original agreement between the parties had called for arbitration under one of the rule systems, the parties elected to design their own arbitration. Consider first the detailed arbitration agreement that the parties employed in place of a standard arbitration clause and then consider the tribunal's interpretation of this agreement and development of its own arbitral rules.

B.   *Kuwait v. American Indep. Oil Co. (The "AMINOIL Case")*, 66 I.L.R. 518 (1984).

1.   Excerpts from the Arbitration Agreement

.   .   .

## II

1.    The arbitral tribunal (hereinafter referred to as "the Tribunal") shall be composed of three members, one appointed by each Party as recited in paragraph 2 of this Article, and a third member who shall act as president, to be appointed by The President of the International Court of Justice.

2.    The member of the Tribunal appointed by the Government shall be Professor Doctor Hamed Sultan. The member appointed by the Company shall be Sir Gerald G. Fitzmaurice, G.C.M.C., Q.C.

3.    If at any time a vacancy shall occur on the Tribunal by reason of death, resignation, or incapacity for more than sixty days of any member, such vacancy shall be filled in the same manner as for the original appointment to that position. If the vacancy is not so filled within sixty days after its occurrence, either Party may request the President of the International Court of Justice to make the necessary appointment, and such appointment shall be final and binding on the Parties. Upon the filling of a vacancy, the proceedings shall be resumed at the point at which the vacancy occurred, after allowing any new member sufficient time to familiarise himself with the proceedings up to that time.

4.    Upon its constitution, the Tribunal shall appoint a secretary who shall possess qualifications as a lawyer in the country of the place of arbitration, who shall assist the Tribunal in the administrative arrangements for the proceedings. The Tribunal may also employ such stenographic and other assistance as it deems necessary.

## III

1.    The Parties recognise that the restoration of the Parties to their respective positions prior to 20 September 1977 and/or the resumption of operations under the 28 June 1948 Agreement (as amended) would be impracticable in any event, and the Company will therefore seek monetary damages instead. Accordingly, the Parties agree to limit their claims against each

other to claims for monetary compensation and/or monetary damages.

The Tribunal shall decide according to law:

i)      The amount of compensation, if any, payable by the Government to the Company in respect of the assets acquired by the Government under Article 2 of Decree Law n° 124.

ii)     The amount of the damages, if any, payable by the Government to the Company in respect of termination of the Agreement of 28 June 1948 by Article I of Decree Law n° 124.

iii)    The amount payable to the Government by the Company, and/or the amount payable to the Company by the Government, in respect of royalties, taxes or other obligations of the Company, in which connection the Tribunal shall determine the validity or invalidity of any amendments or supplements to the 28 June 1948 Agreement which are relevant.

iv)     The amount of interest, if any, payable by either Party to the other, the rate of such interest and the date from which it shall be payable to be awarded at the discretion of the Tribunal.

2.      The law governing the substantive issues between the Parties shall be determined by the Tribunal, having regard to the quality of the Parties, the transnational character of their relations and the principles of law and practice prevailing in the modern world.

IV

1.      Unless otherwise agreed by the Parties, and subject to any mandatory provisions of the procedural law of the place in which the arbitration is held, the Tribunal shall prescribe the procedure applicable to the arbitration on the basis of natural justice and of such principles of transnational arbitration procedure as it may find applicable, and shall regulate all matters relating to the conduct of the arbitration not otherwise provided for herein.

2.     The Tribunal shall hold a first meeting with the Parties as soon as practicable after being constituted, for the purpose of establishing the rules of procedure to govern the arbitration. This meeting, together with any other preliminary meetings held to determine procedural matters, shall not be counted for the purpose of calculating the time limit specified in subparagraph 3(viii) of this Article.

3.     In determining the procedures for the arbitration, the Tribunal shall observe the following provisions:

    i)     The language of the proceedings shall be English. However, the Parties may put forward references to authorities, decisions, awards, opinions and texts (or quotations therefrom) in French without translation.

    ii)    The seat of the arbitration shall be Paris.

    iii)   The Tribunal may, if it deems appropriate, engage experts. The Parties may also call such expert testimony (written or oral) as they wish. Both Parties shall have the right to question any such experts.

    iv)   The Parties shall also have the right to present the oral testimony of witnesses. The Parties undertake to use their best efforts to present witnesses only to the extent necessary to establish their claims and to refrain from calling witnesses where the presentation of documentary evidence will be equally satisfactory. Both Parties hereby express their intention that the oral hearings shall not be unduly prolonged.

    v)    All decisions of the Tribunal shall be by majority vote. All awards, preliminary or final, shall be in writing and signed by each arbitrator and shall state the reasons upon which the award is based. In the event that one arbitrator refuses to sign the award, the two arbitrators forming the majority shall state in the award the circumstances in which the signature of the remaining arbitrator has been withheld.

    vi)   If either Party fails within the prescribed time to appear or to present its case at any stage of the proceedings, the Tribunal may of its own motion or at the request of the other Party proceed with the arbitration and make an award.

vii)   The Tribunal shall keep records of all its proceedings and decisions, and a verbatim record of all oral hearings.

viii)   The final award shall be given within 18 months from the date of the first oral hearing on the substantive issues following the exchange of the Parties' first written submissions on those issues. The Tribunal may extend this period in its discretion. However, such extension shall not exceed 6 months, except that such period shall be extended by the number of days by which the Tribunal may be unable to conduct its business due to unforeseen circumstances beyond the control of the Tribunal or the Parties, such as periods of delay due to the death, resignation or incapacity of any member of the Tribunal, or except with the consent of the Parties.

## V

The final award of the Tribunal shall be binding on both Parties who hereby expressly waive all rights of recourse to any Court, except such rights as cannot be waived by the law of the place of arbitration. Each Party undertakes to comply therewith promptly and in good faith and within 120 days from the date of the final award.

## VI

Each Party will pay its own costs and expenses. The expenses of the Tribunal, including the honoraria of its members, the remuneration of the secretary and staff, and the expenses incurred by them, shall be borne by the Parties in equal shares.

.   .   .

2.      Excerpts from the Award

.   .   .

(iii) As provided by Article VII, paragraph 1, of the Arbitration Agreement, the latter entered into force on the day of its signature.

(iv) In application of its Article II, paragraph 1, the two Parties, on 23 July, 1979, addressed a request to the President of the

International Court of Justice for the appointment of a president of the Tribunal. By a letter dated 1 November, 1979, the President of the Court informed the Parties of the appointment of Monsieur Paul Reuter, Professor of Law at the University of Paris.

(v) On 19 December, 1979, the Tribunal held a first meeting with the Parties in Paris, in order to organize the proceedings. At this meeting each of the Parties submitted to the Tribunal a draft project for the Rules of Procedure. The Tribunal, however, decided to leave the adoption of the Rules until later, but fixed 2 June, 1980 as the date for the simultaneous deposit of the Parties' written Memorials, it being understood that the Counter-Memorials were to be delivered 120 days after that date, and the Replies 60 days after the Counter-Memorials.

(vi) During the same Paris meeting, the Tribunal appointed Monsieur Philippe Cahier, Professor of Law at the Graduate Institute of International Studies, Geneva, as Secretary to the Tribunal, and Monsieur Bernard Audit, Professor of Law at the University of Paris, as Deputy-Secretary.

(vii) At a private meeting of the Tribunal held in Geneva in July 1980, Rules of Procedure were adopted on the 16th of that month pursuant to Article IV, paragraph 2, of the Arbitration Agreement, in order to supplement and complete the procedural provisions of that Article. These Rules are set out in the Annex to the present Section.

(viii) The Parties deposited their Memorials with the Secretary on 2 June, 1980.

(ix) By a letter dated 21 August, 1980, the Government of Kuwait requested an extension of the time-limit for depositing the Counter-Memorials, and Aminoil having been consulted, the Tribunal, by an Order of 12 September, 1980, fixed 5 January, 1981 as the date for the delivery by both Parties of their Counter-Memorials, which were duly deposited on that date.

(x) Aminoil, having on 30 January, 1981 requested an extension of the time-limit for the deposit of the Replies, and the Government of Kuwait having made no objection, the Tribunal, by an Order of 26 February, 1981, fixed 27 April, 1981 as the date for such deposit, and this was duly adhered to by both Parties.

(xi) On 26 June, 1981 the Tribunal held a meeting with the Parties in Geneva in order to settle various points in connection with the forthcoming oral hearings. Following upon this meeting, the Tribunal, by an Order dated 30 June, 1981, fixed 16 November as the date for the opening of the hearings in Paris. It was also provided that a week of the hearings should be devoted to receiving the oral evidence of witnesses and experts. In head Y of the Order it was stated that

(xii) "The Tribunal takes note of the mutual intention of the Parties to direct their respective accountants to produce, if possible, a joint report on questions of *quantum* or, if this is not possible, to produce separate reports for the Tribunal before 1 November."

(xiii) As regards the order in which the Parties were to plead, head IV(a) of the Tribunal's June 30 Order specified that

The questions to be dealt with by the Parties in accordance with the preceding paragraphs, and the Party to speak first on each question, without prejudice to the burden of proof, shall be as follows:

1. The system of law governing the arbitration as a whole and the system of law applicable to the substantive issues in the case: the Government to start.

2. The agreements at any time existing between the Parties before 1973, and the meaning and effect of particular clauses in issue between them: the Government to start.

3. The validity and effect of the instruments of 1973, including the question of the Abu Dhabi formula: Aminoil to start.

4. The validity and effect of the Government's Decree Law n° 124 of 1977: Aminoil to start.

5. The breaches alleged by Aminoil: Aminoil to start.

6.      The breaches alleged by the Government: the Government to start.

7.      In so far as already dealt with under previous heads and in any case exclusive of all questions of pure *quantum*:

   i)      Aminoil's claims: Aminoil to start;

   ii)     the Government's claims: the Government to start.

It was added (head IV(b)) that

The wording of the foregoing questions implies no taking of position by the Tribunal in regard to any of them.

(xiv) On 30 October, 1981, the Chartered Accountant firms of Peat, Marwick, Mitchell and Co., London, and Peat, Marwick, Mitchell and Co., New York, sent the Tribunal a Joint Report on questions of *quantum*. In the absence of agreement on certain points, the first of the above mentioned firms deposited a separate Report on behalf of the Government of Kuwait.

(xv) Under head VIII of its Order of 30 June, 1981, the Tribunal had provided for a second stage of the oral hearings to be devoted exclusively to questions of *quantum*. However, this was eventually found by the Tribunal to be unnecessary, and did not take place.

(xvi) Oral hearings took place in Paris at the Hotel Hilton, from 16 November to 17 December, 1981. . . .

.      .      .

(xviii) The Tribunal wishes to express its great appreciation for the help it has received from the Parties throughout the proceedings in the form of written and oral statements and documentation that have been in conformity with the highest professional standards.

## ANNEX
## THE TRIBUNAL'S RULES OF PROCEDURE

### RULE 1
### PLACE OF ARBITRATION

(a) The Tribunal's Award shall be given at the seat of the arbitration, Paris.

(b) However, the Tribunal may, if it deems it convenient, meet elsewhere for the purposes of its private meetings or deliberations or for consultation with the Parties.

### RULE 2
### VACANCIES IN THE MEMBERSHIP OF THE TRIBUNAL

In the event of a vacancy in the membership of the Tribunal, the Tribunal, as constituted after the filling of the vacancy, shall determine the period necessary for the new member to familiarize himself with the proceedings up to that time before the resumption of the proceedings pursuant to Article II(3) of the Arbitration Agreement.

### RULE 3
### PRESIDENT: FUNCTIONS

(a) The President of the Tribunal shall superintend the administrative arrangements of the Tribunal, and shall preside at all hearings conducted by the Tribunal.

(b) The President, after consultation with the other members of the Tribunal, shall fix time limits, where required, for the various stages of the arbitration and determine the time and date of all hearings conducted by the Tribunal.

### RULE 4
### SECRETARIAT

(a) A Secretary and a Deputy Secretary shall be appointed by the Tribunal in accordance with Article II(4) of the Arbitration Agreement. The Deputy Secretary shall assist, and will have authority, if necessary, to replace the Secretary in those duties; in addition he shall act as a personal assistant to the President.

(b) The Secretary shall, under the direction of the President, make all the necessary administrative and financial arrangements for the conduct of the arbitration, including:

(i)     provision of suitable premises and facilities and

(ii)    the engagement and supervision of such clerical and stenographic staff and other assistance as may be necessary.

(c) The Secretary shall keep the official records of the arbitration, which shall include decisions, rulings, pronouncements, and written communications of the Tribunal or the President; pleadings and all attachments thereto, and written communications submitted by the Parties; and verbatim transcripts of all oral hearings. He shall attend all hearings of the Tribunal, and shall maintain and dispose of the record in accordance with Rule 15 of these Rules.

(d) The Secretary shall, under the direction of the President, have charge of the financial accounts of the Tribunal, shall establish necessary bank accounts and shall make all required disbursements.

(e) Except where otherwise decided by the President, the Secretary shall act as intermediary for communications between the Tribunal and the Parties and between the Parties.

He shall ensure that all communications be duly recorded.

(f) In addition to the foregoing, the Secretary shall perform such other duties as may be directed by the Tribunal or the President.

## RULE 5
## EXPENSES OF THE ARBITRATION

(a) The Tribunal is authorized to incur such expenses for staff and other purposes as may be necessary for the proper conduct of the arbitration.

(b) The Secretary shall request from each Party advance payments sufficient to cover fees and expenses, foreseeable or already incurred.

(c) Each Party shall pay, within three months after the close of the organizational meeting provided for in Article IV(2) of the Arbitration Agreement, an equal share of an amount fixed by the Tribunal as an advance toward the expenses of the arbitration. Further advances shall be made from time to time by both Parties in equal shares within 15 days of their being requested to do so by the

Secretary. If one of the Parties fails to render a payment or payments when requested, the Tribunal shall have discretion and authority to take appropriate measures to ensure the orderly continuance of the arbitration.

(d) Within 60 days after the final Award is rendered, the Secretary shall provide each Party with an accounting, approved by the President, of all expenses of the Tribunal and shall return to the Parties any excess amounts advanced in the proportion in which those amounts were advanced.

## RULE 6
## AGENTS AND COUNSEL

(a)     Each Party shall be represented by an Agent and/or Counsel before the Tribunal.

(b)     All communications from the Tribunal to the Parties shall be sent to the Agents representing the Parties, copies being sent to one other representative of each of the Parties designated by the respective Agents.

(c)     The Parties may communicate to the Tribunal either through their Agent or such other person as may be authorized by the Agent.

(d)     Each Party may also be assisted by advisers and experts.

## RULE 7
## ORGANIZATION OF THE PROCEEDINGS

The proceedings shall consist of two distinct phases: written proceedings and oral hearings.

## RULE 8
## WRITTEN PROCEEDINGS

(a) The written proceedings shall consist of three successive pleadings to be submitted simultaneously:

1)     a memorial, containing a statement of the claims of each Party, the basis of its claims and contentions and the relevant considerations in support thereof;

2)     a counter-memorial, containing the defence of each Party to the claims set out in 1) above;
       and

3)    a reply.

(b)    Documents and other written evidence on which a Party relies shall be submitted with the relevant pleadings.

(c)    A number of twenty copies of each pleading and the attachment thereto, shall be filed by each Party with the Tribunal. The Secretary shall transmit ten copies of each Party's pleadings to the other Party as promptly as possible, and shall similarly furnish each member of the Tribunal with such copies as he may require. When a time limit has been fixed for any such filing, the official date of receipt by the Secretary shall determine compliance with that limit.

(d)    Correction of an error in any written pleading or communication to the Tribunal, after it has been filed, may be made at any time during the arbitration with the consent of the other Party or with the permission of the Tribunal.

## RULE 9
## TIME LIMITS: CLOSURE OF WRITTEN PROCEEDINGS

(a)    The memorials setting out the claims of each Party shall be filed with the Tribunal not later than 2nd June 1980. The counter-memorials shall be filed not later than one hundred and twenty (120) days after the filing date for the memorials. The replies shall be filed not later than sixty (60) days after the filing date for the counter-memorials.

(b)    Upon application of either Party, the President of the Tribunal may, after consultation with the other Party, grant a reasonable extension of any time limit. Any such extension shall be applicable to both Parties. Any application for extension shall be filed with the Secretary not less than twenty (20) days before the expiry of the time limit concerned.

(c)    Unless the Tribunal directs otherwise, the written proceedings shall be considered closed after the time for filing of the replies has expired.

(d)    After the end of the written pleadings, no further documents may be submitted to the Tribunal by either Party, except with the consent of the other Party. In the absence of such consent, the Tribunal may, if it considers the document necessary, authorize its production.

## RULE 10
## ADJUDICATION OF THE CASE

(a)     At the end of the written proceedings, and after deliberation and taking into consideration any views expressed by the Parties, the Tribunal may, for a better regulation of the case, decide that the oral hearings shall be divided into two or more stages, the particular subject-matter of which it will determine. The ultimate stage will include the precise determination of any financial amounts due from either Party to the other.

(b)     At any time during the oral hearings, the Tribunal may give a preliminary ruling concerning matters already debated. Ultimately the Tribunal shall give its final Award, which will bear upon the whole case.

## RULE 11
## ORAL HEARINGS

(a)     After the closure of the written proceedings, the Tribunal shall commence oral hearings on a date to be fixed by the Tribunal after consultation with the Parties.

(b)     The conduct of the oral hearings shall be under the direction of the President who shall rule on all procedural points or questions in accordance with the provisions of Art. IV of the Arbitration Agreement and with the rules of procedure established by it on 16 July 1980.

(c)     The oral hearings shall consist of the hearing by the Tribunal of the arguments of the Parties' agents and counsel and of depositions by experts, of testimony by witnesses, including any exhibits offered in support thereof.

(d)     The order in which the Parties shall be heard shall be decided by the Tribunal after consultation with the Parties.

(e)     The Parties may also call such expert testimony, written or oral, as they wish.

(f)     The Tribunal also may, if it deems appropriate, engage experts who shall submit to the Tribunal oral or written deposition setting out their investigations and conclusions.

(g)     The Tribunal and the Parties shall have the right to question any such experts.

(h)     The Tribunal and each Party shall inform the Secretary in good time, as specified by the Tribunal, of the names, occupations and addresses of the experts that the Tribunal or the Party wishes to produce, with the indication of the points on which evidence, investigations or conclusions will be requested or given. If the Tribunal or either Party wishes to question any of the experts so appointed at an oral hearing, notice shall be given to the Secretary specifying the part or parts of the oral or written evidence in respect of which clarification is sought.

(i)     If either Party wishes to present the testimony of witnesses, it shall inform the Secretary in good time of the names, occupations and addresses of the witnesses that Party wishes to produce with the indication, in general terms, of the points or facts on which evidence will be sought. The Tribunal shall, if necessary, draw the attention of the Parties to their duty to use their best efforts to present witnesses only to the extent necessary to establish their claims and to refrain from calling witnesses where the presentation of documentary evidence will be equally satisfactory. The Tribunal shall have the right and the duty to implement the clause of Art. IV and to conduct the arbitration's oral proceedings accordingly.

(j)     The Tribunal may itself invite the Parties to present witnesses or request them to produce additional evidence on points or facts on which the Tribunal desires further information.

(k)     The President may at any stage of the oral hearings intervene in order to direct the course of the proceedings. The President and the other members of the Tribunal may put questions to or ask for information from agent, counsel, experts or witnesses. Both Parties shall enjoy a similar right.

(l)     Before presenting his deposition before the Tribunal each expert shall declare as follows: "I hereby solemnly declare, on my honour and in all conscience, that my statement will reflect my best professional judgement."

(m)     Before giving evidence, each witness shall declare as follows: "I hereby solemnly declare, on my honour and in all conscience, that I shall say the truth, the whole truth and nothing but the truth."

(n)     When the Tribunal deems that the Parties have completed the presentation of their cases, the Tribunal shall declare the hearings closed.

## RULE 12
## TAKING OF TESTIMONY AND REPORTS

(a)      Witnesses and experts, when giving evidence orally, shall first be questioned by the agent or counsel of the Party presenting them.

(b)      Witnesses and experts may then be examined by the agent or counsel of the opposing Party.

(c)      Further examination by either Party will be allowed in the discretion of the Tribunal on points arising out of, or directly connected with the previous questioning or examination.

(d)      Any objections to questions addressed to witnesses or experts or to any specific line of argument being pursued by counsel shall be allowed or disallowed at the discretion of the President, who may give his ruling immediately or defer it to a later sitting. The ruling may take the form of disallowing the objection for immediate purposes, but noting it as one that the Tribunal may bear in mind for the purposes of its eventual deliberation.

## RULE 13
## PRIVATE NATURE OF THE PROCEEDINGS:
## TRANSCRIPT OF THE RECORD

(a)      The proceedings shall take place in private. Only the Tribunal, the Secretary and Deputy Secretary and members of the Tribunal's staff, the Parties' agents, counsel, experts, witnesses, and officials associated with either Party, shall be entitled to attend the oral hearings or other sessions of the Tribunal with the Parties.

(b)      A verbatim transcript shall be kept of each oral hearing. Copies of the transcript of each hearing shall be furnished in principle daily to the Parties. One copy shall be authenticated by the Secretary for the record.

(c)      The written pleadings, with the attachments thereto, and oral testimony and any exhibits in support thereof, shall be treated as confidential, to be used solely for the purposes of the arbitration, until after the delivery of the final Award.

## RULE 14
## FINAL AWARD

(a)     The final Award shall be in reasoned form with a statement of any minority views, or the text of any minority opinion, annexed.

(b)     Seven original copies of the final Award shall be signed by the members of the Tribunal joining therein and by the Secretary. One such copy shall be retained by each member of the Tribunal and by the Secretary and the Deputy Secretary; and one copy shall be delivered to each Party.

## RULE 15
## DISPOSITION OF THE RECORD

The official record of the arbitration shall be retained by the Secretary under the direction of the President until such time as the President shall have received proof satisfactory to him that the Award has been complied with, or until such time as both Parties give the Secretary written notice that the record no longer be maintained. New expenses incurred for disposition of the record shall be shared by the Parties.

## RULE 16
## RULES PART OF RECORD; AMENDMENT; CLARIFICATION

(a)     These rules shall be made part of the official record of the arbitration.

(b)     These rules may be amended by the Tribunal after consultation with the Parties. The President may issue such clarifications or interpretations of the rules as may be required for the efficient conduct of the arbitration.

## SECTION III
## The Applicable Law

1.     The Parties have approached the question of "the applicable law" by distinguishing the procedural law of the arbitration — or law governing the arbitration as a whole - and the law governing the substantive issues in the case.

2.     On these topics they have furnished rival analyses and concepts which, on the scientific and academic levels, possess very great interest; but the Tribunal, in carrying out the function entrusted to it, has not experienced any difficulty as to the determination of the applicable law. The essential reason for this is twofold: the Parties themselves by their mutual arbitral commitments, have defined with adequate clarity what the applicable law is; and the legal systems that either do, or may, call for consideration in this connection have characteristics such that, for this case, the solution of the problem becomes easy.

3.     With regard to the law governing the arbitral procedure in the broadest sense, it is not open to doubt that the Parties have chosen the French legal system for everything that is implied in the statement in Article IV,1 of the Arbitration Agreement to the effect that the proceedings are subject to "any mandatory provisions of the procedural law of the place where the arbitration is held" (namely Paris); and both Parties "expressly waive all rights of recourse to any Court, except such rights as cannot be waived by the law of the place of arbitration" (Article V).

4.     But this does not in the least entail of itself a general submission to the law of the Tribunal's seat which was designated as Paris. In actual fact the Parties themselves, in the Arbitration Agreement, provided the means of settling the essential procedural rules, when they conferred on the Tribunal the power to "prescribe the procedure applicable to the arbitration on the basis of natural justice and of such principles of transnational arbitration procedure as it may find applicable" (Article IV, 1), which was done by the Rules adopted on 16 July, 1980.

5.     Having regard to the way in which the Tribunal has been constituted, its international or rather, transnational character is apparent. It must also be stressed that French law has always been very liberal concerning the procedural law of arbitral tribunals, and has left this to the free choice of the Parties who, often, have not had recourse to any one given national system. French law has thus befriended arbitrations the transnational character of which has been well in evidence. This tendency has been enhanced for the future by recent French legislation (Decree n° 81-500 of 12 May, 1981) which, even more specifically than before, affords recognition to transnational arbitration.

. . .

6.      Respecting the law applicable to the substantive issues in the dispute, which is what is really at stake between the Parties regarding the applicable law, the question is equally simple in the present case. It can hardly be contested but that the law of Kuwait applies to many matters over which it is the law most directly involved. But this conclusion, based on good sense as well as law, does not carry any all-embracing consequences with it, — and this for two reasons. The first is that Kuwait law is a highly evolved system as to which the Government has been at pains to stress that "established public international law is necessarily a part of the law of Kuwait" (GCM paragraph 3.97(5)). In their turn the general principles of law are part of public international law. — (Article 38,1(c) of the Statute of the International Court of Justice), — and that this specifically applies to Kuwait oil concessions, duly results from the clauses included in these. For instance, in the 1973 Agreement between the Parties, First Annex, Second Part, XII (GM App. I.9) the following provision is to be found (punctuation of second sentence added):

> The parties base their relations with regard to the agreements between them on the principles of goodwill and good faith. Taking account of the different nationalities of the parties, the agreements between them shall be given effect, and must be interpreted and applied, in conformity with principles common to the laws of Kuwait and of the State of New York, United States of America, and in the absence of such common principles, then in conformity with the principles of law normally recognized by civilized states in general, including those which have been applied by international tribunals.

Although the Parties did not, in the course of the present arbitral proceedings, make any reference to this particular text, it is of all the more interest to note that the ideas it embodies are no isolated features of Kuwait practice.

7.      Equally, the Offshore Concession Agreement of the Arabian Oil Company (AOC) . . . contains the same provision, except that reference is made to the principles common to Kuwait and to Japanese law (Article 39). The Oil Concession Agreement with the Kuwait

National Petroleum Company and Hispanica de Petroleos, concluded in 1967 . . ., refers to the principles common to Kuwait and to Spanish law. Yet it would be quite unrealistic to suppose that these three Concessions were governed by three different régimes. Clearly, it must have been the general principles of law that were chiefly present to the minds of the Government of Kuwait and its associates.

8.     But there is a second consideration which has greatly eased the task of the Tribunal, namely that the Parties have themselves, in effect, indicated in the Arbitration Agreement what the applicable law is. Article III,2 of the Agreement provides that

> The law governing the substantive issues between the Parties shall be determined by the Tribunal, having regard to the quality of the Parties, the transnational character of their relations and the principles of law and practice prevailing in the modern world.

Although it may in theory be possible for a litigation to be governed by an assemblage of rules different from that which, before the Arbitration, governed the situations and matters that are the object of the litigation, there must be a presumption that this is not the case. Thus, to the extent that Article III,2 of the Arbitration Agreement calls for interpretation, such an interpretation ought to be based on that provision which not only was freely chosen by the Parties in 1973 (see paragraph 6 *supra*), but also reflects the spirit which has underlain the carrying on of the oil concessions in Kuwait.

9.     Article III,2, with good reason, makes it clear that Kuwait is a sovereign State entrusted with the interests of a national community, the law of which cons[t]itutes an essential part of intracommunity relations within the State. At the same time, by referring to the transnational character of relations with the concessionaire, and to the general principles of law, this Article brings out the wealth and fertility of the set of legal rules that the Tribunal is called upon to apply.

10.     The different sources of the law thus to be applied are not at least in the present case - in contradiction with one another. Indeed, if, as recalled above, international law constitutes an integral part of the law of Kuwait, the general principles of law correspondingly recognize the rights of the State in its capacity of supreme protector of the general interest. If the different legal elements involved do not always

and everywhere blend as successfully as in the present case, it is nevertheless on taking advantage of their resources, and encouraging their trend towards unification, that the future of a truly international economic order in the investment field will depend.

### Notes and Questions

1. In the *Aminoil* case, the parties were at pains to design a choice of applicable law clause that met their specific needs. The tribunal discussed it in Section 3 of its award. Analyze the different components of the choice of law clause and identify which parts were incorporated at the behest of which party. As an arbitrator in this case, ask yourself what message the parties seem to be conveying to the tribunal with regard to the norms they wish to have applied to the case.

2. Prepare a short memorandum for a client who has asked you whether he should design an *ad hoc* arbitration rather than adopting one of the standard arbitration clauses. In your memorandum, weigh the advantages and disadvantages of such a course and the costs that may be involved.

3. As an arbitrator implementing an *ad hoc* arbitration agreement or a judge reviewing an award that has ensued from such an agreement, what precedents or authorities will you turn to for interpretative assistance?

## IX.    SPECIAL PROBLEMS IN STATE CONTRACTS

Contracts between private parties and foreign states that contain arbitration clauses may encounter three difficult problems: (1) internal restrictions on the capacity of the state to agree to arbitration, (2) issues relating to the authority of the person who signs on behalf of the state, and (3) controversy as to whether the state may be deemed to be a party to a set of contracts where it signed early protocols only, and then was replaced by a state entity having a formally separate legal identity.

The Preliminary Award in the *ad hoc* arbitration of *Benteler v. Belgium*, European Commercial Cases, 1985, p. 101, identified four theories for affirming the validity of the arbitration clause in cases involving states:

> (i)    Acknowledging a distinction between internal *ordre public* (public policy) and a less constraining international *ordre public*, and then

holding that a prohibition against the state or state entities' agreeing to arbitration is applicable only in domestic matters.

(ii)    Applying a presumption that, with respect to state or parastatal entities in international contracts, the capacity of the state or its subdivisions to conclude arbitration agreements is governed by the proper law of the contract rather than the internal law of the state.

(iii)   Holding the prohibition of agreements to arbitrate to be contrary to international public order, in the sense that a state which has concluded an arbitration agreement would be held to act contrary to international ordre public if it later tried to affirm that its internal law was incompatible with the undertaking to arbitrate.

(iv)    Allowing the international arbitrator to disregard the state's internal prohibition if, as according to the Preliminary Award, "the circumstances of the case are such that the state would be acting *contra factum proprium* by raising it"—a more moderate variant of the last approach involving an analysis similar to that underlying the notion of estoppel.

Of all the arbitral institutions in the world, one specializes in arbitrations involving private parties and states. It is the International Centre for the Settlement of Investment Disputes (ICSID), established under the aegis of the World Bank pursuant to the 1965 Washington Convention on the Settlement of Investment Disputes between States and Nationals of Other States.[111] The complexity of the issues under consideration is manifest when one peruses ICSID's Model Clauses, of which the following are illustrative.

---

[111] *See supra* p. 239 and note 66.

A.      ICSID MODEL CLAUSES AND COMMENTARIES, ICSID
        Doc. 5/Rev. 1, at 8-10 (1987).

## SECTION 3. - SPECIAL CLAUSES RELATING TO THE PARTIES

A. *Constituent Subdivision or Governmental Agency*

11. When one of the parties to the ICSID Conciliation/Arbitration
clause is not the Contracting State, but is a constituent subdivision or
a governmental agency of the Contracting State, two special
requirements must be fulfilled pursuant to Article 25(1) and (3):

- the subdivision or agency must have been designated to
  ICSID by the State concerned; and
- the consent given by the subdivision or agency must be
  approved by the State concerned unless that State has
  notified ICSID that no such approval is required.

The following clause is intended to show that these conditions
are satisfied:

### CLAUSE VI

[Name of the subdivision or agency] is [a constituent
subdivision] [an agency] of [name of the Host State],
which has been designated to the International Centre
for Settlement of Investment Disputes (ICSID) in
accordance with Article 25(1) of the Convention on the
Settlement of Investment Disputes between States and
Nationals of Other States (the Convention). In
accordance with Article 25(3) of the Convention, [name
of the Host State]:

-[hereby gives its approval to this consent agreement as
recorded in (one of the Basic Clauses) (Article
_____, section _____, _____,
19_____ ) between (name of the subdivision or agency)
and (name of the investor)].

-[has notified ICSID that (name of subdivision or
agency) requires no approval to give its consent to
ICSID (Conciliation) (Arbitration) pursuant to the

provisions of (this Agreement), (the Agreement dated
_____, 19___) between (name of
subdivision or agency) and (name of the investor)].

## B. *Nationality of the Investor*

12. If the investor is a natural person, the Convention requires him to
fulfil the following jurisdictional requirements: he must be a national
of a Contracting State other than the Host State both on the date of
consent and on the date of the registration of the request for
conciliation or arbitration, and he may not on either of these two dates
also have the nationality of the Host State. If the private party is a
juridical person, it must merely have the nationality of a Contracting
State other than the Host State on the date of consent. While the
Convention does not require that nationality be specified in the consent
agreement and a stipulation of nationality cannot correct an actual
disability, it may be useful to specify, by means of a clause such as the
one below, the nationality of the investor:

### CLAUSE VII

For the purposes of Article 25(3) of the Convention, it
is hereby agreed that [name of Investor] is a national of
[name of another Contracting State].

13. If the investor is a juridical person which on the date of consent
has the nationality of the Host State, Article 25(2)(b) of the Convention
provides that ICSID may still have jurisdiction if the parties agree that
"because of foreign control" the entity in question "should be treated
as a national of another Contracting State for the purpose of [the]
Convention." When this is the case, the parties may record their
agreement as to the nationality of the investor in a clause such as the
following:

### CLAUSE VIII

For the purposes of Article 25(2)(b) of the Convention, it is
hereby agreed that, although [name of the Investor] is a national
of [name of the Host State], it is controlled by nationals of
[name(s) of other Contracting State(s)] and shall be treated as
a national of [that] [those] State[s] for the purposes of the
Convention.

\*    \*    \*

To see how these concepts fare in practice, consider the following excerpts from the Interim Award of 24 October 1984 in the ICSID case below.

B.    *Liberian Eastern Timber Corp. ("LETCO") v. Liberia*, 13 YEARBOOK OF COMMERCIAL ARBITRATION, 35, 37-41 (1988).

INTERIM AWARD ON JURISDICTION

1.    The arbitral tribunal referred to Art. 25(1) of the Washington Convention and observed that this article demands three essential requirements in order for the tribunal to exercise jurisdiction.

2.    The first requirement is that there is a legal dispute arising directly out of an investment. The arbitral tribunal had:

> "no doubt that, based on the Concession Agreement, amounts paid out to develop the Concession, as well as other undertakings, this legal dispute has arisen directly from an 'investment' as that term is used in the Convention."

3.    The second requirement is that the parties have consented in writing to submit to ICSID. The content of the arbitration clause in the Agreement was for the arbitral tribunal "clear evidence of the parties' consent in writing to submit to" ICSID.

4.    The third requirement is that there is a dispute between a Contracting State and a national of another Contracting State. That requirement needed, according to the arbitral tribunal closer examination:

> "Art. 25(1) of the Convention requires, for the tribunal's jurisdiction, that the dispute be between a 'Contracting State and a national of another Contracting State.' Since Liberia has signed and ratified the Convention, it qualifies as a 'Contracting State.' LETCO on the other hand, is a company incorporated and registered within the Republic of Liberia. LETCO accordingly appears to have been a Liberian company and a juridical person with Liberian nationality, on the date on which the parties consented to submit the

dispute to arbitration. However, Art. 25(2)(*b*) goes on to define 'national of another Contracting State' as:

'any juridical person which had the nationality of a Contracting State other than the state party to the dispute on the date on which the parties consented to submit such dispute to conciliation or arbitration and *any juridical person which had the nationality of the Contracting State party to the dispute on the date and which, because of foreign control, parties have agreed should be treated as a national of another Contracting State for the purposes of this Convention.*' (Emphasis added)

"As previously indicated, LETCO would appear to have been a juridical person which had the nationality of the Contracting State party to the dispute (Liberia) on the date the parties consented to arbitration. Yet it is necessary to examine whether, because of foreign control, the parties have agreed that LETCO should be treated as a 'national of another Contracting State' (France) for the purpose of this Convention.

[5]    "(a) *Foreign control of LETCO*

"The evidence provided by LETCO clearly indicates that it was under French control at the time the Concession Agreement was signed. This control is not only a result of the fact that LETCO's capital stock was 100% owned by French nationals as indicated by both LETCO and official documents of the Liberian Government, it also results from what appears to be effective control by French nationals; effective control in the sense that, apart from French shareholdings, French nationals dominated the company decision-making structure. It appears from the evidence presented that a majority, if not all, of LETCO's directors, as well as the General Manager, were at all times French nationals.

[6] "(b) *Agreement, because of foreign control, to treat LETCO as a national of another Contracting State*

"In order to exercise jurisdiction the tribunal must determine that, because of French control, the Government of Liberia had agreed to treat LETCO as a French national. This requirement raises a number of difficult questions, in particular: Must there be a causal relationship between effective control and the agreement? If so, how can it be proved? What sort of an agreement, implied or expressed, is required? If the agreement may be implied, what facts are capable of implying such an agreement?

[7] "Clearly, the Convention's use of the word 'because' in Art. 25(2)(*b*) establishes a need to show that the agreement to treat LETCO as a French national was motivated by the fact that it was under French control. However, in most instances the virtually insurmountable burden of proof in showing what motivated a government's actions might well frustrate the purpose of the Convention. Therefore, unless circumstances clearly indicate otherwise, it must be presumed that where there exists foreign control, the agreement to treat the company in question as a foreign national is 'because' of this foreign control.

[8] "In the case at hand, there is no indication whatsoever that an agreement to treat LETCO as a French national resulted from anything other than the fact that it was under French control and we must therefore conclude that the necessary causal relationship exists.

[9] "The next question that must be resolved is that of the required nature of the agreement to treat LETCO as French national. Though it is not necessary to go so far in the case at hand, it could be argued with some force that the mere fact that Liberia and LETCO included an ICSID arbitration clause in the Concession Agreement constitutes an agreement to treat LETCO as a 'national of another Contracting State.' To conclude otherwise would be tantamount to stating that Liberia never intended to honour this part of the Concession Agreement; that Liberia, by agreeing to the ICSID clause, acted in bad faith and contrary to the tenor and purpose of the ICSID Convention.

[10] "When a Contracting State signs an investment agreement, containing an ICSID arbitration clause, with a foreign

controlled juridical person with the same nationality as the Contracting State and it does so with the knowledge that it will only be subject to ICSID jurisdiction if it has agreed to treat that company as a juridical person of another Contracting State, the Contracting State could be deemed to have agreed to such treatment by having agreed to the ICSID arbitration clause. This is especially the case when the Contracting State's laws require the foreign investor to establish itself locally as a juridical person in order to carry out an investment.

[11]     "Though the tribunal is not bound by the precedents established by other ICSID tribunals, it is nonetheless instructive to consider their interpretations of what constitutes an agreement to treat a juridical person which had the nationality of the Contracting State party to the dispute as a national of another Contracting State. In the *Holidays Inns* [sic] case, the tribunal indicated that 'such an agreement should therefore be explicit. An implied agreement would only be acceptable in the event that the specific circumstances would exclude any other interpretation of the intention of the parties, which is not the case here.' In *Amco-Asia et al. v. The Republic of Indonesia*, the claimant apparently applied to the Indonesian investment authorities for the establishment of a 'foreign business.' The parties also inserted an ICSID clause in their agreement. Since the Indonesian Government approved both the investment application and the ICSID clause, the tribunal found that there was an expressed agreement. Citing the *Holiday Inns* case, the tribunal stated:

'To refer to the *Holiday Inns* award — in spite of the same not being a binding precedent in this case here — this agreement is by no means implied; it is expressed, and clearly expressed, no formal or ritual clause being provided for in the Convention, nor needed in order for such an agreement to be binding upon the parties.'

[12]     "In the present case, there is adequate evidence to show that there existed an agreement to treat LETCO as a French national. The actions of the parties indicated that, even if there was no express agreement, there was at least an implied agreement.

[13]     "Both actions and documents show that Liberia agreed to treat LETCO as a foreign national. Perhaps most indicative of such

treatment are the annual certificates of registration which LETCO was required to file with the Liberian Ministry of Commerce, Industry and Transportation. These registrations were signed by such government officials as the Director of Domestic Trade, the Assistant Minister for Commerce and the Deputy Minister for Commerce. From 1975 to 1983 these certificates contained a section for indicating the registrating company's nationality. During all these years such nationality was indicated as 'French.'

[14] "Another indication of Liberia's treatment of LETCO as a foreign national is the appointment of the Minister of Foreign Affairs by the Liberian Head of State to participate in an advisory committee established to consider the questions raised by the dispute. Such an appointment indicates that non-domestic matters were involved despite the fact that LETCO was presumably a Liberian company. Though this Committee's opinions apparently were not binding on the Liberian Government, it is nonetheless interesting to note that the Committee's opinion was that Liberia would, based on the ICSID clause, be obligated to arbitrate.

[15] "These actions, combined with the fact, as indicated in the affidavit of the French Commercial Attaché to Liberia, that LETCO was obligated to form a Liberian company to carry out its investment and the fact that an ICSID arbitration clause was contained in the Concession Agreement, lead the tribunal to the inevitable conclusion that Liberia did agree to treat LETCO as a 'national of another Contracting State.'

"Given the fact that Liberia had failed to file a pleading in this dispute, the tribunal has raised the question of jurisdiction of its own initiative and required LETCO to submit evidence on this question. The evidence submitted has proven beyond a reasonable doubt that this tribunal has jurisdiction within the meaning of Art. 25 of the Convention and that it may now proceed to a consideration of the substance of the dispute between the parties."

### Notes and Questions

1. Of course all of the doctrines considered above, which focused on actions or statements by the State, apply only if one may properly attribute such actions or

statements to the State. Attributing such actions or statements to the state is often a difficult matter in and of itself. What happens if a document purporting to bind a government is signed by an official who is exceeding his authority?

2. The sovereign or state character of one of the parties can be critical in many other phases of the arbitration. See, in this regard, Chapters 3, 4, 5, 9, and especially 10.

> C.　　Jan Paulsson, *May a State Invoke Its Internal Law to Repudiate Consent to International Commercial Arbitration?*, 2 ARB. INT'L, 90, 102-03 n.34 (1986).

[The following excerpt catalogues a number of instances in which a state attempted to avoid arbitration by appealing to its own national law. Many of the defenses included claims that the official of the state who signed the arbitration agreement did not have the authority or competence to bind the state.]

In the 1982 *Aminoil v. Kuwait* award, which applied *inter alia* general principles of law, the distinguished tribunal presided by Paul Reuter stated that 'it is entirely normal and useful that, in transnational economic relations, the capacity of the Minister in charge of economic affairs should be presumed, as is that of a Minister for Foreign Affairs in inter-State relationships,' 21 *International Legal Material*, 1006 (1982). This concept has not been extensively developed in public international law. The following reported precedents may be recalled:

> In *Wauquier et Cie v. Government of Turkey et. al.* (1930), 10 Recueil des Décisions des Tribunaux Arbitraux Mixtes, 65 (1930); 1929-30 *Annual Digest and Reports of Public International Law Cases*, Case No. 262, at p. 434, the French Government argued that the Governor General of Vilayet, who had entered into a supply contract on behalf of the Municipality of Sivas, had no authorisation to contract in the name of the municipality and that therefore the Government did not have to pay the outstanding portion of accounts due on the shipment. The international tribunal rejected this argument, holding that the contractor was entitled to rely on the authority of the Governor General.

In the *Hemming* (GB v. US, 1920); 6 *Rep. Int. Arb. Awards,* 51, and *Trumbull* (*Chile v. US*) Moore, 4 *International Arbitrations,*

3569 (undated, decided under a 1892 convention) inter-State arbitrations, both applying general principles of international law, the US Government was held not entitled to repudiate the engagement of local counsel by the US diplomatic services in India and Chile, respectively; it did not matter that the US Government was correct in arguing that its own consular regulations did not authorise local consuls to employ legal advisers.

Finally, in the well-known 1933 *Eastern Greenland* case (also known as the case of the Ihlen Declaration), the Permanent Court of International Justice held that an oral declaration of the Norwegian Minister of Foreign Affairs to his Danish counterpart to the effect that Norway would never occupy any part of Greenland meant that 'Norway reaffirmed that she recognises the whole of Greenland as Danish; and thereby she has debarred herself from contesting Danish Sovereignty over the whole of Greenland,' PCIJ, Series A/B, No. 53, 70/71.

Considering practice to be 'uncertain,' Nguyen Quoc Dinh, Patrick Daillier and Alain Pellet, in their second edition of *Droit international public* (Paris, 1980) summarise at pp. 180-1 the principal systematic approaches to the problem of 'imperfect ratifications' as follows: First, the dualistic concept, which denies any international effect to national constitutional flaws of the consent to a convention; a treaty concluded in violation of domestic constitutional rules remains valid under international law. Second, the *monistic* theory which would reach the opposite conclusion; national constitutional rules partake of the international order by 'complementing' the international treaty-making process. Third, an attempt to reconcile these theoretical approaches may be referred to as an *empirical approach*, under which only a 'violation manifeste d'une disposition constitutionnelle notoirement connue would invalidate a purported engagement on behalf of the State.' . . . in all other cases, the ratification of a treaty by a head of State constitutes an affirmation that all competent State organs have truly accepted that the treaty become definitive, and then *he should be believed*. Otherwise, in order to prove that the head of State violated a constitutional rule of any trend, it would be necessary that the other parties interpret it themselves, which they do not have the right to do by virtue of the principle of non-interference in international affairs. *Ibid.*, at p. 181 (author's translation; emphasis in the original).

Notes and Questions

1. See, in this regard, Article 46 of the 1969 Vienna Convention on the Law of Treaties, (U.N. Doc. A/Conf.39/27, Fourth Annex):

> 1. A State may not invoke the fact that its consent to be bound by a treaty has been expressed in violation of a provision of its internal law regarding competence to conclude treaties as invalidating its consent unless that violation was manifest and concerned a rule of its internal law of fundamental importance.

> 2. A violation is manifest if it would be objectively evident to any State conducting itself in the matter in accordance with normal practice and in good faith.

2. The issue of capacity to represent a State may arise in very concrete instances. Does the signature of the captain of a warship in distress bind the State when he agrees to a form of contract (including an arbitration clause) handed to him by a salvage crew in a storm on the high seas? *See B.V. Bureau Wijsmuller v. United States*, No. 79 Civ. 4223 (S.D.N.Y. Feb. 2, 1982); 487 F. Supp. 156 (S.D.N.Y. 1979), *aff'd mem.*, 633 F. 2d 202; 702 F.2d 333 (2d Cir. 1983); 72 AM. J. INT'L. L. 411 (1978).

3. Arbitration agreements signed by States may prove ultimately ineffective if sovereign immunity from execution is not neutralized in some manner, *i.e.*, either by contractual waiver or by the law of a relevant enforcement forum. This subject will be considered in further detail in Chapter 10.

## X.  SUMMARY AND CONCLUSIONS

Chapter 1 explained the imperative in international commercial transactions to plan on jurisdiction and elaborated the special advantages of arbitration as one anticipatory method of dispute resolution for resolving the problem of jurisdictional uncertainty. Chapter 2 builds on our previous conclusions from that line of inquiry. It assumes that counsel has elected arbitration as the mode for dispute resolution in an international transaction. The Chapter then systematically considers the various intellectual tasks which a responsible lawyer would address in the design of an arbitral regime: the drafting of the arbitral clause, choice of venue, choice of substantive law (or an invitation to the tribunal to decide by reference to its sense of equity or according to *lex mercatoria*), the choice of arbitral rules, the option of designing an *ad hoc* arbitration, and the special problems that state contracts present in the design of an arbitral regime. This phase of the arbitral process, which is often treated mechanically or ignored, frequently proves to be outcome determinative when a dispute erupts and an arbitration commences. The responsible lawyer must master the material necessary for the performance of these tasks in order adequately to discharge her professional responsibility.

# CHAPTER 3

# ARBITRABILITY

## I.   INTRODUCTION

Freedom of contract, including the freedom to agree to arbitration, is not absolute. Limits on the right to consent to waive recourse to courts in favor of some private arbitration procedure are rationally imposed when courts perceive private disputes as implicating public policy questions so sensitive that it is felt that they should be reserved for decision by community officials. These are the so-called "non-arbitrable" matters. At one time or another, non-arbitrable matters have included disputes concerning competition law, patents, securities regulations and punitive damages. In cases involving subjects deemed by their nature to be non-arbitrable, courts have refused to compel a business enterprise to arbitrate despite the fact that it had previously agreed to do so and, more than likely, received some consideration in exchange for its agreement. The following materials set out the current map of restrictions and explore the rationale for judicially imposed constraints on the right to compel arbitration of certain subject matters. The materials also explore the question of timing: the wisdom of judicial intervention at the beginning of the arbitral process, when one party is seeking to avoid its agreement to arbitrate, rather than after the award has been rendered.

## II.   PRIORITIZING POLICY GOALS

### A.   SCOPE AND PURPOSE

William W. Park, *Private Adjudicators and the Public Interest: The Expanding Scope of International Arbitration*, 12 BROOK. J. INT'L. L. 629, 629-40 (1986).

.   .   .

Legal rules that affect private commercial transactions may benefit the public as well as provide justice between disputing parties. The businessman who brings an action for treble damages for injury due to a violation of the Sherman Act, designed to preserve the free enterprise system, enforces the Act for the benefit of all society. Courts have resisted giving effect to agreements to arbitrate disputes relating to such "core" public law claims, of which antitrust actions are but one illustration, for fear that private adjudicators may under-enforce laws designed to protect all of society.

.   .   .

All laws implicate public interests, in the sense that they further societal goals, such as ensuring respect for contracts or the orderly inheritance of property. Yet some laws appear to bear upon public interests to a greater degree than others.

Private parties may negotiate away some rights by an arbitration clause or choice of law clause — even before any dispute arise[112] — and courts will enforce this bargain. The right to demand payment for goods sold and delivered might, for example, be bargained away. As to other rights, however, courts hesitate to permit a waiver, before the dispute arises, of rights that implicate what might be referred to as "non-negotiable" public interests. Indeed, the vindication of some claims involves widespread effects, external to the parties, which are so significant that adjudication becomes a matter of public concern.

Disputes arising under competition law represent but one of several types of claims as to which courts have refused to compel arbitration, pursuant to an otherwise enforceable predispute agreement to arbitrate. With respect to commercial disputes,[113] American courts, at one time or another, have found at least a half dozen other areas of

---

[112] [16] A distinction between, "predispute" and "post-dispute" arbitration agreements is made in many jurisdictions. For example, in England predispute agreements to exclude judicial review of arbitral awards are still void as to shipping, insurance, and commodities contracts governed by English law. Court review of disputes in these areas was considered a fruitful catalyst for development of English law, long preeminent in maritime, insurance and commodities matters. Prohibition of predispute exclusion agreements in these areas was intended to encourage fertilization of English law by the commercial community through judicially reviewable arbitration. Exclusion of appeal in these "special category" disputes is possible only after the disputes actually arise. . . .

[113] [18] Non-commercial disputes may also be non-arbitrable, for example when they implicate civil rights or employment discrimination, or family law and child custody.

federal law to be "non-arbitrable" because of subject matter, including (1) the 1933 Securities Act, (2) patents,[114] (3) ERISA claims at termination of employment, (4) civil claims under the Racketeer Influenced and Corrupt Organizations Act, (5) bankruptcy matters as to which there is an automatic stay of all actions, (6) the Commodities Exchange Act, and (7) the Civil Rights Act.

Certain areas of state law have also been non-arbitrable, including claims under franchise law, not implicating interstate commerce and thus pre-empted by the Federal Arbitration Act,[115] and claims for punitive damages.

The goal of these "non-negotiable" legal rules is not merely justice between the parties. They also create benefits for all of society — such as a fair stock market or an orderly way to deal with bankruptcies. For this reason, courts consider that these rules implicate what might be called "public rights."

The first refrain that appears in arguments against arbitrability of public disputes is that public dispute resolution will fertilize judicial precedent. The development of the legal system, it may be argued, requires implementation and interpretation of statutes by courts that create precedents open for all to see. However, this argument seems to put the cart before the horse. Public interpretation of statutes does create precedent that may guide businessmen. However, courts elaborate the law to deal with disputes; they do not entertain litigation in order to permit lawyers to elaborate the law.

The second and more central theme that runs through the non-arbitrability cases is a concern that society at large will be injured by arbitration of public law claims. Courts express this fear in a variety of ways. They may say that the legal and factual issues are too

---

[114] [21] *See* cases cited in Davis, *Patent Arbitration: A Modest Proposal*, 10 ARB. J. 35 (1955). In 1982 Congress amended the patent statute to permit arbitration of validity and infringement suits. *See* 35 U.S.C. § 294 (1952).

[115] [28] Recently, it has been held that the Federal Arbitration Act prevails over the California Investment Franchise Law . . . . *See* Southland Corp. v. Keating, 465 U.S. 1 (1984) (involving California franchise of Texas-based owner of "Seven-Eleven" stores, holding that issues arising under State Investment Franchise Law were arbitrable).

complicated for arbitrators; that arbitration proceedings are too informal, providing inadequate discovery; that arbitrators, like foxes guarding the chicken coop, have a pro-business bias and will under-enforce laws designed to protect the public; that arbitrators are less connected to the democratic process than judges; that lack of appeal to arbitral awards makes arbitration a "black hole" to which rights are sent and never heard from again.

No empirical evidence suggests that arbitrators are necessarily any less trustworthy or competent than judges. There may, however, be merit in holding "public law issues" non-arbitrable under a slightly different alternative analysis, which starts with a recognition that arbitrators are paid only to do justice between or among the parties before them. "Public rights" belong not to the litigants, but to society at large. Society never signed the arbitration agreement, and is not a party to the arbitration. If the arbitration, which is a consensual process, affects only the consenting adults who signed the agreement, they alone are hurt by the arbitrators' folly. But if the dispute affects the property of one who never signed the arbitration agreement, the arbitration takes on a different cast. Indeed, the right to proper enforcement of antitrust laws may be analogous to a third person's property right. Furthermore, the societal interest in the vindication of claims relating to matters such as free economic competition and the securities markets belongs not to the businessmen in the controversy, but to a community which never agreed to arbitrate.

The dozen years before the *Mitsubishi* decision saw a chipping away of the judicial resistance to arbitration of public law claims. From one perspective, the *Mitsubishi* case is merely an extension of the doctrine announced in previous cases. Specifically, prior to *Mitsubishi*, the Supreme Court held in *Sherk* [sic] *v. Alberto-Culver*[116] that in an international contract securities law issues were arbitrable, notwithstanding their non-arbitrability in a domestic setting. *Sherk's* [sic] special rule for cross-border transactions, justified as necessary to avoid damaging the "fabric of international commerce and trade," was a logical extension of the Court's opinion in *Bremen v. Zapata*, which had been decided two years previously. In *Bremen*, the Court gave

---

[116] [30] 417 U.S. 506 (1974) (contract for sale of European corporations by a German citizen to an American company pursuant to a contract signed in Austria, closed in Switzerland and providing for I.C.C. arbitration in Paris).

effect to a predispute choice of forum clause that selected the High Court of London to decide a controversy between a German company and an American company.

Moreover, in 1984 the Supreme Court ruled that when interstate commerce is involved, prohibitions on arbitration under state franchise laws are invalid, preempted by the Federal Arbitration Act, as are prohibitions on arbitration of state securities law claims.[117] The trend toward greater arbitrability of subject matter is also manifest in legislative measures. Congress has removed barriers to arbitration of disputes involving the validity and infringement of patents, although the decisions are not binding on third parties.[118]

.  .  .

The *Mitsubishi* case skeletonizes various rival policies, each sound and worthy of recognition by itself, yet conflicting with each other in their application. These competing themes require a hierarchical ordering so that their application to a particular controverted event may be determined. In viewing these policies, one might articulate three competing objectives: (1) freedom of contract to provide for private dispute resolution, which calls for an efficient arbitral process; (2) protection of society against under-enforcement of

---

[117] Dean Witter Reynolds v. Byrd, 470 U.S. 213, 105 S. Ct. 1238, 84 L. Ed. 2d 158 (1985) (investor suit of brokerage firm because securities declined in value). In a footnote the Court suggested that claims under the 1934 Exchange Act, as opposed to the 1933 Securities Act, should be arbitrable. 105 S. Ct. at 1240 n.1.

[118] 35 U.S.C. § 294 (1952). Voluntary Arbitration
     (a) A contract involving a patent or any right under a patent may contain a provision requiring arbitration of any dispute relating to patent validity or infringement arising under the contract. In the absence of such a provision, the parties to an existing patent validity or infringement dispute may agree in writing to settle such dispute by arbitration. Any such provision or agreement shall be valid, irrevocable, and enforceable, except for any grounds that exist at law or in equity for revocation of a contract.
     .  .  .  .
     (c) An award by an arbitrator shall be final and binding between the parties to the arbitration but shall have no force or effect on any other person.
     .  .  .  .
*Id.* (added Pub. L. 97-247, § 17(b)(1), Aug. 27, 1982, 96 Stat. 322).

law by private adjudicators; and (3) meeting the needs of international trade and investment for a system of neutral non-national binding dispute resolution.

Underlying the first objective is the assumption that the enforcement of a freely accepted bargain to arbitrate — entered into by parties with equal negotiating power — will provide the business community with the benefits of confidential, economical and speedy dispute resolution. A different result might be reached in the case of "contracts of adhesion" imposed on weaker parties with little bargaining power. It may have been so in the Mitsubishi relationship with Soler, though the First Circuit based its refusal to compel arbitration on nonarbitrability of subject matter, not on the "adhesive" nature of the contract.

The second goal, protecting the public against under-enforcement of mandatory public norms, relates to a concern of many judges that arbitrators will be less likely than courts to apply our competition law correctly, or at least less likely to find liability and to assess treble damages. Incorrect application of the law may hurt those segments of society that have a stake in the outcome of the arbitration.

The final objective — meeting the needs of international commercial and investment transactions — presumes that business people will be more likely to enter into trans-border contracts, resulting in more efficient allocation of global resources, if they feel confident that potential disputes will be settled in a forum more neutral than the other party's national courts. While trans-border business will continue even if assertion of public law claims can defeat the arbitration agreement, it would seem reasonable to expect that many wealth-creating transactions might fail if business people lack confidence that they can avoid the "hometown justice" of the other party's national courts.

.    .    .

## Notes and Questions

1. The preceding suggests that non-arbitrability is based on fears of "under-enforcement." Courts may accept plea bargains in criminal matters or may enter negotiated settlements as judgments. Is that under-enforcement? Is the concern under-

enforcement or the absence of judicial supervision? To what extent does arbitral review address this problem?

2. Is the fact that a claim is based on "public law" the reason for non-arbitrability? Is that cogent? Are some private law claims non-arbitrable? Should they be?

3. Identify three areas that are susceptible to contract which in your view, should not be arbitrable. Explain your answer.

4. As a Justice of the Supreme Court, draft a general statement about non-arbitrability that can guide lower courts as they grapple with new claims.

## B.    TIMING

William W. Park, *National Law and Commercial Justice: Safeguarding Procedural Integrity in International Arbitration*, 63 TUL. L. REV. 647, 699-703 (1989).

.    .    .

In purely domestic disputes, a case can be made for denying arbitrators the power to decide public law disputes. In international dispute resolution, however, the paramount importance of insuring a neutral forum argues for enforcement of arbitration clauses. The effectiveness of neutral cross-border arbitration requires that arbitrators have the first word in deciding the contract's interpretation, even if judges have the last word on the contract's vital public policy implications.

In large measure the health of arbitration depends on the timing of court interference. To prevent an arbitrator from interpreting the contract, or to require parallel proceedings for public law issues, frustrates the parties' most fundamental expectations about the settlement of their differences. Having thought he agreed to arbitrate before a neutral law professor in Paris or London, the claimant instead finds the dispute decided in whole or in part before a hostile judge in the defendant's country. Whether in Boston or Barcelona, Atlanta or Algiers, Chicago or Cairo, the other side's hometown judge was not the bargained-for adjudicator.

On the other hand, if courts delay intervention until the award has been rendered, the agreement to arbitrate will have been honored. Only if the arbitrator did in fact ignore vital national interests of the relevant jurisdictions will judicial interference be necessary.

.    .    .

Allowing an arbitrator to decide a public law claim, although his award may be refused enforcement on grounds of public policy, is not a perfect accommodation of the competing claims for a neutral forum and for safeguarding the public interest. It does, however, respond to the special needs of international commerce by permitting the legal merits of the dispute to pass through the strainer of neutral arbitration before judges later review the award on the restricted grounds of what the Second Circuit has called our "most basic notions of morality and justice."[119]

International commercial arbitration provides a neutral playing field on which transnational economic law is enforced. Although it is difficult to generalize, the role of arbitration in the process of global wealth creation normally is justified by neither speed nor cost, but rather because its neutrality of forum and delocalized procedure provide a means of avoiding the "hometown justice" of the other party's judicial system.[120] Arbitration also reduces the idiosyncracies of national procedural law in matters such as discovery, the rules of evidence, and examining witnesses.

In a purely domestic context, an unenforceable arbitration clause may result in a trial in New York rather than an arbitration in Boston. In an international dispute, the alternative judicial proceedings may be in a foreign language and before a hostile judge of a country in which political influence makes a fair trial problematic: not a variant of the

---

[119] [181] Parsons & Whittemore Overseas Co. v. Société Générale de l'Industrie du Papier (RAKTA), 508 F.2d 969, 974 (2d Cir. 1974) (rejecting a public policy defense based on break in diplomatic relations between the U.S. and Egypt). . . .

[120] [182] Different considerations (principally arbitrator expertise) may lead to agreements to arbitrate matters of fact (so-called "sniff & feel" arbitrations) or matters arising out of standard form contracts in industries with historical ties to a particular locality (e.g., insurance arbitration in London).

language of Shakespeare used in the Big Apple, but the pure language of the prophet Mohammed in Tripoli.

This special need for neutrality of forum led the Supreme Court to allow a wider scope for subject matter arbitrability in international arbitration than in domestic. Securities law and antitrust claims were arbitrable in international disputes at a time when they could not be submitted to arbitrators in a domestic controversy.

.        .        .

### Notes and Questions

1. What are the effects of early judicial interference in an international arbitration?

2. Should the strategic question of *when* a court ought to intercede in the issue of non-arbitrability vary for international and domestic arbitration? Why? Why not?

3. Can you suggest reasons for early court intervention on some types of non-arbitrability issues in international arbitration? What are they?

## III.    TRENDS IN ARBITRABILITY JUDGMENTS

The subject matters dealt with in the following cases and statutory material have been considered, at one time or another, so sensitive from a public policy perspective that courts were unwilling to compel arbitration. As the cases show, however, there is a growing judicial predilection to expand the ambit of arbitrability and to hold business managers to their agreements to arbitrate even for matters that were formerly considered non-arbitrable. As you study them, ask yourself what is driving this trend. Might there be any merit in a cynic's description of arbitration as the garbage pail into which overcrowded courts throw their unwanted cases?

A.    ANTITRUST

*Mitsubishi Motors Corp. v. Soler Chrysler-Plymouth, Inc.*, 473 U.S. 614 (1985).

[Chrysler Motors (Chrysler) and Mitsubishi Heavy Industries entered into a joint venture to produce cars that would be marketed through Chrysler's distribution network. Chrysler dealers outside the continental United States were to distribute vehicles manufactured by a Japanese company, Mitsubishi Motors, owned jointly by Chrysler, through its Swiss subsidiary Chrysler International S.A., and Mitsubishi Heavy Industries.

Soler entered into two contracts: (1) a "Distributorship Agreement," with Chrysler's Swiss subsidiary and (2) a tripartite "Sales Agreement," binding not only Soler and Chrysler, but also Mitsubishi Motors, which covered the actual sale of the vehicles by the manufacturer.

The Sales Agreement contained a peculiar arbitration clause, which covered only disputes between Soler and Mitsubishi Motors, and only if arising under five of the contract's fifteen articles:

> All disputes, controversies or differences which may arise between [Mitsubishi] and [Soler] out of or in relation to Articles I-B through V of [the Sales Agreement] or for breach thereof, shall be finally settled by arbitration in Japan in accordance with the rules and regulations of the Japan Commercial Arbitration Association.

After Soler ordered the vehicles, business declined in San Juan. Soler asked to transship the vehicles to other markets in North, Central and South America, but Mitsubishi Motors refused to permit the transshipment, purportedly out of concern for the vehicles' suitability in areas outside Puerto Rico, where heaters might be needed or where unleaded high octane fuel could not be obtained. After Soler disclaimed the order, Mitsubishi Motors filed a claim to compel arbitration, to obtain a declaration that the distributorship was terminated, and to receive liquidated damages to reimburse storage costs and interest for the vehicles ordered but not shipped. These claims, as well as Soler's

Sherman Act counter-claims alleging a conspiracy to divide markets, were referred to arbitration by the district court.

Thereafter, the arbitration was interrupted when the First Circuit held that the antitrust counterclaims could not be referred to arbitration, following the doctrine announced in 1968 by the Second Circuit in *American Safety Equipment v. J.P. McGuire*, 391 F.2d 821 (2nd Cir. 1968). To fit the non-arbitrability doctrine into the framework of the New York Convention, the First Circuit linked Article II, relating to enforcement of the arbitration agreement, with Article V, relating to recognition of the award. Language in Article V — "under the laws of [the enforcement] country" — permits refusal of recognition of an award if the subject matter of the difference is not capable of settlement by arbitration under the law of that country where enforcement is sought. This language was read into Article II which mandates enforcement of agreements concerning a subject matter "capable of settlement by arbitration."

The Supreme Court granted certiorari primarily to consider whether an American court should enforce an agreement to resolve antitrust claims by arbitration when that agreement arises from an international transaction. Justice Blackmun delivered the Court's opinion.]

·   ·   · ·

At the outset, we address the contention raised in Soler's cross-petition that the arbitration clause at issue may not be read to encompass the statutory counterclaims stated in its answer to the complaint. In making this argument, Soler does not question the Court of Appeals' application of ¶ VI of the Sales Agreement to the disputes involved here as a matter of standard contract interpretation. Instead, it argues that as a matter of law a court may not construe an arbitration agreement to encompass claims arising out of statutes designed to protect a class to which the party resisting arbitration belongs "unless [that party] has expressly agreed" to arbitrate those claims, see Pet. for Cert. in No. 83-1733, pp. 8, i, by which Soler presumably means that the arbitration clause must specifically mention the statute giving rise to the claims that a party to the clause seeks to arbitrate. See 723 F.2d, at 159. Soler reasons that, because it falls within the class for whose benefit the federal and local antitrust laws and dealers' Acts were passed, but the arbitration clause at issue does not mention these statutes or statutes in general, the clause cannot be read to contemplate arbitration of these statutory claims.

We do not agree, for we find no warrant in the Arbitration Act for implying in every contract within its ken a presumption against arbitration of statutory claims. The Act's centerpiece provision makes a written agreement to arbitrate "in any maritime transaction or a contract evidencing a transaction involving commerce . . . valid, irrevocable, and enforceable, save upon such grounds as exist at law or in equity for the revocation of any contract." 9 U.S.C. § 2. The "liberal federal policy favoring arbitration agreements," *Moses H. Cone Memorial Hospital v. Mercury Construction Corp.*, 460 U.S. 1, (1983), manifested by this provision and the Act as a whole, is at bottom a policy guaranteeing the enforcement of private contractual arrangements: the Act simply "creates a body of federal substantive law establishing and regulating the duty to honor an agreement to arbitrate." *Id.*, at 25, n. 32. As this Court recently observed, "[t]he preeminent concern of Congress in passing the Act was to enforce private agreements into which parties had entered," a concern which "requires that we rigorously enforce agreements to arbitrate." *Dean Witter Reynolds Inc. v. Byrd*, 470 U.S. 213, 221 (1985).

Accordingly, the first task of a court asked to compel arbitration of a dispute is to determine whether the parties agreed to arbitrate that dispute. The court is to make this determination by applying the "federal substantive law of arbitrability, applicable to any arbitration agreement within the coverage of the Act." *Moses H. Cone Memorial Hospital*, 460 U.S., at 24. See *Prima Paint Corp. v. Flood & Conklin Mfg. Co.* 24, 388 U.S. 395, 400-404 (1967); *Southland Corp. v. Keating*, 465 U.S. 1 (1984). And that body of law counsels

> "that questions of arbitrability must be addressed with a healthy regard for the federal policy favoring arbitration. . . . The Arbitration Act establishes that, as a matter of federal law, any doubts concerning the scope of arbitrable issues should be resolved in favor of arbitration, whether the problem at hand is the construction of the contract language itself or an allegation of waiver, delay, or a like defense to arbitrability." *Moses H. Cone Memorial Hospital*, 460 U.S., at 24-25.

See, *e.g.*, *Steelworkers v. Warrior & Gulf Navigation Co.*, 363 U.S. 574, 582-583 (1960). Thus, as with any other contract, the parties' intentions control, but those intentions are generously construed as to issues of arbitrability.

There is no reason to depart from these guidelines where a party bound by an arbitration agreement raises claims founded on statutory rights. Some time ago this Court expressed "hope for [the Act's] usefulness both in controversies based on statutes or on standards otherwise created," *Wilko v. Swan*, 346 U.S. 427, 432 (1953); see *Merrill Lynch, Pierce, Fenner & Smith, Inc. v. Ware*, 414 U.S. 117, 135, n. 15 (1973), and we are well past the time when judicial suspicion of the desirability of arbitration and of the competence of arbitral tribunals inhibited the development of arbitration as an alternative means of dispute resolution. Just last Term in *Southland Corp.*, *supra*, where we held that § 2 of the Act declared a national policy applicable equally in state as well as federal courts, we construed an arbitration clause to encompass the disputes at issue without pausing at the source in a state statute of the rights asserted by the parties resisting arbitration. 465 U.S., at 15, and n. 7, 104 S. Ct., at 860, and n. 7. Of course, courts should remain attuned to well-supported claims that the agreement to arbitrate resulted from the sort of fraud or overwhelming economic power that would provide grounds "for the revocation of any contract." 9 U.S.C. § 2; see *Southland Corp.*, 465 U.S., at 16, n. 11; *The Bremen v. Zapata Off-Shore Co.*, 407 U.S. 1, 15 (1972). But, absent such compelling considerations, the Act itself provides no basis for disfavoring agreements to arbitrate statutory claims by skewing the otherwise hospitable inquiry into arbitrability.

That is not to say that all controversies implicating statutory rights are suitable for arbitration. There is no reason to distort the process of contract interpretation, however, in order to ferret out the inappropriate. Just as it is the congressional policy manifested in the Federal Arbitration Act that requires courts liberally to construe the scope of arbitration agreements covered by that Act, it is the congressional intention expressed in some other statute on which the courts must rely to identify any category of claims as to which agreements to arbitrate will be held unenforceable. See *Wilko v. Swan*, 346 U.S., at 434-435; *Southland Corp.*, 465 U.S., at 16, n. 11; *Dean Witter Reynolds Inc.*, 470 U.S., at 224-225 (concurring opinion). For that reason, Soler's concern for statutorily protected classes provides no reason to color the lens through which the arbitration clause is read. By agreeing to arbitrate a statutory claim, a party does not forgo the substantive rights afforded by the statute; it only submits to their resolution in an arbitral, rather than a judicial, forum. It trades the procedures and opportunity for review of the courtroom for the simplicity, informality, and expedition of arbitration. We must assume that if Congress intended the substantive protection afforded by a given statute to include protection against waiver of the right to a judicial forum, that intention will be deducible from text or legislative history. See *Wilko v. Swan*, *supra*. Having made the bargain to arbitrate, the party should be held to it unless Congress itself has evinced an intention to preclude a waiver of judicial remedies for the statutory rights at issue. Nothing, in the meantime, prevents a party from excluding statutory claims from the scope of an agreement to arbitrate. See *Prima Paint Corp.*, 388 U.S., at 406.

In sum, the Court of Appeals correctly conducted a two-step inquiry, first determining whether the parties' agreement to arbitrate reached the statutory issues, and then, upon finding it did, considering whether legal constraints external to the parties' agreement foreclosed the arbitration of those claims. We endorse its rejection of Soler's proposed rule of arbitration-clause construction.

### III

We now turn to consider whether Soler's antitrust claims are nonarbitrable even though it has agreed to arbitrate them. In holding that they are not, the Court of Appeals followed the decision of the Second Circuit in *American Safety Equipment Corp. v. J.P. Maguire & Co.*, 391 F.2d 821 (1968). Notwithstanding the absence of any explicit support for such an exception in either the Sherman Act or the Federal Arbitration Act, the Second Circuit there reasoned that "the pervasive public interest in enforcement of the antitrust laws, and the nature of the claims that arise in such cases, combine to make . . . antitrust claims . . . inappropriate for arbitration." *Id*. at 827-828. We find it unnecessary to assess the legitimacy of the *American Safety* doctrine as applied to agreements to arbitrate arising from domestic transactions. As in *Scherk v. Alberto-Culver Co.*, 417 U.S. 506 (1974), we conclude that concerns of international comity, respect for the capacities of foreign and transnational tribunals, and sensitivity to the need of the international commercial system for predictability in the resolution of disputes require that we enforce the parties' agreement, even assuming that a contrary result would be forthcoming in a domestic context.

Even before *Scherk*, this Court had recognized the utility of forum-selection clauses in international transactions. In *The Bremen*, *supra*, an American oil company, seeking to evade a contractual choice of an English forum and, by implication, English law, filed a suit in admiralty in a United States District Court against the German corporation which had contracted to tow its rig to a location in the Adriatic Sea. Notwithstanding the possibility that the English court would enforce provisions in the towage contract exculpating the German party which an American court would refuse to enforce, this Court gave effect to the choice-of-forum clause. It observed:

> "The expansion of American business and industry will hardly be encouraged if, notwithstanding solemn contracts, we insist on a parochial concept that all disputes must be resolved under our laws and in our courts. . . . We cannot have trade and commerce in world markets and international waters exclusively on our terms, governed by our laws, and resolved in our courts."

407 U.S., at 9. Recognizing that "agreeing in advance on a forum acceptable to both parties is an indispensable element in international trade, commerce, and contracting," *id.* at 13-14, the decision in *The Bremen* clearly eschewed a provincial solicitude for the jurisdiction of domestic forums.

Identical considerations governed the Court's decision in *Scherk*, which categorized "[a]n agreement to arbitrate before a specified tribunal [as], in effect, a specialized kind of forum-selection clause that posits not only the situs of suit but also the procedure to be used in resolving the dispute." 417 U.S., at 519. In *Scherk*, the American company Alberto-Culver purchased several interrelated business enterprises, organized under the laws of Germany and Liechtenstein, as well as the rights held by those enterprises in certain trademarks, from a German citizen who at the time of trial resided in Switzerland. Although the contract of sale contained a clause providing for arbitration before the International Chamber of Commerce in Paris of "any controversy or claim [arising] out of this agreement or the breach thereof," Alberto-Culver subsequently brought suit against Scherk in a Federal District Court in Illinois, alleging that Scherk had violated § 10(b) of the Securities Exchange Act of 1934 by fraudulently misrepresenting the status of the trademarks as unencumbered. The District Court denied a motion to stay the proceedings before it and enjoined the parties from going forward before the arbitral tribunal in Paris. The Court of Appeals for the Seventh Circuit affirmed, relying on this Court's holding in *Wilko v. Swan*, 346 U.S. 427 (1953), that agreements to arbitrate disputes arising under the Securities Act of 1933 are nonarbitrable. This Court reversed, enforcing the arbitration agreement even while assuming for purposes of the decision that the controversy would be nonarbitrable under the holding of *Wilko* had it arisen out of a domestic transaction. Again, the Court emphasized:

> "A contractual provision specifying in advance the forum in which disputes shall be litigated and the law to be applied is . . . an almost indispensable precondition to achievement of the orderliness and predictability essential to any international business transaction. . . .
>
> A parochial refusal by the courts of one country to enforce an international arbitration agreement would not only frustrate these purposes, but would invite unseemly and mutually destructive jockeying by the parties to secure tactical litigation advantages. . . . [It would] damage the fabric of international commerce and trade, and imperil the willingness and ability of businessmen to enter into international commercial agreements." 417 U.S., at 516-517.

Accordingly, the Court held Alberto-Culver to its bargain, sending it to the international arbitral tribunal before which it had agreed to seek its remedies.

*The Bremen* and *Scherk* establish a strong presumption in favor of enforcement of freely negotiated contractual choice-of-forum provisions. Here, as in *Scherk*, that presumption is reinforced by the emphatic federal policy in favor of arbitral dispute resolution. And at least since this Nation's accession in 1970 to the Convention, see [1970] 21 U.S.T. 2517, T.I.A.S. 6997, and the implementation of the Convention in the same year by amendment of the Federal Arbitration Act, that federal policy applies with special force in the field of international commerce. Thus, we must weigh the concerns of *American Safety* against a strong belief in the efficacy of arbitral procedures for the resolution of international commercial disputes and an equal commitment to the enforcement of freely negotiated choice-of-forum clauses.

At the outset, we confess to some skepticism of certain aspects of the *American Safety* doctrine. As distilled by the First Circuit, 723 F.2d, at 162, the doctrine comprises four ingredients. First, private parties play a pivotal role in aiding governmental enforcement of the antitrust laws by means of the private action for treble damages. Second, "the strong possibility that contracts which generate antitrust disputes may be contracts of adhesion militates against automatic forum determination by contract." Third, antitrust issues, prone to complication, require sophisticated legal and economic analysis, and thus are "ill-adapted to strengths of the arbitral process, *i.e.*, expedition, minimal requirements of written rationale, simplicity, resort to basic concepts of common sense and simple equity." Finally, just as "issues of war and peace are too important to be vested in the generals, . . . decisions as to antitrust regulation of business are too important to be lodged in arbitrators chosen from the business community — particularly those from a foreign community that has had no experience with or exposure to our law and values." See *American Safety*, 391 F.2d, at 826-827.

Initially, we find the second concern unjustified. The mere appearance of an antitrust dispute does not alone warrant invalidation of the selected forum on the undemonstrated assumption that the arbitration clause is tainted. A party resisting arbitration of course may attack directly the validity of the agreement to arbitrate. See *Prima Paint Corp. v. Flood & Conklin Mfg. Co.*, 388 U.S. 395 (1967). Moreover, the party may attempt to make a showing that would warrant setting aside the forum-selection clause — that the agreement was "[a]ffected by fraud, undue influence, or overweening bargaining power"; that "enforcement would be unreasonable and unjust"; or that proceedings "in the contractual forum will be so gravely difficult and inconvenient that [the resisting party] will for all practical purposes be deprived of his day in court." *The Bremen*, 407 U.S., at 12, 15, 18. But absent such a showing — and none was attempted here — there is no basis for assuming the forum inadequate or its selection unfair.

Next, potential complexity should not suffice to ward off arbitration. We might well have some doubt that even the courts following *American Safety* subscribe fully to the view that antitrust matters are inherently insusceptible to resolution by arbitration, as these same courts have agreed that an undertaking to arbitrate antitrust claims entered into *after* the dispute arises is acceptable. See, *e.g.*, *Coenen v. R.W. Pressprich & Co.*, 453 F.2d 1209, 1215 (CA2), cert. denied, 406 U.S. 949 (1972); *Cobb v. Lewis*, 488 F.2d 41, 48 (CA5 1974). See also, in the present cases, 723 F.2d, at 168, n. 12 (leaving question open). And the vertical restraints which most frequently give birth to antitrust claims covered by an arbitration agreement will not often occasion the monstrous proceedings that have given antitrust litigation an image of intractability. In any event, adaptability and access to expertise are hallmarks of arbitration. The anticipated subject matter of the dispute may be taken into account when the arbitrators are appointed, and arbitral rules typically provide for the participation of experts either employed by the parties or appointed by the tribunal.[121] Moreover, it is often a judgment that streamlined proceedings and expeditious results will best serve their needs that causes parties to agree to arbitrate their disputes; it is typically a desire to keep the effort and expense required to resolve a dispute within manageable bounds that prompts them mutually to forgo access to judicial remedies. In sum, the factor of potential complexity alone does not persuade us that an arbitral tribunal could not properly handle an antitrust matter.

For similar reasons, we also reject the proposition that an arbitration panel will pose too great a danger of innate hostility to the constraints on business conduct that antitrust law imposes. International arbitrators frequently are drawn from the legal as well as the business community; where the dispute has an important legal component, the parties and the arbitral body with whose assistance they have agreed to

---

[121] [17] See, *e.g.*, Japan Commercial Arbitration Association Rule 26, reprinted in App. 218-219; L. Craig, W. Park, & J. Paulsson, International Chamber of Commerce Arbitration §§ 25.03, 26.04 (1984); Art. 27, Arbitration Rules of United Nations Commission on International Trade Law (UNCITRAL) (1976), reprinted in 2 Yearbook Commercial Arbitration 167 (1977).

settle their dispute can be expected to select arbitrators accordingly.[122] We decline to indulge the presumption that the parties and arbitral body conducting a proceeding will be unable or unwilling to retain competent, conscientious, and impartial arbitrators.

We are left, then, with the core of the *American Safety* doctrine — the fundamental importance to American democratic capitalism of the regime of the antitrust laws. See, *e.g.*, *United States v. Topco Associates, Inc.*, 405 U.S. 596, 610 (1972); *Northern Pacific R. Co. v. United States*, 356 U.S. 1, 4 (1958). Without doubt, the private cause of action plays a central role in enforcing this regime. See, *e.g.*, *Hawaii v. Standard Oil Co.*, 405 U.S. 251, 262 (1972). As the Court of Appeals pointed out:

> "'A claim under the antitrust laws is not merely a private matter. The Sherman Act is designed to promote the national interest in a competitive economy; thus, the

---

[122] [18] See Craig, Park, & Paulsson, *supra*, § 12.03, p. 28; Sanders, Commentary on UNCITRAL Arbitration Rules § 15.1, in 2 Yearbook Commercial Arbitration, *supra*, at 203.

We are advised by Mitsubishi and *amicus* International Chamber of Commerce, without contradiction by Soler, that the arbitration panel selected to hear the parties' claims here is composed of three Japanese lawyers, one a former law school dean, another a former judge, and the third a practicing attorney with American legal training who has written on Japanese antitrust law. Brief for Petitioner in No. 83-1569, p. 26; Brief for International Chamber of Commerce as *Amicus Curiae* 16, n. 28.

The Court of Appeals was concerned that international arbitrators would lack "experience with or exposure to our law and values." 723 F.2d, at 162. The obstacles confronted by the arbitration panel in this case, however, should be no greater than those confronted by any judicial or arbitral tribunal required to determine foreign law. See, *e.g.*, Fed. Rule Civ. Proc. 44.1. Moreover, while our attachment to the antitrust laws may be stronger than most, many other countries, including Japan, have similar bodies of competition law. See, *e.g.*, 1 Law of Transnational Business Transactions, ch. 9 (Banks, Antitrust Aspects of International Business Operations), § 9.03[7] (V. Nanda ed. 1984); H. Iyori & A. Uesugi, The Antimonopoly Laws of Japan (1983).

plaintiff asserting his rights under the Act has been likened to a private attorney-general who protects the public's interest.'" 723 F.2d, at 168, quoting *American Safety*, 391 F.2d, at 826.

The treble-damages provision wielded by the private litigant is a chief tool in the antitrust enforcement scheme, posing a crucial deterrent to potential violators. See, *e.g.*, *Perma Life Mufflers, Inc. v. International Parts Corp.*, 392 U.S. 134, 138-139 (1968).

The importance of the private damages remedy, however, does not compel the conclusion that it may not be sought outside an American court. Notwithstanding its important incidental policing function, the treble-damages cause of action conferred on private parties by § 4 of the Clayton Act, 15 U.S.C. § 15, and pursued by Soler here by way of its third counterclaim, seeks primarily to enable an injured competitor to gain compensation for that injury.

> "Section 4 . . . is in essence a remedial provision. It provides treble damages to "[a]ny person who shall be injured in his business or property by reason of anything forbidden in the antitrust laws. . . ." Of course, treble damages also play an important role in penalizing wrongdoers and deterring wrongdoing, as we also have frequently observed. . . . It nevertheless is true that the treble-damages provision, which makes awards available only to injured parties, and measures the awards by a multiple of the injury actually proved, is designed primarily as a remedy." *Brunswick Corp. v. Pueblo Bowl-O-Mat, Inc.*, 429 U.S. 477, 485-486 (1977).

After examining the respective legislative histories, the Court in *Brunswick* recognized that when first enacted in 1890 as § 7 of the Sherman Act, 26 Stat. 210, the treble-damages provision "was conceived of primarily as a remedy for '[t]he people of the United States as individuals,'" 429 U.S., at 486, n. 10, quoting 21 Cong. Rec. 1767-1768 (1890) (remarks of Sen. George); when reenacted in 1914 as § 4 of the Clayton Act, 38 Stat. 731, it was still "conceived primarily as 'open[ing] the door of justice to every man, whenever he may be injured by those who violate the antitrust laws, and giv[ing] the injured party ample damages for the wrong suffered.'" 429 U.S., at 486, n. 10, quoting 51 Cong. Rec. 9073 (1914) (remarks of Rep.

Webb). And, of course, the antitrust cause of action remains at all times under the control of the individual litigant: no citizen is under an obligation to bring an antitrust suit, see *Illinois Brick Co. v. Illinois*, 431 U.S. 720, 746 (1977), and the private antitrust plaintiff needs no executive or judicial approval before settling one. It follows that, at least where the international cast of a transaction would otherwise add an element of uncertainty to dispute resolution, the prospective litigant may provide in advance for a mutually agreeable procedure whereby he would seek his antitrust recovery as well as settle other controversies.

There is no reason to assume at the outset of the dispute that international arbitration will not provide an adequate mechanism. To be sure, the international arbitral tribunal owes no prior allegiance to the legal norms of particular states; hence, it has no direct obligation to vindicate their statutory dictates. The tribunal, however, is bound to effectuate the intentions of the parties. Where the parties have agreed that the arbitral body is to decide a defined set of claims which includes, as in these cases, those arising from the application of American antitrust law, the tribunal therefore should be bound to decide that dispute in accord with the national law giving rise to the claim. Cf. *Wilko v. Swan*, 346 U.S., at 433-34.[123] And so long as the

---

[123] [This well-known footnote was numbered 19 in Justice Blackmun's opinion.]

In addition to the clause providing for arbitration before the Japan Commercial Arbitration Association, the Sales Agreement includes a choice-of-law clause which reads: "This Agreement is made in, and will be governed by and construed in all respects according to the laws of the Swiss Confederation as if entirely performed therein." App. 56. The United States raises the possibility that the arbitral panel will read this provision not simply to govern interpretation of the contract terms, but wholly to displace American law even where it otherwise would apply. Brief for United States as *Amicus Curiae* 20. The International Chamber of Commerce opines that it is "[c]onceivabl[e], although we believe it unlikely, [that] the arbitrators could consider Soler's affirmative claim of anticompetitive conduct by CISA and Mitsubishi to fall within the purview of this choice-of-law provision, with the result that it would be decided under Swiss law rather than the U.S. Sherman Act." Brief for International Chamber of Commerce as *Amicus Curiae* 25. At oral argument, however, counsel for Mitsubishi conceded that American law applied to the antitrust claims and represented that the claims had been submitted to the

prospective litigant effectively may vindicate its statutory cause of action in the arbitral forum, the statute will continue to serve both its remedial and deterrent function.

Having permitted the arbitration to go forward, the national courts of the United States will have the opportunity at the award-enforcement stage to ensure that the legitimate interest in the enforcement of the antitrust laws has been addressed. The Convention reserves to each signatory country the right to refuse enforcement of an award where the "recognition or enforcement of the award would be contrary to the public policy of that country." Art. V(2)(b), 21 U.S.T., at 2520; see *Scherk*, 417 U.S., at 519, n. 14. While the efficacy of the arbitral process requires that substantive review at the award-enforcement stage remain minimal, it would not require intrusive inquiry to ascertain that the tribunal took cognizance of the antitrust claims and actually decided them.[124]

---

arbitration panel in Japan on that basis. Tr. of Oral Arg. 18. The record confirms that before the decision of the Court of Appeals the arbitral panel had taken these claims under submission. See District Court Order of May 25, 1984, pp. 2-3.

We therefore have no occasion to speculate on this matter at this stage in the proceedings, when Mitsubishi seeks to enforce the agreement to arbitrate, not to enforce an award. Nor need we consider now the effect of an arbitral tribunal's failure to take cognizance of the statutory cause of action on the claimant's capacity to reinitiate suit in federal court. We merely note that in the event the choice-of-forum and choice-of-law clauses operated in tandem as a prospective waiver of a party's right to pursue statutory remedies for antitrust violations, we would have little hesitation in condemning the agreement as against public policy. . . .

[124] [20] See n. 19, *supra*. We note, for example, that the rules of the Japan Commercial Arbitration Association provide for the taking of a "summary record" of each hearing, Rule 28.1; for the stenographic recording of the proceedings where the tribunal so orders or a party requests one, Rule 28.2; and for a statement of reasons for the award unless the parties agree otherwise, Rule 36.1(4). See App. 219 and 221.

Needless to say, we intimate no views on the merits of Soler's antitrust claims.

As international trade has expanded in recent decades, so too has the use of international arbitration to resolve disputes arising in the course of that trade. The controversies that international arbitral institutions are called upon to resolve have increased in diversity as well as in complexity. Yet the potential of these tribunals for efficient disposition of legal disagreements arising from commercial relations has not yet been tested. If they are to take a central place in the international legal order, national courts will need to "shake off the old judicial hostility to arbitration," *Kulukundis Shipping Co. v. Amtorg Trading Corp.*, 126 F.2d 978, 985 (CA2 1942), and also their customary and understandable unwillingness to cede jurisdiction of a claim arising under domestic law to a foreign or transnational tribunal. To this extent, at least, it will be necessary for national courts to subordinate domestic notions of arbitrability to the international policy favoring commercial arbitration. . . .

Accordingly, we "require this representative of the American business community to honor its bargain," *Alberto-Culver Co. v. Scherk*, 484 F.2d 611, 620 (CA7 1973) (Stevens, J., dissenting), by holding this agreement to arbitrate "enforce[able] . . . in accord with the explicit provisions of the Arbitration Act." *Scherk*, 417 U.S., at 520.

The judgment of the Court of Appeals is affirmed in part and reversed in part, and the cases are remanded for further proceedings consistent with this opinion. . . .

JUSTICE POWELL took no part in the decision of these cases.

JUSTICE STEVENS, with whom JUSTICE BRENNAN joins, and with whom JUSTICE MARSHALL joins except as to Part II, dissenting.

．　　．　　．

This Court agrees with the Court of Appeals' interpretation of the scope of the arbitration clause, but disagrees with its conclusion that the clause is unenforceable insofar as it purports to cover an antitrust claim against a Japanese company. This Court's holding rests almost exclusively on the federal policy favoring arbitration of commercial disputes and vague notions of international comity arising from the fact that the automobiles involved here were manufactured in Japan. Because I am convinced that the Court of Appeals' construction of the arbitration clause is erroneous, and because I strongly disagree with this Court's interpretation of the relevant federal statutes, I respectfully dissent. In my opinion, (1) a fair construction of the language in the arbitration clause in the parties' contract does not encompass a claim that auto manufacturers entered into a conspiracy in violation of the antitrust laws; (2) an arbitration clause should not normally be construed to cover a statutory remedy that it does not expressly identify; (3) Congress did not intend § 2 of the Federal Arbitration Act to apply to antitrust claims; and (4) Congress did not intend the Convention on the Recognition and Enforcement of Foreign Arbitral Awards to apply to disputes that are not covered by the Federal Arbitration Act.

.    .    .

[Justice Stevens' arguments on points 1-3 above are omitted.]

## IV

The Court assumes for the purposes of its decision that the antitrust issues would not be arbitrable if this were a purely domestic dispute, *ante*, at 629, but holds that the international character of the controversy makes it arbitrable. The holding rests on vague concerns for the international implications of its decision and a misguided application of *Scherk v. Alberto-Culver Co.*, 417 U.S. 506 (1974).

### International Obligations of the United States

Before relying on its own notions of what international comity requires, it is surprising that the Court does not determine the specific commitments that the United States has made to enforce private agreements to arbitrate disputes arising under public law. As the Court acknowledges, the only treaty relevant here is the Convention on the Recognition and Enforcement of Foreign Arbitral Awards. [1970] 21 U.S.T. 2517, T.I.A.S. No. 6997. The Convention was adopted in 1958 at a multilateral conference sponsored by the United Nations. This Nation did not sign the proposed convention at that time; displaying its characteristic caution before entering into international compacts, the United States did not accede to it until 12 years later.

As the Court acknowledged in *Scherk v. Alberto-Culver Co.*, 417 U.S., at 520, n. 15, the principal purpose of the Convention "was to encourage the recognition and enforcement of commercial arbitration agreements in international contracts and to unify the standards by which agreements to arbitrate are observed and arbitral awards are enforced in the signatory countries." However, the United States, as *amicus curiae*, advises the Court that the Convention "clearly contemplates" that signatory nations will enforce domestic laws prohibiting the arbitration of certain subject matters. Brief for United States as *Amicus Curiae* 28. This interpretation of the Convention was adopted by the Court of Appeals, 723 F.2d, at 162-166, and the Court declines to reject it, *ante*, at 639-640, n. 21. The construction is beyond doubt.

Article II(3) of the Convention provides that the court of a Contracting State, "when seized of an action in a matter in respect of which the parties have made an agreement within the meaning of this article, shall, at the request of one of the parties, refer the parties to arbitration." This obligation does not arise, however, (i) if the agreement "is null and void, inoperative or incapable of being performed," Art. II(3), or (ii) if the dispute does not concern "a subject matter capable of settlement by arbitration," Art. II(1). The former qualification principally applies to matters of fraud, mistake, and duress in the inducement, or problems of procedural fairness and feasibility. 723 F.2d, at 164. The latter clause plainly suggests the possibility that some subject matters are not capable of arbitration under the domestic laws of the signatory nations, and that agreements to arbitrate such disputes need not be enforced.

This construction is confirmed by the provisions of the Convention which provide for the enforcement of international arbitration awards. Article III provides that each "Contracting State shall recognize arbitral awards as binding and enforce them." However, if an arbitration award is "contrary to the public policy of [a] country" called upon to enforce it, or if it concerns a subject matter which is "not capable of settlement by arbitration under the law of that country," the Convention does not require that it be enforced. Arts. V(2)(a) and (b). Thus, reading Articles II and V together, the Convention provides that agreements to arbitrate disputes which are nonarbitrable under domestic law need not be honored, nor awards rendered under them enforced.

This construction is also supported by the legislative history of the Senate's advice and consent to the Convention. In presenting the

Convention for the Senate's consideration the President offered the following interpretation of Article II(1):

> "The requirement that the agreement apply to a matter capable of settlement by arbitration is necessary in order to take proper account of laws in force in many countries which prohibit the submission of certain questions to arbitration. In some States of the United States, for example, disputes affecting the title to real property are not arbitrable." S.Exec.Doc. E, at 19.

The Senate's consent to the Convention presumably was made in light of this interpretation, and thus it is to be afforded considerable weight. *Sumitomo Shoji America, Inc. v. Avagliano*, 457 U.S. 176, 184-185 (1982).

*International Comity*

It is clear then that the international obligations of the United States permit us to honor Congress' commitment to the exclusive resolution of antitrust disputes in the federal courts. The Court today refuses to do so, offering only vague concerns for comity among nations. The courts of other nations, on the other hand, have applied the exception provided in the Convention, and refused to enforce agreements to arbitrate specific subject matters of concern to them.

It may be that the subject-matter exception to the Convention ought to be reserved — as a matter of domestic law — for matters of the greatest public interest which involve concerns that are shared by other nations. The Sherman Act's commitment to free competitive markets is among our most important civil policies. *Supra*, at 650-657. This commitment, shared by other nations which are signatory to the Convention, is hardly the sort of parochial concern that we should decline to enforce in the interest of international comity. Indeed, the branch of Government entrusted with the conduct of political relations with foreign governments has informed us that the "United States' determination that federal antitrust claims are nonarbitrable under the Convention . . . is not likely to result in either surprise or recrimination on the part of other signatories to the Convention." Brief for United States as *Amicus Curiae* 30.

Lacking any support for the proposition that the enforcement of our domestic laws in this context will result in international recriminations, the Court seeks refuge in an obtuse application of its own precedent, *Scherk v. Alberto-Culver Co.*, 417 U.S. 506 (1974), in order to defend the contrary result. The *Scherk* case was an action for damages brought by an American purchaser of three European businesses in which it was claimed that the seller's fraudulent representations concerning the status of certain European trademarks constituted a violation of § 10(b) of the Securities Exchange Act of 1934, 15 U.S.C. § 78j(b). The Court held that the parties' agreement to arbitrate any dispute arising out of the purchase agreement was enforceable under the Federal Arbitration Act. The legal issue was whether the Court's earlier holding in *Wilko v. Swan*, 346 U.S. 427 (1953) — "that an agreement to arbitrate could not preclude a buyer of a security from seeking a judicial remedy under the Securities Act of 1933," see 417 U.S., at 510 — was "controlling authority." *Ibid.*

The Court carefully identified two important differences between the *Wilko* case and the *Scherk* case. First, the statute involved in *Wilko* contained an express private remedy that had "no statutory counterpart" in the statute involved in *Scherk*, see 417 U.S., at 513. Although the Court noted that this difference provided a "colorable argument" for reaching a different result, the Court did not rely on it. *Id.* at 513-514.

Instead, it based its decision on the second distinction — that the outcome in *Wilko* was governed entirely by American law whereas in *Scherk* foreign rules of law would control and, if the arbitration clause were not enforced, a host of international conflict-of-laws problems would arise. The Court explained:

> "Alberto-Culver's contract to purchase the business entities belonging to Scherk was a truly international agreement. Alberto-Culver is an American corporation with its principal place of business and the vast bulk of its activity in this country, while Scherk is a citizen of Germany whose companies were organized under the laws of Germany and Liechtenstein. The negotiations leading to the signing of the contract in Austria and to the closing in Switzerland took place in the United States, England, and Germany, and involved

consultations with legal and trademark experts from
each of those countries and from Liechtenstein. Finally,
and most significantly, the subject matter of the contract
concerned the sale of business enterprises organized
under the laws of and primarily situated in European
countries, whose activities were largely, if not entirely,
directed to European markets.

Such a contract involves considerations and
policies significantly different from those found
controlling in *Wilko*. In *Wilko*, quite apart from the
arbitration provision, there was no question but that the
laws of the United States generally, and the federal
securities laws in particular, would govern disputes
arising out of the stock-purchase agreement. The parties,
the negotiations, and the subject matter of the contract
were all situated in this country, and no credible claim
could have been entertained that any international
conflict-of-laws problems would arise. In this case, by
contrast, in the absence of the arbitration provision
considerable uncertainty existed at the time of the
agreement, and still exists, concerning the law
applicable to the resolution of disputes arising out of the
contract." 417 U.S., at 515-516.

Thus, in its opinion in *Scherk*, the Court distinguished *Wilko* because
in that case "no credible claim could have been entertained that any
international conflict-of-laws problems would arise." 417 U.S., at 516.
That distinction fits this case precisely, since I consider it perfectly
clear that the rules of American antitrust law must govern the claim of
an American automobile dealer that he has been injured by an
international conspiracy to restrain trade in the American automobile
market.

The critical importance of the foreign-law issues in *Scherk* was
apparent to me even before the case reached this Court. . . . For that
reason, it is especially distressing to find that the Court is unable to
perceive why the reasoning in *Scherk* is wholly inapplicable to Soler's
antitrust claims against Chrysler and Mitsubishi. The merits of those
claims are controlled entirely by American law. It is true that the
automobiles are manufactured in Japan and that Mitsubishi is a
Japanese corporation, but the same antitrust questions would be

presented if Mitsubishi were owned by two American companies instead of by one American and one Japanese partner. When Mitsubishi enters the American market and plans to engage in business in that market over a period of years, it must recognize its obligation to comply with American law and to be subject to the remedial provisions of American statutes.

The federal claim that was asserted in *Scherk*, unlike Soler's antitrust claim, had not been expressly authorized by Congress. Indeed, until this Court's recent decision in *Landreth Timber Co. v. Landreth*, 471 U.S. 681 (1985), the federal cause of action asserted in *Scherk* would not have been entertained in a number of Federal Circuits because it did not involve the kind of securities transaction that Congress intended to regulate when it enacted the Securities Exchange Act of 1934. The fraud claimed in *Scherk* was virtually identical to the breach of warranty claim; arbitration of such claims arising out of an agreement between parties of equal bargaining strength does not conflict with any significant federal policy.

In contrast, Soler's claim not only implicates our fundamental antitrust policies, *supra*, at 650-657, but also should be evaluated in the light of an explicit congressional finding concerning the disparity in bargaining power between automobile manufacturers and their franchised dealers. In 1956, when Congress enacted special legislation to protect dealers from bad-faith franchise terminations, it recited its intent "to balance the power now heavily weighted in favor of automobile manufacturers." 70 Stat. 1125. The special federal interest in protecting automobile dealers from overreaching by car manufacturers, as well as the policies underlying the Sherman Act, underscore the folly of the Court's decision today.

V

The Court's repeated incantation of the high ideals of "international arbitration" creates the impression that this case involves the fate of an institution designed to implement a formula for world peace. But just as it is improper to subordinate the public interest in enforcement of antitrust policy to the private interest in resolving commercial disputes, so is it equally unwise to allow a vision of world unity to distort the importance of the selection of the proper forum for resolving this dispute. Like any other mechanism for resolving controversies, international arbitration will only succeed if it is realistically limited to tasks it is capable of performing well — the prompt and inexpensive resolution of essentially contractual disputes between commercial partners. As for matters involving the political passions and the fundamental interests of nations, even the multilateral convention adopted under the auspices of the United Nations recognizes that private international arbitration is incapable of achieving satisfactory results.

In my opinion, the elected representatives of the American people would not have us dispatch an American citizen to a foreign land in search of an uncertain remedy for the violation of a public right that is protected by the Sherman Act. This is especially so when there has been no genuine bargaining over the terms of the submission, and the arbitration remedy provided has not even the most elementary guarantees of fair process. Consideration of a fully developed record by a jury, instructed in the law by a federal judge, and subject to appellate review, is a surer guide to the competitive character of a commercial practice than the practically unreviewable judgment of a private arbitrator.

Unlike the Congress that enacted the Sherman Act in 1890, the Court today does not seem to appreciate the value of economic freedom. I respectfully dissent.

### Notes and Questions

1. Parties to a commercial dispute always have the right to settle their differences by mutual agreement. Why then should there ever be a question about "arbitrability" of the dispute? In arbitration, the parties to the dispute entrust this task of settlement to third parties wearing hats as arbitrators. What policy considerations justify a legal barrier to arbitral resolution of a controversy that could have been settled privately without either judges or arbitrators? Does it matter whether the arbitration agreement is concluded before or after the dispute arises?

2. Look again at Justice Blackmun's "prospective waiver" doctrine in footnote 19 [text footnote 123] of *Mitsubishi*. Lawyers do not always distinguish between a forum selection agreement (of which an agreement to arbitrate is one example) and the contract's choice of law clause. In thinking about the way the parties' freedom to choose applicable law will effect a court's willingness to enforce an arbitration agreement, look to the discussion of mandatory national norms (what Continental scholars would call *lois de police*) in Section 187 of the Restatement (Second) Conflict of Laws.

Section 187, Restatement (Second) Conflict of Laws provides as follows:

(1)     The law of the state chosen by the parties to govern their contractual rights and duties will be applied if the particular issue is one which the parties could have resolved by an explicit provision in their agreement directed to that issue.

(2)     The law of the state chosen by the parties to govern their contractual rights and duties will be applied, even if the particular issue is one which the parties could not have resolved by an explicit provision in their agreement directed to that issue, unless either

(a)     the chosen state has no substantial relationship to the parties or the transaction and there is no rational basis for the parties' choice, or

(b)     application of the law of the chosen state would be contrary to a fundamental policy of a state which has materially greater interest than the chosen state in the determination of the particular issue and which, under the rule of §188, would be the state of the applicable law in the absence of an effective choice of law by the parties.

(3)     In the absence of a contrary indication of intention, the reference is to the local law of the state of the chosen law.

3. In footnote 18 [text footnote 122] of *Mitsubishi*, the Court focuses on the ability and experience of the arbitrators in denying the presumptions of *American Safety* about the quality of the arbitral process. Should the Court fashion a broad and blunt rule about arbitrability of anti-trust disputes on the basis of the practice of specific arbitral institutions? Why would one presume that experience under the International Chamber of Commerce Rules would be a guide to the practice of the Japanese Commercial Arbitration Association, which governed the arbitration between Soler Chrysler-Plymouth and Mitsubishi?

4. Should the Court have based its decision to allow the arbitration to go forward merely on the vital need for neutrality of forum in trans-border commercial dispute resolution?

5. *Plus ça change, plus c'est la même chose*. Because Soler had filed a petition for reorganization under chapter 11 of the Bankruptcy Code, the District Court in Puerto Rico had to determine the effect of the Code's automatic stay of all actions. (11 U.S.C. § 362). The Court held that the Arbitration Act prevailed over the Bankruptcy Code in *Mitsubishi Motors v. Soler Chrysler-Plymouth*, No. 85-838 (D.P.R. Apr. 14, 1986). See the discussion of arbitrability and bankruptcy *infra* Part III.C.

6. What is meant by the language in Convention Article II(1) that limits mandatory enforcement of arbitration agreements to subject matters "capable of settlement by arbitration"?

7. When will an arbitration agreement be so "affected by fraud, undue influence or overweening bargaining power" as to impeach its enforcement?

### B.       SECURITIES

1.       *Scherk v. Alberto-Culver Co.*, 417 U.S. 506 (1974).

MR. JUSTICE STEWART delivered the opinion of the Court.

Alberto-Culver Co., the respondent, is an American company incorporated in Delaware with its principal office in Illinois. It manufactures and distributes toiletries and hair products in this country and abroad. During the 1960's Alberto-Culver decided to expand its overseas operations, and as part of this program it approached the petitioner Fritz Scherk, a German citizen residing at the time of trial in Switzerland. Scherk was the owner of three interrelated business entities, organized under the laws of Germany and Liechtenstein, that were engaged in the manufacture of toiletries and the licensing of trademarks for such toiletries. An initial contact with Scherk was made by a representative of Alberto-Culver in Germany in June 1967, and negotiations followed at further meetings in both Europe and the United States during 1967 and 1968. In February 1969 a contract was signed in Vienna, Austria, which provided for the transfer of the ownership of Scherk's enterprises to Alberto-Culver, along with all rights held by these enterprises to trademarks in cosmetic goods. The contract contained a number of express warranties whereby Scherk guaranteed the sole and unencumbered ownership of these trademarks. In addition, the contract contained an arbitration clause providing that "any controversy or claim [that] shall arise out of this agreement or the breach thereof" would be referred to arbitration before the International Chamber of Commerce in Paris, France, and that "[t]he laws of the

State of Illinois, U.S.A. shall apply to and govern this agreement, its interpretation and performance."[125]

The closing of the transaction took place in Geneva, Switzerland, in June 1969. Nearly one year later Alberto-Culver allegedly discovered that the trademark rights purchased under the contract were subject to substantial encumbrances that threatened to give others superior rights to the trademarks and to restrict or preclude Alberto-Culver's use of them. Alberto-Culver thereupon tendered back to Scherk the property that had been transferred to it and offered to rescind the contract. Upon Scherk's refusal, Alberto-Culver commenced this action for damages and other relief in a Federal District Court in Illinois, contending that Scherk's fraudulent representations concerning the status of the trademark rights constituted violations of § 10 (b) of the Securities Exchange Act of 1934, 48 Stat. 891, 15 U.S.C. § 78j (b), and Rule 10b-5 promulgated thereunder, 17 CFR § 240.10b-5.

In response, Scherk filed a motion to dismiss the action for want of personal and subject-matter jurisdiction as well as on the basis of *forum non conveniens*, or, alternatively, to stay the action pending arbitration in Paris pursuant to the agreement of the parties. Alberto-Culver, in turn, opposed this motion and sought a preliminary

---

[125] [1] The arbitration clause relating to the transfer of one of Scherk's business entities, similar to the clauses covering the other two, reads in its entirety as follows:

"The parties agree that if any controversy or claim shall arise out of this agreement or the breach thereof and either party shall request that the matter shall be settled by arbitration, the matter shall be settled exclusively by arbitration in accordance with the rules then obtaining of the International Chamber of Commerce, Paris, France, by a single arbitrator, if the parties shall agree upon one, or by one arbitrator appointed by each party and a third arbitrator appointed by the other arbitrators. In case of any failure of a party to make an appointment referred to above within four weeks after notice of the controversy, such appointment shall be made by said Chamber. All arbitration proceedings shall be held in Paris, France, and each party agrees to comply in all respects with any award made in any such proceeding and to the entry of a judgment in any jurisdiction upon any award rendered in such proceeding. The laws of the State of Illinois, U.S.A. shall apply to and govern this agreement, its interpretation and performance."

injunction restraining the prosecution of arbitration proceedings.[126] On December 2, 1971, the District Court denied Scherk's motion to dismiss, and, on January 14, 1972, it granted a preliminary order enjoining Scherk from proceeding with arbitration. In taking these actions the court relied entirely on this Court's decision in *Wilko v. Swan*, 346 U.S. 427, which held that an agreement to arbitrate could not preclude a buyer of a security from seeking a judicial remedy under the Securities Act of 1933, in view of the language of § 14 of that Act, barring "[a]ny condition, stipulation, or provision binding any person acquiring any security to waive compliance with any provision of this subchapter . . . ." 48 Stat. 84, 15 U.S.C. § 77n. The Court of Appeals for the Seventh Circuit, with one judge dissenting, affirmed, upon what it considered the controlling authority of the *Wilko* decision. 484 F.2d 611. Because of the importance of the question presented we granted Scherk's petition for a writ of certiorari. 414 U.S. 1156.

I

The United States Arbitration Act, now 9 U.S.C. § 1 *et seq.*, reversing centuries of judicial hostility to arbitration agreements, was designed to allow parties to avoid "the costliness and delays of litigation," and to place arbitration agreements "upon the same footing as other contracts . . . ." H. R. Rep. No. 96, 68th Cong., 1st Sess., 1, 2 (1924); see also S. Rep. No. 536, 68th Cong., 1st Sess. (1924). Accordingly the Act provides that an arbitration agreement such as is here involved "shall be valid, irrevocable, and enforceable, save upon such grounds as exist at law or in equity for the revocation of any contract." 9 U.S.C. § 2. The Act also provides in § 3 for a stay of proceedings in a case where a court is satisfied that the issue before it is arbitrable under the agreement, and § 4 of the Act directs a federal court to order parties to proceed to arbitration if there has been a "failure, neglect, or refusal" of any party to honor an agreement to arbitrate.

In *Wilko v. Swan*, *supra*, this Court acknowledged that the Act reflects a legislative recognition of the "desirability of arbitration as an

---

[126] [2] Scherk had taken steps to initiate arbitration in Paris in early 1971. He did not, however, file a formal request for arbitration with the International Chamber of Commerce until November 9, 1971, almost five months after the filing of Alberto-Culver's complaint in the Illinois federal court.

alternative to the complications of litigation," 346 U.S., at 431, but nonetheless declined to apply the Act's provisions. That case involved an agreement between Anthony Wilko and Hayden, Stone & Co., a large brokerage firm, under which Wilko agreed to purchase on margin a number of shares of a corporation's common stock. Wilko alleged that his purchase of the stock was induced by false representations on the part of the defendant concerning the value of the shares, and he brought suit for damages under § 12 (2) of the Securities Act of 1933, 15 U.S.C. § 77*l*. The defendant responded that Wilko had agreed to submit all controversies arising out of the purchase to arbitration, and that this agreement, contained in a written margin contract between the parties, should be given full effect under the Arbitration Act.

The Court found that "[t]wo policies, not easily reconcilable, are involved in this case." 346 U.S., at 438. On the one hand, the Arbitration Act stressed "the need for avoiding the delay and expense of litigation," *id.*, at 431, and directed that such agreements be "valid, irrevocable, and enforceable" in federal courts. On the other hand, the Securities Act of 1933 was "[d]esigned to protect investors" and to require "issuers, underwriters, and dealers to make full and fair disclosure of the character of securities sold in interstate and foreign commerce and to prevent fraud in their sale," by creating "a special right to recover for misrepresentation . . . ." 346 U.S., at 431. In particular, the Court noted that § 14 of the Securities Act, 15 U.S.C. § 77n, provides:

> "Any condition, stipulation, or provision binding any person acquiring any security to waive compliance with any provision of this subchapter or of the rules and regulations of the Commission shall be void."

The Court ruled that an agreement to arbitrate "is a 'stipulation,' and [that] the right to select the judicial forum is the kind of 'provision' that cannot be waived under § 14 of the Securities Act." 346 U.S., at 434-435. Thus, Wilko's advance agreement to arbitrate any disputes subsequently arising out of his contract to purchase the securities was unenforceable under the terms of § 14 of the Securities Act of 1933.

Alberto-Culver, relying on this precedent, contends that the District Court and Court of Appeals were correct in holding that its agreement to arbitrate disputes arising under the contract with Scherk is similarly unenforceable in view of its contentions that Scherk's conduct constituted violations of the Securities Exchange Act of 1934 and rules promulgated thereunder. For the reasons that follow, we reject this contention and hold that the provisions of the Arbitration Act cannot be ignored in this case.

At the outset, a colorable argument could be made that even the semantic reasoning of the *Wilko* opinion does not control the case before us. *Wilko* concerned a suit brought under § 12 (2) of the Securities Act of 1933, which provides a defrauded purchaser with the "special right" of a private remedy for civil liability, 346 U.S., at 431. There is no statutory counterpart of § 12 (2) in the Securities Exchange Act of 1934, and neither § 10 (b) of that Act nor Rule 10b-5 speaks of a private remedy to redress violations of the kind alleged here. While federal case law has established that § 10 (b) and Rule 10b-5 create an implied private cause of action, see 6 L. Loss, Securities Regulation 3869-3873 (1969) and cases cited therein; cf. *J.I. Case Co. v. Borak*, 377 U.S. 426, the Act itself does not establish the "special right" that the Court in *Wilko* found significant. Furthermore, while both the Securities Act of 1933 and the Securities Exchange Act of 1934 contain sections barring waiver of compliance with any "provision" of the respective Acts, certain of the "provisions" of the 1933 Act that the Court held could not be waived by Wilko's agreement to arbitrate find no counterpart in the 1934 Act. In particular, the Court in *Wilko* noted that the jurisdictional provision of the 1933 Act, 15 U.S.C. § 77v, allowed a plaintiff to bring suit "in any court of competent jurisdiction—federal or state—and removal from a state court is prohibited." 346 U.S., at 431. The analogous provision of the 1934 Act, by contrast, provides for suit only in the federal district courts that have "exclusive jurisdiction," 15 U.S.C. § 78aa, thus significantly restricting the plaintiff's choice of forum.

Accepting the premise, however, that the operative portions of the language of the 1933 Act relied upon in *Wilko* are contained in the Securities Exchange Act of 1934, the respondent's reliance on *Wilko* in this case ignores the significant and, we find, crucial differences between the agreement involved in *Wilko* and the one signed by the parties here. Alberto-Culver's contract to purchase the business entities belonging to Scherk was a truly international agreement. Alberto-Culver is an American corporation with its principal place of business and the vast bulk of its activity in this country, while Scherk is a citizen of Germany whose companies were organized under the laws of

Germany and Liechtenstein. The negotiations leading to the signing of the contract in Austria and to the closing in Switzerland took place in the United States, England, and Germany, and involved consultations with legal and trademark experts from each of those countries and from Liechtenstein. Finally, and most significantly, the subject matter of the contract concerned the sale of business enterprises organized under the laws of and primarily situated in European countries, whose activities were largely, if not entirely, directed to European markets.

Such a contract involves considerations and policies significantly different from those found controlling in *Wilko*. In *Wilko*, quite apart from the arbitration provision, there was no question but that the laws of the United States generally, and the federal securities laws in particular, would govern disputes arising out of the stock-purchase agreement. The parties, the negotiations, and the subject matter of the contract were all situated in this country, and no credible claim could have been entertained that any international conflict-of-laws problems would arise. In this case, by contrast, in the absence of the arbitration provision considerable uncertainty existed at the time of the agreement, and still exists, concerning the law applicable to the resolution of disputes arising out of the contract.

Such uncertainty will almost inevitably exist with respect to any contract touching two or more countries, each with its own substantive laws and conflict-of-laws rules. A contractual provision specifying in advance the forum in which disputes shall be litigated and the law to be applied is, therefore, an almost indispensable precondition to achievement of the orderliness and predictability essential to any international business transaction. Furthermore, such a provision obviates the danger that a dispute under the agreement might be submitted to a forum hostile to the interests of one of the parties or unfamiliar with the problem area involved.[127]

---

[127] [10] See Quigley, Accession by the United States to the United Nations Convention on the Recognition and Enforcement of Foreign Arbitral Awards, 70 Yale L.J. 1049, 1051 (1961). For example, while the arbitration agreement involved here provided that the controversies arising out of the agreement be resolved under "[t]he laws of the State of Illinois," *supra*, n. 1, a determination of the existence and extent of fraud concerning the trademarks would necessarily involve an understanding of foreign law on that subject.

A parochial refusal by the courts of one country to enforce an international arbitration agreement would not only frustrate these purposes, but would invite unseemly and mutually destructive jockeying by the parties to secure tactical litigation advantages. In the present case, for example, it is not inconceivable that if Scherk had anticipated that Alberto-Culver would be able in this country to enjoin resort to arbitration he might have sought an order in France or some other country enjoining Alberto-Culver from proceeding with its litigation in the United States. Whatever recognition the courts of this country might ultimately have granted to the order of the foreign court, the dicey atmosphere of such a legal no-man's-land would surely damage the fabric of international commerce and trade, and imperil the willingness and ability of businessmen to enter into international commercial agreements.

The exception to the clear provisions of the Arbitration Act carved out by *Wilko* is simply inapposite to a case such as the one before us. In *Wilko* the Court reasoned that "[w]hen the security buyer, prior to any violation of the Securities Act, waives his right to sue in courts, he gives up more than would a participant in other business transactions. The security buyer has a wider choice of courts and venue. He thus surrenders one of the advantages the Act gives him . . . ." 346 U.S., at 435. In the context of an international contract, however, these advantages become chimerical since, as indicated above, an opposing party may by speedy resort to a foreign court block or hinder access to the American court of the purchaser's choice.

Two Terms ago in *The Bremen v. Zapata Off-Shore Co.*, 407 U.S. 1, we rejected the doctrine that a forum-selection clause of a contract, although voluntarily adopted by the parties, will not be respected in a suit brought in the United States "'unless the selected state would provide a more convenient forum than the state in which suit is brought.'" *Id.*, at 7. Rather, we concluded that a "forum clause should control absent a strong showing that it should be set aside." *Id.*, at 15. We noted that "much uncertainty and possibly great inconvenience to both parties could arise if a suit could be maintained in any jurisdiction in which an accident might occur or if jurisdiction were left to any place [where personal or *in rem* jurisdiction might be established]. The elimination of all such uncertainties by agreeing in advance on a forum acceptable to both parties is an indispensable element in international trade, commerce, and contracting." *Id.*, at 13-14.

An agreement to arbitrate before a specified tribunal is, in effect, a specialized kind of forum-selection clause that posits not only the situs of suit but also the procedure to be used in resolving the dispute.[128] The invalidation of such an agreement in the case before us would not only allow the respondent to repudiate its solemn promise but would, as well, reflect a "parochial concept that all disputes must be resolved under our laws and in our courts. . . . We cannot have trade and commerce in world markets and international waters exclusively on our terms, governed by our laws, and resolved in our courts." *Id.*, at 9.

For all these reasons we hold that the agreement of the parties in this case to arbitrate any dispute arising out of their international commercial transaction is to be respected and enforced by the federal courts in accord with the explicit provisions of the Arbitration Act.

Accordingly, the judgment of the Court of Appeals is reversed and the case is remanded to that court with directions to remand to the District Court for further proceedings consistent with this opinion. . . .

[Justices Douglas, Brennan, White, and Marshall dissented.]

### Notes and Questions

1. Is the Court's approach in *Scherk* more or less "internationalist" than that of *Mitsubishi*? Which decision gives greater recognition to the specificity of international transactions?

2. The Court in *Scherk* found that "in the absence of the arbitration provision, considerable uncertainty existed at the time of the agreement, and still exists, concerning the law applicable to the resolution of disputes arising out of the contract." Why does a choice of law problem in a transaction require arbitration for its solution?

3. Justice Stevens, in his dissent in *Mitsubishi*, *supra*, observed that in *Scherk* the Court deemed international arbitration appropriate because foreign laws

---

[128] [13] Under some circumstances, the designation of arbitration in a certain place might also be viewed as implicitly selecting the law of that place to apply to that transaction. In this case, however, "[t]he laws of the State of Illinois" were explicitly made applicable by the arbitration agreement. See n. 1, *supra*.

controlled. In *Mitsubishi*, however, American anti-trust law controlled. Does the substantive law of the transaction determine where it will be adjudicated?

2.       *Rodriguez de Quijas v. Shearson/American Express Inc.*, 490 U.S. 477 (1989).

KENNEDY, J., delivered the opinion of the Court, in which REHNQUIST, C.J., and WHITE, O'CONNOR, and SCALIA joined. STEVENS, J., filed a dissenting opinion in which BRENNAN, MARSHALL, and BLACKMUN, JJ., joined. . . .

.    .    .

The question here is whether a predispute agreement to arbitrate claims under the Securities Act of 1933 is unenforceable, requiring resolution of the claims only in a judicial forum.

I

Petitioners are individuals who invested about $400,000 in securities. They signed a standard customer agreement with the broker, which included a clause stating that the parties agreed to settle any controversies "relating to [the] accounts" through binding arbitration that complies with specified procedures. The agreement to arbitrate these controversies is unqualified, unless it is found to be unenforceable under federal or state law. Customer's Agreement ¶ 13. The investments turned sour, and petitioners eventually sued respondent and its broker-agent in charge of the accounts, alleging that their money was lost in unauthorized and fraudulent transactions. In their complaint they pleaded various violations of federal and state law, including claims under § 12(2) of the Securities Act of 1933, 15 U.S.C. § 77*l*(2), and claims under three sections of the Securities Exchange Act of 1934.

The District Court ordered all the claims to be submitted to arbitration except for those raised under § 12(2) of the Securities Act. It held that the latter claims must proceed in the court action under our clear holding on the point in *Wilko v. Swan*, 346 U.S. 427 (1953). The District Court reaffirmed its ruling upon reconsideration and also entered a default judgment against the broker, who is no longer in the case. The Court of Appeals reversed, concluding that the arbitration agreement is enforceable because this Court's subsequent decisions have reduced *Wilko* to "obsolescence." *Rodriguez de Quijas v. Shearson/Lehman Bros., Inc.*, 845 F.2d 1296, 1299 (CA5 1988). We granted certiorari, 488 U.S. 954 (1988).

## II

The *Wilko* case, decided in 1953, required the Court to determine whether an agreement to arbitrate future controversies constitutes a binding stipulation "to waive compliance with any provision" of the Securities Act, which is nullified by § 14 of the Act. 15 U.S.C. § 77n. The Court considered the language, purposes, and legislative history of the Securities Act and concluded that the agreement to arbitrate was void under § 14. But the decision was a difficult one in view of the competing legislative policy embodied in the Arbitration Act, which the Court described as "not easily reconcilable," and which strongly favors the enforcement of agreements to arbitrate as a means of securing "prompt, economical and adequate solution of controversies." 346 U.S., at 438.

It has been recognized that *Wilko* was not obviously correct, for "the language prohibiting waiver of 'compliance with any provision of this title' could easily have been read to relate to substantive provisions of the Act without including the remedy provisions." *Alberto-Culver Co. v. Scherk*, 484 F.2d 611, 618, n. 7 (CA7 1973) (Stevens, J., dissenting), rev'd, 417 U.S. 506 (1974). The Court did not read the language this way in *Wilko*, however, and gave two reasons. First, the Court rejected the argument that "arbitration is merely a form of trial to be used in lieu of a trial at law." 346 U.S., at 433. The Court found instead that § 14 does not permit waiver of "the right to select the judicial forum" in favor of arbitration, *id.*, at 435, because "arbitration lacks the certainty of a suit at law under the Act to enforce [the buyer's] rights," *id.*, at 432. Second, the Court concluded that the Securities Act was intended to protect buyers of securities, who often do not deal at arm's length and on equal terms with sellers, by offering them "a wider choice of courts and venue" than is enjoyed by participants in other business transactions, making "the right to select the judicial forum" a particularly valuable feature of the Securities Act. *Id.*, at 435.

We do not think these reasons justify an interpretation of § 14 that prohibits agreements to arbitrate future disputes relating to the purchase of securities. The Court's characterization of the arbitration process in *Wilko* is pervaded by what Judge Jerome Frank called "the old judicial hostility to arbitration." *Kulukundis Shipping Co. v. Amtorg Trading Corp.*, 126 F.2d 978, 985 (CA2 1942). That view has been steadily eroded over the years, beginning in the lower courts. See *Scherk, supra*, at 616 (Stevens, J., dissenting) (citing cases). The erosion intensified in our most recent decisions upholding agreements to arbitrate federal claims raised under the Securities Exchange Act of 1934, see *Shearson/American Express Inc. v. McMahon*, 482 U.S. 220 (1987), under the Racketeer Influenced and Corrupt Organizations (RICO) statutes, see *ibid.*, and under the antitrust laws, see *Mitsubishi Motors Corp. v. Soler Chrysler-Plymouth, Inc.*, 473 U.S. 614 (1985). See also *Dean Witter Reynolds Inc. v. Byrd*, 470 U.S. 213, 221 (1985) (federal arbitration statute "requires that we rigorously enforce agreements to arbitrate"); *Moses H. Cone Memorial Hospital v. Mercury Construction Corp.*, 460 U.S. 1, 24 (1983) ("[Q]uestions of arbitrability must be addressed with a healthy regard for the federal policy favoring arbitration"). The shift in the Court's views on arbitration away from those adopted in *Wilko* is shown by the flat statement in *Mitsubishi*: "By agreeing to arbitrate a statutory claim, a party does not forgo the substantive rights afforded by the statute; it only submits to their resolution in an arbitral, rather than a judicial, forum." 473 U.S., at 628. To the extent that *Wilko* rested on suspicion of arbitration as a method of weakening the protections afforded in the substantive law to would-be complainants, it has fallen far out of step with our current strong endorsement of the federal statutes favoring this method of resolving disputes.

Once the outmoded presumption of disfavoring arbitration proceedings is set to one side, it becomes clear that the right to select the judicial forum and the wider choice of courts are not such essential features of the Securities Act that § 14 is properly construed to bar any waiver of these provisions. Nor are they so critical that they cannot be waived under the rationale that the Securities Act was intended to place buyers of securities on an equal footing with sellers. *Wilko* identified two different kinds of provisions in the Securities Act that would advance this objective. Some are substantive, such as the provision placing on the seller the burden of proving lack of scienter when a buyer alleges fraud. See 346 U.S., at 431, citing 15 U.S.C. § 77*l*(2).

Others are procedural. The specific procedural improvements highlighted in *Wilko* are the statute's broad venue provisions in the federal courts; the existence of nationwide service of process in the federal courts; the extinction of the amount-in-controversy requirement that had applied to fraud suits when they were brought in federal courts under diversity jurisdiction rather than as a federal cause of action; and the grant of concurrent jurisdiction in the state and federal courts without possibility of removal. See 346 U.S., at 431, citing 15 U.S.C. § 77v(a).

There is no sound basis for construing the prohibition in § 14 on waiving "compliance with any provision" of the Securities Act to apply to these procedural provisions. Although the first three measures do facilitate suits by buyers of securities, the grant of concurrent jurisdiction constitutes explicit authorization for complainants to waive those protections by filing suit in state court without possibility of removal to federal court. These measures, moreover, are present in other federal statutes which have not been interpreted to prohibit enforcement of predispute agreements to arbitrate. See *Shearson/American Express Inc. v. McMahon, supra* (construing the Securities Exchange Act of 1934; see 15 U.S.C. § 78aa); *ibid.* (construing the RICO statutes; see 18 U.S.C. § 1965); *Mitsubishi Motors Corp. v. Soler Chrysler-Plymouth, Inc., supra* (construing the antitrust laws; see 15 U.S.C. § 15).

Indeed, in *McMahon* the Court declined to read § 29(a) of the Securities Exchange Act of 1934, the language of which is in every respect the same as that in § 14 of the 1933 Act, compare 15 U.S.C. § 77v(a) with § 78aa, to prohibit enforcement of predispute agreements to arbitrate. The only conceivable distinction in this regard between the Securities Act and the Securities Exchange Act is that the former statute allows concurrent federal-state jurisdiction over causes of action and the latter statute provides for exclusive federal jurisdiction. But even if this distinction were thought to make any difference at all, it would suggest that arbitration agreements, which are "in effect, a specialized kind of forum-selection clause," *Scherk v. Alberto-Culver Co.*, 417 U.S. 506, 519 (1974), should not be prohibited under the Securities Act, since they, like the provision for concurrent jurisdiction, serve to advance the objective of allowing buyers of securities a broader right to select the forum for resolving disputes, whether it be judicial or otherwise. And in *McMahon* we explained at length why we rejected the *Wilko* Court's aversion to arbitration as a forum for resolving disputes over securities transactions, especially in light of the relatively recent expansion of the Securities and Exchange Commission's authority to oversee and to regulate those arbitration procedures. 482 U.S., at 231-234. We need not repeat those arguments here.

Finally, in *McMahon* we stressed the strong language of the Arbitration Act, which declares as a matter of federal law that arbitration agreements "shall be valid, irrevocable, and enforceable, save upon such grounds as exist at law or in equity for the revocation of any contract." 9 U.S.C. § 2. Under that statute, the party opposing arbitration carries the burden of showing that Congress intended in a separate statute to preclude a waiver of judicial remedies, or that such a waiver of judicial remedies inherently conflicts with the underlying purposes of that other statute. 482 U.S., at 226-227. But as Justice Frankfurter said in dissent in *Wilko*, so it is true in this case: "There is nothing in the record before us, nor in the facts of which we can take judicial notice, to indicate that the arbitral system . . . would not afford the plaintiff the rights to which he is entitled." 346 U.S., at 439. Petitioners have not carried their burden of showing that arbitration agreements are not enforceable under the Securities Act.

The language quoted above from § 2 of the Arbitration Act also allows the courts to give relief where the party opposing arbitration presents "well-supported claims that the agreement to arbitrate resulted from the sort of fraud or overwhelming economic power that would provide grounds 'for the revocation of any contract.'" *Mitsubishi*, 473 U.S., at 627. This avenue of relief is in harmony with the Securities Act's concern to protect buyers of securities by removing "the disadvantages under which buyers labor" in their dealings with sellers. *Wilko*, *supra*, at 435. Although petitioners suggest that the agreement to arbitrate here was adhesive in nature, the record contains no factual showing sufficient to support that suggestion.

.     .     .

[The judgment of the Court of Appeals was affirmed.]

## Notes and Questions

1. Has the court gone too far in *Rodriguez de Quijas v. Shearson/American Express Inc.*? Should arbitration clauses in consumer transactions be presumed invalid, given the greater sophistication and superior bargaining power often exercised by the seller of goods and services? As a policy matter, what (if anything) would be wrong with a federal statute similar to the Massachusetts regulations struck down on federal preemption grounds in *Securities Indus. Assoc. v. Connolly*, 883 F.2d 1114 (1st Cir. 1989)? Should the Federal Arbitration Act be amended to provide special presumptions about the validity for arbitration clauses in consumer transactions? See proposals to this end in Carbonneau, *Arbitration and the U.S. Supreme Court: A Plea for Statutory Reform*, 5 OHIO ST. J. DISP. RESOL. 231 (1990).

2. Look again at *Scherk v. Alberto-Culver Co.*, 417 U.S. 506 (1974), *Rodriguez de Quijas v. Shearson/American Express Inc.*, 490 U.S. 477 (1989), and *Mitsubishi Motors Corp. v. Soler Chrysler-Plymouth, Inc.*, 473 U.S. 614 (1985). What is driving the Court to abandon the traditional judicial resistance to arbitration of disputes implicating core public policies such as those raised by securities laws and anti-trust statutes? Is it a matter of:

(i)     greater confidence in the integrity and ability of arbitrators?

(ii)    court overcrowding and the litigation crisis ("hypertrophy in the growth of the civil docket in the United States," to use the words of Judge Selya in *Securities Indus. Assoc. v. Connolly*, 883 F.2d 1114, 1116 (1st Cir. 1989))?

(iii)   the relative clarity of policy in these types of disputes and, as a result, the routinization of their decision?

(iv)    All of the above?

3. Does the court in *Rodriguez de Quijas* give sufficient attention to the adhesive, take-it-or-leave-it nature of the contract?

C.    BANKRUPTCY

1.    *Société Nationale Algerienne Pour La Recherche, La Production, Le Transport, La Transformation et La Commercialisation des Hydrocarbures [Sonatrach] v. Distrigas Corp.*, 80 B.R. 606 (Bankr. D. Mass. 1987).

## MEMORANDUM AND ORDER

YOUNG, District Judge

In this appeal, the appellant, Societe Nationale Algerienne Pour La Recherche, La Production, Le Transport, La Transformation et La Commercialisation des Hydrocarbures ("Sonatrach") challenges the ruling of the United States Bankruptcy Court, dated May 15, 1986, denying Sonatrach's Motion to Modify the Automatic Stay to allow Sonatrach to commence arbitration before the International Chamber of Commerce, in Geneva, Switzerland pursuant to the arbitration clause in its contract with appellee Distrigas Corporation ("Distrigas"). The Bankruptcy Court denied Sonatrach's original motion to modify the stay on the ground that the contractual arbitration clause was "moot" in view of the rejection by Distrigas of the contract in its entirety after filing for protection under Chapter 11 of the U.S. Bankruptcy Code, 11 U.S.C. § 101 *et seq.* (1982). Sonatrach, the national energy corporation of the Algerian government and the creditor in this bankruptcy dispute, seeks international arbitration in order to determine the damages resulting from the rejection by the debtor Distrigas of a twenty-year supply contract for the purchase and sale of Algerian liquified natural gas.[129]

---

[129] [2] This dispute is but one battle in a much larger campaign. The parties' tactics here reflect their larger strategy. Sonatrach is the principal—indeed virtually the only—creditor of Distrigas. Sonatrach claims out-of-pocket losses of approximately twelve million dollars. Interestingly, the assets of Distrigas presently in the possession of the bankruptcy trustee are largely sufficient to satisfy this claim and those of the few other creditors as well as pay the costs of administration of the bankrupt's estate. There is no reasonable likelihood that Distrigas will ever have any additional assets or funds to meet any larger claims nor is there any likelihood that the trustee will uncover any additional assets or funds.

What then, as a practical matter of commerce, is all the fuss about?

For the reasons discussed below, this Court rules that Sonatrach is entitled to commence international arbitration, pursuant to the parties' contractual agreement, to resolve any outstanding questions of liability and damages in its breach of contract claim against Distrigas and directs that the automatic stay be modified accordingly.

There are two fundamental prongs to this appeal which must necessarily be addressed *seriatim*. The first presents the threshold issue of whether the arbitration clause contained in Article 17 of the Distrigas-Sonatrach contract survives the contract's rejection by the debtor in bankruptcy. Distrigas argues that its rejection of the contract effectively terminates the contract in its entirety while Sonatrach contends that rejection constitutes a material breach. What may initially appear to be a pointless semantic dispute actually has significant ramifications in this case as both "breach" and "termination" are employed as distinct terms of art under the Bankruptcy Code.

The rejection of an executory contract under the Bankruptcy Code receives explicit treatment in § 365(g). The Court begins its analysis of the statute heeding the familiar principle of statutory construction that requires courts to first examine the language of the statute. *See, e.g., Blue Chip Stamps v. Manor Drug Store*, 421 U.S. 723, 756, 95 S.Ct. 1917, 1935, 44 L.Ed.2d 539 (1974). Section 365(g) provides as follows:

> Except as provided in subsection (h)(2) and (i)(2) of this section, the *rejection* of an executory contract or unexpired lease of the debtor constitutes a *breach* of such contract or lease—
> (1) if such contract or lease has not been assumed under this section or under a plan confirmed under chapter 9,

---

Measuring the damages by the benefit-of-the-bargain, Sonatrach claims 1.2 billion dollars. While Distrigas could never satisfy such an enormous award, were one to be made, Distrigas is the wholly owned subsidiary of Cabot Cabot & Forbes [sic; in reality the parent was Cabot Corporation, unrelated to Cabot Cabot & Forbes, eds.] and Sonatrach seems to believe that it may be better able to lift the corporate veil in an international forum than here at home. For its part, Distrigas prefers to remain veiled before a known Bankruptcy Judge rather than endure the uncertainties of an international tribunal of "three foreigners." Remarks of Distrigas' counsel in Hearing Transcript, November 5, 1986, p. 25.

11, or 13 of this title, immediately before the date of the
filing of the petition. (emphasis added).

Significantly, at other points, including §§ 365(h)(1) and 365(i)(1),
which immediately follow, the Code states that rejected executory
contracts may be considered "terminated" under certain enumerated
conditions. Thus, "[w]here the legal concept of termination is
appropriate that term is used." *In re Storage Technology Corporation*,
53 B.R. 471, 474 (Bankr.D.Colo.1985). The precise use of language
strongly suggests that the relevant statutory provisions merit strict
construction as it appears that "the drafters of § 365 were aware of the
difference between a 'breach' and a 'termination'." *Blue Barn
Associates v. Picnic 'N Chicken, Inc.*, 58 B.R. 523, 525
(Bankr.S.D.Cal.1986). In *Storage Technology*, 53 B.R. at 474, the
court came to a similar conclusion: "A review of the overall structure
of § 365 . . . indicates that the words 'breach' and 'termination' were
intended to have different meanings."

Accordingly, the issue of whether the contract's rejection should
properly be considered "breach" or "termination" may not be
dismissed as a mere technicality. If the contract is terminated upon
rejection the present inquiry must necessarily come to a swift
conclusion as neither party is required to perform under the inoperative
agreement. *See* 5A A.L. Corbin, Corbin on Contracts, §§ 1229-30 (2d
ed. 1964 & Supp. 1984). If, however, the contract is deemed breached,
the nonbankrupt party is entitled to a pre-petition claim for damages
against the bankrupt estate. 11 U.S.C. § 365(g)(1).

While there is not a vast body of case law that analyzes the
semantic distinctions employed in § 365, the two recent bankruptcy
opinions cited above provide well-reasoned interpretations of the
controlling statutory language which comport with this Court's
predilection for narrow and precise statutory construction. In *Storage
Technology*, 53 B.R. at 475, the court, after carefully reviewing § 365
and the existing case law, concludes that "rejection of a lease does not
have the conclusive effect of terminating the lease." Similarly, in its
own careful analysis, the court in *Picnic 'N Chicken*, 58 B.R. at 526,
adopts the *Storage Technology* approach, ruling that "the
better-reasoned decisions hold that rejection by the debtor does not
necessarily terminate a lease agreement for all purposes."

Distrigas' attempt to distinguish these persuasive cases from the instant situation on the basis that they involved leases and not executory contracts is misplaced. A lease agreement, as far as it involves "obligations which continue in the future," *In re Jolly*, 574 F.2d 349, 351 (6th Cir.), *cert. denied*, 439 U.S. 929, 99 S.Ct. 316, 58 L.Ed.2d 322 (1978), is a form of executory contract that may be easily analogized to the present situation. Moreover, as another court has observed, "unexpired leases have been expressly included within Section 365 of the Code to preclude any uncertainty as to whether an unexpired lease is an executory contract." *Hasset v. Revlon, Inc. (In re O.P.M. Leasing Services, Inc.)*, 23 B.R. 104, 117 (Bankr.S.D.N.Y.1982).

This Court is equally unimpressed by Distrigas' reliance upon *Commercial Finance Limited v. Hawaii Dimensions, Inc.*, 47 B.R. 425 (D.Haw.1985), to rebut the sound reasoning employed by *Storage Technology* and *Picnic 'N Chicken*. The court in *Hawaii Dimensions* equates a lease's rejection with its termination based primarily upon a rather cursory statutory analysis driven perhaps more by concerns of equity than by the need to interpret rigorously the breach-termination distinction as identified in § 365(g), the controlling statutory section. The court stated that any contrary statutory interpretation "would unreasonably burden the lessor" under the facts of that case. *Hawaii Dimensions*, 47 B.R. at 427-28. Thus, the explanation offered in *Storage Technology*, 53 B.R. at 474, for the anomalous *Hawaii Dimensions* result rings true: "the potential for inequitable results appears to have [had] a large impact on the ultimate result reached [there]."

To be sure, this Court heartily approves of the general propositions, cited by Distrigas, that an executory contract must either be accepted or rejected in its entirety and the accompanying proposition that the parties to a contract may not selectively revive provisions in order to extract benefits at the other party's expense. Yet, these accepted principles of black letter law notwithstanding, a different tack is more appropriate with respect to arbitration clauses which represent the freely-negotiated method of dispute resolution selected *in advance* by the parties. As in the instant case, it may be safely assumed that arbitration clauses are not thoughtlessly incorporated into complex, international commercial contracts as mere ballast or as a meaningless nod in the direction of international comity. This assumption is further bolstered where both parties have equal bargaining power and are represented in their transactions by experienced and accomplished legal counsel.

In such circumstances, a strong argument can be made for construing arbitration agreements as "separable" from the principal contract even though they are physically embodied in the same instruments. Indeed, the First Circuit has expressed this preference and suggested that allowing an arbitration clause to be automatically invalidated along with the principal agreement would be akin to destroying "precisely what the parties had sought to create" as a dispute resolution device. *Lummus Company v. Commonwealth Oil Refining Company, Inc.*, 280 F.2d 915, 924 (1st Cir.), *cert. denied*, 364 U.S. 911, 81 S.Ct. 274, 5 L.Ed.2d 225 (1960); *see also Prima Paint Corp. v. Flood & Conklin Mfg. Co.*, 388 U.S. 395, 87 S.Ct. 1801, 18 L.Ed.2d 1270 (1967). This notion of separability is implicitly acknowledged in a well-established line of Massachusetts state court decisions which hold that even a contract's *termination* does not necessarily terminate arbitration provisions or other forms of dispute resolution procedure. *Mendez v. Trustees of Boston University*, 362 Mass. 353, 356, 285 N.E.2d 446 (1972) and cases cited therein.[130]

In view of the foregoing, this Court clears the first hurdle in the present appeal and rules that the arbitration provision survives the Distrigas rejection and retains its vitality as a viable method of alternative dispute resolution under the present circumstances.

With the arbitration clause still operational, the second—and certainly more far-reaching-issue raised in this appeal becomes ripe for resolution: the reconciliation of two important federal statutes, the Bankruptcy Code, 11 U.S.C. § 101 *et seq.* and the Arbitration Act, 9

---

[130] [3] In more general terms, a legal commentator has advanced the following conclusion on the "separability" doctrine:

> It is now firmly established in the United States, as well as in many other countries, that an arbitration clause is considered a separable contract between the parties which survives as an obligation of the promisor even if the underlying contract is voidable.

Westbrook, *The Coming Encounter: International Arbitration and Bankruptcy*, 67 Minn.L.Rev. 595, 623 (1983).

U.S.C. § 1 *et seq.* (1982), the underlying policies of each coming here in the instant case into direct conflict. Distrigas argues that the bankruptcy court should properly retain jurisdiction over all matters pertaining to its on-going bankruptcy proceeding. Sonatrach contends, on the contrary, that an international arbitration tribunal be allowed to determine contract damages pursuant to the arbitration provision contained in the rejected supply contract. The statutory interaction inherent in the current dispute presents a conflict of near polar extremes: bankruptcy policy exerts an inexorable pull towards centralization while arbitration policy advocates a decentralized approach towards dispute resolution. Reaching a satisfactory reconciliation between the two is no simple matter especially when each statute advances clear and unassailable legislative policies and comes well-armed with strong judicial approval. When confronted with a question of this nature, the Court is not assisted by the availability of any "bright line test" or controlling precedent. Indeed, in terms of existing precedent on this issue, this Court is left to mine a very thin vein of the law. The touchstones must be balance, pragmatism, and flexibility. Accordingly, any determination concerning the relative priority of conflicting federal statutes must be tailored to the facts of the individual case and, in essence, this Court perceives its role as one of balancing the prospective harms and benefits inherent in favoring any given legislative policy choice with fairness to the parties in reaching the most equitable solution.

At the outset, the respective policy considerations behind each statute merit brief discussion. The Bankruptcy Reform Act, codified at 11 U.S.C. § 101, was enacted in 1978 to promote several well-defined policy goals including the centralization of all bankruptcy matters in a specialized forum—the federal Bankruptcy Court—which was given exclusive jurisdiction over the bankrupt's affairs. *See Northern Pipeline Construction Co. v. Marathon Pipeline Co.*, 458 U.S. 50, 102 S.Ct. 2858, 73 L.Ed.2d 598 (1982). By centralizing all disputes in the bankruptcy courts, Congress sought to ensure the orderly and expeditious rehabilitation or liquidation of debtors, taking special care, in enacting the automatic stay provisions of §362, "to give the debtor and his creditor body a full, fair, speedy, and unhampered chance for reorganization." *Braniff Airways, Inc. v. United Air Lines, Inc.*, 33 B.R. 33, 34 (Bankr.N.D.Tex. 1983).

The Federal Arbitration Act, 9 U.S.C. § 1 *et seq.*, and its subsequent incorporation of the Convention of the Recognition and

Enforcement of Foreign Arbitral Awards, 21 U.S.T. 2517 T.I.A.S. No. 6997 (acceded to by U.S. Sept. 1, 1970), seeks generally to overcome "the anachronistic judicial hostility to agreements to arbitrate" that American courts inherited from their English brethren. *Mitsubishi Motors Corporation v. Soler Chrysler Plymouth, Inc.*, [sic] 473 U.S. 614, 105 S.Ct. 3346, 3354 n. 14, 87 L.Ed.2d 444 (1985). On a more practical level, the Act promotes neutrality and certainty in the adjudication of international commercial disputes and, at its very core, codifies the notion that arbitration agreements be placed "on the same footing" as private contractual arrangements and should be honored even at the expense of a court's being "ousted" from jurisdiction. *Mitsubishi*, 105 S.Ct. at 3353-54.

The federal bankruptcy courts, newly-vested with the requisite authority to deal with the specialized and increasingly complex area of bankruptcy law, are understandably reluctant to part with their broad jurisdictional sweep. Accordingly, the observation that "[t]he bankruptcy court does not ordinarily surrender its jurisdiction except under exceptional circumstances," *In re Brookhaven Textiles, Inc.*, 21 B.R. 204, 206 (Bankr.S.D.N.Y.1982), is amply supported by several bankruptcy court decisions in which the courts have found bankruptcy policy to supersede conflicting federal statutory policies including the pro-arbitration policy advanced under the Arbitration Act. There is no uniform line of decision, however, as other bankruptcy courts have expressed markedly divergent views and have enforced arbitration agreements. Yet, in general terms, it has been fairly stated that "[w]here compelling the arbitration of disputes conflicts with other important federal policies, the courts have frequently refused to order arbitration." *Bache Halsey Stuart, Inc. v. French*, 425 F.Supp. 1231, 1233 (D.C.Cir.1977). . . .

These decisions, however, while helpful and informative, are necessarily limited to their particular facts and do not control under the present factual circumstances, especially where the dispute contains a significant international dimension. The two most salient facts of the present case, as it now stands, which serve to distinguish it from the mainstream are the international character of the transaction and the presence of a failed Chapter 11 debtor. These characteristics are of substantial import. With regard to international arbitration agreements, for example, the United States Supreme Court has recently stated that the "emphatic" federal policy in favor of arbitration "applies with special force in the field of international commerce." *Mitsubishi*, 105

S.Ct. at 3357. Similarly, with the failure of Distrigas to reorganize successfully, one of the Bankruptcy Code's primary goals—"to give debtors a fresh start"—has already been frustrated. *Quinn v. CGR*, 48 B.R. 367, 369 (D.Colo.1985).

Few courts have focused upon the precise interplay between bankruptcy policy and the policy favoring international arbitration. *Allen & Hein*, 59 B.R. 733 (Bankr.S.D.Cal.1986). Fewer still have involved a factual scenario similar to the present case. Only one decision, *Quinn*, bears a reasonably close resemblance and, while it should not control pursuant to this Court's stated philosophy that federal statutory conflicts need be resolved on a case-by-case basis, its reasoning is compelling and worthy of attention.

In *Quinn*, 48 B.R. 367 (D.Colo.1985), the trustee of a bankrupt United States corporation, Life Imaging Corporation, filed suit against a French corporation to collect money damages allegedly due under a distributorship agreement between the parties. Life Imaging's attempt to reorganize under Chapter 11 had not succeeded and it had started to liquidate. The defendant, CGR, moved for an order compelling arbitration of the damages issue under the distributorship agreement's arbitration provision. In support of its motion, CGR contended that Life Imaging's existing bankruptcy should not affect arbitration of the bankrupt's alleged contractual rights when the dispute presented, in the court's words, "no issues of sensitive or pressing public policy." *Id.* at 369.

The court decided in favor of ordering arbitration in that situation for two primary reasons: the Bankruptcy Code's major policy goal of providing the debtor with an opportunity to rehabilitate had been "defeated . . . by the proven inability of the debtor to reorganize and continue a revitalized business life." *Id.* Moreover, the court could not identify any significant bankruptcy or public policy issues present within the dispute over contract damages, stating that international arbitration is indicated especially when no "complex or weighty matters of federal law are present." *Id.*

The *Quinn* situation is similar to the instant case where only the discrete issue of contract damages will be submitted to arbitration. The foreign tribunal will thus not have to interpret and adjudicate any core bankruptcy issues such as creditors' priority, preferential transfers and offsets that were present in other cases where arbitration was denied. *See, e.g.*, *Allegaert*, 548 F.2d 432 (2d Cir.1977); *Braniff*, 33 B.R. 33 (Bankr.N.D.Tex.1983). Further, while an expeditious and economical resolution is always in everyone's interest, the fact that a debtor has failed at Chapter 11 reorganization—much like a critically ill patient who has finally succumbed despite all resuscitation efforts—removes some of the immediate time sensitivity that usually accompanies Chapter 11 situations. Thus, the cases upon which Distrigas relies that have favored the bankruptcy court's retaining jurisdiction—especially *Braniff*, 33 B.R. 33 (Bankr.N.D.Tex.1983), *Banque Francaise du Commerce Exterieur v. Rio Grande Trading Inc.*, 17 B.R. 134 (Bankr.S.D.Tex.1981), and *Kenner Products Company v. Societe Fonciere et Financiere Agache-Willot*, 532 F.Supp. 478 (S.D.N.Y.1982)—stand in stark contrast. The *Braniff* decision, for example, involved a debtor airline that was actively involved in Chapter 11 reorganization. Indeed, in *Braniff*, 33 B.R. at 34, the court, in its lucid exposition of the Bankruptcy Code's broad powers, noted that the legislative intent behind such policy was to provide both debtors and creditors with "an unhampered chance for reorganization," and concluded that this policy superseded arbitration especially when the crux of the dispute involved the fundamental bankruptcy issue of the distribution of debtor's assets and creditor priority. The court further posited that arbitration was not workable since "[r]equiring the debtor to resort to arbitration would delay the efforts to reorganize" and the debtor was on a precariously "tight schedule." *Id.* at 36.

No such constraints exist in the present case which, like *Quinn*, involves a debtor entering liquidation and a dispute primarily concerning the valuation of damages in a breach of contract situation.

The line of decisions which conclusively tip the judicial scale in favor of arbitration, however, are not bankruptcy decisions but are rather a line of United States Supreme Court opinions which enthusiastically endorse an internationalist approach towards commercial disputes involving foreign entities. These decisions—*The Bremen v. Zapata Off-Shore Co.*, 407 U.S. 1, 92 S.Ct. 1907, 32 L.Ed.2d 513 (1972) (forum selection clause in international commercial contract enforced); *Scherk v. Alberto-Culver Co.*, 417 U.S. 506, 94 S.Ct. 2449, 41 L.Ed.2d 270 (1974) (international arbitration clause held enforceable when in conflict with federal securities laws); and most recently, *Mitsubishi*, 473 U.S. 614, 105 S.Ct. 3346, 87 L.Ed.2d

444 (1985) (international arbitration clause held enforceable when in conflict with federal anti-trust laws)—eschew the parochial tendencies of domestic tribunals in retaining jurisdiction over international commercial disputes. The Supreme Court powerfully advocates the need for international comity in an increasingly interdependent world. Such respect is especially important, in this Court's view, when parties mutually agree to be bound by freely-negotiated contracts.

The Supreme Court in *Zapata* employed convincing language decrying provincialism and this language has been influential in guiding the later *Scherk* and *Mitsubishi* decisions where, in fact, it was quoted verbatim:

> The expansion of American business and industry will hardly be encouraged if, notwithstanding solemn contracts, we insist on a parochial concept that all disputes must be resolved under our laws and in our courts. . . . We cannot have trade and commerce in world markets and international waters exclusively on our terms, governed by our laws, and resolved in our courts.

*Zapata*, 407 U.S. at 9, 92 S.Ct. at 1912; *Scherk*, 417 U.S. at 519, 94 S.Ct. at 2457; *Mitsubishi*, 105 S.Ct. at 3356.

Distrigas makes much of the so-called "public policy" exception articulated in *Zapata*, arguing that it applies to the instant case. The "public policy" exception is described as follows:

> A contractual choice-of-forum clause should be held unenforceable if enforcement would contravene a strong public policy of the forum in which suit is brought, whether declared by statute or by judicial decision.

*Zapata*, 407 U.S. at 15, 92 S.Ct. at 1916.

Distrigas' reliance is misplaced as the Supreme Court went on to elaborate that the "public policy" exception, while applicable in strictly domestic situations, would not control in international commercial matters. *Id.* at 16, 92 S.Ct. at 1916. Furthermore, even if the "public policy" exception could apply to the instant international situation, the issues of contract damages which Sonatrach seeks to arbitrate, impinge very little on the Bankruptcy Code. In order to nullify an arbitration clause, the Supreme Court in *Zapata* would demand that the Debtor demonstrate some "compelling and countervailing reason" that it should be dishonored, especially when such choice was "made in an arm's-length negotiation by experienced and sophisticated businessmen." *Id.* at 12, 92 S.Ct. at 1914. Distrigas has failed to meet this standard.

In similar fashion, the Supreme Court in *Scherk*, 417 U.S. at 519, 94 S.Ct. at 2457, chose to respect an international arbitration agreement noting that the invalidation of such an agreement would not only allow the respondent "to repudiate its solemn promise," but could lead to the creation of "a legal no-man's land" that would have an undeniably chilling effect upon international commerce. The Court concluded:

> A parochial refusal by the courts of one country to enforce an international arbitration agreement would not only frustrate [the orderliness and predictability essential to any international business transactions, as well as other purposes,] but would invite unseemly and mutually destructive jockeying by the parties to secure tactical litigation advantages.

*Id.* at 516-17, 94 S.Ct. at 2456.

The trilogy culminates in *Mitsubishi*, 105 S.Ct. at 3356, a decision in which the Supreme Court relied heavily upon the rationale advanced in the preceding decisions, stating that they "establish a strong presumption in favor of enforcement of freely negotiated contractual choice-of-forum provisions." The Court came to the following unequivocal conclusion:

> As in *Scherk*, we conclude that concerns of international comity, respect for the capacities of foreign and transnational tribunals and sensitivity to the need of the international commercial system for predictability in the resolution of disputes require that we enforce the parties' agreement, *even assuming that a contrary result would be forthcoming in a domestic context.*

*Mitsubishi*, 105 S.Ct. at 3355 (citations omitted) (emphasis added).

Taken together, these decisions erect a compelling argument in favor of requiring Distrigas—as a "representative of the American business community," *Mitsubishi*, 105 S.Ct. at 3361 (citing *Alberto-Culver v. Scherk*, 484 F.2d 611, 620 [7th Cir.1973])—to honor its bargain and proceed with international arbitration. Although the Supreme Court has not specifically addressed the clash of *bankruptcy* and international arbitration, it would be unrealistic indeed to argue that bankruptcy principles are qualitatively more fundamental to our capitalistic democratic system than either the securities laws or anti-trust policy.[131]

In weighing the strong public policy favoring international arbitration with any countervailing potential harm to bankruptcy policy upon the present facts, this Court finds the scales weighted in favor of arbitration. As discussed earlier, no major bankruptcy issues will be implicated in valuing contract damages and the international arbitration panel requires no special expertise to accomplish their task. While international arbitration will require a temporary and limited incursion into the Bankruptcy Court's exclusive jurisdictional bailiwick,[132] no bankruptcy policies will suffer adverse impact. Conversely, the very image of the United States in the international business community stands to be tarnished. It is important and necessary for the United States to hold its domiciliaries to their bargains and not allow them to escape their commercial obligations by ducking into statutory safe

---

[131] [8] This is not to say, however, that the Supreme Court's holdings mean that international arbitration is the appropriate remedy in all circumstances. There may be disputes where arbitration is decidedly unsuitable or where Congress has undertaken "to specify categories of claims it wishes to reserve for decision by our own courts without contravening this Nation's obligations under the Convention." *Mitsubishi*, 105 S.Ct. at 3360 n. 21. Neither of these factors exist in the present case.

[132] Once arbitration has commenced, United States courts have the opportunity at the arbitration award enforcement stage "to ensure that the legitimate interest in the enforcement of the . . . laws has been addressed" and are entitled under the Convention "to refuse enforcement of an award" where such enforcement would be "contrary to the public policy of that country." *Mitsubishi*, 105 S.Ct. at 3360. It is not at all clear, for example, that piercing the Distrigas corporate veil is within the scope of the matters referred to international arbitration. It is the Bankruptcy Court in this district that may well have to initially determine that matter. *See* Restatement (Second) of Judgments §84(3)(a) (1982).

harbors.[133] Rather, our country should take special pains to project those qualities of honesty and fairness which are essential parts of the traditional American character and be perceived as a fair and equal player in the global marketplace, particularly in our commercial relations with the underdeveloped world. Any additional time and expense required by the international arbitration process—which is only speculative at this point—will be overshadowed in importance by the virtues of having the parties abide by their commitments.

Therefore, Sonatrach's Motion to Modify the Stay and proceed with international arbitration is ALLOWED for the reasons stated above. . . .

\* \* \*

2.  Jay L. Westbrook, *The Coming Encounter: International Arbitration and Bankruptcy*, 67 MINN. L. REV. 595, 642-644 (1983).

. . . .

. . . The central policy propositions [regarding the role of national courts in transnational commercial disputes] are that U.S. bankruptcy courts should boldly assert their jurisdiction over the issue of arbitration *vel non* whenever a sensible choice of law rule would select the United States as the primary bankruptcy jurisdiction for a particular debtor but, having asserted jurisdiction, the bankruptcy courts should generally enforce international arbitration agreements. The alternative is legal chaos or, at least, incoherence. If our national courts will not fashion sensible rules about the role of international arbitration in the extraordinary circumstances of bankruptcy, can we expect foreign courts to do so? Even if the nonbankruptcy courts of each place of arbitration do assume this burden, they are not as well suited as the bankruptcy courts of the debtor's domicile to adapt an international arbitration agreement to the special circumstances of bankruptcy. Under the best of circumstances, the adoption of varying rules by each judicial system having territorial jurisdiction of a

---

[133] [10] This Court notes that counsel for Distrigas, displaying admirable candor, conceded to using the Bankruptcy Court "as a vehicle to avoid arbitration." Hearing Transcript, December 4, 1986, p. 6.

particular arbitration will hardly serve the goals of predictability and consistency so essential to any international business transaction.

The same problems plague many other aspects of transnational litigation. The general suggestion is that comity and coherence in international commercial relationships will not be achieved by a reflexive refusal to get involved. Only a power which has been asserted can then defer to international cooperation.

We live in a transitional age in which legal principles lag far behind the on-rushing internationalization of commerce. We must rely for now on national legal systems as the primary vehicle for the enforcement of legitimate commercial expectations. Unless the courts of each nation are willing to assert jurisdiction and then defer when appropriate to international legal principles, parties will be left with erratic enforcement or no enforcement at all. The absence of enforceable expectations is the worst possible environment for commerce, especially that commerce which must leap the walls of cultural and political differences.

The creation within national legal systems of sound legal principles to govern international commerce is difficult. It takes, in particular, hard-working and courageous judges to follow a course both assertive and cooperative. Yet the effort should commend itself. If the flow of international commerce may create channels through which law may follow, if the chains of self-interest forged by commerce may restrain the blows too often commanded by politics or religion or ideology, then the lawyers and judges who fashion the law of international commerce may claim some contribution to a larger and better future.

### Notes and Questions

1. *See also Fotochrome Inc. v. Copal Co.*, 517 F. 2d 512 (2d Cir. 1975) (holding that a bankruptcy court in the United States does not have power to relitigate the merits of a contract dispute resolved by arbitration abroad commenced before the filing of a Chapter 11 petition for reorganization under the U.S. Bankruptcy Act). *See also* Lawrence W. Newman & Michael Burrows, *Enforcement of Arbitration Provisions in Bankruptcy*, N.Y.L.J. June 18, 1992, at 3.

2. *Compare Braniff Airways v. United Air Lines*, 33 B.R. 33 (Bankr. N.D. Tex. 1983) (debtor not required to submit to arbitration) *with In re Springer-Penguin*

*Inc.*, 74 B.R. 879 (S.D.N.Y. 1987) (order staying arbitration proceeding in Yugoslavia).

3. As a practical matter, what are the consequences of allowing an arbitration tribunal to liquidate a claim against a party in bankruptcy? Is the problem arbitrability or enforceability of an award? Discuss.

4. In an arbitration against a bankrupt party already subject to a judge in bankruptcy, who will make the strategic decisions (such as nomination of an arbitrator) on behalf of the bankrupt party in the arbitration? Does it depend on what sort of a bankruptcy proceeding (*e.g.*, full Chapter 7 proceeding or only a Chapter 11 reorganization) has developed?

5. In *Sonatrach* the court suggests that Chapter 11 bankruptcies will henceforth trump international arbitration clauses, while a winding up will not, supposedly because time is less important then. In the United States, Chapter 11 is now used as a management tool. Does this aspect of the decision create opportunities for the U.S. side of an international contract to defeat an arbitration clause?

## D.    RICO

*Shearson/American Express Inc. et al. v. McMahon et al.*, 482 U.S. 220 (1987).

JUSTICE O'CONNOR delivered the opinion of the Court.

.    .    .

## I

[Eugene and Julia McMahon, individually and as trustees for various pension and profit-sharing plans, were customers of petitioner Shearson/American Express Inc. (Shearson), a brokerage firm registered with the Securities and Exchange Commission. Two customer agreements signed by Julia McMahon provided for arbitration of any controversy relating to the accounts the McMahons maintained with Shearson. The arbitration provision provided in relevant part as follows:

"Unless unenforceable due to federal or state law, any controversy arising out of or relating to my accounts, to transactions with you for me or to this agreement or the breach thereof, shall be settled by arbitration in accordance with the rules, then in effect, of the National Association of Securities Dealers, Inc. or the Boards of Directors of the New York Stock Exchange, Inc. and/or the American Stock Exchange, Inc. as I may elect." 618 F.Supp. 384, 385 (1985).

In October 1984, the McMahons filed a complaint against Shearson in the United States District Court for the Southern District of New York, alleging that Shearson through its representative Mary Ann McNulty, had violated § 10(b) of the Exchange Act and Rule 10b-5, by engaging in fraudulent, excessive trading on respondents' accounts and by making false statements and omitting material facts from the advice given to respondents. The complaint also alleged a RICO claim, 18 U.S.C. § 1962(c), and state law claims for fraud and breach of fiduciary duties.

Shearson moved to compel arbitration of the McMahons' claims pursuant to § 3 of the Federal Arbitration Act. The District Court granted the motion in part, rejecting the McMahons' contention that the arbitration agreements were unenforceable as contracts of adhesion. The Court also found that the McMahons' § 10(b) claims were arbitrable under the terms of the agreement, but that the McMahons' RICO claim was not arbitrable because of the important federal policies inherent in the enforcement of RICO by the federal courts. 618 F.Supp., at 387.

The Court of Appeals affirmed the District Court on the RICO claims, but it reversed on the Exchange Act claims. With respect to the RICO claim, the Court of Appeals concluded that "public policy" considerations made it "inappropriat[e]" to apply the provisions of the Arbitration Act to RICO suits, which the court reasoned were "not merely a private matter." It distinguished this Court's reasoning in *Mitsubishi Motors Corp. v. Soler Chrysler-Plymouth, Inc.* concerning the arbitrability of antitrust claims on the ground that it involved *international* business transactions and did not affect the law "as applied to agreements to arbitrate arising from domestic transactions."

With respect to the Exchange Act claims, the Court of Appeals noted that under *Wilko v. Swan*, 346 U.S. 427 (1953), claims arising under § 12(2) of the Securities Act of 1933 are not subject to compulsory arbitration. The Court of Appeals observed that it previously had extended the *Wilko* rule to claims arising under § 10(b) of the Exchange Act in *Allegaert v. Perot*, 548 F.2d 432 (2d Cir. 1977), cert. denied, 432 U.S. 910 (1977). The court acknowledged that *Scherk v. Alberto-Culver Co.*, 417 U.S. 506 (1974) had "cast some doubt on the applicability of *Wilko* to claims under § 10(b)," but nevertheless concluded that it was bound by the "clear judicial precedent in this Circuit," and held that *Wilko* must be applied to Exchange Act claims.

The Supreme Court granted certiorari to resolve the conflict among the Courts of Appeals regarding the arbitrability of § 10(b) and RICO claims.]

.   .   .

The Federal Arbitration Act, 9 U.S.C. § 1 *et seq.*, provides the starting point for answering the questions raised in this case. The Act was intended to "revers[e] centuries of judicial hostility to arbitration agreements," *Scherk v. Alberto-Culver Co.*, *supra*, at 510, by "plac[ing] arbitration agreements 'upon the same footing as other contracts.'" 417 U.S., at 511, quoting H. R. Rep. 96, 68th Cong., 1st Sess. 1, 2 (1924). The Arbitration Act accomplishes this purpose by providing that arbitration agreements "shall be valid, irrevocable, and enforceable, save upon such grounds as exist at law or in equity for the revocation of any contract." 9 U.S.C. § 2. The Act also provides that a court must stay its proceedings if it is satisfied that an issue before it is arbitrable under the agreement, § 3; and it authorizes a federal district court to issue an order compelling arbitration if there has been a "failure, neglect, or refusal" to comply with the arbitration agreement, § 4.

The Arbitration Act thus establishes a "federal policy favoring arbitration," *Moses H. Cone Memorial Hospital v. Mercury Construction Corp.*, 460 U.S. 1, 24 (1983), requiring that "we rigorously enforce agreements to arbitrate." *Dean Witter Reynolds Inc. v. Byrd*, *supra*, at 221. This duty to enforce arbitration agreements is not diminished when a party bound by an agreement raises a claim founded on statutory rights. As we observed in *Mitsubishi Motors Corp. v. Soler Chrysler-Plymouth, Inc.*, "we are well past the time when judicial suspicion of the desirability of arbitration and of the competence of arbitral tribunals" should inhibit enforcement of the Act "'in controversies based on statutes.'" 473 U.S., at 626-627, quoting

*Wilko v. Swan, supra*, at 432. Absent a well-founded claim that an arbitration agreement resulted from the sort of fraud or excessive economic power that "would provide grounds 'for the revocation of any contract,'" 473 U.S., at 627, the Arbitration Act "provides no basis for disfavoring agreements to arbitrate statutory claims by skewing the otherwise hospitable inquiry into arbitrability." *Ibid.*

The Arbitration Act, standing alone, therefore mandates enforcement of agreements to arbitrate statutory claims. Like any statutory directive, the Arbitration Act's mandate may be overridden by a contrary congressional command. The burden is on the party opposing arbitration, however, to show that Congress intended to preclude a waiver of judicial remedies for the statutory rights at issue. See *id.*, at 628. If Congress did intend to limit or prohibit waiver of a judicial forum for a particular claim, such an intent "will be deducible from [the statute's] text or legislative history," *ibid.*, or from an inherent conflict between arbitration and the statute's underlying purposes. See *Id.* at 632-637; *Dean Witter Reynolds Inc. v. Byrd*, 470 U.S., at 217.

To defeat application of the Arbitration Act in this case, therefore, the McMahons must demonstrate that Congress intended to make an exception to the Arbitration Act for claims arising under RICO and the Exchange Act, an intention discernible from the text, history, or purposes of the statute. We examine the McMahons' arguments regarding the Exchange Act and RICO in turn.

[The Court's discussion of the Exchange Act is omitted.]

.     .     .

Unlike the Exchange Act, there is nothing in the text of the RICO statute that even arguably evinces congressional intent to exclude civil RICO claims from the dictates of the Arbitration Act. This silence in the text is matched by silence in the statute's legislative history. The private treble-damages provision codified as 18 U.S.C. § 1964(c) was added to the House version of the bill after the bill had been passed by the Senate, and it received only abbreviated discussion in either House. See *Sedima, S. P. R. L. v. Imrex Co.*, 473 U.S. 479, 486-488 (1985). There is no hint in these legislative debates that Congress intended for RICO treble-damages claims to be excluded from the ambit of the Arbitration Act. See *Genesco, Inc. v. T. Kakiuchi & Co., Ltd.*, 815

F.2d 840, 850-851 (CA2 1987); *Mayaja, Inc. v. Bodkin*, 803 F.2d 157, 164 (CA5 1986).

Because RICO's text and legislative history fail to reveal any intent to override the provisions of the Arbitration Act, the McMahons must argue that there is an irreconcilable conflict between arbitration and RICO's underlying purposes. Our decision in *Mitsubishi Motors Corp. v. Soler Chrysler-Plymouth Inc.*, 473 U.S. 614 (1985), however, already has addressed many of the grounds given by the McMahons to support this claim. In *Mitsubishi*, we held that nothing in the nature of the federal antitrust laws prohibits parties from agreeing to arbitrate antitrust claims arising out of international commercial transactions. Although the holding in *Mitsubishi* was limited to the international context, see *id.* at 629, much of its reasoning is equally applicable here. Thus, for example, the McMahons have argued that RICO claims are too complex to be subject to arbitration. We determined in *Mitsubishi*, however, that "potential complexity should not suffice to ward off arbitration." *Id.* at 633. Antitrust matters are every bit as complex as RICO claims, but we found that the "adaptability and access to expertise" characteristic of arbitration rebutted the view "that an arbitral tribunal could not properly handle an antitrust matter." *Id.*, at 633-34.

Likewise, the McMahons contend that the "overlap" between RICO's civil and criminal provisions renders § 1964(c) claims nonarbitrable. See *Page v. Moseley, Hallgarten, Estabrook & Weeden, Inc.*, 806 F.2d 291, 299, n. 13 (CA1 1986) ("[T]he makings of a 'pattern of racketeering' are not yet clear, but the fact remains that a 'pattern' for civil purposes is a 'pattern' for criminal purposes"). Yet § 1964(c) is no different in this respect from the federal antitrust laws. In *Sedima, S. P. R. L. v. Imrex Co.*, *supra*, we rejected the view that § 1964(c) "provide[s] civil remedies for offenses criminal in nature." See 473 U.S., at 492. In doing so, this Court observed:

> "[T]he fact that conduct can result in both criminal liability and treble damages does not mean that there is not a bona fide civil action. The familiar provisions for both criminal liability and treble damages under the antitrust laws indicate as much. *Ibid.* *Mitsubishi* recognized that treble-damages suits for claims arising under § 1 of the Sherman Act may be subject to

arbitration, even though such conduct may also give rise to claims of criminal liability. See *Mitsubishi Motors Corp. v. Soler Chrysler-Plymouth, Inc.*, *supra*. We similarly find that the criminal provisions of RICO do not preclude arbitration of bona fide civil actions brought under § 1964(c).

The McMahons' final argument is that the public interest in the enforcement of RICO precludes its submission to arbitration. *Mitsubishi* again is relevant to the question. In that case we thoroughly examined the legislative intent behind § 4 of the Clayton Act in assaying whether the importance of the private treble-damages remedy in enforcing the antitrust laws precluded arbitration of § 4 claims. We found that "[n]otwithstanding its important incidental policing function, the treble-damages cause of action . . . seeks primarily to enable an injured competitor to gain compensation for that injury." 473 U.S., at 635. Emphasizing the priority of the compensatory function of § 4 over its deterrent function, *Mitsubishi* concluded that "so long as the prospective litigant effectively may vindicate its statutory cause of action in the arbitral forum, the statute will continue to serve both its remedial and deterrent function." *Id.*, at 637.

The legislative history of § 1964(c) reveals the same emphasis on the remedial role of the treble-damages provision. In introducing the treble-damages provision to the House Judiciary Committee, Representative Steiger stressed that "those who have been wronged by organized crime should at least be given access to a legal remedy." Hearings on S. 30, and related proposals, before Subcommittee No. 5 of the House Committee on the Judiciary, 91st Cong., 2d Sess., 520 (1970). The policing function of § 1964(c), although important, was a secondary concern. See *ibid.* ("In addition, the availability of such a remedy would enhance the effectiveness of title IX's prohibitions"). During the congressional debates on § 1964(c), Representative Steiger again emphasized the remedial purpose of the provision: "It is the intent of this body, I am certain, to see that innocent parties who are the victims of organized crime have a right to obtain proper redress . . . It represents the one opportunity for those of us who have been seriously affected by organized crime activity to recover." 116 Cong. Rec. 35346-35347 (1970). This focus on the remedial function of § 1964(c) is reinforced by the recurrent references in the legislative debates to § 4 of the Clayton Act as the model for the RICO treble-damages provision. See, *e.g.*, 116 Cong. Rec. 35346 (statement of Rep. Poff) (RICO provision "has its counterpart almost in haec verba in the antitrust statutes"); *id.*, at 25190 (statement of Sen. McClellan) (proposed amendment would "authorize private civil damage suits based upon the concept of section 4 of the Clayton Antitrust Act"). See generally *Sedima, S. P. R. L. v. Imrex Co.*, 473 U.S., at 489 ("The clearest current in [RICO's] history is the reliance on the Clayton Act model").

Not only does *Mitsubishi* support the arbitrability of RICO claims, but there is even more reason to suppose that arbitration will adequately serve the purposes of RICO than that it will adequately protect private enforcement of the antitrust laws. Antitrust violations generally have a widespread impact on national markets as a whole, and the antitrust treble-damages provision gives private parties an incentive to bring civil suits that serve to advance the national interest in a competitive economy. See Lindsay, "Public" Rights and Private Forums: Predispute Arbitration Agreements and Securities Litigation, 20 Loyola (LA) L. Rev. 643, 691-692 (1987). RICO's drafters likewise sought to provide vigorous incentives for plaintiffs to pursue RICO claims that would advance society's fight against organized crime. See *Sedima, S. P. R. L. v. Imrex Co.*, *supra*, at 498. But in fact RICO actions are seldom asserted "against the archetypal, intimidating mobster." *Id.*, at 499; see also *id.*, at 506 (MARSHALL, J., dissenting) ("[O]nly 9% of all civil RICO cases have involved allegations of criminal activity normally associated with professional criminals"). The special incentives necessary to encourage civil enforcement actions against organized crime do not support nonarbitrability of run-of-the-mill civil RICO claims brought against legitimate enterprises. The private attorney general role for the typical RICO plaintiff is simply less plausible than it is for the typical antitrust plaintiff, and does not support a finding that there is an irreconcilable conflict between arbitration and enforcement of the RICO statute.

In sum, we find no basis for concluding that Congress intended to prevent enforcement of agreements to arbitrate RICO claims. The McMahons may effectively vindicate their RICO claim in an arbitral forum, and therefore there is no inherent conflict between arbitration and the purposes underlying § 1964(c). Moreover, nothing in RICO's text or legislative history otherwise demonstrates congressional intent to make an exception to the Arbitration Act for RICO claims. Accordingly, the McMahons, "having made the bargain to arbitrate," will be held to their bargain. Their RICO claim is arbitrable under the terms of the Arbitration Act.

.　　.　　.

[Justice Blackmun, with whom Justice Brennan and Justice Marshall joined, concurred in part and dissented in part. In a separate opinion, Justice Stevens also concurred in part and dissented in part.]

### Notes and Questions

1. The Court states: "The special incentives necessary to encourage civil enforcement actions against organized crime do not support non-arbitrability of run-of-the-mill civil RICO claims brought against legitimate enterprises." Why would a statute concerned with stopping racketeering be concerned with claims against legitimate enterprises?

2. Whatever the origins and original legislative target of RICO, would not the effect of the statute's application in *Shearson v. McMahon* be simply to provide an additional statutory remedy to a claim for breach of contract? What public policies would militate against arbitrability of such a claim?

### E.　PATENTS

#### 1.　35 U.S.C. § 135(d) — Arbitration of Interferences

Parties to a patent interference, within such time as may be specified by the Commissioner by regulation, may determine such contest or any aspect thereof by arbitration. Such arbitration shall be governed by the provisions of title 9 [9 U.S.C.S. §§ 1 et seq.] to the extent such title is not inconsistent with this section. The parties shall give notice of any arbitration award to the Commissioner, and such award shall, as between the parties to the arbitration, be dispositive of the issues to which it relates. The arbitration award shall be unenforceable until such notice is given. Nothing in this subsection shall preclude the Commissioner from determining patentability of the invention involved in the interference.

## 2.     35 U.S.C. § 294 — Voluntary Arbitration

(a) A contract involving a patent or any right under a patent may contain a provision requiring arbitration of any dispute relating to patent validity or infringement arising under the contract. In the absence of such a provision, the parties to an existing patent validity or infringement dispute may agree in writing to settle such dispute by arbitration. Any such provision or agreement shall be valid, irrevocable, and enforceable, except for any grounds that exist at law or in equity for revocation of a contract.

(b) Arbitration of such disputes, awards by arbitrators and confirmation of awards shall be governed by title 9, United States Code, to the extent such title is not inconsistent with this section. In any such arbitration proceeding, the defenses provided for under section 282 of this title shall be considered by the arbitrator if raised by any party to the proceeding.

(c) An award by an arbitrator shall be final and binding between the parties to the arbitration but shall have no force or effect on any other person. The parties to an arbitration may agree that in the event a patent which is the subject matter of an award is subsequently determined to be invalid or unenforceable in a judgment rendered by a court of competent jurisdiction from which no appeal can or has been taken, such award may be modified by any court of competent jurisdiction upon application by any party to the arbitration. Any such modification shall govern the rights and obligations between such parties from the date of such modification.

(d) When an award is made by an arbitrator, the patentee, his assignee or licensee shall give notice thereof in writing to the Commissioner. There shall be a separate notice prepared for each patent involved in such proceeding. Such notice shall set forth the names and addresses of the parties, the name of the inventor, and the name of the patent owner, shall designate the number of the patent, and shall contain a copy of the award. If an award is modified by a court, the party requesting such modification shall give notice of such modification to the Commissioner. The Commissioner shall, upon receipt of either notice, enter the same in the record of the prosecution of such patent. If the required notice is not filed with the Commissioner, any party to the proceeding may provide such notice to the Commissioner.

(e) The award shall be unenforceable until the notice required by subsection (d) is received by the Commissioner.

<u>Notes and Questions</u>

1. State the policies for and against a regime allowing arbitrability of patent disputes.

2. Compare arbitrability of antitrust claims and of patent claims. Indicate what significant differences would justify or require different approaches to the question of arbitrability.

3. *See generally* Michael F. Hoellering, *New Opportunities for Patent Arbitration*, N.Y.L.J. Dec. 16, 1982, at 1.

### F.     PUNITIVE DAMAGES

Note on *Mastrobuono v. Shearson Lehman Hutton*, 115 S.Ct. 1212 (1995).

Antonio and Diana Mastrobuono brought an action in federal district court for damages arising out of an alleged mishandling of their securities trading account by Shearson Lehman. On the basis of an arbitration clause in Shearson's standard form Client Agreement, Shearson moved to stay the court proceedings and to compel arbitration pursuant to the rules of the National Association of Securities Dealers.

The arbitral award in favor of the Mastrobuonos included $400,000 in punitive damages in addition to the $159,000 of compensatory damages. The district court, upheld by the Seventh Circuit Court of Appeals, vacated the award of punitive damages on the basis of a choice-of-law clause in the Client Agreement specifying application of New York law, which provided that only courts had power to award punitive damages.

In an eight-judge majority opinion written by Justice Stevens, the Supreme Court reversed the lower court decisions, and held that an arbitrator might award punitive damages notwithstanding the New York choice-of-law provision. The Court seems to have interpreted the reference to New York law to include only New York's substantive law, and not the "allocation of power between alternative tribunals."

Justice Thomas dissented, finding no difference between the question raised by the New York choice-of-law clause and the one at issue in *Volt v. Stanford*, discussed in Chapter 4 at Section IV-D.

### G.    CARRIAGE OF GOODS BY SEA ACT

Note on *Vimar Seguros y Reaseguros v. M/V Sky Reefer*, 115 S.Ct. 2322 (1995).

A standard form bill of lading was issued in connection with the transport of a shipload of Moroccan oranges to Massachusetts. The bill of lading contained both arbitration and choice-of-law clauses, providing that any disputes would be governed by Japanese law and would be referred to arbitration in Tokyo by the Tokyo Maritime Arbitration Commission. When the oranges arrived in the United States, the purchaser discovered over $ 1 million in damage.

When the purchaser and its insurers brought suit in the United States, the shipowner moved to stay the court action and compel arbitration in Tokyo. On the basis of Section 3(8) of the Carriage of Goods by Sea Act (COGSA), which prohibits any "lessening of liability" for loss due to negligence or failure in duties provided under the Act, the purchaser and insurer opposed arbitration. The COGSA argument was based on an assumption that arbitrators might misapply the law in a way that reduced the carrier's responsibility for the acts or omissions of the stevedores it had hired.

The Court of Appeals for the First Circuit affirmed the District Court order to arbitrate, resolving the conflict between COGSA and the Federal Arbitration Act on the basis that the latter, more specific, statute controlled the issue. The Supreme Court affirmed the First Circuit's decision, but without assuming arguendo that COGSA nullified the arbitration clause. Rather, the Supreme Court found that arbitration clauses in bills of lading did not "lessen liability" under COGSA, and therefore no conflict existed between the FAA and COGSA.

### IV.    JUSTIFYING A SPECIAL TEST FOR ARBITRABILITY IN INTERNATIONAL CONTEXTS

We have seen that some matters that are not arbitrable in a domestic context may still be arbitrated when the controverted event covered by the arbitration clause has an international aspect. Such a double standard might be justified by the particular need for neutrality in trans-border commercial dispute resolution. The following comment explores the special nature of controversies arising out of international trade and investment.

> William W. Park, *Private Adjudicators and the Public Interest: The Expanding Scope of International Arbitration*, 12 BROOK. J. INT'L L. 629, 664-67, 670-73 (1986).

. . .

In an international context, dramatically disagreeable consequences can result from an unenforceable arbitration agreement. Unenforceability may mean not just litigation in Louisville rather than arbitration in Albany, but perhaps proceedings in Arabic before a judge in Tripoli or in Jeddah rather than before an English-speaking arbitrator in Stockholm or Geneva. Imagine a Libyan enterprise contracting with a New York enterprise under an agreement that provides for arbitration of disputes in Paris under International Chamber of Commerce (I.C.C.) Rules. Nothing would have stopped the parties from excluding local statutory claims from the scope of the arbitration agreement, but they decided not to do so. When the contract became onerous for the Libyan corporation, it asserted a Libyan "statutory claim" before a Libyan court, which in turn refuses on public policy grounds to give effect to the agreement to arbitrate. The American company had expected that the dispute be arbitrated in Paris rather than litigated in Tripoli, and the Libyans had expected arbitration in Paris rather than litigation in New York. Both sides would be more distressed to see these expectations defeated by assertions of statutory counterclaims.

Parties to international transactions should be able to bargain for an arbitration procedure that reduces the risk of potentially hostile "hometown justice" in the other party's national courts. If this goal can be defeated by asserting a local statutory right, then parties to international transactions will be denied the opportunity to provide with any certainty for a neutral dispute resolution process. The absence of this reasonable certainty of a neutral forum may impede or distort international trade and investment, resulting in a less efficient exploitation and allocation of global resources.

Our legal concepts and practice tend to be exported, serving as examples to foreign courts. If the American business community is not made to honor its arbitration bargains, foreign judges may refuse to enforce arbitration agreements and awards against their own nationals, and thus cause American exporters and multinationals to suffer.

Billions of dollars of international trade and investment beg for an effective neutral dispute resolution process. Admittedly, many transactions will be concluded regardless of whether the parties expect dispute resolution to be neutral. But some may not. Uncertainty whether the neutral adjudicatory process, bargained for at the outset of a contractual relationship, will indeed be implemented in the event of a dispute cannot be other than an obstacle to a cross-border business transaction.

.    .    .

Society's interest in assuring the vindication of statutory rights should not be disregarded lightly. Concern that arbitrators will be less likely than judges and juries to enforce the law properly may not be entirely misplaced. The arbitrator is paid to consider the interests of the parties. He may also consider public or societal interests affected by the outcome of the dispute, but this is not the arbitrator's principle job.

Because public law claims can be the object of a private settlement does not necessarily mean they should be capable of resolution by an arbitrator. Settlement occurs *after* the dispute arises, and the amount received in settlement presumably would roughly equal the amount received in litigation, discounted for reduced legal fees. The parties would evaluate their legal chances of success in litigation before settling. On the other hand, because the arbitration clause frequently is included in the main contract and signed before the dispute arises, this clause permits little or no informed evaluation of claims, as no claims have arisen. Furthermore, a pre-dispute agreement may bargain away rights as yet unknown through waiver of liability as to unidentified future offenses. As a result, the public interest in proper enforcement of the law may be frustrated. In at least two capacities the public may suffer when antitrust laws, for example, are under-enforced: *qua* consumer (affected by the particular controverted transactions) and, more generally, qua beneficiary of the political liberty and economic efficiency furthered by the free enterprise system.[134]

. . .

Assuring vindication of public law claims is not society's only concern, however. The competing public interest in permitting development of a neutral transnational dispute resolution system may outweigh the concern for vindication of public law claims by judges rather than arbitrators. In domestic transactions, the imperative of a neutral forum does not present itself with the same force as in a transnational context. The public interest in protection from under-enforcement or misinterpretation of public law issues, which prevails when the transaction is purely domestic, may be outweighed by the interest in permitting a neutral private adjudicatory process when the transaction crosses national boundaries. For an American enterprise, the consequences of finding oneself not before an I.C.C. appointed arbitrator but before Greek, Libyan or French courts, with proceedings in the language not of the playwright Shakespeare, but perhaps of the playwrights Molière or Sophocles or of the prophet Mohammed, are more dramatic than the consequences of ending up in court in New York rather than in an American Arbitration Association (AAA) arbitration.

Even if arbitrators do not enforce statutory rights as well as judges, a special rule of arbitrability for the international realm would be justified under a hierarchy of societal policies that take into account the peculiar need for neutrality in resolution of international contracts disputes. The relative weights one gives to these competing considerations — proper enforcement of the law and neutrality of forum — is obviously a matter on which reasonable folks may differ. Fostering an efficient arbitral process, necessary to freedom to contract for private adjudication, may be outweighed by the goal of protecting the public against under-enforcement of public law statutes. However, the protection of the public against under-enforcement may be outweighed by the goal of increased certainty of neutral dispute

---

[134] [126] In articulating the community/societal interests affected one must identify assumptions about the free enterprise system and the objectives of the antitrust laws. Do we want a free market efficiency for economic reasons? Or is our motivation political, to avoid the untoward consequences of undue concentrations of power and wealth?

resolution for trans-border business. The assumptions of [cases refusing to enforce arbitration of statutory claims] need not be denied; but in a transnational rather than domestic context, the special need for a neutral forum presents an additional overriding consideration.

.   .   .

Assessing the societal interest in arbitration as a viable dispute resolution option depends on the alternatives one may contemplate. Businessmen who regret their decision to arbitrate when they view the alternative of American courts forget that they were motivated to agree to arbitration by a vision of foreign courts. The arbitration agreement is usually drafted into the principle contract out of concern that it will be too late to avoid foreign courts after a dispute arises.

The argument for international arbitration is not that it avoids cost and delay, for the process is usually long and expensive. Rather, the justification is that parties to a dispute that crosses national boundaries need a non-national mechanism for resolution of the controversies. A third nation's courts are not always an option, either because of uncertainty that the courts will accept jurisdiction of a dispute with no connection to the forum state, or because the courts of nations which were formerly colonial powers are unacceptable to developing nations, whose courts in turn are not acceptable to the Western multinational.

Although arbitration may not be a first choice for dispute resolution, it frequently imposes itself on a transaction for want of another alternative for parties that have rejected both non-binding mediation and national judges. To make the arbitral system work, both sides must have a reasonable certainty that the agreement will be enforced. This larger view of the function of transnational arbitration argues for limiting the opportunities of American parties to assert local statutory claims or counterclaims in order to avoid the consequences of their commitments.

If the American judiciary contributes to an erosion of the international business community's confidence in the arbitral process, American corporations will be the losers when the shoe is on the other foot and foreign courts imitate American practice to deny enforcement of the bargain for the more neutral forum afforded by arbitration.

.    .    .

The dissent by Justice Stevens in *Mitsubishi* expresses concern that enforcing commitments to arbitrate may dispatch American citizens "to a foreign land in search of an uncertain remedy for the violation of a public right." Paradoxically, an even more uncertain remedy in a foreign court may be exactly the fate of American business if arbitration agreements are not enforced. The alternative to arbitration depicted by Stevens in the penultimate sentence of his dissent is "consideration of a fully developed record by a jury instructed by a federal judge." Justice Stevens' view of the alternatives, however, might be somewhat incomplete. Another alternative is the specter that haunted the businessman when he signed the arbitration agreement: disposition of disputes by a foreign judge in a foreign language.

Arbitration abroad is rarely as good as hauling the opposing party before one's hometown judges, but usually it is better than appearing before the opposing party's national courts. Requiring American businessmen to honor their agreements to arbitrate international contract disputes is a necessary step in building a binding neutral dispute resolution system that will enable Americans to avoid foreign courts.

The majority in *Mitsubishi* has reached the right result in holding that antitrust claims are arbitrable in an international context. However, its suggestion that courts later examine arbitral awards to determine whether public law claims were addressed may be open to question. A "second look" at the arbitral process might open the door to a merits review that would render the arbitration little more than a precursor to litigation.

The majority in *Mitsubishi* limited its decision to international contracts. The limitation, even if desirable does not necessarily follow from Justice Blackmun's assumption that arbitrators as well as judges can enforce public laws. This assumption would seem to apply equally to domestic arbitration.

The distinction between domestic and international arbitration would seem to flow more logically from a decision based on the policies underlying the New York Convention, to which nations adhere in the hope of assuring for their nationals the opportunity to contract out of the home-town justice of foreign courts. A special rule for international disputes makes arbitration available to parties doing business across national boundaries, but not in a purely domestic context. In the latter domestic context, the need for a neutral forum is not as acute as in international transactions, and non-arbitrability is justified to protect public interests implicated in the dispute.

In international contract disputes, the need for a neutral forum justifies a departure from standards applied to domestic transactions. Domestically nurtured concerns for proper enforcement of public law claims may have to yield to a larger concern that international trade and investment not be frustrated because of routine refusal to honor commitments to arbitrate international contracts disputes.

In a purely domestic context, an unenforceable arbitration clause may mean adjudication in Los Angeles rather than in Boston. As disquieting as the prospect of California justice may be to a New Englander, an unenforceable arbitration agreement can give rise to even more apprehension in an international context, where judicial proceedings may be in a foreign language and in a country where xenophobia or political influence make a fair trial questionable.

Arbitration is not a *summmum bonum*, however, and it seems appropriate to give some discretion to the judge called upon to enforce the agreement to arbitrate. The New York Convention may be too blunt an instrument, with the result that its signatories take lightly their international commitments. The Convention contains no explicit escape hatch whereby a judge may distinguish a contract between two sophisticated multinationals from a contract of adhesion imposed on a small local merchant with little bargaining power. Indeed one troubling aspect of the *Mitsubishi* case is that Soler was just the type of company in need of the paternalistic legislation represented by the Automobile Dealer's Day in Court Act. A special, more liberal, rule for international transactions should be applied only to cases in which there has been a freely bargained-for waiver of rights.

The *raison d'etre* for commercial arbitration in transactions that go beyond our national frontiers is the search for a delocalized dispute resolution in a neutral forum. If American corporations can escape their bargained-for, but inconvenient, arbitration commitments by alleging violations of statutory rights, foreign corporations will attempt to follow suit. The resulting lack of confidence in a neutral adjudicatory process will not enhance the role of international trade and investment in the process of global wealth production and distribution. Rather, an ineffective arbitral system may produce a dramatic irony in which the American businessman is hauled before a foreign judge less appealing to him than the transnational arbitral tribunal whose jurisdiction he first accepted but later sought to avoid. Commercial self-interest, as well as fairness, argue for requiring Americans to respect commitments made in the world marketplace.

### Notes and Questions

1. What about American foreign policy? Will our courts inadvertently embarrass the State Department if they enforce awards that fail to respect laws of foreign states relating to property abroad? What do you think of the wisdom of section 15 of the Federal Arbitration Act? Section 15 provides that American courts may not refuse to enforce arbitration agreements or confirm arbitral awards on the basis of the Act of State doctrine. Section 15 overturns the result in *Libyan American Oil Co. v. Socialist People's Libyan Arab Jamahirya*, 482 F. Supp. 1175 (D.D.C. 1980).

2. Until recently courts were divided over whether arbitrators may award punitive damages if not expressly so empowered under the arbitration clause. However, in *Mastrobuono v. Shearson Lehman Hutton*, 115 S.Ct. 1212 (1995), the Supreme Court reinstated an award involving a contract governed by New York law, where the arbitrator allowed punitive damages notwithstanding that New York law allows only courts to award punitive damages. *Compare Raytheon v. Automated Business Sys.*, 882 F.2d 6 (1st Cir. 1989) (allowing punitive damages even absent specific authorization in the arbitration agreement) *with Garrity v. Lyle Stuart*, 40 N.Y.2d 454 (1976). *See generally* E. Allan Farnsworth, *Punitive Damages in Arbitration*, 7 ARB. INT'L 3 (1991); Hollering, Address to the American Arbitration Association, Arbitration and the Law, at 19, (1984); Glower W. Jones, *Win Punitive Damages in Arbitration*, ABA J., May 1, 1987, at 87; Glower W. Jones, *Punitive Damages in Arbitration in the USA*, INT'L BUS. LAW, June 1986, at 188; Thomas J. Stipanowich, *Punitive Damages in Arbitration: Garrity v. Lyle Stuart Revisited*, 66 B.U.L. REV. 953 (1986).

3. Does it matter whether courts deny the arbitrability of an international dispute before the arbitration, rather than annul an award on public policy grounds after the arbitration? The goal of assuring a neutral forum for a trans-national dispute competes with the objective of safeguarding the public's interest in proper adjudication of statutory claims. An accommodation of these competing claims inheres in legal rules that allow an arbitrator to decide public law claims, even though his award may later be refused recognition or enforcement on public policy grounds. This admittedly imperfect accommodation of two goals is problematic. Permitting the arbitration to go forward may, in the end, result in a waste of arbitral resources. However, allowing the arbitration to proceed does permit the legal merits of a dispute to pass through the strainer of the agreed-upon arbitrators before judges review the

award (one would hope) only on the narrow grounds of conformity to what the Second Circuit in *Parsons & Whittemore* called "our most basic notions of morality and justice." 508 F.2d 969, 974 (2d Cir. 1974).


V.    SUMMARY AND CONCLUSIONS

By the time a dispute subject to an arbitration clause occurs, the business manager who signed the agreement (perhaps several years earlier when the basic commercial relationship was established) may have had a change of mind about the utility of arbitration for her company in the particular case. To avoid the agreement to arbitrate, the managers wishing to avoid their obligations to arbitrate may ask a court to declare the subject matter of the dispute "non-arbitrable" notwithstanding an otherwise valid arbitration clause.

Judges have at one time or another declared various matters non-arbitrable, including competition law, patents, securities regulations, and punitive damages. The rationale behind these cases rests in part on the assumption that the issues at stake are of great public interest and that arbitrators will be less capable than judges in applying the proper law to them. When arbitrators get things wrong in a "purely private" dispute, only the parties who have chosen arbitration are injured. But when arbitrators must interpret a statute that implicates a core public policy, the entire community risks losing out as a result of the arbitrator's failure to understand and apply correctly the law.

Courts have shown increasing concern that the cry of "non-arbitrability" not impair arbitration's effectiveness in providing a neutral forum for adjudication of international business disputes. If American courts fail to uphold arbitration agreements on the basis that the dispute touches on non-arbitrable subject matters under U.S. law, courts of other countries may be tempted to do the same when their nationals are conducting business with Americans. In the end, all parties concerned will suffer, as they may have no alternative but to go before non-neutral courts to argue their cases in foreign languages and under unfamiliar procedures.

The right to arbitrate sensitive public law issues is not absolute, however. Multinationals sometimes seek escape from an onerous restriction of public law by electing to have their contracts governed by the law of a country with no such norms. When there is a risk that such a choice of law clause might be declared invalid as against public policy, one way of trying to avoid the potential invalidity would be to submit future disputes to arbitrators who do not share the judicial respect for the mandatory public norms in question. Such a strategic device, however, may prove to be of limited utility, because judges can still refuse to enforce an arbitration clause that operates in tandem with a choice-of-law clause as a "prospective waiver" of sensitive public legal rights.

CHAPTER 4

# INITIATING ARBITRATION

I.    INTRODUCTION

On the day when a lucrative contract is signed, a multinational enterprise may agree to abandon recourse to the otherwise competent courts to settle differences arising out of the contract. With neither party willing to accept the jurisdiction of the other side's courts, an agreement to arbitrate any future hypothetical disputes seems better than a legal no man's land. When a dispute actually arises, however, the home town justice of local courts may look more appealing, or the uncertainty of foreign arbitrators more frightening, than when the contract was signed. At this point, the party wanting its bargained-for arbitration has no alternative but to enlist the aid of courts to force the recalcitrant party to live up to its commitment. In attempting to compel arbitration, or stay competing litigation, counsel for the party seeking arbitration will have to rely on a complex network of treaty provisions, national statutes and institutional rules.

Examine the following elements of the legal framework that will be invoked in attempts to enforce an agreement to arbitrate.

II.   THE TREATY FRAMEWORK

   A.   CONVENTION ON THE RECOGNITION AND ENFORCEMENT
        OF FOREIGN ARBITRAL AWARDS (THE NEW YORK
        CONVENTION OF 1958), June 10, 1958, art. II, 21
        U.S.T. 2517, 2519; 330 U.N.T.S., 3, 38.

As will be recalled, the Convention on the Recognition and Enforcement of Foreign Arbitral Awards, or "the New York Convention," establishes the duties of national courts of almost ninety states to enforce arbitration agreements. Article II of the Convention uses the mandatory verb "shall" in directing courts of its contracting states to refer parties who have agreed to arbitrate to arbitration.

Yet the scope of the New York Convention with respect to agreements is not as clear as it might be. Arbitration agreements falling under the Convention would seem to include those in contracts calling for arbitration to be conducted abroad (that is, in a country other than the one called on to enforce the agreement), or those that are international in character, in that the contract parties include a foreign person or the underlying transaction implicates international commerce. The following discussion considers the applicability of the Convention to three categories of arbitration agreement.

B.     ALBERT  J.  VAN  DEN  BERG,  THE  NEW  YORK ARBITRATION CONVENTION OF 1958 56-71 (1981).

. . . [T]he New York Convention basically contemplates two actions: the enforcement of the arbitral award and the enforcement of the arbitration agreement. . . .

. . . If a court is to hold the New York Convention applicable to an action for the enforcement of the arbitration agreement, the agreement must meet a certain number of conditions amongst which that the agreement must be in writing as required by Article II(2) of the Convention.

.     .     .

. . . Originally, it was the intention to leave the provisions concerning the formal validity of the arbitration agreement and the obligatory referral to arbitration to a separate Protocol. At the end of the New York Conference of 1958, it was realized that this was not desirable. Article II was drafted in a race against time, with, as consequence, the omission of an indication as to which arbitration agreements the Convention would apply.

For resolving the question which arbitration agreements can be enforced under the Convention, it would be consistent to interpret Article II(3) in conformity with Article I, which is mainly based on the place of rendition of the award. As the place of rendition of the award must be considered also the place of arbitration, we may examine hereafter three categories of arbitration agreements:

(1)     an agreement providing for arbitration in another State than that where the agreement is invoked . . .

(2)     an agreement providing for an arbitration in the State where the agreement is invoked . . .

(3)     an agreement which does not indicate where the arbitration is to take place . . .

.     .     .

In the case of an agreement providing for arbitration in another State, Article I of the Convention could be applied by analogy. As the Convention applies to the enforcement of an award made in another State, it could apply to the enforcement of an agreement providing for arbitration in another State.

An examination of the court decisions in which an application under Article II(3) was made, reveals that the majority of them involved an agreement providing for arbitration in another State. The application of the Convention to this category of arbitration agreements appears to be so self-evident that almost no court gave an explanation why it applied to the Convention. . . .

A question concerning the applicability of Article II(3) of the Convention to an agreement providing for arbitration in another State is whether the agreement should have an international element. An arbitration agreement can be deemed "international" in its broad sense if, seen from the court before which it is invoked, at least one of the parties to it is foreign, or if it involves a relationship (contract) which has legal (*i.e.* connected with legal norms in force in several States) and/or economic (*i.e.* transfer of money, goods or services across national borders) contacts with more than one State. These criteria, in my opinion, should not be used on a mutually exclusive basis, but can be used whenever applicable.

It will rarely happen that an agreement invoked in a State other than the State where the arbitration takes, or is to take, place concerns a subject matter which has legal or economic contacts with the State where the arbitration is to take place only and involves parties who are both subject to the jurisdiction of the latter State. If such a case occurs, it may be pointed out that the Convention does not exclude the enforcement of an award made in another State in respect of a matter which is purely domestic for that State.

It is, however, not so unlikely that an agreement provides for arbitration abroad between two parties who are both subject to the jurisdiction of the State where the agreement is invoked. Some places are quite popular for certain types of arbitration. An example is maritime arbitration in London. What has been observed in respect of an arbitral award made abroad between two nationals of the State where the enforcement is sought can be applied here by analogy. As the Convention excludes the nationality of the parties from its scope for the enforcement of the award, by analogy, the enforcement of an agreement providing for arbitration abroad between two parties from the State where the agreement is invoked may be considered to fall under Article II(3).

.     .     .

The law implementing the Convention in the United States appears to exclude such a case from the Convention's applicability as Section 202 of that law provides that the Convention does not apply to an agreement providing for arbitration abroad between two United States citizens unless it involves a legal relationship which has some reasonable relation with one or more foreign States. It may, however, be argued that even in this case an application by analogy of Article I is justified. The scope of the Convention is not limited to awards with an international element. It also covers the theoretical possibility of an award made abroad concerning an affair which is entirely domestic for the country where the enforcement is sought. If the enforcement of an award made abroad between two United States nationals concerning a purely domestic (U.S.) affair may not be refused for this reason only in the United States, the same would apply to the enforcement of the arbitration agreement. As was argued in respect of the enforcement of the award, Section 202 of the United States Act must be considered to be incompatible with the New York Convention in respect of the enforcement of the arbitration agreement on this point.[135] The Arbitration Act of 1975, which implements the Convention in the United Kingdom, does not provide for the restriction of Section 202 of the United States Act.[136] Rather, this Act applies to the enforcement of any arbitration agreement providing for arbitration abroad,

---

[135] For the text of Section 202, see Supplement at p. 422.

[136] For the text of the Arbitration Act of 1996, see Supplement at p. 163.

irrespective of the nationality of the parties or the internationality of the subject matter. The Act applies therefore to arbitration in Paris between two British nationals concerning a domestic (U.K.) transaction.

.   .   .

In the case of an agreement providing for arbitration in the State in which the agreement is invoked, Article I obviously cannot be applied by analogy. However, this would not be a reason to deny the applicability of the Convention.

.   .   .

The principle being that Article II(3) of the Convention also applies to an agreement providing for arbitration in the State where its enforcement is sought, it remains to be determined to which arbitration agreements of this category Article II(3) applies. An acceptable interpretation would be that these agreements are only those which have an international element. The reason for the limitation in this category of agreements is that the primary goal of the Convention is international commercial arbitration. If any agreement providing for arbitration in the forum's State were to fall under the Convention, quite a number of domestic arbitration laws would be upset as they lay down rules for the formal validity of the arbitration agreement and the referral to arbitration which are different from Article II of the Convention.

.   .   .

. . . However, a certain degree of disagreement exists as to the question when an agreement can be considered as "international." This disagreement is reflected in the court decisions and implementing Acts in regard to the agreement providing for arbitration in the forum's State. We will therefore examine the two main criteria for considering an agreement "international" — the nationality of the parties and the subject matter of the agreement — in the following.

.   .   .

The criterion that at least one of the parties be a foreign national for determining the applicability of Article II(3) to an agreement providing for arbitration in the State in which it is invoked, can be found in the English Arbitration Act of 1975. Section I concerning the "Effect of arbitration agreements on court proceedings" provides in its second paragraph "This section applies to any arbitration which is not a domestic arbitration agreement. . . ".

What is understood by a "domestic agreement" is defined in paragraph 4 of Section 1 as follows:

"In this Section 'domestic arbitration agreement' means an arbitration agreement which does not provide, expressly or by implication, for arbitration in a State other than the United Kingdom *and* to which neither

(a)    an individual who is a national of, or habitually resident in, any State other than the United Kingdom, nor

(b)    a body corporate which is incorporated in, or whose central management and control is exercised in, any State other than the United Kingdom, is a party at the time the proceedings are commenced." (emphasis added)

Therefore, according to the English Arbitration Act of 1975, an arbitration agreement is domestic only if *two* conditions are met: (1) both parties must be British and (2) the agreement must provide for arbitration in the United Kingdom. Consequently, any arbitration agreement which does not meet one or both conditions will be "international" — although the English Act does not use this expression — and will fall under Article II(3) of the Convention.

It means, in the first place, that Article II(3) of the Convention applies to an agreement providing for arbitration outside the United Kingdom without any requirement as to the nationality of the parties or the internationality of the subject matter of the agreement. We need not come back on this (first) category of arbitration agreements as it was already discussed [previously] . . . .

It means for the (second) category of arbitration agreements presently under discussion that where the agreement provides for arbitration within the United Kingdom, such agreement will fall under Article II(3) of the Convention as soon as one of the parties is non-British. This aspect of Section 1(2) <u>to</u> [sic] (4) of the Arbitration Act of 1975 has been applied by the English courts in three cases.

. . . .

. . . [T]he law implementing the New York Convention in the United States is the only one which expressly declares that a court may also direct that arbitration be held within the United States (Sect. 206). This rule is qualified by Section 202, second sentence, which reads as follows:

"An agreement or award arising out of such a relationship which is entirely between citizens of the United States shall be deemed not to fall under the Convention unless that relationship involves property located abroad, envisages performance or enforcement abroad, or has some other reasonable relation with one or more foreign states."

This part of Section 202 read in conjunction with Section 206 implies, in the first place, that Article II(3) of the Convention applies in any case to agreements to arbitrate to which at least one of the parties is non-American, irrespective whether the place of arbitration is within or without the United States. Apparently, it is presumed that such agreement always relates to an international transaction.

Both Sections imply, in the second place, that Article II(3) also applies to agreements between two U.S. parties, irrespective whether the place of arbitration is within or without the United States, provided that the underlying transaction is international. The United States law therefore includes an agreement providing for arbitration in the United States between two American nationals if the agreement relates to a subject matter which is international.

. . . .

. . . [The] parties may have omitted to indicate the place of arbitration in their agreement. It may also be that the parties have referred in their agreement to Arbitration Rules of an arbitration institute which Rules provide that the administering authority has to designate the place of arbitration, and that authority has not yet made the designation. In addition, some arbitral clauses and Arbitration Rules provide that under certain conditions arbitration can be initiated in the country of either party (the so-called "home-on-home" arbitral clause).

For determining whether such an arbitration agreement falls under Article II(3) of the Convention, the same test of internationality as applied to the agreement providing for arbitration in the State where the agreement is invoked, can be adopted. This seems to be the only possible solution as, failing the place of arbitration, Article I cannot be applied by analogy as was possible for the agreement providing for arbitration in another State. On the other hand, the interpretation that any arbitration agreement would fall under the Convention has to be rejected as being too broad.

### Notes and Questions

1. Compare the scope of the Convention with respect to awards discussed in *Bergesen v. Joseph Muller Corp.*, 548 F.Supp. 650 (S.D.N.Y. 1982), *aff'd.* 710 F.2d 928 (2d Cir. 1983), *infra* p. 1034.

2. The New York Convention was not the first attempt at an arbitration treaty of general applicability. Arbitration Conventions signed in Geneva in 1923 and 1927 were earlier efforts in this area. *See* Supplement at pp. 34 & 36. When the New York Convention applies, however, these previous treaties will cease to have effect between parties to the Convention. New York Convention, Art. VII(2).

3. You are a clerk for District Court Judge X. Prepare a memorandum explaining the policy that should determine which sorts of agreements to arbitrate should be compelled by U.S. courts.

### C.    UNITED STATES RESERVATIONS ON ACCESSION TO THE NEW YORK CONVENTION

The New York Convention permits two treaty reservations. First, Article I(3) provides that a state may restrict the Convention on the basis of geographical reciprocity, to cover only awards rendered in the territory of another contracting state. Second, a state may apply the Convention only to commercial disputes. The United States has adopted both reservations, as set forth below.

> The United States of America will apply the Convention, on the basis of reciprocity, to the recognition and enforcement of only those awards made in the territory of another Contracting State. The United States of America will apply the Convention only to differences arising out of legal relationships, whether

contractual or not, which are considered as commercial under the national law of the United States.[137]

<u>Notes and Questions</u>

1. What interests was the United States protecting in taking the reservation with regard to reciprocity?

2. Does the reservation limiting the applicability of the convention to commercial relationships vary in accordance with changes in conceptions of what is "commercial" in U.S. law or is the commitment made by the United States to other parties to the Convention frozen with respect to commerciality as of the moment of U.S. ratification?

## III. WHAT IS A "WRITING"?

Article II of the New York Convention requires an "agreement in writing" for the arbitration agreement to be enforceable under the Convention. What constitutes a "writing" has been subject to discussion. Telegrams are definitely included. What about an unsigned exchange of telexes or facsimiles? Differences in the French and English texts of Article II(2) have complicated analyses, as pointed out in the following excerpt.

### A. ADAM SAMUEL, JURISDICTIONAL PROBLEMS IN INTERNATIONAL COMMERCIAL ARBITRATION 82-83 (1989).

The English and French versions of the paragraph mean quite different things. It is, therefore, impossible to say categorically what the provision actually means. The second group of problems relate to the French text which appears to exclude, from the ambit of the Convention, agreements made by means of communication which are, or are becoming increasingly common in international trade.

.  .  .

---

[137] United States Reservations on Accession to the New York Convention (deposited on September 30, 1970, to take effect December 29, 1970).

The French version, which, translated into English, would read, "the term 'arbitration agreement' shall mean either, . . ." appears to limit the arbitral agreements, to which the Convention applies, to those defined in Article II. The English text, however, has been described as being of "an inclusive character," in that while agreements of the type mentioned in Article II(2) are definitely within the ambit of the Convention, its application is not limited to such agreements. Others which constitute valid agreements in writing under the private international law of the forum are equally included.

\*     \*     \*

The following European judicial decision interprets the "writing" requirement as it applies to arbitration clauses incorporated into an agreement by reference to standard form contracts and general conditions. What policy considerations were driving the courts in this matter?

B.     *Bomar Oil v. Entreprise Tunisienne d'activité petrolière ("ETAP")*, 15 YEARBOOK OF COMMERCIAL ARBITRATION 447 (1990).[138]

By an exchange of telexes in August 1983, ETAP sold Bomar 65,000 metric tons of crude oil. Reference was made in two of ETAP's telexes to ETAP's standard contract which provided for arbitration in Geneva.

A dispute arose concerning an adjustment of the price, whereupon ETAP notified Bomar of its intention to resort to arbitration. Bomar refused to appoint an arbitrator, arguing that there was no valid arbitration agreement between the parties. Pursuant to the provisions of ETAP's standard contract, the President of the ICC designated an arbitrator in lieu of Bomar.

On 2 July 1984, the three arbitrators established Terms of Reference which were signed by both parties. Arbitration was to take place in Paris under French procedural law supplemented by the UNCITRAL Arbitration Rules.

---

[138] The facts of this case are reported in more detail in 13 YEARBOOK OF COMMERCIAL ARBITRATION 466-70 (1988).

By an award of 25 January 1985, the arbitrators rejected Bomar's objection to their jurisdiction over the dispute. Bomar applied for the setting aside of the award to the Court of Appeal of Paris. The Court of Appeal upheld the arbitrators' decision on their jurisdiction to hear the dispute. This decision is reported in XIII YEARBOOK (1988) under France no. 12.

The Supreme Court considered the provisions of Art. II(1) and (2) of the New York Convention, and reasoned:

> According to Art. II(1), each Contracting State recognizes the agreement in writing by which the parties undertake to submit to arbitration all or any differences which have arisen or which may arise between them in respect of a defined legal relationship, whether contractual or not, concerning a subject matter capable of settlement by arbitration. According to Art. II(2), "agreement in writing" means an arbitral clause in a contract or an arbitration agreement, signed by the parties or contained in an exchange of letters or telegrams.

> .   .   .

> The judgment [of the Court of Appeal] holds that the arbitration clause contained in the ETAP standard contract, to which reference is made in the main contract concluded by an exchange of telexes, is binding on the parties, reasoning that Bomar, being conversant with the operations of the oil trade, cannot assert to have not been aware of the usual clauses in contracts concluded in this sector of activity. Further, the Court holds that it was Bomar's duty to consult the standard contract to which the telex of the seller referred expressly, before giving its definite consent to ETAP's offer.

> The above-mentioned rules do not exclude the incorporation of an arbitral clause by reference. However, it is necessary — as it would be in French law — that the existence of the clause be mentioned in the main contract, unless there exists between the parties a longstanding business relationship which ensures that they are properly aware of the written conditions normally governing their commercial relationships.

Since [the Court of Appeal] decided without determining that the clause at issue had been mentioned in the exchange of telexes, or that there existed a longstanding business relationship between the parties, the Court of Appeal violated the above-mentioned norms.

On rehearing, the Court of Appeal stated generally that the party invoking the arbitration agreement was required to prove that the other party knew of the arbitral clause at the time it entered into the principal agreement. Examination of the relevant correspondence between the parties, both merchants by profession, led the Court to hold that the arbitration clause in the standard form contract could be invoked against Bomar. See decision of Cour d'Appel de Versailles, 23 January 1991, reprinted in XVII YEARBOOK OF INTERNATIONAL ARBITRATION 488 (1992), affirmed by the Cour de Cassation, 9 November 1993 (1ʳᵉ Ch. Civ.).

### Notes and Questions

1. How, other than by invocation of an arbitration clause in a standard form contract, would the party seeking arbitration demonstrate that the other party knew of the arbitration clause?

2. From a policy perspective, is the implication of the French decisions likely to contribute to clarification of arbitral obligations in standardized contracts?

3. Consider Dr. Samuel's contention. How significant is the difference between the English and French texts?

4. Unlike the New York Convention, the 1961 European Convention,[139] which was designed to supplement the New York Convention by limiting grounds on which an award may be set aside, applies, by virtue of Article I, on the basis of nationality of parties.

5. The European Convention contains unusually detailed provisions for enforcing agreements to arbitrate according to both institutional and *ad hoc* arbitral procedures. See, in particular, Article IV Organization of the Arbitration.

---

[139] European Convention on International Commercial Arbitration (The Geneva Convention of 1961), Apr. 21, 1961, 484 U.N.T.S. 364. The text is in the Supplement at p. 71.

6. Article 1 of the Panama Convention of 1975, officially called the "Inter-American Convention on International Commercial Arbitration,"[140] provides that agreements to arbitrate are "valid." Unlike the New York Convention, however, the Panama Convention does not impose on the courts of a Contracting State the duty to stay their own proceedings and refer the parties to arbitration. On other differences between the Panama Convention and the New York Convention, see Albert J. van den Berg, *The New York Convention of 1958 and the Panama Convention of 1975: Redundancy or Compatibility?*, 5 ARB. INT'L 214 (1989). Many Latin American countries have also adhered to the New York Convention, as well as the Panama Convention.

C. CONVENTION ON THE SETTLEMENT OF INVESTMENT DISPUTES BETWEEN STATES AND NATIONALS OF OTHER STATES (THE WASHINGTON CONVENTION OF 1965), Mar. 18, 1965, 575 U.N.T.S. 159.

Distinct "writing" requirements may obtain when states are parties to arbitration agreements. Under the aegis of the World Bank, the Washington Convention of 1965 established the "International Centre for the Settlement of Investment Disputes." The Centre's jurisdiction is set forth in Chapter II of the Convention.

Article 25

(1) The jurisdiction of the Centre shall extend to any legal dispute arising directly out of an investment, between a Contracting State (or any constituent subdivision or agency of a Contracting State designated to the Centre by that State) and a national of another Contracting State, which the parties have given their consent, no party may withdraw its consent unilaterally.

.    .    .

(3) Consent by a constituent subdivision or agency of a Contracting State shall require the approval of that State unless that State notifies the Centre that no such approval is required.

(4) Any Contracting State may, at the time of the ratification, acceptance or approval of this Convention or at any time thereafter, notify the Centre of the class or classes of disputes which it would or

---

[140] 14 I.L.M. 336 (1975).

would not consider submitting to the jurisdiction of the Centre. The Secretary-General shall forthwith transmit such notification to all Contracting States. Such notification shall not constitute the consent required by paragraph (1).

### Notes and Questions

1. State commitments to arbitration may have political and constitutional implications. Hence the specification in Article 25. How should Article 25(3) be interpreted with regard to state-owned corporations?

2. As summarized in Chapter 2, the ICSID regime provides no role for national courts in this or subsequent phases of the arbitral process. Why?

3. What functional equivalent to the corresponding role of national courts in the New York Convention does the Washington Convention provide?

### D.  BILATERAL TREATIES: TREATIES OF FRIENDSHIP, COMMERCE & NAVIGATION

Arbitration agreements may also be enforced under provisions of bilateral conventions, such as Article VI of the U.S.-German Treaty of Friendship, Commerce and Navigation, Oct. 29, 1954, 7 U.S.T. 1840, 1845, T.I.A.S. No. 3,593.

## ARTICLE VI

1.   Nationals and companies of either party shall be accorded national treatment with respect to access to the courts of justice and to administrative tribunals and agencies within the territories of the other Party, in all degrees of jurisdiction, both in pursuit and in defense of their rights. It is understood that companies of either Party not engaged in activities within the territories of the other Party shall enjoy such access therein without any requirement of registration or domestication.

2.   Contracts entered into between nationals or companies of either Party and nationals or companies of the other Party, that provide for the settlement by arbitration of controversies, shall not be deemed unenforceable within the territories of such other Party merely on the grounds that the place designated for the

arbitration proceedings is outside such territories or that the nationality of one or more of the arbitrators is not that of such other Party. Awards duly rendered pursuant to any such contracts, which are final and enforceable under the laws of the place where rendered, shall be deemed conclusive in enforcement proceedings brought before the courts of competent jurisdiction of either Party, and shall be entitled to be declared enforceable by such courts, except where found contrary to public policy. When so declared, such awards shall be entitled to privileges and measures of enforcement appertaining to awards rendered locally. It is understood, however, that awards rendered outside the United States of America shall be entitled in any court in any State thereof only to the same measure of recognition as rendered in other States thereof.

<u>Notes and Questions</u>

1. Contrast the regime under the New York Convention with that of Article VI of the U.S.-German FCN Treaty.

2. Are there grounds under Article VI(2) under which the courts of the parties to the Convention may refuse to compel arbitration? What are they?

## IV.   THE INTERSECTION OF NATIONAL LAW AND THE INTERNATIONAL ARBITRAL SYSTEM

### A.   WHAT IS AN "INTERNATIONAL" ARBITRATION?

In practice, national laws may sometimes prove more important than the treaty framework within which they operate. Many national statutes, independent of the treaties, accord special treatment to international arbitration. First, however, national courts must determine whether a particular arbitration is "international." Characterization tests used to determine whether or not an arbitration is international generally have focused on either the parties or the transaction. A party-oriented test looks to the nationality and residence of the litigants. English, Belgian and Swiss legislation follow this mode. A less mechanical test that asks whether the arbitration implicates the interests of international commerce, regardless of who the parties are, has been adopted by the French. The United States takes a middle ground by excluding contracts between Americans from the scope of the New

York Convention unless the transaction has a reasonable relationship to a foreign country.

Consider the following national statutory formulations for determining which arbitrations are international in character. Which criteria are more appropriate to the goals of the New York Convention? Bear in mind that national statutes generally provide more favorable treatment to international arbitration, in the sense of lowering barriers to the enforcement of both agreements to arbitrate and awards. When are the consequences of a failed arbitration agreement most dramatically disagreeable?

## 1.    THE UNITED STATES: A CASE STUDY.

In some cases there may be advantages to bringing an arbitration agreement under Chapter 2 of the Federal Arbitration Act, which enforces agreements and awards falling under the New York Convention. For example, cases covered by the Convention can be removed from state courts to the federal district court of the place of the proceeding. 9 U.S.C. §205 (1988). Moreover, when an award is rendered, the period for judicial confirmation is three years rather than one. 9 U.S.C. §207 (1988). Courts may compel arbitration covered by the Convention whether within or without the United States. 9 U.S.C. §206 (1988).

Agreements between Americans will not normally fall under the Convention as enforced by United States courts.

### 9 U.S.C. §202 (1988)

An arbitration agreement . . . arising out of such a relationship which is entirely between citizens of the United States shall be deemed not to fall under the Convention unless that relationship involves property located abroad, envisages performance or enforcement abroad, or has some other reasonable relation with one or more foreign states. For the purposes of this section a corporation is a citizen of the United States if it is incorporated or has its principal place of business in the United States.

The jurisdiction of federal courts in such a case was tested in the case below, in which the court compelled arbitration between two American entities when their contract had a reasonable relationship to a foreign country.

2. *Fuller Co. v. Compagnie Des Bauxites De Guinée*, 421 F.Supp. 938 (W.D. Pa. 1976).

In this case, the court must interpret the scope and meaning of the Convention on the Recognition and Enforcement of Foreign Arbitral Awards, enacted into law in the United States as 9 U.S.C. 201 et seq. and the extent of the parties' contractual agreement to arbitrate. . . . Fuller Company, a Pennsylvania corporation, and Compagnie Des Bauxites De Guinee [Hereinafter: CBG], a Delaware corporation, executed a contract under which Fuller would design, manufacture and sell a drying and calcining plant for CBG's bauxite plant in the Republic of Guinea. The equipment was to be manufactured in the United States and shipped to Guinea FOB at Philadelphia. [Following a discussion of alleged defects in the equipment, CBG submitted a request for arbitration to the Court of Arbitration of the International Chamber of Commerce on November 5, 1975.]

. . .

This opinion will not resolve the underlying claims and disputes between the parties. Rather, the court at this stage of the proceedings is called upon to determine which of three possible forums should proceed with factual hearings on the merits:

(1)	This court.
(2)	An arbitration panel in Pittsburgh.
(3)	The Court of Common Pleas of Allegheny County.

. . .

Jurisdiction of this court is invoked by CBG pursuant to the terms of the Convention on the Recognition and Enforcement of Foreign Arbitral Awards, enacted into law by Congress on July 31, 1970, as 9 U.S.C. 201-208 (hereinafter: The Convention). As a contract entirely between citizens of the United States, it is clear that the Fuller-CBG contract meets the jurisdictional requirements of the implementing legislation to the Convention if *any one* of four conditions are met: [footnote omitted]

    (1)    The agreement involves property located abroad.
    (2)    The agreement envisages performance abroad.
    (3)    The agreement envisages enforcement abroad.
    (4)    The agreement has some other reasonable relation with one or more foreign states.

No court has yet interpreted the meaning of the Convention as it applies to contracts executed between citizens of the United States. However, some guidance can be obtained from the legislative history of the act.

Mr. Richard D. Kearney, the Chairman of the Secretary of State's Advisory Committee on Private International Law gave the following testimony before the Senate Committee on Foreign Relations (Chaired by Senator Fullbright) on February 13, 1970:

> "We have included in section 202 a requirement that any case concerning an agreement or award solely between U.S. citizens is excluded unless there is some important foreign element involved, such as property located abroad, the performance of a contract in a foreign country, or a similar reasonable relation with one or more foreign states. The reasonable relationship criterion is taken from the general provisions of the Uniform Commercial Code. Section 1-105(1) of the code[141] permits the parties to a transaction that bears a reasonable relationship to any other state or nation to specify that the law of that state or nation will govern their rights and duties.

---

[141] [4] That provision reads as follows:

> "(1) Except as provided hereafter in this section, when a transaction bears a reasonable relation to this state and also to another state or nation the parties may agree that the law either of this state or of such other state or nation shall govern their rights and duties. Failing such agreement this Act applies to transactions bearing an appropriate relation to this state."

In this connection of course, it should be recalled that what we are dealing with under the Convention is solely a situation in which the parties have voluntarily agreed to arbitration. The Convention and implementing legislation will apply to a transaction only because the parties to that transaction have agreed to settle disputes by arbitration. The provision on choice of law in the Uniform Commercial Code is also based on the same kind of voluntary action by the parties to a transaction. Since the Commercial Code is basic law on commercial transactions in the United States it seemed appropriate to incorporate its test of reasonable relationship into the implementing legislation on foreign arbitral awards." .

. .

.      .      .

The statements contained in the affidavits submitted in this case differ sharply in regard to the significance the parties attached to overseas technical services when entering into their contract. Philip Richter, manager for project management of Fuller alleges that this technical advice in Guinea was at most a very minor and insignificant part of the contract while John W. Lambert, chief engineer of CBG and Paul DuPont, chief engineer of Tractionel [a Belgian corporation consulting as an engineer for CBG] allege that overseas technical services of Fuller were relied upon by CBG in entering into the contract and constitute a crucial part of the bargain. [footnote omitted] It is not necessary to resolve this conflict in the evidence. Clearly, extensive overseas technical services were contemplated by Fuller in entering into the contract and were in fact provided. [footnote omitted]

In addition to the substantial amount of performance of this contract in Guinea already mentioned, a number of other foreign contacts serve to create a "reasonable relationship with one or more foreign states":

(1) Under the original agreement, arbitration was to occur in Geneva, Switzerland. Thus, the original agreement envisaged enforcement overseas, although the parties have subsequently agreed to arbitration in Pittsburgh, Pennsylvania.

(2) Section 2(s) of Contract No. 16 requires Fuller to deliver replacement parts to Port Kamsar, Guinea. (Further performance overseas).

(3) Section 2(d)(ii)(1) of Contract No. 16 requires Fuller to be afforded full access and opportunity to recommend modification or adjustments of the equipment in Guinea after the start-up of industrial relations. (Further performance overseas).

(4) Section 2(d)(ii)(5) of Contract No. 16 guarantees Fuller full access and opportunity to recommend improvements of possible defects as to the functioning or manufacturing, during the performance tests of the equipment in Guinea. (Further performance abroad).

(5) To the extent that Fuller had erection responsibilities in Guinea, it is arguable that the contract involves property abroad. But in light of the ambiguity in the contract in this regard and the fact that Fuller shipped the goods FOB Philadelphia, the court places little reliance on this point.

(6) Tractionel [CBG's Belgian engineering consultant] is headquartered in Brussels, Belgium and appears to have had important connections with all phases of this contract as witnessed by their attendance at the January 28, 1975 meeting in Pittsburgh, Pennsylvania. Under Section 8.6.2 of Volume I General Conditions, Fuller was to apply to Tractionel for the issuance from Brussels, Belgium of Provisional and Final Acceptance Certificates. [footnote omitted]

The motion to remand will therefore be denied.

.     .     .

Now that jurisdiction has been determined to properly lie in this court, the question arises as to how it should be exercised. The court will order that arbitration be convened pursuant to the terms of the implementing legislation to the Convention. The defendant's motion to stay trial and all further proceedings pending issuance of final award or determination in the arbitration will therefore be granted.

## Notes and Questions

1. In *Fuller*, the court found six internationalizing factors. What is the *minimum* number of factors that would suffice to establish jurisdiction? Explain your answer.

2. Is the selection of a foreign venue for arbitration *per se* an internationalizing factor?

3. The situation in France is regulated by the Nouveau Code de procédure civile, Article 1492 which provides that "[a]n international arbitration is one which implicates the interests of international commerce."

4. The situation in Switzerland is regulated by the Swiss Private International Law Act, Art. 176(1):

> The provisions of this chapter shall apply to all arbitrations where the seat of the arbitral tribunal is situated in Switzerland and where at least one of the parties was, at the moment when the arbitral agreement was concluded, neither domiciled nor habitually resident in Switzerland.

5. Article 1(3) of the UNCITRAL Model Law defines an arbitration as international if:

a.      the parties to an arbitration agreement have, at the time of the conclusion of that agreement, their places of business in different States; or

b.      one of the following places is situated outside the State in which the parties have their places of business:

      (i)      the place of arbitration if determined in, or pursuant to, the arbitration agreement;

      (ii)      any place where a substantial part of the obligations of the commercial relationship is to be performed or the place with which the subject-matter of the dispute is most closely connected; or

c.      the parties have expressly agreed that the subject-matter of the arbitration agreement relates to more than one country.

6. Criteria for determining whether an arbitration is "international" which are based on nationality are largely self-executing in that public and private international law provide rather clear guidelines for the determination of nationality though there is less certainty about the consequences of such determination. The French and, to an extent, the U.S. approach are more judicially subjective. Given that subjectivity, how can international impartiality be achieved? Is it important?

### B. WHAT IS A COMMERCIAL MATTER?

The United States' reservations to the New York Convention also restrict its application to legal relationships considered as "commercial." The meaning of "commercial" is discussed in the following excerpts from a treatise by Redfern and Hunter and a federal case involving a dispute between Japanese and Greek corporations.

1. ALAN REDFERN & MARTIN HUNTER, LAW AND PRACTICE OF INTERNATIONAL COMMERCIAL ARBITRATION 15-16 (2d ed. 1986).

Whilst there is no universally accepted definition of the term commercial, it has now become part of the language. It serves, for instance, to distinguish international commercial arbitrations from international arbitrations between states concerned with boundary disputes and other political issues. It also serves to distinguish them from arbitrations (which are usually but not necessarily domestic) concerned with such matters as property tenure, employment and family law. Indeed, it may be said that if the term had not existed it would have been necessary to invent it, much as it has been necessary to establish in England a commercial court which deals only with disputes arising out of trading and other commercial relationships.

In a particular case it may be of great importance to know whether the legal relationship out of which the arbitration arose was or was not a commercial relationship. The question will arise, for example, if it becomes necessary to seek recognition or enforcement of a foreign arbitral award in a state which has adhered to the New York Convention, but which had entered the commercial reservation. It will then be necessary to look closely at the law of the state concerned to see what definition it adopts of the term "commercial." Internationally, the approach is to interpret the term "commercial" as widely as possible. Although problems have occasionally arisen because courts of particular countries have adopted a narrow definition of commercial, the general approach of courts of many nations is to define commercial so as to embrace all types of trade or business transactions.

\*     \*     \*

2.      *Sumitomo Corp. v. Parakopi Compania Maritima, S.A.*, 477 F.Supp. 737 (S.D.N.Y. 1979), *aff'd mem.*, 620 F.2d 286 (2d Cir. 1980).

.   .   .

Sumitomo and Oshima are corporations organized and existing under the laws of Japan. Sumitomo has its principal place of business in Tokyo, Japan, and Oshima has its principal place of business in Nagasaki, Japan. Parakopi is incorporated in Panama, and has its principal place of business in Piraeus, Greece.

In September 1975, Sumitomo and Parakopi entered into a contract whereby Sumitomo agreed to construct for and sell to Parakopi a bulk carrier.[142] Oshima, as the builder, agreed to be bound by all the terms and conditions of the contract applicable to it.

Section 1 of Article XIV of the purchase agreement provides for the resolution of all non-technical disputes by arbitration in New York:

Should any dispute arise between the parties in regard to the construction of the VESSEL, her engines and/or materials or to any other technical matters, such dispute shall forthwith be referred to the Principal Surveyor of the Classification Society in Japan, whose opinion shall be final and binding upon both parties hereto. Any other dispute arising under or by virtue of this Contract or any difference of opinion between the parties hereto concerning their rights and obligations under this Contract . . . shall be settled by arbitration in New York, New York in accordance with the rules of the United States Arbitration Act.

Under section 2 of Article XIV, a party seeking arbitration must serve a written demand for arbitration on the other side and designate an arbitrator. The other party is obligated, within 20 days after receiving the written demand, to designate its arbitrator. The two arbitrators are then to select a third arbitrator, and the three arbitrators will constitute the arbitration panel.

---

[142] [1] The contract was negotiated in New York and executed in Greece.

The vessel was completed in 1977 and was delivered to and accepted by Parakopi in June of that year. Under the terms of the contract, the purchase price of the vessel was fixed in terms of Japanese yen. Some 70 per cent of the purchase price was to be paid over a seven-year period in 14 semi-annual installments. Although Parakopi has been paying the installments due to date, it commenced an action in Greece in January 1979 [footnote omitted] seeking to be relieved of its obligations under the contract on the basis of unforeseeable circumstances, *i.e.*, the sharp rise in value of the yen against the dollar, [footnote omitted] and on the ground of fraud, *i.e.*, the petitioners' alleged fraudulent concealment from Parakopi of knowledge that the yen would increase in value. [footnote omitted] See exh. B to Petition To Compel Arbitration and for Appointment of Arbitrator.

Petitioners served a demand for arbitration of the matter in controversy on Parakopi in April 1979 and designated an arbitrator pursuant to section 2 of Article XIV of the contract. Although Parakopi did subsequently select an arbitrator, its arbitrator refused to proceed with the selection of a third arbitrator. Thereafter, it became apparent that Parakopi was not going to voluntarily proceed to arbitration, and petitioners commenced this action.

Parakopi's opposition to the petition is predicated on four arguments: (1) that the parties entered into a stipulation which precludes the petitioners from taking any action to proceed to arbitration until October 19, 1979; (2) that the Court lacks subject matter jurisdiction; (3) that the petitioners' proper remedy is to seek a stay of the suit in Greece from a Greek court; and (4) that even assuming this Court has jurisdiction, it should defer to the Greek litigation for reasons of comity. See Respondent's Mem. of Law in Opp. to Petitioner, at 2.

.   .   .

## B.   *Subject Matter Jurisdiction*

Petitioners commenced this action under the Convention on the Recognition and Enforcement of Foreign Arbitration Awards (the "Convention"), 21 U.S.T. 2517, T.I.A.S. No. 8052. Subject matter jurisdiction is claimed under 9 U.S.C. § 203, which provides:

An action or proceeding under the Convention shall be deemed to arise under the laws and treaties of the United States. The district courts of the United States . . . shall have original jurisdiction over such an action or proceeding, regardless of the amount in controversy.

In contending that this Court lacks subject matter jurisdiction over the instant petition, Parakopi relies on 9 U.S.C. §§ 1 and 202. Section 202 provides that an arbitration agreement or arbitral award falls under the Convention if it "aris[es] out of a legal relationship, whether contractual or not, which is considered as commercial . . . ." Section 1 of Title 9 defines "commerce" as follows:

"commerce," as herein defined, means commerce among the several States or with foreign nations, or in any Territory of the United States or in the District of Columbia, or between any such Territory and any State or foreign nation . . . .

Citing cases holding that "commerce" as defined by 9 U.S.C. § 1 does not include commerce involving only foreign parties, [footnote omitted] Parakopi argues that "commercial" disputes involving only foreign entities should also be excluded from coverage under 9 U.S.C. §§ 202 and 203. I disagree.

The language of the relevant sections of the statute does not support Parakopi's assertion that the definition of "commerce" in section 1 controls the scope of section 202. First of all, section 202 does not use the term "commerce" at all, but utilizes the term "commercial." Secondly, section 202 uses "commercial" in a substantive rather than geographical sense, while section 1 does not substantively define "commerce" at all, defining it only in geographical terms. Section 202 refers to "a legal relationship . . . which is considered as commercial," while section 1 provides that "'commerce' . . . means commerce among the several States or with foreign nations . . . ." Moreover, in limiting the application of the Convention to "commercial" disputes, the United States did not make reference to 9 U.S.C. § 1; instead it referred to "legal relationships . . . which are considered as commercial under the national law of the United States." Convention, n.29. While 9 U.S.C. § 1 is certainly part of the national law of the United States, it does not constitute all of the national law of the United States. In delineating the coverage of the Convention, Congress explicitly excluded purely domestic transactions. 9 U.S.C.

§ 202. Had Congress also intended to exclude purely foreign transactions, it undoubtedly would have done so explicitly as well.

The fact that 9 U.S.C. § 1 is part of Chapter 1 of the Arbitration Act while 9 U.S.C. § 202 is part of Chapter 2 is also an indication that section 1 does not control section 202. Chapter 1 existed prior to the United States' accession to the Convention, and indeed was not designated as "Chapter 1" until the provisions implementing the convention were added to Title 9 as Chapter 2. *See* Act of July 31, 1970, Pub. L. No. 91-368, 84 Stat. 692. The provisions of Chapter 1 apply to proceedings brought under Chapter 2 only to the extent that they do not conflict with the provisions of Chapter 2 or the Convention. 9 U.S.C. § 208.

Concluding that the Court has subject matter jurisdiction over this matter would certainly further the policies underlying the Convention. The Supreme Court has noted that:

> The goal of the Convention, and the principal purpose underlying American adoption and implementation of it, was to encourage the recognition and enforcement of commercial arbitration agreements in international contracts and to unify the standards by which agreements to arbitrate are observed and arbitral awards are enforced in the signatory countries.

*Scherk v. Alberto-Culver Co.*, 417 U.S. 506, 520 n.15 (1974) . . . To hold that subject matter jurisdiction is lacking where the parties involved are all foreign entities would certainly undermine the goal of encouraging the recognition and enforcement of arbitration agreements in international contracts.

Finally, although the issue of whether the scope of Chapter 2 is limited by the definition of "commerce" in Chapter 1 has not been previously addressed, American courts have applied the Convention to situations involving only foreign entities. . . .

[The request for dismissal was denied, arbitration was ordered in New York and a third arbitrator was appointed.]

Notes and Questions

1. Given the Supreme Court's policy goal in *Scherk*, which is adopted by the *Sumitomo* court, is the definition of a "commercial matter" for arbitration purposes still relevant? Discuss.

2. The efforts of a party-appointed arbitrator to obstruct the formation of a tribunal or its operation is a latent possibility in this type of regime. The institutional techniques for controlling its abuse are discussed in Chapter 2, *infra* pp. 253-56.

## C. WHERE SHOULD ARBITRATION BE COMPELLED?

As will be discussed in Chapter 9, the situs of an arbitration is of the utmost importance with respect to control mechanisms applied to awards. Situs is also critical to enforceability of an arbitration agreement by American courts because on accession to the New York Convention the United States reserved its application on the basis of reciprocity only to those awards made in other signatory states.

1.      *National Iranian Oil Co. v. Ashland Oil, Inc.,* 817 F.2d 326 (5th Cir. 1987).

.   .   .

## I.

According to the allegations contained in the pleadings and accompanying memoranda, two Ashland Oil Company (Ashland) subsidiaries, Ashland Overseas Trading Limited (AOTL) and Ashland Bermuda Limited began to use the National Iranian Oil Company (NIOC), an instrumentality of the Islamic Republic of Iran, as their primary supplier of Middle Eastern crude oil in 1973. The parties entered into long-term contracts. Amid the maelstrom of chaos and confusion engendered during the Islamic Revolution in Iran, NIOC allegedly repudiated then renegotiated its contracts with Ashland's two subsidiaries on several occasions in 1978 and 1979. On March 11, 1979, the parties allegedly entered into a two-year, nine-month contract, providing that NIOC was to supply AOTL with 150,000 barrels of crude oil per day. NIOC allegedly repudiated this March contract on April 10, 1979. On April 11, the parties allegedly executed a new contract, providing that NIOC was to supply AOTL with 115,000 barrels of crude per day until December 31, 1979.

On November 12, 1979, following the takeover of the American Embassy in Tehran and the seizure of American hostages on November 4, President Carter banned the importation of all oil from Iran not already in transit. Exec. Order No. 4702, 44 Fed. Reg. 65581 (November 16, 1979). Several cargoes of crude, however, were then en route to AOTL. AOTL received and refined the oil, worth nearly $283,000,000. Despite NIOC's demand, neither Ashland nor its subsidiaries have rendered payment. Ashland, in essence, contends that it is not responsible for the alleged breaches of its subsidiaries and that NIOC itself breached the March and April agreements.

In accord with the terms of the arbitration clause of the parties' April contract, NIOC appointed an arbitrator to resolve the dispute. Despite the forum selection clause contained in the arbitration provision, Ashland refuses to participate in an arbitral proceeding in Iran because of the danger to Americans. Nor has Ashland agreed to participate in an arbitration elsewhere. NIOC thus brought suit against Ashland in federal district court, and alleged breach of contract in the first three counts of its complaint. In count four of its complaint, NIOC sought to compel arbitration in Mississippi, to have the court appoint an arbitrator and to stay litigation pursuant to the United States Arbitration Act (Act), 9 U.S.C. § 1 *et seq.*

Ashland then filed a counterclaim, alleging tortious interference with and breach of contract by NIOC. NIOC responded to the counterclaim by filing an application that also sought to appoint an arbitrator, to compel arbitration, and to stay litigation. Because the terms of the agreement expressly provided for arbitration in Tehran, the district court found that it lacked the power to order arbitration in Mississippi under section 4 of the Act, and thus it denied NIOC's motion. 641 F.Supp. 211 (S.D.Miss.1986). NIOC appeals from that order.

On appeal, NIOC points to the strong federal policy favoring the private resolution of contract disputes, particularly in the international commercial context, and argues that we should reverse the district court and order arbitration in Mississippi because the parties have "waived" the forum selection clause in the contract. Alternatively, NIOC contends that, because it is now impossible to render performance of the contract's terms, we should sever the forum selection clause from the rest of the arbitration provision and order

Ashland to perform the essential part of their bargain, *viz.*, to arbitrate. Finding no merit to these contentions, we affirm the district court's judgment on other grounds. Not only justice and sound policy, but also the law prevents NIOC from holding Ashland hostage to an agreement not contemplated *ex ante*.

.   .   .

### III.

Section 4 of the [Federal Arbitration] Act provides in relevant part that:

> A party aggrieved by the alleged failure, neglect or refusal of another to arbitrate under a written agreement for arbitration may petition any United States district court . . . for an order directing that such arbitration proceed in the manner *provided for in the agreement. . . .* The court shall hear the parties, and upon being satisfied that the making of the agreement for arbitration or the failure to comply therewith is not in issue, the court shall make an order directing the parties to proceed to arbitration *in accordance with the terms of the agreement.* The hearing and proceedings, under such agreement, *shall be within the district in which the petition for an order directing such arbitration is filed.*

9 U.S.C. § 4 (emphasis added). Section 4 thus facially mandates that two conditions must be met before a district court may compel arbitration: (1) that the arbitration be held in the district in which the court sits; *and* (2) that the arbitration be held in accordance with the agreement of the parties. In this case the forum selection clause, found in Article X of the April contract, provides that "the seat of arbitration shall be in Tehran, unless otherwise agreed by the parties." Rec. at 28. Relying on *Snyder v. Smith*, 736 F.2d 409 (7th Cir.), *cert. denied*, 469 U.S. 1037, 105 S.Ct. 513, 83 L.Ed.2d 403 (1984), the district court reasoned that the language of Section 4 deprived it of the power to compel arbitration in Mississippi, because to order arbitration in Mississippi would violate the forum selection clause and thus would not be "in accordance with the terms of the agreement." 9 U.S.C. § 4.

．　　．　　．

NIOC contends that since it is not seeking to compel arbitration in Iran, it has waived its right to the benefit of the forum selection clause. Further, NIOC argues that Ashland also has waived the "benefit" of such clause by refusing to participate in an arbitral proceeding in Tehran or elsewhere. NIOC therefore concludes that, because the putative waivers render the forum selection clause nugatory, we are free to order arbitration in Mississippi without contravening the contract's terms. This argument rings hollow.

In the first place, as NIOC now concedes, it has no right to an order compelling arbitration in Tehran. When the United States adhered to the Convention on the Recognition and Enforcement of Foreign Arbitral Awards (Convention), 21 U.S.T. 2517, T.I.A.S. No. 6997 (1970) (implemented by chapter 2 of 9 U.S.C.), U.S. courts were granted the power to compel arbitration in signatory countries. *See* 9 U.S.C. § 206. But Iran is not one of the 65 nations that have adhered to the Convention, *see* note following 9 U.S.C.A. § 201 at 208-09 (Supp.1986), and thus no American court may order arbitration in Iran. Convention Articles I(1), I(3); Declaration of the U.S. upon accession (Declaration), reprinted in 9 U.S.C.A. at 213 n. 43 (Supp.1986); *see Sedco, Inc. v. Petroleos Mexicanos Mexican National Oil Co. (Pemex)*, 767 F.2d 1140, 1145 (5th Cir.1985); *Ledee v. Ceramiche Ragno*, 684 F.2d 184, 185-86 (1st Cir.1982). Consequently, NIOC has no right that is recognized under U.S. law to compel an arbitration in Iran.

Because a waiver is a voluntary relinquishment of a known right . . . and because NIOC has nothing that it could relinquish in a U.S. court, NIOC could not have waived its "right" to the benefit of the forum selection clause. Moreover, Ashland contends and NIOC does not dispute that NIOC has attempted, and still may be attempting, to compel arbitration through the court system in Iran. Thus, NIOC has not waived its contractual right to arbitration in Iran. NIOC, at most, simply and pragmatically has recognized that it has no legal right in the U.S. courts to compel arbitration in Tehran.

## IV.

NIOC also argues that, because it may be "inconvenient" for Ashland to participate in an arbitral proceeding in Iran, this impossibility (or commercial impracticability) renders the forum selection clause without force. Appellant's brief at 23. NIOC, relying on *Snyder*, 736 F.2d at 419, and *The Bremen*, 407 U.S. at 10-12, 92 S.Ct. at 1913-14, therefore asserts that the forum selection clause should be severed and Ashland compelled to perform the essential term of the bargain, *viz.*, to participate in an arbitral proceeding (in Mississippi). This syllogism too is fatally flawed.

In *The Bremen*, 407 U.S. at 10-12, 92 S.Ct. at 1913-14, the Supreme Court held, in the context of an international admiralty dispute, that forum selection clauses must be strictly enforced, unless the enforcement would be "unreasonable," or unless the resisting party could show "countervailing" or "compelling" reasons why it should not be enforced. But the forum selection clause at issue in *The Bremen* did not relate to the choice of *situs* in an arbitral proceeding, rather it related to the parties' contractual choice of arbitration as opposed to litigation to resolve its disputes. Thus, in *Sam Reisfeld & Son Import Co. v. S.A. Eteco*, 530 F.2d 679 (5th Cir.1976), we held that the test in *The Bremen* was inapposite respecting the enforcement of the choice of situs expressed in an arbitration agreement. In *Reisfeld*, a U.S. company argued that a forum selection clause designating Belgium as the situs of arbitration should not be enforced because "it is so unreasonable that it either vitiates the arbitration clause altogether or requires a transfer to a more neutral situs." *Id*. at 680. We held that the forum selection clause contained in an arbitration provision must be enforced, even if unreasonable. A forum selection clause establishing the situs of arbitration must be enforced unless it conflicts with an "explicit provision of the Federal Arbitration Act." *Id*. at 680-81.

> Under the Act, a party seeking to avoid arbitration must allege and prove that the arbitration clause itself was a product of fraud, coercion, or "such grounds as exist at law or in equity for the revocation of the contract."

*Id*. at 681 (quoting 9 U.S.C. § 2) . . . NIOC does not assert that it has been a victim of fraud or coercion, and its assertion of inconvenience or impossibility fails as a "legal ground" for vitiating the freely chosen forum selection clause.

Under traditional principles of contract law, NIOC's argument that the political atmosphere in Iran renders arbitration there impossible or impracticable certainly supplies an adequate predicate for finding the forum selection clause unenforceable and without effect. *See, e.g. Restatement (Second) of Contracts*, at § 264; U.C.C. 2-615 & comment 4; *see generally* A. Farnsworth, *Contracts* § 95 (1982). "Where only part of the obligor's performance is impracticable his duty to render the remaining part is unaffected if . . . it is still practicable for him to render performance that is substantial." *Restatement (Second) of Contracts* at § 270; *see, e.g., Net Realty Holding Trust v. Franconia Properties, Inc.*, 544 F.Supp. 759, 769 (E.D.Va.1982). But impracticability is an argument upon which NIOC may not rely.

In order to assert the doctrine of impossibility or commercial impracticability, the party wishing to assert such a defense must meet two conditions. First "[t]he affected party must have no reason to know at the time the contract was made of the facts on which he [or she] relies." *Restatement (Second) of Contracts* at § 266, comment a . . . That NIOC—an instrumentality of the Islamic Republic of Iran—could not reasonably have foreseen in April 1979 that an American entity might find it impracticable to participate then or in the near future in an arbitral proceeding in Tehran defies credulity.

By January 16, 1979, the Shah had departed, and by February 1, the Ayatollah Khomeini had returned triumphantly to Iran. On February 14, the American Embassy was attacked for the first time, killing one Iranian civilian employee, wounding an American Marine, and taking some 100 Americans hostage, including Ambassador Sullivan, for approximately two hours. In short, by April 1979, when the contract was executed, the revolutionary government was in place — the same government that took power largely by "mobilizing millions of Iranians against an America equated with satan." B. Rubin, *Paved With Good Intentions: The American Experience and Iran* 255 (1980). Thus, it simply is unimaginable that NIOC, part of the revolutionary government, could not reasonably have foreseen that Tehran would become a forum in which it is indisputably impossible for Americans to participate in any proceedings. *See, e.g., McDonnell Douglas Corp. v. Islamic Republic of Iran*, 758 F.2d 341, 345-46 (8th Cir.1985) (taking judicial notice of the grave difficulties that would confront an American entity were it forced to litigate a dispute in Iran, and collecting cases).

Second, a party may not rely on the doctrine of impossibility or impracticability "[i]f the event is due to the fault of the . . . [party] himself [or herself]." *Restatement (Second) of Contracts* at § 261, comment d; . . . Simply put, "a party may not affirmatively cause the event that prevents . . . [the] performance." *Nissho-Iwai Co. v. Occidental Crude Sales, Inc.*, 729 F.2d 1530, 1540 (5th Cir.1984). Yet, as part of the revolutionary Government, NIOC certainly bears responsibility for creating the chain of events making it impossible for an American entity reasonably to travel to and to engage in quasi-judicial proceedings in Iran. Thus, NIOC cannot assert the doctrine of impossibility.

Even were NIOC able to rely on the fact that it is now impossible for Ashland to arbitrate in Iran, thus vitiating the forum selection clause, NIOC must show that the venue provision is severable from the rest of the arbitration agreement. Whether the agreement to arbitrate is entire or severable turns on the parties' intent at the time the agreement was executed, as determined from the language of the contract and the surrounding circumstances. *See, e.g., Prospero Associates v. Burroughs Corp.*, 714 F.2d 1022, 1026-27 (10th Cir.1983); *Pollux Marine Agencies, Inc. v. Louis Dreyfus Corp.*, 455 F.Supp. 211, 219 (S.D.N.Y.1978). NIOC must therefore show that the essence, the essential term, of the bargain was to arbitrate, while the situs of the arbitration was merely a minor consideration. *See Restatement (Second) of Contracts* at § 184, comment a; § 185(1) & comment b.

But the language of the standard form document—drafted by NIOC—belies any such argument. Not only did NIOC choose Tehran as the site of any arbitration, but the contract also provides that Iranian law governs the interpretation and rendition of any arbitral awards. The arbitration agreement also provides that, should one of the parties fail to appoint an arbitrator or should the two arbitrators fail to agree on a third arbitrator, "the interested party may request the *President of the Appeal Court of Tehran* to appoint the second arbitrator or the third arbitrator as the case may be." Rec. at 27 (emphasis added). Indeed, the contract expressly provides that the entire agreement is to be interpreted by reference to Iranian law. The language of the contract thus makes self-evident the importance of Iranian law and Iranian institutions to NIOC. Therefore, the document plainly suggests that the situs selection clause was as important to NIOC as the agreement to resolve disputes privately through arbitration. The language of the contract demonstrates that the parties intended the forum selection clause and the arbitral agreement to be entire, not divisible.

Finally, even were the forum selection clause severable, we are still not informed how the parties intended to arbitrate in *Mississippi*. NIOC contends, somewhat disingenuously, that because Ashland's corporate offices are in Kentucky, Jackson is far more convenient to Ashland than to NIOC. But NIOC does not dispute Ashland's allegation that NIOC ran to Mississippi because it is one of the few jurisdictions with a six-year, rather than four-year, limitations period for contracts' claims. Thus, by filing when it did in Mississippi, NIOC was able to assert its claim before the statute of limitations had run, and simultaneously to argue that that statute of limitations had run on Ashland's counterclaim, which had accrued earlier.

Notwithstanding considerations of "convenience," one cannot reasonably argue that the parties' contract contemplates arbitration in Mississippi. The contract's provision that arbitration was to be in Tehran "unless otherwise agreed" suggests that, were Iran to become inconvenient or unacceptable to one or both parties, no other forum was to be available unless mutually agreed upon. Because arbitration is a creature of contract, we cannot rewrite the agreement of the parties and order the proceeding to be held in Mississippi. . . .

NIOC could have chosen to negotiate a forum selection clause with a situs in any one of the 65 nations that are signatories to the Convention, thereby permitting extraterritorial enforcement by U.S. courts. It also could have selected any one of 50 states in this country in which we could have compelled Ashland to arbitrate. But it did not. It selected a situs that was unenforceable *ab initio*, and we have no statutory or equitable mandate that allows us to redraft the agreement premised on convenience of the parties *ex post*. . . .

.     .     .

. . .When the United States adhered to the Convention, it expressly chose the option available in Article I(3), to "apply the Convention, on the basis of reciprocity, to the recognition and enforcement of *only* those awards made in the territory of another Contracting State." Declaration (emphasis added). While the House and

Senate Committee reports do not inform us as to the purpose of adopting this reservation, its purpose seems obvious. Concerned with reciprocity, Congress must have meant only to allow signatories to partake of the Convention's benefits in U.S. courts and thus to give further incentives to non-signatory nations to adhere to the Convention. Were we now to order arbitration in Mississippi, despite the forum selection clause designating Tehran into an agreement as the site of arbitration, we would do great violence to this obvious congressional purpose. Were we to order arbitration in the U.S. in the face of a forum selection clause designating a non-signatory forum, which was unenforceable *ab initio*, the non-signatory would have little reason to leave the Hobbesian jungle of international chaos for the ordered and more predictable world of international commercial law.

* * *

Where the parties' agreement on situs is not entirely clear, the sin of equivocation can be costly, as illustrated by the following Ninth Circuit case involving a pathological arbitral clause in a contract between Chinese and Californian entities.

> 2. *Bauhinia Corp. v. China Nat'l Mach.& Equip. Import & Export Corp.*, 819 F.2d 247 (9th Cir. 1987).

. . .

Bauhinia is a California Corporation founded by Mr. Abbies Tsang who fled the People's Republic of China in 1974. CMEC is a Chinese state trading organization.

In 1981 and 1982 Bauhinia contracted to purchase nails from CMEC. The parties executed the contracts in California for delivery to Stockton, San Francisco and Los Angeles, California, and Seattle, Washington. CMEC failed to deliver the nails claiming that an edict from the People's Republic of China prevented performance.

After Bauhinia filed suit in district court, CMEC moved to compel arbitration invoking arbitration clauses in the contracts. The first contract, written in Chinese, provides "[i]n case quality problems occurs, the both sides shall have consultation as soon as possible to resolve it." The other two contracts, written in English, contain the following clause

> All disputes in connection with the execution of this Contract shall be settled through friendly negotiations. In case an arbitration is necessary and is to be held in Peking, the case in dispute shall then be submitted for arbitration to the Foreign Trade Arbitration Commission of the China Council for the Promotion of International Trade, Peking, in accordance with the "Provisional Rules of Procedure of the Foreign Trade Arbitration Commission of the China Council for the Promotion of International Trade." The decision of the Commission shall be accepted as final and binding upon both parties.

> In case the Arbitration is to take place at [BLANK] either party shall appoint one arbitrator, and the arbitrators thus appointed shall nominate a third person as umpire, to form an arbitration committee. The award of the Arbitration Committee shall be accepted as final by both Parties. The Arbitrators and the umpire shall be confined to persons of Chinese or [BLANK] Nationality.

On November 18, 1985, the district court granted CMEC's motion to compel arbitration and further ordered the parties to submit the matter to the American Arbitration Association pursuant to the Association's rules and regulations. In its order, the court noted the "strong federal policy in favor of arbitration in the context of international agreements." The order does not state the court's reason for designating the AAA instead of CCPIT. At the hearing the judge indicated that the contract clearly called for arbitration but was ambiguous as to whether arbitration was mandated in Peking or some other location. He expressed concerns that Mr. Tsang might be subjected to personal danger if forced to return to China and that the CCPIT would not provide a "speedy, thorough, informal, neutral decisionmaking process," consistent with the parties' intent in seeking arbitration.

> CMEC appeals that part of the order designating AAA instead of CCPIT as the arbitration agency. It argues that the district court erred in overriding the parties' choice of arbitrator, CCPIT.

.    .    .

[Despite the district court denial of certification of review, compelling arbitration is appealable; the court of appeals reviews decisions regarding validity and scope of arbitration clauses *de novo*.]

The contract here expressly calls for arbitration. In light of the strong federal policy favoring arbitration, we conclude that the trial court did not err in ordering the parties to submit the matter to arbitration.

The more difficult question, however, is whether the court properly ordered arbitration before the AAA. The clauses do not expressly choose a forum. The clauses consist of two paragraphs. The first paragraph reads "*in case* arbitration is necessary and is to be held in Peking. . . ." (emphasis added). Likewise, the second paragraph begins: "*In case* arbitration is to take place at [BLANK]. . . ." (emphasis added). CMEC argues that by failing to complete the blanks in the second paragraph, the parties implicitly chose the Peking forum. In support, CMEC cites the Arbitration Act's requirement that such clauses be enforced according to their terms. Furthermore, argues CMEC, most of the witnesses, evidence and law are in the People's Republic of China; Mr. Tsang negotiated the contracts in the People's Republic of China; and the CCPIT is an impartial agency.

. . . We agree with the district court that this contract is ambiguous. The two paragraphs are mutually exclusive. The document lacks any indication what forum the parties intended to select. Furthermore the record offers no evidence of an implied agreement to select a particular forum. The record permits only one conclusion, that the parties intended to leave the issue open. *See Oil Basins Ltd. v. Broken Hill Proprietary Co.*, 613 F.Supp. 483, 487 (S.D.N.Y.1985).

At the hearing, the judge indicated that he found the contract ambiguous on the forum issue. He then asked the parties to "resolve the problem of when, where and how without court intervention. . . . If you don't think you can do so, tell me and I'll issue an order that orders arbitration be taken at the forum and under the requirements set forth by the Court." The parties failed to resolve the issue so the court ordered arbitration before the AAA.

In the absence of a term specifying location, a district court can only order arbitration within its district. Chapter 2 of Title 9 codifies the Convention on the Recognition and Enforcement of Foreign

Arbitral Awards. Section 206 empowers a district court to "direct that arbitration be held in accordance with the agreement at any place therein provided for, whether that place is within or without the United States." However, by its terms, section 206 does not permit a court to designate a foreign forum when the agreement fails to designate a place. Chapter 1 of the Arbitration Act applies to international agreements to the extent that Chapter 1 does not conflict with Chapter 2. 9 U.S.C. § 208. Under Chapter 1, the arbitration proceedings "shall be within the district in which the petition for an order directing such arbitration is filed."[143] 9 U.S.C. § 4. Therefore, under the statutory regime, the only place that the district court could order arbitration is the Eastern District of California. *See Oil Basins*, 613 F.Supp. at 488.

We conclude that the court acted reasonably. The contracts left the location open. The judge gave the parties an opportunity to resolve the matter themselves. When they failed to do so, he took the only action within his power.

### Notes and Questions

1. Observe that where a clear shared intention to arbitrate has been foiled by an imperfectly drafted clause, this court assumed it would be appropriate to "repair" the clause so that arbitration could proceed. How far should a national court go in this regard? Consider the contrasting treatment in *NIOC v. Ashland*.

2. The court in *NIOC*, in effect, acknowledged that the forum selection clause was unenforceable and, hence, sought another reasonable and equitable forum for arbitration. Is it appropriate for a national court to "repair" an inoperable arbitral clause when there has been a change of circumstances? Discuss.

3. How would the *Bauhinia* court have approached the *NIOC* case?

---

[143] [1] Section 206 only applies to international agreements. We express no opinion on whether a district court may order arbitration outside the district in cases of interstate agreements that expressly specify location. *See Snyder v. Smith*, 736 F.2d 409, 420 (7th Cir.), *cert. denied*, 469 U.S. 1037, 105 S.Ct. 513, 83 L.Ed.2d 403 (1984); *Management Recruiters of Albany, Inc. v. Management Recruiters, Int'l, Inc.*, 643 F.Supp. 750, 753 (N.D.N.Y.1986).

### D.    FEDERAL/STATE CONFLICTS: WHICH LAW GOVERNS?

Federal/state conflicts are sometimes critical to outcomes of attempts to enforce arbitration agreements, as illustrated by the following U.S. Supreme Court decision and the federal cases in the notes that follow.

*Volt Info. Sciences Inc. v. Board of Trustees of Leland Stanford Junior Univ.*, 489 U.S. 468 (1989).

CHIEF JUSTICE REHNQUIST delivered the opinion of the Court.

Unlike its federal counterpart, the California Arbitration Act, Cal. Civ. Proc. Code Ann. § 1280 *et seq.* (West 1982), contains a provision allowing a court to stay arbitration pending resolution of related litigation. We hold that application of the California statute is not pre-empted by the Federal Arbitration Act (FAA or Act), 9 U.S.C. § 1 *et seq.*, in a case where the parties have agreed that their arbitration agreement will be governed by the law of California.

Appellant Volt Information Sciences, Inc. (Volt), and appellee Board of Trustees of Leland Stanford Junior University (Stanford) entered into a construction contract . . . . The contract contained an agreement to arbitrate all disputes between the parties "arising out of or relating to this contract or the breach thereof."[144] The contract also contained a choice-of-law clause providing that "[t]he Contract shall be governed by the law of the place where the Project is located." App. 37. During the course of the project, a dispute developed, . . . and Volt made a formal demand for arbitration. Stanford responded by filing an action against Volt in California Superior Court, alleging fraud and breach of contract; in the same action, Stanford also sought

---

[144] [1] The arbitration clause read in full as follows:

> "All claims, disputes and other matters in question between the parties to this contract, arising out of or relating to this contract or the breach thereof, shall be decided by arbitration in accordance with the Construction Industry Arbitration Rules of the American Arbitration Association then prevailing unless the parties mutually agreed [*sic*] otherwise. . . . This agreement to arbitrate . . . shall be specifically enforceable under the prevailing arbitration law."
> App. 40.

indemnity from two other companies involved in the construction project, with whom it did not have arbitration agreements. Volt petitioned the Superior Court to compel arbitration of the dispute.[145] Stanford in turn moved to stay arbitration pursuant to Cal. Civ. Proc. Code Ann. § 1281.2(c) (West 1982), which permits a court to stay arbitration pending resolution of related litigation between a party to the arbitration agreement and third parties not bound by it, where "there is a possibility of conflicting rulings on a common issue of law or fact."[146]    The Superior Court denied Volt's motion to compel arbitration and stayed the arbitration proceedings pending the outcome of the litigation on the authority of § 1281.2(c). App. 59-60.

The California Court of Appeal affirmed. The court acknowledged that the parties' contract involved interstate commerce, that the FAA governs contracts in interstate commerce, and that the FAA contains no provision permitting a court to stay arbitration pending resolution of related litigation involving third parties not bound by the arbitration agreement. App. 64-65. However, the court held that by specifying that their contract would be governed by "'the law of the place where the project is located,'" the parties had incorporated the California rules of arbitration, including § 1281.2(c), into their arbitration agreement. *Id.*, at 65. Finally, the court rejected Volt's contention that, even if the parties had agreed to arbitrate under the

---

[145] [2] Volt's motion to compel was apparently brought pursuant to § 4 of the FAA, 9 U.S.C. § 4, and the parallel provision of the California Arbitration Act, Cal. Civ. Proc. Code Ann. § 1281.2 (West 1982); the motion cited both Acts as authority, but did not specify the particular sections upon which reliance was placed. App. 45-46. Volt also asked the court to stay the Superior Court litigation until the arbitration was completed, presumably pursuant to § 3 of the FAA, 9 U.S.C. § 3, and the parallel provision of the California Arbitration Act, Cal. Civ. Proc. Code Ann. § 1281.2(c)(3) (West 1982). App. 45-46.

[146] [3] Cal. Civ. Proc. Code Ann. § 1281.2(c) provides, in pertinent part, that when a court determines that "[a] party to the arbitration agreement is also a party to a pending court action or special proceeding with a third party, arising out of the same transaction or series of related transactions and there is a possibility of conflicting rulings on a common issue of law or fact[,] . . . the court (1) may refuse to enforce the arbitration agreement and may order intervention or joinder of all parties in a single action or special proceeding;  (2) may order intervention or joinder as to all or only certain issues; (3) may order arbitration among the parties who have agreed to arbitration and stay the pending court action or special proceeding pending the outcome of the arbitration proceeding;  or (4) may stay arbitration pending the outcome of the court action or special proceeding."

California rules, application of § 1281.2(c) here was nonetheless pre-empted by the FAA because the contract involved interstate commerce. *Id.*, at 68-80.

The court reasoned that the purpose of the FAA was "'not [to] mandate the arbitration of all claims, but merely the enforcement . . . of privately negotiated arbitration agreements.'" *Id.*, at 70 (quoting *Dean Witter Reynolds Inc. v. Byrd*, 470 U.S. 213, 219 (1985)). While the FAA therefore pre-empts application of state laws which render arbitration agreements unenforceable, "[i]t does not follow, however, that the federal law has preclusive effect in a case where the parties have chosen in their [arbitration] agreement to abide by state rules." App. 71. To the contrary, because "[t]he thrust of the federal law is that arbitration is strictly a matter of contract," *ibid.*, the parties to an arbitration agreement should be "at liberty to choose the terms under which they will arbitrate." *Id.*, at 72. Where, as here, the parties have chosen in their agreement to abide by the state rules of arbitration, application of the FAA to prevent enforcement of those rules would actually be "inimical to the policies underlying state and federal arbitration law," *id.*, at 73, because it would "force the parties to arbitrate in a manner contrary to their agreement." *Id.*, at 65. The California Supreme Court denied Volt's petition for discretionary review. *Id.*, at 87. We postponed consideration of our jurisdiction to the hearing on the merits. 485 U.S. 976 (1988). We now hold that we have appellate jurisdiction [footnote omitted] and affirm.

Appellant devotes the bulk of its argument to convincing us that the Court of Appeal erred in interpreting the choice-of-law clause to mean that the parties had incorporated the California rules of arbitration into their arbitration agreement. See Brief for Appellant 66-96. Appellant acknowledges, as it must, that the interpretation of private contracts is ordinarily a question of state law, which this Court does not sit to review. See *id.*, at 26, 29. But appellant nonetheless maintains that we should set aside the Court of Appeal's interpretation of this particular contractual provision for two principal reasons.

Appellant first suggests that the Court of Appeal's construction of the choice-of-law clause was in effect a finding that appellant had "waived" its "federally guaranteed right to compel arbitration of the parties' dispute," a waiver whose validity must be judged by reference to federal rather than state law. *Id.*, at 17, 30-36. This argument fundamentally misconceives the nature of the rights created by the FAA. The Act was designed "to overrule the judiciary's longstanding refusal to enforce agreements to arbitrate," *Byrd, supra*, at 219-220, and place such agreements "'upon the same footing as other contracts,'" *Scherk v. Alberto-Culver Co.*, 417 U.S. 506, 511 (1974) (quoting H.R. Rep. No. 96, 68th Cong., 1st Sess., 1, 2 (1924)). Section 2 of the Act therefore declares that a written agreement to arbitrate in any contract involving interstate commerce or a maritime transaction "shall be valid, irrevocable, and enforceable, save upon such grounds as exist at law or in equity for the revocation of any contract," 9 U.S.C. § 2, and § 4 allows a party to such an arbitration agreement to "petition any United States district court . . . for an order directing that such arbitration proceed in the manner provided for in such agreement."

But § 4 of the FAA does not confer a right to compel arbitration of any dispute at any time; it confers only the right to obtain an order directing that "arbitration proceed *in the manner provided for in [the parties'] agreement*." 9 U.S.C. § 4 (emphasis added). Here the Court of Appeal found that, by incorporating the California rules of arbitration into their agreement, the parties had agreed that arbitration would not proceed in situations which fell within the scope of Calif. Code Civ. Proc. Ann. § 1281.2(c). This was not a finding that appellant had "waived" an FAA-guaranteed right to compel arbitration of this dispute, but a finding that it had no such right in the first place, because the parties' agreement did not require arbitration to proceed in this situation. Accordingly, appellant's contention that the contract interpretation issue presented here involves the "waiver" of a federal right is without merit.

Second, appellant argues that we should set aside the Court of Appeal's construction of the choice-of-law clause because it violates the settled federal rule that questions of arbitrability in contracts subject to the FAA must be resolved with a healthy regard for the federal policy favoring arbitration. Brief for Appellant 49-52; *id.*, at 92-96, citing *Moses H. Cone Memorial Hospital v. Mercury Construction Corp.*, 460 U.S. 1, 24-25 (1983) . . .; *Mitsubishi Motors Corp. v. Soler Chrysler-Plymouth, Inc.*, 473 U.S. 614, 626 (1985) . . . . These cases of course establish that, in applying general state-law principles of contract interpretation to the interpretation of an arbitration agreement within the scope of the Act, see *Perry v. Thomas*, 482 U.S. 483, 493,

n. 9 (1987), due regard must be given to the federal policy favoring arbitration, and ambiguities as to the scope of the arbitration clause itself resolved in favor of arbitration.

But we do not think the Court of Appeal offended the *Moses H. Cone* principle by interpreting the choice-of-law provision to mean that the parties intended the California rules of arbitration, including the § 1281.2(c) stay provision, to apply to their arbitration agreement. There is no federal policy favoring arbitration under a certain set of procedural rules; the federal policy is simply to ensure the enforceability, according to their terms, of private agreements to arbitrate. Interpreting a choice-of-law clause to make applicable state rules governing the conduct of arbitration—rules which are manifestly designed to encourage resort to the arbitral process—simply does not offend the rule of liberal construction set forth in *Moses H. Cone*, nor does it offend any other policy embodied in the FAA.[147]

The question remains whether, assuming the choice-of-law clause meant what the Court of Appeal found it to mean, application of Cal. Civ. Proc. Code Ann. § 1281.2(c) is nonetheless pre-empted by the FAA to the extent it is used to stay arbitration under this contract involving interstate commerce. It is undisputed that this contract falls within the coverage of the FAA, since it involves interstate commerce, and that the FAA contains no provision authorizing a stay of arbitration in this situation. Appellees contend, however, that §§ 3 and 4 of the FAA, which are the specific sections claimed to conflict with the California statute at issue here, are not applicable in this state-court proceeding and thus cannot pre-empt application of the California statute. See Brief for Appellee 43-50.

---

[147] [5] Unlike the dissent, see *post* at 1259-1260, we think the California arbitration rules which the parties have incorporated into their contract generally foster the federal policy favoring arbitration. As indicated, the FAA itself contains no provision designed to deal with the special practical problems that arise in multiparty contractual disputes when some or all of the contracts at issue include agreements to arbitrate. California has taken the lead in fashioning a legislative response to this problem, by giving courts authority to consolidate or stay arbitration proceedings in these situations in order to minimize the potential for contradictory judgments. See Calif. Civ. Proc. Code Ann. § 1281.2(c).

While the argument is not without some merit,[148] we need not resolve it to decide this case, for we conclude that even if §§ 3 and 4 of the FAA are fully applicable in state-court proceedings, they do not prevent application of Cal. Civ. Proc. Code Ann. § 1281.2(c) to stay arbitration where, as here, the parties have agreed to arbitrate in accordance with California law.

The FAA contains no express pre-emptive provision, nor does it reflect a congressional intent to occupy the entire field of arbitration. . . . But even when Congress has not completely displaced state regulation in an area, state law may nonetheless be pre-empted to the extent that it actually conflicts with federal law—that is, to the extent that it "stands as an obstacle to the accomplishment and execution of the full purposes and objectives of Congress." *Hines v. Davidowitz*, 312 U.S. 52, 67 (1941). The question before us, therefore, is whether application of Cal. Civ. Proc. Code Ann. § 1281.2(c) to stay arbitration under this contract in interstate commerce, in accordance with the terms of the arbitration agreement itself, would undermine the goals and policies of the FAA. We conclude that it would not.

The FAA was designed "to overrule the judiciary's long-standing refusal to enforce agreements to arbitrate," *Dean Witter Reynolds, Inc. v. Byrd*, 470 U.S., at 219-220, and to place such agreements "'upon the same footing as other contracts,'" *Scherk v. Alberto-Culver Co.*, 417 U.S., at 511 (quoting H.R. Rep. No. 96, 68th Cong., 1st Sess., 1, 2 (1924)). While Congress was no doubt aware that the Act would encourage the expeditious resolution of disputes, its passage "was motivated, first and foremost, by a congressional desire to enforce agreements into which parties had entered." *Byrd*, 470 U.S., at 220. Accordingly, we have recognized that the FAA does not require parties to arbitrate when they have not agreed to do so, see *id.*, at 219

---

[148] [6] While we have held that the FAA's "substantive" provisions—§§ 1 and 2—are applicable in state as well as federal court, see *Southland Corp. v. Keating*, 465 U.S. 1, 12 (1984), we have never held that §§ 3 and 4, which by their terms appear to apply only to proceedings in federal court, see 9 U.S.C. § 3 (referring to proceedings "brought in any of the courts of the United States"); § 4 (referring to "any United States district court"), are nonetheless applicable in state court. See *Southland Corp. v. Keating, supra*, at 16, n. 10 (expressly reserving the question whether "§§ 3 and 4 of the Arbitration Act apply to proceedings in state courts"); see also *id.*, at 29 (O'CONNOR, J., dissenting) (§§ 3 and 4 of the FAA apply only in federal court).

(the Act "does not mandate the arbitration of all claims"), nor does it prevent parties who do agree to arbitrate from excluding certain claims from the scope of their arbitration agreement, see *Mitsubishi Motors Corp. v. Soler Chrysler-Plymouth, Inc.*, 473 U.S., at 628 (citing *Prima Paint Corp. v. Flood & Conklin Mfg. Co.*, 388 U.S. 395, 406 (1967)). It simply requires courts to enforce privately negotiated agreements to arbitrate, like other contracts, in accordance with their terms. See *Prima Paint*, *supra*, at 404, n. 12 (the Act was designed "to make arbitration agreements as enforceable as other contracts, but not more so").

In recognition of Congress' principal purpose of ensuring that private arbitration agreements are enforced according to their terms, we have held that the FAA pre-empts state laws which "require a judicial forum for the resolution of claims which the contracting parties agreed to resolve by arbitration." *Southland Corp. v. Keating*, 465 U.S. 1, 10 (1984). See, *e.g.*, *id.*, at 10-16 (finding pre-empted a state statute which rendered agreements to arbitrate certain franchise claims unenforceable); *Perry v. Thomas*, 482 U.S., at 490 (finding pre-empted a state statute which rendered unenforceable private agreements to arbitrate certain wage collection claims). But it does not follow that the FAA prevents the enforcement of agreements to arbitrate under different rules than those set forth in the Act itself. Indeed, such a result would be quite inimical to the FAA's primary purpose of ensuring that private agreements to arbitrate are enforced according to their terms. Arbitration under the Act is a matter of consent, not coercion, and parties are generally free to structure their arbitration agreements as they see fit. Just as they may limit by contract the issues which they will arbitrate, see *Mitsubishi*, *supra*, at 628, so too may they specify by contract the rules under which that arbitration will be conducted. Where, as here, the parties have agreed to abide by state rules of arbitration, enforcing those rules according to the terms of the agreement is fully consistent with the goals of the FAA, even if the result is that arbitration is stayed where the Act would otherwise permit it to go forward. By permitting the courts to "rigorously enforce" such agreements according to their terms, see *Byrd*, *supra*, at 221, we give effect to the contractual rights and expectations of the parties, without doing violence to the policies behind the FAA.

.   .   .

JUSTICE BRENNAN, with whom JUSTICE MARSHALL joins, dissenting.

.    .    .

Contrary to the Court's view, the state court's construction of the choice-of-law clause is reviewable for two independent reasons.

.    .    .

The Court's decision not to review the state court's interpretation of the choice-of-law clause appears to be based on the principle that "the interpretation of private contracts is ordinarily a question of state law, which this Court does not sit to review." *Ante*, at 474. I have no quarrel with the general proposition that the interpretation of contracts is a matter of state law. By ending its analysis at that level of generality, however, the Court overlooks well-established precedent to the effect that, in order to guard against arbitrary denials of federal claims, a state court's construction of a contract in such a way as to preclude enforcement of a federal right is not immune from review in this Court as to its "adequacy."

.    .    .

Arbitration is, of course, "a matter of contract and a party cannot be required to submit to arbitration any dispute which he has not agreed so to submit." *Steelworkers v. Warrior & Gulf Co.*, 363 U.S. 574, 582 (1960). I agree with the Court that "the FAA does not require parties to arbitrate when they have not agreed to do so." *Ante*, at 1254. Since the FAA merely requires enforcement of what the parties have agreed to, moreover, they are free if they wish to write an agreement to arbitrate outside the coverage of the FAA. Such an agreement would permit a state rule, otherwise pre-empted by the FAA, to govern their arbitration. The substantive question in this case is whether or not they have done so. And that question, we have made clear in the past, is a matter of federal law.

Not only does the FAA require the enforcement of arbitration agreements, but we have held that it also establishes substantive federal law that must be consulted in determining whether (or to what extent) a given contract provides for arbitration. We have stated this most clearly in *Moses H. Cone Memorial Hospital v. Mercury Construction Corp.*, 460 U.S. 1, 24-25 (1983):

> "Section 2 [of the FAA] is a congressional declaration of a liberal federal policy favoring arbitration agreements, notwithstanding any state substantive or procedural policies to the contrary. The effect of the section is to create a body of federal substantive law of arbitrability, applicable to any arbitration agreement within the coverage of the Act. . . . [T]he Courts of Appeals have . . . consistently concluded that questions of arbitrability must be addressed with a healthy regard for the federal policy favoring arbitration. We agree. The Arbitration Act establishes that, as a matter of federal law, any doubts concerning the scope of arbitrable issues should be resolved in favor of arbitration, whether the problem at hand is the construction of the contract language itself or an allegation of waiver, delay, or a like defense to arbitrability."

More recently, in *Mitsubishi Motors v. Soler Chrysler-Plymouth, Inc.*, 473 U.S. 614 (1985), we stated that a court should determine whether the parties agreed to arbitrate a dispute "by applying the 'federal substantive law of arbitrability.'" *Id.*, at 626, quoting *Moses H. Cone*, *supra*, at 24. See also *Southland Corp. v. Keating*, 465 U.S. 1 (1984).

The Court recognizes the relevance of the *Moses H. Cone* principle but finds it unoffended by the Court of Appeal's decision, which, the Court suggests, merely determines what set of procedural rules will apply. Ante, at 476. [footnote omitted] I agree fully with the Court that "the federal policy is simply to ensure the enforceability, according to their terms, of private agreements to arbitrate," *ibid.*, but I disagree emphatically with its conclusion that that policy is not frustrated here. Applying the California procedural rule, which stays arbitration while litigation of the same issue goes forward, means simply that the parties' dispute will be litigated rather than arbitrated. Thus, interpreting the parties' agreement to say that the California procedural rules apply rather than the FAA, where the parties arguably had no such intent, implicates the *Moses H. Cone* principle no less than would an interpretation of the parties' contract that erroneously denied the existence of an agreement to arbitrate.[149]

     While appearing to recognize that the state court's interpretation of the contract does raise a question of federal law, the Court nonetheless refuses to determine whether the state court misconstrued that agreement. There is no warrant for failing to do so. The FAA requires that a court determining a question of arbitrability not stop with the application of state-law rules for construing the parties' intentions, but that it also take account of the command of federal law that "those intentions [be] generously construed as to issues of arbitrability." *Mitsubishi Motors*, *supra*, at 626. Thus, the decision below is based on both state and federal law, which are thoroughly intertwined. In such circumstances the state-court judgment cannot be said to rest on an "adequate and independent state ground" so as to bar review by this Court. See *Enterprise Irrigation Dist. v. Farmers Mutual Canal Co.*, 243 U.S. 157, 164 (1917) ("But where the non-federal ground is so interwoven with the other as not to be an independent matter . . . our jurisdiction is plain"). With a proper application of federal law in this case, the state court's judgment might have been different, and our review is therefore not barred. Cf. *Ake v. Oklahoma*, 470 U.S. 68, 74-75 (1985) ("[W]hen resolution of the state procedural law question depends on a federal constitutional ruling, the state-law prong of the court's holding is not independent of federal law, and our jurisdiction is not precluded").

## II

     Construed with deference to the opinion of the California Court of Appeal, yet "with a healthy regard for the federal policy favoring arbitration," *Moses H. Cone*, 460 U.S., at 24, it is clear that the

---

[149] [8] Whether or not "The California arbitration rules . . . generally foster the federal policy favoring arbitration," *ante*, at 476, n. 5, is not the relevant question. Section 2 of the FAA requires courts to enforce agreements to arbitrate, and in *Moses H. Cone* we held that doubts as to whether the parties had so agreed were to be resolved in favor of arbitration. Whether California's arbitration rules are more likely than federal law to foster arbitration, *i.e.*, to induce parties to agree to arbitrate disputes, is another matter entirely. On that question it is up to Congress, not this Court, to "fashio[n] a legislative response," *ante*, at 470, n. 5, and in the meantime we are not free to substitute our notions of good policy for federal law as currently written.

choice-of-law clause cannot bear the interpretation the California court assigned to it.

Construction of a contractual provision is, of course, a matter of discerning the parties' intent. It is important to recall, in the first place, that in this case there is no extrinsic evidence of their intent. We must therefore rely on the contract itself. But the provision of the contract at issue here was not one that these parties drafted themselves. Rather, they incorporated portions of a standard form contract commonly used in the construction industry. That makes it most unlikely that their intent was in any way at variance with the purposes for which choice-of-law clauses are commonly written and the manner in which they are generally interpreted.

It seems to me beyond dispute that the normal purpose of such choice-of-law clauses is to determine that the law of one State rather than that of another State will be applicable; they simply do not speak to any interaction between state and federal law. A cursory glance at standard conflicts texts confirms this observation: they contain no reference at all to the relation between federal and state law in their discussions of contractual choice-of-law clauses. See, *e.g.*, R. Weintraub, Commentary on the Conflict of Laws § 7.3C (2d ed. 1980); E. Scoles & P. Hay, Conflict of Laws 632-652 (1982); R. Leflar, L. McDougal, & R. Felix, American Conflicts Law § 147 (4th ed. 1986). The same is true of standard codifications. See Uniform Commercial Code § 1-105(1) (1978); Restatement (Second) of Conflict of Laws § 187 (1971). Indeed the Restatement of Conflicts notes expressly that it does not deal with "the ever-present problem of determining the respective spheres of authority of the law and courts of the nation and of the member States." *Id.*, § 2, Comment *c*. Decisions of this Court fully bear out the impression that choice-of-law clauses do not speak to any state-federal issue. On at least two occasions we have been called upon to determine the applicability *vel non* of the FAA to contracts containing choice-of-law clauses similar to that at issue here. Despite adverting to the choice-of-law clauses in other contexts in our opinions, we ascribed no significance whatever to them in connection with the applicability of the FAA. *Scherk v. Alberto-Culver Co.*, 417

U.S. 506 (1974); *Bernhardt v. Polygraphic Co.*, 350 U.S. 198 (1956).[150] The great weight of lower court authority similarly rejects the notion that a choice-of-law clause renders the FAA inapplicable. Choice-of-law clauses simply have never been used for the purpose of dealing with the relationship between state and federal law. There is no basis whatever for believing that the parties in this case intended their choice-of-law clause to do so.

Moreover, the literal language of the contract—"the law of the place"—gives no indication of any intention to apply only state law and exclude other law that would normally be applicable to something taking place at that location. By settled principles of federal supremacy, the law of any place in the United States includes federal law. See *Claflin v. Houseman*, 93 U.S. 130 (1876); *Hauenstein v. Lynham*, 100 U.S. 483, 490 (1880) ("[T]he Constitution, laws, and treaties of the United States are as much a part of the law of every State as its own local laws and Constitution"). As the dissenting judge below noted, "under California law, federal law governs matters cognizable in California courts upon which the United States has definitively spoken." App. 82 (opinion of Capaccioli, J.). Thus, "the mere choice of California law is not a selection of California law over federal law. . . ." *Id.*, at 84. In the absence of any evidence to the contrary it must be assumed that this is what the parties meant by "the law of the place where the Project is located."

Indeed, this is precisely what we said when we once previously confronted virtually the same question. In *Fidelity Federal Savings & Loan Assn. v. De la Cuesta*, 458 U.S. 141 (1982), a contract provision stated: "This Deed of Trust shall be governed by the law of the jurisdiction in which the Property is located." *Id.*, at 148, n. 5. Rejecting the contention that the parties thereby had agreed to be bound solely by local law, we held: "Paragraph 15 provides that the deed is

---

[150] [9] In *Scherk*, the contract contained the following clause: "The laws of the State of Illinois, U.S.A. shall apply to and govern this agreement, its interpretation and performance." 417 U.S., at 509, n. 1. Despite discussing the effect of that clause in a different context, *id.*, at 519, n. 13, we did not consider the possibility that the FAA might not apply because of the parties' choice of the law of Illinois. Similarly, in *Bernhardt* the contract provided for arbitration under New York law. While we recognized a choice-of-law problem as to whether New York or Vermont law was applicable, 350 U.S., at 205, we resolved the question of arbitrability under the FAA without any reference to the choice-of-law clause.

to be governed by the 'law of the jurisdiction' in which the property is located; but the 'law of the jurisdiction' includes federal as well as state law." *Id.*, at 157, n. 12. We should similarly conclude here that the choice-of-law clause was not intended to make federal law inapplicable to this contract.

## III

Most commercial contracts written in this country contain choice-of-law clauses, similar to the one in the Stanford-Volt contract, specifying which State's law is to govern the interpretation of the contract. See Scoles & Hay, Conflict of Laws, at 632-633 ("Party autonomy means that the parties are free to select the law governing their contract, subject to certain limitations. They will usually do so by means of an express choice-of-law clause in their written contract"). Were every state court to construe such clauses as an expression of the parties' intent to exclude the application of federal law, as has the California Court of Appeal in this case, the result would be to render the Federal Arbitration Act a virtual nullity as to presently existing contracts. I cannot believe that the parties to contracts intend such consequences to flow from their insertion of a standard choice-of-law clause. Even less can I agree that we are powerless to review decisions of state courts that effectively nullify a vital piece of federal legislation. I respectfully dissent.

### Notes and Questions

1. The majority holds that "where, as here, the parties have agreed to abide by state rules of arbitration, enforcing those rules according to the terms of the agreement is fully consistent with the goals of the FAA, even if the result is that the arbitration is stayed where the Act would otherwise permit it to go forward." Does this, in your view, accurately reflect previous statements by the Court about the public policy in favor of arbitration? Discuss, referring to other cases.

2. The position of United States law on the central issue in *Volt* has been rendered obscure by two recent decisions of the Supreme Court. In *Mastrobuono et al. v. Shearson Lehman Hutton, Inc.*, 115 S.Ct. 1212 (1995) a majority of eight judges reversed two lower courts and reinstated an award, governed by the laws of the state of New York, in which the arbitrators had allowed punitive damages, despite the fact that New York law allows only courts to award punitive damages. Justice Thomas, dissenting, found no difference between the issues raised in this case and in *Volt* and felt that *Volt* should control.

In *Allied-Bruce Terminix Cos., Inc. v. Dobson*, 115 S.Ct. 834 (1995) the Court reversed the Supreme Court of Alabama which had refused to give effect to an arbitration clause because it was against a state statute invalidating pre-dispute arbitration agreements. The Alabama court ruled that the Federal Act only applied if the parties to an arbitration agreement "contemplated" substantial interstate activity. The U.S. Supreme Court reversed, opting for a broad interpretation of the words "evidencing" and "involving commerce" in §2 of the Federal Arbitration Act. Justice O'Connor concurred, but expressed her belief "that Congress never intended the Federal Arbitration Act to apply in state courts." Justice Scalia dissented on the ground that *Southland Corp. v. Keating*, 465 U.S. 1 (1984), perpetuated a continuing "unauthorized eviction of state-court power to adjudicate a potentially large class of disputes." Justice Thomas dissented on similar grounds.

3. In *Securities Indus. Ass'n v. Connolly*, 883 F.2d 1114 (1st Cir. 1989), the court in footnote 3 states that the choice of law clause in *Volt* did not impinge on the arbitration clause. Do you agree? What if the state arbitration law (which the court presumes was chosen by the parties) had unequivocally denied enforceability to *all* pre-dispute arbitration clauses in interstate commerce?

4. What planning techniques, particularly in the realm of contract draftsmanship, might reduce the risk of what might be characterized as the "restrictive" approach to arbitration in *Volt*? Consider Joseph D. Becker, *Choice of Law and the Federal Arbitration Act: The Shock of Volt*, ARB. J., June 1990, at 32, suggesting that choice of law clauses contain an additional proviso that disputes about the arbitration itself "be governed exclusively by the United States Arbitration Act."

5. In *Southland Corp. v. Keating,* 465 U.S. 1 (1984), the Supreme Court had to decide whether the California Franchise Investment Law could invalidate arbitration agreements covered by the Federal Arbitration Act.

The standard franchise agreement of Southland Corporation (owner and franchisor of 7-Eleven convenience stores) contained the following arbitration clause:

> Any controversy or claim arising out of or relating to this Agreement or the breach thereof shall be settled by arbitration in accordance with the Rules of the American Arbitration Association
>
> . . . .

Several 7-Eleven franchisees filed actions against Southland in California Superior Court alleging, among other things, fraud, oral misrepresentation, breach of contract, breach of fiduciary duty, and violation of the disclosure requirements of the California Franchise Investment Law, CAL. CORP. CODE §31000 *et seq.* (West 1977). Southland's answer included the affirmative defense of failure to arbitrate.

The California Supreme Court reversed the lower court ruling that claims asserted under the Franchise Investment Law are arbitrable. *Keating v. Superior Court of Alameda County*, 645 P.2d 1192 (Ca. 1982). The California Supreme Court interpreted the Franchise Investment Law to require judicial consideration of claims brought under that statute and concluded that the California statute did not contravene the Federal Arbitration Act. Southland petitioned the U.S. Supreme Court challenging the California Franchise Investment Law as it was applied to invalidate a contract for arbitration made pursuant to the Federal Arbitration Act. The U.S. Supreme Court reversed the California judgment in a decision containing the following reasoning:

> The California Supreme Court interpreted [the California Franchise Investment Law, Cal. Corp. Code § 31512] to require judicial consideration of claims brought under the State statute and accordingly refused to enforce the parties' contract to arbitrate such claims. So interpreted the California Franchise Investment Law directly conflicts with §2 of the Federal Arbitration Act and violates the Supremacy Clause.

.  .  .

> We discern only two limitations on the enforceability of arbitration provisions governed by the Federal Arbitration Act: they must be part of a written maritime contract or a contract "evidencing a transaction involving commerce" and such clauses may be revoked upon "grounds as exist at law or in equity for the revocation of any contract." We see nothing in the Act indicating that the broad principle of enforceability is subject to any additional limitations under State law.

> .  .  . In *Prima Paint Corp. v. Flood & Conklin Manufacturing Corp.*, 388 U.S. 395, (1967), the Court examined the legislative history of the Act and concluded that the statute "is based upon . . . the incontestable federal foundations of 'control over interstate commerce and over admiralty.'" *Id.*, at 405, (quoting H. R. Rep. No. 96, 68th Cong., 1st Sess. 1 (1924)). The contract in *Prima Paint*, as here, contained an arbitration clause. One party in that case alleged that the other had committed fraud in the inducement of the contract, although not of arbitration clause in particular, and sought to have the claim of fraud adjudicated in federal court. The Court held that, notwithstanding a contrary state rule, consideration of a claim of fraud in the inducement of a contract "is for the arbitrators and not for the courts," 388 U.S. at 400. . . .

.  .  .

> . . . The interpretation given to the Arbitration Act by the California Supreme Court would therefore encourage and reward forum shopping. We are unwilling to attribute to Congress the intent, in drawing on the comprehensive powers of the Commerce Clause, to create a right to enforce an arbitration contract and yet make the right dependent for its enforcement on the particular

forum in which it is asserted. And since the overwhelming proportion of all civil litigation in this country is in the state courts, we cannot believe Congress intended to limit the Arbitration Act to disputes subject only to *federal*-court jurisdiction. Such an interpretation would frustrate Congressional intent to place "[a]n arbitration agreement . . . upon the same footing as other contracts, where it belongs." H. R. Rep. No. 96, 68th Cong., 1st Sess., 1 (1924).

6. In *Securities Indus. Ass'n v. Connolly*, 883 F.2d 1114 (1st Cir.1989), the First Circuit addressed the validity of Massachusetts regulations limiting the use of arbitration clauses in securities disputes. The following are excerpts from its decision that the Massachusetts regulations were pre-empted by the Federal Arbitration Act, and therefore violated the Supremacy Clause of Article VI of the U.S. Constitution.

The contracts to which the Regulations apply implicate interstate and international commerce, as well as the instrumentalities of that commerce, thus subjecting them to the reach of the FAA. See 9 U.S.C. § 1; *see generally Société Générale de Surveillance, S.A. v. Raytheon European Mgmt and Sys. Co.*, 643 F.2d 863, 867 (1st Cir.1981) . . . . Specifically, the Regulations are aimed at broker-dealers who require customers to sign pre-dispute arbitration agreements (PDAAs) as a concomitant of establishing account relationships. Not coincidentally, many of the major brokerage firms prefer to follow some such praxis. . . .

The Regulations not only regulate; they do so in a manner patently inhospitable to arbitration. They (i) bar firms from requiring individuals to enter PDAAs as a nonnegotiable condition precedent to account relationships, § 12.204(G)(1)(a); (ii) order the prohibition brought "conspicuously" to the attention of prospective customers, §12.204(G)(1)(b); and (iii) demand full written disclosure of "the legal effect of the pre-dispute arbitration contract or clause," § 12.204(G)(1)(c).

. . . .

A policy designed to prevent one party from enforcing an arbitration contract or provision by visiting a penalty on that party is, without much question, contrary to the policies of the FAA. But, there is at least one other way in which the Massachusetts policy would erode the goals of the Act. The Regulations are aimed at nonnegotiable "standard-form" PDAAs. Arbitration is a positive good in the eyes of courts and Congress not just because it relieves crowded calendars, but because it relieves an often unnecessary elaboration of social practices. As the Court has stated, resort to arbitration "trades the procedures and opportunity for review of the courtroom for the simplicity, informality, and expedition of arbitration." *Mitsubishi Motors*, 473 U.S. at 628, 105 S.Ct. at 3354. We must, therefore, be vigilant lest we recreate even the beginnings of hypertrophy in the formation of arbitration contracts. The Regulations demand exactly the kind of inefficiency which arbitration and standard-form contracts (generally legitimate under Massachusetts law) are designed to minify. By depriving broker-dealers of the opportunity to employ form contracts, even were there no penalty attached to their use, Massachusetts has acted to undercut the policies of simplicity and expedition that characterize the arbitral alternative.

.    .    .

The Commonwealth may well be correct that PDAAs ought to be arrived at with greater negotiation and disclosure between broker-dealers and customers than currently takes place. That judgment, however, is not the Commonwealth's to make, at least in its current embodiment, for it singles out arbitration in an impermissible way. The states are forbidden from critical scrutiny expressed in a fashion which might mask historic hostility toward arbitration. Congress sought to avoid having that possibility come to fruition, choosing instead to emphasize and endorse arbitral efficiencies. That value judgment was within the congressional domain—and only Congress, not the states, may create exceptions to it.

That is not to say, of course, that a state must permit broker-dealers to sail as close to the wind as their consciences (or lack thereof) might permit. Massachusetts has a plenitude of lawful weapons in its ethical armamentarium to preserve the integrity of the securities business as conducted in the Commonwealth and to protect consumers. *Cf., e.g., Volt*, 109 S.Ct. at 1254. But because the Regulations treat standard-form PDAAs in the securities industry more severely than standard-form contracts are generally treated under Massachusetts law, and because the policies underlying the Regulations, and their method of enforcement, conflict with the national policy favoring arbitration, the state scheme is too discommoding to the federal plan. The Regulations are, therefore, preempted.

7. *New England Energy, Inc. v. Keystone Shipping Co.*, 855 F.2d 1 (1st Cir.1988) held that federal courts have power to order consolidation of arbitrations when the parties' agreements to arbitrate make no express reference to the issue of consolidation and the pertinent state law specifically provides for consolidation. The following excerpts from the court's decision illustrate how thorny this issue can be.

. . . The parties here are signatories to one of two maritime contracts, both of which provide that disputes arising out of the agreements will be referred to arbitration in Boston "pursuant to the laws relating to arbitration there in force." In one contract, appellant New England Energy Inc. (NEEI) and appellee Keystone Shipping Co. (Keystone) created a joint venture known as the New England Collier Company (NECCO), which became owner and operator of a coal carrying ship named the Energy Independence. In the other agreement, appellant New England Power Company (NEP) chartered the Energy Independence from the joint venture. Both NEEI and NEP are part of the New England Electric System, an electric utility holding company. Arbitration #1 is between NEEI and Keystone—the joint venturers — and Arbitration # 2 is between NEP, the ship operator, and NECCO, the joint venture that chartered the ship to NEP.

NEEI and NEP filed an action . . . seeking consolidation of the two arbitrations pursuant to the Massachusetts Uniform Arbitration Act, Mass.Gen.Laws Ann. ch. 251, §2A.[151] Keystone removed the action to federal court based on diversity jurisdiction. After a hearing, the district court ruled that the factual circumstances were appropriate for consolidation, but it nevertheless denied the application for consolidation on the ground that it lacked the power to join the cases. The court interpreted the Federal Arbitration Act and Supreme Court precedent to say that, in the absence of a specific provision in the parties' contracts allowing consolidation, federal courts are without power to consolidate arbitrations. The district court implicitly found both that the Act preempted the Massachusetts statute providing for consolidated arbitrations, and that it deprived the court of its power to order consolidation under Fed. R. Civ. P. 42(a). NEEI and NEP then filed this appeal.

After carefully reviewing the Supreme Court cases and considering the policies of the Act, we conclude that consolidation could be ordered in this case pursuant to the Massachusetts arbitration consolidation statute. We need not decide whether a federal court also has the power, under Fed. R. Civ. P. 42(a), to

---

[151] [1] The statute provides, in relevant part:

A party aggrieved by the failure or refusal of another to agree to consolidate one arbitration proceeding with another or others, for which the method of appointment of the arbitrator or arbitrators is the same . . . may apply to the superior court for an order for such consolidation. . . . [T]he issue shall be decided under the Massachusetts Rules of Civil Procedure governing consolidation and severance of trials and the court shall issue an order accordingly. No provision in any arbitration agreement shall bar or prevent action by the court under this section.

order consolidation in the absence of a state law providing for it. . . .

.    .    .

The Massachusetts arbitration consolidation provision, as appellants seek to enforce it, does not in any way limit "the broad principle of enforceability" of private agreements to arbitrate. There is no attempt here to divert a case from arbitration to court. Massachusetts seeks only to make more efficient the process of arbitrating. Although the Supreme Court has held that agreements to arbitrate must be enforced "even if the result is 'piecemeal' litigation," *Dean Witter Reynolds*, 470 U.S. at 221, 105 S.Ct. at 1242, the Court also has recognized the Act's endorsement of "speedy and efficient decisionmaking," *id.*, at 219, 105 S.Ct. at 1241. We fail to see why a state should be prevented from enhancing the efficiency of the arbitral process, so long as the state procedure does not directly conflict with a contractual provision.

Nor does the Act's general approach indicate that a federal court would overstep its role if it ordered consolidation under state law after determining that the contract does not bar consolidated arbitrations. . . . Federal courts have jurisdiction to decide more than just the question of arbitrability, and if requested to do so, a court has the power to order compliance with an applicable state law.

.    .    .

[Judge Selya dissented on the ground that the parties had made a choice omitting consolidation options and that the courts should not trump that choice.]

8.  In *Doctor's Associates v. Casarotto*, 116 S.Ct. 1652 (1996), the U.S. Supreme Court invalidated a Montana notice provision that required arbitration clauses to be typed in underlined capital letters on the first page of a contract. While accepting that state contract law generally determines the validity of agreements (including agreements to arbitrate), the Court held that states may not single out arbitration clauses for validity requirements more onerous than those imposed on other contracts.

E.    WHAT IS THE RELEVANCE OF INSTITUTIONAL RULES?

Treaties and national statutes are not the only legal norms that come into play when compelling arbitration. As was noted in Chapter 2, the international lawyer must also be familiar with the institutional rules of whatever supervisory institution under the rules of which a claim will be brought. Consider, by way of example:

a.      International Chamber of Commerce Arbitration Rules of Conciliation and Arbitration, Articles 3-8, Supplement at pp. 448-50 & 455-58.

b.      The Arbitration Rules of the United Nations Commission for International Trade Law (UNCITRAL), Articles 1 and 21, Supplement at pp. 623 & 634.

F.      COMPELLING ARBITRATION AND STAYING INCONSISTENT COURT PROCEEDINGS.

1.      UNITED STATES

American courts may be asked to enforce an arbitration agreement in the context of either (i) a motion to compel arbitration or (ii) a motion to stay litigation. Even absent the New York Convention, Chapter 1 of the Federal Arbitration Act, enacted in 1925, provides for enforcement of agreements to arbitrate and stays of proceedings covered by an arbitration agreement, as set out below.

## 9 U.S.C. §§2 - 4 (1988).

§2. A written provision in any maritime transaction or a contract evidencing a transaction involving commerce to settle by arbitration a controversy thereafter arising out of such contract or transaction, or the refusal to perform the whole or any part thereof, or an agreement in writing to submit to arbitration an existing controversy arising out of such contract, transaction, or refusal, shall be valid, irrevocable, and enforceable, save upon such grounds as exist at law or in equity for the revocation of any contract.

§3. If any suit or proceeding be brought in any of the courts of the United States upon any issue referable to arbitration under an agreement in writing for such arbitration, the court in which such suit is pending, upon being satisfied that the issue involved in such suit or proceeding is referable to arbitration under such an agreement, shall on application of one of the parties stay the trial of the action until such arbitration has been had in accordance with the terms of the agreement, providing the applicant for the stay is not in default in proceeding with such arbitration.

§4. A party aggrieved by the alleged failure, neglect, or refusal of another to arbitrate under a written agreement for arbitration may petition any United States district court which, save for such agreement, would have jurisdiction under Title 28, in civil action or in admiralty of the subject matter of a suit arising out of the controversy between the parties, for an order directing that such arbitration proceed in the manner provided for in such agreement. . . .

### 2. ENGLAND

In England courts will stay legal proceedings unless satisfied that the arbitration agreement is "null and void, inoperative, or incapable of being performed." A stay of proceedings will be granted "in respect of any matter which under the [arbitration] agreement is to be referred to arbitration." English Arbitration Act of 1996, Section 9.

### 3. FRANCE

The provisions of the French *Nouveau Code de procédure civile* achieve the same results as English and American law by requiring French courts to rule that they lack jurisdiction over disputes covered by a valid arbitration agreement.

### Nouveau Code de Procédure Civile, Article 1458.

When a dispute which has been referred to an arbitral tribunal by virtue of an arbitration agreement is brought before a court, the latter must rule that it lacks jurisdiction to hear the dispute.

If the dispute has not as yet been referred to the arbitral tribunal, the court again must rule that it lacks jurisdiction, unless the arbitration agreement is manifestly null.

In both cases, the court cannot raise its lack of jurisdiction on its own motion.

### 4. SWITZERLAND

Under the Swiss federal system, parties to international arbitration would normally be subject to the provisions of the "Federal

Private International Law Act" enacted in 1987 and entered into force at the beginning of 1989.

Most of the provisions relevant to arbitration are found in chapter 12 of the Act (Articles 176-194), discussed elsewhere. It is worth noting here, however, that Article 176(2) of the Act gives the parties the right to exclude the provisions of chapter 12. The alternatives they might consider include cantonal law, which would be the Swiss Intercantonal Arbitration Concordat.

At the very beginning of the Act's general provision, Article 7 deals explicitly with arbitration agreements.

<u>Private International Law Act, Article 7</u>.

Where the parties have concluded an arbitral agreement covering an arbitrable dispute, a Swiss court seized of it shall decline jurisdiction unless

(a) the defendant has proceeded with his defence on the merits without raising any objection;

(b) the court finds that the arbitral agreement is void, inoperative or inapplicable; or

(c) the arbitral tribunal cannot be constituted for reasons due clearly to the activity or inactivity of the defendant.

### 5.    UNITED NATIONS COMMISSION ON INTERNATIONAL TRADE LAW (UNCITRAL)

Article 8 of the Model Law adopted in 1985 by the United Nations Commission on International Trade Law (UNCITRAL) contains provisions requiring courts to refer the parties to arbitration in the case of an action dealing with a matter subject to an arbitration agreement.

### Article 8

(1) A court before which an action is brought in a matter which is the subject of an arbitration agreement shall, if a party so requests

not later than when submitting his first statement on the substance of the dispute, refer the parties to arbitration unless it finds that the agreement is null and void, inoperative or incapable of being performed.

(2) Where an action referred to in paragraph (1) of this article has been brought, arbitral proceedings may nevertheless be commenced or continued, and an award may be made, while the issue is pending before the court.

## V. DETERMINING THE EXISTENCE AND SCOPE OF AGREEMENT

At the very outset of any arbitral dispute resolution, questions are often raised about exactly what and how the parties to the dispute agreed to arbitrate. The claimant may have different perspectives than the defendant on questions such as: Is there a valid agreement? May an arbitration agreement ever be applied to non-signatories? May multi-party disputes be consolidated? Which rules govern the arbitral procedure? What issues are covered by the agreement to submit to arbitration? Can the parties be compelled to arbitrate the question of fraud in the very inducement of the contractual arrangement? The following cases deal with a variety of complicated fact patterns under which such issues are raised.

### A. DOES AN AGREEMENT TO ARBITRATE EXIST?

1. *Beromun Aktiengesellschaft v. Societa Industriale Agricola "Tresse" (SIAT)*, 471 F.Supp. 1163 (S.D.N.Y. 1979).

["Beromun", a Liechtenstein corporation commenced suit against respondents SIAT, an Italian partnership, and the American Arbitration Association seeking an order directing SIAT to proceed to arbitration. SIAT cross moved to dismiss Beromun's petition on grounds of lack of subject matter and personal jurisdiction, failure to comply with the statute of frauds, failure to state a claim, and forum non conveniens. Beromun contended that it entered into a contract to sell a quantity of corn to SIAT, that the contract contained an agreement to arbitrate which included a consent-to-personal-jurisdiction clause, and that SIAT breached the contract and must now proceed to arbitration. Alternatively Beromun asserted that several later communications from SIAT to Beromun constituted enforceable agreements to arbitrate the subject matter of the alleged contract. The Court summarized in detail the confusing exchange of telexes and telephone calls in October 1974, among Beromun, its agents in Italy, and SIAT, purporting to provide for the sale of several thousand long tons of American yellow corn to SIAT.]

.        .        .

. . . Beromun's first theory is that the parties incorporated by reference an arbitration clause into a sales contract. Specifically, the agreement to arbitrate, Beromun claims, was incorporated by the reference to "NEWEST NAEGA N.2" during the October 4, 1974 conversation between Marchetti and Dal Ferro, and subsequently within Marchetti's telexes, Exhs. 2 & 3, to Beromun and SIAT.

"NEWEST NAEGA N.2" is an abbreviation for newest North American Export Grain Association (NAEGA) form Number 2. The NAEGA form contains various conditions, rules, and price, payment, delivery, weight and quality terms. It also contains a standard arbitration clause that includes a consent to personal jurisdiction of all the courts of New York State. It provides:

> 3. ARBITRATION. Buyer and seller agree that any controversy or claim arising out of, in connection with or relating to this contract, or the interpretation, performance or breach thereof, shall be settled by arbitration in the City of New York before the American Arbitration Association or its successors, pursuant to the Grain Arbitration Rules of the American Arbitration Association, as the same may be in effect at the time of such arbitration proceeding, which rules are hereby deemed incorporated herein and made a part hereof, and under the laws of the State of New York. The arbitration award shall be final and binding on both parties and judgment upon such arbitration award may be entered in the Supreme Court of the State of New York or any other Court having Jurisdiction thereof. *Buyer and seller hereby recognize and expressly consent to the jurisdiction over each of them of the American Arbitration Association or its successors, and of all the Courts in the State of New York.* Buyer and seller agree that this contract shall be deemed to have been made in New York State

and be deemed to be performed there, any reference herein or elsewhere to the contrary notwithstanding.

Exh. 1 (emphasis added). It appears that the only basis for personal jurisdiction over SIAT is the submission to jurisdiction clause underscored above. Thus, this court must find an enforceable agreement to arbitrate not only as a basis of subject matter jurisdiction, as noted above, but also as a predicate for the exercise of *in personam* jurisdiction over SIAT. *See Avila Group, Inc. v. Norma J. of California*, 426 F.Supp. 537, 541 & n.13 (S.D.N.Y.1977) (Weinfeld, J.).

[The issue of enforceability and validity of the arbitration clause is governed by federal law, which consists of "generally accepted principles of contract law" of which the UCC is part.]

It has been stated that "[a] written agreement for arbitration is the *sine qua non* of an enforceable arbitration agreement," *Garnac Grain Co. v. Nimpex International, Inc.*, 249 F.Supp. 986, 986 (S.D.N.Y.1964), and such a writing is required under the Convention. Article II, § 1. *See also* 9 U.S.C. § 202 incorporating 9 U.S.C. § 2 which requires a writing. It need not be signed, however, and ordinary contract principles dictate when the parties are bound by a written arbitration provision absent their signatures. . . .

.     .     .

Beromun's theory of contract is founded upon U.C.C. § 2-207 (McKinney 1964) which provides in pertinent part:

Additional Terms in Acceptance or Confirmation.

(1) A definite and seasonable expression of acceptance or a written confirmation which is sent within a reasonable time operates as an acceptance even though it states terms additional to or different from those offered or agreed upon, unless acceptance is expressly made conditional on assent to the additional or different terms.

(2) The additional terms are to be construed as proposals for addition to the contract. Between merchants such terms become part of the contract unless:

          (a) the offer expressly limits acceptance to the terms of the offer;

          (b) they materially alter it; or

          (c) notification or objection to them has already been given or is given within a reasonable time after notice of them is received.

Beromun contends that an oral contract was concluded on October 4, 1974 when Marchetti spoke to Dal Ferro; that Marchetti's identical telexes sent to Beromun and Dal Ferro on that day were written confirmations under section 2-207(1) executed for the parties as seller and buyer; that the disputed "one vessel" term may be treated as an additional or different term; that as such the "one vessel" term was a proposal for addition to the contract under section 2-207(2); and that SIAT's October 5 telex, Exh. 5, stating that "one vessel" had not been agreed upon, was a "notification of objection" to the "one vessel" term that resulted in its exclusion from an already consummated contract.

In support of the above theory Beromun relies heavily on the wording used by SIAT in its October 5 telex. Exh. 5. Specifically, Beromun points to SIAT's use of the words "contract dated October 4, 1974," and "what was agreed upon," the reference to the "conclusion of the transaction," and the failure to object to the broker's sending of a confirmation. Beromun memorandum at 9. To further enhance its argument that a contract had been formed and that SIAT was attempting to renege, Beromun cites a newspaper article, Exh. 4, wherein it is reported that former President Gerald Ford issued a "hold order" on two contracts for the sale of 125 million bushels of corn and wheat to the Soviet Union on the evening of October 4, 1974. This is incorporated into the petition apparently to show that as a result of the President's action grain dealers had reason to become apprehensive that additional export controls would be imposed, the market price of American grain became speculative, and SIAT had a motive to withdraw from the deal.

In the absence of more convincing proof that Marchetti and Dal Ferro for SIAT in fact concluded an oral contract on the afternoon of October 4, 1974, I find Beromun's arguments and its proffered application of U.C.C. § 2-207 to the instant set of facts to be specious for the following reasons.

Both Beromun and SIAT have had extensive business dealings in the international corn and grain trade with each other and third parties. Beromun contends that when parties negotiate a transaction through a broker, it is customary that both the buyer and the seller consider themselves contractually bound from the time the broker confirms the transaction by telephone. Beromun petition, ¶ 16. Even assuming *arguendo* that this is the customary means of negotiating a contract of sale in the grain trade, I have determined that no meeting of the minds occurred during Marchetti and Dal Ferro's conversation of October 4. The evidence shows, according to Marchetti, that the terms of the proposed sale, including "NAEGA 2" and "one vessel," were read to Dal Ferro. Again according to Marchetti, Dal Ferro expressed agreement to those terms through the words "make it." Marchetti affid. & reply affid. In contrast, Dal Ferro contends that no deal was ever finalized due to Marchetti's unilateral insistence, subsequent to the oral conversation, on the "one vessel" term a term obviously considered important by SIAT and one to which SIAT has steadfastly denied ever having orally agreed. Dal Ferro affid.; Exh. 5. Faced with this contradictory evidence, I conclude that no oral agreement has been established, Marchetti's impressions and beliefs to the contrary notwithstanding.

There being no prior oral agreement, Marchetti's October 4 confirmation telexes, Exhs. 2 & 3, were not a true confirmation but rather an offer. *See generally* Official Comment 1 to U.C.C. § 2-207. I find this to be so despite SIAT's language in Exh. 5 cited by Beromun to persuade the court that SIAT considered itself contractually bound even before Marchetti forwarded Exh. 3 to SIAT. Further, SIAT's response to Marchetti in Exh. 5 was not "(a) definite and seasonable expression of acceptance," U.C.C. § 2-207(1), but rather an acceptance "expressly made conditional on (Beromun's) assent," *id.*, to SIAT's deviation from the "one vessel" term, or a counteroffer. The telex clearly stated

WHAT WAS AGREED UPON WAS "QUANTITY" NOT THE TERM "ONE VESSEL." THESE ARE THE USUAL TERMS FROM WHICH WE CANNOT DEPART. PLEASE INFORM SELLERS ABOUT IT.

Exh. 5. Before Beromun assented to the above through Marchetti, see Exh. 7, SIAT withdrew from the negotiations when it telexed to Marchetti that it was compelled to consider the "subject contract null" after unsuccessfully attempting to work out the "one vessel" term that morning in Verona. Exh. 6. Consequently, no contract was ever entered into between the parties.

Because no contract existed, SIAT never became contractually bound to arbitrate through Marchetti's written arbitration and consent-to-jurisdiction clause incorporated by reference to NAEGA 2 in Exhs. 2 & 3. Moreover, in light of my holding that no contract was formed, SIAT's subsequent written offers to arbitrate are of no moment since no subject matter existed for arbitration.

In conclusion, since there was no agreement to arbitrate, Beromun's application for an order directing arbitration is denied. The petition is dismissed for lack of subject matter and In personam jurisdiction, and the balance of SIAT's arguments need not be reached.
. . .

### Notes and Questions

1. Note that *Beromun* turns not on the existence of an arbitration clause but on the existence of an underlying contract.

2. On the policy question of whether courts or arbitrators should determine the existence of an underlying contract, see discussion *infra* p. 524.

2.　　*In re Ferrara S.p.A.*, 441 F.Supp. 778 (S.D.N.Y. 1977).

[United Grain Growers agreed to sell 20,000 tons of Canadian wheat to each of the two buyers. The sales were memorialized on standard form contracts of the North American Export Grain Association (NAEGA), which included an arbitration clause.]

There are before the court competing applications to stay or to compel arbitration of disputes arising from two contracts for the sale of wheat by United Grain Growers, Ltd. ("UGG"), a Canadian corporation, to Fratelli Moretti Cereali, S.p.A. ("Moretti"), and Ferrara S.p.A. ("Ferrara"), both of Italy. Arbitration will be ordered.

. 　 . 　 . 　 .

Moretti and Ferrara resist arbitration primarily on the theory that they did not enter into enforceable agreements to arbitrate. It appears that the contracts were negotiated for the buyers by Italian grain brokers. The buyers claim that there was no discussion of, or express assent to, arbitration during the negotiations, and that the arbitration clause in NAEGA 2 was not mentioned. Relying primarily on New York and federal law, they contend that the quoted language on the face of NAEGA 2 referring to the provisions on the reverse side is insufficient to bind them to the arbitration term. Messrs. Remo Moretti, Director of Moretti, and Riccardo Ferrara, Counsellor of the Administrative Council of Ferrara, have averred in virtually identical affidavits that they neither knew nor had reason to know of the arbitration clauses; each states he is familiar with Italian law, under which arbitration agreements are allegedly unenforceable unless they appear above the signatures of both parties, and each claims he therefore saw no reason to examine the reverse side of NAEGA 2, which is unsigned. As will appear, the court may assume *arguendo*, with whatever strain, that these identical accounts are true. Alternatively, the buyers contend that the contracts are governed by Italian law, and that the arbitration clauses are invalid pursuant to the rule mentioned above.

Since this court's jurisdiction over these actions is conferred by Chapter 2 of the Federal Arbitration Act, 9 U.S.C. §§ 201-208, as added P.L. 91-368, 84 Stat. 692 (1970), it would seem that the enforceability of the arbitration clause at issue must be determined in accordance with federal law, i. e., generally accepted principles of contract law. . . In the instant cases, however, it is unnecessary to decide precisely which body of law governs the enforceability of arbitration agreements in actions in federal courts falling under the United Nations Convention implemented in Chapter 2, see n. 2, *supra*. Whether the applicable law is the federal law developed under Chapter 1 of the Arbitration Act; a uniform body of international law embodied in the Convention, see *Scherk v. Alberto-Culver Co.*, 417 U.S. 506, 520-21 n. 15, 94 S.Ct. 2449, 41 L.Ed.2d 270 (1974); or—by virtue of the parties' contractual choice of law provision and their designation of New York as the place for arbitration, . . . the law of New York State, the result is the same, and the alleged rule of Italian law on which the buyers rely does not apply. The purported Italian law rule appears to be a special requirement governing agreements to arbitrate, but inapplicable to other contractual terms and conditions. Federal courts have consistently refused to apply such rules in cases arising under

Chapter 1 of the Arbitration Act. [citations omitted] . . . Similarly, the Supreme Court has noted that "the delegates to the Convention voiced frequent concern that courts of signatory countries in which an agreement to arbitrate is sought to be enforced should not be permitted to decline enforcement of such agreements on the basis of parochial views of their desirability or in a manner that would diminish the mutually binding nature of the agreements." *Scherk v. Alberto-Culver Co.*, *supra*, 417 U.S. at 520-521 n. 15, 94 S.Ct. at 2458. This concern would seem to be equally compelling whether the "parochial view" is that of the forum or of another state with an alleged interest in the controversy.

The buyers do not deny that NAEGA 2 contracts embodying the essential terms of the actual agreements between the parties were duly executed by authorized agents of the respective companies. Since there is no allegation of fraud or duress in the signing or inducement of the contracts, and the cases do not involve parties of substantially unequal bargaining power or sophistication, the buyers' contentions are insufficient to bring them within any exception to the general rule that a person of ordinary understanding and competence is bound by the provisions of a contract he signs whether or not he has read them. [citations omitted] . . . In these circumstances, the question of a "subjective" agreement to arbitrate is irrelevant. *Avila Group, Inc. v. Norma J. of California*, *supra*; *Bigge Crane & Rigging Co. v. Docutel Corp.*, 371 F.Supp. 240 (E.D.N.Y.1973). There is no doubt that the quoted legends on the face of NAEGA 2 are sufficient to give notice to a reasonably prudent person of the arbitration provision and other things appearing on the back. . . . The buyers are therefore bound by these arbitration clauses, and there is no issue of fact requiring a trial.

In light of this finding, it is unnecessary to rule on the buyers' claim that the grain sale contracts themselves are unenforceable because they allegedly fail to comply with certain Italian Foreign Currency Control Regulations. Given the parties' agreements that the contracts should be deemed to have been made in New York State, and that controversies arising out of the contracts "or the interpretation, performance or breach thereof" should be settled under the laws of that State, the contention seems dubious on the merits. But it is in any event a matter to be decided by the arbitrators.

.    .    .    .

Notes and Questions

1. In contrast to *Beromun*, the critical question in *Ferrara* was the validity of the arbitration agreement itself.

2. Note the difference between the law applicable to the merits of the dispute and the procedural law applicable to the arbitration.

B. WHICH RULES GOVERN?

1. *Société Générale de Surveillance S.A. v. Raytheon European Management & Sys. Co.*, 643 F.2d 863 (1st Cir. 1981).

.   .   .

On July 10, 1975, REMSCO, a Massachusetts firm, and SGS, a French company, entered into a sub-contract under which SGS agreed to provide transportation, and other related services, for NATO Hawk missiles. This sub-contract (which we shall call the Basic Contract) was written on a two page Raytheon Purchase Order Form, to which were attached fifteen typewritten pages of provisions and fifty other pages of typed and printed exhibits and addenda. The Purchase Order is numbered 11.1108.02.0144. The typed statements on the form state the basic subject matter ("transportation and . . . other services"), refer the reader to the attached sixty-five pages for the terms of the contract, delete the printed conditions on the back of the form,[152] and state that the number of the Purchase Order (11.1108.02.0144) "shall be used in all references and correspondence regarding to this agreement". The subsequent sixty-five pages set forth a series of Articles [which *inter alia* dealt with disputes]. . . . Article 16 provides that the Basic Contract will be "construed and interpreted in accordance with the law of the Republic of France". Article 17.2 provides that "all disputes . . . arising in connection with" the Basic Contract "shall be finally settled by arbitration" under the rules of the International Chamber of Commerce in Lausanne, Switzerland. The Basic Contract further provides that any future changes must be in writing.

---

[152] [3] "The terms and conditions of purchase on the reverse of the cover page hereto are deleted in their entirety."

Over the next few years, the parties entered into a series of "change orders". Typically, the change order would be written on a Raytheon Purchase Order Form. In the upper left of the form, under the *printed* words "purchase order number" the typed Basic Contract number (11.1108.02.0144) would appear. In a box next to it titled "c.o. number" the typed number of the change order would appear. At the bottom of the page, among other printed statements, the *printed* words "ship subject to the terms and conditions on the face and back hereof" appeared. Apparently often, or at least sometimes, this latter printed instruction was expressly countermanded by a typed statement. For example, Change Order No. Six, entered into on December 16, 1976, has the typed statement on its face that "this change . . . does not change the Terms and Conditions." Thus, even though Change Order No. Six, and subsequent change orders were written on a new Raytheon form—one with printed terms on the back providing for arbitration in Massachusetts—the terms of the Basic Contract, not the printed terms on the back of the form, appeared to govern.

In December 1976 the parties signed a Memorandum of Understanding which set forth certain changes in the work provided by the Basic Contract, . . . The Memorandum states that the subject matter "will form the basis of a firm definitive contract" to be executed before January 31, 1977. That memorandum was attached to Change Order No. 7. That change order has the number of the Basic Contract (11.1108.02.0144) typed in the upper left hand corner; it has "7" typed under the printed legend "c.o. number"; it has the same printed terms on the face and back as No. 6; but the typing on the front simply refers to the Memorandum of Understanding and does not say that other terms and conditions remain the same.

On June 12, 1977, the parties agreed to Change Order No. 8. That change order also has the same Basic Contract number in the upper left hand corner; it has the number "8" typed under the printed legend "c.o. number"; it has the same printed terms on the face and back as No. 6 . . . And, like order No. 6, but unlike order No. 7, it has the typed statement on its face: "All other terms and conditions set forth in this contract remain unchanged."

Subsequently, a dispute arose in which REMSCO claimed that SGS was negligent in its performance under Change Order No. 8. After informal efforts to resolve the dispute failed, REMSCO sought arbitration in Switzerland under Article 17.2 of the Basic Contract. SGS opposed this arbitration, however, arguing in a letter to REMSCO that the testing and other services called for by Change Order No. 8 were different from the transportation and other services described in the Basic Contract to the point where the arbitration clause of the Basic Contract did not apply. REMSCO then sought arbitration in Boston, presumably on the theory that if Article 17.2 of the Basic Contract did not apply, then the printed arbitration clause on the back of Change Order No. 8 must apply. SGS responded by bringing this action in the district court under Massachusetts law seeking to enjoin the Boston arbitration. Judge McNaught entered a temporary restraining order enjoining the Boston arbitration on December 4, 1979. He found that SGS would probably succeed on the merits of its action. He wrote that it is "logical . . . to claim that, if arbitration is to be held at all, it must be held in these circumstances under Article 17.2 of the original contract. It is not inconsistent to urge further that, by reason of the nature of the services called for by the change order, no arbitration is required should a dispute arise."

On December 17, 1979, REMSCO filed a motion to dissolve the temporary restraining order or in the alternative to "condition any . . . injunction . . . upon SGS's participation in . . . arbitration in Lausanne Switzerland" in accordance with the Basic Contract. Judge McNaught denied this motion in July 1980. In September 1980 REMSCO renewed its motion, specifically requesting the court to "dissolve the temporary restraining order and compel arbitration in either Boston, Massachusetts, or Lausanne, Switzerland." This motion was denied on September 16, 1980. At the same time REMSCO filed with the International Chamber of Commerce a demand for arbitration in Switzerland. SGS filed a response in which it denied that the arbitration clause in the original contract applied to the present controversy but apparently was prepared to allow the arbitration to proceed, reserving the right to argue that Article 17 of the Basic Contract does not apply. Thus, at the present time Judge McNaught's restraining order, preventing arbitration before the American Arbitration Association in Boston remains in effect, while some form of arbitration is proceeding (with reservations) in Switzerland.

## II.

In appealing from Judge McNaught's refusal to dissolve or to modify the temporary restraining order, enjoining arbitration before the

American Arbitration Association in Boston, REMSCO makes three basic arguments. First, it claims that the district court erred as a matter of law in issuing the temporary restraining order, for the Federal Arbitration Act, not Massachusetts state law, applies to this proceeding, and that Act does not grant the court the power to stay arbitration proceedings. Second, it claims that, beginning with Change Order No. 7, the parties created a new contract; thus the Basic Contract (and in particular Article 17) does not apply to Change Order No. 8; rather, the printed arbitration provision on the back of Change Order No. 8 applies. Third, in any event, if the Basic Contract applies, the district court should have ordered arbitration in Switzerland under Article 17. We shall consider each of these arguments in turn.

### A.

We agree with REMSCO that the Federal Arbitration Act applies to this dispute . . . [T]he courts have held that the term "commerce" in this provision of the Act refers to interstate or foreign commerce and is to be broadly construed. . . . In this case, both the Basic Contract and Change Order No. 8 "evidenc[e] . . . a transaction involving (foreign) commerce." The contract, prepared in New Hampshire, is between an American and a French company, and it concerns the transportation and testing in Europe of missiles made in California and Massachusetts. It clearly covers trade "between citizens of this country and subjects of a foreign country . . . ." *Caribbean Steamship Co., S.A. v. La Societe Navale Caennaise, supra*, 140 F.Supp. at 21.

We disagree, however, with REMSCO's claim that the Act removes the district court's power to enjoin the Massachusetts arbitration. The Act supplants only that state law inconsistent with its express provisions. . . . There is no such inconsistency here. The Act expressly provides federal courts with the power to order parties to a dispute to proceed to arbitration where arbitration is called for by the contract. 9 U.S.C. § 3. To allow a federal court to enjoin an arbitration proceeding which is not called for by the contract interferes with neither the letter nor the spirit of this law. Rather, to enjoin a party from arbitrating where an agreement to arbitrate is absent is the concomitant of the power to compel arbitration where it is present. *A.B.C., Inc. v. American Federation of Television & Radio Artists*, 412 F.Supp. 1077 (S.D.N.Y.1976). In fact, were the law read to prevent a court from enjoining an arbitration proceeding it might actually interfere with arbitration—in the unusual case, arguably present here, where one such arbitration proceeding may interfere with another. Thus, we conclude that the district court had adequate authority under Massachusetts law to stay the Massachusetts arbitration.

## B.

We agree with the district court that SGS is likely to prevail in its claim that Change Order No. 8 is part of the Basic Contract and that it does not form part of a new contract instituted by Change Order No. 7. We note that this issue, under the terms of both the Basic Contract (Article 16) and the Memorandum attached to Change Order No. 7, is to be decided as a matter of French law. While the parties have not briefed French law, a cursory review of its basic principles suggests that courts are free to look to objective indications of the parties' intentions. Rene David, *English Law and French Law, A Comparison*, pp. 100 *et seq.* (1980). *Compare* Restatement of Contracts §§ 235-236. There are numerous indications that the parties intended Change Order No. 8 to be governed by the Basic Contract.

For one thing, there is the obvious fact that both Order No. 7 and Order No. 8 were referred to as "*change*" orders. Both refer, in their upper left hand corners, to the Basic Contract by its number (11.1108.02.0144). Both have numbers ("7" and "8" respectively) typed under the headings "c.o. number". For another thing, several critical basic matters, such as secrecy, insurance, credit, and audits were dealt with in the Basic Contract but *not* dealt with in the Memorandum attached to Change Order No. 7. These omissions are odd, if the parties had intended Change Order No. 7 to begin an entirely new contractual relationship, but they are not at all odd if the parties intended the Basic Contract to govern except where modified by the terms of the Change Order. Finally, Change Order No. 8, while it refers by number to the Basic Contract, nowhere refers to Change Order No. 7.

On the other hand, Change Order No. 7 does not specifically state that other terms and conditions are to remain the same, and the Memorandum attached to it says that the parties will enter a "definitive contract". Yet, whether Change Order No. 7 was meant itself to constitute that "definitive contract" is unclear. Even if it was so meant, basic terms in the Basic Contract might still be intended to apply. And,

Change Order No. 8 may in any event pick up terms from the Basic Contract, for No. 7 might well have been intended to be "definitive" only as to matters within its specific subject matter: the costs of transportation and related services in 1977. On the basis of the information before the district court and before us, it appears likely, under French law, that Change Order No. 8 would be found to be part of the Basic Contract. If so, Article 17, with its provision for ICC arbitration in Switzerland, at least *arguably* governs the parties' dispute.

Once it is determined that Article 17 of the Basic Contract *arguably* governs this dispute, then it is appropriate to remit the dispute for resolution in the Swiss arbitration. If Article 17, *in fact*, governs the underlying dispute of the parties, then the printed clause on the back of Change Order No. 8 is inconsistent with Article 17. It could not therefore comprise a part of the contract between the parties. Arbitration in Boston, not having been agreed to by the parties, should be enjoined. However, even if Article 17 later turns out not to govern the underlying dispute, referral to Switzerland now is still proper. Whether SGS is correct in contending that the testing of missiles is so different from their transport that Change Order No. 8 (while within the Basic Contract) was meant to be outside the scope of the arbitrability clause is itself a matter for the International Chamber of Commerce arbitrators. The issue of the scope of an arbitration clause in a contract is an appropriate matter for arbitration. *Butler Products Company v. Unistrut Corporation*, 367 F.2d 733 (7th Cir. 1966). In the present instance, the Rules of Conciliation and Arbitration of the International Chamber of Commerce expressly provide that as long as there is in the opinion of the ICC Court of Arbitration "prima facie" an agreement to arbitrate, "the arbitration shall proceed", and "any decision as to the arbitrator's jurisdiction shall be taken by the arbitrator himself." Article 8, Section 3. SGS has entered into arbitration proceedings in Switzerland for the purpose of making this determination. Since the arbitrators there are more likely to be familiar with commercial dealings in this area and with French law, and since the proceedings are under way, the order of the district court enjoining arbitration in Boston is well within its discretion.

## C.

REMSCO argues, however, that if it is determined in Switzerland that Article 17 was not meant to include the *testing* of missiles within its scope, it will be left without recourse to arbitration for the underlying dispute. It is possible that the parties, in agreeing to Change Order No. 8, meant to delete the printed terms on the back of the change order and to make applicable only Article 17 arbitration limited to whatever matters were previously considered to be within Article 17's scope; if Article 17 did not include "testing" disputes, then there would be no arbitration agreement. Yet, REMSCO responds, such an interpretation is inconsistent with its continued efforts to resolve disputes through arbitration, as reflected in the fact that it prints standard arbitration clauses on the back of its forms and that it has made every effort to provide for arbitration in its dealings with SGS.

In support of the view that the back of Change Order No. 8 is deleted no matter what the scope of Article 17 is, the fact that the typed words at the bottom of Change Order No. 8 read "All other terms and conditions set forth in this contract remain unchanged". On the other hand, one might also read the words of Change Order No. 8 as deleting from the back only provisions inconsistent with the Basic Contract. On this view, if Article 17 does not provide for arbitration of Change Order No. 8 disputes, then the printed arbitration clause on the back of the form would be perfectly consistent with Article 17 and thus not necessarily deleted.

It is obviously difficult to determine whether, if Article 17's scope is limited, the contract leaves the parties without recourse to arbitration or makes operative the printed clause on the back of Change Order No. 8 (which would then be *consistent* with Article 17). Presumably evidence relating to the history of the parties' dealings, their use of arbitration, and French law would be relevant. But this issue need not be decided now. The district court remains free to reexamine the issue and the appropriateness of its restraining order should there be an authoritative determination by a competent authority elsewhere that Article 17 is so limited.

Nor need the district court now order arbitration in Switzerland. The parties are proceeding under the ICC rules with arbitration there, at least to determine the scope of Article 17 and presumably, if Article 17 is found to apply, the arbitrators will arbitrate the underlying dispute. Should it appear that an injunction is needed to obtain arbitration there, the parties remain free to request the district court to issue it. . . .

### Notes and Questions

1. Are there ever circumstances in which parties to a complex transaction would assign different parts of the transaction (*i.e.*, disputes arising from different parts of the transactions) to different arbitral regimes? Explain and give examples.

2. In light of your answer, analyze *Raytheon* to determine whether it was plausible to assume that different arbitral regimes were intended.

3. In the conclusion, the Court asserts that a district court is free to reexamine the issue of Article 17. What are the consequences for the system of international arbitration of such a competence?

2.     *Mobil Oil Indonesia Inc. v. Asamera (Indonesia) Ltd.*, 392 N.Y.S.2d 614 (1977), *rev'd on other grounds*, 401 N.Y.S.2d 186 (1977).

In this action involving contract rights to explore and produce vast petroleum reserves, the parties seek a determination of which procedural rules shall govern arbitration of their disputes. The contract, dated July 16, 1968, contained a broad arbitration clause providing that "[a]ny dispute arising out of or relating to this Agreement shall be settled by arbitration in accordance with the Rules of the International Chamber of Commerce" (hereinafter "Rules" or "ICC") and designated New York City as the place of arbitration. At the time the agreement was executed, and indeed at the time of institution on November 6, 1974 of the arbitration, the 1955 Rules were in force. On June 1, 1975, after arbitration had commenced, new Rules were put into effect (1975 Rules). Following several meetings to prepare the "Terms of Reference" which would govern the arbitral proceeding, at which counsel, the parties, and the three arbitrators were present, a majority of the arbitrators ruled that all proceedings thereafter would be conducted under the 1975 Rules.

On October 31, 1975 petitioner-respondent applied to the ICC Court of Arbitration for a direction that the arbitrators apply the 1955 Rules. The Court refused to interfere, held that it was for the arbitrators to decide the procedural issue presented, and directed the arbitrators to formalize their decision. On March 30, 1976 the arbitrators, again by a majority vote, ruled in an interlocutory award that the 1975 Rules were applicable. They concluded the parties intended to refer to the Rules as they were from time to time and that the general principle, as well as New York law, is to apply procedural rules as they exist at the time the procedural issues arise. See *Matter of Clayton v. Clement*, 33 N.Y.2d 386, 390, 353 N.Y.S.2d 173, 175, 308 N.E.2d 690, 692. The dissenting arbitrator, the esteemed former Judge John Van Voorhis, likewise seeking the intent of the parties, found the parties intended the 1955 Rules to apply. It is submitted, as the Court below found, that prehearing discovery is permitted under the 1975 Rules but not under the 1955 Rules.

.     .     .

That the parties agreed to arbitrate is undisputed as is the fact that the issues raised on arbitration bear a reasonable relationship to the contract. Furthermore, that the arbitrators' result is rational, although it may not have been the result others would have reached is beyond peradventure. The parties agreed to be bound by the Rules of the ICC and it was for the arbitrators to determine which Rules of the ICC were intended.

Despite petitioner's position to the contrary, no evidence is presented that greater restriction exists on the authority of an ICC arbitrator than on the authority of any other commercial arbitrator under the Rules of the American Arbitration Association (AAA). See *Parsons & Wh. Ov. Co., Inc. v. Societe G. de L. du P. (R.)*, 508 F.2d 969, 976-77 (2d Cir. 1974). Nor is any limitation of the arbitrators' broad powers found in the agreement itself.

Under the broad arbitration clause in the case at bar, questions of interpretation are for the arbitrators to decide and this is so even if the contract determination affects the very ground rules of the arbitration. If, for example, the agreement provided for arbitration pursuant to New York law, a determination by the arbitrators would not be overturned because the arbitrators applied the substantive law as of the time of arbitration rather than as of the time of agreement, or vice versa. Such determination as to substantive law goes no more nor less to the parties' agreement to arbitrate than a provision as to which procedural rules to apply. It follows logically and naturally that the determination of the parties' intention as to procedural rules is gauged by the same standard applied to substantive rules: Did the parties agree to arbitrate and did the arbitrators make a rational determination of which procedural rules to apply? As the answer to both portions of the question is in the affirmative, it was improper for the Court below to impose its judgment in the place and stead of the arbitrators.

### Notes and Questions

1. *Mobil* holds that if there is a "broad" arbitration clause, then the "intertemporal" question is within the competence of the arbitrators. How is the breadth of a clause determined? Is this a sound way of dealing with this question?

3.     *Maritime Int'l Nominées Establishment v. Republic of Guinea*, 693 F.2d 1094 (D.C. Cir. 1982).

The Republic of Guinea ("Guinea") appeals from, and raises numerous challenges to, the District Court's order confirming an arbitration award rendered by the American Arbitration Association in favor of Marine International Nominees Establishment ("MINE"). The District Court lacked subject matter jurisdiction, Guinea claims, because Guinea was immune under the Foreign Sovereign Immunities Act of 1976 ("FSIA"), Pub.L. No. 94-583, 90 Stat. 2891; because the arbitration clause contained in the parties' contract precluded the exercise of jurisdiction under the FSIA; and because the FSIA does not, and cannot constitutionally be read to, confer subject matter jurisdiction over suits between foreign plaintiffs and foreign states. Guinea also contends that MINE's service of process upon it did not meet the requirements of the FSIA and that the arbitration award itself was defective and unenforceable.

We reach only the first of these arguments, because we conclude that Guinea was immune under the FSIA and therefore that the court lacked subject matter jurisdiction to confirm the award. Accordingly, we reverse.

I

The following facts, unless indicated otherwise, are not disputed by the parties. The Republic of Guinea is a foreign sovereign state, and MINE is a Liechtenstein corporation. On August 19, 1971, Guinea and MINE[153] entered into a contract providing for the creation of a "mixed economy company" that became known as "SOTRAMAR." J.A. 205-27.[154] The purpose of the contract, as seen by both MINE and Guinea, was to establish and provide shipping services to transport Guinean bauxite to foreign markets. Appellant's Br. 4-5; Appellee's Br. 4; J.A. 209. . . . Although Guinean law was to be "applicable" to the contract, the contract stated that the "law between the parties" was the contract itself, and therefore that "Guinean laws shall be used for the interpretation and the implementation of this Agreement only accessorily and only in the case where the Agreement would leave a problem unsolved." J.A. 222-23.

The contract also contained several provisions relating to the settlement of disputes. When disagreements arose, the parties were first to attempt informal conciliation. If that effort failed, the parties were then to submit the conflict to arbitration by means of the method described in the contract—a panel of three arbitrators "selected by the President of CIRDI at the joint request of the parties or, failing this, at the request of the most diligent party." J.A. 226. "CIRDI" is the French acronym for the International Centre for Settlement of Investment Disputes. A codicil to the contract stated that the arbitrators would be chosen by the "President of the International Court of Settlement of International Disputes [sic] in Washington (CIRDI)." J.A. 229.

.    .    .

Although some SOTRAMAR-related activities took place after the contract was signed, SOTRAMAR never became an operating commercial entity. A rift developed between the parties, and in January

---

[153] [1] The signatories to the contract were Guinea and the Inter Maritime Bank, which acted "in the name and on behalf of" MINE. Joint Appendix ("J.A.") 207.

[154] [2] "SOTRAMAR" is an acronym for the "Societe Mixte de Transports Maritimes," Appellant's Brief ("Br.") 4, or the "Société Guinéenne de Transports Maritimes," Appellee's Br. 5.

1975 the parties signed a form purporting to present their differences to an ICSID arbitration. . . .

What took place next is disputed. By Guinea's account, MINE agreed to file with ICSID the consent and a formal arbitration request; MINE took no such action but instead determined that the consent form was technically deficient; MINE mailed a purportedly correct revised form to Guinea; Guinea never received this form; and MINE made no effort to determine whether the revised form had reached Guinea. Appellant's Br. 7. MINE states that it perceived a deficiency in the first consent form and "urged" Guinea to execute a new form, but that Guinea then "broke off all relations and refused to communicate further with MINE." Appellee's Br. 6. ICSID files contain no record of any request for arbitration in connection with the SOTRAMAR contract. J.A. 236 (letter from Acting Secretary-General of ICSID to counsel for Guinea (Dec. 8, 1980), Exhibit 7 to Guinea's Motion to Dismiss and Opposition to Motion to Confirm Arbitration Award and Enter Judgment).

On January 20, 1978—some three years after the first consent form was signed—MINE filed, in federal district court, a petition to compel arbitration under section 4 of the Federal Arbitration Act ("FAA"), 9 U.S.C. § 4 (1976), asserting subject matter jurisdiction under the FSIA and the FAA. J.A. 6. In essence, section 4 of the FAA empowers a federal district court to order arbitration to proceed in accordance with the terms of an arbitration agreement when adequate findings are made that an agreement did exist and that a default under the agreement did occur. Another relevant section of the FAA, section 5, 9 U.S.C. § 5 (1976), sets forth the circumstances when a court is additionally authorized to order arbitration before an arbitrator or arbitrators not named in the agreement. One such instance occurs when a party "fail[s] to avail himself" of the agreed-upon method for naming arbitrators. *Id.*

Drawing on these provisions, the petition to compel set forth a series of allegations, with exhibits attached, to demonstrate that the court should order the parties to proceed to arbitration before the American Arbitration Association ("AAA"). In essential part, MINE maintained that it had prepared the joint consent form "in accordance with the terms" of the SOTRAMAR contract, that it had then prepared a corrected consent form and had mailed it to Guinea, and that Guinea had "failed and refused either to sign the revised submission or to proceed with arbitration." J.A. 8-9. As a result, MINE continued, it could not initiate an ICSID arbitration. J.A. 9.

Because in MINE's view these facts demonstrated that Guinea intended not to abide by the agreed-upon arbitration method, *id.*, the petition went on to assert that no longer was that method available. *Id.* An order to compel arbitration was therefore proper, "since procedures are available [under section 5] to have a court appoint an arbitrator for the non-cooperating party." J.A. 10.

MINE served process upon Guinea by mailing, via registered mail, copies of the relevant documents to the Ministry of Foreign Affairs in Conakry, Guinea. MINE also sent the same documents by certified mail to the Embassy of Guinea in Washington, D.C. J.A. 47. Guinea did not respond to these documents.

The District Court heard argument on the petition on June 15, 1978; Guinea made no appearance. That same day, the court entered an order granting MINE's petition and ordering arbitration before the AAA and in accordance with the rules of the AAA. J.A. 48. The order set forth the court's conclusions that service had been proper under the FSIA, that the existence of an arbitration agreement and the failure to comply therewith were not in issue, and that Guinea's failure to avail itself of the agreed-upon arbitration method had frustrated the intent of that agreement. The order did not specifically state the basis for the court's subject matter jurisdiction. The clerk of the District Court served copies of the order, by registered mail, upon the Ministry of Foreign Affairs in Guinea and upon the Embassy of Guinea in Washington, D.C. J.A. 50.

MINE then filed, on September 5, 1978, a demand for arbitration before the AAA, J.A. 102, serving notice of the demand upon Guinea by the same method it had followed earlier. J.A. 110. The demand alleged several breaches of the SOTRAMAR agreement, including Guinea's failure to give to SOTRAMAR's management the necessary authority to conclude contracts for the carriage of bauxite and the provision of services, as well as Guinea's grant to another company of the bauxite rights reserved to MINE. J.A. 105-06. Arbitration hearings took place on February 5, 6, and 7, 1979; May 25, 1979; and April 14, 1980. J.A. 95-100 (affidavit of James W. Schroeder, Exhibit C to MINE's Motion to Confirm Arbitration Award and Enter Judgment). During these proceedings, the AAA served upon Guinea various documents concerning the arbitration, *id.*; Guinea did not appear or file any response. On June 9, 1980, the arbitrators rendered an award in excess of $25 million, which primarily represented compensatory damages for breach of contract. J.A. 86-87.

MINE then returned to the District Court, filing on August 22, 1980, a motion to confirm and enter judgment on the arbitration award under section 9 of the FAA, 9 U.S.C. § 9 (1976). J.A. 51. Accompanying the motion was a memorandum of points and authorities, with exhibits attached. Once again, MINE served process upon Guinea by the method followed earlier.

On December 9, 1980, Guinea entered the proceedings for the first time, filing a motion to dismiss for lack of subject matter jurisdiction. Record ("R.") 21. Guinea also filed a memorandum of points and authorities in support of the motion to dismiss and in opposition to MINE's motion to confirm. J.A. 125. In brief outline, the memorandum argued that neither the FAA, the commercial rules of the AAA, nor the FSIA provided the court with subject matter jurisdiction to entertain either MINE's earlier petition to compel or the motion to confirm. J.A. 134-40. The memorandum also contended that the court's earlier order to compel rested on an incorrect premise, because an ICSID arbitration had indeed been available.

MINE then filed, on January 5, 1980, a memorandum in reply to Guinea's motion to dismiss and in further support of its own motion to confirm. J.A. 237. Attached to the document were supporting exhibits.

The court heard oral argument from the parties on January 8, 1981, focusing attention on the issue of subject matter jurisdiction under the FSIA. On January 12, 1981, the court entered an order denying Guinea's motion to dismiss, granting MINE's motion to confirm, and entering judgment on the award. R. 25. The court also issued a four-page memorandum opinion primarily discussing its conclusion that it had subject matter jurisdiction under the FSIA. *In re Arbitration between Maritime International Nominees Establishment v. Republic of Guinea*, 505 F.Supp. 141 (D.D.C.1981) (mem. op.) ["*MINE v. Guinea*"].

On January 16, 1981, Guinea filed a motion for a new trial or, in the alternative, for relief from judgment, on the ground that newly discovered evidence showed that MINE's service of process had been invalid under the FSIA. J.A. 305. Also on that day, Guinea moved for a stay of the judgment until the District Court had ruled on the motion for a new trial, or, in the alternative, for shortening the time for MINE to respond to Guinea's motion for a new trial. R. 28. That same day, MINE submitted an affidavit in opposition to both motions. J.A. 322. On January 21, 1981, the District Court entered an order denying both of Guinea's motions but allowing Guinea five days to seek from this court a stay pending appeal. J.A. 325. Also on January 21, Guinea filed a notice of appeal from the January 12 order confirming the arbitration award. The next day, Guinea moved this court for a stay pending appeal; on January 23 that motion was granted and execution of judgment was stayed until a decision on the merits or further order of the court.

## II

Guinea's challenges to the confirmation order fall into three categories. First, it claims that the District Court lacked subject matter jurisdiction because: (1) the court erred in ruling that Guinea was not immune under the FSIA; (2) even assuming non-immunity, the FSIA does not purport to confer subject matter jurisdiction over suits between foreign plaintiffs and foreign states; (3) the FSIA would be unconstitutional if read to confer such jurisdiction; and (4) the signing by both parties of the first ICSID consent form committed them to an ICSID arbitration and therefore deprived the District Court of jurisdiction.

.    .    .

Because we hold that the court lacked subject matter jurisdiction to confirm the arbitration award, we need not address the service of process issue or the validity *vel non* of the arbitration award itself. And, because this jurisdictional holding rests on our conclusion that the condition for subject matter jurisdiction under the FSIA—non-immunity—was not met, we do not reach the second, third, or fourth of Guinea's subject matter jurisdiction arguments.

[Here the court engaged in fourteen pages on analysis of the Foreign Sovereign Immunity Act and reversed the District Court's opinion that it had subject-matter jurisdiction "[b]ecause non-immunity is a condition to subject-matter jurisdiction under the FSIA."]

### Notes and Questions

1. Note that both of the above cases, *Mobil v. Asamera* and *MINE v. Guinea*, have raised other issues of arbitration law in different stages of the controversy.

2. The special problem presented in arbitration by foreign sovereign immunity claims are discussed in Chapter 2, *supra*.

3. In appraising the District Court's decision to refer the dispute to AAA arbitration, consider the decisions in previous cases in which judges selected arbitral rules for the parties.

C.     WHAT DOES THE AGREEMENT COVER?

> *S.A. Mineracao da Trinidade-Samitri v. Utah Int'l, Inc.*, 745 F.2d 190 (2d Cir. 1984).

SWYGERT, Senior Circuit Judge.

Plaintiff S.A. Mineracao da Trinidade-Samitri ("Samitri"), a Brazilian corporation, brought this action in the United States District Court for the Southern District of New York to obtain a declaratory judgment, damages, and other relief against six defendants, corporations in Brazil, Panama, and the United States ("defendants"). Samitri alleges that defendants fraudulently induced Samitri to enter into an international iron ore mining venture. In addition, Samitri alleges seventeen assorted claims under the laws of Brazil and the United States. Defendants moved pursuant to the United States Arbitration Act, 9 U.S.C. §§ 1-14, 201-08 (1982), to stay the prosecution of Samitri's complaint in the district court and to compel arbitration. Samitri cross-moved to enjoin arbitration. The district court ordered arbitration of all of Samitri's claims except two brought under the Racketeer Influenced and Corrupt Organizations Act, 18 U.S.C. §§ 1961-68 (1982) ("RICO"), which the court stayed pending arbitration. *S.A. Mineracao da Trinidade-Samitri v. Utah International, Inc.*, 576 F.Supp. 566 (S.D.N.Y.1983) and 579 F.Supp. 1049 (S.D.N.Y.1984). We affirm.

[The Court summarized the agreements concluded in 1974 which provided for the structure and financing of the mining joint venture.]

. . .

Samitri claims that the arbitration provisions contained in the 1974 Agreements are relatively narrow and do not encompass claims of fraudulent inducement. Samitri relies upon *In re Kinoshita*, 287 F.2d 951 (2d Cir.1961). In *Kinoshita* this court found that a clause requiring arbitration of "any dispute or difference . . . aris[ing] under" the agreement was not sufficiently broad to encompass a claim of fraudulent inducement. *Id.* at 952-53. . . .

Defendants argue that the instant case is controlled by *Scherk v. Alberto-Culver Co.*, 417 U.S. 506, 94 S.Ct. 2449, 41 L.Ed.2d 270 (1974). . . . [The Court summarized *Scherk* and *Parsons & Whittemore*.]

The scope of an arbitration clause, like any contract provision, is a question of the intent of the parties. *See Necchi S.P.A. v. Necchi Sewing Machine Sales Corp.*, 348 F.2d 693, 696 (2d Cir.1965), *cert. denied*, 383 U.S. 909, 86 S.Ct. 892, 15 L.Ed.2d 664 (1966). That principle, however, frequently fails to offer much guidance. A dispute over the scope of a contract provision generally arises when the parties failed to agree beforehand to the meaning of the provision or, as is usually the case, when they failed to consider the intended meaning of a provision.

Nevertheless, we are guided in our decision by a need to protect the intent of the parties. We decline to overrule *In re Kinoshita*, despite its inconsistency with federal policy favoring arbitration, particularly in international business disputes, because we are concerned that contracting parties may have (in theory at least) relied on that case in their formulation of an arbitration provision. We see no reason, however, why we may not confine *Kinoshita* to its precise facts. We are confident that parties who have actually relied on *Kinoshita* in an attempt to formulate a narrow arbitration provision, have adopted the exact language of the arbitration provision involved in *Kinoshita*. The provision involved in *Kinoshita* required arbitration of "any dispute or difference aris[ing] under" the agreement. Thus, to ensure that an arbitration clause is narrowly interpreted contracting parties must use the foregoing phrase or its equivalent, although the better course, obviously, would be to specify exactly which claims are and are not arbitrable.

By contrast, the arbitration provision involved in the instant case requires arbitration of "any *question* or dispute aris[ing] or *occur[ring]* under" the agreement (emphasis added). Defendants argue that a "question" may "occur" under a contract even when a "dispute" does not "arise" under the contract. *Cf. Stateside Machinery Co. v. Alperin*, 526 F.2d 480, 481 (3d Cir.1975) (clause requiring arbitration of "any unresolved issues" held to cover claim of fraudulent inducement); *In re Kinoshita, supra*, 287 F.2d at 953 ("The agreement to arbitrate is limited . . . when it refers to disputes or controversies 'under' or 'arising out of' the contract."); *Griffin v. Semperit*, 414 F.Supp. 1384, 1392 (S.D.Tex.1976) (phrase "or relating to" found unnecessary to render arbitration clause broad enough to cover fraudulent inducement claim). Although the distinction defendants draw is far from overwhelming, we find it at least as reasonable as the distinction drawn in *Kinoshita*, 287 F.2d at 953, between a "dispute or difference aris[ing] under" an agreement and a "controversy or claim arising out of or relating to" an agreement.

Having determined that *Kinoshita* is inapplicable to the instant case, our decision is guided by the federal policy considerations. "The United States Arbitration Act, . . . reversing centuries of judicial hostility to arbitration agreements, was designed to allow parties to avoid 'the costliness and delays of litigation,' and to place arbitration agreements 'upon the same footing as other contracts.'" . . . The federal policy favoring arbitration requires us to construe arbitration clauses as broadly as possible.

> [D]oubts as to arbitrability should be "resolved in favor of coverage," . . . language excluding certain disputes from arbitration must be "clear and unambiguous" or "unmistakably clear" and . . . arbitration should be ordered "unless it may be said with positive assurance that the arbitration clause is not susceptible of an interpretation that covers the asserted dispute."

*Wire Service Guild v. United Press International*, 623 F.2d 257, 260 (2d Cir.1980) . . . .

Unless excluded, claims of fraud in the inducement of a contract are arbitrable. *See Prima Paint Corp. v. Flood & Conklin Manufacturing Co.*, 388 U.S. 395, 402-04, 87 S.Ct. 1801, 1805-06, 18 L.Ed.2d 1270 (1967). As the district court found, 576 F.Supp. at 571, the language of the arbitration clauses contained in the 1974 Agreements did not clearly exclude fraudulent inducement claims. Moreover, as in *Scherk v. Alberto-Culver Co.*, *supra*, 417 U.S. at 515, 94 S.Ct. at 2455, the Agreements involve a "truly international" business transaction. The corporations are of diverse nationality. The product that is the subject matter of the Agreements is produced in one country and sold to various other countries. "[I]n the absence of the arbitration provision considerable uncertainty existed at the time of the agreement, and still exists, concerning the law applicable to the resolution of disputes arising out of the contract." *Id.* at 516, 94 S.Ct. at 2455 (footnote omitted). Samitri alleges violations of federal securities laws. Defendants are sure to contest the application of these laws to this transaction. *Cf. id.* at n. 9. In this case a provision "specifying in advance the forum in which disputes shall be litigated and the law to be applied" is necessary to achieve the requisite "orderliness and predictability." *Id.* at 516, 94 S.Ct. at 2455. Moreover, although we perceive no danger in the instant case that a United States court will be predisposed to favor Samitri over defendants, the district court's lack of familiarity with the subject matter of the Agreement and the law to be applied (Brazilian) presents a problem. We conclude that the arbitration clauses contained in the 1974 Agreements cover Samitri's claims of fraudulent inducement.

.    .    .

Samitri argues that even if its claims based upon the 1974 Agreements are arbitrable, its claims based upon post-1974 Agreements, none of which contain an arbitration clause, are non-arbitrable. The post-1974 Agreements which Samitri claims were fraudulently induced include: (1) stock purchase agreements executed subsequent to the 1974 Agreements which provided for the purchase by Samitri of additional shares of Samarco; (2) the 1979 Agreement with Respect to Guaranty ("1979 Guaranty") under which Samitri agreed to reimburse 51% of defendants' payments pursuant to the 1979 Guaranty; and (3) the 1983 Memorandum of Agreement under which Samitri agreed to continue to contribute to Samarco and to purchase additional shares of Samarco preferred stock. The district court found that the post-1974 Agreements supplement and restate the 1974 Agreements and thus are subject to the arbitration clauses contained in the 1974 Agreements. We find no error in the district court's conclusion.

The 1974 Shareholders' Agreement expressly contemplated and provided for additional stock purchases by the parties "[i]f . . . Samarco requires additional capital in order to complete the Project [or] . . . in order to avoid the existence of an Event of Default Under the Credit Agreements . . . ." Affidavit of Kenneth E. Marklin, Exhibit B, §§ 2(f) & 2(g), at 9-10. In both instances the Shareholders' Agreement requires the parties to hold an extraordinary general meeting of shareholders of Samarco to vote their shares for an increase in the capital of Samarco in the amount called for by Samarco. The Agreement further requires the parties to subscribe for the additional shares of Samarco stock at the rate of 51% for Samitri and 49% for defendants. *Id.* The so-called stock purchase agreements were executed in accordance with the foregoing provisions of the 1974 Shareholders' Agreement and are subject to the latter's arbitration clause. *Cf. Consumer Concepts, Inc. v. Mego Corp.*, 458 F.Supp. 543, 545 (S.D.N.Y.1978) (agreement between parties found subject to arbitration clause contained in umbrella agreement where umbrella agreement "govern[ed] the continuing relationship between" the parties). *Contrast Seaboard Coast Line R.R. v. Trailer Train Co.*, 690 F.2d 1343, 1349 (11th Cir.1982) (contract found not to constitute umbrella agreement where contract was "of limited application" and did "not profess to cover all present and future aspects of the relationship between" the parties). *Necchi S.p.A. v. Necchi Sewing Machine Sales Corp.*, *supra*, 348 F.2d at 698 (disputes concerning contract without arbitration clause found non-arbitrable where contract "remained distinct and separate from" agreement containing arbitration clause).

Similarly, the 1974 Agreements expressly contemplated and provided for a guaranty of Samarco's indebtedness. The 1974 Shareholders' Agreement was amended in 1979 to state: "This Agreement, as amended as of August 16, 1979, has been executed in connection with . . . the Guaranty dated as of the date hereof . . . ." Affidavit of Bruce T. Mitchell, Exhibit G, ¶ 1(b), at 3. Pursuant to the ownership ratio set forth in the 1974 Agreements, Samitri guaranteed 51% and defendants guaranteed 49% of Samarco's liabilities. *See* Affidavit of Stephen K. Brimhall, Exhibit A, at 2. The 1979 Guaranty Agreement supplemented the 1979 Guaranty and both Agreements supplemented the 1974 Agreements. Thus, disputes concerning the

1979 Guaranty Agreement are arbitrable under the arbitration clauses contained in the 1974 Agreements.

Only the 1982 Memorandum of Agreement was not expressly contemplated and provided for in the 1974 Agreements. The 1982 Memorandum, however, expressly refers to two agreements which contain arbitration clauses. In paragraph 3 of the Memorandum Agreement, the parties "confirm[ed] their intention," to continue to contribute additional capital to Samarco "upon call by SAMARCO in accordance with paragraph 2 of the [1974] Shareholders' Agreement . . . ." In paragraph 4 of the Memorandum Agreement, Samitri agreed to purchase additional shares of Samarco preferred stock "subject to Paragraph 2 of the Agreement dated as of October 21, 1977 . . . ." Affidavit of Stephen K. Brimhall, Exhibit C, at 2. The 1977 ("Preferred Stock Purchase") Agreement referred to in the Memorandum Agreement contains an arbitration clause virtually identical to those contained in the 1974 Agreements. *See* Affidavit of Bruce T. Mitchell, Exhibit D, paragraph 8, at 25.[155] As the district court found, the 1982 Memorandum Agreement "'cannot be read apart from the other arbitrable contracts and must be viewed as a supplement' to those contracts." 576 F.Supp. at 574 (quoting *Consumer Concepts, Inc. v. Mego Corp.*, *supra*, 458 F.Supp. at 545). We agree with the district court's conclusion that the 1974 Agreements were an umbrella for the post-1974 Agreements and that disputes arising under the latter are arbitrable.

.    .    .

We find no merit to Samitri's final claim that the litigation of its non-arbitrable RICO claims should be permitted to proceed notwithstanding arbitration of any other claims. The decision to stay litigation of non-arbitrable claims pending the outcome of litigation "is one left to the district court . . . as a matter of its discretion to control its docket." *Moses H. Cone Memorial Hospital v. Mercury Construction Corp.*, *supra*, 103 S.Ct. at 939 n. 23. Particularly because the arbitrable claims were found to dominate the case and the non-arbitrable claims were found to be of "uncertain" validity, the

---

[155] [2] We find it significant that the only post-1974 Agreement that deviated from the structure set forth in the 1974 Agreements, which was the 1977 Stock Purchase Agreement, contained its own arbitration clause.

district court acted well within its discretion in staying litigation of the non-arbitrable claims. *See N.V. Maatsschappij Voor Industriele Waarden v. A.O. Smith Corp.*, 532 F.2d 874, 876 (2d Cir.1976).

.    .    .

KEARSE, Circuit Judge, dissenting:

. . . I do not see a significant difference between "disputes or controversies 'under' or 'arising out of' the contract," at issue in *In re Kinoshita*, 287 F.2d 951, 953 (2d Cir.1961), and "any question or dispute . . . aris[ing] or occur[ring] under" the contract, the arbitration provision in the present case. I would thus rule, as was held in *Kinoshita*, that claims of fraudulent inducement to enter into the contract fall outside the arbitration provision.

### Notes and Questions

1. Note that in *Samitri* the majority did not rely only on the breadth of the language of the arbitration clause. It also took account of the international character of the transaction. Does "internationality" extend the breadth of the language of a clause? Discuss.

2. Compare *Overseas Union Ins. Ltd. v. AA Mutual Int'l Ins. Co.*, 2 Lloyd's Rep. 63 (1988), involving an English reinsurance contract that raised an analogous question of the scope of the arbitration clause.

3. The dissent by Judge Kearse in *Samitri* may make sense as a matter of linguistic consistency. Is it sound policy? The difference between "disputes or controversies arising out of the contract" and "any question or dispute . . . arising or occurring under the contract" may seem slim. However, would a stay of the arbitration (until a court decides the question of fraud in the inducement) further the goals of the Federal Arbitration Act? Did Judge Kearse have the latitude to go the other way?

### D.    MAY MULTIPARTY DISPUTES BE CONSOLIDATED?

When more than one commercial agreement touches related parties or transactions, inconsistent results may arise as to common issues. In his legendary story of the "Macao Sardine Case," Sir Michael Kerr has reminded us that judicial power to join claims presents a considerable advantage over arbitration when multiple transactions all raise the same issue, such as *force majeure* arising from a single event.[156] In Sir Michael's tale, a quarter million tins of sardines secretly filled with mud by a Macao canning company had been sold and resold many times over throughout Asia. Most of the claims gave rise to consistent judgments for damages against the sellers, rendered in one consolidated action before the Hong Kong Commercial Court. However, the original buyer's action against the Macao canning company that had packed sardines ran into trouble. The underlying contract for this initial sale was subject to an arbitration clause that precluded jurisdiction by the Hong Kong court. The arbitration in the proceeding against the Macao company applied *lex mercatoria* to exonerate the Macao supplier, leaving the merchant with substantial damages to pay, and no hope of recovery against the real culprit.

Although the rules of some arbitral institutions provide for joinder of parties even if resisted by one of the existing parties to the arbitration,[157] this does not deal with the need to obtain the consent of the party to be joined. Some jurisdictions provide for statutory consolidation of related arbitrations.[158] Federal case law has held that consolidation of arbitrations pursuant to the state statute is not pre-empted by the Federal Arbitration Act.[159]

When arbitration does not take place in a jurisdiction with a consolidation statute, careful drafting can promote effective joinder of

---

[156] Michael Kerr, *Arbitration v. Litigation*, 3 ARB. INT'L 79 (1987).

[157] *See* London Court of International Arbitration, 1985 Rules, art. 13.1.

[158] *See, e.g.*, MASS. GEN. L., ch. 251, §2A (1994); CAL. CIV. PROC. CODE §1281.3 (West 1994). In the Netherlands and Hong Kong, courts have power to order consolidation of related arbitrations unless the parties stipulate otherwise. *See* Art. 1046, Dutch Civil Code, discussed in PIETER SANDERS & ALBERT J. VAN DEN BERG, ARBITRATION IN THE NETHERLANDS (1989); HONG KONG ARB. ORD., §6B. The Hong Kong Ordinance gives courts power to consolidate two or more arbitration proceedings where it appears to the court (i) that some common question of law or fact arises in both or all of them, (ii) that the rights to relief claimed therein arise out of the same transaction or series of transactions, or (iii) that for some other reason it is desirable to make an order for consolidation.

[159] *New England Energy v. Keystone Shipping*, 855 F.2d 1 (1st Cir. 1988).

related arbitrations.[160] The objection to consolidation is that arbitrators who consolidate actions will thereby exceed their authority. However, if all relevant parties authorize the arbitral tribunal to join two or more proceedings, it is difficult to see why a party consenting to joinder should later be allowed to change its mind when the arbitral process runs counter to the post-dispute preoccupations.[161] When two parties are named as defendants, of course, they may face a dilemma in nominating their party-appointed arbitrator. If the arbitration agreement provides for a three-member tribunal, the parties' options include compromising on a candidate or in the absence of agreement, a default procedure in which a third-party chooses the arbitrator.

> 1.    Pierre Bellet, *The Dutco Case, Siemens A.G. and BKMI Industrielagen GmbH v. Dutco Construction Co.*, 1992 REV. ARB. 470.

If multiple claimants or multiple defendants from the same corporate group voluntarily make a joint nomination of an arbitrator, the constitution of the arbitral tribunal would normally pose no special problem. In some cases, however, defendants or claimants that are not from the same group perceive their interests and arguments to diverge sufficiently that a jointly nominated arbitrator is unacceptable. One such case was *Siemens A.G. and BKMI Industrienlagen GmbH (BKMI) v. Dutco Consortium Construction Co.*,[162] generally referred to as the "Dutco Case." A dispute arose out of a contract for the construction of a cement plant in Oman. After entering into an agreement to build the plant for an Omani party, the German contractor, BKMI, had

---

[160] All relevant arbitration clauses should provide for arbitration in the same country, according to the same substantive and procedural law, under the same institutional rules, and before a tribunal constituted of the same arbitrators.

[161] Even in England, which has long been unfavorable to consolidation, there is a recognition of the validity of a contractual solution. *See* Sir Michael Mustill, *Multipartite Arbitration: An Agenda for Law-Makers*, 7 ARB. INT'L 393 (1991).

[162] Judgment of 7 January 1992, Cass. Civ. 1ère, published in 1992 REVUE D'ARBITRAGE No. 3, page 470, with commentary by Pierre Bellet. See also commentary by C.R. Seppala, *Multi-party Arbitrations at Risk in France*, INTERNATIONAL FINANCIAL LAW REVIEW, March 1992, page 33; Eric Schwartz, *Multi-Party Arbitration and the ICC*, 10 JOURNAL OF INT'L ARB. (No. 3) page 5 (1993); Jean-Louis Delvolvé, *Multipartism: The Dutco Decision of the French Cour de Cassation*, 9 ARBITRATION INTERNATIONAL (No. 2) 197 (1993).

entered into a contract with two other contractors, Siemens and Dutco. This consortium contract provided that all disputes would be finally settled by three arbitrators appointed under the I.C.C. Arbitration Rules.[163] When a dispute arose among the partners, Dutco brought an arbitration against Siemens and BKMI.

The I.C.C. provided that there would be one arbitrator for the plaintiff and one for the defendants. This meant that either the two defendants had to agree on their joint arbitrator, or else the I.C.C. would select an arbitrator for them both. Siemens and BKMI protested. Understandably, each party wanted to maximize its chances of success through nomination of an arbitrator whose doctrinal and procedural predispositions were sympathetic to that party's own particular arguments. In this respect, each defendant wanted the same opportunity as the plaintiff. Challenged in court, the I.C.C. practice was upheld by the Paris *Cour d'Appel*.

The *Cour de Cassation* held that the I.C.C. practice violated the principle of "equality of the parties," which the Court held to be a matter of non-waivable public policy (*ordre public*). Moreover, the Court found this inequality of treatment to violate Article 1502 (2) of the *Nouveau code de procédure civile*, which provides for the setting aside of an award in cases where the arbitral tribunal was irregularly constituted.[164]

## Notes and Questions

1. One might envisage several responses to the problem of appointment of an arbitrator in situations such as the one in the case above. The first, of course, would be for the parties to provide specifically in the arbitration agreement that the I.C.C. would be authorized to appoint one arbitrator for multiple parties. Unfortunately, however, the *Cour de Cassation* explicitly closed this avenue of escape by declaring that since equality of treatment was a matter of *ordre public* (public policy), the parties could not exclude the principle by contract except after the dispute

---

[163] The I.C.C. Rules, of course, require disputes to be decided either by a sole arbitrator or a three-arbitrator panel. See Article 2.2.

[164] Article 1504 permits setting aside of awards rendered in France on grounds provided in Article 1502, one of which is that "le tribunal arbitral a été irrégulièrement composé."

had arisen.[165] This limitation on the parties' freedom of contract would also foreclose an amendment to the I.C.C. Rules which the parties could incorporate by reference into their agreement. However, one might contemplate a solution by which the I.C.C. appointed an arbitrator for the claimant as well as for the defendants. The inequality of which the defendants complained was their inability to nominate a sympathetic arbitrator as the claimants could do. However, if the I.C.C. were to deny both sides the opportunity to participate in the convening of the arbitral tribunal, then neither claimants nor defendants would be unduly favored or penalized.

2.    ADAM SAMUEL, JURISDICTIONAL PROBLEMS IN INTERNATIONAL COMMERCIAL ARBITRATION 106-17 (1989).

A great deal of concern has been caused, in recent years, by the number of arbitrations heard by different tribunals, in which the same or similar issues are raised, which could be more economically and fairly disposed of in a single set of proceedings. These arbitrations risk coming to contradictory results, which sometimes lead to the one participant in the business transaction, who was not responsible for the loss, paying for it and sometimes the other parties' costs as well.[166]

The consolidation issue arises in a number of different contexts. The simplest involves two or more "back-to-back" contracts on identical terms save the price. This typically concerns the sale and resale of goods, the chartering and sub-chartering of ships or aircraft or the reinsurance of an insurance risk. A breach of the contract at the top of the chain is almost invariably going to cause identical breaches down through it. The middle contracting parties will often function as

---

[165] Article 6 of the French Code civile prohibits contractual derogations of laws relating to ordre public.

[166] T. Stipanowich, Arbitration and the Multipartite Dispute: The Search for Workable Solutions, 72 Iowa L. Rev. 473 at p. 480 (1987). See, for an excellent example of this, *Heinrich Hanno & Co., B.I. v. Fairlight Shipping Co. Ltd. Hanse Schiftfahrtskontor G.m.b.H. v. Andre S.A. (The "Kostas A")* [1985] 1 Lloyd's Rep. 231, where the middle charterer in a chain was held liable to the shipowner and unable to recover against the sub-charterer with the result that it had to pay damages and the costs of both arbitrations for the simple reason that two slightly differently constituted tribunals hearing the arbitrations concurrently reached different conclusions on the construction of the identical charterparty terms: see also V.V. Veeder, *ibid.* and X. Tandeau de Marsac, *ibid.*

little more than "post-boxes" between the head and bottom contractor, simply passing various notifications up the chain.

A more complex situation is where one contracting party subcontracts out his obligations under the head-contract to another or, as is more often the case in the construction industry, a number of subcontractors, who may themselves sub-contract out parts of the work. When problems arise with such a project, there is likely to be a series of lawsuits in which the key issue will be broadly the same: was the relevant item properly installed and, if it was not, whose fault was it? Similar problems emerge with guarantees and other contracts which are conditional on performance or even non-performance. In fact, these types of contracts often simply increase by one the length of a string of law-suits.

There is usually relatively little difficulty in organizing the litigation of these types of disputes in municipal courts. The latter will invariably have a discretionary power to consolidate claims or join aspects of them in order to reduce time and the risk of inconsistent results as and when this is appropriate. There are three central features of this power. First, it can be imposed on a party against its will. Secondly, the identity and composition of the tribunal, which will hear the consolidated or joined proceedings, is not determined by the parties. Finally, the power to consolidate or join is often discretionary and can be used on a case-by-case basis to ensure an appropriate result. Not every dispute arising out of a multipartite transaction is suitable for multi-partite trial. (A classic example of proceedings which should not be joined is when one party has a secret which it has a legitimate reason for not wanting someone else in the contractual chain to discover.)

In these three differences between multi-partite court litigation and arbitration lies the source of the problem for the latter. As was seen in Chapter I, arbitration is widely thought to be based on the agreement of the parties. Neither the tribunal nor any of the parties can traditionally impose a solution which contravenes the terms of the arbitral agreement, on another participant in the arbitration against the latter's will. In addition, if every party in a multi-partite arbitration retains his right to appoint an arbitrator, panels can be enormous and the costs will mount correspondingly. In a complex transaction, reducing this right may leave one of the contractors feeling that his background or point of view is not represented on the tribunal unlike that of his opponents. Lastly, the discretionary nature of the court's power to consolidate, while probably not incapable of duplication in the arbitral field, requires extraordinarily flexible draftsmanship of the arbitral clause that will rarely be practicable. It is clear that a clause, which joins wholly unconnected disputes involving different parties into the same arbitral arena, serves little useful purpose.

A number of ways have been suggested to resolve the problem of multiple arbitrations in which the same issues are litigated. These will be examined under three broad headings: the rule of law approach, which basically treats the arbitration as being the same as a court proceeding and imposes on it the court rules relating to consolidation and joinder; the second, as a matter of municipal law, implies a term, into all arbitral agreements governed by its country's law, that the parties to the agreement will submit to consolidation or joinder in accordance with the rules for court litigation: and finally, the draftsmanship solution which places the onus on the parties and arbitral institutions to incorporate consolidation provisions into their arbitration agreements and rules respectively.

**The rule of law approach**

In broad terms, the "rule of law" approach can be seen as representing the attempts by the United States courts and the legislatures of certain US states and Hong Kong to fashion a rule of law permitting the courts to consolidate arbitrations in the absence of any agreement to this effect by the parties. There are a number of state laws permitting courts to join arbitrations which make no reference to the parties' agreement.[167] On a similar basis, the New York Court of Appeals[168] and the United States Court of Appeals for the Second Circuit[169] have held (probably erroneously) that the consolidation provisions of the US Federal Rules of Civil Procedure apply to

---

[167] California Code of Civil Procedure, § 1281.3; Massachusetts Ann. Laws, 251 §2A; see T. Stipanowich, *supra* n. [161] at 519-521.

[168] *Vigo Steamship Corp. v. Marship Corp. of Monrovia*, 257 N.E.2d 624 (1970).

[169] *Compania Espanola de Petroleos S.A. v. Nereus Shipping S.A.*, *supra* n. [170]. See H. Miller, *infra* n. [174] at 63 and *Weyerhaeuser Company v. Western Seas Shipping Co.*, 743 F.2d 635 (1984) for a critical view of this development. See also T. Stipanowich, *supra* n. [166] at 510-511.

arbitrations governed by the Federal Arbitration Act 1925. In a further development, some US courts have implied agreements to permit third parties to participate in arbitral proceedings in situations where such an implication is some way from being necessary to give the contract business efficacy and the U.S. Court Appeals for the First Circuit has ordered consolidation in a Federal Arbitration Act case on the basis of a state statute.[170]

Acting on a recommendation, contained in the English Commercial Court Committee Report of 1978, Hong Kong added a section to their Arbitration Ordinance which permits the courts to consolidate arbitrations even where the parties have not agreed to this course. Section 6B of the Ordinance provides as follows:

(1)     Where in relation to two or more arbitration proceedings, it appears to the court

(a)     that some common question of law or fact arises in both or all of them, or

(b)     that the rights to relief claimed therein are in respect of or arise out of the same transaction or series of transactions, or,

(c)     that for some other reason it is desirable to make an order under this section,

the Court may order those arbitration proceedings to be consolidated on such terms as it thinks just or may order all of them to be heard at the same time, or one immediately after the other, or may order any of them to be stayed until after the determination of any other of them.

(2)     Where the court orders arbitration proceedings to be consolidated under subsection (1) and all parties to the consolidated arbitration proceedings are in agreement as to

---

[170] See, for example, *Long Branch Sewerage Authority v. Molnar Electrical Contractors*, 363 A.2d 917 (NJ Super.1974); *Gavlik Construction Co. v. H.F. Campbell Co.*, 526 F.2d 777 (1975); T. Stipanowich, *supra* n. [166] at 498-500. For the application of the Massachusetts consolidation statute, see *New England Energy, Inc. v. Keystone Shipping Company*, 855 F.2d 1 (1988).

choice of arbitrator or umpire for those proceedings, the same shall be appointed by the Court but if all parties cannot agree the Court shall have power to appoint an arbitrator or umpire for those proceedings.

(3)     Where the Court makes an appointment under subsection (2) of an arbitrator or umpire for consolidated arbitration proceedings, any appointment of any other arbitrator or umpire that has been made for any of the arbitration proceedings forming part of the consolidation shall for all purposes cease to have effect on and from the appointment under subsection (2).

What is of particular interest here is that unlike the probable US federal (but not state law) position, this provision appears to apply even where the parties have expressly agreed to exclude its application. However, assuming that the Hong Kong Courts continue to apply the principles of English law in the arbitration field, it seems most unlikely that the courts will exercise their powers under Section 6B where the parties have expressly agreed to exclude its application.

**The implied term approach**

Article 1046 of the Dutch Burgerlijke Rechtsvordering, added in the 1986 arbitration law reform, gives the President of the Amsterdam Arrondissementsrechtbank the power to join arbitrations whose subject-matter is connected unless the parties have agreed otherwise. Article 1046 lays down a highly sophisticated series of rules that appear to cover most, if not all, of the problems in this area. It provides as follows:

"1.     If arbitral proceedings have been commenced before an arbitral tribunal in the Netherlands concerning a subject matter which is connected with the subject matter of arbitral proceedings commenced before another arbitral tribunal in the Netherlands, a party may request the President of the District Court in Amsterdam to order a consolidation of the proceedings, *unless the parties have agreed otherwise.*

2.     The President may grant the request wholly or partially or refuse the request, after he has given all parties and the arbitrators the opportunity of expressing their opinion. His

decision shall be communicated in writing to all parties and the arbitral tribunals involved.

3.      If the President orders consolidation in full, the parties shall jointly appoint the arbitrators in an uneven number and determine the rules which shall apply to the consolidated proceedings. If, within the period of time determined by the President, the parties have not reached agreement on the foregoing, the President shall, at the request of a party, appoint the arbitrator or arbitrators and, if necessary, determine the rules which shall apply to the consolidated proceedings. The President shall determine the remuneration for the work carried out so far by the arbitrators whose mandate is terminated by reason of the consolidation.

4.      If the President orders partial consolidation, he shall decide which disputes fall thereunder. The President shall, at the request of a party, appoint the arbitrator or arbitrators and determine which rules shall apply to the consolidated proceedings if, within the period of time determined by the President, the parties have not reached agreement thereon. In that event the arbitral tribunals before which the arbitrations have already commenced shall suspend those arbitrations. The award of the arbitral tribunal appointed for the consolidated arbitrations shall be communicated in writing to the other arbitral tribunals involved. Upon receipt of this award, these arbitral tribunals shall continue the arbitrations commenced before them and decide in accordance with the award rendered in the consolidated proceedings.

. . .

8.      An award rendered under the third or fourth paragraph shall be subject to appeal to a second arbitral instance of and to the extent that all parties involved in the consolidated proceedings have agreed to such appeal.[171]

---

[171] Translation from A.J. van den Berg, *Consolidated Arbitrations and the 1958 New York Arbitration Convention*, 2 ARB. INT'L 367, at 369 (1986). The emphasis has been added.

Apart from its comprehensiveness, Article 1046 has the undoubted merit of clearly indicating that its provisions will be excluded by the parties' agreement. In this sense, it differs from the Hong Kong Ordinance and the statutory and caselaw developments in the USA. One can now say categorically that agreements providing for arbitration in the Netherlands contain an implied term agreeing to court-ordered consolidation where the parties have not expressly stipulated otherwise. By indicating to those wishing to arbitrate in Holland the possibility of opting out of the system, Dutch law appears to overcome constitutional objections that may be raised in some countries based on the right not to be judged by a private individual against one's will. It similarly gives a party, who wishes to keep confidential information away from someone, who is not a party to the arbitral agreement, the opportunity to assure this.

### The "draftsmanship" solution

A number of lawyers have expressed disquiet over the imposition by municipal laws of court-ordered consolidation even where the arbitral agreement does not exclude such a course. Objections generally take three forms. First, this type of consolidation overrides the parties' agreement. Secondly, as a result of the first point, any resulting award may not be enforceable under the New York Convention. Finally, the purpose of arbitration is to keep cases out of the municipal courts. Court-ordered consolidation has the opposite effect and exposes the parties to the vagaries and delays inherent in each country's legal system. Each of these points will be looked at in turn before we come to consider the "draftsmanship" alternative.

The most commonly-found argument against consolidation in the absence of express agreement to this effect by the parties, is that the court, in such a case, is rewriting the relevant arbitral agreements. The appointment provisions will almost invariably have to be redrafted by the court wherever some form of joinder is permitted. Since the parties' agreement is treated by many as being the source of arbitration's legitimacy, such a step is regarded as unacceptable. In the case of some of the statutory enactments in the USA and Hong Kong, it is not entirely clear that their strict wording will yield to an expressed intention not to permit consolidation.

Based on the violence almost inevitably done by the court consolidating arbitrations to the words of the arbitral agreement, concern has been expressed as to the enforceability of awards resulting from such a process, on the basis of Article V(1)(d) of the New York Convention:

> "Recognition and enforcement of the award may be refused, at the request of the party against whom it is invoked, only if that party furnishes . . . proof that: . . .
>
>     (d)  The composition of the arbitral authority, or the arbitral procedure was not in accordance with the agreement of the parties. . ."

At least, where tampering with the appointment mechanism is concerned, it seems reasonably clear that the composition of the arbitral authority is "not in accordance with the agreement of the parties. . . ."

.     .     .

At a positive level, the draftsmanship approach provides two options. First, it is possible to draft a multi-partite clause providing for the participation of all the relevant parties. A number of such precedents already exist. Where not all these entities can be persuaded to sign one such agreement, a chain can be established whereby all the parties agree to arbitrate disputes with members of the chain. The fundamental objection to all this is that while the multi-partite clause is draftable, it is extremely cumbersome and often uneconomic to negotiate. In areas of trade where business has to be conducted quickly because profit margins are relatively slight, the multi-partite clause is often a waste of money to prepare. The occasional rather clumsy arbitration is the price to be paid for the profit made under these contracts. In fact, in some fields, one can say that economic efficiency is diminished by the time taken up preparing joinder clauses which would be better spent in more productive activities.

.     .     .

## Conclusion

There is little doubt that substantial savings in costs and an improvement in the quality of arbitral justice can be achieved by some process through which a third party can order consolidation or the linking of arbitral proceedings when this is appropriate. Experience has shown that it is impractical to leave the creation of such devices entirely up to the parties. A change in the rules of the various arbitral institutions to permit joinder or consolidating to be ordered by the institution in suitable cases would certainly be a step forward. In the final analysis, though, municipal court intervention is probably necessary to cope with the vast numbers of ad hoc arbitrations. A provision for court-ordered consolidation on the lines of that contained in the Dutch Burgerlijke Rechtsvordering, which would permit the parties to contract out of the system, seems to be the best solution. Consolidation or joinder can, in this way, be put out of the question if the participants in the arbitrations concerned so wish, which probably will ensure that any resulting award or awards will be enforceable under the New York Convention, although this last point remains a source of concern.

### Notes and Questions

1. Discuss the possibilities — and difficulties — of a national statutory solution to the multi-party problem.

2. For an institutional approach to the question of multi-party arbitration, see ICC GUIDE ON MULTI-PARTY ARBITRATION, PUB. NO. 404 (1982).

### E.    MAY THE AGREEMENT TO ARBITRATE BE APPLIED TO NON-SIGNATORY RELATED PARTIES?

Arbitration is a consensual process. Normally no entity may be compelled to arbitrate if he, she, or the organization has not signed an arbitration agreement. Suppose, however, that a multinational corporate group decides to "park" a contract in a particular subsidiary for the purpose of limiting potential liability if things should go wrong. Courts faced with an award in excess of the assets of the signatory subsidiary will have to deal with the question of when a parent or sister company should answer for the debts of the award debtor. When asked to pierce the corporate veil, courts look, *inter alia*, to factors such as undercapitalization of the signatory company and inter-mixture of management.

The question of respect for the corporate veil may also be raised at the outset of an arbitration when one party seeks to join a non-signatory company related by common ownership to the adverse party. The goal of such a move is often to bind the deep pocket for purposes of making the award enforceable at a later time. A number of justifications for binding non-signatories may be put forward, including agency theory and the parties' expectations. Not surprisingly, approaches taken by judges and arbitrators differ in certain key respects.

## 1.    ARBITRAL ATTITUDES

Joining a non-signatory raises initial jurisdictional questions, as illustrated in the following case.

*Dow Chemical France et al. v. Istover-Saint Gobain*, 110 J. DU DROIT INT'L 899 (1983).

In 1965, Dow Chemical, a multinational corporate group, licensed Istover-St. Gobain to sell its products in France. Only Dow Chemical International S.A., a predecessor of Dow Chemical A.G. of Zurich, signed the contract for the licensors. A similar contract was entered into three years later between Dow Chemical (Europe) S.A., a subsidiary of Dow Chemical A.G. of Zurich. Both contracts contained clauses requiring all disputes arising out of the distributorships to be settled by arbitration in Paris under the I.C.C. Rules. French law was applicable to the merits of the dispute.

In 1981, Dow Chemical Company, the U.S. parent company, Dow Chemical France and Dow Chemical A.G. of Zurich, two of its subsidiaries, and Dow Chemical (Europe) S.A., the Zurich corporation's subsidiary all filed a claim for breach of contract against Istover-St. Gobain with the I.C.C. in Paris. Istover-St. Gobain asked the arbitral tribunal to declare itself to be without jurisdiction to hear claims brought by Dow Chemical Company, the U.S. parent company, and Dow Chemical France, neither of whom has signed any of the contracts. It claimed at the same time that Dow Chemical A.G. of Zurich and Dow Chemical (Europe) S.A., who were undoubtedly parties to one or other of the agreements, had suffered no loss from any breach of contract by them.

The arbitral tribunal ruled that it did have jurisdiction over all the claimants, applying trade usages insofar as they were compatible with French international public policy. Its decision was upheld by the Paris Cour d'appel (1984 *Rev. Arb.* 98).

The arbitrators began by observing that the two contracts had named expressly a predecessor to Dow Chemical France as the source of supplies while nevertheless allowing any other member of the Dow group perform this function. They then considered the negotiations leading up to the 1968 agreement. The early part of these had been conducted mainly by the French subsidiary on the basis that the contract would be concluded with them. In the final stages, the Zurich corporations became further involved and the two sections of the Dow group negotiated as a team. During that time, neither side attached any importance to the precise identity of the parties. The point never seems to have been discussed.

The focus then shifted to the performance of the contract. The French subsidiary had in fact provided all the merchandise under both contracts, set the resale prices and performed Dow's other obligations under the agreements although under these, it could have been done by any member of the group. The tribunal relied on this last point to show that the parent company played the role of pivot in the whole arrangement. The distributors would also have had to use the U.S. corporation's trademarks in selling the merchandise. Finally, the fact that Dow's communication of its ending of the contract had been made by Dow Chemical France was relied upon as showing their key role in the contractual arrangements.

To conclude their analysis, the arbitral tribunal stated that Dow Chemical Company, the U.S. parent, exercised total control over the Dow group which was in fact a single economic entity. Consequently, the parent and any corporation, such as Dow Chemical France, that had played a major role in negotiating and performing the distributorship would along with any subsidiary that had signed the contract be held to be party to the agreement to arbitrate in the absence of any indication that Istover-St. Gobain would have objected to this at the time the agreements were entered into.

### Notes and Questions

1. *See also* ICC Case 2138, 102 J. DU DROIT INT'L 934 (1975); ICC Case 2375, 103 J. DU DROIT INT'L 973 (1976); ICC Case 1434, 103 J. DU DROIT INT'L

978 (1976); W. LAURENCE CRAIG ET AL., INTERNATIONAL CHAMBER OF COMMERCE ARBITRATION, §§5.09-5.10 (2d. ed. 1990); Serge Gravel & Patricia Peterson, *French Law and Arbitration Clauses — Distinguishing Scope from Validity: Comment on I.C.C. Case No. 6519 Final Award*, 37 McGILL L. J. 510 (1992).

2. Compare the above materials with Chapter 6, Part III.C., pp. 680-90.

## 2.    JUDICIAL APPROACHES

The following cases illustrate approaches that French, Swiss and United States courts have taken in situations where they have been asked to enforce arbitration agreements against non-signatories or doubtful signatories, whether before or after arbitrators decided to determine this aspect of their competence. What factors, including the procedural posture in which the issue is presented, affected the courts in deciding who the proper parties were to the arbitration?

a.    *Southern Pac. Properties Ltd. v. Arab Republic of Egypt,* 26 I.L.M. 1004 (Court of Cassation, France, 1987).

[The Court of Cassation was called upon to decide whether the Paris Court of Appeal had erred when it set aside an ICC award rendered against the Arab Republic of Egypt (the "ARE") arising out of the ARE's cancellation of a tourism and hotel development project undertaken by Southern Pacific Properties ("SPP") and its subsidiary, SPP (Middle East) Ltd. ("SPP(ME)"). At issue was whether the ARE had agreed to arbitrate and was subject to arbitral jurisdiction. SPP had entered into a "Heads of Agreement" on September 23, 1974 concerning the project which was to be developed by a joint venture company to be owned 60% by the SPP group and 40% by the Egyptian Government Organization for Tourism and Hotels ("EGOTH"). For the Egyptian parties the Heads of Agreement was signed by Mr. Ibrahim Naguib, the Minister of Tourism, representing the ARE, and by General Ahmed Zaki, representing EGOTH. On December 12, 1974 a more detailed agreement concerning the project and supplementing the Heads of Agreement was entered into entitled "Agreement for the Development of Two International Destination Projects in Egypt (the Pyramids and Ras-El-Hekma Area)". As to this agreement the Arbitral Tribunal had found: "At the commencement of this Agreement it is described as being one between EGOTH, represented by Mr. Ahmed Zaki, Chairman of the Board, and SPP, represented by Mr. David

Gilmour. On the last page of the Agreement, however, following the signature of General Zaki and Mr. Gilmour on behalf of EGOTH and SPP respectively, there followed the words 'approved, agreed and ratified by the Minister of Tourism, His Excellency Mr. Ibrahim Naguib on the 12th day of December 1974'. Against these typed words there was the signature of Mr. Naguib and an official stamp." (Award, para.14) The December 12, 1974 Agreement contained an arbitration clause providing for ICC arbitration. The September 23, 1974 Heads of Agreement had no arbitration clause. Both agreements were subject to Egyptian Law No. 43 of 1974 regulating foreign investment. Upon termination of the project in 1978 by Presidential decree SPP and SPP (ME) brought ICC arbitration proceedings against the ARE and EGOTH. The arbitrators rejected the ARE's objection to their jurisdiction and condemned it to pay to SPP (ME) the sum of $ 12,500,000 as damages.

The ARE's request for annulment to the Paris Court of Appeal was based on violation of Article 1502 of the French New Code of Civil Procedure which provides for judicial recourse in the event that the arbitral tribunal has decided "in the absence of an arbitration agreement or on the basis of a void or expired agreement". The Court of Appeal had found that the Arab Republic of Egypt was not a party to an agreement containing an arbitration clause, had not agreed subsequently to arbitrate by signing the terms of reference, and was not bound to arbitrate by the agreement of EGOTH, alleged to be its agent or instrumentality. *SPP (Middle East) Ltd. & Southern Pac. Properties Ltd. v. Arab Republic of Egypt*, 23 I.L.M 1048 (Court of Appeals, Paris 1984) (note by Emmanuel Gaillard). Comments on the case are found in Alan Redfern, *Jurisdiction Denied: the Pyramid Collapses*, 1986 J. Bus. L., Jan., 1986 at p. 15; Seppala, *The Pyramids of Egypt Case* 2 Int'l Construction L. Rev. 180 (1985).

The Court of Appeal specifically found that it was to make an independent investigation of the grounds existing to sustain arbitral jurisdiction and found "whereas if the arbitrators, whose jurisdiction is challenged, have the power to rule on the existence or validity of the arbitration agreement, it is no less certain that their ruling is subject to review by the Judge competent to set aside the award . . . ." In the exercise of its power of independent review the Court of Appeal rejected the arbitrators' reasoning that the signature of the agreement by the Minister of Tourism could only be explained as the acceptance by the Minister for the State to becoming a party to the agreement, finding instead that the action simply represented his approval of EGOTH's entering into the agreement, an exercise of his Ministerial powers of supervision or "autorité de tutelle" as known in French law. The Court of Appeal likewise refused to give any weight to the arbitrators conclusions based on the testimony of a representative of SPP as to the circumstances of the signature of the contract, finding that such statements constituted "unsatisfactory evidence." The Cour de Cassation, France's highest court, dismissed a challenge to the Court of Appeal decision in the opinion set forth below.]

.    .    .

Whereas the Court of Appeals, seized with a recourse in annulment pursuant to Article 1504 of the New Code of Civil Procedure, in conjunction with Article 1502(1) of the same Code, and holding that the award had been rendered without the consent of the Arab Republic of Egypt, set aside the award.

On the first ground:

Whereas SPP and SPP(ME) contend that the Court of Appeals, having been seized of a recourse in annulment based on the absence of an arbitration clause, could only examine a flagrant violation or distortion of this agreement, the arbitral jurisdiction remaining solely competent to construe the arbitration agreement, and that the Court of Appeals could not reopen this construction in order to determine itself whether the decision had been rendered outside the scope of an arbitration agreement;

But, whereas, if the role of the Court of Appeals, seized by virtue of Articles 1502 and 1504 of the New Code of Civil Procedure, is limited to the examination of the grounds listed in these provisions, there is no restriction upon the power of the court to examine, as a matter o flaw and in consideration of the circumstances of the case, elements pertinent to the grounds in question; and that in particular, it is for the court to construe the contract in order to determine itself whether the arbitrator ruled in the absence of an arbitration clause; that this ground is not well founded;

On the second ground, split into two parts:

Whereas it is claimed that the Court of Appeals failed to apply the clear provision of the terms of reference, pursuant to which, according to this ground, the Republic of Egypt did not challenge the arbitration until the final award, which would mean that it did not wish to reopen the decision of the arbitrators on their own competence, and the Court failed to respond to the claim that the terms of reference constituted an agreement on jurisdiction, and not on the merits;

But whereas the Court of Appeals, in answer to this claim, had correctly ruled on the one hand that the arbitration agreement could only result from the arbitration clause inserted in the contract of December 12, 1974, and not from the terms of reference whose object was only to define the questions subject to litigation and, on the other hand, that the terms of reference, whereby the Republic of Egypt insisted that there was no agreement to arbitrate, cannot take the place of an arbitration agreement; thus, neither of the arguments can be justified.

On the third ground:

Whereas the two corporations also claim that the Court of Appeals, by refusing to consider that a signature of the Egyptian Minister of Tourism preceded by the words "approved, agreed and ratified" in the contract of December 12, 1974, constituted a commitment by the Egyptian state, and failed to draw the legal consequences of such signature according to the principles and usages of international commerce;

But, whereas it is not the duty of the Court of Cassation to control the existence and application of the principles and usages of international commerce; that this ground cannot thus be considered;

And on the fourth ground, split into two parts:

Whereas the appellate brief finally argues that the Court of Appeals did not seek to determine whether, in the same contract of December 12, 1974, EGOTH assuming that it enjoyed an autonomous juridical personality, had not acted on behalf of the Egyptian State, which would constitute both a violation of the contract that used the word "ratified" and a failure to respond to this ground;

But, whereas the excerpts from this brief do not support clearly the arguments presented today to the Court of Cassation and did not call for a ruling on the alleged intent to represent the Egyptian state; that the ambiguity of the terms preceding the signature of the Minister called for al interpretation, which the Court of Appeals gave in ruling that it only involved the intervention of a supervisory authority; that, therefore, neither this ground nor any of its parts can be accepted.

### Notes and Questions

1. Having failed to obtain arbitral jurisdiction over Egypt based on the ICC clause in the contract with EGOTH, SPP and SPP(ME) subsequently brought arbitration against the ARE under the rules of the International Centre for the Settlement of Disputes established under the 1966 Washington Convention on the Settlement of Disputes between States and Nationals of Other States. (For a description of the ICSID regime, see Chapter 2.) Both Egypt and the United Kingdom (which had extended the application of the Washington Convention to its colony, Hong Kong) were signatories of the Convention. Article 25 of the Convention provides that ICSID arbitral jurisdiction extends to investment disputes "which the parties to the dispute consent in writing to submit to the Centre." Claimants alleged that Egypt had consented in advance to ICSID arbitration of all disputes concerning investments authorized pursuant to its foreign investment legislation, Law No. 43 of 1974, which provided for dispute resolution "within the framework of the Convention for Settlement of Investment Disputes between the State and Nationals of other countries . . . ." The ICSID Tribunal agreed that it had jurisdiction over the dispute by virtue of the ARE's foreign investment law. *See* decision of April 14, 1988, *reported in* 16 YEARBOOK OF COMMERCIAL ARBITRATION 16 (1991). An award on the merits in favor of SPP and SPP(ME) was rendered on May 20, 1992, awarding Claimants indemnification in the amount of US$ 27.6 million. *See* 8 MEALEY'S INT'L ARB. REP. A-1 to A-68 (August, 1993). The ARE filed a request for annulment under the ICSID Rules, but prior to a decision on their request a negotiated settlement intervened. *Id.* No. 1, pp. 3-4 (January, 1993). *See generally* Georges Delaume, *L'Affaire du Plateau des Pyramides et le CIRDI: Considerations sur le Droit Applicable*, 1994 REVUE DE L'ARBITRAGE 39.

2. For discussion of the problem of "non-signatories" in arbitration proceedings, as seen through the eyes of arbitrators rather than judges, see Chapter 6, Part III.C, pp. 680-90.

3. Compare the way that United States courts have dealt with intertwined litigation and arbitration among related parties.

b.    *Dale Metals Corp. v. Kiwa Chem. Indus. Co.*, 442 F.Supp. 78 (S.D.N.Y. 1977).

LASKER, District Judge.

[Toyo Menka Kaisha, Ltd. ("TMK") sought a stay of this action, pending completion of the arbitration proceeding that has been commenced in Japan, in which TMK sued Overseas Development Corporation ("ODC") for moneys due under the sales agreement that underlies this case. Dale Metals Corp. ("Dale") and its principal shareholder and affiliate, ODC, claimed to have been fraudulently induced to distribute Kiwalite, a reflective sheeting material used for the construction of highway signs, manufactured by Kiwa Chemical Industry Co., Ltd. ("Kiwa"). They further claimed that after they embarked on the distribution plan, TMK, Kiwa and two other companies (Sakai Trading Co., Inc. and Sakai Trading New York, Inc.) conspired to wrest the United States toehold created by Dale Metals and to appropriate the established paths of distribution so that the two Sakai companies could act as the American distributors of Kiwa products.]

.    .    .

. . . TMK asks, as an alternative to dismissing this case, that the court stay this case pending arbitration. As discussed above, TMK and ODC are parties to an arbitration that has already commenced in Japan, where TMK seeks payment for goods that were delivered under the confirmations of sale. Plaintiffs' opposition to the stay is based on the fact that several of the parties to this action are not subject to the arbitration clause or to the proceeding.

From the papers submitted, it is apparent that the charges against TMK and Kiwa are identical and that the harm alleged to have been suffered by ODC and Dale is also identical. Furthermore, all the defendants are claimed to share responsibility for the wrongdoings allegedly committed by the Sakai companies. In short, it is fair to say that in an arbitration proceeding between TMK and ODC, every issue that is raised here will be vigorously pressed. In such circumstances a stay is appropriate even though it affects parties who are not bound to arbitrate. *Lawson Fabrics, Inc. v. Akzona, Inc.*, 355 F.Supp. 1146, 1151 (S.D.N.Y.), *aff'd* 486 F.2d 1394 (2d Cir.1973). In *Lawson*, the plaintiffs commenced an arbitration proceeding alleging delivery of sub-standard goods and non-payment. Subsequently, the plaintiffs commenced a federal action, naming the arbitration defendant and an additional party as defendants. In reaching the decision to stay the federal proceedings, despite the presence of a "new" party who was a stranger to the arbitration, the court emphasized that, as is true in the instant case, the claims before it and the arbitrators were substantially similar:

> ". . . The claims against Akzona [the stranger to the arbitration] basically involve the allegation that it conspired with and encouraged Blanchard to deliver improper, mislabelled goods in order to defraud Lawson. The decision of the arbitration as to whether, in fact, Lawson has been defrauded will inevitably decide whether non-conforming and mislabelled goods were delivered, and thus will at least partially determine the issues which form the basis of the claim against Akzona. . . .

> "Since the arbitration proceedings are in progress, it cannot be argued that there is likely to be an unreasonable delay of this Federal action . . ." 355 F.Supp. at 1151.

Finally, the court noted that refusal to stay the federal action would thwart the pronounced federal policy in favor of arbitration. The reasoning of the court in *Lawson Fabrics, Inc.*, is applicable to the case before this court and is persuasive.

The motion to remand is denied. The motion to stay is granted on condition that all defendants agree in writing within thirty days to submit to the pending arbitration proceeding and to be bound by any award granted by the arbitrators and to allow Dale to participate as a party in the arbitration if it wishes. In the event defendants do not accept the conditions stated, the motion to stay will be denied upon further application.

## Notes and Questions

1. In *Dale Metals*, Judge Lasker's decision is influenced by concerns for judicial economy and respect for forum selection. Does he take adequate account of the interest in effective arbitration? Discuss.

2. In 1975, Egypt, United Arab Emirates, Saudi Arabia and Qatar set up by treaty the Arab Organization for Industrialization (AOI) to build a unified Arab arms industry. The charter of AOI gave AOI complete legal personality and a share capital of $1 billion. In 1978, AOI and Westland Helicopters, Ltd. (WHL) entered into a contract (the "shareholders agreement") to buy respectively 70% and 30% of an Egyptian company called the Arab British Helicopter Company (ABH) which would construct WHL helicopters in Egypt. WHL also concluded a joint-venture agreement with ABH to build helicopters. Both contracts provided for the arbitration of any disputes in Geneva under the ICC Rules. The contract was governed by Swiss law. This was one of similar agreements made by AOI and companies in the arms trade from all over the world.

In response to Egypt's 1979 peace treaty with Israel, the Saudi Government announced that the three other states were terminating the existence of AOI as of July 19, 1979 and that a liquidation committee would be set up. The next day Egypt passed a law nationalizing AOI turning it into an Egyptian company. It announced that this Egyptian AOI (EAOI) would fulfill AOI's obligations. Many of AOI's business partners agreed to continue to perform the engagements entered into with AOI with EAOI. The following year WHL, having decided not to continue performing its AOI agreement with EAOI, declared the contract to have been discharged by breach and commenced an ICC arbitration against the four Arab states, ABH, and AOI.

The jurisdictional issues were complex. Egypt claimed that it was not a party to the arbitral agreement with WHL and, therefore, that the arbitral tribunal had no jurisdiction over it. WHL claimed that EAOI was not a party to the arbitration. The state of Egypt wished to escape the arbitration to avoid paying WHL any money. To complicate matters, however, EAOI (in effect Egypt under a separate corporate form with no substantial assets) wanted to be a party to the arbitration, since if it could prove it was a party to the 1978 WHL shareholder agreement, it could obtain damages from WHL for the latter's breach of contract. Switzerland's highest court, the Federal Tribunal,[172] reasoned as follows:

> The strict control of a legal entity by the State or the close relationship between that entity and the State is not sufficiently pertinent to overcome the presumption that, when the State has not signed the arbitration clause, the entity which signed it should be regarded as the sole party to the arbitration [referring to *Wetco*].

---

[172] *République arabe d'Egypte et al. v. Westland Helicopters Ltd.*, 28 I.L.M. 687 (1989). Excerpts from decision of the Swiss Federal Tribunal translated by Georges R. Delaume.

In order to accept that the State and the entity are effectively a single entity, it must be shown that the constituent law of that entity might be objectively construed in this way; such is not the case . . . if the constituent law confers upon the entity the status of a national company having its own juridical personality; this consideration, combined with other provisions showing the autonomy of the company, points to the juridical independence of the company and supports the conclusion that can be drawn from the fact that the arbitration clause was not signed by the State [referring to *Wetco*].

If the State is not a party to the instrument containing the arbitration agreement, the approval of that instrument by a Minister—i.e. a representative of the State—is not sufficient to imply the intention of the State to be a party to that instrument and to waive its immunity from suit [referring to the decision of the Court of Appeal of Paris in the S.P.P. case].

When the law provides that public entities engaged in economic and commercial activities have juridical personality, and that such entities have autonomous organizations and separate budgets, and are subject to accounting methods and to taxes applicable to private enterprises, such entities unequivocally have juridical personalities and legal status separate from that of the State, and can, therefore, act in their own names and have their own assets [referring to the same decision].

Furthermore, solving the issue of the "separate juridical entity" is not a prerequisite to resolving a dispute which does not concern the personality of the entity but rather the question whether the State has or has not agreed to bind itself; suffice it to note that by letting the public entity alone subscribe to the agreement involved, the State has clearly intimated that it did not want to be a party to the arbitration agreement [referring to the same decision].

Taking into account the complete juridical independence resulting from the constituent instruments of AOI . . . the application of the aforesaid principles to the instant case leads to the following conclusion: by letting the AOI alone subscribe to the "Shareholders Agreement" with WHL, the founding States (which furthermore have expressly conferred upon AOI authority to sue and to determine with its partners the means to settle disputes) have manifestly shown that they did not want to be bound by the arbitration agreement.

3. Note the strategic and tactical calculations of "shareholders" in the *Westland Helicopters* case.

4. The "Cartier Finance" case illustrates the not uncommon setting in which the related-party problems may arise. In *Vendome Holding S.A., Cartier Munich G.m.b.H. v. Horowitz*,[173] the principal shareholder of the companies making up the Cartier group had, in November 1974, engaged Manfredo Horowitz to be the distributor of Cartier products everywhere except in North and South America and Israel. The contract said that Horowitz would be "entering into the service of the Cartier group in its entirety." The document was headed "Joailliers Paris Cartier" and the agreement was stated to have been concluded with the consent of the board of Cartier International B.V. of Amsterdam. The shareholder, Robert Hocq, purported to sign on behalf of "Cartier." The contract provided for arbitration of all disputes arising out of it. In June 1975, Cartier limited of Nassau agreed to pay Donatella Horowitz, Manfredo's wife, $10,000 a month with respect to expenses incurred as a result of her husband's work.

In January 1976, the distributorship was terminated and in August that year, Horowitz's lawyer notified Cartier S.A. of Paris of his intention to commence an arbitration against that corporation. The latter responded by stating that the contract bound Cartier B.V. and not the Paris corporation. Before the arbitral tribunal, Horowitz claimed damages and various other sums to be jointly and severally assessed against all the corporations in the Cartier group, certain payments allegedly due to his wife under the 1975 agreement and the validation of an attachment granted by the Tessin authorities against Cartier S.A. of Paris. The arbitral tribunal sitting in Geneva essentially accepted Horowitz's claims and ordered the "Cartier group" to pay him certain sums while validating the attachment. The nine companies alleged to be part of the group included Vêndome Holding (Luxembourg), Cartier Munich GmbH, Cartier S.A. of Geneva, Interdicia S.A. (Villars), Cartier Ltd. (Hong Kong), Cartier S.A. of Paris, Cartier International B.V. (Amsterdam) and Cartier Ltd. (Nassau). A cantonal Court rejected an application to set aside the award. Against this decision, the Cartier companies appealed to the Federal Tribunal (the highest court in Switzerland).

The court began by pointing out that there was no such legal entity as the Cartier group. In spite of Hocq's position controlling the group, there was no evidence that he was the agent of any of the corporations either generally or by virtue of a special instruction when the contract was made. Even the sole shareholder of a corporation does not have the power to act on behalf of the company if that power is exclusively entrusted to other people. There was no evidence that any member of the group apart form Cartier N.V. and Cartier S.A. were bound by the arbitral agreement under the applicable law. In the absence of any evidence that Hocq had been authorized to make contracts on these corporations' behalf, the Swiss Federal Tribunal annulled as "arbitrary" the Vaud court's decision refusing to set aside the award as against all but Cartier B.V. of Amsterdam and Cartier S.A. of Paris.

---

[173] *Vendome Holding S.A., Cartier Munich G.m.b.H. v. Horowitz*, 1981 JdT 61-127 (Swiss Federal Tribunal).

5. Cognate problems arose in *Builders Fed. (Hong Kong) v. Turner Constr.*, 655 F.Supp. 1400 (S.D.N.Y. 1987). Builders Federal (Hong Kong) Ltd. and Josef Gartner & Co. (a West German corporation) formed a joint venture in order to bid for certain subcontracting work for the construction of twin office buildings in Singapore in a project called "The Gateway." The Gateway's developer was Gateway Land Ltd. ("Gateway Land"), a Singapore corporation. The main contractor for the project was Turner (East Asia), Ltd. ("TEA"), a Singapore corporation and a wholly-owned subsidiary of Turner International Industries, Inc. Builders Federal and Gartner entered into a subcontract with TEA at Gateway Land's instructions. Both the main contract (between Gateway Land and TEA) and the subcontract (between TEA and Builders Federal/Gartner) provided for arbitration of all disputes in Singapore. In addition, clause XXII of the subcontract provided that:

> . . . if the dispute or difference between the Contractor and the Sub-Contractor is substantially the same as a matter which is a dispute or difference between the Contractor and the Employer under the Main Contract the Contractor and the Sub-Contractor hereby agree that such dispute or difference shall be referred to arbitration pursuant to the terms of the Main Contract.

TEA suspended and then terminated work on the project, which automatically suspended and then terminated work under all the subcontracts. TEA blamed Gateway Land for the termination. Gateway Land blamed TEA. Various litigation and arbitration proceedings commenced in Singapore. Builders Federal and Gartner moved to compel TEA to arbitrate claims arising out of the subcontract before an arbitrator in Singapore. TEA argued that these claims should be submitted to arbitration under the main contract. Builders Federal and Gartner also moved to compel TEA's collective corporate parents to arbitrate claims against TEA, contending that defendants should be regarded as the "alter egos" of TEA. The TEA corporate group moved to stay proceedings in the United States pending arbitration in Singapore. The Court held as follows:

.   .   .

> While the petition does not say so explicitly, plaintiffs' brief in opposition to defendants' motion to dismiss shows that plaintiffs ask this Court to direct defendants to arbitrate in Singapore.

.   .   .

> In a declaration accompanying its accession to the Convention, the United States limited the Convention's application "to differences arising out of legal relationships, whether contractual or not, which are considered as commercial under the national law of the United States." Notes following Convention printed at 9 U.S.C. §201 (West 1986) at 213. Within that limitation, which does not exclude the commercial contract at bar, Congress intended the broadest possible implementation of the

Convention. Thus the Act, in addition to setting up procedural and jurisdictional machinery for the Convention, also provides in §208 that Chapter 1 of the Act applies to proceedings brought under Chapter 2, to the extent that Chapter 1 is "not in conflict" with Chapter 2 or with the Convention as ratified by the United States.

.  .  .

Plaintiffs at bar are entitled to invoke section 4 of the Act, within the framework of the Convention, unless defendants demonstrate that section 4 is "inconsistent" with Article II(3) of the Convention. The defendants do not persuade me of this. In my view, a court of a Contracting State becomes "seized of an action" under the Convention when a party to a written arbitration agreement seeks to compel arbitration in accordance with any procedures available under the internal laws of the Contracting State where enforcement is sought.

Given the Supreme Court's repeated recognition of American public policy favoring arbitration, as embodied in the nation's adherence to and implementation of the Convention (Mitsubishi being only the most recent such declaration), I decline to be the first American judge to impose so significant a limitation upon the Convention's remedies.

.  .  .

In the alternative, defendants ask that proceedings in this Court be stayed pending completion of the arbitration proceedings in Singapore. I will grant that application, subject to the conditions set forth below. . . .

When the existence of any agreement obligating anyone to arbitrate anywhere is at issue, then by definition the section 4 trial must precede the arbitration.[174] But that is not necessarily so when an arbitration agreement concededly exists, undisputedly binding named parties to arbitrate, and the section 4 petitioner claims that non-signatories to the contract are also bound to arbitrate. In those circumstances an arbitration will in any event take place between the named parties to the contract. If the prevailing party's award is not satisfied by the other party, the prevailing party may

---

[174] 9 U.S.C. §4 provides that:

If the making of the arbitration agreement or the failure, neglect, or refusal to perform the same be in issue, the court shall proceed summarily to the trial thereof.

subsequently proceed against the non-signatory, either as guarantor of the named party's obligations or on an alter ego theory. *Orion Shipping & Trading Co., Inc. v. Eastern States Petroleum Corporation of Panama, S.A.*, 312 F.2d 299, 301 (2d Cir. 1963). The precise holding in *Orion* is that a proceeding to confirm an award of arbitrators under section 9 of the Act, a limited proceeding, is "not the proper" time for the District Court to consider "piercing the corporate veil" of the parent. But the Second Circuit's more general holdings, to which I have just referred, prompted Judge Carter of this Court in *Cochin Refineries Ltd. v. Triton Shipping Inc.*, S.D.N.Y. 74 Civ. 216 (decided March 19, 1974), to stay a corporate veil piercing effort until resolution of the arbitration between the named parties.

. . .

In the case at bar, were I to "proceed summarily" at this time to the trial of plaintiffs' petition, it would have a disruptive effect upon the pending judicial and arbitral proceedings in Singapore, the agreed-upon situs of the arbitration. Plaintiffs' brief seeks to minimize that disruption, but it appears to me both real and significant. Plaintiffs' discovery demands in aid of its alter ego theory are far-reaching, in respect of both document production and answers to interrogatories. The taking of depositions of TEA and defendants' officers and employees cannot be far behind. I say this not in criticism of the litigation tactics of plaintiffs' counsel here, but in recognition that such litigation would in all likelihood disrupt and delay the rather stringent procedural deadlines imposed by Mr. Gardam, the Singapore arbitrator. In addition, the Singapore court is currently considering whether plaintiffs are required to submit their claims as part of the arbitration under the main contract, or are entitled to a separate arbitration against TEA. This Court's order, adding three additional corporate parties to the Singapore proceedings, would constitute an intrusive action against which comity counsels.

Quite apart from these considerations, resolution of the issues in the Singapore arbitration may well limit or narrow the issues here. That is a sufficient basis for this Court to exercise its inherent power "to control the disposition of the cases on its docket with economy of time and effort for itself, for counsel and for litigants."

. . .

The concerns this Court addressed in *Hidrocarburos, supra*, are alleviated by the present defendants' willingness, expressed through counsel, to waive any "due process" arguments arising out of their desired non-participation in the Singapore arbitration. I will exact that undertaking as a condition for a stay of these proceedings. Meaning no disrespect to counsel, the undertaking must take the form of corporate resolutions in proper form, given by each of the three corporate defendants. Those resolutions must set forth the defendants' agreements that if plaintiffs prevail on the merits of the petition at bar, defendants will regard themselves as bound by any award rendered in the Singapore arbitration against TEA, as to merits and quantum, precisely as if defendants had participated in that arbitration as parties from its inception. Counsel for defendants are directed to settle the text of such corporate resolutions on notice before they are executed.

6. In *SONATRACH v. General Tire & Rubber Co.*, 430 F.Supp. 1332 (S.D. N.Y. 1977),

[("SONATRACH") an Algerian corporation engaged in the production and marketing of the natural gas and petroleum resources of Algeria, hired the Chemical Construction Corporation ("Chemico") and Chemico (Africa) Incorporated ("Chemico (Africa)") to build a natural gas liquefaction plant in Algeria, for a total price of over $300,000,000. Their agreement provided for dispute resolution by a three member panel of arbitrators appointed under the rules of the ICC. Chemico, a New York corporation, and Chemico (Africa), a Nevada corporation, had their principal places of business in New York.

SONATRACH complained that Chemico's performance was not in accordance with an agreed upon time schedule. Chemico blamed the delays on Algerian suppliers and subcontractors selected by SONATRACH and on the rising cost of local labor. SONATRACH discovered that $15.5 million had been paid by Chemico to several third-parties as commissions for assistance in securing the award of the contract. SONATRACH complained that these monies, which were derived from contract payments, should have been applied to project costs. SONATRACH consequently initiated arbitration and commenced an action in Algiers to attach Chemico's assets.

In New York, SONATRACH commenced an action against Chemico and Chemico (Africa), as well as against two parties that were not party to the arbitration clause, General Tire and Rubber Company ("General Tire") and Aerojet-General Corporation ("Aerojet"), alleging *inter alia* that SONATRACH was fraudulently induced to enter into the contract in that it was unaware that commission payments would be made and that Aerojet and General Tire interfered with Chemico's performance under the contract. Chemico and Chemico (Africa) moved to stay the action pending the ICC arbitration. General Tire and Aerojet have joined in these motions. SONATRACH opposes the stay on the ground that the issues raised in this action are not properly part of the ICC arbitration.

The arbitration clause, translated from the original French, reads

*"ARTICLE 12 — SETTLEMENT OF DISPUTES*

The present contract shall be interpreted according to the legislation in effect in Algeria on the date of signature of the present contract. Any litigation *deriving from* the contract shall be equitably and definitively settled according to the rules of conciliation and arbitration of the International Chamber of Commerce by three arbiters, each of the parties selecting one arbiter; the third one shall be designated according to the rules and shall be a jurist. The arbiters shall meet in Lausanne (Switzerland) and the languages used shall be French or English, at the choice of each of the parties. They shall be bound by the terms of this contract.*"

(emphasis added).

In the French original, the italicized phrase appeared as *"découlant du,"* literally translated as "flowing from" and encompassing terms such as "deriving from," "arising out of," "proceeding from," and "springing from."

The court summarized its conclusions on the effect of the arbitration clause as follows:

Assuming *arguendo* that the fraud in the inducement claim is not properly within the scope of the phrase *"découlant du,"* there still would be no reason to deny a stay. The rationale for permitting a plenary action to proceed prior to arbitration is to allow for a judicial determination of the validity of the agreement to arbitrate. That policy will not be furthered by denying a stay of this action since the plaintiff has already chosen to rely on the arbitration clause by instituting the ICC proceeding prior to commencing this action. The factual assertions which plaintiff first sought to raise in arbitration are the same as the assertions which plaintiff now argues amount to fraud in the inducement and, inferentially, should bar arbitration. Having decided to proceed with the arbitration, the plaintiff cannot now insist on first litigating the validity of the clause.

The only hardship to SONATRACH in granting the stay is to thwart its use of the United States courts to obtain discovery in aid of the arbitration. To deny the stay would be to encourage baseless suits brought by foreign plaintiffs to gain advantage in foreign litigation.

The motion for a stay pending arbitration is granted. To insure that the parties are not prejudiced by an unreasonable delay in the arbitration, should the arbitration not be completed within six months, the plaintiff may move to vacate the stay].

7. Look again at the Massachusetts statute providing for consolidation of arbitrations and *New England Energy Inc. v. Keystone Shipping Co.*, 855 F.2d (1st Cir. 1988), *supra* notes 158-59 and accompanying text.

   a. To what extent does court-ordered consolidation infringe the consensual nature of arbitration? Is a consolidated procedure what the parties bargained for? Might a court at the place where a consolidated award is presented for enforcement refuse to recognize the award on the grounds (set forth in Article V(1)(c) of the New York Convention) that "the award deals with a difference not contemplated by or not falling within the terms of the submission to arbitration . . . or contain[ing] decisions on matters beyond the scope of the submission to arbitration."

   b. Do you see any difficulty in reconciling *New England Energy v. Keystone Shipping* and *Volt v. Stanford* (giving effect to state arbitration statues) with the result in *Southland Corp. v. Keating*, 465 U.S. 1 (1984)? When should state law on arbitration matters have to yield to federal law? How does one determine when state law is more restrictive than federal law?

8. Why are there not more arbitration cases related to international bank loans and other financial disputes? Could it have something to do with the traditional leverage exercised by lenders in imposing their home courts on foreign borrowers? Would an English bank rather have disputes with a Nigerian borrower decided by ICC arbitration in Geneva or by the High Court of London?

9. As a tactical matter, what procedures for securing an effective remedy would have been available to SPP after the decision of the Tribunal fédérale?

c.    *First Options of Chicago v. Manuel Kaplan et ux. and MK Investments, Inc.*, 115 S.Ct. 1920 (1995).

[A Pennsylvania corporation (MK Investments) that acted as a "market maker" in options on the Philadelphia Stock Exchange had entered into a debt restructuring arrangement with a clearinghouse (First Options) to cover losses incurred during the October 1987 stock market crash. The "workout" documents included a subordinated loan agreement signed by the corporation, which contained an arbitration clause, and a letter agreement signed by the company's owners (Manuel and Carol Kaplan), which did *not* contain an arbitration clause.

On non-payment of the loan, the clearinghouse sought arbitration not only against the corporation, but also against its owners. Ultimately the arbitral tribunal decided to pierce the corporate veil, and asserted its jurisdiction over the Kaplans themselves. On the merits of the dispute, the tribunal decided in favor of the clearinghouse in an award that was later confirmed by the Federal District Court. On appeal, however, the Third Circuit found insufficient evidence to pierce the corporate veil, and ordered the district court to vacate the award against the Kaplans. The Supreme Court affirmed.

The Supreme Court distinguished between the standard to be applied to the judicial review of an arbitrators decision on whether a dispute is subject to arbitration, and the arbitrators' decision on the substantive merits of the dispute. Justice Breyer delivered the opinion for a unanimous Court.]

.   .   .

The first question—the standard of review applied to an arbitrator's decision about arbitrability—is a narrow one. To understand just how narrow, consider three types of disagreement present in this case. First, the Kaplans and First Options disagree about whether the Kaplans are personally liable for MKI's debt to First Options. That disagreement makes up the *merits* of the dispute. Second, they disagree about whether they agreed to arbitrate the merits. That disagreement is about the *arbitrability* of the dispute. Third, they disagree about *who should have the primary power to decide the second matter*. Does that power belong primarily to the arbitrators (because the court reviews their arbitrability decision deferentially) or to the court (because the court makes up its mind about arbitrability independently)? We consider here only this third question.

Although the question is a narrow one, it has a certain practical importance. That is because a party who has not agreed to arbitrate will normally have a right to a court's decision about the merits of its dispute (say, as here, its obligation under a contract). But, where the party has agreed to arbitrate, he or she, in effect, has relinquished much of that right's practical value. The party still can ask a court to review the arbitrator's decision, but the court will set that decision aside only in very unusual circumstances. *See, e.g.*, 9 U.S.C. § 10 (award procured by corruption, fraud, or undue means; arbitrator exceeded his powers); *Wilko v. Swan*, 346 U.S. 427, 436-437, 74 S.Ct.

182, 187-188, 98 L.Ed. 168 (1953) (parties bound by arbitrator's decision not in "manifest disregard" of the law), overruled on other grounds, *Rodriguez de Quijas v. Shearson/American Express, Inc.*, 490 U.S. 477, 109 S.Ct. 1917, 104 L.Ed.2d 526 (1989). Hence, who—court or arbitrator—has the primary authority to decide whether a party has agreed to arbitrate can make a critical difference to a party resisting arbitration.

We believe the answer to the "who" question (*i.e.*, the standard-of-review question) is fairly simple. Just as the arbitrability of the merits of a dispute depends upon whether the parties agreed to arbitrate that dispute, see, *e.g.*, *Mastrobuono v. Shearson Lehman Hutton, Inc.*, 514 U.S. __, __, 115 S.Ct. 1212, 1216, 131 L.Ed.2d 76 (1995); *Mitsubishi Motors Corp. v. Soler Chrysler-Plymouth, Inc.*, 473 U.S. 614, 626, 105 S.Ct. 3346, 3353, 87 L.Ed.2d 444 (1985), so the question "who has the primary power to decide arbitrability" turns upon what the parties agreed about *that* matter. Did the parties agree to submit the arbitrability question itself to arbitration? If so, then the court's standard for reviewing the arbitrator's decision about *that* matter should not differ from the standard courts apply when they review any other matter that parties have agreed to arbitrate. See *AT & T Technologies, Inc. v. Communications Workers*, 475 U.S. 643, 649, 106 S.Ct. 1415, 1418, 89 L.Ed.2d 648 (1986) (parties may agree to arbitrate arbitrability); *Steelworkers v. Warrior & Gulf Navigation Co.*, 363 U.S. 574, 583, n. 7, 80 S.Ct. 1347, 1353, n. 7, 4 L.Ed.2d 1409 (1960) (same). That is to say, the court should give considerable leeway to the arbitrator, setting aside his or her decision only in certain narrow circumstances. See, *e.g.*, 9 U.S.C. § 10. If, on the other hand, the parties did *not* agree to submit the arbitrability question itself to arbitration, then the court should decide that question just as it would decide any other question that the parties did not submit to arbitration, namely independently. These two answers flow inexorably from the fact that arbitration is simply a matter of contract between the parties; it is a way to resolve those disputes—but only those disputes—that the parties have agreed to submit to arbitration. See, *e.g.*, *AT & T Technologies*, *supra*, at 649, 106 S.Ct., at 1418; *Mastrobuono*, *supra*, at __, and n. 9, 115 S.Ct., at 1216-1217, and n. 9; *Allied-Bruce Terminix Cos. v. Dobson*, 513 U.S. __, __, 115 S.Ct. 834, 837-838, 130 L.Ed.2d 753 (1995); *Mitsubishi Motors Corp.*, *supra*, at 625-626, 105 S.Ct., at 3353.

We agree with First Options, therefore, that a court must defer to an arbitrator's arbitrability decision when the parties submitted that matter to arbitration. Nevertheless, that conclusion does not help First Options win this case. That is because a fair and complete answer to the standard-of-review question requires a word about how a court should decide whether the parties have agreed to submit the arbitrability issue to arbitration. And, that word makes clear that the Kaplans did not agree to arbitrate arbitrability here.

When deciding whether the parties agreed to arbitrate a certain matter (including arbitrability), courts generally (though with a qualification we discuss below) should apply ordinary state-law principles that govern the formation of contracts. . . .

This Court, however, has (as we just said) added an important qualification, applicable when courts decide whether a party has agreed that arbitrators should decide arbitrability: Courts should not assume that the parties agreed to arbitrate arbitrability unless there is "clea[r] and unmistakabl[e]" evidence that they did so. *AT & T Technologies*, *supra*, at 649, 106 S.Ct., at 1418-1419; *see Warrior & Gulf*, *supra*, at 583, n. 7, 80 S.Ct., at 1353, n. 7. In this manner the law treats silence or ambiguity about the question "*who* (primarily) should decide arbitrability" differently from the way it treats silence or ambiguity about the question "*whether* a particular merits-related dispute is arbitrable because it is within the scope of a valid arbitration agreement"—for in respect to this latter question the law reverses the presumption. See *Mitsubishi Motors*, *supra*, at 626, 105 S.Ct., at 3353 ("'[A]ny doubts concerning the scope of arbitrable issues should be resolved in favor of arbitration'") (quoting *Moses H. Cone Memorial Hospital v. Mercury Constr. Corp.*, 460 U.S. 1, 24-25, 103 S.Ct. 927, 941, 74 L.Ed.2d 765 (1983)); *Warrior & Gulf*, *supra*, at 582-583, 80 S.Ct., at 1352-1353.

But, this difference in treatment is understandable. The latter question arises when the parties have a contract that provides for arbitration of some issues. In such circumstances, the parties likely gave at least some thought to the scope of arbitration. And, given the law's permissive policies in respect to arbitration, see, *e.g.*, *Mitsubishi Motors*, *supra*, at 626, 105 S.Ct., at 3353, one can understand why the law would insist upon clarity before concluding that the parties did *not* want to arbitrate a related matter. See Domke § 12.02, p. 156 (issues will be deemed arbitrable unless "it is clear that the arbitration clause has not included" them). On the other hand, the former question—the "who (primarily) should decide arbitrability" question—is rather arcane. A party often might not focus upon that question or upon the significance of having arbitrators decide the scope of their own powers. Cf. Cox, Reflections Upon Labor Arbitration, 72 Harv. L.Rev. 1482, 1508-1509 (1959), cited in *Warrior & Gulf*, 363 U.S., at 583, n. 7, 80 S.Ct., at 1353, n. 7. And, given the principle that a party can be forced to arbitrate only those issues it specifically has agreed to submit to arbitration, one can understand why courts might hesitate to interpret silence or ambiguity on the "who should decide arbitrability" point as giving the arbitrators that power, for doing so might too often force unwilling parties to arbitrate a matter they reasonably would have thought a judge, not an arbitrator, would decide. *Ibid.* See generally, *Dean Witter Reynolds Inc. v. Byrd*, 470 U.S. 213, 219-220, 105 S.Ct. 1238, 1241-1242, 84 L.Ed.2d 158 (1985) (Arbitrator Act's basic purpose is to "ensure judicial enforcement of privately made agreements to arbitrate").

On the record before us, First Options cannot show that the Kaplans clearly agreed to have the arbitrators decide (*i.e.*, to arbitrate) the question of arbitrability. First Options relies on the Kaplans' filing with the arbitrators a written memorandum objecting to the arbitrators' jurisdiction. But merely arguing the arbitrability issue to an arbitrator does not indicate a clear willingness to arbitrate that issue, *i.e.*, a willingness to be effectively bound by the arbitrator's decision on that point. To the contrary, insofar as the Kaplans were forcefully objecting to the arbitrators deciding their dispute with First Options, one naturally would think that they did *not* want the arbitrators to have binding authority over them. This conclusion draws added support from (1) an obvious explanation for the Kaplans' presence before the arbitrators (*i.e.*, that MKI, Mr. Kaplan's wholly owned firm, was arbitrating workout agreement matters); and (2) Third circuit law that suggested that the Kaplans might argue arbitrability to the arbitrators without losing their right to independent court review, *Teamsters v. Western Pennsylvania Motor Carriers Assn.*, 574 F.2d 783, 786-788 (1978); see 19 F.3d, at 1512, n. 13.

First Options makes several counterarguments: (1) that the Kaplans had other ways to get an independent court decision on the question of arbitrability without arguing the issue to the arbitrators (*e.g.*, by trying to enjoin the arbitration, or by refusing to participate in the arbitration and then defending against a court petition First Options would have brought to compel arbitration, see 9 U.S.C. § 4); (2) that permitting parties to argue arbitrability to an arbitrator without being bound by the result would cause delay and waste in the resolution of disputes; and (3) that the Arbitration Act therefore requires a presumption that the Kaplans agreed to be bound by the arbitrators' decision, not the contrary. The first of these points, however, while true, simply does not say anything about whether the Kaplans intended to be bound by the arbitrators' decision. The second point, too, is inconclusive, for factual circumstances vary too greatly to permit a confident conclusion about whether allowing the arbitrator to make an initial (but independently reviewable) arbitrability determination would, in general, slow down the dispute resolution process. And, the third point is legally erroneous, for there is no strong arbitration-related policy favoring First Options in respect to its particular argument here. After all, the basic objective in this area is not to resolve disputes in the quickest manner possible, no matter what the parties' wishes, *Dean Witter Reynolds, supra*, at 219-220, 105 S.Ct., at 1241-1242, but to ensure that commercial arbitration agreements, like other contracts, "'are enforced according to their terms,'" *Mastrobuono*, 514 U.S., at __, 115 S.Ct., at 1214 (quoting *Volt Information Sciences*, 489 U.S., at 479, 109 S.Ct., at 1256), and according to the intentions of the parties, *Mitsubishi Motors*, 473 U.S., at 626, 105 S.Ct., at 3353. See *Allied-Bruce*, 513 U.S., at __, 115 S.Ct., at 837. That policy favors the Kaplans, not First Options.

We conclude that, because the Kaplans did not clearly agree to submit the question of arbitrability to arbitration, the Court of Appeals was correct in finding that the arbitrability of the Kaplan/First Options dispute was subject to independent review by the courts.

[The Supreme Court went on to discuss what standard was appropriate for the Court of Appeals review of the District Court determination to confirm or to vacate the award.]

.   .   .

The judgment of the Court of Appeals is affirmed.

*It is so ordered.*

## Notes and Questions

1. In *First Options of Chicago v. Kaplan*, the Court implied that in some cases an arbitrator's decision on arbitral authority might be binding:

> "Did the parties agree to submit the arbitrability question itself to arbitration? If so, then the court's standard for reviewing the arbitrator's decision about the matter should not differ from the standard courts apply when they review any other matter that the parties have agreed to arbitrate."

115 S.Ct. 1920, at 1923. Does this dicta imply that the contours of an arbitrator's jurisdiction may sometimes escape judicial scrutiny? Such an "arbitrability agreement" giving arbitrators sole competence to rule on jurisdiction is most plausible in cases where there exists a truly distinct arbitration clause that refers explicitly to disputes about arbitrability arising under the first arbitration clause. An arbitral tribunal so constituted would then be doing no more than deciding a question of fact and/or law: "Was the initial arbitration agreement validly concluded in such a way as to empower the arbitrator to the extent asserted?" One arbitrator would answer that question in a way that would bear on the jurisdiction of another. See generally William W. Park, The Arbitrability Dicta in First Options v. Kaplan, 12 ARB. INT'L 137 (19  ).

2. Could an argument be made that a single arbitration clause properly drafted could do the same job? For example, imagine that the arbitration clause signed by MK Investments in *First Options* included the phrase suggested by the dicta: "The arbitrability question itself [is subject] to arbitration." Could the addition of these eight words change the result if Carol and Manuel Kaplan had not signed that agreement? The logical problem with such a "one stop arbitrability agreement" is that the limits inherent in the arbitration clause (the Kaplans themselves never agreed to arbitrate) will almost inevitably limit the arbitrability portion of the clause as well. If the Kaplans never signed the document containing the combined arbitration/arbitrability agreement, then they could not have submitted the arbitrability question to arbitrators. To state that the arbitral tribunal has jurisdiction to determine whether the Kaplans agreed to arbitrate presumes the conclusion on the very question at issue. An arbitrator deciding his or her own jurisdiction in such an instance suggests an image of Baron Münchhausen pulling himself up by his own pigtail.

## F.     SEPARABILITY OF THE ARBITRATION CLAUSE

The process by which arbitrators determine the limits of their jurisdiction is discussed more fully in Chapter 6. What happens, however, when the contracting party who is resisting arbitration attempts to stop the arbitral process before it has even begun by claiming that the contract — and thus the arbitration agreement contained therein — is void? Should a court enter into the merits of the arguments relating to the alleged fraud and thus the contract validity?

Or is this precisely the question that the contracting parties would normally have intended to be settled by the arbitrator?

One approach to this dilemma, adopted in the United States, has been to separate the arbitration clause from the main contract. Thus if the arbitration agreement itself was not procured by fraud, it would be up to the arbitrators to decide whether or not the representations that induced the principal contract were fraudulent. The next three cases present the leading American authority for the "separability" doctrine. The two English cases take a contrasting approach to analogous issues. Together these cases present a searching examination of the policies and implications of the available alternatives.

      1.     *Prima Paint Corp. v. Flood & Conklin Mfg. Co.*, 388 U.S. 395 (1967).

MR. JUSTICE FORTAS delivered the opinion of the Court.

This case presents the question whether the federal court or an arbitrator is to resolve a claim of "fraud in the inducement," under a contract governed by the United States Arbitration Act of 1925,[175] where there is no evidence that the contracting parties intended to withhold that issue from arbitration.

The question arises from the following set of facts. On October 7, 1964, respondent, Flood & Conklin Manufacturing Company, a New Jersey corporation, entered into what was styled a "Consulting Agreement," with petitioner, Prima Paint Corporation, a Maryland corporation. This agreement followed by less than three weeks the execution of a contract pursuant to which Prima Paint purchased F & C's paint business. The consulting agreement provided that for a six-year period F & C was to furnish advice and consultation "in connection with the formulae, manufacturing operations, sales and servicing of Prima Trade Sales accounts." These services were to be performed personally by F & C's chairman, Jerome K. Jelin, "except in the event of his death or disability." F & C bound itself for the duration of the contractual period to make no "Trade Sales" of paint or paint products in its existing sales territory or to current customers. To the consulting agreement were appended lists of F & C customers,

---

[175] [1] 9 U.S.C. §§ 1-14.

whose patronage was to be taken over by Prima Paint. In return for these lists, the covenant not to compete, and the services of Mr. Jelin, Prima Paint agreed to pay F & C certain percentages of its receipts from the listed customers and from all others, such payments not to exceed $225,000 over the life of the agreement. The agreement took into account the possibility that Prima Paint might encounter financial difficulties, including bankruptcy, but no corresponding reference was made to possible financial problems which might be encountered by F & C. The agreement stated that it "embodies the entire understanding of the parties on the subject matter." Finally, the parties agreed to a broad arbitration clause, which read in part:

> "Any controversy or claim arising out of or relating to this Agreement, or the breach thereof, shall be settled by arbitration in the City of New York, in accordance with the rules then obtaining of the American Arbitration Association . . . ."

The first payment by Prima Paint to F & C under the consulting agreement was due on September 1, 1965. None was made on that date. Seventeen days later, Prima Paint did pay the appropriate amount, but into escrow. It notified attorneys for F & C that in various enumerated respects their client had broken both the consulting agreement and the earlier purchase agreement. Prima Paint's principal contention, so far as presently relevant, was that F & C had fraudulently represented that it was solvent and able to perform its contractual obligations, where as it was in fact insolvent and intended to file a petition under Chapter XI of the Bankruptcy Act, 52 Stat. 905, 11 U.S.C. § 701 *et seq.*, shortly after execution of the consulting agreement. Prima Paint noted that such a petition was filed by F & C on October 14, 1964, one week after the contract had been signed. F & C's response, on October 25, was to serve a "notice of intention to arbitrate." On November 12, three days before expiration of its time to answer this "notice," Prima Paint filed suit in the United States District Court for the Southern District of New York, seeking rescission of the consulting agreement on the basis of the alleged fraudulent inducement. The complaint asserted that the federal court had diversity jurisdiction.

Contemporaneously with the filing of its complaint, Prima Paint petitioned the District Court for an order enjoining F & C from proceeding with the arbitration. F & C cross-moved to stay the court action pending arbitration. F & C contended that the issue presented—whether there was fraud in the inducement of the consulting agreement—was a question for the arbitrators and not for the District Court. Cross-affidavits were filed on the merits. On behalf of Prima Paint, the charges in the complaint were reiterated. Affiants for F & C attacked the sufficiency of Prima Paint's allegations of fraud, denied that misrepresentations had been made during negotiations, and asserted that Prima Paint had relied exclusively upon delivery of the lists, the promise not to compete, and the availability of Mr. Jelin. They contended that Prima Paint had availed itself of these considerations for nearly a year without claiming "fraud," noting that Prima Paint was in no position to claim ignorance of the bankruptcy proceeding since it had participated therein in February of 1965. They added that F & C was revested with its assets in March of 1965.

.     .     .

Having determined that the contract in question is within the coverage of the Arbitration Act, we turn to the central issue in this case: whether a claim of fraud in the inducement of the entire contract is to be resolved by the federal court, or whether the matter is to be referred to the arbitrators. The courts of appeals have differed in their approach to this question. The view of the Court of Appeals for the Second Circuit, as expressed in this case and in others, is that—*except where the parties otherwise intend*—arbitration clauses as a matter of federal law are "separable" from the contracts in which they are embedded, and that where no claim is made that fraud was directed to the arbitration clause itself, a broad arbitration clause will be held to encompass arbitration of the claim that the contract itself was induced by fraud. The Court of Appeals for the First Circuit, on the other hand, has taken the view that the question of "severability" is one of state law, and that where a State regards such a clause as inseparable a claim of fraud in the inducement must be decided by the court. *Lummus Co. v. Commonwealth Oil Ref. Co.*, 280 F. 2d 915, 923-24 (C. A. 1st Cir.), cert. denied, 364 U. S. 911 (1960).

With respect to cases brought in federal court involving maritime contracts or those evidencing transactions in "commerce," we think that Congress has provided an explicit answer. That answer is to be found in § 4 of the Act, which provides a remedy to a party seeking to compel compliance with an arbitration agreement. Under § 4, with respect to a matter within the jurisdiction of the federal courts save for the existence of an arbitration clause, the federal court is instructed to order arbitration to proceed once it is satisfied that "the making of the agreement for arbitration or the failure to comply [with the arbitration agreement] is not in issue." Accordingly, if the claim is fraud in the inducement of the arbitration clause itself—an issue which goes to the "making" of the agreement to arbitrate—the federal court may proceed to adjudicate it. But the statutory language does not permit the federal court to consider claims of fraud in the inducement of the contract generally. Section 4 does not expressly relate to situations like the present in which a stay is sought of a federal action in order that arbitration may proceed. But it is inconceivable that Congress intended the rule to differ depending upon which party to the arbitration agreement first invokes the assistance of a federal court. We hold, therefore, that in passing upon a § 3 application for a stay while the parties arbitrate, a federal court may consider only issues relating to the making and performance of the agreement to arbitrate. In so concluding, we not only honor the plain meaning of the statute but also the unmistakably clear congressional purpose that the arbitration procedure, when selected by the parties to a contract, be speedy and not subject to delay and obstruction in the courts.

.   .   .

In the present case no claim has been advanced by Prima Paint that F & C fraudulently induced it to enter into the agreement to arbitrate "[a]ny controversy or claim arising out of or relating to this Agreement, or the breach thereof." This contractual language is easily broad enough to encompass Prima Paint's claim that both execution and acceleration of the consulting agreement itself were procured by fraud. Indeed, no claim is made that Prima Paint ever intended that "legal" issues relating to the contract be excluded from arbitration, or that it was not entirely free so to contract. Federal courts are bound to apply rules enacted by Congress with respect to matters—here, a contract involving commerce—over which it has legislative power. The question which Prima Paint requested the District Court to adjudicate preliminarily to allowing arbitration to proceed is one not intended by Congress to delay the granting of a §3 stay. Accordingly, the decision below dismissing Prima Paint's appeal is

*Affirmed.*

. . .

MR. JUSTICE BLACK, with whom MR. JUSTICE DOUGLAS and MR. JUSTICE STEWART join, dissenting.

. . .

2. *Ashville Invs. Ltd. v. Elmer Contractors Ltd.*, 2 Lloyd's Rep. 73 (1988).

**Lord Justice MAY**: In these appeals the parties are respectively the buildings owners (Ashville) and the contractors (Elmer) for the construction of six warehouse units in Wokingham. The contract between them was in the JCT form (July 1977 Revision) under seal and was dated Dec 22, 1982. Negotiations for the work began in April, 1982. Ultimately Ashville invited Elmer to tender on the basis of a specification dated Dec 9 and drawings dated Dec 16, 1982. On this basis Elmer quoted a price for the building works on Dec 21, 1982. A meeting then took place between the parties' representatives on Dec 22 at the end of which the contract under seal of that date was entered into for the building work to be done for L715,000, which had been Elmers's tendered price. Appended to the sealed document was an amended version of the conditions forming part of the JCT form together with initialled drawings and specifications relating to the work which was to be done.

It is, however, an undisputed fact that there were substantial differences between the specifications and drawings upon which Elmer tendered and those which were initialled on Dec 22, 1982 and incorporated into the building contract. It is Elmer's contention that they were unaware of these differences until well after the works had begun. The evidence filed on behalf of Ashville is to the effect that the differences were specifically drawn to the attention of Elmer's representatives at the meeting of Dec 22, 1982. Those representatives then considered the cost implications of such differences but decided not to change their tender price. It was only thereafter that the contract was executed.

. . .

The basis of Elmer's claim in the arbitration put shortly is that the work which they agreed to carry out for the tender figure was that which was contained in the specification and drawings upon which they tendered: further, that their design liability under the contract was limited as set out in the minute of the meeting of Dec 22, 1982, which I have already quoted. In these circumstances, if the written contract must be taken as providing otherwise, then Elmer's contention is that it does not represent what was truly agreed between themselves and Ashville. Consequently in their points of claim Elmer seek inter alia rectification of the contract on the ground that it was entered into between themselves and Ashville as a result of either a mutual, or alternatively a unilateral mistake. Elmer also seek damages allegedly sustained by them as a result of an innocent misrepresentation and or a negligent mis-statement made to them by Ashville's representatives which induced them to enter into the contract about which they now complain.

Points of defence were served on June 27, 1985. Paragraph 8 of these denied that the arbitrator had any power under the arbitration clause in the building contract to order rectification of it. Paragraph 9 in its turn denied that the arbitrator had power under the same arbitration clause to grant any relief in respect of the misrepresentation pleaded in the points of claim. I should say at this stage that the points of claim originally alleged in the alternative that Ashville's misrepresentation had been innocent or fraudulent. After Ashville had taken the jurisdictional objections in their points of defence, it was not until Mar 31, 1986 that they suggested that these should be referred to the Commercial Court for decision. Elmer did not agree so Ashville issued an originating summons on May 14, 1986 seeking declarations, first, that the arbitrator did not have jurisdiction under the relevant arbitration clause to hear and determine issues which had arisen in that arbitration involving mutual mistake, innocent misrepresentation and fraudulent misrepresentation; and secondly, that the arbitrator had no power under the agreement to grant the relief claimed in respect of those issues, namely rectification and damages. The originating summons also claimed an appropriate order under §24(2) of the Arbitration Act, 1950 having regard to the allegation of fraud that there then was in the points of claim. On July 11, 1986 Elmer issued a corresponding originating summons for declarations that the arbitrator did have jurisdiction to hear and determine all issues which had arisen in the pleadings in the arbitration and that the arbitrator had power to grant all the relief claimed in the points of claim.

In the event the learned Judge dismissed Ashville's originating summons and granted Elmer the declarations asked in theirs. Ashville now appeal asking that the learned Judge's decision on each originating summons should be reversed.

It is convenient at this point to set out the arbitration clause in the relevant building contract. In so far as is relevant for present purposes it was in these terms:

> Provided always that in case any dispute or difference shall arise between the Employer or the Architect on his behalf and the Contractor . . . as to the construction of this Contract or as to any matter or thing of whatsoever nature arising thereunder or in connection therewith . . . then such dispute or difference shall be and is hereby referred to the arbitration and final decision of a person to be agreed between the parties, or failing agreement . . . appointed . . . by the President or Vice President for the time being of the Royal Institute of Chartered Surveyors.

The learned Judge held that the extent of the arbitrator's jurisdiction and whether he had the power to grant the relief sought depended upon the proper construction of the arbitration clause. He expressed the view that the dispute or difference between the parties about the alleged disparity between the tender documents and the sealed contract documents was not one "as to the construction of the contract." On the other hand, in relation to the issue involving the minute of the meeting of Dec 22, 1982, he thought that there was much more doubt whether that was "as to the construction of the contract" or not. However he found it unnecessary to decide this particular point because he held that both these issues constituted disputes or differences arising "in connection with" the contract. He had been referred to certain observations by Lord Simon in *Heyman v. Darwins Ltd.*, (1942) 72 Ll.L.Rep. 65; [1942] A.C. 356 upon which Ashville relied, but he held that these were obiter and in any event pointed out that the wording of the arbitration submission in *Heyman*'s case was far less wide than the wording of the arbitration clause in the instant case. In any event the learned Judge expressed the view, as he put it in his judgment:

> . . . That the climate has grown milder in relation to
> arbitrations during the last 45 years . . .

and that it was thus right to adopt a broad and liberal approach to the
construction of arbitration clauses rather than too narrow and legalistic
an approach.

On this latter point Counsel for Ashville before us submitted
that the learned Judge had misdirected himself. He accepted that the
question was one of construction of the relevant arbitration submission
but contended that its proper construction could not depend on the
nature of the approach of the relevant tribunal. He argued that the
correct approach was to ask whether on its proper construction, that is
to say on the ordinary and natural meaning of the words used, the
arbitration clause either did or did not cover the disputes or differences
in issue.

On this point I respectfully agree. In seeking to construe a
clause in a contract, there is no scope for adopting either a liberal or
a narrow approach, whatever that may mean. The exercise which has
to be undertaken is to determine what the words used mean. It can
happen that in doing so one is driven to the conclusion that that clause
is ambiguous, that it has two possible meanings. In those circumstances
the Court has to prefer one above the other in accordance with settled
principles. If one meaning is more in accord with what the Court
considers to be the underlying purpose and intent of the contract, or
part of it, than the other, then the Court will choose the former rather
than the latter. In some circumstances the Court may reach its
conclusion on construction by applying the contra proferentum rule.
These are, however, well recognized principles of construction; they
are not the consequences or examples of adopting any particular
approach to the question of construction, save to ascertain the true
intention of the parties and the correct meaning of the words used.

On this question of the construction of the arbitration clause,
Counsel for Ashville referred us to at least three decided cases which
he submitted constituted authority binding on us and requiring us to
decide that neither the issues between the parties in this case nor the
relief claimed by Elmer of rectification and damages arose "in
connection with the contract." On this basis he contended that the

learned Judge must have been wrong and that this appeal should be allowed.

In these circumstances I think that it is necessary carefully to consider the role of precedent and the doctrine of stare decisis in a case such as this, in which a question of construction is in truth the fundamental issue between the parties. In my opinion the doctrine of precedent only involves this — that when a case has been decided in a Court it is only the legal principle or principles upon which that Court has so decided that bind Courts of concurrent or lower jurisdictions and require them to follow and adopt them when they are relevant to the decision in later cases before those Courts. The ratio decidendi of a prior case, the reason why it was decided as it was, is in my view only to be understood in this somewhat limited sense.

Thus, in the present context it has been decided and is a principle of law that an arbitrator does not have jurisdiction, nor can the arbitration agreement be construed to give him jurisdiction to rule upon the initial existence of the contract. On the other hand, given an appropriate arbitration clause, an arbitrator does in general have jurisdiction to rule upon the continued existence of the contract. See *Heyman v. Darwin's Ltd.* and Mustill & Boyd's Commercial Arbitration, pp. 78 et seq.

Similarly it is a principle of law that the scope of an arbitrator's jurisdiction and powers in a given case depend fundamentally upon the terms of the arbitration agreement, that is to say upon its proper construction in all the circumstances.

However I do not think that there is any principle of law to the effect that the meaning of certain specific words in one arbitration clause in one contract is immutable and that those same specific words in another arbitration clause in other circumstances in another contract must be construed in the same way. This is not to say that the earlier decision on a given form of words will not be persuasive, to a degree dependent on the extent of the similarity between the contracts and surrounding circumstances in the two cases. In the interests of certainty and clarity a Court may well think it right to construe words in an arbitration agreement, or indeed in a particular type of contract, in the same way as those same words have earlier been construed in another case involving an arbitration clause by another Court. But in my opinion the subsequent Court is not bound by the doctrine of stare decisis to do so.

If I were wrong, then in any event it must be necessary to compare the surrounding circumstances in each case to ensure that those in the later case did not require one to construe albeit the same words differently when used in the different context.

However before turning to the authorities upon which Counsel for Ashville particularly relied, there are in my opinion some further important considerations to have in mind.

First, it is trite law that the answer to the question whether a particular dispute falls within an agreement to arbitrate depends primarily upon the proper construction of that agreement. Further, given that a dispute is, on that proper construction, within the jurisdiction of the arbitrator, then the latter is not only entitled but bound to grant such relief to one party or the other as and to the extent that the law permits for the resolution of that dispute, provided that the arbitration agreement does not exclude that particular relief. In addition, as this Court made clear in *Northern Regional Health Authority v. Derek Crouch Construction Co. Ltd.*, [1984] 1 Q.B. 644, an arbitrator may well be empowered by the terms of the arbitration agreement to grant wider relief to one party or another than might be available at law.

Secondly, therefore, there is no reason in principle why an arbitrator cannot make an order for the rectification of a contract, provided this is justified at law and by the arbitration agreement, nor why he cannot award damages for misrepresentation or a negligent mis-statement, subject to the same proviso. In so far as rectification is concerned, however, there are as I have said a number of decided cases in which on the proper construction of the arbitration clause the Courts held that such a remedy was not open to an arbitrator. I shall refer to these a little later in this judgment.

Thirdly, this Court also pointed out in the *Northern RHA v. Derek Crouch* case that not only are the powers and duties of the architect, the agent of the building owner, under the JCT forms of contract wide indeed, but it is quite clear that the supervisory powers of the arbitrator are and are intended to be wider still. In construing the latter therefore, I have no doubt that it would be wrong to restrict those powers but in law desirable to hold that they are as wide as the actual wording of the arbitration clause permits.

.    .    .

The issue raised by the claim for rectification is an issue of a totally different description. It is an issue of fact which does not arise out of the particular written agreement in question, but which seeks to substitute for that particular document another agreement in terms different from those set out in the written document. Once that fact is appreciated, it appears to me to be clear, beyond argument, that any attempt by the respondents in the proceedings before the learned arbitrator to raise the issue of rectification could not have been successful without some further agreement by both parties to submit that particular matter of dispute, which lay outside the actual submission that was before him. . . .

.    .    .

[In a separate opinion, Lord Justice BINGHAM ventured the following summary of relevant legal principles:] [An] arbitrator derives his jurisdiction from the agreement of the parties at whose instance he is appointed. He has such jurisdiction as they agree to give him and none that they do not. The only inherent limitation is that he cannot make a binding award as to the initial existence of the agreement from which his jurisdiction is said to derive. When a question arises, as it does here, whether a certain dispute falls within an arbitrator's jurisdiction the Court's task is in principle a simple one: it is to consider the dispute in question, to elicit from the arbitration agreement the parties' intentions concerning the jurisdiction to be conferred on the arbitrator and to decide whether the parties did or did not intend a dispute of the kind in question to be resolved by the arbitrator. As Viscount Simon L.C. succinctly put it in *Heyman v. Darwins* (1942) 72 Ll.L.Rep. 65, at 67; [1942] A.C. 356 at 360:

> The answer to the question whether a dispute falls within an arbitration clause in a contract must depend on (a) what is the dispute and (b) what disputes the arbitration clause covers.

3.    *Harbour Assurance Co. (UK) v. Kansa Gen. Int'l Ins. Co.*, 1 Lloyds Rep. 81 (Q.B. 1992).

[This case involved a reinsurance dispute in which the plaintiffs (English insurance companies) agreed that defendant Finnish insurance companies were carrying on business in the United Kingdom illegally, and therefore the underlying contracts (providing for retrocession of insurance policies to the British companies which agreed to reinsure the Finnish companies for certain risks) were illegal, null and void. The British plaintiffs sought a declaratory judgment that they were not liable under the contracts. The underlying agreement between the parties contained an arbitration clause.]

**Mr. Justice STEYN:** *Introduction:*  On this application for a stay under s. 1 of the Arbitration Act 1975 important questions regarding the jurisdiction of arbitrators arise for decision. At the outset it is important to emphasize that this case has nothing to do with the question whether arbitrators are competent to decide on questions relating to their own jurisdiction. The approach in English law is simple, straightforward and practical. As a matter of convenience arbitrators may consider, and decide, whether they have jurisdiction or not: they may decide to assume or decline jurisdiction. But it is well settled in English law that the result of such a preliminary decision has no effect whatsoever on the legal rights of the parties. Only the court can definitively rule on issues relating to the jurisdiction of arbitrators. And it is possible to obtain a speedy declaratory judgment from the Commercial Court as to the validity of an arbitration agreement before or during the arbitration proceedings.

This case is concerned with a different matter, namely the scope of the principle of the separability of the arbitration clause in an integrated written contract. That principle is legal shorthand for a group of rules which govern the circumstances in which the arbitration clause remains binding despite the invalidity, discharge, termination or rescission of the contract. Mustill and Boyd, Commercial Arbitration, 2nd ed., at 7, note 6, state:

> The doctrine of the separability of the arbitration clause has not been espoused in the wider form in which it is known in other jurisdictions. But the narrower English form leads in many cases to the same result.

Given the fact that it is established that in a number of circumstances the arbitration agreement does not fall to the ground with the principal contract, there is no doubt about the existence in English law of the principle of the separability of the arbitration agreement. But this case raises in acute form the question where precisely the line should be drawn between circumstances which do, and circumstances which do not, render the arbitration clause ineffective. This question cannot be answered by concluding on narrow grounds that the case falls on a particular side of a notional line. It is an important and complicated question, which must be considered in some detail.

[Justice Steyn continued the analysis with respect to a motion to stay any court litigation on the issue of illegality so that matter could be dealt with by the contractually required arbitration.]

. . .

It is clearly established that if a contract is terminated for breach, by an acceptance of repudiation, and by frustration, the arbitrator is still entitled to deal with disputes flowing from the ending of the contract. No similar concession is made in respect of subsequent illegality . . . .

. . .

In no English case has it ever been held, and in no English textbook has it ever been suggested, that an arbitration clause can survive the initial invalidity of the contract. . . .

. . .

At a time when the principle of separability of the arbitration was not recognized, the logic of saying that the arbitration clause necessarily follows the misfortunes of the contract was inescapable. While the arbitration clause was treated as an integral part of one contract, the invalidity of the contract necessarily spelt the invalidity of the arbitration clause. And this argument seemed particularly forceful if one focused on the single written document rather than on the diversity of contractual rights and obligations evidenced by it. Once it became accepted that the arbitration clause is a separate agreement ancillary to the contract, the logical impediment to referring to an issue of the invalidity of the contract to arbitration disappears. Provided that the arbitration clause itself is not directly impeached (e.g., by a non est factum plea), the arbitration agreement is as a matter of principled legal theory capable of surviving the invalidity of the contract. . . .

.        .        .

[Judge Steyn goes on to elaborate reasons for the modern trend toward "full recognition of the arbitration clause, subject to that clause not itself being impeached."]

.        .        .

. . . First, there is the imperative of giving effect to the wishes of the parties unless there are compelling reasons of principle why it is not possible to do so. . . . Secondly, if the arbitration clause is not held to survive the invalidity of the contract, a party is afforded the opportunity to evade his obligation to arbitrate by the simple expedient of alleging that the contract is void. In such cases courts of law then inevitably become involved in deciding the substance of a dispute. Moreover, in international transactions where the neutrality of the arbitral process is highly prized, the collapse of this consensual method of dispute resolution compels a party to resort to national courts where in the real world the badge of neutrality is sometimes perceived to be absent. For parties the perceived effectiveness of the neutral arbitral process is often a vital condition in the process of negotiation of the contract. If that perception is absent, it will often present a formidable hurdle to the conclusion of the transaction. A full recognition of the separability principle tends to facilitate international trade. These considerations are of concern in England since England is a major trading nation and London is a major centre of international arbitrations.

.        .        .

My conclusion is therefore that the separability principle, as applicable also to cases of the initial invalidity of the contract, is sound in legal theory. . . .

.        .        .

It will be recalled that it is the Plaintiffs' pleaded case that the retrocessions were illegal and void ab initio. If the approach, which I have adopted is correct, it would be consistent to say that an issue as to the initial illegality of the contract is capable of being referred to arbitration. There is, of course, the qualification that such initial illegality must not directly impeach the arbitration clause. . . .

.     .     .

. . . In any event, while the distinction between initial invalidity and illegality is not one which in my view should nowadays prevail, I am constrained by high authority to hold that it does prevail. Having come to this conclusion, it follows that the application for a stay must be dismissed.

.     .     .

. . . If I had concluded that the separability principle extends to cases of ab initio illegality of the contract, I would have concluded that the arbitration clause in the present case is wide enough to cover such a dispute.

.     .     .

. . . I conclude that the decision in *Taylor* compels me to hold that the separability principle does not extend to ab initio illegality of a contract in which the arbitration clause is embedded. It follows that the application for a stay of the illegality issue must be dismissed.

### Notes and Questions

1. What are the primary differences between the U.S. and the English approaches?

2. One commentator has noted the following:

> What is of greater significance about the *Ashville* case is the fact that all three judges stated that no arbitral clause can give the arbitrator the power to rule on the initial existence of the main contract. It is clear from the context of these *dicta* that "initial existence" is not confined to cases where there is doubt whether the parties reached agreement at all. Contracts void for public policy reasons are clearly included, and other matters which result in the

agreement never having legally bound the parties. The Court of Appeal makes it clear unanimously that there is no separability doctrine in this area of English law. Adam Samuel, *Developments in English Arbitration Law Since the 1984 Antaios Decision*, 5 J. INT'L ARB. 9, 13 (1988).

### G.     WHO DECIDES JURISDICTIONAL QUESTIONS: COURTS OR ARBITRATORS?

As we noticed in the materials dealing with non-signatories (*see First Options v. Kaplan, supra* p. 502), allocating competence between arbitrators and courts can be particularly troublesome with respect to matters that affect arbitrator jurisdiction. Imagine that a claim is made on the basis of an arbitration clause which the defendant says it never signed. Should the defendant be able to go to court at the outset of the proceedings to contest the arbitrators' jurisdiction, or must it wait until an award is rendered, and then move to have that award set aside? If an arbitral tribunal has already rendered an award against the defendant, what (if any) deference should a reviewing court show to the arbitrators' finding?

Such questions are sometimes analyzed according to a chameleon-like concept referred to as *compétence-compétence* (literally "jurisdiction concerning jurisdiction"), which links together a constellation of disparate notions about when arbitrators can rule on the limits of their own power.

In its simplest formulation, *compétence-compétence* means no more than that arbitrators can look into their own jurisdiction without waiting for a court to do so. In other words, there is no need to stop arbitral proceedings to refer a jurisdictional issue to judges.  See Christopher Brown Ltd v. Genossenschaft Oesterreifchischer Waldbesitzer, [1954] 1 Q.B. 8.  However, the arbitrators' determination about their power would be subject to judicial review at any time, including when a motion is made to stay court litigation or to compel arbitration.

French law goes further, however, and delays court review of arbitral jurisdiction until *after* an award is rendered. If an arbitral tribunal has already begun to hear a matter, courts must decline to hear the case. When an arbitral tribunal has not yet been constituted, court litigation will go forward only if the alleged arbitration agreement is clearly void (*manifestement nulle*). See Article 1458 of the *Nouveau code de procédure civile*.

In Germany *Kompetenz-Kompetenz* has been used to describe a situation in which the parties purport to give an arbitral tribunal power to rule on its own jurisdiction in a binding way — without subsequent judicial review. See decisions of the Bundesgerichtshof discussed in PETER SCHLOSSER, *DAS RECHT DER INTERNATIONALEN PRIVATEN SCHIEDSGERICHTSBARKEIT* (1989) at § 556. The current reform of arbitration law in Germany, however, may change this situation. Section 1040 of the draft arbitration law provides that arbitrators will normally (*in der Regel*) rule on their own jurisdiction in the form of an interim award subject to judicial review.

To some extent, what is at issue here is the timing of judicial review.  Going to court at the beginning of the proceedings can save expense for a defendant improperly joined to the arbitration on the basis of a clause that is either invalid or too limited in scope.  On the other hand, judicial resources may be conserved by delaying review until the end of the process, when the parties may have settled. In this connection, note that Article 16 of the UNCITRAL Model Arbitration Law gives the arbitral tribunal an explicit right to determine its own jurisdiction in the form of an interim award subject to challenge within thirty (30) days.

*Compétence-compétence* analysis sometimes (but not always) achieves results similar to those flowing from notions of "separability" (discussed *supra* p. 508). Separability permits arbitrators to invalidate the main contract (e.g., for illegality or fraud in the inducement) without the risk that their decision will also invalidate the source of their power. The doctrine of *compétence-compétence*, on the other hand, gives the arbitrator the right to pass upon alleged infirmities in the arbitration clause, although not necessarily in a binding way.

To illustrate the difference between separability and *compétence-compétence*, assume that an arbitration clause has been included in a "Consulting Agreement" entered into by an American corporation seeking to obtain a public works contract in a foreign country.  The American company might resist arbitration on two grounds: (i) the person who signed the agreement for the American corporation was not authorized to do so and (ii) the consulting agreement was void because payments thereunder were earmarked to bribe government officials.

Separability notions would permit the arbitrators to find the main contract void for illegality without destroying their power to do so under the arbitration clause, but would not prevent a court from second guessing the arbitrator on whether the individual who signed the agreement was authorized to do so. On the other hand, *compétence-compétence* principles would permit the arbitrators to examine the validity of the signature, but would not save an award declaring the contract void for illegality.

The following two American cases discuss the contours of the proper allocation of jurisdictional decisions between courts and arbitrators. Compare them with the solution adopted by Article 16(3) of the UNCITRAL Model Law, which provides thirty days for an aggrieved party to bring a judicial challenge to an arbitrator's decision on his jurisdiction. *See generally* Carl Svernlov, *What Isn't, Ain't*, J. INT'L ARB., Dec. 1991, at 37. *See also* David W. Rivkin & Frances L. Kellner, *In Support of the FAA: An Argument Against U.S. Adoption of the UNCITRAL Model Law*, 1 AM. REV. INT'L ARB. 535, 547-48 (1990).

1.     *Three Valleys Municipal Water District v. E.F. Hutton & Co.*, 925 F.2d 1136 (9th Cir. 1991).

[Three California municipalities and two governmental agencies opened securities accounts with E.F. Hutton, the predecessor to Shearson Lehman. Each entered into a "Client Agreement" containing an arbitration clause. Alleging wrongful conduct that resulted in more than $8 million in damages, the municipalities and agencies filed a complaint in the Federal District Court for the Central District of California. Shearson responded with a motion to stay the litigation and compel arbitration.]

.     .     .

In its January 11, 1989 order, the district court directed arbitration on plaintiffs' RICO and state law claims, but refused to direct arbitration on plaintiffs' claims under § 10(b) of the Exchange

Act and § 12(2) of the Securities Act. There are two issues in this appeal. First, the plaintiffs' contend that the Client Agreements containing the arbitration clauses are void because the signatory did not have authority to bind the plaintiffs. They argue that the district court erred in determining that the threshold issue whether the Client Agreements bind the plaintiffs must be decided by an arbitrator, rather than the district court. Second, assuming plaintiffs are bound to the contracts—and Three Valleys does not deny that it is—Shearson contends that the district court erred in ruling that plaintiffs' claims under § 10(b) of the Exchange Act and §12(2) of the Securities Act are not arbitrable.

.    .    .

## A.

Plaintiffs opposed Shearson's motion to stay the federal proceeding and to compel arbitration on the ground that the Client Agreements containing the arbitration clauses are void because the individual who signed the agreements, Clarence Wood, did not have authority to bind the plaintiffs. The district court held that the question whether plaintiffs are bound to the Client Agreements must be decided by the arbitrators. We need not address whether Wood had authority to bind the plaintiffs; rather, the issue before this court is who decides whether plaintiffs are bound to the contracts—an arbitrator or the district court.

Federal law preempts state law on issues of arbitrability. *Moses H. Cone Memorial Hosp. v. Mercury Constr. Corp.*, 460 U.S. 1, 24, 103 S.Ct. 927, 941, 74 L.Ed.2d 765 (1983). Under the Federal Arbitration Act ("Act"), 9 U.S.C. §§ 1-15, "any doubts concerning the scope of arbitrable issues should be resolved in favor of arbitration, whether the problem at hand is the construction of the contract language itself or an allegation of waiver, delay, or a like defense to arbitrability." *Id.* But "[a]rbitration is a matter of contract and a party cannot be required to submit any dispute which he has not agreed so to submit." *AT&T Technologies, Inc. v. Communications Workers*, 475 U.S. 643, 648, 106 S.Ct. 1415, 1418, 89 L.Ed.2d 648 (1986) . . . Thus, "as with any contract, the parties' intentions control, but those intentions are generously construed as to issues of arbitrability." *Mitsubishi Motors Corp. v. Soler Chrysler-Plymouth, Inc.*, 473 U.S. 614, 626, 105 S.Ct. 3346, 3354, 87 L.Ed.2d 444 (1985).

Shearson contends that *Prima Paint Corp. v. Flood & Conklin Manufacturing Co.*, 388 U.S. 395, 87 S.Ct. 1801, 18 L.Ed.2d 1270 (1967), controls the threshold issue of who determines whether plaintiffs are bound to the arbitration agreements. In *Prima Paint*, the parties entered into a contract containing an arbitration clause which provided that "[a]ny controversy or claim arising out of or relating to this Agreement, or the breach thereof, shall be settled by arbitration." *Id.* at 398, 87 S.Ct. at 1803. Prima Paint later filed suit seeking rescission of the contract on the ground that Flood & Conklin had fraudulently represented that it was solvent and able to perform its contractual obligations, when in fact it was insolvent. Flood & Conklin sought to submit the issue of fraudulent inducement to contract to the arbitrators pursuant to the contract, and moved the district court for a stay pending arbitration.

The Court held that, under the Federal Arbitration Act, 9 U.S.C. § 1-15, whether there was fraud in the inducement of the contract should be decided by an arbitrator and not by the district court. The Court explained that under § 4 of the Act, a federal court is instructed to direct arbitration "once it is satisfied that 'the making of the agreement for arbitration . . . is not in issue.'" *Id.* at 403, 87 S.Ct. at 1806.

> Accordingly, if the claim is fraud in the inducement of the arbitration clause itself—an issue which goes to the "making" of the agreement to arbitrate—the federal court may proceed to adjudicate it. But the statutory language does not permit the federal court to consider claims of fraud in the inducement of the contract generally. . . . We hold, therefore, that in passing upon a § 3 application for a stay while the parties arbitrate, a federal court may consider only issues relating to the making and performance of the agreement to arbitrate.

*Id.* at 403-04, 87 S.Ct. at 1806.

Under this analysis, a federal court may consider a defense of fraud in the inducement of a contract only if the fraud relates specifically to the arbitration clause itself and not to the contract generally. Furthermore, though *Prima Paint* involved a charge of fraud in the inducement of the contract, the rationale of *Prima Paint* extends to attempts to rescind contracts on other grounds. *See, e.g., Unionmutual Stock Life Ins. Co. v. Beneficial Life Ins. Co.*, 774 F.2d 524, 529 (1st Cir.1985) (frustration of purpose and mutual mistake); *Hall v. Prudential-Bache Sec., Inc.*, 662 F.Supp. 468, 471 n. 1 (C.D.Cal.1987) ("[c]laims concerning duress, unconscionability, coercion, or confusion in signing should be determined by an arbitrator"). The more difficult question is whether *Prima Paint* applies to the issue in this case, i.e., whether the signatory had authority to bind the plaintiffs to the agreement.

Shearson argues that *Prima Paint* extends to all challenges regarding the "making" of a contract as opposed to the making of an arbitration clause. This was the interpretation given *Prima Paint* by the court in *Rhoades v. Powell*, 644 F.Supp. 645 (E.D.Cal.1986):

> The *Prima Paint* doctrine is not limited, however, to rescission based on fraudulent inducement, but *extends to all challenges to the making of a contract*: "The teaching of Prima Paint is that a federal court must not remove from the arbitrators consideration of a substantive challenge to a contract unless there has been an independent challenge to the making of the arbitration clause itself. The basis of the underlying challenge to the contract does not alter the [*Prima Paint*] principle."

*Id.* at 653 (emphasis added) (quoting *Unionmutual Stock Life Ins. Co.*, 774 F.2d at 529).

We do not read *Prima Paint* so broadly. The plaintiffs in *Rhoades* and *Unionmutual* did not challenge the making of a contract, but sought to rescind a contract that admittedly existed. Despite the broad dicta in those cases suggesting that *Prima Paint* extends to "all challenges to the making of a contract," we read *Prima Paint* as limited to challenges seeking to *avoid* or *rescind* a contract—not to challenges going to the very existence of a contract that a party claims never to have agreed to. A contrary rule would lead to untenable results. Party A could forge party B's name to a contract and compel party B to arbitrate the question of the genuineness of its signature. Similarly, any citizen of Los Angeles could sign a contract on behalf of the city and Los Angeles would be required to submit to an arbitrator the question whether it was bound to the contract, even if its charter prevented it from engaging in *any* arbitration.

Under this view, *Prima Paint* applies to "voidable" contracts—those "where one party was an infant, or where the contract was induced by fraud, mistake, or duress, or where breach of a warranty or other promise justifies the aggrieved party in putting an end to the contract." *Restatement (Second) Contracts* § 7 comment b (1981). If the dispute is within the scope of an arbitration agreement, an arbitrator may properly decide whether a contract is "voidable" because the parties have agreed to arbitrate the dispute. But, because an "arbitrator's jurisdiction is rooted in the agreement of the parties," *George Day Constr. Co. v. United Bhd. of Carpenters, Local 354*, 722 F.2d 1471, 1474 (9th Cir.1984); *see also I.S. Joseph Co. v. Michigan Sugar Co.*, 803 F.2d 396, 399 (8th Cir.1986) (an arbitrator "has no independent source of jurisdiction apart from the consent of the parties"); *Smith Wilson Co. v. Trading & Dev. Establishment*, 744 F.Supp. 14, 16 (D.D.C.1990) ("arbitrators derive their authority to resolve disputes only because the parties have agreed in advance to submit such grievances to arbitration"), a party who contests the making of a contract containing an arbitration provision cannot be compelled to arbitrate the threshold issue of the *existence* of an agreement to arbitrate.[176] Only a court can make that decision.

Ample case law supports this holding. *See, e.g., Camping Constr. Co. v. District Council of Iron Workers, Local 378*, 915 F.2d 1333, 1340 (9th Cir.1990) ("The court must determine whether a contract ever existed; unless that issue is decided in favor of the party seeking arbitration, there is no basis for submitting any question to an arbitrator."); *National R.R. Passenger Corp. v. Boston & Maine Corp.*, 850 F.2d 756, 761 (D.C.Cir.1988) ("if there was never an agreement to arbitrate, there is no authority to require a party to submit to arbitration"); *I.S. Joseph Co.*, 803 F.2d at 400 ("the enforceability of an arbitration clause is a question for the court when one party denies

---

[176] [4] Shearson argues that this holding has been rejected by the majority in *Prima Paint*. Shearson notes that Justice Black in his *Prima Paint* dissent made a similar argument with respect to the defense of fraudulent inducement, and it was rejected by the majority. 388 U.S. at 407, 87 S.Ct. at 1808 (Black, J., dissenting). But here Shearson seeks to apply *Prima Paint* one step further to a case where the plaintiffs contend that the parties have given the arbitrator no authority to hear any dispute. The *Prima Paint* majority did not address this question.

the existence of a contract with the other"); *Cancanon v. Smith Barney, Harris, Upham & Co.*, 805 F.2d 998 (11th Cir.1986) (defense of fraud in the factum is not arbitrable). In fact, there are at least four cases, under the Federal Arbitration Act, where a court has held that the question of whether a particular individual has authority to bind a party must be determined by the court, not by an arbitrator. . . .

*Par-Knit Mills, Inc. v. Stockbridge Fabrics Co.*, 636 F.2d 51 (3d Cir.1980), is directly on point. There the documents in question were signed by the production manager of the appellant. The appellant argued that the contracts were not binding on it because they were not signed by a corporate officer. "If the production manager did not have the actual or apparent authority to execute the contract, the corporation cannot be bound. . . ." *Id.* at 55. The Third Circuit reversed the district court's order staying the federal court proceeding pending completion of arbitration. The court explained:

> Before a party to a lawsuit can be ordered to arbitrate and thus be deprived of a day in court, there should be an express, unequivocal agreement to that effect. If there is doubt as to whether such an agreement exists, the matter, upon a proper and timely demand, should be submitted to a jury. Only when there is no genuine issue of fact concerning the formation of the agreement should the court decide as a matter of law that the parties did or did not enter into such an agreement. The district court, when considering a motion to compel arbitration which is opposed on the ground that no agreement to arbitrate had been made between the parties, should give to the opposing party the benefit of all reasonable doubts and inferences that may arise.

*Id.* at 54 (footnotes omitted).

Shearson argues that, notwithstanding the general principle that arbitration is proper only upon agreement of the parties, our opinion in *Teledyne, Inc. v. Kone Corp.*, 892 F.2d 1404 (9th Cir.1990), requires that the dispute in this case over the existence of the contract be submitted to arbitration. In *Teledyne*, the plaintiff Teledyne brought a breach of contract action against the defendant Kone. Kone denied that a valid contract existed because the signed agreement was not "final," and sought to arbitrate the breach of contract dispute pursuant to the terms of the arbitration clause contained in the "non-final" agreement. Teledyne argued that Kone has no right to enforce the arbitration provision because Kone denied that the agreement containing the arbitration clause was a valid contract. We rejected Teledyne's argument. We held that, because Kone "attacked the contract as a whole without making an 'independent challenge' to the arbitration provision," *id.* at 1410, Kone did not waive its right to have an arbitrator determine whether the agreement was final and enforceable.

*Teledyne* is a rare case. In *Teledyne*, the plaintiff (1) asserted the validity of the underlying contract containing the arbitration clause by bringing a breach of contract action and (2) did not make an independent challenge to the arbitration clause. The plaintiff thus had no ground on which to repudiate the arbitration agreement. As we explained in *Teledyne*, to allow the plaintiff to circumvent arbitration in these circumstances by bringing its claims in federal court would lead to an absurd result:

> The district court could grant Teledyne relief on the contract only if it finds that the 1986 Draft was finalized. But if the 1986 Draft were final and valid, the arbitration provision would be valid as well since it has not been the subject of any independent challenge. And if the arbitration provision were valid, Teledyne's claim would not belong in federal court in the first place.

*Id.* at 1410.

Moreover in *Teledyne* the parties did not dispute that they signed an agreement containing an arbitration provision, albeit labeled "draft agreement." The question was only as to the effect of the draft agreement. That was properly a matter for the arbitrator.

*Teledyne* does not apply here. Unlike the plaintiff in *Teledyne*, in this case the plaintiffs deny the existence of the contracts containing the arbitration provisions. By contending that they never entered into such contracts, plaintiffs also necessarily contest any agreements to arbitrate within the contracts. To require the plaintiffs to arbitrate where they deny that they entered into the contracts would be inconsistent with the "first principle" of arbitration that "a party cannot be required to submit [to arbitration] any dispute which he has not agreed so to submit." *AT&T Technologies, Inc. v. Communications*

*Workers*, 475 U.S. 643, 648, 106 S.Ct. 1415, 1418, 89 L.Ed.2d 648 (1986).[177]

. . .

We reverse and remand the district court's order staying the federal proceeding and directing arbitration of plaintiffs' RICO and state law claims (except as to Three Valleys). On remand, the district court must first determine whether the signatory had authority to bind the other plaintiffs to the agreements containing the arbitration clauses. In addition, we find that as to any plaintiffs which are bound to the agreements, the federal securities law claims are arbitrable and those plaintiffs have agreed to submit such claims to arbitration.

\* \* \*

2. *Apollo Computer, Inc. v. Berg*, 886 F.2d 469 (1st Cir. 1989).

The plaintiff appeals from a district court order refusing its request for a permanent stay of arbitration proceedings. The facts of the case are undisputed. On March 23, 1984, Apollo Computer, Inc. ("Apollo") and Dicoscan Distributed Computing Scandinavia AB ("Dico") entered into an agreement granting Dico, a Swedish company having its principal place of business in Stockholm, the right to distribute Apollo's computers in four Scandinavian countries. Helge Berg and Lars Arvid Skoog, the defendants in this action, signed the agreement on Dico's behalf in their respective capacities as its chairman and president. The agreement contained a clause stating that all disputes arising out of or in connection with the agreement would be settled in accordance with the Rules of Arbitration of the International Chamber of Commerce ("ICC"), and another clause that stated that the agreement was to be governed by Massachusetts law.

---

[177] [5] Although this "first principle" of arbitration was set forth in cases involving federal labor law, *see AT&T Technologies*, 475 U.S. at 648, 106 S.Ct. at 1418, it applies with equal force to arbitration in non-labor cases pursuant to the Federal Arbitration Act. *See I.S. Joseph Co. v. Michigan Sugar Co.*, 803 F.2d 396, 399 (8th Cir.1986); *Smith Wilson Co. v. Trading & Dev. Establishment*, 744 F.Supp. 14, 16 (D.D.C.1990); *see also Commercial Metals Co. v. Balfour, Guthrie, & Co.*, 577 F.2d 264, 266 (5th Cir.1978) (the Federal Arbitration Act does not confer jurisdiction on arbitrators absent an agreement of the parties to arbitrate).

The agreement also provided that it could not be assigned by Dico without the written consent of Apollo.

In September 1984, after disputes relating to the financing of Dico's purchases, Apollo notified Dico that it intended to terminate the agreement, effective immediately. Dico then filed for protection from its creditors under Swedish bankruptcy law and subsequently entered into liquidation, with its affairs being handled by its trustee in bankruptcy. The trustee assigned Dico's right to bring claims for damages against Apollo to the defendants. In May 1988, the defendants filed a complaint and a request for arbitration with the ICC.

On August 24, 1988, Apollo rejected arbitration, claiming that there was no agreement to arbitrate between it and the defendants, and that assignment of Dico's contractual right to arbitrate was precluded by the agreement's nonassignment clause. The ICC requested both parties to submit briefs on the issue. On December 15, 1988, the ICC's Court of Arbitration decided that pursuant to its rules, the arbitrator should resolve the issue of arbitrability, and directed the parties to commence arbitration proceedings to resolve that issue and, if necessary, the merits.

On January 11, 1989, Apollo filed the instant action in federal district court under diversity of citizenship jurisdiction. It sought a permanent stay of the arbitration, pursuant to M.G.L. ch. 251, §2(b), on the grounds that there is no arbitration agreement between the parties. The parties submitted a statement of material facts not in dispute. Apollo then moved for summary judgment. On May 11, 1989, the district court denied the request to stay arbitration and the motion for summary judgment.

.        .        .

[The Arbitration Clause (§ 14.13) provides, in pertinent part, as follows:

> All disputes arising out of or in connection with this Agreement which cannot be settled by discussion and mutual accord shall be finally settled by arbitration, in accordance with the rules of arbitration of the International Chamber of Commerce. . . . Judgment upon the award so rendered may be entered in any

court having jurisdiction, or application may be made to such court for a judicial acceptance of the award and order of enforcement, as the case may be.

The Non-Assignment Clause (§ 14.02) provides as follows:

> This Agreement shall inure to the benefit of and be binding upon DISTRIBUTOR and its successors and assigns but shall not be assignable by DISTRIBUTOR without the written consent first obtained of APOLLO. In the event DISTRIBUTOR wishes to delegate the performance of any of its obligations hereunder to a third party the written consent of APOLLO must first be obtained and APOLLO reserves the right to approve all terms of any such delegation. Any such purported assignment or delegation without written consent shall be void and of no effect.

The Termination Clause (§ 12.04) provides as follows:

> Except as otherwise provided herein, termination or cancellation of this Agreement shall terminate all further rights and obligations of APOLLO and DISTRIBUTOR hereunder, provided that: a) neither APOLLO nor DISTRIBUTOR shall be relieved of their respective obligations to pay any sums of money due or payable or accrued under this Agreement; and b) if such termination or cancellation is a result of a breach hereof by a party hereto the other party shall be entitled to pursue any and all rights and remedies it has to redress such breach in law or equity, subject to the limitations [of liability provisions] set forth in Section 9 of this Agreement.]

*Arbitrability*

Having determined that we have jurisdiction over this appeal, we now turn to the merits, beginning with a summary of the opinion below. The district court first decided that the parties had explicitly agreed to have the issue of arbitrability decided by the arbitrator. Notwithstanding this conclusion, the court then proceeded to analyze the issue of arbitrability itself. It determined that Dico would have the right to seek arbitration of the underlying claims if it had pursued them on its own behalf. The only remaining issue, the court reasoned, was whether the agreement's non-assignment clause prevented the defendants from asserting Dico's right to arbitrate. The court ruled that it did not because under Massachusetts law, a general nonassignment clause will be construed as barring only the delegation of duties, not the assignment of rights.

Apollo makes the following claims on appeal. First, it argues that the right to compel arbitration did not survive the termination of the agreement, so that even Dico would not have had the right to compel arbitration of the claims at issue. Second, it argues that even if Dico had the right to compel arbitration of the claims, it had not validly assigned that right to the defendants. Third, it argues that the agreement's nonassignment clause renders the purported assignment unenforceable against Apollo.

We do not reach any of these arguments because we find that the parties contracted to submit issues of arbitrability to the arbitrator. . . .

In this case, the parties agreed that all disputes arising out of or in connection with their contract would be settled by binding arbitration "in accordance with the rules of arbitration of the International Chamber of Commerce." Article 8.3 of the ICC's Rules of Arbitration states:

> Should one of the parties raise one or more pleas concerning the existence or validity of the agreement to arbitrate, and should the [Court of Arbitration of the International Chamber of Commerce] be satisfied of the *prima facie* existence of such an agreement, the [Court of Arbitration of the International Chamber of Commerce] may, without prejudice to the admissibility or merits of the plea or pleas, decide that the arbitration shall proceed. In such a case, any decision as to the arbitrator's jurisdiction shall be taken by the arbitrator himself.

Article 8.4 of the ICC's Rules of Arbitration states:

> Unless otherwise provided, the arbitrator shall not cease to have jurisdiction by reason of any claim that the contract is null and void or allegation that it is inexistent

provided that he upholds the validity of the agreement to arbitrate. He shall continue to have jurisdiction, even though the contract itself may be inexistent or null and void, to determine the respective rights of the parties and to adjudicate upon their claims and pleas.

The contract therefore delegates to the arbitrator decisions about the arbitrability of disputes involving the existence and validity of a *prima facie* agreement to arbitrate.

Both the ICC's Court of Arbitration and the district court determined that a *prima facie* agreement to arbitrate existed. Therefore, they reasoned, Article 8.3 requires the arbitrator to determine the validity of the arbitration agreement in this specific instance—in other words, decide whether the arbitration agreement applies to disputes between Apollo and the assignees of Dico.

Apollo did not discuss this issue in its brief. At oral argument, it averred that Article 8.3 is inapplicable because no *prima facie* agreement to arbitrate exists between it and the defendants. We are unpersuaded by this argument. The relevant agreement here is the one between Apollo and Dico. The defendants claim that Dico's right to compel arbitration under that agreement has been assigned to them. We find that they have made the *prima facie* showing required by Article 8.3. Whether the right to compel arbitration survives the termination of the agreement, and if so, whether that right was validly assigned to the defendants and whether it can be enforced by them against Apollo are issues relating to the continued existence and validity of the agreement.

Ordinarily, Apollo would be entitled to have these issues resolved by a court. *See, e.g., I.S. Joseph Co., Inc. v. Michigan Sugar Co.*, 803 F.2d 396, 399-400 (8th Cir.1986); *American Safety Equipment Corp. v. J.P. Maguire & Co.*, 391 F.2d 821, 828-29 (2d Cir.1968). By contracting to have all disputes resolved according to the Rules of the ICC, however, Apollo agreed to be bound by Articles 8.3 and 8.4. These provisions clearly and unmistakably allow the arbitrator to determine her own jurisdiction when, as here, there exists a *prima facie* agreement to arbitrate whose continued existence and validity is being questioned. *See Société Generale*, 643 F.2d at 869. The arbitrator should decide whether a valid arbitration agreement exists between Apollo and the defendants under the terms of the contract between Apollo and Dico.[178] Consequently, without expressing any opinion on the merits of the issues raised by Apollo, we affirm the district court's order denying a permanent stay of the arbitration proceedings. . . .

### Notes and Questions

1. Compare the approach of the U.S. Supreme Court in *First Options v. Kaplan*, *supra* p. 502.

2. For the arbitral tribunal's interim award on jurisdiction in *Apollo Computers v. Berg*, see Chapter 6, *infra* p. 685. A sequel to this case, *Hewlett Packard v. Berg*, 61 F.3d 101 (1st Cir. 1995), concerned set-off of claims subject to arbitration.

3. In *Overseas Union Ins. Ltd. v. AA Mut. Int'l Ins. Co.*, 2 Lloyd's Rep. 63 (1988), the court seems to imply that judges can construe arbitration clauses without reference to national policy. Justice Evans says that he must "reject the notion that the construction of [particular] arbitration clauses should be influenced by some supposed judicial attitude toward arbitration clauses [generally], whether of disapproval in the earlier days or of greater keenness more recently." Is this "voodoo jurisprudence" in which words may be presumed to have a content apart from their context? Or, is the real problem that arbitral clauses raise *several* competing judicial attitudes and national policies? What are these different attitudes and policies?

4. One issue that arises repeatedly in determining the validity of an arbitration clause is the matter of whether a purported agent actually had, or could be assumed to have had, authority to bind one of the parties to an alleged contract. Should such disputes over the formation of the agreement to arbitrate be dealt with by courts or by arbitrators? See the Memorandum Opinion of Judge Richey in *Smith Wilson Co. v. Trading & Dev. Establishment*, No. 90 Civ. 1125 (D.D.C. Aug. 30, 1990), finding the question of an agent's authority to be one for a court or a jury.

5. Time Limits.

No consensus yet exists on whether courts or arbitrators should have the last word on time bars and other preconditions to arbitration. Certain arbitration rules require disputes to be brought within a fixed time after the controverted events. For

---

[178] [5] The fact that the arbitrability determination turns on complicated legal issues does not alter our conclusion, because contracting parties are at liberty to entrust an arbitrator with the resolution of such issues. *See Local 369, Utility Workers Union v. Boston Edison Co.*, 752 F.2d 1, 3 (1st Cir.1984); *George Day Constr. Co., Inc. v. United Brotherhood of Carpenters*, 722 F.2d 1471, 1475 (9th Cir.1984).

example, the National Association of Securities Dealers Code of Arbitration provide that "no dispute, claim or controversy shall be eligible for submission to arbitration under this Code where six years have elapsed from the occurrence or event giving rise to the act or dispute, claim or controversy." One recent decision held a time bar to be a question for arbitrators, citing language in the NASD Code to the effect that arbitrators could "interpret and determine the applicability of all provisions under this Code." See *Painewebber v. Elahi*, 87 F.3d 589 (1st Cir. 1996). Compare *Merrill Lynch v. Cohen*, 62 F. 3d 381 (11th Cir. 1995), holding that courts, not arbitrators, must decide whether a claim is time barred under arbitration rules.

Analogous questions arise with respect to statutes of limitations imposed by substantive law rather than by arbitration rules. Some courts have held that applying a statute of limitations is for judges in the context of a motion to compel arbitration, but for arbitrators when raised in an arbitration of the underlying claim. See *National Iranian Oil v. Mapco Intern.*, 983 F.2d 485 (3d Cir. 1992); *Avant Petroleum v. Pecten Arabian Ltd.*, 696 F. Supp. 42 (S.D.N.Y. 1988). Such decisions rest on the assumption that there are two separate contracts, subject to two separate statutes of limitations: the principal agreement (to buy, sell, license, lease or lend), whose interpretation is for the arbitrators, and the agreement to arbitrate, whose enforcement is for the courts.


## VI.    SUMMARY AND CONCLUSIONS

Human nature and business relationships being what they are, it is not surprising that companies seeking to initiate arbitration should sometimes meet resistance from their contractual counterparties. The recalcitrant party may believe, in good faith, that the arbitration clause does not cover the specific matters giving rise to the controversy. Or the party resisting arbitration may simply want to stall for time, to obtain a more favorable settlement, or to maneuver the other side into what is perceived as a more favorable (or biased) forum. In either event, the courts are faced with jurisdictional questions. As the materials in this chapter demonstrate, they do not yield to facile analysis.

In the previous chapter, we saw that one argument against permitting an arbitration to go forward is that forum public policy may have characterized the subject matter of the dispute as inappropriate for arbitral resolution. Equally common as a ground for resisting initiation of an arbitral proceeding is the claim that the arbitration clause is deficient as a contractual matter in any of the following ways: (i) the scope of the clause is too narrow to include the controverted events, (ii) the clause was void *ab initio*, or (iii) the clause has become invalid by some event subsequent to its execution, such as attempted rescission of the principal agreement. In such events, principles known under the appellations "separability" and "competence/competence" have been used to allocate between arbitrators and judges the task of deciding whether the arbitration should go forward.

The "separability" doctrine has gained acceptance in all major arbitral centers. The doctrine holds that the arbitration clause itself is separate from the main contract in which it is encapsulated. Therefore, a claim that the contract has become invalid (for example, because of one party's fraudulent inducement to contract) equally raises questions about the validity of the arbitration clause and does not, accordingly, prevent the arbitrators from ruling on the issue of contractual validity. Although sometimes hard to grasp conceptually, this doctrine makes sense from a practical perspective. The alternative could be destructive of arbitration, for it is all too easy for a party seeking to derail an arbitration at its inception to claim that the main agreement was or had become invalid.

The amalgam of motions that has come to be known as *compétence-compétence* or *Kompetenz-Kompetenz* will deal with the prospect of a party wishing to delay arbitration by an early challenge to arbitral jurisdiction, the doctrine holds that arbitrators are competent, at least as an initial matter, to rule on their own competence to hear the dispute. The timing of court review of such jurisdictional rulings will vary from country to country.

The problems of multi-party arbitration and of related parties that are non-signatories continue to vex arbitration. In some jurisdictions courts and legislatures have demonstrated creativity in dealing with both sets of difficulties. For the foreseeable future, however, lawyers will have to show special care at the drafting stage in order to insure that the arbitration will proceed against all relevant parties.

As we shall see in Chapter 9, many of the jurisdictional issues raised at the initial stages of the arbitral process will also be relevant if and when the award is presented for judicial confirmation, or challenged in a proceeding to enforce or to vacate the award.

CHAPTER 5

# CHOOSING ARBITRATORS

## I. INTRODUCTION

One of the more obvious differences between litigation before ordinary courts and arbitration is that in arbitration one may "choose one's judge." In considering the process of nominating arbitrators one should, however, bear in mind that the choice will not be unilateral. Both sides must agree to the manner in which the tribunal is constituted. Since it is generally impractical to name specific arbitrators at the date of signature of the contract containing the arbitration clause, and since such agreement may be unlikely once a dispute has arisen, arbitration clauses normally define a *method* for the nomination of the tribunal. With a three-member tribunal, each side usually designates one arbitrator. The problem then arises with respect to the selection of the third person to serve as the chairman. (The same problem arises when the parties must select a sole arbitrator.) If the parties cannot agree, a third party, an "appointing authority," must choose the chairman. The appointing authority could be a judge but typically is an arbitral institution.

> A.   O. Glossner, *Sociological Aspects of International Commercial Arbitration, in* THE ART OF ARBITRATION 143, 144-46 (Pieter Sanders ed., 1982).

'L'arbitrage vaut ce que vaut l'arbitre!' This phrase has a proverbial quality. To be an arbitrator is to exercise an honourable function. It is not a profession, although there are institutions which train arbitrators aiming more at the non-lawyer as it is not necessary that the arbitrator be a lawyer. He can be just as well a technical expert or an engineer. But he must be a person of knowledge and high moral standard. He must be able to appease parties who may quarrel over a contract. He may possibly have to see that the parties agree to a settlement. It is only natural that the parties listen more attentively to someone who speaks to them from a position of experience, knowledge, or reputation. To be an arbitrator is a noble task, which challenges the whole personality, all of its intellectual and physical capacities. He is entrusted by virtue of a contract with the parties to an arbitration to

541

deal with their property, to decide on their investment, to present conclusions with far-reaching consequences, which can only be challenged, if there is proof that the parties' basic rights of due process have been violated. The responsibility of an arbitrator is immense. If he fails there is practically no remedy available, because most laws do not allow one to sue an arbitrator for a wrong decision and, what is decisive, arbitrators cannot grant compensation for a possible damage caused to a party, even if they could be sued, for lack of means. This is what makes it difficult to believe that amiable composition, a foster child of French legal intellect, where the arbitrator is his own master in the decision making process, but for the mandatory provisions of the law, is in practice a recommendable form of arbitration. No one can finally appraise the arbitrator's sense of justice and feeling for practical needs until decision has been rendered by him. It seems better to have the arbitrator observe controllable legal standards.

*    *    *

Since the quality of an arbitration is profoundly dependent on the quality of the arbitral tribunal, one should not entrust the task of selecting a tribunal to an unknown institution. At great cost, a Canadian company discovered in the following case the importance of choosing a known appointing authority.

B.      *Severe sentences for a bogus "arbitration,"* LE MONDE, July 5, 1988, at 18 (translated by the editors).

STRASBURG - On 1 July the criminal court of Strasburg sentenced Mr. Maurice Vignals, 63, President of the Centre national d'arbitrage (CNA), to three years imprisonment and a 200,000 francs fine for attempted fraud against a Canadian company, Bel Tronics, which has a plant in Cernay in Haut-Rhin.

The case began in 1986 in the aftermath of a commercial dispute between the Canadian company, which specialized in alarm systems and satellite TV antennas, and a Strasburg company, Portex, which one year earlier had signed a contract to become the exclusive distributor of Bel Tronics' products in Europe. The contract provided that in the event of a commercial dispute the two companies would refer the matter to an organization called the Centre national d'arbitrage (CNA), which had an office in Vendenheim in Bas-Rhin.

In May 1986, the conflict between the two companies became so acute that Portex invoked this [arbitration] clause and filed with the CNA a request that Bel Tronics be ordered to pay nearly 5 million francs in damages. There followed a brief procedural battle at the end of which the CNA tribunal, which has its seat in Bordeaux, decided that Bel Tronics should be ordered to pay 91 million francs to Portex and to pay the latter's fees and costs in an amount of nearly 2 million francs.

This caused the Canadian company to worry; to pay such an amount would mean that it would purely and simply have to shut down the factory it had built in Cernay with the help of various Alsatian municipal authorities. It therefore commenced an action before the Court of Appeal of Bordeaux in order to have the award set aside, but on 14 October 1987 that Court rejected the application. Thus in theory the CNA award took on executory force.

At this point, executives of the Canadian company asked for a more in-depth investigation of CNA. It was this investigation that led to the indictment of three men, on the grounds of fraud and attempted fraud and an appearance on 24 June before the criminal court of Strasburg. Mr. Maurice Vignals, President of the CNA, his Alsatian correspondent, Mr Bernard Ardouin, and the general manager of Portex, Mr. Michel Viandier, were accused of having organized a fictitious arbitration to the detriment of the Canadian company.

The investigation revealed that CNA barely existed except on paper and that the supposed members of the "arbitral tribunal" in fact never met to render the decisions that were served on Bel Tronics. The minutes of the meetings were forgeries. The arbitral tribunal was comprised of Mr. Maurice Vignals alone; Mr. Vignals had also succeeded in deluding the judges of the Bordeaux Court of Appeal.

Apart from the sentence against the President of the CNA, the criminal court of Strasburg severely punished the CNA's Alsatian representative, Mr. Bernard Ardouin, by sentencing him to two years imprisonment and a 100,000 franc fine, and the chief executive of Portex, Mr. Michel Viandier, 36, was found to be an accomplice and given a two year suspended sentence and a 100,000 franc fine.

\* \* \*

## II.    PROCEDURES FOR SELECTION

There exists a wide variety of procedures for naming arbitrators. You will recall from the discussion in Chapter 2 the systems created under the following rules (reproduced in the Supplement): Article 2 of the ICC Rules of Arbitration; Article 3 of the LCIA Rules; Articles 6-8 of the UNCITRAL Rules; and Articles 12-16 and 37-40 of the 1965 ICSID Convention, which should be read in conjunction with Rules 2-6 of the ICSID Rules of Procedure for Arbitration Proceedings. When reviewing these provisions, the following crucial and concrete questions should be kept in mind:

-    if the agreement to arbitrate is silent on the number of arbitrators, will there be a sole arbitrator or a three-member tribunal?

-    if there is to be a three-member tribunal, who will appoint the arbitrators?

-    if each of the parties has the possibility of nominating an arbitrator, are there any restrictions on whom they can name?

-    what happens if the agreement to arbitrate or the relevant rules of arbitration require that arbitrators have certain qualifications (such as nationality or training in a given body of law), and a party which has the right to nominate an arbitrator in fact nominates someone who (1) manifestly or (2) arguably does not fulfill that criterion?

-    what happens if a party which has the right to nominate an arbitrator designates someone who is (1) manifestly or (2) arguably disqualified on grounds of conflict of interest or for other ethical reasons?

-    how would the other party or the arbitral institution know the factual circumstances that might raise doubts about the nominee's suitability?

- how do appointing authorities select arbitrators?

Some arbitral institutions, such as the American Arbitration Association and the Netherlands Arbitration Institute, provide for so-called list procedures by which sole arbitrators or chairmen of three-member tribunals may be selected by the institution's communicating to each side a list of names which the parties then rank or reject. The process is designed to result in the appointment of the candidate who both parties respect. Article 14 of the Arbitration Rules of the Netherlands Arbitration Institute provides:

Article 14. List-Procedure

(1) As soon as possible after receipt of the short answer referred to in article 7 or, on [sic] the absence thereof, after expiration of the period of time for filing the short answer, the Administrator shall communicate to each of the parties an identical list of names. If one arbitrator is to be appointed, the list shall contain not less than three names; if three arbitrators are to be appointed, the list shall contain not less than nine names.

(2) Each party may delete from this list the names of persons against whom he has overriding objections, and number the remaining names in the order of his preference.

(3) If a list is not returned to the Administrator within two weeks after its dispatch to a party, it will be assumed that all persons appearing on it are equally acceptable to that party for appointment as arbitrator.

(4) As soon as possible after receipt of the lists, or failing this, after expiration of the period of time referred to in the previous paragraph, the Administrator shall, taking into account the preferences and/or objections expressed by the parties, invite one or three persons from the list, as the case may be, to act as arbitrators.

(5) If and to the extent that the lists which have been returned show an insufficient number of persons who

are acceptable as arbitrator to each of the parties, the Administrator shall be authorised to invite directly one or more other persons to act as arbitrator. The same shall apply if a person is not able or does not wish to accept the Administrator's invitation to act as arbitrator, or if there appear to be other reasons precluding him from acting as arbitrator, and there remain on the lists an insufficient number of persons who are acceptable as arbitrator to each of the parties.

(6) If the arbitral tribunal is composed of three arbitrators, the arbitrators shall choose a chairman from amongst themselves, if necessary, in accordance with the provisions of article 16(3).

(7) If the parties agreed only to the appointment of arbitrator(s) by the NAI, without referring to arbitration by the NAI or arbitration in accordance with the NAI Rules, such appointment shall take place in accordance with the provisions of this article unless the parties agreed to another method of appointment by the NAI.

(8) For the application of the provisions of this article, the Administrator preferably shall draw the names of persons from the General Panel of Arbitrators which is established, expanded and amended by the NAI.

(9) The appointment of the arbitrator(s) in accordance with the provisions of this article shall take place within two months after commencement of the arbitration.

## III.    TACTICAL CONSIDERATIONS

In deciding on an arbitrator, the parties' choice (unless they limit it themselves, for example by requiring or excluding certain nationalities) is virtually unrestricted. Subject to the requirement in some jurisdictions that the arbitrator be a lawyer (for example in Spain — if the dispute is of a legal nature) and other exceptions (for example in Saudi Arabia arbitrators must be Muslim), any natural person may be appointed.

Given such a wide choice, each party should be able to nominate an arbitrator in which it has confidence. What qualities might be important? Consider one discussion:

A.    ALAN REDFERN & MARTIN HUNTER, LAW AND PRACTICE OF INTERNATIONAL COMMERCIAL ARBITRATION 214-17 (2d ed. 1991).

Disputes which may be referred to international arbitration are too varied and too numerous for it to be sensible to lay down any general rule as to the kind of person who should or should not be chosen to act as an arbitrator. Each party must make up his own mind as to the qualifications he requires in an arbitrator in whom he will have full confidence. The most that can be done is to indicate some of the more important considerations.

Sole arbitrator

In international commercial arbitrations (as distinct from purely domestic arbitrations) before a sole arbitrator, it is usual to appoint a lawyer. Even where the dispute is relatively simple, difficult problems of procedure and of conflict of laws frequently arise; and these are problems which a lawyer with suitable experience is better equipped to handle than a person whose expertise lies in another area. As it is expressed in an ICC publication: "Because of the legal nature of international arbitration, most [ICC arbitrators] are lawyers or university professors."

Three arbitrators

Where the arbitral tribunal is to consist of three arbitrators, at least one member of the arbitral tribunal (preferably the presiding arbitrator) should be a lawyer or at least a person specifically qualified as an arbitrator, having studied arbitration law. There is no reason why the other two members of the arbitral tribunal should also be lawyers, unless the dispute is one in which the issues involved are principally issues of law. Part of the attraction of arbitration is the way in which the expertise necessary for the understanding and resolution of the dispute may be found amongst the arbitrators themselves. For example, if a dispute arises out of an international construction contract, involving matters of a technical nature, it may be appropriate that one or more of the members of the arbitral tribunal should be a civil engineer or someone skilled in the particular technical matters which are in issue. However, where the presiding arbitrator is likely to be a lawyer (as in ICC arbitrations) a party should consider his position carefully before being left in a situation in which (the other party having nominated a lawyer) the arbitral tribunal is composed of two lawyers "against" a technical expert arbitrator nominated by him.

### [ ] Language

It is highly desirable (not to say essential) that an arbitrator has an adequate working knowledge of the language in which the arbitration is to take place. This is an obvious requirement, but one which is forgotten not only by parties but by appointing authorities as well. If an arbitrator is appointed who does not have a good knowledge of the language of the arbitration, it becomes necessary to engage an interpreter to translate the evidence of the witnesses and the arguments of the lawyers into a language which can be understood by the arbitrator concerned. Translating oral evidence accurately into another language is a very difficult task, particularly where a witness is being examined in minute detail on his evidence of fact or opinion. It also adds considerably to the expense of the arbitral proceedings; first, because of the interpreter's fees and, secondly, because of the extra time which is taken if everything of importance has to be translated from the working language of the arbitration into a language which the arbitrator himself can understand.

### [ ] Experience and outlook

It is becoming increasingly important for international arbitrators to show their awareness of the world of international trade relations and of the different traditions, aims and expectations of the people of that world. An arbitrator, like anyone else, is inevitably conditioned by the education he has received and the society in which he has grown up. However, an experienced international arbitrator will try to be aware of his own shortcomings in this respect and will endeavour to adopt an outlook free from national or cultural prejudice, so as best to understand the conduct of the parties to the dispute. He will do no service to the parties, or indeed to international commercial arbitration in general, if he allows his personal background and training to dominate his approach to the issues which are in dispute:

> . . . in his conduct of the arbitration and in his awards
> - and this is an essential aspect of his objectivity - the
> international arbitrator of today must show proof of a
> comparative or comparatist mind, open to legal
> pluralism, to various cultures and various political and
> social systems. 'Arbitration will hardly be regarded by
> a party as a suitable way of solving the case' - writes
> Rene David quite rightly - 'if it is to be administered by
> an arbitrator who is imbued with the ways of thinking
> and the prejudices of another culture.'

The problem is a real one; and one of which the international arbitral
institutions have become increasingly aware. Many of the
less-developed nations lack confidence in international commercial
arbitration. This is largely because of the fear that arbitral tribunals,
established under the auspices of arbitral institutions based in the
world's major industrial nations, will have an inbuilt cultural and social
bias against them, however impeccable the intellectual integrity of the
individual arbitrators may be:

> With regard to judges - whose personal integrity cannot
> be called into question - one cannot deny the fact that by
> dint of belonging to a certain hemisphere and a certain
> social system, their conception of law can only be a
> reflection of their own system. They thus have a
> tendency to consider that the arguments of the Third
> World client are devoid of any legal basis, and to hold
> them ineffective once they fail to correspond with their
> own conception of law.

It would be wrong to choose someone as an arbitrator (and
particularly as a sole or presiding arbitrator) solely because of his
country of origin. It is the ability and qualifications of the arbitrator
himself which count, not his national or political background.
Nevertheless, it is also important that arbitrators should be selected
from outside the charmed circle of the industrialised nations. Western
lawyers, particularly those who represent parties from less-developed
countries, should be aware of this important consideration; and they
should recognise the need to assist in the development of a breed of
experienced arbitrators from such countries.

[ ] Education and training

Probably the most important qualification for an international arbitrator is that he should be experienced in the law and practice of arbitration. There is no sense in appointing as a sole or presiding arbitrator someone who is an experienced lawyer if that experience does not include practical experience of arbitration. Nor, for that matter, is it sensible to appoint a civil engineer or a structural engineer or an expert in nuclear physics, however distinguished he may be, and however relevant his experience may be to the issues in dispute, unless at the same time he has practical experience of the arbitral process. This may be less important when there is an arbitral tribunal of three arbitrators, but only if the presiding arbitrator at least has relevant experience of international arbitral practice. This point cannot be over-emphasised. The reputation and acceptability of the arbitral process depends on the quality of the arbitrators themselves. The task of presiding over the conduct of an international commercial arbitration is no less skilled than that of driving a car or flying an aircraft. It should not be entrusted to someone with no practical experience of it.

### Notes and Questions

1. In addition to these considerations, more general factors are often important. In particular, a party might consider the relative merits of appointing a common law as opposed to civil law lawyer or a lawyer as opposed to a technical expert.

2. Occasionally parties are tempted to abuse their right to make nominations, by naming someone manifestly biased, or by selecting a remote-controlled obstructionist, or by appointing someone who can be counted on to resign in a most untimely fashion. The 1985 LCIA Rules seek to deal with this problem in Article 3.5:

> In the event that the Court determines that a nominee is not suitable or independent or impartial, or if an appointed arbitrator is to be replaced, the Court shall have discretion to decide whether or not to follow the original nominating process. If it so decides any opportunity for renomination shall be waived if not exercised within 30 days, after which the Court shall appoint the replacement as soon as practicable.

Under some arbitration rules, the tribunal itself *i.e.*, generally the two remaining members — is given authority to rule on the consequences of an attempted resignation. This authority exists under the ICSID Rules, and in 1976 gave rise to what has become known as the Incident of Sir John Foster, which arose during the course of the first case ever brought under the ICSID Rules, namely *Holiday Inns/Occidental Petroleum v. Morocco*. The Claimants nominated Sir John Foster, an English barrister, and the Respondent nominated the French professor, Paul Reuter. Judge Sture Petrén of Sweden was the Chairman.

B.   *Holiday Inns/Occidental Petroleum v. Morocco*, 11 ICSID Ann. Rep. (W. Bank) 32, 34 (1977).

July 27, 1976. The Secretary-General informs the parties that the President has learned from John Foster that the latter had accepted an appointment as "outside director" on the Board of Occidental Petroleum Corporation, one of the Claimants.

September 27, 1976. Messrs. Sture Petrén and Paul Reuter met to consider Sir John Foster's resignation, which was submitted subject to the condition that the Claimants appoint his successor. They decided (i) that the condition attached to the resignation was not a proper one and should be disregarded, and (ii) to withhold the Tribunal's consent to the resignation. As a result, the proceedings were suspended and the vacancy was to be filled pursuant to Article 56(3) of the Convention by the Chairman of the Administrative Council. The Claimants objected to the Tribunal's decision . . . .

October 28, 1976. Professor J.C. Schultsz (Dutch), appointed by the Chairman of the Administrative Council to fill the vacancy created by Sir John Foster's resignation, accepts his appointment and the proceedings are resumed.

C.     Frédéric Eisemann,[179] *The Double Sanction of the ICSID Convention for Agreements or Understandings between an Arbitrator and the Party Appointing Him*, 23 ANNUAIRE FRANÇAIS DE DROIT INTERNATIONAL 436 (1977) (translation by the editors).

. . . Sir John Foster's change of situation was not strictly speaking incompatible with the declaration he signed at the outset of the case to the effect that he would act impartially and not accept any remuneration "in relation to the case." It thus appears that there must have been something more that caused Chairman Petrén and Professor Reuter, after numerous consultations with the Secretary General, to have condemned their colleague's acceptance of appointment as a board member in such a categorical fashion. Did they suppose that there had been a grave case of dishonest scheming? In our view, this must be the conclusion if one is to stick to the letter of the ICSID Convention. There then remains the "spirit" - a notion which is sufficiently vague that it allows for a number of tests, including, in particular, that of the rule of deontology. The latter does in fact appear to disapprove, for the duration of the proceedings, contacts between an arbitrator and the party which designated him. *A fortiori*, one might take the view, from a deontological point of view, that contacts resulting in a nomination to the board of the company which itself designated the arbitrator are incompatible with the image and function of any arbitration; however, from this point of view, one is simply led to consider that the arbitrator has an ethical duty to make a choice: either to decline the proposal, or to resign as arbitrator.

The arbitrator opted for the latter. . . The other arbitrators, after consultations with the Secretary General of ICSID, concluded that they could not accept the condition to which their colleague had sought to subject his resignation; this was motivated by the gravity of the facts underlying the resignation. What was this "condition"? Sir John Foster had simply insisted that the Claimants be put in a position to name his replacement. In other words, far from conditioning his resignation on something of itself extravagant, the arbitrator asked for nothing more than the application of the general rule in such circumstances. There exists no set of rules outside the ICSID system which envisages any

---

[179] Former Secretary-General of the ICC Court of Arbitration.

other outcome. Byzantine though it may be, the refusal to allow the Claimant to exercise its right to designate the replacement had its foundation in Article 56(3) of the Convention, which authorizes the Arbitral Tribunal to refuse to "approve" a resignation. . . This is purely a fiction, because such a refusal does not obligate the resigning arbitrator to continue to exercise his functions - to the contrary! What is really at work is a double sanction which consists of first removing an arbitrator and then imposing his replacement on the party which designated him. But this double sanction is not the only conceivable result. Even in the system of the ICSID Convention, there must be exceptional circumstances to justify the Arbitral Tribunal's treatment of a resignation as having been given "without its consent" and thus to cause the President of the World Bank to intervene and to name the replacement instead of allowing the concerned party to do so.

. . . [I]t is appropriate to recall the origins of this procedure: what reasons militated in favor of a breach with a principle of the law of arbitration which is generally recognized and, it would seem, applied without damage to the arbitral process?

Inter-State arbitration has often been aborted by the resignation or - which amounts to the same thing - withdrawal of a "national" arbitrator. This tactic of obstructing the arbitration and thus depriving the arbitral agreement of all effect is rare in private international arbitration and poses no particular problem in that context. It is curious to observe that the system of the ICSID Convention contains the same anti-obstructionist provisions as those to be found in private-law institutional arbitration, which in their context have proved able to neutralize all kinds of attempts to block the proceedings, including those made by a State party. In particular, the President of ICSID's Administrative Council is called upon by Article 38 to remedy default by naming the arbitrator or arbitrators not yet designated at the expiry of a relatively short deadline. As this mechanism also applies - once again in conformity with the practice of private-law arbitral institutions - in the same fashion with respect to filling vacancies, the resignation or withdrawal of an arbitrator cannot block the arbitration.

But this weapon was not considered sufficient to ensure that tribunals in the ICSID system would remain "immutable". . . . . In 1958, the Commentary to the [Model Inter-State Arbitration Rules prepared by the International Law Commission of the United Nations] declared bluntly "that it is not practically possible to prevent an arbitrator from resigning or withdrawing if he so desires, and in such an event it is sufficient to provide that the vacancy will be filled in accordance with the procedure used for the initial nomination." It is therefore somewhat surprising to find, ten years later, the ICSID Convention to have reverted almost *verbatim* to the abandoned system of a 1953 [draft] which conditioned the right of the interested party to designate a replacement for the retired arbitrator upon "the consent of the Arbitral Tribunal."

. . . ICSID unquestionably "has jurisdiction which cannot be defeated by the unilateral act of one of the parties": but can one claim that that would not have been the case without the penalizing provision envisaged in 1953 by the International Law Commission and abandoned by the same Commission in 1958? Doubts were expressed on several occasions, during the preparatory sessions, as to the wisdom of the rule in question. Are the explanations which were given then able to throw light on the triggering of this fearful mechanism in [this] case?

A Turkish representative expressed his failure to understand why one should abandon the general principle of Article 56(1) which provided that a vacancy should be filled in accordance with the original mode of designation. An Israeli expert withdrew his objections only after Mr. Broches [the future Secretary General of ICSID, acting as Chairman of the session] gave assurances that the provision would be invoked only "in exceptional circumstances" and indicated that its purpose was to "prevent collusion" between parties and arbitrators designated by them. The same explanation was given by Mr. Broches during the plenary session of 23 February 1965 when Latin American representatives . . . expressed their preference for the solution given by the International Law Commission in 1958. According to the record, Mr. Broches concluded as follows: "If a party could prevail upon an arbitrator to resign in the course of the proceedings without cause, he would be able to frustrate or slow down the proceedings." Although these explanations were not sufficient to cause all delegates to assent to the controversial provision, other participants expressed favorable views; among their statements, one might in particular note the one which gave as the objective of the text "to ensure that the proceedings be conducted in good faith." As can be seen, this leaves a range of possible reasons for not consenting to a resignation - which does not facilitate the task of arbitrators called upon to rule on a request to resign.

One might even query whether the authors of the provision relating to the consent of the Tribunal intended this sanction to be applied without distinction to States and to private parties, to claimants and to respondents. . . . [W]ho did the draftsmen want to discourage? This problem did not of course arise with respect to the draft Inter-State arbitration rules of 1953. As Article 56(3) is borrowed *verbatim* from this draft, it is probably but a matter of pure chance that Professor P. Lalive envisaged only "the withdrawal of an arbitrator on the instructions of the government party" and considered that "the system of the World Bank Convention eliminates these difficulties and would appear well suited to discourage States from having recourse to this tactic". . . . But this supposition cannot be reconciled with the experience of international commercial arbitration between States and private parties, which leads to the conclusion that one may ensure that proceedings are conducted in appropriate fashion; why would the situation be different with respect to "semi-international" arbitrations under the auspices of ICSID?

Be this as it may, it is regrettable that the draftsmen thought it unimportant to define "acceptable" grounds of resignation on the grounds that "the experience of other international arbitral institutions appears reassuring in this regard." This explanation is not very clear: a list of grounds would not have been of the slightest interest in the framework of the 1958 Model Rules where no resignation during the course of proceedings - accepted in principle irrespective of its grounds - could deprive the interested party of its right to designate the replacement, provided only that it respect applicable deadlines for so doing. As we have already emphasized, this is precisely the system adopted by all institutions for international commercial arbitration, to wit the designation of the replacement by the initial nominating method.

We are not of course in a position to criticize the Tribunal's application in this case of a rule which is unprecedented in the contemporary law and institutional practice of arbitration. It is nevertheless permissible to wonder whether this incident serves the interests concerned and, more generally, whether it is likely to enhance the prestige of ICSID. This is not a matter of questioning the good intentions of the authors of Article 56(3), let alone the conviction expressed by Mr. Broches . . . to the effect that the measures adopted by the Tribunal had served an objective of the highest interest for all contracting States: "that the integrity of the arbitral proceedings commenced under the auspices of the Convention be safeguarded." This commendable attitude, however, immediately clashes with a purely pragmatic objection: if one considers that the arbitrator who became a member of the board of the company which had designated him was deontologically bound to withdraw, is that "sanction" not enough to discourage an arbitrator and a party from establishing relations incompatible with the arbitral process?

A final reflection on the advisability of the second sanction: the nomination of a replacement without the participation of the interested party. What would in fact have happened if Sir John Foster had not given his resignation? One might imagine the not inconceivable case that the arbitrator might, in accordance with a widely held view, have considered that his new situation did not prevent him from fulfilling the undertakings contained in the declaration prescribed by Article 6 of the ICSID Rules of Arbitration [to the effect that the arbitrator will respect the secrecy of the proceedings, and will reach his decision equitably without receiving any instructions or remuneration relating to the case except from ICSID]. One might suppose that in such as case, the Tribunal would not have been authorized to make a ruling on the matter unless it had been seized of a challenge by the adverse party, the Government of Morocco, under Article 57 of the Convention. What would have happened? The Tribunal would undoubtedly have ruled that the challenge was well founded and thus have brought about the same vacancy as that created after the resignation of Sir John Foster. Only in this case, the claimants would have been in a position to fill the vacancy by designating within the relevant deadline the replacement of their choice.

[The parties eventually amicably settled the dispute in 1978.]


### Notes and Questions

1. Article 3.5 of the 1985 LCIA Rules, of course, did not exist at the time of this incident. (For the LCIA Rules, see Supplement at p. 513.) What views would the two Secretaries-General (Broches of ICSID, Eisemann of the ICC Court) have taken of this provision? The following is what the two principal draftsmen of the 1985 LCIA Rules had to say:

PARTY APPOINTED ARBITRATORS. The rules are designed to dissuade parties from abusing opportunities to nominate arbitrators. In cases where such an opportunity exists (generally because the parties have agreed that there shall be three arbitrators, of whom two are to be nominated by the parties), it is waived unless it is exercised within 30 days of receipt by the respondent of the Request for Arbitration. (Article 3.4.)

Furthermore, when making such nominations, the parties are discouraged from proposing arbitrators who are not suitable or independent or impartial, or who are otherwise unsuitable, because the Court may refuse to appoint such nominees. (Article 3.3.) Indeed, if an unacceptable nomination has been made (or perhaps more likely if consecutive unacceptable nominations have been made), the Court retains discretion to refuse to allow the party to make a new nomination, and to make the appointment itself. (Article 3.5.)

If an arbitrator is to be replaced after he has been appointed (whether because he resigned or because he was removed for cause), the Court also retains the discretion not to follow the original nominating procedure. (Article 3.5.)

Practitioners having experience of cases where respondents have used the opportunity of naming arbitrators as a dilatory tactic - or, worse, as a chance to designate someone who will reveal everything about the tribunal's deliberations to his "client" - will recognize that these Rules have a lot of teeth. The LCIA hopes that the Rules will seldom have to be applied in their full severity, and that their very existence will cause all parties to behave reasonably, and in the process contribute to the development of a generally acceptable deontology of international arbitration.[180]

2. Contrast the LCIA method for dealing with this problem with that of the ICC, AAA and UNCITRAL Rules. Which appears to be more efficient?

## IV.    PARTY-APPOINTED ARBITRATORS

Arbitrations may be conducted by a tribunal comprised of any number of arbitrators. In important international commercial disputes, however, the tendency is to appoint a three-person tribunal. In most cases, each party will appoint one arbitrator and the third will be appointed by agreement between the parties, by the two

---

[180] *See* Martin Hunter and Jan Paulsson, *A Commentary on the 1985 Rules of the London Court of International Arbitration*, 10 YEARBOOK OF COMMERCIAL ARBITRATION 167 (1985).

party-nominated arbitrators or by the institution under whose auspices the arbitration is being conducted.

To what extent is a party-nominated arbitrator held to standards of objectivity? Must he remain neutral, impartial and independent? Indeed, to what extent is it realistic to apply these terms, which are often used interchangeably to describe the required attributes, to a party-appointed arbitrator? Discussion here will be restricted to the concepts of neutrality and independence. Arbitrators' impartiality is considered in Chapter 8, Section II, *infra*.

The party-appointed arbitrator is not like a judge whose responsibilities are determined by the state; rather the parties and/or the arbitral institution supervising the arbitration determine the arbitrator's responsibilities. Is it therefore optimistic to expect arbitrators not to be influenced by any form of prejudice? The American Arbitration Association and the American Bar Association recognize that on occasion arbitrators will not be neutral. However, with full disclosure of the position, such non-neutrality is considered acceptable:

A.      Robert Coulson, *Do we Know How Arbitration Panels Decide?*, J. INT'L ARB., June 1989, at 7, 10-11.

. . . In the United States, some people suspect that a party-appointed arbitrator will be biased in favor of the appointing party. The Code of Ethics for Commercial Arbitrators adopted by the American Arbitration Association and the American Bar Association confronts that issue, going at some length to tell parties how to protect themselves:

> In all arbitrations in which there are two or more party-appointed arbitrators, it is important for everyone concerned to know from the start whether the party-appointed arbitrators are expected to be neutrals or non-neutrals. In such arbitrations, the two party-appointed arbitrators should be considered non-neutrals unless both parties inform the arbitrators that all three arbitrators are to be neutral, or unless the contract, the applicable arbitration rules, or any governing law requires that all three arbitrators are to be neutral. AAA-ABA Code, page 13.

The Code of Ethics instructs non-neutral arbitrators to act in good faith, with integrity, and with fairness, even though they may be predisposed towards a party. They should not engage in delaying tactics or harass the other party or a witness or mislead the other arbitrators. They should disclose any relationship they may have with the party that appointed them. If they intend to communicate with that party during the arbitration, they should advise the other arbitrators and the other parties.

A leading English lawyer, Martin Hunter, covered that subject in the November 1987 issue of Arbitration:

> The arbitral process is brought into disrepute if the presiding arbitrator finds himself in the middle, between two party-nominated arbitrators taking extreme positions. His choice is to allow the arbitration to collapse by reason of there being no award at all or to select one of the party-nominated arbitrators to negotiate with in the hope of finding some form of compromise that will achieve a majority award. . . it seems clear that a party may nominate an arbitrator who is predisposed towards him personally in a very general sense, or as regards his position in the disputes, provided that the nominee is at the same time capable of applying his mind judicially and impartially to the evidence and arguments submitted by both parties. Indeed, when I am representing a client in arbitration, what I am really looking for in a party nominated arbitrator is someone with the maximum predisposition towards my client, but with the minimum appearance of bias. pp. 222-223

Some advocates might apply Hunter's appointment strategy to the entire panel, attempting to recruit neutral arbitrators who are thought to be predisposed, but with no appearance of bias. Lawyers like to win cases.

The intention of each party in arbitration is to persuade the panel that their position is correct, not to achieve some idealized version of perfect justice. In some situations, a tripartite system of arbitration may serve the interests of the parties more effectively than a panel made up of three totally impartial arbitrators.

Certain kinds of disputes may be better decided by panels that include party-appointed arbitrators who are avowed advocates for their party. When arbitration is used to facilitate continuing negotiations, a tripartite panel may inject an extra motivation to bargain. In such a structure, the umpire must bargain with each party-appointed arbitrator in an effort to achieve a majority. Depending upon the nature of the issues, party-appointed advocate/arbitrators may energize the executive sessions by educating the umpire about the complex background of the dispute or by identifying unsuspected flaws in a proposed award.

### Notes and Questions

1. Coulson's view is that, provided that each party is aware of the status of the other's arbitrator, the notion of so-called "non-neutrals" is accepted in the United States, where the Code applies to domestic arbitrations. Lawyers should undoubtedly recognise this acceptance in appointing arbitrators on behalf of their clients. Do you agree? Why?

2. A general predisposition on the part of the arbitrator towards one's client may be acceptable. But how far can this predisposition go? Can an arbitrator be appointed who is bound to make certain decisions as a representative of the party appointing him? This question is particularly important in bi-national panels or those created by conventions or other international agreements. The issue is discussed in the context of NAFTA, *infra* p. 581.

B.    JOHN BASSETT MOORE, HISTORY AND DIGEST OF THE INTERNATIONAL ARBITRATIONS TO WHICH UNITED STATES HAS BEEN A PARTY (reporting J.G.A. McKenny v. Mexico (Mexico v. U.S.A.) 1876 award of Mixed Commission) (1898).

[I]t is argued by counsel that the act of the United States Government in recognizing Zuloaga is conclusive upon Mr. Commissioner Wadsworth, because he is the "judicial representative of the United States in this Commission," and that for this reason he is precluded from even inquiring into the propriety of the recognition by the United States of the government of Zuloaga. It is scarcely necessary to remark that this view is founded upon a total misconception of the nature and character of the office of a commissioner under the convention between the United States and Mexico. Mr.

Commissioner Wadsworth is not a "judicial representative of the United States in this commission," nor "a judicial officer" of that government. The authority which he possesses he derives from both the United States and Mexico, and is obliged to exercise it impartially for the benefit of both. He would possess neither office nor authority without the consent and concurrence of both nations, and is not more bound by the official acts or municipal regulations of the United States than by those of Mexico. He derives his appointment to a place on the board - a place created by the action of both governments - from the Government of the United States, indeed, but is no more bound by this appointment to represent the interests of the United States than those of Mexico, and no more bound by the acts of that government than his colleague on the board, or their umpire. He is an impartial arbiter selected by the United States, but deriving all his powers from the United States and Mexico, nor more the officer of the former than of the latter.

*     *     *

Whatever may be the debate about neutrality, it is clear that, in nominating an arbitrator, a party should not nominate an individual who lacks independence. Indeed, the question of independence of party-nominated arbitrators is expressly dealt with in the rules of certain arbitral institutions (such as Article 2(4) of the ICC Rules). A party-nominated arbitrator must not, for example, have a financial interest in the outcome of the case or be unilaterally remunerated by the party which appointed him.

In cases where an arbitrator are remunerated by the party who appointed him there can be little debate about their independence. What other grounds may there be for doubting the arbitrator's independence? Stephen Bond, then Secretary General of the ICC Court of Arbitration, in 1988 gave some indication of the factors which lead the ICC Court to refuse to confirm the appointment of arbitrators. His views apply also to chairmen of tribunals, with regard to whom the question of independence is considered in Part V below.

C.      Stephen R. Bond, *The Selection of ICC Arbitrators and the Requirement of Independence*, 4 ARB. INT'L 300, 307-09 (1988).

As with challenges, the reasons for the decisions by the court as to appointments or confirmation are not communicated. This is consistent with the administrative, as opposed to jurisdictional, nature of the court's role. Of course, in virtually every instance the parties and the prospective arbitrator concerned are fully aware of the facts relating to independence which have been placed before the court as they have been set out either in the Statement of Independence of the prospective arbitrator or in the request for non-confirmation of a party and each document would have been notified by the Secretariat to all concerned for comment within a fixed time-period. The comments received are not notified for further comment lest the process continue indefinitely, in order to promote full and frank comments and, again, because the decision is of an administrative nature.

Regarding the source of the court's standards in deciding upon matters of independence, it has correctly been observed that 'The Court certainly does not act as an institutional appendage of any national court system . . . At the same time the Court does bear in mind the general mandate of Article 26 of the Rules that ". . . The Court of Arbitration shall act in the spirit of these Rules and shall make every effort to make sure that the award is enforceable by law."' As stated above, the court members certainly have in mind the desirability of promoting to the greatest extent possible the confidence of the parties in the arbitral tribunal, although such an objective must be balanced to a certain extent with the objective of avoiding unwarranted delays and discouraging dilatory manoeuvres.

Likewise, the ICC Court certainly takes into account in assessing each case whether the particular facts demonstrate a close, substantial, recent and proven relationship between a party and a prospective arbitrator. Great weight is also accorded to the views of the parties. Where, in the face of a Statement of Independence with reservations, the parties raise no objections to the prospective arbitrator, the court almost always confirms or appoints him. (Of course in every one of these instances the prospective arbitrator has stated that the facts disclosed do not affect his independence and that he is, in fact, independent.) Further, in almost every instance where a party has objected to a confirmation of a prospective co-arbitrator based on reservations in the Statement of Independence, the court has refused confirmation. However, the parties' views are not necessarily decisive. Especially as regards a prospective chairman, the court may well refuse appointment without even requesting the views of the parties and, in the few instances where a party has raised objections not based on reservations set out in the Statement of Independence (based on, for example, the arbitrator's nationality or the fact of not having heard of the prospective arbitrator), the court has tended to confirm the arbitrator.

Turning from the general to the more concrete, not surprisingly the most common basis for refusal by the ICC Court to confirm or appoint a prospective arbitrator is a past or present direct professional link between the arbitrator and a party or between a business associate of the arbitrator and a party or an entity connected to a party. Typical in this regard are prospective arbitrators who as lawyers had represented a party in other matters or whose partners had done so, and persons having acted in the past as advisers for a party.

It is essential to take note, however, of the many nuances present in decisions where such links were alleged and/or disclosed. For example, in one case a prospective arbitrator submitted a Statement of Independence with the reserve that another partner in his 800 lawyer firm had acted for a party in an unrelated matter about which the prospective arbitrator knew nothing. The other party to the arbitration did not request non-confirmation and the court did confirm the arbitrator. The court has also confirmed as co-arbitrator, in the absence of objection from the other party, a nominee who had provided legal services to a corporation one of whose officers was also an officer of the party proposing the nominee.

In contrast with the above decisions, there are those where, without seeking the views of the parties, the court refused to confirm a prospective chairman proposed by an ICC National Committee because the person had provided a consultation to one of the parties some time before. In another case, even without an objection raised by the other party, the court refused to confirm a nominee whose law firm was concurrently acting for the party which has proposed the nominee. Nominees have also been refused confirmation in instances where the nominee had professional ties to a party's counsel, ie acted on their behalf. In one case a prospective arbitrator who was a QC ["Queen's

Counsel"] had been retained by defendant's counsel to plead a matter unrelated to the arbitration and the opposing party objected.

The ICC Court has not considered that the fact that a nominee has the same nationality as a party constitutes a lack of independence. This point generally, although not always, arises in connection with nominees coming from Eastern Europe when proposed by a party of the same nationality. The matter has been treated at length elsewhere, including an excellent commentary by Professor Szasz. Suffice it to say that the ICC Court bases its decisions in each case on the concrete facts regarding the relationship of the prospective arbitrator and the parties involved and not on sweeping generalisations about the legal, political or social conditions in particular countries. Obviously, just as in any other case, the ICC Court would not look with favour at the nomination by an enterprise in a socialist country of its General Counsel. Such would also be the case with the same type of nomination by a Western company. So too, there is no justification for presuming automatically that a particular Professor of Law from an Eastern European country is automatically less independent of a steel enterprise in his country than would be his Western counterpart from a steel company in the Western country. National Courts have consistently rejected such generalisations and the ICC Court will no doubt continue in such cases to examine the facts and circumstances relevant to the question of the independence of the specific nominee concerned vis-à-vis the actual parties to the case. On this basis, Eastern European nominees have generally been confirmed and on occasion been refused confirmation, just as have been nominees from Western and developing countries alike.

*     *     *

What, though, is to be done when an arbitrator lacks independence? The other party may challenge him, although a challenge may not be necessary. In an arbitration between the United Kingdom and Saudi Arabia, the arbitrator nominated by the United Kingdom resigned because of the obvious lack of independence of the Saudi nominee.

D.    J. GILLIS WETTER, THE INTERNATIONAL ARBITRAL
      PROCESS 368 (1979) [The Buraimi Oasis Arbitration].

The British Foreign Office issued on October 4 a
statement on the dispute between the United Kingdom
and Saudi Arabia over the ownership of the Buraimi
Oasis area, giving details of the allegations of attempted
bribery by Saudi Arabia which Britain had brought in
September before the international arbitration tribunal
appointed to consider the dispute.

After recalling that the United Kingdom had asked the
tribunal to consider its complaints of repeated violations
by Saudi Arabia of the arbitration agreement of July 30,
1954, in view of the Saudi Government's failure to take
action on British diplomatic representations, the
statement said that "the main charges which the United
Kingdom made against Saudi Arabia were that the latter
had tried to overthrow the Ruler of Abu Dhabi by force
in favour of a Saudi nominee, and that they had been
engaged in a deliberate, systematic, and persistent policy
of large-scale bribery calculated to subvert the people in
the disputed areas from their allegiance to the Ruler of
Abu Dhabi or the Sultan of Muscat." Evidence given by
Sheikh Hazza (the brother of the Ruler of Abu Dhabi),
which counsel for Saudi Arabia had not attempted to
refute, had shown that in 1951 the cadet branch of the
ruling family, which was not well disposed towards the
present ruler, had gone to Saudi Arabia and had been
given a very large sum of money and facilities for
obtaining arms. On their return to Dubai, a sheikhdom
bordering on Abu Dhabi, they had attempted to secure
support for an armed entry into Abu Dhabi with a view
to overthrowing the present Ruler.

Although evidence showed that as much as 5,000 rupees
a month was being paid to certain individuals as the
price of their adherence to the Saudi cause (the
statement continued), the campaign of bribery was
particularly directed against members of the ruling
family of Abu Dhabi, notably Sheikh Zaid bin-Sultan, a
brother of the present Ruler and his representative in

Buraimi. On March 30, 1955, Abdullah al-Qureishi (ostensibly a clerk in the Saudi police at Buraimi, but known to be a high political officer) had promised Sheikh Zaid that if he would throw in his lot with the Saudis he would be assured of his position in Buraimi, and would receive funds from the Saudis and 50 per cent of the profits from any oil that might be discovered there; he had also said that should the arbitration go against the Saudis, they would take the area by force. On Aug. 4 Qureishi had said that King Saud would give Sheikh Zaid 400,000,000 rupees (about £30,000,000) if he would prevent the Iraq Petroleum Company from operating in the disputed territories and leave the field open to Aramco (the Arabian-American Oil Company, which holds the concession for operating in Saudi Arabia). Evidence to this effect had been given before the tribunal both by Sheikh Zaid and by Captain Clayton (the commander of the Abu Dhabi and Muscat police detachment in the Buraimi zone), to whom he had reported these approaches, neither witness being shaken in cross-examination. A similar attempt at bribery had been made against two of the principal sheikhs of the Dhawahir tribe, who had been offered a monthly payment of 100,000 rupees each.

Counsel for Saudi Arabia, the statement emphasized, had not denied that a substantial sum of money had been distributed, and had made no attempt to refute the evidence of Sheikh Hazza or of the two sheikhs of the Dhawahir tribe. Qureishi had admitted in evidence that there had been meetings between himself and Sheikh Zaid, but said that they had been asked for by Sheikh Zaid because he wanted advice about how to make his peace with Saudi Arabia, and had denied that he had ever made any offers of money.

When the British Government had laid their case before the tribunal at Geneva, the statement alleged, Sheikh Yasin (the Saudi member of the tribunal) had had to be called to order by the president for sending a note to the Saudi agent during a sitting of the tribunal, whilst Qureishi had admitted under cross-examination that his first act on arriving in Geneva had been to get in touch with Sheikh Yasin. The statement said that there could be "little doubt that the evidence he (Qureishi) subsequently gave was carefully rehearsed with the Saudi arbitrator," who had made it abundantly clear that he was conducting the proceedings on behalf of the Saudi Arabian Government and "was representing that Government on the tribunal rather than acting as an impartial arbitrator." Although Sheikh Yasin had also stated that Qureishi was his official, for whose acts in Buraimi he accepted responsibility, he nevertheless claimed that he had "forgotten" to take action on three British protests against Qureishi's presence in the Buraimi zone. Finally, confirmation had been secured of the British Government's suspicion that attempts had been made to tamper with the impartiality of the tribunal behind the president's back, and to these circumstances Sir Reader Bullard (the British representative on the tribunal) had had no choice but to declare that he could not continue as a member of the tribunal.

The Saudi Arabian Embassy in London, in a statement issued on October 7, completely denied the British allegations, and accused Sir Reader Bullard of withdrawing in order to prevent the tribunal from recording its judgment.

The statement said that since the sessions had been private and the president of the tribunal had been specially asked by the parties not to make public disclosures of information about its proceedings, it could not reply in detail to the British charges. The allegation that the British witnesses had not been shaken in cross-examination, however, would be shown to be "absolutely false" by the tape-recording of the proceedings. Sir Reader Bullard's resignation had taken place "at the very last moment, after the hearing had been concluded and the decision of the tribunal had been drafted by the three neutral members," and had alone prevented the tribunal from issuing its decision with respect to these "fantastic charges." If the British Government had been truly persuaded of the validity of its accusations, the statement observed, "it might have induced its member to remain for another half-hour, to enable the tribunal to record its judgment." Sheikh Yasin's dual capacity as Saudi arbitrator and Deputy Foreign Minister had been known to the British Government and to the tribunal for more than a year, and had been seized upon at the last minute to justify the British member's resignation and to keep the tribunal's decision from becoming a matter of public knowledge. No evidence had been cited in support of the allegation that attempts had been made to tamper with the impartiality of the tribunal, which the statement described as "utterly untrue and unworthy of the Government of the United Kingdom." In conclusion, the statement observed that although Saudi Arabia had originally wished to settle the dispute by a plebiscite in the disputed area, it had accepted the British proposal for arbitration, and was still willing to proceed with it if Britain would abandon "public recrimination and the campaign of intimidation it has carried on in the areas adjacent to those in dispute."

The Buraimi Oasis was occupied on October 26 by forces of the Ruler of Abu Dhabi and the Sultan of Muscat, which were commanded by British officers and supported by the Trucial Oman levies. Some fighting occurred in which two of the attacking force were killed and three wounded. The Saudi Arabian force of 15 police stationed in the Oasis, two of whom were wounded, were taken prisoner and subsequently repatriated.

Sir Anthony Eden stated in the British House of Commons on October 26 that Dr. Dihaigo, one of the two remaining neutral members of the arbitration tribunal, had resigned, and that as the Saudi Arabian authorities had "systematically disregarded" the agreed conditions of arbitration, a fair and impartial arbitration had not been possible. The British Government had therefore felt obliged "in the exercise of its duty, which is to protect the legitimate interests of the Ruler of Abu Dhabi and the Sultan of Muscat, to advise them that the attempt to reach a just compromise by means of arbitration has failed," and their forces had accordingly resumed control of the Oasis and areas to the west of it. "I regret that this step should have been necessary," Sir Anthony concluded, "but as negotiations and arbitration have both failed, we have no other means of honouring our obligations and standing by our friends."

### Notes and Questions

1. In international arbitrations under the 1958 Convention (*see* Supplement at p. 40), a default instance might have decided this dispute. What methods exist at public international law? *See generally*, W. MICHAEL REISMAN, NULLITY AND REVISION: THE REVIEW AND ENFORCEMENT OF INTERNATIONAL JUDGMENTS AND AWARDS (1971).

## V.     CHAIRMAN OR SOLE ARBITRATOR

Many arbitral tribunals are comprised of a sole arbitrator. The appointment of one individual tends to speed up the arbitration because the amount of administrative coordination is reduced and the time required for the tribunal to consult and reach a decision is eliminated. In addition, the appointment of a sole arbitrator reduces costs because the parties pay only one set of fees and expenses.

But notwithstanding these advantages, the tendency in significant international commercial arbitrations is to appoint a three-person tribunal. The ICC Rules, for example, provide that if the parties have not agreed on the number of arbitrators, a sole arbitrator will be appointed unless "the dispute is such as to warrant the appointment of three arbitrators." The ICC Court of Arbitration generally takes the view that, if the sum in dispute exceeds US $1,000,000, a three-person tribunal is warranted. In a three-person tribunal, one member will be nominated chairman (usually by the other two arbitrators or by the arbitral institution under whose auspices the arbitration is being conducted).

As considered above, while lack of independence is not acceptable, it is recognized that party-appointed arbitrators may be "non-neutral." To be non-neutral allows an arbitrator to have a general predisposition towards a particular party. Non-neutrality, however, requires the arbitrator to refrain from allowing that predisposition to colour his judgment. Yet this rather flexible standard is inappropriate for the chairman of an arbitral tribunal or a sole arbitrator. As one commentator notes:

> If doubts may be entertained as to the party-appointed arbitrators, the situation is different in the case of arbitrators designated otherwise: by an agreement between the parties or by the other arbitrators, or by some third person. The arbitrator is then bound to be independent and impartial in the same manner as a judge. This principle is unanimously recognized; how it is implemented and guaranteed differs however from country to country.[181]

The general practice in international arbitration is that the chairman or sole arbitrator should not be of the same nationality as either of the parties. The ICC Rules and the LCIA Rules are explicit on this score. Article 2.6 of the ICC Rules states:

> The sole arbitrator or the chairman of the arbitral tribunal shall be chosen from a country other than those of which the parties are nationals. However, in suitable circumstances and provided that neither of the parties objects within the time-limit fixed by the Court, the sole arbitrator or the chairman of the arbitral tribunal may be chosen from a country of which any of the parties is a national.

Article 3.3 of the LCIA Rules provides in relevant part:

> The Court alone is empowered to appoint arbitrators and such appointment will be made in the name of the Court by the President or any Vice President of the Court. The Court will appoint arbitrators with due regard for any particular method or criteria of selection agreed by the parties. In selecting arbitrators consideration will be given, so far as possible, to the nature of the contract, the nature and circumstances of the dispute, and the

---

[181] RENÉ DAVID, ARBITRATION IN INTERNATIONAL TRADE 255 (1985).

nationality, location and languages of the parties. Where the parties are of different nationalities, then, unless they have agreed otherwise, sole arbitrators or chairmen are not to be appointed if they have the same nationality as any party (the nationality of parties being understood to include that of controlling shareholders or interests).

. . .

### Notes and Questions

1. To what extent does a nationality provision such as the ones above guarantee independence? In practice, arguably only to a very limited extent. However, at least by appointing a chairman or sole arbitrator of a different nationality from the parties, the appearance of independence is heightened, if not the likelihood of actual independence.

2. Independence is perhaps a more tangible concept than neutrality. Specific factors suggesting a lack of independence can be identified by the sole arbitrator or chairman and by those concerned by appointment of a particular arbitrator. Such factors include being of the same nationality as one of the parties, being previously on the board of directors of one of the party-corporations, or previously serving as legal counsel for one of the parties. Neutrality, although considered a pre-requisite for sole arbitrators and chairmen, is arguably more difficult to ensure.

Mohammed Bedjaoui, *The Arbitrator: One Man-Three Roles*, J. INT'L ARB., Mar. 1988, at 7, 9-10.

Before this theme is expanded a comment should be made about the arbitrator as a "being." He is neither a robot nor an inanimate object. Before considering him as a judge, the arbitrator as a man should be borne in mind. He is a being of flesh and blood, as is an ordinary judge. It is necessary then to deal right from the start with the ethical questions concerning the nature of the man, in the sense that they are not confined solely to the arbitrator. These questions, common to all human beings, confront us with the quasi-metaphysical problem of impartiality in a man who is called on to judge other men. Like all men, an arbitrator has a conscience which gives him a certain outlook on the world. He cannot detach himself from all the emotional ties which, consciously or unconsciously, may influence his thoughts. Whenever men are judged, including judgment by arbitration, as we have already said, a wager is laid on impartiality.

An arbitrator is not a disembodied, floating being, without origins, or ethnic, cultural, religious, social and other attachments. "There are," states a report to the symposium of 20 November 1970 on arbitration, "some indistinct forms which pose a very difficult problem for those who will be demanding about indisputable impartiality. These forms are called Ideology (or that which we name ideology), Religion (or that which we name religion) and History (of more recent inspiration)." I think it would be destructive to exaggerate these considerations, and naive or suspicious to ignore their existence completely in certain East-West or North-South arbitrations. These are the problems of arbitral "neutrality" of the harsh times we live in.

*     *     *

## VI.     DUTY OF DISCLOSURE

It is vital for an arbitrator to disclose at an early stage all and any possible facts which may affect or appear to affect his independence. If an arbitrator fully discloses the relevant facts, he limits the risk of being subsequently challenged and the risk of subsequent refusal by the petitioned forum to enforce the award.

ICSID, the LCIA and the ICC all have a form of Statement of Independence, which the potential arbitrator must complete before his appointment. Article 2.7 of the ICC Rules requires that:

> Before appointment or confirmation by the Court, a prospective arbitrator shall disclose in writing to the Secretary General of the Court any facts or circumstances *which might be of such nature* as to call into question the arbitrator's independence *in the eyes of the parties.*

> An arbitrator shall immediately disclose in writing to the Secretary General of the Court and the parties any facts

or circumstances of a similar nature which may arise
between the arbitrator's appointment or confirmation by
the Court and the notification of the final award.
(Emphasis added.)

This rule, adopted in its present form in the 1988 version of the ICC
Rules, replaced an earlier version that was more subjective. The earlier
version required the arbitrators to disclose facts which in their opinion
might call their independence into doubt in the eyes of the parties.
Some argued that even that 1988 disclosure requirement should have
been interpreted liberally:

A.     Stephen R. Bond, *The Selection of ICC Arbitrators and
       the Requirement of Independence*, 4 ARB. INT'L 300,
       304-05 (1988).

Regarding the phrase 'in the eyes of the parties', this must not
be read as limitative, i.e., as encouraging the potential arbitrator to say
to himself, 'Well, I would consider that fact X is pertinent to an
assessment of my independence, but I doubt the parties would do so
and therefore I won't disclose it.' In the writer's opinion - which may
be shared by the ICC Court - the phrase is intended to encourage the
arbitrator to stretch his mind, to disclose facts that he himself might not
consider as 'calling into question' his independence, but which might
do so 'in the eyes of the parties'. Because in an ICC arbitration the
parties are generally of different nationalities and thus at least one party
is of a nationality other than that of the prospective arbitrator, it is
especially important that the nominee stretch beyond a purely national
and domestic perspective and make a special effort to consider the facts
and circumstances as the parties might view and construe them.

One example of this, perhaps at the far edge and controversial,
was an ICC case where a challenge was raised against the chairman of
an arbitral tribunal during the course of an arbitration on the basis that
the chairman had been an active critic of the human rights situation
under the former régime in the country of the challenging party. In the
event, the ICC Court, taking into account all of the circumstances of
the given case, rejected the challenge. But it may well have been
preferable for the arbitrator to have disclosed these facts before
confirmation so that any comments could have been received and
considered prior to the commencement of the arbitration. Such is

exactly the purpose of having the prospective arbitrator examine the situation through 'the eyes of the parties'.

.    .    .

The 1988 disclosure ICC requirement was further amended in 1990.

> B.    JAN PAULSSON, ETHICS FOR INTERNATIONAL ARBITRATORS: HOW HAVE THE 1987 GUIDELINES FARED?, Speech delivered to the 23rd International Bar Association Conference, at 7-12 (Sept. 1990).

The new text asks the potential nominee to take into account:

> whether there exists any past or present relationship, direct or indirect, with any of the parties or any of their counsel, whether financial, professional or of another kind and whether the nature of any such relationship is such that disclosure is called for. . .

It should be noted that the relationships considered as potentially calling for disclosure include those between the arbitrator and any lawyer appearing in the case. (*Cf.* INTERNATIONAL BAR ASSOCIATION, ETHICS FOR INTERNATIONAL ARBITRATORS art. 4.2, *infra* p. [7], ch. 8). This [provision] caused a well-known Swiss professor and arbitrator, M. Alain Hirsch, to express dissatisfaction in a comment entitled *May arbitrators know the lawyers of the parties?* 1990 BULLETIN 7 (1990). Prof. Hirsch wrote that the new text had been adopted without consulting practitioners, and that in fact it will have deleterious effects. If the potential arbitrator must disclose his contacts with the lawyers involved in the case, that presumably includes all lawyers in any *firm* present in the case. Since the international arbitration world is rather small, it is usual for arbitrators to have had dealings with the lawyers in one or even both sides. The potential arbitrator will not be certain of being able to recall a complete list; sometimes he could not do so in any event for reasons of professional confidentiality.

Prof Hirsch concludes that many arbitrators will be unhappy about making such a list, especially when they consider the likelihood that they may be asked for yet further particulars. Furthermore, parties may seek to recuse arbitrators for tactical motives, and find ostensible grounds for doing so if the arbitrator has made a detailed list. Prof. Hirsch accepts that lawyer-to-arbitrator relationships may have to be disclosed if they have been close and lasting, and particularly if the arbitrator has earned significant professional fees in the context of these relations. He deems however that the new ICC declaration is excessive, and that competent and experienced arbitrators - who are precisely the ones who are best known in the legal community - will be eliminated from the process in favor of inexperienced people in a manner which will reduce confidence in ICC arbitration.

The Secretary-General of the ICC Court, Mr. Stephen Bond, has written a detailed reply to Prof. Hirsch, *The ICC Arbitrator's Statement of Independence*, 1990 BULLETIN 226 (1990). Mr. Bond makes a number of points which are of particular interest in the ICC context. (For example, he dismisses any suggestion that the new form declaration implies any change of ICC standards, and points out that the form does not require a potential arbitrator to make a list of contacts, but simply to search his own mind and take account of such relationships with counsel as might be appropriate to disclose. He also notes that the new form had in fact been prepared after consultation with prospective arbitrators in a number of countries, including Switzerland, without a single objection to the new wording, and reports that he is unaware of a single instance of a refusal to complete the form.)

A number of Mr. Bond's comments are, however, of interest beyond the specific framework of ICC arbitration. For example, he proceeds from the thought-provoking premise that

> if the concept of arbitrator independence is to be a reality upon which the confidence of the parties may legitimately be based rather than a mere theory to be greeted with cynicism, more than blind faith must be demanded of the parties . . . a meaningful procedure

must exist whereby prospective arbitrators may disclose information the parties should be aware of when assessing the independence of the prospective arbitrator concerned.[182]

He then makes the important point that early *disclosure by an arbitrator* is far better than late *discovery by a party*, at a stage when removal of an arbitrator would entail a great waste of time and money.

The fact of disclosing a relationship which the prospective arbitrator does not believe interferes with his independence does not of course necessarily justify an objection to his nomination. Mr. Bond cites the Swiss authors Lalive, Poudret & Reymond to the effect that after years of activity in international arbitration, leading practitioners come to know each other by dint of practical experience, and that this does not automatically cause them to be less independent - *"bien au contraire."*

Mr. Bond cites with approval the example of a prospective arbitrator who wrote as follows on his statement:

> I know well two senior members of the law firm representing the claimants: Dr. X (a fellow examiner at the Law Faculty at the National University) and an Englishman who has now retired out of Singapore. But I have yet to meet Mr. Y who has been handling this case; I have only spoken to him on the phone a few times.
>
> I also know well a senior lawyer (Mr. Z) representing the respondent. Both Singapore and Malaysia are small countries, and it is common for judges and senior lawyers to know each other — some professionally, some socially and some both professionally and socially.[183]

---

[182] *Id.* at 226.

[183] *Id.* at 230.

Notice that such a situation is not unusual in the ICC setting. Mr. Bond reveals that in this instance there was in fact no objection and the nominee was confirmed.

In connection with the observation about the inevitability of close knit legal communities in small countries, Mr. Bond mentions the specific case of Switzerland as an illustration, noting that a paper delivered at the annual American Bar Association conference a few weeks ago, while praising the reform of Swiss law with respect to international arbitration, nonetheless noted that

> The concerns that some Americans have historically felt over the "old-boy network" among Swiss arbitrators and the appointment process in the absence of party agreement, will . . . continue.[184]

As Mr. Bond puts, it is precisely to allay such concerns — whether they are warranted or not — that appropriate disclosure should be made rather than resisted. Apprehensions are inevitable and should be forestalled rather than ignored.

Mr. Bond's principal difference with Prof. Hirsch relates to the latter's apparent view that lawyer-to-arbitrator relations should be viewed as different than party-to-arbitrator relations in that when they are "routine" they are of a different nature and need not be disclosed. In Mr. Bond's analysis, a lawyer is the agent of his party and [consequently] it is illogical to say that

> links which are of such a nature that they should be disclosed if they exist between the prospective arbitrator and the principal (the party) suddenly become irrelevant when they exist between the prospective arbitrator and the agent (the party's counsel). Should the prospective arbitrator actually lack independence vis-à-vis the agent (counsel), can it really be argued that the prospective arbitrator is nonetheless independent of the principal (the party)? As an objective of disclosure is to help assure the parties that the prospective arbitrator is "independent" and thus is free to decide in favor of or

---

[184] *Id.* at 232.

against either party based strictly on the law and facts, creating a distinction such as that suggested in the article between party and counsel, (principal and agent) would seem to be entirely beside the point.[185]

This problem is one of degree and of subjective sensitivity, so we can expect that the discussion will be a continuing one.

C. Maître G. Danet,[186] *News of Arbitration Abroad: Independence of Arbitrators under the ICC System*, 9 BULLETIN SWISS ARB. ASSOC. 45, 47 (1991) (translated by the editors).

. . . I find the new text of the ICC Declaration of Independence to be entirely excessive.

If it were taken literally, it would become absolutely impossible for first-rate lawyers — and in particular former presidents of bar associations — to act as arbitrators because they necessarily have a direct or indirect relationship with one or another counsel.

I therefore believe that the wording is manifestly over-broad, even if at present it is restrictively interpreted by the ICC itself.

It would appear that in light of all the recent developments affecting the structure of law firms in Europe [translator's note: the author doubtless refers to the cross-border expansions, mergers, and associations that flourished in 1989-90], it essentially focuses on organic relationships between an arbitrator and one of the parties' counsel.

Moreover, I think that the reasoning of Stephen Bond is also difficult to accept as it is premised on the view of counsel as a pure and simple agent of a party, which necessarily excludes any notion of independence on the part of counsel with respect to his client.

---

[185] *Id.* at 231.

[186] Former President of the Bar Association of Paris.

## Notes and Questions

1. The way English barristers cooperate in chambers is a source of mystery to many practitioners outside the legal systems of the Commonwealth. The notion that barristers belonging to the same set of chambers may act on opposite sides in a litigation, with no perception that any conflict of interests arises, baffles outsiders. (In England the practice is so well-established that the Court of Appeal dismissed as "wholly without substance and mischievous" an appeal against a decision rendered by a barrister sitting as Deputy High Court Judge in a case where a fellow member of his chambers acted as counsel. *Nye Saunders & Partners v. Alan D. Bristow*, 37 Building Law Reports 92 (1987).

The rationale is, of course, that barristers never enter into partnership. Although they contribute to defray the expenses of their set of chambers, they do not share profits. It is not clear that this explanation would be universally accepted on the continent; in France, for example, the members of a legal société de moyens (association of means) would certainly be barred from representing adversaries in the same case, although such lawyers, like barristers, share expenses only, and not profits. Indeed, the rules applicable to avocats in France even prohibit those who practice in cabinets groupés (*i.e.*, share premises without creating a legal entity) from acting against each other.

2. While the issue of the compatibility of the participation of barristers from the same set of chambers in different roles in the same proceedings has occasionally arisen in the context of international arbitration, it has rarely been the focus of post-award litigation outside England. A decision of June 28, 1991, *Kuwait Foreign Trading Contracting Co. v. Icori Estero Spa.*, of the Paris Court of Appeal (an especially influential court in the specific context of international arbitration, since it is the jurisdiction which directly hears challenges against all awards rendered in Paris) therefore merits special attention.

The dispute arose out of a construction contract. An interim award was rendered in October 1989, by a three-member tribunal presided over by an English barrister, deciding in favor of the Italian builder. KFTCIC applied to the Cour d'appel for the annulment of the award. The grounds of annulment which are of interest for present purposes were the alleged irregularity of the composition of the tribunal and the violation of basic principles of procedural fairness (droits de la défense). More precisely, KFTCIC argued that the chairman of the arbitral tribunal was not independent of Icori due to the fact, revealed to it only subsequently to the hearings in arbitration, that he belonged to the same set of chambers as counsel for Icori. "The business relations that exist between barristers belonging to the same chambers," in Icori's submission, may "influence the independence of one of them when he is named arbitrator in a case where another barrister from the same chambers appears as counsel for one of the parties."

The challenge to the award was rejected. As concerned the issue just defined, the Cour d'appel reasoned as follows:

-     The independence of an arbitrator is an essential characteristic of his jurisdictional function.

-     To show a lack of independence, one must demonstrate "a definite risk of bias."

-     The obligation of an arbitrator to disclose such matters as might cause the parties to examine their right of recusal should be measured both by reference to the "notoriousness of the criticized situation" and its effect on the arbitrator's judgment.

-     As shown by various opinions submitted to the Cour, barristers' chambers comprise an "original institution, specific to the British system," whose members are essentially independent of each other; they share premises and assistants, but unlike French associations they do not create professional connections implying "common interests or any economic or intellectual inter-dependence among its members."

-     Given the specialization of sets of chambers, it often happens that members of the same chambers appear against each other, or participate as arbitrators in cases where another member acts as counsel.

-     No "objective factor" existed in this case that would appear likely to have affected the independence of the Chairman, whose membership in the same set of chambers as counsel to one of the parties did not create any lien de dépendance between the arbitrator and said party.

-     The Chairman cannot be criticized for having failed to disclose a situation which per se was not such as to color his judgment or  "have an effect on the exercise of his jurisdictional function."

-     Therefore, it could not be said that the composition of the tribunal was vitiated, nor that droits de la défense had been violated.

The Cour d'appel of Paris has in this decision proved itself to be impressively open-minded in accepting an institution which is entirely foreign from the perspective of the European continent. On the other hand, it may be questioned whether its solicitude did not go too far when it commented that the arbitrator could not be criticized for having failed to disclose his connection with counsel. (In this particular case the chairman could not have made such a disclosure at the time of accepting his appointment, because counsel had not yet been instructed. In other words, the issue of disclosure arose only upon the appearance as counsel of his colleague in chambers.)

       The legal profession throughout Europe is in a state of evolution. English barristers are not immune to these developments. Several sets of chambers have produced promotional brochures worthy of major law firms. One of the principal guides to the English legal profession, THE LEGAL 500, contains rankings by specialization not only of individual barristers, but indeed of sets of chambers viewed as a unit. So if barristers do not have a connection in the sense of shared profits, it must be admitted that at least some of them have a common interest in that most valuable commodity: the goodwill of their chambers. Even if that interest did not constitute valid grounds of recusal in this case, prudence and sensitivity to the understandable unfamiliarity of non-English parties [with this practice] may, as a general proposition, militate in favor of disclosure.

Consider the dissent in the following case under the United States-Canada Free Trade Agreement in which the U.S. alleged material breach of the Code of Conduct of the Agreement and a serious conflict of interest on the part of two out of three panelists. A majority of the review panel found the United States' "extraordinary challenge" regarding the "late" full disclosure of two of the panelists' past and present relationships with the Canadian parties to the dispute to be unfounded. Canadian Justice Gordon Hart, one of the two members of the majority, acknowledged that certain disclosures had not been made, but suggested a standard that combined subjective intent on the part of the panelist to conceal and an objective test of materiality: whether the information, if it had been revealed, would have led to removal of the panelist concerned. "In this case, it is my view that there was no intentional refusal to reveal any matter that would justify the opposite party in removing either panelist and the request by the U.S. Government for an extraordinary challenge should be rejected." (*See also*, "Panel Rejects U.S. Claim of Lumber Bias," LOS ANGELES TIMES, August 4, 1994, Part D, p. 2:3) The other member of the majority, also Canadian, concurred. The only American member of the panel, Judge Malcolm Wilkey, dissented in terms and with a degree of passion rather unusual in international arbitration.

D.    *In re Certain Softwood Lumber Products from Canada (U.S. v. Can.)*, No. ECC-94-1904-01USA (Extraordinary Challenge Comm., U.S.-Can. Free Trade Agreement, Aug. 3, 1994) at 74-80, 85-86, Dissenting Opinion of Judge Malcolm Wilkey.


.    .    .


There is an obligation for a prospective panelist, at the time he is originally placed on a general list and at the time he is queried as to his willingness and his capacity to serve on a specific Panel, to disclose any and everything which might affect his impartial performance of his duties on the Panel, or affect the judgment of the contending parties as to whether to accept the particular panelist or reject him. The two governments do not send their investigative agencies to pry into the details of the prospective panelist's business and personal affiliations. There is no subpoena of the records of the panelist or his law firm, no review of his business contacts, public or private records to determine his sources of income for past years. The two governments rely exclusively on the honesty — and just as importantly, the diligence — of the prospective panelist to reveal any and everything which could seemingly have an impact on his being chosen to serve or not.

This obligation of disclosure, *properly fulfilled* by prospective panelists, leaves them free from worry of future embarrassment. The argument made in this case that the enforcement of the disclosure of this information will discourage qualified panelists from serving is totally fallacious. The problem in this case arose because of a lack of disclosure. If a panelist is honest and diligent in disclosing *everything*, then he may or may not be selected. Being rejected because of his legitimate business affiliations is no disgrace. Serving on the Panel after full and complete disclosure means that neither side will have any cause whatsoever to challenge his impartiality. To repeat, the problem in this and in future cases comes and will come from a failure to meet the disclosure obligations; the prospective panelist who meets his disclosure obligations has nothing to worry about.[187]

---

[187] Justice Hart chides the United States for not raising the disqualification issue earlier (p. 49), then for acting too swiftly once it was aware (p. 51), and defends the two panelists because facts requiring disqualification are so hard to come by. (p. 57)

. . .

When the exchange of nominees for a specific Panel is made between the two parties, Canada and the United States, either party has the right of a "peremptory challenge" to any name submitted. No reason need be given. In this case the firms to which Hunter and Dearden belonged had a few affiliations with companies or with the timber industry involved. Discounting these few connections, the United States accepted Hunter and Dearden.

It is absolutely impossible to say with total certainty, whether, if the United States had known the full extent of Hunter and Dearden's personal and firm affiliations and representations of not only the timber industry but the Canadian Federal and Provincial Governments, the United States would have accepted or rejected Hunter or Dearden. I have my own opinion which I will elucidate later. Whether we can say precisely what the United States *would have done* in July 1992, if all of this had been revealed, the *fact is* that the United States *immediately did ask* for the disqualification of both Hunter and Dearden and the vacating of the Panel opinion to which their two votes was essential — when it finally learned the full truth.

The key is — the United States had the absolute *right* to accept or to reject Hunter and Dearden. Corollary to this, the United States had the absolute right to know the complete truth as to their and their firm's affiliations, on which to base its decision. The United States was denied those rights guaranteed under the FTA. The United States has no recourse except to ask for the vacating of the Panel judgment and opinion to which the votes of Hunter and Dearden were essential.

It is not possible to argue now that these relationships were harmless. They were not revealed initially when the United States was making its decision to accept or reject the two panelists. The information was obtained from the panelists much later, after specific requests made by the United States at the instigation of interested participants. Only the United States has the power to make the decision on the suitability of the panelists, and it was denied that power by the failure to make the initial disclosures in July 1992 and in a few instances as the work of the Panel progressed. Disclosures made later could not restore that right to its pristine power.

The only remedy now is to set aside the Panel majority judgment and opinion.

.   .   .

Panelists Lawson Hunter materially breached the Code of Conduct by failing to disclose initially and during the course of the Panel proceeding the following:

1.   legal services he *personally* provided to an agency of the Canadian Government, one of the two parties in this proceeding, during the course of this proceeding itself;
2.   his law firm's relationships with eleven Canadian lumber and forest product companies continuing during the proceedings in this case; and
3.   his and his firm's relationships with the Canadian Government during the course of these proceedings.

.   .   .

Last, and somewhat incredible, while he served on the Binational Panel, in the fall of 1992, he himself *personally* did work for an agency of the Canadian Government. Hunter's services sought by the Canadian Government were in the nature of advice and consultation in a field in which he had a rather unique experience. Whatever the nature or value of his services to the Canadian Government, Hunter was an employee of the Canadian Government at the same time he was deciding as a member of the Panel the claims put forth by that Government as one of the two principal litigants.

The lumber companies which Hunter's two firms represented had a direct financial interest in the outcome of the Panel proceedings. These companies were the original subjects of the Commerce Department's investigation on subsidies. As members of associations, the companies were actively interested in and participated in Panel proceedings. These particular companies and their industry stood to gain directly from the decision. As a partner in his two firms, Hunter stood to gain financially from the representation of the lumber companies and the Canadian Government.

Chairman Richard Dearden materially violated the code of conduct by failing to disclose:

1.     his firms' financial interests and relationships with the Governments of Canada, Ontario, British Columbia and the Government of the United States, all of which were parties to the Panel proceedings;

2.     his and his law firms' existing and past relationships with three Canadian lumber and forest product companies;

3.     his firms' relationship with Miranda Inc. and Georgia Pacific, both interested in the lumber Panel proceeding.

Dearden failed to make reasonable efforts to become aware of these relationships. In so failing, both to disclose and to make reasonable efforts to acquire the information and disclose, he created a situation giving rise to the appearance of partiality in his judgments as a member of the Panel.

For Chairman Dearden the nature of these relationships of his firms (not his personally) were heavy on the governmental side. Both initially and in response to the parties' enquiries, he ultimately disclosed that his firm had provided and was providing legal advice to three Provincial Governments and to the Canadian Federal Government, both before and during the Panel proceedings. The Provinces involved, Saskatchewan, Manitoba and Alberta, and most significantly, British Columbia and Ontario, were interested parties to the Panel proceeding. Together they account for over eighty (80) percent of the lumber exports from Canada to the United States. One of the lumber companies filed a separate notice of appearance in the lumber Panel proceeding.

### Notes and Questions

1. Justice Hart, as mentioned above, introduced a two-prong test: subjective intention to mislead by concealing and an objective materiality test, *i.e.*, what was concealed would, if known, have led to the insistence on recusal of the then candidate for the Panel. In light of the details spelled out by Judge Wilkey, what would have constituted, in the view of the majority, material grounds for recusal?

2. Judge Wilkey suggests an absolute test. How practicable is it, in the light of contemporary legal practice? Firms are very large and membership is fluid, with partners and associates leaving for roles in government, returning or moving to other firms. If a candidate for an arbitration or a bi-national panel scrupulously reveals any relevant conflicts or their absence, should he or she be held responsible for

connections to the case by other partners of his firm with whom he does not work? Judge Wilkey's answer is clear. Are you persuaded of his view? Discuss.

3. One of the panelists in the case under discussion was consulted by the Canadian Government on other matters during the arbitration. Judge Wilkey finds this unacceptable under principles of conflict of interest. Is he realistic? If a U.S. panelist in a trade case, in which the Department of Commerce was the moving party, was consulted by the Department of Defense on an unrelated matter and revealed the connection, should the connection require him to recuse himself? If he did not reveal the connection, would you, as a member of a review panel find that objectively and materially that connection should lead to setting aside or annulling the decision or award?

4. Are the criteria proposed by Judge Wilkey here realistic? How many active and experienced lawyers are likely to volunteer for the types of arbitrations concerned if the Wilkey Test becomes dominant?

### E.    BIAS DEFINED IN SWISS PRACTICE

One of the questions raised in *Softwood Lumber* was the material test for bias. Professor Pierre Jolidon,[188] gives the following twenty examples of "appearance of bias," almost all of which are based on actual Swiss cases:

1. The fact that the arbitrator has an indirect interest in the outcome of the dispute because he, or a member of his family, is the presumed heir of one of the parties, or has made an undertaking to his benefit as a guarantor or a joint debtor, or may be implicated in an ancillary action, or is the owner of an object which is surety for the disputed claim.

2. Marked sentiments of animosity, or to the contrary very deep friendship, with regard to the lawyer of one of the parties; to be on a first-name basis is insufficient.

3. Close personal relations between the arbitrator or members of his family and members of the family of one of the parties or, with respect to a corporate entity, with persons who own a majority of its shares or who run it, or with members of the family of such persons.

---

[188] University of Bern and substitute judge of the Swiss Federal Tribunal.

4.    The fact that the arbitrator has had regular close business relations with one of the parties, and that such relations are not too removed in time. (It sufficed that an arbitrator had previously, as a professor or barrister, been consulted, by the liquidators of a company in liquidation which was a party to the arbitration, on the subject of the disputed claims, that he had drafted for them a request to the Federal Tribunal, and that he had moreover been the liquidator of a partnership of which the company in liquidation had been a partner. It was not sufficient that another arbitrator had routine and non-exclusive business relations with one of the parties, nor that he had ten years previously had close professional relations with it.)

5.    The fact that the arbitrator is frequently and regularly designated as such by one of the parties and that he must expect, if said party prevails, that he would be given additional important nominations.

6.    The fact that the arbitrator, whether a sole arbitrator or a member of a panel, has or has had a function within any corporate entity which is a party to the arbitration, or within a related company.

7.    The membership of the arbitrator and one of the parties in the same closed club, or secret society.

8.    The fact that the arbitrator is a barrister and practices in partnership or in shared offices with the lawyer of one of the parties.

9.    The fact that the arbitrator's wife works as a legal assistant in the offices of the lawyer of the party which had appointed him.

10.   The fact that the arbitrator declares that he considers himself to represent, within the arbitral tribunal, the interests of the party which appointed him.

11.   The fact that the arbitrator is employed by one of the parties, or that he is a significant debtor or creditor of one of the parties.

12. The fact that the arbitrator, or a company which he owns or runs, has been an adversary of one of the parties to the arbitration in a relatively recent suit.

13. In a case where general creditors in bankruptcy are a party, the fact that the arbitrator administers the bankruptcy.

14. In a case between heirs and third parties, the fact that the arbitrator is a trustee under the will.

15. The fact that an arbitrator belongs to an enterprise which competes directly with one of the parties, if the case concerns the type of activity which is common to them.

16. The fact that the arbitrator acted or expressed himself, with regard to one of the parties, whether prior to the arbitration or during its course, in a manner that clearly manifests his bias against it with regard to the dispute.

17. The fact that the arbitrator accepted to discuss the case with one of the parties, unbeknownst to or excluding the other party, outside the ordinary proceedings.

18. The fact that the arbitrator accepted imperative instructions from one of the parties with respect to the relevant proceedings.

19. The fact that the arbitrator accepted, from one of the parties, information or documents, unbeknownst to the other parties to the case, with the intent of using them to influence the award.

20. The fact that the arbitrator had been in close contact with another arbitrator, recused in the same case due to an appearance of bias, and had, on that occasion, outside the arbitration, discussed in detail the subject matter of the dispute.[189]

\*    \*    \*

---

[189] PIERRE JOLIDON, COMMENTAIRE DU CONCORDAT SUISSE SUR L'ARBITRAGE 269-271 (1984) (translated by the editors).

The materials above have focused on links between the arbitrator and the parties' legal advisers. What is the position with regard to business or other relations between an arbitrator and one of the parties?

F.    MARTIN  DOMKE,  DOMKE  ON  COMMERCIAL ARBITRATION 326-27 (rev. ed. 1984).

The Supreme Court of the United States has established a standard for determining the extent to which Section 10 of the Federal Arbitration Act requires disclosure of the arbitrator's prior business relationships with either party to the arbitration agreement. In *Commonwealth Coatings Corp. v. Continental Casualty Co.*, the third arbitrator, chosen by the two party-nominees, failed to reveal to the petitioner until after the award had been made that he had performed occasional consulting construction work for the respondent. Although petitioner failed to adduce any proof of actual fraud or bias, the court held that evidence of even the slightest pecuniary interest is sufficient to void the award under Section 10(a) and 10(b) of the Act. It was noted that Congress in enacting Section 10 of the United States Arbitration Act showed desire to provide for impartial arbitration rather than just for any arbitration. The Court further held that "this rule of arbitration and this canon of judicial ethics rests on the premise that any tribunal permitted by law to try cases and controversies not only must be unbiased but must avoid even the appearance of bias. Subsequently, an arbitrator also appointed by the two nominees failed to disclose that his law firm had represented a party to the arbitration in litigation involving issues similar to those in the present case, this omission did not require voiding of the award under Section 10(b) of the Federal Arbitration Act, the Court holding that *Commonwealth* only required that an arbitrator disclose his financial dealings with any party to the agreement and did not mandate that the arbitrator report his entire "business biography." Notwithstanding that the party-appointed arbitrator was attorney for that party, was a stockbroker of the party-corporation, was related to the president of that corporation, and had been contacted during deliberations of the contract, there was no misconduct requiring the vacatur of the award.

G.     *Commonwealth Coatings Corp. v. Continental Casualty Co.*, 393 U.S. 145 (1968).

[After a prime contractor refused to pay a subcontractor the money which the subcontractor claimed was due for a painting job, the controversy was submitted to arbitration. The subcontractor and the prime contractor each appointed an arbitrator, and these two arbitrators selected a third arbitrator, who was supposedly neutral. After the arbitration award was made, the subcontractor discovered that the prime contractor had been a regular customer of the third arbitrator and had paid him several thousand dollars in fees for services as an engineering consultant, including services on the projects involved in the arbitration. Suing the sureties on the prime contractor's bond, the subcontractor challenged the arbitration award, but the United States District Court for the District of Puerto Rico, finding that the arbitration proceedings were fair and impartial, refused to set aside the award, and the Court of Appeals for the First Circuit affirmed.

On certiorari, the United States Supreme Court reversed. In an opinion by BLACK, J., expressing the view of six members of the court, it was held that the arbitration award should be set aside, because, under §10 of the United States Arbitration Act, the failure to disclose the business dealings between the prime contractor and the third arbitrator constituted a manifest violation of the strict morality and fairness which Congress expected of them.]

.    .    .

MR. JUSTICE WHITE, with whom MR. JUSTICE MARSHALL joins, concurring.

While I am glad to join my Brother BLACK'S opinion in this case, I desire to make these additional remarks. The Court does not decide today that arbitrators are to be held to the standards of judicial decorum of Article III judges, or indeed of any judges. It is often because they are men of affairs, not apart from but of the marketplace, that they are effective in their adjudicatory function. Cf. *United Steelworkers v. Warrior & Gulf Navigation Co.*, 363 U.S. 574 (1960). This does not mean the judiciary must overlook outright chicanery in giving effect to their awards; that would be an abdication of our responsibility. But it does mean that arbitrators are not automatically disqualified by a business relationship with the parties before them if both parties are informed of the relationship in advance, or if they are unaware of the facts but the relationship is trivial. I see no reason automatically to disqualify the best informed and most capable potential arbitrators.

The arbitration process functions best when an amicable and trusting atmosphere is preserved and there is voluntary compliance with the decree, without need for judicial enforcement. This end is best served by establishing an atmosphere of frankness at the outset, through disclosure by the arbitrator of any financial transactions which he has had or is negotiating with either of the parties. In many cases the arbitrator might believe the business relationship to be so insubstantial that to make a point of revealing it would suggest he is indeed easily swayed, and perhaps a partisan of that party. But if the law requires the disclosure, no such imputation can arise. And it is far better that the relationship be disclosed at the outset, when the parties are free to reject the arbitrator or accept him with knowledge of the relationship and continuing faith in his objectivity, than to have the relationship come to light after the arbitration, when a suspicious or disgruntled party can seize on it as a pretext for invalidating the award. The judiciary should minimize its role in arbitration as judge of the arbitrator's impartiality. That role is best consigned to the parties, who are the architects of their own arbitration process, and are far better informed of the prevailing ethical standards and reputations within their business.

Of course, an arbitrator's business relationships may be diverse indeed, involving more or less remote commercial connections with great numbers of people. He cannot be expected to provide the parties with his complete and unexpurgated business biography. But it is enough for present purposes to hold, as the Court does, that where the arbitrator has a substantial interest in a firm which has done more than trivial business with a party, that fact must be disclosed. If arbitrators err on the side of disclosure, as they should, it will not be difficult for courts to identify those undisclosed relationships which are too insubstantial to warrant vacating an award.

MR. JUSTICE FORTAS, with whom MR. JUSTICE HARLAN and MR. JUSTICE STEWART join, dissenting.

I dissent and would affirm the judgment.

The facts in this case do not lend themselves to the Court's ruling. The Court sets aside the arbitration award despite the fact that the award is unanimous and no claim is made of actual partiality, unfairness, bias, or fraud.

The arbitration was held pursuant to provisions in the contracts between the parties. It is not subject to the rules of the American Arbitration Association. It is governed by the United States Arbitration Act, 9 U.S.C. §§ 1-14.

Each party appointed an arbitrator and the third arbitrator was chosen by those two. The controversy relates to the third arbitrator.

The third arbitrator was not asked about business connections with either party. Petitioner's complaint is that he failed to volunteer information about professional services rendered by him to the other party to the contract, the most recent of which were performed over a year before the arbitration. Both courts below held, and petitioner concedes, that the third arbitrator was innocent of any actual partiality, or bias, or improper motive. There is no suggestion of concealment as distinguished from the innocent failure to volunteer information.

The third arbitrator is a leading and respected consulting engineer who has performed services for "most of the contractors in Puerto Rico." He was well known to petitioner's counsel and they were personal friends. Petitioner's counsel candidly admitted that if he had been told about the arbitrator's prior relationship "I don't think I would have objected because I know Mr. Capacete [the arbitrator]."

Clearly, the District Judge's conclusion, affirmed by the Court of Appeals for the First Circuit, was correct, that "the arbitrators conducted fair, impartial hearings; that they reached a proper determination of the issues before them, and that plaintiff's objections represent a 'situation where the losing party to an arbitration is now clutching at straws in an attempt to avoid the results of the arbitration to which it became a party.'"

The Court nevertheless orders that the arbitration award be set aside. It uses this singularly inappropriate case to announce a *per se* rule that in my judgment has no basis in the applicable statute or jurisprudential principles: that, regardless of the agreement between the parties, if an arbitrator has any prior business relationship with one of

the parties of which he fails to inform the other party, however
innocently, the arbitration award is always subject to being set aside.
This is so even where the award is unanimous; where there is no
suggestion that the nondisclosure indicates partiality or bias; and where
it is conceded that there was in fact no irregularity, unfairness, bias,
or partiality. Until the decision today, it has not been the law that an
arbitrator's failure to disclose a prior business relationship with one of
the parties will compel the setting aside of an arbitration award
regardless of the circumstances.

I agree that failure of an arbitrator to volunteer information
about business dealings with one party will, prima facie, support a
claim of partiality or bias. But where there is no suggestion that the
nondisclosure was calculated, and where the complaining party
disclaims any imputation of partiality, bias, or misconduct, the
presumption clearly is overcome.

I do not believe that it is either necessary, appropriate, or
permissible to rule, as the Court does, that, regardless of the facts,
innocent failure to volunteer information constitutes the "evident
partiality" necessary under § 10(b) of the Arbitration Act to set aside
an award. "Evident partiality" means what is says: conduct—or at least
an attitude or disposition—by the arbitrator favoring one party rather
than the other. This case demonstrates that to rule otherwise may be a
palpable injustice, since all agree that the arbitrator was innocent of
either "Evident partiality" or anything approaching it.

Arbitration is essentially consensual and practical. The United
States Arbitration Act is obviously designed to protect the integrity of
the process with a minimum of insistence upon set formulae and rules.
The Court applies to this process rules applicable to judges and not to
a system characterized by dealing on faith and reputation for reliability.
Such formalism is not contemplated by the Act nor is it warranted in
a case where no claim is made of partiality, of unfairness, or of
misconduct in any degree.

*     *     *

H. *International Produce, Inc. v. A/S Rosshavet*, 638 F.2d 548 (2d Cir. 1981).

[Hammond L. Cederholm, a Vice President of a management firm retained by owners of commercial vessels (Elwell), was appointed Chairman in an arbitration concerning an admiralty incident in the Mississippi.]

. . .

At the initial September 8, 1977 hearing, each of the arbitrators disclosed possible conflicts of interest. Nelson, Rosshavet's appointee, stated that his firm had a long-standing business relationship with International's parent corporation. Klosty, International's appointee, disclosed that he had previously been appointed as an arbitrator by International and that he had done business with them as a broker. International's counsel, Hill, Rivkins, Carey, Loesberg, O'Brien & Mulroy (Hill Rivkins), accepted Nelson's and Klosty's participation. Cederholm stated that, although he had no dealing with Rosshavet or International, Haight, Gardner, Poor & Havens (Haight Gardner)-who was representing Rosshavet-was also handling a Protection and Indemnity Club matter (the Mary S. Arbitration # 1) for one of Elwell's clients. Cederholm then invited questions from both counsel. International's counsel, J. Edwin Carey, of Hill Rivkins, stated that he had no questions and that the panel was acceptable to International. He did not ask Cederholm the name of the vessel involved in Haight Gardner's representation; if he had, he would have learned that it was the Mary S.

One of Elwell's clients, World Carrier Corporation owned the Mary S. Neither Cederholm nor Elwell had any financial interest in World Carrier, and Elwell received a fixed fee regardless of the Mary S.'s profitability. The Mary S. was protected by a Freight, Defense and Demurrage policy of the Protection and Indemnity Club Assuranceforeningen Gard (Gard), a common type of maritime insurance that covers the legal expenses of any claims involving the vessel but not any ultimate liability on such claims. The law firm of Haight Garnder had represented the Gard in New York since 1936; and when the first arbitration hearing in the Ross Isle dispute was held, Haight Garnder was already representing World Carrier as owner of the Mary S. in an unrelated dispute, the Mary S. Arbitration # 1. The dispute which led to the Mary S. Arbitration # 2 had not yet arisen.

On December 6, 1977, Rosshavet presented its witnesses in the arbitration, which was held in New York: Captain Hjarand Sem, the Master of the Ross Isle, and Captain Walter Durabb, the Branch Pilot in control of the Ross Isle when it went aground. Sem had come from Norway for the hearing and Durabb from Louisiana. The previous afternoon, however, Arbitrator Nelson had become ill and was unable to attend the hearings. Because of the expense of bringing the witnesses to New York and the uncertainty of their future availability, the parties agreed to proceed with only two arbitrators on the understanding that the missing arbitrator would read the transcript.

Two days later, on December 8, 1977, the Mary S. became involved in a dispute related to the closing of the St. Lawrence Seaway. Cederholm, as an officer of the firm that managed the Mary S., was involved in the negotiations which preceded the impasse. The owners of the Mary S. again retained Haight Gardner as recommended by the Gard's New York representatives; the charterers retained Hill Rivkins. Thus, the choice of law firms in the Mary S. Arbitration # 2 left Cederholm in the position of being a non-party witness in a suit between parties who were represented by the same law firms that were appearing before him in the Ross Isle arbitration.

On January 5, 1978, Carey of Hill Rivkins telephoned Cederholm and suggested that he should resign from the Ross Isle panel because a Haight Gardner attorney would "in all likelihood" call Cederholm and prepare him to testify in the Mary S. arbitration and a Hill Rivkins attorney would then cross-examine him. However, only one attorney-Howard Miller, an associate at Haight Gardner-was involved in both the Mary S. and the Ross Isle disputes. That same day, Cederholm wrote to his fellow arbitrators and to both counsel in the Ross Isle arbitration, informing them of the alleged conflict of interest and seeking their recommendations.

Rosshavet's counsel urged that Cederholm stay on the panel to avoid prejudicing their client: if Cederholm withdrew, there would be only one arbitrator who had observed Rosshavet's witnesses. Both of the other arbitrators strongly discouraged Cederholm's resignation, stressing Cederholm's personal integrity as well as the difficulty of finding any arbitrator in relatively small maritime community without some possible speculative conflict. Carey, however, formally requested Cederholm's withdrawal, although he simultaneously expressed confidence that Cederholm could "continue to act judiciously and objectively without partiality or bias."

On January 13, 1978, Cederholm informed Carey that he was remaining on the panel because no aspect of the Mary S. Arbitration # 2 threatened his impartiality in the Ross Isle arbitration: "they are entirely dissimilar cases and there are no inter-relationships between the principles of both cases." Cederholm did condition his decision on the removal of the attorney working on both cases, Howard Miller of Haight Gardner, from one case or the other. Haight Gardner immediately removed Miller from the Mary S. case. Carey acknowledged Cederholm's decision and announced his intention to proceed with the introduction of evidence at the January 17 hearing. Cederholm wrote to Carey on January 26 and proposed that, since Carey had not conceded or acknowledged the propriety of his remaining on the panel, Hill Rivkins should consider withdrawing from the Mary S. arbitration if it perceived a conflict. Carey did not reply.

Thereafter, on May 16, 1978, Cederholm gave 80 pages of testimony in the Mary S. Arbitration # 2, including cross-examination by a Hill Rivkins attorney. One final hearing was held in the Ross Isle arbitration on June 6, 1978. Over a year later, on July 1, 1979, the Ross Isle panel unanimously held that the vessel's grounding was caused by International's breach of its warranty of safe port and awarded Rosshavet $1,194,535.57, including interest to the date of the award, with further annual interest of 9% if payment was not complete by July 31, 1979. On July 27, 1979, International petitioned the district court for an order vacating the award; on August 21, Rosshavet cross-petitioned seeking confirmation.

Judge Broderick, in a memorandum opinion of April 16, 1980, vacated the award under 9 U.S.C. § 10(b), on the ground that the totality of Cederholm's relationship to the Haight Gardner and Hill Rivkins law firms "created the appearance of bias." We disagree.

The United States Arbitration Act of 1925, 9 U.S.C. § 10 (1976), authorizes a district court to vacate an arbitration award under specified circumstances, including "[w]here there was evident partiality or corruption in the arbitrators, or either of them." In believing that the standard for reviewing the award was whether there was an "appearance of bias," the district court was equating that standard with "evident partiality." We do not find support in *Commonwealth*

*Coatings Corp. v. Continental Casualty Co.*, 393 U.S. 145, 89 S.Ct. 337, 21 L.Ed.2d 301 (1968), for the district court's equating of "appearance of bias" with "evident partiality" in view of the facts of that case.

In *Commonwealth Coatings*, the challenged arbitrator had earned about $12,000 in fees over a period of four or five years for consulting services rendered to the prevailing party which included services on the very project there involved. The arbitrator did not disclose this relationship and it was not known to the losing party. Mr. Justice Black's plurality opinion found that the arbitrator's failure to disclose required setting aside the award for "evident partiality." He wrote that an arbitration panel "not only must be unbiased but also must avoid even the appearance of bias." 393 U.S. at 150, 89 S.Ct. at 340.

However, Mr. Justice White, writing for himself and Mr. Justice Marshall, concurred for somewhat different reasons:

> The Court does not decide today that arbitrators are to be held to the standards of judicial decorum of Article III judges, or indeed of any judges. . . [I]t is enough for present purposes to hold, as the Court does, that where the arbitrator has a *substantial interest* in a firm which has done more than trivial business with a *party* [to the arbitration], that fact must be *disclosed*.

393 U.S. at 151-152, 89 S.Ct. at 340 (emphasis added). Thus two of the justices restricted the scope of the Court's ruling to situations where business and financial dealings with a party are not disclosed by the arbitrator and disassociated themselves from Justice Black's dictum about "appearance of bias." Three justices dissented.

We agree, therefore, with the appellant, that the Supreme Court in *Commonwealth Coatings* did not expand the § 10 standard of "evident partiality" to include "appearance of bias." In *Commonwealth Coatings* there was clear, unexplained evidence of "evident partiality." Here we have an assertion of "appearance of bias" which seems to us, at best, to be speculation without substance. Cederholm fully revealed his relationship to Haight Gardner, and Carey did not inquire further. *See Andros Compania Maritima S.A. v. Marc. Rich & Co., A.G.*, 579

F.2d 691 (2d Cir.1978). The Mary S. Arbitration # 2, which only developed into an arbitrable dispute later, did not involve either of the parties in the Ross Isle arbitration. By happenstance, it did involve the same law firms, but Cederholm's role was only that of a witness who testified and was cross-examined by the Hill Rivkins lawyer. There was no claim of bias on the part of Cederholm, or even of any animosity toward any counsel. Thus, the record is completely bare of anything remotely resembling "evident partiality." *See Ilios Shipping and Trading Corp. v. American Anthracite and Bituminous Coal Corp.*, 148 F.Supp. 698 (S.D.N.Y.), *aff'd*, 245 F.2d 873 (2d Cir.1957) (per curiam). We doubt that there is any substantial basis for finding even an "appearance of bias" in Cederholm's position or anything he did. Be that as it may, we are convinced that there is no evidence of "evident partiality."

It is not unusual that those who are selected as arbitrators in maritime arbitrations have had numerous prior dealings with one or more of the parties or their counsel. Cederholm's extensive involvement in the maritime community was not unique; both of the other arbitrators revealed past dealings with one of the parties. Arbitrator Klosty aptly analogized New York's maritime-arbitration community to a busy harbor, where the wakes of the members often cross.

The most sought-after arbitrators are those who are prominent and experienced members of the specific business community in which the dispute to be arbitrated arose. Since they are chosen precisely because of their involvement in that community, some degree of overlapping representation and interest inevitably results. *See e.g.*, *Garfield & Co. v. Wiest*, 432 F.2d 849 (2d Cir.1970), *cert. denied*, 401 U.S. 940, 91 S.Ct. 939, 28 L.Ed.2d 220 (1971). Those chosen as arbitrators in important shipping arbitrations have typically participated in a great number of prior maritime disputes, not only as arbitrators but also as parties and witnesses. They have therefore almost inevitably come into contact with a significant proportion of the relatively few lawyers who make up the New York admiralty bar. Under these circumstances, a decision on our part to vacate arbitration awards whenever a mere appearance of bias can be made out would seriously disrupt the salutary process of settling maritime disputes through arbitration. We are convinced that the goals of the arbitration system would not be served if arbitrators and Article III judges were held to the same high standard. To vacate an arbitration award where nothing more than an appearance of bias is alleged would be "automatically to disqualify the best informed and most capable potential arbitrators." *Commonwealth Coatings, supra,* 393 U.S. at 150, 89 S.Ct. at 340 (White, J., concurring). This we decline to do.

Finally, we see no merit in International's assertion that Cederholm's conduct violated section 9 of the Rules of the Society of Maritime Arbitrators, which requires an arbitrator to disclose, no later than the first hearing, any relationship with counsel for either party. Cederholm fully revealed his connection with Haight Gardner at the first hearing on September 8, 1977. Developments thereafter in the Mary S. Arbitration # 2 were considered by the other arbitrators at Cederholm's request. We think it significant that, after all the relevant facts regarding any possible bias on Cederholm's part were disclosed to counsel and the arbitrators, the other two arbitrators-including, of course, the one selected by International-saw no impediment to Cederholm's continuing as arbitrator and urged him to remain.

We therefore reverse the district court's order which vacated the award on grounds of "appearance of bias," and remand with directions to confirm the award.

\*     \*     \*

I.      *Fertilizer Corp. of India v. IDI Management, Inc.,* 517 F.Supp. 948, 953-55 (S.D. Ohio, 1981).

.     .     .

IDI asserts that enforcement of the Nitrophosphate Award would violate the public policy of the United States, in violation of Article V(2)(b) of the Convention. They allege that Mr. B. Sen, the arbitrator nominated by FCI for the Nitrophosphate case (as well as for the Methanol case) had served as counsel for FCI in at least two other legal or arbitral proceedings and that these facts were not disclosed to IDI. Respondent cites *Commonwealth Coatings Corp. v. Continental Casualty Co.,* 393 U.S. 145, 89 S.Ct. 337, 21 L.Ed.2d 812 (1968), *reh. denied,* 393 U.S. 1112, 89 S.Ct. 848, 21 L.Ed.2d 812 (1969) to support the claim that American public policy demands that arbitrators be not only unbiased but free from even the appearance of bias. Further, they argue, since Mr. B. Sen was remunerated financially by FCI, the nondisclosure of the relationship is fatal to enforcement, despite the fact that the arbitration was unanimous and even though actual fraud or bias may be incapable of proof. IDI also claims that it had no constructive or other notice of Mr. Sen's relationship with FCI, although Indian counsel retained by IDI may have been aware of the arrangement. IDI has submitted affidavits of its responsible officers and past and present counsel (App. 2, Supp. App. C, D, E, F, G) to support this contention.

FCI responds that Mr. Sen was chosen properly under the ICC rules as well as under the Convention. Article V(1)(b) permits a refusal to enforce an award if the losing party was not given proper notice of the arbitrator's appointment or was otherwise unable to present his case; subsection (d) of this Article covers the case where the composition of the arbitral panel was not in accord with the parties' agreement. IDI had proper notice and participated extensively in all sessions, presenting its case thoroughly. The contract between the parties calls for arbitration under the ICC rules by one or more arbitrators appointed in accordance with those rules (Ex. A to petition, ¶12.2). The ICC rules applicable at the time made no mention of neutrality, and not until the 1975 ICC rules became effective was an "independent" arbitrator required. FCI contends that even today it is not clear whether an "independent" arbitrator need be neutral. Moreover, they argue, Mr. Sen is a Senior Advocate and, as such, his relationship with FCI was not that of attorney and client. Rather, Senior Advocates in India are hired by the client's advocate (similar to the retention of a barrister by a solicitor under the British system), are paid by the advocate (who is normally reimbursed by the client), and the Senior Advocate is thus insulated from the client. He is an officer of the Court, like a British Queen's Counsel, and may argue for and against the same client at different times.

FCI answers further that, although not required by the ICC rules, a biographical data sheet on Mr. Sen was furnished to IDI; this indicated that he had a connection with the Indian Government, of which FCI is a wholly-owned entity.

FCI also claims that IDI had actual or constructive notice of Mr. Sen's relationship with FCI. They argue that IDI's Indian counsel, Mr. Pai, was well-acquainted with the facts and that his knowledge should be imputed to IDI. They also claim that an IDI vice-president was given a copy of another arbitration award which clearly revealed that Mr. Sen appeared on FCI's behalf. IDI vigorously denies any such knowledge on its part and strongly protests the propriety of imputing to IDI Mr. Pai's knowledge. IDI supports its denial with affidavits from Mr. Pai and other relevant personnel.

FCI has submitted the affidavit of Colin Ross-Munro, Q.C. (docs. 27-28) which states that there is no impropriety in an Indian Senior Advocate appearing in an arbitration on behalf of a party without disclosing that he had represented that party in another context. IDI has submitted the affidavit of George Mark Waller, Q.C. (doc. 32) which asserts exactly the opposite.

The Court does not take lightly IDI's charge. In view of the unanimity of the Nitrophosphate Award, there is nothing to suggest actual bias or prejudice on Mr. Sen's part, yet we strongly believe that full disclosure of any possible interest or bias is the better rule whenever one is in a position to determine the rights of others. However, we do not find that nondisclosure of Mr. Sen's relationship with FCI has so tainted the proceedings as to nullify the award.

FCI relies upon *Commonwealth Coatings*, *supra*, as the statement of American public policy with respect to neutrality of arbitrators. It is true that in this case a plurality of the Supreme Court found that "any tribunal permitted by law to try cases and controversies not only must be unbiased but also must avoid even the appearance of bias," 393 U.S. at 150, 89 S.Ct. at 340, and stated that "we should, if anything, be even more scrupulous to safeguard the impartiality of arbitrators than judges," *Id.* at 149, 89 S.Ct. at 339. Two Justices concurred but emphasized that arbitrators are not to be held to the standards of Article III judges, or of any judges, 393 U.S. at 150, 89 S.Ct. at 340, White, J., concurring, and three Justices dissented, insisting that, in the absence of a showing of unfairness or partiality, there was no reason to set aside an award for failure to disclose a prior business relationship. 393 U.S. at 153, 89 S. Ct. at 341, Fortas, J., dissenting.

Moreover, *Commonwealth Coatings* is distinguishable on the facts. That case dealt with a so-called tri-partite arbitration where one party chose one arbitrator, the other party chose a second, and those two arbitrators selected the third. The controversy centered on the third arbitrator, "the supposedly neutral member of the panel." 393 U.S. at 146, 89 S.Ct. at 338. In the present case, we are dealing, not with the third member of the panel, but with the member appointed by the party, FCI, with whom the alleged undisclosed relationship existed. The third member of the panel was Lord Devlin. Although IDI claims that Lord Devlin was appointed at Mr. Sen's suggestion, while FCI claims that he was appointed at Mr. Rand's (IDI's former counsel's) suggestion, and each supplies a letter purporting to uphold its claim (IDI's Supp. App. H and FCI's App. I), there is nothing at all to suggest that Lord Devlin was other than totally impartial. In fact, it is undisputed that the identical panel of arbitrators found for IDI in the Methanol arbitration, with Mr. Sen dissenting, but with Lord Devlin and Mr. Wilson favoring IDI.

The Court of Appeals for the Second Circuit has concluded that the Convention's public policy defense should be narrowly construed. "Enforcement of foreign arbitral awards may be denied on this basis only where enforcement would violate the forum state's most basic notions of morality and justice." *Parsons and Whittemore Overseas Co., Inc. v. Societe Generale de l'Industrie du Papier (RAKTA)*, 508 F.2d 969, 974 (2d Cir. 1974). Even in domestic arbitrations, that Court has "viewed the teachings of *Commonwealth Coatings* pragmatically, employing a case-by-case approach in preference to dogmatic rigidity." *Andros Compania Maritima v. Marc Rich & Co.*, 579 F.2d 691, 700 (2d Cir. 1978). And, in a very recent case, the Second Circuit decided specifically that awards should not be vacated because of an appearance of bias. *International Produce, Inc. v. A/S Rosshavet*, 638 F.2d 548 (2d Cir. 1981). We believe, also, that the Court has given wise advice in counselling courts "to invoke the public policy defense with caution lest foreign courts frequently accept it as a defense to enforcement of arbitral awards rendered in the United States." *Parsons and Whittemore*, *supra*, 508 F.2d at 974.

We therefore find that recognition or enforcement of the Nitrophosphate Award would not be contrary to the public policy of the United States, and enforcement may not be denied on this basis. The stronger public policy, we believe, is that which favors arbitration, both international and domestic, as exemplified in *Scherk v. Alberto-Culver Co.*, 417 U.S. 506, 94 S.Ct. 2449, 41 L.Ed.2d 270 (1974) and in the *Steelworkers Trilogy*.

*     *     *

J.      *The State of Israel v. Desert Exploration 1976 Incident*, summarized in Lawrence F. Ebb, *A Tale of Three Cities: Arbitrator Misconduct by Abuse of Retainer and Commitment Fee Arrangements*, THE AMERICAN REVIEW OF INTERNATIONAL ARBITRATION: ESSAYS IN HONOR OF HANS SMIT 3, 177, 181-90 (1992).

.      .      .

In 1980 a contractual dispute between Desert Exploration 1976 (hereafter referred to as "DE '76"), an American partnership, against the State of Israel with respect to a contract for the exploration, development and production of petroleum in an area in the Sinai Peninsula. DE '76 filed a Request for Arbitration and retained an American law firm (hereafter "A") to represent it in the arbitration. It designated its party-appointed arbitrator "B," in January 1980 simultaneously with the entry by firm "A" into a $10,000 "retainer agreement" with him, described below. The agreement was not initially disclosed to the other party; the $10,000 was paid to Arbitrator "B" in February 1980; the first sitting of the Tribunal took place in July 1980.

Israel appointed as an arbitrator a former Supreme Court Judge. He, together with "B," jointly chose as the third arbitrator an English barrister who served as the Chairman. It was agreed that the arbitrators, in this *ad hoc* arbitration, would each receive an equal amount of compensation with the payments being made together with reimbursement of expenses, by the Chairman. It was common ground between the parties that all three arbitrators, however designated or appointed, were required to conduct themselves as impartial and independent.

Arbitration sittings for the examination and hearing of witnesses continued intermittently over a two-year period, for a total of 39 days. Hearings were scheduled for August 9-27, 1982 to complete the examination of witnesses, and oral argument was scheduled for January 1983. But disclosure of the retainer agreement by "B" to the Chairman in January 1982 and thereafter to the arbitrator appointed by the State of Israel at a hearing held on June 4, 1982 led to a swift notification by the Attorney General of Israel to DE '76 counsel "that Israel intended to terminate the arbitration proceedings, based on DE '76's failure to disclose, for more than two years" the "retainer agreement." Israel moved in the Tel Aviv-Jaffa District Court for an order confirming its decision to terminate the arbitration, or, alternatively, a direction to remove "B" as an arbitrator.

### B. *Grounds for Termination of the Arbitration*

1. *A Pre-Existing Relationship.* Several grounds were submitted by the State of Israel to the Tel Aviv-Jaffa District Court in 1982 in support of its motion for a declaratory judgment confirming the State's decision to terminate the arbitration by rescission of the arbitration agreement. Some of these turned on a pre-existing social and professional relationship between Arbitrator "B" and one of the partners of the American law firm and his intermittent professional relationship with the firm for many years preceding the arbitration. These were treated as *de minimis* and swept aside by the Israeli district judge as not providing:

> the slightest basis for disqualifying Second Respondent ["B"] from serving as an arbitrator in the matter before us. It is only natural that a litigant who is entitled to choose one of the Arbitrators to deal with his matter, should prefer a person whom he knows to possess the qualities required for conducting an arbitration in the proper manner, and so long as the arbitrator chosen has no personal interest in the outcome of the deliberations, there is no room for his disqualification. . . . It is a daily occurrence that there are appointed to serve as arbitrators lawyers who represented the litigants' rights up to the time of the appointment as arbitrators, and resigned from such representation with the sole and avowed purpose of serving as arbitrators in matters in which they acted for the litigants until that stage without anyone finding fault therewith.

.    .    .

Given the failure of Israel to have immediately acted on that knowledge and to have requested the removal of "B" as an arbitrator, the court held that it:

> must be deemed to have waived such complaints as it might have had in this connection. A person is not allowed to continue with arbitration proceedings when

he is aware of a complaint that may disqualify an arbitrator or discontinue the arbitration, in the hope that a judgment will be given in his favour, and later pull it out of his sleeve when he later sees reason to apprehend that his expectations will not be realized.

.   .   .

While dismissing the foregoing as irrelevant, or trivial, or waived, the District Judge viewed with the utmost gravity the fact that the $10,000 "retainer fee" that had been paid to "B" by the American law firm had long remained undisclosed.

The "retainer" was described as having been designed to compensate "B" if no arbitration were commenced (*e.g.*, because of settlement by the parties) "as compensation for the loss of the prospect to obtain alternative engagements in consequence of reserving time for the arbitration." On the other hand, if the arbitration proceeding did occur, the arrangement was described by the Court as requiring that the $10,000 be set off against the remuneration." [sic]

The Court ruled that "the retainer agreement itself does not seem to me to be unfair, provided the conditions thereof be transmitted to the opposing party before commencement of the arbitration."

It also ruled that the details of the retainer agreement should be disclosed to the opposing party "at the same time as dispatch of the notice of appointment of "B" as arbitrator, or immediately thereafter," in order to give the opposing party an opportunity to object, should it so desire, to "B's" service as arbitrator. The Judge surmised that the likelihood of objection if disclosure at the outset had occurred was slight as the retainer agreement "merely" entailed a setoff of the $10,000 "against the payment of fees."

However, the retainer agreement was not disclosed to the State of Israel either before commencement of the arbitration or immediately thereafter; and in fact, according to "B's" subsequent affidavit, disclosure was much later: "He mentioned the remuneration agreement in an informal conversation with the arbitration Chairman in January 1982." The date of the conversation was that given in "B's" Affidavit during the 1982 Tel Aviv trial proceedings. Subsequently, in a deposition taken on March 8, 1989, "B" set the date as being in the summer of 1981 during a sightseeing trip with the Chairman.

"B" had not brought the retainer agreement to the hearings with him until May 1982, and the arbitrator appointed by the State of Israel was then informed by the Chairman of the retainer agreement and given a copy in June 1982.

The Israeli Court found that "B" did not himself set off the sum of $10,000 against the fees paid out by the Chairman and "waited for close to two and a half years before actually informing the arbitrator appointed for Israel." The United States District Court in its recapitulation described the delinquent period as being alleged by the Attorney General for the State of Israel to have been "for more than two years."

The Israeli Court ruled that Arbitrator "B" had acted improperly in not disclosing the existence and details of the retainer agreement "at the latest at the time when he received the first payment."

The Court based its determination of arbitrator misconduct, by virtue of the non-disclosure, on Section 30 of the Arbitration Law of Israel, which provides that "an arbitrator who has consented to his appointment shall act loyally towards the parties . . ." The reader may wonder why the Court did not look to and rely upon, at least in the first instance, a set of institutional arbitration rules stated by the Arbitration Clause to be governing. The answer is that, unfortunately for the tidy administration of arbitral procedure, Article VIII of the Arbitration Clause of the Basic Agreement covering the arrangements between DE '76 and Israel provided that any arbitration that might be required to resolve controversies arising with respect to the Agreement should be conducted under the "Rules of Conciliation and Arbitration *of the International Arbitration Association*." [emphasis added]

This appeared to be, and is, an example of what has been termed a "pathological arbitration clause" since it obviously was intended to refer to the "Rules of Conciliation and Arbitration of the International Chamber of Commerce," and there is in fact no "International Arbitration Association," as the Arbitral Tribunal immediately recognized.

Given this ambiguity and potential stumbling block, the Arbitral Tribunal decided at its first meeting in 1980 that the arbitration would be governed by the Arbitration Law of the State of Israel, which embodies the same provision as to independence and non-partisanship of the arbitrators as in the ICC Rules, although it also includes somewhat more severe sanctions to insure compliance with the standards for such independence.

The Court interpreted Section 30 of the Arbitration Law as creating a "duty of trust" on the part of all three arbitrators to both parties. This is typical of international commercial arbitration systems, in contrast to an arbitral system dealing with labor controversies that allows two of the arbitrators "to act as counsel" for each of the parties and to have only the "umpire" be the impartial and independent person of the Tribunal.

The duty of loyalty, Judge Shilo rules, "is subject to each party knowing the nature of the relations that exist between the other party and his chosen arbitrator." In this case, all three of the arbitrators were under an obligation to be independent of each of the parties and owed a "duty of full loyalty towards both parties even if he was chosen by only one of them."

This led the court to the conclusion, based on Section 30 of the Arbitration Law, that "it is incumbent upon every party appointing an arbitrator to disclose any fact or circumstance which is likely to preclude the arbitrator appointed by him from full discharge of the loyalty duty." The existence of the retainer agreement was held to be such a fact or circumstance.

.     .     .

Thus, Judge Shilo concluded that it was the duty of the American law firm, which was the counsel to DE '76, "to make these facts known" about the retainer agreement before the commencement of the arbitration. He found it a source of annoyance, and an illustration of a "stubborn attitude," that DE '76 should have made the disingenuous claim that it had fulfilled its duty of disclosure by including the check for $10,000 (to the order of Arbitrator "B") among the documents required for discovery. The documents, delivered in April 1981, included a photocopy of the $10,000 check with the words "for retainer-arbitration" printed in the margin. "The cheque bears the date 11.2.80" (February 11, 1980).

Counsel for the State of Israel submitted in his affidavit to the Israeli Court that neither he nor anyone else functioning in the matter on behalf of the State of Israel had noted the existence of the $10,000 check among the "many thousands of items among them bank statements and scores of checks" that had been produced by counsel for DE '76 in the discovery of documents.

Judge Shilo ruled:

> I have no reason to disbelieve Advocate Efrat, nor is there any room in the circumstances of the matter for regarding the non-detection of the said check as [indicating] negligence on his part . . . If there was a duty of disclosing the conditions of the retainer imposed on First Respondents' shoulders, and nobody seems to dispute this, such duty was *to make a full, clear and unequivocal disclosure and the inclusion of a photocopy of the check among the many documents discovered without any specification* of the nature of the transaction to which it related along with all the details in a manner focusing the attention of the other side, *does not constitute such a disclosure.* [emphasis added]

### C. *Rescission of the Arbitration Agreement*

Rather than removing Arbitrator "B" under the provisions of Section 11 of the Arbitration Law, the State "lawfully rescinded the arbitration agreement on grounds of the circumstances outlined above," *i.e.*, breach of the duty to fulfill the arbitration agreement in good faith, so that the arbitration was terminated.

Section 12(b) of the Arbitration Law of Israel provides:

> Where an arbitrator has been removed, the court may, if it sees a special reason for doing so, instead of appointing a substitute arbitrator, decide that the dispute which is the subject of the arbitration shall not be dealt with by arbitration.

The court confirmed the State's decision to terminate the arbitration. In doing so, it granted the request of the State of Israel, which in its Application sought confirmation of its view that DE '76 "had materially breached the arbitration agreement." The Court relied upon Article Two of the contracts (Remedies for Breach of Contract) Law for the remedy of rescission, rather than on the remedy in Section 12(b) of the Arbitration Law, although the wrong had originated in the failure to carry out the duty of disclosure under the Arbitration Law. In any event, the two legal bases are intertwined, since the Court cited as the fundamental breach of contract, *i.e.*, the Arbitration Agreement, "the non-disclosure of the retainer conditions prior to the commencement of the arbitration."

.    .    .

Counsel for DE '76 filed an appeal with the Supreme Court of Israel, dated September 2, 1982. However, this was not pursued; instead, a settlement agreement for $10 million was ultimately reached by the parties on May 12, 1983. It provided *inter alia* that each party shall "bear its own expenses including legal costs, both in respect of the Arbitration proceedings" and in respect of the proceedings before the Israeli court and Supreme Court. The appeal was withdrawn, and, in accordance with the settlement agreement, the Tel Aviv-Jaffa District Court decision was vacated.

.    .    .

Two of the original limited partners who entered into the partnership known as DE '76 brought suit derivatively against the defendant law firm "A" several years after the Israeli District Court opinion and the settlement agreement. The defendant law firm had made the "retainer agreement" payment of $10,000 to Arbitrator "B" and were the leading counsel on behalf of DE '76 in the international arbitration. Plaintiffs' allegations, as summarized by the Federal District Court in 1990, were:

> Plaintiffs allege that the law firm defendants breached their fiduciary duty as attorneys (Count I), and acted negligently in their representation of DE '76 (Count II), by making the unlawful payment to the arbitrator and calling for funds to prosecute the arbitration without revealing the payment or the possible negative impact of

its subsequent disclosure on the arbitration. Plaintiffs assert that as a result of defendants' actions they expended large amounts of funds in the terminated arbitration and accepted a settlement considerably lower than the value of their claims. Plaintiffs seek recovery of the difference between the value of DE '76's claims against Israel and the actual amount of settlement received as well as recovery of the expenses incurred by DE '76 in the arbitration . . . .

The plaintiffs had offered "both the required expert testimony" in the form of an affidavit and representations that had earlier been made by the defendant, before the abortive termination of the arbitration, that the recovery for DE '76 would be a minimum of $11,215,000 with a potential range from $15-$25 million. The plaintiffs contended before the Federal District Court that DE '76 "had several claims for recovery in the arbitration proceedings, which, including costs, attorneys' fees and expenses, totalled between $28-30 million."

The plaintiff moved for partial summary judgment, citing the decision by the Israeli District Court in *DE '76 v. The State of Israel*. Because the decision had been vacated in accordance with the settlement agreement in Israel, the United States District Court held in a 1988 Memorandum decision that the Israeli decision could not be considered conclusive.

Subsequently, when the defendant law firm moved for summary judgment in 1990, the District Court issued a memorandum opinion denying that motion. The court stated that the plaintiffs in that suit were seeking as one of a number of claims "recovery of the legal fees and expenses incurred by DE '76 in the arbitration itself as well as costs incurred challenging its termination." The District Court denied the defendant's motion with respect to plaintiff's claims for the costs of the arbitration and the challenge to its termination.

The District Court took note, *inter alia*, in its memorandum opinion of 1990, that with respect to the possible alternative of a suit in the United States that might have been brought against the State of Israel itself, "plaintiffs point out that the scope of relief in the United States would not be as broad as in the arbitration. . . . The prevailing party in the Israeli arbitration would have been entitled to recover its costs, including the fees and expenses of the arbitrators and attorneys, fees not recoverable in an action in the United States."

While no holding eventuated from the District Court proceedings with respect to the amount of arbitration costs (because of entry into a settlement agreement), whether related solely to the arbitration proceedings itself or also to the defense of the arbitration in the Israeli District Court, the amount claimed in the Federal District Court proceedings with respect to the arbitration costs alone was "at least $3,525.031." This included DE '76's 60 percent share of the fees and expenses of the three arbitrators, as well as all of the fees and expenses of attorneys who had represented DE '76 in the arbitration.

Notes and Questions

1. In a case with some similarities to *Desert Exploration*, *Norjarl A/S v. Hyundai Heavy Industries Co., Ltd.*, 3 All E.R. 211 (1991), an English court reviewed the propriety of commitment fees demanded by arbitrators.

2. In *Desert Exploration*, the critical question is not the propriety of an international arbitrator asking a party for a commitment fee before accepting an arbitration commitment that may never eventuate and as a result never generate fees. It is arguable that an arbitrator is entitled to concern himself or herself with opportunity costs. The problem is, however, one of disclosure. If Professor B. had disclosed the arrangement with the party appointing him promptly, would there have been any ground for suit in Tel Aviv?

3. Considering the approach of the Supreme Court in *Commonwealth*, do you think that the judicial standard for arbitrators should allow contingent commitment fees?

## VII.    OBJECTIONS

On what grounds may a party challenge an arbitrator? In ICC arbitrations, the grounds are wide-ranging, going beyond a lack of independence.

A.     W. Laurence Craig, et al., International Chamber of Commerce Arbitration 227-35 (2d ed. 1990).

13.05 Grounds for challenge

i) Grounds not limited to lack of independence

Historically, the grounds for challenge under the Rules have not been specified and the Court of Arbitration has inherent power to grant a challenge on any grounds it deems appropriate. The right to challenge was provided for under the 1955 Rules which contained no specific requirement of independence of the party-appointed arbitrator and no linkage between the right to challenge and any such lack of independence. The 1975 Rules made specific provision for the independence of the party-nominated arbitrator but left the right of challenge in a separate provision, without specification of the grounds, in the same terms as previously stated. The 1988 Rules, after making specific provision first for the independence of the party-nominated arbitrator (Article 2(4)) and then for all arbitrators (Article 2(7)) goes on to provide (in Article 2(8)) that:

> A challenge of an arbitrator, whether for an alleged lack of independence or otherwise, is made by the submission to the Secretary General of the Court of a written statement specifying the facts and circumstances on which the challenge is based. (Emphasis added.)

Although the drafting is awkward, it must be concluded, first, that challenges may be made on grounds other than lack of independence and, second, that for such unspecified grounds the wide discretion exercised by the Court in the past is reaffirmed and reinforced. The awkwardness of the text may stem from the ICC's reluctance, due to the particular circumstances of the party-nominated arbitrator, to specify clearly in its rules, as have other institutions (*see, e.g.*, the UNCITRAL Arbitration Rules, Article 3.1) that an arbitrator shall be independent and impartial. In fact, this requirement is implicit, and has been traditionally applied by the Court in its practice to all arbitrators, taking into account wherever necessary any special circumstances concerning the party-nominated arbitrator.

ii) Party-nominated v. third or sole arbitrators

Except in the case of a challenge on the basis of nationality (see point (iii) below), a party-nominated arbitrator can be challenged on the same grounds as a presiding arbitrator. An ICC tribunal should be composed of arbitrators who have the capacity to render a fair and impartial award based on the evidence before them. Although the grounds of challenge are not defined in the ICC Rules, they may be likened to those that apply to the recusation of a judge in a civil matter.

While the general principle is that all ICC arbitrators should be impartial, there is a substantial difference in application of the rule to party-nominated arbitrators as opposed to presiding arbitrators. In the case of a party-nominated arbitrator, the principle of independence must be weighed against the right of a party to nominate an arbitrator compatible with its national and economic circumstances. No such counterbalancing interests exist with respect to a chairman or sole arbitrator.

iii) Nationality

A party-nominated arbitrator may not be challenged on the basis of his nationality. In the absence of a contrary agreement, parties are free to nominate arbitrators of their own or any other nationality. Under Article 2(6) of the ICC Rules, however, a presiding arbitrator "shall be chosen from a country other than those of which the parties are nationals."

In choosing the National Committee to name a third or sole arbitrator, the ICC Court will frequently go beyond the minimum requirements of Article 2(6) in order to avoid any appearance of national bias. For instance, in a dispute between a Swedish company and an English company, the Court would not be likely to choose the Norwegian National Committee to propose the third arbitrator since a litigant might believe that Scandinavians have a similar outlook. On the other hand, if the Court had determined for special reasons that a Scandinavian third arbitrator was appropriate, it would not sustain a challenge on the mere basis of nationality.

There are occasions where parties challenge presiding arbitrators on the basis of residence in the State of which one of the parties was a citizen and had cultural or family ties with citizens of that State. Such challenges generally seem to fail. However, in one ICC arbitration, revealed in U.S. court proceedings which reviewed a connected case, the Italian Chairman of an arbitral tribunal was found to have dual citizenship; he was also a U.S. national, as was one of the parties. On challenge by the non-U.S. party, he was disqualified by the Court of Arbitration.

Problems can also be caused by the issue of corporate nationality. On the face of it, a corporation is deemed to have the nationality of the State in which it is incorporated. In exceptional circumstances, however, it is necessary to take into account the nationality of its controlling shareholders. Where, for example, an arbitration involves a French subsidiary of an American multinational enterprise, the Court of Arbitration would generally not ask for a proposal for a third or sole arbitrator from either the French or the U.S. National Committees in order to avoid arguments of conflicting national interest. If either the French or U.S. National Committee had been chosen (perhaps due to lack of adequate information), it is entirely possible that the Court would make a new appointment on challenge. However, no case of this kind appears to have been made public. In one case in the authors' practice, the defendant called the Court's attention to the fact that the claimant, a Liechtenstein entity, was in fact the business vehicle of an Egyptian national. In response, the Court recalled its request for nomination of the chairman by the Egyptian National Committee and redirected its request to the Austrian National Committee. Controversy was thus avoided. The advantage of such early consideration of the nationality problem is that it takes place before a specific individual has been nominated; the discussion focuses on general principles rather than personal attributes.

On the one hand, the Court must as a pragmatic matter take into account the national character of the underlying economic interests in issue, just as it pragmatically determines when a business dispute is of an international character under Article 1 of the Rules (see Section 10.02). On the other hand, the Court should not permit nor encourage artificial attempts to bar the appointment of neutral arbitrators by invoking a multiplicity of corporate nationalities within a group. Thus, the fact that a corporate party has a branch in the country from which the neutral arbitrator was chosen should not be accepted per se as grounds for challenge.

### iv) Continuing financial interest or professional or subordinate relationship

Few things are as great an impediment to impartiality than the possibility that the arbitrator has a financial interest in the dispute or a financial relationship with one of the parties. The most obvious example is where the nominee has an ongoing employment relationship with the nominating party; not only does such a nominee have a financial interest in keeping his job, but he is also by definition in a subordinate relationship to his employer.

It is rare that a party nominates one of its employees as an arbitrator. The rule is so basic as to be recognized in all legal systems. The issue arises more frequently with respect to employment by a related company or individual. In such cases, the Court applies common sense rather than a formal rule. It must determine whether the relationship could affect the impartiality of the arbitrator. Challenges have been sustained in cases where the arbitrator was employed by a company belonging to the group of which the nominating party was also a member. In another instance, the general counsel of a large multinational company withdrew after being challenged on the grounds that he was an employee of a holding company which had an indirect interest in the outcome of the arbitration (it owned shares in an operating company having a joint venture interest with one of the litigants).

Lawyers are occasionally challenged successfully. It is generally recognized that the regular counsel for one of the parties may not serve as an arbitrator in the absence of agreement to the contrary. The Court of Arbitration has recognized this ground for challenge and has thereby confirmed the obligatory rules in effect in most countries (see point (vii) below). It is possible, however, that in some cases, the Court may deem the professional relationship to be so occasional or trivial it rejects the challenge.

A more vexing problem may arise in the context of the nomination as arbitrator of a lawyer who is a partner in a large law firm: even though he may be of recognized ability and international reputation and personally independent of both the nominating and opposing parties, he will in most circumstances not be allowed to serve as arbitrator if one of the other members of his firm has counselled the party nominating him, even on completely unrelated matters. The general rule appears to be that in most circumstances a challenge to such a person is upheld. While no doubt the arbitrator is professionally independent of the party, there remains a theoretical financial conflict of interest: the law firm in which the partner has a financial interest will profit from the continued relationship with the party, and an adverse arbitral decision might trouble that relationship.

In an arbitration involving a State entity, on the other hand, it is less likely that the Court will uphold challenges against arbitrators employed by the State (either directly as government bureaucrats, or indirectly as employees of a State enterprise, agency or university) for reasons described in Section 13.03. Unless the entity employing the arbitrator is directly subordinate to the State agency or enterprise involved in the arbitration, it is unlikely that the Court will take into account the indirect influences that are bound to exist. Such grounds, however, have been the basis of successful challenges in the analogous case of multinational enterprises.

### v) Prior financial interest or professional or subordinate relationship

If an arbitrator has a continuing financial interest or a professional or subordinate relationship with a party, one may fear (see (iv) above) that he will be subject to some pressure to render an award favorable to the party appointing him. If such a relationship is in the past, the analysis is somewhat different. The arbitrator can no longer be said to have a subordinate relationship to the party. Nevertheless, financial or personal interests are not necessarily absent. A person who has had previous business with a party may hope to resume such relations in the future. A long prior employment with a party may have given rise to such a close relationship as to make impartiality difficult. A further risk exists if the arbitrator has had a long employment or professional relationship with a party; he may be cognizant of facts relating to the party or the conduct of its business which are not part of the evidence presented before the arbitral tribunal. His opinion on the controversy may thus be influenced by facts not available to the other arbitrators.

While it is difficult to define specifically prior relationships that are disqualifying, it is safe to state that past relationships generally do not create strong grounds for challenge. The Court will not automatically assume that a nominee should be disqualified because of occasional business relationships in the past with the nominating party. Furthermore, the sensitivity of the issue is considerably attenuated by the fact that it arises almost invariably in the context of party-nominated arbitrators. Due to the diversity of national interests and the requirement that the chairman come from a third country, it is rare that an ICC chairman will have had any contacts with either party.

The *Universal Pictures v. Inex Films and Inter-Export* case illustrates some issues of disqualification in ICC arbitrations. In that case, the United States party picked as its arbitrator an American lawyer in independent practice in London. The lawyer had, however, been a salaried corporate counsel of the claimant's parent company five years earlier. The defendants had received through the Secretariat the party-nominated arbitrator's resume, which included a statement of his prior employment and the name of the company he had worked for (which, incidentally, was not the same as that of the subsidiary). In addition, counsel for claimant revealed at the commencement of the proceedings before the arbitral tribunal that the party-nominated arbitrator had previously been employed by the parent company of the party. No objection was made to the arbitral tribunal or to the Court of Arbitration, and an award was subsequently rendered in favor of the claimant. In exequatur and appeal proceedings in France, the defendants alleged, inter alia, that the American arbitrator lacked independence.

The French Court of First Instance, whose decision was upheld on appeal, found (a) that the defendants had been informed of the ties between the arbitrator and the claimant at an appropriate time; (b) that having had the opportunity to protest the confirmation of the arbitrator, they could not claim that they were victims of error or fraud; and (c) that the fact that the party-nominated arbitrator had worked for the parent company of the claimant five years previously was insufficient to justify a conclusion that he was not independent, especially since there had been no proof that he had maintained ties with the corporate group since that time.

vi) Bias or previously expressed opinion

An obvious ground for challenge lies if the arbitrator has previously given his opinion on the matter in dispute; he can no longer address the issues in arbitration with an open mind. Lawyers having previously given their opinion on points at issue in the arbitration to one of the parties should not serve as ICC arbitrators.

The question may take on a wider dimension. May an arbitrator in a nationalization indemnification case be disqualified because he is an ardent supporter and frequent speaker on the necessity of full indemnification, including lost profits? Or because he is a partisan of the Charter of Economic Rights and Duties of States, known to hold the view that no contractual indemnification is required and only local law compensation provisions should be regarded? Here the distinction between party-appointed arbitrators and the presiding arbitrator once again comes into play. Absent aggravating factors, it seems doubtful that the Court would sustain a challenge in such circumstances against a party appointment; a party should be free to choose an arbitrator of a compatible legal "culture."

On the other hand, the Court would want to avoid appointing a presiding arbitrator who had publicly taken extreme and detailed views on political or economic issues central to the arbitration. Nevertheless, the success of a challenge would depend on all the circumstances. The expression of academic views in scholarly publications by a jurist does not necessarily preclude him from deciding a case in a completely impartial manner, based only on the evidence, arguments, and applicable law in the case.

Other allegations of bias have been founded on the conduct of an arbitrator in prior arbitrations. A challenge will not ordinarily succeed simply because an arbitrator has served in the same capacity in prior proceedings involving one of the parties. Such a claim for recusal would not lie against a judge, and it is hard to see why the rule should be different in arbitral proceedings absent additional factors. One such factor may be the fact that the party-nominated arbitrator has frequently and regularly been appointed by that party. He may thus bring to the arbitration superior knowledge concerning one of the parties and his opinion may be influenced by facts outside the arbitration record. Furthermore, the prospect of continued and regular appointment, with the financial rewards that such appointment would bring, could also be of relevance. In the ordinary case, however, prior service as party-nominated arbitrator is not grounds for disqualification. An open question, however, is whether the failure of the arbitrator to reveal such prior appointments would be an independent ground of disqualification.

While bias undoubtedly is grounds for challenge, the burden is on the challenger to demonstrate that real bias does in fact exist. For example, bias has been alleged to be reflected by the arbitrator's comportment in prior business relations of a confrontational type, in prior legal proceedings as counsel, and as arbitrator (alleged offensive and prejudicial conduct).

Such challenges raise delicate problems for the Court of Arbitration. The Court is understandably reluctant to sustain a challenge based on a party's subjective allegation of bias which is denied by the arbitrator. The Court occasionally may seek to avoid ruling on the issue. If it feels that the claims of the challenger, even if somewhat subjective, are bona fides, it may instruct the Secretariat to ask the arbitrator whether he wishes to continue in view of the opposition and possible effect thereof on the proceedings. Thus some challenges are settled informally. On the other hand, the Court will not take this approach if it feels that the challenge is unreasonable or made to cause delay.

vii) The use of national court precedents

A party seeking to justify a challenge will frequently refer to precedents of national courts, since the Court's decisions are kept confidential and the ICC Rules do not define the criteria for challenge. Cognizant of the mandate of Article 26 that all efforts should be made to ensure that an award is enforceable at law, the Court is especially attentive to reasoned arguments that rejecting the challenge may endanger the enforceability of an award in a jurisdiction having some connection with the arbitration. Thus while not binding, national court precedents can be persuasive arguments for the Court of Arbitration.

It should be noted that most national court decisions arise in appeal or execution decisions after an award has been rendered. Thus some of the cases involving allegations of newly discovered disqualifying facts regarding an arbitrator may be nothing more than last-ditch attempts to avoid honoring duly rendered awards. Challenging an arbitrator during the arbitration may therefore have more chances of success than the same challenge by a losing party in court.

It is clear that national precedents may not be blindly transposed to the international arbitration context. As Swiss arbitration experts have noted, the criteria for disqualification of arbitrators in domestic arbitrations may not automatically be applied to international arbitrations. In some countries, domestic arbitration under local procedural laws is subject to stricter criteria than those of the ICC, requiring complete absence of relation or communication between an arbitrator and the parties. Other countries apply more permissive criteria than the ICC; rather than being independent, party-nominated arbitrators are permitted and in fact expected to become the advocate of a party's cause before the third arbitrator who serves as a type of umpire. There exist specialized arbitration associations where an enormous number of disputes are arbitrated by a small group of professional arbitrators, and which therefore are different from ICC arbitrations. Examples are maritime and commodity arbitrations in London and textile industry arbitrations in New York.

Nevertheless, national courts deal with international and domestic arbitrations in a variety of circumstances that may be relevant to the ICC arbitral process. The Court of Arbitration may usefully be referred to precedents relating to the disqualification of arbitration of arbitrators on the grounds of bias, partiality, or the like. Not only may the reasoning of such precedents be persuasive, but the Court will be attentive to the question whether its action (or more usually its non-action) would hamper execution of the award, with particular care as to the standards which might be brought to bear by a national court at the seat of arbitration.

## Procedures for Challenging an Arbitrator

If a party decides to challenge an arbitrator, how exactly should it go about doing so? The process will depend, first, on whether the arbitration is being conducted under the auspices of an arbitral institution (and, if so, which institution) and, second, where the arbitration is taking place.

The approaches to challenges and the procedures for challenges vary among arbitral institutions. Guillermo Alvarez, a general counsel at the ICC Court of Arbitration, has considered the position in relation to the ICC.

\*   \*   \*

B.      Guillermo A. Alvarez, *The Challenge of Arbitrators*, J.
        ARB. INT'L, Jan. 1990, at 203, 204-07.

The great majority of national laws empower the national judge to
decide on an arbitrator's challenge. Article 2.8 of the ICC Rules, on
the other hand, provides for a decision to be taken by the ICC Court.
Consequently, the first question that arises is that of the authority
competent to decide on the challenge.

       The freedom of the parties to refer to rules of an arbitration
institution for settling their disputes is broadly accepted. This freedom
is recognized by many national laws, by international conventions and
by case law. Accordingly, when parties have agreed to apply the ICC
Rules, they must submit the challenge to the ICC Court of Arbitration
in accordance with Article 2.8. Indeed, both the jurisdiction of the
arbitral institution and the application of its Rules result from the will
of the parties.

       As we shall see, however, the particular nature of the
relationship between permanent arbitration institutions and the parties
may well justify the intervention of municipal courts to assess the
contractual liability of the protagonists on the stage of administered
arbitration. Submission of the challenge of an arbitrator to a national
judge by a party that has agreed to an institutional procedure may,
however, be regrettable. Naturally, this kind of practice rewards the
bad faith of parties seeking to sabotage the arbitral procedure.

       Nevertheless even where there is an established procedure for
challenging arbitrators in institutional arbitration, exceptional
circumstances may lead local courts to intervene.

### (a) Procedure in Institutional Arbitration

The procedure for challenging arbitrators in ICC arbitration is provided
by Articles 2.8 and 2.9 of the Rules. The institutional remedy, which
has been recognized by various legislative provisions, and referred to
in case law, is necessitated by the risks resulting from untimely referral
to municipal courts and by the need to respect the procedure chosen by
the parties.

       The advantages of institutional jurisdiction are also confirmed
in practice. Institutions such as the ICC Court of Arbitration are in a
better position to assess the wide variety of factual situations likely to

exist in an international context. Direct intervention by national courts would, on the other hand, be likely to shatter consistent solutions and would introduce the risk of decisions inspired by each country's favourable or unfavourable attitude towards arbitration. Moreover, if one bears in mind the duration of the challenge procedure and its suspensive nature, a party's temptation to act in bad faith is controlled more effectively by the arbitral institution, and the potential resulting disruption is mitigated. We can cite, for example, the case of a defendant who submitted six challenges against the chairman of an arbitral tribunal to the ICC before applying to a national court which also dismissed its claim.

Over the period between January 1983 and December 1989, the Court was seized of 73 challenges against 98 arbitrators. Overall these requests were filed by the claimant in 20 cases (27.4%) and by the defendant in 52 cases (72.6%). As to the merits, 60 challenges (82.1%) considered to be groundless or time barred were rejected. Out of the eight challenges allowed, four were requested by the claimant and four by the defendant (out of a total of 98, that is 7.5%).

The increasing number of challenges (11 in 1986 and 22 in 1987) led to a modification of the Rules of the Court in 1987. The text which came into force on 1 January 1988 reflects a concern both to ensure the independence of the arbitrators, and to guarantee the effectiveness of the arbitral procedure. That is why the challenge procedure provided for in Article 2 (paragraphs 8 and 9) of the Rules was completed to include appropriate time limits. In addition, the distinction between the procedure for challenging the arbitrator (Articles 2.8 and 2.9) and the one provided for his replacement (Articles 2.10 and 2.11) was maintained. Under Articles 2.10 and 2.11 the Court may replace an arbitrator who is not fulfilling his functions in accordance with ICC Rules at the request of the parties or *ex officio*.

### (i) Initiation of the procedure

The modification of Article 2.7 of the former ICC Rules and the introduction of a statement of independence that every arbitrator must complete before his appointment by the Court, will no doubt reduce the number and the frequency of challenges. The reforms have already been felt; only ten challenges were submitted in 1989, compared with 22 in 1987.

Presently, a party wishing to introduce a challenge '. . .whether for precise time limits or the challenge will be time barred: within 30 days from notification of the appointment of the arbitrator by the Court or within 30 days from the date when the party making the challenge was informed of the facts or circumstances on which the challenge is based. Naturally, the Court has a right to assess the difficulties which might result from the application of the time limit in the case of the challenge of an arbitrator based on grounds arising in the course of the arbitration procedure. Not only does the challenge have to be submitted within the time limits specified in the Rules; it also has to specify the facts and circumstances on which it is based. Lastly, the challenge must be sent in writing to the Secretary General of the Court, who is responsible for triggering the challenge procedure.

### (ii) Development

So as to allow an opportunity for presenting their comments to the arbitrator concerned and, if they so desire, the other arbitrators, a copy of the challenge is sent to them by the Secretary General of the Court. The time limit afforded to the arbitrators and the party for making their comments must be 'appropriate' according to their geographic location and to the circumstances. The fact that the Secretary General has a certain discretion in fixing this time limit ensures the submission to the ICC Court of all the parties' opinions while keeping a control over delays which might otherwise be excessive. In any case, it is up to the ICC Court to assess whether the time limits granted by the Secretariat are appropriate within the meaning of the Rules.

The challenge is referred to the Court when the comments of the arbitrator in question and, if they so desire, those of the other arbitrators or parties have reached the Secretariat within the specified time limits.

### (iii) Outcome

The decision on the challenge of an arbitrator is taken by the Plenary Session of the Court. Consequently the challenge of the arbitrator, his reply and, where applicable, the comments of the other arbitrators or parties are referred to the Court. On the report of one of its members, the Plenary Session of the Court discusses the matter and makes a final decision on the challenge. If the challenge is accepted, a substitute arbitrator is appointed in accordance with the procedure laid down by article 2.12 of the Rules. The Court's decision is final and reasons for it are not communicated to the parties (article 2.13 of the Rules).

Despite the theoretical difficulties to which it may give rise the administrative nature of the decision taken by the Court in application of article 2.9 of the ICC Rules is no longer seriously disputed. The non-judicial nature of the ICC Court's decisions, resulting from articles 2.1 and 2.13 of the ICC Rules, has been confirmed by case law which we shall examine when we come to deal with the question of intervention by the State courts.

\*    \*    \*

C.    *AMCO ASIA Corporation and Others v. The Republic of Indonesia* (June 26, 1982).

I.    Facts and procedure

This decision is made in accordance with Rule 9 of the Rules of Procedure for Arbitration Proceedings on the proposal made on June 21, 1982 by the Respondent to disqualify Edward W. Rubin, the arbitrator appointed by Claimants.

The Respondent bases his proposal on the following:

Pursuant to Rule 6 of the Arbitration Rules Edward W. Rubin had, on April 20, 1982, stated:

> . . . I have, and have not had any professional, business or other relationship with the parties, except:
>
> 1.    My law firm, Phillips and Vineberg, through myself, last year rendered some advice on certain Canadian tax matters to Mr. T.K. Tan, who I believe but I am not certain is a shareholder and/or director of one or more of the Claimants.
>
> 2.    My law firm, Phillips and Vineberg, had a joint office and profit-sharing arrangement in Hong Kong for the period 1972-1975 with Messrs. Coudert Brothers, attorneys for the Claimants.

3. My law firm, Phillips and Vineberg, has
and has had dealings with Messrs. White
and Case, attorneys for the Respondent.

The Respondent contends that the contents of this declaration reflect several facts which indicate that the challenged arbitrator has a manifest lack of the qualities required by paragraph (1) of Article 14 of the Convention on the Settlement of Investment Disputes between States and Nationals of Other States (The "Convention" Article 57). The challenged arbitrator has served as attorney for Mr. T.K. Tan, who "controls" Claimant companies and thus Mr. Rubin would be sitting in judgment of his own client. In addition the "Joint Office and Profit-Sharing arrangement" between counsel for Claimant and the challenged arbitrator — even if the character of this arrangement is not fully disclosed — requires that the challenged arbitrator be treated de facto as if he had been a partner of Claimant's counsel in this matter. Taking these facts together, the Respondent contends that "the proposition that Mr. Rubin 'may be relied upon to exercise independent judgment' as to Claimant's charges against Indonesia is untenable." (Page 9 in Respondent's proposal). The Respondent did not, however, question Mr. Rubin's moral character and recognized competence.

The Claimant contends in his memorandum filed on June 23, 1982 that neither Mr. Rubin nor his law firm has any attorney-client relationship with Claimants or any of their officers, directors or shareholders. Once, prior to Mr. Rubin's appointment as an arbitrator, Phillips and Vineberg's Hong Kong office, which is the only Canadian law firm in Hong Kong, rendered minor Canadian tax advice to Mr. Tan, who lives in Hong Kong, has a business in Canada and is an officer and shareholder of Claimants. Total legal fees for such advice were only HK$2280 (less than US$450).

The Claimant further contends that neither Mr. Tan, nor Claimants, were clients of either Phillips and Vineberg or Coudert Brothers during the period from 1972-1975 when Phillips and Vineberg had a profit-sharing arrangement in Hong Kong with Coudert Brothers, attorneys for Claimants. The profit-sharing arrangement was completely terminated at the end of 1975 and there has been no other relationship or sharing of profits since then.

According to Rule 9 of the Rules of Arbitration an informal meeting was held in Washington D.C. on June 23, 1982 between the arbitrators and the attorneys of the Parties.

The challenged arbitrator gave, in accordance with Rule 9 paragraph 3, the following oral explanations:

1. In June or July 1981, Mr. Tan came to see Mr. Rubin in his office, where he spent about 15 minutes giving the facts of the situation of a company in Canada in which he had an interest. He left and a few days later Mr. Rubin sent him a letter of about 1-1/2 - 2 pages. The firm's account was approx. HK$2500. Neither Mr. Rubin nor his firm acted for or counselled Mr. Tan and/or any company with which he was associated in the nearly 10 years he has acted in Hong Kong prior to June/July 1981. Nor has he or his firm rendered any counsel or advice to Mr. Tan and/or any of his companies since that time.

2. Mr. Rubin further stated that, although he now knows that the present Arbitration was filed in January 1981, and was therefore pending at the time of his tax advice to Mr. Tan, he was not approached by Messrs. Coudert Brothers until late August or early September 1981 — well after his letter of advice to Mr. Tan. Accordingly, when he advised Mr. Tan he was in no way aware of the present Arbitration, its status or even that he would be approached to act as an arbitrator.

3. Concerning the profit-sharing arrangement with Messrs. Coudert Brothers, Mr. Rubin explained that this was ended in September/October 1975 although his firm sub-let office space from Coudert Brothers for a few years subsequently. All dealings since 1975 have been on a purely arm's length basis in the same way as his firm deals with any other law firm, including White and Case, counsel for the Respondent. All accounts between his firm and Coudert Brothers with regard to the end of the profit-sharing arrangement were settled at that time, and there was no residual, on-going subsequent fee, profit- or loss-sharing relationship between the two firms since.

4. During the period of the profit-sharing arrangement neither Mr. Tan nor any of his companies were clients of his firm or of Coudert Brothers in Hong Kong.

At the same informal meeting counsel for the Parties developed orally their arguments and presented the legal contentions which will be summarized below.

II.      The legal contentions of the Parties

A preliminary remark is to be made here: according to the chairman's suggestion Mr. Rubin, who had furnished the explanations on facts here above cited, refrained himself from any discussion of the legal contentions of the Parties.

A. The legal contentions of the Respondent

The legal contentions of the Republic of Indonesia may be summarized as follows:

1. In an ICSID arbitration, instituted and conducted according to the provisions of the Convention, all the arbitrators have to be of absolute impartiality, and no distinction can be admitted in this respect between the chairman of the tribunal and the two other arbitrators, be the latter respectively appointed by the parties, pursuant to Article 37-2(b) of the Convention.

Indeed, says the Republic, while the general principles and the common rules of international and municipal laws require such impartiality, the highest standard of impartiality is here required, since sovereign States have agreed to submit themselves to international arbitration, thus waiving the privilege of immunity, and since according to Article 53(1) of the Convention "the award shall be binding on the Parties and shall not be subject to any other remedy except those provided for in (the) Convention," such remedies being the request for revision submitted to the arbitral tribunal itself, or the request for annulment, submitted to an ad hoc Committee appointed from the Panel of Arbitrators: Convention, Articles 51 and 52. Thus, no external judicial control can be exercised on the award.

.   .   .

### B. The legal contentions of the Claimants

1. The Claimants do not deny that the highest standard of impartiality is required from arbitrators acting in an ICSID arbitration, be they chairman or members of the arbitral tribunal.

2. Nevertheless, the Claimants contend that where an arbitrator is appointed by a party, the inescapable consequence is that some relationships not only social, but in some instances professional, will exist or have existed between the arbitrator and the party who appoints him. It is but normal, says the Claimants, that when somebody is called to appoint an arbitrator, he will select a person whom he knows, and in whom he has full confidence, due to the experience the appointing party can have gained, precisely thanks to his relationship with the nominee.

Now, since the Convention provides for party-appointed arbitrators, it can but have taken into account this normal situation, which does not prevent, however, the thus appointed arbitrator from being a person "who may be relied upon to exercise independent judgment."

.    .    .

4. These being, according to Claimants, the legal principles and rules to be applied and such principles and rules not being contradicted by the case law precedents referred to by the Republic, the Claimants contend that the facts stated and explained by Mr. Rubin do not allow to consider that he is not a "person reliable upon to exercise independent judgment."

The Claimants contend that these facts are minor or trivial. None of them is of a kind which allows to cast a doubt on Mr. Rubin's reliability in this respect. As to the precedents invoked by the Republic, none of them concerns a party arbitrator, and the facts involved were of an entirely different kind. Accordingly, the Claimants maintain that the proposal to disqualify should be denied.

## III.    Discussion

1. In all matters concerning the establishment of the Tribunal and the procedure of the arbitration, the only sources of law to which

direct reference is to be made are the Convention, and the Rules adopted by the Administrative Council of the ICSID pursuant to Article 6(1)(c) of the Convention, with no intrusion of any provision or specific precedent of other international conventions, rules of international arbitration established by other international bodies, or national statutes and judicial precedents.

To be sure, the provisions or the precedents found in these other sources of law may be considered as a matter of comparison, and as embodying from time to time the general principles governing international arbitration. Nonetheless, while taking into account, where necessary, such general principles, the Convention and, as the case may be, the Rules are to be construed in accordance with their letter, their spirit, and with the aim which States purported to achieve when signing and ratifying the Convention.

2. This aim is to provide to host-states and investors an international device to settle their disputes, by reaching a decision which is final and binding, and offers the highest possible guarantees of legality, fairness and impartiality. It goes without saying that in this respect, an absolute impartiality of the sole arbitrator or, as the case may be, of all the members of an arbitral tribunal, is required, and it is right to say that no distinction can and should be made, as to the standard of impartiality, between the members of an arbitral tribunal, whatever the method of their appointment.

3. These principles are embodied in Article 14 of the Convention, hereabove reproduced, which defines the conditions to be fulfilled by a person to be appointed as an arbitrator.

As to this provision, the undersigned deem it useful to present the following remarks:

(a) The final phase of the first sentence of paragraph 1, in which it is required that the arbitrator be a person "who may be relied upon to exercise independent judgment" is not to be interpreted as being just an aspect or a consequence of the high moral character previously required. The phrase designates a specific situation and while it may be difficult to imagine that a person of high moral character could not be reliable, it appears that the drafters of the Convention have intended to exclude a person whose particular situation in a given case could create a risk of lack of absolute impartiality.

.    .    .

(b) However, in the view of the undersigned, the independent and specific character of the condition provided for in this last phrase (which may be called "the third condition") does not mean that such condition precludes the appointment as an arbitrator of a person who has had, before his appointment, some relationship with a party. Such relations would be a reason of non-appointment — and as it will be seen, a reason for disqualification — only where they appear as creating a risk of inability to exercise independent judgment, and as a result, a "non-reliability" to such exercise.

In this respect, the undersigned share the views expressed by the Claimants when saying that the mere fact that the Convention has opened the way to the appointment of arbitrators by the party, leads necessarily to the consequence that a person is not excluded from such appointment for the only reason that some relationship existed between that person and a party, whatever the character — even professional — or the extent of said relations.

.    .    .

5. In view of the principles and the interpretation thus established, it does not appear to the undersigned that the facts proven in this case indicate a manifest lack by Mr. Rubin of the "reliability" required by Article 14 of the Convention, and indeed, not even a non-manifest lack of the same.

A legal advice on a minor question which could not have been anything but minor, as the fees received show it, is of no bearance on the "reliability" of the adviser to be an arbitrator appointed by the client to whom he had given this advice.

To give and to receive such an advice does not create an "attorney-client" relationship, and is by no means comparable to the situation of a regular counsel of the appointing party. Similarly, relationships between the law firm of the appointed arbitrator and the counsel for said party, that ceased around six years before the appointment was made, cannot have such significance; not to speak about the sublease of premises and the employment of the same telephone operator (but not on the same telephone number) which are of a purely material kind, and cannot create any psychological risk of partiality.

To be sure, the Respondent has alleged that a combination of facts may have a greater impact than just their suming up. This is a right view, provided each fact has a minimum bearance by its own, which in the view of the undersigned is not the case here.

6. To conclude, it must be said, that not only do such facts not indicate a manifest lack of reliability of Mr. Rubin; in addition, they do not allow a reasonable feeling of non-reliability, which means that whatever the interpretation of the word "manifest" in Article 57, and even if it would mean a non-reliability which is just perceived, they could not justify Mr. Rubin's disqualification.

This conclusion is not contradicted by the international rules on arbitration, nor by the judicial precedents invoked by the Respondent.

For all these reasons, Messrs. Goldman and Foighel decide as follows:

1. The proposal to disqualify Mr. Edward W. Rubin is denied.

\*    \*    \*

VIII.    THE ROLE OF COURTS IN CHALLENGES

A.    Guillermo A. Alvarez, *The Challenge of Arbitrators*, J. INT'L ARB., Jan. 1990, at 203, 208-13.

During the 65 years that the ICC Court of Arbitration has been in existence, there have been profound changes in the landscape of international commercial arbitration. Instituted at a time when both the dimensions of international trade and its practitioners favoured resort to *ad hoc* arbitration, the ICC Court of Arbitration is the pioneer of institutionalisation which currently stands at more than 70 institutions in 44 different countries.

Conversely, judicial intervention becomes rare as certain tasks vested in the courts are transferred to arbitral institutions. Parties wishing to exclude their disputes from State court jurisdiction altogether, aware of the delays and risks involved in drafting a 'self-sufficient' arbitration clause, have found that institutional arbitration provides a significant contribution to the legal security of their contract. Hence, confidential arbitration proceedings will take place under the aegis of an institution with the necessary experience and in accordance with known and mutually agreed rules. But, as this transfer of tasks originally assigned to the State judge preceded the legislative recognition of institutional arbitration, case law (and international conventions) have contributed to the evolution of statutory law.

Furthermore, the national courts remain vigilant in exercising residual jurisdiction in cases of international institutional arbitration. Congruent with the main objective of international arbitration, sanctioned by international conventions, restated by national law, and recognized by case law, normal judicial control occurs *a posteriori*, once the final award is rendered. Nonetheless, the diversity of the supervisory functions exercised by the ICC Court of Arbitration and the contentious attitude of parties, have recently given rise to a new encounter between the institution and the State courts, during the procedure.

### (i) Normal judicial control

Considering that the main objective of arbitration is to reach a final decision rapidly and confidentially, local court intervention defeats the purpose of the procedure chosen by the parties. However, the existence of international public policy and the reality of the world of business make the assistance of municipal courts essential, be it in the assessment of the legality of the award or, when necessary, in ordering its compulsory enforcement.

Fortunately, the supervision exercised by local courts when seized with a challenge to the final award is restricted to limited grounds and occurs only at the end of the procedure, thus avoiding premature State court proceedings. In ruling such a request for intervention admissible, the Paris Cour d'Appel rightly stated that claimants: '. . . may, if necessary, exercise one of the remedies against the future arbitral award provided under articles 1502 and 1504 of the New Code of Civil Procedure; one must also draw from this decision that supervision relates only to the arbitral award. This statement is not devoid of interest since, in a case decided four months earlier, an action for nullity brought by Opinter against both the final award and the decision of the ICC Court to reject a request challenging an arbitrator, the French court declared that the recourse against the ICC decision was not admissible:

> . . . the nullity recourse defined by article 1484 NCCP relates only to 'acts considered to be arbitral awards', and excludes any other act or decision;
> . . . accordingly, a decision of this kind does not have the form of an 'act' considered — albeit formally — as an arbitral award, within the meaning of the said provision.

Moreover, the recourse was directed both against the institutional decision rejecting the challenge and against the final award. This astute formulation led the Court of Appeals to a qualification of the decisions of the ICC Court:

> . . . the decision by the Court of Arbitration of 20 October 1982 to reject the challenge of an arbitrator, was not issued by a judicial body — to which the guiding principles of due process would apply and to which article 1460 NCCP refers in the case of arbitration — and does not constitute a decision that is judicial in its nature and thus subject to the obligation to provide reasoned grounds. . .

> . . . the Court of Arbitration is not itself an arbitrator, and . . . it is simply responsible for organising the arbitration, in particular by appointing the arbitrators; . . . neither the said powers nor the decisions which express them are judicial.

therefore the French judge limited himself to examining whether the ICC Rules had been properly applied:

> Considering, in consequence, that the attacked decision was taken in compliance with the Rules of the ICC Court of Arbitration — that the parties accepted by deciding to submit their disputes to ICC arbitration, so that the said Rules form an integral part of their agreements — did not have to be reasoned, and

whereas, accordingly, it escapes the grounds alleged by
Opinter.

In addition to its spirit, both liberal and very favourable towards
institutional arbitration, this judgment has the merit of fixing the limits
beyond which the activities of arbitral institutions may be subjected to
premature judicial control.

### (ii) Premature judicial control

Modern case law does not warmly welcome the disruption of
arbitration procedures by the introduction of State court proceedings.
Indeed, the disturbance caused by premature intervention of state courts
coupled with the risk of bringing the arbitration procedure to a halt,
strike at part of the contract which the parties will often consider to
have been a determining factor of their acceptance.

Nonetheless, arbitral institutions are bound to carry out all the
tasks entrusted to them by the parties. Thus *subsidiary intervention*
enables State courts to verify whether the ICC Court has complied with
its Rules. Conversely, for the local court to claim *exclusive jurisdiction*
to settle such questions seems unjustifiable, dangerous and unsuitable
to the needs of international arbitration.

### (iii) Subsidiary intervention

When municipal courts limit their intervention in the course of the
arbitral procedure to examining the conditions of application of its
Rules by the arbitral institution, they create the conditions for a new
form of cooperation.

The decision of the French courts in the case *Raffineries d'Homs*
provides a good example. Here a decision by the Court of Arbitration
ordering the replacement of an arbitrator was referred first to the Paris
Tribunal de Grande Instance and subsequently to the Cour d'Appel,
both of which recognized the ICC's jurisdiction to rule on the question
in application of the ICC Rules. Despite the fact that the first instance
court had declared the recourse to be admissible, in its judgment it
restricted itself to examining whether the ICC Rules had been properly
applied by the Court of Arbitration:

> . . . since the ICC Court of Arbitration followed the
> proper procedure laid down in the Rules that the parties
> — in full control of their rights — had mutually and of

their own free will adopted, the ICC Court of Arbitration which informed the parties of its decision, cannot be held to be at fault in its decision which opened up the way to the replacement of an arbitrator . . .

The same applies to the judgment of the Court of Appeals:

> . . . on the question whether the said body's decision was taken in accordance with the due procedure, suffice it to notice that the appellants have not adduced evidence of any breach of the ICC Rules; on the contrary the documents produced prove that the Rules . . . were correctly applied when the challenge in question was examined.

But only the Court of Appeals drew the consequences of the international and institutional nature of ICC arbitration: i.e., that an annulment recourse against the Court of Arbitration's decisions is not admissible:

> . . . the action in nullity against the Court of Arbitration's decision is not admissible since in the context of an entirely contractual international arbitration, there is no need either to investigate if such a decision is judicial in character, or to examine the other grounds put forward, all of which are inoperative;

This detail is important for it does away with the possibility of applying for annulment of an institutional decision '. . .in the context of an entirely contractual international arbitration.' Primarily directed towards ICC arbitration (a contractual and international institution), the statement seems, in our view, to reserve the exercise of judicial control in case of *ad hoc* arbitration.

The liberalism of French law under which this case was decided contrasted with the Swiss Concordat prior to the enactment of the 1987 Swiss Federal Act on Private International law.

### (iv) Exclusive jurisdiction
Clearly restricted by a law inadequate to the realities of 'entirely contractual international arbitration', to use the formula of the Paris

Court of Appeals, the Swiss courts have held themselves to have exclusive jurisdiction to decide on the removal of a challenged arbitrator. . . . we shall restrict ourselves to noting that the compulsory application of certain articles of the Swiss Concordat on Arbitration (CIA) and - before the CIA came into force in the canton of Zurich — provisions of the Zivilprozessordnung (ZPO), has resulted in the length of arbitral procedures approaching the duration of ordinary court proceedings.

In the *Westland* case, a request for the challenge of the three arbitrators was referred to the Geneva first instance court, which rendered a judgment on 7 February 1985 declaring the challenges not admissible on the grounds that the petitioners should first have submitted them to the ICC Court of Arbitration. Alleging a violation of article 21 of the CIA, the petitioners appealed the first instance decision. The Geneva Court of Justice rejected the challenge in the following terms:

> . . . in view of Article 1.3 CIA, if the appellants challenged the arbitrators before the ICC Court of Arbitration, the ICC decision would be subject to recourse before the Geneva courts.

The case was then brought to the Tribunal Fédéral which reversed the judgment of the cantonal Cour de Justice. In so doing, the Federal Court underscored the mandatory nature of Article 21 of the CIA:

> . . . 2.7 of the Rules of the ICC Court of Arbitration . . . clearly contravenes Articles 21 of the CIA (and it) is therefore inapplicable by virtue of article 1 para. 2 CIA.

Under these circumstances, the challenge procedure took place in accordance with the Concordat. After several judicial incidents, the decision rejecting the challenge became final on 19 July 1988, that is nearly four years after the challenge was initially submitted.

Perhaps as a result of the ambiguity of the ZPO, the position in the canton of Zurich is more complex. Although it is only of academic interest now that Zurich applies the new Swiss law, the way in which the Zurich courts have treated cases of challenge and replacement is worthy of comment. When a decision to replace an arbitrator taken by the ICC Court of Arbitration was referred to the Obergericht of the canton of Zurich in the *Clark International* case, the local court restricted its intervention to examining the conditions of application of Article 2.8 of the ICC Rules (1975 version). Hence, Article 244.5 ZPO did not order exclusive local court jurisdiction in case of *replacement* of an arbitrator.

However, the exclusive jurisdiction of the Zurich courts seems indisputable in case of a challenge. Indeed, a judgment of the Kassationsgericht ordered the removal of two arbitrators who had already been unsuccessfully challenged before the ICC Court of Arbitration.

An analysis of Swiss case law does, nonetheless, lay bare the distress of the Swiss courts. On two occasions the federal judges brought to mind essential objective of arbitration and their message was heard in Parliament. The new Swiss Federal Act on Private International Law (article 180.3) now orders compliance with the challenge procedure chosen by the parties. Case law has thus contributed to modernisation of the law. Other laws, in particular the UNCITRAL Model Law of 1985, entrust the final decision on challenges to the courts. Their evolution, as in the example of Switzerland, will require the lucidity of judges, the attentive ear of Parliament and the efforts of practitioners and scholars. The contribution of international arbitral institutions towards the harmonisation of notions of independence and impartiality more appropriate to the wide ranging varieties of factual situations which they are regularly confronted with, will avoid an outburst of regional solutions.

### Notes and Questions

1. It will often be the case that a challenge is made to the appointment of an arbitrator, not because of genuine concern regarding that arbitrator's independence, but for tactical reasons. Thus, a respondent may well pursue an unmeritorious challenge in the hope that it will encumber and delay the arbitration. Can an arbitrator be challenged on the grounds that he no longer fills conditions which were preconditions to his appointment? The issue was addressed in the interlocutory award by the Permanent Court of International Justice in *Losinger & Co. v. Yugoslavia*, 1936 P.C.I.J. (ser. C) No. 78, at 105, 112 (June 27 & Dec. 14.)

> It would be equally absurd to change an arbitrator once he has been properly seized of the matter, under the pretext that he is no longer President of the Federal Tribunal. His Presidency changes every 2

years and if there were two or three individuals who had to be involved successively in the same case, that would go against fair justice.

In addition, the matter has been decided in France where, when the arbitrator is appointed by virtue of his office, for example by being the President of such a Tribunal, the parties are deemed to have appointed the individual who was exercising those duties at the moment when the proceedings commenced ("Arbitrage," page 509, Dalloz, Répertoire Pratique, T. I, no. 140). Once the arbitrator has been seized of the matter, he therefore remains competent.

2. Are these circumstances in which changes of role or other attributes would require the challenge and replacement of the arbitrator?

Does a challenge of an arbitrator mean that the whole arbitral process necessarily comes to a halt? The answer to this question depends on where the arbitration is being held.

B.     RENÉ DAVID, ARBITRATION IN INTERNATIONAL TRADE 263-64 (1985).

287. Competent authority. The impartiality of judges is a fundamental principle in all countries, and everywhere the question whether an arbitrator is disqualified or not, or whether he has been impartial or not, will finally be decided by the courts. An exception is constituted by socialist countries, where it is submitted to, and decided in a final way by, the Court of Arbitration of the competent Chamber of Foreign Trade.

The question which arises is whether, when a party challenges the qualification of an arbitrator, the arbitral tribunal may, if it thinks fit, proceed with the arbitration until an award is made. As in the case when a party raises an objection to the arbitral tribunal's competence there is a risk that a party may endeavour without good reason to stop the arbitration procedure in order to delay the pronouncement of the award. Between the two hypotheses there is however a difference. It may be difficult to decide whether there is a valid agreement, which covers the dispute in hand; it is much easier to decide whether there is a plausible reason why a person ought not to act as an arbitrator. This may explain why the two problems have been approached differently in a number of laws.

In the countries of the Romano-Germanic family it is generally considered that the arbitral tribunal, if an arbitrator is challenged, is bound to postpone the examination of the case until the matter has been decided by a court. To lessen the inconveniences of this solution it is provided by a number of laws that the challenging party must apply to the court within a very short delay after his objection has been rejected by the arbitral tribunal: a delay of ten days according to Belgian law, of five days in Argentina and Colombia. No clear solution is given in other laws. The Swiss Concordat limits itself to saying that the question is within the exclusive jurisdiction of the courts, and Danish law that all disputes regarding the qualification of the arbitrators must be decided by the courts. French law provides only that the objection shall be settled by the president of the court having jurisdiction in the matter (Art. 1463).

In other countries the arbitral tribunal is not bound to suspend the arbitration procedure. Only after an award has been made will a control be exercised by the courts. This rule applies in Austria and probably in Sweden, although it is disputed in this country.

This last rule is certainly to be preferred in the case of international arbitrations, where it is always desirable to avoid the intervention of a national court. A risk is involved however. The party who lacks confidence in an arbitrator will possibly decline to participate in the procedure of the arbitration after his request for the challenge of an arbitrator has been rejected. To act otherwise might be interpreted as an admission that his objection was not serious. But it must be admitted that this is indeed most generally the case and that the objection raised is in most cases purely dilatory. If there is any doubt it is highly probable that the arbitrator who is challenged will decline to remain an arbitrator in the case. He will be encouraged to do so when the arbitral tribunal is composed of more than one arbitrator. More strictness is probably to be expected from the arbitrators than from the court in the matter.

A middle way can be found. The parties' agreement may remit the matter to an Arbitration Court, which is able to dispose of it most rapidly. This practice, especially advisable when there is a single arbitrator, is followed in the socialist countries. The arbitral tribunal must suspend its procedure until the Arbitration Court has given a decision rejecting the challenge of an arbitrator; a provision to this effect is to be found in the Rules of a number of arbitral institutions in non-socialist as well as in socialist countries. In socialist countries the decision of the Arbitration Court settles the matter finally; in non-socialist countries on the other hand it can be appealed again before a court. It is expressly provided by the laws of Ecuador and Peru that the arbitral tribunal can be authorized to continue the procedure or arbitration when the Arbitration Court has decided that the challenge of an arbitrator was not justified.

## IX.    SUMMARY AND CONCLUSIONS

The overall quality of the people chosen is critical in the performance of every role. But in international arbitration, the choice of arbitrators may be the most important single task parties face. Arbitral tribunals have an unusually difficult task in the international arena, given the challenges of conducting proceedings in such a way that they are cost-effective while taking care to ensure that the award will withstand review if its enforcement is challenged before a variety of potential national courts.

The role of party-nominated arbitrators is the most delicate issue facing the international arbitral process. Depending on their legal culture and ethics, some parties will use their right of nomination to appoint unscrupulous agents as arbitrators, while others faithfully respect the principle of independence in making their nominations. Were it perceived that the former gained an advantage by naming biased arbitrators, arbitration would degenerate as parties raced to the bottom:   the lowest common denominator of ethical standards. Fortunately, arbitral institutions and national courts have been aware of this danger and have removed arbitrators whose independence is in doubt. With respect to arbitrators whose bias is not apparent at the moment of appointment but is revealed in the course of proceedings, the most effective sanction tends to be the reaction of co-arbitrators, who discount such an arbitrator's views upon noticing his bias.

# CHAPTER 6

# PRELIMINARY DECISIONS

## I.    INTRODUCTION

Some questions must be determined by the arbitrator prior to others. The most fundamental is the issue of jurisdiction: the arbitrator cannot determine the merits of a dispute unless the dispute lies within the scope of the jurisdiction granted to him by the parties. Other questions, unlike the question of jurisdiction, may not condition the very ability of the arbitrator to proceed but may simply have to be determined before reaching the merits. These include determining the rules and procedures to be followed in the arbitration and deciding diverse choice of law issues, including a determination of the law governing the arbitration, and of the law governing the merits of the dispute. On occasion other questions may also be decided as preliminary issues, such as statute of limitations or other procedural defenses. For purposes of procedural efficiency it may sometimes be useful to establish sequences for deciding, *e.g.*, to decide first the issue of responsibility and only later, if required, the issue of damages. In complex arbitrations containing many claims (particularly in construction cases), arbitrators frequently decide to render a number of partial awards dealing with some, but not all, of the matters. All of these constitute preliminary decisions by arbitrators as well.

Arbitrators' preliminary decisions of the kind just referred to relate to, and anticipate, the final award on the merits. Another kind of preliminary decision deals with provisional measures. They are collateral to the substantive dispute in arbitration and are intended to preserve the status quo pending arbitration, to secure the efficacy of the arbitral award that may be rendered, or to secure evidence to be used in the arbitral proceeding. These measures can be taken both by arbitral tribunals and by courts, but in many cases it is preferable for the arbitral tribunal, which the parties have agreed will decide the merits of any disputes between them, to determine also the matter of preliminary measures. In other cases (such as, for instance, the provisional measure of attachment which involves persons not parties to the arbitration) the assistance of the courts will be required to make provisional measures effective.

to the arbitration) the assistance of the courts will be required to make provisional measures effective.

We will consider, at the end of this chapter, the exercise by arbitrators of powers in relation to provisional measures and the related issue of the granting of provisional measures by courts and their impact on the arbitral process.

We take up in Sections III and IV of this chapter some of the most important preliminary issues — jurisdiction and choice of law — which arbitrators must as a matter of logic take up before dealing with the merits. Before examining how arbitrators decide these issues, however, we should first consider the form in which preliminary decisions should be made in general. May they be made in an interlocutory procedural order or should they be included in a formal award? Where finality is required, as in the case, for instance, of jurisdictional and choice of law issues, an award may be necessary. But should these preliminary decisions simply be made first in the order of issues decided in a final award, thus disposing of them sequentially prior to the decision on the merits but only at the end of the arbitration, or should they be determined earlier in a separate interim or partial award?

II.    WHY PRELIMINARY DECISIONS?

This question was considered in the report of a Working Party to the International Chamber of Commerce ("ICC") Commission on International Arbitration.

> Working Party on Dissenting Opinions, Interim and Partial Awards of the ICC Commission on International Arbitration, Final Reports on Interim and Partial Awards (1989), 1 ICC INT'L CT ARB. BULL. (Dec. 1990) at 26, 27-28.

It is hard to envisage any reason why arbitrators occasionally classify purely procedural orders as awards, other than by error or an imperfect understanding of the arbitration process. The most common reasons for making interlocutory decisions on substantive issues in the form of an award are that:

> - a definitive determination of some (but not all) of the claims may enable a deserving party to collect some money before the

final award deals with all of the remaining issues in dispute; and

- a determination of a particular issue (*e.g.*, liability) may either avoid the need for, or at least simplify, the remaining stages of the arbitration.

In the first case it will normally only be the claimant who has an interest in asking for a partial award in respect of some (but not all) of the claims; it is when the second of the reasons mentioned above applies that it is most likely that the parties themselves will jointly request the arbitrator to make an interim award.

Another, perhaps more nebulous, reason for making an interim or partial award is where the arbitrator wishes to invoke a sense of finality on a particular issue. This may be in a formal sense, in creating a decision which operates as res judicata between the parties. However, there are other aspects of finality. Arbitrators may wish to "lock into place" on an irreversible basis a particular decision on a claim or other issue to be determined. This may have the benefit of streamlining and simplifying the later stages of the arbitration, thus saving time and money as well as avoiding the repetition of "dead" arguments. It also means that the proceedings do not have to go back to the beginning in the event that an arbitrator has to be replaced during a long-running arbitration.

There are also circumstances in which the parties, or at least one of them, may wish to achieve "interim finality." For instance, where there is a jurisdiction issue one of the parties may wish to have a positive decision from the arbitrator in the form of an award for the purposes of recognition under the New York Convention, thus creating a bar to parallel proceedings in national courts. Equally, because decisions on jurisdiction issues are frequently reviewable by the national courts at the place of arbitration, parties may wish to have a decision on jurisdiction in the form of an interim award so that the appellate procedure will not have to wait until the end of the arbitration. This is the philosophy underlying Article 16 of the UNCITRAL Model Law. (The UNCITRAL working papers on this point are particularly thorough and informative.) In a Model Law country it would not matter whether or not the decision is in the form of an award, because the decision would be appealable in any event. But in many countries the courts would only have jurisdiction to review the decision if it is in the form of a reasoned award.

The point is not solely a matter of whether or not any particular decision by an arbitrator can, under the law of every country in the world, be characterized in law as an award: but that in certain instances the arbitrator (or the parties) may wish to have the decision partake of the solemnity and generally accepted consequences of an award.

### Notes and Questions

1. The most fundamental issue which may be determined as a preliminary issue is the issue of arbitral jurisdiction. Where the arbitrator decides that he does not have jurisdiction, the award will be final: a determination that the arbitration cannot proceed. When the decision is positive — in favor of arbitral jurisdiction — it may either be rendered as an interim award on this issue or the issue may be joined with issues on the merits, all of which will then be determined in a final award.

2. Analyze the tactical advantages to one party or the other of preliminary decisions. Do they tend to discriminate against one of the parties in subsequent phases of the arbitration? If they do, how can this consequence be minimized while retaining whatever benefits preliminary decisions contribute to the arbitral process? What are the implications of preliminary decisions for the cost and speed of proceedings? What kinds of preliminary decisions or awards are sought by claimants? By defendants?

3. Consider the effect of an interim award. Suppose that in an arbitral proceeding an interim award had been rendered establishing the liability of the defendant by a majority decision (one of the arbitrators dissenting). In the subsequent proceedings on the issue of damages, would the dissenting arbitrator be bound to consider the issue of damages as if there were no doubt as to liability?

4. Suppose, in the above case, that after the interim award had been rendered, one of the arbitrators had been replaced by a new arbitrator because of the former's death, incapacity, or inability to serve. Would a party be entitled to require a rehearing before the newly constituted tribunal of evidence relating to the issues considered in the interim award? For a discussion of the procedural point, see *Trade & Transport, Inc. v. Natural Petroleum Charterers, Inc.*, 738 F.Supp. 789 (S.D.N.Y. 1990).

III.    JURISDICTION

   A.    ARBITRATORS' JURISDICTION TO DETERMINE THEIR
         OWN JURISDICTION (*compétence-compétence* or
         *Kompetenz-Kompetenz*). *See also* Chapter 4, p. 524.

         1.    IMPLIED POWERS

Arbitral decision making is a private system of justice
authorized and regulated by law which permits arbitral tribunals to
derogate from the state's procedural system of justice before courts as
ordinarily provided in its laws and constitution. As long as the parties
have agreed to arbitrate, there is no reason why this choice and this
derogation should not be respected, and indeed compelled. *See supra*
Chapters 3 and 4. But what if one of the parties contests the
jurisdiction of the arbitrator and alleges that he is not bound to arbitrate
because of the nature of the dispute, because the dispute is outside the
scope of the agreement, because the agreement has lapsed or
terminated, or for some other reason? May the arbitrator rule on this
challenge or must an adjournment be granted so that it can be disposed
of by a court?

   The question is essentially one of sequence and timing: in no
system of law should an arbitrator's determination of jurisdiction be
beyond the scope of review by a court. An arbitrator's determination
in excess of his jurisdiction may be set aside at the seat of arbitration,
according to the provisions of local law, or denied enforcement
elsewhere under the terms of the New York Convention. *See infra*
Chapter 9. The issue is whether the arbitrator can make initial
determinations as to jurisdiction and based thereon proceed to enter a
final and binding award on the merits, subject only to *ex post facto*
powers of review or enforcement by courts.

   Particularly where it is alleged that there is simply no agreement
to arbitrate, or that the arbitration agreement or clause is null and void
*ab initio*, the courts in some countries will accept to rule on the issue
without awaiting an arbitral ruling on the issue. *See supra* Chapters 3
and 4. In other jurisdictions, the determination of whether the initial
decision on jurisdiction will be made by a court or by an arbitrator will
depend on the scope of the agreement to arbitrate, that is whether the
clause is considered to be "broad" or "narrow." *See Prima Paint Corp.*

*v. Flood & Conklin Mfg. Co.*, 388 U.S. 395 (1967), *supra* p. 509. It can be argued that since a court will have the last word on the arbitrator's jurisdiction, there is an economy in having jurisdictional issues decided first by the court, thus avoiding the waste in time and money should an arbitrator, having determined that he had power to go forward, proceed to determine the merits of the dispute only to have his award overturned, in a subsequent judicial review, on jurisdictional grounds. On the other hand, in international transactions the primary motivation of a party in entering into an arbitration agreement is to avoid having to submit his case to a national court, particularly where it is likely to be the foreign court of his opposite party, where his opponent will enjoy the many tactical benefits of the home court advantage. Even if the jurisdictional issue were raised in another foreign court — not the home court of the adversary — a party may be confronted with unfamiliar language, procedures, and judicial attitudes. It could be argued, therefore, that it would be, given the purpose of arbitration, anomalous if the initial procedural step in a dispute arising under a contract with an arbitration clause would be the testing of the validity and scope of the clause in a national court. Moreover, such interim judicial recourse would paralyze the arbitral proceedings and perhaps subsequently could lead to a stop-and-start procedure with the complaining party taking successive actions before the court as successive jurisdictional questions arose. The potential for abuse is obvious. At least where an arbitration clause exists, *prima facie*, it can be argued that it would be contrary both to the intent of the parties and to legislative provisions favoring arbitration to permit any party challenging jurisdiction to have immediate recourse to the courts.

On the other hand, conceptual problems are posed when the arbitrator whose powers can only flow from the parties' contractual agreement makes jurisdictional findings which bind a party, but that party continues to insist that the arbitration agreement does not cover the dispute in question or, indeed, that it even binds him at all. Conceptually the arbitrator is in the position of the remarkable Baron Munchausen who contrived to pull himself out of the bog by tugging on his own suspenders.

Generally, practical considerations have prevailed. There is substantial agreement that in international commercial arbitration the arbitrator should in ordinary circumstances have the power to determine his or her own jurisdiction without prior recourse to the courts. In continental legal systems this has been referred to as *compétence-compétence* or *Kompetenz-Kompetenz*, meaning it is within the jurisdiction of an arbitrator to determine his own jurisdiction. *See* Chapter 4, p. 524.

One rationale used by arbitrators to support their right to rule upon their own jurisdiction has relied on an analog of their role to that of a judge on an international tribunal. International tribunals, particularly the International Court of Justice, are considered to have inherent power to determine their own competence.[190] To what extent may the analogy between an arbitral tribunal in an international commercial dispute and an international court be accepted?

a.    *TOPCO/Calasiatic v. Libya* (the *Texaco-Libya* arbitration), preliminary award of the Sole Arbitrator, Professor Réné-Jean Dupuy, (Nov. 27, 1975), *reproduced in* 1 J. Gillis Wetter, The International Arbitral Process 441 (1979).

[The Texaco-Libya dispute arose out of the nationalization in 1973 by the Libyan Government headed by Colonel Gadhafi of oil

---

[190] For the International Court of Justice this is based on Article 36(6) of the Statute of the International Court which provides: "In the event of a dispute as to whether the court has jurisdiction, the matter shall be settled by decision of the court." Statute of the I.C.J. art. 36 ¶6. This has been argued to mean that the International Court is the final and absolute judge of its own jurisdiction. *See* Sir Gerald Fitzmaurice, *The Law and Procedure of the International Court of Justice, 1951-4: Questions of Jurisdiction, Competence and Procedure, in* 34 Brit. Y.B. Int'l L. 1, 25-28 (1958); Ibrahim F. Shihata, The Power of the International Court of Justice to Determine Its Own Jurisdiction (1965). It has been pointed out, however, that even the International Court of Justice, like international tribunals of limited jurisdiction, must be subject to internal or external control mechanisms in order to remain an accepted dispute resolution device. *See* W. Michael Reisman, Systems of Control in International Adjudication and Arbitration 17 (1992). Where the Court fails to apply internal controls on the exercise of its jurisdiction there will be a greater tendency for parties to refuse to accept its judgments: "[O]ne structural consequence of the breakdown of informal and internalized control mechanisms is their externalization, at greater cost to the system. In the absence of reliable internal controls, states resorting to the court will increasingly fall back upon the classic control device of the unilateral claim of *excès de pouvoir*. This may not help the operation of the court or amplify its contribution to world order." *Id.* at 44-45; *see also infra* Chapter 9.

concessions earlier granted to foreign oil companies under the regime of King Idris. The Texaco concession agreement, like the other Libyan concession agreements, was governed by "the principles of law of Libya common to the principles of international law, and in the absence of such common principles then by and in accordance with the general principles of law as may have been applied by international tribunals" and called for international arbitration of disputes. In default of agreement by the parties, the arbitrator was to be chosen by the President of the International Court of Justice at the Hague. In the *Texaco* case the President named as sole arbitrator Professor René-Jean Dupuy, a French professor of international law. The Libyan Government defaulted in the arbitration but it specifically contested the jurisdiction of the arbitral tribunal in a letter addressed to the President of the International Court of Justice contesting his appointment. The arbitrator considered the letter as setting out a jurisdictional defense.]

9. It is for the Sole Arbitrator, and for him alone, to render a decision on his own jurisdiction by virtue of a traditional rule followed by international case law and unanimously recognized by the writings of legal scholars.

International case law has continuously confirmed that arbitrators are necessarily the judges of their own jurisdiction, since Lord Chancellor Loughborough[191] in the *Betsey* case decided to adopt that rule. That same rule has been expressly confirmed in the contemporary era by several decisions of the International Court of Justice, notably by the judgment in the *Nottebohm*[192] case and by the judgment relating to the *Case concerning the Arbitral Award Made by the King of Spain on December 23, 1906.*[193] It has been formally adopted in a great number of International instruments.[194]

---

[191] J.B. Moore, 4 International Adjudications, Ancient and Modern, History and Documents (1931), at 81 and 179 *et seq.*

[192] [1953] I.C.J. 111 *et seq.*, especially page 119.

[193] [1960] I.C.J. 192 *et seq.*, especially page 206.

[194] In particular, Art. 36(4) of the Statute of the Permanent Court of International Justice and Art. 36(6) of the Statute of International Court of Justice, and also Art. 41(1) of the Washington Convention of 18 March 1965 on the Settlement of Investment Disputes between States and Nationals of Other States, Art. 5(3) of the

10. As for the authors, their opinions can be summarized in saying as Professor David[195] did that "the writings of legal scholars unanimously recognize that arbitrators may decide their own jurisdiction".

11. This solution, which is justified by its necessity, is, moreover, in harmony with the dual nature of arbitration: with respect to the jurisdictional nature ("nature juridictionnelle"), by its function in the sense that the arbitrator is vested with the duty of stating the law and in so doing by resolving the dispute which has been submitted to him, but also with respect to the contractual nature ("nature conventionnelle") if one considers the origin of the arbitrator's duty which is found directly or indirectly in the agreement of parties. One comes to the conclusion that the Sole Arbitrator is competent to decide his own jurisdiction, no matter which of these two aspects one envisions in this case.

12. If one looks at arbitration from its jurisdictional aspect, one is evidently bound to apply to the arbitrator the rule according to which any tribunal and any judge is, in the first place, judge of its own jurisdiction. As Messrs. Cornu and Foyer[196] write:

> "When a judge is entrusted with the duty of deciding a dispute, he necessarily becomes, by this very fact, the judge of certain questions which are directly related to his mission and to his activities and it would be practically inconceivable to submit these questions to another judge. This rule is without exception.

---

1961 European Convention on International Commercial Arbitration, as well as Art. 13(3) of the Rules of Conciliation and Arbitration of the International Chamber of Commerce of 1955 which provisions were reaffirmed by Art. 8(3) of the 1975 Rules which became effective on 1 June 1975. Finally, it is confirmed by the Rules of Arbitration and Conciliation of the Permanent Court of Arbitration for the Settlement of International Disputes between Two Parties of which Only One is a State, of which Art. 4 is worded as follows: "The arbitral Tribunal, which shall be the judge of its own competence, shall have the power to interpret the instruments on which the competence is based".

[195] R. David, L'Arbitrage Commercial International en Droit Comparé, Cours de Doctorat 1968-1969, at 313 and the writers referred to therein.

[196] G. Cornu and J. Foyer, Procédure Civile 138 (1958).

> Every judge is judge of his own jurisdiction. —
> Jurisdiction to decide jurisdiction is one of the
> illustrations of this natural necessity. Even in the
> absence of a text of law in this sense, it is generally
> recognized that every judge is judge of his jurisdiction.
>
> For a judge, whoever he may be, the question of
> his jurisdiction is never a question of an interlocutory
> character. . ."

Thus, if we take into account the jurisdictional character of arbitration, we have here a first reason why we should apply to the Sole Arbitrator the rule which is applicable to "any judge whoever he may be" to the effect that every judge is judge of his own jurisdiction.

13. But, if one looks at the contractual nature of the Arbitration, we would arrive at the same conclusion: this conclusion obviously flows from the letter (reference: 57.029), dated 18 December 1974, sent by the Registry of the International Court of Justice to the Libyan Government to explain to it the reasons which led the President of the International Court of Justice to exercise his power of appointment in the present case. According to the terms of that letter, [footnote omitted]

> "The provisions of Clause 28 of the Deeds of
> Concession reveal that the parties anticipated not only
> the possibility of differences concerning the
> interpretation or performance of the Concession Deeds,
> but also the possibility of a failure to agree as to the
> applicability of the clause, and that they agreed that that
> latter issue should be for determination by any Sole
> Arbitrator appointed by the President of the Court. In
> these circumstances, having regard to the jurisdiction
> conferred by the clause on the Sole Arbitrator with
> regard to questions concerning the applicability of the
> clause, the President feels that it would not be proper
> for him to enter upon such considerations, inasmuch as
> to rule upon such a question would amount to a judicial
> act, prejudging one of the very questions which it has
> been agreed should be for determination by the
> Arbitrator."

The passage of this letter, which has just been quoted, properly draws attention to the rule expressed in paragraph 5, Section 2, of Clause 28 of the Deeds of Concession according to the terms of which

> ". . . the Sole Arbitrator, shall determine the applicability of this Clause and the procedure to be followed in the Arbitration."

For the parties to have provided, as they have, in this Clause 28 that the Arbitrator shall determine the applicability of the arbitral clause is necessarily tantamount to their deciding that it rests with the Arbitrator — and with him alone — to determine the question as to whether he has jurisdiction.

Consequently, not only a customary rule, which has the character of necessity, derived from the jurisdictional nature of the arbitration, confirmed by case law more than 100 years old and recognized unanimously by the writings of legal scholars, but also the terms themselves of the clause by virtue of which the Sole Arbitrator has been appointed, require that the Sole Arbitrator should be competent to decide his own jurisdiction.

[For the second part of the award, see *infra* p. 668.]


### Notes and Questions

1. In *Texaco*, where the dispute involved a state and hence had public international law overtones, the arbitrator analogized his situation to that of a judge of an international tribunal, particularly of the International Court of Justice. The status of the ICJ is quite unique, however. Created by convention, there is no other body which can review its decisions; if it did not determine the extent of its jurisdiction, who would? The only alternative would be that a dispute about jurisdiction would have to be referred back to the parties; effectively the procedure would end. In ordinary international commercial arbitration, however, the arbitrator cannot validly make such a comparison because he cannot plead absolute necessity for making the determination on jurisdiction. If he were not to decide the issue, a court would. Hence the issue is not one of necessity but a policy choice.

2. There are other reasons why the status of an arbitrator cannot be assimilated, without reservation, to the status of a judge of any kind. A judge may not be competent to rule on the merits of a given dispute because of rules of territoriality, the status of the parties before him, or the nature of the dispute. But he remains a judge of the court of which he is a member, having the powers that are vested in him

by law. The arbitrator, on the other hand, is designated only by contract and the very existence of his functions as an arbitrator can only be confirmed after an examination of whether the agreement effectively designates him to rule upon disputes arising thereunder. How can the putative arbitrator claim a status which permits him to make this determination? The doctrine of *compétence-compétence* creates a legal foundation, perhaps better termed a legal fiction, apart from the terms of the contract itself, permitting the arbitrator to make this initial determination. While the philosophical soundness of the *compétence-compétence* construct may be doubted, the comparative economy and utility of having a system where the arbitrator initially rules on his own jurisdiction or competence cannot be contested.

3. The practical advantage of permitting an arbitrator to determine his jurisdiction, at least as an initial matter, was described in an English case as follows:

> It is not the law that arbitrators, if their jurisdiction is challenged or questioned, are bound immediately to refuse to act until their jurisdiction has been determined by some court which has power to determine it finally. Nor is it the law that they are bound to go on without investigating the merits of the challenge and to determine the matter in dispute, leaving the question of their jurisdiction to be held over until it is determined by some Court which had power to determine it. They might then be merely wasting their time and everybody else's. They are not obliged to take either of those courses. They are entitled to inquire into the merits of the issue as to whether they have jurisdiction or not, not for the purpose of reaching any conclusion which will be binding upon the parties — because that they cannot do — but for the purpose of satisfying themselves as a preliminary matter about whether they ought to go on with the arbitration or not.

Christopher Brown Ltd. v. Genossenschaft Osterreichisher Waldbesitzer Holzwirtschaftsbetriebe 1 Q.B. 8, 12-13 (1954).

For further discussion of the relationship between determination by courts and arbitral tribunals of the issue of arbitral jurisdiction, and the timing thereof, see *supra* Chapter 4, p. 524.

4. The international arbitration community has expressed widespread support for the notion of the arbitrator's power to determine his own jurisdiction. *See* Clive M. Schmitthoff, *The Jurisdiction of the Arbitrator in* THE ART OF ARBITRATION 285, 288 (Jan C. Schultsz & Albert Jan Van Den Berg eds., 1982); Julian D.M. Lew, *Determination of Arbitrators' Jurisdiction and the Public Policy Limitations on that Jurisdiction, in* CONTEMPORARY PROBLEMS IN INTERNATIONAL ARBITRATION 73 (Julian D.M. Lew ed., 1987); Berthold Goldman, *The Complementary Roles of Judges and Arbitrators in Ensuring that Commercial Arbitration is Effective, in* INTERNATIONAL ARBITRATION: 60 YEARS OF ICC ARBITRATION 257, 261 (1984). For a detailed review, and the most convincing explanation, of the necessity of the power of the arbitrator to determine his own jurisdiction, see Pierre Mayer, *L'Autonomie de*

*l'arbitre international dans l'appréciation de sa propre compétence*, 217 RECUEIL DES COURS 323 (1989).

## 2.    POWERS PROVIDED BY ARBITRATION CLAUSES

Given that a philosophical rationale exists to permit the arbitrator to make a preliminary determination of his own jurisdiction, the arbitrator faced with a challenge to his jurisdiction will primarily be involved in a determination of whether the parties had agreed that jurisdictional questions would be determined by the arbitrator and only secondarily whether there is any legal impediment to giving effect to that agreement. The parties can facilitate the task of the arbitrator either by drafting an arbitration clause expressly giving him the power to determine the existence and scope of his jurisdiction or by drafting a "broad" arbitration clause which will be deemed to provide the jurisdiction of an arbitrator to determine his own jurisdiction. A "narrow" clause may not. For further discussion, see *supra* Chapter 4.

The analysis of the scope of the arbitration clause is particularly important in *ad hoc* (*i.e.*, non-institutional) arbitration since there will frequently be no arbitration rules, incorporated by reference into the agreements, to supply the missing elements. Institutions also supply model arbitration clauses to be used with their rules and intended to provide wide power to the arbitrator.

Where the arbitration clause does give the arbitrator power to determine his jurisdiction it will then be up to him to determine its scope. This task has been succinctly defined as follows: "The answer to the question whether a dispute falls within an arbitration clause in a contract must depend on (a) what is the dispute and (b) what disputes the arbitration clause covers." Heyman v. Darwins, App. Cas. 356, 360 (C.A. 1942).

### Notes and Questions

Do the following clauses give power to the arbitrator to determine his own jurisdiction? What is the scope of disputes that they cover?

1. "Any controversy or claim arising out of or relating to this contract, or the breach thereof, shall be settled by arbitration in accordance with the Commercial Arbitration Rules of the American Arbitration Association, and judgment on the award rendered by the arbitrator(s) may be entered in any court having jurisdiction

thereof." AAA Standard Commercial Arbitration Clause. *See Prima Paint Corporation v. Flood & Conklin Mfg. Co.*, 388 U.S. 395 (1967), discussed *supra* p. 509, where this clause was interpreted as a broad clause giving the arbitral tribunal jurisdiction to examine whether the contract was void for fraud in the inducement of the contract generally.

2. "Provided always that in case any dispute or difference shall arise between the Employer or the Architect on his behalf and the Contractor . . . . as to the construction of this Contract or as to any matter or thing of whatsoever nature arising thereunder or in connection therewith . . . then such dispute or difference shall be and is hereby referred to the arbitration and final decision of a person to be agreed between the parties, or failing agreement . . . appointed . . . by the President or Vice President for the time being of the Royal Institute of Chartered Surveyors." *See Ashville Invs. Ltd. v. Elmer Contractors Ltd.*, 2 Lloyd's Rep. 73, 74 (1988), excerpted and discussed *supra* p. 513, where the English court was required to determine the scope of the jurisdiction given to the arbitrators by this clause. At issue was whether the arbitrators could consider the effect of misrepresentation by the co-contractants on a party's contractual obligations and the power of the tribunal to order rectification. The court concluded that while the issues of misrepresentation were not caught by the "arising under" language of the clause they were covered by the words "in connection therewith." *See* J. Gillis Wetter, *The Importance of Having a Connection: The Doctrine of 'Separability' of the Arbitration Agreement and Compétence de la Compétence in English Law: A Comment on the Judgment of the Court of Appeal in Ashville Investments v. Elmer Contractors*, 3 ARB. INT'L 329, 336 (1987).

3. "Any and all differences or disputes of whatever nature arising out of this Agreement shall be put to arbitration in the City of New York pursuant to . . . the laws of the State of New York." *See Michele Amoruso et Figli v. Fisheries Development*, 499 F.Supp. 1074 (S.D.N.Y. 1980), where this clause, which does not include "in connection with" language, was found to be sufficiently narrow to require examination by the court, and not the arbitral tribunal, of the issue of fraud in the inducement. *See also In re Kinoshita & Co.* 287 F.2d 951 (2d Cir. 1961).

4. "All disputes arising in connection with the present contract shall be finally settled under the Rules of Conciliation and Arbitration of the International Chamber of Commerce by one or more arbitrators appointed in accordance with the said Rules." ICC Standard Arbitration Clause (1988 ed.). For a review of how this clause has been interpreted by arbitrators and courts, see W. LAURENCE CRAIG ET AL., INTERNATIONAL CHAMBER OF COMMERCE ARBITRATION §6.03 (2d ed. 1990) where it is stated: "The ICC Model Clause, with its three key expressions ("all disputes . . . in connection with . . . finally settled") has stood the test of time."

5. "Any dispute arising out of or in connection with this contract, including any question regarding its existence, validity or termination, shall be referred to and finally resolved by arbitration under the Rules of the London Court of International Arbitration, which Rules are deemed to be incorporated by reference into this

clause." London Court of International Arbitration Standard Arbitration Clause (1985 ed.).

6. "Any dispute, controversy or claim arising out of or relating to this contract, or the breach, termination or invalidity thereof, shall be settled by arbitration in accordance with the UNCITRAL Arbitration Rules as at present in force." Model Clause for use with UNCITRAL Arbitration Rules (1976 ed.).

## 3.    POWERS PROVIDED BY INSTITUTIONAL RULES

Arbitration clauses give some idea of what kind of powers the parties have agreed to give to the arbitrator, but they are by necessity short, and it is difficult to provide for everything in the clause. Where the parties select an institutional arbitration with its own prescribed rules (like the ICC or the AAA) or adopt a set of rules (like UNCITRAL), the rules may provide the missing contractual element.

Among the most carefully drafted international arbitration rules are those prepared by the United Nations Commission on International Trade Law (UNCITRAL) and issued in 1976. See *supra* Chapter 2, for discussion and Supplement at p. 623 for full text. Article 21 of the UNCITRAL Rules provides:

> 1. The arbitral tribunal shall have the power to rule on objections that it has no jurisdiction, including any objections with respect to the existence or validity of the arbitration clause or of the separate arbitration agreement.

> 2. The arbitral tribunal shall have the power to determine the existence or the validity of the contract of which an arbitration clause forms a part. For the purposes of article 21, an arbitration clause which forms part of a contract and which provides for arbitration under these Rules shall be treated as an agreement independent of the other terms of the contract. A decision by the arbitral tribunal that the contract is null and void shall not entail *ipso jure* the invalidity of the arbitration clause.

3. A plea that the arbitral tribunal does not have jurisdiction shall be raised not later than in the statement of defence or, with respect to a counter-claim, in the reply to the counter claim.

4. In general, the arbitral tribunal should rule on a plea concerning its jurisdiction as a preliminary question. However, the arbitral tribunal may proceed with the arbitration and rule on such a plea in their final award.

The most widely used arbitration rules in international commerce are the Rules of the International Chamber of Commerce. Articles 7 and 8(3) through 8(4) of these rules specifically confirm the arbitrator's power to rule on his own jurisdiction, but they also provide an administrative procedure pursuant to which the International Court of Arbitration of the ICC, an administrative body, will not constitute an arbitral tribunal, or send the file to arbitrators if it finds that there is no *prima facie* agreement between the parties to arbitrate.[197] The operation of the procedure provided for in the ICC Rules is illustrated by a partial award on jurisdiction rendered by an arbitral tribunal in 1983.

> a.      ICC Arbitration No. 4402, Partial Award (Mar. 17, 1983) 9 YEARBOOK OF COMMERCIAL ARBITRATION 138 (1984).

[Claimant companies, respectively Bahamian and Luxembourgeois, and referred to as "F.C." and "S.C.," had brought arbitration proceedings against a French company (First Defendant or "F.D.") with which First Claimant had signed an oil field operating agreement containing an arbitration clause. They had joined to the proceedings as Second Defendant ("S.D.") the First Defendant's French parent company which had signed several agreements with claimants but not one specifically providing for arbitration. The French parent had set up First Defendant as a 100% owned subsidiary for the purpose of entering into the operating agreement contemplated under the other agreements. The issue was whether claimants were entitled

---

[197] For full text of the ICC Rules, see Supplement at p. 451.

to join the parent company to the operating agreement arbitration. The issue first arose as an administrative question under Article 8(3) of the Rules; the Chairman of the ICC Court of Arbitration acting under a provision of the Rules that permitted him to act for the Court when decisions were required on an urgent basis determined that *prima facie* there existed an agreement to arbitrate with the parent. The decision is reported in 8 Yearbook of Commercial Arbitration 204 (1983). As a result of the administrative decision, the matter was referred to arbitration. Defendants did not object to First Claimant's parent participating in the arbitration. However, the Second Defendant, the French parent company, was only prepared to sign the Terms of Reference "without prejudice to the questions of jurisdiction." Accordingly, the first task of the arbitral tribunal was to determine the jurisdictional issue.]

1. This arbitration is governed by the Rules of Conciliation and Arbitration of the International Chamber of Commerce, Court of Arbitration, by the Rules of the Swiss Intercantonal Arbitration Convention (SIAC) to the extent that their application is mandatory and the rules ordered by the Arbitrators . . . . The applicable substantive law is the substantive law of Switzerland.

2. There is no doubt that the Arbitral Tribunal may decide on its own jurisdiction; both the ICC — Rules (Article 8(3) [sic] and Article 8 SIAC provide for this power of a Tribunal.

3. Since Claimants request that S.D. be included as a party in this Arbitration under the Rules of Conciliation and Arbitration of the ICC based on an implicit agreement between themselves and S.D., and Defendant contests that there is a valid agreement to arbitrate for S.D., the issue to be decided is:

Whether S.D. is a proper party to this Arbitration.

4. Pursuant to Article 3 SIAC, the Arbitral Tribunal may render a partial award, unless the parties agreed otherwise. Such a partial award is considered in itself a final award for the issues decided in it.

Whether a partial award may be rendered or not, lies in the discretion of the Arbitrators.

The rendering of a partial award is usually conditioned upon the fulfillment of the following requirements:

-   The issue to be dealt with is clearly separable from other parts of the litigation;
-   The question to be decided is liquid, fully exposed by the parties and proved;
-   A partial award will help to decide the remaining questions;
-   There is urgency in clearing this special question.

The issue of jurisdiction over a party to an Arbitration is a classical setting for a partial award. It can be clearly separated from the other issues in the actual case and easily be disposed of by the Tribunal without going into the merits of the case. It is clear that a decision of the question of jurisdiction is helpful for all parties involved in the Arbitration. At [sic] [And] last it is obvious, that the economic advantages call for an early decision on the question who is a proper party to the case.

It is therefore appropriate to render a partial award on the question of jurisdiction over S.D.

5. The question of jurisdiction over a party in an arbitration case has to be examined by the Arbitrators *ex officio*. To decide on that, the validity of the arbitration clause is a preliminary issue and has to be taken into consideration.

6. Neither party contends that S.D. signed the Operating Agreement with the actual arbitration clause. However, Claimants contend that the behavior of S.D. and the contractual relationships at the time of signature of Contract I-80, the Operating Agreement and some other documents constitute enough evidence for the implicit agreement to arbitrate under the rules of the ICC, Court of Arbitration.

7. . . . The seat of this Arbitral Tribunal is Geneva (Switzerland); the Canton of Geneva has ratified the Swiss Intercantonal Arbitration Convention; article 6 of this Convention is mandatory and provides for a written document containing either a compromise [submission agreement] or an arbitration clause. This written document has to fulfill the requirements of article 13 ss. of the Swiss Code of Obligations. If those are not complied with, none [sic] [no one] may be forced to submit a dispute to an Arbitral Tribunal (BGE 102 I a 582; Decision

of the Swiss Federal Court of November 14, 1979, Libyan Republic/Wetco Ltd). Nobody, even non-Swiss citizens, can without his consent be deprived of his own natural judge (art. 58 of the Constitution).

8a. Neither party contends that S.D. signed the Operating Agreement with the actual arbitration clause. It is not contested either that Mr. X, who signed the Operating Agreement on behalf of F.D., acted only for the subsidiary and not for the mother company. It becomes clear from the introduction of the Operating Agreement that only F.D. is a party to it. Claimants do not contend that Mr. X was acting on S.D.'s behalf with special power of attorney or as a member of S.D.'s board of directors. Mr. X therefore had only the power to bind F.D., as he was acting in the Operating Agreement expressly as chairman of F.D.; any other company could not be committed by his signature.

b. Even if Claimants thought that Mr. X was signing on behalf of S.D., the arbitration clause would not have sufficiently been accepted by the mother company. F.D. is a separate legal entity and has its own directors and officers; those have the right and the duty to carry out business for the corporation (cf. unpublished decision of the Swiss Federal Court of October 10, 1979, different companies of the Cartier-group vs. Horowitz, p. 18).

c. Claimants do not contend that S.D. and its subsidiaries are forming a single legal entity for which each of the members of the group are entitled to act. It is obvious from the materials submitted by Defendant that this is not the case. Therefore, F.D.'s chairman could not act on behalf of the concern and had no power to sign an arbitration clause on behalf of the mother company.

9. Claimants do contend, however, that the behaviour of S.D. at the time of the signature of Contract I-80, the Operating Agreement and some other documents relating to the operations in (Country of Central America) constitute enough evidence for an implicit agreement to arbitrate according to the Rules of the International Chamber of Commerce.

10. It is Claimants' obligation to prove that S.D. was a party to the Operating Agreement and consequently to the arbitration clause. Claimants invoke mainly the existing contractual network between themselves and S.D. as basis for its inclusion into this Arbitration.

Such relationships are not sufficient to overcome the requirement of an actual signature to the agreement containing the arbitration clause.

a) All contracts and agreements to which Claimants and S.D. are parties have their own clauses for jurisdiction and applicable law; none of them provide for an arbitration under the rules of the International Chamber of Commerce, Court of Arbitration. Claimants argue that article VII of "Protocol d'Accords No. I" be read in such a way that S.D. did agree to this arbitration clause as contained in the Operating Agreement. But this protocol points out only the main issues to be dealt with in the Operating Agreement; it leaves to S.D. to decide on the structure of the intervention of the Group for the operations in (Country of Central America). By creating F.D. and nominating it as the operator, S.D. acted within the frame of this protocol and complied with the special provisions of article VII by causing F.D. to sign the Operating Agreement.

b) Moreover, at the time of signature of "Protocol I," Claimants already knew that F.D. and not S.D. was the company carrying out the operations in (Country of Central America) as operator (see the introduction of this Protocol d'Accords). If Claimants had wanted to include S.D. in the Operating Agreement, and, therefore, in the arbitration clauses, they could have so requested before signing the Operating Agreement. Having failed to do this Claimants are now precluded from having S.D. included as a party to this Arbitration.

c) And finally, based on the foregoing, the mandatory requirements of the Swiss Intercantonal Arbitration Convention as to this Tribunal's jurisdiction over S.D. have not been met.

DECISION
In view of the foregoing, the following decision is *rendered*:

   1. The jurisdiction of the Arbitral Tribunal over S.D. is denied.

   2. The Arbitration proceedings will continue between Claimants and F.D.

*     *     *

Unless the parties have specifically agreed that the arbitrator shall render an interim award on a preliminary issue, the decision of whether to render an interim award is made by the arbitrator in his discretion. This is illustrated by a decision by the French *Cour de cassation* (France's highest court) which set aside a decision of the court of appeal of Paris. The court of appeal had annulled an ICC arbitration award because the tribunal had rendered a final award on all issues before it and had not rendered a preliminary award on the issue of jurisdiction.

> b. *SOFIDIF et al v. Organization for Investment, Economic and Technical Assistance of Iran (OIETAI) and Atomic Energy Organization of Iran (AEOI)*, Cour de Cassation, Cass. Civ. 1re (Mar. 8, 1988) 1989 REV. ARB. 481.

[The French government and the Iranian government under the Shah had concluded in 1974 a series of agreements providing for cooperation in the peaceful use of atomic energy and the development of an Iranian nuclear energy program. Among the agreements it was provided that Iran would take a shareholding interest in the French company SOFIDIF for the purpose of participating in and providing part of the financing for the construction of a uranium enrichment facility in France, part of whose production would be used to fulfill Iranian requirements for enriched uranium. After the Islamic revolution and Iran's decision to cancel its nuclear energy program, Iran had no further need for enriched uranium and so advised its French partners.

SOFIDIF, together with other French company signatories of the agreements, brought arbitration based on ICC arbitration clauses in two different contracts. The Iranian parties objected from the outset to arbitral jurisdiction, claiming that the two clauses could not be consolidated, and objecting as to the proper parties to the arbitration. The Terms of Reference of the arbitral proceedings provided that the arbitral tribunal would determine its own jurisdiction, the scope thereof, and the receivability of the demands as to the parties concerned. Only upon having made these determinations was the tribunal to adjudicate the merits of the dispute. By a first procedural order, the arbitral tribunal had stated that it would render an interim award on these jurisdictional matters. Subsequently, in view of the relevance of the facts to issues required to be decided both for jurisdiction and on the merits, it decided that the issues of jurisdiction and liability should be decided in the same award and issued a second procedural order to that effect. In its subsequently rendered award, the tribunal found that it had jurisdiction, that the Iranian investment organization, OIETAI, was liable to SOFIDIF on the merits, and provided for further proceedings on the issue of damages. In review proceedings, the Paris Court of Appeal set aside the award on the ground that the arbitrators failed to abide by the agreement of the parties in the Terms of Reference. The Court of Appeal interpreted the Terms to mean that the arbitral tribunal should have determined the preliminary issues by a preliminary award on jurisdiction and should not have joined the jurisdictional issue to the merits and resolved the issues of jurisdiction and liability in the same award. It accordingly annulled the award. This annulment decision was made the subject of a further appeal to the Cour de Cassation.]

In view of articles 1494, 1504, first paragraph, and 1502, third paragraph [which permit the Court of Appeal to set aside an award rendered in France in international arbitral proceedings if "the arbitrator decided in a manner incompatible with the mission conferred upon him."] of the New Code for Civil Procedure;

Whereas it results from these texts that if, in an international arbitration, the mission conferred upon the arbitrators may involve particular obligations in relation to the procedure to be followed, and may require them to rule by distinct awards on competence, on receivability and on the merits, it must be on the condition that these obligations result from explicit and precise clauses of the terms of reference;

Whereas the judgment that has been attacked annulled the arbitral award rendered on 25 April 1985, under the auspices of the International Chamber of Commerce, because, in joining together the issues of jurisdiction and the merits, the arbitrators overstepped their powers; that in fact, this part of the terms of reference reveals the basic preoccupation of the parties involved and their uncertainty concerning the suitable jurisdiction to resolve their disputes as a result of the diversity of arbitration clauses included in their various past contracts, that the court of appeal found in the terms and in the spirit of the terms of reference the outline of the steps to be taken by the arbitrators who were asked to determine the extent of their competence and that this request was necessarily a prerequisite since it controlled the choice of the litigious issues which could be adjudicated;

Whereas, however, if the terms of reference of the arbitrators listed under four categories the litigious issues to be resolved, and if it indicated that certain ones were preconditions to the others, it in no way required that points I and II relating to competence and receivability be decided by a separate award rendered before the award on the merits;

That in deciding as it did, and since no explicit and precise clause of the terms of reference requires the arbitrators to decide by two separate and successive awards on their competence and on the merits, the court of appeal violated the aforementioned texts;

[The decision of the Court of Appeals was quashed and the case remanded.]

### Notes and Questions

1. The requirement that there be some material evidence of an agreement to arbitrate before the ICC will form an arbitral tribunal protects a respondent from the trouble and expense of undertaking a defense before his contractual "judge" when there is no evidence that an agreement to arbitrate existed at all. *See* W. LAURENCE CRAIG ET AL., INTERNATIONAL CHAMBER OF COMMERCE ARBITRATION, Chapter 11 (2d ed. 1990). But the protection is not complete. The ICC Court of Arbitration has found *prima facie* evidence of an agreement to arbitrate, and arbitrators have found in favor of arbitral jurisdiction, in cases where reviewing courts have subsequently found no agreement to arbitrate. *See, e.g.*, *Westland Helicopter v. AOI*, Federal Tribunal (Switzerland), 28 ILM 687, 691 (1989) (English translation) (Agreement to arbitrate entered into by an international organization, the Arab Organization for Industrialization ("AOI"), did not bind its member states to arbitrate).

2. The notion that the arbitrator should initially have the power to determine his jurisdiction as provided in some of the institutional arbitration rules examined earlier has found its way into positive law, particularly in Europe, where it is expressed in numerous national laws governing arbitral procedure. *See, e.g.*, Swiss Federal Law on Private International Law ("LDIP") Art. 186 (1); French New Code of Civil Procedure, Arts. 1458, 1466; Netherlands Arbitration Act of 1986, Art. 1052; UNCITRAL Model Law, Art. 16. Such laws are complementary to the provision of the New York Convention which provide for the staying of court litigation to permit arbitration to proceed. *See supra* Chapter 4. The scope of the power of the arbitrator to determine his own jurisdiction is more reserved in some common law countries, particularly England, at least where the issues are whether a contract containing an arbitration clause was entered into at all, or whether it was void *ab initio*. *See* discussion *supra* Chapter 4, Part V.

3. Institutional arbitration rules also assist in dealing with the problems raised by the invalidity or termination of the agreement in which the arbitration clause is found. Article 21(2) of the UNCITRAL Rules and Art. 8(4) of the ICC Rules provide for the case where the respondent argues that the arbitrator's jurisdictional powers have been terminated by the breach, termination, or nullity of the principal contract in which the arbitration clause is found. Both the UNCITRAL and ICC rules provide for the "autonomy" or "severability" of the arbitration clause so that the arbitrator retains competence to determine the consequences of the breach. This is a problem of considerable conceptual interest and practical consequences.

## B. AUTONOMY AND SEVERABILITY OF THE ARBITRATION CLAUSE

Many years ago, parties would frequently agree, pursuant to the terms of a separate agreement, to arbitrate a dispute which had previously arisen (usually pursuant to an ordinary commercial contract). In fact, legislation in some civil law countries permitted arbitration only by such a separate agreement to arbitrate (called a *compromis*) entered into after a dispute had arisen and not by an arbitration clause calling for the arbitration of all future disputes arising under the commercial contract in which the clause was found. That legislative requirement no longer exists (except, perhaps, in some Latin American countries). Today, the arbitration clause contained within the body of a commercial agreement has become the ordinary way to provide for arbitration.

The inclusion of the arbitration clause in a substantive agreement between the parties has raised problems of its own, however, in addition to those raised by the arbitrator's jurisdiction to determine his own jurisdiction. Even where this initial power is recognized, what happens if a party raises the defense that the entire contract either was void or voidable or has been lawfully rescinded or terminated? If the arguments are correct, must this not inevitably mean that the arbitration clause upon which the arbitrator's jurisdiction is predicated has also been avoided, rescinded or terminated with the consequence that the arbitrator is deprived of the competence he otherwise would have had?

A collective policy decision to assign to the arbitrator the competence to decide this sort of question resulted in a legal theory of the "autonomy" or "independence" of the arbitration clause. The clause is said to be "separable" or "severable" from the main contract.

We will use the terms "autonomy," "separability," and "severability" interchangeably. In Chapter 4, this problem was examined from the perspective of national courts.

The materials that follow revisit the problem from the perspective of arbitral tribunals, encountering the matter as a request for a preliminary decision.

1.    STEPHEN M. SCHWEBEL, INTERNATIONAL ARBITRATION: THREE SALIENT PROBLEMS 1-6 (1987).

## A. *The Question*

Where a contract or a treaty provides for arbitration of disputes which arise thereunder, does the invalidity, termination, nullification or suspension of the contract or treaty vitiate the arbitral obligations of the parties? This a question which has repeatedly — and recently — arisen in arbitral practice, international and national, public and commercial. It is a question in which the trend of legal principle and practice is predominantly in one direction. It may even be said that this classic question of the arbitral process is settled. Nevertheless, in practice the question persists. The defence is recurrently raised by a party seeking to avoid or frustrate an arbitration. On exceptional occasion, the defence succeeds. The question accordingly merits analysis not only because of its jurisprudential subtlety but because of its practical import.

The question will be considered in public international law and in international commercial arbitration. International commercial arbitration cannot be discussed without reference to national arbitration law, and thus there will be some reference to national law, particularly the law of countries in which international commercial arbitration is frequently held. But a survey of relevant national law will not be attempted.

## B. *The Theory*

It may be argued that if an agreement contains an obligation to arbitrate disputes arising under it, but the agreement is invalid or no longer in force, the obligation to arbitrate disappears with the agreement of which it is a part. If the agreement was never entered into at all, its arbitration clause never came into force. If the agreement was not validly entered into, then, *prima facie*, it is invalid as a whole, as must be all of its parts, including its arbitration clause. And if the agreement has been nullified or terminated — or, arguably, suspended — presumably it follows that the obligation to arbitrate disputes arising under the agreement is nullified, terminated or suspended. Now if, in these various contingencies, there is no initial or sustained obligation to arbitrate under an agreement which either never came into force or is no longer in force, then the arbitral tribunal which may be or is constituted pursuant to the arbitration clause of the void or voided agreement has no standing to do anything; it cannot pass upon the validity of the agreement or upon the effect of the tribunal's establishment or upon its jurisdiction or upon the merits of the case because it cannot have a legal status which derives from a vacuum. "Nothing?" said King Lear: "Nothing will come of nothing."

In logic, the foregoing line of argument is plausible. But in law it has been overcome by presumptions and by practice. It has been overcome by necessity. And it has been overcome by the essence of the arbitral process. If it is inherent in the arbitral (and judicial) process that a tribunal is the judge of its own jurisdiction, that it has *compétence de la compétence*, it is no less inherent in that process that an arbitral tribunal shall have the competence to pass upon disputes arising out of the agreement which is the immediate source of the tribunal's creation even where those disputes engage the initial or continuing validity of that agreement. This essential doctrine of modern arbitration is called that of the severability, separability or autonomy of the arbitration agreement. (In this discussion, in which these terms are employed interchangeably, "severability" will mainly be used.) The rationale of the doctrine of the severability of the arbitration agreement has four foundations.

First, when two parties enter into a contract or a treaty providing for arbitration of disputes arising thereunder, and do so as they typically do in comprehensive terms — "any dispute arising out of or relating to this agreement" — they intend to require arbitration of *any* dispute not otherwise settled, including disputes over the validity of the contract or treaty. Had the parties, when concluding the agreement, been asked: "Do you mean, in providing that 'any dispute arising out of or relating to this agreement' shall be submitted to arbitration, to exclude disputes over the validity of the agreement?", surely they would have replied that they did not mean to exclude such disputes. The will of the parties should be given effect.

Second, if one party could deny arbitration to the other party by the allegation that the agreement lacked initial or continuing validity, if by such an allegation it could deprive an arbitral tribunal of the competence to rule upon that allegation, upon its constitution and jurisdiction and upon the merits of the dispute, then it would always be open to a party to an agreement containing an arbitration clause to vitiate its arbitral obligation by the simple expedient of declaring the agreement void.

In the ordinary run of national commercial intercourse, to accord each party the facility of evading its arbitral obligation in this fashion would be serious enough, for the cure would presumably require recourse to a national court, which would determine the validity or invalidity of the agreement between the parties and, if it upheld it, remit the parties to obligatory arbitration. That of itself would prejudice a key object of the agreement's provision for arbitration: namely, speed and simplicity of settlement of disputes, without the time-consuming trouble and expense of recourse to the courts. And it would involve the courts in the substantive determination of an otherwise arbitrable question in a fashion which they generally and rightly eschew. But in the less ordinary run of interstate transactions, the result could be far more serious still: destruction of the arbitral remedy. For normally there is no international court with compulsory jurisdiction to determine and enforce the validity of the international agreement. And even in the sphere of international commercial contracts, which are legion, the procedure of requiring a party to have recourse to a national court to enforce the arbitral remedy against the other party would in many case be, at best, prejudicial to the purposes of the arbitral process. In other cases, in which the agreement runs not between two persons or companies of different nationality but between a foreign contractor and a government, not only would the contractor be loath to seek enforcement of his arbitral remedy in national courts; often national courts would lack the authority to require the executive branch to arbitrate contrary to its will, its executive order or national legislation.

Thus the intention of the parties and the requirements of effective arbitration combine to give rise to the concept of severability. That concept is strengthened by — indeed, it is widely said, is essentially composed of — a third element as well. In reality, or, if not in reality, then in the contemplation of the law and as a matter of legal presumption, the parties to an agreement containing an arbitration clause conclude not one agreement but two: first, the substantive or principal agreement which provides for a certain course of action; second, an additional, separable agreement which provides for arbitration of disputes arising out of the principal agreement. Even if it be argued, or even if it be authoritatively decided, that the principal agreement is invalid, or voided, nullified, terminated, or suspended, nevertheless the arbitral agreement is separable and separated, and, so separated, survives to furnish a viable basis for the arbitration tribunal to rule upon such arguments or arrive at those or other determinations. Historically, in some legal systems, provision for arbitration of disputes arising under a contract was actually contained in (and had to be contained in) a separate piece of paper in order to meet the legal necessity of a clearly identifiable agreement to refer a dispute to arbitration and thereby oust the jurisdiction of the courts. Its severability and survival accordingly were the more plausible. Indeed, even if the arbitration agreement were found not in a separate piece of paper but as a clause of a principal agreement, nevertheless the very concept and phrase "arbitration agreement" itself imports the existence of a separate or at any rate separable agreement, which is or can be divorced from the body of the principal agreement if needs be. Thus when the parties to an agreement containing an arbitration clause enter into that agreement, they conclude not one but two agreements, the arbitral twin of which survives any birth defect or acquired disability of the principal agreement.

In the case of an arbitral tribunal whose procedure is governed by the national law of the place of arbitration, national courts to which appeal is made may uphold or exceptionally strike down the arbitration award which the arbitral tribunal has given in the exercise of its separable capacity. But the courts of most countries will not review the holdings of the arbitrator on the substance of the case and accordingly will not challenge his holding with respect to the validity of the principal agreement which contains the arbitral clause. That most distinguished authority on international commercial arbitration, Professor Pieter Sanders, points out that this is still another — i.e., a fourth — consideration which militates in favour of the rule of the severability of the arbitral clause because, if severability were not the rule, the courts would, contrary to the norm, be drawn into passing upon the substance of the dispute submitted to arbitration.

*     *     *

The principles of severability of the arbitration clause was applied in the *Texaco-Libya* arbitration which we have considered earlier, *supra* pp. 646-52.

> 2.     *Texas Overseas Petroleum Co. v. Libyan Arab Republic*, privately printed edition (Nov. 27, 1975) (preliminary award)(René-Jean Dupuy, Sole Arb.), *reprinted in* 1 J. GILLIS WETTER, THE INTERNATIONAL PROCESS: PUBLIC AND PRIVATE 444-56 (1979).

14. As for the solution of the problem which creates the question of the jurisdiction of the Sole Arbitrator in the present case, that solution is linked to the answer to be given to the two following questions:

A. Supposing that the measures of nationalization could have had the effect of voiding the Deeds of Concession themselves, can this effect extend to the provisions of these Deeds relating to arbitration and, more specifically, to Clause 28?

15. Before examining the argument on this first point, it would be appropriate to emphasize the fact that the premise assumed therein is purely and simply a hypothesis designed merely to make it possible to pursue the argument: it does not prejudge in any way the question of the validity or the effects of the measures of nationalization, which relates solely to the merits of the dispute. It is under the reservation of this essential and preliminary observation that one asks the question if—assuming the measures of nationalization could have the effect indicated above—would this effect extend to the provisions of the Deeds of Concession relating to arbitration?

16. The principle to which it is appropriate to refer in this matter is that of the autonomy or the independence of the arbitration clause. This principle, which has the consequence of permitting the arbitration clause to escape the fate of the contract which contains it, has been upheld by several decisions of international case law. More

particularly, in this connection . . . the *Lena Goldfields* case[198] [and] the *Losinger* case...[199]

17. ...The principle of the autonomy of the arbitration clause has since then been confirmed by several decisions; and one can say that it is now solidly established in French private international law.[200]

18. The writings of legal scholars also recognize the full autonomy of the arbitral clause or the arbitration agreement. [Professor Dupuy quotes the late Judge Jiménez de Aréchega,[201] as well as Kojanec,[202] Weil,[203] and Lalive.[204]]

[The sole arbitrator, by preliminary award, determined that he had jurisdiction to determine the validity and effect of the measures

---

[198] 5 Annual Digest of International Law Cases Nos. 1 and 258 (1929-1930), at 38 and 426, respectively. See also Nussbaum, "The Arbitration between the Lena Goldfields, Ltd. and the Soviet Government," 36 Cornell L. Qu. 31 (1950).

[199] [1936] P.C.I.J., Ser. C., No. 78, at 105.

[200] See three decisions rendered on 18 May 1971 [1972] D. Jur. 37, note Alexandre; Rev. Arb. 2 (1972), note Kahn; 61 Rev. Crit. D. Int'l Privé 124 (1972), note Mezger; 99 Journal du Droit International ("Clunet") 62 (1972), note Oppetit, and the *Hecht* decision of 4 July 1972 (99 Clunet 843 (1972), note Oppetit, and Rev. Arb. 89 (1974)). See also on the *Hecht* decision; Francescakis, "Le Principe Jurisprudentiel de l'Accord Compromissoire après l'Arrêt Hecht de la Cour de Cassation", Rev. Arb. 67 (1974).

[201] "L'Arbitrage entre les Etats et les Sociétés Privées Etrangères", in Mélanges en l'Honneur de Gilbert Gidel 367 (1961), at 375.

[202] "The Legal Nature of Agreements Concluded by Private Entities with Foreign States", in Colloquium on International Commercial Agreements Organized in 1968 by the Hague Academy of International Law 299 *et seq.* (1969), at 330.

[203] Weil, "Problèmes Relatifs aux Contrats Passés entre un Etat et un Particulier", 128 Recueil des Cours de l'Académie de Droit International de la Haye ("R.C.A.D.I.") 95 (1969), at 222; "Les Clauses de Stabilisation ou d'Intangibilité Insérées dans les Accords de Développement Economique", in Mélanges Offerts à Charles Rousseau 301 (1974), at 325.

[204] P. Lalive, "Problèmes Relatifs à l'Arbitrage International Commercial", 120 R.C.A.D.I. 569 (1967), at 593.

taken by Libya to nationalize the oil concession agreement which had been granted to Texaco.]

\*　　\*　　\*

The issue of separability of the arbitration clause was posed with particular acuity in the case of *Sojuznefteexport v. JOC Oil Co.* where an arbitral tribunal of the Arbitration Court of the USSR Chamber of Commerce and Industry rendered an award in favor of a Soviet Foreign Trade Organization against a foreign purchaser for the value of oil purchased even though it was conceded that the sales purchase agreement in which the arbitration clause was contained was invalid and unenforceable. The Russian trade organization had failed to have the agreement executed by two authorized signatories as required for foreign trade agreements under Russian law.

3. *All-Union Export-Import Assoc. Sojuznefteexport (Moscow) v. Joc Oil, Ltd. Bermuda*, Foreign Trade Arbitration Commission at The USSR Chamber of Commerce and Industy, Moscow, Arbitration No. 109/1980 (July 9, 1984) (unpublished) (translation as used in review proceedings).

[Sojuznefteexport (the "Association" or "SNE") was a Soviet foreign trade organization which in 1976 entered into a contract to sell large quantities of oil and fuel oil for delivery during 1977 to JOC OIL Limited ("JOC," "Joc" or the "Firm"), a Bermuda Company. After having made payments for the first six shipments, JOC defaulted and received 33 oil shipments having a claimed value of USD 101 million without paying the contract price or any other amount. The purchase agreements incorporated SNE's standard conditions for FOB sales which provided for arbitration in the following terms:

All disputes or differences which may arise out of this contract or in connection with it are to be settled, without recourse to the general Courts of law, in the arbitration order by the Foreign Trade Arbitration Commission of the U.S.S.R. Chamber of Commerce and Industry in Moscow ["FTAC"], in conformity with the rules of procedure of the above Commission.

SNE brought arbitration. JOC defended principally on the basis that the purchase agreement was not executed by two authorized representatives of SNE and accordingly was void by application of the mandatory provisions of Soviet law. JOC alleged that as a consequence the arbitral tribunal was without competence to adjudicate the dispute either because the arbitration clause was void or, if not, that it could not apply to a dispute relating to a void or nonexistent contract. SNE claimed that the sales agreement was not void and that it had been ratified by partial performance or subsequent agreement; primarily it claimed that even if the sales agreement were void under Soviet law for failure to comply with the two signature rule, the arbitration clause, because of its autonomous nature under Soviet law, had an independent existence and because of its procedural character did not require two signatures to be valid. SNE claimed accordingly that the arbitral tribunal was competent to adjudicate its claim for restitution of the value of the oil received by JOC without payment. JOC denied the ability of the arbitration clause to survive a "non-existent" contract and also offered a number of secondary defenses on the merits of the claims. It also asserted a counterclaim. The facts are further stated in the tribunal's "Reasons for the Award." The tribunal's statement of the "Facts of the Case" is omitted.]

1. The Foreign Trade Arbitration Commission has confirmed the agreement of the parties as to the material law to be applied to the dispute between them. As this law, the parties have agreed upon Soviet law. The Commission has therefore decided the dispute being guided by the corresponding provisions of the Fundamentals of Civil Legislation of the USSR and of the Union Republics of 1961 and the Civil Code of the RSFSR of 1964. In connection with this, it has been borne in mind that on the question of the form of foreign trade transactions completed by Soviet organizations and the procedure for their signature, Soviet law is applied independently of the agreement of the parties (article 125 of the Fundamentals).

2. According to Article 27 of the Civil Procedural Code of the RSFSR in cases contemplated by law or International Treaty, a dispute arising out of civil legal relationships, by agreement of the parties can be referred for resolution by an arbitration body, the Maritime Arbitration Commission or the Foreign Trade Arbitration Commission at the Chamber of Commerce and Industry of the USSR. As stated in the statute on the Foreign Trade Arbitration Commission at the Chamber of Commerce and Industry of the USSR, confirmed by the

Decree of the Presidium of the Supreme Soviet of the USSR of the 16th April 1975, this Commission is a permanently functioning arbitration court and decides disputes arising from contractual and other civil legal relationships, arising between the subjects of law of different countries in relation to the implementation of foreign trade and of other international economic relationships. The Commission considers disputes where there is a written agreement between the Parties to submit for its decision a dispute which has arisen or which may arise. It is further envisaged that the agreement for the submission of a dispute to the Commission can also be expressed on the part of the plaintiff by the filing of a claim and on the part of the defendant by the completion of actions which evidence his voluntary submission to the jurisdiction of the Commission, in particular by communicating to the Commission, in reply to the latter's inquiry, his consent to submit to its jurisdiction. Point 2 of paragraph 1 of the Rules of Procedure of the Foreign Trade Arbitration Commission (hereinafter the Rules) in particular reproduce this formula of the law determining the competence of the FTAC.

The Rules consequently envisage different types of written agreements of the parties as to the submission of a dispute to the FTAC and do not require that this agreement be expressed in an independent document signed by the parties. The Rules also do not require fulfillment of those requirements which Soviet civil law, in accordance with articles 45 and 565 of the CC, require for the conclusion of a foreign trade transaction of which one party is a Soviet Organization. This provision of the Rules does not depart from paragraph 2, article II of the New York Convention of 1958 in which it is stated that an agreement, establishing the arbitration procedure for hearing disputes, "shall include an arbitral clause in a contract or an arbitration agreement, signed by the parties or contained in an exchange of letters or telegrams."

The Commission therefore does not perceive the distinctions between the legal nature of an arbitration clause, included in the text of a material-legal contract concluded by parties, and the legal nature of a separate written agreement as to the submission of a dispute to the jurisdiction of the FTAC. The circumstance that such an agreement is included in the text of a contract by a separate point or is formulated in an independent written document signed by the parties does not change the legal nature of an arbitration agreement. The distinction consists only in the legal-technical methods of expressing the will of the parties who have agreed to submit a dispute to the jurisdiction of arbitrators chosen by the parties.

All this allows the Commission to recognize the arbitration clause contained in the contract signed in the name of the Association "Sojuznefteexport" by the Chairman of the Association V.E. Merkulow and in the name of the firm "Joc Oil" by John Deuss as a written agreement satisfying the requirements of the law — the Statute on the Foreign Trade Arbitration Commission and its Rules as to the form of concluding such an agreement.

So far as the dispute is concerned which arose during the proceedings concerning the inter-relationship of the contract which established the rights and duties of the parties arising out of the sale of oil and oil products (the material-legal contract) and the arbitration agreement (the arbitration clause), that is to say as to whether the agreement is independent (autonomous) in relation to the contract independently of the decision as to the question of the validity or invalidity of the contract, the Commission has come to the following conclusion. In the Rules of the FTAC there are no direct references to the fact that an arbitration agreement (arbitration clause) is autonomous in relation to the contract. But the above analysis of the Statute of the FTAC and of its Rules which have defined the competence of the Commission, and also the practice of the Commission allows the conclusion to be drawn that the independence of an arbitration clause is not subject to doubt. Thus, in the ruling of the FTAC on the 29th January 1974, taken on hearing a dispute between a Soviet and an Indian organization, the arbitration agreement is treated as a procedural contract and not as an element (condition) of a material-legal contract (Arbitration Practice of the FTAC, Moscow 1979, part VII, page 68). The subject of an arbitration agreement (clause) is distinguished from the subject of a material-legal contract (of the contract of purchase and sale). The subject of the agreement is the obligation of the parties to submit the examination of a dispute between a plaintiff and defendant to arbitration (the FTAC) at the place where it sits, that is to say in Moscow, having excluded by that very fact the possibility of the resolution of the dispute in a state court.

Predominant in the literature is the recognition of the autonomy of an arbitration agreement, its independence in relation to the contract. Such is the point of view of the overwhelming majority of Soviet authors who have expressed themselves on this subject [citations omitted]. The opinion of Soviet scholars are not unanimous but the Arbitration Commission considers as correct the opinion of those scholars, and this opinion is dominant, who recognize the autonomy of an arbitration clause, since this opinion relies upon the propositions of Soviet law cited above, from which there flows its autonomy as an independent procedural agreement. The prevalence of the recognition of the autonomy of an arbitration clause in relation to the contract was noted in the report of the well known specialist on questions of arbitration, the Rumanian Professor I. Nestor, "International Commercial Arbitration" in the United Nations Commission on International Trade Law (document A/CN 9/64 1st March 1972).

The principle of the independence of an arbitration clause (in relation to the contract, to which the said clause relates), is now predominant both in doctrine as well as in practice. In a developed form, this principle has received its expression in the Arbitration rules of UNCITRAL (article 21.2) developed by the United Nations Commission on International Trade Law and accepted as a recommendation in the Resolution of the General Assembly of the United Nations of the 15th December 1976 (official reports of the 31st session of the General Assembly of the United Nations, addendum 17, A/31/17/Chapter V, part C).

Taking into account the cited facts and observations as to the nature of an arbitration agreement (clause), the Commission has come to the conclusion that, by virtue of its procedural content and independently of the form of its conclusion, it is autonomous in relation to the material-legal contract. An arbitration clause, included in a contract, means that there are regulated in it relationships different in legal nature, and that therefore the effect of the arbitration clause is separate from the effect of the remaining provisions of the foreign trade contract.

The requirements, laid down for the recognition of the validity of the two contracts, which differ in their legal nature, need not coincide. Different also are the consequences of the recognition of these contracts as invalid. An arbitration agreement can be recognized as invalid only in the case where there are discovered in it defects in will (mistake, fraud and so on), the breach of the requirements of the law relating to the content and the form of an arbitration agreement which has been concluded. Such circumstances leading to the invalidity of an arbitration agreement do not exist and neither one of the parties stated its invalidity referring to such circumstances. The firm considers the arbitration agreement as invalid for other reasons asserting that it is a component part of a contract which, in its opinion, as a whole (together with the arbitration clause) is invalid.

From this there follows the incorrectness in the objections relating to the fact that the New York Convention of 1958 is applicable only to arbitration agreements on the basis of disputes arising out of specific contracts and therefore is inapplicable to contracts recognized as invalid. In article II of the said Convention there is envisaged the enforcement of arbitral awards in relation to disputes which arise and can arise also in connection with other specific legal relationships, the object of which can be the subject of arbitration proceedings. This means, that since in connection with the invalidity of a contract, the applicable law envisages legal consequences, which are determined by a different non-contractual legal relationship but are connected with the invalid contract, the arbitrators have the right to examine the dispute and to rule upon it.

Proceeding from the above analysis of the Soviet material and procedural legislation applicable to the dispute in question, the Commission has recognized that an arbitration agreement (arbitration clause) is a procedural contract, independent from the material-legal contract and that therefore the question as to the validity or invalidity of this contract does not affect the agreement of the parties about the submission of the existing dispute to the jurisdiction of the FTAC. The Commission has come to the conclusion that the arbitration clause, contained in the contract is valid and therefore in accordance with the right assigned to it has recognized itself as competent to hear the dispute as to its essence and to rule upon it.

3. The Commission has examined further the application of the representatives of the firm "Joc Oil" as to recognizing as invalid the contract of 17th November 1976 from which the dispute has arisen and has satisfied this application in view of the failure to observe the procedure for its signing (article 14 of the Fundamentals, article 45 of the CC).

[Having recognized that the sales agreement was invalid because of failure to respect the two-signature rule for foreign trade organizations, mandatory under Russian law, the tribunal went on to deny SNE's arguments that the initial invalidity could be cured by partial performance and that the initial agreement was approved or ratified by a subsequent agreement.]

5. On the question of the consequences of recognizing the contract of the 17th November 1976 as invalid, the representatives of the parties as pointed out in the exposition of the facts of the case, proceeded from a different approach to the question as to whether the recognition of the contract as invalid had any legal consequences and in the case of a positive answer to this question, as to what these consequences are.

In examining this question, the Commission established that according to article 14 of the Fundamentals (article 48 of the CC) under an invalid transaction each of the parties is obligated to return to the other party everything received under the transaction and if it is impossible to return what has been received in kind, to reimburse its value in money if other consequences of the invalidity of the transaction are not set out in the law that is to say bilateral (mutual) restitution must be effected.

The Arbitration Commission has confirmed further that, the recognition of the transaction as invalid does not mean that such a transaction does not give rise to any legal consequences, that it is nothing, legally amounting to a nullity, as asserted by the defendant on the main claim. As is evident from the content of article 48 of the CC, a court of arbitration tribunal in the event of a dispute must discuss the question of the consequences of the invalidity of a transaction and rule upon the same.

The assertion of the representatives of the Firm that the recognition of the contract as invalid must result in the refusal of the Arbitration Tribunal to hear the case on the basis that there has not arisen a legal relationship envisaged by the contract, is mistaken. It contradicts Soviet law applicable in this case, the practice of its application and the very concept of a transaction. In reality, a transaction, being a legal fact, is not always confined only to the expression of the will of the parties, directed to the achievement of a legal result, but gives rise, in the event of the breach of the requirements of the law, in relations to the content and form of the transaction, to other consequences envisaged by the law. It is necessary that there is a strict delineation of the factual elements lying at the basis of the legal relationships, to the establishment of which the will of the parties is directed, and the legal consequences, which the parties were not able to or did not wish to contemplate but which independently of their will are established by law. Such a delineation very distinctly manifests itself in an invalid transaction, the consequences of which are established by law. Therefore the assertion is incorrect that an invalid (null and void) transaction does not result in any consequences. It does not lead to the legal consequences for which it was intended, but it gives rise to other consequences, for example in some cases the duty to transfer what was received to the state (article 49 of the CC), and according to the general rule, set out in article 48 of the CC, the restoration of the parties to the initial position (mutual restitution). The opinion is also mistaken that a transaction is considered as the will of the parties only if it leads to the achievement of the legal result which the parties had in mind.

.     .     .

As the subject of a contract are things having generic characteristics — oil and oil products, and to require their return is impossible, for they have been resold by the Firm to other persons and have long since been consumed, full mutual restitution is also impossible, but part of the goods delivered by the Association were not paid for by the Firm to the Association in the sum value of those goods. The Association has presented a claim for reimbursement of the value of only that part of the oil and oil products which were delivered and which were not paid for by the defendant on the main claim. Therefore the Commission recognizes that the rules of article 48 of the CC are insufficient for the solution of the situation in dispute.

Article 48 of the CC is a general rule envisaging mutual restitution of the parties in the event of the recognition of a transaction as invalid; the duty of each of them to return everything received under the transaction and if it is not possible to do so in kind, to reimburse its value in money. But in article 48 of the CC there is no reference to other consequences connected with restitution, for example in the event that the duty to return to the other party under an invalid contract anything unjustly received in the form of a monetary sum lies only on one of a specific period of time. This takes place when the parties have already partially fulfilled their obligations under contract which they considered valid, but then the contract is recognized as invalid. Therefore, in view of the impossibility of restoring both parties to their initial position, since what has been transferred has already been used up, used in another way, but the value of what has been used has not been paid for, it is necessary to effect unilateral restitution, that is to say the payment of a monetary sum for the goods transferred to the other party, but not paid for by him to the Creditor... The Commission has therefore come to the conclusion that additionally to article 48 of the CC, in this specific case, as the basis for rendering the award, it is necessary to be guided by article 473 of the CC according to which a person who without any basis in law or a transaction has acquired property at the cost of another has the duty to return to the latter the unjustly acquired property.

[The tribunal went on to apply principles of restitution under Russian law to determine that SNE was entitled to receive the value of the oil at the time that it was acquired by JOC at the then prevailing world prices, which were found not to be different from the prices invoiced pursuant to the invalid contract. It was also entitled to receive any profits which JOC would have made on the oil shipments which it wrongfully retained. This was deemed to be equivalent to interest at a commercial rate as used in the oil trade during the period of detention. The tribunal rendered an award of almost $200 million, but rejected the claim for an additional $122 million in lost profits which it found not proven. It also rejected the defendant's counter-claim.]

Notes and Questions

1. Although the *JOC* arbitration award was not subject to judicial review at the seat of arbitration in Russia, its validity was challenged in enforcement proceedings brought at the defendant's domicile in Bermuda. The award was initially refused enforcement by a Bermuda trial court but this decision was reversed by the appellate court in a 2-1 decision that confirmed the award. *Sojuznefteexport v. JOC Oil Ltd.*, (Berm. Ct. App. 1987), *published in* 4 MEALEY'S INT'L ARB. REP. B1 (1989). The majority held the view that while the sales contract was "invalid" because of failure to comply with the two-signature rule, it was not non-existent; accordingly, the independent arbitration clause could be applied to disputes involving the transaction arising from the invalid contract. For the dissenting judge it was evident that the invalid agreement was void or non-existent and that it was "quite ridiculous to suggest that this arbitration clause which formed part of that 'non-existent' contract would nevertheless, somehow, be deemed to have come into existence." What is the distinction at law, generally, between a contract which is "invalid" and one which is "*void ab initio*" or "non-existent"? Can you think of any examples?

2. What significance should be given to the fact that the Arbitration Rules of the Arbitration Court at the USSR Chamber of Commerce and Industry were

amended on March 1, 1988, subsequent to the *JOC Oil* arbitration to read: "An arbitration clause shall be considered having legal force irrespective of the validity of the contract, component part of which it is"? *See* Anthony Gardner, *The Doctrine of Separability in Soviet Arbitration Law: An Analysis of* Sojuzneftexport v. JOC Oil Co., 28 COLUM. J. TRANSNAT'L L. 301 (1989).

3. Do you agree with the comment: "The issue in *JOC Oil* was not the existence of a contract, but rather the legal effect under Soviet law of an improperly signed foreign trade contract. While separating an arbitration clause from an allegedly non-existent contract strains logic, separating an arbitration clause from an allegedly invalid contract is practically and theoretically justifiable as a means of promoting the presumed intent of the parties to arbitrate their disputes." Gardner, *supra*, at pp. 326-27.

4. The arbitrator is frequently called upon to determine the capacity of a party or authority of representatives of a party to enter into an arbitration agreement. (For a discussion of when, pursuant to different legal systems, these issues may initially be determined by an arbitrator, see *supra* Chapter 4, pp. 448-50). The issue is raised with particular acuity in the case of states or state agencies. In the *JOC Oil* case, the Russian state agency, claimant in the arbitration, alleged that its arbitration agreement was valid and relied on the separability doctrine to sustain arbitral jurisdiction over its *quantum meruit* claim. More frequently, government organizations are defendants in international trade and investment organizations and allege that the agreement to arbitrate is void because of their lack of capacity, under their own law, to arbitrate. In such a case, the separability doctrine will not be sufficient to aid the private party. It may, however, be helped by the notion of estoppel. A state, as defendant, having entered into an international trade or investment agreement, should not be allowed, to deny, pursuant to provisions of its internal law, its capacity, or the authority to act for it of its officers and agents who have been clothed with apparent authority, to enter into a dispute resolution provision which has been accepted as a keystone of international commerce. Consider, in this regard, the award in ICC Arbitration No. 1939 (1971) cited by Yves Detrains in 1973 REV. ARB. 122, 145, which states:

> International <u>ordre public</u> would vigorously reject the proposition that a State organ, dealing with foreigners, having openly, knowingly and intentionally concluded an arbitration clause that inspires the cocontractant's confidence, could thereafter, whether in the arbitral proceedings, or in execution proceedings invoke the nullity of its own promise.

5. What is the relationship between the doctrine of *compétence-compétence*, or the power of an arbitrator to determine his own jurisdiction, and the autonomy or severability of the arbitration clause? *See* W. LAURENCE CRAIG ET AL., INTERNATIONAL CHAMBER OF COMMERCE ARBITRATION § 5.04 (2d ed. 1990).

### C. ARBITRATOR'S DECISION CONCERNING NON-SIGNATORIES AND PROBLEMATICAL SIGNATORIES

One of the preliminary jurisdictional decisions that an arbitrator may have to make is whether the injured party bringing the claim can activate an arbitration clause which it has not itself signed but of which it is either an intended beneficiary/obligor, or an explicit or implicit assignee, or when it, in fact, has performed the obligations of the contract. A similar, but distinct, issue is whether a non-signatory parent or related Company, or the state, may be added as a party because of its participation in the activities of its subsidiary company or a state agency or enterprise. The issues have come up in a variety of situations.

> 1. W. LAURENCE CRAIG ET AL., INTERNATIONAL CHAMBER OF COMMERCE ARBITRATION 200-201 (2d ed. 1990).

In recent years, ICC arbitral tribunals have been called upon to decide such varied jurisdictional questions as:

(i) whether representatives of a company which initialed an arbitration agreement on behalf of a company to be formed bound the existing company to arbitrate;

(ii) whether a state agency or entity bound the state itself to arbitral jurisdiction;

(iii) whether a member of a group of corporations could appear as a claimant in regards to injury caused to it as seller under the terms of a distribution agreement entered into by another member of its group and containing an arbitration clause;

(iv) whether a member of a group of companies having played a role in the negotiation of the contract containing an arbitration agreement, and signed by a member of its group, could be joined to the arbitration proceedings as defendant;

(v) whether a company intended to be the beneficiary of an agreement containing an arbitration clause, but not a signatory thereof, could itself claim the benefit of arbitration;

(vi) whether a corporation was bound by an ICC arbitration clause entered into by an officer and employee having general representation powers when it was alleged that certain signature formalities required under the law of incorporation were not complied with;

(vii) whether a state was bound by the acts of its Minister when it was alleged that certain formalities required under the law of the state were not complied with;

(viii)   whether a sub-contractor which had signed an arbitration clause with the main contractor was also bound to arbitrate in a global proceeding with the owner of the works due to incorporation by reference of the arbitration clause between the contractor and the owner; and

(ix) whether state members of a joint venture consortium, in the nature of a partnership, were individually bound to arbitrate pursuant to the terms of an arbitration agreement entered into by the consortium entity with a third party contractor.

The solution to these diverse issues is not evident and requires the resolution by the arbitrators of complex questions of fact and law. Recognized principles of agency and contract under applicable systems of law supply the basis by which a non-signatory may in some cases be obligated under, or may claim the benefit of, an arbitration clause. Yet those cases are few and the burden of the party claiming under such principles is great, particularly where mandatory procedural requirements in force at the place of arbitration may impose additional formal conditions. An enormous amount of time and money may be spent arguing these issues, a disadvantage which is compounded by the knowledge that jurisdictional issues decided by the arbitrators are subject to review by national courts, whether in review proceedings at the place of arbitration or in proceedings brought elsewhere to secure execution of the award.

Occasionally, the circumstances which lead up to jurisdictional claims in behalf of or against a non-signatory party could not have been foreseen at the time of initial contracting. Principles of construction and implication may be invoked to effect what must have been the true intent of the original parties to the arbitration agreement and to parties related to them. More frequently, the issue of the rights or liabilities of non-signatory parties arises because of a failure of contract draftsmen to take the rudimentary precautions in the drafting of the arbitration agreement, and in these circumstances the chances are great that the arbitral tribunal will find it impossible to make for the parties a contract which they failed to achieve by themselves.

*     *     *

2.    *MAP Tankers, Inc. v. Mobil Tankers, Ltd., Society of Maritime Arbitrators, Inc.*, Partial Final Award No. 1510 (Nov. 28, 1980), *reprinted in* 7 YEARBOOK OF COMMERCIAL ARBITRATION 151-55 (1982).

[On April 7, 1978, the parties concluded a charter party on MOBILVOY form pursuant to which MAP Tankers, Inc., the shipowner, chartered to Mobil Tankers, Ltd., the charterer, the *M/T Bonny* to perform a voyage from "one safe port Coryton (England)" to "one safe port Alexandria and one safe port Piraeus in this rotation," with a cargo of lubricating oil. On April 17, 1978, the "Bonny" loaded some 3.5 million tons for Alexandria, consigned for the Societa Cooperative de Petrole [sic] and shipped by Mobil Oil Co. Ltd. for the account of Mobil Export Corp., and some 600,000 tons for Piraeus, consigned for Mobil Hellas and shipped by Mobil Oil Co., Ltd. for the account of Mobil Sales and Supply Corp.]

From May 2-22, 1978, the "*Bonny*" discharged at Alexandria, where the oil was found to be contaminated and otherwise damaged. Mobil Export only invoiced for the sound portion, and had the damaged part reconditioned in Rotterdam at its own expense.

From May 25 to June 6, 1978, discharge took place at Piraeus, and also here damage was ascertained. Mobil Hellas retained the sound portion and some of the unsound oil, the rest being reconditioned at Mobil Sales' expense, which only sent an invoice for the sound portion and a reduced price for the unsound oil retained by Mobil Hellas.

In May 1978, Mobil Hellas filed a lawsuit in Piraeus against MAP Tankers (Owner) for damages. On July 13, 1978, MAP's P & I Club issued a letter of undertaking addressed to Mobil Oil, to MOBIL Tankers (Charterer), to Mobil Export, Mobil Sales and to Mobil Oil

Egypt, in exchange for Charterer's payment of freight which it withheld to secure the cargo claims.

On October 30, 1978, MAP Tankers filed for arbitration pursuant to the arbitral clause in the charter party:

L. Special Provisions:

5. Any dispute arising during execution of this Charter Party shall be settled in New York Owners and Charterers each appointing an Arbitrator — Merchant or Broker — and the two thus chosen, if they cannot agree, shall nominate a third Arbitrator — Merchant or Broker — whose decision shall be final. Should one of the parties neglect or refuse to appoint an Arbitrator within twenty one days after receipt of request from the other party, the single Arbitrator appointed shall have the right to decide alone and his decision shall be binding on both parties. For the purpose of enforcing awards, this agreement shall be made a Rule of Court.

Claimant claimed for demurrage, extra expenses and interest of unpaid freight US $142,877.64 in total, and Defendant claimed US $400,000.00 for damage to the cargo.

[One question in dispute was whether the Charterer was entitled to include the assigned claims which it had introduced for the other MOBIL companies.]

1. First, the arbitrators dealt with MOBIL Tankers bringing forward the claims of its related companies.

We should first state that the Panel unanimously subscribes to the rule set forth in Allied Chemical,[205] stating that the interests of subsidiary and associated companies of the same parent may be entered into the same arbitration proceeding along with its sister company charterer. In this particular case, the evidence

---

[205] *Allied Chemical Inter-American Corp. v. Piermay Shipping Co.*, SMA Award 1168 (1977), relied on by Charterer (Gen. Ed.).

clearly establishes the corporate relationship between Charterer, Mobil Sales, Mobil Export and Mobil Hellas, and their association with the same parent organization. We see no logical basis for denying Charterer the right to introduce the claims of these subsidiary companies into this proceeding.

It has been argued by some that the charter party arbitration clause simply provides for the adjudication of disputes between Owner and Charterer and that no other party may enter the proceedings unless it does so with the express consent of the two so named. This is surely so as respects third parties not in any way associated with the parties to the charter party. However, it is neither sensible nor practical to exclude the claims of companies who have an interest in the venture and who are members of the same corporate family. The practicality of such an approach is apparent. The major shipping organizations often charter through a subsidiary company, ship their cargoes through another and sometimes consign them to other related companies. To consider the arbitration clause as one which limits the right to arbitrate to the chartering subsidiary and to no other company within the same corporate family involved in the venture is to narrowly restrict the parties apparent intention to arbitrate their differences. We consider our conclusion in this respect to be consistent with the more recent court decisions on this matter.

The Panel unanimously finds the relationship of the various Mobil companies to each other to be of such a character as to allow Charterer to include their claims in this proceeding.

It is apparent that Mobil Export assumed the alleged loss for contaminated lube oil at Alexandria when it issued a revised invoice to Coops reflecting only the value of sound oil discharged. All damages associated with the Alexandria discharge, including recondition expenses were assumed by Mobil Export and the claim, therefore belonged to the Mobil group of companies.

The Piraeus shipments were initially consigned to a Mobil interest and once again there were adjustments to the final invoice reflecting Mobil Sales' assumption of the loss. In any case, the Piraeus consignments were at the risk of either Mobil Hellas as consignee of Mobil Sales as shipper, each of which is a member of the Mobil group.

As the Panel has unanimously ruled that Charterer may introduce the claims of the Mobil group of Companies into this arbitration proceeding, it follows that both the Alexandria and Piraeus cargo damage claims set forth by Charterer may be presented here.

\*          \*          \*

3.      *Helge Berg and Lars Arvid Skoog v. Apollo Computer, Inc.*, ICC Arbitration No. 6259, Interim Award on Jurisdiction (Sept. 20, 1990) (unpublished).

[The facts of the case are stated in the decision of the Court of Appeal for the First Circuit, the text of which is found in Chapter 4, *supra* pp. 533-38. The Tribunal was required to determine in the preliminary phase of the arbitration whether it had jurisdiction to hear and determine the merits of the disputes between the parties in view of the defense that there was no arbitration agreement in existence at the time of the procedures. Defendant alleged that a trustee in bankruptcy could not transfer the benefit of an arbitration clause to a party related to the bankrupt company for the purpose of enforcing a debt owed to the bankrupt. It also argued that its termination of the distributorship agreement due to the distributor's non-payment also terminated the arbitration clause, relying, *inter alia*, on the fact that a term of the agreement provided that all rights and obligations under the agreement expired with its termination except for those specifically designated as surviving termination. Although the arbitration clause was not so specified, the arbitral tribunal found that the agreement to arbitrate survived termination of the main agreement based on the language of the contract, the policy of United States law favoring arbitration in international contracts and the notion of autonomy and separability of the arbitration clause.]

Assuming, as we do, that the arbitration clause survives termination of the Agreement, the Claimants must then demonstrate that the assignment of rights was not prohibited by the Agreement and was properly accomplished pursuant to applicable law. Apollo contends that the assignment from Dico to claimants is unenforceable because a) the Agreement precludes any assignment of Dico's rights without the prior written consent of Apollo, and b) Claimants can only enforce an arbitration clause where they assume both the obligations and benefits under the arbitration clause. Apollo also asserts that the assignment to these two Claimants is invalid.

Apollo argues that the 1984 Agreement's "Assignment-Distributor" clause is an overriding non-assignment provision rendering the purported assignment unenforceable against Apollo.

Paragraph 14.02 of the Agreement provides:

This Agreement shall inure to the benefit of and be binding upon [DICO] and its successors and assigns but shall not be assignable by [DICO] without the written consent first obtained of APOLLO. In the event [DICO] wishes to delegate the performance of any of its obligations hereunder to a third party the written consent of APOLLO must first be obtained and APOLLO reserves the right to approve all terms of any such delegation, Any such purported assignment or delegation without written consent shall be void and of no effect.

In construing the above provision, it appears to us that the second sentence amplifies the meaning of the first sentence rather than separately prohibiting the delegation of duties, This construction also comports with Massachusetts law which interprets a general clause prohibiting contract assignment as barring only the delegation of performance and not the assignment of rights. *See* Massachusetts General Laws, Chapter 106, Section 2-210. Further support for this principle is given by Justice Skinner of the U.S. District Court for the District of Massachusetts, who opined:

Under Massachusetts law. . . a general clause prohibiting assignment of contract, is construed as barring only the delegation of contractual duties. Neither is there reason to hold the assignment invalid under applicable federal law.

*Apollo Computer, op. cit.* at 8[206] Justice Skinner also noted that the general assignment clause in the Agreement did not expressly prohibit the assignment of arbitration rights. *Id.*

Apollo's further point regarding the unenforceability of the assignment to Dico is inapposite. Apollo's reliance on *Old Colony Regional Vocational Technical High School Dist. v. New England Contractors*, 5 Mass. App. Ct. 836 (1977), to establish that only an assignee of an entire contract who assumes both its obligations and benefits can enforce an arbitration clause, is misplaced because that case is factually distinguishable from the present situation. In *Old Colony* the court stated, in *dictum*, that a general contractor could not assign an arbitration clause to its subcontractors where the subcontractors had no relationship with the owner. Here, the Claimants are not truly strangers to Apollo — in addition to being directors and primary shareholders of Dico they were the principals who negotiated and signed the 1984 Agreement on behalf of Dico. In *Old Colony*, unlike the present situation, both the contractor and the subcontractor had claims against the owner and the court stated that both parties were able to participate in the arbitration proceedings because they all had a stake in the outcome. Here, Dico is a bankrupt company which must have its rights asserted by another entity or person or else those rights will be lost. In essence, Apollo is not being forced to arbitrate with a new or different party but with the party designated to step in the shoes of Dico as a result of Dico's bankruptcy. Thus, neither the provisions of the 1984 Agreement nor Massachusetts law compel a finding that the assignment is unenforceable.

In support of their contention that the assignment was valid under Swedish law, Claimants have presented an opinion from Advokatfirman of Stockholm, Sweden. The Lindahl law firm opinion states:

---

[206] On appeal, the First Circuit did not reach the merits of this dispute and held that the issue of arbitrability is to be determined by the arbitrators in accordance with ICC rules. *Apollo Computer. Inc. v. Berg et al.*, 886 F.2d 469, 472 (1st Cir. 1989).

A.    The assignment by Sjöstedt of Dicoscan's claim for damages against Apollo was within the powers of Sjöstedt in his capacity as official receiver for Dicoscan.

B.    The assignment was valid and legally binding under Swedish law, and was validly done for the benefit of the individuals to whom it was made.

C.    The assignment constitutes a valid and legally binding obligation of the bankrupt estate even without consideration, as that notion would be commonly understood in common law jurisdictions.

D.    Given the broad powers of the receiver under Swedish law, Sjöstedt would have been entitled to take any actions against Apollo that could have been taken by the company before it was declared bankrupt, including the institution of court proceedings or enforcement of arbitration agreements had he not assigned the claim damages against Apollo as set forth in exhibits A and B.

The assignment of Dico's rights by the receiver in bankruptcy appears to be unequivocal and valid under Swedish law according to the opinion of the law firm of Lindahl noted above. Apart from denying the validity of the assignment as contrary to the terms of the 1984 Agreement and Massachusetts law, Apollo does not address under American or Swedish law the legal authority of the receiver to assign Dico's claims to claimants.

Apollo stresses the fact that the assignment from the receiver does not *in haec verba* grant Dico's right to arbitration to Claimants. However, the broad language of the assignment of "the right to bring claim for damages against Apollo Computer, Inc. due to cancellation of agency contract or otherwise . . . ," appears to us to clearly permit Claimants to pursue those claims in arbitration. The receiver had the right, as the Lindahl opinion states, to pursue any action against Apollo that could have been taken by Dico prior to bankruptcy. In the 1984

Agreement, Dico had agreed to arbitration against Apollo if any disputes arose.

Accordingly, Claimants have the same right to pursue claims in arbitration against Apollo which both Dico and the receiver would have had.

. . .

In conclusion, pursuant to Articles 8(3) and 8(4) of the ICC Rules or Arbitration, we find and award, that:

1.     The right to arbitration of the disputed claims in this proceeding survives the termination of the 1984 Agreement under the terms of the Agreement and applicable law.

2.     The Tribunal has jurisdiction to hear the disputed claims in this proceeding and to render an award for or against Berg and Skoog as assignees of the claims herein held by Dico against Apollo.

### Notes and Questions

1. It is sometimes argued that an arbitrator is more likely than a judge to find in favor of arbitral jurisdiction in a contested case. There may be a natural tendency for the arbitrator to wish to perform the mission which has arguably been confided to him by contract and which at least one of the parties is urging on him. For an articulation of this view, see the dissenting opinion of Lumbard, C.J., in *Trafalgar Shipping Co. v. International Milling Co.*, 401 F.2d 568, 573 (2d. Cir. 1968) ("Moreover, it is not likely that arbitrators can be altogether objective in deciding whether or not they ought to hear the merits. Once they have bitten into the enticing fruit of controversy, they are not apt to stay the satisfying of their appetite after one bite."). The majority found, however, that the issue of laches — whether a delay by a shipowner of five years from the date of injury in bringing arbitration against the ship's charterer rendered the dispute non-arbitrable — was initially for the arbitral tribunal and not for the court. By the same token, he may be receptive to extending arbitral jurisdiction to non-signatories arguably bound by the clause when this is necessary for the arbitral mission to be efficacious. Nor can financial incentives always be excluded. The review powers of the judge are a check on any overreaching. Whether this oversight will be benevolent or otherwise will depend not only on the legislation but also on judicial attitudes at the seat of arbitration.

2. Does an assignee or successor in interest of a contract containing an arbitration clause automatically succeed to the benefits and burdens of the arbitration clause? In the affirmative, does this conflict in any way with the notion of the autonomy of the arbitration clause? Is there any difference between assignees and successors in interest? What if only a <u>part</u> of the contract containing the arbitration clause is assigned? Could the contract partner be required to arbitrate with several different parties? *See generally* Daniel Girsberger and Christian Hausmaninger, *Assignment of Rights and Agreement to Arbitrate*, 8 ARB. INT'L 121 (1992).

3. If the non-signatory corporate affiliates in *MAP Tankers* and *Dow Chemicals* (*supra*, Chapter 4) had not sought arbitration as claimants, but were sought to be joined as defendants, would the tribunal have found they were subject to arbitral jurisdiction? Should there be a different standard for determining whether a related party should be allowed to claim the benefit of an arbitration clause to assert a claim than for determining whether a non-signatory party may be compelled to arbitrate as a defendant against his will? *Compare* République arabe d'Egypte v. Westland Helicopter Ltd. *with* Vendome Holding, S.A., Cartier Munich G.m.b.H. v. Horowitz, *supra*, Chapter 4 (both dealing with non-signatory defendant parties).

## IV.    CHOICE OF LAW

### A.    LAW GOVERNING THE ARBITRATION (*LEX ARBITRI*)

The arbitrator may be required, after his appointment, to consider various issues of choice of law relevant both to the conduct of proceedings and to the merits of the dispute. Sometimes, particularly where the parties have failed to stipulate in the contract the substantive or proper law of the contract, this determination may take the form of an interim award on that issue. It then serves as a guide to the parties for their further submissions and argument. Prior to embarking on this typical choice of law exercise (*see* subparagraph C.3. *infra*), the arbitrator may be required to examine whether there is a law governing the arbitration itself and whether this law will have an effect on how the arbitrator shall conduct the proceedings.

The law governing the arbitration determines the relationship between the arbitral tribunal and national courts. It will, for instance, determine whether, and to what extent, judicial review of the award or court intervention during arbitral proceedings is authorized (*See* Chapter 9, *infra*). It may also prescribe certain mandatory procedures which the arbitral tribunal must respect, at the risk of the possible nullification of its award. It is important not to confuse the law governing the arbitration, or *lex arbitri*, with the proper law of the contract. The latter governs issues of interpretation, performance, non-performance, and liability under the contract and may frequently be stipulated in the contract's choice of law clause.

The distinction between *lex arbitri* and proper law of the contract is well illustrated by a 1970 case in the House of Lords in England. The issue was whether the arbitrator should "state a case" — that is, certify certain questions of law arising in the arbitration for decision by a court — as was required under English arbitration law at the time, or whether he should decide them himself, as was authorized under the law of Scotland.

> *James Miller & Partners, Ltd. v. Whitworth Street Estates (Manchester), Ltd.*, 1 ALL E.R. 796, 801-02, 809-10 (House of Lords Mar. 3, 1970).

[An English company contracted with a Scottish construction company for building work to be done at a site in Scotland for the English company's factory. The contract was concluded on a Royal Institute of British Architects form contract which did not contain a specific choice of substantive law. After disputes arose a Scottish arbitrator was named by the President of the Royal Institute and the arbitration took place in Scotland. During the course of the arbitral proceedings the English company, over the objection of the Scottish construction company, sought to have a case stated to the English High Court under the Arbitration Act 1950 (which did not apply in Scotland). The Court of Appeal, *per* Lord Denning, would have ordered a case to be stated. When the matter reached the House of Lords, the Judicial Committee found by a three to two majority that the proper law of the contract, based on the use of the British Architects form of contract, was English law, but found unanimously that Scottish law governed the arbitration and the application for a stated case failed. Hence the appeal was allowed, and no case could be stated to the English High Court. Each of the five law lords wrote an opinion, of which two are excerpted below.]

LORD HODSON [after finding the proper law of the contract to be English law, the opinion continued]:

I am satisfied, however, that, whether the proper law of the contract is English or Scottish, the arbitration being admittedly a matter of procedure as opposed to being a matter of substantive law is on principle and authority to be governed by the lex fori, in this case Scottish law. Furthermore, the parties have, in my judgment, plainly submitted to the Scottish arbitration on the footing that Scottish procedure was to govern.

The leading case of *Don v. Lippmann* (1837), a Scottish appeal to your Lordships' House, was concerned with the law of prescription and it was held that the sexennial period according to the lex fori prevailed over the lex contractus. Lord Brougham held that there is this distinction between the contract and the remedy that whatever relates to the remedy is to be governed by the lex fori; the law of the country to whose courts application is made for performance. I see no reason why this principle should not be applied to arbitration proceedings. It appears from *Norske Atlas Ins. Co., Ltd. v. London Gen. Ins. Co., Ltd.* (1927) that Mackinnon J. was of this opinion. An opinion to the same effect is to be found in Dicey and Morris: Conflict of Laws (8th edition 1967) . . . .

.   .   .

Here the parties did not, in the first place, choose the law which should govern the arbitration proceedings but they subsequently accepted a Scottish arbiter in Scottish arbitration proceedings. This agreement involved no variation of the original contract for it is not inconsistent with the terms of that agreement that arbitration, if any, should take place in Scotland and be governed by Scottish procedure. That Scottish arbitration procedure was to be followed was accepted by the parties as is shown by the correspondence which took place following the appointment of the arbiter in Glasgow. The arbiter himself made the position abundantly clear by appointing as his clerk a Glasgow solicitor. Scottish procedure was followed throughout without objection until the application was made for a case to be stated. Then for the first time, when it was realized that this procedure was not available in Scotland, was any attempt made to depart from what had previously been agreed. The respondents submit that in agreeing to Scottish procedure they were not contemplating the case stated process which is used in England but not in Scotland. This will not avail them since, as was admitted, stating a case is a procedural matter and the respondents cannot pick and choose from the various operations involved in Scottish procedure. The form of the application made by the appellants for the appointment of an arbitrator does not avail the respondents merely because of the use of the form of words 'where there is a submission to arbitration, within the meaning of the Arbitration Act 1950.' There was in truth a submission within the meaning of the English Act, which does not apply to Scotland, but this does not lead to the conclusion that the English Act was to govern the Scottish arbitration proceedings.

LORD WILBERFORCE [after finding the proper law of the contract to be Scottish law, continued]:

I turn to the second question, what law is to govern the arbitration procedure? If the proper law of the contract is Scottish there could be no argument in favour of the intrusion of English law into the arbitration. But if the proper law is English, an interesting question arises. One must ask first whether, in principle, it is possible for the law governing the arbitral procedure to differ from that governing the substance of the contract. No authority was cited to us which explicitly answers this question one way or the other, but I have no doubt as to the answer. It is a matter of experience that numerous arbitrations are conducted by English arbitrators in England on matters governed by contracts whose proper law is or may be that of another country; and I should be surprised if it had ever been held that such arbitrations were not governed by the English Arbitration Act in procedural matters, including the right to apply for a case to be stated. (I leave aside as a special case arbitrations conducted under the rules of the International Chamber of Commerce, though even these may be governed by the law of the place of arbitration.) The principle must surely be the same as that which applies to court proceedings brought in one country concerning a contract governed by the law of another; and that such proceedings as regards all matters which the law regards as procedural are governed by the lex fori has been accepted at least since Lord Brougham's judgment in *Don v. Lippmann*. In my opinion, the law is correctly stated by Professor Kahn-Freund and Dr Morris in Dicey and Morris *op. cit.* page 1048, where they say:

> It cannot however be doubted that the courts would give effect to the choice of a law other than the proper law of the contract. Thus, if parties agreed on an arbitration clause expressed to be governed by English law but providing for arbitration in Switzerland, it may be held that, whereas English law governs the validity, interpretation and effect of the arbitration clause as such (including the scope of the arbitrators'

jurisdiction), the proceedings are governed by Swiss law. It is also submitted that where the parties have failed to choose the law governing the arbitration proceedings, those proceedings must be considered, at any rate prima facie, as being governed by the law of the country in which the arbitration is held, on the ground that it is the country most closely connected with the proceedings.

## Notes and Questions

1. In *James Miller* it was decided that, as is frequently the case, the *lex arbitri* and the proper law of the contract were governed by different systems of law. Suppose part of the proper law of the contract is inconsistent with the *lex arbitri*. Which prevails?

2. Ordinarily, two legal systems compete for the application as the *lex arbitri*: the law of the place where the arbitration is held (the "seat" of the arbitration), and the law intended by the parties to govern the arbitration. The case for the mandatory application of the law of the forum as being the only system of law which applies either by its own force, or can give force to any agreement by the parties as to procedure (or anything else), is stated in its classic form by the English jurist F.A. Mann:

> Every right or power a person enjoys is inexorably conferred by or derived from a system of municipal laws which may conveniently and in accordance with tradition be call *lex fori*, though it would be more exact (but also less familiar) to speak of the *lex arbitri*.

F.A. Mann, *Lex Facit Arbitrum*, *in* INTERNATIONAL ARBITRATION: LIBER AMICORUM FOR MARTIN DOMKE 157 (Pieter Sanders, ed., 1967), *reprinted in* 2 ARB. INT'L 241, 245 (1986).

Even if Dr. Mann's thesis is accepted, the conflict between the law of the seat of arbitration and the law intended by the parties to govern the arbitration may be more apparent than real since the system of law at the place of arbitration will ordinarily permit the parties to choose the law or laws governing their agreement, including their agreement to arbitrate.

3. While parties frequently insert a clause making a choice of substantive law to govern the agreement, they seldom make specific choices of law to govern the agreement to arbitrate or specifically adopt the procedural law of a state to govern the arbitration proceedings. In these circumstances, the arbitrator is sometimes left to infer the intent of the parties by a presumption flowing from a choice of the place of arbitration (*i.e.*, a party may be presumed to intend that the arbitration law and procedure of the place where he has chosen to arbitrate will apply), or from other indicia in the terms of the contract.

4. When arbitration takes place in the United States, pursuant to international or interstate contracts, the parties ordinarily expect that the procedural law will be governed by the Federal Arbitration Act. However, the case of *Volt Information Sciences, Inc. v. Board of Trustees of Stanford University*, 489 U.S. 468 (1989) (excerpted *supra* Chapter 4, p. 421) finds that the Federal Arbitration Act does not necessarily preempt all provisions of state arbitration law. Would it be desirable for the parties to make a specific choice of the Federal Arbitration Act or the procedural law of the arbitration to the exclusion of any state procedures? If so, would the following clause accomplish this: ". . . provided that any dispute, controversy, question or issue arising out of, or relating directly or indirectly to paragraph __ (Arbitration) of this Agreement shall be governed exclusively by the Federal Arbitration Act as then in force"? *See* Joseph D. Becker, *Choice of Law and the Federal Arbitration Act: The Shock of Volt*, 45 ARB. J. 32-37 (1990).


B.      RULES GOVERNING ARBITRATOR'S CONDUCT OF THE PROCEEDINGS

How the arbitral proceedings will be conducted before the arbitrator will ordinarily depend more on the arbitration rules that have been agreed upon between the parties than on the *lex arbitri* or substantive law. *See supra* Chapter 2, "Designing an Arbitration Regime"). Typically, modern arbitration rules give freedom to the arbitrator to conduct the proceedings according to rules which he will establish. The UNCITRAL Arbitration Rules,[207] while setting out some broad principles of procedure, give wide discretion to the arbitrators to establish the rules for the conduct of proceedings subject only to respect for procedural due process.

Article 15

1.      Subject to these Rules, the arbitral tribunal may conduct the arbitration in such manner as it considers appropriate, provided that the parties are treated with equality and that at any stage of the proceedings each party is given a full opportunity of presenting his case.

---

[207] See Supplement at p. 623, for full text. *See also* John P. Dietz, *Development of the UNCITRAL Arbitration Rules* 27 AM J. COMP. L. 449 (1979); Pieter Sanders, *Procedures and Practices under the UNCITRAL Rules*, 27 AM. J. COMP. L. 453; JACOMIJN J. VAN HOF, COMMENTARY ON THE UNCITRAL ARBITRATION RULES: THE APPLICATION BY THE IRAN-U.S. CLAIM TRIBUNAL (1991).

2. If either party so requests at any stage of the proceedings, the arbitral tribunal shall hold hearings for the presentation of evidence by witnesses, including expert witnesses, or for oral argument. In the absence of such a request, the arbitral tribunal shall decide whether to hold such hearings or whether the proceedings shall be conducted on the basis of documents and other materials.

3. All documents or information supplied to the arbitral tribunal by one party shall at the same time be communicated by that party to the other party.

A similar freedom is found in Article 11 of the ICC Rules of Arbitration, the most frequently used rules in international commerce:

> The rules governing the proceedings before the arbitrator shall be those resulting from these Rules and, where these Rules are silent, any rules which the parties (or, failing them, the arbitrator) may settle, and whether or not reference is thereby made to a municipal procedural law to be applied to the arbitration.

1. W. LAURENCE CRAIG ET AL., INTERNATIONAL CHAMBER OF COMMERCE ARBITRATION 269-70 (2d ed. 1990).

As drafted, [Article 11] leaves the manner in which the arbitral proceedings shall be conducted completely in the hands of the parties and the arbitrators. This is consistent with the aim of the Rules to provide a universal procedure for the settlement of international disputes detached, to the extent possible, from the particularities of national law procedures . . . . Despite their international orientation, the ICC Rules do not take a position as to whether an arbitration may be completely detached from national laws governing arbitration as a legal institution, or governing the arbitration agreement itself . . . . Article 11 carefully distinguishes between the arbitrators' powers to make *rules* governing the proceedings and possible references to provisions of municipal arbitration law. Thus, the ICC Rules allow the arbitrators to settle rules directly and do not require them to choose a national law of procedure, specifically distinguishing the issue of procedural rules from such a choice of law.

. . .

The ICC Rules leave unanswered the question whether the arbitrators' powers to set rules of procedure are derived directly from the agreement of the parties and their incorporation of the ICC Rules into that agreement, or must be found in national laws relating to arbitration in effect at the seat of arbitration.

The fact remains that the users of ICC arbitration generally seek a considerable degree of detachment from local procedural law. If there are any procedural requirements at the seat of arbitration, they would be those relating specifically to arbitration and not to court proceedings generally. As a further limitation, such requirements must relate to international arbitration, and not domestic cases. Generally speaking, most jurisdictions give broad discretion to parties to determine the conduct of private arbitration proceedings, and many give especially wide latitude with respect to disputes that are international. If it is true that every State has the power to regulate and control arbitration activities within the limits of its territory,[208] the inquiry that must be made regarding the rules to be adopted by arbitrators is: has the State exercised this power,[209] and if so to what extent?

### Notes and Questions

1. Many arbitrators find that the agreed arbitration rules (usually institutional rules) provide sufficient guidance for their conduct of the arbitration without the necessity to make specific reference to a national law of procedure. In the same way they feel free to exercise liberty afforded to them by such arbitration rules to decide

---

[208] F.A. Mann, "Lex facit arbitrum," *in International Arbitration* 159, at 162 (Liber amicorum for Martin Domke) (1967). *See* W.W. Park and J. Paulsson, "The Binding Force of International Arbitral Awards," 23 *Virginia Journal of International Law* 253, 254-9 (1983).

[209] Pierre Lalive, "Problèmes spécifiques de l'arbitrage international," 1980 *Rev. arb.* 341; "Les règles de conflit appliquées au fond du litige par l'arbitre international siégeant en Suisse," 1976 *Rev. arb.* 155.

on supplementary procedures to be followed or to make procedural rulings without specific reference to national law.

2. Where, however, one of the parties puts in issue the law applicable to arbitration procedure and its relevance, the tribunal will have to make a decision.

3. For a listing of the kinds of procedural measures taken by arbitrators in this way, see Sigvard Jarvin, *The sources and limits of the arbitrator's powers*, *in* CONTEMPORARY PROBLEMS IN INTERNATIONAL ARBITRATION 50, 55-58 (Julian D.M. Lew, ed., 1987).

2.    *French Contractor v. Egyptian Employer*, ICC Arbitration No. 5029, Interim Award (July 16, 1986) 12 YEARBOOK OF COMMERCIAL ARBITRATION 113 (1987) (extracts from the award).

In 1981 a joint venture called X consisting of the French company A, its 100% French subsidiary B, and two Egyptian companies, C and D, entered into a contract with an Egyptian entity for the construction of certain civil works in Egypt. The contract incorporated the FIDIC conditions (3d edition 1977). Clause 67 of these conditions provides for a two-tier system for resolving disputes: disputes have first to be referred to the Engineer and, if a party is dissatisfied with the Engineer's decision, he can submit the dispute to ICC arbitration.

Following the rejection of a number of claims by the Engineer, the French company A and its subsidiary B filed a request for arbitration against the Egyptian employer in 1984. The place of arbitration was determined by the ICC Court of Arbitration to be The Hague.

The Egyptian defendants object to the jurisdiction of the Arbitral Tribunal on a number of grounds. By an interim award of 16 July 1986 the Arbitral Tribunal rejected the jurisdictional defenses (the Egyptian arbitrator dissenting).

## A. *Law governing the arbitration*

1.      Art. 5(1)(b) of the Contract provided:

> The Contract shall be deemed to be an Egyptian Contract and shall be governed by and construed according to the laws in force in Egypt.

2.      Defendant claimed that the law governing the arbitration proceedings is Egyptian civil procedural law. He argued that the choice of law clause, quoted above, covered not only substantive law aspects but also procedural ones, including arbitration. According to defendant in a letter received by the Secretariat of the Court of Arbitration, the text of Clause 67 of the Contract 'clearly expressed the intention of the parties that arbitration is a local arbitration and not international' and 'that it is internal and not external'. Defendant further asserted that the foregoing is not altered by Art. 11 of the ICC Rules.

3.      Whilst claimant agreed with defendant that Egyptian law rules of interpretation should be applied, claimant asserted that the parties intended to agree and in fact did agree to an international, external arbitration under the auspices of the International Chamber of Commerce in view of various foreign elements connected with the contract. Claimant further contended that a distinction, made in all systems of law, must be made between substantive law and procedural law. The former is governed by the law chosen by the parties (*i.e.*, Egyptian law), whilst the latter is governed by the mandatory provisions of the arbitration law of the place of arbitration, *i.e.*, Dutch arbitration law.

4.      The arbitral tribunal reasoned:

> The choice of law clause contained in Art. 5(1)(*b*) of the Contract means that the Contract must be interpreted in accordance with the rules of contract interpretation of Egyptian law, in particular Arts. 150 et seq. of the Egyptian Civil Code. The Arbitral Tribunal will follow these rules of interpretation in respect of all the jurisdictional issues.

5.    The Arbitral Tribunal holds that the law governing the arbitration is the arbitration law of the Netherlands. The Arbitral Tribunal notes at the outset that the Contract is a truly international contract involving parties of different nationalities (i.e., French and Egyptian), the movement of equipment and services across national frontiers, and the payment in different currencies (i.e., Egyptian Pounds and US Dollars). The international character of the Contract is inconsistent with the defendant's allegation that the parties intended to provide for domestic, internal (i.e., Egyptian) arbitration. Such intent cannot be derived from the choice of law clause contained in Art. 5(1)(b) of the Contract, providing for the applicability of Egyptian law, whilst Clause 67, providing for arbitration under the Rules of the ICC, clearly expresses the contrary. As it is recognized in virtually all legal systems around the world, a basic distinction must be made between the law governing the substance and the law governing the procedure. That distinction is also recognized in Egyptian conflict of laws; whereas Art. 19 of the Egyptian Civil Code provides for the law governing the substance of the dispute, Art. 22 is concerned with the law governing the procedure. Accordingly, if the parties had wished that the arbitration be governed by Egyptian procedural law, they should have made a specific agreement thereon. Art. 5(1)(b) of the Contract is not such a provision as it does not mention specifically that arbitration is governed by Egyptian law. Failing such agreement, the arbitration law of the place governs the arbitration. This principle is in accordance with Art. V(1)(a), (d) and (e) of the New York Convention of 1958 to which Egypt and the Netherlands have adhered. . . .

6.    The agreement of the parties to arbitration under the Rules of the International Chamber of Commerce in Clause 67 meant that, failing their agreement on the place of arbitration, they gave, under Art. 12 of the Rules, a mandate to the Court of Arbitration to fix the place of arbitration on their behalf. It is to be noted that defendant itself proposed in the alternative The Hague as the place of arbitration . . . . The prevailing interpretation of the Rules of the ICC nowadays is also that the mandatory provisions of the arbitration law of the place of arbitration govern the arbitration, irrespective of the law governing the substance. Whereas Art. 13(3) of the Rules contains the contractual conflict of law rules for determining the

law governing the substance of the dispute, Art. 11 is concerned with the rules governing the proceedings. In respect of the latter provision, it is stated in the <u>Guide to Arbitration</u> (ICC Publication no. 382) p. 39:

> To make sure that the award will be enforceable at law, the mandatory rules of national law applicable to international arbitrations in the country where the arbitration takes place must anyway be observed, even if other rules of procedure are chosen by the parties or by the arbitrator.

7.     The Arbitral Tribunal emphasizes that the applicability of Dutch arbitration law in the present case by no means implies that the Dutch rules concerning proceeding [sic] before Dutch State Courts are applicable. According to Dutch arbitration law, parties are free to agree on the rules of procedure and, failing such agreement, the arbitrator determines the conduct of the proceedings, subject to a few necessary mandatory provisions. *See generally* P. Sanders, "National Report Netherlands," 6 Yearbook of Commercial Arbitration, 1981, p. 60 *et seq.*; ARBITRATION LAW IN EUROPE (Paris 1981) p. 277 *et seq.* By referring to the Rules of the International Chamber of Commerce, the parties have 'internationalized' the arbitration within this legal framework.

*     *     *

A determination of the national law governing arbitration procedure does not end the inquiry of the arbitral tribunal. An arbitral tribunal need only apply those provisions of national arbitration law that are *mandatory*. It may supplement procedures unless those supplemental measures are condemned by the letter or spirit of the applicable procedural law.

> 3.     *Wintershall A.G. v. Government of Qatar*, Ad hoc arbitration, final arbitration award (May 31, 1988) 28 I.L.M. 833 (1989).

[Claimant Wintershall entered into an Exploration and Production Sharing Agreement (the "EPSA") with the Government of

Qatar to explore for, drill, produce and market petroleum (including crude oil, gas and other hydrocarbon products). The agreement permitted Qatar to terminate the EPSA if within its initial eight-year term Wintershall had not discovered "Crude Oil" or "economically utilizable non-associated Natural Gas." Disputes arose due to Qatar's refusal to permit Wintershall to explore on a certain part of the area due to a border dispute with Bahrain, and by failing to agree with Wintershall concerning a joint project to permit utilization of non-associated natural gas discoveries made by Claimant. Wintershall sought an award for breach of contract and rescission of the contract due to Qatar's actions which it considered expropriatory. In a partial award, the Tribunal found that Qatar had not breached the EPSA which remained in force and effect. The Tribunal made certain declarations concerning the continuing rights and obligations of the parties including findings as to the date for final relinquishment of the area by Wintershall, and the granting of an extension thereto. Partial Award of 29 January 1988, 28 ILM 795 (1989). Claimant requested that the Tribunal, in its final award, confirm and clarify certain of the declarations made in the partial award.]

3. Claimants have asked the Tribunal to confirm its holdings with respect to relinquishment. Accordingly, the Tribunal wishes to confirm that, under the declarations set forth in . . . the Partial Award, the relinquishment rights of the Claimants are as follows:

    A.    The Claimants are not required to relinquish their rights to exercise their option under the third paragraph of Article XV.3 of the EPSA in any part of the 50% of the Contract Area still held by the Claimants, if not in production, until 8 (eight) years from the date of this Final Award.

    B.    The term for the application of the EPSA Article XI relinquishment provisions to the Structure A area begins on the date the Respondent permits Claimants to develop Structure A under the EPSA.

    C.    With respect to the terms for performance stipulated in other provisions of EPSA, the Tribunal hereby confirms the extension of the performance periods required to make meaningful the relinquishment rights above

provided, as more fully set forth in . . . the Partial
Award.

.    .    .

4. The Tribunal recognizes, as pointed out in Clifford Chance's Further
Observations (the "Further Observations") of May 16, 1988, that the
Netherlands Arbitration Act 1986 does not provide for an interpretation
of an award and that the Minister of Justice's report referred to in
paragraph 11 of the Further Observations indicates that the Minister of
Justice does not propose to insert in the Act the possibility of an
interpretation of an award by the Tribunal. However, the Parties by
their agreement of October 22, 1986, signed by duly authorized
representatives of the Parties, adopted as procedural rules the
UNCITRAL Rules adopted by the United Nations General Assembly
on 15 December 1976, and Article 35 of these Rules provides for an
interpretation of the award and Article 37 for an additional award,
subject to certain notice provisions which have been fully satisfied in
this case. It is the Tribunal's view that this agreement governs the
arbitration since the UNCITRAL Arbitration Rules are not in conflict
with any provision of the Netherlands law from which the Parties
cannot derogate (Article 1-2 of the UNCITRAL Arbitration Rules) and
Article 1036 of the Netherlands Arbitration Act 1986, providing that
"Subject to the provisions of this Title, the arbitral proceedings shall
be conducted in such manner as agreed between the Parties . . . ".
There is no provision in the Netherlands Arbitration Act 1986 expressly
excluding the Parties from agreeing to an interpretation and their
agreement under UNCITRAL Article 35 is, in the Tribunal's opinion,
controlling.

It is the further view of the Tribunal that Article 1059 of the
Netherlands Arbitration Act 1986 providing for the *res judicata* effect
of a partial final award in no sense deprives the Parties of the ability
to agree to an interpretation of a partial award under Article 35 of the
UNCITRAL Rules. The Tribunal agrees with the Claimants that the
"principle of *res judicata* prevents the re-opening of necessarily
decided points. It does not prevent the clarification of a decision nor
the giving of a decision on points which an award has left undecided."

The Tribunal has also noted that in his preface to the
Netherlands Arbitration Act 1986, the Minister of Justice of The
Netherlands, F. Korthals Altes, referred to the new Act duly taking

into account the Model Law on International Commercial Arbitration, adopted in 1985 by the United Nations Commission on International Trade Law (UNCITRAL), which expressly provides in Article 33 for an interpretation of an award if so agreed by the parties (Article 33(1)(b)).

Finally, while in no sense controlling, the Respondent by recognizing in its letter of April 28, penultimate paragraph, that Article 40-4. of the UNCITRAL Rules prohibits the charging of additional fees in respect of an interpretation, in effect recognizes that Article 35 is applicable.

5. Nonetheless, in view of the contention by the Respondent that the Tribunal is without authority under Netherlands law to interpret its award, the Tribunal has determined whether the substance of the attached interpretation could be included in an additional award under Article 37 of the UNCITRAL and Article 1061 of the Netherlands Arbitration Act 1986, and, as required by Article 1061(3) of the Netherlands Arbitration Act 1986, the Tribunal has given to the Parties an opportunity to be heard on this question, in particular, the view of the Claimants as set forth in paragraph 14 of the Claimants' submissions of April 14, 1988 that "the inevitable and logical consequence of the Respondent's counterclaim is that claims and matters related to Article XV.3, Third Alternative, were before the Tribunal for decision." These included clarification of how the cost recovery and production sharing principles of Article XIII of the EPSA apply to a non-associated Natural Gas project under the third paragraph of Article XV.3.

It is the determination of the Tribunal that the substance of the attached interpretation could be included in an additional award under Article 37 of the UNCITRAL Rules and/or Article 1061 of the Netherlands Arbitration Act 1986.

6. The Tribunal hereby incorporates into and makes a part of this Final Award its interpretation of the Partial Award and/or additional award, issued today's date.

[The Tribunal proceeded to issue a ten-page interpretation of its prior award relating to certain economic principles to govern performance under the Exploration and Production Sharing Agreement.]

## Notes and Questions

1. In *French Contractor v. Egyptian Employer Arbitration* (*supra*, p. 698) the tribunal assumed that the parties could have agreed that the arbitration, while taking place in the Netherlands, should be governed by Egyptian procedural law. Suppose the contractually agreed *lex arbitri* and the mandatory provisions of arbitration law at the place of arbitration were inconsistent. Discuss.

2. May the parties, by their agreement, dictate how the arbitrator shall conduct the proceedings? For this purpose would there be a difference between *ad hoc* and institutional arbitration?

3. Where nothing is specifically provided by the parties' agreement or in the applicable institutional arbitration rules, is the arbitrator free to determine how the arbitral proceedings will be conducted?

4. What would be the effect if the parties, or the arbitration rules, gave to the arbitrator powers not recognized at the place of arbitration (such as the power to administer an oath in a jurisdiction where it is reserved to judicial officers)?

5. Consider the effect on the recognition of an award of Article V(1)(b) and (d) of the New York Convention. The first provision permits a Convention state to refuse recognition where the contesting party was not given proper notice of the arbitration proceedings, "or was otherwise unable to present his case." The second provision permits non-recognition where "the arbitral procedure was not in accordance with the agreement of the parties, or failing such agreement, was not in accordance with the law of the country where the arbitration took place."

## C.    SUBSTANTIVE LAW GOVERNING THE DISPUTE

A judge sitting in a national court is subject, in all respects, to the law of the state which appointed him and is expected to apply that law — the law of the forum — to all disputes and parties coming before him. Should he be authorized exceptionally to apply foreign law — the law of another sovereign — it will only be because the conflict of laws rule of his forum authorizes and directs him to do.

An international arbitrator is quite different, for he holds no office by appointment by the state, nor does he exercise public or institutional powers in the name of the state. His powers are derived from the arbitration agreement contained in an international contract, usually between parties from different national states. In a sense, no law is foreign or domestic to him. Hence there is no law of the forum, akin to a judge's, with a body of conflict rules. Without derogating from the role of the seat of arbitration in determining the *lex arbitri* (*supra*, Part IV.A.; *see also* Chapter 9 Part II.E.2.), and the need to respect the seat of arbitration's mandatory procedural provisions, it must be asked whether the same respect should be given to its conflict of law rules.

It may be desirable for the international commercial arbitrator to enjoy more flexibility than a national judge in making choices of law. Moreover, it is frequent that the place of arbitration, whether it be chosen by the parties or an appointing authority, has few or no contacts with the parties or the dispute. As Pierre Lalive has written:[210]

> The arbitrator exercises a private mission, conferred contractually, and it is only by a rather artificial interpretation that one can say that his powers arise from — and even then very indirectly — a tolerance of the State of the place of arbitration, or rather of the various States involved (States of the parties, of the *siège*, of the probable places of execution of the award), which accept the institution of arbitration, or of the community of nations, notably those which have ratified international treaties in the matter. Would it not be to force the international arbitrator into a kind of Procrustean bed[211] if he were assimilated to a State judge, who is imperatively bound to the system of private international law of the country where he sits and from which he derives his power of decision?

The most modern arbitration conventions and modern arbitration institution rules all tend to reinforce the international arbitrator's freedom to choose the applicable substantive law without being required to follow the conflict rules of the seat of arbitration (although, of course, those rules may be chosen if, in the circumstances, they are

---

[210] Pierre Lalive, "Les règles de conflits de lois appliquées au fond du l'arbitre international siégeant en Suisse," 1976 REV. ARB. 155, at 159.

[211] [Author's note: Readers will recall the "myth of Procrustes, who seized unsuspecting travellers and made them fit his bed, cutting off their legs if they were long, stretching them if they were too short," *See* Jan Paulsson, *Arbitration Unbound*, 30 INT'L AND COMP. L. Q. 358, 362 (1981).]

the most appropriate). The freedom of the arbitrator in the choice of law process does not liberate him, however, from applying some system of law to govern the substance of the contract. Consider, in this regard, European Convention of 21 April 1961, 484 U.N.T.S. 349, Article VII (Supplement at p. 71); ICC Rules of Arbitration (1975 ed., as modified 1 January 1988) Article 13 (Supplement at pp. 459-61); UNCITRAL Arbitration Rules Article 33 (Supplement at p. 639).

One survey[212] indicated that arbitrators in international commercial arbitration utilize most frequently the following possible choice of law systems: (i) application of the choice of law system in force at the seat; (ii) cumulative application of the choice of law systems of the countries having a relation with the dispute; (iii) application of general principles of conflict of laws; and (iv) application of a rule of conflict chosen directly by the arbitrator. A fifth solution would be for the arbitrator to choose the material law applicable to the contract directly and without passing through the systemic choice of law process at all. The following additional methods have occasionally been suggested, but by and large have not been used by arbitrators in current international commercial arbitrations: application of the conflict of law rules of the country of which the arbitrator is a national; application of the rules of the country whose courts would have had jurisdiction had there not been an agreement to arbitrate; and application of the rules of the country where it would be likely that the award would be executed.[213]

A recent arbitration award involving a determination of the law applicable in a typical international sale of goods case illustrates the cumulative application of national choice of law provisions.

---

[212] *See* W. LAURENCE CRAIG, ET AL., INTERNATIONAL CHAMBER OF COMMERCE ARBITRATION 288 (2d ed. 1990); *see also* Lalive, *supra* note 209, at 159; Derains, *L'application cumulative par l'arbitre des systèmes de conflits de lois intéressés au litige*, 1962 REV. ARB. 99; Frédéric-Edouard Klein, *The law to be applied by the Arbitrators to the Substance of the Dispute*, *in* THE ART OF ARBITRATION 189-206 (Jan C. Schults & Albert Jan van den Berg eds., 1982).

[213] The difficulties of applying these latter methods to international as opposed to domestic arbitrations are reviewed in Lalive, *supra* note 209 at 160-64.

1. *Egyptian Co. (Buyer) v. Yugoslav Co. (Seller)*, ICC Arbitration No. 6281, Award (Aug. 26, 1989), 15 YEARBOOK OF COMMERCIAL ARBITRATION 96 (1990) (extracts).

On 20 August 1987, the parties concluded a contract for the sale of 80,000 metric tons of steel bars at an average price of US $190.00 per metric ton. The goods were delivered in accordance with the contracts between 15 September 1985 and 15 January 1988 to a suitable Yugoslav port.

Claimant had the option to increase the quantity to 160,000 metric tons at the same price and conditions, provided it declared its option to purchase the additional 80,000 metric tons at the latest by 15 December 1987 and opened its letter of credit for the first delivery at the latest by 31 December 1987.

On 26 November 1987, claimant informed defendant that it would exercise the option and would open the L/C during the second half of December 1987. On 9 December 1987, defendant requested a meeting to be held that month, to discuss the prices for the additional quantity of goods. Claimant insisted on the originally agreed price but was prepared to discuss future business transactions. At the meeting held on 28 December 1987, defendant requested US $215.00 per metric ton for the additional deliveries, but claimant did not agree.

In its letter of 31 December 1987, claimant stated that defendant's behaviour was a breach of contract and requested defendant to announce the beneficiaries of the future letters of credit. If defendant did not agree by 6 January 1988, claimant would hold defendant liable for any and all damage, caused by breach of contract. This period was extended to 25 January 1988.

On 26 January 1988, claimant bought 80,000 metric tons of the same type of steel bars from a Romanian company at a price of US $216.00 per metric ton. Claimant alleged that shipping costs from Romania to Egypt were US $2.00 to US $2.50 per metric ton lower than from Yugoslavia to Egypt.

Claimant initiated arbitration under the arbitration clause in the contract which provided for arbitration at the International Chamber of Commerce, claiming compensation for the loss due to the price difference. The sole arbitrator held that claimant was entitled to damages due to defendant's failure to deliver the additional quantity of goods at the original price.

*Excerpt*

(1) The arbitrator decided that Yugoslav law was applicable

(2) It should be determined, first and foremost, in connection with the alleged unreasonableness, due to an increase in world-market prices, which legal provisions should be applied to evaluate the sales contract and thus also, this central issue. At any rate, the Vienna United Nations Convention of Contracts for the International Sale of Goods of 11 April 1980, cannot be applied as such. The Convention is in force, both in Egypt and in Yugoslavia, as well as in France ; yet, according to Art. 100(2) it applies to such sales contracts only that were concluded after the day the Convention went into force, i.e., 1 January 1988. The present sales contract was concluded on 10 August 1987.

(3) The question, which law applies, must therefore be examined on the basis of the rules on international private law.

(4) According to Egyptian international private law, the law of that country applies, where the contract is signed, unless the parties agree otherwise, and, in addition, if they have their principal offices in different states (Art. 19 of the 1949 Civil Code).

(5) According to Yugoslav international private law, the law of that country applies, where the seller had his principal office at the time when he (or the other party) received the offer, if there is no agreement on applicable law between the parties (Bill on International Private Law of 15 February 1982, Sluzbeni list N° 43/1982).

(6) France is a member of the Convention on the Law Applicable to the International Sales of Goods, done at The Hague on 15 June 1955. Art. 3(2) of the above Convention states that if parties have not chosen another law, the contract is governed by the internal law of the state where the seller has his habitual residence at the time at which he received the order. . . .

(7) Since the principal office and the habitual residence of the seller at the time in question was Yugoslavia, and since the sales contract was

concluded in Yugoslavia, all applicable rules on international private law refer to Yugoslav substantive law.

(8) Paragraphs 1 and 2 of (art. 133 of) the Yugoslav Law on Obligations of 1978 read as follows (in an unofficial translation):

> (1) In case of circumstances occurring after the conclusion of the contract, which are of the nature to render the contractual performance of one of the parties difficult or to prevent the scope of the contract to be attained, both to such an extent that it becomes obvious that the contract ceases to correspond to the expectations of the parties and that it would be generally considered unjust to maintain it in force in the unchanged form, the party whose performance has been rendered difficult or which is prevented to attain the scope of the contract by the changed circumstances, can request that the contract be rescinded.
>
> (2) The rescission of the contract cannot be claimed if the party, which invokes the changed circumstances, should have taken these circumstances into account at the time of the conclusion of the contract or could have escaped or overcome such circumstances.

The above definition corresponds to that of a 'frustration' according to Anglo-American law or of a *Wegfall der geschäftsgrundlage* according to German and Austrian law. Yugoslav commentaries (Blagojevic-Krulj; Vizner) speak of a *clausula rebus sic stantibus*, mainly because of the historical development of Yugoslav law. After all, a genuine *clausula rebus sic stantibus* would sustain (in a positive sense) legal relationships only for as long as there are no changes at all, giving no consideration to predictability and applicability. Such a concept cannot be found in the law of obligations, nor the commercial law, of any country (except, as [sic] the most, for unlimited obligations, such as rent and lease relationships, but mainly for support obligations). Otherwise, any business transaction would be exposed to uncertainty, or even be rendered impossible altogether, whenever the mutual covenants are not performed at the time at which the contract is concluded.

(10) In addition to Art. 133 of the Law of Obligations, Usage N° 56 continues to be in force under Yugoslav law, which lists "economic

events, such as extremely sudden and high increases or decreases of price" as one of the reasons resulting in a frustration.

[The arbitrator subsequently examined whether the increase on the steel price from US $190.00 to $215.00 per metric ton was an extremely sudden and high price increase (Art. 133 (1)) and, if so, whether defendant should have taken such a development into consideration at the time when the contract was concluded (Art. 133(2)). He found that the 13.6% increase in world market price did not exceed ordinary market variation included within entrepreneurial risk and the contractual expectations of the parties. The seller was held liable in damages calculated in accordance with Yugoslav law (additional cost in obtaining cover from an Egyptian seller, reduced by the amount of lower shipping costs from Egypt). The arbitrator remarked that the result would have been the same under the Vienna Sales Convention which he stated "one will soon be able to call universal law, on account of the large number of ratifications and accessions that are intended in the near future."]

*   *   *

A description of the process by which arbitrators choose the applicable substantive law for disputes in international commercial arbitration is found in the commentary by a Danish arbitrator, who concludes that international arbitrators have made extensive use of the freedom that is granted to them in the choise of law process.

> 2.    Ole Lando, *The Law Applicable to the Merits of the Dispute*, *in* CONTEMPORARY PROBLEMS IN INTERNATIONAL ARBITRATION (Julian D.M. Lew ed. 1987) 101, 104-12.

**Choice of law by the parties**

**Express choice of law**

Today many contracts contain clauses which expressly submit them to the law of a certain country. The reported cases show that the arbitrators invariably apply the law selected by the parties. Some do so without reference to any national private international law authorizing the choice of law by the parties. Other awards find an authorization of the choice of law in the conventions or in the conflict-of-law rules of a country.

No case is known in which an arbitrator has set aside the parties' express choice of law on the ground of lack of connection with the intended legal system. Several awards uphold the choice of a law unconnected with the contract. It appears that the parties in these cases often wanted a neutral law or a well-developed law to apply. Choice-of-law clauses which were made with an evasive intention and by which the parties committed what the French call *fraude à la loi* have not been found in the arbitration cases. Nor have I found any court decision which has set aside an award on the ground that the arbitrator had given effect to a choice which was not *bona fide* and legal.

## Choice of the *lex mercatoria*

A choice of the *lex mercatoria* is becoming more and more frequent in international contracts. It takes different shapes.

The parties to an international contract sometimes agree not to have their dispute governed by any national law. Instead they submit it to the customs and usages of international trade, to the rules of law which are common to all or most of the states engaged in international trade or in those states connected with the dispute. Where such common rules are not ascertainable the arbitrator applies the rule or chooses the solution which appears to him to be the most appropriate and equitable. In doing so he considers the law of several legal systems. This judicial process is partly an application of legal rules, partly a selective and creative process. The choice described here is the choice of the *lex mercatoria* as the system of law to govern the contract. A combination of the *lex mercatoria* with one legal system is also frequent. Furthermore parties often choose a combination of the *lex mercatoria* and equity (*amiable compositeur*).

.    .    .

## Tacit choice of law by the parties

The cases of an implied choice of law fall into two categories. One is where the intention is demonstrated with reasonable certainty by the terms of the contract or the circumstances of the case. If, for instance, the parties had used a contract formula which was current in a country, they had chosen an arbitration institution established in that country, which was also the country of the place of performance of the contract, then it is argued there is a tacit choice of law.

The other category is where the facts of the case do not support a tacit choice of law. Formerly British, French and German cases made frequent use of the presumed intention of the parties; often they found that the parties had intended the law of the forum to apply. This practice, which has caused much uncertainty, has also been found in the arbitral case law. The choice by the parties of an arbitrator of a certain nationality, an arbitral institution based in that country which is to be the seat of arbitration, has been regarded by some arbitrators as a presumed choice of the law of the nationality of the arbitrator or of the seat of arbitration.

However, the rule *qui eligit arbitrum eligit jus* does not apply generally to international arbitrations.

[The thought that the choice of the place of arbitration could be construed to imply a choice of that country's substantial law is derived from the maxim *qui elegit judicem elegit jus* applicable to judicial proceedings: if the parties wanted to be judged by the judges of the country chosen as forum they could be presumed to accept that those judges would normally apply their own law and hence that they chose that law. The author describes how the maxim was adapted in early cases to include situations where the parties had agreed to the place of arbitration, particularly in English maritime arbitrations where the choice of a London seat of arbitration was indicative of an intent to apply well recognized principles of English maritime and trade law. After reviewing English, French, German, and other case law, he concludes that in international arbitrations the choice of the place of arbitration does not, in the absence of other factors, support a presumption in favor of the choice of the law of the place of arbitration as the governing law of the contract.]

.     .     .

## Choice of law by the arbitrator

For cases where the parties have not selected the law, the European Convention and the ICC Rules have almost identical texts. The European Convention provides:

> 'Failing any indication by the parties as to the applicable
> law, the arbitrators shall apply the proper law under the
> rule of conflict which the arbitrators deem applicable.'

The ICC Rules have preferred the word 'appropriate' to the word 'applicable.' It is doubtful whether this implies any difference of meaning.

This rule gives the arbitrator a number of possibilities. A great variety of methods and solutions are found in the reported cases on the choice of law by the arbitrators. Most of the cases referred to in the following pages are cases decided by ICC arbitrators.

When giving reasons for the award the arbitrator has a double concern. As the servant of the parties he must persuade them and especially the losing party of the justice of his award. Furthermore, he must make sure that the award is enforceable in the country or the countries where enforcement may be sought. This leads many arbitrators to justify their conclusions by referring not only to the law which they deem applicable to the dispute but also to other laws connected with the parties or the subject-matter of the dispute. The arbitrator will often refer to the law of the unsuccessful party to show that this law confirms his findings.

The differing reasons given by arbitrators for their determination of the applicable law, include the following:

## National conflict of law rules

There are several reported cases in which the arbitrator has applied the conflict-of-law rules of a national legal system. Often the arbitrator applied the conflict rule of the country where the case was tried. If the parties have referred to a national arbitration institution the arbitrator will follow the conflict rules of that institution.

It is doubtful to what extent the arbitrator in other cases is bound to apply the conflict-of-law rules of the country in which he hears the case. Article VII of the European Convention, Article 33 of the UNCITRAL Rules, and Article 13(3) of the ICC Rules, all authorize the arbitrator to select his own conflict-of-law rule. It has been convincingly argued that Article VII should be followed by non-national arbitral tribunals even in countries which have not adhered to the European Convention.

There are also numerous awards in which the arbitrator has made a cumulative application of identical or converging conflict-of-law rules of the countries connected with the dispute. If an arbitrator who is confronted with the choice between the laws of two countries cannot show that their laws agree on the substance of the issue he can sometimes demonstrate that their conflict-of-law rules agree on the application of one of the laws. In some cases the arbitrator has shown how abundantly the legal systems agree. Confronted with two legal systems A and B he first shows that the conflict-of-law rules of A and B both lead to the application of the law of A. Then he points out that the substantive laws of A and B also agree on the issue to be decided.

## General principles of private international law

Awards have been found where the 'general principles' of private international law have been invoked. The arbitrator has alleged that there was unanimity among the private international laws of the world or at least among all the major legal systems on the issue. This has sometimes been done with some audacity. In a case from 1967 it was stated that it was 'in conformity with the constant theory and case law concerning the conflict of laws (. . . that . . .) preference has been given to the law of the place where the contract has been made, and subsidiarily, to that of the place of performance.' This holds true of some legal systems but by no means of all.

## 'International' conflict of law rules

In other cases reference has been made to international conventions on private international law. The Hague Convention on the Law Applicable to International Sale of Goods 1955 has been invoked. This has happened even where none of the states connected with the matter had adhered to the Convention. Reference to this Convention has also been made by state courts of countries which were not parties to the Convention. State courts have also invoked conflict of law rules in texts which do not have legally binding character, such as draft conventions and draft laws. Article VII of the European Convention, Article 33 of the UNCITRAL Rules and Article 13(3) of the ICC Rules allow the arbitrator to make use of such texts.

## Non-national conflict of law rule

In several cases the arbitrator has relied on a conflict-of-law rule without disclosing from which legal system or other source he has derived it. The arbitrator has, for instance, stated that he chooses the law of the country in which the contract was made or was to be performed. In most cases it has been easy to find authorities which support the rule chosen by the arbitrator.

## Direct choice of substantive law

In a number of cases the arbitrator has taken a short cut to the substantive law, thus avoiding the intricacies of private international law.

First, in some cases the arbitrator has compared the substantive rules of the various countries connected with the dispute and has found a happy convergence. All rules led him to the same outcome. In most of these cases this short cut has been justifiable. Any conceivable conflict rule would have led him to one of the converging laws. Secondly, in other cases the arbitrator has stated, without giving reasons, that he applied the substantive law of a certain country. He has not revealed whether the laws of other connected countries would have led him to the same result. It is submitted that the arbitrator chose the law which he found most appropriate for the dispute.

## Apply international substantive law

In some cases the arbitrator, in addition to invoking a rule of national law, has supported his finding by reference to the *lex mercatoria* or to the general principles of law.

(a)     In most of the cases this has been the international trade usages or the prevailing practices of international trade. This reference is in accordance with Article VII(1) of the European Convention, and Article 13(4) of the ICC Rules of Arbitration. In these situations the arbitrator need not search for a proper law of the contract.

(b)     Other cases show that the arbitrator has relied exclusively on a non-national law. In fact more and more arbitrators rely on the general principles of law without having been expressly or tacitly authorized to do so by the parties. This is now permissible under French law and probably also under Austrian law. Whether the courts of other European countries will permit it is open to doubt.

An arbitrator who relies solely on 'the general principles of law' is often unable to find principles which are truly 'general' in the sense that they belong to the common core of all legal systems or even the laws connected with the dispute. He will therefore, to a large extent, have to use his creativity and act as a social engineer.

If the parties direct the arbitrator to apply the *lex mercatoria* they will know its merits and its demerits, one of which is the scarcity of 'authority' on which the arbitrator can base his decision. They will know that the arbitrator cannot make scientific investigations to ascertain the 'common core' of many legal systems and that he will often have to use his *bon sens*.

For the same reason an agreement by the parties to have the case decided by *amiable composition* will also allow the arbitrator to apply the *lex mercatoria*. Whereas a selection of the *lex mercatoria* cannot be regarded as an agreement on *amiable composition*, the elements of the *lex mercatoria*, *ie*, international usages, general principles of law, arbitral case law, are appropriate bases for the decisions of an *amiable compositeur* in an international dispute.

Furthermore, a non-national arbitral tribunal is often selected in an effort to 'denationalize' the arbitration. Therefore such a tribunal should be permitted to apply the *lex mercatoria* to cases where the tribunal finds that the contents of the law applicable has [sic] not been ascertained. In these situations most national arbitral tribunals would do as the courts, and apply the *lex fori*. Non-national tribunals, however, have no real forum. Instead of applying the law of the casual seat of the tribunal it is an appropriate way out of the difficulty to apply the *lex mercatoria*. Also, if in a case where the law applicable to the contract has not been selected by the parties one of them pleads the application of the *lex mercatoria* a non-national arbitral tribunal should be permitted to comply with his request.

In other cases, however, where both parties have pleaded application of a national legal system the arbitrator will, it is submitted, act in excess of his powers if he applies the *lex mercatoria* to the contract.

## Conclusion

.   .   .

. . . Probably one day the arbitrators will coordinate their practices as regards the choice of the law applicable to the merits of the dispute. It is likely — and recommendable — that the arbitrator will then follow the trend of the modern legislations which converge with the case law of several countries. It has the following characteristics:

1       The law chosen by the parties governs the contract. Only a choice which appears clearly from indications in the contract or from the behaviour of the parties counts as a choice of law. The presumed intention is not considered.

2       In the absence of a choice of law by the parties the law with which the contract has its most significant connection will govern. This connection is based upon the relevant contacts notably the place of business or the habitual residence of the parties, and the place of performance. The parties' choice of the place of arbitration or the nationality of the arbitrator may also carry weight.

3       It is to be presumed that the contract has its most significant connection with the country where the party who is to effect the performance which is characteristic of the contract has his place of business. Thus sales of movables are presumed to be governed by the law of the seller's place of business, license contracts with the law of the licensor's place of business, and agency and distributorship contracts with the law of the agent's and the distributor's place of business.

However, employment contracts are presumed to be governed by the law of the place of work and contracts, the subject-matter of which are immovables, by the law of the place where the immovable is situated. Other special presumptions for specific contracts exist or may come into existance [sic].

These rules are as mentioned presumptions which mean that they do not apply if it appears from the circumstances of the case that the contract has its most significant connection with the law of another country.

\*    \*    \*

3.        *1. Westinghouse Int'l Property Co. (USA); 2. Westinghouse Electric, S.A. (Switzerland); 3. Westinghouse Electric Corp. (USA); 4. Burns & Roe Enterprise, Inc. (USA) v. 1. National Power Corp. (Philippines); and 2. The Republic of the Philippines (Philippines)*, ICC Arbitration No. 6401, Preliminary Award (Dec. 19, 1991), 7 MEALEY'S INT'L ARB. REP. B1 (Jan. 1992).

[In *Westinghouse et al v. Philippines*, which is discussed in detail *infra* p. 734, the arbitral tribunal was required to find the law governing the validity of the contract in question and the scope of a contractual agreement as to applicable law.]

The Westinghouse Contract contains the following clause in Article 27, which is entitled "Interpretation":

> The construction and interpretation of the terms and conditions of this Contract shall be in accordance with the laws of the Commonwealth of Pennsylvania, United States of America, not including, however, its Laws with respect to choice or conflict of Laws.

The Parties dispute the breadth of this provision, specifically whether it is intended to govern the choice of law concerning the question of the validity of the contract.

Because this is an ICC arbitration with its situs in Geneva, the Tribunal should consider in addition to the relevant contractual provisions the impact of the ICC rules and the law of Switzerland on the choice of law. Article 13(3) of the ICC Rules provides:

> The parties shall be free to determine the law to be applied by the arbitrator to the merits of the dispute. In the absence of any indication by the parties as to the

applicable law, the arbitrator shall apply the law designated as the proper law by the rule of conflict which he deems appropriate.

This provision has become part of the agreement of the parties by their choice of ICC arbitration and by the adoption of the ICC rules in the terms of reference. Under Article 13(3) of the ICC Rules, it is the duty of the Tribunal to determine the law designated by the rule of conflict that it deems appropriate if the Parties themselves have not made the determination.

Because the situs of the Arbitration is Switzerland, pursuant to Article 13(3) of the ICC rules the Tribunal chooses as the most appropriate rule of conflicts that offered by Chapter 12 of SPILA [Swiss Private International Law Act], which sets forth the Swiss law on international arbitration. Chapter 12 contains Article 187 (1), which provides:

The arbitral tribunal shall decide the dispute according to the rules of law chosen by the parties or, in the absence of such a choice, according to the rules of law with which the case has the closest connection.

Thus, both Article 13(3) of the ICC Rules and Article 187(1) of SPILA recognize that the parties to a dispute are free to select the law to be applied to the merits of their dispute and provide that, if the parties have made a choice, that choice is binding on the Tribunal. Hence, we now turn to the question whether Article 27 of the Construction Contract should be construed as a choice of governing law for all contractual issues, in particular the issue of contract validity and the issue of jurisdiction of the Tribunal.

## 1. The Scope of Article 27 of the Construction Contract

The parties disagree as to the scope of Article 27 of the Construction Contract. Westinghouse argues that a broad reading should be given to that article so as to subject all issues relating to the construction contract to the law of Pennsylvania.[214] The Defendants argue that by its terms, and consistent with its negotiating history, Article 27 applies only to the "construction and interpretation of the terms and conditions" of the contract.

The negotiating history of Article 27, concerning which there is no substantial disagreement between the parties, is not complex. The original draft of the Construction Contract proposed by Westinghouse in November 1974 included the following choice of law clause:

> The validity, construction, and performance of this Contract shall be governed by and interpreted in accordance with the laws of the State of New York, United States of America, not including however, its laws with respect to choice or conflict of laws.

Def. Ex. 80.

This article was discussed at a negotiating session held in Manila on January, 24, 1975, during which the parties agreed to strike the words "validity" and "performance" from the provision. Def. Ex. 87. Moreover, at this point in the negotiations Westinghouse sought to apply the laws of the Commonwealth of Pennsylvania and NPC sought to apply the laws of the Republic of the Philippines.

The wording of Article 27 was again discussed at a negotiating session held on March 24, 1975 in Manila. The minutes of that meeting reflect that the parties reached the following agreement concerning the provision:

> This should read: "The construction and interpretation of this Contract shall be governed by and interpreted in accordance with the laws of the Commonwealth of Pennsylvania, not including, however, its laws with respect to choice or conflict of laws."

---

[214] Article 27 provides that "the laws of the Commonwealth of Pennsylvania . . . not including, however, its Laws with respect to choice or conflict of Laws" shall control. Article 27 thus specifically excludes Pennsylvania's conflict of laws rules. In effect, Article 27 provides that only the internal law of Pennsylvania shall be applied, meaning the law that a Pennsylvania court would apply when a matter before it involves contacts solely with Pennsylvania.

Def. Ex. 94. The Construction Contract as executed contains essentially the same language as that agreed upon at that negotiating session.

The record is thus clear that the parties failed to agree upon the law to govern the validity or performance of the Construction Contract. Accordingly, pursuant to Article 13(3) of the ICC Rules, "in the absence of any indication by the parties" it is the duty of the Tribunal to determine the applicable law by selecting and applying the rule of conflict it deems appropriate.

## 2. Principles Applied in Selecting the Governing Law

Because the Tribunal has freedom of choice under Article 13(3) of the ICC Rules, it has chosen to apply Article 187(1) of SPILA, which provides that the Tribunal shall choose as the governing law "the rules of law with which the case has the closest connection." As the Tribunal has noted, the application of SPILA is most appropriate because Switzerland is the situs of this Arbitration. Under Article 187(1) of SPILA, the question remains with which law this Arbitration is most closely connected. The Tribunal notes that Article 187(1) refers broadly to "the case" and not any specific element thereof. Because Article 187(1) is part of a general codification of Swiss rules of conflict of laws, it is appropriate to examine other provisions of SPILA — even those not directly applicable to international arbitrations — in order to clarify the "closest connection" rule of Article 187(1).

Article 117(1) of SPILA echoes the requirement of Article 187(1) by providing that "[i]n the absence of a choice of law, the contract shall be governed by the law of the State with which it is most closely connected."

Paragraphs two and three of Article 117 of SPILA spell out presumptions as to which country is most closely connected with a contract, providing in substance that (a) there is a presumption that the closest connection is with the country in which the party making the characteristic performance has its habitual residence and (b) in a contract for construction or similar service contracts, the characteristic performance is the service performance.

Thus, Swiss law, unlike the conflict-of-laws rules of many jurisdictions, does not weigh contacts but proceeds on the basis of a statutory presumption.

In the Tribunal's view, the principles expressed in Article 117, though not mandatory with respect to international arbitrations, are nevertheless the best source of clarification of the concept of closest connection contained in Article 187(1) since they are part of the body of generally applicable Swiss rules of conflict of laws. There is no reason why the meaning of "closest connection" in Article 187(1), which is applicable to this arbitration should not be the same as the meaning of the same term in Article 117. In view of the above, the Tribunal has no reason to disagree with the statutory presumption of Article 117.

## 3. Application of the Governing Law to the Contracts

.    .    .

The Westinghouse Contract provided for the study, construction and equipment of a nuclear power plant on a turnkey basis. This type of contract is clearly a construction contract under Article 117(3)(c) of SPILA, in which the characteristic performance is the service provided by Westinghouse. Like the Burns & Roe Contract, the closest connection — and thus the governing law with respect to validity — is with the location where Westinghouse has its principal place of business, *i.e.*, the Commonwealth of Pennsylvania. The choice of the law of Pennsylvania to govern the validity of the Westinghouse Contract should not come as a surprise to the parties, as they had agreed in the contract itself that Pennsylvania's law was to govern the construction and interpretation of the contract. Indeed, common sense and general conflict-of-law principles favor the application of a single system of law to all issues raised in connection with a contract.

### Notes and Questions

1.  Section 187(2) of the Restatement (2d), Conflict of Laws authorizes contracting parties to choose the law applicable to their contractual duties except where the chosen law has no substantial relationship to the parties or to the transaction and there is no other reasonable basis for the parties choice. Would an arbitrator accept this limitation? Should he?

2. Exercise of the power of *amiable composition* is "intended to produce a binding and enforceable award; but one which the arbitral tribunal may reach without applying strict legal principles, if these appear unjust." A. ALLAN REDFERN & MARTIN HUNTER, LAW AND PRACTICE OF INTERNATIONAL COMMERCIAL ARBITRATION 35 (2d ed. 1990). Why do arbitration rules and laws require that an arbitrator may exercise those powers only if the parties have specifically so agreed?

3. It is also possible for parties to agree that the arbitrator shall decide *ex aequo et bono* ("in equity and good conscience"). How different is this from giving the arbitrator powers to adjudicate as *amiable compositeur*? For a provision treating the powers similarly, *see* Article 33 UNCITRAL Rules, and Article 28(3) UNCITRAL Model Law. For the view that the powers are significantly different, *see* M. Kerr, *Equity Arbitration in England*, 2 AM. REV. INT'L ARB. 377, 384 (1993); Mauro Rubino-Sammartano, *Amiable Compositeur (Joint Mandate to Settle) and* Ex Bono et Aequo *(Discretional Authority to Mitigate Strict Law)* 9 J. INT'L ARB. 5 (1992).

4. Can an arbitrator decide to apply principles of *lex mercatoria* to govern a contract even where the parties have not made a specific agreement to this effect? Will a court recognize and enforce the award? *See* Chapter 9, *infra*.

5. For further readings on the criteria used by arbitrators in making choice of law decisions, *see* H. NAON, CHOICE OF LAW PROBLEMS IN INTERNATIONAL COMMERCIAL ARBITRATION (1992); A.F.M. Maniruzzaman, *Conflict of Laws in International Arbitration: Practice and Trends*, 9 ARB. INT'L 371 (1993).

## D. OTHER CHOICE OF LAW PROBLEMS FOR THE ARBITRATOR.

### 1. MANDATORY RULES OF LAW

The dispute before the arbitrator may be affected by laws other than those chosen by the parties. These typically are laws in jurisdictions having a material relationship, and some internationally recognized legislative and/or adjudicative competence over, the transaction (frequently the place of performance). These laws cover such subjects as exchange controls, export limitations, competition law, and others. Should the arbitrator apply or take into consideration the public law desiderata?

> a.   Pierre Mayer, *Mandatory Rules of Law in International Arbitration*, 2 ARB. INT'L 274, 275-77 (1986).

. . . Neither the various international treaties dealing with arbitration (such as the New York and Geneva Conventions), nor such a comprehensive modern national law as the French Nouveau Code de Procédure Civile, contain the slightest provision with respect to the relationship between mandatory rules of law and the arbitral process. On the other hand, no less than four international treaties contain at least one article dealing with the impact of mandatory rules of law before national judges.

Although developments in judicial case-law is not the focus of this article, the abundance of material in this related area may well suggest a definition of mandatory rules of law valid in arbitration as well. There are in fact many definitions. For present purposes, we may be inspired by those given in the various treaties, which yield the following synthesis: a mandatory rule (*loi de police* in French) is an imperative provision of law which must be applied to an international relationship irrespective of the law that governs that relationship.

To put it another way: mandatory rules of law are a matter of public policy (*ordre public*) and moreover reflect a public policy so commanding that they must be applied even if the general body of law to which they belong is not competent by application of the relevant rule of conflict of laws. It is the imperative nature *per se* of such rules that make them applicable. One is thus led to conclude that there is an approach to mandatory rules of law different from the classical method of conflict of laws. In matters of contract, the effect of a mandatory rule of law of a given country is to create an obligation to apply such a rule, or indeed simply a possibility of so doing, despite the fact that the parties have expressly or implicitly subjected their contracts to the law of another country.

Among the mandatory rules of law most frequently encountered the following may be cited: competition laws; currency controls; environmental protection laws; measures of embargo, blockade or boycott; or laws falling in the rather different category of legislation designed to protect parties presumed to be in an inferior bargaining position, such as wage earners or commercial agents.

This list of examples reveals that the dearth of sources is not only surprising but also paradoxical, because all the types of rules just mentioned impinge on relationships that are contractual in nature. The fact is that most international contracts contain arbitration clauses; if they give rise to a dispute, it will more often be brought before an arbitrator than before a judge. How can one then explain that an issue which is essentially of concern to arbitrators is so seldom studied in this perspective, and that international treaties which deal with the issue of mandatory rules of law do not even mention its potential relevance in the context of arbitration?

Three types of reasons have probably been operative. The first is that such scholarly work as has focused on mandatory rules of law has been carried out more from the perspective of classical private international law rather than from that favouring the development of the law of international trade. One finds little willingness in international trade law to welcome the mandatory and possibly disruptive intervention of the State in the conclusion and performance of contracts.

Secondly, the international treaties that relate to arbitrations date from a period when the notion of mandatory rules of law was hardly ever discussed. More recent conventions which deal with mandatory rules have been designed not for arbitration, but for judicial assistance. Their draftsmen, specialists in that particular area, have tended not to venture into a domain relatively unfamiliar to them.

A final reason is to be found in the singular complexity of the problem of applying mandatory rules of law whenever it arises before an arbitrator. Assuming that the arbitrator does not have any reticence of an intellectual nature to abandon the conflict of laws method in favour of that of mandatory rules of law, he would then be confronted, unlike the national judge, with a conflict between the will of the State having promulgated the mandatory rule of law, on the one hand, and, on the other hand, the will of the parties — from which indeed, his authority is derived. Moreover, he must resolve this conflict from two points of view: for the purposes of his own forum, but also taking into account an external forum. He must thus first decide the issue by reference to the contractual freedom which in arbitration is the cornerstone of the process of resolving conflicts of law; this is his own forum. But at the same time, he should concern himself with what may happen to his award, and in particular with the risk that if he does not apply a mandatory rule of law the award will not be recognized by the country having passed the law. The relevant considerations are thus very complex, and all the more so since it is often difficult to anticipate what will happen to an award; there may be several potential execution jurisdictions, and one cannot always predict the attitude of judges who may be called upon to examine the award.

The best way to approach the problem is thus probably to analyze the existing corpus of arbitral awards. One should not however expect too much. First of all, arbitral case-law is not abundant, at least with respect to published awards. Next, arbitrators are not particularly motivated by any desire to contribute to jurisprudence and accordingly tend to proceed by affirmation rather than persuasion. And the affirmations one finds in arbitral awards tend to be inconsistent.

In order to compensate for the insufficiency of *lex lata*, the present author will venture to propose solutions *de lege ferenda*, putting himself in the position of an arbitrator faced with a litigant invoking an alleged mandatory rule of law. Such an arbitrator must deal with three questions :

(1) May he apply mandatory rules of law as a matter of general principle?

(2) If so, *should* he apply them as a matter of general principle?

(3) If so, which specific mandatory rules should he apply?

### Notes and Questions

1. In the United States the international arbitrator must (if his award is to be recognized) apply mandatory public law norms such as those provided by the Sherman Act and its treble damages provision. In *Mitsubishi*, it was determined that the presumption in favor of arbitration and the arbitrability of disputes should be recognized and that the allegations concerning violations of the Sherman Act could be considered by the arbitrators, who were not preempted by federal court jurisdiction. To reach that result, one of the issues considered by the U.S. Supreme Court was whether in fact international arbitral tribunals were capable of adjudicating the complex economic and policy issues involved when mandatory law issues were involved. *See supra* Chapter 3, Part III.

2. Given the operation of concurrent jurisdiction which was discussed in Chapter 1, two or more states may insist that their mandatory wills apply to the arbitration. How shall the arbitrator decide?

A party may sometimes claim that mandatory laws applicable to him at his domicile have the effect of nullifying the arbitration agreement or arbitration procedure or offer him a substantive defense to non-performance of the contract in issue. The international arbitrator must apply choice of law concepts to such clauses but will also take into account the fact that parties choose international arbitration at a neutral site over court proceedings at the defendant's domicile, among other reasons, to reduce, to the extent possible, the effect of hometown procedural measures.

b.      *Dalmia Cement, Ltd. (India) v. National Bank of Pakistan (Pakistan)*, ICC Arbitration No. 1512 (Pierre Lalive, sole arbitrator), Final award (Mar. 1, 1971), 1 YEARBOOK OF COMMERCIAL ARBITRATION 128 (1976) (extracts).

[By a number of agreements concluded between 1962 and 1964, claimant Dalmia, carrying on business in India, agreed to sell cement factories in India to a Pakistani company, which agreed in return to deliver to Dalmia quantities of cement over a period of three years. The National Bank of Pakistan entered into a separate guarantee agreement with Dalmia promising monetary compensation in the event of non-delivery of the cement by the Pakistani company, in the amount of 94 Pakistani Rupees for every ton of cement not delivered. The guarantee agreement contained an ICC arbitration clause. In 1965 there was a period of active hostilities (September 6-22) between India and Pakistan, during which the respective governments adopted legislative measures restricting commercial relations between their nationals. Combat ceased after the Security Council Resolution ordered a cease fire on September 22, 1965. The Soviet Union then offered its good offices which led to the Tashkent Declaration on 10 January 1966, pursuant to which hostilities were ended by agreement among the parties. *See* 5 ILM 320 (1966). During the entire period of the contract, no cement was delivered, and the National Bank of Pakistan did not honor its guarantee. Dalmia commenced arbitration against the Bank, and Professor Pierre Lalive was appointed as sole arbitrator by the ICC. The arbitration took place in Switzerland. The arbitrator rendered two preliminary awards confirming his jurisdiction. The first, in 1967, rejected a claim that a state of war existed between India and Pakistan, putting an end to the arbitrator's jurisdiction. The second, in 1970, found that the Pakistani defendant by its agreement to arbitrate was precluded from seeking from a Pakistani court an injunction against the arbitral proceedings, *see* 5 Yearbook of Commercial Arbitration 170 (1980). The final seventy-page award on the merits of March 1, 1971 was summarized in a Yearbook of Commercial Arbitration extract.]

### 1. *Applicable procedural law*

Considering the parties' absence of choice, the arbitrator followed in the event of no provision being made in the Rules, the law of the country in which the proceedings are taking place, that is to say, in fact, the Code of Civil Procedure of the Canton of Geneva, Switzerland.

As a result of the above, the various references made by the parties to a Pakistani or Indian Code of Procedure, or to the juridical decisions of one or the other of these countries, were held irrelevant and could not be taken into account by the arbitrator.

This does not of course mean that the results obtained by the latter, based on I.C.C Rules and, possibly, on the rules of procedure of Geneva, will necessarily differ from those reached by a judge or arbitrator subject to the Pakistani or Indian Rules of procedure. By virtue of the I.C.C Rules (notably articles 16 et seq., in particular 20, 21 and 31), the arbitrator has a wide discretion in matters of procedure, for instance, he has the right to proceed the hearing of the case 'by all appropriate means' (cf. Article 20, French Text which is somewhat more precise than the English text), having the power (but not the duty) of hearing witnesses, if he believes this is useful. This freedom of decision regarding the proceedings does not, needless to say, signify complete and unfettered discretion. In applying and interpreting the Rules of Conciliation and Arbitration of the I.C.C, in keeping with their spirit and in accordance with the nature and essence of international business arbitration, the arbitrator cannot avoid the duty of abiding by the general fundamental principles of procedure.

[The arbitrator rejected the defense of the Pakistani Bank that because of the intervening hostilities it should be liberated from its guarantee obligations under the English law concept (recognized in India and Pakistan) of frustration of contract due to changed circumstances (*rebus sic stantibus*). The arbitrator found that the conditions for the application of these principles had not been fulfilled in the circumstances of the case.]

.     .     .

## 3. *Applicable law as to the substance of the dispute*

A.     A preliminary question was briefly raised, *i.e.* that of the system of private international law which should be applied by the arbitrator when deciding any question of conflict.

> "The international arbitrator has no *lex fori*, to which he can borrow rules of conflict of laws. The Rules of Conciliation and Arbitration of the International Chamber of Commerce, which governs the present proceedings, do not contain any provision on this point.
>
> The problem has often been debated in doctrinal writings, where various solutions are put forward for instance application of the private international law of the seat of arbitration (in the present case, the Swiss private international law); or application of principles of comparative private international law; or application lastly, of the conflict of laws, if any (which does not seem to be the case for the I.C.C. unless it is thought to be the conflict of laws of the seat of arbitration), which governs the arbitration proceedings, etc.
>
> However this may be, the three or four solutions just mentioned with regard to

the various systems of private international law to be applied by the arbitrator, would, in the present case, lead to the same practical result in all likelihood, since there exists a large measure of agreement and concordance, on the question of applicable law to contracts, not only between the various systems deriving from English conflict of laws, but also, more generally, between the main systems of conflict of laws in the world. In the field of contract, it is possible to speak, to a large extent, of a common or universal private international law, at least whenever the question is that of the law governing the contract when there is an expressed choice by the parties.

There are few principles more universally admitted in private international law than that referred to by the standard terms of the 'proper law of the contract,' according to which the law governing the contract is that which has been chosen by the parties, whether expressly or (with certain differences of variations according to the various systems) tacitly. The differences which may be observed here between different national systems relate only to the possible limits of the parties power to choose the applicable law or to certain special questions or to modalities, but not to the principle itself, which is universally accepted etc."

B.   The Bank Guarantee expressly provided for the application of Indian Law. Since the parties have made an *express* choice, it is irrelevant to examine authorities or doctrinal writings on the question of tacit or implied intention, or of the power of the Court to infer a selection of law, or what facts and incidents of the case should be examined and taken into account in order to decide with which legal system the contract is 'most substantially connected.' The arbitrator has no power to substitute his own choice to that of the parties, as soon as there exists an expressed, clear and unambiguous choice, and no sufficient reason has been put forward to refuse effects to such a choice.

C.      Indian law thus being applicable to the contract, the question arises whether the Pakistani emergency legislation, which considered as illegal any payment to an Indian party by reason of the hostilities, could have freed the Pakistani Bank from its obligation.

The arbitrator first considered what might be in this respect the possible effect of the law of the place of performance ('*lex loci solutionis*'). The arbitrator reasoned: This question is described as 'uncertain' or 'highly controversial' in the leading books on the subject (cf. *Dicey-Morris*, op. cit., Rule 132 p. 761 and Rule 134 pp. 776-77; *Chitty* op. cit., vol. I No. 1283, *Cheshire*, op. cit., 7th ed., p. 211-13). The prevailing trend of opinion, however, in the absence of any direct authority on this point, seems clearly to favor the answer, that the proper law of the contract, and *not* the law of the place of payment determines the questions whether the debtor is discharged by law of his contractual obligation.

To return now to the rules of private international law on the law governing supervening illegality or impossibility of performance. While it is uncertain whether the foreign law of the place of performance ('foreign' in relation to the forum) determines this question, on one point, at least, there appears to exist unanimity; where the contract is legal by its proper law and when such law is the law of the place of performance.

Where is, then, in this case, the 'locus solutionis' or place of performance? Notwithstanding the Defendants argument to the effect that it is in Pakistan, the arbitrator saw no alternative but to give effect to the unambiguous terms of the Bank Guarantee whereby the defendant expressly undertook *to pay in India*.

In summing up the arbitrator concluded that, in spite of its very able and learned arguments, the defendant has not been able to show, and indeed could not possibly succeed in showing, that Pakistani law was or is the proper law of the Bank Guarantee or the '*lex loci solutionis*,' and that it governs the question of discharge by frustration or of supervening illegality or impossibility of performance.

Accordingly the Bank was condemned to pay under its guarantee.

[Recognition proceedings were brought in England, and the award was recognized and given effect in the High Court (*Dalmia Dairy Industries v. National Bank of Pakistan*) Judgment of Mr. Justice Kerr of February 27, 1976, whose judgment was confirmed by the Court of Appeal (decision of May 18, 1977), both reported at 2 Lloyds Rep. 223 (1978).]

\* \* \*

Bribery and corruption raise fundamental policy issues which the arbitrator must address when they are presented in a case before him. In some cases, they may invalidate the agreement obtained by their aid or even (exceptionally) the arbitration agreement itself. Outright bribery is no doubt condemned by all legal systems, but its legal effect on agreements that were secured by it may depend on the applicable law, as well as government regulatory legislation in force at the place of performance of the contract that may interpose itself when the question of the validity and performance of a contract governed by a different law involves allegations of bribery. The whole scale of problems was examined in the *Westinghouse* arbitration.

c.       *1. Westinghouse International Property Co. (USA); 2. Westinghouse Electric, S.A. (Switzerland); 3. Westinghouse Electric Corp. (USA); 4. Burns & Roe Enterprise, Inc. (USA) v. 1. National Power Corp. (Philippines); and 2. The Republic of the Philippines (Philippines)*, ICC Arb. No. 6401, Preliminary Award (Dec. 19, 1991), 7 MEALEYS INT'L ARB. REP.. B1 (Jan. 1992).

[In July 1973, President Ferdinand Marcos announced plans to build the Philippines' first nuclear power plant and, in January 1974, a presidential decree placed National Power Corporation ("NPC"), the state-owned electricity company, under direct supervision of the Office of the President. There was a fierce battle between Westinghouse and General Electric (with lesser competition from French, German, and Japanese companies) to obtain the construction contract, which was eventually awarded to Westinghouse in June of 1974, and a contract containing an ICC arbitration clause was signed on February 9, 1976. Construction was substantially completed in 1985 but the plant was not accepted by the Philippines, did not receive an operating license, and never went into operation. In February 1986, the Marcos Government was overthrown and the new government, headed by President Corazón Aquino, decided not to operate the plant. On December 1, 1988, Westinghouse brought arbitration against both NPC and the Philippines, claiming that it was owed tens of millions of dollars for unpaid items, price adjustments and cost increases resulting from excusable delay. A claim by Burns & Roe under a related consulting contract was consolidated by agreement in the arbitration proceeding (but its role in the arbitration is not considered in this excerpt). The defendants denied all the claims, and, as a preliminary issue, alleged that the contract and its arbitration clause were invalid because they were procured by bribery.[215] It was also alleged as a preliminary issue that the Philippines was not subject to arbitral jurisdiction.]

---

[215] The Philippines would have preferred to have the bribery charges tried in US federal court and brought proceedings before the U.S. district court in New Jersey on the same date that Westinghouse filed its claim in arbitration. The district court stayed the proceeding pending arbitration, however. *See Republic of the Philippines v. Westinghouse Electric Corp.*, 714 F.Supp. 1362 (D.N.J. 1989).

As noted above, the doctrine of *Kompetenz-Kompetenz* gives the Tribunal jurisdiction to determine its own jurisdiction. Whether the Tribunal ultimately has jurisdiction to resolve the disputes that have arisen under the contracts depends upon the validity of the arbitration clauses, which in turn may be influenced by the invalidity of the contracts themselves. Accordingly, in this section the Tribunal will analyze those issues.

Defendants have made several attacks upon the validity of the arbitration clauses and the contracts in an effort to establish that this Tribunal does not have jurisdiction over this dispute. Their major attack is that the arbitration clauses in both the Burns & Roe Contract and the Westinghouse Contract are "invalid and unenforceable" because the contracts were procured by bribery. Def. Br. at 125. Their secondary attack, which is raised only with respect to the Westinghouse arbitration clause, is that that arbitration clause itself is invalid and unenforceable because "NPC was forced to accept the Westinghouse arbitration clause through bribe-induced pressure from President Marcos." *Id.* at 130. In addition, the Defendants also argue, to a lesser extent, that Section 4(a) of the Philippines Anti-Graft and Corrupt Practices Act ("Anti-Graft Act") renders the contracts and the arbitration clauses contained therein void, divesting this Tribunal of jurisdiction.

The Tribunal's analysis of these contentions of Defendants will first consider the issue of bribery with respect to the contracts and the Westinghouse arbitration clause and thereafter the issue of the application of Section 4(a) of the Anti-Graft Act.

## A. The Definition of Bribery Applied by the Tribunal

Before turning to a detailed analysis of the evidence upon which Defendants' position rests, it is convenient to consider the legality of the argument. The initial position of Defendants was that they would establish bribery by showing that Burns & Roe and Westinghouse paid money or other consideration of value to Marcos for his using his influence to have the Consulting Contract and the Construction Contract awarded to them. In the final stages of the preliminary phase of this Arbitration, Defendants modified their position and argued that bribery would be established by showing that Claimants intended to pay money or other consideration of value to Marcos, and that he agreed to accept such payments to have the contracts awarded to them, irrespective of whether or not they could establish that Marcos actually received any payments. It may be said that this new position of Defendants takes a less strict view of bribery than their initial position.

.    .    .

It is clear that, if the Defendants are able to prove that Marcos received a payment, it would be a clear instance of bribery. However, the Tribunal is prepared also to examine whether the Defendants have been able to prove bribery under their own definition. Therefore, in order to establish that the Consulting Contract or the Construction Contract is invalid and void by reason of bribery, Defendants must establish by clear and convincing evidence the following essential elements of their claim of bribery. With respect to each challenged contract, Defendants must show:

(a)    that the alleged briber intended to provide a payment or another thing of value to President Marcos and

(b)    that President Marcos agreed to accept this consideration, either directly or through Disini, in exchange for his directing that NPC enter into the challenged contract with the briber.

Defendants need not show that consideration was actually received by Marcos. However, if Defendants are unable to make such a showing, they must prove the existence of an actual agreement. This is necessary because evidence of payments would imply the existence of an agreement; in the absence of such evidence, there must be additional proof that there was an agreement. Put somewhat differently, Defendants face a higher burden of proof concerning the existence of an agreement if they are unable to prove actual payments.

.    .    .

In order to establish that the Construction Contract was procured by bribery, Defendants must prove by clear and convincing evidence that (a) Westinghouse intended to provide a payment to President Marcos and (b) President Marcos agreed to accept this payment through Disini in exchange for his directing NPC to enter into the contract with Westinghouse.

Defendants have presented a fair amount of evidence supporting the first element of bribery. Even if that evidence does not conclusively establish that Westinghouse actually knew that Marcos would receive some of their SSR payments to Disini, it appears from that same evidence that Westinghouse would not have been surprised or bothered by that fact.

However, Defendants have had a more difficult time establishing the second element of bribery. It is clear that Marcos used his power to push the Westinghouse proposal. . . . However, there is also conflicting evidence on this score. For instance, at the same time Marcos was supporting Westinghouse, he was also considering proposals from other companies, including German nuclear reactor manufacturer Kraftwerk Union. *See, e.g.*, West. Exs. 75. 92.

Most significantly, there is no direct evidence that Marcos supported Westinghouse because he expected to benefit from the SSR payments to Herdis. The circumstantial evidence also fails to prove that Marcos promoted Westinghouse because he expected to receive some of the SSR payments to Herdis. There is no evidence either of any agreement between Marcos and Westinghouse, or that Disini acted as agent for Marcos. At most, the evidence indicates that some Westinghouse employees thought that Marcos owned some of Herdis and that Marcos had documents in his possession that outlines the commissions Herdis was supposed to receive for the contracts. However, there is no evidence that Marcos received any share of those commissions. Although Defendants argue that the circumstantial evidence establishes that Marcos must have received a share of the commissions, the Tribunal is not persuaded.

.        .        .

The Tribunal notes that Defendants have had unusual access to information — far beyond that available to the usual litigant — in order to develop their case in this Arbitration, including information derived from the Swiss government, the Philippines investigation and the United States federal court proceeding. Nonetheless, on the record before it, the Tribunal can only conclude that Defendants have failed to carry their burden of proving Westinghouse's alleged bribery.

## 2. The Westinghouse Arbitration Clause

Because Defendants' strongest attack on jurisdiction rests on their contention that the Construction Contract as a whole was obtained by bribery and that that bribery invalidated the arbitration clause, the Tribunal considered that question first. Having found that the Construction Contract was not obtained by bribery, the Tribunal new turns to a consideration of Defendants' separate argument that the Westinghouse arbitration clause was itself obtained by bribery.[216]

[The tribunal found that NPC had not proved that the arbitration clause had been forced or imposed on it, nor that President Marcos had intervened in respect to the arbitration clause. Even less had it been proved that any such pressure was the result of bribery.]

. . .

The Tribunal does not find in the documents that have been submitted by the parties any trace of a fundamental disagreement on the arbitration provision, except for the usual differences of approach as mentioned above. Moreover, the Tribunal notes that it has become standard practice for important international contracts, such as the Construction Contract to be referred to international arbitration to avoid the submission of future disputes to the national courts of the domicile of the parties. Finally, it appears that in other contracts entered into by NPC with third parties around the same time, the arbitration provisions were as broad in scope as the provision in the Westinghouse Contract and not limited to technical matters. *See, e.g.*, West. Exs. 174, 195.

. . .

On the basis of this analysis of the evidence with respect to the negotiating history of the Construction Contract and of its arbitration clause, the Tribunal finds that Defendants have not established that the arbitration clause was obtained through bribery of Marcos.

---

[216] Defendants do not make a similar argument with respect to the Burns & Roe arbitration clause.

D.    THE ISSUE OF THE ANTI-GRAFT ACT

Defendants also contend that the Burns & Roe Contract and the Westinghouse Contract are void because of violation of a Philippine statute known as the Anti-Graft Act.

1.    THE SCOPE OF THE ANTI-GRAFT ACT

[Article 4(a) of the Philippine Anti-Graft Act prevented any person having a close personal relation with any public official from receiving a gift or other pecuniary advantage from any person profiting from a contract in which the official had to intervene. It was alleged that the statute was violated by the contract between Disini and Westinghouse and that as a consequence the Westinghouse-NPR Construction Contract was void. The Tribunal found that even if Section 4(a) had been violated the consequence would have been that Disini's receipt of payment was unlawful and restitution could have been required. The statute did not provide for invalidation of the Disini-Westinghouse contract. The tribunal also considered, secondarily, that under the controlling Pennsylvania law the Construction Contract would not have been void even if the Commission Agreement between Westinghouse and Disini had been void as a consequence of the Anti-Graft Act. The Construction Contract was not sufficiently connected to the prior Commission Agreement to render it invalid.]

Notes and Questions

1.  In the *Dalmia* case the arbitrator found that since the proper law of the contract was Indian law, and the place of performance of the contract was India, the interdiction of payment by Pakistani law, the law of one of the parties, would not prevent the award of damages by the arbitral tribunal sitting at a neutral place of arbitration. What if the place of performance had been Pakistan?

2.  When the parties have chosen a neutral arbitration site and a proper law other than the law of the place of performance, may the arbitrator apply the mandatory rules of that place of performance? Should he?

3.  If neither party raises the issue of the applicability of a mandatory provision of law may the arbitrator raise it himself? Should he? Does it make any difference if the mandatory provision is found in the law governing the contract or in some other law?

4. In *Westinghouse* the issue before the arbitrator was the validity of a contract allegedly obtained by bribery. Imagine a dispute under a contract *to bribe*, such as a contract between an enterprise and an agent entered into for the purpose of paying bribes or making illicit payments to a third party. What should be the attitude of the arbitrator? *Compare* ICC Arbitration No. 1110 (1963), *reported in* JULIAN D.M. LEW, APPLICABLE LAW IN INTERNATIONAL COMMERCIAL ARBITRATION 553-55 (1978) (refusing to take arbitral jurisdiction over a contract whose purpose was bribery, on the grounds that the contract was void as contrary to public policy and the dispute was non-arbitrable) *with* ICC Arbitration No. 5622 (1988), *reported in* 1993 SWISS BULL. 216 (Agreement subject to Swiss law providing for commission payments in connection with public works project in Algeria which violated provisions of Algerian law forbidding payments to intermediaries. Arbitrator finds agreement null and void in its entirety. Arbitration award set aside, as contrary to Swiss public policy and the applicable Swiss law governing the contract, by Cour de Justice of Geneva whose decision was confirmed by the Federal Tribunal on April 17, 1990, decisions summarized in 1993 SWISS BULL. 250-54; comments in Vincent Heuzé *La Morale, l'Arbitre et le Juge*, 1993 REV. ARB. 179.)

## 2. PRESCRIPTION AND INTEREST

A number of applicable law issues continue to raise troublesome problems in international arbitration: statutes of limitation or prescription, interest to be awarded as damages, and the arbitrator's power to award exemplary or punitive damages. Issues of prescription frequently come up as preliminary questions. Issues of interest and penalties, which are by their nature contingent, usually come up at the time of final award, but they too raise questions of legal principle similar to those involving limitations. In all of these areas, the arbitrator wants to reach a legal solution which is also fair, taking account of the situation of the parties and the facts of a dispute. On the other hand, issues of prescription are based entirely on statutory law, with no apparent play for equitable considerations.

The initial characterization of a prescription problem is fraught with difficulty, for a limitations period may be considered as a question of substance, in which case it would ordinarily be determined by the proper law of the contract, or as a question of procedure, in which case the law of procedure (most likely the law of the seat of arbitration) would apply. Does a procedural limitation period apply to an international arbitration or is it intended only to proscribe actions before local courts? Does the limitation period at the seat of arbitration have a strong connection with the arbitral dispute? What if the seat were chosen, not by the parties, but by an arbitral institution?

ALAN REDFERN & MARTIN HUNTER, LAW AND PRACTICE OF INTERNATIONAL COMMERCIAL ARBITRATION 194-96 (2d ed. 1991).

Time limits for bringing legal proceedings by way of arbitration or litigation are imposed by the law of most, if not all, countries. It is said that the interest of the state is that litigation should be finite; *interest republicae ut sit finis litium*. Whereas contractual time limits are often short, generally a matter of months, those imposed by law are longer, generally a number of years. This in itself creates no special problem. In principle it is right that a claimant should have adequate time in which to prepare and bring a claim. Where problems are likely to arise is in the conflict of laws. In particular, there may be a difference in both the length and the nature of the time limits laid down by different national systems of law. One system of law, for example, may provide that claims under a contract are to be brought within three years, whilst another system may classify time limits as matters of substance, governed by another system of law may allow five years. More importantly, one system of law may classify time limits as matters of procedure, to be governed by the law of the place of arbitration, whilst the same law as that which governs all the other substantive matters in issue, that is to say the proper law of the contract.

Such differences between national laws provide fertile ground for conflict. For example, the proper law of the contract may impose a five-year limit within which a claim must be referred to the courts or to arbitration, whereas the law of the place of arbitration may impose a three-year limit. If a claim is referred to arbitration four years after the cause of action has arise, which time limit should prevail? If it is the proper law of the contract, the three-year limit imposed by the law of the place of arbitration may be ignored; but if the procedural law of the place of arbitration is to be applied, the arbitral proceedings may be barred by lapse of time. This example indicates that, if time is running out, it is advisable to look carefully at the intended place or places of arbitration and to choose one which will give the most favourable result for the claimant; this is sometimes known as "forum shopping."

Civil law countries have tended to classify provisions relating to time limits as matters of substance, whilst the approach of common law countries has been to treat questions relating to time limits as matters of procedure. However, a trend has developed in some common law countries towards classifying foreign laws governing time limits as matters of substance.[217] Where there is likely to be a problem over time limits, the provisions contained in the relevant legal systems (usually those of the proper law of the contract and the law of the place of arbitration) must be studied to see what time limits they impose and whether they classify those limits as substantive or procedural.

. . .

The issues of interest to be assessed by the arbitrator as part of his award raise similar conflict of laws complexities. Three laws must be consulted: the law governing the substance of the dispute (ordinarily the proper law of the contract); the law governing the arbitration (ordinarily the procedural law of the place of arbitration); and the law of the likely place of enforcement. This last criteria is always hypothetical as one can never be sure where an attempt will be made to enforce an award and it is difficult to reconcile with other legal standards the arbitrator may be required to follow. Nevertheless, the practice may have particular importance concerning the issue of interest because in some areas of the world, particularly Moslem countries, the payment of interest may be either forbidden as usury or severely limited. At the same time, it is acknowledged by all modern economic systems that delay in payment causes a damage independent of the original fault, and that the damages caused by long delayed payment may easily exceed in protracted proceedings the original harm itself. This may lead the international arbitrator simply to consider pre-award interest as an element of damages to be evaluated based on factual and economic data pertinent to the parties and the dispute.

### Notes and Questions

1. In *Lex Mercatoria: An Arbitrator's View*, 6 ARB. INT'L 133, 143 (1990), *supra* Chapter 2, p. 233, Professor Lowenfeld suggests that where statutes of limitations of the two relevant jurisdictions have run, but a multilateral treaty to which both jurisdictions are party has a different prescription period, the treaty would govern. Is this *lex mercatoria*? Is this a conflicts analysis? Is this correct? Discuss.

---

[217] This approach was adopted in England by the Foreign Limitation Periods Act 1984.

2. In *Grove Skanska v. Lockheed Aircraft Int'l AG*, ICC Arbitration, No. 3903 (1981) *summarized in* David J. Branson and Richard E. Wallace, Jr., *Awarding Interest in International Commercial Arbitration: Establishing a Uniform Approach*, 28 VA. J. INT'L L. 919, 934 (1988), the defendant, Lockheed, the breaching party, argued that interest should not be awarded on the late-payment sum because the contract did not expressly provide for interest. In rejecting that contention, the tribunal said that "the only damages for failure to pay a sum due on the appointed day is interest," and that "the Agreement provides for a series of dates when payments are due from the Prime Contractor to the Subcontractor." Therefore, the tribunal found that, "failure to allow interest would mean that the stated obligation to comply with the due dates was backed by no legal sanction. . . . Interest is the sanction imposed by law for non-compliance with the due date for payment. 'It is not necessary there should be any agreement for interest in order to permit a party to recover it.'" The arbitrators therefore adopted the widespread view that interest must be awarded whether or not proof of damage due to late payment is proffered. For the rate of interest the arbitrators found that even though the agreement provided that it was governed by "the law of the State of New York (procedural and substantive)" interest would not be limited to the statutory rate in New York (6%) which they found applied only to court actions and not to arbitration proceedings.

3. In marked contrast to the decision in ICC Arbitration No. 3903 is the determination in ICC Arbitration No. 4606 (1985), *Parker Drilling Co. v. Sonatrach*, I.C.C. Case No. 4606 (Award of Jan. 7, 1985) (unreported), *summarized in* David J. Branson and Richard E. Wallace, Jr., *Awarding Interest in International Commercial Arbitration: Establishing a Uniform Approach*, 28 VA. J. INT'L. L, 923, 937 (1988) in which the arbitrators declined to award any interest. The underlying dispute, between an Algerian company, Sonatrach, and a Bahamian company, Parker Drilling Company, Ltd., involved a series of claims arising from the alleged breach of a contract for drilling services in Algeria. The parties had specified that the contract would be governed and interpreted according to Algerian law. The arbitrators therefore determined that only the contract and Algerian law were relevant. The tribunal concluded that the Algerian Civil Code, which clearly deals with compensation of prejudice suffered by a creditor, "remains silent on the question of late-payment interests."

> The arbitrators next found that the absence of an express prohibition of interest in a business context was merely intended by the legislators to permit business to provide for interest in their contracts. In the absence of an express contractual provision, however, the legislators intended Islamic law to apply. The arbitrators supported their interpretation by citing to Article One of the Algerian Civil Code, which provides that "in the absence of any legal disposition, the judge will pronounce according to the principles of Moslem law." Because the contract in question did not contain an express provision for interest and Islamic law "rejects late-payment interests," the arbitrators concluded that Parker was not entitled to any late-payment interest.

With regard to compensatory interest, the arbitrators held that Algerian law required proof of a "<u>special</u> prejudice" resulting from the non-execution of payments. It had not been proved.

4.        In *McCollough & Co., Inc. v. The Ministry of Post Telegraph and Telephone*, 11 Iran-U.S. Cl. Trib. Rep. 3 (1986), the Tribunal entered an award in favor of the U.S. claimant for unpaid invoices and other amounts due under contract with the Iranian Ministry of Post. The Iran-U.S. Claim Tribunal was to apply the legal principles set forth in the Article V of the Claim Settlement Declaration which provided: "The Tribunal shall decide all cases on the basis of respect for law, applying such choice of law rules and principles of commercial and international law as the Tribunal determines to be applicable, taking into account relevant usages of the trade, contract provisions and changed circumstances." Chairman Virally said:

> [t]hat no uniform rule of law relating to interest has emerged from the practice in transnational arbitration, in contrast to the well developed rules regarding the determination of the standard of compensation for damages resulting from a breach of contract where the rule of full compensation usually is applied. No comparable rule has taken form governing the rate of interest or the time from which interest is to be computed. This is illustrated by the frequent use of the word 'fair' to qualify the rate chosen, or by the equally frequent references to the "discretion of the arbitrator." The absence of a uniform rule does not, however, imply the absence of general principles. On the contrary, two principles or guidelines, of general import, albeit of delicate implementation, can be deduced from the international practice briefly described above.

> The first principle is that under normal circumstances, and especially in commercial cases, interest is allocated on the amounts awarded as damages in order to compensate for the delay with which the payment to the successful party is made. . .

> The second principle is that the rate of interest must be reasonable, taking due account of all pertinent circumstances, which the Tribunal is entitled to consider by virtue of the discretion it is empowered to exercise in this field.

>        .     .     .

> [t]he Claimant has not submitted any specific reasons for the higher rate of interest claimed against the Respondent PTT. The Tribunal has further taken into account that at issue in this Case are ordinary contracts of a commercial nature, governed by Iranian law, without any provisions for applicable rates of interest in case of delayed payments, and that the breaches of contract at issue relate largely to non-payment of invoices. On the basis of the foregoing the Tribunal determines that a fair rate of interest to be awarded on all the amounts determined to be due and owing to the Claimant is 10% per annum. . . (Opinion at paras. 97-99, 104)

Consider the concurring and dissenting opinion of Judge C. Brower (at para. 24):

> Conceptually, interest is an item of damage. Its award is intended as compensation for the temporary withholding of money, and its measure is the cost of such deprivation. In a perfect world such measure would be the actual cost to the injured creditor of replacing it, *i.e.*, the interest paid for borrowing substitute funds, or the earnings lost due to its unavailability, *i.e.*, the return on such sums had they been received and reinvested.

> .   .   .

> While, as noted, I believe the work of the tribunal would have been facilitated by this Chamber joining in adherence to the fair standard already established, I recognize that the application of a flat rate of interest of 10%, if not varied, would have the advantage of even more complete automaticity and is not presently unjust.

5. In *Grove Skanska v. Lockheed Aircraft Int'l A.G.*, where interest was allowed at a commercial rate, did the arbitrators apply *lex mercatoria*? In his comment on the arbitration, A. Lowenfeld said of it "The arbitrators, an Englishman, a Canadian and an American, quickly agreed that interest should be awarded: if payments were found to have been due in Year I, to order them made in Year III or IV, without interest would be wrong, commercially unreasonable and therefore contrary to law. Dr. Mann and Lord Justice Mustill might well ask, 'contrary to what law?' and if pressed the arbitrators would have said 'contrary to the law reflecting the normal expectations and usage of enterprises engaged in international construction projects'" Andreas F. Lowenfeld, *Lex Mercatoria: An Arbitrators View*, 6 ARB. INT'L. 133, 143 (1990).

6. Does moratory interest prescribed by law (the "legal rate of interest") necessarily apply to determine or limit damages to compensate time-related losses actually suffered by the Claimant? *See* the J. Tackaberry, *Elementary Economics and the Construction Dispute. An Outsider's Look at the Swiss Law Remedies Available to the Unpaid Contractor*, 7 J. INT'L ARB. 73 (1990) (describing the Swiss law approach).

7. May an arbitrator disguise a monetary allowance which would not be permitted as moratory interest pursuant to the applicable law by determining the "present value" of the claimant's damages as of the date of the award, or within a lump sum determination of damages? *Compare Liberian Eastern Timber Corp. (LETCO) v. Government of the Republic of Liberia*, ICSID Arbitration No. 31 of 1986, 26 I.L.M. 647 (1987) *with* ICC Arbitration No. 5277 (1987), 13 Yearbook of Commercial Arbitration 80 (1988).

8. May arbitrators award compound interest? Explain the juridical method to be used in answering this question. *See* F.A. Mann, *Compound Interest as an Item of Damage in International Law*, 21 U. CAL. DAVIS L. REV. 577 (1988); *On Interest, Compound Interest and Damages* 101 LAW QTLY. REV. (London) 30 (1985); *General*

*Electric Co. (USA) v. Renusagar Power Co., Ltd.*, ICC Arbitration No. 4367, (Rt. Hon. Peter Thomas, Q.C., Chairman, B. Bitker and Dr. K. Dixit, Member), Award (Sept. 12, 1986), 8 MEALEYS INT'L ARB. REP. A2 (Nov. 1993) (compound interest allowed by arbitral tribunal).

### 3.    PUNITIVE DAMAGES

Associated with the issue of interest, which is intended to add an amount to the material damages suffered to take into account the passage of time, is the issue of penalties or treble damages, which are intended to add a component of exemplary punitive damages to the compensatory damages awarded. Punitive damages have become increasingly important as an item of indemnification claim in civil suits, at least in the United States. *See* Chapter 3, p. 372. If the dispute is covered by an arbitration clause, can the arbitrator award punitive damages? The issue is raised at the first level, which we take up here, as to whether the arbitrator should be persuaded to award punitive damages in an appropriate case. At a second level, there always remains the issue of whether a court will enforce such an award. The following excerpt deals with the first issue. In the quoted materials, Professor Farnsworth hypothesizes that an English supplier has committed an aggravated and "bad faith" breach of a sales agreement with a Californian purchaser. The agreement calls for the application of the substantive law of California (where the courts have frequently imposed punitive damages for aggravated breaches) and calls for arbitration in California.

E. Allan Farnsworth, *Punitive Damages in Arbitration*, 7 ARB. INT'L 3, 5-8 (1991).

·    ·    ·

Suppose that a contract is made by an English supplier to furnish and put into operation sophisticated machinery for an American buyer in California. Suppose that the contract contains a broad arbitration clause providing for arbitration in California and incorporating the rules of the American Arbitration Association along with a choice of law clause referring to California law. A dispute arises and the American buyer, asserting that there has been an 'aggravated' breach by the English supplier, initiates arbitral proceedings in California under the clause, and demands, not only compensatory damages of $10,000,000, but punitive damages of another $10,000,000 for the English suppliers 'bad faith breach.' The English supplier might ask four distinct questions:

(1) Will a court in California grant a motion to stay arbitration of the punitive damage claim on the ground that arbitrators have no power to award punitive damages?

(2) If a court will not stay arbitration of the punitive damage claim, will the arbitrators, applying California law, award punitive damages?

(3) If the arbitrators award punitive as well as compensatory damages, will a court in California vacate the part of the award granting punitive damages?

(4) If the court in California refuses to vacate the award and the American buyer seeks to have it enforced by a court in England, will that court refuse to enforce it on grounds of public policy?

(1) *Will a Court Stay Arbitration of the Punitive Damage Claim*?

Even in the United States, we have little authority on this precise question. (Although it is similar to the third question, it is not identical for it is possible that a court might vacate an award of punitive damages once rendered even though it would decline to stay arbitration of the punitive damage claim, presuming that the arbitrators would not exceed their powers.) *Willis v. Shearson/American Express Inc.*,[218] to which I will return later, arose on a motion to stay arbitration proceedings on the ground that a demand for punitive damages was improper in an arbitration. The federal district court in that case rejected this contention and held that the demand for punitive damages could go to arbitration under the federal arbitration law.

---

[218] 569 F.Supp. 821 (M.D.N.C. 1983).

Assuming that an American court would follow this precedent and refuse to stay arbitration of the punitive damage claim, we come to the second question.

### (2) *Will the Arbitrators Grant Punitive Damages?*

This question has two aspects. First, will the arbitrators consider the case at hand an appropriate one for punitive damages under the applicable law, in this case, California? Second, will the arbitrators assume that they — as arbitrators — have the power to award punitive damages assuming that the case is an appropriate one?

As to the first aspect — the appropriateness of punitive damages under the applicable law — there is, I take it, a marked difference between the law in England and that in the United States. While in England, as I understand it, a court may grant punitive damages in some cases of tort and for breach of a fiduciary duty, it is still the case that punitive damages are not available for what are essentially breach of contract actions. As it was put in *Addis v. Gramaphone Co.*:[219] 'damages for breach of contract [are] in the nature of compensation, not punishment.' In this respect American courts have become more generous than British courts, awarding punitive damages — it often seems — not only in furtherance of the traditional goals of punishing a past wrong and deterring similar conduct in the future, but also out of a sense that 'compensatory' damages do not fully compensate an aggrieved party for all the harm that party has suffered.

Our courts generally may award punitive damages in tort actions, and a number of courts have awarded punitive damages for a breach of contract that is in some respect tortious. Some courts have gone to considerable lengths to find the necessary tortious conduct.[220] In this California outdid the other states by creating a new tort of 'bad faith breach' of contract.

---

[219] [1909] A.C. 488, 494 (H.L.) (Lord Atkinson). But see *Rookes v. Barnard*, [1964] A.C. 73 (H.L.).

[220] *See generally* E. Farnsworth, CONTRACTS, §12.8 (2d ed. 1990).

The first sighting of this new tort came during the 1950's and involved actions against insurers that were regarded as having broken contracts with their insured's in bad faith.[221] Not until 1984, however, was there a serious suggestion that this new tort of bad faith breach might be extended beyond the insurance cases. In that year the California Supreme Court decided *Seaman's Direct Buying Service v. Standard Oil Company of California*,[222] a case involving an oil dealership contract. In remanding for a new trial, the court *in dictum* defined a new tort where a party to a contract "in addition to breaching the contract . . . seeks to shield itself from liability by denying, in bad faith and without probable cause, that the contract exists." The court declined to pass on "whether and under what circumstances, a breach of the implied covenant of good faith and fair dealing in a commercial context may give rise to an action in tort," but it said there had to be some "special relationship like that between insurer and insured." "No doubt," it added, "there are other relationships with similar characteristics and deserving of similar legal treatment."

In 1988, however, the California Supreme Court pulled in its horns to a considerable extent by refusing, in *Foley v. Interactive Data Corp.*,[223] to find that an employer's wrongful discharge of an employee involved a bad faith breach of an employment contract under the *dictum* in *Seaman's* case. After criticizing the 'uncritical' extension by lower California courts of the insurance model "without careful consideration of the fundamental policies underlying the development of tort and contract," the court reached this somewhat surprising conclusion: "we are not convinced that a "special relationship" of the kind required by *Seaman's* "analogous to that between insurer and insured should be deemed to exist in the usual employment relationship." (One might well ask where it would exist if not between employer and employee.)

---

[221] See, e.g., *Communale v. Traders & Gen. Ins. Co.*, 50 Cal. 2d 654, 328 P.2d 198 (1958).

[222] 36 Cal. 3d 752, 768-769, 686 P.2d 1158, 1166-1167 (1984).

[223] 47 Cal. 3d 654, 689, 692, 765 P.2d 373, 393, 395 (1988).

Only a few states have been tempted to follow California's lead in *Seaman's* case.[224] And the moderating effect of *Foley* on the spread of the doctrine of bad faith breach remains to be seen. Nonetheless the spectre of punitive damages for bad faith breach of contract continues to stalk the corridors in the courthouses of a significant minority of American states.

This brings us to the second aspect — assuming that the arbitrators consider the case at hand an appropriate one for punitive damages under the applicable law, will they assume that they — as arbitrators — have the power to award such damages? I have found little authority on this precise question.[225] The reports of the Iran-United States tribunal at The Hague shed some light on it. In a separate opinion in one case,[226] an American arbitrator suggested that 'punitive or exemplary damages might be sought' in that tribunal for unlawful expropriation. He saw 'strong reasons why it would be appropriate for an international tribunal to award punitive or exemplary damages for unlawful expropriation, for otherwise the injured party would get only what it would have gotten by lawful expropriation and would receive nothing additional for the enhanced wrong done it and the offending state would experience no disincentive for the repetition of unlawful conduct.' (Parenthetically it is worth noting that in this argument the traditional goal of deterrence is mingled with the sense that traditional 'compensatory' damages do not fully compensate).

This second aspect — whether arbitrators will assume that they have the power — has a somewhat uncertain relation to the third and fourth questions, which go to enforceability,

---

[224] According to footnote in *Foley*, 'In only three cases outside of California have courts held that a breach of the covenant of good faith and fair dealing gives rise to tort damages.' 47 Cal. 3d at 686, n. 26, 765 P.2d, at 391, n. 26.

[225] See WALL STREET JOURNAL, p. 1, June 11, 1990 ('Stock Investors Win More Punitive Awards in Arbitration Cases').

[226] *Sedco, Inc. v. NIOC*, 10 Iran-U.S. C.T.R. 180, 205 (1986) (separate opinion of Brower). *See also Amoco Int'l Fin. Corp. v. Iran*, 15 Iran-U.S. C.T.R. 189, 248 (1983) (Virally, Ch.).

since — in spite of the fact that most arbitral awards are complied with voluntarily and without judicial intervention — prudent arbitrators may decline to render an award of punitive damages if it would not be enforceable. The International Chamber of Commerce Rules[227] state that 'the arbitrators . . . shall make every effort to make sure that the award is enforceable at law.' The Rules are silent, however, with respect to the place where the award is to be enforceable. Is it the place of arbitration? (This raises my third question). Or is it the place or places where enforcement is likely to be sought — or may possibly be sought? (This raises my fourth question). Julian Lew has written that 'an arbitrator must ensure that this award does not offend the national public policy of the place where enforcement is sought.'[228] Putting such a responsibility on the shoulders of the arbitrators raises two practical questions. First, how is this responsibility to be discharged if the place of enforcement is uncertain, as where enforcement is likely to involve a ship that calls in many ports? And second, assuming that the arbitrators can foresee the likely place or places of enforcement, how and at what stage of the procedure are they to be informed by the parties as to possible difficulties in enforcing an award in that place or those places? A satisfactory answer must take account of the circumstance that often the question will not arise until after hearings have concluded and the arbitrators are in the process of preparing their award. One may ask whether the arbitrators' responsibility should not be limited to avoiding an award that they know or at least suspect will be unenforceable in a probable place of enforcement, with the responsibility on the claimant to inform the arbitrators as to potential problems . . . .

## Notes and Questions

1. In a number of arbitration awards made in the United States, arbitrators have, in fact, awarded punitive damages. As Professor Farnsworth points out in his articles, the restrictive grounds upon which an award may be set aside under the

---

[227] ICC Rules, art. 26.

[228] J. Lew, *Applicable Law in International Commercial Arbitration*, p. 537 (1978).

Federal Arbitration Act rule out any possibility of nullification because of misinterpretation of the law by the tribunal. The only permissible grounds for annulment would be that an arbitrator lacks power to award punitive damages, a position which was taken by the highest court of the state of New York in *Garrity v. Lyle Stuart, Inc.*, 40 N.Y.2d 354, 353 N.E.2d 793 (1976), but which generally has not been followed by the federal courts and about which Professor Farnsworth states: "[T]he handwriting on the wall suggests that Garrity's days are numbered — if indeed it retains any vitality at all." 7 ARB. INT'L 3, 9-10.

2. A related issue is whether a foreign court might refuse enforcement of an arbitrator's award of punitive damages based on violation of that forum's policy. While there is little authority on the subject, there are grounds for believing that such an award would be at risk in many jurisdictions (particularly in England, the jurisdiction of Professor Farnsworth's hypothesis, which has displayed, in another context, hostility to United States treble damages awards). *See supra*, 7 ARB. INT'L 3, 11-13. In this respect there are comparisons to be made with the refusal of a United States court to enforce that part of an arbitration award, rendered under French law, which provided for interest at a rate considered by the enforcement court to be a penalty. *See Laminoirs-Tréfileries-Câbleries de Lens, S.A. v. Southwire Co.*, 484 F.Supp. 1063 (N.D. Ga. 1980) (excerpts and discussion of the public policy issue *infra*, pp. 1201-02.

## V.    PROVISIONAL MEASURES ORDERED BY ARBITRATORS

### A.    ARBITRATORS' POWERS IN GENERAL

Before or during the course of the arbitral proceedings, it may be necessary or prudent to act, on a provisional basis, to preserve the rights of the parties or the subject matter of the dispute until a final decision on the merits can be taken. In addition, a party may wish to ensure the enforceability of any final award that may be entered. Examples of the kinds of measures which may be sought would include inspection by the tribunal or by a neutral third party expert of goods or merchandise before it is transferred beyond the control of the parties, sale of perishable goods, orders not to call down a performance bond or letter of guarantee, instructions to continue work prescribed in a contract pending arbitration, deposits of sums in escrow, injunctive remedies, and, in appropriate cases, attachment and other similar measures.

Provisional measures may broadly be divided into three categories:

- those that have to do with the discovery, preservation and production of evidence concerning the dispute;

- those that have to do with preserving the subject matter of the dispute and avoiding prejudice to the rights of the parties during the pendency of the proceedings; and

- those that are destined to permit the effective execution of the award to be rendered on the merits, sometimes called conservatory measures.

The first category will be examined not in this section, but in Chapter 7, concerning the conduct of the arbitral proceedings. Both arbitral tribunals and the courts are concerned with the two other categories, but it will be noted that the third category, ordinarily requiring the exercise of coercion, most frequently arises before courts and is dealt with in Chapter 4. The second category, tied closely to the dispute itself, may be brought up before either arbitral tribunals or the courts.

Where the arbitrator has jurisdiction to act, he is, in many ways, best suited to make provisional orders addressed to parties who are before him and in relation to a dispute over which he has exclusive jurisdiction on the merits. In some circumstances, however, measures available to an arbitrator may be either inefficacious or impossible.

Provisional measures are typically of an urgent nature. If they are needed after a dispute has arisen but prior to the constitution of the arbitral tribunal, it is obviously not possible to seek relief from the yet to be formed tribunal. If the relief requested requires measures to be taken against a third party, as in a typical attachment proceeding, the arbitrator will be unable to act, for he has jurisdiction only over parties to the arbitration agreement. In cases where an arbitrator makes a provisional order applicable to a party before it, but has no power to enforce it, his action may be inefficacious.

The subject of provisional measures to be taken in connection with arbitration raises issues of the exclusive and non-exclusive powers of arbitrators and courts and how they may interact, cooperatively rather than in antagonism.[229] In some cases, the arbitrator may need the assistance of the courts; in others, he would prefer to be insulated from intervention by the courts. The relationship between the arbitrator and the courts, and the degree of assistance or intervention by the courts will depend upon the law of the jurisdiction where the arbitration is held and the wisdom with which it is applied.

Insofar as the parties are concerned, however, it is logical that the arbitrator should have inherent jurisdiction to take all provisional measures appropriate to the dispute that he has been empowered ultimately to decide. Where the parties have agreed that the arbitrator may make a final and binding award on the merits of the dispute, they should accept his power to make interlocutory procedural orders required for the efficacy of the process and of the award. But jurisdiction to make procedural orders does not carry with it any power to enforce them. The arbitrator does not have direct enforcement powers, even over the parties to the arbitration; he cannot punish for contempt, fine, or imprison a contumacious party. Where statutory provisions give him power to order provisional measures, the orders can only be enforced by court action.

Nonetheless, arbitral tribunals routinely order interim measures of protection, which parties before them, concerned not to inconvenience the ultimate trier of fact and law on the merits of the dispute, just as routinely accept. These apparently inherent powers of the arbitrator are reinforced by the specific grant of power to the arbitrators by arbitration rules agreed by the parties. Consider, for example, Article 26 of the UNCITRAL Arbitration Rules (*see* Supplement at p. 636) and Section 34 of the American Arbitration Association, Commercial Arbitration Rules, effective 1 September 1988 (*see* Supplement at p. 485). The London Court of International Arbitration ("LCIA") Rules give specific powers to the arbitral tribunal concerning interim measures and provide that the parties will not apply to a court of law for such measures. (London Court of International Arbitration Rules, effective January 1, 1985 (for the full text, *see* Supplement at p. 513).)

---

[229] Berthold Goldman, *The Complementary Roles of Judges and Arbitrators in Ensuring that International Commercial Arbitration is Effective*, in SIXTY YEARS OF ICC ARBITRATION: A LOOK AT THE FUTURE 257, 279-80 (1984).

Article 8(5) of the ICC Rules of Arbitration in force from January 1, 1988 (*see* Supplement at p. 458), on the other hand, specifically provides that parties may in some circumstances seek provisional measures from courts. The Rules only <u>imply</u> that the power to grant interim measures is ordinarily or concurrently exercised by the arbitrators. In practice, ICC tribunals are prepared to grant provisional measures, unless some mandatory provision of law at the seat of arbitration prevents it, and frequently do so.[230]

An Iran-U.S. Claims Tribunal case provides an example of protective measures that were issued by an arbitral tribunal on an urgent basis. The dispute involved the two governments. The procedure of the Claims Tribunal is governed by a modified version of the UNCITRAL Rules.

1.     *Iran v. United States*, 5 Iran-U.S. Cl. Trib. Rep. 131 (1984).

Within the framework of Claims Nos. A-4 and A-15 (III) filed with the Tribunal by the Government of the Islamic Republic of Iran against the Government of the United States of America, seeking the restitution to the Claimant of immovable and movable properties of the Iranian Embassy and Consulates located in the United States, and damages for an alleged breach by the Respondent of its obligations in this respect under the Declaration of the Government of the Democratic and Popular Republic of Algeria of 19 January 1981, the Claimant submitted on 20 December 1983 a Request for an interim measure to prevent the Government of the United States of America from auctioning the movable properties of the Iranian Embassy and Consulates in the United States and to cancel any transaction entered into pursuant to such auctions.

In an Order filed on 18 January 1984, Chamber Two of the Tribunal, which had been appointed to deal with this request by Presidential Order No. 17 of 5 January 1984, held that the circumstances as presented to the Tribunal at the time were not such as to require the exercise of its power to order the requested interim measure of protection, as these circumstances did not appear to create

---

[230] W. LAURENCE CRAIG, ET AL., INTERNATIONAL CHAMBER OF COMMERCE ARBITRATION § 8.07 (2d ed. 1990).

a risk of an irreparable prejudice, not capable of reparation by the payment of damages. In this Order it was further noted that this decision did not prevent the Party which had made the request from making a fresh request based on new facts.

On 31 January 1984 the Government of the Islamic Republic of Iran filed a Related Request for an interim Order enjoining the United States Government from auctioning movable properties of Iran's Embassy and Consulates in the United States.

In this new request, the Government of the Islamic Republic of Iran asserts the occurrence of new facts, indicating to the Tribunal that a public auction will take place in Washington, D.C., at C.G. Sloan & Company, Inc., from 3 through 5 February 1984, at which, it is stated, specific irreplaceable items of property, "exquisite, historical, and national properties existing in Iran's Embassy and Consulates in the United States," are to be sold. To specify its Request, the Government of the Islamic Republic of Iran has attached to it a telex dated 31 January 1984 from the Iranian Interest Section at the Algerian Embassy in Washington, together with the auctioneer's advertisement published in the "Iran Times" of 20 January 1984 and the relevant pages of the auction's catalogue.

Furthermore, the Government of the Islamic Republic of Iran, on 1 February 1984, has submitted a more specific list of these properties, to wit: items 1736 to 1817 of the relevant pages of the auction's catalogue.

Finally, the Tribunal has received a letter from the Agent of the United States of America, conveying the comments from the U.S. State Department, which states:

> OFM confirmed today with Sloane's that none of the items in question are being sold on consignment from the Department of State. At the December sale in New York at Sotherby Parke Bernet, Sloane's bought all the crested china, crystal and silver offered and is now reselling those items for its own account. Similarly, other items from earlier Sloane's sales are being resold by private individuals, including two rugs, twelve crested platters, and some paintings,

and:

> . . . we have just learned that there will be a 'minor catalogue sale' at Sloane's on February 25-26 which will include lesser items from the Department consignment initially intended for the December 9-11 auction. Some of these items were published in the catalogue prior to the December sale but were not auctioned when other more valuable items were brought into the sale from other sources.

By Presidential Order No. 23 of 1 February 1984, Chamber Two was appointed to deal with this question of interim measures.

The Tribunal notes that the Government of the United States of America, in its Memorial in opposition to Iran's Request for interim measures, filed on 3 January 1984, pertaining to the request dealt with in the Order filed on 18 January 1984, repeatedly asserts that objects which have unique historical, artistic or cultural value are not envisaged to be sold, and,

> that it has made every effort to identify objects among the Iranian properties which possess significant historical, cultural or other unique features and to ensure that such objects are preserved for eventual return to Iran. Objects such as early Persian manuscripts (including Korans), tiles, prints, and pottery from the eighteenth and nineteenth centuries remain in storage and will not be sold.

In the same Memorial, the Government of the United States of America points out, in regard to previous auctions of items of property from the Iranian Embassy and Consulates in the United States, that

> (t)he auction sales were entirely regular and lawful. Title to those properties has passed under United States law. The United States has no basis for suits to rescind the transactions, and no way of compelling the purchasers to relinquish the items they acquired. (p. 19 of the U.S. Memorial).

Under reference to its Order of 18 January 1984, in view of the new facts introduced by the Government of the Islamic Republic of Iran, as well as in view of the above quoted paragraph from the U.S. Memorial of 3 January 1984, it appears to the Tribunal that the items on the list are irreplaceable, and the Tribunal finds it necessary, therefore, to take an interim measure [pending the decision of the Full Tribunal in cases A-4 and A-15].

.     .     .

The Tribunal urgently requests the Government of the United States of America to take all necessary and appropriate measures to prevent the sale of Iran's diplomatic and consular properties in the United States which possess important historical, cultural, or other unique features, and which, by their nature, are irreplaceable.

[The following note is appended in handwriting to the signature of Mr. Aldrich:]

I concur, although I believe only some of the items on the references list are arguably irreplaceable.

*     *     *

In the particular circumstances of the Iran-U.S. Claims Tribunal case, the tribunal might expect voluntary compliance from the government to whom its order was directed. In ordinary international commercial arbitration cases, however, the arbitrators must consider the enforceability of their orders. None of the arbitration institution rules stipulates the form in which provisional measures must be taken by the arbitrators, apparently leaving it to the discretion of the arbitrators whether they should issue a simple procedural order (which by its nature is difficult, if not impossible, to enforce), or a partial award which, is subject to judicial review but also to judicial recognition and enforcement.

In the following case, the arbitral tribunal hesitated between these alternatives, but in the end entered a declaration in the form of an award to which it invited the parties to comply, reserving the possibility to reconsider it, if compliance were not forthcoming.

2.     *French Construction Co. A v. Iranian Gov't Org.*
       *B*, ICC Arbitration No. 3896, 10 YEARBOOK OF
       COMMERCIAL ARBITRATION 47 (1985) (English)
       and 1983 JDI 889, 918-919 (French).

## FACTS

Arbitral proceedings were in progress between French construction company A and the Iranian Government organization B, based on a contract between them dated September 18, 1977. During the course of the arbitration, B instructed an Iranian bank to make a call under the performance guarantee given by a banking syndicate pursuant to A's contractual obligations. A sought interim relief from the arbitral tribunal in the form of a declaration that the bank guarantees were null or had been rendered unenforceable; that the call under them was fraudulent and unjustified; and an order that B suspend any call until a decision was reached on the merits of the dispute. The Tribunal issued a partial award in which it declined to give the declaration requested but proposed instead that in order to preserve the *status quo*, the claimant withdraw its allegation of fraud and that the defendant renounce its call under the guarantees, until the arbitral proceedings on the merits of the underlying contract were concluded.

## EXTRACT

On the tribunal's jurisdiction:

> "The fact that the arbitral tribunal can in no sense, and does not intend to, concern itself with any dispute between the parties to the bank guarantee, does not, however, mean that questions relating to these guarantees, notably whether they are valid or no longer enforceable, between the parties to the present arbitration, cannot be addressed or discussed by the Arbitral Tribunal. . . . The fact remains that, between the parties to the contract and to the present arbitration, the rights and obligations of the contractor and the employer necessarily encompass the guarantee of good performance in the execution of the contractor's duties and the conditions of operation.
>
> From this point of view it is not possible to state that once the contract came into existence, the link between the guarantee and the contract would completely

disappear or, more precisely, such an assertion — however correct it may be in respect of certain types of bank guarantees taken alone, so-called 'automatic' guarantees, as far as relations between the bank and the beneficiary are concerned — cannot be accepted without more with regard to the principal or underlying contract. We are not concerned here with examining the conditions under which the guarantor, according to the terms of the guarantee, must assess its obligation to honour the demand for payment made by the beneficiary. It is rather a case of evaluating, within the framework of the present arbitration, in which the parties to the underlying contract confront each other, whether the call under the guarantee was well founded or not.

(. . .)

"[T]he Arbitral Tribunal considers that, if the question of the 'guarantee,' *as between the giver of the guarantee and the beneficiary*, falls entirely outside the scope of the present arbitration, as the defendant submits, the same would not be true in the context of the underlying contract and the relation between the parties to the present arbitration. By its very nature, this issue is not independent and could never be entirely separated from the problems of performance or non-performance of the obligations under the contract; on the contrary, it is clearly an ancillary or necessary aspect thereof.

(. . .)

"To sum up, it might be the case either that the contract, correctly interpreted, does not impose any condition on the exercise of the right of the Iranian party to make a call under the guarantees in any circumstances; or alternatively that the contract regulates, expressly or implicitly, the exercise of this right by the beneficiary, prohibiting, for example, an abusive or fraudulent call, or at the least correcting the 'automatic' character of the guarantee vis-à-vis the guarantor by the interposition of the liability which the employer beneficiary would incur towards the contractor who authorized the guarantee if the call under the guarantees turned out to be ill-founded.

"Having regard to these factors, the Arbitral Tribunal considers itself competent to pronounce on these questions as between the parties, and to choose between the different hypotheses once the time comes to do so."

On the appropriate form of interim relief:

". . . In the view of the Arbitral Tribunal, what is essential is that the guarantees continue to exist and could be paid to the beneficiary if the need arose, in conformity with what is stipulated in the contract. In abstaining from pursuing a call under the guarantees and exacting payment from the guarantor, the defendant would not in any way be jeopardising its legal position or its legitimate interests, it seems, while its security remained entirely intact.

"As things stand, it will be recalled that no one can pronounce with total certainty upon whether the claimant had correctly fulfilled its contractual obligations, or whether the defendant was right to consider itself discharged from its own obligations by reason of *force majeure*, or finally whether the contract had been terminated or not and on what date. Taking account, also, of the complexity of the legal issues involved, notably as regards the effects of the contractual obligation to provide a guarantee, and the bank guarantees which were given in fulfillment, it is equally impossible at this stage to decide if, according to the contract and given the relations between the parties, the call under the guarantees, once-for-all and irrevocable as it was, was justified on the date in question or not. For all these reasons, the best solution, in the Arbitral Tribunal's opinion, would involve the maintenance, in so far as is possible, of the '*status quo ante*,' that is, the situation which existed at the moment when Terms of Reference no's. 1 and 2 were signed.

"Nor is it desirable in the course of an international arbitration such as this, to allow allegations to stand which are as serious as those of the allegedly abusive and fraudulent call under the guarantee by the defendant.

"In conclusion, the Arbitral Tribunal considers that there exists, undeniably, the risk of the dispute before it becoming aggravated or magnified, and that the parties should, in the same spirit of goodwill that they have already demonstrated in signing the Terms of Reference, refrain from any action likely to widen or aggravate the dispute, or to complicate the task of the Tribunal or even to make more difficult, one way or another, the observance of the final arbitral award."

[The Tribunal went beyond this mere exhortation of principle, and made the following specific proposals to the parties in a conclusionary section of the award which is not reported in the Yearbook of Commerical Arbitration but is reported in the French language summary of the award contained in the JDI, of which the following text is the English translation.]

In this spirit the Arbitral Tribunal proposes to the parties jointly:

- to the Claimant parties to formally withdraw their conclusions seeking a declaration that the call of the bonds by the defendant was abusive and fraudulent and that any pursuit by the defendant of such an action would present the same characteristics, and to refrain from making any further such allegation until the end of the present arbitral procedure.

- simultaneously, the arbitral tribunal proposes to the Defendant party to renounce formally from any calling of the guarantees until the end of the present arbitral procedure, as well.

The arbitral tribunal invites each party to communicate to it, within two months of the present partial award, if it accepts or not the proposition applicable to it and agrees to observe it.

In the event of the failure of any party to accept the proposition applicable to it within the imparted time limit, the arbitral tribunal shall consider that the two propositions cease to have effect.

### Notes and Questions

1. The defendant sought a declaratory award that the bank guarantees were null and void and that a call upon them was fraudulent. Instead, the arbitral tribunal invited the parties to comply with a request. Why did the arbitration tribunal use the precatory form? Would a court have issued a similar request? Is there any reason specific to arbitration which leads to this approach?

2. Did the fact that the arbitration took place in Lausanne, Switzerland, and the procedure was governed by mandatory provisions of the Swiss Intercantonal Concordat (*see* Supplement at p. 399) then in effect, have any influence on the way the tribunal approached provisional measures? *See* Article 26 of the Concordat. Would the arbitrators have acted differently under the Swiss Private International Law Act (*Loi sur le Droit International Privé* or "LDIP") (*see* Supplement at p. 393) which entered into effect in 1989. *See* Article 183 of the LDIP.

3. If the requested declaratory award had been granted, would it have had any effect on the bank which had entered into a separate guarantee agreement of which the defendant was a beneficiary and which did not contain an arbitration clause? Would the consequences have been different in adjudication before a court?

4. If the requested declaratory order had been granted, but the Iranian party had nevertheless drawn down the bank guarantee, would this have constituted a breach of the principal contract subject to arbitration? What would be the fault alleged? What remedy would have been sought?

5. Does an arbitral tribunal have any power to enforce a provisional measure that it orders? How does this differ from the powers of a court? What are the factors that might persuade a party to voluntarily respect provisional measures ordered by an arbitrator?

6. Does the moment of confirmation of jurisdiction have any effect on the ability and/or confidence of an arbitral tribunal to issue a provisional order?

7. For the relationship between arbitration tribunals and the courts for provisional measures and generally, see Berthold Goldman, *The Complementary Roles of Judges and Arbitrators in Ensuring that International Commercial Arbitration is Effective*, *in* SIXTY YEARS OF ICC ARBITRATION: A LOOK AT THE FUTURE 257, 279-

80 (1984).    For a general treatment of provisional measures, see Douglas D. Reichert, *Provisional Remedies in the Context of International Commercial Arbitration*, 3 INT'L TAX & BUS. LAW. 368 (1986); Neil E. McDonell, *The Availability of Provisional Relief in International Commercial Arbitration*, 22 COLUM. J. TRANSNAT'L L. 273 (1984).


Ordinarily, an arbitral tribunal cannot act with the speed and efficiency of a judge acting in motion session with the power to grant injunctive relief. In *Sperry Int'l Trade, Inc. v. Israel*, federal courts had refused to maintain an earlier injunction against a party to an arbitration preventing the calling of a bank guarantee. The arbitral tribunal, however, speedily moved to enter an interim award ordering the defendant party to escrow the funds in issue. This award was then made the subject of recognition and enforcement procedures before the court to which an application for injunctive relief had first been made.

3.      *Sperry Int'l Trade, Inc. v. Israel*, 532 F.Supp. 901 (S.D.N.Y. 1982).


.     .     .


The parties entered into a contract dated July 28, 1978 which contained a broad agreement for arbitration of all disputes arising thereunder or in connection therewith to be settled under the rules of the American Arbitration Association. Sperry was to design and build a communications system for GOI. The contract conditioned GOI's obligation to make certain payments on GOI's receipt of an irrevocable Letter of Credit in its favor. The Letter of Credit was originally in the amount of $11,847,749.00 but was increased to, and became the amount of $15,008,098.00.

The project apparently encountered great difficulties from the start. On August 3, 1981, Sperry filed with the AAA a Demand for Arbitration claiming that GOI had obstructed Sperry's attempts to perform the contract and seeking a declaration that GOI was in breach and also seeking damages of about $10,000,000. GOI denied Sperry's allegations and asserted eleven counterclaims.

On September 11, 1981, Sperry obtained an Order to Show Cause in this Court requiring GOI to show why it should not be required to proceed with the arbitration and why it should not be enjoined meanwhile from drawing under the Letter of Credit.

On October 9, 1981, Sperry halted all work on the project.

On October 16, 1981 this Court heard Sperry's motion to compel arbitration to be proceeded with and for a preliminary injunction and GOI's cross-motions connected therewith. The Court . . . recommended that the AAA proceed on the matter with due dispatch, and stayed GOI from drawing down on the Letter of Credit until April 1, 1982 pending an early ruling of the arbitrators permitting the draw down of the funds.[231]

On January 2, 1982, the Second Circuit reversed that part of this Court's decision concerning the Letter of Credit. It held that this Court had improperly issued a preliminary injunction because Sperry had not, as a matter of law, demonstrated irreparable harm since the potential damage to Sperry was strictly monetary. Whether the contractual condition had arisen for a draw down of the proceeds was not then a subject of litigation. The Court of Appeals expressly stated that it expressed no view as to the other elements that a movant must establish in order to obtain injunctive relief, viz., the merits.

[After the Court of Appeals' decision vacating the injunction Sperry obtained an attachment of the guarantee proceeds in State court and GOI removed the action to Federal court.]

Early in the morning of February 9, 1982, and before the hearing set on the motion to vacate the state court of attachment, the Arbitrators handed down an Award requiring both parties to escrow in a joint account the amount of the proceeds of the Letter of Credit pending resolution of the further issues to be arbitrated or until otherwise dealt with by the Arbitrators or the Courts. They did not reach the issues of liability for breach and damages. Those issues have been set for hearing commencing late in March 1982.

The next day, February 10, being apprised of the Award, Judge Cannella on defendant's motion vacated the Order of Attachment obtained in the state court. [Sperry moved on the same day to confirm

---

[231] [2] The Letter of Credit was also extended to April 1, 1982.

the award and GOI cross-moved to vacate. The parties agreed to block the sums at the bank pending the decision of the court on the motions.]

## The Award

The equitable relief granted by the Arbitrators on February 9, 1982, was in the following terms:

> Upon the motion of Claimant, in an arbitration before this Tribunal commenced by a Demand for Arbitration dated August 3, 1981 (as amended), for injunctive relief with respect to a Letter of Credit (no. WCG-150297) purchased by Claimant from Citibank, N.A., or the proceeds thereof, and for other relief, and upon hearing and considering the arguments presented and the large number of documents submitted (directly or during the month prior to the hearing, through the American Arbitration Association) on behalf of Claimant and Respondent in favor of and in opposition to such injunctive and other relief;

Now, upon due consideration, the arbitrators order as follows:

> 1. The proceeds of said Letter of Credit shall be paid into an escrow account ("Escrow Account") in the joint names of Claimant and Respondent with such bank or other entity in the United States of America as shall be agreed upon in writing by Claimant and Respondent prior to the release of such proceeds by Citibank, N.A. or, in default of such agreement, with Citibank, N.A.

> 2. Claimant and Respondent shall maintain the Escrow Account in their joint names as aforesaid and the moneys or other investments standing to the credit thereof, including all interest or other income which may be earned thereon, shall not be withdrawn or transferred until (and then only in such manner, on such terms and in such amount, whether as to the whole or in part, as) Claimant and Respondent shall so agree in writing or, in default of such agreement, this Tribunal or a Court in the State of New York or Federal Court in the United States of America shall finally so determine.

3. Claimant and Respondent shall not permit the Escrow Account to become subject to any lien or encumbrance without the leave of this Tribunal or of a Court in the State of New York or Federal Court in the United States of America.

.     .     .

8. This order shall constitute an Award of the arbitrators and either party is at liberty to apply forthwith to the United States District Court for the Southern District of New York for confirmation and/or enforcement thereof.

## The objections to confirmation and enforcement and the Award

In brief, GOI contends that confirmation of the Award would be inconsistent with the January 21, 1982, Court of Appeals decision in this matter since, in the view of GOI, the Arbitrators had granted the same preliminary injunctive relief as the Court of Appeals has said is not appropriate or available as a matter of law. GOI argues further that by compelling GOI to "freeze" the amount of the proceeds of the Letter of Credit in a segregated account, the Arbitrators effectively had ordered an attachment of proceeds of the Letter of Credit and in this respect their Award allegedly violates the Foreign Sovereign Immunities Act ("FSIA") 28 U.S.C. § 1610 (d). Thus, GOI contends that the Award reflects a "manifest disregard" by the Arbitrators of the governing law and that they "exceeded their powers." *See* 9 U.S.C. §10 (d). As an added contention GOI suggests that the Award does not purport to finally determine the merits of the conflicting breach of contract claims for the rights of either of the parties to the $15,000,000 proceeds of the Letter of Credit and consequently is interlocutory and not subject to confirmation by Court action at this time.

## The applicable law

.     .     .

The only statutory ground urged by the GOI for vacating and not confirming the Award, and thus the only one relevant to these motions, is 9 U.S.C. § 10(d) which provides that an Award may be vacated where "the arbitrators exceeded their powers, or so imperfectly executed them that a mutual, final, and definite award upon the subject matter submitted was not made." This Circuit has further recognized a non-statutory ground for vacation of such awards, also pressed by the GOI, — i.e., where the arbitrators have shown a "manifest disregard" of the law.

The vacation of arbitration awards is disfavored, and the grounds therefor are to be strictly construed. . . .

.    .    .

## *The Arbitrators did not exceed their powers*

The GOI's argument that the Arbitrators exceeded their powers and ignored the laws of res judicata and collateral estoppel, by redetermining an issue already resolved by the Court of Appeals has fatal flaws. It *assumes mistakenly*, as the record of the Arbitration proceeding and the GOI's own arguments to the Panel and to this Court clearly show, that the Arbitrators were dealing with the same issue and same facts as did the Second Circuit in its decision of January 21, 1982. In point of fact, however, the questions before the Court of Appeals were whether Sperry had shown such overreaching and fraud in the contractual dealings as to entitle Sperry in effect to rescind its Letter of Credit, and such irreparable harm by reason thereof, if the Letter of Credit was allowed to be drawn upon, as to justify the issuance of a preliminary injunction preventing Israel from drawing down on it. The Second Circuit decided that no irreparable harm had been shown because money only was involved and never reached the issue of underlying fraud in the contractual dealings or the satisfaction of the contractual conditions for calling down the proceeds of the Letter of Credit. By the time the parties went before the Arbitrators the GOI, as it repeatedly argued to the Arbitrators and to this Court, had issued the contested certification of entitlement to the proceeds under the Letter of Credit. The issue before the Panel then became whether the GOI was entitled under the terms of the contract to draw at all against the Letter of Credit and whether having drawn thereon violated the contract and intent of the parties and constituted overreaching conduct and an improper certification to the Citibank, N.A. that the GOI was entitled to draw down.

.    .    .

This contract plausibly could be read in accordance with the intent thereof as claimed by Sperry which would imply that the GOI had overreached the terms of the contract and improperly certified that the conditions for drawdown of the proceeds existed. There was no obligation of the bank to go behind such a certification to ascertain its verity. There was an obligation of the GOI to certify only if "in accordance with" Section 59 of the contract, viz., the contemplated "clear and substantial breach". Sperry contended in the arbitration that the certification to the Citibank to obtain the proceeds of the Letter of Credit did not conform to the contract since GOI could not validly claim that Sperry was clearly and substantially in breach of the Agreement.

Sperry presented the Arbitrators with a calendar of alleged faults of the GOI under the contract to support its claim that it was GOI's misconduct which had caused Sperry to halt work on the contract.

.    .    .

Sperry argued that it had already put in $20,000,000 of performance for which it was as yet reimbursed and it had not been paid any of its expected profits on the job of another $10-15 million.

In the light of the foregoing circumstances Sperry argued that it would be inequitable to permit the GOI "to walk away" at this time with an additional $15,000,000, in effect constituting a further investment by Sperry in the project. Sperry pointed out that the GOI had not yet expended or incurred the alleged reprocurement expenses required to complete the project. On no conceivable basis in Sperry's view would Sperry be called upon for another $15,000,000 or the GOI be required to expend that until the accounts between the parties were settled by the Arbitrators.

All these points were vigorously contradicted by GOI.

The Solomonic resolution of the Award to take the money from both parties of course does not decide the merits. The Award makes rational sense at this stage of the Arbitration.

.    .    .

The issues of whether the GOI properly drew down on the Letter of Credit and what equitable treatment should be made of the proceeds were duly and fully submitted to the Arbitrators, who issued an Award constituting a final judgment on those issues. The relief awarded was well within the scope of the Arbitrators' powers under Section 42 of the AAA Commercial Arbitration Rules.

[The award was confirmed.]

\*     \*     \*

The arbitrator who wishes to order interim relief while still reserving the rights of the parties to argue the merits of the underlying issue prior to entering a final award on the merits faces a dilemma: a simple procedural order may not be efficacious, but can he enter an "award" which does not finally dispose of the issue? The arbitral tribunal in the *Messianaki Floga* case followed the interim award route, and its award was sustained in review proceedings.

> 4.     *Southern Seas Navigation Ltd. v. Petroleos Mexicanos*, Society of Maritime Arbitrators, Inc. Interim Award No. 2015 (Aug. 24, 1985), 11 YEARBOOK OF COMMERCIAL ARBITRATION 209 (1986) (extracts).

## FACTS

This arbitration and the related court decision reported below concern the authority of arbitrators to issue interim relief in the nature of a preliminary injunction. Southern Seas Navigation Limited (hereinafter owner) chartered the Messianaki Floga to Petroleos Mexicanos (hereinafter charterer) on the Texacotime form of time charter. Charterer asserted claims near the end of the charter period for a refund of US$ 350,000 in hire for 17.5 days during which it did not have use of the vessel, for reimbursement of costs incurred in feeding the vessel's crew, and for reimbursement of costs incurred in removing dirty ballast water and cleaning the vessel's tanks. Charterer filed a US$ 2 million "notice of lien" (also called "notice of claim" in the award below) on the vessel with the Liberian Registry of Ships in order to obtain security for its claim. Owner had meanwhile defaulted on its mortgage payments and arranged for conveyance of the vessel to a first preferred mortgagee in lieu of foreclosure. Failure to deliver the vessel under the conveyance could have resulted in foreclosure. Owner commenced arbitration with charterer because the conveyance was being held up by charterer's notice of lien, and requested an order requiring charterer to rescind the notice of lien. The arbitrators held that Owner was entitled to have the notice of claim against the vessel reduced to US$ 350,000.

## EXTRACT

The issues before the arbitration panel were whether the relief requested by owner was appropriate and within its authority to grant. After hearing evidence as to the "colorability" of charterer's claims and the likelihood of irreparable harm from granting or denying the requested relief, the arbitration panel ordered charterer to reduce the notice of claim to the amount of its claim for a refund of hire. The panel stated that it had broad remedial authority to issue the kind of relief requested by owner to avoid irreparable harm. Such an award was appropriate insofar as charterer's claims did not appear colorable, because owner's failure to convey the vessel would result in foreclosure. While the claim for a refund of hire was the only one of charterer's claims which appeared colorable, charterer was not precluded from introducing further evidence as of all of its 'claims' in future hearings. The arbitrators stated in particular:

> "This panel has anguished over the wisdom of granting interim relief. Judicial tribunals are more accustomed to segmented proceedings and the creating of flexible remedies. Case law, however, supports our authority as arbitrators to engage in equitable type relief. While the existence of mere financial harm is not usually the basis for exercising extraordinary power or granting interim relief, [it is clear from the case law that] the potential of a bankruptcy or extraordinary financial consequence [which could] not be repaired by a damage award is a valid reason for disturbing the status quo.

> ". . . Based on the unchallenged evidence, it appears the harm to Owner is of sufficient magnitude to invoke this panel's authority . . . . This case involves a financial injury that cannot be recompensed by a damage award. As the relative probability of success on the merits as to the issues discussed favors the party seeking equity relief, we feel an award is justified."

## Notes and Questions

1. The *Southern Seas* award was presented for confirmation: *Southern Seas Navigation, Ltd. v. Petroleos Mexicanos*, 606 F.Supp 692 (S.D.N.Y. 1985). Pemex averred that the award should not be confirmed as "it is not final," but rather, as its title "Interim Ruling" suggests, only an intermediary step in an ongoing arbitral process.

The court held that:

This award is not a partial resolution of the parties' claims as an intermediate step in an ongoing arbitral process but, in effect, a grant of a preliminary injunction. As noted above, the arbitrators themselves perceived the request in such terms.

As our Court of Appeals has expressly stated, not only do arbitrators have traditional powers of equity, "[u]nder New York law [they] have power to fashion relief that a court might not properly grant."[232]

Just as a district court's grant of a preliminary injunction is reviewable as a discrete and separate ruling apart from any decision on the merits, so too is an arbitration award granting similar equitable relief.[233] No undue intrusion upon the arbitral process results from a finding that such an award is ripe for confirmation. . . .

That the arbitrators labeled their decision an "interim" award cannot overcome the fact that if an arbitral award of equitable relief based upon a finding of irreparable harm is to have any meaning at all, the parties must be capable of enforcing or vacating it at the time it is made. Such an award is not "interim" in the sense of being an "intermediate" step toward a further end. Rather, it is an end in itself, for its very purpose is to clarify the parties' rights in the "interim" period pending a final decision on the merits. The only meaningful point at which such an award may be enforced is when

---

[232] [3] *Sperry Int'l Trade, Inc. v. Government of Israel*, 689 F.2d 301, 306 (2d Cir.1982).

[233] [5] Our Court of Appeals has expressed disapproval of review by district courts of interlocutory orders involving only some of the claims submitted to arbitration even where those claims are "separate and distinct." *Michaels v. Mariforum Shipping, S.A.*, 624 F.2d 411, 415 n. 5 (2d Cir.1980); *see Hunt v. Mobil Oil Corp.*, 557 F. Supp. 368, 375 n.22 (S.D.N.Y.), *aff'd without opinion*, 742 F.2d 1438 (2d Cir.1983). Faced with a case involving equitable relief pending arbitration, however, the Court did not find that the district court lacked power to confirm the award. *Sperry Int'l Trade, Inc., v. Government of Israel*, 689 F.2d 301 n. 3 (2d Cir.1982).

it is made, rather than after the arbitrators have completely concluded consideration of all the parties' claims.

2. Because an award is subject to enforcement by the courts, an arbitral tribunal may, as we have seen, seek to grant provisional measures in that form. This somewhat artificial device can be avoided where statutory provisions in force at the seat of arbitration confirm or enhance the arbitrator's jurisdiction and powers to order interim measures. These modern procedural provisions take two forms: either they confirm that the arbitrator has power to issue such orders, or they do that and, in addition, provide a means for direct enforcement by the courts of such procedural orders. Consider, in this regard, Article 17 of the UNCITRAL Model Law (*see* Supplement at p. 126); Article 183 of the Swiss Private International Law Act of 18 December 1987, (*see* Supplement at p. 396).

3. Dutch law allows the parties to agree on summary arbitral proceedings, (*kort geding; référé*), provided for by Article 1051 of the Netherlands Arbitration Act. *See* Supplement at pp. 363-64. Summary arbitral proceedings, like those before the President of the District Court, aim at the ordering of injunctions in urgent cases; they do not yield a decision on the merits.

> The advantage of summary arbitral proceedings is that a party can quickly obtain an injunction to do something or to refrain from doing something from an arbitrator who is familiar with the subject matter of the dispute. Such injunction can be enforced as an arbitral award (see the third paragraph of art. 1051).

> Summary arbitral proceedings are to be distinguished from "speedy arbitrations" which are arbitrations with short periods of time, as provided in some arbitration rules. Speedy arbitrations, like ordinary arbitrations, reach a decision on the merits.

.    .    .

> If, in spite of an agreement for summary arbitral proceedings, the case is brought before the President of the District Court for immediate injunctive relief, the President has the discretionary power to decide whether or not he or the summary arbitral proceedings is better suited for dealing with the application for injunctive relief.

PIETER SANDERS AND ALBERT JAN VAN DEN BERG, THE NETHERLANDS ARBITRATION ACT 1986 29 (1987).

4. In order to maintain the *status quo*, and to prevent an aggravation of the dispute *sub judice*, a party may ask the arbitrators to order another party to the arbitration agreement to refrain from initiating judicial proceedings, whether interlocutory or on the merits, relating to the same subject matter. An arbitrator will be reluctant to make such an order, which he would, in any event, be powerless to enforce. In the first place, as we will see, national courts ordinarily maintain a

concurrent jurisdiction with the arbitrators in respect to provisional measures and indeed have enforcement powers reserved to the state and denied to arbitrators. To the extent that recourse to a court concerning the merits of a matter is inconsistent with an arbitration agreement, the remedy of the aggrieved party is to raise that issue before the court as a defense. At least where the New York Convention is applicable, the court will be required to stay or to dismiss the court proceeding and to enter an order referring the matter to arbitration. *See supra* Chapter 3.

### B.    PROVISIONAL MEASURES IN THE ICSID REGIME

An exception to the general rule of arbitral abstinence from making orders involving parallel court proceedings is found in investment dispute arbitrations brought before the International Centre for the Settlement of Investment Disputes ("ICSID"). Pursuant to the terms of the Washington Convention of 1965, adhered to by 110 states as of July 1, 1993, the signatory nations agreed that for the foreign investment disputes covered, all of which involve a state or state organization and a foreign investor, ICSID arbitration would be the exclusive mode of dispute resolution; recourse to a state court prior to final award is specifically excluded. 17 U.S.T. 1270; T.I.A.S. No. 6090; 575 U.N.T.S. 159. *See* Supplement at p. 91. Article 26 of the Convention provides that "Consent of the parties to arbitration under this Convention shall, unless otherwise stated, be deemed consent to such arbitration to the exclusion of any other remedy."

Once an ICSID arbitration has been initiated, a state party has sometimes moved before its own courts in parallel proceedings, either on the merits or in interlocutory proceedings (expertise or similar measures). Conversely, the private investor may move in the courts of neutral third countries in an attempt to obtain security for the proceedings, by attachment or otherwise. ICSID arbitrators have been asked to issue provisional orders in the circumstances.

In the *Holiday Inns* ICSID arbitration, the private investor sought provisional measures from the arbitral tribunal to prevent the state from taking prejudicial actions in its own courts. The context of the dispute and of the issue is typical of foreign investment arbitrations and therefore excerpts from a description of the case are set out at some length. The awards were not published; the description comes from an article by counsel for the claimant parties.

1.    Pierre A. Lalive, *The First "World Bank" Arbitration* (Holiday Inns v. Morocco) — *Some Legal Problems*, 1980 BRIT. Y.B. INT'L L. 123 (1982).

[The dispute in this case arose out of investment agreements entered into between the Holiday Inn Group ("H.I.") and Occidental Petroleum Corporation ("O.P.C."), on the one hand, and agencies of the Moroccan Government, on the other hand. The agreements called for the foreign investors to pay for, build, equip, and operate four five-star category Holiday Inn hotels at designated sites in Morocco. The Moroccan Government undertook to lend the investors certain amounts of money, to be secured by mortgages on the properties, and to grant them further incentives, such as bonuses, foreign exchange facilities, duties exemptions, and other tax benefits, as well as assistance "in the acquisition of suitable grounds at the lowest possible prices." When the parties encountered irreconcilable disputes, claimants on 13 January 1974 filed, in accordance with the provisions of an arbitration clause in their agreement, a request for arbitration with the International Centre for the Settlement of Investment Disputes ("ICSID"). The Centre is the arbitral institution established by the Convention on the Settlement of Investment Disputes of 18 March 1965 (the "Washington Convention") and the request was the first ever filed with the Centre. While the arbitration eventually was terminated by an amicable settlement in 1978, the tribunal had previously thereto entered an interim award on provisional measures on 2 July 1972, the principal provisions of which are commented on in Pierre Lalive's article.]

. . .    [T]he many difficulties met by the builders in their day-to-day cooperation with various local authorities and bodies (C.I.H. [*Crédit Immobilier et Hôtelier*, a specialized Moroccan lending agency], Ministry of Tourism, customs or exchange control officials, etc.) increased over the years. Long and unexplained delays occurred in the payment of construction draws and bonuses and in the delivery of necessary authorizations, until, in the middle of May 1971, the C.I.H., acting presumably on Government instructions, stopped payment altogether. Meanwhile, the construction of two of the four hotels had been completed and, for the remaining two Holiday Inns, was well advanced. The cessation of the payments due under the Basic Agreement with the Government and the loan contracts with the C.I.H., together with the refusal of foreign exchange and other administrative authorizations, was a serious blow to the foreign builders. Short of adequate financing and of indispensable foreign currency, and confronted with numerous other obstacles, the Holiday group could no longer pay local suppliers and sub-contractors and felt compelled either to stop construction or to provide financing out of its own pocket, contrary in its view to the Basic Agreement. On their side, the Moroccan authorities appear to have felt that the Agreement had to be interpreted as implying a simultaneous personal financial contribution from the builders or, if not, that it was inequitable and should be renegotiated.

A genuine misunderstanding may well have existed as to the economics of the Project and the correct interpretation of the contract. In the claimants' view the whole Project could and should be performed, thanks to H.I. rationalization and special expertise, with Government financing alone. A crisis developed when it was realized on the Moroccan side that the construction was actually proceeding without additional funds from abroad. It can only be said here, in brief, that no clause in the Agreement did expressly provide for such additional funding, as was clearly recognized by the Arbitration Tribunal in a decision of 23 September 1974 on the 'existence and scope of certain liabilities of the Parties deriving from their contractual relations'.

.     .     .

All attempts at conciliation having failed, in spite of negotiations at the highest level, the builders interrupted, in August 1971, the construction of the two Holiday Inns of Casablanca and Tangiers. Negotiations continued, however, but in vain until, on 22 December 1971, the claimants filed their 'request for arbitration.' In the request, the claimants described the dispute as 'a legal dispute arising directly out of an investment within the meaning of Article 25(1)' of the Washington Convention and in particular as relating to (a) the obligation of the Moroccan Government and its agent to resume their loan payments and bonus payments, (b) the compensation due for damages and losses incurred by reason of discontinuance or delays of such payments and (c) the convertibility and transfer of foreign currency used for construction, and of management fees, franchise fees and other compensations for expenses incurred in connection with the establishment and operation of the hotels.

.     .     .

IV.    THE QUESTION OF PROVISIONAL MEASURES

An important practical problem in many international arbitrations, for rather evident reasons, is that of provisional measures or, as they are sometimes called, 'interim measures of protection'.

In commercial arbitration, the general rule appears to be that arbitrators have no power to order provisional measures, which must be requested from ordinary, i.e., State, courts.[234] An arbitration tribunal can do no more, even in case of prior agreement of the parties, than recommend certain acts or abstentions, and draw certain consequences from the compliance, or lack thereof, of the parties. In settlement of disputes under public international law, the matter is largely regulated by specific provisions, at least when 'institutional' tribunals and not *ad hoc* arbitrations are concerned. A well-known example is Article 41 of the Statute of the International Court of Justice.

The magnitude and complexity of most international disputes, involving inescapably long periods of time before any decision or amicable settlement can be reached, give the question of provisional measures considerable significance.

The drafters of the Washington Convention, aware of this practical need, provided in Article 47 that:

> Except as the parties otherwise agree, the tribunal may,
> if it considers that the circumstances so require,
> recommend any provisional measures which should be
> taken to preserve the respective rights of either party.

A large measure of discretion is granted here, as usual, to the arbitration tribunal, who will naturally be inclined, when exercising it, to follow the principles developed in international cases. It is, therefore, of some general interest to outline here how the first Arbitral

---

[234] [Authors' note: In making this comment Professor Lalive relied on, and cited to, Article 26 of the Swiss "Concordat" on Arbitration of 1965 which provided: "The public judicial authorities alone have jurisdiction to make provisional orders proposed by the arbitral tribunal." Compare this with the more recent Swiss statutory provision giving arbitrators jurisdiction to grant provisional orders found in Article 183 of the Swiss LDIP. *See* Supplement at p. 396.]

Tribunal created under the Washington Convention approached and solved the question of provisional measures, when requested to intervene by the claimants, shortly after its own constitution.

The request for provisional measures of 12 May 1972 was based on the following facts, which were, broadly speaking, undisputed: with regard to the two hotels of Casablanca and Tangiers, the building of which had been interrupted in the circumstances related above, the Moroccan Government had taken steps, in February 1972 and the following months, perhaps understandably, in order to have architects appointed, take over the site and complete the construction of the hotels. Although the I.C.S.I.D. arbitration was already pending, the Government did not file any request for provisional measures with the Arbitration Tribunal, but turned to the Moroccan courts.[235] Whether this was due to an oversight or based on the opinion that the Arbitration Tribunal could not act, or would not respond in a practically satisfactory manner, is not known. What is likely is that — as will become apparent below when discussing preliminary objections to jurisdiction — the Moroccan local authorities failed to perceive, or to attach any importance to, the international dimension of the dispute and were thinking only in terms of relations between the C.I.H. and the respective 'H.I.S.A. company'.

As for the two completed hotels of Marrakesh and Fez, somewhat similar local, and unilateral, procedures took place, but the situation was different: the Government's refusal to approve the management contract needed for operating the hotels had led the foreign group, following the breakdown of negotiations, to threaten the closure of the hotels. To prevent this the Moroccan authorities

---

[235] Under the summary procedure known in France and Morocco as *référés*; more precisely, the C.I.H. lodged a unilateral request in February and the Ministry of Finance a similar one in March, with the Tribunal and the Regional Court of Casablanca, respectively. They obtained orders entitling them to take all necessary measures to have construction resumed and completed at H.I. costs. For technical reasons, which need not be detailed here, the H.I. Group was only informed afterwards.

requested, in January 1972, and obtained from the local court, the appointment of a 'judicial administrator'.[236]

In the claimants' view, the unilateral measures taken by the Government or obtained by it from its own courts were not only a violation of their contractual rights under the Basic Agreement (*e.g.*, the rights to build the hotels according to their own specifications and methods, and the rights to operate them as Holiday Inns), but also violated a number of fundamental principles, both of general international law and of the Washington Convention of 1965. As to the latter, reference was made to Article 47, already cited, on provisional measures, and Article 26, providing that:

consent of the parties to arbitration under this Convention shall . . . be deemed consent to arbitration *to the exclusion of any other remedy*.[237]

It followed that the Moroccan courts were totally incompetent in a case pending before the international Tribunal even to order pseudo — or real — 'provisional measures'.

As to the former principles, the requesting party relied on:

The principle universally admitted by international tribunals . . . to the effect that the parties to a case must abstain from any measure capable of exercising a prejudicial effect in regard to the execution of the decision to be given and, in general, not allow any step of any kind to be taken which might aggravate or extend the dispute.[238]

It was submitted that the various measures taken in Morocco, or others about to be taken for the completion or operation of the

---

[236] The two hotels continued thereafter to be operated under the name "H.I." (under the supervision of the Ministry of Tourism) — a fact which led to protests by the claimants; the name was eventually modified.

[237] Emphasis added.

[238] P.C.I.J., *Electricity Company of Sofia and Bulgaria case*, P.C.I.J., Series A/B, no. 79, p. 199; *see also* I.C.J., Case concerning *U.S. Diplomatic and Consular Staff in Teheran*, Order of 15 December 1979, p. 21.

hotels, *did* in fact aggravate the dispute, that they prejudiced the claimants' rights and interests, sometimes in an irreparable manner, and that they would make more difficult, or impossible, the enforcement of an award, if favourable to them on the merits. The claimants were relying also, among other precedents, on the well-known Order of the International Court of Justice in the *Anglo-Iranian Oil Company* case of 5 July 1951 . . . In any case the claimants strongly emphasized the Moroccan courts had no jurisdiction and that the Government, in resorting to them in order to take over the hotels or their building sites, had violated both the Washington Convention and general rules and principles of international law. They insisted, therefore, that after H.I. had stopped construction or closed two hotels, the Moroccan Government was perfectly entitled to seek a way out through provisional measures, but that it ought to have turned to the Arbitration Tribunal.

The Government, announcing its intention to contest in due course the jurisdiction of I.C.S.I.D. and of the Arbitration Tribunal, contended that the Moroccan courts had sole jurisdiction regarding the provisional measures under review, and this not only in relation to the H.I.S.A. companies (subsidiaries organized by the claimants under Moroccan law) but also as a general principle — a more striking assertion in view of the precedents cited above. Such a contention would seem to negate the inherent power of international tribunals to indicate interim measures of protection, quite apart from the direct effect of Articles 26 and 47 of the World Bank Convention. Furthermore — and a mere mention of the fact will suffice, since it is not intended here to dwell on factual aspects — the Government took the hardly surprising view that the measures requested *in casu* by the claimants were 'neither necessary nor useful', but they 'prejudiced the substance of the case', etc., while the Moroccan measures 'assured the protection of the interests of both parties *pendent lite*'.

The difficulty in which an arbitration tribunal, whether *ad hoc* or 'institutional', finds itself when called upon to decide this kind of controversy at the very beginning of arbitration proceedings will be readily appreciated. At such an early stage, when no evidence whatever has yet been adduced, nor any pleadings filed, the tribunal has little or no possibility of ascertaining the truth, but it has to make a quick, though cautious, decision.

The decision given on 2 July 1972 (i.e. immediately following the oral arguments of the parties) can be characterized briefly as a strong one on the legal principles involved while *in concreto* extremely prudent (some would even say timid). On the first aspect, the decision deserves to be cited in full:

> The Parties were in agreement to recognize before the Tribunal that at the date of this Decision contractual relations remain in existence between them based on a series of commitments the foundation of which apparently is the Contract of December 5, 1966. It follows that the Parties are under an obligation to abstain from all measures likely to prevent definitely the execution of their obligations.

> The Tribunal therefore considers that it has jurisdiction to recommend provisional measures according to the terms of Article 47 of the Convention on the Settlement of Investment Disputes between States and Nationals of Other States, the Parties still having the right to express, in the rest of the procedure, any exception relating to the jurisdiction of the Tribunal on any other aspect of the dispute.

Concretely, the Tribunal takes a middle-of-the-road attitude: it declines to recommend a series of measures suggested in the request, and is understandably reluctant to appear to pass judgment even indirectly, at that stage, before the 'respective responsibilities of the Parties regarding the situation of the enterprise in Morocco' have been established. Moreover — and this observation deserves notice — the Tribunal considers that:

> To some extent these requests bear on injunctions which are beyond the framework of provisional measures which the Tribunal could consider.

The interpretation of this rather vague sentence must remain a matter of conjecture and one can only speculate on whether the Tribunal was careful, especially in the first arbitration under the I.C.S.I.D. system, not to assert its authority with regard to a sovereign State too much, or whether it considered that, by their general nature, certain types of provisional measures should as a rule not be recommended by international tribunals. On the other hand, and contrary to the defendants' submissions, the Tribunal did not content itself with affirming its jurisdiction; it did exercise it and considered it 'its duty to make . . . recommendations to the Parties'. The first one is of a general character:

> I. Both parties are invited to abstain from any measure incompatible with the upholding of the Contract and to make sure that the action already taken should not result in any consequences in the future which would go against such upholding.

A second recommendation, formulated in a carefully balanced manner, concerns the exchange of information by the parties regarding the management of the completed hotels and the completion of those hotels still to be constructed.[239] In a third and last recommendation, the Tribunal taking special account of one of the claimants' complaints, recommended consultations 'in order to maintain in the hotels the character of the enterprise which is part of the international chain of Holiday Inns Hotels'.

From the facts summed up above, it should be apparent that the Tribunal took a wise and constructive decision, if somewhat vague and limited in scope. In the nature of things, its practical effects on the site were to depend on the goodwill of the parties, but the jurisdiction of the international Tribunal is strongly affirmed, as well as the general duties of all parties to an arbitration. Nothing is said or implied which could touch the merits of the litigation, but a discreet warning is clearly, if indirectly, given to both parties that the Tribunal could and would take notice of any disregard of its recommendations. In the circumstances, the claimants could hardly expect, and probably did not expect, more from the Tribunal. However, an additional, and perhaps more effective, measure could have been an invitation to both parties to report at regular intervals on their compliance with the recommendations of the Tribunal.

*     *     *

---

[239] The Arbitration Tribunal did not, and could hardly be expected to, invite the Government to stop constructing or operating the hotels, but tried to ensure that the interests of the enterprises would nevertheless be safeguarded.

If the arbitral tribunal's reaction was extremely prudent, if not timid, in this first World Bank arbitration commenced in 1972, the arbitral tribunal in the *MINE v. Guinea* arbitration, thirteen years later, was more robust in its attitude towards what it considered to be improper actions before national courts by the foreign investor.

2.    Paul D. Friedland, *Provisional Measures and ICSID Arbitrations*, 2 ARB. INT'L 335 (1986).

. . . The case of *Maritime International Nominees Establishment* (MINE) *v. Guinea* arose out of a 1971 agreement between MINE, a Liechtenstein corporation, and the Republic of Guinea for the provision of shipping to transport bauxite from Guinea to foreign markets. The agreement, as subsequently amended, contained an ICSID arbitration clause. From 1978 through 1981, one or both of the parties engaged in a series of judicial and arbitral proceedings in the United States, which ultimately resulted *inter alia*, in 1981 in an award in favour of MINE from the American Arbitration Association ('AAA'). The award was not paid.

In May 1984, MINE commenced ICSID arbitration proceedings. Shortly thereafter, MINE instituted proceedings before the courts of Belgium and Switzerland to enforce its AAA award and to secure its ICSID claim against the Republic, and succeeded in obtaining attachments in both Belgium and Switzerland.

In response to the attachments, the Republic of Guinea turned to the ICSID Tribunal, and requested a recommendation that MINE cease its actions before the national courts.

In a decision dated 4 December 1985, the ICSID Tribunal granted the Republic's request, ruling as follows:

(i) The Tribunal recommends that MINE withdraw and terminate any and all judicial proceedings commenced before national jurisdictions and refrain from commencing any further proceedings in connection with this dispute. The judicial proceedings based on the AAA award are considered as connected with the present dispute for the purposes of this provisional measure.

(ii) The Tribunal recommends in addition that MINE withdraw all other provisional measures before national jurisdictions (including any seizures or attachments of the property of the Republic of Guinea whatever their judicial designation and whatever the method) and that MINE refrain from seeking additional provisional measures before any national jurisdiction.

(iii) In view of Article 47 and the applicable ICSID Rules, the Tribunal will take into account in its award the consequences of any failure by MINE to abide by these recommendations.

This decision by the *MINE* Tribunal is a valuable precedent for orders (or recommendations) under Articles 26 and 47 of the Convention curtailing attempts by ICSID parties to secure provisional relief before national courts. In particular, the *MINE* Tribunal's interim ruling makes clear that, where a request for judicial relief bears an undeniable connection to the ICSID arbitration, the request violates the Convention no matter what form the judicial relief might take and whether or not the request for relief has been presented as being unrelated to the ICSID proceedings (*eg*, in this case, notwithstanding the fact that MINE expressly sought enforcement only of its AAA award, rather than security for its ICSID claim).

### Notes and Questions

1. Do you agree with the finding in *Sperry* that an order by an arbitration tribunal to the parties that proceeds of a letter of credit be paid into an escrow account pending a determination of the tribunal on the merits of the case is an award? Does it correspond to the criteria for an interim award set out in the ICC Committee's study, *supra* p. 641? Is it final?

2. "Although piecemeal court applications relating to arbitration are not to be encouraged, there are times when there is a need to enforce the award of the arbitrators even though it may not decide all the issues before them. In some instances, these partial awards may take the form of interim relief, effecting an injunction or conserving property, or they may dispose of a severable issue. Where such awards meet the finality criteria of the various arbitration laws, the courts generally will entertain a petition for enforcement. Where the partial award fails to finally dispose of severable issues, however, it will not be eligible for enforcement." LAWYER'S ARBITRATION LETTER No. 3, Comment 204, 209 (AAA 1986).

3. Under Article 47 of the Washington Convention, ICSID arbitrators have the right to "recommend" provisional measures. In the *MINE* case, the Tribunal said

that it would "take into account in its award the consequences of any failure by MINE to abide by these recommendations." What does this mean? Could a party's refusal to abide by the Tribunal's recommendations as to provisional measures have any incidence on the determination of the merits of the dispute before the arbitrators? On damages?

4. In Charles N. Brower and Ronald E.M. Goodman *Provisional Measures and the Protection of ICSID Jurisdictional Exclusivity Against Municipal Proceedings*, 6 FOREIGN INVESTMENT L. J. (ICSID REV.) 431, 461 (1991), the authors conclude:

> Finally it should be noted that the issue of urgency, normally a prerequisite for the recommendation of provisional measures, has not been discussed in this article, and for good reason. In respect of all categories of provisional measures other than that which form the subject of this article, urgency is a *sine qua non*; an international tribunal must, in effect, be shown the prospective harm it is urged to prevent. In the case of a threat to that tribunal's jurisdiction, however, the harm is inherent and hence indisputable. Furthermore, the threat is posed not simply to the rights of a disputant; it is directed to the very heart of the adjudicative process. Its patent presence dispenses the parties from any burden to demonstrate the same.

Do these considerations have any effect on the power of an ICSID arbitrator to prevent a party from engaging in parallel court litigation? Or on his willingness to recommend a provisional measure on this issue? For an example of how another arbitral institution has handled the issue of competing national court actions, see *E-Systems, Inc. v. The Islamic Republic of Iran*, Award of the Iran-U.S. Claims Tribunal (full tribunal) (Feb. 4, 1983), 2 Iran-U.S. C.T.R. 51, where the Iranian Government had brought a suit in Iranian courts on the merits concerning sales by a U.S. supplier which were the subject of a pending claim before the Tribunal. The Tribunal found:

> This Tribunal has an inherent power to issue such orders as may be necessary to conserve the respective rights of the Parties and to ensure that this Tribunal's jurisdiction and authority are made fully effective. . . . [T]he award to be rendered in this case by the Tribunal . . . will prevail over any decision inconsistent with it rendered by Iranian or United States courts, . . . [and] in order to ensure the full effectiveness of the Tribunal's decisions, the Government of Iran should request that actions in the Iranian Court be stayed until proceedings in this Tribunal have been completed.

The American arbitrators concurred, but insisted that the Tribunal should have referred to its power to order appropriate provisional remedies under the applicable Claims Tribunal arbitration rule (identical to Article 26 of UNCITRAL Rules). The Iranian arbitrators concurred, because the Tribunal admitted that its jurisdiction over the Iranian claim was not exclusive, but objected that the relief requested was not an interim measure and was not authorized by in Article 26 of the Rules.

5. From the examples in the preceding Section, it can be concluded that arbitrators, either through the exercise of powers deemed inherent to the jurisdiction afforded to them by the parties to resolve a dispute or of powers given to them by statute or by arbitration institution rules agreed by the parties, frequently take interim measures either by procedural order or interim award. However, arbitrators have no jurisdiction to make orders of any kind to third parties. The arbitrator cannot enjoin a third party from taking any action, nor may he attach assets of a party to the arbitration in the hands of a third party. Moreover, the interim award mechanism is not a flexible remedy and cannot be used in all circumstances. Finally, many times an urgent need to take interim measures arises at the outset of a dispute between parties to an arbitration agreement and before an arbitral tribunal has been constituted. In these circumstances, and many others, the only meaningful avenue open to a party seeking interim relief is through the courts. This is the subject taken up in Part VI.

## VI.    PROVISIONAL MEASURES ORDERED BY COURTS

### A.    POWER OF COURTS

By agreeing to arbitration, the parties do not necessarily agree to waive or renounce all judicial remedies. The right to seek recognition and enforcement of the award before a court is reserved, as is, arguably, the right to take measures in advance of the award to assure its efficacy. The issue was addressed in *Murray Oil Products* concerning a party's recourse to a judicial anticipatory attachment. Note, however, that the decision was rendered prior to the entry into force of the New York Convention, whose effect on this matter is considered below (*see infra* Part VI.B.1.)

1.    *Murray Oil Prods. Co. v. Mitsui & Co.*, 146 F.2d 381 (2d Cir. 1944).

L. HAND, Circuit Judge.

The defendant, a Japanese corporation, appeals from a summary judgment for the plaintiff, entered upon an award of arbitrators, in an action for damages for failure to deliver a parcel of Manchurian "perilla oil," c.i.f. New York, under a contract of sale. The plaintiff began the action in the state court, and a few days later attached some of the defendant's bank accounts in New York. The defendant appeared and moved for a stay pending the war, which had then broken out; this was granted except that the defendant was required to serve an answer. It then moved the action to the district court and served an answer, pleading, among other defences, that the plaintiff had refused to arbitrate as the contract required. The court stayed the action as to all issues which could not be decided without evidence from Manchuria or Japan; but tried the issue whether the contract contained an arbitration clause, which the plaintiff denied. It found that the contract did contain such a clause; and ordered the parties to arbitrate; they did so, and the arbitrators made an award of $21,840 to the plaintiff, which thereupon moved in the action to confirm the award and for judgement. The defendant — though not disputing the award upon the merits — moved to discontinue the action and vacate the attachment, on the ground that this was the legal effect of the arbitration. The court confirmed the award; directed judgment for the plaintiff to be entered upon it; denied the defendant's motion to discontinue the action and to vacate the attachment; denied a cross-motion of the plaintiff (which we need not describe); and reserved jurisdiction to dispose of the attached property. A judgment was entered on this order, from which the defendant has appealed. The burden of its complaint is that by means of the attachment the plaintiff has obtained an unjust preference over its other creditors; the Alien Property Custodian having now seized its property, which will probably not be enough to pay all in full. It argues that the law of New York treats the submission of a cause to arbitration after an action has been brought as a discontinuance; and that this has been carried over into the Arbitration Act, 9 U.S.C.A. § 1 et seq. It further argues that the court has no power to direct the entry of judgment upon the award under § 9 of Title 9 U.S.C.A., because the contract contained no provision authorizing this to be done.

The contract was made in New York; it purported to submit all controversies to arbitration which might arise under it: "Any dispute arising out of this contract to be settled by arbitration." If this is to be construed as a condition precedent to any action upon the contract, it was illegal in New York at common law. . . . True, arbitration affects only the remedy . . . , and New York decisions do not control, but the doctrine is general, at least in this country. . . . On the other hand the clause at bar was perhaps not a condition precedent. . . .If so, it was not a bar to a suit at common law, regardless of its legality. In either view therefore § 3[240] did not need to remove, and did not remove,

---

[240] [Authors' note:  Section 3 of the U.S. Arbitration Act provides:

If any suit or proceeding be brought in any of the courts of the United States upon any issue referable to arbitration under an agreement in writing for such arbitration, the court in which such

what would at common law have been a bar; on the contrary, it provided the defendant with relief — a stay — under conditions where before he would have been helpless to assert the arbitration clause at all. This was the measure of its change, so far as we can see; had it meant to go further and finally to dispose of the action, as the defendant argues, it would not have chosen the words used, for a stay presupposes that the action shall not abate; and if it does not, it must go to judgment of one kind or another. If a defendant wins before the arbitrators, he must be able to clinch his victory by a judgment; on the other hand, having invoked arbitration, he must also abide the result, if he loses. It would be a lame and impotent conclusion in that event to require the successful plaintiff to begin a new action on the award. Arbitration is merely a form of trial, to be adopted in the action itself, in place of the trial at common law: it is like a reference to a master, or an "advisory trial" under Federal Rules of Civil Procedure, Rule 39(c), 28 U.S.C.A. following section 723c. That is the whole effect of § 3.

The New York decisions on which the defendant relies are irrelevant for several reasons. First, as we have said, the question, being one of the remedy, is not governed by the law of that state; and it is not clear that the federal law recognized the doctrine. Thomton v. Carson, 7 Cranch 596, 3 L.Ed. 451. Second, even if it did, the doctrine applies only where the parties have agreed to arbitrate, and not where, as here, one has been forced to do so. There was some color, in the event of an agreement, for saying that submission to arbitration should effect a discontinuance; but there is none whatever, when both have not agreed. Indeed, that is a situation which could not have arisen while courts refused specifically to enforce an arbitration clause. Last, § 3 would, for the reasons already given, have superseded that practice if it had previously been the law, and if it had applied to this situation. So far as concerned the entry of judgment, the order was plainly right.

---

suit is pending, upon being satisfied that the issue involved in such suit or proceeding is referable to arbitration under such an agreement, shall on application of one of the parties stay the trial of the action until such arbitration has been had in accordance with the terms of the agreement, providing the applicant for the stay is not in default in proceeding with such arbitration.

For the full text of the Act, see Supplement at p. 414.]

Different considerations govern that part of it which refused to vacate the attachment. The strength of the defendant's argument here lies in the fact that, if the attachment stands, the plaintiff will have profited by its refusal to arbitrate, which was a breach of its contract. Since the defendant was willing to do so, the plaintiff could by hypothesis have arbitrated the claim and, either sued upon the award or entered judgment upon it by motion under § 9, if as it contends, that course was open to it in spite of the absence of such a provision in the contract. It did neither for two reasons: it denied that the contract contained such a clause; and it wished to attach the defendant's property. As to the first, it seems to us that there is as much reason for allowing an action to be brought to test the existence of an arbitration clause, as to test the factum of the contract in which the clause occurs. Kulukundis, etc. Corp. v. Amtorg, etc. Co., 2 Cir., 126 F.2d 978. Conceivably, there might be an exception — so far as concerns provisional remedies — if the promisee challenged the existence of the clause, or of the contract, in bad faith, and only to avail himself of attachment, the right to which he would not otherwise have. Since this was a summary judgment and the defendant at least suggests that the plaintiff challenged the existence of an arbitration clause in bad faith, we will assume that such an exception exists, and that the plaintiff's first reason for bringing its action was bad. However, the second was good, because, we think, an arbitration clause does not deprive a promisee of the usual provisional remedies, even when he agrees that the dispute is arbitrable.

As we have seen, § 3 allows such actions to be brought upon contracts containing such clauses, and modifies the procedure only by substituting arbitration as the mode of trial. The promisee retains all those remedies after judgment that he has in any other action; his breach does not prejudice him. If it denies him the provisional remedies which would otherwise be appropriate, it is an unexpressed exception; implied, because to allow them would put a premium upon his wrong, and encourage a disregard of arbitration. But would it do so? If, as we have held, § 3 compels the promisee to arbitrate, he does not escape it by suing in advance of it. And is it clear that to deny him provisional remedies, will promote resort to arbitration? We should assume not. The most common reason for arbitration is to substitute the speedy decision of specialists in the field for that of juries and judges; and that is entirely consistent with a desire to make as effective as possible recovery upon awards, after they have been made, which is what provisional remedies do. Moreover, as we have seen, their denial must in any case be confined to instances in which the promisee does not in good faith challenge the contract or the clause. All these things considered, we cannot think that we should import into the section a limitation, which language does not demand, which could operate over only a part of the field, and which, so far as we can see, would be as likely to defeat as to aid the purpose of the act.

Finally, in one instance at least, the statute specifically provides for attaching the promisor's property in the face of an arbitration clause: § 8 allows a libellant in the admiralty to begin by arresting the ship, or by foreign attachment; the court directs the parties to proceed to arbitration, keeps jurisdiction of the case, enters its decree upon the award, and issues execution upon the ship, or the attached property. It may be objected that the absence of any such provision in § 3 indicates that nothing of the kind was there intended, in accordance with the usual canon. Whatever its force in other situations, that canon applied here, would, however, only serve to mislead us; for it is not too much to say that it would result in an altogether irrational division of the subject matter. The statute is confined to two kinds of claims: "maritime transactions," and transactions in interstate or foreign commerce. Since arbitration clauses are contracts, there will be few instances when the cause of action will not itself sound in contract. Maritime contracts are within the jurisdiction of the admiralty, interstate contracts usually are not. We cannot conceive any reason for giving the remedy of attachment — and arrest — to the first class, and denying it to the second; such a distinction would impute to Congress the merest whimsy, and that too, a whimsy which nothing in the text demands. A possible, and the only rational, explanation for § 8 is that it was adopted out of abundant caution, admiralty procedure being regarded as somewhat apart and esoteric; but that it was implicitly assumed that actions brought under § 3 would proceed throughout in accordance with the practice, applicable to them if arbitration were not the method of trial.

In the view we take it is not therefore necessary to consider the plaintiff's other contention; that it might have proceeded under § 9; and — apparently — that in a proceeding under that section, it might have attached the defendant's property at the outset.

Judgment and order affirmed.

*     *     *

Injunctive relief may also be sought pending arbitration. A court will be more receptive to granting a temporary injunction if the relief is designed simply to preserve the subject matter of the dispute pending the resolution by arbitrators of the merits of the dispute. It will be more reluctant to grant the relief to the extent that the effect of the injunction will be to prejudice the decision on the merits, preempting, as it were, the exclusive jurisdiction of the arbitrators.

> 2.     *Sauer-Getriebe KG v. White Hydraulics, Inc.*, 715 F.2d 348 (7th Cir. 1983, *cert. denied*, 464 U.S. 1070).

CUMMINGS, Chief Judge.

[White Hydraulics ("White"), a United States company, granted Sauer-Getriebe KG ("Sauer"), a German company, an exclusive license to sell White motors outside of the United States and to supply Sauer with technical assistance and know-how to permit it to manufacture the licensed products. The agreement contained an arbitration clause. During the term of the agreement, White commenced negotiations to sell to a third party all of its assets, including the manufacturing rights promised to Sauer. Sauer brought suit in federal court seeking a preliminary injunction preventing the transfer of White's manufacturing assets until the rights of the party had been determined in arbitration. The District Court found that Sauer was not entitled to injunctive relief because it had not established that White had repudiated the contract, found that Sauer had improperly filed its arbitration request (by filing with the ICC in Paris although the arbitration was to be held in London), was required to refile it and that any findings made by the Court would be binding in that arbitration. It dismissed White's counterclaim seeking to find the agreement and its arbitration clause void for vagueness. Both parties appeal.]

.     .     .

. . . For the reasons that follow, we affirm the dismissal of White's counterclaim but vacate the remainder of the judgment and direct the district court to enjoin White from repudiating the contract and from transferring any of Sauer's contractual rights to a third party until the arbitration requested by Sauer is completed and this lawsuit (including any appeals) is terminated.

## *Arbitration Waiver*

White makes two attacks on Sauer's right to arbitrate this dispute. First, White claims that before this dispute may be submitted to arbitration, a court must decide that the contract containing the arbitration clause is valid and enforceable. White argues that if there is no contract to buy and sell motors there is no agreement to arbitrate. The conclusion does not follow its premise. The agreement to arbitrate and the agreement to buy and sell motors are separate. Sauer's promise to arbitrate was given in exchange for White's promise to arbitrate and each promise was sufficient consideration for the other. *See Hellenic Lines, Ltd. v. Louis Dreyfus Corp.*, 372 F.2d 753, 758 (2d Cir.1967). Moreover, there is nothing that requires that courts rather than arbitrators decide the validity of contracts, see, e.g., *In Re Oil Spill By The "Amoco Cadiz,"* 659 F.2d 789, 794-795 (7th Cir.1981) (fraud in the inducement), nor is there anything to suggest that when Sauer and White executed their contract they intended to limit in any way the kind of disputes to be settled by arbitration. The language of the arbitration clause in the contract could not be broader. It expressly provides that

> Any and all disputes arising out of and in connection with this Agreement shall be finally settled by arbitration under the rules of Conciliation and Arbitration of the International Chamber of Commerce by three arbitrators appointed in accordance with the Rules. The arbitration shall take place in London, United Kingdom of Great Britain.

This provision covers Sauer's claim that White repudiated the contract as well as White's claim that the contract is invalid. It is too late for White to argue that arbitrators appointed under ICC rules lack the competence to adjudicate the validity of its contract. Had White thought so when it entered the contract, it would not have agreed to arbitrate "any and all claims" before them.

Second, White argues that by filing this lawsuit, Sauer waived its right to arbitrate. We disagree. Sauer's right to seek injunctive relief in court and its right to arbitrate are not incompatible — Sauer need not have abandoned one to pursue the other — and White cannot in good faith claim that it was misled by Sauer's filing this suit into believing that Sauer intended to forego arbitration. See *Erving v. Virginia Squires Basketball Club*, 468 F.2d 1064 (2d Cir.1972). Sauer alleged in its complaint that it intended to submit a request for arbitration of its claims and Article 8, Section 5 of the internal rules of the ICC court of arbitration expressly authorizes parties to seek the interim relief Sauer sought in its complaint:

> Before the file is transmitted to the arbitrator, and in exceptional circumstances even thereafter, the parties shall be at liberty to apply to any competent judicial authority for interim or conservatory measures, and they shall not by so doing be held to infringe the agreement to arbitrate or to affect the relevant powers reserved to the arbitrator.

Sauer waited four more months before filing an arbitration request with the ICC but, in part at least, the delay was due to White's slowness in responding to Sauer's request for transfer of the manufacturing rights and at any rate, Sauer took no action during those four months inconsistent with its original position. It pleaded its arbitration right in defense to White's counterclaim and it reasserted that in its supplemental complaint.

Judge Sharp did not find that Sauer had waived its right to arbitration. Nonetheless he enjoined Sauer from pursuing the arbitration request it had filed with the ICC in Paris on the ground that the contract required that the request be filed in London. The contract, however, requires that the arbitration "take place in London," not that the request for arbitration be filed there. The contract also provides that the arbitration shall be conducted in accordance with ICC rules. Article 3, paragraph 1 and Article 1, paragraph 5 of those rules in effect require that requests for arbitration be filed in Paris with the Secretariat of the ICC Court of Arbitration. It does not follow that because Sauer filed its request in Paris the arbitration will take place there. Sauer did not request that it take place there — in fact the arbitrator Sauer selected lives in London — and Article 12 of the ICC arbitration rules provides that "the place of arbitration shall be fixed by the Court [of Arbitration], *unless agreed upon by the parties*" (emphasis supplied). There is therefore no reason to suppose that because Sauer filed its arbitration request as required by ICC rules, the arbitration will not be held in the place specified in the contract. Sauer is therefore not required to refile its request in London. Finally, because the arbitration request was filed properly, we also reverse Judge Sharp's order directing Sauer to nominate a new arbitrator.

### District Court Findings Regarding
### the Validity of the Contract

Although the district court found "insufficient evidence to establish the invalidity of the contract . . .," the court did find the contract "vague and ambiguous . . . [and] not certain nor reasonably ascertainable." The court also found that the contract should be strongly and strictly construed against Sauer and most favorably for White and that the arbitrators must therefore construe any uncertain, ambiguous, and vague terms against Sauer and in favor of White. Since the parties agreed to arbitrate all disputes arising from the contract, these findings are not binding and should be disregarded by the arbitrators in any subsequent arbitration proceeding. . . .

### Injunction Against White's Selling
### Trade Secrets and Manufacturing Rights

The district court refused to grant Sauer's request to enjoin White's sale of its manufacturing contractual rights pending resolution of the arbitration. Since Sauer seeks only an injunction pending arbitration, we will consider whether the four factors justifying a preliminary injunction are present. *Wesley-Jessen Division v. Bausch & Lomb, Inc.*, 698 F.2d 862, 867 (7th Cir.1983).

Sauer has shown that it has made a substantial investment in White's hydraulic motors and that it cannot obtain the necessary trade secrets and manufacturing rights from others. Sauer has also shown that without equitable relief, there would be a substantial injury to its reputation, good will and prestige not compensable in damages. Thus it has adequately demonstrated irreparable harm.

White might suffer some hardship if it is enjoined from transferring its manufacturing rights but, by the same token, Sauer's right to arbitration will not be worth much if White transfers those rights before arbitration is settled. Moreover, Sauer is willing to supply a security bond to guarantee White's financial recovery should it be forced to sell its business at a lower price after the injunction is lifted (Sauer Br.22). That would protect White against any financial loss, so that the balance of hardship is in Sauer's favor.

Although it is improper for a court to decide a contractual dispute relegated to arbitration, so far as the issuance of an injunction is concerned Sauer has demonstrated enough probable success on the merits to warrant relief. Sauer will be entitled to specific performance if it convinces the arbitrators that the contract entitles it to the trade secrets and manufacturing rights claimed. The contractual events prerequisite to the transfer of those rights have ostensibly occurred — Sauer has ordered over 15,000 motors, 18 months expired from the signing of the contract and the placing of those orders, and as of August 31, 1981 the Deutschmark-U.S. dollar ratio had been above 2.20 for four months. White bases its case solely on the alleged invalidity of a contract it freely signed three years ago even though it performed under the contract during those three years. Despite Judge Sharp's March 12, 1982, finding that the contract is valid on its face and his March 31 decision that Sauer [sic] [White] failed to establish its invalidity (White App. 52, 57), White is now endeavoring to repudiate that agreement on four separate grounds (White App. 37-39). In these circumstances, Sauer has sufficiently shown likely success.

Finally, the public interest is served by granting this injunctive relief because there is a strong policy in favor of carrying out commercial arbitration when a contract contains an arbitration clause. Arbitration lightens courts' workloads, and it usually results in a speedier resolution of controversies. Since Sauer has satisfied the requisites for obtaining injunctive relief of this type, the district court's refusal to grant it was erroneous.

*       *       *

The standard for obtaining a temporary injunction from a court, including the need to demonstrate irreparable harm, may be higher than the standard required to obtain equitable relief from the arbitrator. This is made clear in the Court of Appeals phase of *Sperry Int'l Trade Inc. v. Israel*, which was decided <u>before</u> the arbitral award and recognition proceedings that we have considered in connection with preliminary decisions by arbitrators in Chapter 6. The circumstances in *Sperry* should be compared and contrasted with those in *Rogers Burgun, Shahine & Descler, Inc. v. Dongsan Construction Co., Ltd., infra* p. 799, where the district court granted exactly the kind of relief which has been denied in *Sperry*.

3. *Sperry Int'l Trade, Inc. v. Israel*, 670 F.2d 8 (2d Cir. 1982).

KEARSE, Circuit Judge:

[Sperry International Trade, Inc. ("Sperry") entered into a contract with the Govenment of Israel ("Israel") to design and construct a communications system for the Israeli Air Force. The contract, which contained an arbitration clause, required Sperry to supply Israel with an irrevocable letter of credit of $15 million as a guarantee of its performance obligations. The letter of credit was payable upon certification by Israel that it was "entitled to the amount covered by such draft by reason of a clear and substantial breach" by Sperry. Disputes arose under the contract. Sperry filed for arbitration and requested the federal district court to enjoin Israel from drawing on the letter of credit. The District Court granted the injunction and the Government of Israel appealed.]

The standard in this circuit for granting a preliminary injunction clearly requires

> a showing of (a) irreparable harm and (b) either (1) likelihood of success on the merits or (2) sufficiently serious questions going to the merits to make them a fair ground for litigation and a balance of hardships tipping decidedly toward the party requesting the preliminary relief.

. . . The rule thus recognizes two tests; as we have previously observed, however, "[b]oth require a showing of irreparable harm." *Union Carbide Agricultural Products*, 632 F.2d at 1017. Under the first test, the movant may succeed if he shows irreparable harm plus a likelihood of success on the merits. Under the second test, the movant may succeed if he shows irreparable harm, plus sufficiently serious questions going to the merits to make them a fair ground for litigation and a balance of hardships tipping decidedly toward the movant.

In the present case, it does not appear that the district court gave recognition to the fact that the second test, like the first test, requires a showing of irreparable injury. The court stated that its injunction was based on

> a probability of [S]perry's success on the merits and possibility of irreparable harm were not such a stay o[f] certification granted, or as a minimum, on a balancing of the hardships tipping decidedly toward Sperry and sufficiently serious questions going to the merits to make them a fair ground for litigation (arbitration).

The statement suggests that the court viewed the second test as obviating proof of irreparable harm. To the extent that the district court ruled under this view of the second test it applied an erroneous standard of law.

This conclusion, however, does not require us to remand the matter for reconsideration under the proper legal standard, for our review of the record persuades us that the proof as to irreparable injury was insufficient as a matter of law. For potential injury to justify the granting of injunctive relief if must be irreparable; that is, it must be the kind of injury for which an award of money cannot compensate. *See Jackson Dairy, supra:*

> it has always been true that irreparable injury means injury for which a monetary award cannot be adequate compensation and that where money damages [are] adequate compensation a preliminary injunction will not issue.

596 F.2d at 72. Thus, if it appears that the potential harm to the moving party is simply a monetary loss, the potential injury is normally not deemed irreparable and hence does not justify injunctive relief. *E.g., KMW International v. Chase Manhattan Bank, N.A., supra,* 606 F.2d at 14-15. Although there may be exceptional cases in which a monetary loss could not be compensated by an award of money damages, as where, for example, the movant shows that the loss would force him into bankruptcy, *see NMC Enterprises, Inc. v. Columbia Broadcasting System, Inc.,* 14 UCC Rep. Serv. 1427 (Sup.Ct.N.Y.Co.1974), in general a preliminary injunction is inappropriate where the potential harm is strictly financial.

In the present case the district court made no express finding as to the nature of the possible injury to Sperry, and Sperry's offer of proof of potential injury was unusually sparse. It consisted only of the following assertion:

If [Israel] were to now to draw down this letter of credit, Sperry's already severe cash flow problems would be aggravated to an extent such that Sperry's performance of the Contract would be hamstrung even if [Israel] were otherwise to fulfill its contractual obligations.

(Affidavit of Sperry Senior Contracts Administrator Gordon O. Lamb ¶ 9, dated September 9, 1981.) There was no elaboration whatever of the nature of the alleged cash flow problems, nor any suggestion that they could not be alleviated in some way even if Israel drew on the letter of credit. To the extent that this statement was intended to cast Sperry's overall financial condition in a light of imminent bankruptcy, it was wholly inadequate to justify the granting of injunctive relief. And to the extent that the statement described cash flow problems related only to Project 6977, it shortly became irrelevant: the only suggested consequence of the cash flow problems — the hindrance of Sperry's performance of the Contract — was obviously mooted when, two days after execution of the affidavit (and more than a month prior to the district court's decision), Sperry elected to cease work on the Contract.

At the hearing in the district court, Sperry apparently attempted, without presenting any additional evidence, to bolster the Lamb affidavit. Its counsel described Sperry as a $6 billion corporation that could quickly pay a $15 million judgment and asked the district court to take judicial notice that the profits of Sperry's parent corporation were "only $15 million" for the first quarter of 1981. Counsel argued that "knocking off a parent company's first quarter profits does irreparable harm to the company in the financial world with the price that money is at." Far from supporting Sperry's claim that its injury would be irreparable, these assertions make it clear that the potential damage to Sperry was strictly monetary and was highly unlikely to have the kind of disastrous effect that could justify the granting of injunctive relief.

.     .     .

The order of the district court is . . . reversed insofar as it enjoined Israel from drawing on the letter of credit.

*     *     *

4.    *Rogers, Burgun, Shahine & Descler, Inc. v. Dongsan Construction Co.*, 598 F.Supp. 754 (S.D.N.Y. 1984).

KRAM, District Judge.

[Rogers, Burgun, Shahine & Descler, Inc. ("RBSD"), a United States corporation and an architectural designer of hospitals, entered into a subcontract, containing an arbitration clause, with Dongsan Construction Company, Ltd., a Korean corporation acting as general contractor for construction projects, to perform architectural and engineering design works for a hospital project in Saudi Arabia. RBSD furnished to Dongsan a bank guarantee to secure Dongsan's payment to it of a 20% advance payment on the contract price. After most of the works were completed, disputes arose between the parties. RBSD commenced suit in federal district court for sums allegedly due to it under the sub-contract, and for a preliminary injunction enjoining Dongsan from calling the Letter of Guarantee. Dongsan filed a motion to dismiss or stay the action pending arbitration. In its opinion the court reviewed the milestones of federal policy in favor of international arbitration prior to addressing Dongsan's motion to stay the proceedings and RBSD's defenses to the motion and its application to continue the preliminary injunction.]

Plaintiff's only other claim in opposition to Dongsan's motion to stay is that Dongsan has not proceeded to arbitration and RBSD chooses not to proceed there either. Essentially, therefore, RBSD is waiving its right to enforcement of the arbitration provision and asserting that Dongsan has waived its right, too, by failing to commence the arbitration.

Dongsan moved to stay or dismiss this action relying on the arbitration provision in its first court filing in this action.[241] This hardly evinces an intent on Dongsan's part to waive its right to arbitrate this dispute. *See I.T.A.D. Assocs., Inc. v. Podar Bros.*, 636 F.2d 75, 77 (4th Cir.1981) (issue of arbitration was raised in first pleading in court, held not waived). Dongsan must, however, move

---

[241] [7] Dongsan's motion predated even an answer to the complaint herein. Since the motion is being granted no answer will be necessary until the arbitration is concluded.

toward arbitration or the Court will find its conduct tantamount to a waiver.

Accordingly, Dongsan's motion to stay these proceedings is granted. Dongsan shall file proof that it has commenced arbitration proceedings pursuant to Article XVI of the Subcontract with this Court within thirty days of the date of this Order and RBSD is directed to proceed to such arbitration. If Dongsan does not institute arbitration proceedings within thirty days, this action will resume and Dongsan shall answer the complaint by January 10, 1985, or be deemed in default.

## RBSD's Motion for a Preliminary Injunction

The fact that this dispute is to be arbitrated does not deprive the Court of its authority to provide provisional remedies. . . . The Court must therefore, decide if this is "a proper case" for an injunction. *Erving*, 468 F.2d at 1067.

The standards governing the issuance of a preliminary injunction are well established in this Circuit. A preliminary injunction will issue only upon

> a showing of (a) irreparable harm and (b) either (1) likelihood of success on the merits or (2) sufficiently serious questions going to the merits to make them a fair ground for litigation and a balance of hardships tipping decidedly toward the party requesting the preliminary relief.

*Jackson Dairy, Inc. v. H.P. Hood & Sons, Inc.*, 596 F.2d 70, 72 (2d Cir.1979); *see also, e.g., Jack Kahn Music Co. v. Baldwin Piano & Organ Co.*, 604 F.2d 755, 758 (2d Cir.1979). I find that the second prong test has been met in the present case.

The relief sought in this case is minimal. RBSD seeks only to preserve the *status quo* with respect to the Letter of Guarantee. "The *status quo* has been frequently defined as the last uncontested status which preceded the pending controversy." *Flood v. Kuhn*, 309 F.Supp. 793, 798 (S.D.N.Y.1970), *aff'd,* 443 F.2d 264 (2d Cir.1971), *aff'd,* 407 U.S. 258, 92 S.Ct. 2099, 32 L.Ed.2d 728 (1972), *quoted in*

*Erving*, 349 F.Supp. at 719. The last uncontested status in this case found Dongsan holding a Letter of Guarantee for $155,766 with RBSD holding that sum to indemnify Bank Al-Jazira for the letter should it be called. Dongsan's argument that the status quo would be preserved by allowing it to call the letter and take the $155,766 secured thereby is unavailing.[242] RBSD seeks only to prevent Dongsan from calling this letter.[243]

The contract dispute involves nearly one million dollars. Dongsan is a Korean corporation with apparently no fixed assets in the United States. Dongsan does maintain an office in New Jersey and a large amount of liquid assets in bank accounts in New York and New Jersey. Those assets, however, because they are all liquid, could easily be depleted or removed from the United States. If that were to occur, RBSD's ability to recover in this Court on any arbitration award obtained in Paris would be frustrated.

With respect to the Letter of Guarantee, the potential for frustration of RBSD's recovery is doubled. The monies securing the letter are currently in RBSD's possession. If Dongsan is permitted to call the letter, those assets would be transferred, essentially from RBSD to Dongsan. Any arbitral determination that RBSD is entitled to recover from Dongsan, or that Dongsan was not entitled to call the letter, would be meaningless if Dongsan were to transfer its liquid assets, increased by the monies securing the letter, out of the reach of this Court. Since there would then be no adequate remedy at law for RBSD in this Court, the Court finds that there could be irreparable harm to RBSD if Dongsan is not enjoined from calling the letter.

---

[242] [8] Dongsan also argues that the status quo will be upset if it "is unable to *maintain* its security in the form of the Letter of Guarantee" (emphasis added), presumably because the Letter might expire by its own terms and Dongsan would be left with nothing. RBSD has, however, agreed to secure an extension of the Letter for the duration of the arbitration. RBSD is directed to do so and to file proof of such extension with the Court by December 15, 1984. Thus, the status quo will be *maintained*.

[243] [9] The underlying dispute involves nearly one million dollars, RBSD has not attempted to restrain Dongsan from doing anything with assets valued near that amount to secure any potential judgment. Rather it has merely sought to avoid *increasing* the amounts potentially unrecoverable from Dongsan.

Dongsan's argument that RBSD would be able to enforce any arbitration award in Korea does not change this finding. RBSD would still have no adequate remedy at law here, in this Court. *See Petroleum Exploration, Inc. v. Public Service Comm'n*, 304 U.S. 209, 217, 58 S.Ct. 834, 838, 82 L.Ed. 1294 (1938); *Di Giovanni v. Camden Fire Ins. Ass'n*, 296 U.S. 64, 69, 56, S.Ct. 1, 3, 80 L.Ed. 47 (1935); *United States v. State of New York*, 708 F.2d 92, 93 (2d Cir.1983). In those cases, the federal courts held that legal remedies in *state* courts did not suffice to make injunctive relief in *federal* courts unavailable. The absence of legal remedy is to be determined in this Court. If the availability of legal remedies in state court is not sufficient to preclude injunctive relief here, *a fortiori* the availability of a legal remedy in a foreign country is not sufficient.[244]

The parties are in hot dispute about the underlying contractual claims. Plaintiff claims it is due nearly $1,000,000. Defendant asserts that plaintiff's obligation to indemnify could total $10,000,000. Certainly this is sufficient to establish serious questions going to the merits for the arbitrator's decision.

Finally, the Court finds that the balance of hardships tips decidedly toward RBSD. If the status quo is maintained, defendant feels no hardship whatsoever. Dongsan maintains security in the sum of $155,766 should the arbitrators determine that it is entitled to any or all of that sum (or more), and loses nothing that it currently has. If the status quo is not maintained, and Dongsan is permitted to call the letter, RBSD stands to lose its own money (the $155,766) without recourse here.

Accordingly, RBSD's motion is granted. RBSD is to file proof of extension of the Letter of Guarantee for one year (to be extended further if necessary) by December 15, 1984. Dongsan, and any of its officers, directors, controlling persons, parents, affiliates, and/or

---

[244] [10] The Court notes that there is some question about the availability of prejudgment attachment under the Convention. *Compare Carolina Power & Light Co. v. Uranex*, 451 F.Supp. 1044 (N.D.Cal.1977) (yes) *with Metropolitan World Tanker Corp. v. P.N. Pertambangan Minjaklangas Bumi Nasional*, 427 F.Supp. 2 (S.D.N.Y. 1975) (no). However, the relief sought here is not an attachment. Dongsan is in no way restricted in its use or possession of its assets, but only in its power to gather more assets from RBSD leaving RBSD with only the recourse of recovery in Korea.

subsidiaries, is hereby enjoined from directing the Bank Al-Jazira to honor or pay the Letter of Guarantee involved herein.

*          *          *

As opposed to the fragile powers of an arbitrator in ordinary commercial arbitration to make orders to protect its jurisdiction, a court does have constitutional status, and statutory powers, to act. In an extreme case a federal court has felt free to enjoin a party defendant in arbitral proceedings from continuing to bring inconsistent actions in state courts for the purpose of interfering with the arbitration.

5.     *Hunt v. Mobil Oil Corp.*, 583 F.Supp. 1092 (S.D.N.Y. 1984).

EDWARD WEINFELD, District Judge.

In its ruling entered upon its opinion dated February 15, 1983, this Court, among other matters, held that under an exception to the Federal Anti-Injunction Act, 28 U.S.C. § 2283, it was empowered to enjoin an action commenced by the Hunts in the New York State Supreme Court in order to effectuate any judgment with respect to a pending arbitration.[245] The Court enjoined the Hunts "from prosecuting their pending state action" and directed them to "continue with the pending arbitration." In its affirmance the Court of Appeals expressly noted that this Court "correctly found that the stay order comes within one of the exceptions to section 2283 because it was necessary 'to effectuate the judgment' compelling arbitration" and further observed that the Hunts' "contention that the stay was not necessary to effectuate the arbitration order because the state court action would not interfere with the arbitration is meritless."[246]

Seemingly, with such definitive determinations one would have assumed that the arbitration went forward. Instead, thereafter the Hunts commenced two additional state court actions. One was instituted in the

---

[245] [1] *Hunt v. Mobil Oil Corp.*, 557 F.Supp. 368, 372 (S.D.N.Y. 1983). Familiarity is assumed with the other rulings in this matter, noted by the Court in *Hunt*, 557 F.Supp. 368, 370 n. 1.

[246] [2] *Hunt v. Mobil Oil Corp.*, No. 83-7201, *slip op.* at 4 (2d Cir. Aug. 15, 1983).

New York State Supreme Court against the American Arbitration Association ("AAA") and Grace Petroleum Libya, Inc. The essence of the Hunts' claim is that the AAA violated its fiduciary and other alleged duties properly to administer the arbitration, failed to render an accounting of fees paid to arbitrators for their services, permitted the arbitrators to charge excessive fees, and failed to disclose facts with respect to alleged conflicts of interest and appearances of impropriety by one or more arbitrators.

The Hunts also commenced a state court action in the District of Columbia against Kenneth W. Dam, a former arbitrator. In that action the Hunts allege the charging by Dam of exorbitant fees, double bills, improper charges of expenses, and seek an accounting of all fees received during his services as arbitrator; in addition, they seek information relating to his alleged conflict of interest.

In the first state action, which was enjoined, the principal thrust of the charges was that each of the original three arbitrators, including Dam, had failed to disclose actual or potential conflicts of interest and that the AAA had failed in its supervisory duties and by various conduct had denied the Hunts fundamental fairness in the arbitration proceeding.

The Hunts now seek an order from this Court clarifying its earlier order of February 15, 1983, to the effect that it does not enjoin the Hunts from continuing these subsequently instituted lawsuits. The order entered by this Court is explicit and clear and requires no clarification. The new state actions in substance do not differ from the first New York State action, which was enjoined and found to be interlocutory. However variously phrased, in an effort to avoid the effect of the stay of the first state suit, they parallel the allegations of that action. In effect, the Hunts again are seeking interlocutory review of arbitration related matters that were inherent in and advanced in the first state action which, among other matters, charged the arbitrators with alleged conflicts of interest and appearances of impropriety and the AAA with breach of its duty to oversee the administration of the arbitration.

The current allegations in the latest lawsuits are clearly designed to lay the ground work of an attack upon a final award by the arbitrators in an effort to establish the now oft repeated assertions of the Hunts that the arbitrators by reason of alleged conflicts of interest were disqualified and that the Hunts were deprived of their right to fair and impartial judgment of the arbitrators.

To permit the continuance of the current state actions with the avowed purpose of extensive discovery of facts from Dam, other arbitrators, third parties and the AAA as to the fees and alleged bases for disqualifications would unduly delay and interfere with the pending arbitration. Judicial rulings by those courts with respect to alleged conflicts of interest, excessive and unauthorized fee charges, and the AAA's alleged breach of duty would amount to unwarranted interference with this Court's order directing that the arbitration proceed.

The arbitration should proceed forthwith. Upon the rendition of a final award by the arbitrators, Hunt or any other aggrieved party may raise any claim that the arbitrators acted improperly, were involved in conflicts of interest, or were engaged in any conduct that impairs the validity of the award. Similarly, an alleged impropriety by the AAA that tainted the award may then be raised.[247] With respect to the Hunts' claims as to exorbitant fees, double billing and the like, the Hunts and the other parties entered into a Compensation Stipulation which contained specific amounts to be paid for services and under which the parties to the arbitration were to advance payments to defray the anticipated cost to the AAA subject to final apportionment by the arbitrators in their award. That agreement provides the award shall include an allowance of all fees and expenses, including arbitration compensation incurred in the conduct of the arbitration. The various claims with respect to exorbitant fees and the like may also be determined in an attack upon the final award.[248]

It is beyond cavil that the Hunts' current state actions, however thinly disguised to avoid a plea of collateral estoppel, are not only interlocutory in nature, but if not stayed, as was their prior action, would only further delay this arbitration, already too long delayed, and would serve to interfere with this Court's power to effectuate any judgment that may be warranted under the arbitration.

---

[247] [4] 9 U.S.C. §§ 9, 10(a)-(c), 11(a) (1976).

[248] [5] *Id.* § 10; *Wright-Austin Co. v. International Union*, 422 F.Supp. 1364, 1370-71 (E.D.Mich. 1976).

The plaintiffs' motion for clarification is denied. The defendants' motion to enjoin the Hunts, their agents, employees and attorneys from proceeding with their new state actions and any other interlocutory court or administrative action relating to the arbitration is granted. The parties are directed to continue with the arbitration of the claims arising out of the Libyan Producers Agreement dated January 15, 1971, pending before the American Arbitration Association in accordance with the terms of the agreement and the prior orders of this Court.

So ordered.

### Notes and Questions

1. Do the cases suggest that the courts see themselves as assisting in the arbitral process or do they consider arbitration as an adjunct to the judicial process?

2. Is a court more likely to take interim measures if a request is made to it before the arbitral tribunal is formed?

3. Measures, such as attachment, which are directed against third parties can only be taken by a court. Is there any reason to assume, where nothing is said in the arbitration agreement or rules, that by agreeing to arbitration the parties have waived their rights to this judicial remedy? If not, how can it be avoided that parties who have agreed to arbitrate sometimes find that the first step in dispute resolution is in court?

4. Outside of the United States, the jurisdiction of national courts to attach property and take other interim measurers in support of arbitration is well recognized and is ordinarily set out in specific legislative provisions. In England the Arbitration Act of 1996 which provides that in regard to specified interim measures the High Court shall have in relation to a reference to arbitration the same powers as it enjoys in relation to an action or matter in the High Court. Included in these powers is the issue of so-called *Mareva* injunctions restraining the respondent from moving his assets from the jurisdiction of the English courts as security for the enforcement of any award to be rendered. *See* David W. Shenton, *Attachment and other Interim Court remedies in Support of Arbitration: The English Courts*, in INTERIM COURT REMEDIES IN SUPPORT OF ARBITRATION (David W. Shenton & Wolfgang Kuhn eds., 1987). International Bar Association, London (1987). In France, the interim measures in connection with arbitration are authorized as part of the general powers of the judge sitting *en référé* (in chambers) to order urgent or conservatory measurers, attachments or provisional payments (*référé provision*), as long as they do not prejudice the merits of the dispute. *See* Jacques Buhart, *Attachments and Other Interim Court Remedies in Support of Arbitration: French Law*, in INTERIM COURT REMEDIES IN SUPPORT OF ARBITRATION, *supra*. In Switzerland, the relationship

between arbitrators and the courts and their concurrent powers to take provisional measures is spelled out in the recent legislation provisions of Article 183 of the Law of December 18, 1987 on private international law (*"loi sur le droit international privé"* or "LDIP"). *See* PIERRE A. LALIVE ET AL., LE DROIT DE L'ARBITRAGE INTERNE ET INTERNATIONAL SUISSE, 360-69 (1989).

### B. EFFECT OF INTERNATIONAL CONVENTIONS ON POWER OF COURTS TO TAKE PROVISIONAL MEASURES

#### 1. NEW YORK CONVENTION

If it is generally accepted that courts have inherent powers to take provisional measures in connection with arbitration, the question nevertheless arises whether international conventions relating to arbitration inhibit the exercise of such powers. In the international context, the desire to avoid national court adjudication is perhaps the strongest motivation for the parties' agreement to arbitrate. The purpose of international conventions, it may be argued, is to assure, where they have agreed to arbitrate, that the parties are referred to arbitration and that an award so obtained is entitled to recognition and enforcement in national courts. The issue of the role of national courts in respect to provisional measures has come up both in regard to the New York Convention and the Washington Convention. Article II (3) of the New York Convention (for the full text, *see* Supplement at p. 40) provides:

> The court of a Contracting State, when seized of an action in a matter in respect of which the parties have made an agreement within the meaning of this article, shall, at the request of one of the parties, refer the parties to arbitration, unless it finds that the said agreement is null and void, inoperative or incapable of being performed.

As was said by a contemporaneous commentator:

> The reasonable interpretation of that language is that the court should not only refer the parties to arbitration but should also stay any conflicting court proceedings pending the outcome of the arbitration. Leonard

V. Quigley, *Convention on Foreign Arbitral Awards*, 58
A.B.A. J. 821 (1972).

To what extent, however, should provisional measures be
considered to "conflict" with the arbitration proceeding? Are
provisional measures an aid to arbitration or do they constitute
unwanted and unwarranted interference by national courts with the
forum chosen by the parties -arbitration? These are questions which
have been considered by courts which have been requested, on the
basis of the New York Convention, not only to stay or dismiss court
proceedings on the merits so that arbitral proceedings could go
forward, but also to dismiss provisional measures such as attachments
on the same basis. The issues have come up both in the United States
and in foreign proceedings, but appear to have raised problems
principally in the United States.

The United States ratified the New York Convention in 1970,
and the conditions for its application were supplied by the addition of
Chapter 2 to the United States Arbitration Act originally enacted in
1925 and codified in Title 9, U.S. Code, of which Sections 201 and
206 of the United States Arbitration Act are pertinent to this
discussion.

Not long after the entry into effect of these provisions the
federal court of appeal for the third circuit in Philadelphia was called
upon, in *McCreary*, to determine whether the obligation to "refer" a
matter to arbitration carried with it the obligation to dissolve a
preexisting attachment obtained by the U.S. claimant concerning a
claim which it had first raised in court proceedings and which was now
to be referred to arbitration.

      a.     *McCreary Tire & Rubber Co. v. CEAT
             S.p.A.,* 501 F.2d 1032 (3d Cir. 1974).

GIBBONS, Circuit Judge.

[McCreary, a U.S. distributor of CEAT, an Italian
manufacturer, had brought suit against CEAT in the federal district
court for Massachusetts, which suit was stayed in view of the parties'
arbitration agreement. A second suit, together with an attachment of
CEAT's accounts in a local bank, was brought in a federal district
court in Pennsylvania. The District Court denied CEAT's motion to

dissolve the attachment and to stay the suit in court. CEAT appealed. The Court of Appeal first referred to the findings of the district court and after having found that the orders were appealable considered the issues of the stay of court proceedings and the continuation of the attachment.]

. . . Attached to McCreary's complaint as Exhibit A is a copy of a contract dated November 16, 1970 whereby CEAT appointed McCreary its exclusive distributor in the United States of pneumatic tires and tubes manufactured by CEAT in Italy bearing the CEAT label or having the same tread design as tires bearing that label. Section 3 of the contract also provides, in relevant part:

> "(b) During the period this agreement is in effect, CEAT shall not appoint any other distributor or any other agent for the sale of Products in the Territory, and CEAT shall not itself otherwise sell or distribute the Products directly and indirectly in the Territory. . . .

> .     .     .

> (i) CEAT warrants that all Products delivered by it to or for the account of the Distributor shall be free from defects in material or workmanship (which phrase as used in this Agreement shall include ply and tread separation resulting from any such defects, and substantial visual defects) and shall conform to all safety and other standards established by the United States Department of Transportation or any other Federal governmental agency having jurisdiction over the Products."

Count I of the complaint alleges that CEAT has breached the exclusivity clause quoted above by selling to Duddy's Inc., a Massachusetts corporation, radial tires bearing a different trade name but having the same tread design. This count seeks $2,000,000 in damages. Counts III and IV allege breaches of the express warranty quoted above, and of an implied warranty of merchantable quality. Each of these counts seeks $250,000 in damages. The allegations of Counts I, III and IV relate to disputes which quite plainly fall within the arbitration clause in section 7(b) of the agreement:

"This agreement shall be governed by the laws of the Republic of Italy. Any controversy arising out of or in connection with this agreement shall be finally settled under the Rules of Arbitration of the International Chamber of Commerce, by three arbitrators appointed in accordance with said Rules. The arbitration shall be held in Brussels, Belgium, and shall be conducted in English. Judgment upon the award rendered may be entered in any court having jurisdiction for a judicial acceptance of the award and an order of enforcement, as the case may be.

Count II of the complaint realleges the existence of the November 16, 1970, exclusive distributorship contract, Exhibit A. It then refers to Exhibit B, a letter dated November 5, 1970 from CEAT to McCreary, which provides:

"As you know, CEAT tires are manufactured in India by a corporation partly owned by us. We will give that Indian corporation a copy of the proposed Distributor Agreement under which you are made the exclusive distributor in the United States for CEAT passenger car and truck tires. We will use our best efforts to obtain the agreement of the Indian corporation that if it should ever export passenger car or truck tires to the United States, it will appoint you the exclusive distributor for such tires on the same terms and conditions (other than minimum quantities) as the terms and conditions specified in the Distributor Agreement between us. If you do not receive the agreement of the Indian corporation specified above, and if thereafter, at a time that the Distributor Agreement between us is in force, it seeks to sell tires (other than in a nominal or negligible amount) intended to be delivered or sold in the United States, we agree that we will use our efforts to prevent the importation into the United States or sale there under the trademark CEAT owned by us.

We represent that except in India, CEAT tires are not made outside of our plants in Italy. We agree that if at any time we manufacture CEAT tires outside of Italy or we grant the right to any company, whether

or not controlled by us, to manufacture CEAT tires, we
will require that you be designated exclusive distributor
in the United States on the same terms (except for
minimum quantities) as those in the Distributor
Agreement between us."

Count II alleges, further, that since October 1972 CEAT brand tires
manufactured by CEAT Tyres of India, Ltd. (CEAT-India) have been
imported into the United States and sold in the states of California and
Arizona, and that on information and belief CEAT has failed to use its
best efforts to have CEAT-India appoint McCreary as its exclusive
distributor for CEAT brand tires in the United States nor has it used its
best efforts to prevent CEAT brand tires manufactured by CEAT-India
from being imported and sold in the United States. Count II seeks
$250,000 in damages. A fair reading of the count is that the damages
alleged arise out of the existence of the distributorship agreement. Thus
prima facie Count II as well as Counts I, III and IV would seem to
involve a "controversy arising out of or in connection with" that
agreement and to be covered by the arbitration clause. In its motion for
a stay pending arbitration CEAT so alleged, and further alleged:

> "The arbitration agreement between plaintiff and
> defendants must be enforced pursuant to the Convention
> on the Recognition and Enforcement of Foreign Arbitral
> Awards of June 10, 1958."

The district court was also informed of the undisputed fact that
McCreary had started a suit in October 1972 in the United States
District Court for the District of Massachusetts by attempting to attach
debts owed CEAT. In that suit, which joined Duddy's, Inc. as a
defendant, McCreary alleged the same breaches as are alleged in
Counts I and II. CEAT appeared in the Massachusetts action and its
motions for a stay and an order compelling arbitration of the alleged
breach of the exclusive distributorship were granted. Thus when the
stay was denied in this action arbitration had already been ordered, and
is now underway.

McCreary urges that the denial of the stay pending arbitration
should be affirmed since the district court acted within the bounds of
a permissible discretion. . . . But this is not a case in which a stay
pending arbitration was discretionary.

The district court was bound by the terms of the Convention on Recognition and Enforcement of Foreign Arbitral Awards, [1970] 3 U.S.T. 2517, T.I.A.S. No. 6997 (reprinted following 9 U.S.C.A. § 201 (1974 Supp.)). That treaty was ratified by Italy on January 31, 1969 and by the United States on September 30, 1970. Congress passed implementing legislation on July 31, 1970. Pub.L. No. 91-368, 84 Stat. 692 (codified at 9 U.S. C. §§ 201-208). That statute provides in part:

> "An arbitration agreement or arbitral award arising out of a legal relationship, whether contractual or not, which is considered as commercial, including a transaction, contract, or agreement described in section 2 of this title [§2 of the Federal Arbitration Act of 1925, 9 U.S.C. § 2], falls under the Convention." 9 U.S.C. § 202.

The same statute provides that an action or proceeding falling under the Convention shall be deemed to arise under the laws and treaties of the United States and that the district courts of the United States shall have original jurisdiction over such proceedings without regard to amount in controversy. 9 U.S.C. § 203. Although this case was removed on diversity grounds it was also removable on the authority of 9 U.S.C. § 205, which provides for such removal. Moreover 9 U.S.C. § 206 makes clear that the federal court may order arbitration of a dispute to which the Convention applies at the place agreed upon by the parties, within or without the United States. *See also* Agreement Supplementing the Treaty of Friendship, Commerce and Navigation, United States and Italy, article VI, [1961] 1 U.S.T. 131, 136, T.I.A.S. No. 4685. *Compare with* 9 U.S.C. § 4.

. . . .There is nothing discretionary about article II(3) of the Convention. It states that district courts *shall*, at the request of a party to an arbitration agreement refer the parties to arbitration. The enactment of Pub.L. 91-368, providing a federal remedy for the enforcement of the Convention, including removal jurisdiction without regard to diversity or amount in controversy, demonstrates the firm commitment of the Congress to the elimination of vestiges of judicial reluctance to enforce arbitration agreements, at least in the international commercial context. *See* Scherk v. Alberto-Culver Co., 417 U.S. 506, n. 15, 94 S.Ct. 2449, 41 L.Ed.2d 270 (1974). It was error to deny the motion for a stay in disregard of the convention.

## III. THE CONTINUANCE OF THE ATTACHMENT

[The court found that the order refusing to vacate the attachment was properly before the Court of Appeal because sufficiently connected to the appeal from the order denying a stay of the judicial proceedings pending arbitration. McCreary's request for attachment violated its agreement to submit the underlying disputes to arbitration.]

. . . Quite possibly foreign attachment may be available for the enforcement of an arbitration award.[249] This complaint does not seek to enforce an arbitration award by foreign attachment. It seeks to bypass the agreed upon method of settling disputes. Such a bypass is prohibited by the Convention if one party to the agreement objects. Unlike § 3 of the federal Act, article II(3) of the Convention provides that the court of a contracting state shall "refer the parties to arbitration" rather than "stay the trial of the action." The Convention forbids the courts of a contracting state from entertaining a suit which violates an agreement to arbitrate. Thus the contention that arbitration is merely another method of trial, to which state provisional remedies should equally apply, is unavailable. That contention, accepted by Judge Learned Hand as a justification for prearbitration attachment in Murray Oil Products Co. v. Mitsui & Co., 146 F.2d 381, 384 (2d Cir. 1944), was rejected, in a diversity context, by the Supreme Court in Bernhardt v. Polygraphic Company of America, Inc., 350 U.S. 198, 202, 76 S.Ct. 273, 100 L.Ed. 199 (1956). Here, although the suit is in the federal court after removal from a state court, the governing law with respect to arbitration is the Convention. In the district court CEAT, after referring to the Treaty, alleged:

"4. Contrary to the terms of both the Distributor Agreement and of the Convention, no arbitration has been had of the claims asserted by the plaintiff in this action against the defendant, and defendant is not aware of any demands by plaintiff for such arbitration."

---

[249] [3] Article III of the Convention provides:

Each Contracting State shall recognize arbitral awards as binding and enforce them in accordance with rules and procedure of the territory where the award is relied upon, under the conditions laid down in the following articles. . . .

CEAT then asked for an order releasing all property from the foreign attachment and permitting arbitration. The obvious purpose of the enactment of Pub. L. 91-368, permitting removal of all cases falling within the terms of the treaty, was to prevent the vagaries of state law from impeding its full implementation. Permitting a continued resort to foreign attachment in breach of the agreement is inconsistent with that purpose. The relief requested, a release of all property from the attachment, should have been granted.

Since we conclude that the Convention requires discharge of the foreign attachment, we have no occasion to pass upon CEAT's attack on the constitutionality of the Pennsylvania foreign attachment procedures.

The order of the district court will be reversed and the case remanded for the entry of an order (1) discharging the foreign attachment and (2) referring the disputed claims to arbitration pursuant to Article 7(b) of Exhibit A attached to the complaint.

\*     \*     \*

The *McCreary* case is not the exclusive federal court position on attachment in Convention arbitration cases. Three year later in 1977, an opposite and parallel line of federal cases was initiated by the decision of the federal district court for the Northern District of California in the *Uranex* case.

b.     *Carolina Power & Light Co. v. Uranex*,
451 F.Supp. 1044 (N.D. Cal. 1977).

PECKHAM, Chief Judge.

In 1973 Carolina Power & Light Company ("CP&L"), a North Carolina public utility company, contracted with defendant Uranex for the delivery of uranium concentrates to CP&L during the period 1977 to 1986. Uranex is a French *groupement d'intérêt économique* that markets uranium internationally. Following the recent and dramatic rise in the price of uranium fuel in the world market, Uranex either would not or could not deliver at the contract price, and requested renegotiation. CP&L has refused to enter any discussions aimed at contract modifications.

Earlier this year CP&L filed the present action against Uranex, and proceeded *ex parte* to attach an 85 million dollar debt owed to Uranex by Homestake Mining Company ("Homestake"), a San Francisco based corporation that markets uranium throughout the United States. The 85 million dollars is due to Uranex pursuant to a uranium supply contract between Homestake and Uranex, and has no relationship to the present litigation except as a potential source for CP&L to satisfy any judgment that might issue. But for the attachment the funds would have been transferred out of the country in the ordinary course of business.

The contract between CP&L and Uranex provides that disputes are to be submitted to arbitration in New York. At the time this lawsuit was filed CP&L sought to compel Uranex to enter arbitration. Since that time, however, Uranex voluntarily has entered arbitration and those proceedings are now going on in New York. Both parties agree that because of the arbitration agreement this court cannot adjudicate the merits of the dispute, but CP&L contends that the court should stay this action and maintain the attachment in order to protect any award that CP&L might receive in the New York arbitration. CP&L claims that Uranex has no other assets in this country with which to satisfy a judgment, and Uranex apparently does not dispute this proposition. Uranex has moved the court on several grounds to dismiss the complaint and quash the writ of attachment.

[The court first decided that since the rendering by the Supreme Court of the then very recent decision of *Shaffer v. Heitner*, 433 U.S. 186 (1977), it did not have jurisdiction over defendant *quasi in rem* based on the presence in the jurisdiction of the property subject to the attachment. However, it accepted the plaintiff's argument that it should have jurisdiction to attach that property as security for a judgment being sought in a forum where the litigation could be maintained consistently with *International Shoe*. Accordingly it accepted to take jurisdiction over the defendant on the issue of the attachment provided that plaintiff would have within 30 days filed proceedings before a court that had *in personam* jurisdiction over the defendant (presumably such a court would have stayed proceedings during the pendency of arbitration). The court then went on to consider whether maintaining the attachment was contrary to the provisions of the New York Convention.]

In 1970 the United States became a party to the Convention on the Recognition and Enforcement of Foreign Arbitral Awards (hereafter cited as Convention), 9 U.S.C. §§ 201 *et seq.* (1970), . . . .

The Convention and its implementing statutes contain no reference to prejudgment attachment, and provide little guidance in this controversy. Article II of the Convention states only that a "court of a Contracting State . . . shall, at the request of one of the parties, refer the parties to arbitration." To implement this aspect of the Convention, section 206 of Title 9 provides that "[a] court having jurisdiction under this chapter may direct that arbitration be held in accordance with the agreement at any place therein provided for, whether that place is within or without the United States." The language of these provisions provides little apparent support for defendant's argument.

Uranex, however, relies upon the decisions of the Third Circuit in *McCreary Tire & Rubber Co. v. CEAT, S.p.A.*, 501 F.2d 1032 (3d Cir. 1974). . . . At least one district court has chosen to follow the rationale of the *McCreary* opinion in applying the Convention to prejudgment attachments. *See Metropolitan World Tanker, Corp. v. P.N. Pertambangan Minjakdangas Bumi Nasional (P.M. Pertamina)*, 427 F.Supp. 2 (S.D.N.Y. 1975).

This court, however, does not find the reasoning of *McCreary* convincing. As mentioned above, nothing in the text of the Convention itself suggests that it precludes prejudgment attachment. The United States Arbitration Act, 9 U.S.C. §§ 1 *et seq.* (1970), which operates much like the Convention for domestic agreements involving maritime or interstate commerce, does not prohibit maintenance of a prejudgment attachment during a stay pending arbitration:

> After declaring (§ 2 [of the Arbitration Act]) such agreements [to arbitrate] to be enforceable, Congress, in succeeding sections, implemented the declared policy. By § 3 it provided that "if any suit or proceeding be brought in any of the courts of the United States upon any issue referable to arbitration under any agreement in writing for such arbitration, the court . . . shall on application of one of the parties stay the trial . . . until such arbitration has been had" if the applicant is not in default in proceeding with such arbitration. The section obviously envisages action in a court on a cause

of action and does not oust the court's jurisdiction of the action, though the parties have agreed to arbitrate. And, it would seem there is nothing to prevent the plaintiff from commencing the action by attachment if such procedure is available under the applicable law. This section deals with suits at law or in equity. The concept seems to be that a power to grant a stay is enough without to power to order that the arbitration proceed, for, if a stay be granted, the plaintiff can never get relief unless he proceeds to arbitration.

*Barge "Anaconda" v. American Sugar Refining Co.*, 322 U.S. 42, 44-45, 64 S.Ct. 863, 865, 88 L.Ed. 1117 (1944). *See also Murray Oil Products Co. v. Mitsui & Co.*, 146 F.2d 381 (2d Cir. 1944).[250] The *McCreary* court makes two rather elliptical comments to distinguish the United States Arbitration Act from the Convention. First, the court notes that the Arbitration Act only directs courts to "stay the trial of

---

[250] [3] In *McCreary* the Third Circuit commented that the approach taken in *Murray Oil Products Co. v. Mitsui & Co., supra,* was rejected "in a diversity context" by the Supreme Court in *Bernhardt v. Polygraphic Co. of America, Inc.,* 350 U.S. 198, 76 S.Ct. 273, 100 L.Ed. 199 (1956). This comment is inaccurate. *Murray Oil Products* concerned a contract in interstate commerce with an arbitration clause and the United States Arbitration Act clearly applied. On defendant's motion the district court had stayed the action pending arbitration, and after the arbitrators had found for the plaintiff, the district court entered summary judgment for plaintiff pursuant to the arbitral decision. Writing for the Second Circuit, Judge Learned Hand held that it was appropriate for the district court to enter summary judgment on the arbitral award without requiring plaintiff to initiate a separate action for confirmation of the arbitral award. With respect to this decision he observed that "[a]rbitration is merely a form of trial, to be adopted in the action itself, in place of the trial at common law . . ." 146 F.2d. at 383. He then went on to determine, as a second and separate issue, that the United States Arbitration Act allowed the district court to maintain a prejudgment attachment pending arbitration. In *Bernhardt v. Polygraphic Co. of America, Inc., supra,* the Supreme Court first determined that the contract in question did not involve interstate commerce, and hence that the rules of the United States Arbitration Act could not be applied directly as substantive law. The court also decided that rules concerning the validity of arbitration agreements were substantive and not procedural, and that therefore in a diversity case not involving interstate commerce state rules of law on arbitration were to be applied. It was in that context that the Supreme Court quoted and "rejected" Learned Hand's comment that arbitration was "merely a form of trial." None of the questions actually decided in *Murray Oil Products* were involved in *Bernhardt v. Polygraphic Co. of America, Inc., supra.*

the action," while the Convention requires a court to "refer the parties to arbitration." 501 F.2d at 1038. From this difference the *McCreary* court apparently concludes that while the Arbitration Act might permit continued jurisdiction and even maintenance of a prejudgment attachment pending arbitration, application of the Convention completely ousts the court of jurisdiction. The use of the general term "refer," however, might reflect little more than the fact that the Convention must be applied in many very different legal systems,[251] and possibly in circumstances where the use of the technical term "stay" would not be a meaningful directive. Furthermore, section 4 of the United States Arbitration Act grants district courts the power to actually order the parties to arbitration, but this provision has not been interpreted to deprive the courts of continuing jurisdiction over the action.

Second, the *McCreary* court found support for its position in the fact that the implementing statutes of the Convention provide for removal jurisdiction in the federal courts. *See* 9 U.S.C. § 205 (1970). The Third Circuit concluded that "[t]he obvious purpose [of providing for removal jurisdiction] . . . was to prevent the vagaries of state law from impeding its [the Convention's] full implementation. Permitting a continued resort to foreign attachment . . . is inconsistent with that purpose." It must be noted, however, that any case falling within section 4 of the United States Arbitration Act also would be subject to removal pursuant to 28 U.S.C. § 1441. Furthermore, removal to federal court could have little impact on the "vagaries" of state provisional remedies, for pursuant to Rule 64 of the Federal Rules of Civil Procedure the district courts employ the procedures and remedies of the states where they sit. Finally, it should be noted that in other contexts the Supreme Court has concluded that the availability of provisional remedies encourages rather than obstructs the use of agreements to arbitrate. *See Boys Market, Inc. v. Retail Clerks Union*, 398 U.S. 235, 90 S.Ct. 1583, 26 L.Ed.2d 199 (1970).

In sum this court will not follow the reasoning of *McCreary Tire & Rubber Company v. CEAT, S.p.A.*, *supra*. There is no indication in

---

[251] [4] There are over 50 contracting nations to the Convention, and "equally authentic" texts in five different languages. *See* Convention on the Recognition and Enforcement of Foreign Arbitral Awards, Art. XVI.

either the text or the apparent policies of the Convention that resort to prejudgment attachment was to be precluded.

\*     \*     \*

The *Uranex* case was settled and was not made the subject of decision by a Court of Appeal. Nevertheless it has set out in a well reasoned decision the basis for allowing pre-award attachment in arbitration covered by the Convention and sets up a split of authority between the federal circuits on this issue which will have to be resolved by the Supreme Court.

In the meantime, in *Cooper v. Ateliers de la Motobécane S.A.*, the Court of Appeal of New York (New York's highest court) weighed in with its own views. It went beyond *McCreary*, questioning whether attachment was ever appropriate in arbitration matters and suggesting that, even in domestic cases in New York, attachment might not be available once a stay of judicial proceedings had been granted in favor of arbitration.

c.      *Cooper v. Ateliers de la Motobécane*, 442 N.E.2d 1239 (1982).

COOKE, Chief Judge.

. . . . .

I

Plaintiff and others not here involved entered into a contract with defendant, a French corporation, to establish a New York corporation to distribute defendant's products. The agreement provided that plaintiff and others could each tender his or her shares for repurchase to defendant or the New York corporation, the two being jointly and severally obligated to buy such shares according to a price-setting formula. Disputes over valuation were to be resolved by arbitration in Switzerland.

In April, 1978, plaintiff tendered his shares for repurchase. Negotiations ensued until defendant finally demanded arbitration. In September, 1978, plaintiff sought a permanent stay of arbitration in Supreme Court (Action I). Special Term denied the petition, but the

Appellate Division reversed and issued a stay. The Court of Appeals, relying on *Matter of United Nations Dev. Corp. v. Norkin Plumbing Co.*, 45 N.Y.2d 358, 408 N.Y.S.2d 424, 380 N.E.2d 253, reversed and denied the stay in a one-sentence decision (49 N.Y.2d 819, 427 N.Y. S.2d 619, 404 N.E.2d 741).

During the pendency of Action I, in January, 1979, plaintiff commenced this action for a money judgment (Action II) and obtained an ex parte attachment of a debt owed by the New York corporation to defendant. Plaintiff sought to confirm the attachment and was opposed by defendant, who moved to dismiss the complaint and vacate the attachment. Supreme Court confirmed the attachment after the Appellate Division had granted a stay of arbitration in Action I. Defendant renewed its motion to dismiss and vacate after the Court of Appeals reversed in Action I. Special Term granted the motion, relying on Federal cases that interpret the UN Convention as stripping a court of jurisdiction to entertain an attachment action. The Appellate Division reversed in a 4-1 decision, rejecting the loss-of-jurisdiction argument and holding that there could be prearbitration attachment. The dissenting Justice relied on Special Term's decision.

## II

[The Court reviewed the history of international conventions favoring international commercial arbitration and emphasized the efficacity of the New York Convention which requires the party opposing enforcement to prove the award's invalidity and also permits (Art.VI) a party after the award to request a court to order that the other party be ordered to give suitable security.]

## III

The provisional remedy of attachment is, in part, a device to secure the payment of a money judgment (see McLaughlin, Practice Commentaries, McKinney's Cons Law of NY, Book 7B, CPLR 6201:1, p. 11). It is available only in an action for damages (see CPLR 6201; McLaughlin, *op. cit.*). Under the appropriate circumstances, it can be obtained in a matter that is subject to arbitration: an order of attachment will remain valid if it was obtained with notice or has been confirmed in a contract action before a defendant obtains a stay of proceedings because the underlying controversy is subject to arbitration (see *American Reserve Ins. Co. v. China Ins. Co.*, 297 N.Y. 322,

326-327, 79 N.E.2d 425). It should be noted, however, that attachment would not be available in a proceeding to compel arbitration (see CPLR 7503, subd. [a]), as that is not an action seeking a money judgment.

It is open to dispute whether attachment is even necessary in the arbitration context. Arbitration, as part of the contracting process, is subject to the same implicit assumptions of good faith and honesty that permeate the entire relationship. Voluntary compliance with arbitral awards may be as high as 85% . . . . Moreover, parties are free to include security clauses (e.g., performance bonds or creating escrow accounts) in their agreements to arbitrate. The UN Convention apparently considered the problem and saw no need to provide for prearbitration security (cf. USCS Administrative Rules, Foreign Arbitral Awards Conv, Art. VI [security available when party opposes enforcement of award]). Moreover, the list of signatory countries provides that it will be able to enforce an arbitral award almost anywhere in the world (see *id.*, at Appendix: List of Participants, Declarations and Reservations).

IV

More important here, however, is the injection of uncertainty — the antithesis of the UN Convention's purpose — that would occur by permitting attachments and judicial proceedings. Once again, the foreign business entity would be subject to foreign laws with which it is unfamiliar.

The UN Convention was implemented in the United States in 1970 (Public L. 91-368, codified at U.S.Code, tit. 9, § 201 *et seq.*). This act amended the Federal Arbitration Act by re-enacting the earlier sections and denominating them "Chapter 1," and adding "Chapter 2" to provide a vehicle for enforcing the UN Convention (see Aksen, *op. cit.*, at p. 16). In *McCreary Tire & Rubber Co. v. CEAT*, 501 F.2d 1032 the Third Circuit ruled that the language "refer the parties to arbitration" (USCS Administrative Rules, Foreign Arbitral Awards Conv, art. II, § 3) precludes the courts from acting in any capacity except to order arbitration, and therefore an order of attachment could not be issued. To hold otherwise would defeat the purpose of the UN Convention . . . .

Plaintiff relies on a number of cases to the contrary (*see Paramount Carriers Corp. v. Cook Inds.*, 465 F.Supp 599 [SDNY];

*Compania de Navegacion y Financiera Bosnia, S.A., v. National Unity Mar. Salvage Corp.*, 457 F.Supp. 1013 [S.D.N.Y.]; *Atlas Chartering Servs. v. World Trade Group*, 453 F.Supp. 861 [S.D.N.Y.]; *Carolina Power & Light Co. v. Uranex*, 451 F.Supp. 1044 [N.D. Cal]. Most of these cases are distinguishable, however. The implementing statute provides that normal Federal arbitration law applies to the extent it is not inconsistent with the UN Convention (see U.S. Code, tit. 9, § 208). That law specifically permits attachment to be used in admiralty cases (see U.S. Code, tit. 9, § 8). In all of the cases relied on by plaintiff, except for *National Unity Mar.* and *Carolina Power*, the courts relied on section 8 in approving attachment in a case arising out of a maritime contract. In *National Unity Mar.*, the court discussed neither section 8 nor the UN Convention in approving attachment in a maritime contract case. Only in *Carolina Power* did the court allow attachment in a case not involving a maritime contract falling under the UN Convention. That court rejected *McCreary*'s reasoning that it must divest itself of jurisdiction. Instead, concerned that the plaintiff would be unable to enforce an eventual arbitral award, the District Court approved the security attachment, a rationale that, as discussed above, is not compelling.

The controversy now before this court demonstrates the soundness of the decisions reached by the Third and Fourth Circuits. Defendant agreed to arbitrate disputes, but instead has become embroiled in two lawsuits. Action II, the instant case, is nothing more than plaintiff's attempt to circumvent Special Term's ruling in Action I denying the stay of arbitration. Indeed, the chronology of events indicates that the order of attachment should never have issued at all, as the underlying dispute is subject to arbitration.

## V

Whenever a matter of foreign relations is involved, one must consider the mirror image of a particular situation. Is it desirable to subject American property overseas to whatever rules of attachment and other judicial process may apply in some foreign country when our citizen has agreed to arbitrate a dispute? It can be assumed that American business entities engaging in international trade would not encourage such a result. Permitting this type of attachment to stand would expose American business to that risk in other countries.

The essence of arbitration is resolving disputes without the interference of the judicial process and its strictures. When international trade is involved, this essence is enhanced by the desire to avoid unfamiliar foreign law. The UN Convention has considered the problems and created a solution, one that does not contemplate significant judicial intervention until after an arbitral award is made. The purpose and policy of the UN Convention will be best carried out by restricting prearbitration judicial action to determining whether arbitration should be compelled.

Accordingly, the order of the Appellate Division should be reversed, with costs, and the order of Supreme Court, New York County, reinstated.

MEYER, Judge (dissenting).

. . . .

In response to the majority I add that: (1) nothing in the UN Convention or in the history of its negotiation or its implementation by Congress suggests that the word "refer" as used in section 3 of article II of the UN Convention was intended to foreclose the use of attachment where permitted by the law of the jurisdiction in which the attachment is obtained; (2) in light of the majority's concessions that foreign arbitration awards are enforced on the same terms as domestic awards . . . that there are circumstances under which a domestic award may be enforced under our law through use of a preaward attachment . . . and that the UN Convention speaks only in terms of postaward security . . ., and of the fact that the UN Convention does not specifically address the subject of preaward attachment, the UN Convention cannot properly be said to have proscribed such an attachment by implication; and (3) the use of attachment in maritime contract cases arbitrated under the Federal statute cannot properly be distinguished from arbitration related attachment permitted under State statutory and decisional law, for the UN Convention makes no distinction; it either permits or proscribes both. In my view, absent more specific language of proscription in the UN Convention, it permits both.

\*     \*     \*

d.      ALBERT J. VAN DEN BERG, THE NEW
        YORK ARBITRATION CONVENTION OF
        1958 139-40 (1981).

### Pre-award attachment not precluded

The Convention contains no provision on the matter of attachment; thus the availability and procedure depend on the law of the court before which the attachment is sought.

No court has doubted that an attachment in connection with the enforcement of an arbitral *award* in order to secure payment under the award, is compatible with the New York Convention.

There also seems to be no doubt as to the possibility of a pre-award attachment, that is to say an attachment before or during the arbitration, in order to secure the subject matter in dispute or the payment under the award if rendered in favor of the party who has applied for the attachment. In virtually all countries, attachment, like other provisional remedies involving coercion, cannot be ordered by the arbitrator, but has to be applied for at the court. The availability and procedure here also depend on the law of the court before which the attachment is requested, the Convention being silent on the matter of attachment.

Accordingly, the Italian Supreme Court has not hesitated to validate a pre-award attachment pursuant to Italian law in a case in which the arbitration agreement fell under the New York Convention.[252]

The English Admiralty Court had no difficulty, either, in upholding the arrest of a vessel in connection with an action *in rem* when it stayed the court proceedings on the merits in virtue of Section 1(1) of the Arbitration Act of 1975 (i.e., the implementing legislation of the Convention in the United Kingdom).[253] The Judge said:

---

[252] Corte di Cassazione (Sez. Un.) May 12, 1977, No. 3989, Scherk Enterprises A.G. v. Société des Grandes Marques (Italy no. 28), validating attachment pending arbitration in Zurich.

[253] Admiralty Court (Queen's Bench Division), January 13, 1978, *The Rena K* (U.K. no. 6).

> "There is nothing in Section 1(1) of the 1975 Act which obliges the Court, whenever it grants a stay of action *in rem* in which security has been obtained, to make an order for the unconditional release of such security."

[The author goes on to comment on United States practice and to criticize *McCreary* and those cases relying on it.]

### Notes and Questions

1. Were the decisions in *McCreary* and *Cooper* denying the right to attachment influenced by the fact that in both cases the attachments which were dissolved had been granted in favor of parties who had brought other judicial proceedings in violation of an agreement to arbitrate and were seeking to evade their arbitration obligations?

2. In the *Cooper* case, did Motobécane have the right to remove the proceeding to federal court? If so, would the outcome have been different?

3. In *Cooper*, was the assumption of the majority correct that, in the "mirror image" situation, an American party in a foreign jurisdiction and benefiting from an arbitration agreement would not be subject to attachment? Albert J. van den Berg indicates in a 1981 commentary that the case law developed under the Convention to date confirms his earlier observation (*supra*, p. 824) that the Convention is no impediment to attachment. Other foreign observers accept the premise, and have debated whether the Convention should be amended to prevent pre-award attachment. *See* Sigvard Jarvin, *Is Exclusion of Concurrent Courts' Jurisdiction over Conservatory Measures to be Introduced by a Revision to the Convention?*, J. INT'L ARB, (Mar. 1989), at 171 (1989); Bernardo M. Cremades, *Is Exclusion of Concurrent Courts' Jurisdiction over Conservatory Measures to be Introduced through a Revision of the New York Convention?*, J. INT'L ARB, (Sept. 1989), at 105.

4. The rationale of the decisions in *McCreary* and *Cooper*, as well as other cases denying attachments in New York Convention arbitrations, appears to be that it is the context of the reciprocal rights and obligations arising under the Convention, including the state's obligation to refer parties to arbitration and to recognize and enforce arbitration awards, which makes inconsistent the grant of preaward attachment. Where the party to an international arbitration against whom attachment is sought is not a national of a Convention country, the rationale for judicial abstention from attachment fails.

5. The possible effect of state law on attachments relating to international disputes subject to New York Convention arbitrations should not be neglected. Except as otherwise provided by the Constitution of the United States or an applicable federal statute, the attachment will be granted by a federal court under the same circumstances and in the same manner as it would have been granted under the law

of the state in which the federal court sits. This applies to actions brought directly before federal courts under the Federal Arbitration Act or to actions removed from state courts pursuant to Section 205 of the Act. This is the result of Rule 64 Federal Rules of Civil Procedure which provides:

> At the commencement of and during the course of an action, all remedies providing for seizure of person or property for the purpose of securing satisfaction of the judgment ultimately to be entered in the action are available under the circumstances and in the manner provided by the law of the state in which the district court is held, subject to the following qualifications: (1) any existing statute of the United States governs to the extent to which it is applicable; (2) the action in which any of the foregoing remedies is used shall be commenced and prosecuted or, if removed from a state court, shall be prosecuted after removal, pursuant to these rules. The remedies thus available include asset attachment, garnishment, replevin, sequestration, and other corresponding or equivalent remedies, however designated and regardless of whether by state procedure the remedy is ancillary to an action or must be obtained by an independent action.

The provisions in the Federal Rules of Civil Procedure reflect the principles of federalism provided by the United States Constitution. The application of these principles in the field of international arbitration raises some interesting issues in view of the constitutional dimension (supremacy through the Constitution of international treaty obligations) and the presence of a federal statute (the Federal Arbitration Act) whose provisions preempt any directly conflicting provisions of state law.[254] *See supra* Chapter 4, Part IV.D., p. 421. For a review of the background of the federal-state relationship relevant to attachment and a summary the present state of disagreement as to whether the New York Convention impedes the granting of attachments in relation to arbitration covered by the Convention, see R. Hulbert, *The Role of the Courts: The American Law Perspective in* CONSERVATORY AND PROVISIONAL MEASURES IN INTERNATIONAL ARBITRATION, Ninth Joint Colloquium on International Arbitration (ICC, AAA ICSID) (Paris 1992).

6. Based on a desire to reverse the rule of the *Cooper* case *see* Committee on Arbitration and Alternative Dispute Resolution of the Association of the Bar of the

---

[254] While Rule 64, Federal Rules of Civil Procedure provides the basic requirement for referring to state law of attachment and execution, the possibility of federal preemption is set out in Rule 81(a)(3) which states:

> [i]n proceedings under Title 9, U.S.C., relating to arbitration [the Federal Arbitration Act] or under [the federal statute providing for arbitration of railway labor disputes] these rules [of civil procedure] apply only to the extent that matters of procedure are not provided for in those statutes.

City of New York, THE ADVISABILITY AND AVAILABILITY OF PROVISIONAL REMEDIES IN THE ARBITRATION PROCESS, 39 The Record 625 (1984). Section 7502 of the New York Civil Practice Law and Rules was amended to add a new subsection (c) that, in pertinent part, provides as follows:

> The supreme court in the county in which an arbitration is pending, or, if not yet commenced, in a county specified in subdivision (a), may entertain an application for an order of attachment or for a preliminary injunction in connection with an arbitrable controversy, but only upon the ground that the award to which the applicant may be entitled may be rendered ineffectual without such provisional relief. . . .

The state legislation was effective to confirm that attachment was available in connection with arbitration as a matter of state law, and to correct any misapprehension in that regard. It could not, however, correct the state court's interpretation of the New York Convention as forbidding attachment which as a matter of federal and constitutional law would remain binding on the state court. Recognizing this, the Association of the Bar of the City of New York proposed a specific amendment to the Federal Arbitration Act recognizing that the Convention did not prohibit the granting by courts of provisional remedies in connection with arbitration. *See* Joseph D. Becker, *Attachments and international arbitration — an addendum*, 2 ARB. INT'L. 365 (1986). As of September 1994, no affirmative legislative action had been taken on the proposed amendment of the Federal Arbitration Act.

7. As was seen in *Rodgers, Burgun, Shahine & Deschler, Inc. v. Dongsan* (*supra* p. 799), a federal court has the power to grant an injunction to preserve the *status quo* and assure the efficacy of arbitration, and may be persuaded to do so even in Convention cases. Since injunction is an equitable remedy, federal courts apply their own standards in determining the conditions in which an injunction will be granted and are not required to refer to state law. *See also Sauer Getriebe KG v. White Hydraulics, Inc.* (*supra* p. 791). While there is substantial authority for the granting of injunctions by federal courts in connection with arbitrations subject to the Convention, some federal courts have followed the *McCreary/Cooper* rationale and extended it to the field of injunctions. As in the field of attachments, the Supreme Court has not ruled on the split.

8. In the maritime field, Section 8 of Chapter 1 (domestic arbitration) of the Federal Arbitration Act specifically permits a party, even where an arbitration clause is involved, to begin proceedings by libel and seizure of the vessel according to usual admiralty proceedings and the court, while referring the parties to arbitration shall retain jurisdiction over the property and to enter its decree upon the award. Section 208 of Chapter 2 (international arbitration) of the Federal Arbitration Act provides that the provisions of Chapter to the extent "that chapter is not in conflict with this chapter or the Convention as ratified by the United States." A number of federal courts have sustained provisional measures in maritime cases where proceedings on the merits were subject to arbitration and found no impediment in the New York

Convention. *E.A.S.T. Inc. v. M/V Alia*, 876 F.2d 1168 (5th Cir. 1989); *Construction Exporting Enterprises, UNECA v. Nikki Maritime, Ltd.*, 558 F.Supp. 1372 (S.D.N.Y. 1983); *Atlas Chartering Services, Inc. v. World Trade Group, Inc.*, 453 F.Supp. 861 (S.D.N.Y. 1978); *Andros Compania Maritime S.A. v. André & Cie S.A.*, 430 F.Supp. 88 (S.D.N.Y. 1977). This appears to extend to attachments and injunctive relief for the purpose of assuring the efficacy of the arbitration and not to obtain jurisdiction. For an express finding that Section of the Federal Arbitration Act is not inconsistent with the Convention, *see*, *E.A.S.T. Inc. v. M/V Alaia, et al.*, 876 F.2d 1168 (5th Cir. 1989).

9. Further readings on the effect of the New York Convention on attachments and court ordered provisional remedies: Joseph D. Becker, *Attachments in Aid of International Arbitration — the American Position*, 1 ARB. INT'L 40 (1985); Charles N. Brower & W. Michael Tupman, *Court Ordered Provisional Measures and the New York Convention*, 80 AM. J. INT'L L. 24 (1986); Douglas D. Reichert, *Provisional Remedies in the Context of International Commercial Arbitration*, 3 INT'L TAX & BUS. L. 368 (1986); Lawrence F. Ebb, *Flight of Assets from the Jurisdiction in the Twinkling of a Telex: Pre-and Post-Award Conservatory Relief in International Commercial Arbitration*, 7 J. INT'L ARB. 9 (1990); Neil E. McDonell, *The Availability of Provisional Relief in International Commercial Arbitration*, 22 COLUM. J. TRANSNAT'L L. 273 (1984).

## 2.   WASHINGTON CONVENTION

We have already seen several examples of the view of international arbitrators in ICSID proceedings that pre-award measures before national tribunals are inconsistent with the exclusive nature of the arbitral remedy provided by the Washington Convention (*supra*, Part V.B., p. 774). What is the position taken by the courts?

The issue was raised before the courts of Antwerp, Belgium and Geneva, Switzerland in the complicated case of *MINE v. Guinea*, a brief summary of which is set out above in connection with the ICSID arbitral proceedings (*supra* pp. 783-84). In that case, MINE had obtained an American Arbitration Association award against Guinea in 1980, confirmation of which was subsequently refused (on the ground of sovereign immunity) by a United States Court of Appeal in 1982, *MINE v. The Republic of Guinea*, 693 F.2d 1094 (D.C. Cir. 1982), *reprinted in* 21 I.L.M. 355 (1982), *as amended*, 22 I.L.M. 86 (1983), *cert. denied* 104 S. Ct. 71 (1983). In May 1984, MINE initiated ICSID arbitral proceedings and in May and June 1985 brought attachment proceedings before the Tribunal of the Canton of Geneva in Switzerland and the Tribunal of Antwerp in Belgium. The 1986 Swiss decision lifting the attachment is set out in Chapter 9 (*infra* p. 1017).

The 1985 Antwerp decision also set aside the attachment on the succinct ground that an attachment was a "remedy" and that where the parties had agreed to ICSID arbitration Article 26 of the Washington Convention provided that such arbitration was agreed to the exclusion of any other remedy.

> a. *Guinea v. Maritime Int'l Nominees Establishment (MINE)*, Case No. 6.551, Decision of the Tribunal of Antwerp[261] Public Hearings Case No. 6.551 of the Judge for Attachment Matters (Sept. 27, 1985), 1 FOREIGN INVESTMENT L. J. (ICSID REV.) 380 (1986).

*The Judge for Attachment Matters Decides the Following*:

. . .

Considering articles 2, 34, 36, 37 and 41 of the law of June 15, 1935;

. . .

Considering that the demand of the Plaintiff is for the immediate lifting of the attachment for security requested by the Defendant against the Plaintiff and of goods in the hands of third parties effected as regards the S.A. Banque Belgo-Zairoise at Brussels and the N.V. Bank Brussel Lambert at Brussels by bailiff S. Sacre at Brussels, and as regards the N.V. Hansamar, the P.V.B.A. Anhamar, the N.V. Westcott Shipping, the N.V. Unamar and the N.V. Senexomar, all of them established at Antwerp, by bailiff Briers at Antwerp, on June 17, 1985;

To condemn the Defendant *ex aequo and bono* and provisionally to pay to the Plaintiff an amount of BF 5,000,000 as indemnity;

To condemn the Defendant to pay interest at the rate set by law and the cost of proceedings;

---

[261] Based on a translation published at 24 ILM 1639 (1985).

Considering that the Defendant voluntarily lifted the attachment for security realized by bailiff S. Sacre at Brussels on June 17, 1985 with the Bank Brussel Lambert;

That the claim of the Plaintiff with respect to that point has become without purpose;

Considering that the parties agreed that disputes arising between them would be settled by the International Centre for Settlement of Investment Disputes (ICSID) by virtue of the Washington Convention, as appears from the agreement entered into by the parties on August 19, 1971, on December 6, 1974, and January 23, 1975;

That the present Defendant, after having introduced proceedings against the present Plaintiff before the ordinary courts, referred the matter to ICSID in 1984, and that ICSID declared itself competent (p. 68 of the report of the ICSID arbitral hearing on July 3, 1985);

That ICSID thus is exclusively competent and excludes the intervention of the national courts of a State which ratified the Washington Convention;

That Belgium ratified the Washington Convention by law of July 17, 1970;

That Article 26 of the Washington Convention reads as follows:

Consent of the parties to arbitration under this Convention shall, unless otherwise stated, be deemed consent to such arbitration to the exclusion of any other remedy;

That the term "remedy" means: The means by which a right is exercised or the violation of a right is prevented, redressed or compensated. Remedies are of four kinds: by act of the injured party, the principal of which are prohibition, recaption, security, entry, abatement and attachment, according to the texts submitted by the Plaintiff and not seriously contested by the Defendant;

That the parties did not declare, as allowed by Article 26 of the Washington Convention, that a remedy other than arbitration provided for by the Convention was allowed;

That, consequently, according to Article 26 of the Washington Convention of March 18, 1965, any possibility to introduce an action before the national courts of one of the contracting States, in this case Belgium, is excluded for the contracting parties including the possibility to institute proceedings to obtain an attachment (see above, concerning "remedy") (Court of Appeals of Rennes, France, October 26, 1984, News from ICSID, Vol. 2, No. 2, Summer 1985, p. 6-9);

That the other criteria, i.e., the urgency (Article 1413 of the Judicial Code) and the certainty, the exigible and fixed nature of the claim of the seizing defendant party, do not have to be examined; the same applies to the question of the applicability of the principle of the immunity of the State;

Consequently that, as said above, it is established that we are not competent as a result of the agreement between the parties to submit all disputes arising between them to the International Centre for Settlement of Investment Disputes established by the Convention on the Settlement of Investment Disputes between States and Nationals of other States, done at Washington on March 18, 1965 and ratified by Belgium by law of July 17, 1970, especially Article 26 of this Convention;

Consequently, that the claim of the Plaintiff is founded insofar as it seeks to obtain the lifting of the attachment of goods in the hands of third parties;

That the reckless and vexatious character of the above attachments is not proved;

That the claim of the Plaintiff for an indemnity thus is not founded;
*For these Reasons*: . . . [the Court decides to]

Declare the claim of the Plaintiff for an indemnity admissible but unfounded and reject the claim;

Declare the other elements of the claim of the Plaintiff admissible and founded;

Declare that the following attachments for security made at the request of the Defendant are lifted: the attachment for security made by bailiff S. Sacre at Brussels of goods with the S.A. Banque Belgo-Zairoise and made by M. Briers at Antwerp on June 17, 1985, of goods with the N.V. Hansamar, the P.V.B.A. Anhamar, the N.V Westcott Shipping, the N.V. Unamar and the N.V. Sanexomar, all of which are established in Antwerp;

Declare that in the absence of a voluntarily lifting, the present decision shall be considered as lifting the attachments;

Condemn the Defendant to pay the costs of proceedings.

\*    \*    \*

In making its determination, the Antwerp Tribunal referred to a decision of the Court of Appeal of Rennes, France which also found that an attachment constituted a "remedy," the granting of which by a national court was barred in view of the exclusive jurisdiction of ICSID tribunals to grant remedies under the Washington Convention. The French case arose out of the attachment of three fishing boats belonging to a Guinean state organization granted in connection with an arbitrable dispute involving their construction and repair (the dispute had nothing to do with the MINE case also involving Guinea).

b.    *Guinea and Soguipêche v. Atlantic Triton Co.*, Rennes Court of Appeal (Oct. 26, 1984), *in* 24 I.L.M. 340 (1985).

[The Minister of Fisheries of the Revolutionary People's Republic of Guinea entered into a management agreement in 1981 with the Norwegian company Atlantic Triton, who undertook to convert three ships for use as fishing vessels to establish a fishing industry in Guinea, and to provide for their operation and management. The vessels proved totally unsuitable for the purpose, and, after having received advice from appropriate specialized international agencies, Guinea arranged with Atlantic Triton that two of the ships should be rehabilitated by works at a shipyard in Concarneau, France. After reaching some provisional agreement as to the sharing of the rehabilitation costs, disputes arose between Guinea and Atlantic Triton concerning payment of the costs and of previously owing Norwegian shipyard costs and administrative expenses. Atlantic Triton cancelled the agreement as of June 30, 1983, and when no further payments had been received, obtained an attachment of the three ships from the

President of the Quimper Commercial Court on October 12, 1983, as security for its claim of US $571,311, plus penalties and interest, and Guinea's motion to vacate the attachment was dismissed. On January 9, 1984, Guinea filed a request for arbitration with ICSID. It appealed from the lower court's confirmation of the attachment on the grounds, *inter alia*, that the attached property was subject to sovereign immunity from execution and that the attachment violated the Washington Convention.]

The Convention on the Settlement of Investment Dispute between States and Nationals of Other States established under the auspices of the International Bank for Reconstruction and Development (IBRD) on May 18, 1964, which came into effect on October 14, 1966, and was ratified by a large number of states, including France, Norway and Guinea, set up an International Center for Settlement of Investment Disputes (ICSID) which includes conciliation and arbitration machinery (in this case a tribunal).

Article 26 provides that the consent to arbitration shall "unless otherwise stated" be deemed consent to such arbitration to the exclusion of any other remedy, although "a Contracting State may require the exhaustion of local administrative or judicial remedies as a condition of its consent to arbitration under this Convention." Article 47 provides that "except as the parties otherwise agree, the tribunal may, if it considers that the circumstances so require, recommend any provisional measures which should be taken to preserve the respective rights of either party."

The rules applicable to ICSID's arbitration proceedings, which is an official document drawn up by the Administrative Council of the Center pursuant to Article 6 of the Convention, provide, in Rule 39 entitled "provisional measures", that at any time during the proceeding a party may request that provisional measures for the preservation of its rights may be "recommended" by the tribunal, which shall give priority to the request. The tribunal may also recommend provisional measures on its own initiative or recommend measures other than those specified in a request. In cases of urgency the tribunal may take decisions by correspondence among its members; the President may also call special meetings of the tribunal.

The ICSID rules specify that unless otherwise agreed by the parties, consent to arbitration by ICSID is exclusive of any other remedy, and therefore the parties cannot apply to local administrative or judicial authorities to obtain provisional measures, but must have recourse only to the arbitration tribunal.

The purpose of the Convention was to set up a machinery that would be widely accepted for conciliation and arbitration purposes, to which the Contracting States and the nationals of other Contracting States can submit disputes on matters of private international investments, rather than to local jurisdictions.

As this rule regarding arbitration makes the purpose of the Convention clear, it follows that the arbitration tribunal has the general and exclusive power to rule not only on the merits of the dispute but also on all provisional measures. The terms used, such as "remedy" (Article 26 of the Convention) have a general application that dispels any possible ambiguity. . . . If local jurisdictions had the power to consider requests for provisional measures, this would restrict the competence of the tribunal and would entail the serious risk of decisions being taken that could complicate the task of the arbitrators, who in this case must reach equitable decisions. Under international law it is agreed that the parties must refrain from any steps that might have prejudicial effects on the enforcement of a future decision (of an international tribunal) and, in general terms, must not engage in any activities that could aggravate or extend the scope of dispute.

From the start of the dispute bringing into effect the clause providing consent to ICSID arbitration, the parties to the agreement are compelled to have recourse to such arbitration.

*     *     *

The decision of the Rennes Court of Appeal was not, however, the last word on the subject. The Cour de Cassation, France's highest court, annulled the decision and took the position that Article 26 of the ICSID Convention does not prevent a party from seeking provisional remedies from a French court in relation to an ICSID arbitration proceeding.

c. *Guinea and Soguipêche v. Atlantic Triton Co.*, Cour de cassation (Nov. 18, 1986), *in* 26 I.L.M. 373 (1986).

[Atlantic Triton requested the Court of Cassation to set aside the decision of the Court of Appeals of Rennes which had lifted the attachment of the fishing vessels in the French port. Neither the People's Republic of Guinea nor Soguipêche appeared in the Court of Cassation proceeding since, during the time that the attachment had been lifted, the fishing vessels had sailed to Guinea. The issue before the Court of Cassation was accordingly one of principle. The views of the French Government were presented by its Solicitor General ("*Procureur de la République*"). Atlantic Triton attacked the decision of the Rennes Court on these grounds: i) that the Guinean parties had failed to preserve their right to appeal to that Court on grounds of lack of jurisdiction; ii) that the Rennes Court had exceeded its jurisdiction in making a ruling which required the interpretation of a treaty, which is within the exclusive competence of the French Government; and iii) that the Rennes Court had misinterpreted the obligations of the Washington Convention. The Court of Cassation rejected the first two procedural grounds and proceeded to decide on the Convention issue.]

But on the second part of the second ground:

Given Article 26 of the Washington Convention of March 18, 1965;

Whereas in providing that in the framework of this Convention the consent of the parties to arbitration is, unless otherwise stipulated, considered as implying waiver to any other recourse, this text did not intend to prohibit recourse to a judge to request conservatory measures designed to guaranty the execution of the anticipated award;

Whereas the Court of Appeal decided that the goal and the spirit of the Convention implied that the Arbitral tribunal had general jurisdiction, not only to decide the merits but even to take provisional measures;

Whereas in thus holding, given that the power of national courts to order conservatory measures, which is not preempted by the Washington Convention, can only be excluded by express consent of the parties or by implied Convention resulting from the adoption of arbitral Rules calling for such waiver, the Court of Appeal has violated, by misapplication, the text above mentioned;

<u>And on the fourth part of the same ground</u>:

Given article 29, paragraph 2, of the Decree of October 27, 1967;

Whereas according to the provisions of this text, the authorization of the seizure of the ships can be granted once the probable existence of a right has been shown;

Whereas in founding its decision to refuse such an authorization on the absence of urgent reasons, and in therefore subordinating the application of this text to a condition which is not provided therein the Court of Appeals had violated the above mentioned text;

FOR THESE REASONS, and without having to rule on the third part of the second ground:

QUASH AND ANNUL the decision rendered October 26, 1984 between the parties by the Court of Appeal of Rennes, reinstating, consequently, the dispute and the parties, to the condition existing before the rendering of the above decision and, to be so reinstated, the case is sent to the Court of Appeals of Angers, to (address) by special deliberation held in the Chamber of Council . . . .

<u>Notes and Questions</u>

1. The Geneva and Antwerp tribunals and the Court of Appeal at Rennes all took an extensive view of the Convention's prohibition on the grant of remedies by any body other than the ICSID arbitral tribunal, and of the effect of the arbitral tribunal's power to recommend provisional measures. The French Cour de Cassation, on the other hand, viewed the Convention provisions as having a more limited effect, which did not preempt the powers of its courts from granting provisional measures, and took a more pragmatic view as to the desirability of such national court provisional measures. The Cour de Cassation pointed out that the availability of national court measures could be excluded by express agreement by the parties, or by their being subject to Arbitration Rules so providing.

2. On the issue of the desirability *vel non* of judicial interim measures in connection with international arbitration, what are the similarities between the situations encountered in ICSID arbitration and those encountered in cases like *McCreary* and *Uranex*? What are the differences?

3. The *MINE v. Guinea* and *Soguipêche v. Atlantic Triton* arbitrations were subject to ICSID Arbitration Rules in effect prior to September 26, 1984, at which time Rule 39 was amended to add sub-paragraph 5 and to provide:

(1) At any time during the proceeding a party may request that provisional measures for the preservation of its rights be recommended by the Tribunal. The request shall specify the rights to be preserved, the measures the recommendation of which is requested, and the circumstances that require such measures.

(2) The Tribunal shall give priority to the consideration of a request made pursuant to paragraph (1).

(3) The Tribunal may also recommend provisional measures on its own initiative or recommend measures other than those specified in a request. It may at any time modify or revoke its recommendations.

(4) The Tribunal shall only recommend provisional measures, or modify or revoke its recommendations after giving each party an opportunity of presenting its observations.

Arbitration Rules adopted on September 26, 1984, revised Rule 39 to add a new paragraph providing:

(5) Nothing in this Rule shall prevent the parties, provided that they have so stipulated in the agreement recording their consent, from requesting any judicial or other authority to order provisional measures, prior to the institution of the proceedings, or during the proceeding, for the preservation of their respective rights and interests.

Does the revision of the rule settle the conflict between the extensive theory and the limited theory of the effect of the exclusive remedy provision of the Washington Convention on the grant of provisional measures by national courts? Is it clear that national courts may now not grant provisional measures in respect of disputes subject to ICSID arbitration unless the parties have specifically so agreed?[262]

## VII.  SUMMARY AND CONCLUSIONS

A number of questions must be determined by the arbitrator. One of the most urgent is the determination of whether or not there is arbitral jurisdiction. Other issues involve choice of law matters: the law

---

[262] *See e.g.*, Charles N. Brower & Ronald E.M. Goodman, *Provisional Measures and the Protection of ICSID Jurisdictional Exclusivity Against Municipal Proceedings* 6 FOREIGN INVESTMENT L. J. (ICSID REV.) 431, 436 (1991); Bertrand P. Marchais, *ICSID Tribunals and Provisional Measures — Introductory Note to Decisions of the Tribunals of Antwerp and Geneva in MINE v. Guinea*, 1 ICSID REV. 372 (1986); Antonio R. Parra, *Revised Regulations and Rules*, 2 NEWS FROM ICSID 6 (1985).

governing the arbitration; rules governing the arbitrator's conduct of the proceedings; substantive law governing the dispute; the application of mandatory rules of law; prescription, interest and punitive damages. Legal and policy issues with respect to the competence of the arbitrator to issue provisional measures are complex. In some arbitral regimes, some of those competences are shared with courts.

# CHAPTER 7

# ARBITRAL PROCEEDINGS: THE TRIAL

## I. INTRODUCTION

Established rules of procedure strictly bind the conduct of court proceedings, whereas in arbitration the parties have considerable discretion in setting their own rules of procedure. This discretion is subject to the mandatory rules of law where the arbitration will take place and to the assent of the tribunal or governing institution.

In some cases, in particular in maritime arbitrations, the parties conduct the proceedings through the exchange of documents only. The absence of an oral hearing is the exception, however. It is generally accepted in international arbitration that either party may insist upon an oral hearing.

Are the considerations which make an oral hearing an integral part of adjudication by courts similar to those present in arbitrations? Do any factors suggest that the ability to demand a hearing in arbitration is simply an artifact of long-standing dependence upon judicial remedies rather than a feature which furthers the goals of arbitration? Lord Wilberforce considers below some of the advantages of what he describes as "the principle of orality."

Wilberforce, *Written Briefs and Oral Advocacy*, 5 ARB. INT'L 348, 348-55 (1989).

The principle of orality has historical origins in England. Only clerks could read: the common man or woman probably could not. The judge of fact was a common man — the juryman. So everything had to be orally presented; documents had to be read aloud; everything explained three times. All the juryman had to do was to say "yes" or "no." When people became better educated and the majority could read, we did not change the system: we insisted on it. Juries were not allowed to see documents, or make notes; the principle was maintained in civil as well as criminal proceedings, even after juries had been practically abolished, and was defended for its own sake. "This was the best way of reaching the truth." But is it? And if it is, can we afford it?

. . .

The advocate plays an important part here. You cannot expect to get oral, immediate, stylish and accurate judgments without good and intelligent advocacy. The advocate will supply much of the order, of the analysis, indeed much of the wording of the judgment. As an advocate I was often conscious of the fact that it was necessary to keep speaking for enough time to allow judges to arrange their thoughts; and as a judge I was grateful to advocates who did this. No written brief can serve the same purpose.

Orality has a wide general importance. . . . Orality is the means by which the people are brought face to face with their law. They can go into a court and see a case from A-Z and, if it is a case with a jury, can follow it just as the jury does. The commuter in the train from Surbiton can read the best parts of counsel's opening, of his cross-examination, of the judgment or summing-up and reflect on social values. It is very necessary that from time to time there should be a gripping entertainment — this is a kind of social catharsis, which our dull life demands and must have if it is not to seek relief in war.

The converse follows. The less the subject-matter is of social interest, or importance, the less necessary it is to preserve orality. The Commercial Court, or the Chancery Division, can safely work with written statements and affidavits and can save time by doing so. And similarly commercial arbitrations. Arbitrations are private — that is one of their selling points. So there is no social need to allow any more orality than efficiency requires. So much for generality.

Let us now look at orality more concretely. Is the belief in its merits justified? First, is it a good way of getting at the truth — or even of persuading people? We may think so, but our belief is instinctive rather than scientific — should we not be more scientific? People differ very greatly in the way they listen to things. With some, listening is the only way of communicating — the only way of remembering. With others, oral communication is no use unless a note can be taken — they only register on the writing. Others again cannot take in written material unless it is orally explained. What sort is your judge, your mixed jury, your arbitrator, or your lay magistrate? Commercial arbitrators are not necessarily trained listeners. They are selected for a variety of reasons: expertise in the subject matter [sic] acceptability to the nominating parties — and they may never have acted as arbitrators before (others of course are highly professional). On the European Continent, arbitrators are very often professors not used to analysing oral arguments — probably more accustomed to analysis of written words. How should we train people to listen to, to absorb and to extract kernels? People differ very much in the period for which they can listen. Some need a rest after one hour — or less. Some can absorb for quite a long period but then switch off for the rest of the day. This factor is capable of scientific assessment. Are we wise to leave it to chance or guesswork?

About witnesses — oral or written evidence. English judges entertain the belief that they can tell if a man — or even a woman — is speaking the truth. This is a Palladium: and it has comforting consequences: "The judge saw the witness in the box — observed his demeanour." "He was disbelieved by the judge — or the jury." "We (the appeal court) cannot interfere." But there is not much scientific basis for this. Such studies, as I know of, show that liars are believed as often as truth-tellers are disbelieved. And one can test it with multiple tribunals — arbitrators, whether all British or from different nations. I can give several instances where exactly opposite views as to credibility were confidently given by members of such tribunals — *e.g.*, a fact which of course encourages people to avoid oral evidence before them. Indeed, one often finds foreign arbitrators irritated with the English style of examination and cross-examination — it is not a good way of getting at the truth or persuading the tribunal.

Oral evidence can be very extravagant in time. For this reason it attracts a number of technical rules — rules of evidence — as to hearsay, leading questions, etc. — which are often not understood and which are often abused. . . . And one has to ask whether it would be better for the judge to take the evidence rather than the advocates.

In some cases oral evidence is counterproductive — it leads to divergence from the truth. Particularly true of expert witnesses who may be judged . . . according to demeanour . . . . So the case is strong, and is being increasingly accepted, for expert evidence to be given in writing, with limited cross-examination. A corollary of this would be a procedure . . . by which expert evidence is sifted outside the trial, either by the judge, or by an expert . . ., and only the findings brought into the [proceedings]. . . .

There is room in the endless diversity of legal proceedings, for written, or at least partly written, procedures. This is particularly true of arbitrations (i) because of their private character, (ii) because they are often concerned with technical matters rather than with A's word against B's, (iii) particularly if they are held before more than one arbitrator. What of the cost? My own belief is that oral proceedings are more expensive. Days in court can be more visibly charged than days in a study. Witnesses, I believe, cost more if they are kept waiting about than if they are asked for a written statement. Oral presentation presupposes employment of more than one lawyer, written briefs not necessarily so. But one cannot generalise too much. Some continental professors charge honoraria which compare very favourably with those of a distinguished English silk and US lawyers know how to charge for a written brief.

Can one say anything about effectiveness — the comparative effectiveness of oral or written presentations? Here one tends to get anecdotes. Oral advocacy has some clear advantages. We can all recall brilliant openings — those which create prejudice, never later dispelled, those which acutely focus attention on one issue, openings after which the defence realises it must settle; brilliant cross-examination — but remember that many of them depend for success on the possession of material which might go in anyway in written form; brilliant replies which swing the case at the end of the oral hearing. The really skilled advocate knows how to evaluate his tribunal. Even with unknown arbitrators he can soon estimate the intelligence and capacity of the members and adapt to them. A written brief is less adaptable — it presupposes a level of reception which may differ from that which actually exists.

But I, too, can recall brilliant written briefs, and a US lawyer could recall many more. So I am not sure that the effectiveness argument is conclusive. . . . [B]ut for the process of justice one wants to know which produces the most just result rather than which is the best at winning the most cases — perhaps wrongly.

It is possible to arrive at some tentative conclusions: Belief in the virtue of the oral process is largely instinctive and unscientific. . . . Commercial arbitrations, being private, and especially multi-member tribunals, lend themselves to written procedures. In England, we have a traditional and special skill in oral presentation and oral testing of evidence. At its best, or when well controlled, it is probably as good as you can get. But a well conducted Commercial Court case, or commercial arbitration, partly run on written documents, is impressive too and may — one can only say may — be cheaper and quicker. Healthy competition and criticism does no harm.

Lastly, decisions or orders controlling orality ought to be made on the basis of a scientific appraisal rather than on grounds of administrative expediency. We should not allow ourselves to slide, or be slid, into an abandonment of methods which have proved their virtue.

*     *     *

## II.     GATHERING EVIDENCE

If a hearing is to be held, what precisely is its purpose? In common law systems the hearing is used to develop facts raised in perfunctory fashion in pleadings already submitted and to introduce documentary evidence. The continental approach is rather to use the hearing to argue about facts already revealed and developed in written submissions.

A.     W. LAURENCE CRAIG, ET AL., INTERNATIONAL CHAMBER OF COMMERCE ARBITRATION 387-89 (2d ed. 1990).

The continental system of proof is characterized by the exchange of documents between the parties. Hearings serve principally as an occasion for arguments based on facts revealed in written evidence already submitted. The common-law system, on the other hand, uses hearings to develop facts and to introduce documents into evidence.

The governing principles of the ICC Rules and the particularities of international disputes, where the parties and the arbitrators may be domiciled in different countries, favor the continental approach. Pursuant to Articles 3 and 4 of the ICC Rules, the Request for Arbitration and the Answer should contain not only the particulars of the claim and defense, but also the agreements relied on and other documents necessary to establish clearly the circumstances of the case. After the signature of the Terms of Reference, ICC arbitrators will ordinarily provide for further exchanges of written submissions. Communication of documents is usually arranged seriatim, with each side also contributing briefs analyzing the evidence presented. These may take the form of an initial memorial to which the defendant will have the right to file a "counter-memorial" (memorandum of defense) in which the grounds of counterclaim, if any, are also set forth. A further exchange, consisting of a "replique" and a "duplique" accompanied by documents, is often necessary.

Proponents of oral proceedings argue that the examination of witnesses at length and at leisure by skilled counsel is a most important means of revealing the truth. The most fervent proponents of extensive hearings would even argue that documents should be read into the record by counsel, as has been the tradition before the High Court in English practice.

Such tedious practices are largely unknown in ICC arbitration, and would hardly be tolerated by continental arbitrators. Many experienced international arbitrators consider that a witness' essential contribution to the establishment of facts rarely requires more than a few hours of testimony. Arbitrators skeptical of the value of lengthy testimony in commercial cases would maintain that when all is said and done, after many days of observing an intelligent witness on the stand, one knows little more than whether or not one likes him.

In any event, full-blown oral hearings are very lengthy. Examination of witnesses in a major commercial case in English courts frequently takes many weeks, sometimes months. The process is somewhat less time-consuming in the United States, where there is extensive pre-trial deposition of witnesses by counsel prior to hearings. But even such depositions demand enormous amounts of time of witnesses and counsel, although not of the court.

In international arbitration, such extensive hearings are not practical. The site of arbitration will be foreign to at least one of the parties and usually to some or all of the arbitrators. The problems of arranging facilities for the hearing, hotel rooms, translators and stenographers (where required), and the discomfort for counsel working away from home offices contribute to make long hearings an unpleasant chore. The arbitrators usually have other functions which make it impossible for them to be exclusively available for long periods of time. As a result, hearings are seldom scheduled for a period of more than one or two weeks. If further hearings are required, they ordinarily have to be separated in time.

It should not be forgotten that documents are of primary importance in commercial matters. They are relied on heavily even in court litigation. Whatever may be the arguments in favor of oral proceedings in criminal litigation or in tort cases, they are far less relevant to an efficient system for the settlement of international commercial disputes by arbitration.

*     *     *

B.     Richard J. Medalie, *The Libyan Producers' Agreement Arbitration: Developing Innovative Procedures in a Complex Multiparty Arbitration*, J. INT'L ARB., June 1990, at 18-21.

From May 1981 through September 1985, one of the largest and most complex commercial arbitrations in the history of the American Arbitration Association (AAA) — the Libyan Producers' Agreement (LPA) Arbitration — took place. This study is based upon the author's experience as Chairman of the Panel of Arbitrators. . . .

1. Hearsay Documents. Usually, in arbitration, the legal rules of evidence used in the courtroom do not apply. As stated in AAA Rule 31: "The arbitrator shall be the judge of the relevancy and materiality of the evidence offered, and conformity to legal rules of evidence shall not be necessary." All evidence, regardless of its character is normally admissible. The "guiding principle" to be applied, according to the AAA, is that "everything that could further understanding of the case should be heard." Unfortunately, the "guiding principle" was insufficient to resolve the hearsay problems in the LPA Arbitration.

From December 1981 to June 1982, the Hunts submitted into evidence their thousands of documents and their thousands of pages of testimony from the previous trial transcript and pretrial depositions. At the outset, the other parties vigorously objected to the substantial secondary, and even tertiary, hearsay evidence included within many of the documents. The discord and the time the discussion took on each document threatened to slow down the process to a near standstill. On the other hand, for the Panel to have admitted the documents into evidence on a wholesale basis would have created serious problems in gaining the confidence of the parties.

. . . The hearsay issues led to a breakdown in the taking of evidence, in which objections to certain documents led to hours of wrangling.

The wrangling continued for a number of hearing days. Finally, the Arbitrators decided to produce evidentiary guidelines applicable to all document submissions, which they entitled "General Principles of Admissibility of Documents into Evidence."

The Arbitrators believed that their rules of evidence, combined with the issue-by-issue approach, increased their credibility and heightened the willingness of the parties to permit the arbitration to progress at a reasonable tempo. As the Panel stated in the General Principles: "[T]hese principles will help obviate any misunderstanding as to the Panel's rulings on admissibility."

The General Principles specified how the Arbitrators would limit and restrict the use of the submitted evidence. Thus, as an initial matter, all documents admitted into evidence were deemed to be authentic, relevant, material and within the scope of authority of the agent preparing them. The documents could only be admitted, however, "with respect to a particular party or parties and only for the specific issue or issues stated." Moreover, they could not be admitted to contradict any stipulation of the parties, or any "finding . . . previously determined to be binding by way of collateral estoppel," or to establish any "claim . . . previously determined to be precluded by res judicata." Hearsay documents were to be initially admitted into evidence only as the perception by the author or its principle of any statements, actions, conduct, attitudes or view of third parties. Thereafter, following briefing and argument, the Panel propounded new "General Principles of Expanded Admissibility for Certain Documents." This expanded admissibility applied to reports of meetings or negotiations, "whether in the form of official, unofficial or draft minutes, or of contemporaneous notes or reports by an attendee at such meetings" or negotiations.

At an appropriate time, any party was permitted to move to expand or strike the use of any evidence. "In determining whether the use of any document may be so expanded," the Panel ruled that it would "consider such criteria as indicia of reliability, circumstantial guarantees of trustworthiness, and fairness of use." Thus, after all of the Hunts' documents were submitted into evidence pursuant to the General Principles, the Hunts moved to expand the use of some 200 of their documents, many of which were permitted by the Panel to be so treated.

On the basis of the General Principles, the parties were able to understand what evidence helped their claims and how to present further needed evidence to facilitate those claims.

2. *Settlement Documents*. During the course of the LPA Arbitration, one of the parties offered certain documents in evidence to support one of its liability claims. The Panel excluded the documents on the ground that "they recorded internal company discussions that were made during the course of settlement negotiations." The Panel's exclusion of the documents was based on Rule 408 of the Federal Rules of Evidence, which makes inadmissible evidence as to compromise or offers of compromise "to prove liability for or invalidity of the claim or its amount," as well as evidence "of conduct or statements made in compromise negotiations." The Hunt Court, in confirming the Award, held that "[t]he ruling by the Panel was not erroneous."

3. *Affidavits*. In AAA Rule 31, in effect during the LPA Arbitration, an arbitrator was *required* to "receive and consider the evidence of witnesses by affidavit, but shall give it only such weight as he deems it entitled to after consideration of any objections made to its admission." In the LPA Arbitration, various parties submitted affidavits in lieu of live testimony and as a supplement to the documentary evidence. Many of the submissions were met with motions to strike.

The Panel refused to strike any affidavit, but noted that the admission of the affidavits into evidence did not mean that each affidavit would be given full, or even any, weight. In fact, the Panel, before making its ultimate decisions, examined each sentence and each paragraph of the affidavits in order to determine the weight to be assigned to the various portions of the affidavits. In doing so, the Arbitrators were guided by the following criteria:

- statements in affidavits are less reliable than statements
subject to cross-examination;

- affidavits made without a basis of personal knowledge carry little weight;

- only opinion testimony that would be admissible at the actual trial should be given weight in an affidavit;

- speculative statements in an affidavit will be given no weight;

- conclusions of law in an affidavit may be disregarded;

- conclusions of ultimate fact may also be disregarded.

On the basis of these criteria, the Panel assigned either full weight, moderate weight, slight weight or no weight to the various sentences or paragraphs in the affidavits submitted into evidence.

During the confirmation proceeding in Court, one of the parties contended that the Arbitrators had not given certain affidavits the consideration they deserved. The Court rejected the contention as being "without merit," holding that the Arbitrators had determined that the affidavits in question "were conclusory, contained matters of opinion, and therefore [were] not probative or entitled to little weight. This clearly was within the arbitrators' function as fact-finders. This determination was not only in accordance with law, but specifically within [AAA] Rule 31."

## Notes and Questions

1. Whatever the purpose of the hearing, an arbitral tribunal is obliged to give each party an equal and fair opportunity to make its case. In so doing, the parties will present evidence which may relate to the determination of disputed facts, questions of foreign law, or technical issues requiring expert involvement. What exactly though is this evidence intended to do? Is the objective to elicit the truth or to present the case in such a way as to win it?

2. The material selected above all argues for hearings. A number of adversarial procedures do not allow for hearings. Discuss the systemic advantages that non-hearing regimes have.

C.     Arthur  L.  Marriott,  *Evidence  in  International Arbitration*, 5 ARB. INT'L 280 (1989).

It is sometimes said that lawyers are not interested in the truth, but only in what they can prove. Although they perhaps did not express it as bluntly, this was the view of the Court of Appeal and the majority in the House of Lords when they differed from Mr Justice Bingham (as he then was) in a case brought by Air Canada and other airlines against the Secretary of State for Trade. In that case the plaintiff airlines sought discovery from the Secretary of State of documents which in the airlines' view would demonstrate that the Secretary of State was acting unlawfully in giving certain financial directions to the British Airports Authority which had led to a massive increase in landing charges at Heathrow.

> At first instance the Judge had held that:

> The concern of the court must surely be to ensure that the truth is elicited, not caring whether the truth favours one party or the other but anxious that its final decision should be grounded *on a sure foundation of fact* . . . In my judgment documents are necessary for fairly disposing of a cause or for the due administration of justice if they give *substantial assistance* to the court *in determining the facts upon which the decision in the cause will depend.* (Emphasis added.)

In the Court of Appeal, however, Lord Denning remarked that due administration of justice does not always depend on eliciting truth; it often depends on the burden of proof. For Lord Denning the due administration of justice meant the just decision of the case. In the House of Lords, Lord Wilberforce remarked that:

> in a contest between one litigant and another . . . the task of the court is to do and be seen to be doing justice between the parties . . . There is no higher additional duty to ascertain some independent truth.

*     *     *

Consider too the following statement to the effect that the discovery of the truth is the primary objective.

D.    *Parker v. United Mexican States* (*U.S. v. Mex.*), 4
      R.I.A.A. 35, 39 (General Claims Commission 1926).

5. For the future guidance of the respective Agents, the
Commission announces that, however appropriate may be the technical
rules of evidence obtaining in the jurisdiction of either the United
States or Mexico as applied to the conduct of trials in their municipal
courts, they have no place in regulating the admissibility of and in the
weighing of evidence before this international tribunal. There are many
reasons why such technical rules have no application here, among them
being that this Commission is without power to summon witnesses or
issue processes for the taking of depositions with which municipal
tribunals are usually clothed. The Commission expressly decides that
municipal restrictive rules of adjective law or of evidence cannot be
here introduced and given effect by clothing them in such phrases as
"universal principles of law," or "the general theory of law," and the
like. On the contrary, the greatest liberality will obtain in the admission
of evidence before this Commission with the view of discovering the
whole truth with respect to each claim submitted.

6. As an international tribunal, the Commission denies the
existence in international procedure of rules governing the burden of
proof borrowed from municipal procedure. On the contrary, it holds
that it is the duty of the respective Agencies to cooperate in searching
out and presenting to this tribunal all facts throwing any light on the
merits of the claim presented. The Commission denies the "right" of
the respondent merely to wait in silence in cases where it is reasonable
that it should speak. To illustrate, in this case the Mexican Agency
could much more readily than the American Agency ascertain who
among the men ordering typewriting materials from Parker and signing
the receipts of delivery held official positions at the time they so
ordered and signed, and who did not. On the other hand, the
Commission rejects the contention that evidence put forward by the
claimant and not rebutted by the respondent must necessarily be
considered as conclusive. But, when the claimant has established a
*prima facie* case and the respondent has offered no evidence in rebuttal
the latter may not insist that the former pile up evidence to establish its
allegations beyond a reasonable doubt without pointing out some reason
for doubting. While ordinarily it is incumbent upon the party who
alleges a fact to introduce evidence to establish it, yet before this
Commission this rule does not relieve the respondent from its

obligation to lay before the Commission all evidence within its possession to establish the truth, whatever it may be.

7. For the future guidance of the Agents of both Governments, it is proper to here point out that the parties before this Commission are sovereign Nations who are in honor bound to make full disclosures of the facts in each case so far as such facts are within their knowledge, or can reasonably be ascertained by them. The Commission, therefore, will confidently rely upon each Agent to lay before it all of the facts that can reasonably be ascertained by him concerning each case no matter what their effect may be. In any case where evidence which would probably influence its decision is peculiarly within the knowledge of the claimant or of the respondent Government, the failure to produce it, unexplained, may be taken into account by the Commission in reaching a decision. The absence of international rules relative to a division of the burden of proof between the parties is especially obvious in international arbitrations between Governments in their own right, as in those cases the distinction between a plaintiff and a respondent often is unknown, and both parties often have to file their pleadings at the same time. Neither the Hague convention of 1907 for the pacific settlement of international disputes, to which the United States and Mexico are both parties, nor the statute and rules of the Permanent Court of International Justice at The Hague contain any provision as to a burden of proof. On the contrary, article 75 of the said Hague convention of 1907 affirms the tenet adopted by providing that "The parties undertake to supply the tribunal as fully as they consider possible, with all the information required for deciding the case."

\*     \*     \*

E.     *Kling v. United Mexican States (U.S. v. Mex.)*, 4 R.I.A.A. 575 (General Claims Commission 1930).

[It is well recognized that Governments who have agreed to arbitrate are under obligation in entire good faith to try to ascertain the real truth.]

Notes and Questions

1. Whatever the objective of the evidence to be produced, care must be taken to ensure that it is not ruled inadmissible. What is the risk of such a ruling? Generally, it is considered to be minimal. Arbitral tribunals are keen to establish the facts of a dispute and are reluctant to be hampered by technical rules on the admissibility of evidence.

2. *Parker* dismisses "restrictive rules of adjectival law or of evidence" as, in effect, municipal atavisms, to be replaced internationally by the "greatest liberality." Are there any "universal" or "general" values to, *e.g.*, restrictive rules of evidence?

F.      *Western Co. of North America v. Oil and Natural Gas Comm'n*, (ad hoc arbitration, Ian Kinnell, umpire 1985) 13 YEARBOOK OF COMMERCIAL ARBITRATION 5, 13-14 (1988).

[This was an ad hoc arbitration in London, governed by Indian law. The umpire, on appeal from the arbitrators, stated]

As to evidential matters, according to a telex dated 11 June 1985, sent to both parties by the arbitrators, both parties had, at a meeting for directions held on the preceding day, agreed a procedure for the reception of evidence from witnesses which involved the exchange of witness statements with the opportunity given to each party to call for the production of the witness concerned for cross-examination while his statement would stand, subject to all proper questions of admissibility and weight, as his evidence in chief. Although the respondent made no protest prior to the oral hearings, it was suggested on its behalf at the beginning of the relevant part of the first session of oral hearings that the arbitrators had not entirely accurately recorded what had previously been agreed. Moreover, prior to the commencement of the second session of oral hearings (by which time the substance of Claim no. 1 had been heard), the respondent went so far as to submit that Indian law in any event prohibited the reception of statement evidence on the ground that the arbitrators were strictly bound by the Code of Civil Procedure. That suggestion was rejected by the arbitrators but, having no wish myself to act upon inadmissible material, I have given consideration to it. I have, however, no hesitation in expressing my concurrence in the arbitrators' ruling. The only authority cited by the respondent in support of its submission that arbitrators are strictly bound by the Code of Civil

Procedure (AIR 1985 ORISSA 103 following ARI 1982 ORISSA 277) was to no extent compelling. The passage in the earlier case that was relied upon in the latter was not even remotely connected with any question in issue in that case and, in my view, cannot be regarded as even persuasively authoritative. Moreover, it is inconsistent with the view of the Supreme Court expressed in at least one case (see AIR 1967 Supreme Court 1030). While I entirely accept that arbitrators (and umpires) are bound to have regard to certain fundamental evidential precepts they are clearly not in my view bound either by the letter of the Code of Civil Procedure or by the strictly procedural rules of evidence which may apply elsewhere. It is the observance of the rules of natural justice that is paramount in the proper conduct of a reference to arbitration.

In the present case the respondent was given every latitude to require an opportunity to cross-examine all those witnesses of the claimant whose statement evidence was read. In so far as the respondent failed to avail itself of that opportunity — and in so far as the respondent later took the position (in relation to claims other than Claim no. 1) of standing upon its own submission that all statements were inadmissible, reserved its position, and declined to put in evidence on its own behalf — it must in my opinion bear the consequences.

\* \* \*

Further examples of the liberal approach to questions of admissibility are readily available.

G.     *Shufeldt v. Guatemala (Guatemala v. USA)*, 2 R.I.A.A. 1083 (Sir Herbert Sisnett, sole arbiter 1930).

On the question of evidence over which there was some argument, I may point out that in considering the cases quoted on both sides it is clear that international courts are by no means as strict as municipal courts and can not be bound by municipal rules in the receipt and admission of evidence. The evidential value of any evidence produced is for the international tribunal to decide under all the circumstances of the case.

\* \* \*

Indeed, this less strict approach to rules of admissibility is enshrined in the rules of certain arbitral institutions. Thus, Article 14(3) of the 1985 LCIA Rules provides that the tribunal may ". . . receive and take into account such written or oral evidence as it shall determine to be relevant, whether or not strictly admissible in law." Similarly, Rule 33(1) of the ICSID Rules provides that:

"The Tribunal shall be the judge of the admissibility of any evidence adduced and of its probative value."

The note to this Rule leaves no doubts, stating that the rule "reflects long-standing international practice. It confers on the Tribunal the power to determine the admissibility, relevance and materiality of evidence. Hence the Tribunal has full power to decide whether particular evidence (*e.g.*, documents, interrogatories, written depositions, oral evidence by witnesses and experts given before the Tribunal or before a Commissioner) should be admitted."

\*   \*   \*

## III.   EVIDENTIARY WEIGHT OF DOCUMENTS

Redfern and Hunter list four basic methods of presenting evidence to the arbitral tribunal. They are:

(i) production of contemporary documents;
(ii) testimony of witnesses of fact (written or oral);
(iii) opinions of expert witnesses (written or oral);
(iv) inspection of the subject matter of the dispute.

Of these, they consider the production of contemporary documents to be generally the most effective method:

A.   ALAN REDFERN & MARTIN HUNTER, LAW AND PRACTICE OF INTERNATIONAL COMMERCIAL ARBITRATION 329-30 (2d ed. 1991).

In international commercial arbitrations, the best evidence that can be presented in relation to any issue of fact is almost invariably contained in the documents which came into existence at the time of the events giving rise to the dispute. This contrasts with the presentation of evidence in the courts in the common law system, where most facts are proved by direct oral testimony, and even documentary evidence must in principle be introduced by a witness in oral evidence.

It is not difficult to appreciate why reliance on documentary evidence is favoured by international arbitral tribunals. Its presentation is easier and less time consuming; and, in an environment in which cross-examination is regarded as an unreliable method of testing the evidence of a witness, the evidentiary weight of documentary evidence is clearly more substantial than that of oral evidence which is not tested by an effective challenge, either through lack of expertise on the part of the opposing party's advocate or lack of time during the course of the hearings.

However, the best reason for the practice of international arbitration tribunals in relying primarily upon evidence contained in contemporary documents is that the application of the so-called "best evidence rule" applies primarily to the weight of the evidence rather than to its admissibility, and the evidence of contemporary documents will invariably be regarded as being of great weight. The authenticity of documents must be capable of proof if challenged by the other party; but it is not usually necessary to produce original documents, or certified copies, unless there is some special reason for examination of the original.

*     *     *

B.      *Studer v. Great Britain (U.S. v. U.K.)*, 6 R.I.A.A. 149, 152 (American and British Claims Arbitration Tribunal 1925).

[Though the possibility of faulty memory and the preparation of documents solely in anticipation of arbitration grows with the passage of time, no general principles exist to guide a tribunal in weighing subsequent documents. In the *Studer* case, the tribunal found although it did not doubt the "absolute sincerity and perfect good faith" of the party, the party's correspondence written almost twenty years after the event could not be the basis of its judgment.]   The tribunal held that:

[W]here a case rests so largely upon ex parte statements prepared many years after the event by the party in interest, for the express purpose of presenting his claim in the best possible light, allowances must be made for infirmities of memory as well as for a claimant's natural sense of grievance amounting sometimes to almost an obsession. Studer's letter to the Acting Governor of the Straits Settlement and his communication to the Department of State were both written nearly 20 years after the transactions took place. Neither of these statements possesses the solemnity of a sworn declaration. They are merely the attempts of an individual who truly believed that he had been wronged, and perhaps had been unjustly treated, to recall and set down acts and circumstances of long ago. In effect, the Government of the United States asks the Tribunal to accept these statements without substantial corroboration and to found its judgment upon them. Without regarding many, if not most, of the essential facts as duly established in this way, it is difficult to see how any judgment could be rendered; and even so, much would be left to inference and conjecture.[263]

*     *     *

Thus although the tribunal admitted into the evidence the correspondence produced after the event, it treated the evidence with considerable circumspection.

### Notes and Questions

1. Although Redfern and Hunter persuasively argue why contemporaneous documents would be preferred over oral evidence, they do not suggest how a tribunal should weigh documents produced some time after the event. For example, how long is too long? Should the tribunal give weight to internal memoranda written six months after the event? One year afterwards? Ten years later?

2. Problems of authentication might also face a tribunal considering the evidentiary weight of contemporaneous documents. For example, if a party submitted a document into evidence that had not been authenticated by the terms of one of the parties' domestic law, should the lack of authentication in this legally prescribed manner detract from its evidentiary value? Read the following example and consider under what circumstances a tribunal should limit the weight it gives to evidence presented as contemporaneous. Does a tribunal's lack of concern for compliance with procedural rules detract from its ability to ascertain the truth or render a just decision?

3. What constitutes the strongest form of documentary evidence? If the evidence is contemporaneous with the matters raised in the dispute, this will give it added force. But does this exclude correspondence produced some time after the event?

---

[263] *Id.*

4. In *Studer*, although correspondence produced after the event was admitted into evidence, it was treated with considerable circumspection by the tribunal. Even if the evidence is contemporaneous, can it be utilized when it does not comply with the formalities of domestic law? For example, if a receipt submitted in evidence had not been authenticated as required by the law of the place of the transaction, should that detract from its evidential value?

C.    *Hatton v. United Mexican States (U.S. v. Mexico)*, 4 R.I.A.A. 329, 331 (General Claims Commission 1928).

.    .    .

The United States presented as evidence a copy of a receipt said to have been given to the claimant by General Lucero which reads as follows:

> "Vale a la Hda de San Gregorio por 7 siete caballos
> para la tropa que es a mi mando.
> San Gregorio 2 de Marzo - 924 El Gral de B.
>                                         H. Lucero."

The Government of Mexico presented a statement from Francisco Ibarra, who it is said acted as guide for General Lucero. This man asserts that a horse and a mule were taken from the San Gregorio Ranch, but that the horse was returned. As against such testimony it is proper to take account of the fact that the claimant had been allowed to remain in possession of a receipt, evidencing that a larger number of animals was taken and that none was returned. The Commission cannot properly disregard the evidential value of that receipt. And it may be particularly pertinent to note with respect to this point that receipts for military requisitions have been given important standing and recognition in international law and practice. The convention of The Hague of 1907 respecting the law and customs of war on land contains provisions with regard to receipts for military requisitions and contributions.

It was stated in behalf of Mexico that the receipt had not been "authenticated" as required by Mexican law. And furthermore it was urged that the receipt may either have been altered or indeed may have been a fraud, since on the one hand, it refers to "siete caballos" whereas the claimant asked compensation for two mules and five saddle horses, and on the other hand, the body of the receipt was written in pencil and the signature in ink.

It is unnecessary to cite legal authority in support of the statement that an alien in the situation of the claimant is entitled under international law to compensation for requisitioned property. No formalities required by domestic law as to the form of authentication of a receipt for requisitioned property, or the failure of a military commander to comply with those formalities could render such a receipt nugatory as a record of evidential value before this Commission.

### Notes and Questions

1. How then may a party exclude documents from evidence?

D.     *K/S A/S Bill Biakh and K/S A/S Bill Biali v. Hyundai Corp.*, 1 Lloyd's Rep. 187, 188-90 (1988).

[Plaintiffs had agreed to purchase two ships from defendant builders. In a dispute regarding the inferior quality of part of the ships, defendants tried to exclude from evidence certain documents prepared for a technical investigation which took place some time before arbitration proceedings were commenced. Defendants argued that these documents had been agreed to be "without prejudice" (which, under English law, would in appropriate circumstances mean that they could not be relied on in evidence). This contention was rejected by the tribunal, and defendants sought a declaration that the decision was invalid. Mr Justice Steyn in the Commercial Court found that the tribunal had not misconducted itself and that, in any event, even if the arbitrators' ruling was made in error, it could not in law amount to misconduct.]

The central question which arises on rival summonses in two Commercial Court actions is whether the Court has jurisdiction, in relation to two duly constituted arbitrations and during the course of the references to intervene by declaration or injunction to correct an allegedly wrong interlocutory ruling by the arbitrators as to the admissibility of evidence.

A brief outline of the background is necessary. Pursuant to two separate contracts of sale made in May, 1983, K/S A/S Bill Biakh and K/S A/S Bill Biali purchased two new buildings from Hyundai Corporation. The contracts are governed by English law and contain London arbitration clauses. The two vessels were delivered in September and December, 1985, respectively. Disputes arose as to the performance of the vessels as measured against the contractual terms. The disputes related to the fitness for service of the hatch covers. In March, 1986, both vessels were taken out of service. In May, 1986, the buyers commenced London arbitration proceedings under both contracts. In each arbitration the buyers claimed substantial damages on the ground that the builders failed to rectify defects in the hatch covers pursuant to the guarantee clauses in the contracts. The builders contend that the guarantee clauses preclude liability in respect of the claims made, that the buyers did not afford them reasonable opportunity to rectify the defects, and that the buyers were, at least in part, responsible for the design of the hatch covers. Technical issues are of fundamental importance.

Fortunately, the parties secured the appointment in each of the arbitrations of an experienced three-man tribunal well versed in such matters. Pleadings have been exchanged; substantial mutual discovery has taken place. And the hearing date has been fixed for January, 1988. In order to maintain that hearing date, it is now essential that the parties comply with the tight procedural timetable which has been set by the arbitrators. But a problem has arisen as to the evidence which may be adduced at the arbitration hearing.

The genesis of the problem is the documentation relating to agreed technical investigations which took place in 1986 and thereafter; that is, after the arbitrations had commenced. The builders assert that the investigations were conducted to enable the parties to form a basis for negotiations which, it was hoped, would lead to a settlement of the dispute.

Initially, there was a dispute as to whether the documents relating to the investigations were privileged in the sense that they were immune from production on discovery. These documents have now been produced, and the current dispute centres on the question whether such documents may be adduced in evidence. At a preliminary hearing held on Sept. 15, 1987, the builders contended that the exchanges regarding the investigations and all technical documentation relating to such investigations were agreed to be "without prejudice," and that in the context those words mean that the documents cannot be given in evidence. The buyers made a contrary submission. By telex dated Sept. 16, the arbitrators ruled that they were not persuaded that an agreement had been made to exclude these documents and that, as far as they are relevant, they may be relied upon by either side. In other words, the arbitrators have in principle ruled against the builders on their contention that such documents may not be adduced. But they have not yet ruled on the admissibility of any particular documents.

. . .

The builders' first contention is that the arbitrators' ruling was wrong and that it amounted to "misconduct." The nature of the builders' allegation required them to join and serve the arbitrators, and they have done so. Rightly, the arbitrators have simply indicated that they will abide by the judgment of the Court. The usual way in which an assertion of misconduct comes before the Court is either by way of an application for the revocation of the authority of the arbitrator under s. 1 of the Arbitration Act, 1950, or by an application for the removal of the arbitrator under s. 23(1) of the 1950 Act, or as a ground for subsequently seeking to set aside the award under s. 23(2). The builders here seek altogether different and, in my experience, novel relief.

The builders do not want the arbitrators removed. On the contrary, it is accepted on behalf of the builders that the arbitrators are men of integrity and competence. Moreover, it is of fundamental importance to bear in mind that the application is made during the course of the references and that its sole purpose is to achieve a reversal by the Court of an adverse procedural ruling made by the arbitrators. And, I would add, it is a ruling which may depend partly on issues of fact and partly on issues of law.

In an extreme case it is conceivable that an arbitrator's failure to observe the principles of natural justice in the making of interlocutory rulings may lead either to the revocation of the mandate of the arbitrator under s. 1 of the 1950 Act or the removal of the arbitrator under s. 23(2), but it follows from the decision in Bremer Vulkan Schiffbau und Maschinenfabrik v. South India Shipping Corp. Ltd., [1981] 1 Lloyd's Rep. 253; [1981] A.C. 909 that the Court has no inherent jurisdiction to correct procedural errors, even if they can be categorised as misconduct, during the course of the reference, and that the statutory scheme of the Arbitration Acts does not authorize such corrective measures. The remedies are therefore revocation of the authority of the arbitrator or removal of the arbitrator in the exceptional cases where that might be appropriate, or resisting enforcement of the award.

This is not a lacuna in our law. In the interests of expedition and finality of arbitration proceedings, it is of the first importance that judicial intrusion in the arbitral process should be kept to a minimum. A judicial power to correct during the course of the reference procedural ruling of an arbitrator which are within his jurisdiction is unknown in advanced arbitration systems, as is clear from the valuable Year Books published by the International Council of Commercial Arbitration, and the creation of such a power by judicial precedent in this case would constitute a most serious reproach to the ability of our system of arbitration to serve the needs of users of the arbitral process. For these reasons I reject the builders' first argument.

But there is another fundamental objection to the builders' first argument. The builders accept that the arbitrators are honourable men and competent to discharge their duties as arbitrators. The builders do not suggest that they were not given a fair hearing at the preliminary meeting. They simply say that the arbitrators committed misconduct because they came to the wrong conclusion. That is an unsustainable proposition. In relation to post award remedies, the decision of the Court of Appeal in Moran v. Lloyd's, [1983] Q.B. 542 is the clearest authority for the proposition that an error of law or fact cannot by itself amount to misconduct. If that is the case in relation to errors of law or fact as to substantive rights, it would be surprising if a different rule applied to errors regarding admissibility of evidence. That does not, of course, mean that the admission of, for example, utterly irrelevant evidence and reliance on it in the reasons for the award might not afford evidential material for a broader attack on the award itself alleging misconduct on the part of an arbitrator, but a mere error in relation to the admissibility of evidence does not by itself amount to misconduct, and I so rule.

On behalf of the builders, Mr. Millet in his helpful speech realistically recognized the difficulties in his way. He submitted, however, that the position was different in the present case because the arbitrators made what he described as a "gross" error. If an error was made, I find it difficult to see how it can be categorized as gross. After all, it depended to some extent on an assessment of less than compelling evidence of fact adduced by affidavit, and it was acknowledged on behalf of the builders that the phrase "without prejudice" is capable of different meaning, one of which, in my judgment, would be that the results of the investigations would simply bind no-one. In any event, given that one is dealing with nothing more than a possible bona fide error, I am satisfied that the eptithet "gross" cannot alter the position. I accordingly conclude that the arbitrators' ruling of Sept. 16, 1987, even if it was made in error, cannot in law amount to misconduct. For this further reason I conclude that the builders' argument based on misconduct must fail.

### Notes and Questions

1. It would be unusual for a witness whose statement had been submitted in evidence not to be called to give oral evidence if one of the parties so desired. Nonetheless, the tribunal may refuse to hear the witnesses if it considers that it can properly decide the dispute on the basis of the documents submitted to it and the arguments of counsel. Although such a refusal in ICC Case No. 1512 between a Pakistani bank and an Indian cement company was vigorously attacked by the losing company, the arbitrator's approach was upheld by the Court of Appeal in England. *See Dalmia Cement Industries Ltd. (India) v. National Bank of Pakistan*, 2 Lloyd's L. Rep. 223 (1978), *supra* p. 728.

2. One commentator has suggested the following guidelines for treatment of the presentation of evidence by witnesses:

(1)     A party should have the right to be heard in support of its own case.

(2)     Written affidavits signed by a witness (whether or not under oath) should be accepted as evidence, provided that the arbitrator or any party other than the one presenting the witness shall have the right to ask the witness to appear personally to be questioned with respect to the affidavit, failing which the affidavit may be wholly or partially disregarded.

(3)     As for witnesses called for by a party, their identity and the subject of their testimony should be disclosed in advance and the arbitrator should have the full authority to limit their appearance on the grounds of irrelevance or redundance.

> (4)     The arbitrator should have full authority to control the
>          taking of oral testimony, including the right to limit or
>          deny the right of a party to examine, cross-examine or
>          re-examine a witness if he determines it to be unlikely to
>          serve any further relevant purpose.

HANDBOOK OF ARBITRATION PRACTICE 358 (Ronald Bernstein ed. 1987)

## IV.   EVIDENTIARY WEIGHT OF TESTIMONY

Factual evidence may be presented to the tribunal by the
testimony of witnesses. Such testimony may be given in the form of a
written statement or, alternatively or in addition, orally at the hearing.

### A.   FORMALITIES

Written statements of witnesses play an increasingly significant
role in the presentation of evidence. Generally, these statements do not
have to comply with any formalities of presentation or content, nor
must they generally comply with local municipal law. Again, the
hesitancy of an international arbitral tribunal to insist upon formalities
comports with the institution's desire to shed the cumbersome
limitations of domestic courts and instead deal with the substantive
issues expeditiously and fairly. One should continually question
whether this distinction between substance and procedure is one that
tribunals can consistently and principally maintain. Consider the
following case in which the tribunal decided that the international
nature of the dispute marshalled against the requirement that written
statements comply with domestic law.

> *The Steamer Montijo (U.S. v. Columbia)*, *in* REPERTORY OF
> INT'L ARBITRAL JURISPRUDENCE 411-12 (V. Coussirat-Coustère
> & P.M. Eisemann eds. 1989).

To the first of the allegations the undersigned replies that,
although independent testimony of any fact is always desirable, there
are many cases in which it can not be procured. But this is no reason
for excluding the evidence of eye witnesses and of participators in a
transaction on the ground that they may be interested, pecuniarily or
otherwise, in its solution. To render such testimony invalid it would be
necessary to prove a notorious absence of credibility in the witnesses,
or a manifest combination or conspiracy on their part to swear falsely.

It would surely not be held that in a trial for mutiny committed on board of a ship on the high sea, the evidence of a portion of the crew could not be received against another portion because the informants might expect a reward from the owners, or a share in the property which they might have contributed to save by their resistance to the mutineers.

But it is to be borne in mind that there is another and independent witness of the capture; the affidavit of Agustin Castellanos, a native of Cuba, but a naturalized citizen of the United States, who was on board of the Montijo, and who did not in any way belong to her crew, distinctly states that the hoisting of the American flag by order of Herrero and Diaz as a signal to a schooner which was lying in the offing, and which proved to be laden with men and supplies for the revolutionists, was done in absolute opposition to the wish of the captain of the Montijo, who even put the flag away in his own cabin to insure its safety. It is true that the arbitrator of Colombia asserts that this affidavit, being only made before the Consul of the United States, without the intervention of any Colombian authority, would not be valid before a tribunal of the republic. But this court of arbitration is not a Colombian tribunal, but an international one. It consequently rests with the arbitrators alone to decide what evidence they will receive or reject, and the undersigned, as final referee can not see any reason for setting aside the declaration, on oath, of a respectable person, entirely impartial in the matter, against whose right to be believed, on oath, no allegation is or has been made. The undersigned is of opinion that, even if there were no other evidence that the Montijo was taken possession of against the consent of her owner and commander, the affidavit of the Senor Castellanos would of itself suffice to prove that such was the case.

\* \* \*

B. WEIGHING CREDIBILITY

Most significantly, even if testimony is admitted into evidence, what weight will it bear? Will it be of no value simply because the witness is a party in interest in the proceedings or because he has not been available to be questioned?

1.    ALAN REDFERN & MARTIN HUNTER, LAW AND
      PRACTICE OF INTERNATIONAL COMMERCIAL
      ARBITRATION 336-37 (2d ed. 1991).

An arbitral tribunal has a discretion to determine the evidentiary weight to be given to witness evidence. This arises from the general principles applicable to arbitration proceedings, and is expressly affirmed, for example, in the UNCITRAL Arbitration Rules.

In general, arbitral tribunals tend to give less weight to uncorroborated witness evidence than to evidence contained in contemporary documents. Arbitral tribunals also give greater weight to the evidence of a witness which has been tested by cross-examination, or by an examination by the arbitral tribunal itself. Similarly, although in some legal systems a party cannot give evidence, the evidence of a party is rarely excluded in international commercial arbitration, although the untested evidence of a witness who has a clear interest in the result of the case may be given less evidentiary weight than the evidence of a witness who is truly independent.

. . . [A]rbitral tribunals normally reject any submission that they should not hear the evidence of any particular witness, even if it is secondary evidence. However, an arbitral tribunal will give less weight to secondary evidence if, in its opinion, the party calling that evidence could have produced a witness who would have been able to give direct evidence on the factual issue in question.

*     *     *

These general principles are supported by the Walfish Bay Boundary case:

2.    *Walfish Bay Boundary* (*Germany v. UK*) (sole
      arbitrator 1911), *in* 11 Reports of Int'l Arb.
      Awards 267 (UN, NY 1948-1980).

XLVI. Considering that the evidence constituted by the sworn declarations of Messrs. Boehm, Sichel, Evensen, and Belck, cited in the German memorandum to show that until 1885 both the British authorities and the colonists resident in Walfish Bay who were acquainted with the boundary question understood that the eastern frontier of the territory passed close to the church at Scheppmansdorf, is evidence like that advanced by Great Britain in the opposite sense, the value of which, being in favour of the High Party which invokes it, should be weighed more carefully than is necessary when it is unfavourable to that party, and, starting from the basis, as has been done till now, that this method is in accordance with the rules of sane criticism, in conformity with the leading system in modern law, and the only one acceptable in the proceedings of an international arbitration, in which no principle or positive rule imposes any other limit on the powers of the arbitrator;

XLVII. Considering that all the evidence alluded to has been produced out of Court, in the sense that the arbitrator has not been able to conduct any cross-examination and without being disputed, inasmuch as the party prejudiced by it has not cross-examined the witness either, circumstances which, though they do not deserve blame, and appear easily explicable in the present case, certainly diminish the value of the evidence;

XLVIII. Considering that to judge by the respective assertions of the two parties, the witnesses brought forward by one or the other depend in some way or other by reason of nationality, residence, or office, on the State in whose favour they are giving evidence - a fact which, though it does not properly constitute a legal objection, is a ground for a reasonable presumption that they may accentuate their assertions, whether they wish it or not, in a definite sense. . . .

*   *   *

C.    PARTIES AS WITNESSES

In particular, the rule that parties to the dispute may not give evidence (as is the case in court proceedings in, for example, Germany) is generally disregarded.

> 1.    Michael Straus, *The Practice of the Iran-U.S. Claims Tribunal in Receiving Evidence from Parties and from Experts*, J. INT'L ARB., Sept. 1986, at 57, 58-62.

There is no uniform practice among legal systems whether to receive the testimony of parties as witnesses, or whether to accept the testimony of individuals so closely-related to the parties as to be said to have a financial interest in the outcome of the dispute. *See* SANDIFER, EVIDENCE BEFORE INTERNATIONAL TRIBUNALS 349ff. (1975). Modern arbitral practice, however, seems to be that where an individual party or, in the case of juridical persons, a party's officers and employees, have knowledge of the facts in issue, it would be unreasonable for an arbitral tribunal to refuse their testimony, since all testimony is ultimately subject to the arbitrators' judgment as to its probative value based on such factors as credibility and relevance. Thus, as concluded by Professor Sandifer:

> A rule denying any weight to the testimony of interested parties or excluding it altogether may have some justification in municipal procedure, where other evidence will usually be available. . . In international procedure, where the claimant through no fault of his own so frequently has no evidence except his own or that of parties intimately interested in the case upon which to base a claim for redress, such a rule is surely inequitable and unsound. *Id.* at 364.

*See also*, J. SIMPSON AND H. FOX, INTERNATIONAL ARBITRATION: LAW AND PRACTICE 192 (1959) ("In International law there are no general rules requiring the exclusion of categories of evidence").

The Tribunal's actual use of the testimony of parties to a dispute (so-called "interested" witnesses) has essentially followed Sandifer's observations, but within a procedural framework of greater or lesser complexity depending on the Chamber involved. For example, Chamber Two at an early stage in its hearings apparently allowed individual claimants to testify as fact witnesses on central elements of their claims, without regard to their interest in the outcome. Thus, in *Leila Danesh Arfa Mahmoud v. Islamic Republic of Iran*, Award No. 204-237-2 (November 27, 1985), the Chamber received oral testimony from the claimant as to the factual basis for her allegations regarding her status as a U.S. national, and the expropriation of her real property in Iran. Although the claim was ultimately dismissed for lack of jurisdiction based on the Chamber's conclusion that Mrs. Mahmoud did not have "dominant and effective" U.S. nationality during the time period relevant to her claim, there was never any question raised either of her capacity to testify as a "witness," or whether to classify her testimony in some other manner merely because she was also the claimant.

Chamber Three, however, developed a somewhat more involved procedural approach, allowing individual parties or parties' "representatives" to give "information" about the parties contentions, but not formally as witnesses. Under this guideline, parties or current employees of corporate parties — regardless of their level of authority in the company — are regarded as "interested" in the outcome of the claim, and may therefore only give "statements." At times such individuals are referred to by the Tribunals as "party witnesses" — perhaps a rather hybrid term, but an accurate description of the practical operation of the guidelines. Non-employees or former employees with no continuing ties to the company may, however, give testimony. Following these guidelines, Chamber Three heard a claimant engineer's statement at a hearing regarding the extent of his performance of engineering services, the reasons he was forced to leave Iran before completing his contract, and his efforts to mitigate damages caused by the early termination of the contract. Those statements, together with written evidence, then became the basis for an award in the claimant's favor. *Alan Craig v. Ministry of Energy of Iran*, 3 Iran-US C.T.R. 280 (September 2, 1983).

Chamber One of the Tribunal apparently followed the same approach as Chamber Three. . . . In a similar fashion, Chamber Two has more recently refined the distinctions it makes so that while senior company officials are generally regarded as party representatives who may give information but not as witnesses, lower-level employees may be heard in the latter capacity. *See, e.g.*, Minutes of Hearing in Case No. 49 (contract director of claimant company heard as party-witness; field engineer heard as ordinary witness).

Chamber One, it should be noted, was strongly criticized in the *Economy Forms* case by the dissenting arbitrator, Dr. Mahmoud Kashani, for allowing in the form of information evidence given by a party's representative. Kashani pointed out that Economy Forms had not provided written documentation as to the citizenship of holders of more than 50% of the company, and that the Chairman's oral "statement" based on personal knowledge that he knew those holders to be U.S. citizens was thus crucial to the proof of jurisdiction over the claim based on the U.S. nationality of the company. Kashani objected:

Although the Tribunal acknowledges that the Claimant has presented no evidence or documentation in order to establish its nationality, the majority has exempted the Claimant from the obligation to do so. Without the slightest legal basis, it has accepted the assertions solely on the basis of the statements of Mr. Jennings himself, who is an interested party in his claim and thus it has made it clear that its Award is invalid. Is it not unfair and oppressive that the unsubstantiated statements by the Claimant in an international forum be accepted as establishing its allegations, and that such a considerable sum be awarded against a sovereign government merely on the basis of an allegation brought against it? Indubitably, those persons with an interest in the Tribunal's arbitration will not relax their vigilance and will not readily overlook such high-handed decisions, nor will the international legal system, closely following the Tribunal's decision. 5 Iran-U.S. C.T.R. at 23.

Kashani's position is obviously wrong, since if accepted it would unfairly eliminate credible evidence from consideration even where no substitute is available. But the rationale behind the approach taken by Chambers One and Three seems at first also to be obscure, given the Chambers' actual use in deciding cases both of party "statements" and of witness' testimonial evidence. Lawyers accustomed to common law proceedings may thus be unable to perceive a logical basis for the distinction. For example, there seems no reason to believe that an expert witness retained by a party to give testimony to a tribunal as to such matters as the value of the company's shares is more "neutral" than a relatively junior current employee who is nevertheless the most knowledgeable available witness as to acts taken by revolutionary forces in seizing management power over the company. The witness/representative distinction might have substantive value if the Tribunal credited or discounted "testimony" or "statements" by virtue of that difference alone — but it doesn't and shouldn't.

The reason for the distinction seems to lie — at least judging from the presence of civilian lawyers on the Tribunal — in the reluctance of some civil law traditions to accept testimony from a witness who is also the claimant or the claimant's employee. For example, arbitrators from a German tradition will be reluctant to hear a managing director of a company or a chief executive officer since he will be considered "too close" to the party itself. Moreover, under a more extreme civil law view, perhaps represented in *Economy Forms* by Dr. Kashani's dissent, such persons might be entirely disqualified from providing evidence which will form the basis for an award.

Despite this reluctance, it has become clear through the Tribunal's practice that the Tribunal will accept *all* evidence presented to it, whether styled as witness "testimony" or as party "information," and will weigh it for probative value taking into consideration factors such as the evidence-provider's truthfulness, the likelihood that he had personal knowledge of the facts, and of course his interest in the outcome of the dispute. This practice has developed to the point where, despite early concerns whether the distinction might work to the prejudice of U.S. claimants who were unable to supply evidence other than that available through party-witnesses, the U.S. Government has taken the position

> that the Tribunal's practice of allowing testimony by all persons who possess relevant factual information, whether they are denominated witnesses or party witnesses, is both consistent with the Tribunal Rules of Procedure and sound as a matter of general [international arbitral] practice.

Letter from the Agent for the United States to Judge Willem Riphagen, Chairman, Chamber Two, dated May 15, 1984 (also enclosing a memorandum of law).

\* \* \*

In addition, the tribunal will give greater or lesser weight to testimony depending on the nature of the particular fact or facts it is intended to prove. Thus, in the following case, affidavit evidence to show grave misconduct had to be of a most conclusive character.

> 2. *McCurdy v. United Mexican States* (*U.S. v. Mex.*), 4 R.I.A.A. 418, 421 (General Claims Commission 1929).

Although, in other cases, (*William A. Parker*, Docket No. 127, and *G.L. Solis*, Docket No. 3245), the Commission has stated that it would consider certain facts as proved, even if they were only supported by affidavits, it declared likewise, that in each case the value attached to such affidavits would be estimated in accordance with the circumstances surrounding the fact under consideration. In this case it is endeavoured to prove misconduct, in a grave degree, of Mexican officials and therefore the Agency advancing the charge should submit evidence of the highest and most conclusive character.

\*     \*     \*

One of the most characteristic differences between the common law and civil law approaches to procedure relates to the use of witnesses.

D.     EXPERT TESTIMONY

1.     *Lehigh Valley RR Co. v. Germany* (*Sabotage Cases*) (*U.S. v. Germany*) (Mixed Claims Commission 1932), *in* 8 Reports of Int'l Arb. Awards 107 (UN, NY 1948-1980).

It remains to consider whether these doubts can be resolved by recourse to the expert testimony. This consists of about one thousand pages. The questions submitted to the experts are in my belief novel. They involve at the foundation certain known qualities of ink and paper. But as one reads the testimony on both sides one is impressed with the fact that the experts themselves had to resort to experiments with lemon-juice writing on new and old paper in order to reach their conclusions. Many of the opinions of the experts on the one side are countered by diametrically opposite results stated by those on the other. I agree with the arguments of both Agents that certain of the experiments and tests which they criticize are not beyond fair criticism and fail to carry conviction. I entertain no doubt that all the experts retained by both litigants were inspired by a desire to do their honest best with a very difficult problem. Both sets of experts evidently believe in the soundness of their conclusions, for they challenge the Commission to make certain experiments and examinations for itself, and it is hardly conceivable that they would do so unless they felt that the results of such experimentation by laymen would justify their confidence. My experience in this behalf has, however, been most unsatisfactory and has only tended to confirm the feeling that on the expert evidence alone my judgment would be left in balance as to the authenticity of the document. Expert evidence is often an aid in determining questions of the sort here presented; but is it far from an infallible guide, as witness the fact that several of the experts for the claimants convinced themselves of the authenticity of the Wozniak letters. This comment does not by any means apply to all of the experts who testify about the Herrmann message, and it is not to be taken as indicating that I have the slightest doubt that all of the expert's opinions are honestly entertained. It is mentioned merely as an illustration of the fact above stated, that, at best, expert evidence can usually be only an aid to judgment, and not always in and of itself so conclusive as to carry conviction.

\*     \*     \*

2.    Jan    Paulsson,    *International    Commercial Arbitrations*, *in* RONALD BERNSTEIN & DEREK WOOD, HANDBOOK OF ARBITRATION PRACTICE 425, 454-55 (1993).

Use of experts

In common-law court cases involving technical matters, any party may call expert witnesses on its own behalf to provide evidence on technical questions in issue. "Battles of experts" ensue, with detailed examination and cross-examination by counsel. Oral testimony of experts presented by the parties is rare in civil-law countries, where tradition and applicable procedural codes provide for the appointment of one or more neutral experts by the court.

Under Article 12 of the LCIA Rules and Article 14(2) of the ICC Rules, arbitrators may appoint neutral experts. With reference to less specific institutional rules, such as those of ICSID, one may conclude that authority to make such appointments is encompassed in more general powers to resolve the dispute expeditiously. Such is certainly the trend, as witnessed by Article 27 of the UNCITRAL Rules; Article 7 of the IBA Rules of Evidence; and Article 26 of the UNCITRAL Model Law. In major cases involving technical issues, however, both parties frequently wish to present evidence and testimony by experts whom they have consulted, whether the tribunal desires to be aided by a neutral expert or not. This occurs irrespective of whether the parties come from civil-law or common-law jurisdictions. In fact, when the issues in dispute include the evaluation of construction, engineering, design or mechanical and chemical processes, it is often indispensable for a party to consult experts outside its own organisation. Such experts, while paid for their work, do not have the same interest in the outcome of the litigation as a party's employee. Detached from the dispute, they can evaluate the issues more objectively. Their testimony may lend additional credibility to the party's case.

Even if they intend to appoint a neutral expert, arbitrators are not well-advised to reject the presentation of expert testimony by the parties. In particular, parties from common-law countries view with great misgiving a procedure whereby the arbitrators receive all their technical briefing from someone who, perhaps by unfortunate accident, may turn out to be incompetent: such an "expert" could not easily be challenged because, while perfectly mistaken, he is also perfectly neutral in the sense that his erroneous conclusions were not intended to benefit either side.

Since the information to be given by a party's expert is ordinarily both detailed and technical, the expert's report is generally filed as a document with other written evidence in the case. The consultation should provide a résumé of the qualifications of the expert as well as a summary of his modus operandi and the evidence examined in preparing his report.

The written report is the foundation upon which the expert's oral examination is built. He should be able to defend his views in response to questions from both the tribunal and opposing counsel. The flexible procedure of international arbitration and its relaxation of evidentiary rules provide a receptive framework for hearing party-produced experts, who can make significant contributions to the resolution of complex technical disputes.

The rules of ICSID and the ICC are flexible in allowing the parties to present expert witnesses, and allowing the arbitral tribunal to be assisted by its own appointed expert, but they do not guarantee that such an opportunity will be available, nor that a tribunal-appointed expert would be subject to questioning.

## Notes and Questions

1. The 1976 UNCITRAL Arbitration Rules provide for in Article 27(4)

> At the request of either party the expert, after delivery of the report, may be heard at a hearing where the parties shall have the opportunity to be present and to interrogate the expert. At this hearing either party may present expert witnesses in order to testify on the points at issue.

This concept, by and large reflected in Article 26(6) of the UNCITRAL Model Law, as well as in Article 12(2) of the LCIA Rules, would appear to be best suited to international cases. If a technical issue is important enough that the tribunal decides to appoint an expert, it is important enough that the parties should have full opportunity to examine and if necessary to challenge the views of the expert.

2. *Parsons & Whittemore Overseas Co. v. Société Générale de l'Industrie du Papier (RAKTA)*, 508 F.2d 969, 975-76 (2d Cir. 1974). [The facts are set out in Chapter 1, *supra* p. 136.]

> Under Article V(1)(b) of the Convention, enforcement of a foreign arbitral award may be denied if the defendant can prove that he was "not given proper notice . . . or was otherwise unable to present his case." This provision essentially sanctions the application of the forum state's standards of due process . . .

> Overseas seeks relief under this provision for the arbitration court's refusal to delay proceedings in order to accommodate the speaking schedule of one of Overseas' witnesses, Davis Nes, the United States Chargé d'Affairs in Egypt at the time of the Six Day War. This attempt to state a due process claim fails for several reasons. First, inability to produce one's witnesses before an arbitral tribunal is a risk inherent in an agreement to submit to arbitration. By agreeing to submit disputes to arbitration, a party relinquishes his courtroom rights — including that to subpoena witnesses — in favor of arbitration "with all of its well known advantages and drawbacks." . . . Secondly, the logistical problems of scheduling hearing dates convenient to parties, counsel and arbitrators scattered about the globe argues against deviating from an initially mutually agreeable time plan unless a scheduling change is truly unavoidable. In this instance, Overseas' allegedly key witness was kept from attending the hearing due to a prior commitment to lecture at an American university - hardly the type of obstacle to his presence which would require the arbitral tribunal to postpone the hearing as a matter of fundamental fairness to Overseas. Finally, Overseas cannot complain that the tribunal decided the case without considering evidence critical to its defense and within only Mr. Nes' ability to produce. In fact, the tribunal

did have before it an affidavit by Mr. Nes in which he furnished, by his own account, "a good deal of the information to which I would have testified." Appendix to Brief of Appellant at 184a. Moreover, had Mr. Nes wished to furnish all the information to which he would have testified, there is every reason to believe that the arbitration tribunal would have considered that as well.

The arbitration tribunal acted within its discretion in declining to reschedule a hearing for the convenience of an Overseas witness. Overseas' due process rights under American law, rights entitled to full force under the Convention as a defense to enforcement, were in no way infringed by the tribunal's decision.

### E.     CROSS-EXAMINATION

As can be seen from D.W. Shenton's introduction to the IBA Rules of Evidence in Arbitration International 1985 (Part V below), there exist fundamental differences between the common law adversarial approach to proceedings and that of the civil law's inquisitorial system. Thus, the common law firmly favours the cross-examination of witnesses, while the civil law rejects it. What happens in international arbitrations? René David considers that, in practice, the two systems are reconciled without difficulty.

### 1.     RENÉ DAVID, ARBITRATION IN INTERNATIONAL TRADE 296 (1985).

Different techniques are used in civil law and in common law countries for the examination of witnesses (including the parties themselves). In common law countries witnesses are subjected to examination-in-chief and cross-examination by the advocates of the parties; in civil law countries the leading role is played by the judge himself, who examines the witnesses. The opposition between the two methods is much less marked in the arbitration procedures where there is much less formalism. The witnesses will ordinarily be asked questions there both by the parties' advocates and by the arbitrator in as friendly an atmosphere as possible. No jury is present, and the strictness of the English rules of procedure can therefore be departed from. Much has been said and written about the difficulty of finding a way to reconcile the practices followed in civil law and in common law countries; in truth this reconciliation occurs without difficulty in practice. It is regarded as a matter of course that the arbitrator will play a larger role than a common law judge would, and also that examination-in-chief and cross-examination will not be separated into two phases as distinct as they are in common law procedures.

*   *   *

This statement is perhaps unduly sanguine. What will a party from a common law country think when, having entered into an arbitration agreement (which refers to rules of arbitration which are silent as to how evidence will be taken) discovers that he will neither be able to examine or cross examine witnesses, nor be heard as a witness, nor obtain fully discovery? On the other hand, what if the reverse is true and the party from the civil system finds himself facing common law procedures? Will the parties be satisfied?

It is to limit such problems that, in 1983, the IBA produced Article 5 of its Rules of Evidence.

### 2. INTERNATIONAL BAR ASSOCIATION, RULES OF EVIDENCE, 1983, ARTICLE 5.

Article 5. Witnesses

(1) Within 60 days of the delivery of the last Introductory Submission made by the Defendant or by the date agreed between the parties or determined by the Arbitrator, all parties shall deliver their Witness Statements to the Arbitrator only.

(2) Each Witness Statement shall:

(a) contain the full names and address of the Witness, his relationship to or connection with any of the parties, and a description of his background, qualifications, training and experience if these are relevant to the dispute or to the contents of his Statement;

(b) contain a full statement of evidence it is desired by that party to present through the testimony of that witness;

(c) reflect whether the witness is a witness of fact or an expert, and whether the witness is testifying from his own knowledge, observation or experience, or from information and belief, and if the latter, the source of his knowledge; and

(d) be signed by the witness, and give the date and place of signature.

(3) When the Arbitrator has received the Witness Statement(s) of each party he shall simultaneously deliver copies of all the Witness Statement(s) to all the other parties to the arbitration.

(4) Within 40 days of the receipt of any Witness Statement from another party a party may submit further or supplementary Witness Statements or Oral Evidence Notices in response to evidence submitted by such other party.

(5) Within 20 days of the receipt of any Witness Statement any party may by notice to the Arbitrator and all other parties (an "Oral Evidence Notice") request the right himself to give oral evidence at the hearing, or for any of his own witnesses or the witnesses of any other party to give oral evidence at the hearing. An Oral Evidence Notice shall stipulate the issues to which that evidence is to relate.

(6) Within 20 days of the receipt of any Oral Evidence Notice all parties shall reply thereto. If a party fails to reply he shall be deemed to have agreed to the request contained in that Oral Evidence Notice. If all parties agree, or are deemed to have agreed, to a particular Oral Evidence Notice, the witness named therein shall give oral evidence at the hearing in accordance with the Oral Evidence Notice. The Arbitrator may himself order that any witness gives oral evidence.

(7) If a party objects to an Oral Evidence Notice he shall state his reasons, and the questions whether the witness shall give oral evidence and, if so, the issues upon which the evidence shall be given, shall be determined by the Arbitrator in his discretion. The Arbitrator may give his decision on this question on the

basis of the documents submitted or after hearing the parties, as he may decide.

(8) A party may be heard in support of his own case. It shall be proper for a party or his legal advisers to interview witnesses or potential witnesses.

(9) Any witness who gives oral evidence shall in the first place be questioned by the Arbitrator, and thereafter submit to examination by the party calling him, cross-examination by all other parties and re-examination by the party calling him.

(10) The Arbitrator shall at all times have complete control over the procedure in relation to a witness giving oral evidence, including the right to limit or deny the right of a party to examine, cross-examine or re-examine a witness when it appears to the Arbitrator that such evidence or examination is unlikely to serve any further relevant purpose.

(11) The testimony of any witness not giving oral evidence or of a witness in respect of any portion of his evidence not subject to oral testimony, shall be taken by means of his Witness Statement only.

(12) A party shall be entitled to stipulate the name of a witness in his Oral Evidence Notice even if no Witness Statement has been produced for that witness, provided that the party states in writing that he has requested the witness to give a Witness Statement but that the witness has refused to do so and that the party has no power to compel him to provide such Statement. If the witness has given the party an informal or partial statement or other document (whether signed or not) the party shall deliver a copy thereof to the Arbitrator and to the other parties at the time he delivers the Oral Evidence Notice relating to that witness.

(13) The Arbitrator shall decide what weight to attach to the evidence or Statements of any witness or party.

(14) Nothing herein shall preclude the Arbitrator in his discretion from permitting any witness to give oral or written evidence.

\*     \*     \*

Article 5 of the Rules of Evidence in fact represents a compromise.

> 3.     David W. Shenton, *An Introduction to the IBA Rules of Evidence*, 1 ARB. INT'L 118, 123-24 (1985).

Article 5 provides a somewhat novel compromise between the common law and civil law approaches. Verbal testimony is presented to the tribunal prior to the hearing in the form of a written deposition. The right of a party to cross-examine exists only on those matters that are directly in issue and in respect of which advance notice is given by means of an oral evidence notice. The arbitrator has the unfettered power to decide whether oral testimony will be heard and cross-examined. The witness is first questioned by the arbitrator. He may thereafter be examined, cross-examined and re-examined by the parties in the common law manner. The procedure can be stopped by the arbitrator at any stage if he considers that it is unlikely to serve any further relevant purpose. Witnesses can be called without the prior filing of a witness's statement only if it can be shown that the witness has refused to give one and cannot be compelled to do so but is, apparently, prepared to give oral testimony at the hearing (Article 5.12). It is felt for obvious reasons that such occasions are likely to be extremely rare.

\*     \*     \*

## V.     DISCOVERY

The role of discovery in arbitration depends largely upon the rules of the various arbitral institutions, the domestic procedural rules of the place of the arbitration, and in the case of ad hoc arbitrations, the provisions of the arbitration agreements as written by the parties themselves. Philosophies about the advantages of discovery are roughly divided between common law jurisdictions and civil law jurisdictions. Disagreement does exist, however, within these two broad divisions.

In court proceedings in common law countries, a discovery procedure exists under which the parties are obliged to disclose to each other all relevant documents, whether or not those documents are favourable to their cases. This procedure is acknowledged to be time-consuming and often expensive. Consider then why it has been adopted by common law countries and whether such a model is appropriate for international commercial arbitration.

A.      David W. Shenton, *An Introduction to the IBA Rules of Evidence* 1 ARB. INT'L 118, 120-22 (1985).

It is an integral requirement of . . . [the] system [of common law] that the parties disclose to each other in advance the documentation comprising the written part of the evidence. It is also fundamental that each party disclose to the other side all the relevant written material, whether such material is supportive of that party's case or not. This is the procedure known as discovery, and under the common law system it is regarded as of paramount importance. It is a cornerstone of the system that the basic evidence is called in the form of verbal testimony of witnesses, including the testimony of the parties to the dispute. It is equally fundamental that such evidence be tested by cross-examination. As Mr Robert Goff, QC (as he then was), stated in his presentation at the Symposium referred to above: 'It is a strong conviction of English practising lawyers that, on a contested question of fact, the most satisfactory way to get to the bottom of the matter is, if possible, to see and hear the actual witnesses and to test their evidence by cross-examination in the light of all relevant matters, including contemporary documents.' He did, however, go on to say, '. . . but cross-examination is only likely to happen in substantial, closely contested disputes, in which lawyers are instructed. In most arbitrations, matters do not come to that stage.' The United States view was not dissimilar and the importance of cross-examination was stressed. In arbitrations, however, United States' practitioners do not see the necessity for elaborate pre-trial discovery of facts or documents; nor for elaborate (if any) pleadings, holding that it is sufficient that the facts and issues be fully explained by the lawyer opening his case and before calling or deploying his testimony. As Mr Robert Coulson, President of the AAA explained, 'Ordinarily, arbitrators will expect the parties to provide all testimony and evidence necessary to decide the case.' However, he did not imply that any party is under an obligation to provide testimony or evidence detrimental to his case as with English discovery procedures.

In civil law systems, whether arbitrators are expected to apply the rules of evidence and procedure of their national courts, or whether they are themselves left to determine the procedure for examining and taking evidence, the approach is inquisitorial. Lawyers having presented written arguments, allegations and documents in advance, it is for the judge or the arbitrator adjudicating on the matter to determine how the testimony will be received, how evidentiary matters that remain unclear will be investigated, and where or whether verbal testimony is required. It is the tribunal that questions the witness of its own motion or, at best, at the instance of the lawyers of one or other of the parties. As Professor Roger Perrot, Deputy Director of the Institute of Legal Studies, Paris, put it: 'The technique of "direct examination" and of "cross-examination" of the parties, witnesses or experts is totally unknown in our legal systems in Continental Europe. The arbitrator is the person in charge of the investigation. It is he who conducts the hearing of witnesses, who puts questions to them and who challenges them if necessary in order to obtain further details.' He goes on to allow, however, '. . . if the hearing proceeds in a serene and courteous atmosphere, it is often the case, even, that each counsel directly questions the witnesses summoned by the opposing party. But this only amounts to a simple measure of tolerance to which the arbitrator can always put an end.' It seems that the arbitrator not only conducts the reception of evidence by himself from materials and testimony tendered by the parties, but may also have new witnesses appear on his own motion; indeed, in the case of conflicting testimony, he may order an enquiry *ex officio*. As Professor Perrot pointed out: 'Once arbitrators have the power to order that witnesses be heard *ex officio*, they can at the same time appoint any third party whom they wish to hear.'

\* \* \*

Mustill and Boyd argue that properly used, discovery is "a powerful instrument of justice."[264] They continue: "In cases where all the information as to a particular event or fact lies in the hands of one party, discovery may provide the only means of ascertaining the

---

[264] MICHAEL J. MUSTILL & STEWART C. BOYD, THE LAW AND PRACTICE OF COMMERCIAL ARBITRATION IN ENGLAND 285 (1982).

truth."[265] On the other hand, the authors do acknowledge that the process has disadvantages for

> [I]f it is employed without discrimination, the procedure can have serious practical disadvantages. In complex cases, a full order for discovery may require the parties to list and produce large quantities of documents, all but a small fraction of which are of no interest or value to either party. If carried out thoroughly, the preparation of a list of documents involves the parties and their legal advisers in a great expenditure of time and money, much of which could be more usefully employed in preparing the evidence for the hearing.
>
> Moreover, the making of an order for discovery takes it for granted that both sides will thoroughly comply with the order. If this assumption is falsified, and one party gives full discovery while the other does not, the former may be placed at a serious disadvantage. If injustice is to be avoided, the arbitrator must take care to see that the process is carried out fairly, if it is carried out at all. This means, in practice, that an order for discovery will often be useless unless the parties are represented by English solicitors. Many foreigners view with incredulity a system which requires them to produce (for example) documents passing within their own organisation, which were never intended for general distribution; and they point out with justice that the possibility of disclosure must serve to inhibit their freedom to express themselves frankly in writing.[266]

It is for these reasons that discovery is regarded by most civil law lawyers as being unnecessary. In order to do justice in a case, civil law lawyers prefer simply to produce those documents upon which the parties rely, leaving the tribunal to draw any adverse inference if a party fails to produce a document which is harmful to its position.

---

[265] *Id.*

[266] *Id.*

In English court proceedings, there are two types of discovery, general and specific. As Mustill and Boyd explain:

> A general order for discovery requires a party to produce a list of all documents which are or have been in his possession, custody or power . . . .
>
> Any document is disclosable which it is reasonable to suppose contains information which may enable a party either to advance his own case or to damage that of his adversary, or if it is a document which may fairly lead him to a train of enquiry which may have either of these two consequences.
>
> In a High Court action, discovery of documents takes place automatically, after the exchange of pleadings, unless the Court makes an order to the contrary.
>
> .   .   .
>
> The procedure for specific discovery is available where a party has reason to believe that his opponent has not fully complied with his obligations as regards discovery — for example, where the disclosed documents refer to other documents which have not themselves been disclosed, or where it is obvious from the nature of the transaction that documents must have come into a party's possession or power, which are not included in the list. . . .[267]

Given the virtual automaticity of discovery in English High Court proceedings, the question arises as to how this rule of procedure affects arbitration in that jurisdiction. A number of jurists have disagreed about the applicability of this rule of discovery as the next article indicates. Consider the impact of applying the rule indiscriminately to the desirability of England as a site for arbitration for parties both from common law jurisdictions and civil law

---

[267] *Id.* at 284-85.

jurisdictions. Does the application further or frustrate the intentions of the parties in choosing arbitration as their method of dispute resolution?

B. W.G.O. Morgan, *Discovery in Arbitration*, J. INT'L ARB., Sept. 1986, at 9, 12-14, 22-24.

It is perhaps the fact that discovery is so wide-ranging and takes place automatically in most High Court actions that has given rise to the quite unfounded notion, even among lawyers, that it is a necessary element in English arbitrations as well as in English civil litigation, even to the extent of being automatic and applying to documents detrimental to a party's case. So distinguished a judge as Lord Denning gave increase to this misapprehension when, as the then Master of the Rolls, he implied in *Alfred Crompton Amusement Machines, Ltd., v. Customs and Excise Commissioners*, a case decided as comparatively recently as 1971, that a party to an arbitration was just as entitled to discovery as if he had been one to a High Court civil action. Small wonder, therefore, that in construction industry arbitrations, both the arbitrators, who are more often than not laymen, and the parties unhesitatingly agree to full discovery, which frequently involves the production of an excessive number of documents!

Far from being an automatic event in English arbitrations, discovery is a procedure which the parties can, if they so wish, exclude altogether. Even if they do not expressly exclude it, they have no obligation to adopt it unless the arbitrator makes a specific order that they should do so. There is no provision in the Arbitration Acts that requires the making of such a direction by an arbitral tribunal, although it has power to do so, if such has not been excluded by agreement. This follows from the fact that the Rules of the Supreme Court, under which the function of the judge is pre-determined and restricted, do not apply to arbitrations, in which the role of the arbitrator gives scope for, and sometimes demands, initiative that would be wholly out of place in a court, e.g. the examination of the parties.

If every arbitration agreement defined specifically the manner in which the arbitral tribunal should carry out its function, discovery would present no great problem. Such perfection is, however, rarely achieved and, in practice, the best one can normally hope for is that arbitration rules have been incorporated in the contract by reference. Not infrequently, even such a reference is lacking. If no procedure or interlocutory powers are agreed upon, either specifically or by reference to rules, then a measure of implication may become necessary. It was suggested by Diplock, J., as he then was, in *London Export Corporation v. Jubilee Coffee Roasting Co., Ltd.*, a decision subsequently upheld in the Court of Appeal, that, in such circumstances, an arbitrator's powers may be implied (i) from the language of the reference, i.e., the reference to arbitration, (ii) by statute, (iii) from surrounding circumstances, and (iv) by trade or custom.

Unfortunately, the assistance provided by statutory enactments in the above context is not impressive. The Arbitration Acts say very little about the powers of arbitrators, and what they do say tends to confuse rather than to enlighten. Thus, Section 12(1) of the Arbitration Act, 1950, empowers them to examine witnesses on oath or affirmation, to call for documents and to compel the parties to do all such other things as they may require during the proceedings on the reference. "Prima facie," these provisions, and the last of them in particular, invest arbitrators with wide powers, but they have been interpreted as being limited to such things as may be required to assist them in arriving at a determination of the dispute referred. The sub-section does not confer upon an arbitrator all the powers of a judge. He cannot, for example, commit for contempt or issue injunctions, nor can he order security for costs to be furnished by either party. The maximum effect of Section 12(1) is to allow an arbitrator, where no contrary intention is expressed in the arbitration agreement, a discretion to order full discovery on the High Court model. Equally, of course, it permits him to direct that there should be no discovery at all.

Just as Section 12(1) of the Act appears, "prima facie," to grant greater powers to arbitrators than it, in fact, does, so a later sub-section — 12(6) — is less restrictive in its effect than one might suppose at first sight. Under that sub-section specific powers are given to the court in relation to arbitration proceedings, including, by virtue of paragraph (b) thereof, that of making an order in respect of discovery of documents and interrogatories. One might reasonably deduce from the wording of the sub-section that those powers are granted to the court because the arbitrator does not possess them himself. That, however, is not so, for it is well-established that an arbitrator has power to order discovery and/or interrogatories.

The practical position of an arbitrator in an English arbitration, in which discovery has not been expressly excluded, may then be summarised as follows, viz:

1) It is for him in his discretion, to decide what degree of discovery, if any, is necessary to enable him to perform his function properly.

2) He may order only limited discovery. For instance, if it is apparent at the outset of the arbitration that the hearing will take place in stages because the case falls into clearly defined parts, he may restrict his order for discovery to the documents material to the first stage. Again, if the issues are few and clear-cut, he may dispense with general discovery altogether and merely order specific discovery in relation to those issues.

3) He may decide not to order discovery at all. If, for example, the (voluntarily produced) documents are especially numerous, but he is satisfied that he can rely upon the parties to make as full a disclosure as he requires, he may omit discovery altogether and order the parties to proceed straightaway to inspection, simply directing that each party should have all his relevant documents available at a specified time and place (generally the office of the solicitor of one of the parties), so as to enable the other party to look at them and take copies of those that are of interest to him. Since he is the master of the arbitral procedure he will not be regarded as having erred, or misdirected himself, if he does not order the discovery of a particular document or class of documents.

4) Although his power to order discovery and inspection of documents is, like that of the High Court, subject to the usual rules as to privilege, the latter are, like strict rules of procedure, somewhat relaxed in the case of arbitrations. Thus it was held, in *Mitchell Construction Kinnear Moodie Group v. East Anglia Region Hospital Board* that an arbitrator had acted properly in ordering the disclosure of the personal files of the employees of one of the parties. The "ratio

decidendi" of the case was that, since arbitration proceedings are private, confidentially is less likely to be a good ground for refusing discovery than it would be in a publicly heard court action.

5) Whenever he feels obliged to make a discovery order of any kind he should also make an order for inspection. Without the latter the former would serve little purpose. The order for inspection should not, however, extend beyond what is really necessary. Thus, in *James Laing, Son & Co. (M/c) Ltd., v. Eastcheap Dried Fruit Co.*, it was held that arbitrators were entitled to refuse a party's inspection of certain documents after they had satisfied themselves that that party had copies of them in his possession.

. . .

[In a dispute between a party from a civil law country and one from a common law country, how are the two conflicting views on the discovery process dealt with? Morgan continues in this article to discuss one institution's attempt to settle this conflict.]

The conflicting principles and attitudes that exist, not only as between the Civil and Common Law jurisdictions but also within the latter, make it extremely difficult to achieve a general code of practice applicable to discovery and ancillary procedures in international commercial arbitrations. For that reason, efforts so far made to that end have not been outstandingly successful.

The UNCITRAL Arbitration Rules, published in 1976 and so called because they had been prepared by the United Nations Commission on International Trade Law ("UNCITRAL") were intended, in the words of their principal draftsman, Professor Sanders, of the Netherlands, "to be acceptable in both capitalist and socialist systems, in developed and developing countries and in common law as well as civil law jurisdictions." Despite this magisterial claim the Rules do not constitute anything like an evenly balanced compromise between the different jurisdictions, being heavily slanted towards continental practice, and do not empower the tribunal to order general discovery of relevant documents. Indeed, the only power that exists in this context is a very limited one of ordering discovery in relation to matters on which expert evidence may be called.

A further, and potentially more important, development was the UNCITRAL Model Law on Arbitration, which appeared in its final form in 1985 but has yet to be formally adopted in any jurisdiction and will almost certainly not be so by the United Kingdom. The Model Law again, however, bears the heavy imprint of continental practice and does not empower any court functioning under its provisions to order either the attendance of a witness to give oral testimony or the production of documents. Indeed, the deficiency goes deeper still, for the Model Law does not permit even the arbitral tribunal to order general discovery of documents. The best thing that can be said of it, in this connection, is that it provides that parties are obliged to disclose to a tribunal's expert all documents relevant to his enquiry and that, if there is a dispute as to relevance, the tribunal shall decide it. The provisions is, however, a "paper tiger," for there is no sanction if the tribunal's order is disobeyed.

Both the UNCITRAL Rules and Model Law, of course, enjoy an official status. Unofficial, and rather more satisfactory, efforts have also been made by responsible private bodies to deal with discovery as part of an international code of rules. The latest of these was that of the Council of the International Bar Association [IBA]. The latter, in May, 1983, after extensive discussion, adopted by resolution, and recommended to its members and others a set of Supplementary Rules of Evidence (for use only when they were not in conflict with either the general rules of the arbitration or any mandatory applicable principles of law), which concentrated upon the manner in which evidence should be received. Broadly speaking, these Rules too tend to favour the Civil Law system although . . . quite important concessions are made to the Common Law. Those who drafted them no doubt had it well in mind not only that there is nothing in either the English or American law of arbitration which specifically prohibits an inquisitorial approach but also that as distinguished an English authority as Kerr, L. J., had expressed approval of its use in certain arbitrations.

It is made plain, by inference, in Article 4.1 of the Supplementary Rules of Evidence that there is no obligation on a party to disclose documents other than those on which he wishes to rely. There is, however, a provision against surprise, requiring parties to exchange lists of documents in advance and prohibiting, subject to the consent of the arbitrator, the production at the hearing of documents that have not been so listed. A further concession to Common Law discovery procedure appears in Article 4.4, which permits one party to serve on the other, in the circumstances therein set out a notice to produce a document relevant to the dispute but not listed. (This provision is, however, of only limited value because the party can only serve his notice when he knows of the existence of the particular document and when it has previously passed between the parties or between a third party and the opposing party.) If the notice is not complied with, production can be ordered by the arbitrator who, in the event of a failure to produce, may draw the appropriate conclusion - normally the ultimate sanction in a Civil Law arbitration.

*     *     *

The Rules of Evidence are recommended by the IBA for incorporation in procedural rules governing international commercial arbitrations. Even if not specifically adopted by the parties, it is suggested in the Preamble to the Rules that they be used as a guide for arbitrators conducting proceedings between parties from different legal systems. Article 4 of the IBA Rules of Evidence sets forth guidelines for document discovery.

C.    INTERNATIONAL BAR ASSOCIATION, RULES OF EVIDENCE, 1983, ARTICLE 4.

(1) Each party shall make Production of Documents in respect of all documentation on which such party desires to rely.

(2) No later than 60 days after delivery of the last Introductory Submission made by the Defendant or by the date agreed between the parties or determined by the Arbitrator, each party shall exchange his List with every other party and deliver his List to the Arbitrator. Unless a document has been so listed it shall not be produced at the hearing without the consent of the Arbitrator. All documents in the List shall be numbered consecutively, and shall be produced in their entirety unless otherwise agreed or ordered. Each party shall provide the Arbitrator with a copy of each document in his List.

(3) A party shall at any time be entitled to a copy of any document listed by another party upon offer of payment of the reasonable copying charge. Such document shall be supplied within 15 days of the request.

(4) A party may by Notice to Produce a Document request any other party to provide him with any document relevant to the dispute between the parties and not listed, provided such document is identified with reasonable particularity and provided further that it passed to or from such other party from or to a third party who is not a party to the arbitration. If a party refuses to comply with a Notice to Produce a Document he may be ordered to do so by the Arbitrator.

(5) The Arbitrator shall have the power, upon application by one of the parties or of his own volition, to order a party to produce any relevant document within such party's possession, custody or control.

(6) If a party fails to comply with the Arbitrator's order to produce any relevant document within such party's possession, custody or control, the Arbitrator shall draw his conclusions from such failure.

## VI. REPRESENTATION/RIGHTS OF AUDIENCE

In court proceedings it is usually the case that the litigants must, if they are represented at all, hire local counsel who are qualified to practice local law. In international arbitration, in contrast, the parties may select counsel on the basis of their expertise in the arbitration field or their pre-existing knowledge of the file; the fact that such counsel has no connection whatsoever with the place of arbitration is generally of no import. Indeed, it may be that the team representing a disputant may include not only lawyers, but also, say, engineers or other professionals. In some cases, in particular those involving commodity associations, representation by lawyers at arbitration hearings is not permitted. (The English Court of Appeal has found that this restriction is not contrary to public policy. *Henry Bath v. Burgby Products*, 1 Lloyd's Rep. 389 (1962).)

This so-called "open door" policy is widely accepted in practice though it is sometimes resisted by members of the local bar who may prefer a more protectionist regime. It has, however, received little attention in legislation. The Australian International Arbitration Amendment Act (1989) is an exception. Sections 29(2) and (3) of that Act provide that:

> (2) A party may appear in person before an arbitral tribunal and may be represented . . .

> (b) by a duly qualified legal practitioner from any legal jurisdiction of that party's choice; or

> (c) by any other person of that party's choice.

> (3) A legal practitioner or a person, referred to in paragraphs (2)(b) or (c) respectively, while acting on behalf of a party to an arbitral proceeding to which Part III applies, including appearing before an arbitral tribunal, shall not thereby be taken to have breached any law regulating admission to, or the practice of, the profession of the law within the legal jurisdiction in which the arbitral proceedings are conducted.[268]

A.    *Lawler, Matusky & Skeller v. Attorney General of Barbados*, Civ. Case No. 320 of 1981 (High Court Barbados Aug. 22, 1983).

The Agreement between the parties provided for the claimant — applicants, as engineering consultants to the Government of Barbados, to perform certain professional engineering services in connection with the construction of the Bridgetown Sewerage Project. Article 16 of the Agreement provides —

> 16.01    This Agreement shall be governed in all respect by the laws of Barbados.

---

[268] International Arbitration Amendment Act 1989, 1989 Austl. Acts. 25, §§29(2) & (3) (amending Arbitration (Foreign Awards and Arguments) Act 1974).

16.02    All disputes, differences or questions between the Parties to this Agreement with respect to any matter or thing arising out of or relating to the Agreement which are not settled by negotiation or other agreed method of settlement may, after written notice by either party to the Agreement of the other Party, be submitted to arbitration in accordance with the provisions of the Arbitration Act 1958 (Act 1958 - 23) Chapter 110 of Barbados.

It is clear therefore that from the outset the parties agreed that the law governing the contract would be the law of Barbados and the law governing the arbitration proceedings, the lexi fori, would be the Arbitration Act, Chapter 110, of Barbados.

When an arbitral tribunal is ordered to state a question of law arising in the course of the reference in the form of a special case for the decision of the High Court, there is a division of function between the tribunal and the Court. It is for the Court to decide the question of law and it is for the tribunal to make findings on all matters of fact which are relevant to the decision of the question of law: see Donaldson J. in Rolimpex v. Dossa & Sons Ltd. (1971) 1 Ll.L.R. 380 at p. 304.

In this case the arbitrator has set out his findings as follows:

a.    Mr. Kannry is both an engineer and an attorney, licensed in those professions in the State of New York, and has had extensive experience for several years in representing Claimant, in those capacities, in dealings with the Government of Barbados on the matters at issue to be resolved in this Arbitration.

b.    The Government's several legal representatives, with whom Mr. Kannry, dealt on contract negotiations, earlier claims resolution and other matters of legal representation for Claimant, did not object, as far as I know, in any manner to such representation, and Claimant extensively relied upon the experience so acquired by Mr. Kannry in that capacity. To deprive Claimant of the right to such continued representation in the Arbitration hearings could be prejudicial to that party.

c.    My experience in international engineering and construction contracts, and my personal involvement in arbitrations to resolve disputes arising therefrom, has been that there exists a well recognised practice of permitting parties in arbitration hearings, as separate and distinct from the litigation process in Court, to be represented by a person of their own choosing, and not necessarily one who is admitted to practice law in the particular jurisdiction where the hearings are to be held.

d.    Inasmuch as the nature of the dispute between the parties is technical, involving engineering and construction matters, Mr. Kannry's background in those areas and familiarity with the technical facts from several years of experience in this matter, and wholly independent of any legal credentials, justifies his appointment as Claimant representative for the arbitration hearings.

e.    The fact that this Court appointed me as Arbitrator evidenced its recognition of the importance of technical expertise over local legal expertise in this matter. The same standard is proper in connection with the parties' representatives.

f.    The Arbitration Act of Barbados, which governs the procedures agreed to by the parties as applicable to the resolution of disputes, is silent on this subject and, therefore, does not either require representation of a party by a Barbados attorney or preclude representation of a party by other than a Barbados attorney.

g.   The provision of the Legal Profession Act, which Respondent has cited as the sole basis for objecting to Mr. Kannry as Claimant representative in the Arbitration, is neither incorporated by reference in the Arbitration Act, nor does it specifically refer to arbitration proceedings. Both the distractions made by Mr. Kannry in the papers submitted to me, and not contested by respondent, and the conduct of Respondent attorneys and other Government legal representatives during the several years of direct dealing with Mr. Kannry, as Claimant representative, are consistent with the common and usual meaning ascribed to the term "practice of law" in English-speaking countries throughout the world.

h.   Article 16, paragraph 16.01 of the Agreement, provides that "this Agreement shall be governed in all respects by the laws of Barbados." Inasmuch as this requirement, separate and distinct from the procedural matter of disputes resolution under paragraph 16.02, will likely necessitate consideration of other Barbados laws relating to the rights, duties and obligations of the parties in the performance of the Agreement, I directed that Claimant representative be assisted by a Barbados attorney at all hearings to advise on those points.

These findings disclose the complete reasoning on which the arbitrator proceeded in giving his ruling on the 21st of January, 1982. And I must clarify from the outset how certain aspects of these findings must be approached.

· · ·

. . . [W]ith respect to the arbitrator's reference to the existence of a well recognised practice permitting parties in arbitration hearings to be represented by a person of their own choosing, no such practice can supersede the law of Barbados which governs the arbitration proceedings. In *Orion Cia. Espanola de Seguros v. Belfort Maats* [1962] 2 Ll. L.R. 25, Megaw J., said:

> The conclusion which I draw from those judgments is that it is the policy of the law in this country that, in the conduct of arbitrations, arbitrators must in general apply a fixed and recognisable question of law, which primarily and normally would be the law of England and that they cannot be allowed to apply some different criterion such as the view of the individual arbitrator or umpire on abstract justice or equitable principles.

Adapting this approach to the instant case the law of Barbados is the law to be applied and effect can be given to the practice of which the arbitrator speaks only if the law of Barbados permits it. If the Legal Profession Act excludes representation in arbitration hearings in Barbados by a person who is not an attorney-at-law registered thereunder, the international practice must yield to the law.

Third, if it is against the law for Mr. Kannry to represent the claimants in arbitration hearings in Barbados, the conduct of the legal representations of the Government in dealing with Mr. Kannry as the claimant's representative cannot preclude the Attorney General from raising the illegality. The arbitrator, like everyone else, would have to obey the law and could not authorise or condone its breach. . . .

. . . ..

Lord Diplock in his speech in *Bremer Vulkan v. South India Shipping Corp.* [1981] 1 All E.R. 209, considered what the mutual obligations of the parties are in a private arbitration. He said at (p. 301) —

> By appointing a sole arbitrator pursuant to a private arbitration agreement which does not expressly or by reference specify any particular rules, the parties make the arbitrator the master of the procedure to be followed in the arbitration. Apart from a few statutory requirements under the Arbitration Act 1950 (the Arbitration Act Cap. 110 is the local equivalent) which are not relevant to the instant case, the arbitrator has a

complete discretion to determine how the arbitration is to be conducted from the time of his appointment to the time of his award, so long as the procedure he adopts does not offend the rules of natural justice.

Over a century earlier Erle C.J. in *Re Macqueen* (1851) C.B. (U.S.) 312 dealt with the argument that the interests of justice required that arbitrators acting under the Friendly Societies Act should be compelled to hear the parties by Counsel, the substance of the complaint being the refusal of the arbitrators to allow the complainant to be so represented. Some of his remarks have relevance beyond the circumstances of the case with which he was dealing. He said at pp. 313, 314 —

> . . . the only charge is that the arbitrators in their discretion thought to fit to decide that the Claimant had no right to introduce counsel. Mr. Yeatman puts it on the ground that it was an unfair exercise of discretion on the part of the arbitrators to refuse to allow the party the assistance of counsel; and he contends that the interests of justice require that the parties upon such an arbitration as this should be heard by counsel. I am of the opinion that the argument fails. I am not aware of any authority for it, and none has been cited.

After stating that allowing counsel to appear in all cases could hinder rather than advance justice in arbitrations under the Friendly Societies Act, he continued —

> . . .[I]n the absence of ancient usage to the contrary, every tribunal has a discretion as to who shall be permitted to appear as advocates before it. And I see the same point substantially came under consideration of this Court in . . . where the court refused to set aside the award on the ground that the arbitrator had declined to permit a stranger to be present for the purpose of assisting the defendant's attorney with practical hints for the conduct of the defence holding that an arbitrator has a general discretion as to the mode of conducting the inquiry before him. Maule J. in that case observes — "It is a very proper, and in some cases a very indispensable thing that arbitrators should within proper limits, be

allowed to deviate from the ordinary rules which govern courts of justice . . . It is, therefore, evidently quite fallacious to say that any suspicion of misconduct is to fix upon an arbitrator because he has thought fit to depart from the ordinary course in conducting the proceeding before him." I am of opinion that the authorities as well as the reason of the thing are opposed to this application.

In the same case Williams J. said at p. 314 —

> . . . Without therefore saying as a general rule that an arbitrator may decline to hear counsel, it is enough to say that in the particular case the refusal was justified.

> As I understand it, it is the common law right of everyone who is sui juris to appoint an agent for any purpose. . . .

. . .

An arbitrator in a private arbitration is, in the words of Lord Diplock in the Bremer Vulkan case, the master of the procedure to be followed in the arbitration so long as the procedure he adopts does not offend the rules of natural justice. It would seem to follow that it is within his competence to rule that he would in his discretion allow a party to the proceedings to be represented at hearings in Barbados by someone chosen by the party.

Moreover since a party has the right at common law to appoint an agent for any purpose whatever, it would seem to follow too that, if he is permitted by the arbitrator to be heard, he can legitimately appoint someone to represent him at hearings in Barbados. But these propositions are challenged by the Attorney General who submits that in Barbados only a person registered as an attorney-at-law can represent a party at hearings in Barbados. Three affidavits are filed in support of this submission.

[The affidavits, all by prominent members of the local bar, asserted that it would be improper and contrary to Barbadian law to allow lawyers who were not admitted to practice to represent parties in international arbitrations heard in Barbados.]

. . .

From this evidence it seems that the view of the profession is based on the practice in Barbados over the last 30 years as well as on their interpretation of the Legal Profession Act. Later in this judgment I will examine the provisions of the Act in order to determine the true meaning and effect of its provisions. As to the other ground for their view such a conclusion ought not in my view to be drawn from what a number of arbitrators have done over a relatively short period of time. There are various types of arbitration and, as seen earlier, the procedure to be followed in each arbitration is determined by the individual arbitrator. . . .

. . .

[The court then set out the provisions of the Legal Profession Act which defines who may practice law in the jurisdiction and sets forth the penalties for the unauthorized practice of law.]

It is submitted on behalf of the Attorney General that if Mr. Kannry were to represent the claimants at the arbitration hearings in Barbados, he would be practising law in breach of section 12(1) (a); and that the arbitrator cannot authorise or permit Mr. Kannry to do any act which would be in contravention of the law of Barbados. My task therefore is to determine whether representation of a party at a hearing in Barbados in a private arbitration constitutes the practice of law within the meaning of the Act.

[The Court reviews comparatively "restrictive or extensive" definitions of the practice of law.]

. . .

Far from the Legal Profession Act disclosing in clear and unambiguous terms the intention to reserve exclusively to attorneys-at-law advocacy and like functions, the indications are that it was not Parliament's intention to make such a significant change in the law. In my judgment the Act did not affect the powers of an arbitrator in a private arbitration to regulate its procedure or the common law right of a party, if permitted by the arbitrator, to be represented by someone chosen by him.

The findings of the arbitrator disclose that, in giving his ruling, he took into account Mr. Kannry's qualifications and references, general as well as in the particular case, his own experience and the possibility of prejudice being caused to the claimants if they were deprived of Mr. Kannry's continued assistance. In my opinion these were all matters which he could properly take into consideration and it cannot be said that he exercised his discretion in any improper manner.

I would answer the first question in this way: The Arbitrator had and still has, the power in law to determine and has correctly and validly determined that the applicants are entitled to be represented at hearings in Barbados by Mr. Jack Kannry, a person not registered under the provisions of the Legal Profession Act.

The Arbitration Act. Cap. 110 governs the proceedings and the High Court of Barbados has jurisdiction under the Act and common law to control them. The Court may set aside an award where the arbitrator misconducts himself or the proceedings or where an arbitration or award has been improperly procured (Section 26). The court may on application give relief where an arbitrator is not impartial or there is a dispute whether a party has been guilty of fraud (Section 27). And at common law the court may intervene if there is a breach of the rules of natural justice. There are good reasons therefore for requiring an attorney-at-law registered in Barbados to be associated with Mr. Kannry. Any applications to the court would be dealt with by someone acquainted with the case. The reasons given by the arbitrator for directing that Mr. Kannry be assisted by a Barbados attorney-at-law at all hearings were to enable Mr. Kannry to be advised on Barbadian law. It seems to me that the considerations I mentioned earlier are more to the point. However that may be, the arbitrator's direction is in my opinion concible. I would therefore answer the second question by saying that the arbitrator could permit the applicants to be represented by Mr.

Kannry and could also permit such representation subject to the proviso that Mr. Kannry be associated with an attorney-at-law registered under the Legal Profession Act.

*     *     *

This liberal approach was confirmed by the High Court of Malaysia in *Zublin Mukibbah Joint Venture v. Malaysia*, No. R8-24-41-89 June 19, 1989. In that case, a U.S. lawyer assisted lawyers admitted to the Malaysian bar in an arbitration in Malaysia. The respondent in the arbitration objected to the presence of the foreign lawyer on the basis that he was not a member of Malaysia's bar, nor an advocate or lawyer under Malaysia's Legal Profession Act 1976. The Court found that the US lawyer was entitled to act and, on the basis that an arbitration was private and "not a Court of Justice in Malaysia as envisaged by the Legal Profession Act," that there had been no breach of that Act.

It is against this background that the Singaporean decision in *Builders Federal (Hong Kong) Ltd. and Josef Gartner & Co v. Turner (East Asia) Pte. Ltd.* March 30, 1988 stands out. In that case, Judicial Commissioner Chan Sek Keong ruled that the representation of the foreign respondents by foreign counsel contravened Singapore's Legal Profession Act.

B.      Michael Polkinghorne, *The Right of Representation in a Foreign Venue*, 4 ARB. INT'L 333, 334-37 (1988).

The arbitration itself concerned a building dispute brought against Turner ("the applicant") for wrongful termination of a construction project by their subcontractors, Builders Federal and Gartner ("the respondents"). The latter had engaged the New York law firm of Debevoise & Plimpton ("Debevoise") to commence arbitration proceedings on their behalf in 1987. Turner subsequently brought High Court proceedings (after obtaining a temporary injunction) seeking a permanent injunction to restrain Debevoise from acting on behalf of the respondents. Turner maintained that Debevoise's involvement in the arbitration proceedings constituted a breach of Sections 29 and 30 of the Legal Profession Act.

The relevant parts of Sections 29-30 read:

29. - (1) Subject to this Part, no person shall practice as an advocate and solicitor or do any act as an advocate or solicitor unless his name is on the roll and he has in force a practising certificate and a person who is not so qualified is referred to in this Act as an unauthorised person.

30. - (1) Any unauthorised person who —

(a)     acts as an advocate or a solicitor or agent for any party to proceedings or as such advocate, solicitor or agent sues out any writ, summons or process, or commences, carries on, solicits or defends any action, suit or other proceeding in the name of any other person or in his own name in any of the courts of Singapore or draws or prepares any document or instrument relating to any proceeding in the courts in Singapore

— shall be guilty of an offence [fine, imprisonment, or both] (*emphasis added*)

Judge Chan gave judgment for Turner and, accordingly, issued a permanent injunction barring Debevoise from taking further part in the arbitration.

The primary object of the Act is to protect the public from claims to legal services by unauthorised persons. Parties who prefer to have their disputes resolved through arbitration rather than by court proceedings are no less members of the public. Their common law right to retain whomsoever . . . they desire or prefer for their legal services in arbitration proceedings in Singapore has, in my view, been taken away by the Act.

In reaching his decision, Judge Chan developed a two-pronged test to determine whether a person or firm "acted as an advocate or solicitor" in contravention of the Act. He postulated that "(a) . . . an act is an act of an advocate and solicitor when it is customarily (whether by history or tradition) within his exclusive function to provide, eg giving advice on legal rights and obligations [and/or] . . . pleading in a court of law; [and] (b) a person acts as an advocate and/or solicitor if, by reason of his being an advocate or solicitor, he is employed to act as such in any matter connected with his profession." In the instant case, in the Judge's opinion, these points were beyond any doubt.

Counsel for the respondents sought to avoid that conclusion by stressing the "fundamentally different" nature of arbitration proceedings, and by arguing that the Act, accordingly, had no application in the area of international arbitration. Counsel raised further arguments concerning the wording of the relevant provisions, including a submission that the word "practise" in section 29(1) of the Act implied regularity in the manner in which one offered one's services to the public. Accordingly, it was argued, Debevoise were not "practising" law by representing the respondents in a single arbitration.

Judge Chan was not impressed by these arguments and gave sections 29 and 30 a more expansive interpretation, despite certain canons of interpretation cited by the respondents. While saying little about the respondent's assertions as to the particular nature of arbitration proceedings, he expressed the view that representing a client on an extended litigation or arbitration battle "would not be doing an isolated act but a series of acts over a period of time in respect of an isolated matter . . . There is no principle which says a person cannot practise as an advocate and solicitor in respect of only one case."

Counsel's final submission, that the Act was intended to protect the public but not persons voluntarily agreeing to resolve their disputes by arbitration, received similarly short shrift. Judge Chan felt that these people (including, of course, the respondents) nevertheless remained part of the "public" to whom the Act was intended to extend.

In this case, the respondents, and accordingly, the "public" enjoying the dubious benefit of the Act's protection, were Hong Kong and West German companies. It is difficult to perceive of these entities as pertaining to the same type of public as the subjects in the cases referred to by the judge in coming to his decision: persons who engage debt collectors and accountants to chase debts or sell land. In effect, the "protection" afforded the international parties in this case effectively denied them representation by counsel of their choice.

The judge stated towards the end of his judgment that his decision "does not mean that only advocates and solicitors of the Supreme Court may appear in arbitration. But it means that only those with [local] practising certificates may practise law in arbitration proceedings." This reflection provides little comfort. Whilst those with certificates may represent a potentially broader class than that of "advocates and solicitors of the Supreme Court," any party still needing or wishing to arbitrate in Singapore, and desirous of enlisting lawyers from outside the jurisdiction, cannot know if and when his counsel may be entitled to appear. The fact that the Law Society of Singapore itself supported Turner's application enhances one's pessimism.

Whilst the Turner decision evidently cannot augur well for Singapore's development as a centre for international arbitration, there is, further, the depressing possibility that it might have ramifications in other jurisdictions where the question has not been judicially considered. Will we now see a rash of similar applications for injunctions brought by other parties wishing to take advantage of this new found restriction?

### Notes and Questions

1. The decision in the *Turner* case was roundly criticised. A typical comment was that of Andreas Lowenfeld, whose view is that it is important "not only for the international arbitration community, but for the much larger international business community, for international arbitration not to become clogged by the vested interests of a local bar. Only if it fends off or limits the spread of localism will arbitration live up to its promise of assistance and support to the continuing growth of international trade, finance, and investment." Andreas F. Lowenfeld *Singapore and the Local Bar: Aberration or Ill Omen?*, J. INT'L ARB., Sept. 1988, at 71.

2. Following much criticism in the wake of this decision, the Singapore Legal Profession Act was amended to enable foreign lawyers to appear in arbitration proceedings in two situations — where the law applicable to the dispute is not Singapore law or, where Singapore law does apply, when a Singapore lawyer appears jointly with the foreign attorney. This provision came into effect in March 1992. The amendment falls short, however, of allowing unrestricted rights of audience.

C.     David Rivkin, *Keeping Lawyers out of International Arbitrations*, INT'L FIN. L. REV., Feb. 1990, at 11, 11-14.

National laws and institutional rules concerning who may act as a representative at an arbitration may be grouped into three categories:

countries and institutions with no limitations; those requiring that the representative have legal training; and those requiring that the designated representative be a member of the local bar.

**No requirements.** The majority of countries do not require that parties be represented by lawyers in international arbitrations. For example, corporations may frequently be represented by members of their management or non-lawyers may represent parties in arbitrations in specialised areas, such as construction or engineering disputes. Moreover, if a party does choose to be represented by a lawyer in these countries, it is not typically limited to a lawyer admitted to practise in the forum state. To the contrary, it is common for foreign lawyers to represent parties in arbitration centres such as the UK, France, Sweden, Switzerland and the US. And if foreign counsel is retained, it is usually from the country whose law governs the dispute, not from the forum state (although sometimes the two may be the same).

Although this flexible standard is the most common, attention must be paid to individual particularities of national practice. For example, even where a party's choice of representative is virtually unrestricted, national laws may require that the representative present a power of attorney to the arbitral panel. In some countries, including Argentina, Austria, the German Democratic Republic, and Greece, a power of attorney is required for all representatives, regardless of the profession or nationality of the representative. In others, including The Netherlands, a power of attorney is required only when the representative is not a lawyer. Finally, in some countries, including Italy and Denmark, as well as in arbitrations held under the auspices of the London Court of International Arbitration, a power of attorney may be required by the arbitrators but is not mandatory. Such proof of authorisation to act on behalf of a party may be demanded, for example, when the arbitrators have doubts about whether a party has authorised its representative.

Rules adopted by various arbitration institutions may also affect the parties' freedom of choice of counsel. For example, the rules of the Korean Commercial Arbitration Board provide that the arbitration tribunal may determine that a person chosen by one of the parties as a representative is not a "proper" one, although this possibility seems to be limited to cases where the designated representative is not a lawyer. The Japan Commercial Arbitration Association's rules provide that "a party may be represented by a lawyer or such other person as shall be recognised to be justified in taking proceedings under these Rules."

The rules of some UK trade associations do not permit representatives of the parties — lawyers, in particular — to appear before an arbitration tribunal at all. Counsel may only advise their clients outside the tribunal.

**Legal training.** While it is common for non-lawyers to represent parties at an arbitration proceeding, the laws of several countries, including Indonesia, Israel, Saudi Arabia and Spain, require that persons representing parties be lawyers, although not necessarily nationals of the country. One expressed justification for this requirement is that only persons subject to ethical rules should be admitted to represent parties in court proceedings. Thus, in Belgium, business representatives (*agents d'affaires*) are not allowed to represent parties before arbitration tribunals. Foreign legal counsellors have occasionally fallen under the rubric of *agents d'affaires* and have been prohibited on this ground from appearing before Belgian arbitration tribunals.

**Admission to the local bar.** Most restrictive are laws that require not only that a representative of a party at an arbitration be a lawyer, but also that the representative be a member of the local bar. Fortunately, Japan and Singapore seem to be the only countries which at present require that the representatives of parties to an arbitration proceeding be lawyers admitted to practise in and residing in the forum state. In Yugoslavia, a party may retain foreign counsel only if the party is itself located outside the country.

In Japan, this practice appears to be based on Article 72 of the law governing the legal profession, according to which persons who are not *bengoshi* may not handle legal affairs relating to litigation cases, non-litigious cases and legal cases against administrative agencies including advice, representation, arbitration and settlement. It has become standard practice in recent years for a Japanese *bengoshi* to use Article 72 to object to a foreign lawyer's representation of a party before an arbitral tribunal. In such cases, rather than risk an eventual holding overturning the outcome on the grounds that the party was improperly represented, parties have agreed to replace the foreign lawyer with a Japanese lawyer. This practice represents a shift from past practice in which foreign lawyers have been involved in commercial arbitrations held in Japan, but it has not yet been challenged in Japanese courts.

\* \* \*

D.   Charles Ragan, *Arbitration in Japan: Caveat Foreign Drafter and Other Lessons*, 7 ARB. INT'L 93, 104-07 (1991).

(b) *Language*

Although the contract (and all its precedents) were written in English, the agreement did not specify the language of the arbitration. In many arbitral régimes, if there is no agreement of the parties, the tribunal determines the language or languages to be used in the proceedings.[269]

The JCAA [Japan Commercial Arbitration Association] Rules do not specifically cover the question. They do state that the award shall be written in Japanese, but, where there has been a request by one of the parties, the award shall be written in both Japanese and English and both versions shall be authentic (Rule 37). The Rules further provide for interpretation or translation if the Tribunal has so ordered, or there has been a request by one of the parties (Rule 29). Finally, the Rules provide that, absent an order from the Tribunal, the cost of various expenses (including interpretation and translation) shall be borne by the requesting party. These rules in the aggregate have the appearance of reasonableness.

In our case, there was *no* interpretation through more than two years of proceedings. Although the American party was permitted to submit initial responsive pleadings and briefs in English, all oral proceedings (and there were about 10 sessions in that time period) were conducted in Japanese. House counsel for the American party complained that he was never quite certain in these sessions that he had a complete grasp of what was unfolding before him.

---

[269] *See, e.g.*, UNCITRAL Rule 22; LCIA Rule 8; Article 11(8) of the ICC-CMI Rules for International Maritime Arbitration.

During the evidence-taking, because of obvious irregularities in some interpretation services, we experimented with tape recordings, simultaneous translation, consecutive translation, and finally consecutive translation with stenographers for both languages.[270] No ideal solution was found. Similar problems also occurred in the exchange briefs: whenever one opponent submitted a brief, we had it translated into English; before responding, we then sought to determine the adequacy and sufficiency of the translation, and whether there were any special clues or messages 'between the lines' of the opponent's brief. The perils and costs of this process are obvious.[271]

From this experience it seems fair to conclude that: (i) The language determination is parochial. (ii) The parties are not treated equally. (iii) The foreign party does not have an equal chance to present its case without being subject to substantial additional costs.

## (c) *Trial counsel*

The ability to be represented in an international arbitration by the counsel of a party's choice is another feature of international arbitration that is often trumpeted as a major advantage over litigation of international disputes in national courts. In international arbitration, clients frequently and understandably prefer to employ counsel from their home base, as it may be more convenient and economical to develop the facts of the case. (In our case, this decision seemed even more logical since California law governed.)

The JCAA Rules appear to recognize and incorporate this common sense principle. They state:

---

[270] The quality of interpreter services provided by the JCAA was uneven. Often, there would be long and apparently significant exchanges in Japanese which either went untranslated or had such abbreviated translations as to leave one with concern about the adequacy of the translation. It does not seem reasonable to expect local Japanese counsel to serve as local counsel and interpreter during these proceedings. Lawyers are paid to be counsel.

[271] At the conclusion of the arbitration, the Rules of the JCAA were interpreted to require that the American party bear the cost of English interpretation and translation, and to share the cost of Japanese stenographers, in the arbitration. Total costs to the American client for translation and interpretation, in and outside the arbitration chamber, approached $100,000.

'A party may be represented by a lawyer or such other person as shall be recognized to be justified in taking procedure under these Rules' (Rule 6).

The Rules also provide for the submission of powers of attorney (Rule 7). This in itself is not surprising, because it is typical for lawyers who appear in Japan to submit powers of attorney, and a similar practice often obtains in Europe.[272] Mr. Michida's comments were in response to a questionnaire propounded to representatives of approximately 10-12 different countries about how a hypothetical case would be handled in their country. Mr. Michida gave no answer to the question whether foreign parties would usually include a lawyer from the place of arbitration on their legal team (Question 7)).

I made my first trip to Japan in October 1987, shortly before the evidence-taking phase was to begin. The objective was to develop before the evidence-taking or 'trial' began, a good working relationship between Japanese local counsel and my firm, which the client had always regarded as lead strategists and trial counsel. In advance of that trip, one of my partners inquired of the JCAA about the kind of power of attorney we should present. I have preserved the response, which was short but (I was soon to learn) most meaningful: 'It is very difficult to answer through the phone.'[273] When I arrived in Tokyo, however, I was informed that I could not attend the scheduled arbitration session.

The reason for this was that, until very recently, the JCAA and the Japanese bar have interpreted the Lawyers' Law to prohibit *all* foreign lawyers from acting as arbitration counsel of record. This view in fact derived from two separate laws. Article 801 of the Japanese Code of Civil Procedure provides that an arbitration award may be

---

[272] S. Michida, The Amicable Texture of Japanese Arbitration, Comments Delivered at the VIIIth International Congress of the International Council for Commercial Arbitration, May 6, 1986 (hereinafter cited as "S. Michida").

[273] At the time, I considered myself moderately knowledgeable about international arbitration but basically ignorant about Japanese business or culture. Based on the available literature, I (wrongly) assumed the former sufficient. I was later enlightened as to the linguistic significance of the JCAA response. I discovered that "If someone allows that something is difficult, it is a good bet that he is really saying 'forget it.'" NY Times, "Some Japanese (One) Urge Plain Speaking" (March 27, 1989) at 3.

cancelled where the 'parties were not represented in accordance with the law.' Article 72 of the Lawyers' Law prohibits, as unauthorized practice of law, the participation for remuneration of an unlicensed lawyer in an arbitration proceeding. The coupling of these two makes it impracticable for a foreign lawyer, who is not licensed to practice in Japan, to take on the exclusive representation of any party in a Japanese arbitration.[274] The reason is simple: a knowledgeable Japanese party may hold the traditional view as a trump card, with which it would seek to upset an unfavourable award.

In our case, we did not appear as counsel of record. We attended approximately 20 arbitral sessions as a 'guest'; we participated in the preparation of all fact and law submissions; with the consent of the arbitrator and opposing party, we made numerous comments (some might say 'arguments'), but these comments were in English and, for the reasons mentioned above, may not have been effective even after translation. In any event, we were not permitted to examine any witness directly.

The law was also unclear as to whether the many foreign lawyers recently granted limited licences to serve as foreign legal consultants in Japan may represent a party at an arbitration. Recently, the Japanese Federation of Bar Associations (the 'Nichibenren') voted to allow foreign legal consultants (or 'gaikokuho jimu bengoshi') to represent parties in Japanese arbitrations where the lawyer is qualified to practice the governing or applicable substantive law of the arbitration.[275]

To date, however, no Japanese court has endorsed such representation (and the Nichibenren's interpretation makes clear that the

---

[274] Numerous arguments may be made in different circumstances for not applying the traditional view. Moreover, the prohibition on foreign representation apparently does not extend to a lawyer working without compensation, or who happens to be an employee of one of the parties to the arbitration. Japan is one of only a handful of countries that require the participation of lawyers who are licensed in the forum state; the vast majority of countries do not have such requirement. . . .

[275] See summary translation published by the Committee on Gaikokuho-Jimu-Bengoshi of the Nichibenren in *A Guide to Rules for Foreign Special Members* (1990). The traditional view had also been used to challenge foreign counsel serving even as *arbitrators*. Under the recent proposal, foreign legal consultants would be permitted to serve as arbitrators.

foreign legal consultant acting as arbitration counsel is *not* permitted to file a motion in a Japanese court or appear before a public agency).[276] No foreign lawyer has attempted to represent a party in an arbitration without qualified local counsel, and it is unlikely that one will attempt to do this when the possibility of the cancellation of an award remains.[277] Moreover, the Nichibenren's recent promulgation concludes with the observation 'it is desirable that [a gaikokuho jimu bengoshi representing a party in a Japanese arbitration] will [nonetheless] have a [Japanese] bengoshi participate in the arbitration proceedings held in Japan.'[278]

Thus, even with the recent bar association vote, the implications of the restrictive Japanese rules on the practice of law are profound: The foreigner can either flout the law and risk having a favourable award upset, or maintain an appearance of parochial propriety and incur substantially greater legal costs than his Japanese opponent.

\* \* \*

Whenever the right of audience is challenged, the question may be raised as to whether the arbitral tribunal should finally decide upon the challenge (because the parties generally wished their dispute to be resolved in arbitration) or whether that authority must repose in the ordinary courts (as the guarantors of fundamental principles of the judicial process). This issue was confronted in the following case.

> E. W. LAURENCE CRAIG, ET AL., INTERNATIONAL CHAMBER OF COMMERCE ARBITRATION 279 (2d ed. 1990)

In England and Wales, where, with a legal profession divided between solicitors and barristers, the local bar enjoys a near-monopoly on appearance rights before domestic courts, the issue has presented itself in a different manner. There are no restrictions on appearance

---

[276] *Ibid.*

[277] *See* R. Greig, *International Commercial Arbitration in Japan: A User's Report* . . . .

[278] *See* summary translation in *A Guide to Rules for Foreign Special Members* (1990).

before arbitral tribunals in England and Wales by foreign counsel, local solicitors, or lay persons. However, foreign parties wishing to retain local barristers have had problems. Until 1985 in all cases, domestic or otherwise, there was no direct right of access to local barristers; they could be retained only through a local solicitor who would then retain the barrister. This was considered expensive and unwieldy by parties who, having already engaged their own (foreign) advisors, would then have to incur fees in respect not only of the barrister, but further of a local solicitor as his conduit. Recent changes in the Overseas Practice Rules of the English bar make it clear that local barristers may now be retained through foreign qualified lawyers in the same manner as through a local solicitor. Foreign parties now have the choice whether to engage local solicitors or not . . . Note that the changes do not allow parties to engage barristers directly but rather give foreign lawyers the right of direct access to them.

There are only a limited number of cases where the courts have ruled on the question of rights of audience. The French Cour de Cassation has expressly ruled that the monopoly of the French bar does not extend to arbitrations sitting in France (Judgment of June 19, 1979, Cass. Civ. 1re, 1979 Rev. Arb. 487 (Fr.).)

[The High Court of Barbados was asked to rule in *Lawler, Matusky & Skeller v. Attorney General of Barbados*, No. 320 of 1981 (August 22, 1983) on whether a member of the New York bar could act in an international arbitration held in Barbados and governed by the law of Barbados. The Court found that Barbados' Legal Profession Act did not prevent a party from being represented by a U.S. lawyer, although it also held that the arbitrator could require that the foreign lawyer be assisted by a Barbados lawyer at all hearings in order to obtain advice on Barbadian law.]

\*   \*   \*

F.   *Bidermann Indus. Licensing, Inc. v. Avmar N.V.*, N.Y.L.J., Oct. 26, 1990, at 23 (N.Y.Sup.Ct.).

Petitioner Bidermann Industries, Inc. ("BILI"), makes this application for an order pursuant to CPLR §7503 staying the arbitration demanded by respondents, Avmar N.V. ("Avmar"), Leit Motif, Inc. ("LMI") and Karl Lagerfeld ("Lagerfeld"), as to the issue of whether BILI's counsel, Coudert Brothers, should be disqualified from representing them in the arbitration proceeding pending between BILI and the respondents.

The issue represented is one of apparent first impression: May the issue of attorney disqualification be determined on an arbitration, or is it a matter exclusively within the province and jurisdiction of the courts?

[An order denying as moot a motion to disqualify Coudert Brothers as attorneys in an arbitration was confirmed on appeal.]

. . .

After the appeal was decided, the respondents moved ahead on the arbitration with BILI. A panel of three arbitrators was appointed to conduct the arbitration proceeding regarding a dispute involving trademark licensing and design services agreements. Respondents, by letter dated April 26, 1990, notified the arbitrators that they would make an application to the panel to disqualify Coudert Brothers as BILI's counsel at the proceedings.

## Discussion

BILI now moves to stay arbitration of that disqualification question, contending that the issue is not arbitrable. Respondents oppose the application a) on the procedural ground that it should have been brought on a separate special proceeding with the requisite notice of petition and petition rather by than motion: b) based on my decision and order, contending that I directed that the issue be brought before the arbitrators; and c) arguing that the issue is properly before the arbitrators. The second argument, has already been discussed and decided and the remaining arguments of the parties may now be considered.

[The Court went on to explain that the special proceeding was still pending as long as the arbitration continued and therefore a separate action need not be commenced.]

. . .

## Arbitrability of Attorney Disqualification

BILI next argues that the issue of disqualification is not arbitrable because it is not within the scope of the arbitration agreement executed between BILI and the respondents. Further, BILI contends it is against public policy to arbitrate the ethical obligations of attorney's, since that is within the exclusive jurisdiction of the courts. Respondents argue that the arbitration provision encompasses any dispute arising out of the agreements or their alleged breach. They also contend that the issue of disqualification is a procedural issue in the arbitration and as such is clearly within the province of the arbitrators to decide.

Pursuant to the license agreements executed by the parties, BILI and respondents agreed that:

> Any controversy, dispute or claim arising out of or relating to this Agreement, or the breach thereof, shall be settled by arbitration which shall be held in the City of New York in accordance with the rules of the American Arbitration Association and judgment upon the award rendered by the arbitrator(s) may be entered in any court having jurisdiction thereof. (Notice of Motion, Exs. B and C, para 21).

The license agreements between BILI and respondents deal with the contractual obligations and aspects of trademark use and design services (Notice of Motion, Exs. B and 6) as well as designating arbitration as the means of resolution of disputes between the parties.

Generally, New York favors arbitration. "[T]hose who agree to arbitrate should be made to keep their solemn written promises." Matter of Grayson-Robinson Stores, Inc., (Iris Constr. Corp.), 8 N.Y.2d 133, 138 (1960). It is the strong policy of this state to encourage use of arbitration as an easy expeditious method of settling disputes which, ideally, dispenses with the need for protracted litigation. . . .

It is a threshold question for the courts, however, upon application pursuant to CPLR §7503(C) "to determine whether the parties agreed to submit their disputes to arbitration, [and] if so, whether the particular disputes come within the scope of their agreement." County of Rockland v. Primiano Construction Co., Inc.,

51 N.Y.2d 1 (1980). Generally, an arbitration agreement will be enforced by the courts provided it does not transgress a provision or statute or violate public policy. . . . "Public policy, whether derived from, and whether explicit or implicit in statute or decisional law, or in neither, may also restrict the freedom to arbitrate." Susquehanna Valley Central School Dist. v. Susquehanna Valley Teacher's Ass'n, 37 N.Y.2d 614, 616-617 (1975). It is for the courts to decide whether the enforcement of an agreement to arbitrate would contravene an important public policy. . . .

Where an important interest of the public at large is likely to be affected by the resolution of a dispute, decision by arbitration is inappropriate, notwithstanding agreement by parties to the dispute. For example, even if child custody and visitation agreements provide for arbitration as the forum for dispute resolution, the courts have jurisdiction to consider the issues de novo. . . . Violations of state antitrust laws are not arbitrable, . . . nor are violations of criminal law . . . and matters involving civil penalties. . . .

Similarly, the regulation of attorneys, and determinations as to whether clients should be deprived of counsel of their choice as a result of professional responsibilities and ethical obligations, implicate fundamental public interests and policies which should be reserved for the courts and should not be subject to arbitration. As the New York Court of Appeals has recognized in the context of disputes regarding attorney disqualification:

. . . although an individual possesses no absolute right to representation by an attorney of his choice, any restriction imposed on that right will be carefully scrutinized. An individual's right to select an attorney who he believes is most capable of proving competent representation implicates both the First Amendment Guarantees of freedom of association (N.Y Const., art. I, §9) and the Sixth Amendment right to counsel (N.Y. Const., art I, §6) and will not yield unless confronted with an overriding competing public interest.

Matter of Abrams, 62 N.Y.2d 183, 196 (1984).

Among the competing public interests which must be balanced against a client's right to counsel of her choice is "the courts' duty to protect the integrity of the judicial system and preserve the ethical standards of the legal profession." Matter of Abrams, supra, at p. 197.

The general policy favoring arbitration . . . must be balanced against the important policy favoring judicial determination of attorney disqualification. While jurisdiction to discipline an attorney for misconduct is vested exclusively in the Appellate Division, disqualification in a particular matter should be sought in the court in which the motion is pending, or, if no action is pending, at a Special Term of the Supreme Court. . . . The court has the inherent power to disqualify an attorney for a party upon a finding that it is improper for him to represent the litigant or to participate in a proceeding. . . .

Although no New York case specifically precludes arbitration of attorney disqualification issues, a number of cases imply that attorney conduct is the exclusive province of the courts. A New York City Council regulation involving the sale of taxicabs, which limited the usual and normal privileges of attorneys, was held invalid because regulation of conduct of attorneys was found to be vested in the courts. . . . In Erdheim v. Selkowe, 51 AD2d 705 (1st Dept. 1976), the Appellate Division, First Department held that arbitrators have no jurisdiction to discipline attorneys, as this is within the exclusive jurisdiction of the Appellate Division.

In Erlanger, the Supreme Court denied a motion which sought to disqualify counsel from representing the other party at arbitration on the grounds of conflict of interest on the merits. The Court of Appeals did not address the appropriateness of raising the issue in court rather than in the arbitration. Although not dispositive, this decision suggests that the issue may be litigated in court rather than in the arbitration. Erlanger v. Erlanger, 20 N.Y.2d 778-9 (1967).

Based on these cases which indicate that attorney regulation questions should be addressed in the courts, I hold that the issue of attorney disqualification is not appropriate for arbitration.

## Conclusion

Accordingly, the motion is granted only to the extent of staying arbitration of the issue of whether Coudert Brothers should be disqualified. This decision does not determine the issue of disqualification on the merits. Defendants are granted leave to move this court for a ruling on the disqualification issue.

<u>Notes and Questions</u>

1. Do the judicial interpretations of the legal profession in Barbados and Singapore do damage to the institution of international arbitration? Do the rules matter as long as they are well-established and parties can factor the requirement of local counsel into their decisions about choosing a venue?

2. Are there any persuasive justifications for national restrictions on choice of attorney in international arbitrations in the national jurisdiction?

## VII.   SUMMARY AND CONCLUSIONS

Arbitrators and counsel participating in international arbitrations have seen that it is possible to marry the best elements of disparate traditions relating to the taking of evidence, and to do so in an efficient way that also conforms to legitimate expectations.

The ICSID Arbitration Rules reflect a conscious attempt to combine features of the major legal systems with respect to procedural rules. The ICC Rules and the 1985 LCIA Rules are not as detailed, but clearly allow for an intelligent integration of various modes for trying cases that should leave all parties with the feeling they have been given full opportunity to present their case in a manner with which they are comfortable.

The 1983 IBA Rules of Evidence show that the effort of harmonisation need not require extensive and obscure definitions, but can be put as a short series of simple and concrete propositions covering the major issues that have long caused controversy with respect to the taking of evidence in international arbitration.

Thus, the right of the tribunal to appoint an independent expert need not be perceived as a denial of the philosophy and traditions of the adversarial process as long as an opportunity is given to question and challenge the findings of the expert, including the use of party-produced expert testimony.

Likewise, full submissions prior to hearings, and a corresponding de-emphasis of tedious formalities regarding the "introduction" of evidence at oral hearings, have been understood as indispensable in most international arbitral proceedings.

On the other hand, civil lawyers have been able to accept the concept that it is important for witnesses to appear, and that the parties should be given an opportunity to question them. Whether this questioning is called "cross-examination" is merely cosmetic. Lawyers unfamiliar with the techniques of cross-examination are understandably reluctant to accept a situation where their adversary may destroy their witnesses but they are unable to retaliate; in addition, they often justifiably feel that cross-examination in international arbitration with witnesses expressing themselves in a second language may degenerate into a humiliating and unseemly exercise. Accordingly, a middle ground can be found in the concept that "questioning" by parties takes place under the control of the arbitrators, who would curtail abuse.

Similarly, discovery may be tailored to the realities and requirements of international arbitration. It is perfectly possible to accept the notion that a party has the right to identify documents in the probable possession of an adversary and request the arbitral tribunal to order the production of these documents. The objection that arbitrators have no powers of coercion is not persuasive; the threat of drawing adverse inferences from the fact of non-production is not an idle one. On the other hand, proponents of the adversarial process are unlikely to get their way if they want to go on fishing expeditions on the basis of vague and over-comprehensive definitions of the documents they seek. They are also likely to have to accept the fact that they will not be able to obtain orders for the production of purely internal documents from the adversary; practitioners in most countries feel this is overreaching. Moreover, it is hard for the arbitrator to know whether the party responding to such an order is really complying, given the totally hypothetical existence of many internal documents. It would hardly be appropriate to penalize parties who keep good records and whose personnel are unwilling to engage in selective shredding. Finally, deposition of adverse witnesses is unlikely to become commonplace in international arbitration.

The unavailability of discovery of internal documents or the deposition of adverse witnesses is not to be deplored. Whatever the merits of these discovery techniques in domestic litigation, they are impractical in international arbitration, where in most cases one party will be in a superior position in terms of its ability to resist discovery. If the language of the arbitration is French, what would be the practical value of being allowed to depose witnesses who refuse to speak anything but Greek (as practitioners who have tried to cross-examine a witness through an interpreter well know) or to be told one may have access to documents located in Piraeus and written in Greek, and, most importantly, the revelation of which ultimately depends on the good faith of the producing party? More likely than not, one will get exactly what one did not want to see, and be carefully steered away from smoking guns.

Perfect homogeneity in the international arbitral process is not going to be brought about in the near future. A case conducted by an English arbitrator in London will continue to have an English flavor, and the advocate will indeed notice a difference if the next month he is involved in a case heard under the direction of a chairman in Zürich. But the various approaches to the taking of evidence may in fact be successfully combined. This should not be surprising since the purpose — namely the objective establishment of the circumstances of the case — is always the same. Furthermore, bringing to bear some of the rigors of adversarial process may often allow a greater depth of critical inquiry than the continental system, while the freedom of the arbitrator to take inquisitorial initiatives may happily steer the case out of the doldrums of evidentiary overkill occasionally permitted under the common-law system, and so unsuitable to international arbitration given the variety of relevant legitimate expectations, as well as the practical requirements of cost-efficiency.

# CHAPTER 8

# COMPORTMENT OF ARBITRATORS

## I.   INTRODUCTION

Arbitrators may have specific duties imposed on them by the parties. In an ad hoc arbitration, these may be included in the arbitrators' terms of appointment. In institutional arbitration, whatever specific requirements the parties impose will be extended by the rules of the particular institution. These duties are, in turn, further supplemented by duties imposed by the law or laws governing the arbitration. From time to time, many of these norms come under stress when arbitrators are pressed to act pragmatically and economically to facilitate the arbitration.

Thus, the arbitrator may be under a duty to act with due care and skill (although he may be immune from liability if that duty is breached) and a duty to act with due diligence and to take the arbitration forward with reasonable expedition. If this latter duty is breached, some jurisdictions allow an action against the tribunal. Further, an arbitrator is under a duty to act "judicially." This means that the arbitrator must treat each party equally and allow each party the same opportunity to present its case.

If an arbitrator fails to fulfill these duties, what is the injured party's remedy? To challenge the offending arbitrator and secure his removal from the panel? Or should the injured party be able to go further than this and recover from the arbitrator any loss that he has incurred as a result of that arbitrator's faults? If so, where should the line be drawn? How serious must be the arbitrator's breach to render him liable to the injured party? This chapter will examine the standards of comportment of arbitrators, the procedures and range of remedies available in respect of remedies for their violation, and the tactical considerations parties must bring to bear in deciding whether and which to pursue.

In addition to these specific duties arising from contracts, rules, and governing laws, arbitrators also have what have been described as "moral and ethical" obligations. The extent of these obligations has been much debated by those involved in international commercial arbitration. As discussed in Chapter 5, some steps have been taken towards setting formal standards. Thus, in 1977, the American Arbitration Association and the American Bar Association produced a Code of Ethics for Arbitrators in Commercial Disputes.[279] (This Code only applies to domestic arbitration in the United States.) More significantly for present purposes, the International Bar Association produced in 1987 a set of guidelines entitled *Ethics for International Arbitrators*.[280]

The IBA Ethics for International Arbitrators was produced in response to the growth of international commercial arbitration and the increasing sophistication of parties and their legal counsel. These changes increased the pressures on arbitrators, making a more formal framework of guidelines indispensable. The IBA guidelines address issues of ethics generally. They deal, for example, with questions such as when an arbitrator should decline an appointment (*e.g.*, if he is not suitably qualified or does not have the time to commit to the case), and an arbitrator's duty of confidentiality. They are, however, primarily concerned with the question of impartiality of arbitrators.

## II.    IMPARTIALITY OF CONDUCT

The terms "impartial," "independent" and "neutral" are those most used to describe the requisite attributes of an arbitrator. The sometimes variable meaning of these terms has already been discussed in Chapter 5, in connection with party-appointed arbitrators. On occasion, it will be recalled, party-appointed arbitrators may be "non-neutral." They must, of course, remain independent, in the sense of having no financial relations with the parties, but they may be "predisposed" (this is the word used in the ABA/AAA Code of Ethics) towards the party which appointed them. While the suggestion that party-appointed arbitrators are totally impartial has been labelled a "fiction" by Robert Coulson,[281] the IBA Ethics for International Arbitrators draws no distinction between arbitrators who are

---

[279] ABA CODE OF ETHICS FOR ARBITRATION IN COMMERCIAL DISPUTES (1977), *reprinted in* 10 Yearbook of Commercial Arbitration 131 (1985).

[280] Reprinted in Supplement at p. 763.

[281] Robert Coulson, *An American Critique of the IBA's Ethics for International Arbitration*, J. INT'L ARB., June 1987, at 103, 105.

party-appointed and those who are not. The basic principle set out at Section 2.1 of the IBA Ethics for International Arbitrators is that "[a] prospective arbitrator shall accept an appointment only if he is fully satisfied that he is able to discharge his duties without bias." The criteria for assessing "bias" are impartiality and independence. Partiality, in this conception, arises where an arbitrator favors one of the parties, or where he is prejudiced in relation to the subject matter of the dispute.

It is, of course, imperative in arbitral proceedings that each party receives equal treatment before the tribunal. This principle is enshrined in Article 18 of the UNCITRAL Model Law:

> The parties shall be treated with equality and each party
> shall be given a full opportunity of presenting his case.

What, though, does equality of treatment mean? It has been suggested that, in ICC proceedings, arbitrators will respect general principles as set out in the following passage.

> A.     W. LAURENCE CRAIG, ET AL., INTERNATIONAL
>        CHAMBER OF COMMERCE ARBITRATION 240 (2d ed.
>        1990).

- An arbitrator communicating with a party in writing should address a copy of the communication to the other party, the other arbitrators, and the Secretariat of the Court.

- An arbitrator should not discuss the merits of the case or receive evidence or legal argument from a party in the absence of the other party and his fellow arbitrators, if any.

- An arbitrator may communicate with a party regarding the fixing of procedural dates or other practical and material aspects of the arbitration, but the contents of such communication should immediately be made known to the other party and arbitrators.

- An arbitral tribunal should generally allow the parties to modify or adopt procedural rules, including ones that may be reached in the course of proceedings. For instance, if both parties agree, each party may communicate ex parte with the arbitrator it   has named, particularly where the parties agree that such communication may favor a settlement.

- An arbitrator should not discuss the merits of the arbitration with another arbitrator in  the absence of the third arbitrator, unless the latter has agreed and is informed of the   subject of the discussion.

### Notes and Questions

1. What does it mean to have a "predisposition" towards one party? Does it inevitably mean that the arbitrator is partial?

2. From the standpoint of the preferred dynamics of international commercial arbitration, is the ABA/AAA approach, tolerating a "predisposition" better than the IBA approach calling for strict impartiality? What are the different consequences of the two standards for international commercial arbitration?

Others have noted that the necessity for arbitrators to administer equal treatment to the parties applies to impartiality of expression and personal contacts with the parties, as well as the making of procedural decisions.

B.    MICHAEL J. MUSTILL & STEWART C. BOYD, THE LAW AND PRACTICE OF COMMERCIAL ARBITRATION IN ENGLAND 253-54 (2d ed. 1989).

In a long arbitration, the tribunal may have to make numerous rulings on issues of procedure. In the nature of things, it will occasionally happen that the majority of the decisions will be in favour of one particular party. This may lead the opponent to feel such a sense of grievance as to suspect that the arbitrator is not approaching the matter impartially. This is of course illogical, since the arbitrator may be right in his decisions, or (even if wrong) may still be acting impartially. This is obvious, and we mention it only because arbitrators have sometimes seemed to become nervous in situations like this, and to run the risk of what is a real injustice, namely to redress an apparent imbalance by deciding points in favour of the aggrieved party contrary to the true merits of the issue. This temptation must be avoided at all costs, although the arbitrator may think it wise to take particular care, if he foresees such a situation developing, to demonstrate that he is approaching each procedural issue in a strictly judicial manner. (We do not, of course, suggest that any responsible arbitrator would consciously decide to give a procedural consolation prize to a party who seemed to be doing rather poorly on interlocutory rulings. Unlike a trial in court, however, arbitration is a consensual procedure, as regards the choice of tribunal and of the method of resolving the dispute. There is sometimes an unrecognised pressure on arbitrators to ensure that parties who have made this choice do not go away dissatisfied. There is an element of humorous exaggeration in the adage that the decision most likely to be right is the one which leaves both parties dissatisfied; but neither is the contrary proposition true. The arbitrator's function is to decide the issue on its merits as he sees them. If, in doing so, he happens to please both sides, this is gratifying, but of only secondary importance.)

There is one particular instance of conduct during the reference which calls for particular mention. It occasionally happens that the reference becomes the subject of proceedings in the High Court: for example, to remove or reconstitute the tribunal; to restrain by injunction the further conduct of the reference; or to set aside or remit the award. It is often the right and on occasion the duty of the arbitrator to provide evidence for the Court as [to] the circumstances which have given rise to the procedural dispute. This does not in itself disqualify him from the reference, even if the evidence strongly favours one of the parties, for the duty of impartiality cannot require the arbitrator to do otherwise than give his own version of the facts, and (where relevant) state his opinions upon them. He should, however, do his best to ensure that he does not give the appearance of having become partisan, so as to lead the Court to feel that the matter will best be dealt with by another arbitrator: a course which will put the parties to unnecessary expense. (*G W Potts Ltd v. MacPherson, Train & Co* (1927) 27 LI L REP 445; *Fratelli Schiavo de Gennaro v. Richard J Hall Ltd* [1953] 2 LLOYD'S REP 169.)

\*     \*     \*

In determining whether there has been a violation of the rules of arbitral comportment, is it *actual* impartiality or the *appearance* of impartiality which is important?

C.     Alan Shilston, *The Evolution of Modern Commercial Arbitration*, J. INT'L ARB., June 1991, at 45, 55-6.

A cornerstone of the private commercial arbitration service is that not only should arbitrators be impartial, but also that they should manifestly be seen to be free of bias. The latter requirement is important since cultural perceptions of what constitutes independence of outlook vary widely. Impartiality in arbitrators should not be taken for granted.

The forces of change linked with political and competitive pressures are wreaking major changes in the structural pattern of public, commercial and professional life. In this climate the topic of conflicts of interest arises from regroupings in areas of service activity in which hitherto independence has not been questioned. The nature of the inter-relationships between subsidiaries and parent holding companies can generate doubts. Such potential conflicts arise in the changing patterns of commercial life.

A recent example from the world of civil engineering construction demonstrates the broad point at issue. The Board of Directors of Eurotunnel, the organisation established to build the Channel Tunnel, has joint chairmen. A successor to the current British co-chairman of the Board of Directors was under consideration. An already non-executive English member of the board was put forward as a possible replacement chairman. The board member under discussion, in his executive capacity, is the chairman of a well-known U.K. construction group, not involved in, but apparently keen to become a participating member of, the consortium of five U.K. contractors engaged in the Eurotunnel project. The co-chairman heading the French side of the consortium interviewed on British television on 8 February 1987, said he was against the idea of the non-executive director being appointed as co-chairman. The French side, he said, attached considerable importance to avoiding conflicts of interest. "I don't think you can be both a contractor, ambitious to have a piece of the action and be a chairman."

Some might say that the French co-chairman's view was merely the application of universal commercial common sense. Others from the U.K., on the other hand, might contend the British have a long tradition of displaying an ability to wear two hats, being capable of, and exercising, independent judgment according to which hat is worn on a particular occasion. Applied to commercial arbitration, the second view is inadmissible. Independence must be seen to be exercised.

Against the background of recent problems with maintaining the independence of advisers acting in City of London mercantile transactions, the Governor of the Bank of England stated, in a recent newspaper interview, that the pressure of competition was partly to blame for lapses in hitherto traditional standards. "The anxiety about retaining clients, let alone finding new ones, has put our old ethos under strain, pushing people across accepted boundaries."

It is crucial to the upholding of the arbitration process integrity that at no stage, however disquieted a disputant may be at the outcome of an arbitration, can serious doubts exist that the arbitrator has been other than procedurally even-handed, objective and seen to be free of bias. It is a requirement, in the face of pressures that formerly did not exist, that needs perpetual vigilance. The best way to reassure the parties is for the arbitrator to communicate freely with them, both orally and in writing, from the start of the arbitration until the concluding stage of the issue of the reasoned award, in which document the arbitrator's thought processes and the quality of his appraisal should be revealed. The arbitrator must be seen to be wholly independent and not associated with business organisations which might involve him or her, directly or indirectly, in what might appear to some to be potential conflicts of interest.

\*    \*    \*

D.    *Tracomin S.A. v. Gibbs Nathaniel (Canada) Ltd. & George Jacob Bridge*, 1 Lloyd's Rep. 586 (Q.B. 1985).

Mr. Justice STAUGHTON: On Jan. 14, 1983, Tracomin S.A. (Tracomin) agreed to buy peanuts from Gibbs, Nathaniel (Canada) Ltd. (the sellers) under two contracts providing for shipment in monthly instalments during the second half of 1983. The December portions were not shipped; the sellers apparently took the view that in the circumstances, whatever they were, their obligation to ship had been discharged. Tracomin disagreed. By telex dated Jan. 10, 1984, they claimed arbitration, and appointed Mr. Sean Armstrong as arbitrator. The sellers replied on Jan. 12, 1984, appointing Mr. George Jacob Bridge, the second respondent in these proceedings, as their arbitrator. Tracomin made efforts to persuade the sellers that they should replace

Mr. Bridge with some other arbitrator, but those efforts were unsuccessful. By this motion, issued on Apr. 12, 1984, they apply for an order that he be removed as arbitrator pursuant to s. 23 (1) of the Arbitration Act, 1950. That sub-section reads:

> Where an arbitrator or umpire has misconducted himself
> or the proceedings, the High Court may remove him.

The misconduct alleged is in accepting an appointment as arbitrator, or continuing to hold that appointment, when disqualified by bias. I should make it clear at once that Tracomin do not allege or seek to prove that Mr. Bridge is in fact biased against them. Their case is that an objective observer of the situation would conclude that there is a significant risk of bias on his part. I shall have to consider later the precise test to be applied when an allegation of bias takes that form, sometimes called "imputed bias." But it is not disputed that bias may be proved in that way, or that if it is proved, a case of misconduct is made out within s. 23 (1). This is yet another instance, and a particularly serious one, where the word "misconduct," as it is used in the law relating to arbitration, is misleading if it be thought to convey moral reproach. As Mr. Grace for Tracomin pointed out in argument, when an arbitrator is removed on the ground of imputed bias the Court does not make any finding which reflects on his integrity in any way. At most the Court concludes that he would have been wiser not to accept the appointment or continue in it, and that he has made an error of judgment.

. . . . .

But these departures from the model of justice which Courts of law seek to maintain make it the more important that arbitrators should in all other respects act with the utmost propriety. . . .

Many arbitrators would agree that the task of avoiding the slightest appearance of partiality is more difficult for them than for magistrates and Judges, because they are so much closer to the parties. Sometimes it is a more difficult task than that of deciding the case before them.

Where the reference is to two arbitrators, and to an umpire if they should disagree, it is clear that the arbitrators are functi officiis once disagreement has taken place. Thereafter they have no judicial function to perform, and are presumably not bound to act judicially. But equally it is clear that, until there has been disagreement, they do perform a judicial function and are bound to act judicially. That is so even if subsequent disagreement is probable or even certain. The contrary has not been argued in this case, or in any other so far as I am aware.

### The facts

With that introduction, I turn to the facts of this case. They are to be found in three separate actions where Tracomin and Mr. Bridge have previously been involved. The first was *Tracomin S.A. v. Sudan Oil Seeds Co. Ltd.*, (1982) T No. 1211. Tracomin, as buyers, were in dispute with Sudan Oil Seeds Co. Ltd. ("S.O.S.") about two contracts for the sale of peanuts. Arbitrators were appointed under the auspices of FOSFA [Federation of Oils, Seeds and Fats Associations Ltd.], S.O.S. appointing Mr. Bridge. They had not considered the claim or disagreed at the time when the following relevant events occurred. Tracomin started proceedings arising out of the dispute in Switzerland. The facts as to those proceedings are set out in my judgment, reported at [1983] 1 LLOYD'S REP. 560 and [1983] 1 W.L.R. 662, and I can summarize them. S.O.S. applied to the Swiss Court for a stay of the Swiss proceedings, on the ground that there was an agreement to arbitrate at FOSFA. That application failed. The decision of the Swiss Court was upheld on appeal. Tracomin then in the English action applied for a declaration and injunction, on the ground that the issue as to whether the arbitration clause formed part of the contract was res judicata and that S.O.S. were estopped from contending that it did. The action was tried before me on June 17, 22, 23 and 24 and Sept. 15, 1982. On Oct. 6, 1982, I gave judgment for S.O.S., holding that they were not estopped from asserting that the arbitration clause was part of the contract. An appeal from my decision was dismissed - [1983] 2 LLOYD'S REP. 384; [1983] 1 W.L.R. 1026.

Further proceedings arising out of the same dispute took place in *Tracomin v. Sudan Oil Seeds Co. Ltd.* (No. 2), (1982) T No. 2531. In that action Tracomin asked for leave to revoke the authority of the FOSFA arbitrators, or for an order that Mr. Bridge be removed as arbitrator. S.O.S. counterclaimed for an injunction restraining Tracomin from continuing or prosecuting or commencing any further proceedings in Switzerland.

So far as the claim was concerned, that action came before Mr. Justice Bingham on Dec. 9, 1982. It was supported by an affidavit of Mr. Michael Robinson, solicitor for Tracomin, sworn on Nov. 15, 1982. That affidavit referred to a number of aspects of the conduct of Mr. Bridge in connection with the action (1982) T No. 1211 and the Swiss proceedings, which were said to show that he had not behaved in an impartial manner. Those matters are of crucial importance to the present case, and I shall have to consider them in detail later. In answer there was an affidavit of Mr. Charles Deans, solicitor for S.O.S. Mr. Bridge was not present or represented before Mr. Justice Bingham initially; but he too had sworn an affidavit setting out the facts as he saw them.

.   .   .

[Mr. Justice Staughton then summarized the course of the proceedings before Mr. Justice Bingham. After establishing the facts, Mr. Justice Bingham called Mr. Bridge's solicitor to the Bar and suggested that he] take instructions from Mr. Bridge as to whether or not he was prepared to stand down voluntarily as Arbitrator in the case . . . . [Mr. Justice Bingham] said that he accepted . . . that there was no question of Mr. Bridge having misconducted himself and that it was a question of appearances, particularly bearing in mind the fact that Tracomin were foreign litigants. [Mr. Justice Bingham] went on to express the view that . . . it was a case in which it would be advantageous to both parties that there should be no question of doubt as to the impartiality of the Arbitrators . . . . [He accordingly adjourned] the application to remove Mr. Bridge to await news as to whether or not Mr. Bridge was prepared to stand down voluntarily.

[Mr. Bridge stated in due course that, having considered Mr. Justice Bingham's views, he was happy to resign voluntarily.]

.   .   .

There is only one fact in that affidavit which seems to me open to doubt — the statement attributed to Mr. Justice Bingham that he accepted that there was no question of Mr. Bridge having misconducted himself. If there was no misconduct in any form, there was no jurisdiction to remove him under s. 23(1) and no point in adjourning the application; it could have been dismissed at once. It seems to me more likely, if I may say so, that Mr. Justice Bingham said that there was no question of actual bias on the part of Mr. Bridge. That was indeed the case. At all events, Mr. Bridge resigned as arbitrator and the application was adjourned sine die.

. . .

Next there was the action *Tracomin S.A. v. Continentale Produkten Gesellschaft Ehrhardt-Renken (G.m.b.H) & Co. and George Bridge and others*, (1983) T No. 853. In those proceedings Mr. Bridge featured not as a first-tier arbitrator appointed by either of the parties, but as a member of two Boards of Appeal. Again Tracomin were buyers, under two contracts for the purchase of Sudanese groundnuts. They went to arbitration at FOSFA and lost at first instance; then they appealed. A Board of Appeal is composed of five members, of whom three are elected by the members of the Appeal Panel and two are appointed by the Federation. In the case of each appeal Mr. Bridge was one of the elected members.

Tracomin and their solicitors made efforts to secure that Mr. Bridge should not be a member of the Boards of Appeal. . . .

The action came before Mr. Justice Lloyd in open Court on July 26, 1983. Tracomin and Mr. Bridge were each represented by Counsel, as were the other members of the Boards of Appeal, the sellers were not represented. I have been provided with a transcript of the proceedings. The learned Judge evidently appreciated at an early stage that the problem would be resolved if Tracomin were to withdraw their allegations against Mr. Bridge, and Mr. Bridge were thereupon to resign as a member of the Boards of Appeal. The difficulty that arose was that Tracomin wanted an undertaking that Mr. Bridge would not sit in any future case on a Board of Appeal if Tracomin were a party to the dispute — or, I think, as an arbitrator. Mr. Bridge felt unable to give that undertaking.

Considerable discussion took place between Counsel and the learned Judge. In the course of that discussion Mr. Justice Lloyd said:

> . . . I think it exceedingly improbable that this situation will ever arise again . . . [p. 17E].

It seems to me highly unlikely that he would allow himself ever to be put again in the position in which this situation would occur. [p. 17H].

. . . if [Mr. Bridge] should ever sit again, which I think you can take it with 99.99 per cent. certainty that he never will . . . [p. 21C].

But there is not going to be a future occasion, if Mr. Bridge is a sensible man, which I find and believe him to be. [p. 28C].

The Judge's conviction that the situation would not occur again may have stemmed from his belief, expressed at three points of the transcript, that nobody wanted to be an arbitrator, and that Mr. Bridge would prefer to have been earning his living as a trader. That may not have been well-founded, since Mr. Bridge had retired from active trading in 1981.

At all events, agreement was eventually reached. By consent, no order was made on the summons save that Tracomin pay the costs of the other members of the Boards of Appeal. Tracomin wrote a letter to Mr. Bridge dated Aug. 15, 1983, which stated that they withdrew all allegations of bias, lack of impartiality and misconduct made against him. Mr. Bridge agreed to and did resign from membership of the two Boards of Appeal.

There were thus two occasions on which application was made to remove Mr. Bridge; on each occasion the Judge who heard the application, in my view rightly if I am permitted to say so, encouraged the parties to reach an amicable solution; and in each case Mr. Bridge did agree to resign. Then in January, 1984, less than six months later, a third commercial concern which had agreed to sell goods to Tracomin appointed Mr. Bridge as arbitrator, and he accepted the appointment. They were Gibbs Nathaniel (Canada) Ltd., the first respondents to this motion. But they have taken no part in the hearing. I have not felt it to be my duty to encourage the parties towards any compromise of the present dispute. It is too late for that. The matter must be decided according to law.

It seems to me that the key to this unhappy dispute lies in the conduct of Mr. Bridge which Tracomin complain about in connection with the Sudan Oil Seeds arbitration and the Swiss and English proceedings directly related to it. If that conduct would justify a finding of imputed bias, then I do not see that anything which happened in the proceedings before Mr. Justice Bingham or Mr. Justice Lloyd can have cured it; in those other proceedings Mr. Bridge offered to resign, now he does not; if anything, the situation has escalated for the worse. If, on the other hand, the conduct of Mr. Bridge in the Sudan Oil Seeds case would not have justified a finding of imputed bias, I do not see that the subsequent proceedings would justify one. On that hypothesis Tracomin have in the past twice made an unfounded allegation of bias against Mr. Bridge; on each occasion, after initial reluctance, he agreed to resign.

Thus far I have not set out the conduct complained of; I must now do so in some detail. It is comprised under three heads:

> (i) While the SOS arbitration was pending, Mr. Bridge wrote a letter dated May 6, 1982, to Maitre Wanner, the lawyer acting for S.O.S. in the Swiss proceedings. That letter read as follows:

>> Dear Maitre Wanner,

>> Re: Dispute between Sudan Oilseeds Co. & Tracomin S.A.

>> I have been requested by Sudan Oilseeds Co. to write to you in connection with a claim made by Tracomin against them and its position under the rules of arbitration of the Federation of Oilseeds & Fats Association Ltd.

>> Tracomin telexed to Sudan Oilseeds Co. on the 14th May 1981 as follows . . . .

> and then there is set out the text of the telex which claimed arbitration and appointed Mr. Beaton as Tracomin's arbitrator. The letter continues:

>> The above telex constituted a claim for arbitration by Tracomin against Sudan

Oilseeds Co. Whether the claim is a valid one is immaterial. The fact is that the claim was made and an arbitrator appointed by Tracomin which makes it a valid claim under the rules and my understanding in accordance with the rules and the law of England is that at that point an arbitration commences.

The party against whom a claim is made is obliged to appoint an arbitrator in return and this was done promptly by Sudan Oilseeds Co. by their telex of the 18th May 1981 when they telexed to Tracomin as follows:

The letter then sets out the telex of Sudan Oilseeds in which they appointed Mr. Bridge as arbitrator. The letter continues:

It is by no means unusual for the respondents to reject the claim of the buyers as has been done in this telex by Sudan Oilseeds Co. but nevertheless to comply with the rules they appointed an arbitrator in reply.

I hope that the above explains the position of a claim to your satisfaction but should there be any questions which you wish to put, I should be happy to answer them.

I am informed that you also wish a comment on this matter from an English lawyer and accordingly I have requested Messrs. William Crump & Sons to write to you which letter you should receive about the same time as this one.

Messrs. William A. Crump & Sons will probably be known to you as they are a highly regarded firm of lawyers (solicitors) specialising in the commercial, maritime and admiralty field.

Yours sincerely,

Mr. Bridge did not send a copy of the letter to Tracomin nor, apparently, to his co-arbitrator. The first that Tracomin heard of it was when it was produced as expert evidence, so to speak, on behalf of S.O.S. in the Swiss proceedings.

(ii) Early in 1982 correspondence took place between Tracomin's English solicitors and Mr. Bridge, as to whether there should be an adjournment of the arbitration between Tracomin and S.O.S., in which Mr. Bridge and another were the arbitrators. In that correspondence Mr. Bridge referred to S.O.S. as "my principals," and said that he was going "to seek instructions from them."

(iii) This ground is set out in par. 15 of Mr. Robinson's affidavit sworn on Nov. 15, 1982:

> The hearing of Action 1982-T-No. 1211 before the Hon. Mr. Justice Staughton lasted from 17th June 1982 to 24th June 1982. There was a further hearing on 15th September 1982. I attended the hearings. Mr. Bridge attended the whole or substantially the whole of the proceedings also. He sat behind Counsel for the First Defendants with their Solicitors and appeared to be discussing the case with them and indeed participating in the instruction of Counsel. Mr. Marcel Dumani, a Director of the Plaintiffs who attended part of the hearing, remarked to me that Mr. Bridge was "sitting in the enemy camp." This is

the Plaintiffs' view and it was the impression that Mr. Bridge gave.

Mr. Deans, the solicitor for S.O.S., answered that in par. 8 of his affidavit sworn on Dec. 7, 1982:

> The third ground is that Mr. Bridge attended much of the hearing before the Honourable Mr. Justice Staughton which was in open Court, and that he gave the impression of "sitting in the enemy camp." Mr. Bridge did indeed attend much of the hearing; he is now retired from active trading and was interested in the proceedings. Outside Court he talked to Mr. Marcel Dumani and to Mr. Robinson and Counsel for the Plaintiffs as well as myself and Counsel for the First Defendants. In Court, it is true, he sat next to me. Again, I respectfully suggest, that this is not misconduct. The hearing was not concerned with the merits of the dispute between the parties but with a procedural matter.

It will be observed that Mr. Deans does not comment on Mr. Robinson's evidence as to Mr. Bridge discussing the case with him and participating in the instruction of Counsel. However, Mr. Bridge does, in par. 3 (b) of his affidavit sworn on Dec. 8, 1982:

> As to the contents of paragraph 15 of Mr. Robinson's Affidavit I would only add to the statements made in paragraph 8 of the Affidavit of Mr. Deans to say that at no time did I give any instructions to Mr. Deans or to Counsel. I attended the majority of the hearings before the Honourable Mr. Justice Staughton and from time to time I asked Mr. Deans to clarify certain arguments which were being advanced but I myself was in no

position nor would I have presumed to give instructions to Mr. Deans or to Counsel.

I will consider those three allegations separately in the first instance, although, of course, it is Mr. Bridge's conduct as a whole which matters. As to (i), Mr. Bridge says, and I accept, that he did not understand that his letter to Maitre Wanner was to be used as expert evidence in the Swiss proceedings. On that basis, I would not regard it as sufficient by itself to establish a case of imputed bias. It seems to me to be within the practice, described earlier in this judgment, whereby a FOSFA arbitrator may advise those who appoint him on the procedure prevailing in FOSFA arbitrations.

Nor would I consider that point (ii) by itself would justify a finding of imputed bias. Mr. Deans, who is the doyen of the Commercial Court solicitors and who has more experience of commodity trade arbitrations than any other practitioner, says in par. 7 of his affidavit:

> In many years experience in dealing with arbitrations under the auspices of FOSFA (to whom I have acted as a legal adviser for some years) I have regularly come across the use of the expression "instructions" in the context explained and I believe it to be a normal expression for the reasons set out above, with no sinister implication as suggested by Mr. Robinson.

Of course, it would be better if an arbitrator did not refer to his appointors as his principals, or say that he was taking instructions from them rather than seeking their comments. But it would be imposing too high a standard on trade arbitrators if the law were to insist on the precise use of language in this context.

Point (iii) — Mr. Bridge's conduct at the hearing before me — is much the most serious of Tracomin's allegations. For an arbitrator, while still seized of judicial functions, to sit in Court behind Counsel for one party and next to the solicitor for that party is, in my judgment, wrong. It is still more wrong for him to appear (and I emphasize that word) to be participating in the instruction of Counsel for one party. That was the impression received by Mr. Robinson, and perhaps by Tracomin's director who remarked that Mr. Bridge was "sitting in the enemy camp." Neither could know what words were in fact passing between Mr. Bridge, Mr. Deans and Counsel — they could only form a view from what they saw. Mr. Deans does not deny that Mr. Robinson might have received that impression. Nor, in terms, does Mr. Bridge, although he says that he would not have presumed to give instructions to Counsel.

.    .    .

*The law*

Mustill and Boyd on Commercial Arbitration has this passage at p. 215:

Antecedent bias

Bias may arise either from a relationship between the arbitrator and one of the parties, or from a relationship between the arbitrator and the subject matter of the dispute. The former is the instance which comes more readily to mind. It can take the shape of a favouritism or antipathy towards one of the parties which can actually be shown to exist. Actual bias of this kind is almost impossible to prove, in the absence of some incautious remark by the person nominated, either before or after the reference begins. It is not, however, necessary to go as far as establishing actual bias, for the Court will in appropriate cases intervene if facts are proved which would lead a reasonable person, not knowing the arbitrator's true state of mind, to think it likely that there was bias.

At p. 216:

It is impossible to lay down any principle more precise that the test of what a reasonable man would think, for ascertaining whether the relationship is close enough to be objectionable. With the exercise of common sense, a situation should never arise in which the arbitrator's personal impartiality is put in question. A person who is approached with a request to act, and knows that he has some kind of relationship with one of the parties, should remember that there is no keener sense of injustice than is felt by someone who has doubts about whether the arbitrator is doing his honest best. He should also bear in mind that the question is not just whether he really is impartial, but whether a reasonable outsider might consider that there is a risk that he is not. If the person nominated considered that a reasonable outsider might (not should) take this view, he should decline to act. If he considers that the case is on the borderline, he should disclose the circumstances which might give rise to suspicion: and he will very often find that no objection is taken to his appointment: candour is always the best way to prevent misunderstandings.

There are, in my judgment, three points of importance to the present case which emerge from the authorities. First, the test is objective, as to what a reasonable man would think; it is not an enquiry into what the party alleging bias thinks, or as to the actual views of the arbitrator who is challenged (*Metropolitan Properties Co. (F.G.C.) Ltd. v. Lannon*, [1969] 1 Q.B. 577, *Hannam v. Bradford Corporation*, [1970] 1 W.L.R. 937, *Hagop Ardahatian v. Unifert International S.A.*, [1984] 2 Lloyd's Rep. 84).

Secondly, the reasonable man forms his view "with no inside knowledge" (per Lord Justice Cross in *Hannam's* case at p. 949). In its context, that statement was directed at inside knowledge of the character of the persons who were accused of bias: see the judgment of Mr. Justice Mustill in *Bremer Handelgesellschaft m.b.H. v. Ets Soules et Cie*, [1985] 1 Lloyd's Rep. 160, at p. 168. But the principle must, in my view, be wider than that, since the Court looks at appearances, "at the impression which would be given to other people" (per Lord Denning, M.R., in the *Metropolitan Properties* case at p. 599). While I respectfully agree with Mr. Justice Mustill that, in some circumstances, the Court may take into account an innocent explanation of facts which at first sight were suspicious, particularly when the challenge to an arbitrator is made before rather than after he has adjudicated, I do not think that this is always the case. Suppose that a reasonable man would have grounds for believing that the arbitrator was the majority shareholder in one of the parties; I do not see why it should not be established by evidence that the shareholder was not the arbitrator, but another person of the same name, or why the Court should not allow the reasonable man to revise his opinion with the benefit of that knowledge. By contrast, if an arbitrator is proved to have conferred with one of the parties about the dispute in circumstances which appear improper, I do not think that the reasonable man's view should be revised by reference to subsequent evidence of what was in fact said. Given that there is a reasonable inference of impropriety in the first place, it would be wrong in my judgment that an application to remove the arbitrator should thereafter fail if the inference is displaced by inside knowledge which was not available to all at the time. Lord Hewart's famous observation is still the law. I am conscious that there must be a dividing line between the two examples that I have given, and a test to determine on which side of that line a particular case lies. With the greatest respect to what may have been the view of Mr. Justice Mustill, I cannot accept that the test is solely whether the application for relief is made before or after the arbitrator has adjudicated. But wherever else the test is to be found, it need not be determined on this motion: I am convinced that in the present case, so far as it concerns the conduct of Mr. Bridge in Court during the S.O.S. case, the view of the reasonable man ought not to be revised in the light of subsequent evidence which was not available to an observer at the time. It will be noted that, in considering another of Tracomin's complaints (the writing of Mr. Bridge's letter to Maitre Wanner) I have paid heed to Mr. Bridge's evidence that he did not know that the letter was going to be used as evidence in Switzerland. But I express no view as to whether it is right to take that evidence into account.

.    .    .

Thirdly, there is some difference of view in the cases as to the precise degree of probability needed to found a charge of imputed bias. In the *Metropolitan Properties* case Lord Denning, M.R., (at p. 599) favoured real likelihood of bias, Lord Justice Danckwerts (at p. 602) reasonable doubt as to the chairman's impartiality. Lord Justice Edmund Davies (at p. 606) rejected real likelihood, and adopted, as a less stringent test, reasonable suspicion of bias . . . .

In many if not most cases it will make no difference which test is applied. That is so in the present case, and I am content to adopt real likelihood, which appears to lay the heaviest burden on the person alleging bias. But I do not, with great respect, share the view of Lord

Justice Cross (in *Hannam's* case) and Lord Justice Ackner (in the *Liverpool City Justices* case) that there is little if any difference between the two tests. If it had been necessary to decide the point, I would have followed what was said by Lord Justice Edmund-Davies in the *Metropolitan Properties* case (1969) 1 Q.B., at p. 606:

> With profound respect to those who have propounded the "real likelihood" test, I take the view that the requirement that justice must manifestly be done operates with undiminished force in cases where bias is alleged and that any development of the law which appears to emasculate that requirement should be strongly resisted. That the different tests, even when applied to the same facts, may lead to different results is illustrated by *Reg. v. Barnsley Licensing Justices* itself, as Devlin L.J. made clear in the passage I have quoted. But I cannot bring myself to hold that a decision may properly be allowed to stand even although there is reasonable suspicion of bias on the part of one or more members of the adjudicating body.

## *Conclusion*

In my judgment a reasonable man, acquainted with the practice at FOSFA, would conclude that there was a real likelihood of bias on the part of Mr. Bridge from the appearance of his conduct during the hearing of the S.O.S. case in this Court. That impression would not be dispelled, but rather slightly fortified, by the letter to Maitre Wanner, the reference to taking instructions from his principals, and the two occasions on which application was made to remove him. But it is on the appearance of Mr. Bridge's conduct during the S.O.S. case in this Court that my conclusion is founded.

Accordingly, I am prepared to make the order sought.

[The parties later came to terms. No order was made because Mr. Bridge agreed to resign.]

Notes and Questions

1. Are you persuaded by Judge Staughton's conclusion with regard to the behavior of Mr. Bridge? Consider each of the allegations made with regard to the arbitrator's conduct and conclude whether, in real-world terms, they would have created an impression of partiality.

2. Consider, in this regard, the behavior of the party-appointed arbitrator in *Desert Exploration*, discussed in Chapter 5, *supra* p. 602. Would that conduct have met the standard prescribed by Judge Staughton?

3. In a domestic arbitration in the United States, the Wall Street Journal reported that Chief Counsel for one of the parties was seen entering the hotel room of the chairman of the panel and, apparently, spending the night there. Would that constitute an impression of impartiality under the standard of Judge Staughton?

4. In *Desert Exploration*, the district court judge of Tel Aviv-Jaffa rejected the allegation of the protesting party that the party-appointed arbitrator had asked aggressive questions from the Bench, indicating a partiality in favor of the party that had appointed him. Discuss.

## III.   COMMUNICATIONS

The impartiality of the tribunal as between the parties must therefore be assured. Equally important though is the appearance of impartiality.

Is such an appearance maintained where there are communications or contacts between the tribunal and the parties? Mustill and Boyd refer to the English case of *Re Hopper*, 2 Lloyd's Rep. 367 (Q.B. 1867).[282] In that case, the arbitrators dined with one of the parties and its lawyer after the hearing. "Much wine was drunk," there was some discussion of the arbitration and, eventually, the arbitrators apparently retired to bed drunk. The High Court was critical of the arbitrators' behavior, but was not prepared to set aside the award because of it.

Would a similar judgment be given today? Is there any risk that the prevalent practice of arbitrators and parties eating lunch together could constitute a problem? Mustill and Boyd think not, but, while they

---

[282] MICHAEL J. MUSTILL & STEWART BOYD, THE LAW AND PRACTICE OF COMMERCIAL ARBITRATION IN ENGLAND 255 (2d ed. 1989).

find the practice "harmless," take the view that it places on the arbitrator "a particular responsibility to dilute his affability with a strict impartiality of manner."

A.    MICHAEL J. MUSTILL & STEWART C. BOYD, THE LAW AND PRACTICE OF COMMERCIAL ARBITRATION IN ENGLAND 255 (2d ed. 1989).

Finally, there is the question of personal contacts during the reference between the arbitrator and the parties. These are not a problem in litigation, nor as a rule in most formal arbitrations. The arbitrator appears at the beginning of the day, and leaves at the end. There is no occasion for personal contact between himself and the parties, and the performance of the procedural rituals itself ensures a proper detachment. A commercial arbitration is often quite different. Procedural niceties are abjured in the interests of speed and economy. Often, many of those involved in the reference are on close professional terms. Informality is the order of the day. This absence of a rigid procedural framework has many advantages, but it means that the arbitrator must form his own view of how to behave. Arbitrators who justifiably take for granted the probity of themselves and their colleagues sometimes forget that those who do not know either them or the system so well may not make the same assumptions. The arbitrator must therefore be alert to see that a friendly and informal way of conducting the reference does not lead an uninformed party to the mistaken conclusion that the arbitrator is not maintaining a truly judicial approach. It goes without saying that social contacts should take place in the presence of both parties.[283]

*    *    *

There must, of course, be communication between the tribunal and the parties in order to facilitate the proceedings. Must such communication involve all parties and all members of the tribunal? For example, to what extent is a party-appointed arbitrator entitled to communicate solely with the party which appointed him? Although the instinctive reaction may be to reject such behavior, it should be recognized that it occurs and, as in the AAA/ABA Code of Ethics, is on occasion expressly permitted.

---

[283] *Id.*

In sharp contrast, Article 5 of the IBA Ethics for International Arbitrators frowns on unilateral communication.

B.    JAN    PAULSSON,    ETHICS    FOR    INTERNATIONAL ARBITRATORS: HOW HAVE THE 1987 GUIDELINES FARED? Speech at the 23rd IBA Conference (Sept. 1990).

Shortly after the promulgation of the guidelines, Robert Coulson, President of the American Arbitration Association, wrote an article entitled "An American Critique of the IBA's Ethics for International Arbitrators," Journal of International Arbitration 1987. 103. Making the case for the rather uniquely American concept of "non-neutral" arbitrators, Mr. Coulson, albeit in his impeccably courteous way, criticized the IBA guidelines as lacking in realism and pragmatism. There is no proof, he wrote, of a worldwide consensus that arbitrators nominated by one party should be impartial and detached from the party that appointed them, so why be hypocritical? Mr. Coulson highlighted three areas of divergence between the IBA guidelines and the American norms exemplified by the 1977 AAA/ABA Code of Ethics, all related to unilateral communications between an arbitrator and the party that nominated him or her:

1.  with respect to issues in dispute,
2.  with respect to fee arrangements, and
3.  with respect to possible terms of settlement.

Regarding the two latter categories, the distinction is simple: The IBA guidelines say no, the AAA/ABA Code allows them. Mr. Coulson argues that arbitrators are like other professionals and should not necessarily be subject to uniform fee structures; and that unilateral probing may improve the chances for settlement. But in the international community countervailing considerations seem paramount: An arbitrator whose remuneration is a secret matter between him and one of the parties will harm the credibility of the process, and so will an arbitrator who has privileged conferences with one party as the case develops.

As for unilateral communications relating to issues in dispute, the IBA guidelines do recognize that they cannot be avoided on two occasions: When a party first contacts a potential arbitrator to ask him if he is willing to serve, and when a party gives its nominee indications as to its preferences or aversions as to the choice of chairman. It would seem rather obvious that the fitness of a particular arbitrator for a particular case can be determined only if the nature of the case is disclosed and discussed.

From Mr. Coulson's point of view, this kind of discussion will necessarily degenerate to a discussion of the merits of the case of a type which the IBA guidelines wish to avoid. To this I have two answers, one practical and the other idealistic. First, these potential discussions take place prior to the constitution of the tribunal, and therefore by definition before the issues have crystallized or even been joined; from that point on, the IBA position is to bar any unilateral communication of the case. Therefore, any lapse into a discussion of the merits at such a preliminary stage is unlikely to be prejudicial. Second, as the introductory note puts it, the guidelines "will attain their objectives only if they are applied in good faith."

I would submit that the American position remains a minority one. Two commentaries published in 1990, the first by a Geneva lawyer, the second by the Secretary General of the ICC International Court of Arbitration, seem to confirm that the option chosen by the IBA in 1987 accurately reflected an emerging consensus; they conclude that the international arbitration community appears to be swinging decisively toward the view that all arbitrators, including those proposed by the parties, should be neutral and independent. J. Werner, Editorial, Journal of International Arbitration 1990. Vol. 5; S. Bond, "The ICC Arbitrator's Statement of Independence," Swiss Arbitration Bulletin No. 3 p. 226.

### Notes and Questions

1. Is Paulsson correct in the limits that he sees in the IBA Guidelines with regard to unilateral communications? When a lawyer is approached by a party looking for an arbitrator, must not the lawyer ask enough about the case to determine whether he or she has a conflict? Does this not involve reading the basic contract and understanding the nature of the dispute? Can activities such as these avoid the type of exchange that Coulson believes inevitable? Discuss.

2. Can you think of circumstances in which a party-appointed arbitrator might feel compelled to speak to the party having made the appointment?

IV.   DELIBERATIONS

After the final hearing or, in a "documents only" arbitration, when all evidence has been submitted, the tribunal will (unless, of course, there is a sole arbitrator) meet to deliberate. In certain jurisdictions, the tribunal is required by law to deliberate. Even in the absence of explicit law, there is general agreement that deliberation is required.

It is unanimously admitted that, if there is more than one arbitrator, the award must be made after a deliberation in which all the arbitrators have taken part. This is expressly stated in the Swiss Concordat: "All arbitrators must participate in each deliberation and decision of the arbitral tribunal." All arbitrators must participate in the deliberation and decision leading to the arbitral award, but the decision itself can be taken by a majority and the award can be made even if an arbitrator refuses to participate in the deliberation or to concur with the decision made by the majority. Unanimity is required in only a few laws: Brazil, Peru, Venezuela.[284]

What then happens if, for whatever reason, one of the arbitrators refuses to participate in deliberations? Moreover, can a failure to deliberate be a ground for setting aside an award on the basis that the arbitrators have misconducted themselves?

A.   *Bank Mellat v. GAA Development & Construction Co.*, 2 Lloyd's Rep. 44, 49-51 (1988).

An application was made by Bank Mellat to set aside a majority award given against it by a three man tribunal. A draft majority award had been prepared and, together with the third arbitrator's dissenting view submitted to the ICC Court of Arbitration. In accordance with the ICC Rules, the Court remitted the draft award to the tribunal and asked it to strengthen certain elements of the award, believed to relate to the arbitrators' reasoning, but in any event being matters of form rather than substance. The following passage comes from the judgment of Justice Steyn.

---

[284] RENÉ DAVID, ARBITRATION IN INTERNATIONAL TRADE 315 (1985).

On the same day the chairman sent a revised majority award to the ICC Secretariat. On Apr. 20 the secretary to the tribunal informed Mr. Djahromi that the chairman was on holiday, and that the revised draft majority award had been sent to the ICC. Mr. Djahromi thereupon telexed the Secretariat of the ICC, stating that he had not been consulted and requesting that the matter should not be placed before the court until he had an opportunity to comment. On Apr. 22 a member of the ICC Secretariat (Mr. M. Buehler) replied by telex, confirming receipt of the revised majority draft award "for information," and adding that

> The revised draft will only be submitted to the court once I am instructed to do so by the chairman of the tribunal. The next plenary session of the court will be held on May 20.

Thereafter, and in April, the dissenting arbitrator received a copy of the revised majority award. On Apr. 28 the chairman, with the approval of Mr. Wright, Q.C., sent a telex to the dissenting arbitrator stating inter alia:

> 2. In the letter it is stated that the court has felt — no doubt under the impression of your dissenting opinion which we had not had in our hands when drafting the majority award and had therefore not been able to take into account — that certain explanations and clarifications were desirable. These have been given in the amended version of the majority award which should now be in your hands. As you will see, the reasons have not been changed in substance but have been elaborated upon with regard to the two points raised in Mr. Buehler's letter.

> 3. The views expressed in the majority award are well known to you as well as your views — expressed during our deliberations, in the dissenting opinion and in your last telex — are known to Mr. Wright and myself. I therefore see no need to convene again the arbitrators for further deliberations.

> 4. In case you have any comments to make in regard to the amended version of the majority award I would be grateful if you would let me and Mr. Wright have these not later than May 7.

That was, of course, a clear invitation to Mr. Djahromi to comment in writing by May 7 on the revised majority award. He did not respond to that invitation. On May 13 the ICC received Mr. Djahromi's "Further dissenting remarks." The ICC sent a facsimile of that document to the chairman and Mr. Wright, and Mr. Djahromi was so informed. On May 19 the chairman sent a final telex to Mr. Djahromi (and copied it to the ICC). The final part of this telex read as follows:

. . . In the telex of April 28, I asked you to send to Mr. Wright and myself any comments you might have not later than May 7. I heard nothing from you and thought the matter was closed.

The revised version was prepared by myself and naturally in the first instance sent to Mr. Wright who had resolved the case in the same manner as myself. After having taken into account some of his views the revised draft was agreed and typed and sent to you and the court. There has been no meeting between Mr. Wright and myself but — as is customary in international arbitrations — the text was prepared by correspondence.

It would seem that your "further dissenting remarks" only contain arguments and views which have already been discussed and considered. I have spoken yesterday afternoon with Mr. Wright on the telephone and he is of the same opinion. Thus, we both find that your further dissenting remarks do not call for any alterations in the draft award.

This award is now considerably overdue, and I think the time has come when the award should be considered by the court and published to the parties. I therefore consider the deliberations closed.

This telex records that Mr. Djahromi's "Further dissenting remarks" were considered. And it authorized the ICC secretariat to place the majority award before the court for approval. It was approved by the court on June 17. The letter from the ICC Secretariat dated July 31, 1987 records that the court took into account the exchange of correspondence (which included the dissenting arbitrator's request for a meeting), but that the court was satisfied that the revised draft award submitted by the majority had been made by the arbitral tribunal in a proper way.

In other words, the court took the view that there was no need for the chairman to convene another meeting.

The question is whether the majority committed misconduct. The principal contract is governed by Iranian law but the law governing the arbitration is English law. It was submitted that the fact that the ICC court took the view that there was no procedural irregularity is irrelevant. I accept that the view of the ICC court cannot in any way be determinative of the issue. But it is in my view unrealistic to describe it as entirely irrelevant. For example, it may be helpful as throwing light on the question whether a further face-to-face meeting between the arbitrators was necessary. That question cannot entirely be divorced from what is usual in ICC practice.

It will be recalled that in the ICC Secretariat's letter of July 31, 1987 the view was expressed that the amendments to the draft majority award were matters of form rather than substance within the meaning of art. 21 of the ICC rules. In a careful and helpful speech Mr. David Hunt, Q.C., for Bank Mellat, contended that the contrary was the case. It is sometimes difficult to draw the line between amendments of form and substance. Without deciding the question I will assume that the amendments which the majority made to their draft award must rank as matters of substance.

It is not disputed that the parties were given a fair hearing, and that after the hearing the arbitrators fully and fairly considered the issues. The charge of misconduct is that the majority failed to consult Mr. Djahromi after the Court of Arbitration referred the draft majority award back for reconsideration. It is submitted, in the first place, that the face-to-face meeting, which Mr. Djahromi requested, was essential. Alternatively, it is submitted that the written communication should have been exchanged before the majority revised their majority award. None of the authorities, cited in argument on behalf of Bank Mellat, afforded any direct support for these particular submissions. Mr. Hunt attempted to derive his concrete submissions from the general proposition that all members of an arbitral tribunal must participate jointly in all stages of the arbitral proceedings. That proposition can be accepted. On the other hand, in the terminology of Dworkin, it is clearly a principle rather than a rule. And it is too general to afford the answer to many concrete problems. This is illustrated by the express concession, which was rightly made on behalf of Bank Mellat, that the majority were not obliged, after the close of deliberations, to discuss the draft majority award with Mr. Djahromi. And it is perhaps more pertinent to the facts of this case, and more helpful, to say that the governing principle is that, after the end of the hearing, parties are entitled to an impartial and fair consideration and resolution by the arbitrators, acting together, of all the issues in the case.

In my judgment there are several answers to the charge of misconduct. The first question is whether there was any duty, owed by the majority to Mr. Djahromi or to the parties, to consult with Mr. Djahromi about the revision of the majority award. This question cannot be viewed in the abstract. It has not been suggested at any time that any of the observations of the ICC court, or amendments to the reasons for the award, involved anything that had not been canvassed at the hearings, and discussed at meetings between the arbitrators. And it is not in every international commercial arbitration of the scale and scope of this arbitration, that the opportunity exists for such extensive oral deliberations as took place in the present case. Moreover, it would be fanciful to suggest that a further meeting or consultation would have afforded Mr. Djahromi an opportunity to convert the majority to his point of view. The sole purpose of a further meeting or consultation would have been to enable Mr. Djahromi to discuss with the majority the redrafting of the reasons of their majority award. Mr. Djahromi disagreed fundamentally and comprehensively with the majority award and its reasons, and it is difficult to conceive of the utility, at that late stage, of a discussion with him of a drafting exercise which was intended to strengthen those reasons. No doubt courtesy between colleagues required a further reference to him, but in my view the governing principle, which I have stated, did not require it as a matter of law. On his ground alone the application must fail.

On the assumption that the majority ought to have consulted with Mr. Djahromi, I turn to what actually happened. The majority declined Mr. Djahromi's request for a face-to-face meeting. The chairman pointed out to Mr. Djahromi that the revisions were agreed between her and Mr. Wright in correspondence. She clearly took the view that Mr. Djahromi should be able to explain his views in the same manner. In the real world of international commercial arbitration, and notably in the case of ICC arbitrations with a tribunal drawn from different countries, arbitrators often have to communicate with one another by telephone, telex or letter. That is particularly so after the hearing, after the arbitrators have met to discuss the issues, and in the subsequent process of drafting reasons. A ruling that the chairman should have called such a meeting in April or May, 1987, months after the hearing and after lengthy meetings between the arbitrators, would in my judgment impose unrealistic, unworkable and time wasting procedures on ICC arbitrators. While I have independently reached this conclusion, I note that the court by the clearest implication took this view when it approved the award in June 1987. That leaves for consideration the alternative submission that the majority should only have revised the draft majority award, which had previously been submitted for approval, *after* written consultations between the three arbitrators. In April, 1987 the revised majority award was sent to the ICC Secretariat for information, and Mr. Djahromi was informed that it would not be placed before the Court until the chairman had authorized it. In April Mr. Djahromi received a copy of the revised majority award. The chairman asked for Mr. Djahromi's comments on the revised majority award by May 7. He failed to respond. But his "Further Dissenting Remarks," commenting on the revised majority award, were seen and taken into account by the majority before the chairman brought matters to a close. The chairman no doubt took the view that while in a Judge or arbitrator an open mind is essential, it must also be able to shut eventually. And she brought matters to a close by her telex of May 14 to Mr. Djahromi, which was copied to the ICC. In my view Mr. Djahromi's views were fully and fairly considered, and no breach of the governing principle has been established. For these reasons too the application must fail.

Finally, if I had been persuaded that there was a procedural flaw in that further consultation with Mr. Djahromi should have taken place as submitted by Bank Mellat, I would nevertheless in the particular circumstances of this case have declined to set aside the award on the ground of misconduct. My reason for this conclusion is that, on the stated hypothesis, the flaw was a technical one and the inference is irresistible that such further consultation would not have been productive of any material changes to the revised majority award. In other words, if there was a procedural flaw, I am satisfied beyond any reasonable doubt that no injustice resulted from it. For this further reason the application must be dismissed. *Bank Mellat v. GAA Dev. & Const. Co.*, 2 LLOYD'S REP. 44, 49-51 (1988).

* * *

B.     *Fertilizantes Fosfatados Mexicanos S.A. v. Chem.
       Carriers, Inc.*, 751 F.Supp. 467 (S.D.N.Y. 1990).

Duffy, J.

[An arbitration clause in a charter party provided for three arbitrators
in New York; a decision by a majority of the panel would be binding.]

## DISCUSSION

Apparently a number of disputes arose and the parties
voluntarily complied with the arbitration clauses of the charters.
Pursuant to those clauses, Chemical chose its designated arbitrator,
Fertilizantes chose its arbitrator, and the two arbitrators so chosen
mutually agreed upon the third arbitrator. At the end of arbitration, one
of the arbitrators submitted a series of extraordinary dissents from the
majority awards. Chemical now seeks to upset the awards in reliance
on statements by the dissenting arbitrator, who has accused the other
members of the panel of misfeasance and malfeasance. Given the
serious nature of the charges, I conducted a hearing on November 15,
1990 to allow Chemical to substantiate its allegations.

In support of its application, Chemical presented the testimony
of the dissenting arbitrator, who testified at great length. In addition,
the several hundred page dissenting "awards," with several hundred
pages of exhibits annexed thereto, were submitted. In opposition,
Fertilizantes called the other two arbitrators, who also testified as to the
deliberations of the arbitration panel.[285]

The only grounds permitted under the statute to set aside an
award are enumerated in 9 U.S.C. § 10:

(a)     Where the award was procured by corruption, fraud, or undue
means.

---

[285] [1] This case should not be viewed as a precedent in any way for inquiry into
the deliberations of an arbitration panel. Such matters should remain confidential and
inviolate. The only reason it was permitted here was because of the seriousness of the
charges made by the dissenter against the other two arbitrators.

(b)      Where there was evident partiality or corruption in the arbitrators, or either of them.

(c)      Where the arbitrators were guilty of misconduct in refusing to postpone the hearing, upon sufficient cause shown, or in refusing to hear evidence pertinent and material to the controversy; or of any other misbehavior by which the rights of any party have been prejudiced.

(d)      Where the arbitrators exceeded their powers, or so imperfectly executed them that a mutual, final, and definite award upon the subject matter submitted was not made.

After an examination of the entire record, and a review of the dissenter's testimony, I am convinced that there is nothing more to the extraordinary charges levelled by the dissenter than frustration in failing to convince the majority of his position. Specifically, on September 15, 1988, a majority of the arbitration panel found against Chemical and in favor of Fertilizantes on its claims for liability. On January 24, 1989, the majority ruled that Chemical did not have the right to raise additional issues for consideration by the panel. On August 30, 1990, a majority of the panel awarded Fertilizantes $5,728,044.13, with interest to accumulate if the award was not paid within 30 days. In addition, Chemical was assessed its share of the arbitrator fees. The arbitrator named by Chemical concurred in the denial of Chemical's claims, but dissented from each of the other findings in a series of decisions dated November 10, 1988, February 27, 1989, and August 28, 1990.

Using hyperbole and extreme language, the dissenter charges the majority with "bias". The dissenter inter alia also claimed that he was excluded from deliberations. I find however, that his claims are not substantiated by the facts. Indeed, portions of the dissenter's testimony became long-winded and unfair broadside attacks upon the majority. In fact, all of the arbitrators had an open line among themselves to voice their concerns, albeit at times in writing. Although the dissenter did not join the majority opinion or assist in its drafting, his positions were made clear at the deliberative sessions. He had a full opportunity to discuss and exchange ideas at those times. Chemical wholly fails to prove any of the statutorily provided grounds for opposing the arbitration award.

This entire affair is quite unfortunate. Indeed, I am convinced that all three arbitrators are honorable men and that nothing untoward occurred during this arbitration. I hope that in the future, feelings of frustration will not lead to such extreme and ill-considered charges.

This memorandum is not intended to indicate that cross-petitioner's position was frivolous within the meaning of Rule 11. Counsel for the cross-petitioner, upon being presented with the dissents, had no other choice than to proceed with their application. It was handled in a thoroughly professional manner and did not descend into an ad hominem attack on the arbitrators. Nonetheless, the parties should note that any further litigation in this matter would be of no benefit. . . .

### Notes and Questions

1. It is universally acknowledged that deliberation is required and the failure of the arbitrators to deliberate before issuing an award is a ground for annulment. *See* KENNETH SMITH CARLSTON, THE PROCESS OF INTERNATIONAL ARBITRATION (1972). There is, however, little explicit authority on what constitutes sufficient deliberation. If a member of the three-person tribunal arrives with his or her mind made up, will there have been deliberation? The burden would appear to be on the chairman of the tribunal to ensure that the *in camera* meetings of the tribunal are so structured that there can be a genuine and searching examination of the positions espoused by the parties and even points taken for granted can be reviewed.

2. Advances in telecommunications now mean that arbitrators (as well as litigants and tribunals) can conduct many of their transactions by teleconference. What is the effect of exchanges by telephone on deliberations? Even when such deliberations are conducted telephonically, should there also be a face-to-face meeting?

3. In three-person tribunals, should all deliberations take place in the presence of all of the arbitrators or may one arbitrator contact another with an interest in developing a joint position? What are the consequences for tribunal deliberation?

## V.   SECRECY

In contrast to litigation in the ordinary courts of law, arbitration is conducted in private. For many parties who use arbitration, this privacy is its greatest advantage.

The tribunal is under a duty not to disclose information obtained during the course of the proceedings. This restriction clearly covers disclosure of the award and the tribunal's deliberations but also less obvious matters. For instance, an arbitrator should not, without the parties' consent, publicize information contained in a witness statement produced for the purposes of the arbitration.

> Ronald Bernstein, *General Principles*, *in* HANDBOOK OF ARBITRATION PRACTICE, 101 (1987).

In almost every arbitration the arbitrator is appointed personally, and not as a member or representative of his firm or of a company which employs him. This applies whether or not the arrangements between him and the firm or company result in his fees being paid over. So he should retain personally his arbitration file; it should not be put into the possession or control of his firm or company.

### Notes and Questions

1. How tightly drawn are the restrictions? For example, may an arbitrator who is a partner in a law firm disclose information to one of his partners? At least one commentator argues that an arbitrator should not disclose information to the members of his firm.

2. How is the obligation of confidentiality enforced? Can an arbitrator be enjoined from disclosing information relating to an arbitration? Do the rules of the arbitral institutions prohibit disclosure? The IBA Ethics for International Arbitrators set out the rule very clearly at least insofar as the deliberations of the tribunal and the award itself are concerned. Where does this leave the arbitrator's obligation as regards other information obtained by him during the course of the proceedings? *See* Article 9 of the IBA Ethics.

## VI.   DISSENTING OPINIONS

Tribunals are often unable to reach a unanimous decision. An arbitrator may endorse an award but disagree with the reasoning behind it; or, more seriously, he may dissent not only from the reasoning in the award but from the result itself. In this case, can the dissenting arbitrator make his views known?

Traditionally, civil law countries have regarded maintaining complete secrecy with regard to a court or tribunal's deliberations as fundamental. In France, for example, an arbitrator in a domestic arbitration who disagrees with a majority decision is not permitted to attach a dissenting award to the majority award. In contrast, it appears that dissenting opinions are permitted in Switzerland, provided that the arbitrator complies with his general duty of diligence. This proviso effectively means that the dissenting opinion should not endanger the validity and enforceability of the award.

A.    Laurent Levy, *Dissenting Opinions in International Arbitration in Switzerland*, 5 ARB. INT'L 35, 35-39 (1989).

An arbitrator whose views did not prevail may wish to let them be known, through a separate opinion which is either "dissenting," (if he disagrees with the decision) or "concurring" (if he approves of the decision but disagrees with its reasoning). Each is termed a "separate opinion" to distinguish it from the "majority opinion" reflecting the reasoning of the arbitrators whose views prevailed.

In Continental Europe, dissenting opinions were traditionally unknown. They were perceived as being in conflict with the collegial nature of the courts; it was felt that a decision should be made by the court as a whole rather than be produced as the mathematical sum of the judges' opinions. The notion of the "confidentiality of the deliberation" (or secret du délibéré) was a corollary: judges could not discuss their deliberations, could not indicate if there was a dissent within their ranks and, a fortiori, could not dissent. In international arbitration, however, dissenting opinions appear with increasing frequency.

As discussed below, Swiss law does not prohibit dissenting opinions; nor does it provide a framework for the minority arbitrator desirous of expressing his concerns about an award.

## I. ADMISSIBILITY OF DISSENTING OPINIONS

Dissenting opinions are not forbidden in Switzerland provided the dissenting arbitrator abides by his *"devoir de diligence"* (general duty of diligence).

### (a) *No rule forbids dissenting opinions*

International arbitration in Switzerland is governed by the Federal Act on Private International Law (PIL) of 18 December 1987 which came into force on 1 January 1989. Article 182 of the PIL provides for the parties to determine the arbitral procedure, directly, indirectly or by submission to a procedural law. Should the parties fail to agree on the procedure, the arbitral tribunal will do so "to the extent necessary"; the only limit to the freedom of the parties (or the arbitrators) is that equal treatment must be ensured as well as the parties' right to be heard in an "adversarial" procedure. Article 189 of the PIL provides that the award shall be made in the form agreed by the parties. In the absence of such an agreement, the award is made in the form chosen by majority decision, or failing that, the form chosen by the Chairman alone.

If the arbitration is governed by the Intercantonal Arbitration Concordat ("Concordat"), there is no prohibition of dissenting opinions. Except for a few mandatory rules, the parties may determine the procedure by agreement or, failing such agreement, the Concordat provides that the arbitrators are to establish the procedure by decisions (Art. 24). Subsidiarily, the 1947 Federal Act on Federal Civil Procedure (Loi fédérale de procédure civile fédérale of 4 December 1947) is applicable to fill procedural gaps (Concordat, Article 24, §2) as is the 1943 Federal Act on Judicial Organisation. Neither of these statutes provide for "confidentiality of deliberation"; rather, federal judges deliberate, deliver their opinion and render their decision in public (1943 Federal Act, Art. 17).

Under either the PIL or the Concordat, the parties or the arbitrators may submit the arbitration to one of the cantonal procedures. About a third of these procedures have no concept of "confidentiality of deliberation" and provide for public opinions.

The parties (or the arbitrators) may agree to use the rules of an institution: UNCITRAL rules neither foresee dissenting opinions nor rule them out. These elections of procedural laws by reference are enforceable.

The admissibility or exclusion of dissenting opinions, both in the practice of arbitration and in the applicable rules of law, are rare enough in Switzerland that it is impossible to conclude that one or the other prevails. This is also the ICC position as will be seen below.

A notion of *secret du délibéré* would not *ipso facto* forbid arbitrators' dissenting opinions; in some national jurisdictions, that notion and dissenting opinions co-exist. The goal of *secret du délibéré* is to preserve the collegial nature of the courts, to keep the judges immune from the parties' grudges, and so to bolster their independence. Such considerations are largely foreign to arbitration where the parties appoint the "judges."

### (b) *General duty of diligence*

The arbitrators are bound to the parties by a duty of confidentiality, which is part of their general duty of diligence arising out of the agency character of the arbitration agreement. This should prohibit undue disclosure of the arbitration process to third parties.

A dissenting opinion may be an attempt, sometimes successful, to pave the way to an annulment recourse or to the blocking of exequatur in some countries. The admissibility of dissenting opinions, therefore, should depend on a balance of interest test in the context of the arbitrators' duty of diligence: on the one side, the efficacy of the award, which is what the parties commissioned and paid the arbitrators for, and on the other side, the usually legitimate desire of an arbitrator to express his disagreement with a majority award. Such a balancing test occurs, for instance, when an arbitrator communicates his dissenting opinion to the ICC Court of Arbitration. The Court considers it when it reviews the award and may decide to attach it to the award (ICC Rules, Art. 21 and Rule 22 of the ICC Internal Rules of the Court). The ICC, however, may decide not to communicate the dissent if it would impair the enforceability of the award.

Questions do arise about the future of the practice of dissenting opinions. In countries where the tradition favours dissenting opinions, is it possible to transpose that tradition to arbitration, especially international arbitration, when the tradition originated in domestic court procedure? Is there a risk of a "cultural gap" between arbitrators coming from different countries which have different views about dissenting opinions and also about the role of a party-appointed arbitrator? Some arbitrators, after all, are expected by a losing party to dissent. The arbitrator himself may need this face-saving device if his view does not prevail, especially in politically-tinted arbitrations (*i.e.*, arbitrations where a State is involved) or when the arbitrator is linked to a party.

Is escalation to be feared with each arbitrator feeling obligated to express a separate opinion for the sake of a party? Will arbitrators spend more time and effort on the drafting of "their" opinions than on the awards, at the expense of the latter's quality and homogeneity? It should be noted that while this would not necessarily be a danger for scholarship, as dissenting opinions may be masterpieces of jurisprudence, it may indeed be an invitation to oppose enforcement. Indeed, this is exactly what some dissenting arbitrators are hoping to accomplish. One may answer that forbidding dissenting opinions will not prevent arbitrators from communicating them and certainly will not put an end to other well-known dilatory or obstructive tactics (*e.g.*, refusal to attend deliberations or to sign the award). Furthermore, to forbid dissenting opinions because they might jeopardise awards would be to legislate with those instances in mind when an arbitrator distorts the arbitral process to undermine the award. Yet prohibiting dissenting opinions only because they might be used abusively is not sound policy; it is preferable to eliminate or penalise abuses rather than the means, otherwise useful, which are used to commit them.

Scientific reasons or a jurist's pride may not be a good reason to render separate opinions. An arbitrator's refusal to be silent in the face of a patent violation of the equality of the parties will justify his dissent, at least as an ultima ratio if the other arbitrators refuse to modify their position. Annulment of the award (or the denial to enforce it) may follow but the dissent may in such circumstances be less the cause of the annulment than the evidence of such cause. The existence, after all, of a dissenting opinion itself cannot be a ground for recourse against an award or its enforcement as it is not contrary to *ordre public*.

\*     \*     \*

As with Switzerland, common law countries allow dissenting opinions. As for the arbitral institutions, ICSID expressly permits dissenting opinions by rule 47(3):

> Any member of the Tribunal may attach his individual opinion to the award, whether he dissents from the majority or not, or a statement of his dissent.

Contrast the practice of the ICC as explained in the following passage.

B.    W. Laurence Craig, et al. International Chamber of Commerce Arbitration 332-35 (2d ed. 1990).

### 19.06 Dissenting opinions

Whether it is a majority award or an award of the chairman alone, an ICC award must contain all the elements of an enforceable award. While the award may indicate that a particular arbitrator did not concur in the decision, a dissenting opinion *per se* does not ordinarily become part of the award, even though its contents may be made known to the parties. A dissenting arbitrator may make his views known to the Court of Arbitration for its use in its scrutiny of the award. These views usually take the form of correspondence addressed to the Court, but they may be incorporated in a dissenting opinion.

Nothing in the Rules specifically prevents annexing a dissenting opinion to the award. The only inhibiting factor may be Article 26. Since Article 26 provides that both the tribunal and the Court of Arbitration shall make every effort that the award be enforceable at law, the award should conform as much as possible to the requirements of the jurisdictions in which arbitrations take place as well as those where awards may be enforced. As in the civil-law tradition there is no place for dissenting opinions in either judicial decisions or arbitral awards (apparently due to the fact that the deliberations of arbitrators and judges are secret and dissenting opinions tend to reveal the inner workings of the tribunal), the practice of making dissenting opinions a part of an ICC award is discouraged. This is all the more true since a great number of parties to ICC arbitration come from civil-law countries and there is always the possibility that an award may be presented for execution in a civil-law country where the defendant has assets. The silence of the Rules themselves regarding dissenting opinions, added to the notions in Article 19 that there may be a "majority decision" in the absence of unanimity, or a "sole decision" by the chairman in the absence of a majority, support the view that there is only one award: the one that disposes of the case. A dissenting opinion is thus extraneous to *the* award.

On the other hand, the procedural laws in many common-law countries permit dissenting opinions by arbitrators as well as by judges. Where the arbitration takes place in one of these countries, a common-law arbitrator may seek to have his dissenting opinion made known. The proper procedure in such a case is for the dissenter to obtain the agreement of his fellow arbitrators, expressed in the latter's majority decision, that the dissenting opinion may be annexed to the award.

As part of its review process, the Court of Arbitration may then decide to approve the annexation of the dissenting opinion to the award, provided always that the enforceability of the award is not jeopardized. Accordingly, Article 17 of the Internal Rules of the Court states explicitly:

> [T]he Court of Arbitration pays particular attention to the respect of the formal requirements laid down by the law applicable to the proceedings and, where relevant, by the mandatory rules of the place of arbitration, notably with regard to the reasons for awards, their signature and *the admissibility of dissenting opinions.* (Emphasis added.)

In general, the Court of Arbitration makes its own determination of whether it considers that there is a legal impediment to communication of the dissenting opinion. However, it also considers that the arbitrators are free to interpret the law of the place of arbitration with regard to the communication of dissenting opinions. Where the majority of the tribunal considers the communication inadmissible under such law, the Court does not communicate the dissenting opinion with the award. When the Secretariat, acting for the Court, communicates the dissenting opinion to the parties with the award, it makes clear that it is not part of the award. Where the dissent is not communicated officially, there is nothing to prevent the dissenting arbitrator communicating his opinion to the parties, provided that it takes place after the official notification of the award.

Because of the diversity of approaches of arbitral tribunals in dealing with dissenting opinions, and particularly because of conflict between civil law and common law concepts, a working committee of the ICC Commission on International Arbitration has conducted a survey of the subject. The opponents of dissenting opinions pointed out their disadvantages within the framework of the ICC Arbitration Rules, which provide for party-nominated arbitrators and scrutiny of awards by the Court of Arbitration. They argued that dissenting opinions underscore the link between the arbitrator and the party who nominates him, weaken the search for a unanimous position, and threaten to draw the Court of Arbitration into a debate — which is not its role — on the respective merits of the majority and dissenting views. Despite these negative views, a large majority of the Committee was strongly of the opinion that an arbitrator had a right to make his dissenting views known and that no steps should be taken to suppress dissenting opinions. It was recognized that it would nevertheless be desirable that a more uniform administrative approach be taken towards such opinions.

The Commission (whose views are only recommendatory and not binding on the ICC Court) confirmed the Report encompassing the views of the majority. The Report provides that the dissenting opinion is not part of the award and that the Court of Arbitration is not required to scrutinize it under Article 21 of the Rules. It recommended, nevertheless, that the Court should continue its current practice of looking at the dissenting opinion at the same time that it scrutinizes the award, for any assistance that it may lend to such scrutiny. The submission of a dissenting opinion should not occasion delay, and the chairman of the arbitral tribunal should fix appropriate time periods for the dissenting opinion to be rendered so that it may be dispatched simultaneously with the award to the Court of Arbitration. Frequently the majority arbitrators wish to see the dissenting opinion so that they may be sure to treat all questions raised in the draft award submitted. Once again, this should not be permitted to be the cause of needless delay.

The Report concluded that the general rule should be that the Court of Arbitration should notify dissenting opinions to the parties. In rare instances where such notification might imperil the award (and the Committee's survey found no country where this was certain to be the case), the current practice of permitting a dissenting arbitrator informally to send his opinion to the parties should be maintained.

The institution of the dissenting opinions from ICC awards will remain controversial. There will continue to be cases where an arbitrator, as a matter of conscience, feels required to make known his views, especially if he believes that the award results in a miscarriage of justice. However, it would be unfortunate if these exceptional instances became commonplace. Party-nominated arbitrators should avoid the temptation of writing dissents only to justify their position.

Ordinary issues of fact and law are not susceptible to judicial review; nor should they be if the institution of arbitration is to retain its vigor. The common-law rationale for dissenting opinions, namely that they usefully frame issues which appellate courts will settle in the interest of establishing the uniform application of legal principles throughout the jurisdiction, is thus inoperative, or at least greatly reduced, in the context of arbitration. In these circumstances, one may feel that the Committee's view that "the ICC should neither encourage nor discourage the giving of such opinions" is too weak, and that, by its apparent neutrality, it might in fact lead to more dissenting opinions. The view of the present authors is that while dissenting opinions may exceptionally be justified, they are generally to be discouraged.

### Notes and Questions

1. A dissenting opinion then is not part of the award. Should it be annexed to the award and, if not, can the dissenting arbitrator send his dissenting opinion to the parties without breaching his duties of confidentiality?

2. Is the arbitrator under an obligation to communicate his opinion, in the form of a dissent, if he knows that the tribunal failed to take into account certain evidence important to the losing party's case?

C.    ALAN REDFERN & MARTIN HUNTER, LAW AND PRACTICE IN INTERNATIONAL COMMERCIAL ARBITRATION 401 (2d ed. 1991).

A special problem arises where the dissenting arbitrator has in his possession knowledge which, if communicated to the unsuccessful party, could form the basis for challenge of the award, or a basis for resisting an action for enforcement by the winning party. A dissenting arbitrator might know, for instance, that the majority arbitrators had refused to look at, or to give any consideration to, relevant written evidence submitted by the unsuccessful party. Alternatively the dissenting arbitrator might know of some material procedural defect which gave rise to a fundamental unfairness, such as the lack of opportunity for the unsuccessful party to present his case properly. In these circumstances, the effect of a properly formulated dissenting opinion might well be to invite a challenge of the award.

This situation is very different from that of simply letting the parties know why one arbitrator disagreed with the rest. It might be argued that it would be improper (and indeed an abuse of the arbitral process) for a minority arbitrator to formulate a dissenting opinion which would assist the losing party in challenging the award of the majority. However, if an arbitrator knows of some material procedural unfairness, which would otherwise remain hidden from the losing party, it is suggested that he has a duty of conscience to disclose it. If he does not do so, an injustice may take place. To permit injustice does no service to the reputation and stature of arbitration as the primary means of resolving international trade disputes.

## VII.   SUMMARY AND CONCLUSIONS

The themes of this chapter are aptly summarized by Ottoarndt Glossner, for many years the Chairman of the ICC's Commission on International Arbitration, the body responsible for revisions of the ICC Arbitration Rules, as well as Chairman of the International Bar Association Committee which developed the Ethics of International Arbitrators that appears at the outset of this chapter.

Ottoarndt Glossner, *Sociological Aspects of International Commercial Arbitration*, *in* THE ART OF ARBITRATION 143, 144-46 (Jan C. Schultsz & Albert Jan Van Den Berg eds., 1982).

. . . The challenge of an arbitrator is an important correcting institution in favor of the parties. In the case of a conflict of interest, whether existing before or during the arbitration proceedings, an arbitrator can be challenged. That arbitrator who decides before being officially challenged to give up his function deserves credit. Even after a challenge procedure has been started, it is laudable for an arbitrator to withdraw voluntarily from his function, as there are certain ethical standards involved. Thus an arbitrator has to avoid any suspicion of being corrupt. When large amounts are involved, the corruption may lie in the very amount of the arbitrator's fees which because of their magnitude can be corruptive per se. The arbitrator should also avoid that the parties have an influence over him which may give cause, however ill-founded, to believe that he is unduly influenced. This may be true for an employee of one party who acts as arbitrator. It would be inadmissible for an arbitrator during the proceedings to accept a directorship in the company which has appointed him as arbitrator.

Last but not least, the arbitrators' attitude amongst themselves is one of the subtle aspects of arbitration. The arbitrator as a chairman or umpire in proceedings must align himself and the fellow-arbitrators to the common goal, the solution of the subject in litigation. He must overcome differences of many kinds, for example, education, nationality quite apart from the latent inclination of arbitrators toward the party who has nominated them.

Thus, it seems that slowly, but steadily certain rules develop from a given moral background of a general nature which command respect in principle, rules, in themselves perhaps not enforceable, but leading to the good example, from which emerge accepted standards for the quality and qualification as an arbitrator.

# CHAPTER 9

# CONTROL MECHANISMS

## I. INTRODUCTION

### A. FUNCTIONS OF CONTROL

W. MICHAEL REISMAN, SYSTEMS OF CONTROL IN INTERNATIONAL ADJUDICATION AND ARBITRATION 1-10 (1992).

Arbitration is a delegated and restricted power to make certain types of decisions in certain prescribed ways. Any restricted delegation of power must have some system of control. Controls are techniques or mechanisms in engineered artifacts, whether physical or social, whose function is to ensure that an artifact works the way it was designed to work. In social and legal arrangements in which a limited power is delegated, control systems are essential; without them the putative restrictions disappear and the limited power may become absolute. The impulse to establish control systems, one might add, is animated neither by cynicism nor by fear of initiative. It rests on a heathy grasp of reality, indeed, one on which the United States constitutional experiment is based. Nor should controls be conceived in a negative sense. Controls are necessary not only for efficient operation. Effective controls are the only assurance of limited government. In this sense controls are a sine qua non of liberty.

.    .    .

All control systems involve costs. Judicial control systems have costs in terms of the funds needed to establish and maintain them and in terms of the time which must be expended in the successive levels of appeal before a dispute is finally resolved. It is arguable that the more hierarchical layers of protection a bureaucracy has, the more likely it is to get things right. But here, as elsewhere, there is no free lunch. The expenses of establishing and maintaining the vast control superstructure are "passed through" to users, raising the costs of justice, in terms of money and time, and, for some marginal actors, pricing them out of the very system which is supposed to offer them

965

the opportunity to protect their rights. At the same time, other actors, calibrating the rising nuisance value provided by the sequential appeal options, may be encouraged to start dubious actions with the not implausible expectation that settlement, at an early stage, will appear more cost-effective to those they are harassing than a perforce lengthy and expensive vindication of their rights.

Added layers of control also increase time costs: the length of the interval between claim and disposition. The old adage "justice delayed is justice denied" is often true in the sense that a delayed victory may deprive the winner of substantial economic value. The costs generated by control systems are imposed on the parties who must pay, at many levels, to defend their positions and whose treasure may be immobilized pending final decision and on the community which must finance the control system and may, itself, be deprived, pending the final decision, of many of the benefits of the values frozen in dispute.

Considerations such as these generate a tension between two control system policies: justice and finality. The old Roman maxim said *interesse rei publicae ut sit finis litium*, "the public interest requires that there be an end to disputes," which imports a clear cutoff point, an arbitrary "enough-is-enough" point. Abraham Lincoln's statement that "nothing is final until it's right" rejects any arbitrary cutoff point. That statement may have been based as much on political realism as on moral conviction; for, right or wrong, diffused popular indignation can acquire a common vector and become political power. New arrangements to regain social stability may then be required. The interest in finality means that an arbitrary limit for control systems must be established. The interest in justice means simply that justice must be done, no matter what the cost nor how long it takes. Control systems perforce strike compromises between these interests. The compromises themselves will often reflect larger political configurations.

.    .    .

For a new and rapidly growing category of events which we often call, for lack of a better term, "transnational," international commercial arbitration, broadly understood, now performs many of the functions of domestic adjudication. But international arbitration lacks a set of bureaucratic institutions comparable to its domestic

commercial arbitration, broadly understood, now performs many of the functions of domestic adjudication. But international arbitration lacks a set of bureaucratic institutions comparable to its domestic counterparts which might perform its control functions, and the international political environment has not been conducive to their creation. Hence international arbitration has approached the control problem in an entirely different way.

In international law the basic theory of arbitration is simple and rather elegant. Arbitral jurisdiction is entirely consensual. As in Roman law and the systems influenced by it, arbitration is a creature of contract. The arbitrator's powers are derived from the contract. Hence, an arbitrator is not entitled to do anything not authorized by the parties: in its classical formula in the Digest of Justinian, *arbiter nihil extra compromissum facere potest*. An arbitral award rendered within the framework of the common agreement of the parties is itself part of the contract and hence binding on them. But an award which is produced in ways inconsistent with the shared contractual expectations of the parties is something to which they had not agreed. The arbitrator has exceeded his power or committed what French law and international doctrine calls an *excès de pouvoir*. If an allegation of nullity can be sustained, the putative award is null and may be ignored by the "losing" party.

A theory like this is quite advantageous to parties, for it gives them an additional contractual option for resolving disputes without engaging the community's courts. It is also advantageous to the community. Private disputes are essentially diversions from productive activity. An arbitral control mechanism facilitates their economical resolution without more general disruption and without direct cost to the community. The doctrine of *excès de pouvoir* is supposed to function as a control mechanism in this theory. Without it, <u>whatever</u> an arbitrator did, no matter how inconsistent it might have been with his instructions, would have produced a binding award. The arbitrator would become an absolute decision-maker and arbitration would lose its character of restrictive delegation. *Excès de pouvoir* is the conceptual foundation of control for arbitration. It is not, however, without certain problems.

This kind of control mechanism can work well in an organized political-legal system, with a hierarchical control system equipped with an effective compulsory jurisdiction to review allegations of excessive jurisdiction and to decide impartially the alleged nullity of the award. But it is susceptible to abuse in a system, like the international one, in which there is no such permanent and effective and hierarchical structure. In the absence of a reviewing authority, a party alleging that an arbitrator did something not authorized by the agreement to arbitrate is simultaneously prosecutor, judge, and jury *in sua causa*. The potential for abuse is obvious. Ironically, the very theory of nullity which serves, in domestic contexts, to police the arbitrator and thus encourages arbitration tends, in the international setting, to undermine it. But the alternative to the risk of unilateral abuse, no control, is also unacceptable.

As long as arbitration was infrequently used and parties could discount losing beforehand, this system, while hardly optimal, worked. But as modern transnational arbitration increased as a function of the expansion of transnational activity, the inadequacy of this control mechanism in this new context became more apparent. Arbitration was in danger of being undermined.

The apparent solutions were unsatisfactory. Efforts to make awards binding without regard to their possible *excès de pouvoir* — in effect, abandoning all control systems — may well have discouraged resort to arbitration. Legal decision without control runs the danger of reducing predictability, and rational actors are unlikely to submit matters that are important to them to a voluntary dispute system that ranges from uncertain to capricious. Efforts to allow claims of nullity and to try to control them by making them precise have been countered by fears of abuse, for it has been assumed (and not unreasonably) that the more precise the grounds for nullifying, the more claims for nullification there will actually be. A leitmotif of modern international arbitration has been the search for a way of breaking free of the unsatisfactory consequences of each of these alternatives by devising some sort of new institutional device that could provide responsible and predictable control, while minimizing the potential for abuse of claims of nullity.

.    .    .

Contemporary international arbitration must literally adopt or invent its own control system. In doing so it faces a number of intertwined practical and policy problems that are different from domestic adjudication and which tend to make a direct and unqualified co-optation of domestic control institutions counterproductive. A major incentive for international commercial arbitration is its promise of simplicity, economy, supranational neutrality, and speed. The fact that the parties can shape the tribunal and, if they so decide, individually appoint one of the arbitrators with the expectation that he or she will be sympathetic to their view certainly makes arbitration attractive, certainly more attractive than adjudication in an alien national court system. Many would say that properties such as these are arbitration's raison d'être.

But many of these same attractive features militate against an elaborate control mechanism; for, as in domestic practice, such a mechanism would temporarily extend and raise the cost of dispute resolution. The desirable properties of international arbitration also militate against exclusive or heavy reliance on domestic courts as control institutions. Yet, without these familiar control mechanisms, can one rely exclusively on the social controls inherent in face-to-face relationships, small groups, and "old boy networks?" The very scale and wide dispersal of transnational events reduce the efficacy of these social controls. National, legal, and general cultural heterogeneity, the larger number of actors and the increased randomness of arbitrator combinations, all of which are characteristic of contemporary international arbitration, make latent social controls such as peer pressure and common values of personal conscience more ephemeral and marginal and, on the whole, less effective than in more homogeneous national settings.

The diminished effect of all these latent control devices could encourage violations and ultimately undermine resort to international arbitration. The absence of controls would leave the international arbitral system prey to "moral hazard,"[286] unable to correct those potentially serious injustices whose probability of occurrence is increased by the very absence of controls.

In national judicial bureaucracies, key parts of the control system may be lodged in the hierarchical bureaucracies, key parts of the control system may be lodged in the hierarchical network of courts hearing appeals. The fact that the same role may be assigned both

---

[286] Grubel, *Risk, Uncertainty and Moral Hazard*, 38 J. RISK AND INSURANCE 99, 106 (1971).

review and control functions is confusing, but hardly unusual, especially in international law. There, the phenomenon of *dédoublement fonctionnel*, the doubling of functions of particular actors, is the rule rather than the exception. But the consolidation of functions is not without problems.

The conflation of appeal and control should not lead students or actors to assume that the functions are identical. Appeal is a form of control, but it is not identical with it. Appeal, viewed from within the system, is concerned with rectifying any of a broad range of errors in order to put the decision in question in conformity with the key policies of the community. Control is concerned with the very existence of the community, its decision process, and its continuing efficient operation. In most general terms, discharge of the control function requires a broader macro-organizational perspective. Appeal is concerned with what is right for the parties. Control is concerned with the minimum conditions for the continuation of the process of decision itself.

The control and appeal functions may sometimes apply similar criteria and reach identical conclusions. But in many cases, issues of concern on appeal will not be relevant to the control function, in the sense that however the appeal may be decided, none of the concerns of control will be implicated. The point, which is elusive in a national setting because of the location of control functions in part of the judicial bureaucracy, is clearer in international arbitration. The comparatively limited grounds on which an award may be attacked in a review procedure, as opposed to the broader grounds on which an appeal may be lodged, signal different concerns. Indeed, a control system may enforce an award that would (indeed, should) be struck down had it been a judgment on appeal. Such an anomaly is characteristic of arbitral review.

The functional distinctions between and different responsibilities of appeal, review, and control raise acute problems in international commercial arbitration. Where there are widely differentiated institutions, as, for example, in the French municipal legal system, it might be possible to lodge these different functions in separate institutions. But internationally there are relatively few institutions with which to work. Some candidates, such as national courts, would impose costs on the functioning of international commercial arbitration that could price it out of the business.

For all of these reasons, modern international commercial arbitration, in its broad acceptance, continues to experiment with a number of types of unique control systems. Though each was devised at a different moment in the past, in a different institutional context, and with a different *Problematic*, they have interacted and interstimulated, for many of the problems are the same and the experience of one effort has been pertinent and of value to the other. Because most of the control systems are still in operation, they, together, constitute a type of living museum of comparative law and organization, its successes and its pathologies. For different reasons, most of the experiments are in crisis. Some of them are in danger of failing.

*   *   *

### B.    A Note on Taxonomy

Courts, scholars and counsel to litigants often show less precision than they might with respect to the various overlapping, yet distinct, procedures through which judges may exercise control over an arbitration. The materials in this chapter deal principally with control exercised after an award has been rendered, rather than when the arbitration is initiated. On control mechanisms at the earlier stages of the arbitral process, see Chapters 3 and 4. Courts exercise control over an award when asked to take any of four different actions:

(i)    confirm the award by a judgment making it enforceable as such or to validate the award by granting it a recognition order (called *exequatur*, in some Continental legal systems);

(ii)    vacate the award (sometimes called "setting aside," *vacatur* or "annulment"), pronouncing it of no effect either in whole or in part;

(iii)    recognize the award as having a *res judicata* or collateral estoppel effect that precludes inconsistent court decisions between the same parties or on the same issues; and

(iv)    execute the award by attaching assets of the award debtor.

In modern international commercial arbitration, problems can arise from failure to distinguish *vacatur* (whether referred to as such, or called annulment or setting aside) from confirmation. The New York Convention gives a broader effect to *vacatur* of an award at the place where rendered, than to mere lack of judicial confirmation. Prior to adoption of the New York Convention, however, many countries required that a foreign award be confirmed by a foreign court at the place where rendered before it could be enforced in the forum state. One goal of the New York Convention was to do away with this "double *exequatur*" requirement. In place of a requirement of prior foreign homologation of an award, Article V (l) (e) of the New York Convention provides that recognition and enforcement of an award may be refused if the award "has been set aside or suspended by a competent authority of the country in which . . . that award was made." Mere failure to have an award confirmed where rendered is no longer a ground for refusal of recognition of an award under the Convention.

Motions to confirm awards and motions to vacate awards may be, and frequently are, made in the same case. The following two cases address a question of central importance to the arbitral process: what should be the consequence of an arbitrator's alleged failure to respect either (i) public policy or (ii) the law selected by the parties to govern the dispute? The themes evoked by the courts' treatment of the question arise again and again at various stages of the control process.

C.    THE MECHANISMS OF JUDICIAL CONTROL

1.    *Northrop Corp. v. Triad Int'l Marketing, S.A.,* 811 F.2d 1265 (9th Cir. 1987).

JAMES R. BROWNING, Chief Judge:

In October, 1970 Northrop and Triad entered into a "Marketing Agreement," under which Triad became Northrop's exclusive marketing representative to solicit contracts for aircraft and related maintenance, training, and support services for the Saudi Air Force, in return for commissions on sales. Northrop made substantial sales to Saudi Arabia and paid Triad a substantial part of the commissions due under the Marketing Agreement.

On September 17, 1975, the Council of Ministers of Saudi Arabia issued Decree No. 1275, prohibiting the payment of commissions in connection with armaments contracts.[287] Northrop ceased paying commissions to Triad. Triad protested, and demanded payment of the commissions remaining due under the Agreement. The dispute was submitted to arbitration. The arbitrators sustained Triad's claim in part, denied it in part, and entered an award in Triad's favor.

Triad filed an action to confirm the arbitrators' award, and Northrop filed suit to vacate it. The district court vacated the award in some respects. 593 F.Supp. 928, 942 (C.D.Cal.1984). Triad appealed. We reverse.

I

The arbitrators noted that the essence of Northrop's defense was that Saudi Arabia's Decree No. 1275 applied to the Marketing Agreement, and made illegal any commission payment to Triad under the Agreement. "This contention," the arbitrators said, "necessitates a consideration of the meaning and effect of paragraph 13 of the Marketing Agreement." First Arbitrators' Decision at 19.

Paragraph 13 of the Marketing Agreement provided: "[T]he validity and construction of this Agreement shall be governed by the laws of the State of California." It further provided: "Any controversy or claim between the parties hereto arising out of or in connection with this Agreement . . . shall be settled by arbitration," and "[t]he award

---

[287] [1] That Decree provides in relevant part:

*First*: No company under contract with the Saudi Arabian government for the supply of arms or related equipment shall pay any amount as commission to any middleman, sales agent, representative or broker irrespective of their nationality, and whether the contract was concluded directly between the Saudi Arabian government and the company or through another state. Any commission arrangement already concluded by any of these companies with any other party shall be considered void and not binding for the Saudi Arabian government;

*Second*: If any of the foreign companies described in Article I (one) were found to have been under obligation for the payment of commission, payment of such commission shall be suspended after notifying the concerned companies of this decision. Relevant commissions shall be deducted from the total amount of the contract for the account of the Saudi Arabian government.

of a majority of the arbitrators . . . shall be final and binding upon the parties."[288]

The arbitrators noted that Northrop had proposed inclusion of paragraph 13 in the Marketing Agreement to make it

> unnecessary for Northrop to make an in-depth study of the law of countries such as Saudi Arabia, Iran, etc., to know what its rights and obligations would be. Instead of having varying and even inconsistent results under the same contractual provisions as a result of applying different laws, depending on where the marketing was to occur, this clause resulted in uniformity of interpretation and application of the contract. Northrop was familiar with the law of California and knew what to expect from it.

*Id.* at 19-20. Accordingly, the arbitrators interpreted paragraph 13 as requiring that the local law of California determine the effect of Saudi Arabia Decree No. 1275 on Northrop's obligation to pay commissions to Triad pursuant to the Marketing Agreement.[289] Northrop does not disagree with this determination.

---

[288] [3] Paragraph 13 of the Marketing Agreement states in full:

> The validity and construction of this Agreement shall be governed by the laws of the State of California in the United States of America. Triad agrees not to institute any litigation or proceedings against Northrop outside the continental United States. Any controversy or claim between the parties hereto arising out of or in connection with this Agreement which might be the subject of any action at law or suit in equity shall be settled by arbitration in the City of Los Angeles, State of California, in the United States of America, under the rules then obtaining of the American Arbitration Association. The award of a majority of the arbitrators, including the apportionment of the expenses of the arbitration, shall be final and binding upon the parties, and judgment upon the award rendered may be entered in any court having jurisdiction.

[289] [4] The arbitrators noted that if paragraph 13's choice of California law were to be read as including California's conflict-of-law rules, the effect would be to inject "the laws of various other countries into the resolution of these disputes, thereby causing the uncertainty and lack of uniformity which the parties sought to avoid." First Arbitrators' Opinion at 21. *See* Restatement (Second) of Conflict of Laws, §§ 186 comment b, 187(3) & comment h.

Northrop argued the Marketing Agreement was invalid under California Civil Code § 1511. This statute provides "performance of an obligation . . . is excused . . . [w]hen such performance . . . is prevented . . . by the operation of law . . . ." Cal.Civ.Code § 1511(1). Northrop reasoned Saudi Decree No. 1275 rendered the Marketing Agreement unlawful under California Civil Code § 1511 because the Decree "prevented" payment of commissions to Triad and thus "excused" Northrop's performance of its obligations under the Agreement.

The arbitrators pointed out that the decisions interpreting California Civil Code § 1511 principally relied upon by Northrop, including *Baird v. Wendt Enterprises, Inc.*, 248 Cal.App.2d 52, 56 Cal.Rptr. 118 (1967), and *Johnson v. Atkins*, 53 Cal.App.2d 430, 127 P.2d 1027 (1942), did not look to the law of the foreign jurisdiction to determine whether performance of the contract was unlawful, but instead examined the legal action the foreign jurisdiction had taken to determine whether in fact it prevented performance of the contract. In *Baird*, the court concluded that a foreign jurisdiction's adoption of a building code precluding issuance of a permit to construct a building "prevented" performance of the contract within the meaning of section 1511. In *Atkins*, the court held a foreign jurisdiction's cancellation of entry permits for copra "prevented" performance of a contract to sell copra for delivery in the foreign jurisdiction.

The arbitrators concluded there "was no comparable governmental action in this case." The building in *Baird* could not be built without a building permit; the copra in *Atkins* could not be delivered without an entry permit; but in this case despite the issuance of Decree No. 1275, Northrop could still pay Triad the commissions the Marketing Agreement called for, and Triad could still give advice, translate documents, make local arrangements, and perform the other services the Agreement required. Moreover, as Triad points out, before Decree No. 1275 issued, Triad had successfully solicited the sales contracts Northrop sought and thus had already completed performance of its principal obligation under the Marketing Agreement.

Northrop argued that to honor its obligation to Triad, Northrop would be required to violate Decree No. 1275. The arbitrators adopted Judge Hamley's statement for this court in a similar case and responded: "It may be that Boeing has gotten itself into some trouble with the government of Kuwait by setting up and terminating a selling agency in a manner allegedly violative of Kuwait law. But as between Boeing and Alghanim, we think the contract provision must govern." *Alghanim v. Boeing Co.*, 477 F.2d 143, 150 (9th Cir.1973).

## II

The district court reviewed the arbitrators' decision *de novo*, rather than under a deferential standard, on the ground that the question presented was whether the Agreement was "contrary to law and public policy," 593 F.Supp. at 936. We consider later whether the arbitrators' interpretation and application of the Agreement is unenforceable because it is contrary to public policy. As the district court correctly stated, this was a question for the court alone to decide. *W.R. Grace & Co. v. Local 759, Int'l Union of United Rubber Workers*, 461 U.S. 757, 766 . . . .

The question the arbitrators decided, however, was one of contract interpretation. That issue was the proper interpretation of the requirement of paragraph 13 of the Marketing Agreement that claims arising in connection with the Agreement be settled by arbitration and that California law be applied in resolving them. More specifically, the question was whether paragraph 13 required the arbitrators to apply California Civil Code § 1511 to determine the effect of Saudi Arabia Decree No. 1275 on the obligations of the parties under the Agreement, and, if so, what that determination should be. This issue arose from the very terms of the Marketing Agreement. Its resolution was an inescapable part of the arbitrators' task of interpreting and applying the Agreement and resolving the dispute between these parties. Courts are bound to enforce an award based upon the arbitrators' resolution of such an issue "even in the face of 'erroneous findings of fact or misinterpretations of law.'" *French v. Merrill Lynch, Pierce, Fenner & Smith*, 784 F.2d 902, 906 (9th Cir.1986) (quoting *American Postal Workers*, 682 F.2d at 1285).

. . .

The arbitrators' conclusions on legal issues are entitled to deference here. The legal issues were fully briefed and argued to the arbitrators; the arbitrators carefully considered and decided them in a lengthy written opinion. To now subject these decisions to *de novo* review would destroy the finality for which the parties contracted and render the exhaustive arbitration process merely a prelude to the judicial litigation which the parties sought to avoid.[290]

## III

In stating the rule of deferential review afforded arbitration awards, the Supreme Court also noted a limitation: "the interpretations of the law by the arbitrators *in contrast to manifest disregard* are not subject, in the federal courts, to judicial review for error in interpretation." *Wilko v. Swan*, 346 U.S. 427, 436-37 (1953) (emphasis added). Although the "manifest disregard of law" standard is not easily defined, *see San Martine Compania de Navegacion, S.A. v. Saguenay Terminals Ltd.*, 293 F.2d 796, 801 n. 4 (9th Cir.1961), it is clear it has not been met in this case.

By the very terms of the rule of deferential review, mere error in interpretation of California law would not be enough to justify refusal to enforce the arbitrators' decision. Moreover, it is far from evident that the arbitrators misread California law at all. No California case clearly contrary to the arbitrators' interpretation has been called to our attention. It was not unreasonable for the arbitrators to distinguish the cases upon which Northrop relied on the ground stated by the arbitrators.[291] The district court's analogy to *Industrial Development & Land Co. v. Goldschmidt*, 56 Cal.App. 507, 206 P. 134 (1922), was misplaced; in that case the law claimed to make performance illegal was not foreign law but the eighteenth amendment,

---

[290] [6] Courts asked to enforce arbitrators' agreements have reviewed some legal issues *de novo*. *See, e.g., American Postal Workers v. United States Postal Serv.*, 682 F.2d at 1285; *Broadway Cab Coop. v. Teamsters 7 Chauffeur Local*, 710 F.2d 1379, 1383 (9th Cir.1983). Questions falling in this category are not clearly defined. What is clear is that legal questions resolved in an award that "draws its essence from the collective bargaining agreement," as did the award in this case, are for the arbitrators to decide and those decisions are entitled to deferential review. *United Steelworkers v. Enterprise Wheel & Car Corp.*, 363 U.S. 593, 597, 80 S.Ct. 1358, 1361, 4 L.Ed.2d 1424 (1960).

[291] [7] The interpretation of Section 1511 the arbitrators adopted appears to be consistent with the general rule. "Impossibility based on foreign law does not fall within the same class as that occasioned by domestic law, and it has generally been held no excuse for breach of contract." W. Jaeger, 18 Williston on Contracts § 1938 at 42-43 (3d ed. 1978). Such impossibility is not treated as impossibility of law, but as impossibility "of fact." *Id.* at 43.

which was as controlling in California as if it had been a California statute or constitutional provision.

The district court examined the language and history of Saudi Arabia Decree No. 1275 in some detail and concluded that it prohibited the payment of the commissions involved in this case. 593 F.Supp. at 938. But as we have said, the question was whether payment was prohibited under California law, not Saudi law, and the answer to that question turned not upon whether Decree No. 1275 stated a rule of Saudi law under which the payment would be illegal, but rather upon whether the existence of such a rule in Saudi law excused performance under California Civil Code § 1511.

Northrop also argues that if the Saudi Decree did not excuse performance of the Marketing Agreement under California Civil Code § 1511, the choice-of-law clause in the Agreement should be set aside and the Saudi Decree should be applied directly to invalidate the Marketing Agreement under the principle announced in Restatement (Second) of Conflicts § 187(2)(b) (1971).[292] However, choice-of-law and choice-of-forum provisions in international commercial contracts are "an almost indispensable precondition to achievement of the orderliness and predictability essential to any international business transaction," and should be enforced absent strong reasons to set them aside. *Scherk v. Alberto-Culver Co.*, 417 U.S. 506, 516-20, 94 S.Ct. 2449, 2455-57, 41 L.Ed.2d 270 (1974); *The Bremen v. Zapata Off-Shore Co.*, 407 U.S. 1, 92 S.Ct. 1907, 32 L.Ed. 513 (1972). We agree with the arbitrators that the general principle of conflicts Northrop cites is not sufficient standing alone to overcome the strong policy consideration announced in *Scherk* and *Bremen*.

---

[292] [8] The Restatement provides:

§ 187.  Law of the State Chosen by the Parties

(2)  The law of the state chosen by the parties to govern their contractual rights and duties will be applied . . . unless . . .
(b)  application of the law of the chosen state would be contrary to a fundamental policy of a state which has a materially greater interest than the chosen state in the determination of the particular issue . . . .

## IV

Northrop argues the courts should not enforce the Marketing Agreement because to do so would be contrary to public policy. As noted earlier, this is a question for the courts alone to decide. *W.R. Grace*, 461 U.S. at 766, 103 S.Ct. at 2183.

Northrop contends the central question upon which this appeal turns is one of public policy. Northrop argues "that California law, as a matter of public policy, prohibits enforcement of a contract where performance of the contract would be illegal under the law of a foreign state. This rule is codified in California Civil Code § 1511. . . ." Appellee's Brief at 29.

Section 1511 appears in California's codification of the law of contracts, under the heading "Extinction of Obligations." Cal.Civ.Code § 1511 (West 1982). We do not regard section 1511 as a declaration that it is the public policy of the state of California that contracts unenforceable under the laws of any other jurisdiction shall not be enforced in California. Section 1511 is a codification of a rule of purely private law embodying a common-law defense in an action between contracting parties for breach. If the statutory codification of such rules of contract law were regarded as converting them into principles of public policy cognizable only in courts, the capacity of arbitrators to resolve contract disputes would be seriously diminished.

Northrop's argument that the courts should decline to enforce the Marketing Agreement because it conflicts with the public policy Saudi Arabia announced in Decree No. 1275 flies in the face of the parties' agreement that the law of California, and not Saudi Arabia, would determine the validity and construction of the contract. Northrop has cited no California regulation, statute, or court decision demonstrating that enforcement of a contract to pay commissions to a marketing representative is contrary to the public policy of California, whether such commissions are illegal under the law of a foreign state or are not.

Northrop's most substantial argument is that the public policy reflected in Decree No. 1275 was also the policy of the United States Department of Defense. In its opinion the district court said "it is clear [the Department of Defense] wished to conform its policy precisely to that announced by Saudi Arabia." The court concluded that the

Department's "enforcement of Saudi policy was coercive rather than voluntary, and is properly characterized as U.S. public policy." 593 F.Supp. at 936 n. 13.

To justify refusal to enforce an arbitration award on grounds of public policy, the policy "must be well defined and dominant." *W.R. Grace*, 461 U.S. at 766, 103 S.Ct. at 2183. The Saudi Arabian policy the Department of Defense arguably adopted was neither. It is clear the Department wished to accommodate Saudi Arabian interests and sensibilities. It is also clear, however, that the Department was interested in encouraging sales to Saudi Arabia of American manufactured military equipment, and considered the efforts of Triad critical to that end. It is not clear from the evidence before the arbitrators and the district court what policy the Department of Defense adopted in pursuit of these sometimes inconsistent goals.

Northrop calls attention to evidence indicating Saudi Arabia and the Department of Defense adopted a policy of prohibiting payment of commissions whether or not ultimately charged to the Saudi Arabian government. Triad argues from evidence indicating both Decree No. 1275 and Department of Defense policy were aimed at prohibiting commissions that added to the cost of Saudi procurement, and that in any event the Department of Defense was unable to determine the Decree's exact application, even assuming the Department wished to mirror its policy. The district court resolved the conflict in Northrop's favor, 593 F.Supp. at 936 n. 13, 937-38, but even if we were to agree, we could not say on this record the policy the Department adopted was "well defined and dominant." The district court's refusal to enforce the arbitrators' decision on the ground that it conflicted with the policy of the Department of Defense was, therefore, unwarranted.

2.       Rosemary S. Page, *Res Judicata, Collateral Estoppel, Arbitration Awards*,[293] in AAA ANNUAL REPORT: ARBITRATION AND THE LAW 39 (1987-88).

Recently, three courts in New York examined the doctrines of res judicata and collateral estoppel as applied to arbitration awards.

The Latin phrase res judicata means simply "a matter adjudged." The doctrine of res judicata bars the readjudication of a matter that has been decided. This doctrine, derived from English common law, was developed because it was "expedient and because there should be an end to litigation." Even in England, the doctrine of res judicata applied to arbitration awards as well as to court decrees.

Collateral estoppel, an outgrowth of the res judicata concept, is the conclusiveness of a determination in a prior proceeding where the subsequent proceeding is upon a different cause of action.

In the United States, both federal and state law acknowledge the preclusive effect of decisions rendered by an arbitrator. For example, "arbitration and award" may be pleaded as an affirmative defense under New York procedure and under the Federal Rules of Civil Procedure.

.     .     .

*Gemco Latinoamerica, Inc. v. Seiko Time Corp.*[294] . . . Gemco presents a classic example of how the doctrine of res judicata not only bars a second suit involving the same parties based upon the same cause of action but even "precludes the parties or their privies from relitigating issues that were or could have been raised in the prior proceeding.

---

[293] ROSEMARY S. PAGE, RES JUDICATA, COLLATERAL ESTOPPEL, ARBITRATION AWARDS (1988). The New York Law Publishing Co. Reprinted with the permission of the New York Law Journal.

[294] [6] *Gemco Latinoamerica, Inc. v. Seiko Time Corp.*, 671 F.Supp. 972 (S.D.N.Y.1987).

In *Gemco*, a watch and clock distributor sued its supplier, with whom it had a distributorship agreement, and also sued the parent and grandparent of the supplier with whom the distributor had no contract. Among the distributor's claims against all three defendants were allegations of breach of contract, unfair competition, and other violations of Puerto Rico's Law 75 and federal statutes.

The distributorship agreement between the distributor and the supplier contained an arbitration clause. Previously the distributor had arbitrated with the supplier the same issues which the distributor now raised in litigation. The distributor who had been the respondent in that arbitration had lost, on the merits, all of its counterclaims raised against the supplier. The award was confirmed and judgment was entered upon it with no opposition from the distributor. Neither the parent nor the grandparent of the supplier had been parties to this arbitration since the distributor's motion for a court order to compel the parent and grandparent to join in the arbitration as alter egos to the supplier had been denied by the court.

The *Gemco* court found that the distributor's claims against the supplier for breach of contract, breach of duty to deal in good faith, and violation of Puerto Rico's Law 75 were clearly barred by the arbitration award. These claims, which the distributor had raised as counterclaims in the arbitration, had been dismissed by the arbitrators on the merits.

While the supplier defended, in the litigation, on the grounds of res judicata, the parent and the grandparent relied on collateral estoppel to block these same claims against themselves. First, the court dismissed the breach of contract claims against the parent and the grandparent for failure to state a cause of action. Next, the *Gemco* court noted that the parent and the grandparent were not parties to the arbitration so the award was not res judicata as to any claims against them. The parent and the grandparent urged the court to dismiss the remaining claims against them under the doctrine of collateral estoppel, however, theorizing that defensive use of collateral estoppel prevents a plaintiff from asserting against a second defendant a claim that the plaintiff has previously litigated and lost against another.

The *Gemco* court found that the criteria in New York for the invocation of collateral estoppel are

(1) the factual and legal issues in question were necessarily raised and decided in the prior action; (2) such issues are identical to those concerned in the present action; and (3) the party against whom the doctrine is asserted had a full and fair opportunity to litigate the prior proceeding.

The distributor's claim in the arbitration did include allegations concerning the conduct of the parent and the grandparent acting in concert with the supplier. However, the *Gemco* court denied the motion of the parent and the grandparent to apply the collateral estoppel doctrine, saying that the violation of law claims against them were not necessarily resolved unfavorably to the distributor in the arbitration. "[T]he wholly separate question of whether the other defendants took independent action which may have violated Law 75 could not have been addressed by the arbitrators, who were in no way concerned with the possible liability of parties who were not before them . . . ."

### Notes and Questions

1. In *Northrop v. Triad* the court cites precedent in footnote 6 relating to awards rendered in labor arbitration. The issue is the appropriateness of *de novo* review of the arbitral tribunal's decision. To what extent, if at all, should labor arbitration be relevant to such a question in commercial arbitration? What do you make of the language in Section 1 of the Federal Arbitration Act providing that the Act does not apply to "contracts of employment?" Is a collective bargaining agreement a "contract of employment?"

2. If decisions related to labor arbitration are not precedent in commercial arbitration, should they be considered as persuasive by analogy, to guide judges dealing with similar issues that arise in commercial dispute resolution? And vice versa? Are the statutory and policy underpinnings of labor arbitration and of commercial arbitrationcomparable? Discuss.

3. In *Northrop*, the Court holds that it should not examine whether the arbitrators correctly applied California law. But does it, in fact, do so? Assuming that the correct law was applied but incorrectly, would enforcement of the ensuing award be consistent with public policy? With constitutional requirements?

4. Compare *Brandeis Intsel Ltd. v. Calabrian Chemicals Corp.*, 656 F.Supp. 160 (S.D.N.Y. 1987). In *Brandeis* the Court refuses to read into the New York Convention "manifest disregard of the law" (a judicially-created ground for vacatur of awards rendered in the U.S.) as a defense to enforcement of an award. One part of its reasoning was that a U.S. judge would have difficulty when foreign law was concerned. How significant is this "difficulty-factor" as the basis for the decision?

II. INTERNAL INSTITUTIONAL REVIEW

Even before national judges are asked to look at an arbitrator's work, there may have been a supervisory or control function exercised at the level of the institution whose rules govern the arbitral process.

A. THE INTERNATIONAL CHAMBER OF COMMERCE

The ICC Arbitration Rules provide for scrutiny of the form of an award by the ICC Court of Arbitration. The "Court" of the ICC, of course, does not actually decide the merits of the dispute, but merely exercises a limited supervisory role over the work of the arbitrators, who are selected on a case by case basis. *See generally* W. LAURENCE CRAIG, ET AL., INTERNATIONAL CHAMBER OF COMMERCE ARBITRATION, (2d ed. 1990), at section 2.03.

1. INTERNATIONAL CHAMBER OF COMMERCE, RULES OF ARBITRATION, ARTICLE 21.

*Article 21 Scrutiny of award by the Court*

Before signing an award, whether partial or definitive, the arbitrator shall submit it in draft form to the Court. The Court may lay down modifications as to the form of the award and, without affecting the arbitrator's liberty of decision, may also draw his attention to points of substance. No award shall be signed until it has been approved by the Court as to its form.

2. INTERNAL RULES OF THE ICC COURT OF ARBITRATION, RULE 17.

Arbitral Awards: Form

When it scrutinizes draft arbitral awards in accordance with Article 21 of the ICC Rules of Arbitration, the Court of Arbitration pays particular attention to the respect of the formal requirements laid down by the law applicable to the proceedings and, where relevant, by the mandatory rules of the place of arbitration, notably with regard to the reasons for awards, their signature and the admissibility of dissenting opinions.

B.      ICSID AND INTERNATIONAL INSTITUTIONAL REVIEW

1.      W. MICHAEL REISMAN, SYSTEMS OF CONTROL IN INTERNATIONAL ADJUDICATION AND ARBITRATION 50 (1992).

In designing their control system, the drafters of the ICSID Convention drew upon the experience of both the League and the United Nations International Law Commission. But they modified it in one critical way. Rather than incorporating the International Court of Justice, as had the abortive proposals of Rundstein and then Scelle, the new convention created its own internal, international review instance.

ICSID Convention Article 52(1) broke no new ground in setting out the grounds for annulment of an ICSID award. It stated:

Either party may request annulment of the award by an application in writing addressed to the Secretary-General on one or more of the following grounds:

(a) that the Tribunal was not properly constituted;

(b) that the Tribunal has manifestly exceeded its powers;

(c) that there was corruption on the part of a member of the Tribunal;

(d) that there has been a serious departure from a fundamental rule of procedure; or

(e) that the award has failed to state the reasons on which it is based.

Article 52 thus authorizes either party to request by application to the secretary-general of the Arbitration Centre annulment of an award rendered by an ICSID tribunal for a limited number of specified reasons, comprised of the familiar terms of art of arbitral utility (as quoted above). The application for annulment had to be made within 120 days of the date on which the award was rendered.

The innovation in ICSID was the control entity to which claims for nullification were to be submitted. Once the request has been lodged, the chairman of the ICSID Administrative Council (ex officio the president of the World Bank) appoints an ad hoc committee of three persons from a panel of names proposed by states' members and kept by the secretary-general, none of whom may have the nationality of the state-party or the foreign investor. Name notwithstanding, the committee is, in effect, another tribunal, following the same procedures prescribed in the convention for the original tribunal, though its mandate is more circumscribed than the tribunal whose award it is reviewing. In the course of its proceedings, the committee may stay enforcement of the award. If it finds that there has been a violation of one or more of the standards, the ad hoc committee is authorized to annul the award in whole or in part. If the award is nullified by the committee, either party may submit the dispute to a new tribunal, constituted in accordance with the convention.

### 2. *Klöckner Industrie Anlagen GmbH v. United Republic of Cameroon*

[Summary of the Phases of the Case from W. MICHAEL REISMAN, SYSTEMS OF CONTROL IN INTERNATIONAL ADJUDICATION AND ARBITRATION 51-65 (1992).]

The essential relationships between the parties in this case were concisely described by the tribunal in the first phase of the case:

> This was a joint venture between Kloeckner, a multinational European Corporation, and a developing country. The plant to be built was an example of imported modern technology and engineering. Cameroon had no experience in manufacturing fertilizer products. The factory was to be acquired with the Government's guarantee of payment; its output being of major importance for the country's agriculture, and agriculture being in turn the very foundation of Cameroon's economic ambitions. Cameroon counted on Kloeckner to supply all that was necessary to ensure the success of the project. Kloeckner had carried out the initial feasibility study. It had designed the plant and carried out the technical studies. Kloeckner had undertaken to organize the long-term financing, over ten years, of the project. It built or bought from others all the machinery and all the material. It coordinated the work of suppliers

and sub-contractors. It was to execute, operate, and manage the project, procure necessary raw materials, and organize the marketing of output. By accepting — and indeed seeking out — these responsibilities, Kloeckner had taken on a serious obligation. Kloeckner claimed to be capable of supplying all the know-how, all the material, and all the management skills necessary to ensure the project's success, the Government's only role being to supply a site and to guarantee payment of the contract price.

These relationships were concretized in a network of agreements. In 1971 Klöckner, the West German multinational, and the West African government of Cameroon, had concluded a so-called "Basic Agreement," which created a type of joint venture in the form of a Cameroonian company, SOCAME, which was to construct and manage a fertilizer plant. Klöckner, owning 51 percent of SOCAME, would control it; the government was to hold the remaining 49 percent. The Basic Agreement assigned to Klöckner the responsibility "for the technical and commercial management of the Company (SOCAME) under a management contract for at least five years, beginning with the start-up of operations." The agreement also contained an arbitration clause, referring disputes to ICSID.

Three months later, Klöckner and Cameroon concluded another agreement, this one a turnkey contract for the factory to be built or supplied by Klöckner; in the subsequent disputes, this was referred to as the "Supply Contract." SOCAME would pay Klöckner for the factory, but the government of Cameroon guaranteed SOCAME's payments. This turnkey or supply contract also contained an ICSID arbitration clause.

In 1973 the Cameroon government and SOCAME, now in operation and controlled by Klöckner, concluded another agreement, the so-called "Convention," defining additional rights and obligations of the parties and referring to all the previous agreements. The convention also contained an ICSID clause. In 1977 Klöckner and SOCAME, which Klöckner still controlled, concluded a management contract. This new contract referred to the previous contracts in which the fundamentals of the management agreement had been set out and further elaborated those management responsibilities.

While each of the other contractual documents chose ICSID arbitration, the management contract contained an arbitration clause referring disputes to the International Chamber of Commerce. Now this was rather unusual, but one can imagine complex transactions in which there might be cogent reasons for using several different dispute resolving institutions. In agreeing to build and manage a port for a government, the prime contractor might wish an ICSID clause in agreements with the government, except for jurisdiction over maritime collision disputes that could be assigned to a tribunal specialized over maritime matters. Contracts with foreign subcontractors might include an ICC clause. Contracts with local subcontractors might refer to the local arbitration system. But the rich variety of contractual partners in this hypothetical was hardly matched in the Klöckner-Cameroon relationship. In fact, this curious and belated reassignment of part of the dispute-resolving competence of this particular integrated operation to a different arbitration system may not have been an act of caprice or an accident, as we will see in a moment. Certainly, by the time the management contract was concluded, arbitration was no longer a remote contingent possibility. Klöckner had known for some time that there were serious difficulties with the project, that some facts on which original projections of profitability had been based had changed drastically and that, in fact, the factory could not be profitable. (In the arbitration, Cameroon presented evidence, which apparently persuaded the tribunal, that throughout its life, the factory barely attained 30 percent of its promised capacity.) Klöckner did not share this new information with the Cameroonian government.

After the factory started up, output fell far below original projections. In 1978 the Cameroonian government sought the views of an outside consultant, who recommended that the factory be redesigned in order to modify its processes. Money, of course, would be required. Cameroon invited Klöckner to participate, but Klöckner refused to make any additional capital contributions to SOCAME and instead yielded its majority shareholding.

Even after the supplementary investment and redesign, the factory proved unworkable and SOCAME refused to pay Klöckner for it. Klöckner then initiated ICSID arbitration against the government of Cameroon for payments it had guaranteed. Because the various arbitration clauses now referred different parts of the transaction to two different arbitral systems — ICSID and ICC — Klöckner confined its claim to a demand for the guaranteed payment for the turnkey delivery of a factory (the supply contract), a matter subject to ICSID jurisdiction, while contending that any counterclaims based on allegations about violation of its management obligations that Cameroon might want to raise had been assigned by the parties to another arbitral system (ICC) and, hence, could not be heard in ICSID. With regard to the factory's performance, Klöckner insisted that it had no obligations with regard to its workability. Cameroon counterclaimed for violations of obligations under the various agreements. It insisted that it was entitled to a factory that worked and not just a factory. Its counterclaims also raised matters concerning management of the enterprise. Klöckner insisted that these matters had been assigned to the International Chamber of Commerce in Paris and not to ICSID in Washington.

Klöckner's demurrer to these counterclaims was one of the most interesting aspects of the case. The final management contract, which spelled out the details of the management relationship that had been expressed more generally in some of the previous instruments, incorporated, as mentioned earlier, an ICC rather than ICSID arbitration clause. Klöckner, as the then majority owner and effective manager of SOCAME, was, in one sense, concluding an agreement with itself. Why did it elect ICC arbitration? Conceivably, it may have thought that ICSID was inappropriate, for SOCAME was not the host state. But, then, other agreements with SOCAME had incorporated ICSID clauses. It is also possible that this was the result of carelessness or error. But if the factual account in the first award is accepted, Klöckner may have realized, as early as 1973, that the original projections of profitability which it had prepared for the Cameroonian government, and were apparently the basis for the decision about the transaction, were obsolete. Even with additional funds, it was not at all certain that the planned enterprise could turn a profit. Klöckner, at this time in control of SOCAME, did not share this information with the government. In a sense, the success or failure of the factory may not have been of central urgency to Klöckner, for its payments were guaranteed by the government of Cameroon and backed up, as it were, by an ICSID clause.

It is possible — this is pure speculation — that Klöckner, in 1977, still in charge of SOCAME, inserted the ICC clause in the management contract as a worst-case contingency. It may have hoped that if Cameroon concluded that it had been treated unfairly and refused to pay its guarantee and Klöckner initiated arbitration under the

ICSID clause, the only issue over which ICSID would have jurisdiction, if the strategy worked, was the question of whether or not a factory was built and delivered. All of the questions about Klöckner's management behavior and, in particular, whether it concealed vital information which might have permitted Cameroon to reduce its exposure or even to cut its losses terminally by aborting the project earlier, would not be subject to ICSID jurisdiction, if, according to this gambit, they had been assigned to the ICC. A favorable jurisdictional decision that the issue properly before an ICSID tribunal was the factory and not the quality of its management would have been virtually outcome-determinative.

If this was Klöckner's strategy, it was confounded by the ICSID tribunal, which concluded, over the strong dissent of Klöckner's party-appointed arbitrator, that the tribunal had jurisdiction over management issues by virtue of the Basic Agreement. Klöckner's second line of defense to Cameroon's complaints about the quality of the factory was that its only obligation was to supply a factory. It had no obligation to supply a factory that worked.

In turning to this latter question, the tribunal held that Cameroonian law applied. Because Cameroon had been divided, during the colonial period, between Britain and France and had inherited systems of British common law and French civil law which continued to operate in its two component regions, the tribunal applied Cameroonian conflicts of law and concluded that French civil law, as incorporated in Cameroonian law, applied.

This law, the tribunal held, included the obligation of a party to disclose to the other party material information of interest to it.

> We take for granted that the principle according to which a person who engages in close contractual relations, based on confidence, must deal with its partner in a frank, loyal and candid manner, is a basic principle of French civil law, as is indeed the case under the other national codes which we know of. This is the criterion that applies to relations between partners in simple forms of association anywhere. The rule is particularly appropriate in more complex international ventures, such as the present one.

Within that normative framework, the tribunal concluded:

> In the present case, as we have suggested, we do not feel that Kloeckner had dealt frankly with Cameroon. At critical stages of the project, Kloeckner hid from its partner, information of vital importance. On several occasions, it failed to disclose facts which, if they had been known to the government, could have caused it to put an end to the venture and cancel the contract before the expenditure of the funds whose payment Kloeckner now seeks to obtain by means of an award. When a partner in a financially complex international venture learns of certain facts which could influence the attitudes and the actions of the other partner with respect to the project; when the first partner fails to disclose this information to the other; and the second thereupon continues with the project and incurs additional costs, the first partner has not acted frankly and loyally vis-a-vis his partner, and he cannot rightly present a claim to funds whose expenditure would perhaps never have been necessary if he had been frank and candid in his dealings. In a very significant sense, the fault is his. The fact that the funds were spent becomes his responsibility and not that of his partner. In this respect, we decide that Kloeckner violated its fundamental contractual obligations and may not insist upon payment of the entire price of the Turnkey Contract.

Cameroon argued that Klöckner's failure to perform had relieved Cameroon of its own obligation to pay Klöckner. It invoked the French contracts law principle of *exceptio non adimpleti contractus*, which permits one party to a contract to refrain unilaterally and lawfully from performing its obligations under the contract when faced with material nonperformance by the other party. Klöckner, according to the majority of the tribunal, had failed to perform in a way which justified the application by Cameroon of the *exceptio*.

The issue of adequacy of performance turned on whether the obligation was to supply a factory that worked or simply to supply a factory, without regard to whether it was operable. Klöckner argued that it fulfilled its requirements under the contract by supplying a factory. The tribunal held:

In order to perform the relevant contracts correctly, it was not sufficient to supply a fertilizer factory; the factory had to have the required capacity and had to be managed in the manner necessary to obtain the proposed goals. . . . Kloeckner had undertaken to ensure continuous functioning and maintenance of the factory (technical management) as well as to perform its commercial management. . . . The most conclusive proof of Kloeckner's failure to perform its duty of technical and commercial management results simply from the shutdown of the factory in December 1977, by decision of Kloeckner personnel sent to Cameroon, after 18 months of underproduction and operating losses.

Accordingly, the tribunal decided by majority to reject Klöckner's claim as well as Cameroon's counterclaim. In effect, the award was a victory for Cameroon.

Klöckner's party-appointed arbitrator, Professor Dominique Schmidt, appended an unusual fifty-three-page dissenting opinion. Ordinarily, dissenting opinions express a different legal view, leading to a different outcome but acknowledge the authority of the award. Professor Schmidt did not dissent in this sense. He stated that the award was null, because of, in the words of its author, "important mistakes, the numerous contradictions and failures to state the grounds, and the misrepresentation of contractual clauses."

Klöckner promptly applied to the secretary-general of ICSID for nullification of the award under Article 52 of the ICSID Convention, essentially on the grounds spelled out in Professor Schmidt's dissent. The chairman of ICSID's Administrative Council (who is, by virtue of Article 5 of the convention, the president of the World Bank) appointed a three-person ad hoc committee composed of distinguished professors and eminent arbitrators from Switzerland, Austria, and Egypt.

The ad hoc committee's decision was extremely long (176 typed pages) elaborate, and careful. In places it is stunning and brilliant, but it is also marked by a tendency toward hairsplitting, or "legal purity," as the committee put it, without, it would appear, any intended irony. It justified its purist approach on theoretical grounds. There are good arguments to be made for strict application of a review procedure. But, as is often the case, any legal approach which resolutely tries to avoid reality runs the danger of colliding head-on with it.

As the first ad hoc committee operating under the convention, its members were manifestly sensitive to the fact that their decision would profoundly shape expectations about control systems of arbitration, in general, and ICSID review, in particular. On its own motion, the committee purported to issue an authoritative interpretation of the control procedure of ICSID. It took up this burden, it said, in view of the fact that this was "the first Application for Annulment ever lodged against an ICSID award" and in view of the "interest to the parties and to the new Tribunal that may be constituted under Article 52(6)."

The committee's appreciation of its longer-term mission was not modest. Even after nullifying the award, it appended a long obiter dictum, comprising almost two-thirds of its decision. The purpose of the excursus was explained in a grandiloquent style, by now familiar to readers of this unusual document. "While it is superfluous here to return to each criticism of the Award, it is incumbent upon the Committee, in the interest of the Tribunal itself and in the higher interest of the arbitration system set up by the Washington Convention, not to leave any of the claimant's essential complaints unanswered." The fact that a matter had nothing to do with its mandate under the convention was apparently no reason to refrain from commenting on it. Even matters such as "particularities of structure and presentation of the Award" were favored with gratuitous evaluations. Nor was it only the award that was graded by the committee. The states-parties to the ICSID Convention themselves were graciously advised about how they might go about revising the rules.

## Constitutive Rulings

At the most basic level, the committee made what amount to four constitutive rulings about ICSID review. These rulings, which would have a decisive effect on the disposition of the Klöckner case, were also designed to shape all future procedures under Article 52. Let us consider them briefly.

*A presumption in favor of the validity of the award under review*. The committee posited a presumption in favor of the validity of the award under question. In cases in which doubts were raised, "analysis should be resolved *in favorem validitatis sententiae.*" This particular holding, to which the committee returned on a number of occasions in its decision, appears to be mandated by the structure of ICSID review. The alternative, that the award does not enjoy such a presumption, would, in effect, transform the procedure under Article 52 into a de novo arbitration. If the award did not enjoy a presumption of validity and the burden of proof was not on the challenging party, the procedure would be rearbitration.

*Hair trigger: the automatic technical discrepancy standard.* The second constitutive holding was that review was to be technical and mechanical; the ad hoc committee was to have no prudential competence. In keeping with that conception, the committee posited an automatic requirement of nullification if a defect were established. The gravity or significance of a particular defect was not to be taken into account. In effect, this requirement made Article 52 into a hair trigger, a mechanism of extraordinary sensitivity that would set off nullification at the slightest provocation, without regard to the magnitude of the defect established.

In terms of legal theory, the committee had elected, in effect, to adopt a "rule" rather than a "standard" approach. Where a large number of similar cases come to a decision-maker and the value of any case is substantially less than the transaction costs involved in deciding it, considerations of economy may dictate that each case be decided by a "binary" rule in which many variables are fixed a priori and only two choice options, on the order of "a" or "not-a," are allowed the decision-maker. A rule approach is effected by evidentiary limitations on everything except what is needed to establish the relevance of the binary rule to the case at hand. All other evidence is simply inadmissible. A rule approach may also be dictated by intense policy demands. Some defects, for example corruption of a chairman, may be deemed per se to require nullification even if the consequences are minimal.

The "rule" approach may be contrasted with a "standard" approach, in which each case is examined in terms of its special facts and related to and decided in accord with the full array of community policies. A much wider array of evidence is perforce admissible in a standard approach. In many contexts the preferability of a "rule" over a "standard" approach is arguable. But the principle of economy, the proliferation of similar cases, and the need for economy on which the rule approach is based can hardly apply to the limited number of cases with widely varying and complex fact-patterns that come to ICSID tribunals.

Choosing whether to use a rule or standard approach is a constitutive decision. Like all such decisions, one would expect a canvassing of the aggregate consequences of the alternatives in terms of the fundamental goals and objectives of arbitral review in the ICSID system. But the Klöckner committee's constitutive decision was not based on this sort of exercise nor was it inferred from jurisprudence nor tested by reference to past practice. It was derived essentially from textual interpretation which the committee derived from the convention. Article 52(3) of the ICSID Convention states that "the Committee shall have the authority to annul the award." From this the committee concluded that if it found a defect, it was obliged to nullify the award.

This is a doubtful interpretation. It would appear from the language of that provision, in the context of the convention as a whole, that its purpose was not to install a rule of compulsory nullification but simply to confirm *who* nullifies. Article 52(3) establishes that the committee *does not* report back to the secretary-general with a recommendation or opinion, for the provision does not assume that the actual competence to annul is located in the permanent administrative apparatus of ICSID. Rather, it is the committee which makes the decision on annulment.

Such an interpretation would have allowed a committee some discretion as to whether or to what extent to nullify. The Klöckner committee construed the provision as an injunction to it to annul an award even if there were no injury to the other party or no substantial cause for grievance.

*The expansion of grounds for annulment.* In a third constitutive ruling, the committee rejected the notion that its role and competence were limited to testing the award only in terms of the grounds listed in Article 52. Article 52, it will be recalled, does not simply say that *any* departure from any of the prescriptions of the convention warrants annulment. Instead, it lists specific grounds, some of which differ in language and scope, from coordinate sections of the convention. For example, a party may request annulment under Article 52(1)(e) on the ground that "the award has failed to state the reasons on which it is based." Article 48, which is comprised of a series of instructions to the tribunal seised of the case, states in subparagraph 3 that "[t]he award shall deal with every question submitted to the Tribunal, and shall state the reasons upon which it is based." Article 52(1)(e) is plainly narrower than Article 48(3). *Stricto sensu*, nullification would be inappropriate under Article 52(1)(e) if the reasons for the award reached were stated, but the award did not deal with every question submitted to the tribunal nor did it set out the reasons for the particular disposition of each question.

The committee decided to ignore the clear differences between the language of Article 52(1) and other sections of the convention and, instead, chose to coordinate sections of the convention with Article 52(1) by reading that provision as a type of *renvoi* to the rest of the convention. In effect, the committee interpreted the convention as authorizing and requiring it to examine a challenged award's compliance with *all* the standards set out in the rest of the convention.

. . . A strict reading would have limited the ambit of the control function to the enumeration in Article 52(1). The committee's interpretation greatly enlarged its own work as well as expanded future possibilities for challenging awards. Implicitly, it also affected the latent compromising function of arbitration, a matter which will be considered below.

*A formal rather than substantive test of reasons*. In a fourth constitutive ruling, the committee adopted a formal rather than substantive requirement for adequacy of reasons. In the committee's view, as long as the tribunal's "answers seem tenable and not arbitrary, *they do not constitute a manifest excess of powers*." In case of doubt, as noted earlier, "analysis should be resolved *in favorem validitatis sententiae*."

This formalistic approach, which seemed to have been designed to help sustain challenged awards, actually reduces the effect of the presumption in favor of validity, for it produces a curious passivity and unwillingness to try to penetrate the thinking of the tribunal whose award is under attack. Thus, in elaborating its conception of its mandate, the committee said:

> [I]t is not for the Committee to imagine what might or should have been the arbitrators' reasons any more than

it should substitute "correct" reasons for possibly "incorrect" reasons, or deal "*ex post facto*" with questions submitted to the Tribunal which the Award left unanswered. The only role of the Committee here is to state whether there is one of the grounds for annulment set out in Article 52 of the Convention, and to draw the consequences under the same Article. In this sense, the Committee defends the Convention's legal purity.

What emerges, then, is a formalistic approach which eschews a real effort at reconstruction of the objectives or deeper ratiocination of the award under review. Under such an approach, a committee would theoretically nullify an award for faults in logic somewhere between first premise and conclusion, even though it might be arguable, even clear, that the conclusion was correct.

This particular construction of the convention is textually plausible and consistent with the core idea animating arbitral review. The alternative, a substantive test, runs the danger of sliding into appeal. But the committee's construction is not informed by any sense of the control function in arbitration and, as a result, poses certain risks for the future of ICSID arbitration. Due to varying levels of personal ability and the diversity of legal cultures, different arbitrators perceive and analyze legal questions differently, reason differently and at extraordinarily different lengths, and write judgments with greatly varying degrees of skill and elegance, often in a language to which they are not native. If a subsequent ad hoc committee, composed in part of people from still different legal cultures, decided that it is not obliged to try to "get into the skin" of the tribunal and reconstruct the reasoning of the award it is reviewing, and does not approach its task with full recognition of the difficulties of construing any human communication, a fortiori, transnational legal communications, the probability of nullifying on grounds of inadequate reasons increases. And if the committee is unwilling to try to determine whether, reasons notwithstanding, a plausible and defensible (if not wise) answer was reached, nullifications with formal but no material justification will occur.

*Appeal rather than review consequences.* The committee postulated constitutive rulings that restricted substantive inquiry and was at pains to emphasize that it was involved in a review of particular grounds established in Article 52 of the ICSID Convention and not an appeal on the wisdom or "correctness" of the award. This is a proper concern of everyone engaged in arbitral review. Notwithstanding, the committee tended to slip into appeal. In addition to finding that there were defects in the award which warranted nullification, the committee made certain key decisions on some legal issues of the merits, some of which it even suggested might be used by a subsequent tribunal. This is a radical and interesting redefinition at the constitutive level of the review function. We will consider its implications below.

Although the ad hoc committee reaffirmed a commitment *in favorem validitatis sententiae*, the net consequence of its constitutive holdings was, as we will see, a weakening of that presumption and a marked tilting in review in favor of the challenging party.

*Substantive Holdings*

Klöckner, it will be recalled, had challenged the validity of the entire award on jurisdictional grounds, contending that the tribunal had, among other things, exceeded its jurisdiction by basing its award on alleged violations of management responsibilities. Klöckner averred that allegations about those matters were subject to the ICC jurisdictional clause in the management contract. Because the tribunal had purported to decide them, it had exceeded its jurisdiction and its award was null.

The committee purported to examine every possible construction of the two jurisdictional clauses. It did not conceal its serious doubts about the tribunal's jurisdictional conclusions. Nevertheless, the committee did not substitute its own judgment for that of the tribunal and did not find a ground for nullification here. "Such an interpretation of the agreements and especially of the two arbitration clauses, whether correct or not, is tenable and does not in any event constitute a manifest excess of power. To this extent, the complaint, while admissible, is unfounded." Although the committee did not find the tribunal's reasons persuasive, they were, it found, not implausible. Hence they benefited from the presumption in favor of validity.

> [T]he Tribunal refused to accept, in the absence of completely precise and unequivocal contractual provisions, that the parties to the Management Contract wanted to "derogate" from the Protocol's ICSID clause. The Tribunal may have implicitly accepted that the

ICSID clause constituted for both parties an "essential jurisdictional guarantee," the relinquishment of which could neither be presumed nor accepted in the absence of clear evidence.

This was a liberal and extremely tolerant holding. In light of the analytic method of the rest of the committee's decision, it is puzzling. The tribunal's jurisdictional decision was probably the most questionable part of its award. After all, the parties had decided to structure their transaction in four agreements and to assign arbitral jurisdiction over different parts of the agreements to different arbitral institutions. Yet the tribunal, rather than accept the legal characterization the parties had jointly selected, had looked at the integrated transaction as a factual matter and then used that perspective to override contractual options plainly adopted by the parties. In doing this, the committee only asked itself whether this arrangement was "tenable," without determining whether governing legal systems might make other judgments. "Tenability," absent reference to an encompassing system of law, can become quite subjective.

The committee's conclusion in this part of the decision is all the most puzzling in that a contrary finding on the tribunal's jurisdictional decision would have produced an annulment for *excès de pouvoir*, in a more economical fashion than the methods actually selected by the committee. It also would have done less injury to the review function of ICSID. One may note in passing that arbitrators at the present time rarely find themselves without jurisdiction. As we saw earlier, that development may have long-term implications for both willingness to submit to arbitration and, at the international level, the lawmaking process.

The minimum standard of plausibility and the presumption in favor of validity did not avail the award on other matters. Klöckner had attacked the award on the ground that the tribunal had not applied the proper law. The tribunal, as will be recalled, had explicitly designated that part of Cameroonian law based on French law as the applicable law. Klöckner had been particularly offended by the tribunal's use of the "obligation to disclose everything to a partner." The tribunal had said: "We assume that the principle according to which a person who engages in close contractual relations, based on confidence, must deal with his partner in a frank, loyal and candid manner is a basic principle of French civil law, as is indeed the case under other national codes which we know of." Klöckner's gravamen, it appeared, was not the selection of the proper law as such, but whether the tribunal had made a mistake in applying that proper law.

In an arbitral review format, this was a difficult, even tricky argument for Klöckner to make. The usual practice of review instances has been well summarized by a U.S. federal court. "To vacate an arbitration award for manifest disregard of the law there must be 'something beyond and different from a mere error in the law or failure on the part of the arbitrators to understand or apply.' . . . Plaintiff has not demonstrated, as it must, that the majority arbitrators deliberately disregarded what they knew to be the law in order to reach the result they did." The Klöckner tribunal had certainly *identified* the proper law (or laws). The claim that it might have mistakenly applied that law, a legitimate ground for appeal, would not have been admissible in review, for it would have required the committee to redecide the merits.

In light of the committee's tolerant treatment of the tribunal's jurisdictional holding, one might have thought that the tribunal's holding would satisfy the requirements of the ICSID Convention, especially if it were buttressed by the presumption in favor of validity. But the committee found it wanting. "It may immediately be noticed that here the Tribunal does not claim to ascertain the existence (of a rule or a principle) but asserts or postulates the existence of such a 'principle' which (after having postulated its existence) the Tribunal *assumes* or takes for granted that it 'is a basic principle of French civil law.'" The committee was particularly troubled by the award's observation that "this is the criterion that applies to relations between partners in simple forms of association anywhere," that "the rule [sic] is particularly appropriate in more complex international ventures, such as the present one," and that the arbitrators declared that they were "convinced that it is particularly important that *universal requirements* of frankness and loyalty in dealings between partners be applied in cases such as this one."

The committee felt that it was insufficient to refer to a "basic principle" without more specific references. It was also troubled by the failure to distinguish between "rule" and "principle." In keeping with its own constitutive holdings, the committee did not attempt to discover, for itself, whether the tribunal's reference to a "basic principle" could in fact be related to rules in the governing law which would have established that the tribunal was correct but careless in its method of citation. (The tribunal's sweeping proposition, one may note, is problematic in arms-length commercial transactions.) The defect, in the view of the committee, was fatal.

> [I]n the absence of any information, evidence or citation in the Award, it would seem difficult to accept, and impossible to *presume*, that there is a general duty, under French civil law, or for that matter other systems of civil law, for a contracting party to make a *"full disclosure"* to its partner. If we were to "presume" anything, it would instead be that such a duty (the basic idea of which may, of course, be accepted as it follows from the principle of good faith; cf. Article 1134, para. 3 of the French Civil Code) must, to be given effect in positive law, have conditions for its application and limits!

As a result, the committee concluded that a ground for annulment had occurred.

> [I]n its reasoning, limited to postulating and not demonstrating the existence of a principle or exploring the rules by which it can only take concrete form, the Tribunal has not applied "the law of the Contracting State." Strictly speaking, it could not be said that it made this decision without providing reasons, within the meaning of Articles 48(3) and 52 (1)(e). It did, however, act outside the framework provided by Article 42(1), applying concepts or principles it probably considered equitable.

The committee concluded that the award was a single unit and that this ground necessitated a total annulment.

Citation method is certainly an important part of our science, but international commercial law draws perforce on lawyers trained in many different legal systems, each of which has a different style or dialect of citation, ratiocination, and redaction. Some systems redact judgments in what Karl Llewellyn called "the grand style"; this is the style of the International Court, for example, of which the chairman of the Klöckner tribunal had been the president. Other systems, for example, the United States in its current practice, use idiosyncratic and highly particularistic citation methods. Citations are sprinkled to support even the most self-evident of propositions with the abandon of a Northwest Coast indian throwing an epic potlatch.

Strictly speaking, the tribunal had fulfilled the requirements of both Article 52 and Article 42. It provided reasons for its judgment which sounded in the applicable law. The tribunal's reference to other systems of law was neither optional nor incorrect. By referring to international and "general principles," the tribunal would have demonstrated that Cameroonian law was not inconsistent with international law and hence continued to apply. If there had been a conflict, Cameroonian law, under one theory of interpretation of the ICSID Convention, might have had to yield to international law.

This part of the decision of the committee is cast in terms of inadequate reasons and thus avoids the appearance of an appeal of a mistaken application of law. Though the committee was at pains to distinguish this claim from a claim of an erroneous application (*error in judicando*), it is difficult to escape the impression that the real thrust of the committee's concern was that the tribunal's legal conclusion of an obligation imposed on Klöckner *de tout reveler* constituted a mistake in law. Of course, the committee could not frame its objections in those terms, for that would have manifestly transformed the review into an appeal. Perhaps that accounts for the tortured and ultimately unpersuasive formulation of inadequacy of reasons.

·     ·     ·

Because the ad hoc committee nullified the entire award, a second arbitration initiated by Klöckner was, in principle, obliged to relitigate everything again. There was no res judicata, however fragmentary, remaining from the first award. A second tribunal was empaneled. It was chaired by Carl Salans and included Juan Antonio Cremades and Jorge Casteñeda. It rendered an award in January 1988 which has not been published. It has been reported to have been in favor of Klöckner though giving it only a fraction of the amount it claimed. That award has been challenged in another Article 52 procedure. The ad hoc committee in this case, chaired by Ambassador Sompong Sucharitkul and composed of Judge Mbaye of the International Court and Professor Giardina of Italy, rendered a decision which has not been published but has been reported to have nullified partially the award.

*   *   *

3.    *AMCO Asia Corp. et al. v. Indonesia*, 1 INT'L ARB. REP. 649 (1986).

[Summary of the Phases of the Cases from W. MICHAEL REISMAN, SYSTEMS OF CONTROL IN INTERNATIONAL ADJUDICATION AND ARBITRATION 66-78 (1992).]

.   .   .

The AMCO case was in many ways the paradigmatic dispute about contemporary direct foreign investment. Indonesia was in the hapless but classic position of a developing country: resource rich and capital poor and thus desperately seeking foreign capital to jump-start productive economic activity. Indonesia had developed a broad program to attract foreign investment by awarding licenses with concessions and incentives for approved foreign investors. Each foreign investment was negotiated separately, but they were all similar in general terms. In return for a commitment to invest a prescribed amount of foreign capital in Indonesia for an approved project, the government would grant a package of concessions, tax holidays, and other inducements.

AMCO, a U.S. company, negotiated this type of model agreement with Indonesia. AMCO committed itself to build and manage a hotel in Jakarta, in collaboration with an Indonesian joint venturer, a private company largely organized by military officers. AMCO promised to invest $3 million of foreign currency in Indonesia as part of its program. The agreement contained an ICSID arbitration clause.

After the hotel was built, the Indonesian joint venturer lodged many complaints. At the same time, the Indonesian government alleged, in various forms, nonpayment of the capital sums which AMCO had agreed to introduce into Indonesia. AMCO did not respond. On the night of March 30, 1980, police and military personnel seized the hotel and expelled the management. Shortly afterward, the competent Indonesian government agency concluded that AMCO had not fulfilled its foreign capital obligations and terminated its license. After unsuccessful efforts to have the decision reversed in Indonesian courts, AMCO exercised its right to ICSID arbitration, claiming not less than $9 million plus interest.

The ICSID tribunal's award considered two basic claims: expropriation and breach of contract. The tribunal concluded as a matter of fact that:

> [O]n or about the critical period there was a taking of Claimants' rights to the control and management of the land and all the Kartika Plaza Building. . . . [A] number of army and policy personnel were present at the hotel premises on the Ist [*sic*] April, 1980 and by their very presence assisted in the successful seizure from P.T. AMCO of the exercise of its lease and management rights. . . . As a taking per se is not necessarily an unlawful act attributable to a state, the tribunal proceeded to examine whether this taking "amounts to an expropriation which according to Indonesian Law and to International Law can give rise to a claim for compensation." The first question was whether Indonesia itself was the agent of the taking. The tribunal held that the Indonesian government had not expropriated: . . . The taking was instigated by P.T. Wisma and was carried out for the benefit of the same. . . . The Tribunal was not provided with any evidence that the takeover of the hotel and thereby the taking of the Claimants' exercise of their rights to control and management was due to a governmental decision.

This may have been a courtesy to sovereign sensibilities, for the award still concluded that Indonesia had failed to protect an alien from suffering these acts, that the takeover was unlawful, and that the Indonesian Court ruling did not purport to legitimize the act.

With regard to AMCO's claim for breach of contract, the tribunal found that the relationship between AMCO and Indonesia was more in the nature of a license, though "not alien to the general concept of contract."

> Being an agreement aimed at producing legal effects in the economic field, creating obligations for the applicant

and obligations for the State, even if in the latter case they are conditional, the legal combination formed by the application and by the approval thereof is not alien to the general concept of contract according to Indonesian law. Nor is it alien to general principles of law.

However, it is not *identical* to a private law contract, due to the fact that the State is entitled to withdraw the approval it granted *for reasons which could not be invoked by a private contracting entity, and/or to decide and implement the withdrawal by utilizing procedures which are different from those which can and have to be utilized by a private entity.* (Italics in original)

Indonesia was entitled, according to the tribunal, to terminate such a relationship for, among other things, nonfulfillment of its terms. But in order to be lawful, the termination had to meet procedural requirements and be substantively justified. AMCO had not met its full requirement of foreign capital, which was a violation, but the tribunal found that it was immaterial. Even if the violation had justified termination, Indonesia had to terminate in accord with international due process and, under its own law, had to give certain prescribed warnings. If Indonesia had violated due process, it was liable, even if the termination had been substantively justified. And Indonesia had violated due process, the tribunal held, for though written warnings had been given, they had not emanated from the right agency nor used the proper language.

The tribunal decided not to inquire into the cogency of other grounds for revocation that had been considered by the appropriate Indonesian authority, for the act was, in its view, already unlawful.

But the tribunal awarded the claimant only $3,200,000 plus 6 percent interest, a sum considerably less than it had claimed. Indonesia had counterclaimed for all the monies, which, except for the tax holiday granted by the license, the claimants should have paid as taxes and import duties. The tribunal rejected the counterclaim: "[S]ince the Tribunal finds that the revocation of the license was unlawful, as a consequence, the revocation of the tax facilities was unlawful as well."

The award was unanimous and, given the fraction of the claim actually awarded, bore the signs of an internal tribunal compromise. Compromise is a curiously unstable phenomenon in arbitration. There are structural pressures both for and against it and structural costs when a compromise is struck for all or part of a decision. The option in three-party arbitration of selection of party-appointed arbitrators introduces and implicitly endorses certain intracameral dynamics for compromise, while the requirement of a thoroughly motivated judgment restrains it. If reasons are viewed as, in key part, a ritual rather than as a real record of the actual ratiocination of the tribunal, the compromise dynamic can operate. But if the reasons requirement is transformed into a ritual, then the control function which operates through the requirement of manifest reasons is lost.

If the AMCO award was a compromise, it would help to explain the award's curious reasoning which was laconic in some parts and opaque and puzzling in others. To cite one dramatic example, the tribunal found that AMCO indeed had not invested the $3 million of foreign currency it had committed itself to bring into the project as part of the terms of the license it had secured. The shortfall, according to the tribunal's calculation, was some 16 percent. Under its own theory, this would have justified the termination. The tribunal summarily concluded that this was not "material," without explaining why or under what legal system materiality was being tested.

If compromise is to work, its crafters must correctly identify and accommodate the essential concerns of each of the parties to it. When more than money is involved, a viable compromise will be more than a matter of numbers. It is precisely in this sense that the AMCO compromise proved problematic. The award was unanimous, was for substantially less than AMCO had claimed, and might have been viewed from Indonesia's perspective as amounting to less than the general transaction and nuisance cost of continuing the dispute. Indonesia apparently felt that it had to challenge the award, for if a country establishes a program to induce foreign investment and grants licenses on the basis of that program but discrepancies of as much as 16 percent of the foreign commitment to invest are internationally determined to be irrelevant such that the government may not terminate the license, the host country will find itself in the position of being unable to enforce its own law.

On Indonesia's application, the chairman of ICSID's Administrative Council established an ad hoc committee. Its chairman, Professor Seidl-Hohenveldern of Austria, had been a member of the Klöckner ad hoc committee. A prominent Philippine lawyer, now a justice on the Philippine Supreme Court, and an Italian professor were the other members of the committee. In 1986 the committee annulled the original award in part. It found that the shortfall of 16 percent had been understated. Of the $3 million which AMCO had been expected to invest, the committee believed that less than $1 million had actually been invested. But the committee did not nullify the entire award. It confirmed many of the factual and legal holdings of the tribunal.

## Constitutive Rulings

The fact that the case immediately after Klöckner was also being challenged was plainly not lost on the AMCO committee. The Klöckner committee had been sensitive to and, indeed, had explicitly addressed the constitutive dimension of its operation. Yet it developed a theory that facilitated challenges to awards, thanks to its constitutive holdings and, in particular, the large number of detailed grounds it made available. Without acknowledging Klöckner's authority or openly entering the lists against it and without enunciating its own explicit constitutive principles, the AMCO committee also addressed the constitutive dimension in its decision, making constitutive rulings, some explicit, some implicit, that revised Klöckner.

By implication, the AMCO committee confirmed the presumption *in favorem validitatis sententiae*. It appears to have ignored the Klöckner committee's expansion of the grounds for nullification and moved quite far from Klöckner's technical and formal approaches. It will be recalled that the Klöckner committee had rejected a prudential competence: after posing the question of whether it could refrain from annulling if it found that the first tribunal's departure was of no consequence, it concluded that the convention gave it no discretion in the matter and established instead a hair trigger. The AMCO ad hoc committee did not accept this theoretical position. In a number of places, as we will see, the AMCO committee found certain things in the award to be technical discrepancies in terms of one of the grounds specified in Article 52 but refused to nullify because it found that the matter was obiter dictum. In other places, the committee noted the existence of a ground of nullity but refused to nullify because the discrepancy was *de minimis*.

Thus the ad hoc committee refused to nullify on the ground that an alleged international principle of due process was violated. The committee found that the tribunal had made the wrong choice of law and had based this part of the award on a norm from the wrong legal system, but the committee found that the *content* of the international principle the tribunal had applied was materially the same as the applicable law, Indonesian law. This time the relevance of the tribunal's holding was not minimized by calling it obiter dictum. The tribunal's failure to apply the law prescribed by the ICSID Convention was confirmed. It was technically a violation of Article 52. But since the committee concluded, from the testimony of the parties, that the proper law, had it been applied, would have yielded exactly the same result, it refrained from nullifying on that ground.

In a sense, Klöckner and AMCO join issues here, presenting, *grosso modo*, two different interpretations of the competence and functions of an ICSID ad hoc committee. One approach may be referred to as the "technical discrepancy" approach. It is highly technical and rests on the conviction that a committee must declare nullification if it finds a technical discrepancy from the convention without regard to whether the technical discrepancy caused injury to the party alleging it or distorted the award. The other approach may be referred to as the "material violation" approach. It would ignore a technical discrepancy if, in the context of the case, it did not constitute a material violation of the standards of the convention. This approach, akin to the American appellate practice of harmless error, is consequentialist and consistent with the doctrine *de minimis no curat praetor*.

Each of these approaches has a different modus operandi. In the technical discrepancy approach, the committee does no more than determine if something done by the tribunal that rendered the award sounds in one of the grounds itemized in Article 52(1). Any confirmed technical violations of the convention require nullification per se. There is no need to explore whether the "mistake" causes an injury to the party alleging nullity nor, in such an inquiry, to assess whether the correct discharge of the arbitral function would have yielded the same result. There is also no reason for an ad hoc committee to assess what the correct answer would have been in order to determine whether the violation of Article 52(1) is significant. By definition there can be no violation of the convention that is not significant. Nor is there need or authorization to think in terms of control function.

In terms of the theory of arbitral review, there is something to be said for the technical discrepancy approach. It keeps the review agency from getting too deeply into the merits of the award and exercising (or reexercising) judgments about them. And it restrains the reviewer from making comparative judgments about which parts of a tribunal's statute or of arbitral procedure are more important than others. (Some of these apparent advantages may be illusory, for the use of the *ratio decidendi-obiter dictum* distinction seems to permit a reviewer applying the technical discrepancy approach to ignore some technical discrepancies and to refrain from nullifying because of them.) But appraised in terms of the control function, the technical discrepancy approach may, as we will see, prove deficient.

In contrast, the material violation approach explores what the correct component of the award, in terms of its premises, would have been in order to determine whether or not a ground of nullity of sufficient consequence and injury to the party initiating the review warrants a total or partial nullification of the award or may be ignored. This approach necessitates not merely interpretation of the explicit award, but requires efforts at reconstruction of the ratiocination of the tribunal whose award is under review. While classical arbitral review prohibits examination of the merits of the dispute, the material violation approach does involve an inquiry into the "right" answer. But the examination is purely instrumental and is undertaken only if a preliminary finding of a technical violation has been made. Klöckner, it will be recalled, would nullify at that moment, without regard to whether or not the technical discrepancy led to a material discrepancy. AMCO, in contrast, would examine whether the technical discrepancy constituted a material violation. The purpose of this investigation is not to substitute a committee's view for that of the tribunal. It is only to stop the committee from nullifying an award on technical grounds when the award itself is materially correct. Yet because of the doctrine of res judicata, these instrumental findings may have consequences in possible subsequent phases of the dispute.

The method of inquiry of the material violation approach is marked by both negative and affirmative formulations and perforce statements of correct answers that would be revisory in consequence were the committee endowed with the competence to substitute its view as a new award binding on the parties.

*Substantive Holdings*

A central part of the dispute was whether Indonesia could lawfully revoke AMCO's license. A core question here was the substantive lawfulness of the revocation. That lawfulness depended, according to the original tribunal and to both of the parties, on compliance by AMCO with its commitments to Indonesia.

The award found compliance; discrepancies between obligations of investment in Indonesia and actual performance were deemed not to be material.

The ad hoc committee nullified this part of the award for failing to apply fundamental provisions of Indonesian law and failing to state reasons. The award had established a number of common points as between the parties:

> [If] the failure to fulfill their obligations, as alleged by Respondent, could be established, the revocation of the license could be justified. . . . [A] contract can be terminated by one of the parties where the other party does not fulfill its obligations. . . . [T]he revocation of the investment application's approval by the host State can be justified only by *material* failures on the part of the investor. . . . [T]he sub-lease agreements between P.T. AMCO ASIA and P.T. AEROPACIFIC were not, in any event at the date of the revocation, a material failure justifying the same. . . . [T]he applicant undertook to invest the sum of US $3,000,000. . . . [T]he full capital of P.T. AMCO INDONESIA (that is to say the investment to be made) was to be paid within ten years.

The critical question with regard to the lawfulness of Indonesia's revocation was whether these requirements, which both parties accepted, had been complied with.

The parties agreed that there had not been compliance. Issue was joined over the magnitude of the discrepancy between the investment required and the funds actually committed, and this discrepancy's legal significance. Of the two versions presented, the tribunal, it will be recalled, had accepted the smaller shortfall and found that it was legally immaterial. The ad hoc committee nullified this portion of the award:

> [I]t was firmly established, in the view of the ad hoc Committee, firstly that according to relevant provisions of Indonesian law, only investments recognized and definitely registered as such by the competent Indonesian authority (Bank Indonesia) are investments within the meaning of the Foreign Investment Law. . . . It was also clearly established . . . that P.T. Amco failed to obtain definitive registration with Bank Indonesia of all the amounts claimed to have been invested by it in the Hotel project. . . . The evidence before the Tribunal showed that as late as 1977, Amco's investment of foreign capital duly and definitely registered with Bank Indonesia in accordance with the Foreign Investment Law, amounted to only US $983,992. . . . The Tribunal in determining that the investment of Amco had reached the sum of US $2,472,490 clearly failed to apply the relevant provisions of Indonesian law. The ad hoc Committee holds that the Tribunal manifestly exceeded its powers in this regard and is compelled to annul this finding. . . . If it be assumed that BKPM's finding that P.T. Amco's share capitalization figure of US $1,399,000 had in fact included US $1,000,000 of loan funds, was correct, then the Tribunal had effectively failed to apply Article 2 of the Foreign Investment Law which limits qualified foreign investment to investment of equity capital. The Tribunal, in any case, failed to state reasons for counting the entire US $1,399,000 as equity capital and not merely US $399,000. . . . If, upon the other hand, it be assumed that the BKPM finding was *not* correct and the entire US $1,399,000 had somehow become "equity capital," then the Tribunal had still failed to apply Article 2 of the Foreign Investment Law and to state reasons. . . . [T]he ad hoc Committee feels obliged to consider that the Tribunal manifestly exceeded its powers in failing to apply fundamental provisions of Indonesian law and failed to state reasons for its calculation of P.T. Amco's investment.

The method used here is a good example of the material violation approach. It necessarily generates affirmative conclusions, for it tests claims of nullity not on the purely technical grounds of Article 52(1) but on grounds of whether the alleged nullification really makes any difference in the context of the case. The nullity of the award is established by reference to the substantively accurate position. Hence the AMCO committee concluded not simply that the award was null on the formal ground of absence of express reasons. Insofar as the committee could have reconstructed the tribunal's ratiocination, it might have found that the tribunal's conclusions had been at least substantively plausible, if not substantively correct. But the ad hoc committee found that the tribunal's ruling was wrong on material grounds, for the investor actually brought an amount far less than required (indeed far less than the award found). Hence the license had been properly revoked.

A number of consequences flowed directly from nullification of this part of the award. The first, obviously, was the nullification by necessary implication of the award's finding of nonmateriality of the discrepancy between AMCO's obligation and AMCO's performance. The tribunal's conclusion that BKPM (the Indonesian financial control agency) was unjustified in revoking AMCO's license also had to be annulled. This, too, was the result of a materiality test. For the ad hoc committee, Indonesia's failure to protect adequately against a taking by unauthorized personnel, though procedurally defective, was substantively justified.

Consider the contrasting consequences of the different methods with regard to the procedural defects in the license termination. If the Klöckner committee's theory had been applied, this probably would have been decided otherwise for, in a technical sense, it was a violation. Under the AMCO committee's theory, though, it was not. The committee also found that a material approach in this part of its inquiry was mandated by Indonesian law: "The fundamental character of Indonesian administrative law seems, to the ad hoc Committee, to be such that a conclusion on the legality of an act of an Indonesian public authority, and on its implications for responsibility for damages, can be reached only after an over-all evaluation of the act, including consideration of its substantive bases." Because the revocation was substantively lawful, the ad hoc committee found that the tribunal's award of compensation for procedural violations also had to be nullified.

The previous nullifications appeared to entail nullifications with regard to the temporal extent of AMCO's claim to manage the hotel. This too nullified a key part of the award and established, by implication, the temporal limits of any subsequent claim.

Indonesia had contended that the award should be nullified because the tribunal should have accepted Indonesia's warnings to AMCO as sufficient within the meaning of Indonesian law. The ad hoc committee rejected this contention. But the "warning" and "hearing" issues were then deprived of legal consequence, for they constituted a technical rather than material violation.

As a consequence of the method the committee developed, part of the AMCO award was nullified. The only issue remaining to be relitigated by a new tribunal, were it established, would have seemed to have been the question of damages (if any) for the nonfeasance from the time of the taking until the time of the justified and lawful revocation of the license. But, as is often the case, things proved to be more complex.

## AMCO II

Shortly after the ad hoc committee in AMCO partially annulled the award, AMCO, as it was entitled under the ICSID Convention, applied for a new arbitration. It will be convenient to refer to this new phase of the case as AMCO II. A new tribunal was established, chaired by Professor Rosalyn Higgins of London. One of the first issues the AMCO II tribunal had to deal with was just how much of the dispute before the first tribunal would be heard again. This was a matter of interpreting what issues had been nullified by the ad hoc committee and what issues had not and were hence res judicata and not available for relitigation. The framework within which this interpretation was to take place was the scope to be attributed to the concept of res judicata in international arbitration. The question was, it soon became clear, to be treated in large part as one of policy.

These questions were hardly theoretical or academic. Their resolution would have major impacts on the parties in the case no less than on parties in future arbitrations. How the matter was to be resolved had the potential for shifting the ICSID structure from one of symmetrical party equality in the context of the speed and economy of arbitration to one inclining in favor of successive losers. Though there were a few analogies in older cases, this was, in many ways, a case of first impression.

The first question posed to the second AMCO tribunal was the extent of the res judicata effect to be accorded the premises and reasoning of the ad hoc committee. If the mode of nullification adopted by the AMCO committee were endorsed and effect were given to its explicit as well as implicit confirmations of parts of the original tribunal's award, the scope of the new arbitration would be quite narrow. AMCO would be allowed, in this second phase of the case, to argue for little more than compensation for the period from March 31-April 1 when the unlawful taking occurred, until the time when the license was terminated, some three months later, by the competent Indonesian court. Damages would, accordingly, be quite small. At the same time, Indonesia would be entitled to bring counterclaims for reimbursement of many of the concessions it had made to AMCO under the license, which the first tribunal had concluded AMCO had violated. Indonesia also had substantial tax claims.

Thus, a broad conception of res judicata would limit what the plaintiff could get, but posed so many dangers in the form of counterclaims to the plaintiff that it might have deterred it from reinitiating the arbitration entirely. The broad conception of res judicata would also have had consequences for future cases, for the margin for relitigation in successive tribunals would always be narrower.

If, in contrast, res judicata were to be interpreted narrowly to exclude reasoning and its premises as well as implied confirmations, the margin for relitigation would, in many cases, be much broader. This could provide a greater incentive to the losing party to seek recourse under Article 52. The implications for the ICSID control system are plain.

The AMCO II tribunal grappled with this problem in the first phase of the case. It showed great sensitivity to the issue of the scope of its own future jurisdiction, but appeared to be oblivious to the control dimension of the decision it was making. It adopted a narrow approach to the findings of the ad hoc committee.

> If the present Tribunal were bound by "integral reasoning" of the *ad hoc* Committee, then the present Tribunal would have bestowed upon the *ad hoc*

Committee the role of an appeal court. The underlying reasoning of an *ad hoc* Committee could be so extensive that the tasks of a subsequent Tribunal could be rendered mechanical, and not consistent with its authority — as indicated in Article 52(6), which speaks of "the dispute" being submitted to a new Tribunal.

The reasoning in this statement is not without problems. It rests on two grounds to support its conclusion. The first ground concerns a fear of transformation of review into appeal. Arbitral review can slide into an appeal on the merits and, given the structure of international arbitration, this may not be desirable. But is that the issue at stake here? It is not an ad hoc committee's reasoning in support of its conclusions (which is explicitly required by the convention) that transforms a review into an appeal. Nor is there a transformation of review into appeal because effect is given by subsequent tribunals to the integrated reasoning of the ad hoc committee. We encounter an appeal, rather than a review, when an ad hoc committee moves beyond an examination of the probity of procedures to an examination of the "correctness" of legal application and nullifies for that reason, substituting its own view for that of the original tribunal. That may be improper or, at the least, undesirable, but it is not related to the question of giving effect to reasons.

The second reason invoked by the AMCO II tribunal is that assigning res judicata effect to the ad hoc committee's reasoning could drastically reduce the scope of relitigation for a subsequent tribunal. There is a logical pathology here. A consequence of a choice cannot be a reason for a choice until one has established by reference to law or policy that the consequence is a desirable or undesirable legal or policy consequence.

AMCO II does not address the policy issue but reasons that giving effect to the reasoning of the committee by means of a broad conception of res judicata would be inconsistent with the convention which allows either party to resubmit the "dispute." As part (and possibly a large part) of the dispute would not be resubmittable, convention-granted rights, this line of reasoning goes, would be violated.

Consider the difficulties in this line of reasoning. If it is valid, there can be no place for res judicata in the ICSID control scheme, for any res judicata effect, whether broad or narrow, must reduce the arbitrability of what constituted the "dispute," whatever its parameters may have been, in the first phase. But there must be a place here for res judicata by virtue of a committee's convention-granted power to annul only partially. Otherwise, we must ignore the explicit power of a committee to annul only part of an award and conclude that even when a committee annuls partially, a subsequent tribunal must treat it as a total nullification and hear the dispute de novo, lest the convention-granted right to bring the "dispute" to a new tribunal be infringed. AMCO II's reasoning here leads it into a cul-de-sac in which it seriously undermines the convention power of partial nullification.

The reasoning of the AMCO II tribunal is not only defective on its own terms, but also begs the real issue, which is one of policy. AMCO II rejects a broad conception of res judicata including integral reasoning because it fears that this could limit its own jurisdiction and, more generally, the ambit of functioning of subsequent tribunals, impaneled after a nullification. This is, of course, true. The question is whether it is desirable on policy grounds. I submit that it is, for it would focus the control system and prevent its abuse by attenuating, at each successive phase, the matter in dispute, obviating the rehearing of matters that were not defective, not nullified, and hence not entitled to rehearing, thereby limiting the scope of rehearing and reducing the incentive of abusive review. In the absence of such a restrictive approach, each successive tribunal would have to decide *pro hac vice* how much res judicata effect to accord to the previous decision. As litigants will not know in advance, one party will have good reason to try its luck.

Given the fact that ICSID Article 52 procedures are more likely to proliferate, the efficacy of ICSID and its survival as a meaningful dispute-resolving mechanism will depend upon preserving this balance. In my view the balance will be seriously disturbed if an award deemed by an ad hoc committee to be defective in severable part necessarily and automatically entails the nullification of a greater part of the labor of the parties and the first tribunal. The net result will be to require the parties to invest major resources in a relitigation of matters which, in the view of the first tribunal and in the view of an ad hoc committee that scrutinized its work, are untainted, directly or indirectly, by a ground of nullity and hence had been decided within the terms of arbitral jurisdiction.

One must bear in mind that even an institutionalized system of review, if wrongly designed or wrongly interpreted, is susceptible to abuse. The losing party to a second arbitration may request the installation of an ad hoc committee in the hope that even a minor, technical defect will, *pace* the Klöckner committee, entail the nullification of the entire award and provide a potentially infinite series of opportunities to win or, at least, to stave off losing and paying. The utility of the convention's system of partial nullifications and its implied corollary of a broad res judicata is that each subsequent arbitration will be permitted to hear only the annulled portions of the preceding award, thereby reducing, at each successive stage, the incentive and rewards for abuse.

Nor should the financial consequences of mandatory total relitigation be minimized. Arbitral costs may total millions of dollars, sums which developing countries can ill afford. If the prospective costs are so great as to require the country to settle in ways adverse to its rights, then Article 52 becomes a weapon for extortion and undermines ICSID's mission. Investors, as well, may be prejudiced, for heavy litigation costs may make private investors decide that ICSID and, possibly, a particular private investment in a foreign country are no longer attractive.

To contend, as a matter of policy, that the doctrine of res judicata should insulate those matters decided by a first tribunal which were not nullified as well as the broader reasoning of the ad hoc committee addresses, of course, only part of the problem. The question of how a subsequent tribunal discharges its obligations under the convention and under international law and how, in particular, it interprets those parts of the prior award which are deemed to have survived the partial nullification decision of an ad hoc committee no less than how the committee decision itself is to be interpreted is another matter.

Although the merits of these decisions are of far less interest to us in this discussion than are the evolving control dimensions, it may be of interest to note that the tribunal in AMCO II rendered its decision on the merits on May 31, 1990, awarding AMCO $2,567,966.20 plus 6 percent interest. Because AMCO I and the ad hoc committee had confirmed that AMCO had violated the terms of the license and, *pace* AMCO I, such a violation warranted Indonesia's termination of the license, compensation for procedural violations by the Indonesian administration could not sustain an award of $2.5 million. Instead, the tribunal developed a rather innovative theory of the "tainted background," according to which, certain undefined tainting factors in the background (or foreground, as it developed) of the impugned national decision could render it a violation of law, even if it were substantively correct. If a tainting factor were found, full compensation could be ordered as if the substantive claim were well-founded.

The theory apparently dispenses with traditional tests of the required actionability of the alleged taint and thus functions as something of an *ex aequo et bono* formula. With its flexible notion of background, it dispenses with traditional tests of relevance and causality. It could prove to be difficult for defendants to argue against it.

At the time of this writing, both AMCO and the Republic of Indonesia have applied for the annulment of the AMCO II award. An ad hoc committee has been impaneled.

. . .

[The final decision of the ad hoc Committee has not been reported, but it is understood that AMCO was again awarded a sum in the neighborhood of the award of AMCO II.]

> 4. Note on *Maritime Int'l Nominees Establishment (MINE) v. Guinea*, W. MICHAEL REISMAN, SYSTEMS OF CONTROL IN INTERNATIONAL ADJUDICATION AND ARBITRATION 79-86 (1992). [The various stages of the case are reported in 5 ASA BULLETIN 24-40 (1987).]

. . .

In 1963 the government of Guinea and the Harvey Aluminum Company established a joint venture called Compagnie des Bauxites de Guinée or CBG. Its purpose was to mine bauxite. Harvey's interest was subsequently transferred to Halco, a company owned by six major aluminum producers who contracted to purchase bauxite from CBG. Article 9 of the Harvey Agreement authorized Guinea to transport up to 50 percent of the exported material, but at rates not exceeding market rates.

On the basis of its Article 9 rights, Guinea contracted, in 1971, with the Maritime International Nominees Establishment or MINE, a Liechtenstein company, to create another joint venture, whose purpose was "l'armement et la gestion de navires au long-cours sous forme d'achat, de location-vente our d'affrétement dans des conditions conformes aux interêts des parties." Governance of the joint venture was by an administrative council of ten members, five appointed by each of the venturers, with the president to be appointed by the Guinean government, the vice president by MINE. The council could be convened by the president and had to be if three members of the council requested it. Article 5 of the joint venture agreement provided that all formal decisions, all policy and implementation decisions, and all administrative decisions having a value of more than one million Guinean francs were to be taken by "double signature" of the president and vice president. Article 12 obliged MINE to make available to the joint venture, at its request, "le personnel technique nécessaire à son bon fonctionnement, personnel ne pouvant être fourni par le GOUVERNEMENT." A joint venture company called SOTRAMAR was formed. Thus MINE undertook to provide the necessary technical personnel and to charter and make available to the joint venture the necessary ships as well as to guarantee them financially. The 1973 agreement contained a dispute resolution clause calling for ICSID arbitration.

By 1973 no charter parties had been concluded and Guinea notified the bauxite takers in CBG that they would have to make their own transport arrangements for that year. There was considerable disagreement between Guinea and MINE as to the responsibility for this state of affairs. MINE asked for a meeting of the administrative council, which the president did not call. Guinea, for its part and without notifying MINE, concluded that MINE was unwilling to carry out its obligations and, in 1974, contracted with another company, AFROBULK, for the execution of its Article 9 rights for a period of two years and, thereafter, for the creation of a joint venture.

MINE thereupon invoked the arbitration procedure, alleging breach of contract, with two general grievances: first, failure to perform internal obligations, specifically Guinea's alleged failures to take the measures necessary to make SOTRAMAR viable; and second, external violations, specifically, Guinea's unilateral notification to the bauxite takers that they should make their own arrangements for transportation in 1973 and its unilateral agreement with AFROBULK to execute the Article 9 rights. Guinea defended that it was MINE that had breached the agreement by failing to conclude freight contracts and to charter vessels and that, therefore, the contract with AFROBULK was a lawful measure mitigating damages.

The request for arbitration was submitted on May 7, 1984, but the arbitration tribunal was only constituted in June 1985. Curiously, all of its members were American nationals. The tribunal rejected Guinea's defense that MINE had breached the contract. It found that Guinea's contract with AFROBULK "was contrary to the spirit, and express provisions of the Convention" and that "Guinea's conduct in secretly negotiating the AFROBULK arrangement, and in denying its existence to MINE thereafter, exhibits bad faith on its part, violating the principle of good faith set forth in the French Civil Code." A unanimous award was rendered on January 6, 1988, ordering Guinea to pay MINE $12,249,483, a total that was arrived at after setting off a $210,000 counterclaim that was awarded to Guinea.

On March 28, 1988, within the statutory 120-day period for filing annulment requests, Guinea applied for a partial annulment on the basis of Article 52(1), paragraphs e, b, and d. Specifically, with regard to Article 52(1)(e), Guinea alleged that the tribunal had failed to state any reasons for its decision on damages and that it had failed to address certain allegedly pivotal questions. With regard to Article 52(1)(b), Guinea alleged that the tribunal failed to apply "any law, much less the correct law" as to both liability and damages. With regard to Article 52(1)(d), Guinea alleged that the tribunal had departed from a fundamental rule of procedure by adopting a measure of damages that had not been advanced or discussed by the parties.

On December 14, 1989, an ad hoc committee was formed composed of Judge Keba M'baye of the International Court of Justice, Aron Broches, the former general counsel of the World Bank and the first secretary-general of ICSID, and Professor Sompong Sucharitkul, who served as president. The implications for the ICSID system of the lengthening series of nullifications was explicitly put into issue in the proceedings. MINE, as part of its defense and surely with no small measure of self-interest, urged a restrictive approach because "a series of annulments of ICSID awards might impair the effectiveness and integrity of ICSID as an international institution for settlement of disputes." While the committee dismissed, without further explanation, such a "pure statistical approach . . . as a wholly inappropriate measure of ICSID's effectiveness," the committee's decision shows a deep concern with the role of the annulment procedure within the ICSID system. Almost a fifth of the operative parts of the award represents a considered examination of this issue.

*Reduced range of annulments.* The emphasis is decidedly on closing the aperture and introducing restrictions. The first restriction has to do with the Klöckner ad hoc committee's conception of the range of grounds for annulment. Thus, in paragraph 4.06, the MINE committee states

> Article 52(1)(b) does not provide a sanction for every excess of its power by a tribunal but requires that the excess be *manifest* which necessarily limits an *ad hoc* Committee's freedom of appreciation as to whether the tribunal has exceeded its powers. Again, the text of Article 52(1)(d) makes clear that not every departure from a rule of procedure justifies annulment; it requires that the departure be a *serious* one and that rule of procedure be *fundamental* in order to constitute a ground for annulment. (Italics in original)

*Rejection of mandatory annulment.* The committee also rejected Klöckner's conception of mandatory annulment on the finding of a ground of nullity. Basing itself on textual interpretation, the MINE committee stated that an ad hoc committee is *not* obliged to nullify an award simply because one of the grounds of annulment is established.

> Article 52(3) provides that an *ad hoc* Committee "shall have the authority to annul the award or any part thereof on any of the grounds set forth in paragraph (1)." The Convention does not require automatic exercise of that authority to annul an award whenever a timely application for its annulment has been made and the applicant has established one of the grounds for annulment. Nor does the Committee consider that the language of Article 52(3) implies such automatic exercise.

The choice available to an ad hoc committee, according to the MINE committee, derives from an inherent discretion.

An *ad hoc* Committee retains a measure of discretion in ruling on applications for annulment. To be sure, its discretion is not unlimited and should not be exercised to the point of defeating the object and purpose of the remedy of annulment. It may, however, refuse to exercise its authority to annul an award where annulment is clearly not required to remedy procedural injustice and annulment would unjustifiably erode the binding force and finality of ICSID awards.

*Confirmation of res judicata.* The committee was also at pains to emphasize the res judicata effect of any portion of a previous award which was not annulled.

*Ex aequo et bono decisions must be manifest.* Having assigned itself a discretionary power, the committee's general analysis on particular grounds of nullity, did not (indeed, did not have to) depart markedly from the earlier case law. The committee confirmed that "a tribunal's disregard of the agreed rules of law would constitute a derogation from the terms of reference within which the tribunal has been authorized to function. Examples of such a derogation include the application of rules of law other than the ones agreed by the parties, or a decision not based on any law unless the parties had agreed on a decision *ex aequo et bono*. But, the committee immediately added, the derogation must be "manifest," an adjective which is puzzling in this context. If the original tribunal goes out of its way to conceal an *ex aequo et bono* decision in what appears to be a legal formula, it will not be manifest. Such concealment is usually the case. One rarely finds in the annals of international arbitration, statements on the order of the New Testament: "this is the law, but *I* say unto you." I would assume that the committee's intention here is that, however concealed the decision *ex aequo et bono* is, when it is exposed in an ad hoc committee procedure, it is its nonlegal quality that must be manifest. Consistent with prior holdings, the committee emphasized that this pathology was to be distinguished from erroneous application of the law in order to prevent ICSID review from becoming a form of appeal.

*A higher threshold for procedural pathologies.* The committee also tried to restrict the ambit for nullifications for procedural pathologies by postulating that Article 52(1)(d) required "quantitative and qualitative criteria." "The departure must be substantial and be such as to deprive a party of the benefit or protection which the rule was intended to provide." But "even a serious departure from a rule of procedure will not give rise to annulment, unless that rule is 'fundamental'" and, most significantly, "[t]he term 'fundamental rule of procedure' is not to be understood as necessarily including all of the Arbitration Rules adopted by the Centre."

*Reduced reasons requirement.* The MINE committee also introduced some drastic restrictions on the reasons requirement. It summarily discharged a tribunal from having to produce an award dealing with "every question" submitted to it. Only a failure to state reasons for those grounds on which the award is actually based will, in its view, constitute a ground for annulment. And, as far as the requisite substance of the reasons themselves are concerned, the committee held that

> the requirement that an award has to be motivated implied that it must enable the reader to follow the reasoning of the Tribunal on points of fact and law. It implies that, and only that. The adequacy of the reasoning is not an appropriate standard of review. . . . [T]he requirement to state reasons is satisfied as long as the award enables one to follow how the tribunal proceeded from Point A to Point B and eventually to its conclusion.

On the other hand, "the minimum requirement is in particular not satisfied by either contradictory or frivolous reasons." One would assume that this means that if a tribunal cites, as its reason for a proposition, a case which is plainly not in point, that will not be deemed to meet the reasons test. Any other interpretation would reduce the role of reasons to empty formality and could hardly fulfill the objects and purposes of this requirement of the convention. And while every question need not be answered, "a tribunal's failure to address a question submitted to it may render its award unintelligible and thus subject to annulment for failure to state reasons."

## Substantive Holdings

*Failure to cite correct law.* The constitutive rulings were reflected in the specific treatment of the applicant's claims. Guinea contended that the tribunal "failed to apply any law, let alone the correct law" and that there was an "almost total lack of citation to legal authorities." The committee stated, as its baseline for appraisal, its independent view of the applicable law: "When the Agreement is silent or incomplete, recourse must be had to Guinean law in its entirety, subject to the qualification that the only rules of Guinean law (public or private) that are applicable are those that were in existence at the date of the Agreement." On this basis the committee dismissed the tribunal's error in citing to Article 1134 of the French Civil Code instead of to the identical Article 1134 of the Code Civil de l'Union Francaise. Because the provisions are identical, the discrepancy was technical and there was no material violation. "[T]he Committee does not consider that this error warrants annulment." In fact, the citation density of the MINE award under review was very low, but the committee appears to have validated the material components of the award by reference to its own view of the proper law.

*Failure to state reasons*. If one were to take as a normative standard the style of citation in an American student law journal, in which the requirement for footnotes seems to follow the linear rather than some notional criterion, the pages of arbitral awards would consist largely of footnotes. In practical application, the MINE committee reduced the requirement to provide reasons for every statement with its own "rule of reason" which was given a number of applications.

Guinea had cited as an example of the tribunal's alleged failure to give reasons its statement that changed commercial circumstances brought about during the 1973 Middle East war did not make it "legally impossible for either side to perform" the agreement." This was, Guinea alleged, unsupported and inconsistent with the tribunal's finding "that neither short-term nor long-term contracts of affreightment were available, through no fault of the parties."

The statement is quite conclusory and does jump over some necessary reasoning, especially if it is accompanied by a statement that there was a state of commercial impossibility. But the committee rejected Guinea's argument on the factual ground that neither party had argued legal impossibility or implied a legal impediment. This holding is puzzling, for it seems to suggest that when a tribunal adduces its own legal view, which it is entitled to do, rather than adopt a view of one of the parties over which issue has been joined, the reason requirement is either suspended or is lower. In fact, the committee appears to be using its own test of material accuracy and internal relevance, for it says that "there was no necessity for the Tribunal to give reasons for stating an obvious truth from which it drew no conclusions."

Guinea also argued that key arguments it had lodged had not been addressed by the tribunal. The committee contended, rather weakly, that the tribunal had been "aware" of the arguments, but it could only point to those sections of the award in which "Guinea's Assertions" had been recapitulated. But ultimately, the committee acknowledged that "[t]he Tribunal did not explicitly address and decide either of Guinea's arguments." But again the committee avoided a technical discrepancy by applying a material violation approach: "The Tribunal did not have to address these specific conflicting contentions of the parties because it did address and resolved [sic] Guinea's principal argument to the effect that after the July 1973 agreement ('arbitration') with the bauxite receivers, MINE, in the Tribunal's paraphrase, 'demonstrated its lack of will and competence to put SOTRAMAR in operation, thereby breaching its obligations under the Convention.' [sic] By rejecting Guinea's factual assertions and stating, albeit rather summarily, that many conditions of the package still had to be negotiated, the committee was able to conclude that "the award," in the words of the committee, "is supported by reasons which can be followed without great difficulty." This conclusion also obviated the need to address other Guinean arguments, for, by the disposition of this issue, they had become "irrelevant." The same analysis discharged the tribunal from any obligation to deal with Guinean arguments about the limits of good faith and rights of mitigation, for it had already decided that MINE had not been in breach.

*Damages.* The tribunal's statement of law regarding damages was terse and devoid of, in the language of the committee, "statutory or case law references." According to the tribunal: "The Tribunal accepts the general principle that MINE is entitled to be compensated for the profits it would have earned if Guinea had not breached the Convention. The lost profits need not be proven with complete certainty, nor should recovery be denied simply because the amount is difficult to ascertain." In applying this conception, the tribunal rejected summarily, at best, the three alternative theories of damages proffered by MINE. Two of the theories were not deemed "usable." The third was not considered. Instead, the tribunal used the figures in the two-year AFROBULK contract which Guinea received, since it had already determined that this rightly belonged to SOTRAMAR, and extended them over a period of ten years. The reasons for this abbreviated period were explained by the tribunal in the following terms: "While the Convention was to last 30 years, the Bauxite Receivers under the Harvey Agreement were bound to CBG for only 20 years, and 10 years appears to be a reasonable period considering that the Convention contained provisions for early termination." The tribunal awarded simple interest on each year's estimated lost profits at the average U.S. prime rate.

The committee annulled the portions of the award relating to damages for failure to state the reasons on which they were based and the failure to address issues. Article 16 of the agreement between Guinea and MINE had limited damages in case of breach to one year. The tribunal either failed to consider this argument or considered it but thought it should be rejected. But "[t]hat did not free the Tribunal from its duty to give reasons for its ejection as an indispensable component of the statement of reasons on which its conclusion was based." The committee also found that to the extent that the tribunal did purport to state reasons, they were inconsistent and in contradiction with its own analyses of the adduced alternative damage theories.

*Costs.* The tribunal had awarded $275,000 to MINE as costs, but without reasons, for which Guinea challenged it. The committee held that the awarding of costs is discretionary and is subject to no obligation to state reasons. Since Guinea did not allege abuse of discretion, that challenge failed. But because the basis for costs, that Guinea was the losing party, no longer remained, a domino-effect required that part of the award as well be nullified.

### Notes and Questions

1. For further discussion, *see* D.A. Redfern, *ICSID — Losing its Appeal?*, 3 ARB. INT'L 98 (1987). *See generally* Mark B. Feldman, *The Annulment Proceedings and the Finality of ICSID Arbitral Awards*, 2 FOREIGN INVESTMENT L.J. (ICSID REV.) 85 (1987); Philippe Kahn, *Le contrôle des sentences arbitrales rendues par un tribunal CIRDI*, *in* LA JURIDICTION INTERNATIONALE PERMANENTE 363 (1987); Flavia Lattanzi, *Convenzione di Washington sulle Controversie Relative ad Investimenti e Invalidatà delle Sentenze Arbitrali*, 70 RIVISTA DI DIRITTO INTERNAZIONALE 521 (1987); Bjorn Pirrwitz, *Annulment of Arbitral Awards under Article 52 of the Washington Convention on the Settlement of Investment Disputes Between States and Nationals of Other States*, 23 TEXAS INT'L L.J. 74 (1988); Ignaz Seidl-Hohenveldern, *Die Aufhebung von ICSID Schiedsprüchen*, JAHRBUCH FÜR DIE

PRAXIS DER SCHIEDSGERICHTBARKEIT 100 (1989); Thibaut de Berranger, *L'article 52 de la Convention de Washington du 18 mars 1965 et les premiers enseignements de sa pratique*, REVUE DE L'ARBITRAGE 93 (1988).

2. One criticism of the Klöckner annullment decision states:

> Had it been as sensitive to the formative effect of its work on the ICSID control system as it said it was, the committee might have reflected that the route it was taking might well be tantamount to the worst of possible worlds. It served as precedent for review of the wisdom and correctness of an award *as well as* for a very detailed technical examination of awards. If its conception of the proper role of the ad hod committee in the ICSID system were to become authoritative, the probability of future nullifications would increase without a corresponding increase in desirable control.

W.M. REISMAN, SYSTEMS OF CONTROL IN INTERNATIONAL ADJUDICATION AND ARBITRATION 65 (1992). Contrast the broad approach of review, almost tantamount to appeal, in *Klöckner*, with *Northrop v. Triad, supra*.

3. The same author has criticized the Klöckner's ad hoc committee's approach to procedural violations:

> An inadequate conception of control function is also apparent in the ad hoc committee's treatment of procedure. Klöckner had petitioned for nullification on grounds of procedural violations. The committee implied that some of the procedures undertaken by the tribunal may have compromised Klöckner's procedural rights, but felt that Klöckner's claim was barred since Klöckner had not promptly raised objections. Such a holding could act to increase procedural factiousness in future ICSID arbitrations, since it seems to require a litigant to argue each procedural matter it feels is or may be improper the moment it arises. If it does not, *pace* the committee, it may be barred from raising it at the review phase. Happily, this implication appears to have abeen decisively revered by the secretariat of ICSID, which reportedly rejected a request for an ad hoc committee to review an interim award in a subsequent case and indicated that the proper moment for review al all issues was at the end of the procedure.

REISMAN *op. cit. supra* at 65.

The *Klöckner* case has been widely discussed in the literature, *see supra* at Note 1.

### C.   INTERPLAY BETWEEN JUDICIAL REVIEW AND INSTITUTIONAL RULES

Many arbitration rules provide explicitly for the exclusion of recourse to national judicial authorities. For example, the Arbitration Rules of the International Chamber of Commerce provide in Article 24 that the parties "shall be deemed to have . . . waived their right to any form of appeal insofar as such waiver can validly be made." The China International Economic and Trade Arbitration Commission, Arbitration Rules (Version of 1 January 1989) provide in Article 36 that "neither party may bring a suit before a law-court or make a request to any other organization for revising the arbitral award."

The extent to which national courts implicated in the arbitral process will accept exclusion of judicial recourse has often been problematic. The case below deals with control exercised by courts at the arbitral seat in the context of the 1979 English legislation enacted to provide greater autonomy in international arbitration. Similar principles apply under Section 69 of the 1996 Arbitration Act that has now superseded the 1979 statute.

1.     *Arab African Energy Corp. Ltd. v. Olieprodukten Nederland B.V.*, 2 Lloyd's Rep. 419 (Q.B. 1983).

[The contract between the parties was confirmed by two telex messages which included a provision stating "English law — arbitration, if any, London according I.C.C. Rules." An appeal was sought against the award.]

. . .The question for me is whether, if the parties incorporated the I.C.C. rules by reference, they have (whether they appreciated it or not) made a valid exclusion agreement for purposes of s. 3 of the Arbitration Act, 1979. That section reads, so far as material, as follows:

(1) Subject to the following provisions of this section and section 4 below — (a) the High Court shall not, under section 1 (3) (b) above, grant leave to appeal with respect to a question of law arising out of an award . . . if the parties to the reference in question have entered into an agreement in writing (in this section referred to as an "exclusion agreement") which

excludes the right of appeal under section 1 above in relation to that award . . . (2) An exclusion agreement may be expressed so as so [sic] relate to a particular award, to awards under a particular reference or to any other description of awards, whether arising out of the same reference or not; and an agreement may be an exclusion agreement for the purposes of this section whether it is entered into before or after the passing of this Act and whether or not it forms part of an arbitration agreement. (4) Except as provided by sub-section (1) above, sections 1 and 2 above shall have effect notwithstanding anything in any agreement purporting — (a) to prohibit or restrict access to the High Court; or (b) to restrict the jurisdiction of that court; or (c) to prohibit or restrict the making of a reasoned award.

Section 4 of the Act provides for exclusion agreements not to apply in certain cases. It is common ground between the parties that it had no application for the purposes of this case. The provision of the I.C.C. rules which is relied upon as an exclusion agreement is art. 24, which reads as follows:

> 1. The arbitral award shall be final. 2. By submitting the dispute to arbitration by the International Chamber of Commerce, the parties shall be deemed to have undertaken to carry out the resulting award without delay and to have waived their right to any form of appeal insofar as such waiver can validly be made.

.   .   .

Arbitration "according" I.C.C. rules must in my judgment mean "in conformity with" them. No process is envisaged whereby the procedural rules have to be winnowed out from the remainder for the purpose of administering the conduct of the arbitration but not its effect. Such a process would itself be a fruitful source of dissension.

Section 3 (1) of the 1979 Act does not require the overt demonstration of an intention to exclude the right of appeal. True it is, that formerly the Court was careful to maintain its supervisory jurisdiction over arbitrators and their awards. But that aspect of public policy has now given way to the need for finality. In this respect the striving for legal accuracy may be said to have been overtaken by commercial expediency. Since public policy has now changed its stance, I see no reason to continue to adopt an approach to the construction of exclusion agreements which might well have been appropriate before it had done so. In my judgment, the phrase "an agreement in writing which excludes the right of appeal" is apt to apply to an exclusion agreement incorporated by reference. I reach this conclusion unpersuaded to the contrary by the decisions of the European Court which I consider might be misleading in this essentially domestic context. Whatever considerations of good sense may support those decisions and however much one might be impressed by them if approaching the matter a priori, the pursuit of homogeneity should not deter me from the broader approach hitherto adopted by the common law. It is more important that commercial men should know that the English Courts are consistent than that the Courts should turn towards Luxembourg when Parliament has not directed them to do so.

While recalling Sir Alan Herbet's dictum about "deeming," I am quite unable to hold that if parties agree that they should be deemed to have waived their right to any form of appeal they have not thereby done so. It also seems to me that the exclusion (in effect) of every right of appeal which can lawfully be excluded, not only achieves that result but achieves it in a way which is harmonious with the 1979 Act and allows for those particular matters in which the right of appeal cannot be excluded.

For these reasons the applicant is disentitled from applying for leave to appeal and there will be judgment for the respondent. The conclusion is, as I venture to think, one which would have been reached directly by commercial men without having to tread the lawyers' maze.

### Notes and Questions

1.  The Arafenco decision has been followed by the Court of Appeal in *Marine Contractors Inc. v. Shell Petroleum Development Co. of Nigeria Ltd.*, 2 Lloyd's Rep. 77 (1984).

2.  Whether the rules of an arbitral institution have been followed will also be relevant in a treaty context. The New York Convention in Article V(1)(d) provides that awards may be refused recognition if the arbitral procedure was not in accordance with the agreement of the parties. In this connection, consider the

Thompson Memorandum on arbitrator independence in *Fertilizer Corporation of India v. IDI Management, Inc.*, 530 F.Supp. 542 (S.D. Ohio 1982), discussed *infra* p. 1033, Note 1.

The effect of institutional arbitration rules also arose in the following case decided in the Swiss canton of Geneva.

2. *Maritime Int'l Nominees Establishment (MINE) v. Guinea*, Tribunal de 1ere instance, Geneva (Mar. 13, 1986), 1 FOREIGN INVESTMENT L. J. (ICSID REV.) 383, 383-391 (1986).

[The facts of the *MINE v. Guinea* case are summarized *supra* p. 1017. In this phase of the case, MINE sought an interim remedy from the District Court of Geneva.]

. . .

Whereas considering that according to the instrument signed December 6, 1974, and January 23, 1977, the parties agreed to submit their difference to ICSID,

Whereas a proceeding is pending before the ICSID Arbitral Tribunal, which was initiated by MINE on May 7, 1984, and

Whereas according to Article 26 of the Convention on the Settlement of Investment Disputes between States and Nationals of Other States, dated March 18, 1965, the consent of the parties to arbitration under the Convention is, unless otherwise agreed, considered as implying a waiver of all other remedies,

Whereas Switzerland ratified the Convention of March 18, 1965,

Whereas the Convention is thus Swiss law . . . ,

Whereas it should be recognized that in referring to this Tribunal, the applicant is not acting in conformity with Article 26 of the Convention,

Whereas in the order dated December 4, 1985 (p. 7) the Federal Tribunal noted the exclusivity of the ICSID arbitration proceeding,

Whereas the ICSID Arbitral Tribunal itself held that the litigation instituted by MINE in national courts constitutes a violation of its request for ICSID arbitration and constitutes "other remedy" as defined in Article 26 of the Convention,

Whereas in its decision on provisional measures dated December 4, 1985, the ICSID Arbitral Tribunal recommended to MINE that it withdraw and permanently discontinue all pending litigation in national courts, as well as dissolve all other provisional measures (see respondent's exhibit 1),

Whereas on February 5, 1986, the ICSID Arbitral Tribunal rejected MINE's request for rehearing and modification relating to the provisional measure rendered December 4, 1985 (see respondent's exhibit 35).

Whereas recourse to ICSID arbitration should be considered as an implied waiver of all other means of settlement (Art. 26) — when a State agrees to submit a dispute to ICSID arbitration and to thereby give an investor access to an international forum, this State should not be exposed also to other means of pressure or to other remedies (Revue de l'Arbitrage 1983, ICSID and Sovereign Immunity, Georges R. Delaume, p. 144, 145, 157),

Whereas in a case between the parties, relating to their dispute relative to the Agreement of August 19, 1971, the Attachment Judge of Antwerp upheld the exclusivity of ICSID, which had determined that it had jurisdiction, and held that the intervention of national courts of a State which has ratified the Washington Convention is excluded (see respondent's exhibits 11, 12),

Whereas it may be pointed out that in its response to the public law appeal (p. 22, 23), MINE emphasized that the lifting of provisional measures, if granted, should be ordered by the Arbitral Tribunal, because the question is directly linked to the competence of ICSID,

Whereas the ICSID Arbitral Tribunal has ruled on these provisional measures, and recommended their withdrawal in its decision of December 4, 1985,

Whereas according to the Message of the Federal Council, concerning the approval of the Convention on the Settlement of Investment Disputes between States and Nationals of other States, by virtue of a general principle of international law, a claim may only be brought before an international authority after the exhaustion of all local remedies. This rule is equally valid when the parties choose arbitration as the means of settling their dispute. With regard to arbitration as provided for by the Convention, the consent of parties must be considered as indicating waiver of all other remedies (F.F. 1967 2, p. 1466),

Whereas the request which MINE filed with the Tribunal is contrary to the exclusive nature of ICSID arbitration as provided in Article 26 of the Washington Convention of March 18, 1965,

Whereas MINE thus could not appear before this Tribunal,

Whereas in addition, for the same reasons, the award invoked by MINE cannot be considered binding (Art. 5, ch. 1 of the New York Convention).

15.     Whereas there is yet another reason why the request cannot be acted upon,

Whereas the American Arbitration Association tribunal award invoked by MINE was rendered in June 1980,

Whereas for this same dispute with the Republic of Guinea, MINE commenced a new arbitration proceeding before ICSID in May 1984,

Whereas this arbitration proceeding is currently pending,

Whereas the award invoked by MINE in support of its request may not be considered final,

Whereas following the conduct of MINE, which has initiated a new arbitration proceeding, the dispute between the parties may not be considered definitively settled,

Whereas whether an award is binding is a question first of all of the law governing the arbitration proceedings. In their autonomy, the parties freely designate the law of the proceedings (see Art. 5(1)(d) of the New York Convention). As a consequence of the preeminence which the New York Convention gives to their free will, the parties may establish their own rules of procedure or may adopt pre-existing rules, either official or private (see J d T 1982, p. 369, 370),

Whereas the parties agreed to submit their disputes to the ICSID Arbitral Tribunal,

Whereas following the American Arbitration Association's award, the applicant went before ICSID,

Whereas this, request for arbitration by MINE indicates that MINE has accepted Article 26 of the Washington Convention of March 18, 1965, which governs the arbitration proceeding,

Whereas MINE has thus acknowledged that the award of June 1980 had no binding effect, and above all did not have the right to come before this Tribunal,

Whereas for all the foregoing reasons, the request filed October 23, 1985, by MINE is dismissed.

### Notes and Questions

1. In *Fertilizer Corporation of India v. IDI Management*, 530 F.Supp. 542 (S.D. Ohio 1982), enforcement of the award was unsuccessfully resisted on the grounds that lack of arbitrator independence violates public policy under New York Convention Article V(2)(b). The memorandum of William Thompson, formerly with the Secretariat of the International Chamber of Commerce, stated that lack of independence was grounds for arbitrator disqualification. In light of this aspect of the I.C.C. Rules, would IDI have been better off basing its opposition to enforcement of the award on Convention Article V(1)(d), which provides for refusal of recognition to awards when "the arbitral procedure was not in accordance with the agreement of the parties?"

2. Look again at the synopsis of the AMCO award and the decision of the Ad Hoc Committee on pages 1002-17.

    a.    In the Tribunal's award, was Indonesia held to have expropriated AMCO? Explain your answer and, insofar as possible, explain the motives of the Award in making its characterization.

b.      The Tribunal decided that an appropriate warning "was not given to AMCO." What was an appropriate warning? If there had been an appropriate warning, would this have been designed to allow the investor to fulfill its obligations?

c.      What were Indonesia's reasons for withdrawing the license?

d.      Discuss the evidentiary standards which the Tribunal applied.

e.      Do you think that this award is based on strict law or would more accurately be called a decision ex aequo et bono?

f.      What do you think would be an equitable decision in this case?

g.      In the decision of the Ad Hoc Committee, does the Committee make an effort to determine the correct answer? Is this appropriate?


D.      TREATY FRAMEWORK

        1.      NEW YORK CONVENTION

                a.      SCOPE AND SCHEME

        The New York Arbitration Convention gives parties to international contracts a reasonable expectation that their arbitration agreements will be rendered effective. Article III requires recognition and enforcement of foreign arbitral awards subject to carefully specified defenses set forth in Convention Article V. In contrast to the 1961 European Convention, the New York Convention does not require parties to the arbitration to have the nationality of Convention states. Rather it takes a territorial approach with respect to its scope, and covers primarily foreign awards — which is to say, awards rendered in a country other than the one in which enforcement is sought. New York Convention coverage also extends to awards "not considered domestic" in the state where recognition or enforcement is sought. The contours of a "non-domestic" award are dealt with below in the Bergesen case.

                        (i)     *Bergesen v. Joseph Muller Corp.*,
                                710 F.2d 928 (2d Cir. 1983).

        [Sigval Bergesen, a Norwegian shipowner, and Joseph Muller Corporation, a Swiss company, entered into three charter parties providing for the transportation of chemicals from the United States to Europe. Each charter party contained an arbitration clause providing for arbitration in New York, and the Chairman of the American Arbitration Association was given authority to resolve disputes in connection with the appointment of arbitrators.

In 1972, after disputes had arisen during the course of performing the 1970 and 1971 charters, Bergesen made a demand for arbitration of claims for demurrage and shifting and port expenses. Muller denied liability and asserted counterclaims. The initial panel of arbitrators chosen by the parties was dissolved because of Muller's objections and a second panel was selected through the offices of the American Arbitration Association. This panel held hearings in 1976 and 1977 and rendered a written decision on December 14, 1978 in favor of Bergesen, with a net award to Bergesen of $61,406.09 plus interest.

Bergesen then sought enforcement of its award in Switzerland where Muller was based. For over two years Muller successfully resisted enforcement. On December 10, 1981, shortly before the expiration of the three-year limitations period provided in 9 U.S.C. §207, Bergesen filed a petition in the United States District Court for the Southern District of New York to confirm the arbitration award. In 1982 the District Court for the Southern District of New York confirmed Bergesen's award, holding that the Convention applied to arbitration awards rendered in the United States involving foreign interests.

On appeal from this judgment, Muller contended that the Convention did not cover enforcement of the arbitration award made in the United States because it was neither territorially a "foreign" award nor an award "not considered as domestic" within the meaning of the Convention.]

CARDAMONE, Circuit Judge:

.    .    .

Whether the Convention applies to a commercial arbitration award rendered in the United States is a question previously posed but left unresolved in this Court. *See Andros Compania Maritima, S.A. v. Marc Rich & Co.*, A.G., 579 F.2d 691, 699 n. 11 (2d Cir.1978); *I/S*

*Stavborg v. National Metal Converters, Inc.*, 500 F.2d 424, 426 n. 2
(2d Cir.1974). The two district courts that have addressed the issue
have reached opposite conclusions, with little in the way of analysis.
*Compare Transmarine Seaways Corp. of Monrovia v. Marc Rich &
Co., A.G.*, 480 F.Supp. 352, 353 (S.D.N.Y.) (Haight, J.) (finding the
Convention applicable), *aff'd mem.*, 614 F.2d 1291 (2d Cir.1979),
*cert. denied*, 445 U.S. 930, 100 S.Ct. 1318, 63 L.Ed.2d 763 (1980)
*with Diapulse Corporation of America v. Carba, Ltd.*, No. 78 Civ.
3263 (S.D.N.Y. June 28, 1979) (Broderick, J.) (Convention did not
apply "by its terms"), *remanded on other grounds*, 626 F.2d 1108 (2d
Cir.1980). The facts of the instant case make it necessary to resolve
what this Court earlier termed an "intriguing" issue, *see Andros
Compania Maritima, S.A.*, 579 F.2d at 699 n. 11.

To resolve that issue we turn first to the Convention's history.
Under the auspices of the United Nations, the Convention on the
Recognition and Enforcement of Foreign Arbitral Awards was
convened in New York City in 1958 to resolve difficulties created by
two earlier treaties—the 1923 Geneva Protocol on Arbitration Clauses,
27 L.N.T.S. 157 (1924), and the 1927 Geneva Convention on the
Execution of Foreign Arbitral Awards, 92 L.N.T.S. 301 (1929).
Because of the legal and practical difficulties which arose from
application of these earlier treaties, one commentator wrote, "The
formidable amount of highly qualified labor which went into their
preparation has not been rewarded by any perceptible progress in
international commercial arbitration." Nussbaum, *Treaties on
Commercial Arbitration—A Test of International Private-Law
Legislation*, 56 HARV.L.REV. 219, 236 (1942).

A proposed draft of the 1958 Convention which was to govern
the enforcement of foreign arbitral awards stated that it was to apply
to arbitration awards rendered in a country other than the state where
enforcement was sought. *See* G. Haight, *Convention on the Recognition
and Enforcement of Foreign Arbitral Awards* 1 (1958) (Haight). This
proposal was controversial because the delegates were divided on
whether it defined adequately what constituted a foreign award. On one
side were ranged the countries of western Europe accustomed to civil
law concepts; on the other side were the eastern European states and
the common law nations. Contini at 292. For example, several
countries, including France, Italy and West Germany, objected to the
proposal on the ground that a territorial criterion was not adequate to

establish whether an award was foreign or domestic. These nations believed that the nationality of the parties, the subject of the dispute and the rules of arbitral procedure were factors to be taken into account in determining whether an award was foreign. *Id.*; Haight at 2. In both France and West Germany, for example, the nationality of an award was determined by the law governing the procedure. Thus, an award rendered in London under German law was considered domestic when enforcement was attempted in Germany, and an award rendered in Paris under foreign law was considered foreign when enforcement was sought in France. Contini at 292. As an alternative to the territorial concept, eight European nations proposed that the Convention "apply to the recognition and enforcement of arbitral awards other than those considered as domestic in the country in which they are relied upon." Haight at 2. Eight other countries, including the United States, objected to this proposal, arguing that common law nations would not understand the distinction between foreign and domestic awards. These latter countries urged the delegates to adopt only the territorial criterion.

A working party composed of representatives from ten states to which the matter was referred recommended that both criteria be included. Thus, the Convention was to apply to awards made in a country other than the state where enforcement was sought as well as to awards not considered domestic in that state. The members of the Working Party representing the western European group agreed to this recommendation, provided that each nation would be allowed to exclude certain categories of awards rendered abroad. At the conclusion of the conference this exclusion was omitted, so that the text originally proposed by the Working Party was adopted as Article I of the Convention. A commentator noted that the Working Party's intent was to find a compromise formula which would restrict the territorial concept. Contini at 293. The final action taken by the Convention appears to have had the opposite result, i.e., except as provided in paragraph 3, the first paragraph of Article I means that the Convention applies to all arbitral awards rendered in a country other than the state of enforcement, whether or not such awards may be regarded as domestic in that state; "*it also applies to all awards not considered as domestic in the state of enforcement, whether or not any of such awards may have been rendered in the territory of that state.*" *Id.* at 293-94 (emphasis supplied).

To assure accession to the Convention by a substantial number of nations, two reservations were included. They are set forth in Article I(3). The first provides that any nation "may on the basis of reciprocity declare that it will apply the Convention "only to those awards made in the territory of another contracting state." The second states that the Convention will apply only to differences arising out of legal relationships "considered as commercial under the national law" of the state declaring such a reservation. These reservations were included as a necessary recognition of the variety and diversity of the interests represented at the conference, as demonstrated, for example, by the statement of the delegate from Belgium that without any right of reservation his country would not accede. Haight at 16; Quigly at 1061.

## III

With this background in mind, we turn to Muller's contentions regarding the scope of the Convention. The relevant portion of the Convention, Article I, is set forth in the margin.[295] The territorial concept expressed in the first sentence of Article I(1) presents little difficulty. Muller correctly urges that since the arbitral award in this case was made in New York and enforcement was sought in the United States, the award does not meet the territorial criterion. Simply put, it is not a foreign award as defined in Article I(1) because it was not rendered outside the nation where enforcement is sought.

Muller next contends that the award may not be considered a foreign award within the purview of the second sentence of Article I(1) because it fails to qualify as an award "not considered as domestic." Muller claims that the purpose of the "not considered as domestic" test was to provide for the enforcement of what it terms "stateless awards," i.e., those rendered in the territory where enforcement is sought but considered unenforceable because of some foreign component. This argument is unpersuasive since some countries favoring the provision

---

[295] [2] This Convention shall apply to the recognition and enforcement of arbitral awards made in the territory of a State other than the State where the recognition and enforcement of such awards are sought, and arising out of differences between persons, whether physical or legal. It shall also apply to arbitral awards not considered as domestic awards in the State where their recognition and enforcement are sought.

desired it so as to preclude the enforcement of certain awards rendered abroad, not to enhance enforcement of awards rendered domestically.

Additionally, Muller urges a narrow reading of the Convention contrary to its intended purpose. The Convention did not define nondomestic awards. The definition appears to have been left out deliberately in order to cover as wide a variety of eligible awards as possible, while permitting the enforcing authority to supply its own definition of "nondomestic" in conformity with its own national law. Omitting the definition made it easier for those states championing the territorial concept to ratify the Convention while at the same time making the Convention more palatable in those states which espoused the view that the nationality of the award was to be determined by the law governing the arbitral procedure. We adopt the view that awards "not considered as domestic" denotes awards which are subject to the Convention not because made abroad, but because made within the legal framework of another country, e.g., pronounced in accordance with foreign law or involving parties domiciled or having their principal place of business outside the enforcing jurisdiction. *See generally* Pisar at 18. We prefer this broader construction because it is more in line with the intended purpose of the treaty, which was entered into to encourage the recognition and enforcement of international arbitration awards, *see Scherk v. Alberto Culver Co.*, 417 U.S. 506, 520 n. 15, 94 S.Ct. 2449, 2457 n. 15, 41 L.Ed.2d 270 (1974). Applying that purpose to this case involving two foreign entities leads to the conclusion that this award is not domestic.

## IV

Muller also urges us to interpret the Convention narrowly based on the fact that, as stated in a Presidential Proclamation dated September 1, 1970, 21 U.S.T. 2517, T.I.A.S. No. 6997, the 1970 accession by the United States to the Convention adopted both reservations of Article I(3). The fact that the United States acceded to the Convention with a declaration of reservations provides little reason for us to construe the accession in narrow terms. Had the United States acceded to the Convention without these two reservations, the scope of the Convention doubtless would have had wider impact. Comment, *International Commercial Arbitration Under the United Nations Convention and the Amended Federal Arbitration Statute*, 47 Wash.L.Rev. 441 (1972). Nonetheless, the treaty language should be interpreted broadly to effectuate its recognition and enforcement purposes. *See Scherk*, 417 U.S. at 520 n. 15, 94 S.Ct. at 2457 n. 15 (the Convention's goal was "to encourage the recognition and enforcement of commercial arbitration agreements in international contracts"); *Reed v. Wiser*, 555 F.2d 1079, 1088 (2d Cir.), *cert. denied*, 434 U.S. 922 (1977); *cf. Parsons & Whittemore Overseas Co. v. Societe Generale de L'Industrie du Papier (Rakta)*, 508 F.2d 969, 974 (2d Cir.1974) (defenses to enforcement of foreign awards under the Convention are narrowly construed).

## V

We now turn to the argument that the implementing statute was not intended to cover awards rendered within the United States. Section 202 of Title 9 of the United States Code which is entitled "Agreement or award falling under the Convention," provides in relevant part:

> An agreement or award arising out of such a relationship which is entirely between citizens of the United States shall be deemed not to fall under the Convention unless that relationship involves property located abroad, envisages performance or enforcement abroad, or has some other reasonable relation with one or more foreign states.

The legislative history of this provision indicates that it was intended to ensure that "an agreement or award arising out of a legal relationship exclusively between citizens of the United States is not enforceable under the Convention in [United States] courts unless it has a reasonable relation with a foreign state." H.R.Rep. No. 91-1181, 91st Cong., 2d Sess. 2, *reprinted in* 1970 U.S.Code Cong. & Ad.News 3601, 3602. Inasmuch as it was apparently left to each state to define which awards were to be considered nondomestic, *see Pisar* at 18, Congress spelled out its definition of that concept in section 202. Had Congress desired to exclude arbitral awards involving two foreign parties rendered within the United States from enforcement by our courts it could readily have done so. It did not. *See Sumitomo Corp. v. Parakopi Compania Maritima*, 477 F.Supp. 737, 741 (S.D.N.Y.1979), *aff'd mem.*, 620 F.2d 286 (2d Cir.1980); Aksen, *American Arbitration Accession Arrives in the Age of Aquarius: United States Implements United Nations Convention on the Recognition and Enforcement of Foreign Arbitral Awards*, 3 Sw.U.L.Rev. 1, 16 (1971) (Under implementing legislation Convention should apply when foreign contacts are substantial, i.e., "where a foreign person or corporation is a party to an agreement involving foreign performance, or where the business deal has some other 'reasonable relation with one or more foreign states.'"); *see also* McMahon at 740-43 (questioning whether section 202 covers awards similar to that in the present case).

Additional support for the view that awards rendered in the United States may qualify for enforcement under the Convention is found in the remaining sections of the implementing statute. It has been held that section 203 of the statute provides jurisdiction for disputes involving two aliens. *See Sumitomo Corp.*, 477 F.Supp. at 740-41. Section 204 supplies venue for such an action and section 206 states that "[a] court having jurisdiction under this chapter may direct that arbitration be held . . . at any place therein provided for, *whether that place is within or without the United States*" (emphasis supplied). It would be anomalous to hold that a district court could direct two aliens to arbitration within the United States under the statute, but that it could not enforce the resulting award under legislation which, in large part, was enacted for just that purpose.

Muller's further contention that it could not have been the aim of Congress to apply the Convention to this transaction because it would remove too broad a class of awards from enforcement under the Federal Arbitration Act, 9 U.S.C. §§ 1-13, is unpersuasive. That this particular award might also have been enforced under the Federal Arbitration Act is not significant. There is no reason to assume that Congress did not intend to provide overlapping coverage between the Convention and the Federal Arbitration Act. Similarly, Muller's argument that Bergesen only sought enforcement under the terms of the Convention because it has a longer statute of limitations than other laws under which Bergesen could have sued is irrelevant. Since the statutes overlap in this case Bergesen has more than one remedy available and may choose the most advantageous. . . .

\*    \*    \*

The following article by an expert on the New York Convention uses the Bergesen case as the point of departure for a systematic examination of exactly what is meant by a "non-domestic" award.

(ii)    Albert Jan van den Berg, *Non-domestic arbitral awards under the 1958 New York Convention*, 2 ARB. INT'L 191 (1986).

The question what constitutes a non-domestic award within the meaning of the New York Convention is one of the most complicated issues posed by this treaty . . . . The Bergesen case is not only troublesome for the question what constitutes a non-domestic award. To complicate matters further, one of the parties also argued that the award in question could be considered 'stateless.' The question what constitutes a 'stateless award,' and whether such an award comes within the Convention's purview, is the subject of the seventh and last section of this article.

.      .       .

The Court of Appeals in Bergesen stated that the Convention applies in any case to the recognition and enforcement of an arbitral award made in the territory of another state. This observation conforms to the legislative history reviewed above. In fact, the compromise reached at the New York Conference was in favour of the territorialists. The non-domestic award defined in the second criterion was intended as an extension of the Convention's field of application. This is also made clear in the text of the Convention itself. The second criterion provides: 'It shall also apply to arbitral awards not considered as domestic awards in the State where their recognition and enforcement are sought' (emphasis added). In other words, the Convention always applies to the recognition and enforcement of an arbitral award made in another State (ie, the first criterion), whilst it may, in addition, apply to the recognition and enforcement of an arbitral award made in the State where the recognition and enforcement are sought if such an award is considered non-domestic (ie, the second criterion). As a result, the second criterion of the Convention's scope applies only to the recognition and enforcement of an arbitral award made in the territory of the State where recognition and enforcement are sought.

. . . . Further, in order to appreciate the Convention's scope in relation to the non-domestic award, it is also necessary to make some observations regarding the distinction between recognition and enforcement on the one hand and setting aside on the other.

. . .

As a general rule, whilst recognition and enforcement merely have a territorial effect, setting aside (also known as vacatur or annulment) has, according to the Convention, an extra-territorial effect.

When a court recognises and enforces an arbitral award, whether made within its territory or abroad, it accepts that the award has the same force and effect as a domestic court judgment within its jurisdiction. The legal basis for recognition and enforcement of an arbitral award made within a court's jurisdiction is to be found in the arbitration law of that jurisdiction. For the recognition and enforcement of a foreign arbitral award, the legal basis is the New York Convention or, if it exists, municipal law regarding the recognition and enforcement of a foreign arbitral award. The granting or refusal of recognition and enforcement is territorially limited to the court's jurisdiction. The decision of a national court to grant or refuse recognition and enforcement does not affect foreign courts because such a decision is not under the Convention a ground for which recognition or enforcement may be respectively granted or refused.

Different rules apply, according to the New York Convention, to the setting aside of the arbitral award. First, the court of the country in which, or under the law of which, the award is made ('country of origin') is exclusively competent to entertain the action for setting aside the award. A foreign court may not entertain such an action since the Convention refers to a setting aside only by the court of the country of origin. A foreign court may refuse recognition and enforcement of an arbitral award within its jurisdiction if one or more of the grounds of refusal for recognition and enforcement are present. Second, if the arbitral award has been set aside in the country of origin, foreign courts are in principle bound by that decision. In that case they may refuse recognition and enforcement of the award, if the recognition and enforcement are sought under the Convention.

An example may clarify the above distinction between the recognition and enforcement of an arbitral award on the one hand and the setting aside of an award on the other. An arbitral award made in Sweden under Swedish arbitration law can be set aside by a Swedish court only. Foreign courts may merely refuse recognition and enforcement of that award within their jurisdiction, but have no authority to set it aside. However, if a Swiss court has refused recognition and enforcement of the Swedish award, an Italian court is not bound by such refusal and may still grant recognition and enforcement. Such conflicting decisions are rare in practice. If the Swedish court has set aside the award, a Swiss or Italian court may, under the Convention, refuse recognition and enforcement on the grounds of that Swedish decision.

The West German Law quoted above deals with an award made in another country under German procedural law. If the award is made under German procedural law, German courts consider the award to be domestic. West Germany therefore is the country 'under the law of which' the award is made, in other words, the country of origin. The West German Law rightly provides that the West German courts are competent to decide on the setting aside of the award.

.     .     .

[One view has] considered an award as non-domestic if it is governed, on the basis of an agreement of the parties to this effect, by the arbitration law of another country. For example, parties may agree to arbitrate in France on the basis of West German arbitration law. If the request for enforcement is based on the Convention, French courts will indeed apply the Convention since they consider the award as non-domestic, although it is made within their own territory.

.     .     .

The foregoing interpretation may be called the traditional interpretation. This interpretation is not only based on the legislative history of the Convention but is also confirmed by the text of the Convention. The Convention refers to arbitral awards not only made in another country but also under the law of another country. If the Convention is applied only to arbitral awards made in another State, there was no need to refer to awards made under the law of a country. This aspect will be discussed below. It should also be noted that commentators outside the United States have affirmed that the non-domestic arbitral award is an award made in the enforcing State under the arbitration law of another State.

In practice, however, parties rarely agree to arbitrate in one country under the arbitration law of another country. To do so would be to introduce a hazardous complication. One would have to ascertain

— or hope! — that both the country where the arbitration takes place and the country whose arbitration law is chosen would recognise the capacity to agree to arbitrate under the law of a country other than that where the arbitration takes place. The law governing the arbitration determines which country's courts are competent to render assistance in the arbitration, for example by appointing arbitrators. That law also determines which country's courts are competent to control the lawfulness of the arbitration and the award, ordinarily carried out in an action for setting aside the award. If the parties agree to arbitrate in country A under the arbitration law of country B, it may happen that country A does not recognise the capacity to designate a foreign arbitration law. In such a case, the courts in country A will hold the award made within its territory to be domestic and would consequently hold themselves competent to entertain an action for setting aside the award. But if, at the same time, country B allows arbitration abroad under its arbitration law, its courts will also consider the award to be domestic and may hold themselves equally competent to entertain an action for setting aside the award. This may end up in an undesirable situation where the courts of two countries decide on the setting aside of the award, with possibly conflicting decisions. The reverse situation may be equally undesirable: if country A recognises the capacity, but country B does not allow arbitration abroad under its arbitration law, the setting aside cannot be sought in either country.

·    ·    ·

If the foregoing interpretation, based on the legislative history and text of the Convention, is applied to Bergesen, the conclusion must be that the award was not a non-domestic award within the meaning of the Convention. The arbitration clause provided expressly that 'The arbitration . . . shall be governed by the laws of the State of New York . . . .' The reference to the laws of the State of New York must be deemed a reference to New York State arbitration law. Even if this reference is construed as a reference to the law applicable to the substance, ie, the law to be applied by the arbitrators to the merits of the dispute, the Bergesen arbitration was not governed by the arbitration law of another Contracting State because there was no indication that the parties expressly or implicitly agreed to a foreign arbitration law.

The Court of Appeals thus went beyond the legislative history and text of the Convention. If the second criterion of non-domestic awards is read in isolation, a court can be deemed to be free to do so because the text gives a court a discretionary power: the Convention can be applied to an arbitral award if a court 'considers' it non-domestic. The reason the Court of Appeals preferred the 'broader construction,' was that 'it is more in line with the intended purpose of the treaty.' The court described the purpose as being 'to encourage the recognition and enforcement of international arbitration awards.' It referred in this respect to the famous decision of the US Supreme Court in Fritz Scherk v. Alberto Culver Co. While the sentiment is laudable, it should not be allowed to obscure the question of whether the 'broader construction' is justified by a reading of the second criterion in isolation.

The Court of Appeals interpreted awards 'not considered as domestic' to be awards which are 'made within the legal framework of another country.' It gave as examples of 'the legal framework of another country,' awards which are 'pronounced in accordance with foreign law' or which involve 'parties domiciled or having their principal place of business outside the enforcing jurisdiction.' The reference by the Court of Appeals to 'the legal framework of another country' is at first sight somewhat puzzling. The examples given by the Court of awards 'pronounced in accordance with foreign law' is equally mystifying. Does the foreign law mean the law applicable to the arbitration or the law applicable to the substance, or both? What the court presumably had in mind was that the award involved some foreign element with respect to either the law applicable to the arbitration or the law applicable to the substance. Neither was present in Bergesen. As observed before, the arbitration clause referred to New York State law.

## The parties' nationality

What in fact motivated the Court of Appeals to hold the award to be non-domestic was quite clearly the foreign nationality of both parties involved (ie, Norwegian and Swiss). This consideration finds no basis in the New York Convention, as far as the first criterion for its field of application is concerned. The Convention's scope does not depend on the nationality of the parties. Such a condition was imposed by the Geneva Convention of 1927, the New York Convention's predecessor, which required that the parties be subject to the jurisdiction of different Contracting States. The expression 'subject to the jurisdiction' of a

State had caused uncertainty, as some courts interpreted it as referring to nationality, while others construed it as domicile.

Consequently, the nationality requirement was left out of the New York Convention. The Convention, therefore, applies in theory to the enforcement of an arbitral award made in another country between two nationals of the enforcing State. The Italian Supreme Court, for example, has recognised this rule and held that it supersedes the principle of Italian law that two Italians are not allowed to arbitrate abroad. As will be discussed below, the US implementing legislation is in this respect not in conformity with the Convention.

As far as the first criterion (ie, awards made abroad) is concerned, the foreign nationality of the parties is irrelevant for the Convention's applicability. But may the foreign nationality of the parties satisfy the second criterion (ie, non-domestic awards made within the enforcing State)? The second criterion read in isolation would permit a court to do so because, as observed before, it gives a court discretionary power whether or not to regard an award as non-domestic. Although according to the traditional interpretation a non-domestic award is an award made in the enforcing State under the arbitration law of another State, a court may go further and deem an award to be non-domestic because of the foreign nationality of the parties regardless of the applicable arbitration law. Such an expansive interpretation is apparently adopted by the Court of Appeals in Bergesen.

## The US implementing legislation

The Court of Appeals obviously came to this broader construction on the basis of the legislation implementing the Convention in the United States. The Court referred to the provision by which the Convention should not apply to an agreement or award arising out of a legal relationship exclusively between citizens of the United States, unless that relationship has some reasonable relation with one or more foreign States. The court then stated that Congress spelled out its definition of non-domestic awards in the just mentioned provision.

The legislative history of the implementing legislation suggests that its drafters were not concerned with a definition of a non-domestic award within the meaning of the Convention. Their concern was:

> [W]e were faced with the problem that section 1 of the [Federal Arbitration] Act, which defines commerce, specifically includes both interstate and foreign commerce, while the implementation of the Convention should be concerned only with foreign commerce. Consequently, it was necessary to modify the definition of commerce to make it quite clear that arbitration arising out of relationships in interstate commerce remains under the original Arbitration Act and is excluded from the operation of the proposed chapter 2.

> To achieve this result we have included in section 202 the requirement that any case concerning an agreement or award solely between US citizens is excluded unless there is some important foreign element involved . . . .

In other words, the drafters were concerned about a delineation of the ambit of Chapter One and Chapter Two of the Federal Arbitration Act. The legislative history contains no indication that the provision was intended to be a definition of non-domestic awards.

The core of the problem seems to be that in an arbitration between two aliens within the United States it is often difficult, if not impossible, for the parties to obtain jurisdiction in the Federal courts under Chapter One of the Federal Arbitration Act with regard to matters connected with the arbitration. Chapter One does not create an independent basis for federal jurisdiction. Two aliens cannot satisfy the requirement of diversity jurisdiction which requires that at least one of the parties be a citizen of the United States. The implementing legislation, Chapter Two of the Federal Arbitration Act, has cured this unsatisfactory situation. It provides for original jurisdiction of the Federal courts in an 'action or proceeding falling under the Convention.' The diversity requirement does not apply in this case. Although the Court of Appeals did not explicitly mention the problems caused by Chapter One for two foreign parties arbitrating within the United States, it did indeed refer to the provision in Chapter Two, creating original jurisdiction, in support of its view that awards rendered in the United States may qualify for enforcement under the Convention.

Viewed within this perspective, the interpretation by the Court of Appeals makes the United States a more hospitable forum for foreign parties intending to arbitrate within the United States. They can now be assured that the ensuing award can be enforced in the Federal courts. However, the legal basis is scant. Neither the text nor the legislative history of the Convention indicates that recognition and enforcement of an award made between two foreign parties under the arbitration law of the country in which recognition and enforcement are sought should fall under the Convention. The same applies to the legislative history of the US implementing legislation. Even the provision relating to the original jurisdiction of the Federal courts in the implementing legislation cannot be deemed to constitute an indication to this effect. That provision can be invoked only if the award falls under the Convention; to do so would be a petitio principii: assuming the answer to the very question that is being analysed. In fact, a legal basis can be found only if the text of the second criterion is read in isolation. As mentioned, that text gives courts in Contracting States a discretionary power to consider awards made within their jurisdiction as non-domestic. But can the text of the second criterion be read in isolation?

.     .     .

If the expansive interpretation is followed, enforcement of an arbitral award containing a foreign element and made in the United States may become more difficult. Enforcement of an award falling under Chapter One of the Federal Arbitration Act is almost automatic. Objections to an award must be raised through an action for setting aside the award. The same applies to the arbitration laws of most of the constituent States of the United States. In contrast, enforcement of an award under Chapter Two of the Federal Arbitration Act and the Convention can be resisted on a number of grounds. Many of these grounds for refusal of enforcement correspond in essence to the grounds for setting aside under Chapter One of the Federal Arbitration Act and most of the arbitration laws of the constituent States.

One is then faced with the rather undesirable situation where the same award may be subject to resistance by a losing party on the basis of similar grounds in two different procedures. First, in proceedings initiated by the winning party aiming at the enforcement of the award under Chapter Two of the Federal Arbitration Act and the Convention, the losing party may invoke all grounds for refusal of enforcement listed in the Convention. Second, in proceedings initiated by the losing party aiming at the setting aside of the award under Chapter One of the Federal Arbitration Act or under State arbitration law the losing party may assert grounds for setting aside the award which are similar to the Convention's grounds for refusal of recognition and enforcement.

It may be argued that the doctrine of collateral estoppel controls this situation and that a losing party is estopped from challenging the award in the second procedure if he has already asserted these grounds in a first procedure. However, an action for the enforcement is essentially different from an action for the setting aside of the award. As mentioned before, this distinction is clearly made by the Convention itself. In addition, the grounds for refusal of enforcement under the Convention are not identical to, but only similar (in most cases) to the grounds for setting aside under Federal and State arbitration law. Crafty pleaders may not have to stretch their imagination too far to establish grounds for setting aside that are prima facie distinguishable from grounds for resistance to enforcement.

.    .    .

## STATELESS AWARDS

Muller also argued before the Court of Appeals that the notion of non-domestic covers awards which Muller called "stateless awards," and that the award in question failed to qualify as such. Muller defined the stateless award as one 'rendered in the territory where enforcement is sought but considered unenforceable because of some foreign component.' The Court of Appeals found this argument unpersuasive:

> [S]ince some countries favouring the provision [ie, the second criterion] desired it so as to preclude the enforcement of certain awards rendered abroad, not to enhance enforcement of awards rendered domestically.

This reasoning of the court is unclear. Either the court understood Muller's argument incorrectly or Muller presented its argument badly. Muller presumably referred to a third category of awards. It can be questioned whether this category falls under the Convention and, especially, under the second criterion of non-domestic awards.

### Concept of stateless awards

Until now two types of awards have been discussed here, (i) an arbitral award governed by the arbitration law of the place of arbitration (most cases), and (ii) an arbitral award governed, on the basis of an agreement between the parties, by the arbitration law of a country other than the place of arbitration (rather theoretical, corresponding to the second criterion under the traditional interpretation). Some authors identify a third category, which Muller apparently had in mind: an arbitral award not governed by any arbitration law at all, but solely by an agreement of the parties. Various names are invented for this category of awards: a-national, supra-national, transnational, expatriate, de-nationalised or floating awards. The attractiveness of an arbitration and award detached from the ambit of any national arbitration law, is that domestically influenced particularities of a national arbitration law are in principle eliminated. The parties are free to organise the arbitration themselves or, to authorise the arbitrators to do so, as they deem fit. The arbitration may take place anywhere, as the place of arbitration would not entail the applicability of the arbitration law of the country concerned.

However, the legal status of de-nationalised arbitration is uncertain. If the arbitration agreement does not provide, in sufficient detail, for the constitution of an arbitral tribunal and the arbitral procedure, difficulties will rise as no recourse may be had to a national arbitration law. Furthermore, arbitration, international as it may be, needs at least a supporting judicial authority which, failing an international authority competent in this respect, must necessarily be the court of some country. The judicial support may, for example, be needed for the challenge of an arbitrator. Supervision by a judicial authority over at least the validity of the arbitration agreement and the fundamental rules of due process must also be ensured. Such supervision is carried out by entertaining such actions as those aiming to set aside the award. It is a generally accepted principle that the courts of the country under the arbitration law of which the arbitration takes place or took place are the competent judicial authority in relation to the foregoing matter. Such competence would be excluded in the case of de-nationalised arbitration. There are few international arbitrations where parties have agreed to a de-nationalised arbitration. There exists an appalling example of the difficulties encountered in enforcing an arbitral award resulting from an allegedly de-nationalised arbitration.

It should be noted at this point that for a long time it was thought that arbitration under the Rules of the International Chamber of Commerce ('ICC') was de-nationalised. This belief induced the

Court of Appeal of Paris to decide, in 1980, that an ICC award made in Paris between a Swedish shipyard and a Libyan State-owned corporation was not governed by French arbitration law. The court therefore dismissed the action for setting aside the award. Subsequent to this decision, two developments occurred. First, in 1981 France adopted a new arbitration law specifically applicable to international arbitrations. According to this law, awards rendered in an international arbitration in France must always be subject to an action for setting aside before the French courts. Second, the ICC issued a new commentary on its Rules, in which it is expressly stated that 'the mandatory rules of national law applicable to international arbitrations in the country where the arbitration takes place must anyway be observed, even if other rules of procedure are chosen by the parties or by the arbitrator.'

A de-nationalised arbitration must be distinguished from an arbitration which is internationalised within the limits imposed by a national arbitration law. Such internationalisation can be achieved referring to arbitration rules geared to international arbitration, such as the ICC Rules, the 1985 Rules of the London Court of International Arbitration or the UNCITRAL Arbitration Rules. The limits imposed by a national arbitration law are those provisions which are mandatory. It is therefore important in international arbitrations to designate a place of arbitration in a country which has a liberal arbitration law.

## Convention not applicable to stateless awards

After the foregoing explanation as to what constitutes a stateless award, it is appropriate to return to the argument made by Muller before the US Court of Appeals. The Court of Appeals rightly rejected Muller's argument that the second criterion covers stateless awards, although the court's reasoning is somewhat confusing. The New York Convention must be deemed to apply only to arbitral awards which are governed by a specific national arbitration law. This principle applies to both the first and second criterion of the Convention's field of application. It is true that the text of the Convention, as far as its field of application is concerned, does not require that the award be governed by a national arbitration law.

However, if the Convention's scope is read in conjunction with the Convention's other provisions, it becomes evident that this requirement is implied. Enforcement of an award may be rejected if the respondent can prove that the arbitration agreement is invalid 'under the <u>law</u> to which the parties have subjected it, or failing any indication thereon, under the <u>law</u> of the country where the award was made' (emphasis added). Enforcement of an award may also be refused if the respondent can prove that the award has been set aside by a court of 'the country in which, or under the <u>law</u> of which, that award was made' (emphasis added). Although another basis for refusal of enforcement, which concerns irregularities in the composition of the arbitral tribunal and the arbitral procedure, refers in the first place to the agreement of the parties on these matters, and failing such agreement, to the law of the place of arbitration, this provision cannot be deemed to alter the principle that the Convention may apply only to arbitral awards which are governed by a specific arbitration law.

The New York Convention not being a basis for enforcement of stateless awards, the only realistic approach to giving this category of awards a sufficient legal backing is an appropriate international convention. Such a treaty exists for investment disputes: The 1965 Washington Convention on the Settlement of Investment Disputes Between States and Nationals of Other States. This Convention provides for a self-sufficient system of truly international arbitration which is solely governed by the provisions of the Convention and the rules and regulations issued thereunder. There is no other international convention comparable to the Washington Convention. Specifically, the New York Convention regulates only two aspects of international arbitration: the enforcement of the arbitration agreement and that of the arbitral award. All other aspects are by necessity governed by some national arbitration law, which, as explained before, is normally the arbitration law of the place of arbitration.

### Notes and Questions

1. With respect to United States Application of the Convention, whether an award is foreign or "non-domestic," the United States excludes from Convention coverage awards arising out of relationships entirely between American citizens that have no reasonable foreign link in the form of property located abroad, performance or enforcement abroad, or some other reasonable relation with one or more foreign states. *See* 9 U.S.C. § 202.

2. The United States, like many other nations, applies the Convention to foreign awards on the basis of geographical reciprocity. Only foreign awards rendered in the territory of another contracting state benefit from the Convention enforcement

scheme. This reservation looks to the place where the award is rendered rather than to the parties' nationality.

b.     THE INTERACTION OF NEW YORK
CONVENTION ARTICLES III, V AND VII

Note the interaction of New York Convention Articles III, V and VII, set forth below. Article III mandates recognition of arbitral awards. Article V sets forth the grounds on which an award may be refused recognition or enforcement under the Convention. Article VII provides that the Convention will not deprive any interested party of the opportunity to enforce an award under dispositions of law that may be more favorable to it than the Convention.

The first part of Article V includes five defects that must be asserted and proven by the party resisting enforcement of the award. They include lack of a valid arbitration agreement, denial of an opportunity to be heard, an excess of jurisdiction by an arbitrator who has decided matters beyond the scope of the submission agreement and annulment of the award in the country where rendered. These defenses permit a court to avoid lending its power to support a procedurally defective, fraudulent or unfair arbitration, but are not intended to justify judicial review of the merits of the underlying disputes.

In addition, a court on its own motion, without any proof by the party resisting the award, may refuse recognition or enforcement on the basis of the forum law's "public policy" and non-arbitrability of subject matter. While all Convention defenses might be said to relate to public policy in some way, these last defenses serve as explicit "catch-all" escape hatches from enforcement and recognition.

The following commentary on how the Article V defenses are supposed to work was written shortly after the Convention was drafted, and discusses several of the competing positions in the drafting process.

(i)     Leonard V. Quigley, *Accession by the United States to the United Nations Convention on the Recognition and Enforcement of Foreign Arbitral Awards*, 70 YALE L.J. 1049, 1066-71 (1961).

Enforcement of Foreign Arbitral Awards — Grounds for Refusal

Article V lists five grounds upon which the award may be refused recognition and enforcement upon the request of the defendant, and two further grounds upon which the competent authority of the forum State may on its own motion refuse recognition and enforcement. Two important themes run through the seven grounds of invalidity. The first is that of ultimate judicial control over enforcement of the award, the problem of the "double exequatur." The ultimate authority was placed in the enforcing State, but Article V 1. (e) allows the defendant to attack the award on the ground that it has not yet become binding or has been set aside or suspended by a competent authority "of the country in which, or under the law of which, that award was made." The second important theme is contractual autonomy. The representatives of the International Chamber of Commerce advocated a proposal which would allow the parties to select the law of any country to pick principles of decision to govern the arbitration without regard to such law. Only the first of these was accepted, and is reflected throughout Article V. Complete divorce of the arbitral process from the law of some State was thought to be too revolutionary a concept for a Convention which was intended to be ratified by a large number of nations.

·     ·     ·

## Article V 1.(e): The Award Is Not Binding or Has Been Set Aside or Suspended.

·     ·     ·

This paragraph reflects the inability of the Conference to agree on the solution to the problem of the "double exequatur." No one wanted the Convention to require judicial proceedings in confirmation of the award in both the rendering and enforcing State. At the same time, an award which had been set aside by competent authority in the

State where rendered should hardly be granted enforcement in another State.

The hardest question is the status in the enforcing State of an award that has not been set aside but is still subject to review in the rendering State by appeal or other procedures. The Conference rejected the requirement that the award be "final and operative" in the rendering State, yet was unwilling to make awards enforceable as soon as rendered.

In the confusion over the word "binding," there was no discussion of the phrase "or under the law of which." While this parallels the provision in Article V 1. (a) granting the parties the power to pick the law governing their agreement, the matter of setting aside the award is an entirely different matter. This phrase provides that when an award is rendered in one state under the law of a second state, the courts of that second state may set aside or suspend the award. Such a debatable result is probably not provided for under the national law of most of the States under whose law the award might have been made.

Significantly, the paragraph fails to specify the grounds upon which the rendering State may set aside or suspend the award. While it would have provided greater reliability to the enforcement of awards under the Convention had the available grounds been defined in some way, such action would have constituted meddling with national procedure for handling domestic awards, a subject beyond the competence of the Conference.

## Article V 2.(a): Subject Matter Not Arbitrable

.  .  .

This ground, and the following one, may be raised either by the defendant or by the competent authority before which the award is brought for enforcement.

This paragraph carries over the similar provision in Article 1. (b) of the Geneva Convention. France opposed its inclusion in the Convention on the ground that domestic standards of arbitrability should not be applied to international awards. Germany agreed, pointing out that matters which sharply conflicted with strong local policies could be handled under the public policy clause. The paragraph was adopted, however, and the enforcing State is thus empowered to decide the "arbitrability" of the dispute under its local standards. A certain degree of forum-shopping by successful parties is thus assured.

\*    \*    \*

(ii)    *Pabalk Ticaret Ltd. Sirketi v. S.A. Norsolor*, D.S. Jur. 101 (Cour de cassation Oct. 9, 1984); 24 I.L.M. 663 (1986).

Considering jointly Article VII of the Convention on the Recognition and Enforcement of Foreign Arbitral Awards, signed in New York on June 10, 1958, and Article 12 of the New Code of Civil Procedure;

Whereas, according to Article VII of the New York Convention, the Convention does not deprive any interested party of any right he may have to avail himself of an arbitral award in the manner and to the extent allowed by the law or the treaties of the country where such award is sought to be relied upon; as a result the judge cannot refuse enforcement when his own national legal system permits it, and, by virtue of Article 12 of the New Code of Civil Procedures, he should, even sua sponte, research the matter if such is the case;

Whereas Pabalk Ticaret Limited Sirketi (Pabalk), a Turkish company incorporated in Turkey, and Ugilor, a company incorporated in France, which has since become Norsolor, were parties to an agency agreement which contained an arbitration clause referring to the Rules for the International Chamber of Commerce (ICC) Court of Arbitration and in particular to Article 13 of these Rules prescribing that in the absence of any indication by the parties as to the applicable law, the arbitrators should apply the law designated as the proper law by the rule of conflict which they deem appropriate, it being specified that they shall take account of the provisions of the contract and the relevant trade usages;

Whereas in their award rendered on October 26, 1979, the arbitrators stated that, faced with the difficulty of choosing a national law the application of which is sufficiently compelling, it was appropriate, given the international nature of the agreement, to leave aside any compelling reference to a specific legal system, be it Turkish or French, and to apply the international lex mercatoria, of which one of the fundamental principles is that of good faith which must govern the formation and performance of contracts;

Whereas the arbitral tribunal found that the termination of the agreement was attributable to Ugilor and that Ugilor's conduct caused unjustified damages to Pabalk, which equity required to be compensated;

Whereas this award, in its four-point decree, ordered Norsolor to pay various sums to Pabalk;

Whereas the award was held enforceable in France by an order dated February 4, 1980, of the President of the Tribunal de Grande Instance of Paris, which Norsolor sought to attack on the basis of Article 1028 of the Code of Civil Procedure, since repealed but nonetheless applicable here, claiming that the arbitrators had acted as amiables compositeurs and thus had exceeded the bounds of their authority;

Whereas by judgment dated March 4, 1981, the Tribunal de Grande Instance rejected the demand that the enforcement order be retracted;

Whereas, to amend this decision and retract the order in that it granted enforcement of parts III and IV of the arbitral award, the judgment under attack applied Article V(1)(e) of the New York Convention, ratified both by Austria and France, and according to which the recognition and enforcement of an award would be refused only if the award had been set aside by a competent authority of the country in which, or under the law of which, that award was made, and the judgment under attack relied on the fact that these parts III and IV of the decree of the award had been set aside by a decision dated January 29, 1982 of the Vienna Court of Appeals on the ground that the arbitral tribunal, in violation of Article 13 of the Rules for the ICC Court of Arbitration, had not determined the national law applicable and limited themselves to refer to the international lex mercatoria, a "world law of questionable validity";

Whereas by ruling in this manner, where the Court of Appeals had a duty to determine, even sua sponte, if French law would not allow Pabalk to avail himself of the award at stake, the Court of Appeals violated the above mentioned provisions.

## FOR THESE REASONS:

We reverse and set aside the decision rendered November 19, 1982, by the Court of Appeals of Paris and send the case to the Court of Appeals of Amiens . . . .

### Notes and Questions

1. For a discussion of *lex mercatoria*, see *supra* p. 202.

2. One problem with any Convention drafted in several languages that are equally authentic is that the different versions may not be entirely congruent. For example, the English version of Article V of the New York Convention is permissive, stating that an award "may" be refused recognition and enforcement on the basis of the article's litany of defenses. The French text, however, is more forceful, providing that "recognition and execution of an award will not be refused unless" (La reconnaissance et l'éxécution de la sentence ne seront refusées que si la sentence a été annulée ou suspendue). This has led at least one court — rightly or wrongly — to consider itself under an obligation to refuse recognition to a defective award. *See Berardi v. Clair*, (Cour d'appel, Paris June 20, 1981), Rev. Arb. 424, 426, in which a Paris Appeal Court refused recognition in France to an award set aside in Geneva, the place of the arbitration.

3. In some cases (such as *Pabalk v. Norsolor, supra* p. 203), this difference may not really matter, since Convention Article VII provides that any interested party may avail itself of an award to the extent allowed by the national law of the enforcement forum.

2.     EUROPEAN CONVENTION ON INTERNATIONAL COMMERCIAL ARBITRATION, Apr. 21, 1961, art. 9, 484 U.N.T.S. 349.

### Setting Aside Of The Arbitral Award

1. The setting aside in a Contracting State of an arbitral award covered by this Convention shall only constitute a ground for the refusal of recognition or enforcement in another Contracting State where such setting aside took place in a State in which, or under the

law of which, the award has been made and for one of the following reasons:

(a)     the parties to the arbitration agreement were under the law applicable to them, under some incapacity or the said agreement is not valid under the law to which the parties have subjected it or, failing any indication thereon, under the law of the country where the award was made; or

(b)     the party requesting the setting aside of the award was not given proper notice of the appointment of the arbitrator or of the arbitration proceedings or was otherwise unable to present his case; or

(c)     the award deals with a difference not contemplated by or not falling within the terms of the submission to arbitration, or it contains decisions on matters beyond the scope of the submission to arbitration, provided that, if the decisions on matters submitted to arbitration can be separated from those not so submitted, that part of the award which contains decisions on matters submitted to arbitration need not be set aside;

(d)     the composition of the arbitral authority or the arbitral procedure was not in accordance with the agreement of the parties, or failing such agreement, with the provisions of article IV of this Convention.

2.     In relations between Contracting States that are also parties to the New York Convention on the Recognition and Enforcement of Foreign Arbitral Awards of 10th June 1958, paragraph 1 of this article limits the application of Article V (1)(e) of the New York Convention solely to the cases of setting aside set out under paragraph 1 above.

### Notes and Questions

1. We have seen that the New York Convention permits non-recognition of any award set aside where rendered, regardless of the grounds on which the award was annulled. Contrast the approach contained in the European Convention on

International Commercial Arbitration (Geneva, 1961), which limits the cases in which the setting aside of an award will constitute a ground for refusal of recognition. Which approach is better? Why?

### 3. CONTROL THROUGH ENFORCEMENT MECHANISMS NOT PROVIDED BY MULTILATERAL ARBITRATION TREATIES

#### a. TREATIES OF FRIENDSHIP, COMMERCE AND NAVIGATION

In some cases, the party seeking to enforce an award may find that it is not covered by any multilateral arbitration treaties. At this point bilateral treaties may come into play. See, for example, Article 6(2) of the U.S.-German Treaty of Friendship, Commerce and Navigation (FCN), 29 October 1954, 7 U.S.T. 1840, 1845, T.I.A.S. No. 3593. This treaty is discussed in *Landegger v. Bayerische Hypotheken und Wechsel Bank*, 357 F.Supp. 692 (S.D.N.Y. 1972).

Lionel Kennedy, *Enforcing International Commercial Arbitration Agreements and Awards Not Subject to the New York Convention*, 23 VA. J. INT'L L. 75 (1982).

The first U.S. attempts to govern international arbitration agreements took the form of provisions in bilateral FCN treaties. At the heart of these treaties is the notion that one party's nationals should not suffer discrimination in the other party's territory. The arbitration provision in the 1954 U.S.-German treaty[296] is typical in providing that an agreement to arbitrate shall not be considered invalid merely because the arbitration is to occur abroad or that it is to use foreign arbitrators.[297] The provision further states that if an award made

---

[296] Treaty of Friendship, Commerce and Navigation, Oct. 29, 1954, U.S.-F.R.G., 7 U.S.T. 1840, 1845, T.I.A.S. No. 3593 [hereinafter cited as U.S.-German FCN Treaty].

[297] The U.S. German-FCN treaty provides:

Contracts entered into between nationals or companies of either party and nationals or companies of the other party that provide for settlement by arbitration of controversies shall not be deemed unenforceable within the territories of such other party merely on the grounds that the place

pursuant to such an agreement is final where rendered, it is enforceable in both nations unless a court finds that it contravenes public policy.

There are two reasons why an FCN treaty might cover arbitration that the Convention does not. First, the United States has FCN treaties with a number of countries that are not parties to the Convention.[298] Thus the Convention's reciprocity provisions would not necessarily prevent a U.S. court from honoring an arbitration agreement or award from one of those countries. Second, because it does not have the same reservations as the Convention, an FCN treaty might cover a broader range of agreements. For example, by relying on the arbitration provision of an FCN treaty a party could circumvent the Convention's requirement of reciprocity with the State of the *locus arbitri*.[299] The FCN treaties have limited use for U.S. parties, however, because they have no specific implementing legislation conferring a basis for U.S. jurisdiction independently of the contract itself.

．　　．　　．

---

designated for arbitration proceedings is outside such territories or that the nationality of one or more of the arbitrators is not that of such other party. Awards duly rendered pursuant to any such contracts which are final and enforceable under the laws of the place where rendered shall be deemed conclusive in enforcement proceedings brought before the courts of competent jurisdiction of either party, and shall be entitled to be declared enforceable by such courts, except where found contrary to public policy.

Id. art. 6, para. 2.

[298] The United States has signed FCN treaties containing arbitration provisions with the following countries: Belgium, Denmark, France, Greece, Iran, Ireland, Israel, Italy, Japan, Luxembourg, the Netherlands, Nicaragua, Pakistan, South Korea, Taiwan, Thailand, Togo, Vietnam, and West Germany. Iran, Nicaragua, Taiwan, Togo, and Vietnam have not signed the New York Convention; Pakistan has signed but not ratified the Convention. Multilateral Treaties Deposited with the Secretary General . . . .

[299] Thus an award resulting from a dispute between U.S. and West German nationals where the arbitration was held in a non-Convention country would be unenforceable under the Convention because of the U.S. reciprocity reservation. The U.S.-German FCN Treaty, however, would encompass it because it applies to the two countries' nationals, regardless of where the arbitration takes place . . . .

ENFORCING A FOREIGN ARBITRAL AWARD NOT COVERED BY
THE NEW YORK CONVENTION

The chance of enforcing a foreign arbitral award is much better than the chance of compelling arbitration. The 1925 Act, the FCN treaties, and state law all offer useful possibilities. It is also possible to convert the award to a judgment in the country where it was rendered and then sue on that judgment in the United States.

*The 1925 Act*

On its face the 1925 Act offers little support for the domestic enforcement of arbitral awards rendered in foreign arbitrations. Under section 9, awards are enforceable only if the contract provides for entry of judgment on the award by a specific federal court. The judicial applications of section 9 reveal some doubt, however, over whether a court should take the provision literally, or whether an implicit intention to allow for the enforcement of an award in U.S. courts could satisfy the section.

*Splosna Plovba v. Agrelak Steamship Corp.*[300] concerned an English arbitration that occurred before Britain had ratified the New York Convention. The underlying contract provided that "for the purpose of enforcing any award, this agreement may be made a rule of the Court."[301] The U.S. Court held that the contract was not explicit enough to constitute an authorization for enforcement of the award in a court outside the place of arbitration.[302] It said that a British judgment was required and that any shortcutting of the appropriate procedure should be discouraged.[303] On the other hand, the court in *Audi v. Overseas Motors*[304] took a broader view. It looked instead to the intent of the parties concerning the finality of the arbitration and

---

[300] 381 F.Supp. 1368 (S.D.N.Y. 1974).

[301] Id. at 1369-70.

[302] Id. at 1371.

[303] Id.

[304] 418 F.Supp. 982 (E.D. Mich. 1976).

their invocation of federal jurisdiction.[305] The absence of a clause in the original contract providing for the entry of judgment by a specific U.S. court did not cause the arbitration to fail. In reaching this result the court took the same approach as the circuit courts in several recent domestic arbitration cases. It is important to remember that the 1925 Act also sets forth a number of grounds for refusing to enforce an arbitral award. These include such defects in the arbitration process as corruption, fraud, partiality, and the failure of the arbitrators to hear evidence or carry out their duties. Courts construe these defenses narrowly, however, so as to avoid frustrating the parties' purposes in resorting to arbitration. Thus an award will not be set aside solely because the arbitrator misinterprets the law or makes erroneous findings of fact.[306]

.  .  .

### The FCN Treaties

The FCN treaties can offer support for a party seeking to enforce an arbitral award in the United States that was rendered in a foreign jurisdiction provided he can satisfy three criteria: the other party is a citizen of a signatory FCN country; the award is "final and enforceable" under the laws of the place where rendered; and subsequent proceedings for enforcement are brought before a court of competent jurisdiction. The typical FCN treaty provisions include no clear enforcement mechanism and lack the benefit of implementing legislation that might provide guidance as to how these criteria are satisfied. Nonetheless, in *Landegger v. Bayerische Hypotheken und Wechsel Bank*,[307] the court enforced an award under the U.S.-German treaty even though an appeal from the arbitration was pending in a German court. The U.S. court reasoned that the treaty did not prevent it from enforcing an award that was not final in Germany. If the

---

[305] Id. at 985.

[306] See Orion Shipping & Trading Co. v. Eastern States Petroleum Corp., 312 F.2d 299, 300 (2d Cir.), *cert. denied*, 373 U.S. 949 (1963) ("[T]he law is clear that an arbitration award based upon a misinterpretation of law or an insufficiency of supporting facts will not be overturned."); Frances Jalet, Judicial Review of Arbitration: The Judicial Attitude, 45 Cornell L.Q. 519 (1960).

[307] 357 F.Supp. 692 (S.D.N.Y. 1972).

German appeal later revealed some reason for vacating the award, the defendant could reopen the U.S. judgment. In reaching this conclusion the court endorsed the principle that the treaty did not prohibit it from giving broader recognition to a foreign adjudication than was strictly required by the treaty itself.

As for defenses, the typical FCN treaty contains only the public policy clauses as a defense to the enforcement of arbitral awards. This public policy defense is broad enough, however, to encompass all the defenses in the 1925 Act against enforcing an award resulting from a procedurally defective arbitration.

### Enforceability of Awards in State Courts

In many states the local law may offer the best chance of enforcing a foreign award. For example, New York's arbitration statute provides for the enforcement of arbitral awards without distinction as to their origin.[308] Moreover, New York state courts have continued

---

[308] Section 7501 of the New York Act, the general jurisdictional provision, provides that:

> A written agreement to submit any controversy thereafter arising or any existing controversy to arbitration is enforceable without regard to the justiciable character of the controversy and confers jurisdiction on the courts of the state to enforce it and to enter judgment on an award. In determining any matter arising under this article, the court shall not consider whether the claim with respect to which arbitration is sought is tenable, or otherwise pass upon the merits of the dispute.

N.Y. Arbitration Law §7501 (McKinney 1980). On its face, section 7501 presents a constitutional problem: it gives a New York court jurisdiction to enforce any arbitral award regardless of its connection with New York. At the very least, another basis for New York jurisdiction should be required. For instance, if the execution of the contract were in New York or the defendant was a New York domiciliary, this would probably suffice as a basis of jurisdiction. See Swan v. Sit'n Chat Restaurant, Inc., 43 A.D.2d 949, 950, 352 N.Y.S.2d 31, 34 (N.Y. App. Div. 1974) (court enforced award because defendant was domiciled in New York and by-laws of organization that conducted the arbitration provided for its confirmation there). The predecessor to § 7501, however, provided that New York courts would only have jurisdiction if the parties had agreed to arbitrate in New York. There is some support for the view that the new statute was not intended to change this. N.Y. Arbitration Law §7501 comment C7501:1 (McKinney 1989).

to follow the classic case of *Gilbert v. Burnstine*,[309] in which the Court of Appeals held that an agreement to arbitrate abroad does not offend public policy, and that an award rendered in accordance with local laws is enforceable.[310]

\* \* \*

### b.    AWARDS REDUCED TO JUDGMENTS

Judicial confirmation of an arbitrator's decision sometimes may make the decision enforceable not as an arbitral award, but as a foreign court judgment. In the United States, the enforcement of a foreign judgment may depend on whether federal or state law is applicable. Enforcement of the arbitrator's decision, qua judgment rather than qua award, may give a losing party the right to assert defenses that might have been raised in the original action — and thus present the court of the enforcement forum with a much larger role than merely examining the limited defenses provided in Article V of the New York Convention. The following cases and model statute illustrate that an award may be enforced as a judgment, and suggest some of the problems that may arise if enforcement of the arbitrator's decision is sought qua judgment rather than qua award.

(i)    *The Island Territory of Curacao v. Solitron Devices, Inc.*, 489 F.2d 1313 (2d Cir. 1973).

[Appeal by an American manufacturer from a judgment confirming an arbitration award made in favor of the Island Territory of Curacao and enforcing a judgment entered thereon in the courts of Curacao. The arbitration itself arose out of a dispute over a contract, the parties to which were the Central Government of the Netherlands Antilles and The Island Territory of Curacao, both of these political entities being a part of the Kingdom of the Netherlands, and Solitron Devices, Inc. (Solitron), a manufacturer of electronic products from Rockland County, New York. The contract related to the construction of an industrial park in Curacao and the installation of a Solitron

---

[309] 255 N.Y. 348, 174 N.E. 706 (1931).

[310] Id. at 357-58, 174 N.E. at 708-09.

manufacturing facility in the park. Solitron did not participate in the arbitration proceeding in Curacao or in the judicial proceedings in confirmation of the award in Curacao. The underlying agreement between Curacao and Solitron provided that Curacao would establish an industrial park of about 60 acres and to construct two factory buildings pursuant to Solitron-approved plans and to build an access road and sea water pipes to the building sites; Solitron was to lease the buildings for 20 years at a specified rent and to operate in the larger building and to use or sublease the smaller one, agreeing to put its electronic manufacturing industry into operation within 12 months of completion of the larger building and to create at least 100 jobs. Solitron also undertook to establish prior to January 1974 manufacturing industries in the Netherlands Antilles which in total would provide employment for at least 3,000 persons. It was agreed that the laws of the Netherlands Antilles would be applicable to the agreement and that all disputes as a consequence of or in connection with it, legal as well as factual, should be submitted to a board of arbitration, the decision of which would be binding. The arbitrators were enjoined to give an award "like good men and true" — "ex aequo et bono." Curacao completed the two buildings as agreed, but Solitron failed to enter into a lease agreement and had otherwise treated the agreement as terminated. Solitron declined to proceed to arbitration on the basis that there had been express representations made regarding the favorable economic climate of Curacao in respect to wage rates of 45 United States cents per hour due to a change in government and a revision upward of the minimum hourly rate of wages.

The arbitration proceeded without Solitron's participation, but Solitron was duly informed at all times of the time and dates of hearings and the other procedures followed. The award was made and signed by the arbitrators in Curacao on 13 August 1970, in substance in favor of Curacao's position. The arbitrators found that Solitron was in breach of contract by omission to lease the completed buildings, and awarded 192,482 Dutch Guilders for loss of rent on the two buildings.

The award was converted into a judgment under the law of the Netherlands Antilles, and Curacao obtained "writ of execution" on the basis of the award, declaring the award enforceable in the Curacao Court of First Instance. The award and the judgment entered thereon were final under the law of Antilles.]

.    .    .

. . . Solitron claims that the arbitral award is not enforceable under the Convention on Recognition and Enforcement of Arbitral Awards (Convention on Recognition), as implemented in 9 U.S.C. § 201 et seq., for the following reasons: (1) the construction of an industrial park is a 'governmental' and not a 'commercial' function, so that the Convention does not apply; (2) the arbitration award is not final and definite and is contrary to the public policy of the United States; and (3) the contract and the arbitration agreement terminated by reason of impossibility and, as a result of this termination, there was lack of jurisdiction in Curacao over Solitron. The claim is also made here, as it was below, that the judgment on the arbitral award is not enforceable under Article 53, the New York statute, because the Convention on Recognition and its implementing legislation have preempted the New York statute and because, under the terms of the New York statute as it has been construed, enforcement is not permitted here. In its reply brief Solitron also argues for the first time that the whole matter is governed by the Convention on the Settlement of Investment Disputes between states and nationals of other states which was ratified and adhered to both by the United States, [1966] 1 U.S.T. 1270, TIAS No. 6090, and the Netherlands, [1966] 1 U.S.T. 1355; 55 Dept. St. Bull 596 (1966).

We deal first with the question under New York law, whether the foreign judgment is enforceable. The first question is whether Article 53, permitting the enforcement of a foreign money judgment, has been preempted by the overriding federal law implementing the Convention and relating to the enforcement of foreign arbitral awards, 9 U.S.C. § 201 et seq. The Convention on Recognition in no way purports to prevent states from enforcing foreign money judgments, whether those judgments are rendered in the enforcement of an arbitration award or otherwise. This is not to say that Solitron's argument is not, indeed, ingenious, since it apparently was not made in the sole case decided under Article 53 or any prior thereto in which the courts of New York State have granted enforcement to foreign judgments based upon foreign arbitration awards arising after the United States Senate's accession to the Convention, albeit with reservations, on October 4, 1968, and the adoption by the Congress of 9 U.S.C. ch. 2 on July 31, 1970. . . .

.    .    .

It remains then to be seen whether under New York law the Curacaoan judgment may be enforced and, in this respect, it is helpful to recall, . . . that Article 53 itself represents a codification of pre-existing common law on the subject. Thus, for example, the district court was plainly correct in its holding, not contested on appeal, that a claim of fraud in the inducement of the contract generally—alleged here on the basis of supposed representations that the wage structure in Curacao would remain stable—is a question for the arbitrators. Prima Paint Corp. v. Flood & Conklin Manufacturing Co., 388 U.S. 395, 87 S.Ct. 1801, 18 L.Ed.2d 1270 (1967); Weinrott v. Carp, 32 N.Y.2d 190, 194, 344 N.Y.S.2d 848, 298 N.E.2d 42 (1973). This carries with it as the district court quite properly held the claims that the contract itself terminated or was frustrated by virtue of the changes in wage rates in Curacao and legislation changing the minimum wages for non-electronic industry employees as well as by the supposed riots and change in personnel of government.

We thus turn to the other points on the basis of which the appellant claims that under New York law and under Article 53 enforcement of the Curacaoan judgment would not be granted. Concededly one of the bases on which New York would not enforce a foreign judgment would be if it were made without jurisdiction. NYCPLR § 5304(a)2. Appellant argues that jurisdiction over it ended in March of 1970, but the basis for this argument is that the contract terminated as a matter of law by reason of impossibility of performance, and this again goes to the change of the minimum wage law imposed by Curacao. The March, 1970, date for 'termination' is based upon Solitron's counsel's self-serving letter of May 15 to the effect that performance had by then become economically impossible. We would point out again that this was, under the broad arbitration clause, initially a question for the arbitrators and was ruled upon and rejected by them. There is nothing in the contract to indicate that Solitron's obligations were predicated on the continued existence of any particular wage rate. Only recently the Fifth Circuit held in Eastern Marine Corp. v. Fukaya Trading Co., 364 F.2d 80, 84-85 (5th Cir.), cert. denied, 385 U.S. 971, 87 S.Ct. 508, 17 L.Ed.2d 435 (1966), that, as a matter of federal substantive law, an arbitration clause survives the frustration of a contract for the purposes of settling, among other things, whether the contract has in fact been frustrated. See also Heyman v. Warwins, [1942] A.C. 356, 366, relied upon by Judge Augustus Hand in In re Pahlberg, 131 F.2d 968 (2d Cir. 1942); Prima Paint Corp. v. Flood & Conklin Manufacturing Co., *supra.* In re Kramer & Uchitelle, 288 N.Y. 467, 43 N.E.2d 493 (1942), heavily relied upon by appellant for the proposition that, at least as a matter of New York law, a proceeding to enforce an arbitration contract presupposes the existence of a valid and enforceable contract at the time the remedy is sought, has been limited, In re Exercycle Corp., 9 N.Y.2d 329, 335-336, 174 N.E.2d 463, 465-466, 214 N.Y.S.2d 353, 356-358 (1961), to the situation in which public policy as embodied in a statute forbids the performance which is the subject of dispute, a policy and statute which are as binding upon the arbitrators as upon the courts. That, of course, is not the situation here, where the defense of frustration is one asserted purely as a common law contractual defense.

On its jurisdictional point, Solitron also argues, however, that its contractual concession of jurisdiction on the basis of the provision that it 'invariably' or irrevocably chose domicile at the offices of its attorney-notary public in Willemstad cannot of itself be sufficient. The argument is not that its consent to jurisdiction was revoked, and indeed could not be because Curacao had already invoked arbitration under the agreement by the time of Solitron's attempted revocation of its consent to jurisdiction on May 12, 1970. Rather, the Solitron argument is to the effect that the document in the nature of a 'marshal's writ,' which was issued after the 'Court of First Instance' 'declared executed' the 'arbitral verdict,' contained language to the effect that 'respondent (Solitron) is no longer domiciled in the Netherlands Antilles,' and that this language represents a concession on the part of Curacao that Solitron's domicile terminated no later than March, 1970. There are at least three answers to this argument:

1. If Solitron's domicile had terminated in March of 1970, why did it wait until May 12, 1970, to cable its agent for service of process to revoke 'such authority if any as you may still retain to represent us,' confirming this by cable and letter dated May 13, 1970?

2. Solitron's attempt to claim that its domicile was terminated because of impossibility of performance assumes, incorrectly, that it, rather than the arbitrators, had the power to decide that issue, a matter which we have already held adversely to Solitron above.

3. The language of the Curacaoan marshal's writ in context at most constitutes an acknowledgment of the fact that the attempted revocation in May of 1970 had become effective by the date of the marshal's writ in April of 1971 (a matter which we need not and do not

affirmatively decide here). That is to say, the marshal's language to the effect that the respondent is no longer domiciled in the Netherlands Antilles relates to the time of the issuance and presentation of the writ in April, 1971.

[The Court then addressed and dismissed Solitron's arguments that the award was unenforceable because it was "completely irrational" and/or contrary to public policy.]

. . .

The last point made in reference to the Curacaoan judgment is that under NYCPLR § 5302 only a final and conclusive judgment may be enforced in New York. The judgment, it is claimed, is not conclusive or final since the arbitration award left it open to either party, after January 1, 1974, to demand further arbitration and possibly to obtain further and more extensive damages. But this is a point that was not raised before the Curacao courts . . . . We must recognize that the judgment itself is definite in amount, was conclusive and enforceable in Curacao, and, indeed, is final to the extent that it specifies precisely what Solitron is to pay; nothing remains to be calculated.

Thus we conclude that the judgment of Curacao was enforceable under Article 53 of the New York Civil Practice Law and Rules and affirm the district court on this ground. In so holding we need not determine the correctness of the alternative ground advanced by the district court that the arbitration award was independently enforceable under the Convention on the Recognition and Enforcement of Foreign Arbitral Awards, by virtue of 9 U.S.C. § 201 et seq. The argument that Solitron may counterclaim for its investment in Curacao is absurd, since credit was already given for this in the arbitral award.

\* \* \*

(ii) *Svenska Handelsbanken v. Carlson*, 258 F.Supp. 448 (D. Mass. 1966).

[A Swedish bank brought an action against the estate of Elmer H. Carlton to recover on a judgment entered in a Swedish court. On 9 February 1959, Carlton, a New Jersey resident engaged in the export-import business, had executed a guarantee for a Swedish firm, Linden & Lindstrom AB, pursuant to which Svenska Handelsbank released funds from the firm's block account for payment of a debt owed to Carlton by Linden & Lindstrom.

In 1963, Linden & Lindstrom Export AB went into liquidation, owing Svenska Handelsbank debts totalling more than 500,000 kronor. Svenska Handelsbanken filed suit in the Gothenburg Magistrate's Court against Carlson's estate to recover the full amount of the guarantee. The defendant was served with process and handed a copy of the complaint at his home in Massachusetts. Carlson failed to answer the complaint and judgment was entered against him by the Swedish court.]

.        .        .

[The Court summarized the law then in force in Massachusetts as follows.]

. . . Plaintiff's first contention is that the judgment of the Swedish court should be given conclusive effect and judgment entered upon it. It appears that the judgment of the Swedish court is a valid one under Swedish law, entered after actual notice and opportunity to defend was given to defendant, by a court which had jurisdiction under Swedish law. It is not clear, however, that it is entitled to conclusive effect in this court. In Hilton v. Guyot, 159 U.S. 113, 16 S.Ct. 139, 40 L.Ed. 95 the United States Supreme Court held that a judgment of a court of a foreign country would be given conclusive effect only if the courts of that nation would give similar effect to judgments rendered in the United States. Where such reciprocity does not exist the foreign judgment is only prima facie evidence of the correctness of the underlying claim. While the court in Banco Nacional de Cuba v. Sabbatino, 376 U.S. 398, 84 S.Ct. 923, 11 L.Ed.2d 804, did not accept the broad language of the Hilton opinion, it did not disturb the specific ruling of that case as to the effect to be given to foreign judgments. However, Massachusetts rather than federal law seems to be properly applicable here. Erie Railroad Co. v. Tompkins, 304 U.S. 64, 58 S.Ct. 817, 82 L.Ed. 1188. Although the Massachusetts cases are very old, the Massachusetts rule appears to be that a judgment of a court of a foreign country is only prima facie evidence of the underlying claim, and that defendant is entitled to all the defenses he might have made to the original action. Bissell v. Briggs, 9 Mass. 462;

Buttrick v. Allen, 8 Mass. 273. There is no decision that would support giving a conclusive effect to the Swedish judgment sued upon here.

On the merits of plaintiff's claim, in addition to the prima facie effect of the Swedish judgment, it is clear on the evidence that plaintiff is entitled to recover to the full amount of the guarantee. The making of the guarantee is not denied. The obligations of Linden & Lindstrom at the time of the execution of the guarantee and at all times since then have been in excess of the amount of the guarantee.

The interpretation and effect of the guarantee, are, of course, governed by Swedish law. Plaintiff has put in evidence certain extracts from Swedish legal materials (with translations) and the testimony of a Swedish legal expert which the court finds correctly state the applicable Swedish law. Under Swedish law the instrument executed by Carlton was an unconditional personal obligation making Carlton primarily liable, equally with Linden & Lindstrom for all obligations of the latter. This guarantee continued until the principal obligation had been discharged. It was not affected by the substitution of new notes for the original ones, it was not terminated by Carlton's death but remained an obligation of his estate, and it covered new loans made after Carlton's death.

.      .      .

[The court examined the merits of the Svenska Handelsbank claim, and rejected defenses, inter alia, that recovery was barred by the six year Massachusetts statute of limitations.]

*      *      *

Subsequent to the Carlson decision, Massachusetts adopted the Uniform Foreign Money Judgments Recognition Act, set forth *infra*, p. 1076.

(iii)    *Seetransport Wiking Trader Schiffahrtsgesellschaft MBH & Co. v. Navimpex Centrala Navala (The Sea Transport Viking Trader Case)*, 29 F.3d 79 (2d Cir. 1994).

. . . . .

. . . Navimpex was a Romanian government trading company engaged in the business of shipbuilding. In 1980, Navimpex contracted to build four ships for Seetransport, but disputes arose and the ships were never built. The parties arbitrated their disputes before the Court of Arbitration of the International Chamber of Commerce in Paris. On March 26, 1984, the arbitral tribunal rendered an award in favor of Seetransport, ordering Navimpex to pay six million deutsche marks, plus interest at the rate of eight percent per year from January 1, 1981. The award also required Navimpex to pay Seetransport $72,000 as reimbursement for Navimpex's unpaid share of the cost of the arbitraton. Navimpex sought to annul the award in the Court of Appeals in Paris, but the Court dismissed the application on March 4, 1986.

By the time that Seetransport sued Navimpex in the United States in 1988 to collect on the arbitral award, the statute of limitations to enforce an award under the Convention had run. This was our holding in the prior appeal, in which we reversed a grant of summary judgment in favor of Seetransport on its action to enforce the arbitral award under the Convention. *See Seetransport I*, 989 F.2d at 581. However, Seetransport had sued not only to enforce the arbitral award, but also to enforce, under New York's Article 53, what it believed to be a French judgment confirming the award. We accordingly remanded to the District Court to consider whether Seetransport could succeed on its New York cause of action. We directed the Court to allow the parties to supplement the record on the issue of "whether the decision of the Court of Appeals of Paris is enforceable in France and thus should be enforced by the district court." *Id.* at 583. After accepting supplemental affidavits on this issue, the District Court ruled that the Paris Court of Appeals' dismissal of Navimpex's application had conferred *exequatur* on the award, making it enforceable in France. It then reinstated the judgment in favor of Seetransport that the District Court had originally granted before the prior appeal. Navimpex and Uzinexportimport appeal.

The central dispute on this appeal is over the significance of the decision of the Paris Court of Appeals dismissing Navimpex's application to annul the award. According to Seetransport, this dismissal conferred *exequatur* on the award. Seetransport further contends that the decree conferring *exequatur* constituted a French judgment awarding the sums specified in the award. New York will enforce a foreign decree under Article 53 only if that decree is a "foreign country judgment which is final, conclusive and enforceable where rendered. . . ." N.Y.Civ.Prac.L. & R. 5302 (McKinney 1978). Appellants contend that even if the Paris Court of Appeals' ruling conferred *exequatur* on the arbitral award, that action did not create a French "judgment." Thus, appellants reason, there is no foreign country judgment that can be enforced under Article 53.

Because questions of foreign law are treated as questions of law under Fed.R.Civ.P. 44.1, we subject the District Court's determinations on the foreign law issues to *de novo* review.

Preliminarily, we agree with the District Court that the Court of Appeals' decision conferred *exequatur* on the arbitral award. Article 1490 of the French New Code of Civil Procedure provides that "[r]ejection of an appeal or a motion to set aside confers *exequatur* on the arbitral award, or on such of its dispositions as are not censored by the Court of Appeal." This provision applies to international arbitrations by operation of Article 1507 of the French code. Seetransport's French law expert, Judge Simone Rozes, who retired in 1988 from her position as the Chief Judge of the *Cour de Cassation*, the highest judicial tribunal in France, testified through her affidavits that the Court of Appeals' rejection of Navimpex's challenge to the award conferred *exequatur*. She cited two cases in which French Courts of Appeal concluded that declaring *exequatur* on an arbitral award at the request of a successful party to an arbitration was unnecessary because the earlier rejection of a challenge to the award by the losing party had automatically conferred *exequatur* by operation of Article 1490.

The issue is whether the ruling conferring *exequatur* merely made the arbitration award enforceable or was itself an enforceable judgment wihtin the meaning of Article 53. We agree with the District

Court that, for purposes of Article 53, the decree conferring *exequatur* on the award was the functional equivalent of a French judgment awarding the sums specified in the award. French courts use the device of *exequatur* to make a decision of an outside tribunal enforceable in France. . . .

(iv)  UNIFORM FOREIGN MONEY JUDGMENTS RECOGNITION ACT OF 1962, 13 U.L.A. 417.

## §1.  [Definitions]

As used in this Act:

(1)  "foreign state" means any governmental unit other than the United States, or any state, district, commonwealth, territory, insular possession thereof, or the Panama Canal Zone, the Trust Territory of the Pacific Islands, or the Ryukyu Islands;

(2)  "foreign judgment" means any judgment of a foreign state granting or denying recovery of a sum of money, other than a judgment for taxes, a fine or other penalty, or a judgment for support in matrimonial or family matters.

## §2.  [Applicability]

This Act applies to any foreign judgment that is final and conclusive and enforceable where rendered even though an appeal therefrom is pending or it is subject to appeal.

## §3.  [Recognition and Enforcement]

Except as provided in section 4, a foreign judgment meeting the requirements of section 2 is conclusive between the parties to the extent that it grants or denies recovery of a sum of money. The foreign judgment is enforceable in the same manner as the judgment of a sister state which is entitled to full faith and credit.

§4.     [Grounds for Non-recognition]

(a)     A foreign judgment is not conclusive if

(1)     the judgment was rendered under a system which does not provide impartial tribunals or procedures compatible with the requirements of due process of law;

(2)     the foreign court did not have personal jurisdiction over the defendant; or

(3)     the foreign court did not have jurisdiction over the subject matter.

(b)     A foreign judgment need not be recognized if

(1)     the defendant in the proceedings in the foreign court did not receive notice of the proceedings in sufficient time to enable him to defend;

(2)     the judgment was obtained by fraud;

(3)     the [cause of action] [claim for relief] on which the judgment is based is repugnant to the public policy of this state;

(4)     the judgment conflicts with another final and conclusive judgment;

(5)     the proceeding in the foreign court was contrary to an agreement between the parties under which the dispute in question was to be settled otherwise than by proceedings in that court; or

(6)     in the case of jurisdiction based only on personal service, the foreign court was a seriously inconvenient forum for the trial of the action.

§5.     [Personal Jurisdiction]

(a)     The foreign judgment shall not be refused recognition for lack of personal jurisdiction if

(1)     the defendant was served personally in the foreign state;

(2)     the defendant voluntarily appeared in the proceedings, other than for the purpose of protecting property seized or threatened with seizure in the proceedings or of contesting the jurisdiction of the court over him;

(3)     the defendant prior to the commencement of the proceedings had agreed to submit to the jurisdiction of the foreign court with respect to the subject matter involved;

(4)     the defendant was domiciled in the foreign state when the proceedings were instituted, or, being a body corporate had its principal place of business, was incorporated, or had otherwise acquired corporate status, in the foreign state;

(5)     the defendant had a business office in the foreign state and the proceedings in the foreign court involved a [cause of action] [claim for relief] arising out of business done by the defendant through that office in the foreign state; or

(6)     the defendant operated a motor vehicle or airplane in the foreign state and the proceedings involved a [cause of action] [claim for relief] arising out of such operation.

(b)     The courts of this state may recognize other bases of jurisdiction.

§6.     [Stay in Case of Appeal]

If the defendant satisfies the court either that an appeal is pending or that he is entitled and intends to appeal from the foreign judgment, the court may stay the proceedings until the appeal has been determined or until the expiration of a period of time sufficient to enable the defendant to prosecute the appeal.

§7.    [Savings Clause]

This Act does not prevent the recognition of a foreign judgment in situations not covered by this Act.

§8. [Uniformity of Interpretation]

This Act shall be so construed as to effectuate its general purpose to make uniform the law of those states which enact it.

§9.    [Short Title]

This Act may be cited as the Uniform Foreign Money-Judgments Recognition Act.

#### Notes and Questions

1. When no treaty applies to an award, state law may be more hospitable than federal law to foreign awards. *See* NYCPLR, Section 7501 and *Gilbert v. Burnstine*, 255 N.Y. 348 (1931), finding a foreign award enforceable even absent a treaty obligation. *Compare Splosna Plovba v. Agrelak Steamship Corp.*, 381 F.Supp. 1368 (S.D.N.Y. 1974), refusing to enforce an award made in England at a time before British ratification of New York Convention. The Convention was held not to cover awards made in the United Kingdom. (Recall, in this regard, the reciprocity reservation of Convention Article I). *Compare* UNICTRAL Model Law, Article 36 and French N.C.P.C., Article 1502.

2. Does a successful challenge of an award at the place of arbitration necessarily uproot the award and make it unenforceable everywhere in the world? Note that Article V of the New York Convention (at least the English version) is permissive, not mandatory, providing that recognition and enforcement of an award "may" be refused if the award has been set aside where rendered. What happens if the country in which enforcement of the award is sought has rules more generous to awards than the New York Convention, and will enforce a foreign award under its domestic law regardless of whether this enforcement is required by the New York Convention?

Dr. Van den Berg states (*supra* p. 1042) that "in principle" the setting aside of an award at the place where rendered binds foreign courts to refuse recognition of the award. But the possibility that the enforcement forum may enforce the award under domestic law regardless of the New York Convention seems to be contemplated by Convention Article VII. *See Pabalk Ticaret v. Norsolor*, *supra* p. 203. Van den Berg seems to foresee this possibility later in the same article.

Note that the French language version of Convention Article V, unlike the equally authoritative English version, is not necessarily permissive. The French text provides that recognition "will not be refused unless . . . the award has been set aside where rendered." ("La reconnaissance et l'exequatur ne seront refusées que si . . . la sentence a été annullée . . . .")

3. Imagine that parties choose to arbitrate in Ruritania, but select New York law to apply to the interpretation of their contract. Could New York courts set aside the Ruritanian award? What is the implication of the New York Convention language in Article V(1)e permitting refusal of recognition to an award set aside "under the law of which [the] award was made?" *See Int'l Standard Electric Corp. v. Bridas Sociedad Anonima Petrolera*, 745 F.Supp. 172 (S.D.N.Y. 1990), which held that by selection of Mexico as the arbitral seat, the parties to the dispute submitted the arbitration to Mexican procedural law notwithstanding their choice of New York law to govern the substance of the dispute. Is this legally correct? Is it good policy?

4. What are the policy implications for international arbitration of *Bergesen v. Joseph Muller*, 710 F.2d 928 (2d Cir. 1983)? Does the case cast doubt on the proposition that all awards rendered in the United States may be subject to challenge on the grounds set forth in Section 10 of the U.S. Arbitration Act? Can a "non-domestic" award benefit from the New York Convention enforceability and yet still be subject to standards of procedural integrity set forth in Section 10 of the U.S. Arbitration Act?

### E. JUDICIAL CONTROL MECHANISMS AT THE PLACE OF THE PROCEEDINGS

### 1. COMPETING MODELS

Under the enforcement scheme of the New York Convention, the arbitral situs has power to give, or to take away, the international currency of an award provided by the Convention. It can "kill" or "uproot" an award by denying it the benefit of the presumptive validity conferred by the Convention. Recall that Article III of the Convention requires recognition and enforcement of foreign awards, subject to Article V(1)(e) of the Convention, which permits refusal of recognition and enforcement to awards annulled where rendered.

For better or for worse, however, the New York Convention does not spell out acceptable grounds for annulment. Specific grounds for setting aside awards are neither mandated nor prohibited by the Convention. The arbitral seat is free to vacate awards for any reason it sees fit, or for none at all.

At least three competing models for judicial review of international arbitral awards have evolved: (1) review of the legal merits; (2) review for defects in procedural integrity; and (3) absence of judicial review. Some legal systems, such as the English and the Swiss, are in fact hybrids of these models. For example, English courts may hear an appeal on questions of law if the parties have not in writing excluded appeal. Even if appeal has been excluded, courts may still annul an award for arbitrator "misconduct." In Switzerland, federal law provides generally for judicial review only to insure the procedural integrity of the arbitral process, while giving parties the option in some cases to exclude judicial review altogether, or to select cantonal procedural law and subject the award to challenge for "arbitrariness" on the basis of a "clear violation of law or equity." The following materials illustrate the options open to national legal systems with respect to control of the award exercised at the place where the award is rendered.

### a.     MERITS REVIEW

In England, parties may appeal on questions of law unless otherwise agreed. *See* §69, English Arbitration Act, Supplement at pp. 203-05.

In Switzerland, parties to international arbitration can elect to substitute cantonal law for the otherwise applicable rules of the Federal Conflict of Laws Act. The Swiss Intercantonal Arbitration Concordat, Article 36 (f) provides

> An action for annulment of the arbitral award may be brought . . . where it is alleged that:

> f.     the award is arbitrary in that it was based on findings which were manifestly contrary to the facts appearing on the file, or in that it constitutes a clear violation of law or equity.

### Notes and Questions

1. On Swiss cantonal procedure, *see generally*, P. Neyroud & W. W. Park, *Predestination and Swiss Arbitration Law: Geneva's Application of the Intercantonal Concordat*, 2 B.U. INT'L L.J. 1 (1983).

2. Note that excluding appeal on the merits of the dispute will not affect the availability of judicial review on matters of arbitrators' excess of authority or serious irregularity in the proceedings. *See* §§67-69, English Arbitration Act 1996, Supplement at pp. 201-05.

b.     REVIEW FOR DEFECTS IN PROCEDURAL INTEGRITY

(i)     UNITED STATES-FEDERAL ARBITRATION ACT, §10

§10. Same; Vacation; Grounds; Rehearing

In either of the following cases the United States court in and for the district wherein the award was made may make an order vacating the award upon the application of any party to the arbitration —

(a)     Where the award was procured by corruption, fraud, or undue means.

(b)     Where there was evident partiality or corruption in the arbitrators, or either of them.

(c)     Where the arbitrators were guilty of misconduct in refusing to postpone the hearing, upon sufficient cause shown, or in refusing to hear evidence pertinent and material to the controversy; or of any other misbehavior by which the rights of any party have been prejudiced.

(d)     Where the arbitrators exceeded their powers, or so imperfectly executed them that a mutual, final, and definitive award upon the subject matter submitted was not made.

(e)     Where an award is vacated and the time within which the agreement required the award to be made has not expired the court may, in its discretion, direct a rehearing by the arbitrators.

Recall the distinction between vacating an award and merely refusing to confirm an award, discussed above in the Introduction. Note that under section 207 of the Federal Arbitration Act, "confirmation" of an award covered by the New York Convention may be refused on grounds set forth in the list of Article V defenses to an award's enforcement. The litany of Article V defenses does not, however, provide a basis for vacatur. The prospect that an award may be set aside for "manifest disregard" of the law by an arbitrator was raised in dicta in Wilko v. Swan, 346 U.S. 427, 436 (1953).

(ii)    ENGLISH ARBITRATION ACT 1996,<br>§§67-68

**67.**—(1) A party to arbitral proceedings may (upon notice to the other parties and to the tribunal) apply to the court—

    (a)     challenging any award of the arbitral tribunal as to its substantive jurisdiction; or

    (b)     for an order declaring an award made by the tribunal on the merits to be of no effect, in whole or in part, because the tribunal did not have substantive jurisdiction.

A party may lose the right to object (see section 73) and the right to apply is subject to the restrictions in section 70(2) and (3).

(2) The arbitral tribunal may continue the arbitral proceedings and make a further award while an application to the court under this section is pending in relation to an award as to jurisdiction.

(3) On an application under this section challenging an award of the arbitral tribunal as to its substantive jurisdiction, the court may by order—

    (a)     confirm the award,

    (b)     vary the award, or

    (c)     set aside the award in whole or in part.

(4) The leave of the court is required for any appeal from a decision of the court under this section.

**68.**—(1) A party to arbitral proceedings may (upon notice to the other parties and to the tribunal) apply to the court challenging an award in the proceedings on the ground of serious irregularity affecting the tribunal, the proceedings or the award.

A party may lose the right to object (see section 73) and the right to apply is subject to the restrictions in section 70(2) and (3).

(2)  Serious irregularity means an irregularity of one or more of the following kinds which the court considers has caused or will cause substantial injustice to the applicant—

(a)    failure by the tribunal to comply with section 33 (general duty of tribunal);

(b)    the tribunal exceeding its powers (otherwise than by exceeding its substantive jurisdiction; see section 67);

(c)    failure by the tribunal to conduct the proceedings in accordance with the procedure agreed by the parties;

(d)    failure by the tribunal to deal with all the issues that were put to it;

(e)    any arbitral or other institution or person vested by the parties with powers in relation to the proceedings or the award exceeding its powers;

(f)    uncertainty or ambiguity as to the effect of the award;

(g)    the award being obtained by fraud or the award or the way in which it was procured being contrary to public policy;

(h)    failure to comply with the requirements as to the form of the award; or

(i)    any irregularity in the conduct of the proceedings or in the award which is admitted by the tribunal or by any arbitral or other institution or person vested by the parties with powers in relation to the proceedings or the award.

(3)  If there is shown to be serious irregularity affecting the tribunal, the proceedings or the award, the court may—

(a)    remit the award to the tribunal, in whole or in part, for reconsideration,

(b)    set the award aside in whole or in part, or

(c)    declare the award to be of no effect, in whole or in part.

The court shall not exercise its power to set aside or to declare an award to be of no effect, in whole or in part, unless it is satisfied that it would be inappropriate to remit the matters in question to the tribunal for reconsideration.

(4)  The leave of the court is required for any appeal from a decision of the court under this section.

### Notes and Questions

1.  When does an error of law amount to a matter of procedural irregularity of excess of authority? The following discussion by two leading British arbitration scholars analyzes the matter under the laws of England.

MICHAEL J. MUSTILL & STEWART C. BOYD, THE LAW AND PRACTICE OF COMMERCIAL ARBITRATION IN ENGLAND 646-48 (2d ed. 1989).

### Judicial Review

As we have already stated, it appears to be well established law that direct intervention through the medium of what used to be known as the prerogative orders, and is now called judicial review, is not available as a means of controlling arbitral proceedings, however gross the abuse.

### Misconduct

At first sight it appears that there would be no ground for the Court to hold that a decision contrary to law could ever amount to misconduct, founding an application to set the award aside. It has been clear for at least 200 years that it is not misconduct for an arbitrator to make a mistake of law or fact. It makes no difference that the error is obvious, in the absence of a jurisdiction to set aside for error on the face. Nor does it matter if the error is gross; the Court has never allowed itself to be drawn into admitting extrinsic evidence of error, merely because of an allegation that the error is more serious than usual.

There is, however, another way of approaching the matter. Instead of concentrating on the erroneous nature of the law applied by the arbitrator, the Court might be persuaded to enquire why the error took place. Once the motives of the arbitrator became open to question, there would be the possibility of treating a studied decision by the arbitrator to disregard his obligation to apply the law as an instance of bad faith, and this would make an attack on the award much easier to mount. Perhaps English law will develop a doctrine similar to that of 'manifest disregard' which is tentatively believed to exist in the law of the United States.

Three questions arise here. First, would the Court have jurisdiction to intervene, if the conduct of the arbitrator could be characterised as male fides? There can be no doubt as to an affirmative answer. The precise judicial mechanism is open to doubt. Perhaps the doctrine could be borrowed from administrative law, so as to hold that the award is void. But it would be more in conformity with the general approach of the law of arbitration to treat the award as voidable.

Second, would there be room for the Court to treat a studied disregard of the mandate as bad faith, if for reasons of policy it was desired to adopt this line of reasoning? There is a real difference between an unintentional and a deliberate departure from the law. The former concerns the substance of the award, and the latter the process by which it is arrived at. A number of scattered dicta support the view that deliberate departure from the law is in a category of its own.

Finally, there is the question whether the Court would in practice be willing to treat a conscious disregard of the law as an example of the type of bad faith which founds an application to set aside. No doubt it will be urged, in support of the view that the Court should not take this step, that the legislature and the courts have in recent years been solicitous to give the parties to arbitration agreements what they want, and that what they want is a speedy process coupled with the elimination of opportunities for delay; and it will be said that it would be contrary to current policy to reintroduce even a small part of the judicial control which the legislature has been at pains to take away. It will be said that it is an offensive misuse of language to characterise as bad faith a decision by the arbitrator not to apply a law which seems to him out of touch with commercial reality. It will also be said that from a practical point of view a distinction between accidental and deliberate mistake will often be impossible to draw.

These are impressive arguments, but we believe them to be misconceived. The proponents of an entirely liberated system of arbitration overlook the essential fact that commerce is concerned with transactions, not with disputes, and that a reasonable degree of certainty lies at the heart of the ordinary conduct of business. Where a contract is governed by English law, the promisor ought to perform the promises expressed or implied by the contract, in the sense given to them by English law; for this forms the consideration given for the reciprocal performance undertaken by the promisee. Unless the bargain proceeds on the assumption that the promisee can insist on a full performance of the promise, understood in accordance with the governing law, he will receive less than value for his price, and the commercial structure of the bargain will be distorted. So also, if the matter comes to a dispute. Just as disputed bargains form only a tiny proportion of those which are entered into, so also do concluded arbitrations amount to a small minority of those which are begun. Business people need to be able to settle their disputes by assessing the likely outcome of the arbitration. This they can only do if they are confident that the arbitrator will at least try to apply an objectively ascertainable system of law. They must, of course, recognize the possibility that the arbitrator will make a mistake, but this is not fatal to the settlement. The parties can accommodate error, but not chance. Moreover, when one comes to regard the arbitrator himself, it is seen that he is appointed to ascertain the rights of the parties. These are the rights which, for good consideration, they have chosen to confer on each other. It is not a proper discharge of his trust to give them, not the rights for which they bargained, but a reformulated set of rights of his own choosing. It is no answer to say that the arbitrator acts with the best of intentions. If he deliberately transgresses his mandate, he is knowingly doing something which he should not do. An award made in such circumstances should not stand, and if the likelihood that such an award will be made is detected whilst the reference is still in progress, the arbitrator should not be allowed to continue in his office.

Nor in our submission is it an answer to say that the distinction between deliberate transgression and an honest error is unworkable. It has been long established in the English law, and judges are well capable of giving effect to it. Certainly, the utmost caution will need to be used, if allegations of manifest disregard are not to be used as an expedient for delay. Relief is likely to be granted on the most sparing basis, if it is ever granted at all. But the maintenance of a right to intervene, in the rare cases where the arbitrator knowingly steps outside his proper function, is in our submission an essential safeguard, now that the more traditional methods of control have been so greatly attenuated.

\* \* \*

*Moran v. Lloyd's*, 1 Law Reports 542, 550-51 (Q.B. 1983).

[T]he authorities established that an arbitrator or umpire does not misconduct himself or the proceedings merely because he makes an error of fact or of law.

. . . .

We stress this aspect in order to make it clear to all who are concerned in and with arbitration that neither section 22 [remission of award to arbitration for reconsideration] nor section 23 [setting aside of an award for misconduct] is available as a backdoor method of circumventing the restrictions upon the court's power to intervene in arbitral proceedings which have been created by the Act of 1979.

. . . [W]e doubt whether, as such, inconsistency between one part of an award and another could ever constitute or evidence misconduct on the part of an arbitrator. The overwhelming likelihood is that it would merely constitute or evidence error of law or of fact or of both and these do not amount to misconduct. *Halsbury's Laws of England*, 4th ed., vol. 2 (1973), para. 622, suggests the contrary and cites *Ames v. Milward* (1818) 8 Taunt. 637 as authority. But that was a case not of misconduct, but of error of law upon the face of the award at a time when this was a ground for setting aside.

. . . Inconsistency of *reasoning* may betray an error of fact, but it is in the nature of arbitral proceedings that this must be accepted by the parties. Alternatively it may betray an error of law. That may give rise to a right of appeal, but it has no other effect. Inconsistency or ambiguity in the operative parts of the award—the parts which would "be enforced in the same manner as a judgment or order to the same effect" if application were made under section 26 of the Act of 1950—may be another matter. The executive power of the state to enforce an award is not to be invoked in an inconsistent or ambiguous form and in such an event it might well be right to remit the award to the arbitrator or umpire under section 22 to enable him to resolve the ambiguity or inconsistency.

*     *     *

*K/S A/S Bill Biakh v. Hyundai Corp.*, 1 Lloyd's Rep. 187 (Q.B. 1987).

[In May, 1983 Bill Biakh and Bill Biali purchased two vessels from Hyundai Corporation. The contracts were governed by English law and contain London arbitration clauses. The two vessels were delivered in September and December, 1985, respectively. Disputes arose as to the performance of the vessels as measured against the contractual terms, related to the fitness for service of the hatch covers. The buyers commenced London arbitration proceedings under both contracts. In each arbitration the buyers claimed substantial damages on the ground that the builders failed to rectify defects in the hatch covers pursuant to the guarantee clauses in the contracts. A problem arose as to the evidence which may be produced at the arbitration hearing. The buyers contended that the exchanges regarding the investigations and all technical documentation relating to such investigations were agreed to be "without prejudice," and that in the context those words mean that the documents cannot be given in evidence. The arbitrators in principle ruled against the builders on their contention that such documents may not be adduced, but did not rule on the admissibility of any particular documents.]

Mr. Justice STEYN: The central question which arises on rival summonses in two Commercial Court actions is whether the Court has jurisdiction, in relation to two duly constituted arbitrations and during the course of the references, to intervene by declaration or injunction to correct an allegedly wrong interlocutory ruling by the arbitrators as to the admissibility of evidence.

.     .     .

The builders' first contention is that the arbitrators' ruling was wrong and that it amounted to "misconduct." The nature of the builders' allegation required them to join and serve the arbitrators, and they have done so. Rightly, the arbitrators have simply indicated that they will abide by the judgment of the Court. The usual way in which an assertion of misconduct comes before the Court is either by way of an application for the revocation of the authority of the arbitrator under §1 of the Arbitration Act, 1950, or by an application for the removal of the arbitrator under §23(1) of the 1950 Act, or as a ground for subsequently seeking to set aside the award under §23(2). The builders here seek altogether different and, in my experience, novel relief.

The builders do not want the arbitrators removed. On the contrary, it is accepted on behalf of the builders that the arbitrators are men of integrity and competence. Moreover, it is of fundamental importance to bear in mind that the application is made during the course of the references and that its sole purpose is to achieve a reversal by the Court of an adverse procedural ruling made by the arbitrators. And, I would add, it is a ruling which may depend partly on issues of fact and partly on issues of law.

In an extreme case it is conceivable that an arbitrator's failure to observe the principles of natural justice in the making of interlocutory rulings may lead either to the revocation of the mandate of the arbitrator under §1 of the 1950 Act or the removal of the arbitrator under §23(2), but it follows from the decision in Bremer Vulkan Schiffbau und Maschinenfabrik v. South India Shipping Corpn. Ltd., [1981] 1 Lloyd's Rep. 253; [1981] A.C. 909 that the Court has no inherent jurisdiction to correct procedural errors, even if they can be categorised as misconduct, during the course of the reference, and that the statutory scheme of the Arbitration Acts does not authorize such corrective measures. The remedies are therefore revocation of the authority of the arbitrator or removal of the arbitrator in the exceptional cases where that might be appropriate, or resisting enforcement of the award.

This is not a lacuna in our law. In the interests of expedition and finality of arbitration proceedings, it is of the first importance that judicial intrusion in the arbitral process should be kept to a minimum. A judicial power to correct during the course of the reference procedural rulings of an arbitrator which are within his jurisdiction is unknown in advanced arbitration systems, as is clear from the valuable Year Books published by the International Council of Commercial Arbitration, and the creation of such a power by judicial precedent in this case would constitute a most serious reproach to the ability of our system of arbitration to serve the needs of users of the arbitral process. For these reasons I reject the builders' first argument.

But there is another fundamental objection to the builders' first argument. The builders accept that the arbitrators are honourable men and competent to discharge their duties as arbitrators. The builders do not suggest that they were not given a fair hearing at the preliminary meeting. They simply say that the arbitrators committed misconduct because they came to the wrong conclusion. That is an unsustainable proposition. In relation to post award remedies, the decision of the Court of Appeal in Moran v. Lloyd's, [1983] Q.B. 542 is the clearest authority for the proposition that an error of law or fact cannot by itself amount to misconduct. If that is the case in relation to errors of law or fact as to substantive rights, it would be surprising if a different rule applied to errors regarding admissibility of evidence. That does not, of course, mean that the admission of, for example, utterly irrelevant evidence <u>and reliance on it</u> in the reasons for the award might not afford evidential material for a broader attack on the award itself alleging misconduct on the part of an arbitrator, but a mere error in relation to the admissibility of evidence does not by itself amount to misconduct, and I so rule.

.     .     .

It is now appropriate to revert to the central question which I posed at the beginning of this judgment. In my view, the answer to it is an unequivocal 'No.' The Courts will not allow the policy of judicial restraint which was enshrined in the 1979 Act to be subverted by a misuse of the concepts of misconduct or excess of authority . . . . Consequently, the parties are bound to observe the arbitrators' interlocutory rulings as set out in their telex in Sept. 16.

### Notes and Questions

1. In an ICC arbitration involving a building project in Iran, the loser alleges arbitral "misconduct" because majority arbitrators refused a face-to-face meeting with a dissenting arbitrator to discuss modification of the award. *See Bank Mellat v. GAA Development and Construction Co.*, 2 Lloyd's Rep. 44 (Q.B. 1988). The decision by Mr. Justice Steyn, discussed *infra*, p. 944, found the flaw merely "a technical one" and dismissed the motion for setting aside the award.

2. In view of the view expressed by Mustill & Boyd and Judge Steyn, are there effective control mechanisms for arbitration in England?

> (iii)  FRANCE—NOUVEAU  CODE  DE
> PROCÉDURE CIVILE, ARTICLES 1502 AND
> 1504

### Article 1502

A decision granting recognition or enforcement to an award is subject to appeal only in the following cases:

(1)   If the arbitral tribunal ruled when there was no arbitration agreement or on the basis of an agreement which was null and void or expired;

(2)   If the arbitral tribunal was irregularly formed or if the sole arbitrator was irregularly appointed;

(3)   If arbitral tribunal ruled without conforming itself to the terms of reference which was entrusted to it;

(4)   When the principle of basic procedural justice (<u>contradiction</u>) has not been observed;

(5)   If recognition or enforcement is contrary to French international public policy.

### Article 1504

An arbitral award rendered in France in matters of international arbitration can be challenged by an action to annul the award on the basis of the grounds provided for in article 1502.

The order granting enforceability to this award is not subject to any means of recourse. However, the action to annul an award entails as a matter of law, within the limits of the court's jurisdiction, recourse against the ruling of the judge for enforcement matters or his jurisdictional divestiture.

> (iv)   NETHERLANDS

Compare the Dutch statute, which is based on the French model, Burgerlijke rechtsvordering, Art. 1065 (1). 12 YEARBOOK OF COMMERCIAL ARBITRATION 370, 383 (1987).

Burgerlijke rechtsvordering, Art. 1065(1)

Grounds for setting aside

1.    Setting aside of the award can take place only on one or more of the following grounds:

(a)    absence of a valid arbitration agreement;

(b)    the arbitral tribunal was constituted in violation of the rules applicable thereto;

(c)    the arbitral tribunal has not complied with its mandate;

(d)    the award is not signed or does not contain reasons in accordance with he provisions of article 1057;

(e)    the award, or the manner in which it was made, violates public policy or good morals.

(v)    SWITZERLAND — FEDERAL PRIVATE INTERNATIONAL LAW ACT, ARTICLE 190(2)

(2)    [An award] shall be capable of being set aside only where

(a)    a sole arbitrator has been incorrectly appointed or the arbitral tribunal has been incorrectly constituted:

(b)    the arbitral tribunal has wrongly declared itself to have or not to have jurisdiction;

(c)    the arbitral tribunal has decided on claims which were not submitted to it or has omitted to decide on any claim that was submitted to it;

(d)    the principles of the equality of treatment of the parties and their right to be heard in a contested proceeding have not been observed; or

(e)    the award is incompatible with public policy.

(vi)    UNICTRAL MODEL LAW, ARTICLE 34(2)

(2)    An arbitral award may be set aside by the court specified in article 6 only if:

(a)    the party making the application furnishes proof that:
(i) a party to the arbitration referred to in article 7 was under some incapacity; or the said agreement is not valid under the law to which the parties have subjected

it or, failing any indication thereon, under the law of this State; or

(ii) the party making the application was not given proper notice of the appointment of an arbitrator or of the arbitral proceedings or was otherwise unable to present his case; or

(iii) the award deals with a dispute not contemplated by or not falling within the terms of the submission to arbitration, or contains decisions on matters beyond the scope of the submission to arbitration, provided that, if the decisions on matters submitted to arbitration can be separated from those not so submitted, only that part of the award which contains decisions on matters not submitted to arbitration may be set aside; or

(iv) the composition of the arbitral tribunal or the arbitral procedure was not in accordance with the agreement of the parties, unless such agreement was in conflict with a provision of this Law from which the parties cannot derogate, or, failing such agreement, was not in accordance with this Law; or

(b)     the court finds that:

(i) the subject-matter of the dispute is not capable of settlement by arbitration under the law of this State; or

(ii) the award is in conflict with the public policy of this State.

### c.     ABSENCE OF JUDICIAL REVIEW

#### (i)     BELGIAN CODE JUDICIAIRE, ARTICLE 1717(4)

Willliam W. Park, *National Law and Commercial Justice: Safeguarding Procedural Integrity in International Arbitration*, 63 TUL. L. REV. 647, 694-95 (1989).

In 1985, Belgians moved toward arbitral autonomy by amending their Code judiciaire to provide that if all parties are non-Belgian, an award rendered in Belgium is not subject to an action for annulment. Article 1717 of the Belgian Code judiciaire provides:

Courts of Belgium may hear a request for annulment only if at least one of the parties to the dispute decided by the award is

> either a physical person having Belgian nationality or residence, or a legal entity created in Belgium or having a Belgian branch or other seat of operation.[311]

The provision is mandatory. Unlike Switzerland, Belgium permits no possibility for foreigners to opt for local judicial review.

Belgian "verve and panache" has been greeted as "salutary" by commentators who favor giving international businessmen the alternative of an arbitration that is "totally unbound."

Such exuberance may be questioned, precisely because arbitration in Belgium is <u>not</u> totally delocalized. Belgian courts may intervene at pre-award stages to assist the arbitration in matters such as nomination of arbitrators, gathering evidence and provisional measures to preserve property. And awards rendered in Belgium continue to benefit from recognition and enforcement under the New York Convention. Winners of defective arbitral awards that have not been annulled can be expected to try to enforce the awards wherever the loser has assets. Even if not ultimately successful, such enforcement attempts will cost the loser time and expense that can hardly be reconciled with the fair operation of a private adjudicatory system. When the victim of procedural irregularities is the losing claimant, the results of arbitral autonomy are even more unfair. If denied the opportunity to have the award set aside where rendered, the unsuccessful claimant has no enforcement forum in which to contest the defective award, since there is nothing to enforce. Its only path to justice will be litigation, notwithstanding the bargain to arbitrate.

---

[311] Law of March 27, 1985 (Belg.), enacting *Code Judiciaire* art. 1717. The French text reads:

> Les tribunaux belges ne peuvent connaître d'une demande en annulation que lorsqu'au moins une partie au différend tranché par la sentence arbitrale est soit une personne physique ayant la nationalité belge ou une résidence en Belgique, soit une personne morale constituée en Belgique ou y ayant une succursale ou un siège quelconque d'opération.

In cases where actions for annulment are permitted (*i.e.*, when a Belgian is a party to the arbitration), grounds include violation of *ordre public*, excess of jurisdiction, an award's lack of reasons, fraud, and violation of due process. *See Code judiciaire* art. 1704(2) (Law of July 4, 1972, Aug. 8, 1972).

The Belgian state thus directly and indirectly assists the arbitrator in his creation of legal rights and duties, but refuses to take responsibility for insuring the integrity of the process. The loser in a defective arbitration in Belgium may be required to resist enforcement wherever in the world it has assets or, if a claimant, may be denied any recourse at all through the arbitral process.

(ii)   SWISS   FEDERAL   PRIVATE   INTERNATIONAL   LAW   ACT, ARTICLE 192(1)

The Swiss federal arbitration statute provides for the possibility of explicit written waiver of review, as set out below:

> If neither party is domiciled, habitually resident or has a place of business in Switzerland, they can, by an express declaration in the arbitral agreement or in a subsequent agreement in writing, exclude the right to bring proceedings to set aside the arbitral award; they can also exclude the right to bring setting aside proceedings on the basis of any one or more of the grounds set out in Article 190(2) [of the Act].

### Notes and Questions

1. Which model of "non-review" — Belgian or Swiss — presents the greater drawbacks? advantages? What are they?

2. Consider, in this regard, the following comment:

> The dangers presented here are more than particularized instances of injustice to one party in an arbitration. In a larger sense, the adoption by potential primary jurisdictions of "hands-off" policies as a way of attracting arbitral business increases the work load of already overtaxed courts in secondary jurisdictions. The jurisdiction that fails to perform its duty, like all economic externalizers, simply requires someone else to shoulder it. In this it threatens to erode the intricate but fragile network of reciprocation upon which jurisdiction in international law is ultimately based.

> The point bears emphasis. One should remember that the allocation of international jurisdiction does not rest on an explicit "full-faith and credit" clause, policed by some international Supreme Court. It rests, instead, on an ongoing reciprocating

process in which the responsible decision institutions of one territorial community give effect within their ambit of operation to the acts of decision institutions of other territories on the assumption that they have in fact behaved responsibly in discharging their own functions. As Max Huber long ago observed, the recognition of another's jurisdiction in international law is part of a compact, based on the expectation that that jurisdiction will be exercised in ways that protect the rights of others. The "hands-off" policies of primary jurisdictions in international arbitration violate that compact and undermine the network of reciprocal expectations and trust that is the ultimate basis of international jurisdiction.

W. MICHAEL REISMAN, SYSTEMS OF CONTROL IN INTERNATIONAL ADJUDICATION AND ARBITRATION 133-34 (1992).

### 2. THE PROPER ROLE OF THE ARBITRAL SEAT: POLEMIC AND PERSPECTIVE

Scholars and practitioners alike have spilled considerable ink in discussing "delocalizing" international arbitration — which is to say, a decreased role for the legal system at the place of the proceedings. Before entering into the debate, consider the following summaries of issues related to the proper role of the arbitration law of the arbitral seat.

### a. WHAT IS AT STAKE?

William W. Park, *National Law and Commercial Justice: Safeguarding Procedural Integrity in International Arbitration*, 63 TUL. L. REV. 647, 684-89 (1989).

'Delocalization' from Two Perspectives

The role of the arbitral seat may be viewed from two different policy perspectives: that of the country in which the award is rendered, and that of the country asked to enforce the award. The perspective of the arbitral situs will be concerned with grounds for review. Should the arbitral seat ever review awards in international commercial disputes? If so, should courts at the situs intervene to correct errors of law on the merits of the dispute? Or should the place of the arbitration limit itself to examining the arbitrator's respect for his mission and for the proceedings' basic fairness, called due process in the United States and natural justice in England?

The observer at the enforcement forum, on the other hand, will ask whether an award, annulled where rendered, should be enforceable in other countries in which the loser has assets. If so, under what circumstances? While the enforcement forum may always impose its own standards for review (as long as these are consistent with treaty obligations), it is less than clear in both law and policy whether the enforcement forum should always, or ever, recognize nullification of an award by courts of the place of the arbitration.

Both sets of questions are prompted by an understandable desire to further a more uniform system of international dispute resolution. Both inquiries essentially ask to what extent arbitral awards should be subject to the jurisdiction of judges at the place of the proceedings. And from both perspectives, the policy dilemma derives in large measure from the New York Convention's failure to define acceptable grounds for annulment at the place where the award is made.

Continental scholars who favor 'floating' awards and delocalized arbitration will see reduction or elimination of judicial review of awards by courts of the arbitral situs as a trend that promotes the wishes of the parties without necessarily violating the vital interest of the arbitral seat. In a transnational dispute, the arbitration usually will have its economic or social impact outside the borders of the place of the proceedings.

This trend toward delocalized arbitration may pose its own problems, however, if carried so far as to eliminate all scrutiny of awards at the seat of the arbitration, as has been done in Belgium. Unless an award is subject to challenge where rendered for violation of minimum standards of procedural fairness (such as excess of authority or fraud), the loser may be forced to challenge the defective award in any country in which assets may be subject to execution of the award. And a losing claimant may have no recourse at all through the arbitral process for the simple reason that there will be no award to enforce.

The 'shift in the control function' from the arbitral situs to the execution forum also involves an increased role for courts in the loser's home country, where the loser most likely will have assets. The implications of this migration toward non-neutral judges have been recognized, although not necessarily accepted, by arbitration lawyers.

### Grounds for Review: The Perspective of the Arbitral Seat

Judicial review of awards where rendered generally falls into two categories: full review on the legal merits; and limited review for conformity to basic procedural fairness, including arbitrator fraud and excess of authority. The former seeks to maximize legal certainty concerning the merits of the dispute; the latter looks to ensure an arbitration's integrity while minimizing judicial meddling with the substantive results.

Recently, a third model has emerged in Belgium, under which the arbitral situs will not set aside an award for any reason, including an arbitrator's fraud or excess of authority. Under this system of 'non-review,' an entity that never signed the arbitration agreement (perhaps joined in the arbitration merely because of its relationship to another party) will not have a chance to litigate the arbitrator's jurisdiction when the award is rendered. Nor would there then be an opportunity to review errors on choice of law or arbitral rules. If the parties agreed on English law to govern the contract and UNCITRAL Rules to govern procedure, the arbitrator might apply French law and AAA rules without the loser being able to challenge these defects unless the award is presented for enforcement at a later time. In this model, a legal system supports arbitration within its borders without providing minimum safeguards of basic justice.

### Effect of Annulled Awards: The Perspective of the Enforcement Forum

Delocalization raises questions for the enforcement forum as well as the arbitral situs. Suppose an arbitral award rendered in Azania is set aside there on the ground that the parties did not validly consent to arbitration. Should the award be enforceable in the United States, where the loser has assets, if the United States takes a contrary view from that of Azania regarding the validity of the arbitration agreement? What should an American court do if an Azanian judge sets aside the award for reasons that are not grounds for annulment in the United States, such as mere error of law or fact, or refusal by a minority arbitrator to sign the award?

Deference to Azanian nullification would be required if the arbitration were covered by the European Convention on International Commercial Arbitration. Known as the Geneva Convention of 1961, this treaty applies to disputes between nationals of different contracting states, which the United States at present is not. Annulment of an award in its country of origin constitutes a ground for refusal of recognition under the 1961 Geneva Convention only when the annulment was for specifically enumerated reasons. Thus, awards rendered in a state that adheres to the 1961 Geneva Convention may occasionally have greater 'international currency' than those of other countries, remaining enforceable under the treaty even after annulment by local courts. The Convention provides that an award annulled where rendered shall nevertheless be enforced unless annulment was for treaty-enumerated reasons: (1) a void agreement, (2) lack of proper notice or inability to present a case, (3) excess of authority (decisions on matters beyond the scope of the submission agreement), and (4) irregular composition of the arbitral tribunal. The European Convention applies only to awards rendered in another contracting state arising from agreements between residents of contracting states. Thus when an award rendered in Paris between a Frenchman and an Italian is presented for enforcement in Italy after annulment for a violation of French ordre public, the Italian court would not be entitled to refuse to enforce the award on the grounds of the French annulment alone. If, however, the other party in the arbitration was an American or an Englishman, the annulled award could be refused recognition, since neither the United States nor the United Kingdom adheres to the European Convention.

Enforcing an award annulled in its country of origin would seem appropriate when the local judiciary dishonestly annulled the award. But if the award were set aside by an honest judge, although on grounds peculiar to the law of the place of the proceedings, it is questionable whether enforcement by a forum not sharing these grounds for review would further or defeat the goal of efficient trans-border dispute resolution.

.    .    .

Not all national constraints impede fair and efficient arbitration. Unless judges at the seat of the arbitration possess clearly defined power to correct fraud, arbitrator excess of authority, and infringement of basic due process, the loser may be required to defend against an unfair award everywhere in the world where it has assets. When the victim of procedural irregularities is the losing claimant, the results of arbitral autonomy are even more dramatically unfair. If denied the opportunity to have the award set aside where rendered, the unsuccessful claimant has no enforcement forum in which to contest the defective award, for the simple reason that there is nothing to enforce. The losing claimant's only recourse would be to commence litigation and to deny the award's res judicata effect — a solution hardly compatible with the bargain to resolve disputes through arbitration rather than the courts.

Commercial arbitration is a consensual waiver of recourse to the courts that would otherwise have jurisdiction. It differs from the heteroclite forms of nonbinding conciliation now in vogue, in that courts are expected to enforce the arbitrator's decision. Most legal systems support such renunciation of judicial jurisdiction either by enforcing agreements and awards, ordering attachments of assets to secure payment of awards, or making defective arbitration clauses workable. However, the support is granted only on the condition that mandatory procedural safeguards be available to protect against arbitrators who exceed the limits of their mission or corrupt the arbitral process. Indeed, national assistance to arbitration would seem to carry with it an obligation to insure the integrity of the decisionmaking process.

One Lord Justice of Appeal in England [Sir Michael Kerr] has argued that judicial review is a 'bulwark against corruption, arbitrariness, bias . . . and . . . sheer incompetence, in relation to acts and decisions with binding legal effect for others. No one having the power to make legally binding decisions in this country should be altogether outside and immune from this system.'

.     .     .

Whether a national legal framework can be called favorable to arbitration depends in large part on whether one adopts the viewpoint of a potential winner or loser. The claimant with a strong case will usually look for speed, economy, and finality. The perspective of the potential loser is also understandable, however. Fearing that his arguments are not self-evident, he will look for judicial review to ensure that all aspects of the case have been fairly considered. It would be misguided and irresponsible to pursue the goals of speed and finality sought by winners at the expense of the procedural fairness expected by losers.

The role of the arbitral situs is vital in supporting international commercial arbitration. Under the New York Convention, the place of the arbitration gives the arbitrator's decision a presumptive validity in any of the countries that have ratified the Convention. Therefore, freeing arbitration from all control over its basic fairness at the place of proceedings may in its own way prove as unfortunate as the opposite extreme of merits review of awards.

From the business manager's perspective, what is called for is assurance that the arbitration agreement and award will be enforced, but with balanced court review: freedom from judicial meddling with the dispute's legal merits, combined with judicial procedures to insure that the arbitrator respected the limits of his authority and basic due process. The arbitral seat should concern itself with the bounds of the arbitrator's mission and the fair play expected by the parties, but not with the correct interpretation of the contract or marginal procedural niceties.

To this end, international treaties might require enforcement of foreign arbitral awards only when rendered in countries providing a nonwaivable right of review of awards for violation of (1) the arbitrator's jurisdiction, both as to the parties and the applicable law, (2) fundamental procedural fairness, including the right to be heard and to present one's case, and (3) international public policy. Nations seeking to attract arbitration business would want local awards to benefit from treaty enforcement, and thus would be encouraged to provide safeguards for the basic integrity of proceedings conducted within their borders.

Keeping review within acceptable limits admittedly is not easy to put into practice. There is no bright line nor intellectually satisfactory test to distinguish between an arbitrator who exceeds his authority, and one who merely makes a mistake and renders a bad award. In some cases an arbitrator may even be justified in disregarding the parties' choice of law in favor of the mandatory norms of the place of performance. But some measure of discernment is possible, and an awareness of the consequence of either too much or too little scrutiny of awards should facilitate the process.

The elaboration of workable definitions of fundamental due process will be similarly difficult. Through a long and perhaps complex articulation of cohesive notions of fairness, parochial peculiarities must be abandoned in favor of an international consensus on the essential elements inhering in the right to effective presentation of one's case.

Even more challenging will be the task of defining the common interests and values to be given effect in delimiting international, as contrasted to internal, public order. Terms such as 'public policy' and 'ordre public' are malleable, and represent ill-defined concepts that risk lending themselves to court scrutiny on the merits of the award.

The winner of an arbitration will not usually warm to judicial review of an award in his favor. Review adds delay and expense, and compromises the privacy that the parties expected from arbitration. But the loser and the public are also affected by the arbitration. Respect for their interests calls for some measure of court scrutiny of awards at the place of the proceedings.

Without some local court supervision of international commercial arbitration, the application of transnational norms may turn arbitration into a businessman's nightmare worse than a Texas jury: a dispute resolution system lacking the predictability necessary to permit informed decisions about the legal risks of commercial choices. Neither the parties to the dispute nor the public interests affected by the arbitration will be well served by letting arbitration drift free of national legal constraints designed to insure that arbitrators fulfill the shared expectations of those who entrusted them with their mission.

### Notes and Questions

1. In 1979 England abolished the "case stated" procedure by which courts excercised control over the arbitrator's decision on the merits of the dispute. The background of the Act is enlightening with respect to the perceived economic advantages of subjecting international arbitration to less rather than more guidance at the place of the proceedings. *See generally*, William W. Park, *Judicial Supervision of Transnational Commercial Arbitration*, 21 HARV. INT'L L.J. 87 (1980). Evaluations of the pound sterling benefits in attracting to England more "invisible exports" (arbitrators' and lawyers' fees in particular) by a laissez-faire attitude toward arbitration appear in statements of Lord Lloyd of Kilgerran, 398 PARL. DEB., H.L. (5th ser.) 536 (1978) and Lord Cullen of Ashborne, 392 PARL. DEB., H.L. (5th ser.) 99 (1978).

2.    To understand how delocalization can make a difference in the enforcement forum, consider the 1984 Dutch decision in *Southern Pacific Properties*

*v. Egypt* (July 12, 1984), reproduced in 24 I.L.M. 1042 (1985), and discussed in Chapter 4, *supra* p. 487. The case involving an aborted construction project in Egypt near the Pyramids also illustrates the influence of the law of the place of arbitration. An award for more than $12 million had been rendered against Egypt by an arbitral tribunal sitting in France. On the 12th of July 1984, the award was both annulled by a court in Paris and recognized by a court in Amsterdam. The Dutch court did not know of the French annulment. One can only speculate as to what the result would have been if the French decision had come a day earlier or the Dutch decision a day later. The Paris annulment led the parties to agree to stay further proceedings in the Netherlands until disposition of the appeal to the annulment in France.

### b.     THE OPTIMUM LEVEL OF JUDICIAL CONTROL

The arbitration lawyers who made us think about an arbitral process largely independent of the law at the place of arbitration suggested both theoretical and practical arguments in favor of what has come to be called (without much precision) "a-national," "delocalized" or "floating" arbitration. The pioneers were principally French, and included Philippe Fouchard and the late Berthold Goldman. *See* Berthold Goldman, *Les conflits de lois dans l'arbitrage international de droit privé*, 109 II RECUEIL DES COURS 347 (1963), and Philippe Fouchard, L'ARBITRAGE COMMERCIAL INTERNATIONAL, Dalloz, Paris 1964. In England, however, articulate protagonists have emphasized the more traditional view that national judges at the place of arbitration should exercise control over the integrity of an arbitration conducted within their borders, even if the arbitration is international in character. The classic English position has been set forth by the late Dr. Francis Mann and Sir Michael Kerr.

The extent to which arbitrators should be autonomous from the legal order of the country in which they render their awards is discussed in the following articles. In evaluating the various models of judicial review at the arbitral situs, ask how the goals of the New York Convention are affected by a balanced rather than an "all or nothing" approach to delocalization.

(i) William W. Park, *The* Lex Loci Arbitri *and International Commercial Arbitration*, 32 INT'L & COMP. L. Q. 21 (1983).

The country where the award is rendered traditionally has legitimised arbitral authority subject to conditions, in the form of mandatory procedural rules imposed on the arbitral proceedings. The proper scope of these local curial norms — commonly known as the lex loci arbitri — has been problematic. In England, prior to 1979, national courts supervised arbitral proceedings to ensure legally correct results. According to another model, however, arbitration is subject to judicial control only to safeguard its fundamental fairness. Yet a third model would free arbitration from any constraints imposed by the legal system of the place where the award is rendered.

These alternative patterns for judicial intervention implicate competing values that do not yield to facile analysis. The commercial community desires finality in private dispute resolution. Yet, national judicial systems may wish to further rival goals, such as the integrity of the adjudicatory process and respect for the rights of third parties.

.  .  .

F.A. Mann has articulated this traditional view with force, arguing that the pronouncements of an arbitral tribunal are not binding unless linked to a specific system of national law:

Every right or power a private person enjoys is inexorably conferred by or derived from a system of municipal law which may conveniently and in accordance with tradition be called lex fori, though it would be more exact (but also less familiar) to speak of the lex arbitri.[312]

The mandatory rules imposed by the lex loci arbitri do not yield to neat classification. Many legal systems prohibit arbitration of disputes involving sensitive public interests, such as the protection of investors in corporate securities or contracts with state agencies. Some

---

[312] F.A. Mann, *Lex Facit Arbitrum*, in INTERNATIONAL ARBITRATION: LIBER AMICORUM FOR MARTIN DOMKE 157, 159 (P. Sanders, ed., 1967).

require arbitrators to state the reasons for their awards, or provide for the removal of arbitrators who are inept or unfair. A few legal systems have provided for appeal from arbitrator error on matters of law.

. . .

The traditional role of the lex loci arbitri has been questioned by scholars and practitioners who suggest that an international commercial arbitral award may "float" free from the constraints of the national law of the place of the proceedings. Such denationalized arbitration, producing an "a-national" arbitral award, marries well with the commercial motive behind the trend toward greater arbitral autonomy in modern arbitration law: to increase a country's attractiveness as a situs for arbitral proceedings. This approach also permits national tribunals to concern themselves less with disputes not implicating national interests, and accommodates international business transactions in which the parties' divergent nationalities create a special need for a neutral and private forum for dispute resolution.

"Denationalized" arbitration, however, has come to mean more than self-restraint by the country of the proceedings in the imposition of local procedural law. "Floating" awards, it has been argued, are and should be enforceable outside the country of proceedings despite annulment where rendered. For example, suppose arbitration is conducted in Azania, where the award is set aside on the ground that the parties did not validly consent to arbitration. Should a court in Ruritania, where the loser has assets, nevertheless enforce the award if it comes to a different conclusion about the validity of the arbitration agreement? What if Azanian courts set aside the award for error of law, a ground for annulment unknown to Ruritanian law?

Varying degrees of floating arbitration might be contemplated. For instance, Ruritania might take the position that annulment in Azania is never relevant to enforcement in Ruritania. A less extreme position might take annulment of an award in Azania as an impediment to enforcement in Ruritania if the annulment was made for reasons considered appropriate under Ruritanian law. For example, Ruritania might accept annulment for arbitrator corruption, but not for arbitrator error of law.

Ruritanian courts, of course, may always deny recognition to an arbitration defective under their own standards. So much is accepted by both traditionalists and proponents of floating arbitration. The divisive issue is whether Ruritanian courts should also defer to Azanian nullification for violation of the latter's procedural norms.

Critical to the viability of "a-national" arbitration is the legal effect of an arbitral award not linked to a national legal system. The distinguished arbitration lawyer, Jan Paulsson, has written recently that "the binding force of an international award may be derived . . . without a specific legal system serving as its foundation."

.     .     .

The paradox of a legal obligation independent of a legal order suggests Athena springing full-blown from the head of Zeus: a binding commitment, free from any municipal law, just appears. Grasp of Paulsson's thesis requires a conceptual leap to a document labelled "obligation" enforced without respect to whether the document constitutes a valid obligation under the legal system normally selected by the enforcement forum's choice of law principles. In other words, the document receives contractual force from the enforcement forum itself regardless of the otherwise governing law.

.     .     .

The 1958 New York Arbitration Convention leaves open the theoretical possibility that the lex arbitri may be other than the law of the place of the proceedings. Under Article V(1)(e), a non-domestic arbitral award may be refused recognition on proof that it has been set aside by "a competent authority of the country in which, or under the law of which, that award was made." Annulment by an authority of the country "under the law of which" an award is made could be construed as a supplementary, rather than substitute, ground for refusal of recognition.

.     .     .

This tension between legality and finality represents a rivalry between the two types of certainty: one related to the uniform application of legal norms; the other concerned with the adjudicatory forum. The value of a uniform application of legal principles perhaps is strongest when there is a danger that private dispute resolution may become a means for the strong to oppress the weak through disproportionately unequal bargaining power, or when the interests of third parties may be affected by the dispute. In such cases, courts arguably may have a duty to examine the legal substance of the dispute and other matters that bear on the award's basic integrity, such as arbitrator fraud, impartiality or excess of authority.

To put it another way, the judiciary need not concern itself with the correctness of an arbitrator's conclusions merely to ensure a correct interpretation of the parties' contract. Court intervention on the merits of a dispute voluntarily submitted to arbitration is required only if an arbitrator's decision directly implicates national or third party interests. Intervention may be justified, for example, if an arbitrator's misinterpretation of an oil supply contract would result in injury to the consumers of the fuel, or when an arbitrator's interpretation of company law frustrates a national policy of protecting the integrity of the market for corporate securities. If national policies are not implicated, courts should limit their role to ensuring that the award is not obtained through violation of fundamental norms of procedural fairness, such as arbitrator fraud, partiality or excess of authority.

.    .    .

Unless deficiencies in the award's integrity are dealt with by the legal system of the place of the proceedings, the losing party must attack an invalid award in each of the many States where the award might be enforced against its property. In the case of a claimant who "loses" an arbitration due to a procedural defect such as arbitrator corruption or excess of authority, the consequences of a completely delocalized arbitration are even more dramatically disagreeable: there will be no opportunity at all to attack the award at the enforcement forum, for the simple reason that there will be no award at all to enforce! Fairness and efficiency alike require that a contesting party should have an opportunity to expose procedural irregularities at the place of the arbitration, which will normally have as great a claim as any other forum to being mutually convenient to the parties.

.    .    .

Wisdom dictates that the State of arbitration exercise some control over the integrity of the proceedings and the interests of third parties. Prima facie validity is accorded foreign arbitral awards under the 1958 New York Arbitration Convention. Fairness requires that a procedurally defective arbitration be susceptible to being annulled at the place where rendered. The loser should not be forced to litigate issues such as arbitrator corruption in all States where it has assets. Nor should an award benefit from the presumptive validity accorded by the New York Convention when there exists a fundamental disaccord between how the arbitrator decided and how the parties to the dispute authorised him to decide. Control by the lex loci arbitri, however, should be limited to ensuring respect for traditional standards of fairness, the limits of the arbitral mission and the rights of third parties.

*     *     *

(ii)    Jan Paulsson, *Delocalisation of International Commercial Arbitration: When and Why It Matters*, 32 INT'L & COMP. L. Q. 53 (1983).

Why should parties to an arbitration not be bound by all the consequences of having the proceedings take place in a particular situs?

Practitioners whose experience is with arbitral institutions firmly entrenched under the aegis of a trade association in a particular locale — whether it be Hamburg or London or Rotterdam — may not appreciate the situation of parties in the context of international ad hoc arbitrations, or arbitration under the Rules of the International Chamber of Commerce (ICC).

Consider the case of ICC proceedings. In 1981, the ICC Court of Arbitration fixed the place of arbitration in 245 cases. That place turned out to be Paris in only 72 cases: less than three times in ten. Of the total 245 cases, 134 involved situations where the ICC merely confirmed the parties' contractual choice of a situs. In the remaining 111 cases (45 per cent), the ICC Court selected a place for the parties, based on criteria of fairness, appropriateness, and convenience. In this category of situs chosen by the ICC Court, the leading places of arbitration were: France (34 times), Switzerland (24 times) and Belgium (12 times). Other places chosen by the ICC Court included

Greece, Egypt, Tunisia, Singapore, Columbia, and the United States. A total of 23 countries were selected by the ICC Court as arbitral situs.

The ICC Court does not select a place solely on the basis of its degree of confidence in the local legal system's proven compatibility with the ICC Rules of Arbitration. Like the UNCITRAL Rules, the ICC Rules have been designed for international proceedings characterised by universality and adaptability.

Accordingly, the situs is chosen for its geographic appropriateness given the context of a particular case, with the respective domiciles of the parties being of central importance. Unless there are objective reasons to conclude that a situs is hostile to awards rendered in compliance with the Rules agreed between the parties, it is assumed that the whole world is a possible situs.

If this were not so, and if the international currency of awards depended ineluctably on their treatment in the hands of local magistrates in their countries of origin, the hopes for a more open and more universal system of international arbitration would be disappointed. Their attention riveted on the attitude of local magistrates, parties and arbitration institutions would have to give absolute priority to legal procedural considerations rather than to the factors of fairness, convenience, and neutrality. Institutions having the choice of selecting seats of arbitration would feel constrained never to venture beyond the tried and true. Perhaps the de facto rule of the ICC would thus become that the place of arbitration in the absence of a contractual stipulation — or perhaps even irrespective of the parties' preference — is invariably Paris. In sum, the world would be a smaller place; the range of mechanisms available to parties to international transactions would be reduced; a pall would be cast over the presently encouraging perspectives of including in the process areas of the world previously left out.

.      .      .

It would appear that the opponents of delocalised arbitration are perplexed, to use Professor Park's image, by the "paradox" of a legal obligation independent of a legal order springing like Athena "full-blown from the head of Zeus." What this critique misses is that the delocalised award is <u>not</u> thought to be independent of any legal order. Rather, the point is that a delocalised award may be accepted by the legal order of an enforcement jurisdiction although it is independent from the legal order of its country of origin. This is no stranger than the analysis of a contract signed at Munich airport between a Japanese consortium and an American subcontractor selected to perform engineering services on a project in the Middle East. Legal consequences may flow from this contract because of the importance attributed to it by the legal orders represented by municipal courts in San Francisco, Tokyo, Alexandria, or elsewhere, depending on a multitude of potentially relevant jurisdictional criteria. I submit that it would occur to no-one to complain that the birth of the legal obligation in Munich airport was impermissibly miraculous because it sprang from the brow of the parties and was thus "independent" of the German legal order.

Hence — and without getting into the complex debate of the contractual versus the jurisdictional genesis of arbitral authority — it scarcely seems revolutionary to give parties the possibility of opting for an arbitral process free from the domestic constraints of the law of the place of arbitration, the effects of the process to be limited only by the minimum norms of transnational currency such as those reflected in the major international conventions.

Having thus reaffirmed that arbitration may be detached from the law of the situs, I hasten to add that I doubt this feature of international arbitration has much of an impact in practice. Competent counsel will in all cases seek to have the process conform to local rules as a matter of prudence. And here they will be sensitive to — and greatly benefit from — the kind of attention to local law given by Professor Park (in the second part of his article) and Mr. Hunter. Even if they do not make a special attempt to inform themselves as to local procedural law, the chances are that they and the arbitrators will not violate fundamental legal provisions. In other words, their award will not be subject to annulment in the place of arbitration.

.     .     .

We are all conditioned by our experience; the road to persuasion is more readily travelled in life than in logic. My purpose is therefore perhaps better served if I refer to the kind of experience that makes a practitioner of ICC or international ad hoc arbitration disposed to accept the notion of detachment from the law of the situs.

Say that the parties have been given as a seat of arbitration the capital of country A, or that they have agreed on it as a neutral and convenient place. Neither party has any connection whatsoever with country A. Not one of the arbitrators is a national of country A. The litigious contract has no nexus with country A.

A majority award is rendered. The losing party moves to set it aside on the grounds that the dissenting arbitrator — who one might suppose was nominated by the said party — had not signed the award. The winning party retorts that the contractually stipulated ICC Rules of Arbitration accept majority awards, and do not require a signature by the dissenting arbitrator. The argument would appear to fail, however, since the law of country A not only requires that all arbitrators sign the award, but provides that any contractual stipulation to the contrary is invalid.

There is no a priori reason to criticise the law of country A. The local legal culture may be such that the rule is quite reasonable. Preparing the local arbitration law many years ago, the legislature had in mind national cases, where all arbitrators would be nationals of country A. And, in fact, the men of the law in country A are known for their reasonable nature. Even when one arbitrator disagrees, it is unthinkable that he would frustrate the effectiveness of the judgment of his two colleagues by refusing to sign the award. His signature is deemed necessary as proof that all three arbitrators participated in the deliberations.

An unfortunate result may be obtained when this rule is applied to international arbitration, where the legitimate expectation of the parties is that the majority rule will prevail, and that the effectiveness of the process cannot be sabotaged by one arbitrator. It is unfortunately true that in some international cases the dispute may be very bitter, and misunderstanding complete. One is far from the atmosphere of the deliberations of three courteous and respectful arbitrators of the same nationality and culture. The losing party's arbitrator may be in collusion with his "client."

I would certainly not favour a situation where the only solution would be that all arbitrators must be of a given nationality, or be selected from an institutional list. This would work against the goals of openness and inclusiveness of the system, and would be a barrier to general recognition of its legitimacy. On the other hand, one cannot count on the courts of country A to follow the French example and make a jurisprudential exception for international cases. As for the legislature, it may have other preoccupations, particularly in countries which do not frequently host international arbitrations.

So the award is set aside in country A. Why does this necessarily have to mean that the award is annulled erga omnes? Could not a country B recognise the award simply by holding that under its law the result of the arbitration is perfectly valid and the reason for annulment in country A is so peculiar to country A that the annulment is properly deemed to be limited to that country? Might not country A in fact be relieved that whilst it has been able to uphold its local law, the international consequences thereof have been limited in a case which in fact had no local connection?

Very simply, the international businessman who had chosen arbitration under a simple set of rules he thought he understood, having ended up at a seat of arbitration selected only for convenience and not out of admiration for any local legal principles, would be deeply shocked to find that the end result of an expensive process in which he had justly prevailed is the utter nullity of his effort, based on a quirk which could not possibly have been in the parties' minds at the time of contracting. He would feel betrayed. I think he would be right, and that it would be proper for a judge in a country B to disregard this particular annulment.

\*    \*    \*

(iii)    F.A. Mann, *Private Arbitration and Public Policy*, 4 CIV. JUST. 257, 262 (1985).

.    .    .

[T]he degree of judicial control of arbitration brought about by the legislation of 1979 as interpreted by the House of Lords has radically changed English law and legal policy. It is no longer true that arbitrators are necessarily bound by the law. Where an exclusion agreement has been concluded they are entirely free to decide in whatever sense they think fit, even to decide in an arbitrary manner. And even in the absence of an exclusion agreement the severe restrictions of the right of appeal may result in awards contra legem.

This is an almost sensational development which constitutes a break with long-established tradition and is, it is submitted, far removed from Kerr L.J.'s requirements of judicial review:

> No-one having the power to make legally binding decisions in this country should in my view be altogether outside and immune from this system. No-one below the highest tribunals should have unreviewable legal powers over others. I believe this to be as necessary in relaxation to arbitral tribunals as in all other contexts, and I speak from experience, both in relation to arbitrations here and abroad.

The change is such that hopefully arbitration will no longer be resorted to where, for the sake of certainty or clarity, a decision on standard contracts or standard terms is required. In such a case the sensible course is to forget the arbitration clause and the vicissitudes arising from the need for leave to appeal and to apply direct to the court for a decision. In the light of events it is necessary to give the same advice in cases in which a problem of pure law arises.

The consequences of the change is that the public policy of establishing uniformity of law, of which Lord Atkin spoke, can hardly be said to continue. Though in matters of procedure the court's power of control is undiminished the assertion that arbitration in England is a judicial process is subject to far-reaching qualifications. In short English law is now very much more in line with the law of arbitration abroad, where procedural rectitude is almost invariably required, but in matters of substantive law a system prevails that may be characterised as semi-judicial, as aiming at speedy but indifferent finality (which in fact is usually far from speedy). Almost everywhere arbitrators are free to commit any error of law, though in the United States of America an award is liable to be set aside if it discloses "manifest disregard of the law," in the Swiss Cantons which have adopted the Concordat a clear violation of law or equity entitles the court to set the award aside, and in Germany it is only the willful miscarriage of justice (Rechtsbeugung) that permits the award to be set aside. Almost everywhere on the Continent express provisions may empower arbitrators to act as "amiables compositeurs" in which event they usually are free to disregard the law altogether; in other words they can act as if an exclusion agreement had been concluded. The exclusion agreement is the English equivalent of the clause expressly providing for the appointment of amiables compositeurs.

. . .

The [UNCITRAL] Model Law provides in Article 16 that the arbitral tribunal has power to rule on its own jurisdiction. In other words it has what is called "Kompetenz-Kompetenz." If such ruling were conclusive it would, of course, be totally unacceptable, for how can lay arbitrators decide on the validity and effect of a contract or an arbitration clause, on the sufficiency of writing, on the question whether a contract has in fact been concluded and so forth? So it is envisaged by Article 16(3) that the arbitrators' ruling may be contested in an action for setting aside the award. This means that, pending the award, the parties are compelled to continue the arbitration proceedings to the bitter end, — at great expense and the loss of much time and effort. Yet Article 34 provides for the circumstances in which "only" the award may be set aside. Lack of jurisdiction is not one of these circumstances, an almost unbelievable omission which characterises the sloppy drafting of the Model Law . . . .

In conclusion it is necessary once more to emphasize Kerr L.J.'s words: "No-one below the highest tribunals should have unreviewable legal powers over others." This is, indeed, the great principle of State that requires us to prefer the system of judicial review which the legislation of 1979 has continued in an amended form. Whether it is the last word, whether further reform is not needed, whether, in particular, the ambit of arbitral misconduct does not need extension, these are minor questions of policy which in due course will no doubt be solved by the judiciary and legislature. The message of this lecture is that it is in the highest interest of the State, that it is a matter of public policy of great import to maintain the principle of judicial review of arbitration not only to develop the law, but also to ensure the administration of justice and thus to avoid the risk of arbitrariness.

*     *     *

(iv)    Michael Kerr, *Arbitration and the Courts: The UNCITRAL Model Law*, 34 Int'l & Comp. L.Q. 1 (1985).

## THE ROLE OF THE COURTS

Although arbitration is a purely consensual process for the resolution of disputes in private, the process has legal consequences for everyone involved in it. Leaving aside statutory arbitrations, with which this article is not concerned, neither the establishment of arbitral tribunals nor the arbitral process itself provides any means of giving effect to these legal consequences. The necessary powers to give binding effect to the legal consequences of arbitration, which is the whole raison d'etre of the arbitral process, is invariably vested in the national courts by legislation. So far as known to this author, this is the position in all legal systems throughout the world. In the ultimate analysis the effectiveness of the private process must therefore rest upon the binding, and even coercive, powers which each State entrusts to its courts. It is the exercise of these powers which determines whether the acts of arbitral tribunals are to be recognised and enforced or are rendered nugatory and ineffective. This is why any discussion about the law of arbitration can only be concerned with the role of the courts in relation to arbitration. There is no other law of arbitration. As stated in one sentence on the first page of the great new work in this field, Mustill and Boyd on <u>Commercial Arbitration</u>: "The law of private arbitration is concerned with the relationship between the courts and the arbitral process." The purpose of this article is to discuss this relationship under the English system in the light of the UNCITRAL Model Law . . . .

.    .    .

## The Balance of the Power of the Courts

Have we got this balance right? In recent years there has already been a clear shift away from the courts towards a philosophy of increasing laissez-faire by allowing the arbitral process to become much more autonomous and free from judicial intervention. This has been due to three main factors.

First there is the pragmatic objective of seeking to encourage international arbitrations to come to this country —- not so much those arising under standard forms of contract which come here anyway, but those which stem from arbitration clauses in "one-off" contracts or from ad hoc references after disputes have arisen. In the same way as every other State which holds an important position in international commerce, we would like to promote the choice of this country, with its laws, institutions and the expertise available, as a desirable venue. This is the first factor which has given rise to the recent trend towards greater arbitral autonomy. There is nothing discreditable in this policy. In so far as it may appear to be chauvinistic, it is no different from what is happening in many other countries, because the whole world of commerce is experiencing something in the nature of an explosion in the demand for international arbitrations for which markets are sought and put forward in different countries.

A second factor which produced a shift away from the courts towards the autonomy of arbitral tribunals was the realisation that under the English system the powers of the courts in controlling the decisions of arbitrators on issues of law were far too great, and far too open to abuse, to be acceptable to the customers whom it was sought to attract and satisfy. This situation was seen as something of a crisis when Lord Diplock gave the Alexander Lecture in 1978 and by April 1979 most of the recommendations of the Commercial Court Committee to deal with this situation were on the statute book in the form of the 1979 Act. The special case procedure was swept away forever. Rightly or wrongly — and I think rightly — there is no question of going back to the system which made the courts the ultimate masters over arbitrations on virtually all issues of law.

Today there is a third factor which is tending to shift this balance still further: the pressure towards harmonisation and virtual unification of national laws and procedures concerning international arbitrations. This development is not a crisis of the kind which became increasingly felt to exist before 1979. But the concept of the UNCITRAL Model Law faces us with a choice, a policy decision, which is likely to have to be made very soon, while the effectiveness of the changes introduced by the 1979 Act is still unclear. The Act has produced a series of compromise solutions, and like most compromises it may have few overt admirers. But its critics are concerned about the procedural effectiveness of the Act rather than about its substance. There appears to be a surprising absence of any strong body of opinion in favour of tilting the balance further towards arbitral autonomy and away from supervision by the courts. There does not even appear to be any great pressure to widen the right to enter into exclusion agreements under standard forms of contract, except perhaps in relation to insurance. On the contrary, a number of the "customers" and arbitral organisations appear to remain strongly in favour of a measure of court control over issues of law, at any rate in arbitrations under standard forms.

.   .   .

Powers of "review" over the decisions of tribunals outside the hierarchy of the courts now lie at the centre of the English legal system. They do not comprise rights of appeal as such, and rights of appeal are being increasingly modified into powers of review. "Judicial review" over the decisions of tribunals outside the hierarchy of the courts is exercised when the principles of natural justice have been infringed or when the ultimate conclusion was one which no reasonable tribunal could have reached. The surviving rights of appeal on issues of law in relation to arbitration are similarly circumscribed by the decisions which have interpreted the 1979 Act. It is significant that the marginal heading of section 1 of the Act does not refer to rights of appeal but to "judicial review of arbitration awards."

It is submitted that the explicit principles of the power of judicial review provide the key to the necessary adaptation of English law if the Model Law gains general acceptance. With the exception of the Sovereign and the Judicial Committees of the House of Lords and Privy Council, there is virtually no body, tribunal, authority or individual in England whose acts or decisions give rise to binding legal consequences for others, but who are altogether immune from judicial review in the event of improper conduct, breaches of the principles of natural justice, or decisions which clearly transcend any standard of objective reasonableness. Such islands of immunity as remain are constantly shrinking. These limited powers of judicial review are exercised by judges whose decisions are themselves controllable by the Divisional Court or the Court of Appeal, sitting in divisions of two or three, and ultimately by the House of Lords sitting in divisions of five, with each member of the higher courts exercising considerable influence over the views of the others. This system is our bulwark against corruption, arbitrariness, bias, improper conduct and — where necessary — sheer incompetence, in relation to acts and decisions with binding legal effect for others. No one having the power to make legally binding decisions in this country should be altogether outside and immune from this system. No one below the highest tribunals should have unreviewable legal powers over others. Speaking from experience, I believe this to be as necessary in relation to arbitrations in England and abroad as in all other contexts.

\*   \*   \*

(v)     Arthur T. von Mehren, *To what Extent Is International Commercial Arbitration Autonomous?*, LE DROIT DES RELATIONS ÉCONOMIQUES INTERNATIONALES: ETUDES OFFERTES À BERTHOLD GOLDMAN 217, 222-24 (Philippe Fouchard ed., 1982).

Dr. Mann's position that "every arbitration is necessarily subject to the law of a given State" — that there is no lex mercatoria — is correct only to the extent that a linkage exists between a given arbitration and a given national or municipal legal order either because of the latter's active intervention or because the arbitrator or a party asks for assistance of public authorities in connection with the conduct of the arbitration or the enforcement of the award. And, even where such linkage is established, the arbitration cannot, except in a most attenuated sense, be said to be subject to the law of the legal order in question unless that legal order is prepared to substitute, in the case of disagreement, its view of what is just or appropriate for the view held by the arbitrator. To what extent does this phenomenon occur?

Active intervention by a State on its own motion with an arbitration being conducted on its territory or by individual over some or all of whom the State could exercise power is presumably extremely rare. Accordingly, the discussion that follows is limited to situations where a linkage is established because a party or arbitrator seeks assistance from public authorities either in conducting the arbitration or in enforcing an award.

In this perspective, the arbitral process and the resulting award can be considered anational or autonomous to the extent that the legal order whose assistance is sought is, in deciding whether to extend that assistance, uninterested in whether the arbitrations will apply, or have applied, rules and principles that derive from a national legal order. The rules applicable to arbitrations within the scope of the U.N. Convention on the Recognition and Enforcement of Foreign Arbitral Awards indicate that national legal orders will often be indifferent to the anational character of the arbitral process or award.

Thus, in the case of the United States, arbitrators in proceedings falling under the Convention can, by virtue of §208 of Chapter 2(19) of Title 9 of the United States Code, "summon in writing any person to attend before them . . . as a witness and in a proper case to bring with him . . . any book, record, document, or paper which may be deemed material as evidence in the case." If this summons is not obeyed, "upon petition the United States district court for the district in which such arbitrators . . . are sitting may compel the attendance of such persons . . . before said . . . arbitrators, or punish said person or persons for contempt in the same manner provided by law for securing the attendance of witnesses or their punishment for neglect or refusal to attend in the courts of the United States." This assistance will presumably be accorded an arbitral proceeding even though it is conducted under the [1975] I.C.C. Rules of Conciliation and Arbitration which provide in Article 11 that

> The rules governing the proceedings before the arbitrator shall be those resulting from these Rules and, where these Rules are silent, any rules which the parties (or, failing them, the arbitrator) may settle, and whether or not reference is thereby made to a municipal procedural law to be applied to the arbitration.

Where recognition or enforcement of an award is sought under the U.N. Convention, Article V of the Convention forbids consideration by the State addressed of the merits of the award. Accordingly, recognition and enforcement will not turn on whether the rules and principles used by the arbitrators were anational or, conversely, derived from a system of national or municipal law.

Similarly, where a party, invoking Article II of the U.N. Convention, requests the "court of a Contracting State, . . . seized of a matter in respect of which the parties have made an agreement within the meaning of this article, . . . [to] refer the parties to arbitration," the fact that the parties had, as permitted by Article 13(4) of the [1975] I.C.C. Rules, given the arbitrator "the powers of an amiable compositeur" does not justify a refusal to refer the matter to arbitration unless the court were to conclude that, because the arbitrator had these powers, the "agreement is null and void, inoperative or incapable of being performed."

On some issues the U.N. Convention does contemplate a linkage between the arbitration and a municipal legal order. Thus Article V(1) provides that recognition and enforcement of an award may be refused if

> (a) The parties to the [arbitral] agreement . . . were, under the law applicable to them, under some incapacity, or the said agreement is not valid under the law to which the parties have subjected it or, failing any indications thereon, under the law of the country where the award was made; or . . .

> (d) The composition of the arbitral authority or the arbitral procedure was not in accordance with the agreement of the parties, or, failing such agreement, was not in accordance with the law of the country where the arbitration took place . . . .

Furthermore, Article V(2) — under which recognition and enforcement can be refused on the ground that "(a) The subject matter of the difference is not capable of settlement by arbitration . . . or (b) The recognition or enforcement would be contrary to public policy . . ." — of course recognizes that the law or views of the State addressed are decisive on these issues.

The foregoing strongly suggests that, as a practical matter, the procedural and substantive law used in international commercial arbitration can, if the parties and arbitrators so desire, be largely autonomous or anational. Furthermore, the view is widely accepted that linking either the arbitral process or the award fully and effectively to a system or national or municipal law would seriously undermine or even destroy the efficacy of arbitration as a dispute-resolving mechanism.

## Notes and Questions

1. For further reading in "delocalization" see W. Laurence Craig, *Uses and Abuses of Appeal From International Arbitration Awards*, PRIVATE INVESTORS ABROAD - PROBLEMS AND SOLUTIONS IN INTERNATIONAL BUSINESS IN 1987 (J. Moss & Matthew Bender, eds., 1988). Craig notes:

> The ingenuity of lawyers is not to be underestimated. If there is a step available in the appeals process, sophisticated litigants will find a way to use them. These procedures will most likely have a very substantial cost even where the arbitration award is not dislodged. As for judicial review in the United States, it is not enough to congratulate ourselves on the excellent record of federal courts in sustaining international arbitration awards. The foreigner not used to heavy American litigation and pretrial discovery will be happy that the arbitration award is eventually sustained but will rue the cost of getting to that result. Also, the ingenuity of lawyers is, of course, not limited to any particular nationality. It can be brought to bear by the legal profession in any country where arbitration takes place. Wherever a jurisdiction permits review of an arbitration award, appeals will be taken, and they will be taken in ever-larger numbers and on increasingly creative grounds.

2. Look again at Professor von Mehren's argument that an arbitrator is subject to a national legal system "only to the extent that a linkage exists between a given arbitrator and a given national legal order either because of the latter's active intervention or because the arbitrator or a party asks for assistance . . . ." *Supra* p. 1119. What about a linkage based on a nation's _non_-active assistance, in the form of allowing an award to benefit from the enforcement scheme of the New York Convention by abstaining from "uprooting" the award under Convention Article V(1)(e) by setting the award aside where rendered?

3. Compare the position of Berthold Goldman, *Les conflits de lois dans l'arbitrage international de droit privé*, 109 II RECUEIL DES COURS 347 at 379-380, 479-480 (1963).

> Unless one adopts the irrational and unjustifiable system of attaching the arbitral process to its seat . . . any search for a way of grounding the arbitration in some system leads one unavoidably to the need for an autonomous non-national system.

> . . . If the common rules of international commerce can, according to us, be described as rules of law, there is no doubt that they do not as yet form a complete legal system. They may be completed by the general principles of law in general or a major part of the trading nations, gradually articulated and clarified by the various anational sources . . . such as international arbitration "caselaw" itself. But it is true that they must also be supplemented sometimes by rules taken from municipal laws.

However, the need — in part, doubtless temporary — for this combination of general rules and municipal laws cannot, we believe, reduce the importance of the former, nor allow one to refuse to give them the description of rules of law. Consequently, to the extent that they suffice to provide the solution to disputes submitted to international arbitration, these rules permit one to go beyond the conflict of laws. One should also note that that where this is not possible and where it is necessary to choose a municipal law rule, its selection should take place in private international arbitration on the basis of a system for solving for conflicts of laws which is itself autonomous and able to move progressively in the direction of uniformity. In the absence then of a complete unification of the substantive law of international relations (that is to say, of a genuinely systematic and complete private international law) at least, one can rely on private international arbitration to arrive at the creation of a system of attachment of its own, particularly in the field of contract law.

4. See also Philippe Fouchard, L'ARBITRAGE COMMERCIAL INTERNATIONAL 22-23 (1964). Professor Fouchard explains the internationality of arbitration in part as an attempt to ensure to international commercial arbitration "a really international framework where the particularities of the conflict of laws and substantive laws will no longer play any role."

3.    VARIATIONS ON THE THEME OF "CURIAL" JUDICIAL REVIEW

a.    *Outhwaite v. Hiscox*, 3 W.L.R. 297 (1991); 17 YEARBOOK OF COMMERCIAL ARBITRATION 599 (1992).

[A dispute arose between two Lloyd's underwriters with regard to the liabilities of the syndicates under a contract of reinsurance entered into in 1982. That contract, governed by the law of England, contained an arbitration clause providing for arbitration in London by two arbitrators and their umpire. In fact, the agreement was varied by the parties who agreed to refer the dispute between them to Mr. R.A. MacCrindle Q.C. as sole arbitrator. The hearings took place in London. An award in the first stage of the arbitration, made in June 1989, the draft award on 6 August 1990 and the final interim award signed on 20 November 1990 were all signed by Mr. MacCrindle in Paris and each concluded with the words "Dated at Paris, France" followed by the date and Mr. MacCrindle's signature, witnessed by his secretary and giving an address in Paris.

On 10 December 1990 the respondent made several motions for judicial review: for leave to appeal to the High Court pursuant to Sect. 1(3)(b) of the Arbitration Act 1979, for an order directing the arbitrator to state further reasons for his award pursuant to Sect. 1(5) of the 1979 Act and for remission of the award pursuant to Sect. 22 of the Arbitration Act 1950. The High Court held that, since the arbitration was an English arbitration the central point of which was in London, the award was 'made' in London, although signed in Paris. Accordingly, the High Court had jurisdiction to entertain the respondent's motions. The Court of Appeal held that the award was made in Paris, but further held that the appellant was estopped from objecting to the Court's jurisdiction to review the award.

Before the House of Lords the respondent contended that even if the award was governed by the New York Convention English courts had jurisdiction to review the award. The House of Lords dismissed the appeal on the following grounds, as worded by Lord Oliver of Aylmerton.]

[T]he Arbitration Act 1975 was passed in order to give effect to the United Kingdom's obligations under the New York Arbitration Convention of 1958 . . . . Sect. 3(1) provides that:

A convention award shall, subject to the following provisions of this Act, be enforceable — (a) in England and Wales, either by action or in the same manner as the award of an arbitrator is enforceable by virtue of section 26 of the Arbitration Act 1950. . . .

The expression 'Convention award' is defined in Sect. 7(1) as:

an award in pursuant of an arbitration agreement in the territory of a State, other than the United Kingdom, which is a party to the New York Convention; . . . .

Sect. 3(2) is of crucial importance having regard to the arguments addressed to the House. It provides:

Any Convention award which would be enforceable under this Act shall be treated as binding for all purposes on the persons as between whom it was made, and may accordingly be relied on by any of those persons by way of defence, set off or otherwise in any legal proceedings in the United Kingdom; and any reference in this Act to enforcing a Convention award shall be construed as including references to relying on such an award.

.    .    .

In support of their arguments for and against the proposition . . . that the arbitrator's award was made in London, both counsel have made reference, as an aid to construction of the Act of 1975, to the travaux préparatoires leading up to the Convention. In so far as it can properly be said that there is any ambiguity in the Act, this is, of course, perfectly permissible as indicating the difficulty with which the Convention, and thus the Act, was seeking to contend. Speaking for myself, however, I have not found this reference of any assistance. It is evident that in the negotiations leading to the Convention there emerged divergent views between the delegates about the appropriate criterion for determining to what awards the Convention should apply and that the school of thought which favoured the simple, if arbitrary, geographical test of where the award was made ultimately won the day, but subject to a compromise addition which included also awards not considered as 'domestic' in the enforcing state. Save to the extent, however, that these discussions indicate a general realisation that the geographical test might produce anomalous results, the travaux do not really help. In particular, they go nowhere towards indicating what satisfies the geographical test and constitutes the 'making' of an award.

.    .    .

In my judgment, therefore, the Court of Appeal were right to hold that the award was a Convention award. The critical question is what is the effect of that holding. Mr. Colman submits that, contrary to the conclusion reached both by McCowan and Leggatt L. JJ. in the Court of Appeal, this is not fatal to him but that nevertheless the English court, as both the enforcing court and the court of the seat of the arbitration, remains entitled, as it certainly would if the award had been made here, to entertain proceedings to set aside or suspend it. The argument may be summarised as follows. It is perfectly true that Sect. 3(1) of the Act of 1975 provides that the Convention award shall be enforceable in England but it does so 'subject to the following provisions of this Act' (i.e. subject to Sects. 4 and 5). Equally it is true that Sect. 3(2) provides that the Convention award shall be 'treated as binding for all purposes,' that it may be 'enforcing' the award is to be construed also as a reference to relying upon it. Thus, since 'any legal proceedings' is as wide a term as can readily be imagined and includes as much proceedings for leave to appeal against an award or for remission as any other proceedings, the mere recital of the fact that the award is a Convention award and thus binding for all purposes prima facie provides a complete bar to any such proceedings being successfully pursued. It has, however, to be borne in mind that subsection (2) applies only to a Convention award 'which would be enforceable under this Act' and that throws one back to subsection (1) where the enforceability is subject to Sects. 4 and 5; and Sect. 5(2)(f) contains the important provision enabling the enforcing court to refuse enforcement/reliance if it is proved that 'the award . . . has been set aside or suspended by a competent court of the authority . . . under the law of which the award was made' — which can conveniently be referred to as 'the curial country' and which is, of course, in the instant case, England, it being beyond dispute that English law is the law of arbitration.

Thus, the argument proceeds, the Act of 1975 clearly contemplates that a position may arise where that [award] which is prima facie binding and unchallengeable before the enforcing court may yet be set aside or suspended by the curial court and whilst it does not expressly deal with the improbable position which may arise where the enforcing country and the curial country are the same, there is nothing in the Act which excludes the arbitral jurisdiction of the curial court in the case where it turns out to be also the court charged with enforcing/recognising the award.

.    .    .

Both the Convention and the Act clearly contemplate that the curial court is or may be invested with capability of exercising a supervisory power whilst leaving to the enforcing court a discretionary power (a) to permit a pending supervisory process to continue and (b) to refuse enforcement of the award if its result in the award being suspended or set aside. Subject to Mr. Sumption's point that no court in a Convention country other than that in the award country can ever be a competent authority (which, for the reasons which I have endeavoured to explain, I cannot accept) the section presents no difficulty at all where the enforcing court and the curial court are in different countries. The only difficulty lies in the limited power conferred by Sect. 5(5) where the same court is both the curial and the enforcing court and the only 'proceedings' consist of the application to the curial court in which, necessarily, the award is being 'relied upon' by the other party. The plain purpose of the subsection was to enable the application to the curial court to catch up with the enforcement of the award and that purpose is achieved where there are no 'proceedings' for enforcement on foot, by the adjournment by the enforcing court of the consideration of the issue of the enforcement of or reliance on the award. Now it is true that this may be thought to give an extended meaning to the word 'proceedings' by applying it to what is, in fact, merely an issue in proceedings, but it gives a sensible meaning to the subsection and a meaning which, as it seems to me, is supported by the Convention. As previously mentioned, subsection 5 gives effect to Art. VI and Art. VI refers to 'the authority before which the award is sought to be relied upon' adjourning 'the <u>decision</u> on the enforcement of the award' [emphasis added].

It is argued that to apply such a purposive construction would defeat the policy of the Convention and of the Act, which is to avoid the need for the enforcing court to do more than enforce or recognise the award by excluding the application of that court's own arbitral rules and procedure. Whilst clearly that is the case where the enforcing court is in a country different from that of the country of the seat of the arbitration — which would be the normal situation, since the likelihood would be that the country of the award and the country having jurisdiction over the conduct of the arbitration would be the same — I can see no clear policy reason for excluding altogether the arbitral jurisdiction of the seat of the arbitration in the improbable case of the award resulting from the arbitration being made elsewhere and thus falling to be enforced in the curial country. Clearly the framers of the Convention contemplated the case of the arbitration and the resulting award occurring in different countries, and intended in Art. VI to provide for the possibility of the continued supervision by the courts of the curial country. Whilst it is doubtful whether they contemplated the unusual case of the curial country and the enforcing country being the same, I can see no good reason why they should have desired or sought to exclude that country's curial jurisdiction in a case where its continuance would otherwise have been appropriate. There is nothing in the Convention that compulsively leads to the conclusion that the enforcing country's curial jurisdiction is to be ignored in all circumstances and indeed Art. I itself contemplates its implication in determining whether any given award is to be considered as a domestic or non-domestic.

In agreement with the Master of the Rolls, therefore, I would hold that the High Court remains capable of exercising its curial jurisdiction over the arbitration and of adjourning, if it thinks fit, any decision on the enforceability of the award until the pending proceedings for review have been determined. Accordingly, I would dismiss the appeal on this ground.

### Notes and Questions

1. *See generally*, Claude Reymond, *Where Is An Arbitral Award Made?* 108 L. Q. REV 1 (1992); John Timmons, *Where is an Arbitration Award Made and What are the Consequences?*, 58 ARB. 124 (1992); Fraser Davidson, *Where Is An Arbitral Award Made?* 41 INT'L & COMP. L.Q. 637 (1992); Michael Schnieder, *Le lieu où la jurisprudence est rendue*, 9 A.S.A. BULLETIN 279 (1991). *Cf.* Francis A. Mann, *Where is an Award Made?*, 1 ARB. INT'L 107 (April, 1985).

2. Is the metaphor of "localization" a useful way of posing the policy problem here? Is the question whether an award has a "location" or is it which, among a number of jurisdictions, will exercise control functions over the process and the award that eventuates and what degree of control will be exercised? In the preceding discussions, is the notion of the locality of an award a metaphysical question which can never be answered?

b.     *Int'l Std. Elec. Corp. v. Bridas Sociedad Anonima Petrolera, Industrial y Comercial*, 745 F.Supp. 172 (S.D.N.Y. 1990).

CONBOY, District Judge:

[The parties on one side sought to vacate a foreign arbitration award and on the other side to enforce that award pursuant to an international convention. International Standard Electric Corporation ("ISEC"), a wholly owned subsidiary of the International Telephone and Telegraph Company ("ITT"), entered into a "Shareholders Agreement" with an Argentinean corporation, Bridas Sociedad Anonima Petrolera, Industrial Y Comercial ("Bridas") providing for sale to Bridas of a 25% interest in ISEC's wholly owned Argentinean telecommunications subsidiary, Compania Standard Electric Argentina

S.A. ("CSEA"). The Shareholders Agreement provides that "[a]ll disputes connected to this Agreement . . . shall be settled or finally decided by one or more arbitrators appointed by the International Chamber of Commerce in accordance with the Rules of Conciliation and Arbitration," and provided that the Agreement would be "governed by and construed under and in accordance with the laws of the State of New York."

In 1985 Bridas filed with the International Chamber of Commerce a Request for Arbitration. In 1989, the arbitral tribunal signed the final Award, which was released and issued to the parties on January 16, 1990, granting Bridas damages of $6,793,000 with interest and granted Bridas $1 million in legal fees and expenses plus $400,000 for the costs of the arbitration.

On February 2, 1990, ISEC filed a petition in New York to vacate and refuse recognition and enforcement of the Award. Bridas cross-petitioned to dismiss ISEC's petition to vacate on the grounds that this Court lacks subject matter jurisdiction to grant such relief under the Convention.]

.    .    .

We will first address the question of whether, under the binding terms of the New York Convention, we lack subject matter jurisdiction to vacate a foreign arbitral award. The situs of the Award in this case was Mexico City, a location chosen by the ICC Court of Arbitration pursuant to rules of procedure explicitly agreed to by the parties. Since the parties here are an American Company and an Argentine Company, it is not difficult to understand why the Mexican capital was selected as the place to conduct the arbitration.

[1] Bridas argues that, under the New York Convention, only the courts of the place of arbitration, in this case the Courts of Mexico, have jurisdiction to vacate or set aside an arbitral award. ISEC argues that under the Convention both the courts of the place of arbitration and the courts of the place whose substantive law has been applied, in this case the courts of the United States, have jurisdiction to vacate or set aside an arbitral award.

Under Article V(1)(e) of the Convention, "an application for the setting aside or suspension of the award" can be made only to the courts or the "competent authority of the country in which, *or under the law of which*, that award was made." (Emphasis added). ISEC argues that "the competent authority of the country . . . under the law of which [the] award was made," refers to the country the substantive law of which, as opposed to the procedural law of which, was applied by the arbitrators. Hence, ISEC insists that since the arbitrators applied substantive New York law, we have jurisdiction to vacate the award.

ISEC cites only one case to support this expansive reading of the Convention, *Laminoirs-Trefileries-Cableries de Lens v. Southwire Co.*, 484 F.Supp. 1063 (N.D.Ga.1980). That case, however, did not involve a foreign award under the Convention, and did not implicate the jurisdictional question here raised, since there the parties' substantive and procedural choice of law, and the situs of the arbitration were both New York. It seems plain that the Convention does not address, contemplate or encompass a challenge to an award in the courts of the state where the award was rendered, since the relation of the courts to the arbitral proceedings is not an international, but a wholly domestic one, at least insofar as the Convention is concerned. Whether such an arbitration would be considered international because of the parties' nationalities under the Federal Arbitration Act, is irrelevant. *See* A. Van den Berg, *The New York Arbitration Convention of 1958* 19-20, 349-50 (Kluwer 1981).

Bridas has cited a case decided by our colleague Judge Keenan, *American Construction Machinery & Equipment Corp. v. Mechanised Construction of Pakistan Ltd.*, 659 F.Supp. 426 (S.D.N.Y.), *aff'd*, 828 F.2d 117 (2d Cir.1987), *cert. denied*, 484 U.S. 1064, 108 S.Ct. 1024, 98 L.Ed.2d 988 (1988), as authority against the ISEC position. This case involved a dispute between a Cayman Islands Company and a Pakistani company, arguably controlled by Pakistani substantive law and arbitrated in Geneva. Judge Keenan was asked to decline enforcement of the award on the ground that a challenge to it was pending in the courts of Pakistan. He ruled that "[t]he law under which this award was made was Swiss law because the award was rendered in Geneva pursuant to Geneva *procedural* law." 659 F.Supp. at 429. This analysis was expressly affirmed in the Court of Appeals, and the Supreme Court declined to review it.

[The Court proceeded to discuss *Cooper v. Ateliers De La Motobecane, S.A.*, 57 N.Y.2d 408, 410, 456 N.Y.S.2d 728, 729, 442 N.E.2d 1239, 1240 (1982), *supra* p. 819, and *Bergesen v. Joseph Muller Corp.*, 710 F.2d 928 (2d Cir. 1983), *supra* p. 1034.]

.   .   .

We conclude that the phrase in the Convention "[the country] under the laws of which that award was made" undoubtedly referenced the complex thicket of the *procedural* law of arbitration obtaining in the numerous and diverse jurisdictions of the dozens of nations in attendance at the time the Convention was being debated. Even today, over three decades after these debates were conducted, there are broad variations in the international community on how arbitrations are to be conducted and under what customs, rules, statutes or court decisions, that is, under what "competent authority." Indeed, some signatory nations have highly specialized arbitration procedures, as is the case with the United States, while many others have nothing beyond generalized civil practice to govern arbitration. *See* Lowenfeld, *The Two-Way Mirror: International Arbitration as Comparative Procedure*, 7 Mich.Y.B.Int'l Legal Studies 163, 166-70 (1985), *reprinted in* 2 *Craig, Park and Paulsson, International Chamber of Commerce Arbitration*, App. VII at 187 (1986).

This view is confirmed by Professor Van den Berg to the effect that the language in dispute reflects the delegates' practical insight that parties to an international arbitration might prefer to equalize travel distance and costs to witnesses by selecting as a situs forum A, midpoint between two cities or two continents, and submit themselves to a different procedural law by selecting the arbitration procedure of forum B.

The "competent authority" as mentioned in Article V(1)(e) for entertaining the action of setting aside the award is virtually always the court of the country in which the award was made. The phrase "or under the law of which" the award was made refers to the theoretical case that on the basis of an agreement of the parties *the award is governed by an arbitration law which is different from the arbitration law of the country in which the award was made.*

A. Van den Berg, *The New York Arbitration Convention of 1958* 350 (Kluwer 1981) (emphasis added). This view is consistent with a commentary on the circumstances under which the Soviet delegate offered the amendment embracing the language in issue. *See* United Nations Conference on International Commercial Arbitration, Summary Record of the 23rd Meeting, 9 June 1958, E/CONF. 26/SR.23 at 12 (12 Sept. 1958), *reprinted in* G. Gaja, *International Commercial Arbitration: New York Convention* III C. 213 (Oceana Pub.1978).

It is clear, we believe, that any suggestion that a Court has jurisdiction to set aside a foreign award based upon the use of its domestic, substantive law in the foreign arbitration defies the logic both of the Convention debates and of the final text, and ignores the nature of the international arbitral system. This is demonstrated overwhelmingly by review of cases in foreign jurisdictions that have considered the question before us.

.   .   .

Finally, we should observe that the core of petitioner's argument, that a generalized supervisory interest of a state in the application of its domestic substantive law (in most arbitrations the law of contract) in a foreign proceeding, is wholly out of step with the universal concept of arbitration in all nations. The whole point of arbitration is that the merits of the dispute will *not* be reviewed in the courts, wherever they be located. Indeed, this principle is so deeply imbedded in American, and specifically, federal jurisprudence, that no further elaboration of the case law is necessary. That this was the animating principle of the Convention, that the Courts should review arbitrations for procedural regularity but resist inquiry into the substantive merits of awards, is clear from the notes on this subject by the Secretary-General of the United Nations. *See* Bermann Aff., *supra*, at 32-33.

Accordingly, we hold that the contested language in Article VI(e) of the Convention, ". . . the competent authority of the country under the law of which, [the] award was made" refers exclusively to procedural and not substantive law, and more precisely, to the regimen or scheme of arbitral procedural law under which the arbitration was conducted, and not the substantive law of contract which was applied in the case.

In this case, the parties subjected themselves to the procedural law of Mexico. Hence, since the situs, or forum of the arbitration is Mexico, and the governing procedural law is that of Mexico, only the courts of Mexico have jurisdiction under the Convention to vacate the award. ISEC's petition to vacate the award is therefore dismissed.

\*    \*    \*

c.      Jan Paulsson, *The New York Convention's Misadventures in India*, 6 INT'L ARB. REP. 3-8 (1992).

In two salient recent cases involving arbitral awards rendered in London, the courts of India have revealed an alarming propensity to exercise authority in a manner contrary to the legitimate expectations of the international community.

In Oil & Natural Gas Commission v. Western Company of North America [ONGC], 1987 All India Reports SC 674, excerpted in XIII Yearbook Commercial Arbitration 473 (1988), the Supreme Court held not only that the Indian courts had jurisdiction to hear an action brought by the losing Indian party to set aside the award, but upheld an Indian court's order that the winning American party desist from enforcement actions in the United States pending the Indian action. The basis for the Court's decision was that Indian law applied to the arbitration agreement, and that the courts of the country whose law governs the arbitration agreement must have jurisdiction to deal with the subsequent award in the same way that it might deal with domestic awards.

In National Thermal Power Corporation v. The Singer Corp. et al., 1992(3)7 Judgements Today SC 198, [Singer] the same Court on 7 May 1992 similarly decided that the Indian courts had jurisdiction to hear an action to set aside a partial award rendered in London. The award had held that while Indian law was the proper law of the contract, English law governed matters of procedure; that the arbitration was not prevented by contractual time bars; and that neither the claims nor the counterclaim were barred by time limitations under Indian law. Again, the Court focused on the fact that Indian law was substantively applicable, and that this applicability extended to the arbitration clause itself.

The Court writes, at paragraph 23: "The proper law of the arbitration agreement is normally the same as the proper law of the contract." This is unremarkable. But after embroidering on this theme, the judgment suddenly makes a quantum leap in paragraph 26:

> the overriding principle is that the courts of the country whose substantive laws govern the arbitration agreement are the competent courts in respect of all matters arising under the arbitration agreement, and the jurisdiction exercised by the courts of the seat of arbitration is merely concurrent and not exclusive and strictly limited to matters of procedure. All other matters in respect of the arbitration agreement fall within the exclusive competence of the courts of the country whose laws govern the arbitration agreement.

This, it is submitted, is simply untrue. At the end of the just-quoted passage, the Court cites four well-known English treatises: Mustill and Boyd, Redfern and Hunter, Russell on Arbitration, and Cheshire & North. But it does so without referring to specific pages. The fact is that none of these authorities support the radical thesis propagated by the Indian court. The scholarly references are, to put it charitably, window dressing.

Under Article V(1)(a) of the New York Convention, it would be open to a losing party to argue before the enforcement court that the arbitration agreement was invalid "under the law to which [the parties] have subjected it." That might mean that evidence of Indian law would be relevant to an enforcement court in, say, New York. It does not mean that Indian courts have competence by virtue of some "overriding principle."

.    .    .

It is submitted that these two Indian decisions misunderstood the New York Convention in a dangerous fashion, ONGC in subverting general principles of the post-award process which have emerged as international consensus over the course of the last 30 years and Singer in disregarding the text of the Convention. These are examples of parochial overreaching by a national legal system. It is to be hoped that the trend will be reversed in India, and not copied elsewhere. For now, India stands alone in this respect; no other legal system has adopted such an aggressively nationalistic posture. The position elsewhere is illustrated by the French Minister of Justice's Report to Parliament introducing what was to become the 1981 Decree on international arbitration, where it is flatly stated:

> the possibility to bring before a French judge an action for annulment against an award made abroad is excluded. (Quoted in J.L. Delvolve, Arbitration in France, at 96 (1982).

.    .    .

[O]ne need look no further than Article I(1) of the Convention to find the following relevant provision:

> This Convention shall apply to the recognition and enforcement of arbitral awards made in the territory of the State other than the State where the recognition and enforcement of such awards are sought, and arising out of differences between persons, whether physical or legal. It shall also apply to arbitral awards not considered as domestic awards in the State where their recognition and enforcement are sought.

This language would clearly cover an award rendered abroad, even if — as was the case in Singer — the applicable substantive law was that of the enforcement jurisdiction.

.    .    .

The unfortunate potential consequences of these two decisions can hardly be exaggerated. They could lead to dangerous and doubtless escalating rivalry between competing legal systems. As the Singer decision recognizes in paragraph 53, they would result in "concurrent" jurisdiction between the courts of the place of arbitration and those of the country whose law governs the arbitration agreement. Doubtless such a conception of the international arbitral process would ultimately lead some arbitrators not to confront the issue of applicable law until they have decided the merits of the case, and then to exercise their imagination to find that the law applicable to the arbitration agreement was not that of the losing party — so as to protect the award from attacks in that party's home courts. That would regrettably put expediency before principle. Furthermore, it could provoke courts into disregarding arbitrators' findings of applicable law. The result would be a grave erosion of the authority of arbitrators. Much of the international acceptance of arbitration, achieved by painstaking efforts since 1958, would be imperilled.

These kinds of reactions would likely be but the beginning of a spiral of one-upmanship, irreversibly damaging the valuable mechanisms of the international arbitral process.

It would be an unfortunate mistake to view this as a matter of favouring "Western" arbitration over Third World court systems. Rather, what is at stake is the reliability of <u>neutral</u> mechanisms for the resolution of international commercial disputes. That such mechanisms can be made to work in the interest of parties from developing countries should be beyond cavil.

.   .   .

[A]lthough Article V(1)(e) of the New York Convention allows non-recognition of awards set aside by "a competent authority of the country in which, <u>or under the law of which</u>, that award was made," there are few illustrations in practice of international contracts that contemplate arbitration in country A all the while providing that the law of country B shall govern the conduct of the arbitration and that its courts shall have "exclusive jurisdiction."

The six just underlined words in Article V(1)(e) do not <u>grant</u> jurisdiction to the courts of the country whose laws govern the arbitration.[313] Jurisdiction would have to be <u>asserted</u> by those courts. The thrust of this commentary is that it would be grievously wrong for them to do so in the absence of an unusual contractual stipulation giving them such authority.

---

[313] Note that Article V(1)(e) does not recognize any role for the courts of the country whose law governs the arbitration <u>agreement</u> (usually the same as that which governs the contract in general). What is contemplated here is a stipulation to the effect that the <u>arbitration</u> shall be conducted in accordance with the law of country X. Article V(1)(e) thus accommodates the rare cases where such a stipulation refers to a law other than the one of the place of arbitration.

## Notes and Questions

1.   Judicial corruption can be just as much a problem as arbitrator corruption. A right to challenge an arbitral award for violation of some fundamental aspect of procedural integrity (such as fraud or excess of arbitral authority) arguably makes sense in a country where the judiciary is honest. What if, however, the national courts of the place of arbitration are known to be corrupt? In such a case, might a policy-maker or practitioner be concerned that judges would abuse their power to set aside awards? Does the balancing of the rights of winners and losers in arbitration come out differently on the question of judicial review in a country where courts are honest? Are there places in the world where business managers would fear court misconduct more than arbitrator misconduct?

2.   Professor von Mehren writes that the traditional position which holds that every arbitration is necessarily the subject of the law of some state is true only when there is a "linkage" between an arbitration and a national legal order. *See supra* p. 1119. When would there not be such a "link"? When does arbitration not take place in the shadow of a threat to invoke state power? Would this threat of state power always mean a "linkage" between the award and the national courts?

3.   In discussions of the proper role of courts at the place of arbitration, one hears much talk about "the parties' desire." How easy is it to ascertain how much finality the parties really want for an award? Do parties to arbitration always expect to be winners in an arbitration with an interest in enforcing the award? What happens when an arbitrator makes a mistake or denies due process? What happens when one side to a dispute changes its mind about the wisdom of arbitration rather than litigation? Having signed an arbitration clause at a time when both sides were optimistic about the future of the commercial relationship, one party may later regret having submitted the dispute to private adjudication rather than a judge. Should courts be "paternalistic" and protect the parties against their own folly?

4.   If an arbitration is held in Switzerland, could the parties elect to have their contract interpreted according to English law, and yet have French procedural law apply to the arbitral process itself? Could all aspects of Swiss law be avoided? See the Swiss LDIP, Articles 190 and 192.

## F.   JUDICIAL REVIEW IN THE ENFORCEMENT FORUM

### 1.   TREATY FRAMEWORK

It is less than self-evident how New York Convention Article V defenses to enforcement of foreign awards should be applied by courts asked to implement an award through recognition or enforcement. Which of the litany of Article V defenses discussed in the following cases and notes is most malleable in the hands of the judge? Which is the most essential to maintaining the integrity of the enforcement forum, for relieving its judges of the duty to lend state power to the implementation of a corrupt arbitral process?

*Deutsche Schachtbau-und Tiefbohrgesellschaft v. Ras Al Khaimah Nat'l Oil Co.*, 2 Lloyd's Rep. 246 (C.A. 1987).

[Note: This case was subsequently reversed on other grounds by the House of Lords. See 2 A.E.R. 833 (1988). The facts are set out in Chapter 2, *supra* p. 215]

.   .   .

The Geneva award is a "Convention Award" within the meaning of the Arbitration Act, 1975, being an award made in pursuance of an arbitration agreement in the territory of a State, other than the United Kingdom, namely Switzerland, which is a party to the New York Convention on the Recognition and Enforcement of Foreign Arbitral Awards. It follows that it is enforceable in England either by action or under s. 26 of the Arbitration Act, 1950, and that such enforcement is mandatory, save in the exceptional cases listed in s. 5 of the 1975 Act.

Section 5 provides, so far as is material, that:

Refusal of enforcement.

5.-(1) Enforcement of a Convention award shall not be refused except in the cases mentioned in this section.

(2) Enforcement of a Convention award may be refused if the person against whom it is invoked proves — . . . (b) that the arbitration agreement was not valid under the law to which the parties subjected it or, failing any indication thereon, under the law of the country where the award was made; or . . . (d) (subject to subsection (4) of this section) the award deals with a difference not contemplated by or not falling within the terms of the submission to arbitration or contains decisions on matters beyond the scope of the submission to arbitration; or . . .

(3) Enforcement of a Convention award may also be refused if the award is in respect of a matter which is not

capable of settlement by arbitration, or if it would be contrary to public policy to enforce the award.

(4) A Convention award which contains decisions on matters not submitted to arbitration may be enforced to the extent that it contains decisions on matters submitted to arbitration which can be separated from those on matters not so submitted.

.     .     .

### Public policy in relation to the enforcement of the award

In pursuance of their duty under art. 13.3 of the I.C.C. rules, the arbitrators determined that the proper law governing the substantive obligations of the parties was "internationally accepted principles of law governing contractual relations." The arbitrators prefaced this decision with the following statement:

The Arbitration Tribunal holds that:

The Concession Agreement, the Assignment Agreement and the 1976 Operating Agreement are contracts between, on one hand, a number of companies organised under various laws, and, on the other hand, a State respectively a company which is actually an agency of such state.

Reference either to the law of any one of the companies, or of such State, or of the State on whose territory one or several of these contracts were entered into, may seem inappropriate, for several reasons.

The Arbitration Tribunal will refer to what has become common practice in international arbitrations particularly in the field of oil drilling concessions, and especially to arbitrations located in Switzerland. Indeed, this practice, which must have been known to the parties, should be regarded as representing their implicit will. Reference is made in particular to the leading cases of Sapphire International Petroleums Ltd. v. National Iranian Oil Company (INTERNATIONAL LAW REPORTS

1967, 136ff), Texaco Overseas Petroleum Company v. The Government of the Libyan Arab Republic (INTERNATIONAL LAW REPORTS 1979, 389ff). See also Lalive, LES RÈGLES DE CONFLIT DE LOIS APPLIQUÉES AU FOND DU LITIGE PAR L'ARBITRE INTERNATIONAL SIÈGEANT EN SUISSE, L'ARBITRAGE INTERNATIONAL PRIVÉ ET LA SUISSE, 1977; see also Derains, "L'application cumulative par l'arbitre des systèmes de conflit de lois intéressés au litige," in REVUE DE L'ARBITRAGE 100 (1972), p. 100.

Mr. Longmore submits that it would be contrary to English public policy to enforce an award which holds that the rights and obligations of the parties are to be determined, not on the basis of any particular national law, but upon some unspecified, and possibly ill defined, internationally accepted principles of law.

.   .   .

[Quoting Mr. Justice Goddard in Maritime Insurance Company, Ltd. v. Assecuranz-Union von 1865, (1935) 52 Lloyd's List L. Rep. 16, 20.]

I agree with Mr. Evans's submission that parties can validly provide for some other system of law to be applied to an arbitration tribunal. Thus, it may be, though perhaps it would be unusual, that the parties could validly agree that a part, or the whole, of their legal relations should be decided by the arbitral tribunal on the basis of a foreign system of law, or perhaps on the basis of principles of international law; for example, in a contract to which a Sovereign State was a party. It may well be that the arbitral tribunal could properly give effect to such an agreement, and the Court in its supervisory jurisdiction would also give effect to it, just as it would give effect to a contractual provision in the body of the contract that the proper law of the contract should be some system of foreign law. Indeed, it might be another way of achieving the same result, and I see no reason why an arbitral tribunal in England should not, in a proper case, where the parties have so agreed, apply foreign law or international law.

Of course, also, as Mr. Evans again suggested, the parties can by their contract, either in the arbitration clause itself or in the rest of the contract, provide that certain incidents of law which would otherwise attach should not attach, such as the exclusion or alternation of the statutory period of limitation, or the exclusion of the implied terms of Sect. 14 of the Sale of Goods Act, 1893, or suchlike matters. There is no possible objection to that, so long as there is nothing contrary to public policy in the exclusion or alteration of the provisions which, in the absence of agreement, would attach.

But this is not such a case. If the parties choose to provide in their contract that the rights and obligations shall not be decided in accordance with law but in accordance with some other criterion, such as what the arbitrators consider to be fair and reasonable, whether or not in accordance with law, then, if that provision has any effect at all, its effect, as I see it, would be that there would be no contract, because the parties did not intend the contract to have legal effect to affect their legal relations. If there were no contract, there would be no legally binding arbitration clause, and an "award" would not be an award which the law would recognize.

A clause in the same terms was considered in this Court in Eagle Star Insurance Co. Ltd. v. Yuval Insurance Co. Ltd., [1978] 1 Lloyd's Rep. 357, where Lord Denning, with the agreement of Lord Justice Goff and Lord Justice Shaw, said at p. 362L:

I do not believe that the presence of such a clause makes the whole contract void or a nullity. It is a perfectly good contract. If there is anything wrong with the provision, it can only be on the ground that it is contrary to public policy for parties so to agree. I must say that I cannot see anything in public policy to make this clause void. On the contrary the clause seems to me to be entirely reasonable. It does not oust the jurisdiction of the Courts. It only ousts technicalities and strict constructions. That is what equity did in the old days. And it is what arbitrators may properly do today under such a clause as this. Even under an ordinary arbitration submission, it was a mistake for the Courts in the beginning to upset awards simply for errors of law. See what Mr. Justice Williams and Mr. Justice Willes said in Hodgkinson v. Fernie, (1857) 3 C.B.N.S. 189 at pp. 202, 205. That mistake can be avoided by such a clause as this: for, as Lord Justice Scrutton said in Czarnikow v. Roth, Schmidt & Co., (1922) 12 LLOYD'S REP. 195; [1922] 2 K.B. 478, the parties can, by express provision, authorise arbitrators to depart from the strictness of the law.

So I am prepared to hold that this arbitration clause, in all its provisions, is valid and of full effect, including the requirement that the arbitrators shall decide on equitable grounds rather than a strict legal interpretation. I realise, of course, that this lessens the points on which one party or the other can ask for a case stated. But that is no bad thing. Cases stated have been carried too far. It would be to the advantage of the commercial community that they should be reduced: and a claim (sic? clause) of this kind would go far to ensure this.

In my judgment there are three questions which the Court has to ask itself when confronted with a clause which purports to provide that the rights of the parties shall be governed by some system of "law" which is not that of England or any other State or is a serious modification of such a law:

1.      <u>Did the parties intend to create legally enforceable rights and obligations?</u>

If they did not, there is no basis for the intervention of the coercive power of the State to give effect to those "rights and obligations." An intention not to create legally enforceable rights and obligations may be expressed — "this agreement is binding in honour only" — or it may be implied from the relationship between the parties or from the fact that the agreed criteria for the determination of the parties' rights and obligations are too vague or idiosyncratic to have been intended as a basis for the creation of such rights and obligations.

2.     Is the resulting agreement sufficiently certain to constitute a legally enforceable contract?

This question assumes that the parties intended to create a legally enforceable relationship, but is addressed to the problem of whether the terms of their agreement are too uncertain to produce such a result. However, given that this was the intention of the parties, the Courts will not be —

> too astute or too subtle in finding defects; but, on the contrary, the court should seek to apply the old maxim of English law, Verba ita sunt intelligenda ut res magis valeat quam pereat (per Lord Wright in Hillas & Co. v. Arcos Ltd., (1932) 43 Lloyd's Rep. 359 at p. 367; (1932) 147 L.T.R. 503 at p. 514).

In this context another maxim is relevant — "id certum est quod certum reddi potest" — and there is a vital distinction between an agreement to agree in future and an agreement to accept terms to be determined by a third party. The former cannot and the latter can form the basis for a legally enforceable agreement.

3.     Would it be contrary to public policy to enforce the award, using the coercive powers of the State?

Considerations of public policy can never be exhaustively defined, but they should be approached with extreme caution. As Mr. Justice Burrough remarked in Richardson v. Mellish, (1824) 2 Bing. 229 at p. 252 "It is never argued at all, but when other points fail." It has to be shown that there is some element of illegality or that the enforcement of the award would be clearly injurious to the public good or, possibly, that enforcement would be wholly offensive to the ordinary reasonable and fully informed member of the public on whose behalf the powers of the State are exercised.

Asking myself these questions, I am left in no doubt that the parties intended to create legally enforceable rights and liabilities and that the enforcement of the award would not be contrary to public policy. That only leaves the question of whether the agreement has the requisite degree of certainty. By choosing to arbitrate under the rules of the I.C.C. and, in particular, art. 13.3, the parties have left proper law to be decided by the arbitrators and have not in terms confined the choice to national systems of law. I can see no basis for concluding that the arbitrators' choice of proper law — a common denominator of principles underlying the laws of the various nations governing contractual relations — is outside the scope of the choice which the parties left to the arbitrators.

### Notes and Questions

1. Look again at *Parsons & Whittemore Overseas Co., Inc. v. Société Genérale de l'Industrie du Papier (RAKTA)*, 508 F.2d 969 (2d Cir. 1974), *supra* p. 136, in which an American company (Parsons & Whittemore Overseas, Inc.) resisted unsuccessfully the enforcement of an award arising out of a contract for construction of a paperboard factory in Alexandria, Egypt that was terminated during the 1967 Arab-Israeli War. Parson & Whittemore presented, and the Court rejected, almost the entire spectrum of defenses to award enforcement under Article V of the New York Convention public policy: non-arbitrability, lack of opportunity to present a defense, excess of jurisdiction and "manifest disregard of the law." Is the last of these defenses only a subset of excess of jurisdiction? The Court deals with "manifest disregard of the law" as follows:

Both the legislative history of Article V, *see supra*, and the statute enacted to implement the United States' accession to the Convention are strong authority for treating as exclusive the bases set forth in the Convention for vacating an award. On the other hand, the Federal Arbitration Act, specifically 9 U.S.C. §10, has been read to include an implied defense to enforcement where the award is in "manifest disregard" of the law. *Wilko v. Swan*, 346 U.S. 427, 436, 74 S. Ct. 182, 98 L. Ed. 168 (1953); *Saxis Steamship Co. v. Multifacs International Traders, Inc.*, 375 F.2d

577, 582 (2d Cir. 1967); *Amicizia Societa Navegazione v. Chilean Nitrate and Iodine Sales Corp.*, 274 F.2d 805, 808 (2d Cir. 1960).

This case does not require us to decide, however, whether this defense stemming from dictum in Wilko, supra, obtains in the international arbitration context. For even assuming that the "manifest disregard" defense applies under the Convention, we would have no difficulty rejecting the appellant's contention that such "manifest disregard" is in evidence here. Overseas in effect asks this court to read this defense as a license to review the record of arbitral proceedings for errors of fact or law — a role which we have emphatically declined to assume in the past and reject once again. "Extensive judicial review frustrates the basic purpose of arbitration, which is to dispose of disputes quickly and avoid the expense and delay of extended court proceedings." *Saxis Steamship Co.*, *supra*, 375 F.2d 577 at 582; *see also*, *Amicizia Societa Navegazione*, *supra*, 274 F.2d 805 at 808.

Insofar as this defense to enforcement of awards in "manifest disregard" of law may be cognizable under the Convention, it, like the other defenses raised by the appellant, fails to provide a sound basis for vacating the foreign arbitral award. We therefore affirm the district court's confirmation of the award.

2. In *Imperial Ethiopian Gov't v. Baruch-Foster Corp.*, 535 F.2d 334 (5th Cir. 1976), the case arose out of a petroleum development contract made with the Ethiopian government. The chairman of the arbitral tribunal that rendered an award in favor of Ethiopia (for breach of contract to drill an oil well) had been a draftsman of the Ethiopian Civil Code. The award was confirmed notwithstanding this alleged lack of independence. Ask yourself what types of links between the arbitration and a party — financial, professional and social — ought to justify refusal to recognize an award? When should the arbitrator's links with a party's counsel be relevant to award recognition?

## 2.    INTERACTION OF ENFORCEMENT FORUM AND ARBITRAL SEAT

The previous section looked at a "delocalization" of arbitration primarily from the perspective of the law of the place of proceedings, asking what grounds are appropriate for annulment by courts at the arbitral situs. It also explored the effect that a court at an enforcement forum might give to an award annulled where rendered. The following Swedish case raises questions about the role of the arbitral seat from a slightly different perspective, asking what a court at the enforcement forum should do when faced with an unresolved foreign proceeding challenging the award at the place of the arbitration.

*General Nat'l Maritime Transport Co. v. Société Götaverken Arendal A.B.* 13 August 1979 (Sweden) (Translated into English in J. Paulsson, *The Role of the Swedish Courts in Transnational Commercial Arbitration*, 21 VA. J. INT'L L. 211, 244-48 (1981).

The buyer on appeal has demanded principally that the Supreme Court should reverse the decision of the Court of Appeal and dismiss the shipyard's application for enforcement, and alternatively that the decision should be postponed until a final decision regarding the complaint filed by the buyer in France has been rendered there. In support of these prayers, the buyer has reaffirmed the grounds it relied upon before the Court of Appeal.

The shipyard has responded that the appeal should be dismissed and that the order for enforcement given by the Court of Appeal should be affirmed.

Grounds

. . .

In support of the claim that the award should not be enforced in this country, the buyer has further argued (cf. paragraph 4 of the decision of the Court of Appeal): Submitting in France an "Opposition à Ordononnance d'Exequatur de Sentence Arbitrale" (sic) under French law automatically prevents and postpones all enforcement until the Tribunal de Grande Instance de Paris has ruled on the enforceability of the award. Under French law the submission of an "opposition" to said authority is the way in which enforcement is postponed until judgment has been rendered on specific alleged grounds for invalidity of the award. . . .

The buyer has submitted considerable evidence to show that as a consequence of the initiation of the challenge procedure, the award cannot be enforced in France pending the court's decision there.

Under Section 7, paragraph one, subparagraph 5 of the Act concerning Foreign Arbitration Agreements and Awards, a foreign award is not valid in this Kingdom if the party against whom the award is invoked shows that the award "has not yet become enforceable or otherwise binding" on the parties in the State in which or under the law of which it was made or that the award has been set aside or suspended by a competent authority of said State. This text, which was promulgated in 1971, is based on Article V(1)(e) of the 1958 New York Convention on the Recognition and Enforcement of Foreign Arbitral Awards. The text of the Convention merely reads "not yet become binding" on the parties etc. The wording "enforceable or otherwise" was added at the initiative of Lagradet (the "Law Council"). As is evident from the legislative history, no material deviation from the Convention was intended (see prop. 1971:131 pages 13, 69 et seq., and 71). The legislative history contains unequivocal statements to the effect that the fact that there remains the possibility of a motion to set aside the award shall not mean that it is not considered binding. That the rules have this meaning has even been admitted by the buyer. One case in which a foreign award is not binding is when its merits can be subject to appeal to a higher jurisdiction. The choice of the word binding was intended to give relief to the party relying on the award. The intent was, inter alia, to avoid the necessity for double exequatur, or the need for the party relying on the award to prove that it is enforceable according to the authorities of the country in which it was rendered.

By the arbitration clause of the shipbuilding contracts (Article 13), the parties agreed to comply with the award as finally binding and enforceable in matters submitted to the arbitrators. Further, the ICC rules of arbitration, under which the now relevant proceedings were conducted, contain a provision (Article 24) that the arbitral award shall be final.

In consideration of the aforesaid, the present arbitral award must be considered to have become enforceable and binding on the parties in France, in the meaning intended by Section 7, paragraph one, subparagraph 5 of the Act concerning Foreign Arbitration Agreements and Awards, as of the moment and by virtue of the very fact that it was rendered. The fact that that buyer has subsequently challenged the award in France by "opposition" thereto has no effect in this respect.

As seen, the buyer has further maintained that under French law the challenge procedure automatically barred and suspended enforceability of the award pending the competent court's judgment on its validity. In the point of view of the buyer, this would constitute such suspension of execution as is referred to in Section 7, paragraph one, subparagraph 5 of said Act. According to the letter of the law as well as its drafting history (prop. 1971:131, page 34), the Article refers in this respect to a situation where the foreign authority after specific consideration of the matter orders that an already binding and enforceable award be set aside or that its enforcement be suspended. The buyer has not even claimed that such a decision has been rendered in the challenge procedure or otherwise.

. . .

In view of the general purposes of the New York Convention and the legislation of 1971 based thereon, to expedite the enforcement of foreign arbitral awards (see prop. 1971:131, pages 1 and 15, compare pages 14 and 42), it cannot be deemed that such circumstances exist as would justify a suspension of the decision in this enforcement case on the grounds of the procedures initiated by the buyer in France.

[Dissenting opinion of Judge Bengtsson omitted.]

### Notes and Questions

1. *General Nat'l Maritime Transport*, the French judicial challenge to an award rendered in Paris was found insufficient ground for refusing enforcement in Sweden. Note that the case was decided in 1979, when a challenge in France did not have suspensive effect on enforcement under French law. This changed with the 1981 French Arbitration Decree.

2. Look at Article 1506 of the Nouveau Code de procédure civile (suspending enforcement of an arbitral award pending an action in France to challenge the award), and ask yourself whether this result is — or should be — changed by a French stay of execution during the period in which the award is subject to challenge.

## 3. STAYING ENFORCEMENT

The enforcement forum is not necessarily faced with the choice of either enforcing or not enforcing an arbitral award. It may be appropriate to suspend enforcement in some cases with an order for the party resisting enforcement to give "suitable security." See, for example, *Fertilizer Corporation of India v. IDI Management, Inc.*, 517 F.Supp. 948, at 962 (S.D. Ohio 1981), involving a motion to enforce a foreign award, and *Oil and Natural Gas Commission v. Western Company of North America*, 2 INT'L ARB. REP. 168 (1987) where the issue was enjoining enforcement.

Article VI of the New York Convention provides:

> If an application for the setting aside or suspension of the award has been made to a competent authority referred to in article V(1)(e), the authority before which the award is sought to be relied upon may, if it considers it proper, adjourn the decision on the enforcement of the award and may also, on the application of the party claiming enforcement of the award, order the other party to give suitable security.

Issues raised by motions to stay enforcement are discussed in the following two commentaries.

> a.      W. Michael Tupman, *Staying Enforcement of Arbitral Awards under the New York Convention*, 3 ARB. INT'L 209, 215-17 (1987).

In *Fertilizer Corporation of India v. IDI Management, Inc.*[314] an ICC tribunal had rendered an award in India in favour of FCI, a state corporation. Afterwards IDI, an American company, petitioned an Indian court to set aside the award, while FCI petitioned another Indian court for confirmation. FCI then sought to enforce the award in the United States. IDI opposed enforcement on several grounds, in particular that the award was not yet binding under Indian law because it had not been confirmed. Alternatively IDI sought a stay of enforcement pending the outcome of the court proceedings in India.

The U.S. District Court rejected all of IDI's arguments against enforcement. As for the binding nature of the award, the court held that 'the award will be considered "binding" for the purposes of the [New York] Convention if no further recourse may be had to another arbitral tribunal (that is, an appeals tribunal). Although there might still

---

[314] 517 F.Supp. 948 (S.D. Ohio 1981).

be recourse to a court of law to set aside an award, this fact does not prevent the award from being "binding."

The District Court did grant IDI's request to stay the enforcement proceeding in the United States. Even though the New York Convention does not contain 'any standard on which a decision to adjourn should be based,' it does give the court petitioned with enforcement 'an unfettered grant of discretion.' The District Court decided to exercise its discretion 'in order to avoid the possibility of an inconsistent result' should an Indian court hold the award was invalid.' The court, however, invited FCI to apply 'for suitable security, as provided by Article VI' of the New York Convention. Subsequently FCI did make such an application, and the court ordered IDI to post a bond to secure the full amount of the award.

In the second case in which a court granted a stay of enforcement, the lengthy saga of *Société Norsolor c. Société Pabalk Tikaret Ltd, Sirketi*, an ICC arbitral tribunal had rendered an award in favour of a Turkish claimant (Pabalk) in Vienna. Pabalk then obtained leave from a French court to enforce the award in France. Norsolor meanwhile had petitioned the Commercial Court of Vienna to set aside the award, but that court upheld the award in full.

Both of those judgments [French and Austrian] were appealed. The Court of Appeals of Paris decided to stay enforcement pending an outcome of the parallel proceeding in Vienna. The French court noted that the Austrian court 'will render its decision at the end of this year or, at the latest, during the first month of next year.' Most important was the concern about the possibility of conflicting results: 'if the arbitral award is set aside by the Court of Appeal of Vienna, the present request for leave of enforcement shall become meaningless.' [I]n these circumstances' the French court decided it was 'appropriate to adjourn the decision on enforcement.'

A complete procedural history of the *Norsolor* case well illustrates the frustration of delay caused by parallel proceedings. After a stay of enforcement in France, the Court of Appeal of Vienna set aside two of the operative parts of the arbitral award. The Court of Appeals of Paris then reversed the decision of the lower French court granting leave to enforce with respect to those parts of the award. The Austrian Supreme Court, however, reversed the decision of the Court of Appeal of Vienna and reinstated the parts of the award which it had set aside. The French Supreme Court in turn reversed the decision of the Court of Appeals of Paris. Only after six years from the date of the award was the claimant at long last free to enforce it.

\*     \*     \*

b.     ADAM SAMUEL, JURISDICTIONAL PROBLEMS IN INTERNATIONAL COMMERCIAL ARBITRATION 307-09 (1989).

There are indications that an English court might grant an injunction restraining the enforcement of an award in respect of which a setting aside application is pending or has been granted. Without hearing any argument on the point, the Court of Appeal has, on one occasion, upheld the granting of such an injunction in connection with an award which had been declared void in England for want of jurisdiction.

. . .

Although it might appear that the granting of an injunction would put the United Kingdom in defiance of Articles III and VII(1) of the New York Convention, an English judge might well take the view that a void award, not having any juridical status under English law, did not come within the ambit of either Article. If, before the setting aside application has been disposed of, the applicant can show an arguable case that he will succeed, a court could justify restraining enforcement on the grounds that a null award is void ab initio, its nullity not being purely the result of a decision to set it aside. If our analysis of the state of English law is correct, no exception is likely to be made for purely transnational awards in view of the Court of Appeal's recent affirmation that English "jurisprudence does not recognize the concept of arbitral procedures floating in the transnational firmament."

A further way in which the setting aside forum may be able to mitigate the effects of the award's enforcement, on a party who has had the award set aside, is by ordering his opponent to make restitution of the sums received as a result of the exequatur. There are three problems with this. First, again, the granting of a restitutionary remedy would appear to be a direct contravention of Articles III and VII(1) of the New York Convention. The setting aside jurisdiction would not be recognizing or enforcing the award in accordance with the rules of procedure of the territory where the award was relied upon, under the conditions laid down in Articles IV and V of the Convention and would be effectively stopping the defendant from relying on a more favourable municipal law. The second difficulty is that it may be impossible, under some laws, to order the restitution of property handed over pursuant to a court order. The final problem is that the setting aside forum (which alone will be prepared to order restitution) may well not have jurisdiction over the party who has obtained payment under the award.

### Notes and Questions

1.  Are there strategies which an award creditor can take that might obviate the problems elaborated in these two articles?

2.  Would an injunction restraining enforcement of an award subject to a foreign "setting aside application" _always_ violate Article III of the New York Convention, as Adam Samuel suggests?

### 4.    "STATELESS" AWARDS

We have already seen that the contours of judicial control in the enforcement forum will depend on whether or not the award is presented for enforcement under the New York Convention. After winning an arbitration, an award creditor will usually want both belt and braces when seeking enforcement of the award. Although many countries will enforce foreign arbitral awards in the appropriate circumstances, even without a treaty obligation, it is always better to avoid having the loser argue that the New York Convention does not cover the award, as happened recently with respect to an award of the Iran-U.S. Claims Tribunal, discussed in the following case.

a.    _Ministry of Defense (Iran) v. Gould, Inc._,
        887 F.2d 1357 (9th Cir. 1989).

O'SCANNLAIN, Circuit Judge:

We are asked to determine whether an award against an American corporation entered by the Iran-United States Claims

Tribunal can be enforced in federal court. The district court ruled that subject matter jurisdiction to enforce such award vests under the New York Convention and the Federal Arbitration Act. We agree.

[The Court summarized the events leading to the overthrow of the Shah of Iran, the seizure of hostages in Iran in 1979, and the agreement that provided for the release of the American hostages. This agreement, known as the Algiers Accords ("the Accords"), comprised the Declaration of the Democratic and Popular Republic of Algeria (Jan. 19, 1981) ("General Declaration") and the Declaration of the Government of the Democratic and Popular Republic of Algeria Concerning the Settlement of Claims by the Government of the United States of America and the Government of Islamic Republic of Iran, *reprinted in* Dept. of State Bull. No. 2047 ("Claims Settlement Declaration").

The Claims Settlement Declaration set up the mechanism by which nationals of either country could present their claims against the government of the other, and established the Iran-United States Claims Tribunal, in which it vested jurisdiction over such claims and any counterclaims arising out of the same transaction. The General Declaration, inter alia, provided that an escrow bank would hold some Iranian assets for the purpose of satisfying awards of U.S. nationals who prevailed on claims against Iran.

By Executive Order President Reagan suspended all claims within the jurisdiction of the Tribunal, and mandated that the Tribunal's determination on the merits of any claim validly before it "shall operate as a final resolution and discharge of the claim for all purposes." The Supreme Court upheld the authority of the President to issue this Executive Order in *Dames & Moore v. Regan*, 453 U.S. 654 (1981).

The dispute in this case arose from contracts between Iran and Hoffman Electric Corporation later merged into Gould Marketing, Inc. ("Gould"), a wholly-owned subsidiary of Gould International, Inc. ("GII"), whereby Hoffman agreed to provide and install certain military equipment.

Hoffman filed claims with the Hague Tribunal seeking damages from Iran for breach of contract, and Iran filed counterclaims for breach of contract. By way of counterclaim, Iran also sought to obtain certain military radio equipment in Hoffman's possession.

The Tribunal eventually issued a consolidated final award in which it ruled that Gould was to pay $3.6 million and return the military radio equipment to Iran.

In contrast to the provision creating the escrow account to secure claims against Iran, the Algiers accords provide no specific vehicle for the enforcement of awards in favor of Iran. Thus Iran moved to enforce its award against Gould in U.S. court. Gould argued that the award did not satisfy the terms of the New York Convention.]

.     .     .

Under the plain meaning of the statute then, three basic requirements exist for jurisdiction to be conferred upon the district court: the award (1) must arise out of a legal relationship (2) which is commercial in nature and (3) which is not entirely domestic in scope. These three conditions are clearly satisfied here.

Congress has provided that the New York Convention, with minor modifications, shall be enforced in United States Courts. 9 U.S.C. § 201. Article I discusses the scope of the Convention, stating that it "shall apply to the recognition and enforcement of arbitral awards made in the territory of a State other than the State where the recognition and enforcement of such awards are sought, and arising out of differences between persons, whether physical or legal . . . [and those awards] not considered as domestic awards in the State where their recognition and enforcement are sought." Article I, ¶ 1. The Convention defines "arbitral awards" to include those "made by permanent arbitral bodies." Article I, ¶ 2. The United States imposes an additional related condition on the award: it must be "made in the territory of another Contracting State." 21 U.S.T. 2566, *reprinted* at notes following 9 U.S.C.A. § 201. Because of the "shall apply" language of Article I, we read these requirements into the jurisdictional mandate of section 203.

The Tribunal's award satisfies these requirements as well. That is, the Tribunal sits at The Hague, which is in the Netherlands, which is a contracting State. In addition, the award is obviously not domestic in nature because Iran is one of the parties to the agreement.

IV

Gould sets forth two basic arguments to support its position that the district court lacks jurisdiction over the enforcement of the award under the Convention. First, relying on language in Articles II and IV, Gould argues that the Convention applies, and hence, jurisdiction to enforce exists, only as to those awards that derive from an arbitral agreement in writing to which the parties voluntarily submitted. It contends that the Accords documents themselves do not satisfy this requirement. Second, Gould argues that the arbitral award was not arrived at in compliance with the Convention's supposed requirement that the proceedings be subject to a "national" arbitration law.

A

The Convention does make several pronouncements concerning the form of the agreement leading up to the award. For example, it places upon each contracting State the obligation to recognize an arbitral agreement in writing between the parties. Convention, Article II, ¶ 1. In addition, the party seeking enforcement must file with the court "[t]he original agreement referred to in article II . . . or a duly certified copy thereof." Convention, Article IV, ¶ 1(b). These provisions do indeed seem to indicate that the award referred to in section 203 emanate from a written agreement.

We construe the Accords themselves as representing the written agreement so required, on the strength of the President's authority to settle claims on behalf of United States nationals through international agreements. "[I]nternational agreements settling claims by nationals of one state against the government of another 'are established international practice reflecting traditional international theory.'" *Dames & Moore*, 453 U.S. at 679, 101 S.Ct. at 2986 (quoting L. Henkin, Foreign Affairs & the Constitution (1972)). More specifically, the Court in *Dames & Moore* held that the President possessed the authority to nullify attachments and order the transfer of Iranian assets, *id.* at 674, 101 S.Ct. at 2983-84, and to suspend claims of American citizens against Iran. *Id.* at 686, 101 S.Ct. at 2990.

Gould contends that *Dames & Moore* should be more narrowly construed. Indeed, the Court itself chose to "re-emphasize the narrowness of our decision. We do not decide that the President possesses plenary power to settle claims, even as against foreign governmental entities." *Id.* at 688, 101 S.Ct. at 2991. Nevertheless, the Court went on to make clear that its holding extends broadly enough to encompass the authority of the President to settle claims under the facts before us. *Id.* Thus, because the President acted within his authority on behalf of United States citizens, the real question is not whether Gould entered into a written agreement to submit its claims against Iran to arbitration, but whether the President—acting on behalf of Gould—entered into such an agreement. The answer is clearly yes. Deputy Secretary of State Warren Christopher initialed the Accords in his role as an agent for the President; and thus, the requirements of Article II, ¶ 1 are satisfied. In addition, the Final Tribunal Rules of Procedure state that "[t]he Claims Settlement Declaration constitutes an agreement in writing by Iran and the United States, on their own behalfs *and on behalf of their nationals* submitting to arbitration within the framework of the Algiers Declarations and in accordance with the Tribunal Rules." Final Tribunal Rule of Procedure 1.3 (emphasis supplied).

Gould urges further that the only court to have considered the issue, the High Court of England, ruled that the Accords do not satisfy the "agreement in writing" standard of the Convention. *See Dallal v. Bank Mellat*, 1 All E.R. 239 (Q.B.1986). This is a mischaracterization of the High Court's opinion, however. First, the High Court in *Dallal* engaged in a ruling on the merits of whether a Tribunal award barred a proceeding in English courts as res judicata based on the same claim; the Court was not ruling on whether it possessed jurisdiction under the Convention. Second, the Court's analysis focused on an evaluation of whether the "conduct of the parties in the arbitration and, in particular, their written pleadings"—not, as argued here, the Accords themselves—constituted the "agreement in writing." *Id.* Finally, the Court's entire discussion appears to be dictum. "*If it were necessary* for me to decide the question at this stage, *I would decide* that the proceedings were a nullity in Dutch law." *Id.* (emphasis supplied).

Moreover, even if the United States government lacked authority to enter into the agreement in writing required under the Convention, we find persuasive the argument that Gould, in filing its claim and arbitrating it before the Tribunal, "ratified" the actions of the United States. *See id.* at 254; Lewis, What Goes Around Comes Around: Can Iran Enforce Awards of the Iran-U.S. Claims Tribunal in the United States?, 26 Colum.J.Transnat'l L. 515, 546 (1988).

## B

The second basic argument Gould makes is premised on language contained in Article V, which lists the defenses available to the party against whom enforcement of a Tribunal Award is sought. Gould asserts that these defensive provisions contain an implicit requirement that the Convention applies only to arbitral awards made in accordance with the national arbitration law of a Party State. In particular, Gould seeks to buttress its position by looking to Article V ¶ 1(e), which provides that the party against whom enforcement is sought may establish that enforcement should not be granted if it can show that "the award has not yet become binding on the parties, or has been set aside or suspended by a competent authority of the country in which, or *under the law of which*, that award was made." New York Convention, Article V ¶ 1(e) (emphasis supplied). Gould argues that this subparagraph would be rendered devoid of practical meaning if the Convention calls for the recognition of awards other than those which are made under a foreign municipal law. Thus, it concludes that because the Tribunal's award in favor of Iran was a creature of international law, and not national law, it does not "fall under" the Convention pursuant to section 203.

Section 203 does not contain a separate jurisdictional requirement that the award be rendered subject to a "national law." Language pertaining to the "choice of law" issue is not mentioned, or even alluded to, in Article I, which lays out the Convention's scope of applicability. In addition, although it is a close question, the fairest reading of Convention itself appears to be that it applies to the enforcement of non-national awards. Indeed, a Dutch court has so held. *See Societe Europeenne d'Etudes et d'Enterprises v. Socialist Federal Republic of Yugoslavia*, HR (Hoge Raad der Nederlanden) NJ 74, 361 (1974) (hereinafter "*Societe*"). In *Societe*, the Hoge Raad, the highest court of the Netherlands, reversed the Court of The Hague, which had ruled that the Dutch trial court erred in recognizing an arbitral award that was not issued according to the law of Switzerland. The Hoge Raad held that the strictures of Article V do not come into effect unless and until "the party against whom the award is invoked furnishes proof of the existence of one of the impediments specified under (a) to (e) [in Article V]." *Id.* at 1006-07. "The relationship between the award and the law of a particular country need only be examined in the framework of an investigation to be carried out following a plea that the impediments mentioned in Article V(1) exist . . . in respect of which questions may arise which can be answered only with reference to the law of a particular country." *Id.*

In addition, allowing the parties to untether themselves from a pre-existing "national law" still leaves certain safe-guards in place to guard against enforcement of an otherwise unfair arbitration award. The Convention contains several due process protections requiring notice and the opportunity to be heard as well as a defense to guard against enforcement of awards contrary to public policy. Article V, ¶¶ 1(b), 2(b). Also, while the Tribunal at times may function as a forum for the resolution of interstate disputes, e.g., when it is called upon to render an opinion as between the United States and Iran under Article II, § 2 of the Claims Settlement Declaration, it primarily is concerned with the resolution of private law rights based on contractual arrangements relating to the provision of goods and services. Article II, ¶ 1. It certainly has served this latter function in this case.

Finally, as they are laid out, the defenses seem to apply to arbitral awards made pursuant to municipal domestic law *or* those made pursuant to law of the parties' choosing, as in this case. In particular, Article V ¶ 1(d) allows a party against whom enforcement is sought to defend against enforcement if "the arbitral procedure was not in accordance with the agreement of the parties, *or*, failing such agreement, was not in accordance with the law of the country where the arbitration took place" (emphasis supplied).

Although this language seems to be at loggerheads with that of Article V ¶ 1(e) concerning "the country . . . under the law of which, [the] award was made," it is possible to reconcile the two provisions in accordance with an interpretation that holds that the Convention applies to "non-national law" awards. That is, if the parties choose not to have their arbitration governed by a "national law," then the losing party simply cannot avail itself of certain of the defenses in subparagraphs (a) and (e).

Thus, we conclude that an award need not be made "under a national law" for a court to entertain jurisdiction over its enforcement pursuant to the Convention.

The district court properly denied that portion of Gould's motion to dismiss for lack of jurisdiction over this matter under 9 U.S.C. § 203, because the award of the Iran-United States Claims

Tribunal that Iran seeks to enforce "falls under" the New York Convention. Because we conclude that jurisdiction exists under section 203, we do not reach the question of whether there was jurisdiction under 28 U.S.C. § 1331. Therefore, we do not consider Iran's cross-appeal on the question of whether the Algiers Accords are self-executing. . . .

[For the subsequent history of Gould, see *Gould v. Iran*, 969 F.2d 764 (9th Cir. 1992).]

\* \* \*

The following comments further explore the problem of "stateless" awards that may or may not be covered by the New York Convention. Since terms like "a-national" and "stateless" are sometimes thrown around in arbitration literature rather carelessly, the first comment deals with taxonomy. The next two look at the problematic SEEE and Bergesen cases. The problem for the practitioner, of course, is to maximize award enforceability through Convention coverage.

b. William W. Park, *National Law and Commercial Justice: Safeguarding Procedural Integrity in International Arbitration*, 63 TUL. L. REV. 647, 663-67 (1989).

### The Nationality of Awards

During the quarter century since talk of 'a-national' arbitration has made its way from Professor Goldman's Hague lectures to the more common conversation of international lawyers, the 'nationality of awards' has been the subject of unnecessary mystification. Much of the confusion in characterizing awards and arbitrations has come from a tendency to apply labels without regard to their context.

The New York Arbitration Convention covers awards characterized as either 'foreign' or 'non-domestic.' Foreign awards are those rendered outside the enforcement forum. Nondomestic awards may be rendered locally, but are nevertheless covered by the Convention because they involve transactions and/or parties that are almost or entirely foreign.

Foreign arbitration overlaps international arbitration. The latter deals with disputes having an international element, and may be delocalized procedurally within the limits of national arbitration law. In countries such as Belgium, England, France, and Switzerland, statutes either limit or permit the parties to restrict judicial review of awards that implicate international commerce. But such awards are neither foreign nor non-national. They are usually subject to national statutory rules concerning vacatur and confirmation, even if related to an international dispute. An award may be nondomestic for purposes of the New York Convention, and yet subject to national procedures for confirmation because it was rendered locally.

The terms 'a-national' and 'stateless' have been used loosely to describe those awards that, for a variety of reasons, are not subject to review under any national law except that of the place in which the award is ultimately presented for enforcement. This characterization might be applied to include awards refused registration in courts of the place where rendered, and awards made in places like Belgium that provide no review of arbitrations between foreigners. Awards under the aegis of the World Bank's International Center for the Settlement of Investment Disputes (ICSID) might also be characterized as a-national. Sui generis public law arbitration under treaty, such as the U.S.--Iran Claims Tribunal, is a problematic category.

Commentators and judges are divided over whether so-called stateless awards are enforceable under the New York Convention. The leading scholar on the Convention [A.J. van den Berg] takes the view that they are not, based on his reading of the Convention's explicit scope in conjunction with its provision relating to defenses to enforcement of awards.

The thirty-year saga of Société Européenne d'Etudes et d'Entreprises v. Yugoslavia (S.E.E.E.) offers a spectacular example of the divergence of opinion on stateless awards. An award rendered in Switzerland on July 2, 1956, disposed of claims arising out of an agreement to build a railroad in Yugoslavia before World War II. The award was filed, but refused registration, in the Cantonal Court of Vaud, the place where rendered. Registration was refused because the arbitral tribunal did not include an uneven number of arbitrators, as required by Vaud law. The award was ultimately denied recognition in the Netherlands, apparently on the grounds of its statelessness. Later, however, the award was granted recognition in France, notwithstanding that it fell 'beyond the judicial sovereignty' of the place where rendered.

Awards such as S.E.E.E. that have merely been refused court registration under the law of the situs are sometimes confused with awards that have been explicitly vacated where rendered. An annulled award is anything but stateless. Indeed, annulment proves the award's link with the place where rendered, as recognized under New York Convention article V.

The term 'a-national arbitration' has also been applied to arbitration in which the arbitrators decide the merits of the dispute without reference to a fixed national system of law, a practice prohibited in some arbitral centers. The arbitrator may decide according to trade usage and lex mercatoria, may take on powers of amiable composition, or may apply 'general principles of law.' Such arbitration is more likely to occur, and is more justified, when it is difficult for the arbitrator to ascertain the exact content of the otherwise applicable law.

For clarity in analysis, it is important to describe what an anational arbitration is not. The term would be misapplied to an award deemed nondomestic under the New York Convention if subject to local judicial review, as in the Bergesen case[315] Nor would it be appropriate to apply the term to an award that is unenforceable because of the sovereign immunity of the loser, as in the Swiss stage of the LIAMCO saga.[316] Such arbitrations are international but not stateless,

---

[315] *Bergesen v. Joseph Muller Corp.*, 548 F.Supp. 650, 654 (S.D.N.Y. 1982), aff'd, 710 F.2d 928 (2d Cir. 1983).

[316] In Switzerland, the Federal Tribunal overturned the attachment order that LIAMCO had secured from the Zurich District Court against Libyan assets in six local banks. The federal court did not challenge the validity of the arbitral award itself, but ruled rather that the Zurich tribunal had no jurisdiction to order attachments against a state when the litigation lacks a 'sufficient domestic relationship.' Such relationship might be established, for example, by activities that justify jurisdictional venue in Switzerland. Neither the location of assets in Switzerland, nor the choice of Geneva as the arbitral seat, established a 'sufficient domestic relationship' in the *LIAMCO* case. *See* Note, *Socialist People's Libyan Arab Jamahirya v. Libyan Am. Oil Co.*, 75 Amer. J. Int'l L. 153 (1981).

since they are subject to judicial confirmation or annulment where rendered.

> c.      Georges   R.   Delaume,   *SEEE   v.*
> *Yugoslavia*: *Epitaph  or  Interlude?*  4  J.
> INT'L ARB., 3, 25 (1987).

.     .     .

Before World War II, the SEEE, a French company, had agreed to build a railroad in Yugoslavia. The agreement between SEEE and Yugoslavia provided for payments to be made over a twelve year period. After war broke out, payments ceased in 1941. After the war, the French Government, taking over the SEEE's claims, negotiated a settlement with Yugoslavia. The SEEE accepted payment. However, a few years later, the SEEE contended that the sums received from Yugoslavia under the French/Yugoslavian agreement did not exhaust the amount of its claim. The SEEE instituted arbitration proceedings in Lausanne, Switzerland, pursuant to an arbitration clause in its contract with Yugoslavia. Yugoslavia objected to the proceedings on the ground that the SEEE's claim had been fully settled and refused to participate in them.

A default award was rendered against Yugoslavia by a panel of two arbitrators. The SEEE filed the award with the registrar of the Cantonal Tribunal of Vaud. The Yugoslav Government brought action in the same Tribunal to have the award declared null and void on various grounds, including the fact that the arbitral tribunal did not include an uneven number of arbitrators, as required by the law of the Canton of Vaud. This was the beginning of a series of judicial proceedings which were to last for the next thirty years.

.     .     .

## The Swiss Decisions

Following the action for annulment of the award brought by Yugoslavia, the SEEE demurred that it should be dismissed because the award was not subject to the law of the Canton of Vaud, the situs of arbitration. The Tribunal agreed and held that, since the award was not a Vaud award, it could not be registered in the Canton, and consequently the earlier registration should be canceled and the award remitted to the parties. In reaching this decision, the Tribunal stated in an interesting dictum that:

> The [Tribunal] which holds that it lacks jurisdiction in respect of the action directed against an arbitral award not subject to Vaud's judicial sovereignty, does not intend to preclude the validity and binding character of such award in accordance with the intention of the parties or under such legal system as would be applicable to [the award]. (as translated)

The SEEE appealed to the Swiss Federal Tribunal, but the appeal was dismissed on the ground that:

> The [Cantonal] Tribunal did not annul, even in part, the award, since all that it did was to hold that the award did not constitute an arbitral award within the meaning of Article 516 of the Code of Civil Procedure, and that it should, therefore, be handed back to the parties. (as translated)

Noting in particular the dictum quoted above in the lower court's judgment, the Federal Tribunal held that since the Tribunal of Vaud had not passed judgment on the binding character of the award or its enforceability "outside the Canton of Vaud," the judgment did not prejudice any rights that the SEEE might have under the award.

These decisions seem to imply that the 1956 award, while it was not a "Vaud" award, might nevertheless be an "international" or a "non-Swiss" one, subject to some non-identified legal system. Under these circumstances, the question arises whether the 1956 award passes the tests set forth in Article I(1) of the New York Convention and qualifies for recognition in other countries which are parties to the Convention. This is the question which was subsequently submitted to the Dutch and French courts.

### The Dutch Proceedings

Before the decisions rendered in The Netherlands in connection with recognition proceedings brought by the SEEE are discussed, it should be mentioned that the New York Convention applies to awards "made in the territory" of a Contracting State as well as to awards "not considered as domestic awards" by the recognizing <u>forum</u> (Article I(1)). However, this double-barrelled test applies only in the absence of a contrary declaration, and such a declaration had been made by both Switzerland and the Netherlands, to the effect that they would apply the Convention only to awards "made in the territory" of another Contracting State.

The question whether the 1956 award could be considered as "made" in Switzerland was not uniformly decided by the Dutch courts.

According to the Hague Court of Appeal, the "making" of an award should not refer only to the geographical location of the seat of arbitration; this concept should include also a reference to the municipal law of the State in which the award was rendered. Since the Swiss courts had held that the 1956 award did not satisfy the requirements of Vaud law, the Court of Appeal felt that the award was not "Swiss" and therefore not entitled to recognition in the Netherlands.

On appeal, the Hoge Raad quashed the decision of the Hague Court on the ground, inter alia, that neither the provisions of Article I(1) of the Convention, nor the "Travaux Préparatoires" justified the construction adopted by the lower court. According to the Hoge Raad:

> [N]either the text nor the history of the Convention gives an indication — apart from a plea of the impediments mentioned in Article V(1) — that the competent authority of the country where recognition and enforcement are sought of an arbitral award given in the territory of another State should, before giving its decision, investigate the relationship between the award and the law of the country where it was made and, failing such relationship, refuse recognition and enforcement.

Upon remand from the Hoge Raad, the Hague Court of Appeal persisted in refusing to recognize the 1956 award, but this time on another ground, namely that the award was contrary to Dutch public policy, because to give effect to it in The Netherlands would be contrary to the terms of the 1950 settlement agreed upon by France and Yugoslavia. A new appeal was taken to the Hoge Raad, which entertained the appeal insofar as it concerned the public policy argument. However, it held that in the final analysis, recognition of the award should be denied on the basis of Article V(1)(c) of the Convention, because following the decisions of the Swiss courts, the 1956 award could no longer be executed in Switzerland, nor recognized in The Netherlands.

The exact significance of the Hoge Raad decision is somewhat uncertain. The 1973 decision seems to support the view that an "international" award may qualify for recognition under the Convention as long as it is "made" in the territory of a Contracting State. However, the 1975 decision reverts to considerations which, in addition to the place of making of the award, would seem to "renationalize" it by bringing it within the legal system of the country in which it is "made." Whichever interpretation is correct, the Dutch decisions make it apparent that attempts to remove the arbitration proceedings from the lex loci arbitri and to "internationalize" or "delocalize" the proceedings may have their price. They may deprive the parties of benefitting from the liberal provisions of "foreign" as opposed to "international" awards.

However, this remark must be qualified as a result of the solution which has prevailed in France in connection with the same case.

## The French Proceedings

Parallel to the Dutch proceedings, the SEEE sought recognition and enforcement of the 1956 award in France. In a 1969 decision, apparently unpublished, the SEEE succeeded in obtaining a judgment of exequatur recognizing the award and then promptly sought to garnish the proceeds of World Bank loans to Yugoslavia by serving notice on the European Office of the World Bank. However, the Paris Tribunal revoked the earlier exequatur judgment on the ground that the award was contrary to public policy, since in rendering the award the arbitrators had ignored the existence of the French Yugoslav settlement of 1950. The Tribunal reasoned that since the SEEE had been kept informed of the negotiations by the French Government, and had accepted payment from Yugoslavia, the SEEE was bound by the terms of the settlement which it had, implicitly if not expressly, agreed to. Consequently, the Tribunal vacated the garnishment order. This decision was affirmed by the Court of Appeal of Paris. Appeal was taken to the Cour de Cassation which quashed the decision of the Court of Appeal, but solely on the ground that the Court had erred when it held the SEEE was bound by the 1950 settlement. According to the Cour de Cassation, the 1950 settlement made between sovereigns, and in particular France, exercising its right of diplomatic protection, had only sovereign rights and could not deprive the SEEE of its own rights against Yugoslavia arising out of the original contract between the SEEE and Yugoslavia.

Following this decision, the case was remanded to another court of Appeal, in Orlèans, for determination on the merits. The decision of the Orlèans Court denied recognition to the award on the ground that it offended French public policy because in rendering it, the arbitrators had made a gross error of calculation and awarded the SEEE as a "balance" remaining due to it, a sum in excess of the "principle" of SEEE's claim. On appeal this judgment was quashed by the Cour de Cassation and the case remanded to the Court of Appeal of Rouen.

The Rouen Court granted recognition to the award. It held, inter alia, that the award fell within the scope of the New York Convention to which both France and Switzerland are parties. Contrary to the reasoning of the Dutch Supreme Court, the Rouen Court held that the decisions of the Swiss courts did not "annul or deprive the award of juridical existence" and merely established that the award was not subject to the Canton of Vaud's "judicial sovereignty."

Consistent with the French idea, the Court noted that the arbitral process is not necessarily governed by the law of the seat of arbitration and can be subject to some other domestic law, or to no law at all if the parties have so provided in their agreement. The Court found that the case in question fell within the last category because the ad hoc arbitration clause between the parties provided that the arbitrators were freed from any "requirements" (formalités), and could decide as amicable compositors whose decision was binding upon the parties. In other words, the Court took the view that the Convention is applicable to "anational" awards "made" (in the geographical sense of the term) in a Contracting State. This is a debatable proposition.

The Court went on to say that, even if the New York Convention was not applicable because of the declaration made by Yugoslavia when it acceded to the Convention, i.e. that the Convention would not apply retrospectively, the award should be recognized under the Geneva Convention of 1927, which had been ratified by Yugoslavia, France and Switzerland prior to the date of the award.

Although these statements seem to be pure dicta since the court held that the New York Convention was applicable, it nevertheless appears that both statements were wrong.

In the first place, for the purposes of the New York Convention, the sole relevant consideration was that the award was "made" in Switzerland and that recognition was sought in France. The fact that, when the award was made Yugoslavia was not party to the Convention and that at the time of recognition Yugoslavia, then a party, had made the above-mentioned declaration, was totally immaterial. This point had been clearly made in the Dutch proceedings.

In the second place, reliance on the Geneva Convention was clearly wrong since the Court held that the award was "anational." Indeed, Article 1(2)(c) of the Geneva Convention provides that it applies to awards made "in conformity with the law governing the arbitration procedure." That expression had already been defined in the Geneva Protocol of 1923 (Article 2(1) as referring to "the law of the country in whose territory the arbitration takes place." In the present case, that would have been the law of the Canton of Vaud. However, the Swiss courts had held that the award was not a Vaud award and the Rouen Court had accepted that characterization. It could not, therefore, without contradicting itself, rely on the Geneva Convention to give recognition to the award, but the contradiction is there.

These are issues which were not raised at the new appeal to the Cour de Cassation. The appeal was dismissed on other grounds, in particular the consideration that courts of arbitration, unlike judicial courts, are not bound by the interpretation given by the French Government to treaties or executive agreements, such as the 1950 French Yugoslavian settlement involved in this case. In no uncertain terms, the Court upheld the freedom of transnational arbitrators to give international agreements the construction they consider appropriate under the circumstances. This decision may constitute a landmark decision in transnational arbitration, which is viewed in France with particular favour. Nevertheless it may be felt that, in this instance, the Court has carried its liberal approach towards transnational arbitration to its limits.

·    ·    ·

## Article VII of the New York Convention and Domestic Law: The more-favorable-right provision

The decision of the Court of Appeal of Rouen, left unanswered the question whether the French courts can, in accordance with Article VII of the New York Convention, recognize an "international" award in accordance with French law, to the extent that the French rules are more liberal than those set forth in the New York Convention. Curiously enough, this question was not submitted to the Cour de Cassation on appeal from the decision. The Cour de Cassation, therefore, could not rule on the issue. However, another decision of the Cour de Cassation in Société Pabalk Ticaret Ltd. Sirkati v. Société Norsolor, supplies an answer. This case concerned the recognition in France of an ICC award rendered in Austria, which had been the subject of an annulment proceeding in the Austrian courts. Recognition was initially granted, but following a decision of the Court of Appeal of Vienna invalidating the award, the Court of Appeal of Paris held that the order granting recognition should be retracted. The Court relied on Article V(1)(e) of the New York Convention according to which recognition and enforcement of an award may be refused if it has been "set aside" in the country in which it was made. This decision was quashed by the Cour de Cassation. The judgment of the Cour is based on two considerations, one of which relates to the New York Convention and the other to French law.

Referring to Article VII(1) of the New York Convention, the Cour holds that, under this provision, a French recognizing court may not refuse recognition when it is authorized to grant it under French law.

Turning its attention to French law, and in particular Article 12 of the New Code of Civil Procedure, according to which:

> the judge decides the case in accordance with the rule of law applicable thereto . . . .
> He may take judicial notice of purely legal issues whatever the juridicial basis relied upon by the parties[.]
> (as translated)

The Cour holds that the Court of Appeal of Paris should have determined, if necessary ex officio, whether the award could be recognized under French law.

This decision significantly curtails the application of the New York Convention, in particular of Article V, in France. In fact, since the provisions of the New Code of Civil Procedure are more favourable to the recognition of "international" awards, than those of the Convention regarding the recognition of "foreign" awards, the decision means that French law will prevail over the Convention. This is because the award creditor is likely to rely on French law, rather than on the Convention, or it will be mandatory for the judge to apply French law ex officio if the award creditor fails to invoke it.

\*     \*     \*

d.     Pierre-Yves Tschanz, *International Arbitration in the United States: The Need for a New Act*, 3 ARB. INT'L 309, 314-19 (1987).

.     .     .

In the *Bergesen* case [*see supra* p. 1034] the Second Circuit decided that the New York Convention applies to awards made in the United States as soon as they have certain international contacts. Under this test, practically all awards made in the United States in international cases are 'not considered as domestic' for purposes of applying to them the New York Convention. The arbitration clause in Bergesen provided for arbitration in New York under New York law. There was no suggestion that the arbitration might have been governed by any other law than New York or United States law.

.     .     .

Section 202 of the USAA is similarly inconsistent with the desirable uniform interpretation of what constitutes a 'non-domestic' award falling under the New York Convention. Under Section 202, the scope of application of the New York Convention in the United States goes far beyond awards made in an arbitration governed by a foreign arbitration law. It embraces any award made in the United States in an arbitration having an international nature by reason of the parties involved or of the underlying transaction.

As demonstrated above, it would be inconsistent for courts in the United States to review the same award twice, once upon a motion to vacate, and again for purposes of its recognition under the New York Convention. <u>Therefore, awards falling under the New York Convention pursuant to Bergesen and Section 202 of the USAA appear not to be subject to vacatur in the United States</u> even though they are governed by United States law. In other words, the implication of the Bergesen case is that awards made in the United States in international cases would only be subject to review for purposes of recognition in the United States. One might wonder whether this far-reaching implication was intended by the Second Circuit or by Congress when enacting Section 202 of the USAA.

Interestingly, the Bergesen court did not actually examine whether any of the grounds of Article V of the New York Convention was met. Thus, the Bergesen case was in fact more akin to a confirmation case, and only borrowed the longer time limit provided by Section 207 of the USAA for recognition of foreign awards. This could have been prompted by the desire to help the winning party in the arbitration, which had failed to apply for confirmation within the one-year period provided by Section 9 of the FAA. The implications described above remain, however, and the uncertainty with it.

.   .   .

The unavailability of vacatur implied by Bergesen . . . presents a drawback. If no vacatur is available, the only remedy of a party having lost an arbitration as a result of fraud or other serious defect in the conduct of the arbitration is to resist enforcement of the award under the New York Convention. If the losing party was the defendant, denial of enforcement might be sufficient to protect the party victim of the fraud. However, when the losing party is the claimant, and its claim has been dismissed as a result of a fraud in the arbitration, then denial of enforcement of the award will hardly protect the party victim of the fraud. The award rejecting the claims as a result of a fraud will not come under the New York Convention because the Convention can come into play only to the extent that there is something to be enforced. Thus, the losing claimant is left with no recourse.

.    .    .

While it appears essential to avoid confusing vacating awards and denying them recognition, the concept of applying the same grounds to deny recognition of awards made in a foreign country and to vacate awards made at home in an international case is not devoid of merits. UNCITRAL's Model Law and the French Decree of 1981 both adopted this solution, and so did the German Law of 15 March 1961 for awards made outside Germany under German arbitration law. While the grounds are the same, however, the distinction between the two kinds of review remains. Contrary to a misconception, arbitration in France of international cases, even if between two foreign parties, is not considered as being 'non-domestic' for purposes of the New York Convention; resulting awards remain subject to vacatur in France.

### Notes and Questions

1.   As already mentioned, awards not enforceable under treaty may be enforced under national law. *See* New York Convention Article VII(1) and *Pabalk Ticaret Ltd. Sirketi v. S.A. Norsolor, supra* p. 203. When considering national control mechanisms, ask how they differ from their treaty analogues. *See, e.g.*, French Nouveau Code de procédure civile, Articles 1502-04 and UNCITRAL Model Law, Article 36, both set forth in the Supplement.

2.   In some cases, domestic control mechanisms may go beyond those provided under the New York Convention. What problems do you see in fitting Justice Blackmun's "second look" doctrine (announced in *Mitsubishi Motors*, excerpted below) into the New York Convention framework? What happens if the award is never presented for enforcement against assets in the United States? Would the "second look" doctrine prevent an award from having res judicata effect if the unhappy loser commenced litigation in the United States on the same issues decided by the arbitrator? The "second look" doctrine was formulated as follows in *Mitsubishi Motors Corp. v. Soler-Chrysler-Plymouth, Inc.*, 473 U.S. 614, 638 (1985):

> Having permitted the arbitration to go forward, the national courts of the United States will have the opportunity at the award enforcement stage to ensure that the legitimate interest in the enforcement of the antitrust laws has been addressed. The Convention reserves to each signatory country the right to refuse enforcement of an award where the "recognition or enforcement of the award would be contrary to the public policy of that country." Art. V(2)(b), 21 U.S.T., at 2520; see Scherk, 417 U.S., at 519, n.14, 94 S. Ct. at 2457 n.14. While the efficacy of the arbitral process requires that substantive review at the award enforcement stage remain minimal, review would not require intrusive inquiry

to ascertain that the tribunal took cognizance of the antitrust claims and actually decided them.

3. *Look at Iran v. Gould* and think about the "reciprocity requirement" of the U.S. reservation to the New York Convention, which provides that the Convention shall only apply to awards rendered in the territory of Convention contracting states. If an award rendered in the Netherlands is not subject to scrutiny by Dutch courts for procedural fairness, there will be no "primary" judicial control of the arbitral process at the place of arbitration. Does this matter? Why should the enforcement forum care about "primary" judicial control at the arbitral seat? Is it because awards benefit from presumptive validity and enforceability under the convention? Would concern over "stateless" awards make more sense if, as a condition for the award's enforcement, the Convention prescribed specific grounds for annulment (such as arbitrator corruption and excess of authority) at the place of arbitral proceedings?

4. To what extent are control mechanisms at the place of arbitration bound up with the enthusiasm of an enforcement forum to recognize foreign awards? Would judges in Azania be more likely or less likely to recognize an award rendered in Ruritania if it became known that Ruritanian judges affirmed awards procured by bribery?

5. The United States supported the Iranian position in *Iran v. Gould* in an Amicus Brief. Why? What would have happened if the Iranians did not replenish the escrow account with enough money to satisfy all awards in which U.S. nationals prevailed against Iran? Would there be a risk that the dissatisfied winner would sue the United States? *See Dames & Moore v. Reagan* discussed *supra* p. 1155.

6. Is the Tschanz article correct that awards covered by the New York Convention pursuant to Bergesen are not subject to vacatur in the United States? Why is it impossible for the same court to review an award both on a motion to vacate and a motion to recognize the award? Compare the reasoning and result in *Hiscox v. Outhwaite*, *supra* p. 1123.

7. For another case in which United States courts held Iranian Claims Tribunal awards subject to the New York Convention, see *Iran Aircraft v. Avco Corp.*, 980 F.2d 141 (2d Cir. 1992).

## G. ISSUES COMMON TO BOTH PRIMARY AND SECONDARY CONTROL OF AWARDS

In looking at national control mechanisms in the arbitral process, one should distinguish between the "primary" control of awards at the place where the award is rendered, and the "secondary" control exercised by courts in the country where the award is presented for enforcement or recognition. In large measure, national laws dealing with foreign arbitration have evolved separately from laws dealing with arbitration conducted locally.

Yet many of the issues facing courts at the place of the proceedings are (or should be) of concern to authorities asked to enforce the award at the situs of the parties' assets. For example, the arbitrators' fidelity to their mission has traditionally been a matter of common concern to judges at both the arbitral seat and the enforcement forum. The overlap between the bases for primary and secondary control can be seen in section 207 of the United States Arbitration Act. Confirmation of an award where rendered may refused for any of the defenses to enforcement of foreign awards under the New York Convention.

Some of the issues discussed below have also been mentioned in connection with judicial intervention at the time an arbitration is initiated. See Chapters 3 and 4. However, judicial controls exercised at the time the agreement is enforced are qualitatively different from those exercised after the award has been rendered. Courts asked only to enforce the arbitration agreement can only speculate as to what mischief arbitrators may do with a particular dispute. Judges asked to enforce or to recognize an award, however, have the benefit of seeing the mischief that the arbitrator may have already done.

## 1.  EXCESS OF AUTHORITY

Arbitration is a consensual process. This means first that for there to be an arbitration, the parties must agree to renounce recourse to ordinary courts in favor of a non-judicial resolution of the dispute. Second, because they derive their powers from the arbitration agreement, arbitrators must respect the parties' mandate as to the scope of the subject matter falling within their mission. Finally, the arbitrator must decide the dispute in the manner the parties authorized, in particular with respect to the application of substantive law and arbitral procedure.

Questions asked by judges faced with a request to annul or to refuse to enforce an award because of arbitral excess of jurisdiction have related to (i) parties (ii) subject matter and (iii) process.

(i) Did the parties agree to arbitrate?

(ii) Does the subject matter of the disputed issue fall within the scope of the agreement?

(iii) Did the arbitrator decide according to the substantive law set forth in the parties' mandate, and in the manner contemplated by the parties, including procedural aspects covered by the legal system (such as cross-examination) and procedural aspects of a more informal nature (hearings and meetings)?

Controlling an arbitrator's excess of authority may be the most important of these national judicial functions. A legal system will not normally support an arbitrator who renders an award against a person who did not sign the arbitration agreement, or an arbitrator who decides a dispute differently from the way the parties agreed he should. If two merchants agree that an arbitrator will settle disputes arising out of the sale of peaches, but have not agreed to arbitration for a later contract to sell pecans, then an award on pecans ought not to stand. Similarly, if the merchants agree that the arbitrator will apply English law, and he explicitly applies provisions of the Swiss Code des obligations, such a decision normally falls outside the arbitrator's jurisdiction.

Once courts get involved in correcting errors of arbitral jurisdiction, it may be difficult to keep them from deciding matters of contract interpretation. It is not always easy to trace the line separating mere error of law from an excess of adjudicatory authority. Indeed, there may be no intellectually satisfactory test for distinguishing between an arbitrator's excess of authority and an arbitrator's mere mistake in making a "bad award." The judge who corrects excess of authority risks imposing his own conclusions about the merits of the dispute.

If the arbitration agreement in the above example (about sale of peaches) instead vaguely referred to sales of "fruit," the scope of the arbitration agreement would be more problematic. A judge reviewing the award would be asked to consider whether the word "fruit" was used with its botanical meaning to include not just peaches, but also the contents of any seed plant's developed ovary, including pecans. Likewise, if the merchants absent-mindedly referred to the "laws of the United Kingdom," the judge might be called upon to determine whether that ambiguous designation was intended to refer to the law of

England, Scotland, or Northern Ireland. Finally, the arbitrator might argue that he was justified in applying mandatory norms (loi de police) of the place of performance that supersede the chosen law.

The following case illustrates how slippery an issue "excess of authority" can be.

a.    *Mobil Oil (Indo.) v. Asamera Oil (Indo.),*
       487 F.Supp. 63 (S.D.N.Y. 1980).

### OPINION

MacMAHON, Chief Judge.

[Asamera secured a concession agreement, the "Sumatra B Agreements," from Indonesia. In 1968 Asamera, in an "Assignment Agreement," assigned its interests to Mobil in return for an outright payment plus continuing ongoing royalty payments on crude oil production from the contract area. The Agreement chose New York law and ICC arbitration in New York. After Mobil discovered a rich deposit of natural gas, a dispute arose as to whether it was obliged to pay royalties on that or only on crude oil. In 1974, arbitration commenced. In 1979, a majority award was rendered requiring Mobil to pay royalties on all hydrocarbon production from the contract area in amounts equal to the royalty on crude oil. The panel also fixed a royalty on crude oil of $.04 per barrel, even though the assignment agreement had not specifically done so. Mobil sought to annul the award.]

.    .    .

Under § 10(d) of the Federal Arbitration Act, we may vacate the award if the arbitrators "exceeded their powers." Mobil contends that the majority here exceeded their powers in four respects: they (1) rewrote the Assignment Agreement by substituting new royalty provisions for the royalty provisions contained in Clause V(B)(1) of the Agreement; (2) failed to determine the dispute in accordance with New York law, as required by Clause XIV; (3) acted in manifest disregard of undisputed facts; and (4) made an award that is wholly irrational and inconsistent.

Before turning to these specific contentions, we must reiterate our Court of Appeals' recent injunction to accord the "narrowest of readings" to the excess-of-powers provision of § 10(d), especially where the contention is that the arbitrators failed correctly to decide a question conceded to have been properly submitted. Indeed, in *Andros Compania Maritima v. Marc Rich & Co.*, the court held:

> "When arbitrators explain their conclusions . . . in terms that offer even a barely colorable justification for the outcome reached, confirmation of the award cannot be prevented by litigants who merely argue, however persuasively, for a different result."

The reason for this rule is simply that in such a case it is the arbitrators' construction of the contract that was bargained for, not the courts,' presumably because the parties preferred at least the theoretical speed, informality, inexpensiveness and expertise of the arbitrators.

Here, there is no dispute that questions as to the nature and amounts of royalty payments were properly before the panel. The arbitration clause here was even broader than the one involved in *Andros Compania* in that it encompassed not only all disputes "arising out of" the contract, but also all those "relating to" the contract. Thus, the arbitrators had jurisdiction to decide the subject matter of the dispute. The only limitations on the exercise of this power were the Assignment Agreement's requirements that the arbitrators follow ICC rules and that the Agreement was to be "governed by" and "construed in accordance with" New York law.

We hold that the majority's 43-page statement of reasons gave at least a "barely colorable" justification for the outcome. Indeed, for each conclusion the majority gave several reasons, all of them based exclusively on New York law.

As to Mobil's obligation to pay a royalty on natural gas and liquid hydrocarbons other than crude oil, the majority stated, among other things, that the Assignment Agreement was ambiguous. Specifically, the term "crude oil," on which royalties were explicitly required, was never defined. The Agreement required Asamera and Benedum to give up all hydrocarbon rights in return for a cash payment and royalties on "crude oil," thus suggesting the possibility that "crude oil," despite its commonsense definition, was intended to be synonymous with "all hydrocarbons." In short, it was not entirely clear what definition the parties intended to give to the term.

The arbitrators were thus entitled, under New York rules of contract construction, to look to parol evidence of all the surrounding facts and circumstances and to construe the Agreement most strongly against the drafter, Mobil. The majority construed the term, in light of the negotiations underlying the Agreement and Mobil's occasional broad use of the term, to include natural gas and all liquid hydrocarbons. While we might make a different construction, we cannot say that the panel failed to apply New York rules of construction or gave reasons for its construction that did not rise to the low level of the "barely colorable."

Having decided that such a royalty was payable, the arbitrators made it substantially equivalent in amount to that required by Clause V(B)(1) of the Agreement, a result that seems not only colorable but eminently sensible, if indeed not logically required by the broad construction of the term "crude oil." As for the fixing of the crude oil royalty at 4 cents per barrel, this was proper since a contract "governed by" New York law is subject to reformation on grounds of mistake and unjust enrichment. The arbitrators found such grounds here.

The provision that royalty requirements extend through any extension of the Sumatra B Agreements simply resolves an ambiguity as to the duration of the Assignment Agreement. This provision is reasonable in that any benefit to Mobil resulting from any extension of the Sumatra B Agreements is ultimately traceable to respondents' transfer of their rights under those Agreements.

Finally, as to the provision that in order to effectuate the royalty payments respondents were to have access to Mobil's records, this remedial provision lay within the arbitrators' discretion under a broad arbitration clause such as this one to mold the remedy to the particular facts.

Thus, we conclude that the award cannot be vacated under 9 U.S.C. § 10(d). Mobil's first two contentions are belied by the arbitrators' application of principles of New York law to the dispute. The "undisputed facts" to which Mobil points were in fact in dispute, and the disputes were simply resolved against Mobil on conflicting evidence. Finally, we cannot say that the award is infested with "complete irrationality" or inconsistency. It is rather based on principles of contract interpretation, unjust enrichment and mistake. The amounts of the royalties required are derived from the provisions of the Assignment Agreement.

*    *    *

Compare the following British perspective on arbitrator excess of authority.

b.    MICHAEL J. MUSTILL & STEWART C. BOYD, THE LAW AND PRACTICE OF COMMERCIAL ARBITRATION IN ENGLAND 554-55 (2d ed. 1989).

### Excess of jurisdiction

An award will be entirely void if the parties never made a binding arbitration agreement; if the matters in dispute fell outside the scope of the agreement; if the arbitrator was not validly appointed, or lacked the necessary qualifications; or if the whole of the relief granted lay outside the powers of the arbitrator. The award will be partially void if the relief granted related to a matter which was not referred, or if for some other reason it was outside the jurisdiction of the arbitrator. In all these situations, the primary active remedy is for the Court to declare that the award is void, in whole or in part. Alternatively, the complaining party may wait until the time comes for enforcement of the award, and then rely on the want of jurisdiction as a defence.

It is, however, clearly established that the Court may, as an alternative to granting declaratory relief, set aside or remit the award. This is illogical. Want of jurisdiction makes an award void, not merely voidable; and the Court cannot set aside something which has no legal existence. Nevertheless, there is no doubt that the jurisdiction has been asserted. Whether the making of an award in excess of jurisdiction amounts to misconduct, or is a separate ground for relief, is not clear; the cases tend to suggest that the latter view is correct.

It is not always easy to distinguish between instances where there is a want of jurisdiction, and those where there is error of law or fact. A particular difficulty arises where the contract prescribes the remedy which must be granted in the event of a breach. In such a case if the arbitrator, having found a breach, mistakenly proceeds to award a remedy other than the one prescribed by the contract, is this outside his jurisdiction, so as to render the award void, or is it simply a mistake of law which, like a mistake as to the primary rights and obligations under the contract, does not amount to an excess of jurisdiction? It seems that the latter is the correct view, and that there is no distinction to be drawn in this connection between a mistake as to primary rights and obligations and a mistake as to the remedies prescribed by the contract. If, however, he applies the correct remedy, but does so in an incorrect way — for example by miscalculating the damages which the submission empowers him to award — then there is no excess of jurisdiction. An error, however gross, in the exercise of his powers does not take an arbitrator outside his jurisdiction and this is so whether his decision is on a matter of substance or procedure.

Where the award is made entirely without jurisdiction, in the sense that there has never been an effective arbitration at all, the appropriate remedy is to set the award aside. On the other hand, where there has been a valid arbitration, but the arbitrator has merely given relief which is outside his powers, the Court has a choice. Often, remission will be chosen, because it is cheaper to return to the same arbitrator than to begin the entire proceedings again. Where the award is defective only in part, and the good can be severed from the bad, the better course is to set aside the defective part rather than remit. Where severance is not possible, an order for remission should be made, with directions to the arbitrator to make a proper award.

When deciding whether there had been an excess of jurisdiction, the Court is not limited to the matters which appear on the face of the award. The scope of the disputes submitted to arbitration may be proved by extrinsic evidence. Where the allegation is made that there was no authority to make an award, there is no presumption in favour of the validity of the award, and the person relying upon it must show that it is valid. Where the dispute is merely whether the arbitrator has acted in excess of an admitted jurisdiction, it is for the party asserting the invalidity to prove it. The decision of the arbitrator as to the extent of his own jurisdiction has no binding effect.

## Notes and Questions

1. *Compare Inter-City Gas Corp. v. Boise Cascasde Corp.*, 845 F.2d 184 (8th Cir. 1988), concerning a dispute over the supply of natural gas. The arbitration awarded damages both to the supplier for under charges due to errors in quantity measurements and to the purchases for overcharge due to application of rates not permitted under the relevant regulatory framework. Each party moved to confirm the parts of the award in its favor and to vacate the adverse award. The Court concluded that the award against the supplier Inter-City should be vacated because it exceeded the arbitrator's powers, but that the award in its favor should be upheld. The Court stated that the arbitrator may "interpret ambiguous language [but] may not disregard plain and unambiguous contract provisions." *Id.*

2. Divergent interpretations of how well the arbitrator applied the law selected by the parties provide rich soil for controversies over arbitral excess of authority. One particularly troublesome matter has been the distinction between an arbitrator's deviation from the fundamental limits set on his authority by "manifestly" disregarding the law, and what might be called merely a "bad award" in which the arbitrator came to a different conclusion about the effect of the applicable law than the court that is reviewing the award. "Manifest disregard of the law" made its way into the arbitration vocabulary in dicta in the now overruled case of *Wilko v. Swan*, 346 U.S. 427, 436 (1953). At least one case, *Brandeis Intsel Ltd. v. Calabrian Chemicals Corp.*, 656 F.Supp. 160 (S.D.N.Y. 1987), has said that the concept of manifest disregard has not worked its way into the defenses to enforcement of an award under Article V of the New York Convention. Is this correct as a matter of policy? Does it matter in view of the wording of Article V(1)(c)? Does the absence of "manifest disregard" as a Convention defense mean that it is not or should not be grounds for setting aside an award where rendered?

3. Note the discussion of excess of authority in *Re Racal Communications Ltd.*, [1981] A.C. 374 at p. 383 per Lord Diplock:

> The break-through made by Anisminic [1969] 2 A.C. 147 was that, as respects administrative tribunals and authorities, the old distinction between errors of law that went to jurisdiction and errors of law that did not, was for practical purposes abolished. Any error of law that could be shown to have been made by them in the course of reaching their decision on matters of fact or of administrative policy would result in their having asked themselves the wrong question with the result that the decision they reached would be a nullity.

Why might this "breakthrough" for administrative proceedings turn out to be a disaster for commercial arbitration?

### 2.     "MANDATORY NORMS" (LOIS DE POLICE)

An arbitrator's intentional refusal to apply the law selected by the parties would, in theory, seem a clear excess of authority leading a court to set aside, or to refuse to recognize or enforce, the improper award. But in some cases, an arbitrator may actually be obligated to ignore the contract's choice of law clause, at least for some issues, in order to respect mandatory norms of the place of contract performance. The general choice-of-law principle that justifies disregard of party autonomy in the matter is set forth in Section 187 of RESTATEMENT (2ND) CONFLICT OF LAWS.

When the place of performance is also the enforcement forum, the arbitrators may find themselves between the Scylla of the arbitral seat (concerned about fidelity to the parties' intent) and the Charybdis of the enforcement forum (feeling compelled to safeguard the public's interest in compliance with mandatory norms). Such mandatory norms — often called lois de police in European legal literature — have already been mentioned earlier (*see supra* Chapter 3, Part III.) when we looked at the "prospective waiver" set forth in footnote 19 of *Mitsubishi Motors v. Soler Chrysler Plymouth* and the "second look" doctrine also announced in Mitsubishi. Recall that in footnote 19 of *Mitsubishi* the U.S. Supreme Court assumed (perhaps naively) that the arbitration would apply U.S. law to the antitrust issue notwithstanding that the contract by its express terms was governed by Swiss law, as set forth below:[317]

> In addition to the clause providing for arbitration before the Japan Commercial Arbitration Association, the Sales Agreement includes a choice-of-law clause which reads: "This Agreement is made in, and will be governed by and construed in all respects according to the laws of the Swiss Confederation as if entirely performed therein." App. 56. The United States raises the possibility that the arbitral panel will read this provision not simply to govern interpretation of the contract terms, but wholly to displace American law even where it otherwise would apply. Brief for United

---

[317] *Mitsubishi Motors Corp. v. Soler Chrysler-Plymouth, Inc.*, 473 U.S. 614 (1984).

States as Amicus Curiae 20. The International Chamber of Commerce opines that it is "[c]onceivabl[e], although we believe it unlikely, [that] the arbitrators could consider Soler's affirmative claim of anti-competitive conduct by CISA and Mitsubishi to fall within the purview of this choice-of-law provision, with the result that it would be decided under Swiss law rather than the U.S. Sherman Act." Brief for International Chamber of Commerce as Amicus Curiae 25. At oral argument, however, counsel for Mitsubishi conceded that American law applied to the antitrust claims and represented that the claims had been submitted to the arbitration panel in Japan on that basis. Tr. of Oral. Arg. 18. The record confirms that before the decision of the Court of Appeals the arbitral panel had taken these claims under submission.

The following materials explore the proper role of mandatory norms that might displace an otherwise valid choice of law in international commercial arbitration.

§187. Law of the State Chosen by the Parties

(1)    The law of the state chosen by the parties to govern their contractual rights and duties will be applied if the particular issue is one which the parties could have resolved by an explicit provision in their agreement directed to that issue.

(2)    The law of the state chosen by the parties to govern their contractual rights and duties will be applied, even if the particular issue is one which the parties could not have resolved by an explicit provision in their agreement directed to that issue, unless either

(a)    the chosen state has no substantial relationship to the parties or the transaction and there is no other reasonable basis for the parties' choice, or

(b)     application of the law of the chosen state would be contrary to a fundamental policy of a state which has a materially greater interest than the chosen state in the determination of the particular issue and which, under the rule of §188, would be the state of the applicable law in the absence of an effective choice of law by the parties.

(3)     In the absence of a contrary indication of intention, the reference is to the local law of the state of the chosen law.

\*     \*     \*

Article 7, European Convention on Laws Applicable to Contractual Obligation

## Mandatory Rules

1.     When applying under this Convention the law of a country, effect may be given to the mandatory rules of the law of another country with which the situation has a close connection, if and in so far as, under the law of the latter country, those rules must be applied whatever the law applicable to the contract. In considering whether to give effect to these mandatory rules, regard shall be had to their nature and purpose and to the consequences of their application or non-application.

2.     Nothing in this Convention shall restrict the application of the rules of the law of the forum in a situation where they are mandatory irrespective of the law otherwise applicable to the contract.

William W. Park, *National Law and Commercial Justice* 63 TUL. L. REV. 647, 668-70 (1989).

Application of the parties' chosen law may lead to an unenforceable award if that law violates the public policy of the country of performance. But an arbitrator who ignores the parties' choice of law, in order to respect mandatory norms of the country of performance, may invite challenge at the place of arbitration for excess of authority. The landmark Supreme Court decision in Mitsubishi Motors Corp. v. Soler Chrysler-Plymouth, Inc. illustrates the arbitrator's dilemma.

In Mitsubishi, the dispute arose out of an automobile distribution agreement between a Japanese manufacturer and an American automobile dealer. Swiss law governed the contract, but the dispute raised an antitrust counterclaim under the United States Sherman Act. The United States Supreme Court ordered arbitration in the case, but warned that in the future it would condemn, as against public policy, a choice of law clause that operated as a "prospective waiver" of the right to pursue Sherman Act claims. The Supreme Court ordered arbitration on the assumption (perhaps naive, and perhaps incorrect) that the arbitrator would apply the Sherman Act to the antitrust counterclaims, even though the contract contained a Swiss choice of law.

More importantly, three sentences of dicta at the end of the majority opinion predicted, on the basis of the New York Convention's explicit "public policy defense," that American courts will have another bite at the arbitration apple when the time comes to enforce the award, to determine whether claims under American antitrust law were addressed. This dicta has come to be known as the second look doctrine. It is uncertain if the second look involves a broad examination of whether the arbitrator properly applied the law, or merely involves a mechanical examination of whether the arbitrator in fact considered the American statute.

Mitsubishi thus exacts a problematic price for arbitrability of antitrust matters. Judicial review of the contents of awards, at least for their conformity with public policy, is the cost for letting the dispute go to arbitration.

In a situation like Mitsubishi the arbitrator is in a bind. If a contract includes a choice of law clause explicitly selecting the legal system of a country whose competition law fundamentally differs from that of the enforcement forum, the arbitrator, mindful of Justice Blackmun's caveat, may nevertheless decide the antitrust claims according to United States law. This departure from the parties' express choice of Swiss law might increase the award's chances of enforcement in the United States, but could open the door to a challenge of the award outside the United States not once, but twice. First, the loser in an arbitration in which the Sherman Act was applied could be expected to seek annulment of the award where rendered, on the theory that the arbitrator decided inconsistently with his mission, which is a ground for review in most major arbitral centers. Annulment would make the award more difficult to enforce throughout the world, because the New York Convention permits refusal of recognition to awards set aside in the country where made.

Departure from the parties' chosen law also might result in a challenge to enforcement of the award against assets outside the jurisdiction in which the award is rendered. Article V(1)(c) of the New York Convention permits the refusal of enforcement to awards when arbitrators decide matters not submitted to them, which is not a totally unreasonable characterization of an adjudication of Sherman Act claims under a Swiss governing law clause.

Because the mandatory national norms of the enforcement forum, often called lois de police, arguably may apply notwithstanding the parties' choice of law clause, the arbitrator could be required to choose whether to give effect to the will of the parties, or to respect the imperative rules of a country with a vital interest in the subject of the dispute. Such an interest might exist in matters such as competition law, currency controls, trade boycott, environmental protection, and bribery. Even if compatible with the policy of the place of arbitration, an award might run afoul of the mandatory public law of the place of performance, thus giving rise to a refusal of recognition of the award under article V(2) of the New York Convention.

\*     \*     \*

The problem of finding the thin line between merits review by courts to correct errors, and review for excess of authority, plagues judges even in non-arbitral contexts. For purposes of illustration, consider the following English cases concerning county courts and administrative tribunals.

## Notes and Questions

1. Recall that Article V(l)(d) of the New York Convention permits refusal of recognition and enforcement to an award when the composition of the arbitral authority was not in accordance with the parties' agreement. In the *MINE* case (*supra* p. 460), involving a Liechtenstein entity and an African government, courts in the United States and Switzerland had to decide whether to enforce an award rendered pursuant to one set of institutional rules (those of the AAA) rather than the rules agreed on by both of the parties (ICSID), when one party unilaterally decided to institute an arbitration under the former rather than the latter. *See Maritime Int'l Nominees Establishment v. Republic of Guinea*, 693 F.2d 1094 (1983) and its Swiss sequel decided by the Geneva Tribunal de première instance, March 13, 1986, 5 ASA BULLETIN 24, 28 (1987); 1 FOREIGN INVESTMENT L.J. (ICSID REV.) (1986).

2. Refer back to Chapter 6 Part IV.C.3 and the materials in discussion there. In the *Westinghouse v. Republic of the Philippines* arbitration, did the tribunal take account of mandatory rules of law?

## 3.    FUNDAMENTAL PROCEDURAL FAIRNESS

Whether referred to as "due process" in the United States, "natural justice" in England, or "adversarial procedure" in France, most countries have notions of fundamental fairness without which a dispute resolution process lacks legitimacy. In some cases concern for procedural fairness overlaps concern about respect for the arbitrator's mission. For example, many courts would label intentional application of the wrong law as a violation of fundamental fairness expected by the parties. One could also reverse the characterization, and label lack of fairness as an excess of authority by the arbitrator, since the parties presumably never authorized a procedure in which fundamental fairness would be disregarded. The following cases deal with allegations of two of the most frequently encountered forms of procedural unfairness: duress and fraud.

*Biotronik v. Medford Medical Instrument Co.*, 415 F.Supp. 133 (D.N.J. 1976).

BROTMAN, District Judge.

This is an action to enforce an arbitration award entered by the International Chamber of Commerce Court of Arbitration at Berne, Switzerland, on December 30, 1974. The petitioner, Biotronik Mess-und Therapiegeraete GmbH & Co., (hereafter 'Biotronik') is a West German manufacturer of implantable cardiac pacemakers and accessories. The respondent, Medford Medical Instrument Co. (hereafter 'Medford'), a New Jersey corporation with its principal place of business in Medford, New Jersey, served as Biotronik's American distributor from December 1969 until January 1972.

The action arises under the United Nations Convention on the Recognition and Enforcement of Foreign Arbitral Awards, [1970] 3 U.S.T. 2517, T.I.A.S. No. 6997, and 9 U.S.C. § 201. The application to confirm the award is brought pursuant to 9 U.S.C. § 207, and is before the court by motion. Jurisdiction of the court is conferred by 9 U.S.C. §203 and 28 U.S.C. § 1331.

## Facts

Medford's distributorship arrangement consisted of two written agreements. In the First Agreement, executed on December 20, 1969, Biotronik granted Medford the exclusive right to market its products in the United States until February 1, 1971. On January 16, 1971, the parties negotiated a second exclusive-distributorship agreement that was to run for a period of twelve months beginning February 1, 1971. In October of 1971, Biotronik exercised its right to terminate the Second Agreement at the end of one year. Biotronik subsequently appointed another firm, Concept Inc., to be its new American distributor.

Six months later, in June, 1972, a dispute arose over several shipments of products that Biotronik had made to Medford immediately prior to the termination of the Second Agreement. Biotronik demanded payment for four shipments of goods in the amount of $65,403.60. Medford did not deny its liability for the shipments, but by letter dated July 17, 1972 claimed to possess breach-of-contract claims arising out of alleged oral promises by Biotronik to renew Medford's distributorship, and other grounds. Medford proposed a mutual renunciation of claims, which Biotronik rejected. . . .

. . .

The Second Agreement contained the following provision for the resolution of such disputes:

> 13.    In the event of any controversy or claim arising out of or related to any provision of this agreement, or the breach thereof, the parties shall attempt to reach an amicable settlement. If they fail to agree, the dispute shall be settled under the Rules of Conciliation and Arbitration of the International Chamber of Commerce, Paris, France, by three arbitrators appointed in accordance with the laws then prevailing. The arbitration shall take place in Berne, Switzerland. German material law (Materielles Recht) and German law of procedure (Prozessrecht) must be applicated [sic]. The award shall be final and binding and may be entered in any court having jurisdiction or application may be made to any court for judicial acceptance of the award or an order for enforcement, as the case may be.

When the parties were unable to reach a settlement, Biotronik, on February 14, 1973, submitted the matter to arbitration pursuant to the above contractual provision. Medford apparently had notice of the pendency of the arbitration, since it submitted to the panel a copy of its July 17, 1972 letter which served as a denial of Biotronik's claims. Opinion of the Arbitrators ¶ 5. In any event, Medford pointedly does not attack the adequacy of notice in this court. Biotronik ultimately prevailed in the arbitration and was awarded the sum of $56,306.78 together with interest and costs.

### The Third Agreement

Medford's opposition to the enforcement of the arbitration award is based on a document that it characterizes as the 'Third Agreement.' This agreement was purportedly executed on January 31, 1972, one day prior to the termination of Medford's distributorship. Written in the handwriting of Medford's president on a sheet of its stationery, the Third Agreement reads in its entirety:

Stating that a 5% Commission is to be paid to Medford
Medical Instrument Co. on the total sales of Biotronik
Pacemakers in the United States for the first year 1972
and a 3% Commission will be paid for the second year
1973. This is to Medford Medical for helping Concept
get started in the U.S. market.

According to Medford, this agreement entitled it to commissions
on the total sales of Biotronik's pacemakers in the United States for
two years after the termination of the distributorship. Medford further
alleges that the parties agreed to credit the commissions against any
outstanding sums owed by Medford to Biotronik. Medford maintains
that it never owed Biotronik the amount awarded in the arbitration
proceeding because the commissions, which were never paid, either
offset or exceeded Biotronik's original claim.

.     .     .

## Medford's Defenses, Part I

Medford's first two defenses consist of alternative legal
theories, both of which are based upon Biotronik's failure to offer any
evidence concerning the Third Agreement to the arbitration panel.
Firstly, Medford argues that Biotronik's non-disclosure renders the
award 'procured by . . . fraud' within the meaning of § 10(a) of the
United States Arbitration Act, 9 U.S.C. § 10(a), and that fraud, even
though not one of the defenses enumerated in Article V of the
Convention, became a defense through the incorporation provision of
9 U.S.C. § 208. Secondly, Medford argues that fraud, even if not
available as a defense through the operation of § 208, constitutes a
defense within the 'public policy' defense of Article V(2)(b) of the
Convention. For these reasons Medford urges this court to stay the
enforcement of the award and order another arbitration proceeding
pursuant to 9 U.S.C. § 3.

It is apparent that both of Medford's defenses turn upon whether
there is an adequate basis to hold that the award was procured through
fraud. Medford contends that Biotronik, when it appeared alone at the
arbitration hearing, knowingly withheld evidence concerning the Third
Agreement and engaged in a calculated attempt to mislead the
arbitrators. Biotronik responds by arguing that, in an adversary system
of justice, the failure of one side to prove the other side's case cannot

constitute a fraud. On this record, the court concurs with Biotronik, and is unable to conclude that Biotronik's conduct should be denominated fraud within § 10(a).

Most courts have held that an arbitration award is not fraudulently obtained within the meaning of § 10(a) of the United States Arbitration Act when the protesting party had an opportunity to rebut his opponent's claims at the arbitration hearing. *E.g., Kirschner v. West Co.*, 247 F.Supp. 550 (E.D.PA.), *aff'd per curiam*, 353 F.2d 537 (3rd Cir. 1965), *cert. denied*, 383 U.S. 945, 86 S.Ct. 1202, 16 L.Ed.2d 208 (1966); *Karppinen v. Karl Kiefer Machine Co.*, 187 F.2d 32 (2nd Cir. 1951). *Karppinen* was one of the earliest discussions of this issue; there the party resisting enforcement alleged that the award had been obtained through the knowing use of perjured testimony. The court responded to this argument by saying:

> We note only in passing that if perjury is "fraud" within the meaning of the statute then, since it necessarily raises issues of credibility which have already been before the arbitrators once, the party relying on it must first show that he could not have discovered it during the arbitration, else he should have invoked it as a defense at that time. 187 F.2d at 35.

Similar reasoning is applicable here. If, in fact, Biotronik knowingly concealed evidence—that is, the Third Agreement—from the arbitration panel, such misrepresentation would be analogous to perjured testimony. While fraud may arise from an omission of material fact as well as an affirmative statement, *Gibbons v. Brandt*, 170 F.2d 385, 391 (7th Cir. 1948), *cert. denied*, 336 U.S. 910, 69 S.Ct. 511, 93 L.Ed. 1074 (1949); *Northwest Airlines, Inc. v. Air Line Pilots Ass'n, International*, 385 F.Supp. 634, 637 (D.D.C.1974), *Karppinen* suggests that the focus under § 10(a) is upon whether the protesting party had an opportunity to discover and reveal the purported fraud at the arbitration hearing. Since Medford was certainly aware of the pendency of the arbitration proceedings, see note 7, *supra*, it was capable of invoking fraud as a defense at that time.

*Catz American Co. v. Pearl Grange Fruit Exchange, Inc.*, 292 F.Supp. 549 (S.D.N.Y.1968) presents another analogous situation. In that case the plaintiff offered the testimony of two alleged brokers in the disputed transaction. The arbitration panel, however, never called for their production. The defendant claimed that the arbitrator's failure to call these witnesses was sufficient to vacate the award, even though the defendant had never attempted to compel the witnesses to testify. The court rejected the defendant's theory:

> It does not appear, on the other hand, that Pearl requested Catz to produce Imperial. If Pearl believed Imperial's testimony to be relevant or essential, it could have requested the arbitrators to summon Imperial by exercising their powers pursuant to 9 U.S.C. § 7, which it did not do, with the result that its real objection now is that Catz should have produced Imperial regardless of the arbitrators' decision in the matter. 292 F.Supp. at 553.

Medford's complaint is the same; it urges fraud when its real objection is that Biotronik should have presented evidence favorable to Medford's case. The court's holding in Catz, that a party cannot complain about the nonproduction of evidence when it failed to offer such evidence itself, is applicable with equal force in this case.

Policy considerations similarly point in the same direction. In Karppinen, supra, Judge Augustus N. Hand wrote that

> It goes without saying that there should be great hesitation in upsetting an arbitration award. The award . . . must stand unless it is made abundantly clear that it was obtained through "corruption, fraud or undue means." 187 F.2d at 34 (footnote omitted).

More recently, the Third Circuit observed that the fact that an arbitration award may be vacated upon a showing of fraud

> does not obliterate the hesitation with which courts should view efforts to re-examine awards. [Citing Karppinen.] To do otherwise would defeat the primary advantages of speed and finality which led to the development of arbitration in business disputes . . . . Newark Stereotypers' Union No. 18 v. Newark Morning Ledger Co., 397 F.2d 594, 598 (3rd Cir.) (footnote

omitted), *cert. denied*, 393 U.S. 954, 89 S. Ct. 378, 21
L. Ed. 2d 365 (1968).

*See generally* Annotation, *Vacation of Arbitration Awards*, 20 A.L.R.
Fed. 295 §§ 2(b), 5 (1974). The stated advantages of arbitration apply
equally to the international context, *see, e.g.*, Contini, *International
Commercial Arbitration*, 8 Am.J.Comp.L. 283 (1959), and so the court
will likewise require a convincing showing before upsetting an
international arbitration award.

Furthermore, in international commercial arbitration
considerations of international reciprocity furnish an additional reason
to construe defenses narrowly. The Second Circuit in *Parsons &
Whittemore, supra*, 508 F.2d at 973, noted the 'pro-enforcement bias
informing the Convention,' and, first addressing the public policy
defense in Article V(2)(b) of the Convention, concluded that

> considerations of reciprocity—considerations given express
> recognition in the Convention itself—counsel courts to invoke
> the public policy defense with caution lest foreign courts
> frequently accept it as a defense to enforcement of arbitral
> awards rendered in the United States. *Id.* at 973-74 (footnote
> omitted).

*See also Scherk v. Alberto-Culver Co.*, 417 U.S. 506, 516-17, 94 S.Ct.
2449, 41 L.Ed.2d 270 (1974). The court in *Parsons & Whittemore*
went on to hold that other defenses should be narrowly construed for
the same reasons, 508 F.2d at 976, and so Medford's novel defense
here should be likewise narrowly construed.

It is evident that Biotronik merely presented its best theory for
recovery before the arbitration panel; there is no allegation, nor could
there be, that its actions prevented Medford from presenting its case.
If the true state of affairs was contrary to Biotronik's version,
Medford, which had contradictory evidence in its possession, should
have come forward with it. The court determines, therefore, that the
facts cannot sustain Medford's defense of fraud.

Since the court fails to find fraud in the procurement of the
arbitration award, the court does not reach, and therefore expresses no
opinion upon, Medford's contention that the defense of fraud within 9

U.S.C. § 10(a) may be asserted in an enforcement action under the Convention by reason of 9 U.S.C. § 208. *See Parsons & Whittemore, supra*, 508 F.2d at 977.

Medford's alternative fraud defense is based on the public policy defense of Article V(2)(b) of the Convention which states:

> 2.    Recognition and enforcement of an arbitral award may also be refused if the competent authority in the country where recognition and enforcement is sought finds that:
>
> .    .    .
>
> (b)    The recognition or enforcement of the award would be contrary to the public policy of that country.

Medford reasons that since fraudulent procurement of an arbitration award would be grounds for vacating an award in domestic arbitration under § 10(a), this is tantamount to a declaration that the enforcement of any fraudulently obtained award is contrary to the public policy of the United States. As such, Medford argues, enforcement should be denied through Article V(2)(b).

Because Medford has been unable to establish fraud under § 10(a), the public policy defense of Article V of the Convention is *a fortiori* inapplicable. For the reasons reviewed *supra*, the Second Circuit has held with respect to the public policy defense that '[e]nforcement of foreign arbitral awards may be denied on this basis only where enforcement would violate the forum state's most basic notions of morality and justice.' *Parsons & Whittemore, supra*, 508 F.2d at 974 (2nd Cir. 1974); *Fotochrome, Inc. v. Copal Co., Ltd.*, 517 F.2d 512, 516 (2nd Cir. 1975). Since the court did not find fraud within § 10(a), it is distinctly incapable of finding that the award violated our 'most basic notions of morality and justice.'

*Medford's Defenses, Part II*

Medford also argues that enforcement should be denied under Article V(1)(b) of the Convention which provides:

1.      Recognition and enforcement of the award may be refused, at the request of the party against whom it is invoked, only if that party furnishes to the competent authority where the recognition and enforcement is sought, proof that:

.      .      .      .      .

(b) The party against whom the award is invoked was not given proper notice of the appointment of the arbitrator or of the arbitration proceedings or was otherwise unable to present his case.

Medford does not contend that it received inadequate notice or was otherwise prevented from participating in the proceedings. Rather, it argues that it was 'unable to present its case' within the meaning of Article V(1)(b) because its rights and liabilities did not mature, and could not be calculated, under the Third Agreement, until that agreement expired at the end of 1973.

[5] This theory misconceives the thrust of the exception. 'This provision essentially sanctions the application of the forum state's standards of due process.' *Parsons & Whittemore, supra*, 508 F.2d at 975. The primary elements of due process are notice of the proceedings and the opportunity to be heard thereon. *Fuentes v. Shevin*, 407 U.S. 67, 80, 92 S.Ct. 1983, 32 L.Ed.2d 556 (1972); *Goldberg v. Kelly*, 397 U.S. 254, 267, 90 S.Ct. 1011, 25 L.Ed.2d 287 (1970); *Sniadach v. Family Finance Corp.*, 395 U.S. 337, 89 S.Ct. 1820, 23 L.Ed.2d 349 (1969).

[6] Medford's due process rights under American law were not infringed under the facts of this case. It received notice of the proceedings; it offers no explanation of its failure to participate. If, as Medford alleges, the Third Agreement prevented its rights from maturing until 1973, it had every opportunity to offer that document and any other extrinsic evidence in support of its position. If Biotronik's initiation of arbitration was untimely, Medford easily could have made this fact known to the arbitration panel. Neither the actions of Biotronik nor the actions of the panel had any effect upon Medford's ability to present its case.

Accordingly, the motion to confirm the award will be granted. Counsel for petitioner to submit an appropriate order.

## Notes and Questions

1. Should there be a double standard — one for domestic and another for international transactions — in notions of fairplay? Fears of American-style discovery have been reported to account for much of the traditional reluctance of non-Americans to choose the United States as a situs for arbitration. Should arbitrators be held to standards appropriate for court litigation? *See Hunt v. Mobil Oil Corp.*, 583 F.Supp. 1092 (S.D.N.Y. 1984); *Coastal State Trading, Inc. v. Zenith Navigation S.A.*, 446 F.Supp. 330 (S.D.N.Y. 1977); *and Commercial Solvents Corp. v. Louisiana Liquid F. Co.*, 20 F.R.D. 359 (S.D.N.Y. 1957).

2. What about cross-examination, which is virtually unknown in non-criminal proceedings in many European countries? Should arbitrators sitting in international cases be given latitude to fashion less parochial and more universal procedural norms? What about arbitrator independence? Is it sufficient that an arbitrator show lack of a financial interest in the outcome of the arbitration? Or should the arbitrator be impartial to the extent of being free from social and professional links with the parties?

3. In *Transmarine Seaways Corp. v. Marc Rich*, 480 F.Supp. 352 (S.D.N.Y. 1979), an arbitral award arising out of a charterparty dispute gave rise to a motion to vacate the award because of allegations of duress in conclusion of the agreement and bias in an arbitrator. Both allegations were rejected. Portions of the case are set forth *supra*, p. 1036.

## 4.    PROPER PARTY

In Chapter 4, we saw how the identity of the party that agreed to arbitrate becomes relevant when courts are asked to compel arbitration, particularly if related corporate entities are involved. Similar issues arise when the arbitration is over and an award has been rendered against someone who claims never to have consented to the abandonment of the jurisdiction of any courts that would otherwise have jurisdiction. "Will the real party please stand up?" was asked by French courts in the following case.

*Southern Pacific Properties v. Arab Republic of Egypt* (Cour de cassation 1987), 26 ILM 1004 (1987)

For the text of this case, see Chapter 4, *supra* p. 487.

### Notes and Questions

1. The question "Who are the proper parties to the arbitration?" is also asked at other stages in the arbitral process, notably when a court is asked to enforce an agreement to arbitrate and when the arbitrators determine their jurisdiction.

## 5. PUBLIC POLICY

The catch-all phrase "public policy" might serve as a justification for all judicial control of the arbitral process.

For example, it should be against a forum's public policy to enforce an award rendered in excess of the arbitrator's jurisdiction, covering matters not within the arbitrator's mandate. Similarly, a court would be justified on public policy grounds in refusing to enforce an award rendered without any respect for fundamental notions of procedural fairplay, including fraud and duress.

"Public policy" may also have an existence of its own, however. For example, violation of public policy constitutes an independent ground for refusal of recognition to a foreign award under Article V(2)(b) of the New York Convention. Look again at *Parsons & Whittemore Overseas Co., Inc. v. Societe Generale De L'Industrie Du Papier (RAKTA)*, 508 F.2d 969 (2d Cir. 1974) and then consider the following cases and comment which explore the meaning of "public policy" for American courts.

a. *Antco Shipping Co., Ltd. v. Sidermar S.p.A.*, 417 F.Supp. 207 (S.D.N.Y. 1976).

*Memorandum*

HAIGHT, District Judge:

[A contract of affreightment for transport of oil from Libya to the Bahamas included a clause excluding Israel from possible Mediterranean loading ports. An arbitration clause specified New York as the venue. A motion was brought to stay the arbitration.]

. . .

Assuming that Antco has correctly described the derivation of the "excluding Israel" phrase, I hold that its presence and effect in this contract do not offend the public policy of the United States as declared in the Export Administration Act of 1969 and its accompanying regulations. That is because the Sidermar/Antco contract of affreightment does not involve, in any meaningful sense, United States exporters, or exports from the United States. This is a contract between an Italian shipowner and a Bahamian charterer for the ocean carriage of cargoes from Mediterranean ports to Caribbean or, at Antco's option, American ports, in which event the contract would give rise to imports, not exports, in respect of the United States. Antco attempts to endow the contract with a U.S. export flavor by reference to the provision in Article 9 that Sidermar intended to perform the contract "with combined carriers which will load dry cargoes for their own account as back-haul voyage to Mediterranean." But even if I assume that the eastbound dry cargo voyages were from United States ports (there is no evidence on the point before me), they do not bear so close a relationship to the obligations of the parties before the Court as to bring the export statute into play, or to invalidate the contract in consequence. The only purpose of referring to the back-haul trade in the Sidermar/Antco contract is to explain why Sidermar might not be able to give Antco "exact scheduling" in respect of loading dates in the Mediterranean.

Antco argues that certain phrases in the statute are so broad that they should be regarded as declaring a public policy entirely independent of the export context. It is true that Section 3(5) of the statute, 50 U.S.C.App. § 2402(5), contains phrases that, considered in isolation, would appear to declare a general policy against any "restrictive trade practices or boycotts fostered or imposed by foreign countries against other countries friendly to the United States." However, the *implementation* given by statute and regulations alike to the statute's declarations of policy relate solely to control of exports from the United States. I am not disposed to extend the boundaries of that implementation beyond what the Congress and executive branch themselves have done, particularly where the effect of such an extension would be to deprive parties of bargained-for contractual benefits and remedies.

Furthermore, Sidermar is right in saying that the United States favors arbitration clauses in contracts touching upon international commerce. The nation speaks in different tongues and at different

CHAPTER 9 CONTROL MECHANISMS

times; cases arise where the determination of "public policy" must be a distillation of several governmental utterances.

. . .

In the case at bar, Sidermar directly invokes the Convention, as implemented by Chapter 2 of the United States Arbitration Act, 9 U.S.C. §§ 201-208. I hold that Sidermar's reliance is well founded. The arbitration agreement in the contract between two foreign corporations falls within the Convention. 9 U.S.C. § 202. This Court has jurisdiction to entertain Sidermar's cross- petition. 9 U.S.C. § 203. Venue is properly laid here, since the arbitration is to take place within the district. 9 U.S.C. § 207. The Court has the power to compel arbitration under 9 U.S.C. § 206 . . . .

To be sure, Article II(3) of the Convention provides:

"The court of a Contracting State, when seized of an action in a matter in respect of which the parties have made an agreement within the meaning of this article, shall, at the request of one of the parties, refer the parties to arbitration, *unless it finds that the said agreement is null and void,* inoperative or incapable of being performed." (emphasis added)

The phrase "null and void" opens the door to an argument for non-enforcement based on illegality; but I construe the phrase to require a showing by the party resisting enforcement of the agreement that the essence of the obligation or remedy is prohibited by a pertinent statute or other declaration of public policy. . . .

. . .

No such showing is made in the case at bar. The "performance which is the subject of the dispute" is Antco's obligation to furnish cargoes to Sidermar's vessels at Mediterranean (or, at *Antco's* option, Nigerian) ports. Israeli ports are excluded; but assuming arguendo that the exclusion in some manner contravenes public policy as expressed in the Export Regulation Act, it still falls far short of entirely forbidding Antco's performance under the contract.

A narrow construction of the Convention's "public policy" defense is supported by *Parsons & Whittemore Overseas Co., Inc. v. Societe Generale de L'Industrie du Papier*, 508 F.2d 969 (2d Cir. 1974), in which we find a more recent consideration by the Second Circuit of the Convention. In *Parsons* enforcement was sought in this court of a foreign arbitral award. While the present case involves enforcement of the arbitration agreement rather than enforcement of the award, comparable questions of public policy arise; thus Article V(2)(b) of the Convention allows the court in which enforcement of a foreign arbitral award is sought to refuse enforcement if "enforcement of the award would be contrary to the public policy of [the forum] country." Enforcement of the arbitration award in Parsons was resisted on the theory that the public policy of the United States would be offended by enforcement. This court confirmed the award, and the Second Circuit affirmed. After reviewing the purposes and drafting of the Convention, the Second Circuit stated:

> "We conclude, therefore, that the Convention's public policy defense should be construed narrowly. Enforcement of foreign arbitral awards may be denied on this basis only where enforcement would violate the forum state's most basic notions of morality and justice. Cf. 1 Restatement Second of the Conflict of Laws § 117, comment c, at 340 (1971); *Loucks v. Standard Oil Co.*, 224 N.Y. 99, 111, 120 N.E. 198 (1918)." 508 F.2d at 974.

This rationale applies with equal force to considerations, within the context of enforcement of the arbitration agreement itself, of whether the contract in question is "null and void" under Article II(3) of the Convention.

Furthermore, in *Parsons* the Second Circuit emphasized that the adherence of the United States to the Convention constitutes, in itself, a significant statement of public policy. The Court stated:

> "To read the public policy defense as a parochial device protective of national political interests would seriously undermine the Convention's utility. This provision was not meant to enshrine the vagaries of international politics under the rubric of 'public policy.' Rather, a circumscribed public policy doctrine was contemplated

by the Convention's framers and every indication is that
the United States, in acceding to the Convention, meant
to subscribe to this supra-national emphasis. Cf. *Scherk
v. Alberto-Culver Co.*, 417 U.S. 506, 94 S.Ct. 2449, 41
L.Ed.2d 270 (1974)." 508 F.2d at 974.

The contract in *Parsons*, between an American construction
company and an Egyptian company, called for the building of a paper
mill in Egypt. The project was funded by the United States State
Department, through the A.I.D. program. Before completion of
construction, the Egyptian government broke off diplomatic relations
with the United States, and ordered all Americans out of Egypt. The
State Department instructed the American company to cease
performance of the contract, in accordance with the provisions of 22
U.S.C. § 2370(p), (q), (t), which prohibited the furnishing of
assistance to the United Arab Republic subsequent to the cessation of
diplomatic relations with that country. The American company
complied; the Egyptian company demanded arbitration before the
International Chamber of Commerce, as provided for in the agreement;
and that tribunal held the American company in breach of contract.
Against this background, the American company contended in this
court that enforcement of the award would contravene United States
public policy. The Second Circuit held that the American company's
argument erroneously equated "national" policy with United States
"public policy"; and concluded:

> "To deny enforcement of this award largely because of
> the United States' falling out with Egypt in recent years
> would mean converting a defense intended to be of
> narrow scope into a major loophole in the Convention's
> mechanism for enforcement. We have little hesitation,
> therefore, in disallowing Overseas' proposed public
> policy defense." 508 F.2d at 974.

I conclude that, in the circumstances of this case, enforcement
of the arbitration agreement in the Sidermar/Antco contract would not
contravene the public policy of the United States.

*       *       *

b.      *Laminoirs-Trefileries-Cableries de Lens, S. A. v. Southwire Co.*, 484 F.Supp. 1063 (N.D. Ga. 1980).

TIDWELL, District Judge.

[Action to vacate an award rendered between a French company and a Georgia corporation.]

.    .    .

It is also contended that the award of interest should not be enforced as being usurious and against public policy. In making their award, the arbitrators determined that under the French law, the applicable annual rate for the time periods in question should be 10½% and 9½% (depending upon the date of maturity of the underpaid invoice), "increasing to fifteen and a half percent and fourteen and a half percent respectively after two months from the date of notification of the award

.    .    .

Article V, par. 2(b) of the United Nations Convention on the Recognition and Enforcement of Foreign Arbitral Awards, 9 U.S.C.A. § 201 *et seq.*, provides that enforcement of an award may be refused if such enforcement would be contrary to the public policy of the country where enforcement is sought. However, enforcement of foreign arbitral awards may be denied on this basis only where enforcement would violate the forum country's most basic notions of morality and justice. *Parsons & Whittemore Overseas Co. v. Societe Generale De L'Industrie Du Papier (RAKTA)*, 508 F.2d 969, 974 (2d Cir. 1974). *See also Gulf States Telephone Co. v. Local 1692, International Brotherhood of Electrical Workers*, 416 F.2d 198, 201 (5th Cir. 1969).

While the exaction of usury (". . . [taking] a greater sum for the use of money than the lawful interest." *Ga. Code Ann.* § 57-102) has been characterized by the Georgia Supreme Court as "odious, illegal, and immoral," *First Federal Savings & Loan Assoc. of Atlanta v. Norwood Realty Co.*, 212 Ga. 524, 527, 93 S.E.2d 763 (1956), the arbitrators concluded that the Georgia legal rate (7% per annum where the rate is not named in the contract, *see Ga. Code Ann.* § 57-101

(1979)) was not applicable under the governing law clause. In Georgia, rates of interest of 9½% and 10½% are not prohibited per se. The legal rate may be as high as 10 1/2% per annum where the parties agree to such in writing, *Ga. Code Ann.* § 57-101 (1979); the rate of interest on a principal sum exceeding $3,000 loaned to a profit corporation may be set without limit by the parties in writing, *Ga. Code Ann.* § 57-118 (1979); interest rates on loans of $100,000 or more are limited only by the agreement of the parties in writing, *Ga. Code Ann.* § 57-119. The existence of these statutes sufficiently convinces the Court that the exaction of interest rates of 9½% and 10½% per annum are not such as would violate this country's or this state's most basic notions of morality and justice. *See Parsons & Whittemore Overseas Co. v. (RAKTA), supra*, 508 F.2d at 974. We cannot have trade and commerce in world markets and international waters exclusively on our terms, governed by our laws, and resolved in our courts. *Scherk v. Alberto Culver Co.*, 417 U.S. 506, 519, 94 S.Ct. 2449, 41 L.Ed.2d 270 (1973).

In applying the French law, however, the arbitrators held that the interest rates assessed should rise 5% per annum after two months from the date of the award, to rates of 14½% and 15½% per annum, respectively. (The French statute relied upon provides: "In the case of a judgment, the rate of legal interest shall be increased by 5 points upon the expiration of a period of two months from the day on which the court decision has become enforceable, even if only provisionally." French Law No. 75-619, July 11, 1975.)

.    .    .

.   .   . [t]he imposition of an additional 5% interest by the arbitrators in accordance with the French statute is penal rather than compensatory, and bears no reasonable relation to any damage resulting from delay in recovery of the sums awarded. Therefore, that portion of the award which purports to assess the rates of interest at 14½% and 15½% will not be enforced or recognized by this Court. 9 U.S.C.A. § 201, Art. V, par. 2(b), Convention on the Recognition and Enforcement of Foreign Arbitral Awards. The rates of 9½% and 10½%, as imposed by the arbitrators, will continue to accrue until the date of Judgment.

*    *    *

> c.     William W. Park, *Private Adjudicators
> and the Public Interest: The Expanding
> Scope of International Arbitration*, 12
> BROOK. J. INT'L. L. 629, 646-48 (1986).

United States courts generally have interpreted the public policy defense as applicable only to a breach of what the Second Circuit has called our "most basic notions of morality and justice." American cases have construed the public policy defense narrowly in order to avoid disrupting the international dispute resolution process. The explicit Convention public policy defense would seem narrower than the non-Convention public policy defense courts may apply in domestic cases.

.     .     .

The dearth of American cases on public policy leaves much to speculation and surmise. One might suggest a tripartite classification of cases in which the public policy defense would be appropriate with respect to: (i) arbitrations involving transactions tainted in their substance, such as contracts for sale of drugs or for sale of military equipment to enemies; (ii) arbitration to enforce contracts entered into under duress; or (iii) arbitrations in which the arbitrator is corrupt.

The contours of these categories cannot be drawn with precision. But they can be drawn narrowly. To construe the public policy broadly would seriously undermine the goal of the arbitral process, which is to avoid extensive court proceedings.

.     .     .

Public Policy as a Ground for Setting Aside Commercial Awards

What happens if a court at the place where an award is rendered is asked not merely to refuse recognition to an arbitrator's decision, but rather to vacate the award that violates public policy? The New York Convention says only that a foreign or non-domestic award may be refused recognition and enforcement if it violates public policy. The Convention says nothing about annulment or vacatur.

Imagine, for example, that an arbitrator in New York renders an award ordering an American multinational corporation to pay $5 million in damages to a French manufacturer. The multinational believes that the arbitrator intentionally disregarded applicable provisions of American anti-trust law, and the award therefore violates a fundamental public policy of the United States. The American defendant is concerned that the French company will attempt to enforce the award outside the United States by attaching the multinational's assets held in countries that do not share the American vision of proper free competition policy. Therefore the American company wants to have the award set aside by courts in New York, in the hope of triggering application of Article V(1)(e) of the New York Convention, which permits refusal of enforcement to awards set aside where rendered.

This is not a case of asking the American court to refuse to recognize or enforce an award, nor merely a failure to "confirm" an award under the Federal Arbitration Act. Rather, the court is being asked to uproot the award by vacatur at the place where rendered.

A quick examination of the Federal Arbitration Act reveals that a violation of public policy as such is not listed in Section 10 as a basis on which an award may be set aside. This lacuna contrasts with the arbitration statutes recently enacted in France, the Netherlands and Switzerland, as well as the UNCITRAL Model Law, which provide explicitly that commercial arbitration awards may be annulled for violation of public policy.

In labor arbitration the United States Supreme Court has long recognized a public policy ground for vacating arbitral awards, the contours of which are discussed below. The implications of this public policy vacatur for commercial arbitration are unclear. See Revere Copper & Brass v. OPIC, 628 F.2d 81 (D.C.C. 1980); Domke on Commercial Arbitration, Ch. 33.03. (G. Wilner, ed., 1990). Could it be argued that because courts may set aside awards in labor arbitration, a similar result should obtain in commercial arbitration? When the arbitrator has offended the forum's basic public policy, should courts in commercial matters assist the arbitral process even indirectly by refraining to exercise the power of judicial annulment?

Judicial review of labor arbitration rests on a different statutory foundation than does commercial arbitration. Section 1 of the Federal Arbitration Act specifically excludes from its coverage "contracts of employment." The extent of this exemption is not entirely clear. See

Matthew Finkin, Commentary on 'Arbitration of Employment Disputes Without Unions,' 66 CHI. KENT L. REV. 799 (1990); Samuel Estreicher, "Reply to Professor Finkin," Id. at 817. Moreover, labor arbitration has its roots in concerns quite apart from those that justify commercial arbitration. While commercial arbitration is usually conceived of as a neutral method for vindicating particular private rights according to a defined legal standard, labor arbitration has been seen as a way to avoid class warfare through mediation.

The body of federal common law applied to collective bargaining agreements has its origin in the Supreme Court decision in Textile Workers Union v. Lincoln Mills, 353 U.S. 448 (1957). The Court's power to enforce an arbitration agreement was based on §301(a) of the Labor Management Relations Act of 1947 (29 U.S.C. §185(a)):

> Suits for violation of contracts between an employer and a labor organization representing employees in an industry affecting commerce . . . may be brought in any district court of the United States having jurisdiction over the parties, without respect to the amount in controversy or without regard to the citizenship of the parties.

Lincoln Mills was decided at a time when courts were often hostile to commercial arbitration, as was evidenced in the 1953 decision in Wilko v. Swan [discussed in Chapter 4, *supra* p. 503] declaring securities law questions non-arbitrable. Lincoln Mills involved an agreement to arbitrate a collective bargaining grievance in Alabama, even though Alabama state law held contracts to arbitrate future disputes to be unenforceable. Because of the judicial hostility to commercial arbitration, the labor union decided to rely on Section 301 of the Taft-Hartley Act.[318] The heart of the union's argument was that labor arbitration and commercial arbitration were different animals.

---

[318] *See* David Feller, *End of the Trilogy: The Declining State of Labor Arbitration*, 48 ARB. J. 18 (1993).

Labor arbitration was more than a mechanism for adjudicatory contract disputes; it was an alternative to industrial strife and strikes.[319]

The comparativist, of course, will contrast the American position when compared to European labor law where individual work-related disputes generally are considered non-arbitrable, and consigned to mandatory labor courts.[320]

In any event, the Supreme Court in Lincoln Mills interpreted Section 301(a) as more than a grant of jurisdiction. The Court said that Section 301 "authorizes federal courts to fashion a body of federal law for the enforcement of these collective bargaining agreements . . . ." 353 U.S. at 451. On judicial review of labor arbitration, see generally Kaden, Judges and Arbitrators: Observations on the Scope of Judicial Review, 80 COLUM. L. REV. 267 (1980); Kaster, Note on the Consequences of a Broad Arbitration Clause Under the Federal Arbitration Act, 52 BOSTON UNIVERSITY L.REV. 571 (1972); and the 1960 trilogy of Steelworkers cases, United Steelworkers v. Enterprise Wheel & Car, 363 U.S. 953 (1960), United Steelworkers v. Warrior & Gulf, 363 U.S. 574 (1960) and United Steelworkers v. American Mfg., 363 U.S. 564 (1960). See generally, Symposium on Labor Arbitration Thirty Years After the Steelworkers Trilogy, 66 CHI. KENT L. REV. 531 (1990); in particular, see Harper, LIMITING 301 PREEMPTION: THREE CHEERS FOR THE TRILOGY, ONLY ONE FOR LINGLE AND LUECK, Id. at 685.

---

[319] Messrs. Feller and Goldberg, counsel to the union, argued that only "as a back-up" that the exclusion of contracts of employment from the Federal Arbitration Act applied only to individual employment contracts, and not to collective bargaining agreements. *Id.* at 19. Presumably court litigation was not an alternative: partly due to time and cost constraints; partly because of perceived judicial hostility to employees; and partly because grievances subject to arbitration were often not major enough to merit court proceedings.

[320] *E.g.*, the *prud'hommes* tribunals of France. *See* Art. 511, French Code du Travail, giving the Conseils de Prud'hommes exclusive jurisdiction to hear individual labor grievances. *See Wattelet c. Getaba & Lorquin*, Cour d'appel de Paris (1ʳᵉ Ch. suppl.), 4 June 1992, 1993 REV. ARB. 449. For an example of an Italian refusal to order arbitration of a labor dispute, *see* Pret. Genova, 30 April 1980, *Quaglia v. Daros in Riv. Dir. Internaz. Priv. E. Proc.* (1980) 458, *reprinted in* 7 Yearbook Commercial Arbitration 342 (1982).

Despite its separate statutory basis, the public policy defense elaborated in labor cases need not necessarily be confined to labor arbitration. Community force is rarely justified to sustain, directly or indirectly, private choices that violate public policy. In United Paperworkers v. Misco, 484 U.S. 29 (1987), the Supreme Court characterized the limitation as "a specific application of the more general doctrine, rooted in the common law, that a court may refuse to enforce contracts that violate law or public policy." Misco, 484 U.S. at 42. The doctrine derives, said the Court, "from the basic notion that no court will lend its aid to one who founds a cause of action upon an illegal or immoral act." Id. Such an overarching public policy limitation arguably cuts across the whole body of law.

Misco arose out of the vacatur of an arbitral award reinstating an employee dismissed for alleged possession of illegal drugs on plant premises, which arguably impaired the employee's ability to operate dangerous machinery used in cutting paper rolls. The Supreme Court admitted public policy grounds for setting aside labor awards, but reversed the lower court's vacatur of the award. In Misco, the Court found the award invulnerable to attack, both for the inadequacy of the asserted policy and the absence of conflict between the policy and the award. The Court stated that "the parties [to the arbitration agreement] did not bargain for the facts to be found by a court, but by an arbitrator chosen by them who had the opportunity to observe [the dismissed employee] and to be familiar with the plant and its problems." Id.

Annulment of an award for a violation of public policy arguably justifies itself more easily in labor arbitration, whose legal framework rests almost entirely on judge-made law, that in a commercial arbitral context is constrained by a specific legislative enactment. Statutory standards contained in the Federal Arbitration Act may be less susceptible to judicial control than the general common law of labor arbitration. Section 10 of the United States Arbitration Act may be read as exhaustive of grounds for vacating awards. However, an implicit limitation stemming from conflict with the external law seems unavoidable. What is at issue is its precise configuration. While some have argued that in many respects labor and commercial arbitration have ceased to differ significantly,[321] it is unclear why vacatur (as contrasted with a simple refusal to enforce the award) for violation of public policy should necessarily carry over from labor grievance arbitration to commercial arbitration.

Those who are troubled by the potential for broad court control of arbitration awards may be comforted by the Supreme Court's rejection of looseness in identifying public policy and in perceiving conflict between such policy and the award. The policy must be "well defined and dominant;" it is not to be drawn from "general considerations of supposed public interests," but from "laws and legal precedents," and "the violation of such a policy must be clearly shown if an award is not to be enforced." See Misco, 484 U.S. at 43.

In an international context, of course, courts must be particularly sensitive to the fact that a public policy ground for vacatur cuts against not only an award's finality, but also the neutrality of the arbitral process, by injecting an unanticipated degree of meddling by national courts. The better course may well be to delay judicial invocation of public policy until a time when courts are asked to take positive action to enforce an award, rather than when asked to pronounce on the award as in a vacatur proceeding. In any event, congruence between standards for judicial review in labor and commercial arbitration cannot be assumed.

### Notes and Questions

1. The issue of public policy may work itself into a judge's "confirmation" of an award through 9 U.S.C. § 207, and thus into judicial discussion of vacatur when courts deal with both issues together without too much discrimination. See Northrop Corp. v. Triad Int'l Marketing S.A., 811 F.2d 1265 (9th Cir. 1987), cert. denied, 108 S. Ct. 261 (1987).

2. There is some evidence that with respect to motions to compel arbitration American courts recognize a qualitative distinction between the policy implications of trans-border and domestic transactions. See, for example, the reasoning of cases dealing with whether arbitration will be compelled: Scherk v. Alberto Culver, 417 U.S. 506 (1974); Mitsubishi Motors Corp. v. Soler-Chrysler-Plymouth, Inc., 473 U.S. 614 (1985), and Sonatrach v. Distrigas, 80 B.R. 606 (D. Mass. 1987). Does the logic

---

[321] See David Feller, End of the Trilogy: The Declining State of Labor Arbitration, supra note 319.

of these decisions show that the United States, like France, is beginning to recognize a double standard for the public policy defense to award enforcement, even though little theoretical scholarship has yet to announce any precise doctrinal underpinnings for these positions?

3. In England, the scope of public policy was tested in a domestic context in *Deutsche Schachtbau-und Tiefbohrgesellschaft (DST) v. Ras Al Khaima National Oil Co.* 2 Lloyd's Rep. 246, (C.A.1987) *supra* p. 1138. The *DST* case held that the absence of any specific legal system applied to the merits of the dispute did not constitute a violation of English public policy. The court placed emphasis on the effects of the enforcement, rather than the award itself.

4. Contracts with foreign states and state entities raise public policy questions with respect to the Act of State and sovereign immunity defenses. *See, e.g., Liberian Eastern Timber Corp. v. Government of Republic of Liberia*, 650 F.Supp. 73 (S.D.N.Y. 1986) and 659 F.Supp. 606 (D.D.C. 1986); *and Libyan American Oil Co. (LIAMCO) v. Socialist People's Libyan Arab Jamahirya*, 482 F.Supp. 1175 (D.D.C. 1980), *vacated* Order No. 80-1207 (D.C. Cir., May 6, 1981). Note that the *LIAMCO* case was statutorily overruled in 1988 by Section 15 of the Federal Arbitration Act.

5. In some developing countries, concepts of sovereignty over foreign investment have occasionally constituted a special public policy leading host states to refuse to recognize foreign arbitral awards. *See* Article 2(2)(c) of the Charter of Economic Rights and Duties of States, providing that "where the question of compensation [for nationalized property] gives rise to a controversy, it shall be settled under the domestic law of the nationalizing state and its tribunals . . . ." G.A. Res. 3281, U.N. Doc. A/9631 (1974), discussed in William W. Park, *Legal Issues in the Third World's Economic Development*, 61 B.U. L. REV. 1321 (1981).

6. How should American foreign policy impact upon enforcement of arbitration awards? Might our courts inadvertently embarrass the State Department if they enforce awards that fail to respect laws of foreign states relating to property abroad? Section 15 of the Federal Arbitration Act calls for enforcement of awards notwithstanding that the awards refuse recognition to foreign acts of state. *See* Justice Harlan's discussion in *Banco Nacional de Cuba v. Sabbatino*, 365 U.S. 398 (1963).

7. An arbitrator sitting in Paris has been charged with deciding a dispute between a Dutch seller and a Saudi buyer of electronic equipment. The arbitrator finds that the buyer has been late in paying for the goods. The contract provides that late payments will bear interest at 20%, clearly a violation of usury laws in France, the place of the arbitration, but not the law of Azania, which has been chosen by the parties to govern their contractual rights and duties.

     i.        If the arbitrator applies the 20% rate, might his award be set aside in Paris for violation of international public policy (ordre public international) under N.C.P.C. Article 1502?

ii. If the arbitrator does <u>not</u> apply the 20% rate, could the award be set aside in Paris for excess of authority, on the theory that by applying a rate of interest other than the one provided in the contract, the arbitrator has in effect re-written the parties' agreement?

iii. Could an award bearing the contract interest rate be refused recognition in the United States (the place where the buyer has assets) under New York Convention Article V(2)(b) for violation of public policy?

iv. Could an award that did <u>not</u> apply the contract interest rate be refused recognition for a violation of Article V(1)(c) of the New York Convention, as a "decision beyond the scope of the submission"?

8. French caselaw has long distinguished between internal and international public policy. See, the following excerpt from H. Battifol & P. Lagarde, 1 DROIT INTERNATIONAL PRIVÉ 423-24 (7th ed. 1981) (translation by the editors).

The heterogeneous nature of the concept of public policy appears even within the field of private international law in that it does not have the same scope depending on whether one is concerned with the acquisition of rights in France or the effect in France of rights acquired abroad where it would prevent their acquisition in France . . . .

However, it is important to note that one is not talking about excluding the application of public policy to the consequences in France of rights acquired abroad. One is dealing with its attenuated effect. That is to say that it comes into play in the most serious cases. In this way, the courts have decided that it is not possible to rely in France on an expropriation without compensation conducted under local law. Public policy prevents the expropriation having any effect in France. The Cour de cassation finally adopted the expression "the attenuated effect" — therefore not void — in its decision of 7 January 1964.

This distinction between ordre public in international rather than domestic contexts has been elaborated in French cases examining alleged violations of usury limits, bankruptcy rules and exchange controls. In *Société Iro-Holding v. Société Sétilex* (Cour d'appel de Paris June 9, 1983) Rev. Arb. 497 (1983), the court stated:

[O]ne should in fact note that the interest rate condemned as being usurious, 19.20% according to the applicant, barely exceeds the top rate published in France for the second half of 1973 and the first half of 1974 — respectively 17.42% and 18.06% — and that it has not been shown nor even alleged that the excessive amounts here would render the rate agreed to in this case higher than those found in the foreign countries concerned or that this has occurred in a situation where it infringes international public policy in the sense understood by French private international law . . . .

*See also Société des grands Moulins de Strasbourg v. Compagnie Continental France* (Cour de cassation Mar. 15, 1988) JOURNAL OFFICIEL REPUBLIQUE FRANÇAISE 47 (sale of wheat; France's highest court refused to recognize an arbitral award rendered in London that disregarded French and European Community regulations in the nature of exchange and price controls); *Thinet & Cie v. Labrely* (Cour de cassation Feb. 2, 1988), Dalloz 1988 IR 81 (construction contract in Saudi Arabia; French court set aside an arbitral award for failure to respect the automatic stay of claims to the French bankruptcy statute).

## III.   SUMMARY AND CONCLUSIONS

International arbitration awards are monitored at a number of critical points. Even before national judges are asked to review an award, a limited control may have been exercised at an institutional level. The rules of the International Chamber of Commerce, for example, provide for scrutiny by the ICC Court over the award as to matters of form. ICSID awards are subject only to internal control mechanisms.

The New York Arbitration Convention provides the basic framework by which international commercial arbitration agreements and awards are recognized and enforced. The Convention requires recognition and enforcement of arbitral awards, subject to a limited litany of defenses designed to safeguard the procedural integrity of the arbitration. The Convention takes a territorial approach with respect to its scope, generally covering foreign awards, which is to say, awards rendered outside the territory where enforcement is sought.

National legal systems implicated in the arbitral process will often recognize a non-waivable right to judicial challenge of awards, notwithstanding arbitration rules that provide explicitly for the exclusion of recourse to national judicial authorities. National arbitration laws often apply less restrictive control standards to international arbitration than to arbitration of purely domestic disputes.

National judicial control of arbitral awards may for ease be discussed either as "primary" control, exercised at the place where the award is rendered, or "secondary" control, exercised by courts in the country where the award is presented for enforcement or recognition.

Issues facing courts asked to enforce the agreement to arbitrate, such as subject matter arbitrability, often are also of concern to courts asked to enforce the award. Judges asked to enforce or to recognize an award have the benefit of seeing the mischief that the arbitrator may have already done, and thus play a much greater role in the arbitral process, both at the place of the proceedings and the situs of the assets that may be used to enforce the claim. In particular, to avoid lending their power to support a procedurally fraudulent or unfair arbitration, courts grapple with the following three principal issues when asked to recognize an award.

(1) Proper Party. Arbitration is a consensual process by which the parties renounce recourse to ordinary courts in favor of a non-judicial resolution of the dispute. The identity of the party that agreed to arbitrate becomes relevant when courts are faced with an award against a related company that claims never to have abandoned its right to have a day in court.

(2) Scope of Arbitrator's Mission. The arbitrators derive their powers from the arbitration agreement, and must respect the parties' mandate as to the subject matter falling within their mission. They must decide the dispute in the manner the parties authorized, in particular with respect to the application of substantive law and arbitral procedure.

(3) Adversarial Process. There must be proper notice and an opportunity for the parties to present their case.

In addition, a court may refuse recognition or enforcement of an award on the basis of its "public policy." While all defenses to enforcement of awards might be said to relate to public policy in an indirect way, the New York Convention contains an explicit "catch-all" escape hatch from enforcement and recognition in that violation of public policy constitutes an independent ground for refusal of recognition to a foreign award under Article V (2) (b) of the New York Convention.

The Convention also permits refusal of recognition and enforcement to awards annulled where rendered. This recognition of the key role of "primary" control mechanisms means that the arbitral situs has the power to give, or to take away, the international currency of an award. Judicial review at the arbitral situs can uproot the award by denying it the benefit of the presumptive validity conferred by the Convention. Some countries, of course, might enforce foreign arbitral awards even if set aside where rendered. However, they would not be under any treaty obligation to do so. Whether recognition of an annulled award would normally constitute sound policy remains open to debate.

In contrast to its explicitly enumerated grounds for refusing recognition or enforcement to a foreign award, the New York Convention does not spell out acceptable grounds for annulment of an award where rendered. Specific grounds for setting aside awards are neither mandated nor prohibited by the Convention. The arbitral seat is free to vacate awards for any reason it sees fit, or for none at all. National legislatures are left to their own devices in determining the degree to which arbitral awards should be subject to judicial review where rendered.

At least three competing models for primary judicial review of international arbitral awards have evolved: review of the legal merits, review for defects in procedural integrity, and no judicial review at all. The different forms of review have led to a vigorous debate over "delocalizing" international arbitration. Both "a-nationalists" and "territorialists," however, are coming to see the importance of balance and context in evaluating the role of the law of the arbitral situs.

# CHAPTER 10

# ENFORCEMENT OF AWARDS

## I.  INTRODUCTION

One of the most interesting aspects of the international arbitral process is the fact that arbitral awards as a whole enjoy a higher degree of transnational currency than judgments of national courts. Considering the fact that winning parties are seldom in the game for the intellectual satisfaction of a perfectly reasoned decision, but for the practical prospects of getting paid, this is a significant feature.

It may seem odd that awards — the results of a voluntarily agreed process pronounced by persons having no official judicial standing — should be more readily enforced around the world than judgments. With the exception of intra-European agreements, the international network of treaties for the recognition of foreign judgments is notoriously deficient. Arbitral awards, in contrast, may in principle be enforced practically anywhere in the world under the 1958 New York Convention on the Recognition and Enforcement of Foreign Arbitral Awards. The New York Convention has been ratified by some 100 countries (some Latin American countries remain the principal group of remaining holdouts).[322] It makes it obligatory for the courts of signatory States to recognize and enforce foreign awards (irrespective of the nationality of the parties) unless the party opposing enforcement establishes the existence of one of the grounds provided by the Convention.

The reader should at this point carefully re-examine Articles III through VI of the Convention[323] which define the specific and limited grounds upon which a Convention Award may be denied recognition and enforcement. This regime has been said by United States courts to demonstrate a "pro-enforcement bias" which is reflected in United States case law applying the Convention, and which is generally followed in foreign court decisions as well. This is not to say that the

---

[322] For the current list of ratifying states, see Supplement at p. 50.

[323] *See* Supplement at pp. 41-3.

States case law applying the Convention, and which is generally followed in foreign court decisions as well. This is not to say that the principles of the Convention have been invariably and efficaciously applied throughout the world. In this chapter we therefore take up not only the undoubted success story of enforcement of international commercial arbitration awards but also some of the problems which have been encountered along the way.

The fact remains that lawyers are often uncomfortable with international sources of law. The very notion of obligations created outside the national context disturbs a common feeling that "the law" is what the legislature has edicted — or perhaps what has been firmly established in a body of familiar cases. It requires an effort to accept that rights and obligations may be just as definitively established by virtue of a treaty originally drafted by foreigners in a foreign language, or by an arbitral tribunal which conducted its business and rendered its award abroad — and was entirely comprised of foreigners.

There is another factor which is at least as significant an obstacle with respect to the enforcement of foreign awards, namely the fact that in almost all cases the party wishing to enforce the award is a foreigner, and the one resisting the award is a national of the enforcement state. It would be pointless and naive to seek to deny the reality of parochialism in many situations.

These twin obstacles — unfamiliarity with the non-national source of the obligation to enforce, and a tendency to sympathize with the party opposing enforcement — go a long way to explaining why there have been so many slips between the cup of adhering to the New York Convention and the lip of its effective incorporation into national legal systems.

The responsibility for assimilating the New York Convention into a national legal system is twofold. First, the legislature must take whatever measures are called for by the relevant State's constitutional requirements in order that the Convention is recognized as part of the State's domestic law. This provides an initial occasion for difficulty: after a State has signed the Convention, its national legislature may fail to integrate it into a domestic law at all, or may do so incorrectly. Second, supposing the Convention to have been correctly integrated into a State's domestic law, local courts have responsibility for its interpretation and application. They, too, may instinctively favor the local party and distrust a law of foreign inspiration, and are also therefore vulnerable to the temptation to interpret and apply the Convention unduly restrictively.

## Notes and Questions

1. Note the possibility that Article I(3) offers ratifying States to make either or both of two permissible reservations. The first reservation has the effect of making the Convention applicable only with respect to awards rendered in countries which have also ratified the Convention. The second limits the Convention's scope to legal relationships characterized as commercial.

2. The New York Convention has been called the most remarkable example in history of international consensus as to common principles of commercial transactions. Capital importing countries, however, were often reluctant in the early years to give it full effect, perhaps because they saw it as a mechanism which operated essentially in favor of foreign nationals. With time, as it became apparent that the Convention is a two-way street and is just as useful to one's own nationals when they wish to enforce an award in their favor as it may be inconvenient when they have lost, the attitudes of national courts shifted. The result is that most national legal systems which have had experience with the Convention may now be said to have a strong bias in favor of enforcement, and no longer seek loop-holes in the text of the Convention. The evolution of judicial attitudes in India, illustrated by the materials in Section III of this Chapter, furnishes an excellent example of this transformation.

3. To understand the remarkable achievement of the New York Convention, however, one should consider what a radical step it was from the very beginning for some countries to yield their sovereign discretion to refuse to enforce awards with which their domestic courts might not agree (and which typically order local citizens to make payments in hard currency to award creditors abroad).

II.    DO THE LEGISLATIVE PROVISIONS IN THE ENFORCEMENT STATE INSURE THAT ITS COURTS RESPECT THE NEW YORK CONVENTION?

A.     *Navigation Maritime Bulgare v. P.T. Nizwar*, Judgment of the Supreme Court of Indonesia, Aug. 20, 1984, 11 YEARBOOK OF COMMERCIAL ARBITRATION 508-09 (1986).

## FACTS

On 12 July 1978, in an arbitration in London brought by Navigation Maritime Bulgare of Bulgaria ("NMB") against P.T. Nizwar of

Indonesia, a sole arbitrator awarded NMB US$ 72,576.39 plus interest of 7.5 per cent per year from 1 January 1975 until date of payment, and arbitration costs of UK £250.

NMB then applied to the Central Jakarta District Court to enforce the award. On 10 June 1981, the District Court ordered P.T. Nizwar to pay the award (Jakarta Court Decision no. 229/PdT.P/1979).

P.T. Nizwar petitioned for cassation to the Indonesian Supreme Court. Because it subsequently failed to file any brief in support of its petition, the Supreme Court refused the cassation request for failure to proceed with the petition. Nevertheless, the Supreme Court announced in its decision refusing cassation that because of the importance of the underlying issue, to wit enforcement of foreign arbitral awards, if would pronounce on the subject anyway. It then proceeded to hold that, notwithstanding Indonesia's ratification of the New York Convention (Presidential Decree No. 34/1981 dated 5 August 1981), foreign arbitral awards are not yet enforceable in Indonesia.

EXTRACT

1. The Court began its analysis by stating that, as a general rule, foreign judgments and foreign arbitral awards cannot be enforced in Indonesia unless a treaty requires enforcement. It then took up the question of whether Indonesia was bound by the 1927 Geneva Convention on the execution of foreign arbitral awards, and concluded that it was not. The Court reasoned that although the Dutch Government acceded to the 1927 Convention on behalf of the Netherlands Indies in 1931, and although Art. 5 of the Agreement on Transitional Measures of 1949 (containing the terms upon which Indonesia obtained independence) provides that Indonesia will be bound by all international agreements entered into by the Dutch Government on behalf of the Netherlands Indies, nevertheless new principles of international law respecting State succession have emerged since World War II with the result that Indonesia is no longer bound by treaties acceded to during the colonial times.

2. The Court then addressed the question of whether Indonesia is bound by the 1958 New York Convention, and concluded that it was not. While acknowledging that Indonesia ratified the New York Convention in 1981, the Court stated that "in accordance with Indonesian practice it is still necessary for the Government to promulgate implementing regulations concerning whether a request to enforce a foreign award

should be made to a District Court (and if so, which District Court) or whether such request should be made directly to the Supreme Court for a determination as to whether the award is contrary to the Indonesian legal order. Pending promulgation of such implementing regulations, Indonesian courts cannot enforce foreign arbitral awards.

*     *     *

As a result of sharp criticism in the international business community, Indonesia took steps in 1990 to ensure judicial compliance with the New York Convention by enacting Supreme Court Regulation No. 1 for 1990.

B. THE SUPREME COURT OF THE REPUBLIC OF INDONESIA, SUPREME COURT REGULATION NO. 1 FOR 1990 ON THE PROCEDURE FOR ENFORCING FOREIGN ARBITRAL AWARDS (TRANSLATION)

Considering: 1. Whereas as a result of the ratification of the Convention on the Recognition and Enforcement of Foreign Arbitral Awards (New York Convention of 1958) by Decree N° 34 of 1981 of the President of the Republic of Indonesia, dated 5 August 1981, it is deemed necessary to promulgate rules respecting procedures for enforcing foreign arbitral awards.

2. Whereas the provisions of the Indonesian Law on Civil Procedures as set forth in the "Revised Indonesian (Procedural) Regulations" (State Gazette 1941 N° 44), the "(Procedural) Regulations outside Java and Madura" (State Gazette 1927 N° 227), as well as the provisions of the "Reglement op de Rechtsvordering" (State Gazette 1847 N° 52 yuncto State Gazette 1849 N° 63) contain no provisions respecting the enforcement of foreign arbitral awards.

3. Whereas, therefore, it is considered necessary to establish procedures for the

enforcement of foreign arbitral awards in
a Regulation of the Supreme Court.

.     .     .

## CHAPTER I
## GENERAL

### Article 1

Authority to deal with matters related to the recognition
and enforcement of foreign arbitral awards is conferred
on the Court of Central Jakarta.

### Article 2

A foreign arbitral award is defined as a decision by any
arbitral tribunal, or by an individual, rendered outside
the jurisdiction of the Republic of Indonesia, or a
decision by any arbitral tribunal, or individual, which
under Indonesian law is deemed a foreign arbitral award
having final force in accordance with Presidential
Decree N° 34 of 1981, "Lembaran Negara" 1981 N°
40, dated 5 August 1981.

### Article 3

Foreign arbitral awards shall be recognized and enforced
in the jurisdiction of the Republic of Indonesia only if
the following conditions are fulfilled :

(1)    The award was rendered by an arbitral tribunal,
       or by an individual, in a State to which the State
       of Indonesia or which together with the State of
       Indonesia is bound by an international
       convention respecting the recognition and
       enforcement of foreign arbitral awards.
       Enforcement shall be based on reciprocity.

(2)    Foreign arbitration awards referred to in Article
       1 above are to be understood as being only those

which according to Indonesian law are rendered within the framework of commercial law.

(3)     Foreign arbitral awards referred to in Article 1 may be enforced in Indonesia only to the extent they are not contrary to public order.

(4)     Foreign arbitral awards may be enforced in Indonesia only after having obtained exequatur from the Supreme Court of the Republic of Indonesia.

## CHAPTER II
## E X E Q U A T U R

### Article 4

(1)     Exequatur is to be granted by the President of the Supreme Court, or by the Vice President of the Supreme Court, or by the Deputy Chairman, Civil Law Division as delegated by the President or Vice President of the Supreme Court.

(2)     Exequatur shall not be granted with respect to a foreign arbitral award clearly inconsistent with the basic principles of the entire Indonesian legal system and the entire Indonesian social order (public order).

## CHAPTER III
## PROCEDURES FOR APPLYING FOR EXEQUATUR

### Article 5

(1)     Applications for enforcement of foreign arbitral awards may be submitted only after being registered with the Secretariat of the Court of Central Jakarta, in accordance with the procedure set down in Articles 377 of the Revised Indonesian (Procedural) Regulations and 705 of the (Procedural) Regulations outside Java and Madura.

(2)    The President of the Court of Central Jakarta referred to in Article 1 above, shall transmit files pertaining to applications for the enforcement of foreign arbitral awards to the Registrar/Secretary General of the Supreme Court to obtain Exequatur.

(3)    Transmittal of the file of the application shall be effected within 14 days from the date of receipt of such application.

(4)    The file as transmitted shall be accompanied by:

a.    An original of the award, or a copy of the award authenticated in accordance with the requirements respecting authentication of foreign documents, and an official translation thereof complying with the requirements of Indonesian law.

b.    An original of the agreement upon the basis of which the foreign arbitral award was rendered, or a copy thereof authenticated in accordance with the requirements respecting authentication of foreign documents, and an official translation thereof complying with the requirements of Indonesian law.

c.    A certification of the Indonesian diplomatic mission in the country where the award was rendered, certifying that the applicant's country is bound with Indonesia by a bilateral or multinational convention regarding the recognition and enforcement of foreign arbitral awards.

## CHAPTER IV
## PROCEDURES FOR ATTACHMENTS AND ENFORCEMENT OF AWARDS

### Article 6

(1) Once the Supreme Court has granted the exequatur, further enforcement falls within the authority of the President of the Court of Central Jakarta.

(2) In case of enforcement in another jurisdiction than that of the Court of Central of Jakarta, the latter shall delegate such task to the Court having enforcement authority in accordance with Article 195 of the Revised Indonesian (Procedural) Regulations, Article 20(2) of the (Procedural) Regulations outside Java and Madura and following.

(3) Executory attachment may be effected on the property and assets owned by the party against whom the award is enforced. Procedures for attachment and enforcement of awards shall follow the procedures set out in the Revised Indonesian (Procedural) Regulations and the (Procedural) Regulations outside Java and Madura.

## CHAPTER V
## COSTS

### Article 7

Applications for the enforcement of any foreign arbitral award shall consist of two parts :

a. Costs for granting Exequatur are set at Rp.250.000 payable through the Registrar/Secretary of the Court of Central Jakarta for remittance to the Registrar/Secretary

General of the Supreme Court of the Republic of Indonesia. Such costs may be reviewed.

b.      Cost for attachment and enforcement of awards shall be paid to the Registrar/Secretary of the Court of Central Jakarta. In case attachment and enforcement is to be effected pursuant to Article 195 of the Revised Indonesian (Procedural) Regulations / article 206(2) of the (Procedural) Regulations outside Java and Madura and following, the cost shall be paid to the Court whose involvement is requested.

### CHAPTER VI
### Article 8

Matters as yet not dealt with will be defined in subsequent regulations.

### CHAPTER VII
### Article 9

This Regulation shall be effective as of its date of promulgation.

Promulgated at : JAKARTA
on the date : 1 MARCH 1990

---

PRESIDENT OF THE SUPREME COURT"

Notes and Questions

1. In reviewing the text of this Regulation, consider whether the procedures and requirements are consonant with the Convention. What in particular is one to make of Articles 4(2) and 5(4)(c)?

As to the latter, the applicability of the New York Convention does not depend on the nationality of the parties, but on the seat of arbitration. The test of reciprocity is whether the country of the place of arbitration has signed a convention with Indonesia - not that of the party seeking enforcement. (Article 3(1) of the Regulation seems to understand this quite well.) It makes no sense that the Indonesian diplomatic mission in the country where the award was rendered should certify whether the applicant's country is bound by a relevant convention, because that may be a different country.

2. Why should one have to rely on any diplomatic missions (not Indonesian ones in particular) to make certifications of this nature? Imagine that a German party has won an award against an Indonesian party, and the award is rendered in Hong Kong. It is well known that the New York Convention is in force in Hong Kong. (This is not only listed in innumerable legal publications, but can be determined by official communication from the United Nations, which keeps the formal record of ratifications.) The German party asks the Indonesian diplomatic mission in Hong Kong to certify that the New York Convention is in force in Hong Kong. (Leave aside the fact that Article 5(4)(c) seems to call for the Indonesian mission in Hong Kong to determine whether Germany is a party to the New York Convention.) Imagine further that the Indonesian mission does not answer the German party, because no one there knows how to get the answer, or because it does not understand how the U.K. ratification extends to Hong Kong. (Or imagine that there is no diplomatic mission in the country.)

It would seem that the German party would be stuck, because it must have this certification (which in fact is futile because the signatories to the New York Convention are well known). At the least, enforcement may be enormously delayed.

One would have to hope that Article 5(4)(c) could be corrected by a subsequent regulation. The proper approach would seem to be that the Indonesian Supreme Court should be satisfied by any reliable proof.

3. What does it mean that costs in Article 7(a) may be "reviewed"? One of the complaints about Thailand's way of enforcing the New York Convention is that the local courts demand a big percentage fee to grant exequatur — which may be a very bad investment if it turns out that the respondent has no money. For similar reasons, Article 7(b) might generate difficulties.

C.  Alberto Mora, *The Revpower Dispute: China's Breach of the New York Convention?*, *in* DISPUTE RESOLUTION IN THE PRC: A PRACTICAL GUIDE TO LITIGATION AND ARBITRATION IN CHINA 153-58 (1995).

[The United States company Revpower in 1988 entered into a Compensation Trade Agreement with the Shanghai Far-East Aero-Technology Import and Export Corporation ("SFAIC"), a state owned corporation under the control of China's Ministry of Aviation, pursuant to which the Chinese company was to manufacture industrial batteries according to Revpower's specifications, and using machinery and equipment and expertise supplied by Revpower. The batteries were then to be purchased by Revpower. When SFAIC was unable to supply a Bank of China performance guarantee and was unable to guarantee fixed prices, Revpower claimed breach of the contract by SFAIC and, after fruitless negotiations for settlement, brought arbitration in Stockholm, under the rules of the Arbitration Institute of the Stockholm Chamber of Commerce, pursuant to the contract's arbitration clause.]

The parties and the Institute selected an illustrious three-person panel to preside over the arbitration: Jeremy A. Cohen, an internationally recognized US expert in the field of Chinese Law (who was appointed by SFAIC); the late Dr. J. Gillis Wetter, considered one of the world's leading experts in international arbitration; and Lars Rahm, a distinguished Swedish attorney.

SFAIC initially responded to the arbitration by objecting to the proceedings on jurisdiction grounds, an argument that was unanimously rejected by the Tribunal in July 1992. Subsequently, on December 11 1992 [sic], SFAIC filed a statement of defence and a counterclaim in the amount of US$3.9 million, to which Revpower responded on March 1 1993 [sic]. SFAIC's defence throughout the arbitration was that virtually everything provided by Revpower during the course of the relationship - including machinery, materials, products, expertise, and letters of credit - was faulty.

Notwithstanding the pending arbitration proceedings and the clause in the Agreement stipulating the use of arbitration to settle all disputes, SFAIC improperly filed a lawsuit against Revpower in the Shanghai Intermediate People's Court on March 25 1993 [sic].

SFAIC's claim in the lawsuit was based on the same Agreement and the same issues that were the subject of the arbitration. Revpower immediately objected to the suit and filed a motion to dismiss. The motion remained pending for over two years despite the requirement under Article 135 of the PRC, *Civil Procedural Law* that the court respond to any such motion within 180 days.

On April 21 1993 [sic], less than two months before the scheduled June 14 final hearing, SFAIC notified the tribunal without explanation that it had decided to withdraw from the arbitration proceedings. The arbitral panel, having earlier decided that it had jurisdiction to consider Revpower's claim, proceeded with the arbitration in SFAIC's absence. On July 13 1993 [sic], after four days of hearings, a unanimous arbitral panel granted Revpower an award in the amount of approximately US$4.49 million, plus interest from the date the case was submitted in 1991, and attorney's fees. At the time of writing, the value of the award with interest is about US$7 million in total.

SFAIC refused Revpower's demand that it abide by the results of the arbitration and pay the award. Thus, Revpower was faced with the need to seek the assistance of the Chinese courts to enforce the award.

Revpower attempted to file its enforcement action on December 6 1993 [sic], well within the six-month filing deadline established by Article 219 of the PRC, *Civil Procedure Law*, in the Shanghai Intermediate Level People's Court, the same court which had refused to dismiss SFAIC's lawsuit. Revpower was required to apply to the Shanghai court for enforcement based on the provisions of the *Supreme People's Court Notice on the Implementation of China's Accession to the Convention on the Recognition and Enforcement of Foreign Arbitral Awards* ('Supreme Court Notice'), which states that an application to a Chinese court for the recognition or enforcement of an arbitral award rendered in the territory of another contracting state shall be heard by the Intermediate People's Court in the following Chinese localities:

.      where the person against whom enforcement of the award is sought is a natural person, the location of his household registration or place of residence;

.      where the person against whom enforcement of the award is sought is a legal person, the location of its principal place of business;

.      where the person against whom enforcement of the award is sought has no place of domicile, place of residence, or principal place of business, but has property in China, the location of the property.

This provision has been criticized by commentators for increasing the potential impact of local protectionism on the enforcement process. In 1991, the problem of local protectionism among some courts was recognized by Mr. Ren Jianxin, the President of the Supreme People's Court, who stated in an address to the National People's Congress that: 'In recent years, local protectionism has seriously affected the judicial work of the courts ... In order to protect local interests, some courts deviated from the principle of basing their judgment on the facts and using the law as the basis of their decision and were partial to local parties.'

Revpower's experience in attempting to enforce the award against SFAIC bears out Mr. Ren's fears regarding local protectionism. Under Article 112 of the PRC, *Civil Procedure Law*, the Shanghai Court was required to acknowledge Revpower's request for enforcement of the award within seven days of filing. However, court officials refused, without explanation or apparent justification, to accept the filing fee proffered by Revpower in order to satisfy the requirement that filing fees be paid in advance. For Revpower, this refusal provided a signal that the doors of the Shanghai Intermediate People's Court were closed to any attempt by Revpower to obtain justice against SFAIC.

Despite the efforts of the US State Department through the US Consul General in Shanghai, letters to the Chinese Ambassador to the United States by several members of Congress, and personal contracts by US Embassy officials in Beijing with officials of the China International Economic and Trade Arbitration Commission, CCPIT and the Ministry of Foreign Trade and Economic Cooperation ('MOFTEC'), all during the first three months of 1994, the Shanghai Court refused to adjudicate Revpower's enforcement action or even acknowledge that the suit had been filed. Repeated calls from the US Consul General to the Chief Judge of the Shanghai Court went unanswered, and subsequent repeated efforts by Revpower officials to file the enforcement action failed to result in any judicial action. Soon afterwards, Revpower received reports that SFAIC, safe behind the shield unlawfully erected by the Shanghai Court, was in the process of secreting or divesting assets by way of obtaining further protection against any collection action by Revpower.

Having exhausted all available avenues in China, Revpower turned to the United States Congress and administration for help in bringing this matter to the attention of the Chinese officials who could right this obvious wrong. Through counsel, Revpower has presented the case that this is no longer primarily a commercial dispute, but rather a state-to-state dispute stemming from China's clear violation of the New York Convention that gains additional significance because of the overwhelming reliance placed on international arbitration by US and other foreign investors in China. China is represented as having signalled by its actions in this case that it is no longer bound by the terms of the Convention, thereby jeopardizing the impartiality of the dispute resolution mechanisms protecting foreign investors. Revpower has further argued that until the dispute is resolved—which it now believes can only occur if the PRC government satisfies the award—and China re-establishes its commitment to honour the terms of the Convention, every US investor runs a greater risk of loss from arbitrary action.

Revpower's argument has found ready acceptance in Washington. To date, Vice President Al Gore, Secretary of State Warren Christopher, and Commerce Secretary Ron Brown have all personally raised the case with Chinese officials, as have lower level officials in the Office of the United States Trade Representative ('USTR') and the Departments of State, Commerce, and Treasury. The US embassy in Beijing and the consulate in Shanghai are both fully involved.

To further cite examples of involvement by the administration, in April 1994, the case was raised by the US delegation in a meeting of the US-China Joint Commission on Commerce and Trade in Washington. In June 1994 Undersecretary of Commerce Jeffrey E. Garten wrote to MOFTEC Minister Gu Yongjiang transmitting a White Paper in which he made specific reference to Revpower's claim to illustrate complaints by US firms concerning the enforcement of China's treaty obligations and its own laws. Mr. Garten also raised the Revpower matter directly with Chinese trade officials while in China in July 1994. Secretary of Commerce Ron Brown's involvement came when he raised the dispute with MOFTEC Minister Wu Yi during his last trip to China. The USTR's involvement in the dispute was first publicly revealed when Deputy USTR Charlene Barshefsky testified before a joint hearing of the Subcommittees on Asia and the Pacific and International Economic Policy and Trade of the House Committee on International Relations on February 2 1995 [sic], of China's practice of 'selectively' upholding its trade agreements with the United States and its difficulty in 'accepting international arbitration judgments.' Later, on April 4, USTR Mickey Kantor testified before the Trade Subcommittee of the Senate Finance Committee, in response to a question on China's compliance with international arbitral commitments, that China would be expected to comply with such commitments.

Congressional involvement in the dispute has also been significant. At present, over 30 Members of Congress have written to the administration or the Chinese government to register their concern and interest in the case. Legislation (S. 1083) has been introduced in the Senate which would require the administration to oppose the entry into the World Trade Organization of any signatory to the New York Convention that causes injury to 'United States persons' as a result of a violation of the Convention. It is expected that counterpart legislation will be introduced in the House of Representatives in the near future. If this legislation is enacted, China's current behavior in this dispute would almost certainly trigger its provisions. Another draft bill creating a civil remedy in favor of parties injured as a result of foreign nations' violation of the New York Convention is also being evaluated by staff on the Senate Judiciary Committee.

The Chinese government still maintains that there has been no violation of the New York Convention and that the Revpower dispute is a matter for the Chinese courts to decide. Even so, it appears that the government is beginning to appreciate the damage caused to its international reputation resulting from the case. On April 24 1995 [sic], the Foreign Affairs Office of the Shanghai Municipal Government telephoned the US Consul General in Shanghai to notify him that the court was preparing to take up the case 'in the near future.' In July, the Shanghai Intermediate People's Court finally dismissed the long-pending SFAIC counterclaim against Revpower, a decision that was almost immediately upheld by an appellate court. Chinese court officials have recently invited Revpower to reinitiate the enforcement action.

While the decision of the Chinese courts would have been welcomed two years ago, they may no longer be of significance to Revpower. Credible information received by company officials over the last two years suggests that SFAIC has been transferring or divesting assets. Thus, pursuit of the enforcement action at this late date may simply result in the additional waste of corporate resources. Revpower officials maintain that the only effective remedy for the Chinese government's breach of international law would be for the government to acknowledge its obligations under the New York Convention and fulfill the award on behalf of its instrumentality. This view has been communicated to the government. In the meantime, Revpower is pursing its efforts with the US government. On August 4 1994, a Super 301 action was filed with the USTR complaining of China's failure to observe its obligations under the New York Convention. Further potential remedies are also under evaluation with Congress and the administration.

## Notes and Questions

1.      Note that the commentary on the Revpower dispute was prepared by the company's US attorney. Is there any legal basis for the claim that China might be directly liable to the contracting partner of its state owned corporation due to failure of Chinese courts to enforce a Convention award? Could there be a public international law obligation on the part of an enforcement state towards another Convention state if the legislation or courts of the enforcement state fail to adequately enforce a Convention award?

2.      The commentator criticizes Chinese legislation for establishing the venue of enforcement actions at the domicile of the defendant where local courts could be prejudiced against enforcement. Where else could venue be fixed?

## III.    WILL THE COURTS OF THE ENFORCEMENT STATE CONSIDER THE AWARD TO BE A CONVENTION AWARD?

The purposes of the New York Convention would be defeated if losers in arbitration could seek to have awards rendered in a foreign neutral venue set aside by their own national courts. Such an attempt was nevertheless rewarded with success by the Indian Supreme Court in *National Thermal Power Corp. v. The Singer Co. & Others*, where an award rendered in London, the seat of the arbitration, was found not to be a foreign award and was not protected by the Convention.

A.      *The National Thermal Power Corp. Ltd. v. The Singer Co.*, (Supreme Court of India May 7, 1992), 3 Supreme Court Cases 551-573 (1992).

On 17 August 1982, National Thermal Power Corporation (NTPC) and The Singer Company (Singer) concluded two agreements at New Delhi. The "General Terms and Conditions of Contract" were expressly incorporated in the agreements. The "General Terms" stated that:

[t]he laws applicable to this Contract shall be the laws in force in India. The Courts of Delhi shall have exclusive jurisdiction in all matters arising under this Contract.

The General Terms further provided in clause 27(6) regarding dispute resolution that in respect of an Indian contractor, the arbitration shall be conducted in New Delhi in accordance with the provisions of the

Arbitration Act, 1940. Dispute resolution in respect of a foreign contractor was provided for in clause 27(7) as follows:

> In the event of foreign Contractor, the arbitration shall be conducted by three arbitrators, one each to be nominated by the Owner and the Contractor and the third to be named by the President of the International Chamber of Commerce, Paris. Save as above, all Rules of Conciliation and Arbitration of the International Chamber of Commerce shall apply to such arbitrations. The arbitration shall be conducted at such places as the arbitrators may determine.

When a dispute arose, it was referred to ICC arbitration and the ICC Court designated London as the place of arbitration. On 9 August 1989, the arbitrators issued an interim award deciding certain preliminary issues. They held that English law applied to the arbitral procedure, that the request for arbitration had been filed in a timely fashion, and that claims and counterclaims were not time-barred.

NTPC applied to the Delhi High Court to have the interim award set aside under the Indian Arbitration Act 1940. The High Court rejected its application, holding that the award was not governed by the Arbitration Act 1940: the arbitration agreement on which the award was made was not governed by the law of India; the award fell within the ambit of the Foreign Awards (Recognition and Enforcement) Act, 1961; London being the seat of arbitration, English Courts alone had jurisdiction to set aside the award, and, the Delhi High Court had no jurisdiction to entertain the application filed under the Arbitration Act, 1940.

The Supreme Court in upholding NTPC's appeal from this judgment found that the award was not a foreign award and set it aside.

*Judgment*

.    .    .

The point for consideration is whether the High Court was right in rejecting the appellant's application filed under the provisions of the Arbitration Act, 1940 and in holding that the award which was made in London on an arbitration agreement was not governed by the law of

India and that it was a foreign award within the meaning of the Foreign Awards Act and beyond the jurisdiction of the Indian Courts except for the purpose of recognition and enforcement under the latter Act.

The award was made in London as an interim award in an arbitration between the NTPC and a foreign contractor on a contract governed by the law of India and made in India for its performance solely in India. The fundamental question is whether the arbitration agreement contained in the contract is governed by the law of India so as to save it from the ambit of the Foreign Awards Act and attract the provisions of the Arbitration Act, 1940. Which is the law which governs the agreement on which the award has been made?

.    .    .

Dicey and Morris in *The Conflict of Laws*, 11th edn., Vol. II ('Dicey') refer to the 'proper law of a contract' thus:

Rule 180 - The term 'proper law of a contract' means the system of law by which the parties intended the contract to be governed, or, where their intention is neither expressed nor to be inferred from the circumstances, the system of law with which the transaction has its closest and most real connection. (pp. 1161-62)

.    .    .

In a case such as the present, there is no need to draw any inference about the intention of the parties or to impute any intention to them, for they have clearly and categorically stipulated that their contract, made in India to be performed in India, is to be governed by the 'laws in force in India' and the courts in Delhi are to 'have exclusive jurisdiction in all matters arising under this contract' (cl. 7). The cardinal test suggested by Dicey in rule 180 is thus fully satisfied.

As regards the governing law of arbitration, Dicey says:

Rule 58 - (1) The validity, effect and interpretation of an arbitration agreement are governed by its proper law.

(2) The law governing arbitration proceedings
is the law chosen by the parties, or, in the absence of
agreement, the law of the country in which the
arbitration is held. (Vol. I, pp. 534-535)

The principle in rule 58, as formulated by Dicey, has two
aspects — (a) the law governing the arbitration agreement, namely,
its proper law; and (b) the law governing the conduct of the
arbitration, namely, its procedural law.

The proper law of the arbitration agreement is normally the
same as the proper law of the contract. It is only in exceptional
cases that it is not so even where the proper law of the contract is
expressly chosen by the parties. Where, however, there is no
express choice of the law governing the contract as a whole, or the
arbitration agreement as such, a presumption may arise that the law
of the country where the arbitration is agreed to be held is the
proper law of the arbitration agreement. But that is only a rebuttable
presumption. See Dicey, Vol. I, p. 539; see the observation in
*Whitworth Street Estates (Manchester) Ltd. v. James Miller &*
*Partners Ltd.*, 1970 AC 583, 607, 612 and 616).

The validity, effect and interpretation of the arbitration
agreement are governed by its proper law. Such law will decide
whether the arbitration clause is wide enough to cover the dispute
between the parties. Such law will also ordinarily decide whether the
arbitration clause binds the parties even when one of them alleges
that the contract is void, or voidable or illegal or that such contract
has been discharged by breach or frustration. See *Heyman & Aur. v.*
*Darwins, Ltd.*, 1942 (1) All E.R. 337. The proper law of arbitration
will also decide
whether the arbitration clause would equally apply to a different
contract between the same parties or between one of those parties
and a third party.

The parties have the freedom to choose the law governing an
international commercial arbitration agreement. They may choose
the substantive law governing as well as the procedural law
governing the conduct of the arbitration. Such choice is exercised
either expressly or by implication. Where there is no express choice
of the law governing the contract as a whole, or the arbitration
agreement in particular, there is, in the absence of any contrary

indication, a presumption that the parties have intended that the proper law of the contract as well as the law governing the arbitration agreement are the same as the law of the country in which the arbitration is agreed to be held. On the other hand, where the proper law of the contract is expressly chosen by the parties, as in the present case, such law must, in the absence of an unmistakable intention to the contrary, govern the arbitration agreement which, though collateral or ancillary to the main contract, is nevertheless a part of such contract.

Whereas, as stated above, the proper law of arbitration (i.e., the substantive law governing arbitration) determines the validity, effect and interpretation of the arbitration agreement, the arbitration proceedings are conducted, in the absence of any agreement to the contrary, in accordance with the law of the country in which the arbitration is held. On the other hand, if the parties have specifically chosen the law governing the conduct and procedure of arbitration, the arbitration proceedings will be conducted in accordance with that law so long as it is not contrary to the public policy or the mandatory requirements of the law of the country in which the arbitration is held. If no such choice has been made by the parties, expressly or by necessary implication, the procedural aspect of the conduct of arbitration (as distinguished from the substantive agreement to arbitrate) will be determined by the law of the place or seat of arbitration.

Where, however, the parties have, as in the instant case, stipulated that the arbitration between them will be conducted in accordance with the ICC Rules, those rules, being in many respects, self-contained or self-regulating and constituting a contractual code of procedure, will govern the conduct of the arbitration, except insofar as they conflict with the mandatory requirements of the proper law of arbitration, or of the procedural law of the seat of arbitration. See the observation of Kerr, L.J., in *Bank Mellat v. Helliniki Techniki SA*, (1983) 3 All E.R. 428; See also *Craig, Park and Paulsson, International Chamber of Commerce Arbitration*, 2nd ed. (1990).

To such an extent the appropriate courts of the seat of arbitration, which in the present case are the competent English courts, will have jurisdiction in respect of procedural matters concerning the conduct of arbitration. But the overriding principle is that the courts of the country whose substantive laws govern the arbitration agreement are the competent courts in respect of all matters arising under the arbitration agreement, and the jurisdiction exercised by the courts of the seat of arbitration is merely concurrent and not exclusive and strictly limited to matters of procedure. All other matters in respect of the arbitration agreement fall within the exclusive competence of the courts of the country whose laws govern the arbitration agreement. See Mustill & Boyd, *Commercial Arbitration*, 2nd ed.; Allen Redfern and Martin Hunter, *Law & Practice of International Commercial Arbitration*, 1986; *Russell on Arbitration*, Twentieth ed., 1982; Cheshire & North's *Private International Law*, eleventh ed. (1987).

The proper law of the contract in the present case being expressly stipulated to be the laws in force in India and the exclusive jurisdiction of the courts in Delhi in all matters arising under the contract having been specifically accepted, and the parties not having chosen expressly or by implication a law different from the Indian law in regard to the agreement contained in the arbitration clause, the proper law governing the arbitration agreement is indeed the law in force in India, and the competent courts of this country must necessarily have jurisdiction over all matters concerning arbitration. Neither the rules of procedure for the conduct of arbitration contractually chosen by the parties (the ICC Rules) nor the mandatory requirements of the procedure followed in the courts of the country in which the arbitration is held can in any matter supersede the overriding jurisdiction and control of the Indian law and the Indian courts.

This means, questions such as the jurisdiction of the arbitrator to decide a particular issue or the continuance of an arbitration or the frustration of the arbitration agreement, its validity, effect and interpretation are determined exclusively by the proper law of the arbitration agreement, which in the present case, is Indian Law. The procedural powers and duties of the arbitrators, as for example, whether they must hear oral evidence, whether the evidence of one party should be recorded necessarily in the presence of the other party, whether there is a right of cross-examination of witnesses, the special requirements of notice, the remedies available to a party in respect of security for costs or for discovery etc. are matters regulated in accordance with the rules chosen by the parties to the extent that those rules are applicable and sufficient and not

repugnant to the requirements of the procedural law and practice of
the seat of arbitration. The concept of party autonomy in
international contracts is respected by all systems of law so far as it
is not incompatible with the proper law of the contract or the
mandatory procedural rules of the place where the arbitration is
agreed to be conducted or any overriding public policy.

.    .    .

Clause 27 of the General Terms of the Contract shows that it
was the intention of the parties that disputes with a foreign
contractor should be referred to arbitration in accordance with the
ICC Rules; while disputes with an Indian contractor should be
settled by arbitration in New Delhi on an *ad hoc* basis.

.    .    .

An international commercial arbitration necessarily involves a
foreign element giving rise to questions as to the choice of law and
the jurisdiction of courts. Unlike in the case of persons belonging to
the same legal system, contractual relationships between persons
belonging to different legal systems may give rise to various private
international law questions such as the identity of the applicable law
and the competent forum. An award rendered in the territory of a
foreign State may be regarded as a domestic award in India where it
is sought to be enforced by reason of Indian law being the proper
law governing the arbitration agreement in terms of which the award
was made. The Foreign Award Act incorporating the New York
Convention, leaves no room for doubt on the point.

.    .    .

A 'foreign award' as defined under the Foreign Awards Act,
1961 means an award made on or after 11.10.1960 on differences
arising between persons out of legal relationships, whether
contractual or not, which are considered to be commercial under the
law in force in India. To qualify as a foreign award under the Act,
the award should have been made in pursuance of an agreement in
writing for arbitration to be governed by the New York Convention
on the Recognition and Enforcement of Foreign Arbitral Awards,
1958, and not to be governed by the law of India. Furthermore such
an award should have been made outside India in the territory of a

foreign State notified by the Government of India as having made reciprocal provisions for enforcement of the Convention. These are the conditions which must be satisfied to qualify an award as a 'foreign award' (Sect. 2 read with Sect. 9).

An award is 'foreign' not merely because it is made in the territory of a foreign State, but because it is made in such a territory on an arbitration agreement not governed by the law of India. An award made on an arbitration agreement governed by the law of India, though rendered outside India, is attracted by the saving clause in Sect. 9 of the Foreign Awards Act and is, therefore, not treated in India as a 'foreign award'.

A 'foreign award' is (subject to Sect. 7) recognised and enforceable in India 'as if it were an award made on a matter referred to arbitration in India' (Sect. 4). Such an award will be ordered to be filed by a competent court in India which will pronounce judgment according to the award (Sect. 6).

Sect. 7 of the Foreign Awards Act, in consonance with Art. V of the New York Convention which is scheduled to the Act, specifies the conditions under which recognition and enforcement of a foreign award will be refused at the request of a party against whom it is invoked.

.   .   .

The Foreign Awards Act contains a specific provision to exclude its operation to what may be regarded as a 'domestic award' in the sense of the award having been made on a[n] arbitration agreement governed by the law of India, although the dispute was with a foreigner and the arbitration was held and the award was made in a foreign State. Sect. 9 of this Act says:

Nothing in this Act shall —
(a) . . .
(b) apply to any award made on an arbitration
agreement governed by the law of India.

Such an award necessarily falls under the Arbitration Act, 1940, and is amenable to the jurisdiction of the Indian Courts and controlled by the Indian system of law just as in the case of any other domestic award, except that the proceedings held abroad and leading to the award were in certain respects amenable to be controlled by the public policy and the mandatory requirements of the law of the place of arbitration and the competent courts of that place.

It is important to recall that in the instant case the parties have expressly stated that the laws applicable to the contract would be the laws in force in India and that the courts of Delhi would have exclusive jurisdiction 'in all matters arising under this contract'. They have further stated that the 'Contract shall in all respects be construed and governed according to Indian laws'. These words are wide enough to engulf every question arising under the contract including the disputes between the parties and the mode of settlement. It was in Delhi that the agreement was executed. The form of the agreement is closely related to the system of law in India. Various Indian enactments are specifically mentioned in the agreement as applicable to it in many respects. The contract is to be performed in India with the aid of Indian workmen whose conditions of service are regulated by Indian laws. One of the parties to the contract is a public sector undertaking. The contract has in every respect the closest and most real connection with the Indian system of law and it is by that law that the parties have expressly evinced their intention to be bound in all respects. The arbitration agreement is contained in one of the clauses of the contract, and not in a separate agreement. In the absence of any indication to the contrary, the governing law of the contract (i.e. in the words of Dicey, the proper law of the contract) being Indian law, it is that system of law which must necessarily govern matters concerning arbitration, although in certain respects the law of the place of arbitration may have its relevance in regard to procedural matters.

It is true that an arbitration agreement may be regarded as a collateral or ancillary contract in the sense that it survives to determine the claims of the parties and the mode of settlement of their disputes even after the breach or repudiation of the main contract. But it is not an independent contract, and it has no meaningful existence except in relation to the rights and liabilities of the parties under the main contract. It is a procedural machinery which is activated when disputes arise between parties regarding their rights and liabilities. The law governing such rights and liabilities is the proper law of the contract, and unless otherwise provided, such law governs the whole contract including the arbitration agreement, and particularly so when the latter is contained not in a separate agreement, but, as in the present case, in one of the clauses of the main contract.

Significantly, London was chosen as the place of arbitration by reason of Art. 12 of the ICC Rules which reads:

> The place of arbitration shall be fixed by the International Court of Arbitration, unless agreed upon by the parties.

The parties had never expressed their intention to choose London as the arbitral forum, but, in the absence of any agreement on the question, London was chosen by the ICC Court as the place of arbitration. London has no significant connection with the contract or the parties except that it is a neutral place and the Chairman of the Arbitral Tribunal is a resident there, the other two members being nationals of the United States and India respectively.

The decisions relied on by counsel for the Singer do not support his contention that the mere fact of London being the place of arbitration excluded the operation of the Arbitration Act, 1940 and the jurisdiction of the courts in India.

[The Court reviewed the decision of the House of Lords in *James Miller & Partners Ltd. v. Whitworth Street Estates (Manchester) Ltd.* (1970) AC 583.]

.   .   .

It is true that the procedural law of the place of arbitration and the courts of that place cannot be altogether excluded, particularly in respect of matters affecting public policy and other mandatory requirements of the legal system of that place. But in a proceeding such as the present which is intended to be controlled by a set of contractual rules which are self-sufficient and designed to cover every step of the proceeding, the need to have recourse to the municipal system of law and the courts of the place of arbitration is reduced to the minimum and the courts of that place are unlikely to interfere with the arbitral proceedings except in cases which shock the judicial conscience. See the observations of Kerr L.J. In *Bank Mellat v. Helliniki Techniki SA*, (1983) 3 All E.R. 428.

Courts would give effect to the choice of a procedural law other than the proper law of the contract only where the parties had agreed that matters of procedure should be governed by a different system of law. If the parties had agreed that the proper law of the contract should be the law in force in India, but had also provided for arbitration in a foreign country, the laws of India would undoubtedly govern the validity, interpretation and effect of all clauses including the arbitration clause in the contract as well as the scope of the arbitrators' jurisdiction. It is Indian law which governs the contract, including the arbitration clause, although in certain respects regarding the conduct of the arbitration proceedings the foreign procedural law and the competent courts of that country may have a certain measure of control. See the principle stated by Lord Denning, M.R. in *International Tank and Pipe SAK v. Kuwait Aviation Fuelling Co. KSC*, (1975) 1 All E.R. 242.

The arbitration clause must be considered together with the rest of the contract and the relevant surrounding circumstances. In the present case, as seen above, the choice of the place of arbitration was, as far as the parties are concerned, merely accidental in so far as they had not expressed any intention in regard to it and the choice was made by the ICC Court for reasons totally unconnected with either party to the contract. On the other hand, apart from the expressly stated intention of the parties, the contract itself, including the arbitration agreement contained in one of its clauses, is redolent of India and matters Indian. The disputes between the parties under the contract have no connection with anything English, and they have the closest connection with Indian laws, rules and regulations. In the circumstances, the mere fact that the venue chosen by the ICC Court for the conduct of arbitration is London does not support the case of the Singer on the point. Any attempt to exclude the jurisdiction of the competent courts and the laws in force in India is totally inconsistent with the agreement between the parties.

In sum, it may be stated that the law expressly chosen by the parties in respect of all matters arising under their contract, which must necessarily include the agreement contained in the arbitration clause, being Indian law and the exclusive jurisdiction of the courts in Delhi having been expressly recognised by the parties to the contract in all matters arising under it, and the contract being most intimately associated with India, the proper law of arbitration and the competent courts are both exclusively Indian, while matters of procedure connected with the conduct of arbitration are left to be regulated by contractually chosen rules of the ICC to the extent that such rules are not in conflict with the public policy and the mandatory requirements of the proper law and of the law of the place of arbitration. The Foreign Awards Act, 1961 has no application to the award in question which has been made on an arbitration agreement governed by the law of India.

The Tribunal has rightly held that the 'substantive law of the contract is Indian law'. The Tribunal has further held 'the laws of England govern procedural matters in the arbitration'.

All substantive rights arising under the agreement including that which is contained in the arbitration clause are, in our view, governed by the laws of India. In respect of the actual conduct of arbitration, the procedural law of England may be applicable to the extent that the ICC Rules are insufficient or repugnant to the public policy or other mandatory provisions of the laws in force in England. Nevertheless, the jurisdiction exercisable by the English courts and the applicability of the laws of that country in procedural matters must be viewed as concurrent and consistent with the jurisdiction of the competent Indian courts and the operation of Indian laws in all matters concerning arbitration in so far as the main contract as well as that which is contained in the arbitration clause are governed by the laws of India.

The Delhi High Court was wrong in treating the award in question as a foreign award. The Foreign Awards Act has no application to the award by reason of the specific exclusion contained in Sect. 9 of the Act. The award is governed by the laws in force in India, including the Arbitration Act, 1940. Accordingly, we set aside the impugned judgment of the Delhi High Court. . . .

\*     \*     \*

B.     *International Jurist Flays India for Overstepping Bounds*, THE PIONEER (Delhi), October 6, 1992, at 3.

A PARIS-BASED expert in business arbitration has flayed India's Supreme Court for two judgements pertaining to arbitral awards given abroad, accusing it of overstepping its jurisdiction and violating international norms as laid down by the New York Convention.

Jan Paulsson, who is also a Vice-President of the London Court of International Arbitration, has after analysing these judgements also cautioned foreign practitioners to avoid "by all means" subjecting their contracts to Indian laws till the legal system in India reverses these trends.

This feeling, if it represents the general impression of foreign legal experts on arbitration proceedings in India, could have serious implications for the country's attempts to globalise through increased foreign collaboration and direct investment.

Writing in the June issue of monthly International Arbitration Report, Mr. Paulsson says that in these two cases involving arbitral awards given in London, "the courts of India have revealed an alarming propensity to exercise authority in a manner contrary to the legitimate expectations of the international community."

The two cases being referred to are Oil and Natural Gas Commission (ONGC) versus Western Company of North America in 1987 and National Thermal Power Corporation (NTPC) versus Singer Corporation and others on May 7 this year.

In the ONGC case, the Supreme Court had held that Indian courts had jurisdiction to hear an action brought by the losing Indian party to set aside the award and also upheld an Indian court's order that the winning American party should desist from enforcement actions in the US.

The basis for this judgement, according to the article, was that Indian law applied to the arbitration agreement and hence the Indian court must have jurisdiction to deal with the subsequent award in the same way as they would with domestic awards.

The Supreme Court decision held that the New York Convention was irrelevant in this context, since the Indian courts had not been asked to enforce a foreign award.

They were only hearing an application to set aside an award which, though rendered in London, was governed by Indian law.

Hence, it argued, the only question was whether the courts had jurisdiction to do so as per Indian law.

In the NTPC case, the Supreme Court similarly decided that Indian courts had jurisdiction to hear an action to set aside a partial award rendered in London. The judgement held that "the proper law of the arbitration agreement is normally the same as the proper law of the contract." Mr. Paulsson has no quarrel with this.

But, the judgement goes on to add that "the over-riding principle is that the courts of the country whose substantive laws govern the arbitration agreement are the competent courts in respect of all matters arising under the arbitration agreement." Maintaining that the jurisdiction of the seat of arbitration (in this case London) is strictly limited to matters of procedure, the judgement held that "all other matters in respect of the arbitration agreement fall within the exclusive competence of the courts of the country whose laws govern the arbitration."

Mr. Paulsson [states] this contention as being "simply untrue" and points out that while the judgement cites four well-known English treatises in support of its positions, "the fact is that none of these authorities support the radical thesis propagated by the Indian court." In a strongly-worded comment, he says the "scholarly references are, to put it charitably, window dressing."

Mr. Paulsson points out that under the New York Convention, a losing party could argue *before the enforcement court* that the arbitration agreement was invalid under the law to which (the parties) have subjected it (emphasis Mr. Paulsson's). "That might mean that evidence of Indian law would be relevant to an enforcement court in, say, New York. It does not mean that Indian courts have competence by virtue of some 'over-riding principles'", he observes.

The two Supreme Court decisions misunderstand the New York Convention — the ONGC judgement by "subverting general principles of the post-award process which have emerged as international consensus over 30 years" and the NTPC verdict by "disregarding the text of the Convention — says the article.

Mr. Paulsson goes on to add: "These are examples of parochial over-reaching by a national legal system. It is to be hoped that the trend will be reversed in India and not copied elsewhere. For now, India stands alone in this respect: no other legal system has adopted such an aggressively nationalistic posture."

After a series of quotations from the text of the Convention and arguments in support of his point, Mr. Paulsson concludes with a warning: "It is to be hoped that the Indian legal system will find a way to reverse this deleterious holding and to reassure the international legal community of its intent to apply the New York Convention faithfully."

"Meanwhile, practitioners must be advised to attempt by all means, if they wish to ensure that contractual disputes may be resolved by arbitral awards enforceable anywhere under the New York Convention, to avoid subjecting their contracts to Indian law — or more specifically to subject the arbitration agreement to another law. Such is the practical effect of the ONGC and Singer decisions."

"Whether this evolution is in India's national interest would seem a fit subject of serious debate within its legal community."

### Notes and Questions

1. It has been pointed out that the much criticized result of the *Singer* decision should be laid less at the doorstep of the Indian courts than of its legislature. As set out in the decision, Section 9 of the Foreign Awards Act implementing the New York Convention provides: "Nothing in this act shall . . . apply to any award made on an arbitration agreement governed by the laws of India."

2. That an award rendered abroad pursuant to an arbitration clause contained in an agreement subject to Indian law should be found to be a domestic Indian award must be considered an artificial construct. A doctrinal defense has been offered for the Indian position favoring the judicial review powers of the courts whose law governs the arbitration agreement. V.S. Deshpande *'Foreign Award' in the 1958 New York Convention*, 9 J. INT'L ARB. 51 (1992). However, the Indian position has been considered out of line with international practice. Lawrence Ebb, *Developing Views on What Constitutes a Foreign Arbitration Agreement and a 'Foreign Award' Under the New York Convention*, 1 AM. REV. INT'L. ARB. 364 (1990) and has been much criticized. *See* Jan Paulsson, *The New York Convention's Misadventures in India*, 6 INT'L ARB. REP. 3-8 (1992). A

philosophical view of the problems and progress of India is found in F.S. Nariman, *Finality in India: The Impossible Dream*, 10 ARB. INT'L 373 (1994).

3. In view of India's ongoing economic liberalization programs since 1991 and its desire to further attract foreign trade and investment, as well as its recognition of justified criticism of India's international commercial arbitration regime, India's arbitration statutes of 1937, 1940 and 1961 were repealed in 1996. They were replaced by the Arbitration and Conciliation Ordinance of 1996 based on the UNCITRAL Model Law and designed to provide a modern arbitration regime for India. The application of these new statutory provisions is expected to remedy the situation described above.

4. In view of the transient nature of arbitral tribunals it is sometimes difficult to determine the seat of arbitration and where the award was made. The determination that an award is domestic will have consequences as to the courts entitled to review the award. It will also affect whether or not the award is entitled to Convention protection, Article 1(1) of the New York Convention providing:

> This Convention shall apply to the recognition and enforcement of arbitral awards made in the territory of a State other than the State where the recognition and enforcement of such awards are sought, and arising out of differences between persons, whether physical or legal. It shall also apply to arbitral awards not considered as domestic awards in the State where their recognition and enforcement are sought.

Review Chapter 9 at pp. 1054-59 concerning the circumstances where awards rendered in the enforcement state have nonetheless been considered as Convention awards.

5. It will be recalled that the fact that an award is not a Convention award is not a bar to its enforcement. However, the criteria will be uniquely those of the enforcement state which may be more restrictive, or occasionally more liberal, than those of the Convention. *See supra* Chapter 9, pp. 1061-65.

## C.     NEW YORK CONVENTION: ARTICLE I — FIELD OF APPLICATION (ARBITRAL AWARDS)

3. When signing, ratifying or acceding to this Convention, or notifying extension under article X hereof, any State may on the basis of reciprocity declare that it will apply the Convention to the recognition and enforcement of awards made only in the territory of another Contracting State. It may also declare that it will apply the Convention only to differences arising out of legal relationships, whether contractual or not, which are considered as commercial under the national law of the State making such declaration.

\*       \*       \*

Article I(1) of the Convention provides that recognition and enforcement shall be granted to an arbitral award made in the territory of "a State other than the State where the recognition and enforcement of such awards are sought", hence to an award rendered in <u>any</u> other State, whether a signatory of the Convention or not. Article I(3) permits a signatory to limit the field of application of the award by using the so-called <u>first reservation</u>. When it does so it will be obliged only to recognize and enforce awards made in the territory of another <u>Contracting</u> State. Approximately two-thirds of Contracting States have subscribed to the Convention's first reservation.

The <u>second reservation</u> provided in Article I (3) permits a Contracting State to limit its recognition and enforcement obligation to awards arising out of legal relationships "which are considered as commercial under the national law of the State making such declaration".

This reservation was included because of concerns that civil law countries, which draw a distinction between commercial and non-commercial transactions, would not be able to adhere to the Convention. To date, less than half of the signatories to the New York Convention have in fact availed themselves of the commercial reservation.

In general, the commercial reservation has not been problematic because national courts have adopted a broad definition of the word "commercial." In India, however, the Court in the following dispute narrowly defined "commercial," thereby inhibiting execution of the award.

D.    *Indian Organic Chemicals Ltd v Chemtex Fibres, Inc. et al.*, 4 YEARBOOK OF COMMERCIAL ARBITRATION 271-73 (1979).

By three agreements made in New York, the Chemtex Group sold to Indian Chemicals a polyester staple fibre plant to be erected in India. The first agreement was concluded between subsidiary 1 (first defendant in the present suit) and Indian Chemicals. Under this agreement subsidiary 1 was to supply the machinery, equipment, drawings, etc. as well as the technical information and data relating not only to the machinery and equipment but also the installations to be made in connection therewith. The agreement contained an arbitral clause providing, inter alia, for 'arbitration in London, England' and 'to be governed by the rules of the International Chamber of Commerce, Paris, France', and further providing that 'the provisions of the Indian Arbitration Act, 1940, shall apply, save and except that where the rules of the said International Chamber of Commerce conflict with the Indian Arbitration Act 1940, the said rules of the International Chamber of Commerce shall prevail'.

The second agreement was concluded between subsidiary 2 (second defendant in the present suit) and Indian Chemicals. Under this agreement subsidiary 2 was to supply certain machinery, equipment, technical designs etc. as well as the technical information 'required for the implementation of the project'. Under this agreement subsidiary 2 was also to provide training facilities to the engineers or technicians designated by Indian Chemicals. This agreement also contained the same arbitral clause as the one just mentioned, except that this time it provided 'arbitration in India.'

The third agreement (captioned 'Four Party Agreement') was concluded between the parent corporation of the Chemtex Group (third defendant in the present suit) and the two subsidiaries on the one hand and Indian Chemicals on the other. In this agreement the parent corporation guaranteed the proper performance of its two subsidiaries. This agreement also contained an arbitral clause, providing for arbitration in London and the applicability of the rules of the ICC.

When, following a dispute, Indian Chemicals initiated a law suit against all three defendants before the Indian Court, the defendants applied for a stay of the action under Sect. 3 of the Foreign Awards (Recognition and Enforcement) Act of 1961, which implements the New York Convention in India. The High Court rejected the application for the reasons summarised below.

Extract

1. The Judge first of all observed that the 1961 Act, which implements the New York Convention in India, was applicable. This Act applies to foreign awards, a definition of which is given in Sect.

2. This definition refers to awards rendered on differences
'considered as commercial under the law in force in India' and made
in pursuance of an arbitration agreement to which the New York
Convention applies.[324] Pursuant to Sect. 3 of the Act, any party to
an agreement to which Art. II of the Convention applies, may, when
court proceedings have been initiated, apply to the court to stay the
proceedings.

The Judge argued that it therefore follows that not only must
the relationship be commercial but such a relationship must,
pursuant to Sect. 2 of the Act, be considered as commercial under
the law of India. If the expression 'commercial relationship' is

---

[324] (1)      Sec. 2 of the 1961 Act reads:

In this Act, unless the context otherwise requires, "foreign award"
means an award on differences between person arising out of legal
relationships, whether contractual or not, considered as commercial
under the law in force in India, made on or after the 11th day of
October, 1960

(a)      in pursuance of an agreement in writing for arbitration to
which the Convention set forth in the Schedule applies, and

(b)      in one of such territories as the Central Government, being
satisfied that reciprocal provisions have been made, may,
by notification as in the Official Gazette, declare to be
territories to which the said Convention applies.

(2)      Sect. 3 (as amended by Law no. 57 of 1973, see YB I (1976) India
no. 1 Note) of the 1961 Act reads:

'Notwithstanding anything contained in the Arbitration Act, 1940 or
in the Code of Civil Procedure, 1908, if any party to an agreement
to which Article II of the Convention set forth in the Schedule
applies, or any person claiming through or under him commences
any legal proceedings in any court against any other party to the
agreement or any person claiming through or under him in respect
of any matter agreed to be referred, any party to such legal
proceedings may, at any time after appearance and before filing a
written statement or taking any other step in the proceedings, apply
to the court to stay the proceedings and the court, unless satisfied
that the agreement is null and void, inoperative or incapable of
being performed or that there is not in fact any dispute between the
parties with regard to the matter agreed to be referred, shall make
an order staying the proceedings.'

interpreted as normally understood in legal parlance, it would render the words 'under the law in force in India' nugatory.

2. The Judge then examined the agreements between Indian Chemicals and the three defendants, and rejected the argument of Indian Chemicals which relied on an earlier decision of the High Court of Bombay, *Kamani Engineering Corp. v. Société de Traction*. In that case it was held that an agreement which provides for technical assistance and know-how is not an agreement of commercial character. The Judge, however, distinguished the agreement in question from that involved in the *Kamani*-case:

> 'These agreements cannot be said to be agreements for providing for mere technical know-how. These agreements partake the character of what may be called turn-key jobs. These agreements cover a broad spectrum of commercial activity needed for the establishment of the facility for production of polyester staple fibre in India by the plaintiffs. The consideration mentioned in the agreement is the price for the goods as also the amounts payable for the services to be rendered including furnishing of the technical information. The provision as to the technical information is merely a part of the bargain between the parties. It is not the whole of it.'

3. However, the Judge considered further:

'The inescapable conclusion that agreements are commercial however does not clinch the issue. Such a characterisation does not amount to saying that the agreements between the plaintiffs and the defendants come within the purview of Sect. 2 read with Sect. 3 of the 1961 Act. The expression occurring in Sect. 2 is legal relationships, whether contractual or not, considered as commercial *under the law in force in India*' (emphasis supplied by the Judge)....
In other words, before provisions of Sect. 3 can be invoked, the agreement must be an agreement embodying a relationship considered commercial under a provision of law. In my opinion, in order to invoke the provisions of Sect. 3, it is not enough to establish that an agreement is commercial. It must also be established that is [sic] is commercial by virtue of a provision of law or an operative legal principle in force in India'.

The Judge concluded that the counsel for defendants

'is unable to call in aid any statutory provision or any operative legal principle in India (according to which the transaction could be considered as commercial).... In these circumstances, I must hold that the agreements though commercial do not fall within the coverage of Sect. 3 of the 1961 Act.'

\* \* \*

The appellate branch of the Indian High Court subsequently took a different view.

E. *European Grain & Shipping, Ltd. (U.K.) v. Bombay Extractions Ltd. (India)*, 8 YEARBOOK OF COMMERCIAL ARBITRATION 371-76 (1983).

By a contract dated September 18, 1976, and signed by both parties, Bombay Extractions agreed to ship to European Grain 250 tons of groundnut extractions at a price of U.K. Pounds 99 per ton. One of the terms of the contract provided that "this contract is made under the terms and conditions effective at the date of the Grain and Feed Trade Association (GAFTA), Baltic Exchange Chambers, 28 St. Mary Axe., London, Contract no. 119."

GAFTA Contract no. 119 contains an arbitration clause, the material part of which reads as follows:

"Any dispute arising out of or under this contract shall be settled by arbitration in London in accordance with the Arbitration Rules of the Grain and Feed Trade Association Ltd. No. 125 such Rules forming part of this contract and of which both parties shall be deemed to be cognisant."

Following a dispute over the damages to be paid for non-shipment by Bombay Extractions, European Grain resorted to arbitration in accordance with the Rules of GAFTA. Notwithstanding having been repeatedly notified, Bombay Extractions neither appointed its arbitrator nor participated in the arbitration proceedings. By an award made on September 8, 1979, the arbitrators awarded to European Grain UK Pounds 12,000, [sic] that being the price difference, and US Dollars 4,812 [sic] on account of dead freight, as

well as interest of 8% per year from April 27, 1977, to the date of
the award.

The request for enforcement by European Grain under the
Indian Arbitration Act 1961, which is the legislation implementing
the New York Convention in India, was rejected by the single Judge
of the High Court of Bombay. The Judge refused enforcement
reasoning that the provisions of the 1961 Act could not be availed on
the basis of an earlier decision by a single Judge of the High Court
of Bombay. In that decision it was held that for Sect. 3 of the 1961
Act to apply, an agreement must be commercial not as normally
understood, but commercial by virtue of a provision of law or an
operative legal principle in force in India.

European Grain appealed against the decision of the single Judge to
the appellate branch of the High Court.

The appellate branch of the High Court (consisting of two Judges)
reversed the decision of the single Judge and granted enforcement
for the following reasons:

EXTRACT

1. After considering the legislative history of the Convention and
quoting Art. I, para. 3, and Art. II, para. 1, of the Convention, the
Court said:

> The declaration contemplated by clause 3 of Article I
> of the New York Convention that a Contracting State
> would apply the Convention only to differences arising
> out of legal relationships, whether contractual or not,
> which were considered as commercial under the
> national law of the State making such declaration and
> the declaration made while declaring India's accession
> to the New York Convention that 'They (Government
> of India) further declare that they will apply the
> Convention only to differences arising out of legal
> relationships, whether contractual or not, which are
> considered as commercial under the Law of India,'
> were given effect to in the definition of 'foreign
> award' in Section 2 [of the 1961 Act], the material
> part of which reads as follow:-

'In this Act, unless the context otherwise requires, "foreign award" means an award on differences between persons arising out of legal relationships, whether contractual or not, considered as commercial under the law in force in India, made on or after the 11th day of October, 1960 -

(a) in pursuance of an agreement in writing for arbitration to which the Convention set forth in the Schedule applies, and

(b) in one of such territories as the Central Government, being satisfied that reciprocal provisions have been made, may, by notification in the Official Gazette, declare to be territories to which the said Convention applies.'

2.	"There is no dispute that United Kingdom is one of the countries which has been notified. The definition of foreign award will show that in order to fall within that definition, the award must satisfy certain requirements. Firstly, it must be an award on differences between persons who have legal relationship with one another, such relationship may be contractual or not, and secondly, the legal relationship must be considered as commercial under the law in force in India, and thirdly, the award must be made on or after 11th October 1960, and lastly, the award must be in pursuance of an agreement in writing for arbitration to which the New York Convention applies.

3.	"Now, for the purposes of this case, it is not necessary to go into the width of the meaning of the word 'commerce' because admittedly, a trading activity like buying and selling, which is involved in the instant case, will be covered by commerce. 'Commercial' will mean pertaining to commerce, on which there can hardly be any dispute. In Black's Law Dictionary, 'commercial' is defined as 'relates to or is connected with trade and traffic or commerce in general' and it is stated that 'commercial' is a 'generic term for [al]most all aspects of buying and selling.'

. . .

5.    "Now, when the definition of foreign award refers to 'legal relationship ... considered as commercial under the law in force in India' we cannot overlook the fact that the 1961 Act was intended to give effect to the New York Convention. The New York Convention made reference to the national law and the declaration of accession to the New York Convention by India made reference to the law of India. Now, the words 'national law' or 'the law of India' no doubt will take in a particular statute, but these words are of such wide import that they will envelope the entire body of laws which are effective or operative in India. Indeed when the statute uses the words 'law in force in India', such use of words could never have contemplated a reference to any particular law and while it may in a given case in the context refer to a law on that particular subject, generally such words are used when reference is made to the general body of laws operative in India.

. . .

"The nature of the relationship will depend on the nature of the transaction and whether the nature of the transaction is commercial or not will have to be determined with reference generally to the law in force in the country inclusive of what the learned Judge, who decided the *Indian Organic Chemicals Ltd.'s* case referred to as an operative legal principle in force in India. The mere use of the word 'under' preceding the words 'law in force in India' would not, in our view, necessarily mean that you have to find a statutory provision or a provision of law which specifically deals with the subject or particular legal relationships being commercial in nature."

"It is no doubt true that the use of the word 'under' in a given case may require a reference to a particular provision of law, but the meaning of the word 'under'

also is 'according to.' (See Black's Law Dictionary).
If the word 'under' is construed in the sense of
meaning 'according to the law of India' or 'according
to the law in force in India' or in the sense of a legal
relationship being regarded as commercial by the law
in force in India, such construction cannot mean, as
was contended, that the court is not giving a meaning
to all the words used in Section 2 or that any part of
that Section being ignored."

6. Counsel for European Grain had referred to two decisions of the
U.S. District Court in New York in which the question of the
meaning of "commercial" was considered.

7. The first was *Island Territory of Curaçao v. Solitron Devices Inc.*
The case concerned a contract to operate an electronics
manufacturing industry on the Island Curaçao which would result in
the creation of several thousands of local jobs. The District Court
had observed:

"Research has developed nothing to show what the
purpose of the 'commercial' limitation was. We may
logically speculate that it was to exclude matrimonial
and other domestic relations awards, political awards,
and the like.

"Judged by any test, however, the contract of January
12, 1968 seems clearly to be 'commercial.' It has
been said in this connection (Quigley, Convention on
Foreign Arbitral Awards, 58 A.B.A.J. 821, 823
(1972)): 'In the case of the United States reservation it
seems clear that the full scope of "commerce" and
foreign commerce as these terms have been broadly
interpreted, is available for arbitral agreements and
awards.'"

8. As regards the second case the Court stated:

The other decision is also of the United States District
Court, Southern District of New York and the extract
is taken out of the *Yearbook of Commercial
Arbitration*, Volume V, 1980, page 271. The dispute

in that case was between two corporations, one from
Chile and the other from New York, and the
arbitration award was made in Chile. It was held that
a dispute arose out of a classic commercial
relationship involving purchase and sale of goods by
two corporations and, therefore, the arbitration
agreement was within the meaning of the New York
Convention. We quote the extract below:-

> 'After having referred to Art. II, para.
> 1, of the New York Convention, and
> having observed that the "United States
> has limited the scope of Art. II, para.
> 1, by adopting the reservation that the
> Convention applies only to arbitration
> agreements 'arising out of legal
> relationships... which are considered as
> commercial.'... Art. I, para. 3 the
> Court concluded that the submission
> agreement provided for arbitration of
> the dispute as to the quality and
> condition of goods purchased. Since the
> dispute arose out of a *classic
> commercial relationship* - one involving
> the purchase and sale of goods by two
> corporations - the submission agreement
> was an arbitration agreement within the
> meaning of the Convention'." (emphasis
> by High Court)

9. The Court inferred from these two American decisions:

> "We have already pointed out above that paragraph 3
> of Article I of the New York Convention refers to
> 'legal relationships . . . which are considered as
> commercial under the national law of the State making
> such declaration.' *The United States District Court has
> thus understood the declaration to mean that if under
> the general law a relationship can be considered as
> commercial, the Convention on the Recognition and
> Enforcement of Foreign Arbitral Awards will be
> attached.*" (emphasis by High Court)

10. The Court dealt with the single Judge's opinion as follows:

"With great respect to the learned Judge, not only are
we unable to agree with the view taken by him, but it
appears to us that the observations made by the
learned Judge that the relationship must be 'considered
as commercial under the provisions *of a law*
(emphasis by High Court) in force in India' seem to
run counter to what the learned Judge himself
observed in the earlier paragraph when he took the
view that the legal relationship must be commercial
'by virtue of a provision of law or *an operative legal
principle in force in India.*' (emphasis by High Court).
Now, an operative legal principle in force in India
would also be a principle flowing from any law
already in force. In any case, it is not possible for us
to accept the construction that the words 'law in force
in India' were intended to mean a particular law
specifically enacted for the purposes of the provisions
of the 1961 Act."

11. The Court concluded:

"We have no doubt that the contract in the instant
case, which was for the sale and purchase of a
commodity, was clearly a contract which brought
about legal relationship which was commercial in
nature under the Indian law."

\*        \*        \*

IV.     RECOGNITION AND ENFORCEMENT UNDER THE CONVENTION: PROCEDURES AND DEFENSES

A.     Jan Paulsson, "The New York Convention in International Practice - Problems of Assimilation", Speech delivered at the ASA (Swiss Arbitration Association) Conference on the New York Convention of 1958 (Feb. 2, 1996) pp. 6-10.

.     .     .

B.     Enforcement of arbitral awards

Once a dispute has been referred to arbitration and an award has been rendered by the tribunal, the second objective of the Convention comes into play, namely to ensure recognition and enforcement of the foreign arbitral <u>award</u>. A foreign award, of course, is an award which either was made in the territory of another State, or was made in the State where enforcement is sought, but has a foreign or international element. This aim of the Convention is set out in Article I, and the general obligation upon contracting states to recognize foreign arbitral awards as binding and to enforce them is set out in Article III. The Convention imposes a clear <u>obligation</u> on member States to enforce awards, if various conditions are fulfilled by the party seeking enforcement. These conditions are found in Article IV. If the conditions are fulfilled, the award must be enforced unless one of the grounds for refusal of enforcement exists. The grounds for refusal of enforcement are set out in Article V.

1.     Conditions for enforcement of awards

The burden of proof on the party seeking enforcement is not an onerous one. The whole purpose of Article IV is to facilitate enforcement. Thus a minimum of conditions are required to be met. These are that:

> "the party applying for recognition and enforcement shall, at the time of the application, supply:
>
> (a)     The duly authenticated original award or a duly certified copy thereof; and

       (b)      The original agreement referred to in Article II
                  or a duly certified copy thereof."

These conditions are the <u>only</u> obligations which the Convention
places on the party seeking enforcement, and in fulfilling them, he
produces *prima facie* evidence entitling him to obtain enforcement of
the award.

There have been a number of cases in a variety of countries where
the party seeking enforcement has failed to meet one or more of the
Article IV conditions. It is interesting to note, however, that in many
of these cases, the courts have taken a flexible approach as to what
in fact constitutes compliance with Article IV and have granted
enforcement even in situations where the conditions have not been
strictly adhered to.

The following examples are evidence of this purposive approach.

In Austria, where a German petitioner sought to enforce an award
given by an arbitral tribunal in Rotterdam, the Austrian Supreme
Court allowed enforcement despite the fact that the petitioner had
only submitted the arbitral award to the Court and had omitted to
provide the underlying arbitration agreement. The Supreme Court
held that the petitioner's non-compliance with Article IV did not
justify a refusal to enforce the award and the Court allowed the
petitioner to cure the defect by producing the agreement at court
subsequently to the filing of the original application for
enforcement.[325]

Similarly, the courts of Hong Kong have been prepared to overlook
such procedural errors. In a case heard by the Hong Kong Supreme
Court in 1991,[326] the Court allowed a Plaintiff who had previously
failed to provide the original award to the Court, to submit this
award during the course of the proceedings.

---

[325] OGH 17-11-1965, 3 Ob. 128/65; Zeitschrift für Rechtsvergleichung Vol. 9 p.
123 (1968), reported in 1 YEARBOOK OF COMMERCIAL ARBITRATION 182 (1976).

[326] *Guangdong New Technology v. Chiu Shing*, Supreme Court of Hong Kong,
High Court, Miscellaneous Proceedings, 23 August 1991, No. MP 1625
(unpublished), reported in 18 YEARBOOK OF COMMERCIAL ARBITRATION 385 (1993).

These and other such decisions seem to be in line with the general spirit of the Convention which is to facilitate enforcement. As the Handelsgericht (Commercial Court) in Zurich reasoned in 1990 in a case concerning the enforcement of an award rendered by the *Chambre Arbitrale Maritime de Paris*:

> "one should not apply too strict a standard to the formal requirements for the submission of documents ... when the conditions for recognition are undisputed and materially beyond doubt."[327]

Other countries, however, appear to have used the existence of such procedural defects as an excuse for refusing to enforce awards, in situations where these defects could easily have been cured.

Some Italian courts have taken what may seem an unduly rigid approach. The Court of Appeal in Bologna[328] refused to enforce a final arbitral award on the ground that the petitioner, although it had provided the Court with the final award of the arbitral tribunal, had failed to submit an original or a certified copy of the partial award which preceded the final award.

Other Italian courts have continued their strict approach in their interpretation of the words "shall at the time of application" in Article IV. In a case where a petitioner had not supplied the court with the arbitration agreement when the application for enforcement was made, the Italian Supreme Court refused to enforce the award for non-compliance with Article IV.[329] The Supreme Court later confirmed this view in another case by holding that if the petitioner fails to supply the arbitration agreement and the arbitral award <u>at the time</u> of making the application for enforcement, the court will not allow this procedural defect to be cured during the course of the

---

[327] Published in <u>Swiss Arbitration Association Bulletin</u> (1990, No. 2) pp. 183-186, and reported in 17 YEARBOOK OF COMMERCIAL ARBITRATION 584 (1992).

[328] Corte di Appello [Court of Appeal (of Bologna)], 4 February 1993 (unpublished), reported in 19 YEARBOOK OF COMMERCIAL ARBITRATION 700 (1994).

[329] *Viceré Livio v. Prodexport*, Corte di Cassazione (SEZ.I) May 26, 1981, No. 3456, published in 31 <u>Giustizia civile</u> (1981) I, cols. 1910-1912, and reported in 7 YEARBOOK OF COMMERCIAL ARBITRATION 345 (1982).

enforcement proceedings, and enforcement will be refused on the grounds that Article IV has not been complied with.[330]

Additional problems are caused by the fact that once an Italian court has refused a request for enforcement (for failure to comply with Article IV, or for any other reason), this decision becomes *res judicata*. Italian courts have thus created a situation where petitioners seeking enforcement of a foreign arbitral award in Italy must beware, because if they fail to follow the Convention to the letter, they risk refusal of enforcement without the opportunity to reapply.

Such a literal interpretation of Article IV thwarts the Convention's uniform application. Fortunately, the courts in most other countries have instead taken a "pro-enforcement" stance on the enforcement of awards.

. . .

## 2.      Grounds for refusal of enforcement

Once the petitioner has complied with the conditions in Article IV, the court must enforce the award <u>unless</u> the party against whom enforcement is sought can prove that one or more of the grounds for refusal, set out in Article V(1), exists. In addition, Article V(2) allows the court to refuse enforcement on its own motion for reasons of public policy.

Article V by its very nature favors enforcement. The burden of proof rests on the party resisting enforcement of the award. The grounds for refusal are also exhaustive, so that enforcement may be refused <u>only if</u> the party resisting enforcement can prove one of the grounds, <u>or if</u> the court finds that the enforcement of the award would result in a violation of its public policy.

---

[330] *Jassica SA v. Ditta Gioacchino Polojaz*, Corte di Cassazione [Supreme Court], 12 February 1987, No. 1526 and 26 May 1987, No. 4706, published in <u>Rivista di diritto internazionale privato e processuale</u> (1988) pp. 515-519 and pp. 529-534, and reported in 17 YEARBOOK OF COMMERCIAL ARBITRATION 525 (1992).

In addition to being exhaustive, the grounds for refusal are meant to be interpreted narrowly. This means that the existence of the grounds in Article V(1) should be accepted in serious cases only and the public policy violation required by Article V(2) should only be asserted by courts in extreme cases. The proper functioning of Article V and the Convention as a whole relies heavily on the national courts' willingness to follow such a narrow interpretation. It is this Article of the Convention which is most prone to misinterpretation and most open to abuse by national courts, displaying skepticism of non-national sources of law and bias against foreigners who wish to enforce awards in their territories.

*     *     *

The five grounds for refusal of enforcement under Article V(1) are, in summary: a) incapacity of the parties or invalidity of the arbitration agreement under applicable law; b) violation of procedural due process; c) the award deals with matters beyond the scope of the submission to arbitration; d) irregularity in the composition of the arbitral tribunal or arbitral procedure; and e) the award has been set aside or suspended by a competent authority of the country in which, or under the law of which, the award was made.

The two additional grounds upon which an enforcement court may refuse recognition are a) that the subject matter is not considered arbitrable under the law of the country of the enforcement court, and b) "[T]he recognition or enforcement of the award would be contrary to the public policy" of the country where recognition and enforcement is sought.

The reader should review Chapter 9 at pp. 1137-72 for examples of the approach to judicial control in the country of enforcement. Three principles can be noted in the enforcement of awards under the Convention: the grounds upon which an award may be refused are intended to be exhaustive; the merits of the arbitral award are in no circumstances to be reexamined; and, the burden of proof for refusal of enforcement is on the respondent. Accordingly, while enforcement may sometimes be refused this is much more likely to occur when a fundamental error of procedural due process or a lack of arbitral jurisdiction can be found rather than where an award is attacked on more general grounds including the

allegation that the award offends the public policy of the
enforcement state.

B.      *Iran Aircraft Industries and Iran Helicopter Support
        and Renewal Company v. Avco Corporation*, 980
        F.2d, 141 (2d Cir. 1992)

[Avco, a United States party, brought arbitration before the
Iran-United States Claims Tribunal on claims arising out of contracts
for the repair and replacement of helicopter engines and replacement
parts with Iranian parties the performance of which was interrupted
by the Iranian revolution. The Iranian parties counterclaimed and a
final award was rendered allowing a net balance of $3,513,086 in
favor of the Iranian parties. The favorable balance was arrived at
largely because of the disallowal of a large part of Avco's claims on
the basis that they were not sufficiently supported by invoices. Avco
obtained summary judgment from the District Court declining to
enforce the award and the Iranian parties appeal.]

.    .    .

On May 17, 1985, the Tribunal held a pre-hearing conference
to consider, *inter alia*, "whether voluminous and complicated data
should be presented through summaries, tabulations, charts, graphs
or extracts in order to save time and costs." *See Avco Corp. v. Iran
Aircraft Indus.*, Case No. 261, 19. Iran-U.S.Cl.Trib.Rep. 200, 235
(1988) (Brower, J., concurring and dissenting). At the conference,
Avco's counsel, Dean Cordiano, requested guidance from the
Tribunal as to the appropriate method for proving certain of its
claims which were based on voluminous invoices, stating:

In the interest of keeping down some of the
documentation for the Tribunal we have not placed in
evidence as of yet the actual supporting invoices. But
we have those invoices and they are available and if
the Tribunal would be interested in seeing them we
can obviously place them in evidence or we can use a
procedure whereby an outside auditing agency, uh,
certifies to the amount of the, uh, summaries vis-a-vis
the underlying invoices. Both of those approaches can
be taken. But I want to assure the Tribunal that all of

the invoices reflected in our exhibits to the memorial .
. . exist and are available.

*Id.* at 235-36. After noting that the Iranian parties "obviously have
had those invoices all along," Cordiano stated that he would:

> like the Tribunal's guidance as to whether, uh, you
> would like this outside certifying agency to go through
> the underlying invoices and certify as to the summary
> amounts or that the Tribunal feels at this point that
> the, uh—that you would rather have the, uh, raw data,
> so to speak—the underlying invoices. Uh, we're
> prepared to do it either way.

*Id.* at 236.

The Chairman of the Chamber Three, Judge Nils Mangard of
Sweden, then engaged in the following colloquy with Cordiano:

| | |
|---|---|
| Mangard: | I don't think we will be very, very much enthusiastic getting kilos and kilos of invoices. |
| Cordiano: | That, that's what I thought so . . . |
| Mangard: | So I think it will help us . . . |
| Cordiano: | We'll use . . . |
| Mangard: | To use the alternative rather. |
| Cordiano: | Alright . . . |
| Mangard: | On the other hand, I don't know if, if any, if there are any objections to any specific invoices so far made by the Respondents. But anyhow as a precaution maybe you could . . . |
| Cordiano: | Yes sir. |
| Mangard: | Get an account made. |

*Id.* at 236. Neither counsel for the Iranian parties nor the Iranian
Judge attended the pre-hearing conference.

On July 22, 1985, Avco submitted to the Tribunal a
Supplemental Memorial, which stated in part:

> In response to the Tribunal's suggestion at the Pre-
> hearing Conference, Avco's counsel has retained

Arthur Young & Co., an internationally recognized
public accounting firm, to verify that the accounts
receivable ledgers submitted to the Tribunal accurately
reflect the actual invoices in Avco's records.

Attached to the Supplemental Memorial was an affidavit of a partner
at Arthur Young & Co. which verified that the accounts receivable
ledgers submitted by Avco tallied with Avco's original invoices,
with the exception of one invoice for $240.14. *Id.* at 237.

The Tribunal held its hearing on the merits on September 16-17,
1986. By that time, Judge Mangard had resigned as Chairman of
Chamber Three and had been replaced by Judge Michael Virally of
France. At the hearing, Judge Parviz Ansari of Iran engaged in the
following colloquy with Cordiano:

| | |
|---|---|
| Ansari: | May I ask a question? It is about the evidence. It was one of the first or one of the few cases that I have seen that the invoices have not been submitted. So what is your position on this point about the substantiation of the claim? |
| Cordiano: | Your Honor, this point was raised at the pre-hearing conference in May of last year. |
| Ansari: | I was not there. |
| Cordiano: | I remember that you weren't there. I think we were kind of lonely that day. We were on one side of the table, the other side was not there . . . We could have produced at some point the thousands of pages of invoices, but we chose to substantiate our invoices through . . . the Arthur Young audit performed specifically for this tribunal proceeding. |

*Id.* at 237.

The Tribunal issued the Award on July 18, 1988. Of
particular relevance here, the Tribunal disallowed Avco's claims
which were documented by its audited accounts receivable ledgers,
stating, "[T]he Tribunal cannot grant Avco's claim solely on the
basis of an affidavit and a list of invoices, even if the existence of

the invoices was certified by an independent audit." *Id.* at 211
(majority opinion).

Judge Brower, the American judge and the only judge of the
panel who was present at the pre-hearing conference, filed a separate
Concurring and Dissenting Opinion in which he stated:

> I believe the Tribunal has misled the Claimant,
> however, unwittingly, regarding the evidence it was
> required to submit, thereby depriving Claimant, to
> that extent, of the ability to present its case. . . .
>
> \*       \*       \*       \*       \*       \*
>
> Since Claimant did exactly what it previously was told
> to do by the Tribunal the denial in the present Award
> of any of those invoice claims on the ground that
> more evidence should have been submitted constitutes
> a denial to Claimant of the ability to present its case
> to the Tribunal.

*Id.* at 231, 238.

### A.    *"Direct" Enforceability of the Award*

> [The Court of Appeal denied the Iranian parties argument that
> under the Algiers Accord all Claims Tribunal awards are
> "final and binding" and must be "directly" enforced by U.S.
> courts without regard to the New York Convention and
> defenses thereunder.]

.  .  .

### B.    *The New York Convention*

Avco argues that the district court properly denied
enforcement of the Award pursuant to Art. V(1)(b) of the New York
Convention because it was unable to present its case to the Tribunal.
The New York Convention provides for nonenforcement where:

> The party against whom the award is invoked was not
> given proper notice of the appointment of the

> arbitrator or of the arbitration proceedings or was
> *otherwise unable to present his case* . . .

New York Convention, Art. V(1)(b) (emphasis added).

We have recognized that the defense provided for in Art. V(1)(b) "essentially sanctions the application of the forum state's standards of due process," and that due process rights are "entitled to full force under the Convention as defenses to enforcement." *Parsons & Whittemore Overseas Co., Inc. v. Societe Generale de l'Industrie du Papier (RAKTA)*, 508 F.2d 969, 975-76 (2d Cir.1974). Under our law, "[t]he fundamental requirement of due process is the opportunity to be heard 'at a meaningful time and in a meaningful manner.'" *Mathews v. Eldridge*, 424 U.S. 319, 333, 96 S.Ct. 893, 902, 47 L.Ed.2d 62 (1976) (quoting *Armstrong v. Manzo*, 380 U.S. 545, 552, 85 S.Ct. 1187, 1191, 14 L.Ed.2d 62 (1965)). Accordingly, if Avco was denied the opportunity to be heard in a meaningful time or in a meaningful manner, enforcement of the Award should be refused pursuant to Art. V(1)(b).

At the pre-hearing conference, Judge Mangard specifically advised Avco not to burden the Tribunal by submitting "kilos and kilos of invoices." Instead, Judge Mangard approved the method of proof proposed by Avco, namely the submission of Avco's audited accounts receivable ledgers. Later, when Judge Ansari questioned Avco's method of proof, he never responded to Avco's explanation that it was proceeding according to an earlier understanding. Thus, Avco was not made aware that the Tribunal now required the actual invoices to substantiate Avco's claim. Having thus led Avco to believe it had used a proper method to substantiate its claim, the Tribunal then rejected Avco's claim for lack of proof.

We believe that by so misleading Avco, however unwittingly, the Tribunal denied Avco the opportunity to present its claim in a meaningful manner. Accordingly, Avco was "unable to present [its] case" within the meaning of Art. V(1)(b), and enforcement of the Award was properly denied.

Affirmed.

CARDAMONE, Circuit Judge, dissenting:

The issue before us is whether Avco was denied an opportunity to present its case before the Iran-United States Claims Tribunal at the Hague. To rule, as the majority does, that it was denied such an opportunity renders the Tribunal's award unenforceable under Art. V(1)(b) of the [New York Convention, 1958]. I respectfully dissent because it seems to me that a fair reading of this record reveals that Avco was not denied such an opportunity. Thus, in my view the arbitral award is enforceable under the New York Convention.

I

Avco's focus is on a pre-trial colloquy between its counsel and Judge Mangard of the Tribunal regarding the use of summaries in place of some of the invoices Avco needed to prove its claim. Judge Mangard stated the panel would not be very "enthusiastic about getting kilos and kilos of invoices," and added that there appeared to be no objection to using summaries of certain invoices, and suggested to counsel that "as a precaution" Avco might get an account summary made. Based on this brief exchange, Avco now makes the dubious argument that this colloquy constituted a binding pre-trial ruling by the Tribunal that summaries of those particular invoices could substitute for the invoices and would be sufficient evidence at trial.

At the time of trial Judge Mangard was no longer a member of the Tribunal. Another judge who was present at the pre-trial had also been replaced. The three-judge panel hearing the case retained therefore only one of the original judges present at the pre-trial exchange. These trial judges had different concerns than had the earlier panel. One of the new judges, Judge Ansari, questioned the adequacy of Avco's proof based only on summaries of invoices. He noted that it was "the first or one of the few cases" he had heard of in which none of the invoices were produced as evidence. In response, Avco's counsel stressed the massive number of invoices involved, mentioning that Avco "*chose* to substantiate [the] invoices through other methods," and stated, "we simply *chose* not to put in thousand of pages of documents." (emphasis added.) Concluding that Avco's proof did not establish its claim, the Tribunal declined to grant Avco an award based only on summaries of its invoices.

## II

The New York Convention obligates U.S. courts to enforce foreign arbitral awards unless certain defenses provided in Art. V(1) of the Convention are established. The specific defense with which we deal in the case at hand appears in Art. V(1)(b). That section states that enforcement of an arbitral award may be denied if the court is satisfied that the party against whom the award is sought to be enforced was unable to present its case before the arbitration panel.

Based on the facts before us, Avco fails to meet the legal standard of being unable to present its case before the arbitral Tribunal so as to render the award unenforceable under the New York Convention. That standard, as the majority points out, essentially involves a due process inquiry to see whether the party against whom enforcement is sought has been put on notice and has had an opportunity to respond. *See Parsons & Whittemore Overseas Co. v. Societe Generale de l'Industrie du Papier (RAKTA)*, 508 F.2d 969, 975-76 (2d Cir.1974). Unfortunately, only limited case law exists on this issue, and those cases that can be found merely note, in applying Art. V(1)(b), that due process serves as an interpretive guide.

One of the reasons for this dissent is because until today no federal or foreign case appears to have used Art. V(1)(b)'s narrow exception as a reason to refuse to enforce an arbitral award due to the arbitration panel's failure to consider certain evidence. Moreover, some decisions have rejected the Art. V(1)(b) defense under other, somewhat analogous circumstances. For example, in *Parsons & Whittemore Overseas Co.*, 508 F.2d at 975-76, we refused to use the defense to bar enforcement based on an arbitral Tribunal's refusal to accommodate a key witness' schedule, stating that the inability to present one's witness was "a risk inherent in an agreement to submit to arbitration." Similarly, another court has held that a party was not denied the opportunity to present its defenses under Art. V(1)(b) when it had notice of an arbitration, but chose not to respond. *See Goetech Lizenz AG v. Evergreen Systems*, 697 F.Supp. 1248, 1253 (E.D.N.Y.1988). The court in *Evergreen Systems* ruled that the defendant's "failure to participate was a decision that was reached only after the Company had full knowledge of the peril at which it acted." *Id.* In the face of Judge

Ansari's repeated questioning of Avco's counsel, Avco was plainly placed on similar notice of the possible risk that the panel would choose not to rely on invoice summaries in determining whether to grant it an award.

Further support for finding that Avco was not denied due process arises from a like exception to enforceability that appears in the Federal Arbitration Act, 9 U.S.C. § 10 (1988). That Act also provides an exception to enforcement for the inability to present one's case at arbitration. The more extensive case law available under § 10 supports the conclusion that Avco was not denied due process before the Iran-U.S. Claims Tribunal. Avco's protests that the events in this case was more "egregious" than in other cases involving the inability to present one's case at arbitration are unpersuasive. The ruling by the Hague Tribunal in the instant matter was not high-handed or arbitrary as are those cases, upon which Avco relies, arising under the Federal Arbitration Act. A reading of those cases reveals that they either involve arbitration hearings actually cut short and not completed before an award was rendered, *see Confinco, Inc. v. Barkie & Bros, N.V.*, 395 F.Supp. 613, 615 (S.D.N.Y.1975); *Teamsters, Local Union No. 506 v. E.D. Clapp Corp.*, 551 F.Supp. 570, 577-78 (N.D.N.Y.1982), *aff'd*, 742 F.2d 1441 (2d Cir.1983), or a panel's outright refusal to hear certain relevant evidence at all, *see Harvey Aluminum Inc. v. United Steelworkers*, 263 F.Supp. 488, 493 (C.D.Cal.1967).

The present picture is vastly different. Avco had a full opportunity to present its claims, and was on notice that there might be a problem with its proof, especially given Judge Ansari's concerns voiced at trial. The earlier panel surely had never said that the invoices themselves would not be accepted or considered as evidence at trial. Nor did the pre-trial colloquy clearly indicate that the earlier panel had issued a definitive ruling that account summaries would be sufficient substitute proof for the invoices. Avco did not declare, after hearing Judge Ansari's comments, that it had been precluded by the pre-trial colloquy from producing the invoices, nor did it then attempt to introduce them before the panel. Rather than address Judge Ansari's concerns through producing the invoices themselves, Avco reiterated its "choice" to produce only a summary of the invoices. In so doing it took a calculated risk. Under these circumstances, Avco can scarcely credibly maintain that it was prevented from presenting its case before the Tribunal.

## III

When reviewing the grant of summary judgment which dismissed the action to enforce the award, we must view the facts in the light more favorable to the Iranian parties. When so viewed those facts fail to demonstrate that Avco was denied the opportunity to present its claims to the Tribunal. For the reasons stated I think the district court erred in reaching the opposite conclusion. Accordingly, I dissent and vote to enforce the award.

\*   \*   \*

Ever since the U.S. Supreme Court's affirmation in *Scherk v. Alberto-Culver Co.*, 417 U.S. 506 (1974), of its pro-arbitration bias, it has been exceedingly difficult to resist enforcement of foreign awards under the New York Convention. The following case, among many set out in previous chapters, is typical.

C.    *Int'l Standard Electric Corp. v. Bridas Sociedad Anonima Petrolera*, 745 F.Supp. 172 (S.D.N.Y. 1990).

CONBOY, District Judge:

[International Standard Electric Corporation (ISEC), a wholly owned subsidiary of ITT sought to enforce an award, rendered in Mexico, against Bridas, an Argentine company. Bridas sought to vacate the award.]

On December 20, 1989, the Panel, in accordance with the rules which require the advance review and approval by the ICC International Court of Arbitration, signed the final Award, which was released and issued to the parties on January 16, 1990.

The Arbitral Award ("Award") (Bridas Notice, Ex. A.), found unanimously by the Panel, concluded that Bridas had not established that ISEC had made misrepresentations or committed fraud in connection with the sale of certain stock to Bridas in 1979 (Award at 17); that Bridas had not established that ISEC had unlawfully mismanaged CSEA (Award at 18); that Bridas had established that in July of 1984 ISEC breached its fiduciary obligations to Bridas in connection with a 1984 recapitalization of CSEA (Award at 19-20); and that Bridas had established that in March of 1985 ISEC breached its contractual and fiduciary obligations to Bridas by selling, over Bridas' objection, its 97% interest in CSEA to Siemens, the German multinational corporation and a major competitor of Bridas in Argentina. The Panel also concluded that ISEC had failed to "comply with the norms of good faith demanded of a fiduciary" by not giving Bridas adequate notice of the proposed sale and its terms (Award at 21-24). Though describing these findings against ISEC as erroneous, ISEC concedes that they are beyond this Court's review. Memorandum of Law in Support of ISEC's Petition to Vacate and in Opposition to Bridas' Cross-Petition to Enforce Arbitration Award, dated April 27, 1990 ("ISEC Mem."), at 5, 7. The Panel awarded Bridas damages of $6,793,000 with interest at 12%, compounded annually, from March 14, 1985. Bridas was also granted $1 million in legal fees and expenses plus $400,000 for the costs of the arbitration.

On February 2, 1990, ISEC filed a petition in this Court to vacate and refuse recognition and enforcement of the Award. Respondent Bridas has cross-petitioned to dismiss ISEC's petition to vacate on the grounds that this Court lacks subject matter jurisdiction to grant such relief under the Convention, and for failure to state a claim pursuant to Fed.R.Civ.P. 12(b)(1) and (6). Bridas further cross-petitions to enforce the Award pursuant to Article III of the Convention.

## ANALYSIS

We will first address the question of whether, under the binding terms of the New York Convention, we lack subject matter jurisdiction to vacate a foreign arbitral award. The situs of the Award in this case was Mexico City, a location chosen by the ICC Court of Arbitration pursuant to rules of procedure explicitly agreed to by the parties. Since the parties here are an American Company and an Argentine Company, it is not difficult to understand why the Mexican capital was selected as the place to conduct the arbitration.

Bridas argues that, under the New York Convention, only the courts of the place of arbitration, in this case the Courts of Mexico, have jurisdiction to vacate or set aside an arbitral award. ISEC argues that under the Convention both the courts of the place of arbitration and the courts of the place whose substantive law has been applied, in this case the courts of the United States, have jurisdiction to vacate or set aside an arbitral award.

Under Article V(1)(e) of the Convention, "an application for the setting aside or suspension of the award" can be made only to the courts or the "competent authority of the country in which, *or under the law of which*, that award was made." (Emphasis added). ISEC argues that "the competent authority of the country . . . under the law of which [the] award was made," refers to the country the substantive law of which, as opposed to the procedural law of which, was applied by the arbitrators. Hence, ISEC insists that since the arbitrators applied substantive New York law, we have jurisdiction to vacate the award.

ISEC cites only one case to support this expansive reading of the Convention, *Laminoirs-Trefileries-Cableries de Lens v. Southwire Co.*, 484 F.Supp. 1063 (N.D.Ga.1980). That case, however, did not involve a foreign award under the Convention, and did not implicate the jurisdictional question here raised, since there the parties' substantive and procedural choice of law, and the situs of the arbitration were both New York. It seems plain that the Convention does not address, contemplate or encompass a challenge to an award in the courts of the state where the award was rendered, since the relation of the courts to the arbitral proceedings is not an international, but a wholly domestic one, at least insofar as the Convention is concerned. Whether such an arbitration would be considered international because of the parties' nationalities under the Federal Arbitration Act, is irrelevant. *See* A. Van den Berg, *The New York Arbitration Convention of 1958* 19-20, 349-50 (Kluwer 1981).

Bridas has cited a case decided by our colleague Judge Keenan, *American Construction Machinery & Equipment Corp. v. Mechanised Construction of Pakistan Ltd.*, 659 F.Supp. 426 (S.D.N.Y.), *aff'd*, 828 F.2d 117 (2d Cir.1987), *cert. denied*, 484 U.S. 1064, 108 S.Ct. 1024, 98 L.Ed.2d 988 (1988), as authority against the ISEC position. This case involved a dispute between a Cayman Islands Company and a Pakistani company, arguably controlled by Pakistani substantive law and arbitrated in Geneva. Judge Keenan was asked to decline enforcement of the award on the ground that a challenge to it was pending in the courts of Pakistan. He ruled that "[t]he law under which this award was made was Swiss law because the award was rendered in Geneva pursuant to Geneva *procedural* law" 659 F.Supp. at 429 (emphasis added). This analysis was expressly affirmed in the Court of Appeals, and the Supreme Court declined to review it.

· · ·

[The Court proceeds to review the history of the treatment of the Convention in the Second Circuit, discussing *Parsons & Whittemore*, *supra* Chapter 1, p. 136; *Cooper v. Ateliers de la Motobecane*, *supra* Chapter 4, p. 819; and *Bergensen v. Muller Corp.*, *supra* Chapter 9, p. 1034.]

We conclude that the phrase in the Convention "[the country] under the laws of which that award was made" undoubtedly referenced the complex thicket of the *procedural* law of arbitration obtaining in the numerous and diverse jurisdictions of the dozens of nations in attendance at the time the Convention was being debated. Even today, over three decades after these debates were conducted, there are broad variations in the international community on how arbitrations are to be conducted and under what customs, rules, statutes or court decisions, that is, under what "competent authority." Indeed, some signatory nations have highly specialized arbitration procedures, as is the case with the United States, while many others have nothing beyond generalized civil practice to govern the arbitration. *See* Lowenfeld, *The Two-Way Mirror: International Arbitration as Comparative Procedure*, 7 Mich.Y.B.Int'l Legal Studies 163, 166-70 (1985), *reprinted in* 2 Craig, Park and Paulssou, [sic] *International Chamber of Commerce Arbitration*, App. VII at 187 (1986).

This view is confirmed by Professor Van den Berg to the effect that the language in dispute reflects the delegates' practical insight that parties to an international arbitration might prefer to equalize travel distance and costs to witnesses by selecting as a situs forum A, midpoint between two cities or two continents, and submit themselves to a different procedural law by selecting the arbitration procedure of forum B.

The "competent authority" as mentioned in Article
V(1)(e) for entertaining the action of setting aside the
award is virtually always the court of the country in
which the award was made. The phrase "or under the
law of which" the award was made refers to the
theoretical case that on the basis of an agreement of
the parties *the award is governed by an arbitration
law which is different from the arbitration law of the
country in which the award was made.*

A. Van den Berg, *The New York Arbitration Convention of 1958* 350
(Kluwer 1981) (emphasis added). This view is consistent with a
commentary on the circumstances under which the Soviet delegate
offered the amendment embracing the language in issue. *See* United
Nations Conference on International Commercial Arbitration,
Summary Record of the 23rd Meeting, 9 June 1958, E/CONF.
26/SR.23 at 12 (12 Sept. 1958), *reprinted in* G. Gaja, *International
Commercial Arbitration: New York Convention* III C. 213 (Oceana
Pub.1978).

It is clear, we believe, that any suggestion that a Court has
jurisdiction to set aside a foreign award based upon the use of its
domestic, substantive law in the foreign arbitration defies the logic
both of the Convention debates and of the final text, and ignores the
nature of the international arbitral system. This is demonstrated
overwhelmingly by review of cases in foreign jurisdictions that have
considered the question before us.

Decisions of foreign courts deciding cases under the
Convention uniformly support the view that the clause in question
means procedural and not substantive (i.e., in most cases contract)
law. See the Affidavit of Professor George A. Bermann of Columbia
Law School, sworn to June 18, 1990 at 22-29 ("Bermann Aff."),
citing for this proposition and discussing rulings of the Supreme
Court of India (*Oil and Natural Gas Commission v. The Western
Company of North America*, decision of January 16, 1987, 12
Y.B.Com.Arb. 473 [1988]); the Brussels Court of Appeals (*S.A.
Mines, Minérals et Métaux v. Mechema, Ltd.*, decision of October
14, 1980, 7 Y.B.Com.Arb. 316 [1982]); the Supreme Court of
France (Cour de Cassation) (*Maatschappij voor Industriële Research
en Ontwikkeling B.V. v. Henri Liévremont and M. Cominassi,*

decision of May 25, 1983, 12 Y.B.Com.Arb. 480 [1987]); the West German Supreme Court (*Bundesgerichtshof*, decision of February 12, 1976, 2 Y.B.Com.Arb. 242 [1977]); the Spanish Supreme Court (Tribunal Supremo) (*Cominco France S.A. v. Soguiber S.L.*, decision of March 24, 1982, 8 Y.B.Com.Arb. 408 [1983]); and the Supreme Court of South Africa (*Laconian Maritime Enterprises Ltd. v. Agromai Lineas Ltd.*, decision of August 27, 1985, 14 Y.B.Com.Arb. 693 [1989]).

Finally, we should observe that the core of petitioner's argument, that a generalized supervisory interest of a state in the application of its domestic substantive law (in most arbitrations the law of contract) in a foreign proceeding, is wholly out of step with the universal concept of arbitration in all nations. The whole point of arbitration is that the merits of the dispute will *not* be reviewed in the courts, wherever they be located. Indeed, this principle is so deeply imbedded in American, and specifically, federal jurisprudence, that no further elaboration of the case law is necessary. That this was the animating principle of the Convention, that the Courts should review arbitrations for procedural regularity but resist inquiry into the substantive merits of awards, is clear from the notes on this subject by the Secretary-General of the United Nations. *See* Bermann Aff., *supra*, at 32-33.

Accordingly, we hold that the contested language in Article V(1)(e) of the Convention, ". . . the competent authority of the country under the law of which, [the] award was made" refers exclusively to procedural and not substantive law, and more precisely, to the regimen or scheme of arbitral procedural law under which the arbitration was conducted, and not the substantive law of contract which was applied in the case.

In this case, the parties subjected themselves to the procedural law of Mexico. Hence, since the situs, or forum of the arbitration is Mexico, and the governing procedural law is that of Mexico, only the courts of Mexico have jurisdiction under the Convention to vacate the award. ISEC's petition to vacate the award is therefore dismissed.

We now turn to Bridas' cross-petition to enforce the award. ISEC apparently concedes, as it must, that this Court has jurisdiction under the Convention to enforce the Award, and that to avoid enforcement ISEC must establish one of the authorized defences under Article V of the Convention. Unfortunately, ISEC's papers are insufficiently rigorous in structure, substance and argument to determine with precision what provisions of the Convention it is proceeding under in resisting enforcement of the Award.

We assume that ISEC is, in substance, asserting defences under Article V(1)(b), in that it was unable to present its case because "the parties must be given the identity of the expert and the expert's opinion, as well as a meaningful opportunity to rebut that opinion," Supplemental Memorandum of Law In Support of ISEC's Petition to Vacate and Deny Enforcement of the Arbitral Award dated July 23, 1990 ("ISEC Supp.Mem.") at 1.; under Article V(1)(c) in that the Arbitral Panel decided matters beyond the scope of the submission to it, because the arbitrators "exceeded their authority by awarding damages based on equitable norms, rather than on law," ISEC Mem. at 28; and under Article V(2)(b) in that enforcement of the Award would be contrary to the public policy of the United States because "the secret procedures utilized by the arbitrators when they appointed an expert violated due process standards . . ." *Id.* at 11.

In connection with the first defense, an inability to present its case, ISEC asserts that its rights under the Convention were subverted by the panel's use of a "secret expert" in New York Law, ISEC Mem. at 11-28, and by the acceptance and presumed consideration by the panel of a brief in Spanish, on the question of the interest award, submitted out of time by Bridas, Affidavit of David Branson, Esq., sworn to April 25, 1990, at 9-12 ("Branson Aff.").

Following closure of the record and voluminous submissions by the parties, the panel sent a letter to counsel on December 14, 1988 advising of its interest in having four points of New York Law addressed at oral argument. The panel also announced its intention of appointing "an independent recognized expert on New York corporate and contract law," to advise on the four legal points identified. Branson Aff., Ex. 4. Bridas objected to the appointment, and did so in the clearest, most emphatic, and unequivocal terms. The record on this point is set forth in the Reply Memorandum of Law In Support of Bridas' (A) Motion to Dismiss ISEC's Petition to vacate and (B) Cross-Petition to Enforce the Arbitration Award

("Bridas Reply Mem."), at 27-30. These objections, which counsel
for ISEC saw as they were submitted to the panel, explicitly
complained of the failure to grant the parties access to the expert's
credentials and report.

ISEC's counsel responded to the panel in a five sentence
telex dated December 21, 1988, only the last sentence of which
deals with the subject of the expert. This single, neutral and wholly
uncritical sentence reads as follows: "Finally, I believe that the
parties should be informed concerning the selection of the legal
expert, his role and the issues to be put to him." Branson Aff., Ex.
5. It should be noted that no objection is raised to non-disclosure of
the expert's name. It is clear on reading the text of the panel's
response of December 29, 1988 to the Branson telex, that the panel
did indeed inform ISEC on the selection, the role of and the issues
to be addressed by the expert. Branson Aff., Ex. 7. On February 14,
1989, ISEC's counsel wrote to the panel, and advised as follows:

> There is another point regarding the retention of the
> expert. ITT is the owner of hundreds of corporations.
> It is possible that a New York lawyer could be in a
> firm that has represented one of these subsidiaries but
> he/she might not be aware of its connection to ITT.
> Should one later be found to exist, it might jeopardize
> the award. If the parties are given the name of the
> expert, they could assure that no conflict exists. Of
> course, it goes without saying that neither party,
> directly or indirectly would have any contact with the
> expert or the firm.

Branson Aff., Ex. 10.

Now what does the plain meaning of this representation to
the panel tell us? It tells us, of course, that ISEC accepts the panel's
response to its telex as broadly satisfactory. Nowhere is the word
secrecy mentioned, and certainly the grim shadow of star chamber is
nowhere invoked, as indeed nowhere is an imminent traducing of
American due process standards mentioned. What we have is a
modest and helpful suggestion, an afterthought really, that the panel
may wish to avert a wholly theoretical and speculative possibility
that a conflict of interest might exist for the expert selected. No
concern is expressed about nor demand made for access to the

expert's report, his formal credentials, and most importantly, his role in the proceedings.

By letter of February 21, 1989, the panel advised the parties in response to the "suggestion" (an excellent choice of word, we believe) of ISEC on the conflict matter that it favored "the selection of a university professor, totally detached from any law firm." Branson Aff., Ex. 11.

This completely satisfied ISEC, in that it expressed itself no more on the matter. We further note, *although we in no way rely upon*, the fact that ISEC promptly remitted its portion of the expert's fee, in contrast to its shameless footdragging on paying its fair share of expenses associated with *every other aspect* of this long and expensive proceeding. Bridas Reply Mem. at 30-32.

We also find that having abandoned whatever objection to the expert that can be said to have been made in its telex of December 21, 1988, ISEC cannot now seek the refuge of its adversary's arguments when, during the heat of that engagement, it stood utterly silent on the merits of the matter, lent no voice or encouragement, and by tactics and tone sought to thereby ingratiate itself with the panel. We can, sadly, divine no other purpose, since counsel now insists that his profound, substantive objections to the process, unvoiced in the record, mirrored those of his opponent.

Such cleverness is the bane of judges the world over. This is what led Hamlet as he reflected on the scull [sic] of Yorick to mock the profession so cruelly. We understand our obligation not to allow a party to impeach on later review a decision of a trial judge, or as here, an arbitral panel, where that party had full opportunity to contest it, and full notice of the vigorous argument of an adversary contesting it, and chose instead not to associate himself with the argument, and not to contest the matter. We thus find as a fact that ISEC never objected to the consultation of an expert by the panel and never demanded access to his report.

Accordingly, we hold that no objection to the appointment procedure used in the selection and consultation of the expert on New York law was made, that any objections ISEC in fact had were waived, and ISEC will not now be heard to complain about it.

As Judge Weinfeld observed in *Hunt v. Mobile Oil Corp*, 654 F.Supp. 1487, 1518 (S.D.N.Y.1987):

> If this [objection] were upheld, it would mean seven
> years of arbitral activities of the parties, of their
> lawyers and the huge legal expenses incurred would
> go down the drain . . . [a party cannot] wait in
> ambush and then render wasteful years of effort at an
> expenditure of millions of dollars. A party cannot
> remain silent, raising no objection during the
> arbitration proceeding, and when an adverse award to
> him has been handed down complain of the situation
> of which he had knowledge from the first,' . . . .

As our colleague Judge Duffy stated in *La Société Nationale pour La Recherche, La Production, Le Transport, La Transformation et la Commercialisation des Hydrocarbures v. Shaheen Natural Resources*, 585 F.Supp. 57, 62, 65 (S.D.N.Y.1983), *aff'd*, 733 F.2d 260 (2d Cir.), *cert. denied*, 469 U.S. 883, 105 S.Ct. 251, 83 L.Ed.2d 188 (1984), a case in which he rejected asserted "procedural deficiencies" in an ICC arbitration as defences to enforcement of a foreign arbitral award, the party resisting enforcement

> should have presented its objection to the arbitration
> panel. . . . To deny recognition and enforcement to
> the arbitration award . . . at this stage would be to
> violate the goal and the purpose of the Convention,
> that is, the summary procedure to expedite the
> recognition and enforcement of arbitration awards.
> See *Imperial Ethiopian Government v. Baruch-Foster
> Corp.*, 535 F.2d [334] at 335 [(5th Cir.1976)].

ISEC asserts that the action by the panel constitutes (a) a violation of the due process standards of the United States; (b) a violation of the public policy of the United States; and (c) a violation of arbitration procedures under the Convention. Since we will not pass upon the appropriateness of the appointment of the legal expert for the reasons stated, these arguments are dismissed. Furthermore, the objection to the receipt by the panel of a memorandum of law from Bridas as out of time is dismissed as frivolous.

We turn now to the remaining defence under the Convention, the assertion by ISEC that the Award dealt with matters or decided differences beyond the scope of the parties' submission to arbitration. ISEC Petition, ¶¶ 17-19, 24. In its legal argument, however, ISEC had made a somewhat different claim, that "the arbitrators exceeded their authority and acted as *amiables compositeurs*, in that they awarded damages" based on equitable norms, rather than on law," ISEC Mem. at 28. This argument is based almost wholly upon one sentence quoted from the Award:

> All in all, the combined guidance of the relevant legal principles, applied in the context of the *equitable nature of the norms which govern our task*, lead us to conclude that Bridas is entitled to the "restitution" of its May 1979 investment of $7.5 million . . . .

Award at 28-29 (emphasis added).

The Award further states, in the very next paragraph, which is not quoted in ISEC's brief:

> [a]lthough New York law awards interest of 9% for violations post 25 June 1981, it further stipulates that this statutory provision is not binding in actions of an equitable nature. CPLR sec. 5001. *See also, Branson & Wallace, [Awarding Interest in International Commercial Arbitration Establishing a Uniform Approach*, 28 Va.J.Int'l L. 919 (1988)]. We exercise the discretion granted by law by establishing an interest rate of 12% *per annum*, annually compounded.

*Id.* at 29.

We note, parenthetically, that the co-author of the law review article cited by the Panel is ISEC's counsel in this case. We will not repeat here the extensive quotations from this article, in great measure at odds with the legal position taken by its author in this action, that fill his adversary's brief. Nor will we comment upon the barely restrained glee of counsel for Bridas in unearthing these nuggets. We observe only that the panel at least here relied upon a distinguished legal expert on the matter in issue.

ISEC disputes the factual findings of the arbitrators, ISEC Mem. at 29-31, in that "the damages that they awarded were neither foreseeable losses flowing from the breaches of fiduciary duty that they found, nor amounts necessary to put Bridas in the position it would have been in had the contract not been breached," *id.* at 28, and concludes that because they made the factual findings that they did, the arbitrators *ipso facto* acted as *amiables compositeurs*, *id.* at 31-36.

ISEC then quotes the ICC Rules to the effect that "'the arbitrator shall assume the powers of an amiable compositeur if the parties are agreed to give him such powers,'" ISEC Mem. at 31 (quoting ICC Rules, Art. 13(4)). This *amiable compositeur* argument is a not especially elegant masque that seeks to conceal the fatal weakness of ISEC's defense: we are forbidden under the Convention to reconsider factual findings of the arbitral panel. Sensing this, ISEC once again transfers its argument to the more conventional, and usually unconvincing "manifest disregard of the law" complaint. ISEC Mem. at 37-40.

However, as ISEC's counsel concedes, ISEC Mem. at 37, the Convention, in Article V(2)(b), authorizes refusal of enforcement of an award only where ". . . enforcement would be contrary to the public policy of [the] country [where the award is to be enforced]." We observe that the Convention says nothing about "manifest disregard of the law."

Our colleague Judge Haight considered this question in *Brandeis Intsel Ltd. v. Calabrian Chemicals Corp.*, 656 F.Supp. 160, 163-68 (S.D.N.Y.1987), and found that the manifest disregard doctrine is a creature of domestic arbitration cases, and that whatever the concept means, it "does not rise to the level of contravening 'public policy' as that phrase is used in Article V of the Convention," and that "the 'manifest disregard' defense is not available to [respondent] within the context of the Convention." *Id.* at 165. *See also Merrill Lynch v. Bobker*, 808 F.2d 930, 933-34 (2d Cir.1986); *Parsons & Whittimore Overseas Co., supra*, 508 F.2d at 977.

We observe that it is only coincidence that the substantive law selected by the parties to be applied in this dispute happens to be the domestic law of a jurisdiction which we from time to time are called upon to apply. It could just as fortuitously have been the domestic law of Botswana or the Ukrainian Soviet Socialist Republic, both countries being contracting members under the Convention at the time of its ratification by the United States. We cannot understand how the Convention, created to assure consistency in the enforcement of foreign arbitral awards, would not be gravely undermined, if judges sitting in each of the many jurisdictions where enforcement may be obtained, were authorized by the Convention to undertake a de novo inquiry into whether the law the arbitrators said they were using was or was not properly applied by them. The plain answer is that the Convention does not, and could not, contemplate such a chaos.

We find no merit in ISEC's claim that the interest component of the Award is penal in nature, ISEC Mem. at 43-45. In this court arbitral awards containing comparable and even higher rates of interest have been enforced as non-penal. *See American Construction Machinery, supra*, 659 F.Supp. at 428; *Brandeis Instel Ltd., supra*, 656 F.Supp. at 170.

ISEC next argues, relying largely upon a 31 year old case in which the New York Civil Court interpreted the German American Treaty of Friendship, Commerce and Navigation of 1956, and entered a money judgment in which it fixed the interest, that the grant in this case of post-Award interest through the date of payment, was not proper. The case is inapposite, for entirely obvious reasons. In any case, we note that in *American Construction Machinery, supra*, the Court enforced a foreign arbitral award under the Convention which provided for "interest at the rate of 17% on [the damages] until the date of payment." 659 F.Supp. at 428.

ISEC also argues that, should this court enforce the Award, "the rate of interest after the Court's entry of judgment is a matter of federal law and is determined by the federal statutory rate of interest, 28 U.S.C. § 1961." ISEC Mem. at 45. We disagree. The statute by its terms applies to "any money judgment in a civil case recovered in a district court." Bridas is not here seeking entry of a money judgment, nor have the parties provided in their arbitration agreement, as is often done, that judgment may be entered upon an award in a particular court. Rather, Bridas has cross-petitioned for entry of an order enforcing a foreign arbitral award under the New York Convention. "[A] confirmation proceeding [under the Convention] is not an original action, it is, rather in the nature of a post-judgment enforcement proceeding." *Fertilizer Corp. of India v. IDI Management, Inc.*, 517 F.Supp. 948, 963 (S.D.Ohio 1981). We note that Judge Haight, in *Brandeis Instel Ltd.*, *supra*, 656 F.Supp. at 170, concluded that section 1961, "absent a showing that under foreign law the interest is penal in nature," did not preclude, in a case under the Convention, a pre-award interest rate of 11.25%.

We therefore find no merit to any defenses raised by ISEC to defeat enforcement of the Award.

### Notes and Questions

1. In *ISEC*, the court construes Article V(1)(e) narrowly. Nevertheless, even under its construction, two legal systems apparently have the competence to set aside or suspend an award, with general suspensive effects under the Convention: the country in which the award was made or the country under whose law the award was made. Whether "law" in the provision is interpreted as substance or procedure, two jurisdictions have a competence which may be exercised inconsistently. How should this be resolved?

2. The *ISEC* case manifests a strong policy in favor of the validity of an award. Contrast the operation of that presumption here with a comparable presumption in the *Klöckner* ad hoc Committee decision, discussed in Chapter 9, *supra* p. 985.

3. The court in ISEC quotes, with approval, Judge Weinfeld to the effect that "a party cannot remain silent, raising no objection during the arbitration procedure, and when an adverse award to him has been handed down complain of a situation of which he had knowledge from the first." As a practical matter, what must a party in an arbitration do in order to reserve its objection for post-award procedures? If the petitioner in that case had lodged a document saying "I protest this matter . . .," would that have reserved his right? Or, given Judge Weinfeld's concern about the amount of money that may have been spent in a proceeding, is the court really saying that a class of objections will simply not be given weight in the post-award procedure? Discuss.

4. In *ISEC*, an apparently critical expert opinion, solicited by the tribunal, was prepared by a professor, whose identity was not revealed to the parties. The Court found this unexceptionable because, it said, a professor is "totally distanced from any law firm." If this is true (whatever it means), is it a justification for

denying the parties the identity of the person preparing the critical opinion? Discuss.

5. The *ISEC* Court notes that the potentially substantive ground for vacating an award under domestic law, because of its "manifest disregard of the law," does not obtain under the Convention. Does this mean that an international award that manifestly disregards the law selected by the parties or the proper law, under principles of private international law, is unassailable?

D.      Håkan Berglin, *The Application in United States Courts of the Public Policy Provision of the Convention on the Recognition and Enforcement of Foreign Arbitral Awards*, 4 DICKINSON J. INT'L L. 167, 179, 183-84 (1986).

While the inevitable conclusion to be drawn from the court's reasoning in *Parsons & Whittemore* [*Parsons & Whittemore Overseas Co., Inc. v. Société Générale de l'Industrie du Papier (RAKTA)*, 508 F.2d 969 (2d Cir. 1974) (reproduced in Chapter 1 at p. 136)] is that enforcement, in principle, should be granted even where it would conflict with national foreign policy interests, the facts presented in the case fell far short of putting this principle to a real test. Far from being a declared, well-established congressional policy, the circumstances relied on by the American corporation were of quite a temporary character. The court also considered the alleged policy conflict incidental rather than substantial and the outcome of the dispute between the parties as being of no vital interest to the United States.

.    .    .

By repeatedly declaring that enforcement should be denied only where enforcement would violate the "most basic notions of morality and justice," United States federal courts undoubtedly have indicated a firm willingness to give the public policy provision of the New York Convention the narrow construction that seems to have been intended by its framers. In fact, it is striking to note the similarity between this phrase and the one employed by the Ad Hoc Committee of the Economic and Social Council of the United Nations during the preparatory work for the Convention when declaring its intent to limit the application of the public policy clause to situations in which enforcement would be "distinctly contrary to

the basic principles of the legal system of the country where the
award was invoked."

The case law, however, is still sparse. As yet it is still quite
possible to argue that the facts of the cases decided so far may not
have really tested how far the courts would be willing to go to
enforce foreign awards in situations where such enforcement would
be in direct and substantial conflict with fundamental domestic legal
or moral concepts or with statutes embodying such concepts.
Moreover, not only have the courts, and most particularly the United
States Supreme Court in its only decision on this point, left a
number of questions unanswered, they have also indicated and even
explicitly pointed out situations in which the question of enforcement
would require considerations other than those that have been
necessary in the cases decided to date. Consequently, it can fairly be
inferred that many issues still remain to be decided before it can be
authoritatively concluded when the courts will deny enforcement of a
foreign arbitral award on the basis of the public policy provision of
the New York Convention and, underlying that, what the courts
ultimately will consider to be the "most basic notions of morality
and justice."

*    *    *

## V.    SPECIAL PROBLEMS IN STATE ARBITRATIONS

It was for many centuries undisputed that States were not
subject to the jurisdiction of any foreign court. A restrictive theory
of sovereign immunity has, however, emerged in the course of this
century. Under this theory, a distinction is drawn between acts of a
State in its sovereign capacity and acts of a State in its commercial
capacity, and between property used in the former as opposed to the
latter context.

Regarding the proceedings themselves, the distinction
between the restrictive and absolute theories is largely irrelevant
because the State is deemed to have waived immunity from
jurisdiction by signing the arbitration agreement. Difficulties may,
however, arise when a party attempts to enforce an award against
the State because a waiver of immunity from jurisdiction is not
necessarily tantamount to a waiver of immunity from execution.
Compare Articles 25(1), 54, and 55 of the 1965 Convention on the

Settlement of Investment Disputes between States and Nationals of Other States (*see* the Supplement at p. 91), the U.S. Foreign Sovereign Immunities Act (*see* Supplement at p. 784) and the United Kingdom State Immunity Act 1978 (*see* Supplement at p. 799).

A.      Jan Paulsson, *Sovereign Immunity From Jurisdiction: French Caselaw Revisited*, 19 INT'L LAWYER 277, 282-85 (1985).

·   ·   ·

## II. Eurodif v. Iran

The case arose out of the Iranian withdrawal from the Eurodif nuclear fuel enrichment project for the construction of a large plant at Tricastin in the south of France. Eurodif was created in 1973 as a joint venture with four European countries as participants. The lead participant was the French *Commissariat à l'Energie Atomique* (CEA). In late 1974, Iran negotiated a 10 percent participation in the project, thereby assuring itself access to a high-technology enrichment process, which the then Iranian government desired as an element of its ambitious nuclear-industry program.

Following the revolution that created the Islamic Republic of Iran, that country's nuclear program was abandoned by governmental decision; Iran ceased payments to Eurodif and repudiated its undertaking to take or pay for its share of Eurodif's output. A capital-intensive venture, Eurodif considered its shareholders' purchase agreements to be a cornerstone of its financial structure and essential to the servicing of its debt.

Eurodif along with Sofidif, a French company established to channel the Iranian participation in Eurodif, as well as CEA, accordingly commenced International Chamber of Commerce arbitration proceedings against Iran as stipulated in the contract. Furthermore, pending the arbitration, Eurodif and Sofidif sought and obtained a conservatory attachment from the Tribunal of Commerce of Paris as security for its claim, which was provisionally evaluated in the amount of 9 billion French francs. The attachment order authorized Eurodif and Sofidif to seize a debt owed by CEA (and secondarily by the French state as guarantor) under a U.S. $1 billion loan granted by the State of Iran in 1975 as part of the overall accords of cooperation in the nuclear area.

Iran appealed, and obtained a favourable decision on 21 April 1982 from the Court of Appeal of Paris, which held that Iran was entitled to sovereign immunity of execution. It noted that the attached debt was owed to the Iranian state whose future use of monies repaid as principal and interest was not subject to any restriction, and therefore the Iranian government would be in a position to exercise its sovereign discretion as to the allocation of these funds to whatever government activities it chose. Under these circumstances, the Court held, immunity applied.

The *Cour de cassation* reversed in a brief decision which begins by articulating the following basic proposition:

> Whereas a foreign State in principle benefits from immunity of execution; but whereas this immunity may exceptionally be ruled out; whereas this is the case whenever the seized asset has been allocated to economic or commercial activity governed by private law and which gave rise to the legal action.

Having announced this as being the general rule, and characteristically omitting any mention that it was in fact creating a *new* rule, the *Cour de cassation* reviewed the general framework of the litigation and the Court of Appeal's decision to accord immunity on the sole basis that the attached assets were "public funds." It noted that the Court of Appeal had deemed it irrelevant to determine "whether the activities of production and distribution of enriched uranium in which the Iranian State had undertaken to participate were of a commercial character that subject them purely to private law," and concluded, in light of the statement of principle quoted above, that:

> . . . in so holding, even though its decision makes clear that the attached claim was one held by the State of Iran against CEA and the French State under the loan agreement of 23 February 1975, and it thus followed that the origins of said claim were the same funds that had been allocated to the accomplishment of the Franco-Iranian program of production and distribution of nuclear energy, the rupture of which by

the Iranian party had given rise to the action, the Court of Appeal, on which it was thus incumbent to determine the nature of this activity in order to decide the issue of immunity of execution, had not given a legal basis for its decision.

The *Cour de cassation* thus overruled the Court of Appeal of Paris and, in conformity with French practice, referred the case to the Court of Appeal of Versailles, to which Iran would have to turn to pursue its challenge of the attachment. (The decision of the Paris Court of Appeal having been reversed, the original attachment order of the Tribunal of Commerce of Paris was reinstated.)

## III. The Consequences

One now knows that if assets of a state have been used for or allocated to the same economic or commercial activities that gave rise to the claim, they are not immune from execution. The only restriction on this rule would seem to be that the transactions must be such that they are of a "private law" character. In practice, much depends on whether French courts in the future interpret the notion of "private law" activities broadly or restrictively. One might reasonably expect that with regard to activities carried out in pursuance of international contracts, French courts would tend to view them as having a private law character whether or not they would have been considered administrative contracts as a matter of French domestic law if they had been concluded between the French state and one of its nationals.[331] With one blow, French jurisprudence may thus be said to have unambiguously aligned itself with the generally restrictive approach to sovereign immunity of

---

[331] Professor Hervé Synvet, in the first French academic commentary on the *Eurodif c. Iran* case, expressed the view that in reproaching the Court of Appeal of Paris for not having determined whether the activity in the context of which the attached loan arose was of a commercial nature, the *Cour de cassation* "in truth implies a preference for a positive answer." M. Synvet lists the following elements as militating against the conclusion that a contract is concluded in the exercise of sovereign functions: contractual form modeled on typical instruments used in international trade, contractual stipulation of a national applicable law, absence of clauses that are *exorbitantes du droit commun* (i.e. containing provisions that two private parties could not *legally agree*), and reference to commercial arbitration in the event of dispute. . . .

execution reflected in U.S. and U.K. legislation, as well as in the
European Convention on State Immunity of 1972 (which France has
not ratified).

The *Eurodif v. Iran* case leaves open the question of the
conditions, if any, under which a private claimant may obtain
execution against a state's assets even though they were not used in
connection with the transaction that gave rise to the claim, by
showing that those assets have their origin in activities of a private
law character. Would the claimant in this situation be required to
make the difficult demonstration that the assets were also intended in
the future to be used in activities of a private law character? To
draw such a conclusion now would doubtless be hasty. One notes
that the *Avocat Général*'s brief before the *Cour de cassation* - which
to some extent may be considered to reflect an official view, if not
directly that of the Ministry of Justice—had criticized the Court of
Appeal for having based its decision only on the destination of the
funds, without taking into account their origin. The *Cour de
cassation*, whose weighing of words is legendary, was careful not to
say that cases where state assets are allocated to the activity
underlying the claim constitute the *only* exceptions to sovereign
immunity of execution.

One might, for example, consider that any state asset
allocated to non-sovereign use may be subject to execution
irrespective of its connection with the claim, and that with respect to
sums of money, the fact that they originated in a commercial
transaction would give rise to a presumption that their destination
would also be non-sovereign. It will surely be argued that there is no
justification in principle for the result that a claimant who happens to
find a state asset in France that is connected with the activities out of
which the claim arose achieve complete success, while an equally
deserving claimant fail [sic] completely because the assets, although
used for non-sovereign activities, do not have such a connection. Of
course, difficulties remain. For example, it remains to be confirmed
that French courts would consider that funds have a commercial
"origin" because their last *use* was in a commercial transaction,
rather than allowing a defendant state to invoke immunity by
pointing to an earlier public source (ultimately leading to the general
revenues of the state, which might be expected to be dominated by
income from taxes and other levies). Nevertheless, it will doubtless

not be long before private claimants seek to avail themselves of the openings suggested by the *Eurodif v. Iran* holding.

B.     *Libyan American Oil Company ("LIAMCO") v. Socialist People's Libyan Arab Jamahirya*, 482 F.Supp. 1175 (D.D.C. 1980)

[Oil concessions entered into between LIAMCO and Libya were nationalized by the latter in 1973 and 1974. LIAMCO brought arbitration under an arbitration clause in the concession agreements and obtained from an arbitral tribunal in Geneva an award in its favor for in excess of $60 million. Libya refused to participate in the arbitration. LIAMCO brought suit in the District of Columbia for confirmation of the award. Libya did not challenge the validity of the award but argued that the court was without jurisdiction and, second, that even if the court had jurisdiction, it should refrain from exercising it because of the act of state doctrine. Jurisdiction was predicated upon the provisions of the Federal Sovereign Immunities Act of 1976.]

. . .

*The jurisdictional question*

Libya is a foreign state, 28 U.S.C. § 1603(a), and therefore entitled to immunity from the jurisdiction of the United States courts according to the FSIA, 28 U.S.C. § 1604, unless some exception set forth in sections 1605-1607 of the same title applies. If an exception to immunity can be demonstrated, then this Court has jurisdiction pursuant to section 1330, provided all the requirements of subsections (a) and (b) are met.

The legislative history clarifies that before United States courts may exercise jurisdiction over a foreign sovereign, the FSIA requires a showing not only of particular reasons for denying sovereign immunity (§ 1330(a)), but also of the traditional requirements for in personam jurisdiction, including the requirement of due process (§ 1330(b)).

(b) *Personal Jurisdiction.*-Section 1330(b) provides in effect, a Federal longarm statute over foreign states . . . . . The requirements of minimum jurisdictional

contacts and adequate notice are embodied in the
provision . . . For personal jurisdiction to exist under
section 1330(b), the claim must first of all be one over
which the district courts have original jurisdiction
under section 1330(a), meaning a claim for which the
foreign state is not entitled to immunity. Significantly,
each of the immunity provisions in the bill, sections
1605-1607, requires some connection between the
lawsuit and the United States, or an express or
implied waiver by the foreign state of its immunity
from jurisdiction. These immunity provisions,
therefore, prescribe the necessary contacts which must
exist before our courts can exercise personal
jurisdiction. Besides incorporating these jurisdictional
contacts by reference, section 1330(b) also satisfies
the due process requirement of adequate notice by
prescribing that proper service be made under section
1608 of the bill. . . .

.   .   .

As noted in the legislative history quoted above, original
jurisdiction under subsection (a) may be established either by "some
*connection* between the lawsuit and the United States, or an express
or implied *waiver* by the foreign state." (emphasis added). Section
1605(a)(1) provides that a foreign state is not immune if it has
"waived its immunity either explicitly or by implication." 28
U.S.C. § 1605(a)(1). Petitioner LIAMCO maintains that Libya
implicitly waived its sovereign immunity by expressly agreeing to
the arbitration and choice of law clauses negotiated in 1966 and
1967, more than ten years after the concessions were originally
entered into. LIAMCO supports its interpretation of the effect of
those clauses by reference to another passage in the legislative
history of the FSIA.

With respect to implicit waivers, the courts
have found such waivers in cases where a foreign
state has agreed to arbitration in another country or
where the foreign state has agreed that the law of a
particular country should govern a contract. . . .

A recent case in this Court also supports this view. In *Ipitrade Int'l, S.A. v. Federal Republic of Nigeria*, 465 F.Supp. 824 (D.D.C.1978), an action for enforcement of an arbitral award based on breach of contract, the Court held that the foreign sovereign's "agreement to adjudicate all disputes arising under the contract in accordance with Swiss law and by arbitration under International Chamber of Commerce rules constituted[d] a waiver of sovereign immunity under the Act." 465 F.Supp. at 826. . . .

Libya thus waived its defense of sovereign immunity for the purposes of § 1330(a) and because there is no suggestion that the requirement of notice under § 1330(b) have not been met, this Court has jurisdiction to recognize and enforce the award. The question of whether to exercise that jurisdiction remains.

*The act of state doctrine*

The Convention under which LIAMCO would have this Court confirm the arbitral award plainly favors enforcement of foreign awards in this forum.

> The court *shall* confirm the award unless it finds one of the grounds for refusal or deferral of recognition or enforcement of the award specified in the said Convention. 9 U.S.C. § 2087. (emphasis added)

Of the seven exceptions listed in Article V of the Convention, one is determinative of the issue before the Court. Subsection 2(a) of Article V provides that recognition and enforcement of an award may be refused if the competent authority in the country where enforcement is sought determines that "[t]he subject matter of the difference is not capable of settlement by arbitration under the law of that country." 9 U.S.C. § 201.

The "subject matter of the difference" in this case is Libya's nationalization of LIAMCO's assets and the rate at which LIAMCO should be compensated for the assets taken under that nationalization. Should that rate be determined according to the terms of the original concessions (by arbitration), or should it rather be determined according to the provision of the nationalization laws themselves (by Libyan committee)?

Had that question been brought before this Court initially, the Court could not have ordered the parties to submit to arbitration because in so doing it would have been compelled to rule on the validity of the Libyan nationalization law. That law by its terms abrogated the concessions entirely and vested exclusive determination of any compensation in a special committee provided for in the same law. The practice that counsels this judicial abstention from passing on the effectiveness of the acts of foreign sovereigns is termed the act of state doctrine. It finds its classic American expression in the Supreme Court case of *Underhill v. Hernandez*, 168 U.S. 250, 18 S.Ct. 83, 42 L.Ed. 456 (1897).

> Every sovereign state is bound to respect the independence of every other sovereign state, and the courts of one country will not sit in judgment on the acts of the government of another, done within its own territory. 168 U.S. at 252, 18 S.Ct. at 84.

The doctrine does not deny courts jurisdiction once it has been acquired.

> It requires only that when it is made to appear that the foreign government has acted in a given way on the subject-matte of the litigation, the details of such action or the merit of the result cannot be questioned, but must be accepted by our courts as a rule for their decision. *Ricaud v. American Metal Co.*, 246 U.S. 304, 309, 38 S.Ct.312, 314, 62 L.Ed. 733 (1917).

Since the ruling in *Underhill*, courts have consistently found a foreign state's act of nationalization to be the classic example of an act of state. "Expropriations of the property of an alien within the boundaries of the sovereign state are traditionally considered to be public acts of the sovereign removed from judicial scrutiny by application of the act of state rubric." *Hunt v. Mobil Oil Corp.*, 550 F.2d 68, 73 (2d Cir.1977), *cert. denied*, 434 U.S. 984, 98 S.Ct. 608, 57 L.Ed.2d 477. Furthermore, other nationalization decrees by the state of Libya identical to the decrees affecting LIAMCO have been considered as sovereign acts for the purposes of the act of state doctrine. As the Court noted in *Hunt*,

We conclude that the political act complained
of here was clearly within the act of state doctrine and
that since the disputed pleadings inevitably call for a
judgment on the sovereign acts of Libya the claim is
non-justiciable. 550 F.2d at 73.

[The court denied petitioner's argument that the terms of the
Hickenlooper Amendment of 1964 barred the application of the act
of state doctrine.]

* * *

For the reasons set forth above, the Court declines to
recognize or enforce the arbitral award. An order consistent with the
memorandum follows.

### Notes and Questions

1.    Following the rendering of the arbitration award in its favor,
LIAMCO sought the attachment of Libyan assets in a number of European
countries. In France, while the attachments were lifted, an expert was ordered by
the court to determine the commercial or non-commercial nature of Libyan assets
in France, for the purpose of possible further execution action. While the expert
was proceeding, the matter was settled on a negotiated basis. Would such judicial
proceedings have an effect on negotiations for settlement?

2.    Following the settlement of LIAMCO's claims, the proceedings
in the District Court of the District of Columbia, and the appeal taken therefrom
by LIAMCO, became moot. Upon petition by LIAMCO, joined by the U.S.
Department of Justice, the District Court's decision was vacated by the Court of
Appeal, without opinion, 684 F.2d 1132 (D.C. Cir. 1981), thus preventing the
District Court's decision from having value as a precedent. The act of state
decision by the District Court has been declared by many commentators to be
"clearly wrong." What is your opinion?

C.    AMERICAN ARBITRATION ASSOCIATION, ARBITRATION
      AND THE LAW: AAA GENERAL COUNSEL'S ANNUAL
      REPORT 233-35 (1988-89).

Section 4(a) of Public Law 100-669, effective November 18,
1988, amends the Federal Arbitration Act by adding a new section
15 to chapter 1. It provides that "[e]nforcement of arbitral

agreements, confirmation of arbitral awards and execution upon judgments based on orders confirming such awards shall not be refused on the basis of the Act of State doctrine."

A defense based on act of state is occasionally raised by a foreign state to bar enforcement of arbitration agreements and awards. The doctrine mandates that courts not pass upon the validity of a foreign state's act of expropriation of property within its territory. The thrust of the defense of act of state in an arbitration context is to bar enforcement of an award on the ground that the dispute arises from an act of state that is not capable of settlement by arbitration.

The new law should put an end to situations in which a government entity may unilaterally repudiate its arbitral agreement and render an award a nullity. It reinforces the effectiveness of arbitration as a means of resolving disputes in contracts and investment agreements between American enterprises and foreign governments and fulfills U.S. obligations under the 1958 United Nations Convention on the Recognition and Enforcement of Foreign Arbitral Awards.

.    .    .

Sections 4(b) and 4(c) of Public Law 100-669 amend the Foreign Sovereign Immunities Act of 1976 (FSIA), 28 U.S.C. §1330 *et seq.*, to enhance arbitration as a means of resolving international commercial disputes between private parties and governments and their parastatal agencies.

The FSIA is a codification of U.S. law governing the adjudication of actions between private parties and foreign states and their agencies. As a rule, foreign states are immune from the jurisdiction of the U.S. federal and state courts. However, there are exceptions to this rule; under 28 U.S.C. §1605, for example, a foreign state is not immune when it has "waived its immunity either explicitly or by implication." Prior to the enactment of the FSIA, the issue of whether a foreign state was subject to the jurisdiction of American courts was determined by either the courts or the U.S. State Department.

The new law specifies that a foreign state and its instrumentalities can no longer use the defense of sovereign immunity in actions by private parties to enforce arbitration agreements and awards against it by adding 28 U.S.C. §1605(a), a new exception to the jurisdictional immunity of a foreign state. It provides that a foreign state is not immune from the jurisdiction of U.S. courts in any case

> in which the action is brought, either to enforce an agreement made by the foreign State with or for the benefit of a private party to submit to arbitration all or any differences which have arisen or which may arise between the parties with respect to a defined legal relationship, whether contractual or not, concerning a subject matter capable of settlement by arbitration under the laws of the United States, or to confirm an award made pursuant to such an agreement to arbitrate, if (A) the arbitration takes place in the United States, (B) the agreement or award is or may be governed by a treaty or other international agreement in force for the United States calling for the recognition and enforcement of arbitral awards, (C) the underlying claim, save for the agreement to arbitrate, could have been brought in a United States court under this section or section 1607, or (D) paragraph (1) of this subsection is otherwise applicable.

Section 1610(a) of title 28 has also been amended to include a new exception to the immunity from attachment or execution of commercial property owned by a foreign state. Previously, section 1610(a) provided that a judgment can be executed against the property of a foreign state only when that property was used for the same commercial activity on which the claim was based. Under the new amendment, however, this requirement no longer applies to arbitration awards. Specifically, section 4(c) provides that property of a foreign state "used for a commercial activity in the United States" shall not be immune from execution if

> the judgment is based on an order confirming an arbitral award rendered against the foreign State, provided that attachment in aid of execution, or execution, would not be inconsistent with any provision in the arbitral agreement.

*   *   *

VI.    RECOGNITION AND ENFORCEMENT WITHOUT RIGHT OF
       EXECUTION

A.    *Hewlett-Packard Company, Inc. v. Helge Berg*, 61
      F.3d 101 (1st Cir. 1995).

[The prior decision of the Court of Appeals finding that
issues of arbitrability (effect of bankruptcy, transfer of claims to
assignees of the bankrupt company, effect of Massachusetts non-
assignability law) were for the arbitral tribunal is reported in
Chapter 4 at p. 533. The preliminary award of the arbitrators is
found in Chapter 6 at p. 685. The final award of the arbitral tribunal
in favor of claimants Helge Berg, et al., allowed certain set-offs
claimed by Respondent, arising under the same 1984 Contract under
which Claimants claimed but did not allow set-offs due to
Respondent arising from payments due under an earlier 1982
Contract which had not been claimed as a basis of arbitral
jurisdiction in the Terms of Reference established by the parties and
the arbitrators. Hewlett Packard, the successor in interest to Apollo
Computers, Inc., commenced a new arbitration under the 1982
Contract in respect of the set-off claims. In the meantime the District
Court denied Hewlett Packard's opposition to recognition and
enforcement, as well as its request for a declaration that it was
entitled to the set-off and, in the alternative, to stay the confirmation
proceeding pending the outcome of the second arbitration. Hewlett
Packard appeals.]

BOUDIN, Circuit Judge.

Hewlett-Packard appeals from an order of the district court
confirming an arbitration award rendered in a business dispute with
appellees Helge Berg and Lars Skoog and rejecting Hewlett-
Packard's requests for a stay of the confirmation proceeding or a
declaration that it is entitled to a set-off for the award. The case
presents several difficult legal issues which can be understood only
after a brief description of the facts and prior proceedings.

### I. Background

In March 1982, Apollo Computer, now owned by Hewlett-
Packard, entered into a two-year distributorship contract with a
Swedish company called Dicoscan Distributed Computer Scandinavia

to sell Hewlett-Packard products in several Nordic countries. The 1982 contract included an agreement to submit any dispute under the contract to binding arbitration. In March 1984, the parties executed a new distributorship contract, which also contained an arbitration clause.

In the meantime, during 1983 and 1984, Dicoscan experienced financial problems. In mid-1984, Apollo claimed that Dicoscan was far behind in its payments. In September, Apollo terminated the 1984 agreement. The following month, Dicoscan filed for bankruptcy. The bankruptcy court assigned to Berg and Skoog, directors and officers of Dicoscan, the right to bring claims against Apollo based on the contracts.

Berg and Skoog filed a request for arbitration with the International Chamber of Commerce Court of Arbitration, claiming millions of dollars of damages arising out of Apollo's unilateral termination of the 1984 agreement. Apollo counterclaimed in the arbitration by asserting that the Swedish company had failed to pay about $10,000 due on the 1984 contract and about $207,000 due under the 1982 contract. After a dispute about Berg and Skoog's right to invoke arbitration, *see Apollo Computer, Inc. v. Berg*, 886, F.2d 469, 473 (1st Cir.1989), an arbitration proceeding was begun.

The arbitrators were required by the parties' contracts to apply Massachusetts law. Ultimately, the arbitrators awarded around $700,000 plus interest to Berg and Skoog, but allowed a set-off for the $10,000 that Dicoscan still owed Apollo under the 1984 contract. To both parties' surprise, the tribunal held that it was without jurisdiction to decide Apollo's more substantial claim based on the 1982 contract, ruling that the 1982 contract was not within the Terms of Reference issued by the arbitrators at the beginning of the proceeding.

As a result, Apollo was left with a sizable obligation to Berg and Skoog on the 1984 contract without a determination of its claim for more than $207,000 on the 1982 contract. Apollo unilaterally decided to pay the arbitration award amount but subtracted the $207,000 plus interest (together, about $300,000) as a "set-off in recoupment," which, it said, is a time-honored common law doctrine embraced in Massachusetts courts. Apollo also filed a request with the tribunal for a second arbitration regarding the 1982 contract. That tribunal has indicated that it will hear the arbitration.

In January 1993, Apollo (later succeeded as the plaintiff by Hewlett-Packard) filed the complaint in this action with the Massachusetts district court. Hewlett-Packard requested that the district court (1) declare that Hewlett-Packard was entitled to the $207,000 set-off and that the arbitration award is fully satisfied, and (2) vacate the tribunal's award and correct it. Hewlett-Packard later withdraw its second claim for relief.

Berg and Skoog moved to dismiss the complaint, arguing that such declaratory relief is unavailable as to foreign arbitration awards. Later, Berg and Skoog moved for confirmation of the arbitration award. Hewlett-Packard opposed confirmation of the award on the ground that, by failing to include its 1982 set-off, the award was contrary to public policy. In the alternative, Hewlett-Packard moved to stay confirmation, pending the outcome of the second arbitration. Hewlett-Packard also asked the court to compel arbitration as to its 1982 claim.

On November 7, 1994, the district judge filed a memorandum, together with a separate order, disposing of all of these motions. The court's order compelled arbitration under the 1982 contract but it confirmed the award previously made by the tribunal on the 1984 contract. The court said that it was without power to stay the confirmation proceeding, as Hewlett-Packard had requested, and that the request for a set-off was an improper attempt to modify the tribunal's award.

Apparently ready to enforce the now-confirmed arbitration award, Berg and Skoog moved the court for entry of final judgment, and proffered a detailed judgment specifying the award, interest and attorney's fees. Four days later, Hewlett-Packard filed its notice of appeal and thereafter filed a response disputing certain aspects of the proposed judgment. The district court has not acted on the motion for entry of final judgment; and no such judgment has been entered.

## II. Discussion

Hewlett-Packard purports to appeal all three of the district court's adverse actions: the confirmation of the arbitration award, the refusal to stay that confirmation proceeding pending the outcome of the second arbitration; and the rejection of Hewlett-Packard's set-off claim declaration. Commendably, Hewlett-Packard has alerted us to a possible jurisdiction problem, which this court is obliged to consider. We do so but caution future panels that the jurisdictional problems have not been briefed in this case.

[The Court found that the District Court's order confirming the award was appealable as a "final order" despite the fact that a final judgment had not been entered thereon, and that also appealable was Hewlett-Packard's claim that the confirmation proceedings should have been stayed.]

.   .   .

We turn now to the merits. Hewlett-Packard does not object to the confirmation of the award in all respects; it says it has paid the award except the disputed amount including interest. But Hewlett-Packard says that the district court erred by confirming the award in full instead of either allowing a set-off or granting a stay of the confirmation pending the results of the new arbitration.

We agree with the district court's rejection at this time of the first alternative. Whether Hewlett-Packard has a valid claim under the 1982 contract is subject to arbitration, we agree with the district court—and Hewlett-Packard—that the tribunal has never resolved the merits of that claim. Whatever the Massachusetts law on set-offs, the district court could not allow the set-off at present without determining that Hewlett-Packard had a valid claim, which is the very subject of the arbitration.

It is hard to imagine a step that would be more offensive to the pro-arbitration policies reflected in Congress' endorsement of the 1958 Convention on the Recognition and Enforcement of Foreign Arbitral Awards, often called the New York Convention. The New York Convention was approved by Congress, and implementing legislation was codified at 9 U.S.C. §§ 201-08. The statute enlists the aid of federal courts to compel arbitration. 9 U.S.C. § 206. By contrast, the judicial set-off requested here would circumvent the 1982 contract to arbitrate and the now-pending arbitration under that contract.

The request to defer confirmation of the award under the 1984 contract stands on a different footing. However the case might stand absent the bankruptcy, Dicoscan's bankruptcy gives Hewlett-Packard a very substantial prudential argument. If the existing award were confirmed in full and reduced to judgment, Hewlett-Packard would have to pay the full award to the defendants as successors-in-interest of an insolvent company. If in due course Hewlett-Packard then prevailed on its claims against the insolvent company on a closely related transaction, it would have no assurance of collecting anything.

Further, Hewlett-Packard cannot be blamed for the discrepant timing in the resolution of its claim, or at least no argument to that effect has been made. After it was told that the defendants did have arbitration rights despite an anti-assignment clause in the contracts, Hewlett-Packard apparently made a reasonable effort to have both the defendants' claim and its own counterclaim resolved in one proceeding at the same time. Only the arbitrators' surprising interpretation of their mandate frustrated this attempt.

Under these circumstances, the seemingly fair solution would be to confirm the award in its uncontested part, reserving confirmation of the balance until the 1982 contract dispute is arbitrated. The district court refused to consider a stay of confirmation on the ground that it was without power to do so. We fully understand the basis for the district court's doubt about its authority, but we conclude that it does have the power to issue a stay in the peculiar circumstances of this case.

Ordinarily there could be no doubt that a court, although obliged to decide a claim, would retain discretion to defer proceedings for prudential reasons. Indeed, a typical reason is the pendency of a related proceeding in another tribunal. "[T]he power to stay proceedings is incidental to the power inherent in every court to control the disposition of the causes on its docket with economy of time and effort for itself, for counsel and for litigants." *Landis v. North Amer. Co.*, 299 U.S. 248, 254, 57 S.Ct. 163, 166, 81 L.Ed. 153 (1936).

The question here is whether this traditional authority is curtailed by the new York Convention and its implementing legislation. The statute provides that, upon a petition for confirmation, a district court "*shall* confirm the award unless it finds one of the grounds for refusal or deferral of recognition or enforcement of the award specified in the said Convention." 9 U.S.C. § 207 (emphasis added). Article VI of the Convention is the only provision that deals with staying confirmation. Article VI states:

> If an application for the setting aside or suspension of the award has been made to a competent authority [in the country where the award has been made], the authority before which the award is sought to be relied upon may, if it considers it proper, adjourn the decision on the enforcement of the award [and require a security].

The circumstances outlined in Article VI do not appear to exist in this case. The question is whether a district court may grant a stay in circumstances other than those authorized in Article VI.

The fact that section 207 uses the word "shall" is not decisive, because a stay is a deferral rather than refusal. But the fact that the statute refers to the Convention and the Convention lists a single ground for a stay could be taken to exclude all other grounds under the principle of *expressio unius est exclusio alterius*. That was, in substance, the reasoning of the district court. However, *expressio unius* is an aid to construction and not an inflexible rule. *See, e.g., United States v. Massachusetts Bay Transport, Auth.*, 614 F.2d 27, 28 (1st Cir. 1980). Whatever we might think if the question were entirely open, precedent informs our decision in this case. Domestic arbitrations are governed by the United States Arbitration Act (chapter 1 of Title 9) but not by the Convention (chapter 2 of Title 9). The Act states that, upon application, "the court *must* grant [a confirmation] order unless the award is vacated, modified, or corrected as prescribed in sections 10 and 11 of this title." 9 U.S.C. § 9 (emphasis added). But courts routinely grant stays in such cases for prudential reasons not listed in sections 10 and 11. *E.g., Middleby*, 962 F.2d at 615-16.

Similarly, this court has held that district courts have discretion to stay an action to *compel* arbitration pending the outcome of related litigation, even though the Act states that on a motion to compel the court "shall hear the parties" and "shall proceed summarily to trial." 9 U.S.C. § 4; *see Acton Corp. v. Borden, Inc.*, 670 F.2d 377, 383 (1st Cir.1982). In *Acton*, then-Judge Breyer held that, in drafting the statute, Congress did not "intend[ ] a major departure from the ordinary rule allowing one federal court to stay litigation when another federal court is on the process of deciding the same issue." We take the same view of Congress' intentions in implementing the Convention.

Of course, a stay of confirmation should not be lightly granted. A central purpose of the Convention—an international agreement to which the United States is only of approximately one hundred signatories—was to expedite the recognition of foreign arbitral awards with a minimum of judicial interference. But the risk that the power to stay could be abused by disgruntled litigants—real though that risk is, *see Spier v. Calzaturificio*, 663, F.Supp. 871, 873 (S.D.N.Y.1987)—argues more for a cautious and prudent exercise of the power than for its elimination.

Because the district court acted under a misapprehension of its authority, we vacate the confirmation order and remand for further proceedings. Whether confirmation or collection of the award should be partially deferred pending the resolution of the 1982 contract arbitration is a matter for the district court to determine in the first instance. Still, we think it would require some explanation if, in the face of the equities of this case, the district court concluded that the full award should be confirmed and collected now.

The confirmation order is *vacated* and the matter is *remanded* to the district court for further proceedings consistent with this opinion.

*          *          *

B.      *National Oil Corporation v. Libyan Sun Oil Company*
        733 F.Supp. 800 (D.Del. 1990).

[The court's citations to the arbitration record and a number of its footnotes have been omitted.]

## OPINION

LATCHUM, Senior District Judge.

In this case the Court has been called upon to examine and evaluate, among other things, the legal significance of the current state of relations between Libya and the United States. The facts and arguments presented by the parties have put this Court in the unenviable and precarious position of having to place legal labels on the foreign policy maneuvers of the Bush administration. Unfortunately, the Court has no choice but to proceed.

Petitioner, National Oil Corporation ("NOC"), seeks to have this Court enter an order confirming a foreign arbitral award rendered in NOC's favor against respondent, Libyan Sun Oil Company ("Sun Oil"). . . . NOC brings this action pursuant to the Convention on the Recognition and Enforcement of Foreign Arbitral Awards ("the Convention"), a treaty ratified by the United States and implemented through Congressional legislation. *See* 9 U.S.C. §§ 201-208 (1970). Sun Oil has moved to dismiss the petition or, in the alternative, to deny recognition of the award. . . . This Court has jurisdiction pursuant to 28 U.S.C. § 1331 as this case arises under federal law. *See* 9 U.S.C. § 203 (West Supp. 1989).[332]

## FACTUAL BACKGROUND

NOC is a corporation organized under the laws of the Socialist People's Libyan Arab Jamahiriya ("Libya"), and wholly owned by the Libyan Government. . . . Sun Oil is a Delaware corporation and a subsidiary of Sun Company, Inc. . . . The dispute currently before the Court stems from an Exploration and Production Sharing Agreement ("EPSA") entered into by the parties on November 20, 1980. The EPSA provided, *inter alia*, that Sun Oil was to carry out and fund an oil exploration program in Libya.

---

[332] [1] The arbitral award in dispute here was issued in Paris, France, under the auspices of the International Chamber of Commerce. France is a signatory of the Convention, and hence the requirement of reciprocity is satisifed. *See* 9 U.S.C. § 201 (West Supp.1989).

Sun Oil began exploration activities in the first half of 1981. On December 18, 1981, Sun Oil invoked the *force majeure* provision[333] contained in the EPSA and suspended performance. . . . Sun Oil claimed that a State Department order prohibiting the use of United States passports for travel to Libya[334] prevent its personnel, all of whom were U.S. citizens, from going to Libya. . . . Thus, Sun Oil believed it could not carry out the EPSA "in accordance with the intentions of the parties to the contract." . . . NOC disputed Sun Oil's claim of *force majeure* and called for continued performance. . . .

In March of 1982, the U.S. Government banned the importation into the United States of any oil from Libya and severely restricted exports from the United States to Libya. 47 Fed.Reg. 10,507 (1982); 47 Fed.Reg. 11,247 (1982). Export regulations issued by the U.S. Department of Commerce required a license for the export of most goods, including all technical information. Because it "had planned to export substantial quantities of technical data and oil technology to Libya in connection with the exploration program," Sun Oil claims that it filed for such an export license "so as to be prepared to resume operations in Libya promptly in the event the U.S. Government lifted the passport prohibition." . . . The application for a license was denied. . . . Thereafter, in late June of 1982, Sun Oil notified NOC that it was claiming the export regulations as an additional event of *force majeure*. . . .

---

[333] [2] That clause reads as follows:

22.1 *Excuse of Obligations*

Any failure or delay on the part of a Party in the performance of its obligations or duties hereunder shall be excused to the extent attributable to force majeure. Force majeure shall include, without limitation: Acts of God; insurrection; riots; war; and any unforeseen circumstances and acts beyond the control of such party.

(D.I. 3, Exhibit A, Annex 1, EPSA ¶ 22.1, at 45-46).

[334] [3] The passport regulation, issued pursuant to an executive order, stated that "United States passports shall cease to be valid for travel to, in, or through Libya unless specifically validated for such travel under the authority of the Secretary of State." 46 Fed.Reg. 60,712 (1981).

On July 19, 1982, NOC filed a request for arbitration with the Court of Arbitration of the International Chamber of Commerce ("the ICC") in Paris, France, pursuant to the arbitration provision contained in the EPSA.[335] . . . The members of the arbitration panel ("the Arbitral Tribunal") were chosen in accordance with the arbitration clause. Each party picked one arbitrator; the third was chosen by the International Chamber of Commerce. Sun Oil selected Edmund Muskie, a former United States Senator and Secretary of State. NOC selected Professor Hein Kotz, Director of the Max Planck Institute in west Germany. Robert Schmelck, a former chief justice of France's supreme court (*la Cour de Cassation*), was selected as the third arbitrator by the ICC Court of Arbitration.

The arbitration proceedings were held in Paris, France. In May and June of 1984, the Arbitral Tribunal held hearings on the issue of *force majeure*. It issued an initial award on May 31, 1985, that stated there had been no *force majeure* within the meaning of the EPSA. . . . The Arbitral Tribunal later held further hearings, and on February 23, 1987, it rendered a second and final award in favor of NOC and against Sun Oil in the amount of twenty million U.S. dollars. . . . NOC has since been unable to collect payment from Sun Oil. . . .

NOC filed this petition for confirmation of the Tribunal's award on July 24, 1989. . . . On September 15, 1989, Sun Oil moved to dismiss the petition. . . . The Court heard oral argument on November 29, 1989 and January 26, 1990.

---

[335] [4] The arbitration clause states:

23.2    *Arbitration*

Any controversy or claim arising out of or relating to this Agreement, or breach thereof, shall, in the absence of an amicable arrangement between the Parties, be settled by arbitration, in accordance with the Rules of Conciliation and Arbitration of the International Chamber of Commerce, in Paris, France, by three arbitrators. Each Party shall appoint its arbitrator, and the International Chamber of Commerce shall appoint the third arbitrator who must be in no way related to either Party and who will be the chairman of the arbitration body.

(D.I. 3, Exhibit A, Annex 1, EPSA ¶ 23, at 47.)

## THE MOTION TO DISMISS

Sun Oil makes numerous arguments regarding why NOC's petition for recognition of this arbitral award should be dismissed. For the reasons stated below, the Court will deny Sun Oil's motion.

[The Court found that Libya, whose government was recognized by the United States, was not denied access to United States Courts despite a rupture of diplomatic relations between the countries, particularly since the executive Branch of the government had granted a Treasury Department License to NOC to engage in the United States judicial proceedings.]

II.  *Treasury Regulations As A Bar To This Suit*

In January of 1986, President Reagan declared that the policies and actions of the Libyan Government posed a sufficient threat to U.S. national security and foreign policy so as to constitute a "national emergency." Thus, pursuant to his delegated authority under the International Emergency Economic Powers Act (IEEPA), 50 U.S.C. §§ 1701-1706 (West Supp.1989),[336] the President issued two executive orders imposing economic sanctions on Libya, and authorizing and directing the Secretary of the Treasury to

---

[336] [8] When the President has declared a national emergency pursuant to 50 U.S.C. § 1701 of the IEEPA, he is authorized, "under such regulations as he may prescribe, by means of instructions, licenses, or otherwise," to:

> (A)    investigate, regulate, or prohibit—
> (i) any transactions in foreign exchange,
> (ii) transfers of credit or payments between, by, through, or to any banking institution, to the extent that such transfers or payments involve any interest of any foreign country or a national thereof,

> (B)    investigate, regulate, direct and compel, nullify, void, prevent or prohibit, any acquisition, holding, withholding, use, transfer, withdrawal, transportation, importation or exportation of, or dealing in, or exercising any right, power, or privilege with respect to, or transactions involving, any property in which any foreign country or a national thereof has any interest; by any person, or with respect to any property, subject to the jurisdiction of the United States.

50 U.S.C. § 1702 (a)(1).

promulgate implementing regulations. *See* Exec. Order No. 12543, 51 Fed.Reg. 875 (Jan. 7, 1986); Exec. Order No. 12544, 51 Fed.Reg. 1235 (Jan. 8, 1986).[337] The regulations subsequently issued by the Secretary, which are those at issue in the instance case, are called the Libyan Sanctions Regulations ("the Regulations"). 51 Fed.Reg. 1354-59 (Jan. 10, 1986); 31 C.F.R. pt. 550 (1986). The Regulations provide, in pertinent part, as follows:

> *Unless licensed* or authorized pursuant to this part, any attachment, *judgment*, decree, lien, execution, garnishment, or other judicial process is *null and void* with respect *to any property in which* on or since 4:10 p.m. E.S.T., January 8, 1986, *there existed an interest of the Government of Libya.*[338]

51 Fed.Reg. 2462 (Jan. 16, 1986); 31 C.F.R. pt. 550, § 550.210(e) (1987) (emphasis added). Licenses are issued by Treasury Department's Office of Foreign Assets Control ("OFAC").

    a.    License for Initiating Suit

Sun Oil argues that NOC's petition should be dismissed because NOC filed this action without a license. Even though OFAC has now granted NOC a license to cover this proceeding, Sun Oil claims that the Regulations' alleged requirement for a license *before* suit can be filed is jurisdictional in nature, and hence cannot be circumvented by issuance of a license that does not specifically provide for retroactive effect.

NOC argues precisely the opposite. It contends that the Regulations did not require it to obtain a license to initiate this proceeding. It did, however, procure such a license without conceding that it was required to do so. Thus, NOC maintains that

---

[337] [9] On January 4, 1990, in accordance with the requirements of the National Emergencies Act, 50 U.S.C. § 1622(d) (West Supp.1989); *see also* IEEPA, 50 U.S.C. §§ 1703(d) & 1706 (West Supp.1989); President Bush continued the state of emergency previously declared with respect to Libya. 55 Fed.Reg. 589 (1990).

[338] [10] Under the Regulations, the term "Government of Libya" specifically includes a corporation that, like NOC, is "substantially owned or controlled" by the Libyan Government. *See* 31 C.F.R. pt. 550, § 550.304(2).

the issue of whether a license is necessary for initiation of suit is now moot.

Sun Oil's arguments are without avail. Although it is true that a license meant to have retroactive effect must state as much, *see* 31 C.F.R. § 550.501(a), the fact is that the license issued to NOC does just that. License number 00595 specifically authorizes all of the transactions or acts necessary for initiating this particular lawsuit in this particular Court. A license could hardly be more specific.

Sun Oil's claim that a license to initiate suit is a jurisdictional requirement that cannot be cured retroactively is similarly without merit, and has been rejected by numerous courts. *See, e.g., Dean Witter Reynolds, Inc. v. Fernandez*, 741 F.2d 355, 360 (11th Cir.1984); *cf. National Airmotive v. Gov't & State of Iran*, 499 F.Supp. 401, 404-05 (D.D.C.1980). The regulations do not deprive this Court of jurisdiction. Rather, to the extent they apply, they merely effect a change in the governing substantive law. Here, the Court need not decide what, if any effect the lack of a license for initiating a lawsuit would have because the Court finds, as NOC urges, that this issue is now moot.

b.     License for Entry of Judgment

Sun Oil argues that even if NOC's license is valid for *initiating* suit, judgment cannot be *entered* in favor of NOC without a further license. Sun Oil contends that, since judgment cannot be entered, NOC lacks standing because its claim cannot be redressed by this Court.

To support its position that the Regulations forbid the entry of judgment in this case, Sun Oil relied on the language contained in the Regulations, especially in section 550.210(e), as well as the language in the specific license obtained by NOC. The license issued to NOC on October 6, 1989, by OFAC, grants permission for "[a]ll transactions necessary for the initiation and conduct" of these and related legal proceedings begun in the Eastern District of Pennsylvania. . . . However, the license also expressly states that it is not to "be construed as authorizing the transfer of any blocked funds, or *entry* or execution of *any judgment*." (*Id.* [emphasis added].) A letter from the director of OFAC that accompanies the license, and is addressed to counsel for NOC, also states that *"no entry of judgment* or execution thereon may be made with respect to either case without a *further specific license"* from OFAC. (Letter of October 6, 1989 from R. Richard Newcomb, Director of OFAC, to Preston Brown, Esq., Attorney for NOC), [emphasis added].)

NOC argues that the Regulations do not require a license to allow a judgment to be entered in its favor in this case. It contends that the Regulations bar only the unlicensed execution of any judgment entered by this Court. According to NOC, Sun Oil's interpretation, that mere *entry* of judgment is barred, would render the Regulations unconstitutional. NOC acknowledges that OFAC's position is, like Sun Oil's, that any judgment entered by this Court will be null and void, unless NOC obtains a license for this particular purpose. . . . But NOC maintains that OFAC's interpretation of the effect of the Regulations is incorrect. . . .

In support of its reading of the Regulations, NOC proffers cases interpreting analogous foreign asset control regulations. All of these cases support the proposition that foreign blocking regulations bar only those judicial proceedings that effect a transfer of foreign property or property interests. *See, e.g., Dean Witter Reynolds, Inc.,* 741 F.2d at 361-62. Not too surprisingly, therefore, in none of these cases were the applicable blocking regulations found to bar the mere entry of judgment.[339]

Sun Oil does not cite a single case to support its interpretation of the Regulations. More importantly, it does not distinguish, or even discuss, the long line of authority relied on by NOC. The Court's own research uncovered numerous cases, in addition to those cited by NOC, that interpreted analogous blocking regulations as barring only judicial acts that would effect a transfer of foreign property or property interests. *See, e.g., Itek Corp. v. First National Bank of Boston,* 704 F.2d 1, 9-10 (1st Cir.1983). In only one case did a court read blocking regulations as prohibiting an

---

[339] [11] Although apparently this is the first time the Libyan Regulations have been interpreted, the cases relied on by NOC are persuasive because the language of the pertinent provisions is so similar to that interpreted by these other courts. *Compare* 31 C.F.R. § 550.210(e) (Libyan Regulations) *with* 31 C.F.R. § 535.203(c) (Iranian Regulations).

unlicensed entry of judgment. *See Chase Manhattan Bank v. United China Syndicate, Ltd.*, 180 F.Supp. 848, 849 (S.D.N.Y.1960) (construing Foreign Assets Control Regulations as prohibiting the entry of a default judgment against Chinese defendant). That court's reasoning has been severely criticized, *see* Goodman, *United States Government Foreign Property Controls*, 52 Geo.L.J. 767, 796-98 (1964) (characterizing the decision as "erroneous"); *Vishipco Line v. Chase Manhattan Bank*, No. 77 Civ. 1251 (RLC), slip op. at 15 (S.D.N.Y. Nov. 3, 1978) ("this case is no longer consistent with the weight of authority"), and does not apply to the facts of this case.

The sheer volume of cases supporting NOC's view is impressive. But its constitutional arguments are equally compelling. NOC contends that since only Congress can interfere with this Court's jurisdiction, any reading of the Regulations that would prevent the entry of judgment would be unconstitutional. *See National Airmotive*, 499 F.Supp. at 405, n. 9. NOC further argues that Congress has not and cannot delegate its exclusive constitutional authority to expand or abridge the jurisdiction of the federal courts. Whether Congress can ever delegate its power over the jurisdiction of the federal courts need not be addressed. In this case the Court finds, as NOC urges, that Congress has not attempted to do so.

[The court went on to deny Libyan Sun's claim, based on *Dames & Moore v. Regan*, 453, U.S. 654 (1981) (Iran claims litigation) that the International Emergency Economic Powers Act (IEEPA) and the President's actions thereunder had the effect of ordering the suspension of Libyan claims in United States courts, and that for the court to adjudicate such claims would interfere with the President's power to settle international claims and to make new substantive rules of law governing such claims. The court found that the Act and the regulations only limited the transfer of foreign property or property interests.]

.     .     .

III.     *Denial of Sun Oil's Motion to Dismiss*

Having rejected all of the arguments offered by Sun Oil in support of its interpretation of the Regulations, the Court will read the language here in dispute as virtually every court before it. The

Libyan Regulations prohibit only those judicial acts that transfer Libyan property or property interests. Thus, the Libyan Regulations do not bar this Court from entering judgment in this case, and Sun Oil's standing arguments must fail. Furthermore, for the reasons previously mentioned, this Court has already determined that NOC should not be barred from U.S. courts because of the state of U.S.-Libyan relations. Therefore, having found all of its arguments without merit, the Court will deny Sun Oil's motion to dismiss NOC's petition.

## THE MOTION TO ENFORCE THE ARBITRAL AWARD

The Convention on the Recognition and Enforcement of Foreign Arbitral Awards attempts "to *encourage* the recognition and enforcement of commercial arbitration agreements in international contracts and to unify the standards by which agreements to arbitrate are observed and arbitral awards are enforced in the signatory countries." *Scherk v. Alberto-Culver Co.*, 417 U.S. 506, 520 n. 15, 94 S.Ct. 2449, 2457 n. 15, 41 L.Ed.2d 270 (1974) (citations omitted) (emphasis added). This Court must recognize the award rendered by the ICC Arbitral Tribunal in NOC's favor unless Sun Oil can successfully assert one of the seven defenses enumerated in Article V of the Convention. *Cf. Parsons & Whittemore Overseas Co., Inc. v. Societe Generale de l'Industrie du Papier (RAKTA)*, 508 F.2d 969, 973 (2d Cir.1974). Sun Oil has invoked three of the seven defenses against recognition. . . . It bears the burden of proving that any of these defenses is applicable. *Imperial Ethiopian Gov't v. Baruch-Foster Corp.*, 535 F.2d 334, 336 (5th Cir.1976); *Al Haddad Bros. Enterprises, Inc. v. M/S Agapi*, 635 F.Supp. 205, 209 (D.Del.1986), *aff'd without opinion*, 813 F.2d 396 (3d Cir.1987).

After considering the evidence and arguments of the parties, this Court, for the reasons outlined below, rejects Sun Oil's defenses and concludes that the arbitral award is entitled to recognition and enforcement under the Convention.

## I.     *Use of "False and Misleading" Testimony*

Sun Oil's first ground for asserting that the arbitral award should not be recognized revolves around the Arbitral Tribunal's reliance on the testimony of a Mr. C. James Bolm, a witness for

NOC. Essentially, Sun Oil claims that Mr. Blom's testimony was false and misleading, that this testimony was critical to the Arbitral Tribunal's decision, and, therefore, that recognition of the award would violate Sun Oil's due process rights.[340] Mr. Blom's testimony was misleading, according to Sun Oil, because the Arbitral Tribunal was given the incorrect impression that Mr. Blom, a former vice president of Occidental Petroleum Corporation ("Occidental"), was in charge of Occidental's Libyan operations during the time period at issue. Sun Oil also charges that Mr. Blom's testimony, "on the central issue of the case", . . . was false. Specifically, Sun Oil challenges Mr. Blom's assertion before the Tribunal that Occidental replaced its 230 American employees in Libya primarily with Canadians from its Canadian subsidiary. According to Sun Oil, this assertion was critical because one of NOC's main contentions during the arbitration was Sun Oil's alleged ability to perform under the EPSA by drawing on its Canadian subsidiary for personnel, as Occidental had allegedly done.

Intentionally giving false testimony in an arbitration proceeding would constitute fraud. *Cf. Dogherra v. Safeway Stores, Inc.*, 679 F.2d 1293, 1297 (9th Cir.), *cert. denied*, 459 U.S. 990, 103 S.Ct. 346, 74 L.Ed.2d (1982). But "in order to protect the finality of arbitration decisions, courts must be slow to vacate an arbitral award on the ground of fraud." *Id.* (citation omitted). Accordingly, "[t]he fraud must not have been discoverable upon the exercise of due diligence prior to the arbitration." *Id.* (citation omitted). The alleged fraud must also relate to a material issue. *See Newark Stereotypers' Union No. 18 v. Newark Morning Ledger Co.*, 397 F.2d 594, 600 (3d Cir.) (perjury does not justify vacation of an arbitral award if it relates to "an issue remote from the question to be decided"), *cert. denied*, 393 U.S. 954, 89 S.Ct. 378, 21 L.Ed.2d 365 (1968); *cf. Dogherra*, 679 F.2d at 1297.

---

[340] [19] Sun Oil claims this first argument for urging non-recognition of the award is based on two of the Convention's enumerated defenses, namely sections 1(b) and 2(b) of Article V. Section 1(b) provides a defense against recognition of an award upon proof that "[t]he party against whom the award is invoked was not given proper notice of the appointment of the arbitrator or of the arbitration proceedings or was otherwise unable to present his case. . . ." Section 2(b) provides that an award may be refused recognition if its enforcement or recognition "would be contrary to the public policy" of the country in which recognition is sought.

### a. Mr. Blom's Credentials

Sun Oil's first challenge, regarding the alleged misrepresentation of Mr. Blom's credentials, borders on the frivolous. It is true that the Tribunal appears to have misunderstood the extent of Mr. Blom's actual duties.[341] But there is no reason to conclude that NOC was at fault for this misapprehension.

Mr. Blom's testimony was completely accurate. During the 1984 hearings, he stated, on direct examination by counsel for NOC, that he lived and worked in Libya from 1967 to 1969, when he was transferred to Bakersfield. . . . He also stated that after his transfer he was eventually promoted to vice president of Eastern Hemisphere Exploration, although he continued to reside in Bakersfield. . . . If the tribunal got the wrong impression about Mr. Blom's relationship with Occidental's Libyan operations or the meaning of his area of responsibility (the "Eastern Hemisphere"), it is Sun Oil's own fault.

Counsel for Sun Oil had ample opportunity to cross-examine Mr. Blom regarding the extent of his duties. . . . Counsel simply chose not to do so. Moreover, Mr. Blom's appearance as a witness was not a surprise. NOC had provided Sun Oil with its list of witnesses over six months before Mr. Blom testified. . . . That list not only identified Mr. Blom as an NOC witness, but also noted his credentials and relationship to Occidental, and stated as to which matters he would testify. . . .

Sun Oil emphasizes Mr. Bolm's *second* appearance before the Tribunal, after the First Award had already been entered. Sun Oil argues that at this point, since the Tribunal's misapprehension of Mr. Blom's credentials was apparent from its statements in the First Award, NOC should have informed the Tribunal of the "error" if it was going to rely on Mr. Blom's testimony again. Although perhaps NOC should have corrected the Tribunal's misperception,[342] it did

---

[341] [20] The Arbitral Tribunal concluded Mr. Blom's position as head of Eastern Hemisphere Exploration meant he was in charge of Occidental's Libyan operations. (*See* D.I. 3, Exhibit B, First Award at 51.)

[342] [23] Even if this were viewed as an impropriety on NOC's part, such misconduct would not be sufficient grounds for refusing to recognize the Tribunal's award. In light of all of the facts, the Court finds that NOC's failure to act

not present any false testimony, even at Mr. Blom's second appearance. Tus, there was no "knowing use of false testimony," as Sun Oil defines the alleged fraud. (D.I. 12 at 32.)

b.    Alleged Use of Canadian Personnel

Sun Oil's second challenge to Mr. Blom's testimony has more force, but is nonetheless not sufficient to warrant non-recognition of the Tribunal's award. Mr. Blom's statement that Occidental replaced its American personnel with Canadians does in fact appear to have been inaccurate. (*See* D.I. 12A, Exhibits 5 & 6. *Compare* Aff. of Mr. Blom, D.I. 15A, Exhibit 6 *with* Transcript of Mr. Blom's Testimony, D.I. 15A, Exhibit 6B.) But, as with its first challenge, Sun Oil has not produced any evidence to show that this inaccuracy was anything other than unintentional.

Mr. Blom testified that about half of Occidental's 230 American employees in Libya were replaced primarily by Canadians from its Canadian subsidiary and British citizens from Occidental's London office. . . . Mr. Blom now states that those 230 American employees were replaced with "non-Americans," half of whom came from within the Occidental organization. . . . Therefore, the essential point of Mr. Blom's testimony is reaffirmed in his affidavit: Sun Oil could have replaced its personnel in Libya with non-Americans, as Occidental did. . . . The affidavits offered by Sun Oil to counter Mr. Blom's testimony do not controvert this critical point. . . .

The most important consideration of all, however, is that Sun Oil was able to present all of these arguments to the Arbitral Tribunal. . . . Mr. Blom's affidavit, which recounts what transpired during his second appearance before the Tribunal in June of 1986, attests to the fact that all of Sun Oil's current arguments were made to, and hence implicitly rejected by, the Tribunal. . . .

---

affirmatively to correct the Tribunal's misunderstanding regarding Mr. Blom's credentials is hardly the type of misconduct that would deprive Sun Oil of a fair hearing. *Cf. Apex Fountain Sales, Inc. v. Kleinfeld*, 818 F.2d 1089, 1094 (3d Cir.1987) ("[M]isconduct apart from corruption, fraud, or partiality in the arbitrators justifies reversal only if it so prejudices the rights of a party that it denies the party a fundamentally fair hearing.").

The Court therefore accepts Mr. Blom's description of the second hearing, and concludes that Sun Oil was not prevented from presenting its case. *See* Convention, art. V., sec. 1(b). In addition, Sun Oil has not proven fraud. Alternatively, even assuming the alleged fraud did occur, it did not relate to a material issue in the arbitration, and Sun Oil could have discovered it during the proceedings.

## II.    *Damage Award Not Supported by the Evidence*

Sun Oil's second challenge to confirmation of the award focuses on the $20 million the Tribunal granted in damages. According to Sun Oil, confirmation of the award should be denied based on article V, section 1(c),[343] because the arbitrators exceeded their authority, and based on article V, section 2(b), the Convention's public policy defense, because confirmation would violate due process. Sun Oil argues that the Tribunal exceeded its authority because it did not base its damage award on the evidence presented and instead acted as an *amiable compositeur*, which tries to reach merely an equitable, and not necessarily legal, result.[344] Sun Oil also argues that the Tribunal did not have jurisdiction to consider NOC's claims based on Article 8.2 of the EPSA because such claims were outside the scope of the Terms of Reference to which the parties agreed before submitting their dispute to arbitration.

Article V, section (1)(c) of the Convention, on which Sun Oil relies, "tracks in more detailed form § 10(d) of the Federal Arbitration Act, 9 U.S.C. § 10(d), which authorizes vacating an award '[w]here the arbitrators exceeded their powers.'" *Parsons &*

---

[343] [27] Recognition may be denied if "[t]he award deals with a difference not contemplated by or not falling within the terms of the submission to arbitration, or it contains decisions on matters beyond the scope of the submission to arbitration. . . ." Convention, art. V, sec. 1(c)

[344] [28] When submitting a dispute to arbitration, the parties can request that the arbitrators act as *amiable compositeurs*, which means that the arbitrators can "tak[e] into consideration not only legal rules, but also what they believe justice, fairness, and equity direct[]." Lecuyer-Thieffrey & Thieffrey, *Negotiating Settlement of Disputes Provisions in International Business Contracts: Recent Developments in Arbitration and Other Processes*, 45 Bus.Law. 577, 591 (1990).

*Whittemore Overseas Co.*, 508 F.2d at 976. Like other Convention defenses to enforcement of a foreign arbitral award, this defense "should be construed narrowly." *Id.* Its counterpart, section 10(d) of the Federal Arbitration Act, has also been given a narrow reading. *Andros Comania Maritima, S.A. v. Marc Rich & Co., A.G.*, 579 F.2d 691, 703 (2d Cir.1978).

The Third Circuit recently addressed a claim that an arbitral award should be vacated because the arbitrators exceeded their powers in violation of section 10(d) of the Federal Arbitration Act. That case, *Mutual Fire, Marine & Inland Insurance Co. v. Norad Reinsurance Co.*, 868 F.2d 52 (3d Cir.1989), describes the inquiry a court should undertake as follows:

> It is . . . well established that the "court's function in confirming or vacating a commercial [arbitration] award is severely limited." In conducting our review we must examine both the form of relief awarded by the arbitrator as well as the terms of that relief. We must determine if the form of the arbitrators' award can be *rationally derived* either from the agreement between the parties or from the parties submissions [sic] to the arbitrators. In addition, the terms of the arbitral award will not be subject to judicial revision unless they are "*completely irrational*."

*Norad Reinsurance Company*, 868 F.2d at 56 (citations omitted) (emphasis added). For the reasons stated below, the Court finds that the Tribunal's award of damages was "rationally derived" from the parties' agreement and that the terms of the award are not "completely irrational."

a.    Jurisdiction of the Tribunal

The arbitration clause contained in the EPSA is very broad. It provides, *inter alia*, that "*[a]ny controversy or claim* arising out of or relating to this Agreement, or breach thereof, shall, in the absence of an amicable arrangement between the Parties, be settled by arbitration. . . ." (emphasis added) The Terms of Reference, pursuant to which the dispute underlying this case was submitted to arbitration, specifically state that one of the "issues to be determined" at arbitration was "[t]o what relief, if any, is each party entitled?" . . . In addition, as stated in the Terms of Reference, NOC's claims included the allegation that Sun Oil was "liable to NOC for all remedies and amounts available under the EPSA and the applicable law. . . ." Thus, the issue of damages, under Article 8.2 or any other provision of the EPSA, was properly before the arbitrators.[345]

b.      The Tribunal's Rationale for Damages

After evaluating whether and to what extent Sun Oil was liable for damages, the Arbitral Tribunal concluded that Article 8.2 of the EPSA constituted a liquidated damages provision. Article 8.2 states in pertinent part:

8.2    *Failure to complete Exploration Program*

In the event that any part of the Exploration Program for any Area is not properly completed by the end of the Exploration Period applicable to such Area, Second Party [Sun Oil] shall immediately pay to First Party [NOC] the costs of such uncompleted part at the end of such Exploration Period.

(D.I. 3, Exhibit A, Annex 1, EPSA ¶ 8.2, at 23-24.)  Article 8.1 of the EPSA, which immediately precedes the language quoted above, states:

8.1    *Exploration Program*

Second Party [Sun Oil] undertakes, as a minimum exploration commitment, to spend such amounts on the Exmoratio Program as may be necessary to complete the Exploration Program properly. The Parties currently anticipate that the Exploration Program will cost *at least one hundred million U.S. Dollars (U.S. $100,000,000)*.

---

[345] [29] Sun Oil made the same jurisdictional argument before the Tribunal.  It was rejected for reasons similar to those stated by this Court. (*See* D.I. 3, Exhibit C, Final Award at 17-20.)

(*Id.* ¶ 8.1, at 23 [emphasis added].) The Tribunal found that this language in the contract made Sun Oil liable "for the costs of the uncompleted part of the exploration program . . . [without any] finding that the First Party [NOC] suffered actual loss."[346] The Tribunal went on, however, to consider the effects of Libyan law, which governs the EPSA.[347]

The Tribunal noted that, under Libyan law, liquidated damages provisions are valid; however, "damages fixed in advance by such [liquidated damages] clauses are not due 'if the debtor establishes that the creditor has not suffered any loss'[ ]" whatsoever. (*Id.* at 31 [discussing Articles 226 and 227 of the Libyan Civil Code].) The Tribunal concluded that "the debtor," Sun Oil, failed to establish that NOC had not suffered a loss:

> The Arbitral Tribunal is however unable to accept SUN-OIL's contention that no damages whatsoever were suffered by N.O.C. as a result of SUN-OIL's non-completion of the exploration program . . . it is clear that N.O.C. did suffer some loss by losing its chance, *within the exploration period*, to discover oil in the Contract Area and, *within the exploration period*, to obtain all the information and data needed to assess the petroleum resources in the Contract Area.

---

[346] [30] The Tribunal commented that although Article 8.2 of the EPSA could "lead to rather her severe and rigid consequences for the party undertaking exploration operations . . . it must be kept in mind that . . . the EPSA is a *risk contract*." (D.I. 3, Exhibit C, Final Award at 32 [emphasis added].) In return for a "tax-free percentage share" of any crude oil discovered and produced, Sun Oil "undertook an unconditional and absolute duty to render a counter-performance which consisted either in the timely completion of the exploration operations or, if SUN-OIL did not complete these operations within the prescribed time, in the payment by SUN-OIL of the costs of the uncompleted part thereof." (*Id.*) Although this was a "heavy commitment," it was not a burden sufficient "to deter one dozen other petroleum companies from entering into more or less identical EPSA's with N.O.C. in or about 1980." (*Id.*)

[347] [31] Article 21 of the EPSA states: "This Agreement shall be governed by an interpreted in accordance with the laws and regulations of the Socialist People's Libyan Arab Jamahiriya, including the Petroleum Law." (D.I. 3, Exhibit A, Annex 1, EPSA ¶ 21, at 45.)

(*Id.* [emphasis in the original]; *see also id.* at 37 ["(T)he actual loss suffered by N.O.C. . . . consists of the damages flowing from the fact that N.O.C. did not receive, within the exploration period, the geophysical information and data needed to assess the petroleum resources in the Contract Area and to make decisions accordingly."].)

Having concluded that Sun Oil failed to make out the requisite showing under Libyan law that NOC did not suffer any loss at all, the Tribunal then went on to consider whether the entire sum called for by the contract as liquidated damages should in fact be awarded. The Tribunal focused again on Libyan law, which provides that "[t]he Judge may reduce the amount of these [liquidated] damages if the debtor establishes that the amount fixed was grossly exaggerated or that the principal obligation has been partially performed." (Id. at 31 [quoting Article 227(2), Libyan Civil Code].) For several reasons—including its conclusions that Sun Oil, although incorrect in claiming *force majeure*, nevertheless acted in good faith, that NOC did not make reasonable efforts to mitigate its loss, and that the cost of NOC's actual loss decreased because of the drop in global crude oil prices—the Tribunal found that NOC's recovery of liquidated damages should be limited to $ 20 million. (*Id.* at 36-40.)

In fashioning its damages award, the Tribunal carefully considered both the EPSA and Libyan law, as well as the submissions and arguments of the parties. The Court finds that there is nothing "completely irrational" about the Tribunal's award or its reading of the parties' contract. Thus, mindful of the fact that "[i]t is not this Court's role . . . to sit as the panel did and reexamine the evidence under the guise of determining whether the arbitrators exceeded their powers," *Norad Reinsurance Company*, 868 F.2d at 56 (citation omitted), the Court will not inquire any further.

c.     Sun Oil's Due Process Rights

Sun Oil argues that its due process rights would be violated by confirmation of this damages award. Hence, it asks that the award not be recognized based on the Convention's public policy defense. Because the Court has already concluded that the Tribunal's award is rationally derived from the language contained in the EPSA and Libyan law, Sun Oil's due process argument does not have any merit.[348]

## III.     *Violation of U.S. Public Policy*

Sun Oil's final challenge to confirmation of the award rests solely on the public policy exception contained in article V, section 2(b), of the Convention. Both parties in this case agree that the public policy defense "should be construed narrowly," and that confirmation of a foreign award should be denied on the basis of public policy "only where enforcement would violate the forum state's most basic notions of morality and justice." *Parsons & Whittemore Overseas Co.*, 508 F.2d at 974 (citations omitted); *see also Waterside Ocean Navigation Co., Inc. v. International Navigation Ltd.*, 737 F.2d 150, 152 (2d Cir. 1984). Not too surprisingly, however, the parties do not agree as to whether this particular case fits within such a definition of the public policy defense.

Sun Oil argues that confirmation of the award in this case would violate the public policy of the United States for three reasons. First, Sun Oil contends that because confirmation would "penalize Sun for obeying and supporting the directives and foreign policy objectives of its government," other companies and individuals would be less likely to support U.S. sanctions programs, thereby diminishing "[t]he ability of the U.S. government to make and enforce policies with economic costs to U.S. citizens and corporations. . . ." . . . Secondly, Sun Oil contends that confirming the award would simply be "inconsistent with the substance of United States antiterrorism policy" . . ., and thirdly, that it would also "undermine the internationally-supported antiterrorism policy . .

---

[348] [32] To some extent, Sun Oil's due process argument is really a claim that the Tribunal erred in its interpretation of Libyan law. A mere error of law would not, however, be sufficient grounds to refuse recognition of the award. Restatement (Third) of the Foreign Relations Law of the United States § 488 comment a (1987); *see Northrop Corp. v. Triad Int'l Mktg. S.A.*, 811 F.2d 1265, 1269 (9th Cir.), *cert. denied*, 484 U.S. 914, 108 S.Ct. 261, 98 L.Ed.2d 219 (1987); *cf. Brandeis Intsel Limited v. Calabrian Chemicals Corp.*, 656 F.Supp. 160, 165 (S.D.N.Y.1987) (not even "manifest disregard of the law" would be sufficient to deny recognition of a foreign arbitral award based on the Convention's public policy exception). Moreover, here there is no reason to believe the Tribunal made any error whatsoever.

. by sending a contradictory signal concerning U.S. commitment to this policy and by making possible the transfer to . . . Libya . . . funds which could be employed to finance its continuing terrorist activities." . . . Sun Oil also presents much statistical and historical information designed to demonstrate the character of the Qadhafi Government. . . .

The problem with Sun Oil's arguments is that "public policy" and "foreign policy" are not synonymous. For example, in *Parsons & Whittemore Overseas Company*, 508 F.2d at 974, the Second Circuit addressed this very issue, saying: "To read the public policy defense as a parochial device protective of national political interests would seriously undermine the Convention's utility. This provision was not meant to enshrine the vagaries of international politics under the rubric of 'public policy.'"

In *Parsons*, the court faced a situation similar to the one in this case. There, a U.S. corporation claimed *force majeure* when, following the outbreak of the Arab-Israeli Six Day War, the Egyptian government severed diplomatic ties with the U.S. and ordered most Americans out of Egypt. The U.S. corporation contended that "various actions by United States officials subsequent to the severance of American-Egyptian relations . . . required Overseas [the U.S. corporation], as a loyal American citizen, to abandon the project." *Id.* Sun Oil argues that this case is different because Libya's terrorist activities, which have been condemned internationally, are hardly just a parochial interest of the U.S. On the other hand, the U.S. Government's policy towards Egypt in the 1960's, the foreign policy at issue in *Parsons*, was just "an outgrowth of an important but nonetheless conventional regional conflict." . . .

Despite Sun Oil's attempts to distinguish *Parsons*, it is clear that the policy objectives at issue here and the ones at issue in *Parsons* differ, at most, in degree and not in kind. This Court does not doubt that the ugly picture of the Qadhafi Government painted by Sun Oil's papers is accurate. The Court is similarly cognizant of the fact that Libya itself is not a signatory to the Convention; and hence, "if the tables were turned," as Sun Oil points out, a U.S. company would not necessarily be able to enforce an arbitral award against NOC in the Libya courts. . . . But Libya's terrorist tactics and opportunistic attitude towards international commercial arbitration are simply *beside the point*.[349]

The United States has not declared war on Libya, and President Bush has not derecognized the Qadhafi Government. In fact, the current Administration has specifically given Libya *permission* to bring this action in this Court. Given these facts and actions by our Executive Branch, this Court simply cannot conclude that to confirm a validly obtained, foreign arbitral award in favor of the Libyan Government would violate the United States' "most basic notions of morality and justice."[350]

Although Sun Oil argues that confirmation of this award would mean that U.S. dollars would end up financing Qadhafi's terrorist exploits, the Court has already pointed out that the President is empowered to prevent any such transfer through the Libyan Sanctions Regulations. Furthermore, Sun Oil's argument that U.S. companies will be less likely to support sanctions if this award is confirmed *assumes* that Sun Oil is correct on the central issue in the arbitration underlying this petition for confirmation: that is, that Sun Oil was justified in suspending performance under the EPSA. The Arbitral Tribunal, however, concluded that Sun Oil was *not* justified in suspending performance because of U.S. actions at that time. Because Sun Oil was able to present all of these arguments, regarding *force majeure* and Sun's attempts to support U.S. policy,

---

[349] [33] The Court would also note that Sun Oil has revealed its own brand of hypocrisy. It portrays its behavior as an attempt to cooperate with the anti-terrorist foreign policy of the United States. But what Sun Oil conveniently overlooks is the fact that the Qadhafi Government was *already* considered to be hostile to U.S. interests when the EPSa was negotiated. For example, Sun Oil's own papers underscore that almost one year *before* the EPSA was entered into, the U.S. Embassy in Tripoli was set on fire by a Libyan mob, and the Libyan authorities did not respond to protect the Embassy. Numerous other Libyan guerilla and terrorist efforts were also known and documented. (*See generally* D.I. 16, Exhibit 1, *Libya Under Qadhafi: A Pattern of Aggression* at A1-A13 [State Department documents outlining Libyan activities].)

[350] [34] In light of the circumstances presented here, the Court need not express any opinion as to whether, when or to what extent a foreign policy objective or dispute might ever be sufficiently compelling to warrant invocation of the Convention's public policy defense against confirmation of a foreign arbitral award.

before the Arbitral Tribunal, this Court will not reexamine that issue here.[351]

.   .   .

## CONCLUSION

The Court will recognize and enforce the Tribunal's award in favor of NOC and against Sun Oil in the amount of 20 million U.S. dollars, with prejudgment and postjudgment interest as described above.

A final judgment will be entered in accordance with this opinion; but execution on the judgment will be stayed, and the judgment may not be registered and transferred in accordance with 28 U.S.C. § 1963 unless the Libyan Sanctions Regulations are complied with, particularly 31 C.F.R. §§ 550.210, 550.413, and 550.511.

## FINAL JUDGMENT

For the reasons set forth in the Court's Opinion entered in this action on this date, it is

ORDERED:

1.      Libyan Sun Oil Company's motion to dismiss National Oil Corporation's petition (for recognition and confirmation of the arbitral award) is hereby denied.

---

[351] [35] It is also important to note that the U.S. Government has demonstrated that it is more than able to indicate when a company such as Sun Oil must abandon its international contractual obligations for the good of our country. In early 1986, over four years *after* Sun Oil first invoked the *force majeure* defense and suspended performance, the President of the United States directed the promulgation of the Libyan Sanctions Regulations. *See supra* pp. 807-808. These regulations expressly prohibit, *inter alia*, the performance by any U.S. person of any unauthorized "contract in support of an industrial or other commercial or governmental project in Libya." 31 C.F.R. § 550.205.

2.     Final Judgment is hereby entered in favor of National Oil Corporation and against Libyan Sun Oil Company in the amount of Twenty Million United States Dollars ($20,000,000,000).

3.     Post-award, prejudgment interest is awarded at the average rate of interest paid on blocked accounts from July 24, 1989 to date of this judgment.

4.     Postjudgment interest is awarded as provided by 28 U.S.C. § 1961 from the date of this judgment until such time, if ever, when the arbitral award and post-award, prejudgment interest is paid into a blocked account; and once this occurs, postjudgment interest will then be only the rate of interest earned on the funds so deposited in the blocked account.

5.     Execution on this Final Judgment is hereby stayed, and the judgment may not be registered and transferred in accordance with 28 U.S.C. § 1963 unless the Libyan Sanctions Regulations are complied with, particularly 31 C.F.R. §§ 550.210, 550.413, and 550.511.

#### Notes and Questions

1.     In the Hewlett Packard case would the court have stayed confirmation if the set off claim had not been subject to arbitration and would have to be established in judicial proceedings?  What if the set off arose out of an unrelated matter?  What is the legal authority on which the power to stay confirmation is based?

2.     In respect to the Libyan Sun case think of other situations where an award may be granted recognition and enforcement but where execution cannot be obtained. Where the making of payment outside the enforcement state is subject to exchange control authorization may the enforcement state deny authorization for payment without infringing its New York Convention obligations?

## VII.     SUMMARY AND CONCLUSIONS

The arbitral remedy is effective only if national courts are willing to give it teeth - whether by enforcing awards or granting conservatory measures in aid of arbitration. The 1958 New York Convention is a singular example of a transnational common law with respect to the enforcement of awards. Yet the Convention necessarily contains some backstops of control of abuse of the arbitral process, and losing parties are naturally tempted to use them as loopholes.

In this connection, it should escape no one's notice that, as a practical matter, the judge who is asked to defer to international standards is likely to be of the same nationality as the party which is urging him to find a way around them. (Enforcement actions usually take place in the defendant's country, where its assets are located.) The protectionist reflex thus works against the goals inherent in the New York Convention. It is overcome not as a matter of altruism, but as a matter of enlightened self-interest. If one country seeks to protect its nationals by refusing to apply the New York Convention, the end result will be (A) that parties dealing with that country will end up refusing to trade, or enter into contracts only on terms that reflect the legal uncertainty of their rights and (B) that the courts of other countries will ultimately be tempted to protect their own nationals by way of retortion.

# Index

---

References are to Pages

---

†